Pocket
Italian
Dictionary

Italian ›English English ›Italian

D0250828

MONDADORI

Collins
An Imprint of HarperCollins*Publishers*

third edition/terza edizione 1999

© HarperCollins Publishers 1996, 1999
© William Collins Sons & Co. Ltd. 1990

latest reprint 2000

HarperCollins Publishers
Westerhill Road, Bishopbriggs, Glasgow G64 2QT, Great Britain

The HarperCollins website address is
www.**fire**and**water**.com

Collins® and Bank of English® are registered trademarks
of HarperCollins Publishers Limited

ISBN 0-00-470772-9

HarperCollins Publishers, Inc.
10 East 53rd Street, New York, NY 10022

ISBN 0-06-095663-1

CIP information is available on request

The HarperCollins USA website address is
www.harpercollins.com

Pubblicato in Italia dalla
Arnoldo Mondadori Editore, Milano
ISBN 88-04-41581-9

Typeset by Morton Word Processing Ltd, Scarborough

*Printed and bound in Great Britain by
Omnia Books Ltd, Glasgow, G64*

general editors/a cura di
Catherine E. Love • Michela Clari

with/hanno collaborato
Gabriella Bacchelli • Loredana Riu
Bob Grossmith

editorial staff/segreteria di redazione
Joyce Littlejohn • Isobel Gordon

series editor/collana a cura di
Lorna Sinclair Knight

INDICE/CONTENTS

I marchi registrati

I termini che a nostro parere
costituiscono un marchio
registrato sono stati designati
come tali. In ogni caso, né la
presenza né l'assenza di tale
designazione implicano alcuna
valutazione del loro reale stato
giuridico.

Note on trademarks

Words which we have reason to
believe constitute trademarks have
been designated as such. However,
neither the presence nor the
absence of such designation should
be regarded as affecting the legal
status of any trademark.

INTRODUZIONE

Il dizionario Tascabile Collins Mondadori è stato concepito e scritto per chi vuole imparare l'inglese per motivi di studio, lavoro o turismo.

La modernità e la ricchezza del lemmario e della fraseologia, l'elegante presentazione delle voci, l'uso del colore e il pratico formato fanno di questo dizionario un'opera unica nel suo genere.

Grazie ai giochi e agli esercizi che troverete nell'originale supplemento vi riuscirà facile e divertente imparare ad usare il dizionario così da trarne il massimo vantaggio.

I dizionari Collins Mondadori sono sinonimo di qualità e modernità: vi ringraziamo di aver scelto il dizionario inglese Tascabile che siamo certi si rivelerà uno strumento di lavoro utile e piacevole da usarsi in ogni occasione.

COME USARE IL DIZIONARIO

Per imparare ad usare in modo efficace il dizionario è importante comprendere la funzione delle differenziazioni tipografiche, dei simboli e delle abbreviazioni usati nel testo. Vi forniamo pertanto qui di seguito alcuni chiarimenti in merito a tali convenzioni.

I lemmi
Sono le parole in **rosso** elencate in ordine alfabetico. Il primo e l'ultimo lemma di ciascuna pagina appaiono al margine superiore.

Dove opportuno, informazioni sull'ambito d'uso o sul livello di formalità di certe parole vengono fornite tra parentesi in corsivo e spesso in forma abbreviata dopo la trascrizione fonetica (es. (*comm*), (*inf*)).

In certi casi più parole con radice comune sono raggruppate sotto lo stesso lemma. Tali parole appaiono in rosso ma in un carattere leggermente ridotto (es. **dolce, dolcezza; accept, acceptance**).

Esempi d'uso del lemma sono a loro volta in neretto ma in un carattere diverso dal lemma (es. **to be cold**).

La trascrizione fonetica

La trascrizione fonetica che illustra la corretta pronuncia del lemma è in parentesi quadra e segue immediatamente il lemma (es. **mezzo** ['mɛddzo]; **knead** [niːd]). L'elenco dei simboli fonetici è alle pagine xiv-xv.

Le traduzioni

Le traduzioni sono in carattere tondo e se si riferiscono a diversi significati del lemma sono separate da un punto e virgola. Spesso diverse traduzioni di un lemma sono introdotte da una o più parole in corsivo in parentesi tonda: la loro funzione è di chiarire a quale significato del lemma si riferisce la traduzione. Possono essere sinonimi, indicazioni di ambito d'uso o di registro del lemma (es. **party** (*POL*) (*team*) o (*celebration*), **laid back** (*inf*) etc.).

Le "parole chiave"

Un trattamento particolare è stato riservato a quelle parole che, per frequenza d'uso o complessità, necessitano una strutturazione più chiara ed esauriente (es. **da, di, avere** in italiano, **at, to, be, this** in inglese). Il simbolo ♦ e i numeri sono usati per guidarvi attraverso le varie distinzioni grammaticali e di significato. Dove necessario, ulteriori informazioni sono fornite in corsivo tra parentesi.

Informazioni grammaticali

Le parti del discorso (noun, adjective ecc.) sono espresse da abbreviazioni convenzionali in corsivo (*n, adj* ecc) e seguono la trascrizione fonetica del lemma.

Eventuali ulteriori informazioni grammaticali, come ad esempio le forme di un verbo irregolare o il plurale irregolare di un sostantivo, precedono tra parentesi la parte del discorso (es. **fall** (*pt* **fell**, *pp* **fallen**) *n*; **man** (*pl* **men**) *n*).

INTRODUCTION

We are delighted that you have decided to buy the Collins Pocket Italian Dictionary, and hope you will enjoy and benefit from using it at home, at school, on holiday or at work.

The innovative use of colour guides you quickly and efficiently to the word you want, and the comprehensive wordlist provides a wealth of modern and idiomatic phrases not normally found in a dictionary this size.

In addition, the supplement provides you with guidance on using the dictionary, along with entertaining ways of improving your dictionary skills.

We hope that you will enjoy using it and that it will significantly enhance your language studies.

USING YOUR COLLINS POCKET DICTIONARY

A wealth of information is presented in the dictionary, using various typefaces, sizes of type, symbols, abbreviations and brackets. The conventions and symbols used are explained in the following sections.

Headwords
The words you look up in a dictionary — "headwords" — are listed alphabetically. They are printed in **red type** for rapid identification. The two headwords appearing at the top of each page indicate the first and last word dealt with on the page in question.

Information about the usage or form of certain headwords is given in brackets after the phonetic spelling. This usually appears in abbreviated form and in italics (e.g. (*fam*), (*COMM*)).

Where appropriate, words related to headwords are grouped in the same entry (**illustrare, illustrazione; accept, acceptance**) in a slightly smaller red type than the headword.

Common expressions in which the headword appears are shown in a different bold roman type (e.g. **aver freddo**).

Phonetic spellings

Where the phonetic spelling of headwords (indicating their pronunciation) is given, it will appear in square brackets immediately after the headword (e.g. **calza** ['kaltsa]; **knead** [ni:d]). A list of these symbols is given on pages xiv-xv.

Translations

Headword translations are given in ordinary type and, where more than one meaning or usage exists, these are separated by a semi-colon. You will often find other words in italics in brackets before the translations. These offer suggested contexts in which the headword might appear (e.g. **duro** (*pietra*) or (*lavoro*)) or provide synonyms (e.g. **duro** (*ostinato*)).

"Key" words

Special status is given to certain Italian and English words which are considered as "key" words in each language. They may, for example, occur very frequently or have several types of usage (e.g. **da, di, avere; at, to, be, this**). A combination of lozenges and numbers helps you to distinguish different parts of speech and different meanings. Further helpful information is provided in brackets and in italics.

Grammatical information

Parts of speech are given in abbreviated form in italics after the phonetic spellings of headwords (e.g. *vt, av, cong*).

Genders of Italian nouns are indicated as follows: *sm* for a masculine and *sf* for a feminine noun. Feminine and irregular plural forms of nouns are also shown (**dottore, essa; droga, ghe**).

Feminine adjective endings are given as are plural forms (**opaco, a, chi, che**).

ABBREVIAZIONI

ABBREVIATIONS

abbreviazione	**abbr**	abbreviation
aggettivo	**adj**	adjective
amministrazione	**ADMIN**	administration
avverbio	**adv**	adverb
aeronautica, viaggi aerei	**AER**	flying, air travel
aggettivo	**ag**	adjective
agricoltura	**AGR**	agriculture
amministrazione	**AMM**	administration
anatomia	**ANAT**	anatomy
architettura	**ARCHIT**	architecture
articolo indeterminativo	**art indet**	indefinite article
attributivo	**attrib**	attributive
ausiliare	**aus, aux**	auxiliary
l'automobile	**AUT**	the motor car and motoring
avverbio	**av**	adverb
aeronautica, viaggi aerei	**AVIAT**	flying, air travel
biologia	**BIOL**	biology
botanica	**BOT**	botany
inglese della Gran Bretagna	**BRIT**	British English
consonante	**C**	consonant
chimica	**CHIM, CHEM**	chemistry
commercio, finanza, banca	**COMM**	commerce, finance, banking
comparativo	**compar**	comparative
informatica	**COMPUT**	computers
congiunzione	**cong, conj**	conjunction
edilizia	**CONSTR**	building
sostantivo usato come aggettivo, non può essere usato né come attributo, né dopo il sostantivo qualificato	**cpd**	compound element: noun used as adjective and which cannot follow the noun it qualifies
cucina	**CUC, CULIN**	cookery
davanti a	**dav**	before
articolo determinativo	**def art**	definite article
determinativo: articolo, aggettivo dimostrativo o indefinito etc	**det**	determiner: article, demonstrative etc
diminutivo	**dimin**	diminutive
diritto	**DIR**	law
economia	**ECON**	economics
edilizia	**EDIL**	building
elettricità, elettronica	**ELETTR, ELEC**	electricity, electronics
esclamazione	**escl, excl**	exclamation
femminile	**f**	feminine
familiare (! da evitare)	**fam(!)**	informal usage (! particularly offensive)
ferrovia	**FERR**	railways
figurato	**fig**	figurative use

ABBREVIAZIONI

ABBREVIATIONS

fisiologia	FISIOL	physiology
fotografia	FOT	photography
(verbo inglese) la cui particella è inseparabile dal verbo	fus	(phrasal verb) where the particle cannot be separated from main verb
nella maggior parte dei sensi; generalmente	gen	in most or all senses; generally
geografia, geologia	GEO	geography, geology
geometria	GEOM	geometry
impersonale	impers	impersonal
articolo indeterminativo	indef art	indefinite article
familiare (! da evitare)	inf(!)	informal usage (! particularly offensive)
infinito	infin	infinitive
informatica	INFORM	computers
insegnamento, sistema scolastico e universitario	INS	schooling, schools and universities
invariabile	inv	invariable
irregolare	irreg	irregular
grammatica, linguistica	LING	grammar, linguistics
maschile	m	masculine
matematica	MAT(H)	mathematics
termine medico, medicina	MED	medical term, medicine
il tempo, meteorologia	METEOR	the weather, meteorology
maschile o femminile, secondo il sesso	m/f	either masculine or feminine depending on sex
esercito, linguaggio militare	MIL	military matters
musica	MUS	music
sostantivo	n	noun
nautica	NAUT	sailing, navigation
numerale (aggettivo, sostantivo)	num	numeral adjective or noun
	o.s.	oneself
peggiorativo	peg, pej	derogatory, pejorative
fotografia	PHOT	photography
fisiologia	PHYSIOL	physiology
plurale	pl	plural
politica	POL	politics
participio passato	pp	past participle
preposizione	prep	preposition
pronome	pron	pronoun
psicologia, psichiatria	PSIC, PSYCH	psychology, psychiatry
tempo passato	pt	past tense
qualcosa	qc	
qualcuno	qn	
religione, liturgia	REL	religions, church service
sostantivo	s	noun
	sb	somebody

ABBREVIAZIONI

ABBREVIATIONS

insegnamento, sistema scolastico e universitario	SCOL	schooling, schools and universities
singolare	sg	singular
soggetto (grammaticale)	sog	(grammatical) subject
	sth	something
congiuntivo	sub	subjunctive
soggetto (grammaticale)	subj	(grammatical) subject
superlativo	superl	superlative
termine tecnico, tecnologia	TECN, TECH	technical term, technology
telecomunicazioni	TEL	telecommunications
tipografia	TIP	typography, printing
televisione	TV	television
tipografia	TYP	typography, printing
inglese degli Stati Uniti	US	American English
vocale	V	vowel
verbo	vb	verb
verbo o gruppo verbale con funzione intransitiva	vi	verb or phrasal verb used intransitively
verbo riflessivo	vr	reflexive verb
verbo o gruppo verbale con funzione transitiva	vt	verb or phrasal verb used transitively
zoologia	ZOOL	zoology
marchio registrato	®	registered trademark
introduce un'equivalenza culturale	≈	introduces a cultural equivalent

TRASCRIZIONE FONETICA

PHONETIC TRANSCRIPTION

Consonants   Consonanti

NB p, b, t, d, k, g are not aspirated in Italian/sono seguite da un'aspirazione in inglese.

puppy	p	*padre*
baby	b	*bambino*
tent	t	*tutto*
daddy	d	*dado*
cork kiss	k	*cane che*
chord		
gag guess	g	*gola ghiro*
so rice kiss	s	*sano*
cousin buzz	z	*svago esame*
sheep sugar	ʃ	*scena*
pleasure beige	ʒ	*garage*
church	tʃ	*pece lanciare*
judge general	dʒ	*giro gioco*
farm raffle	f	*afa faro*
very rev	v	*vero bravo*
thin maths	θ	
that other	ð	
little ball	l	*letto ala*
	ʎ	*gli*
rat brat	r	*rete arco*
mummy comb	m	*ramo madre*
no ran	n	*no fumante*
	ɲ	*gnomo*
singing bank	ŋ	
hat reheat	h	
yet	j	*buio piacere*
wall bewail	w	*uomo guaio*
loch	x	

Vowels   Vocali

NB The pairing of some vowel sounds only indicates approximate equivalence./La messa in equivalenza di certi suoni indica solo una rassomiglianza approssimativa.

heel bead	iː i	*vino idea*
hit pity	ɪ	
	e	*stella edera*
set tent	ɛ	*epoca eccetto*
apple bat	æ a	*mamma amore*
after car calm	ɑː	
fun cousin	ʌ	
over above	ə	
urn fern work	əː	
wash pot	ɔ	*rosa occhio*
born cork	ɔː	
	o	*ponte ognuno*
	ø	*föhn*
full soot	u	*utile zucca*
boon lewd	uː	

Diphthongs   Dittonghi

ɪə	*beer tier*
ɛə	*tear fair there*
eɪ	*date plaice day*
aɪ	*life buy cry*
au	*owl foul now*
əu	*low no*
ɔɪ	*boil boy oily*
uə	*poor tour*

Miscellaneous   Varie

* per l'inglese: la "r" finale viene pronunciata se seguita da una vocale.

ˈ precedes the stressed syllable/precede la sillaba accentata.

ITALIAN PRONUNCIATION

Vowels

Where the vowel **e** or the vowel **o** appears in a stressed syllable it can be either open [ɛ], [ɔ] or closed [e], [o]. As the open or closed pronunciation of these vowels is subject to regional variation, the distinction is of little importance to the user of this dictionary. Phonetic transcription for headwords containing these vowels will therefore only appear where other pronunciation difficulties are present.

Consonants

c before "e" or "i" is pronounced *tch*.

ch is pronounced like the "k" in "kit".

g before "e" or "i" is pronounced like the "j" in "jet".

gh is pronounced like the "g" in "get".

gl before "e" or "i" is normally pronounced like the "lli" in "million", and in a few cases only like the "gl" in "glove".

gn is pronounced like the "ny" in "canyon".

sc before "e" or "i" is pronounced *sh*.

z is pronounced like the "ts" in "stetson", or like the "d's" in "bird's-eye".

Headwords containing the above consonants and consonantal groups have been given full phonetic transcription in this dictionary.

NB All double written consonants in Italian are fully sounded: e.g. the "tt" in "tutto" is pronounced as in "ha*t t*rick".

ITALIANO – INGLESE
ITALIAN – ENGLISH

A, a

A *abbr* (= *autostrada*) ≈ M (= *motorway*)

PAROLA CHIAVE

a (*a+il* = **al**, *a+lo* = **allo**, *a+l'* = **all'**, *a+la*
= **alla**, *a+i* = **ai**, *a+gli* = **agli**, *a+le* = **alle**)
prep **1** (*stato in luogo*) at; (: *in*) in; **essere
alla stazione** to be at the station; **essere
~ casa/~ scuola/~ Roma** to be at home/
at school/in Rome; **è ~ 10 km da qui** it's
10 km from here, it's 10 km away

2 (*moto a luogo*) to; **andare ~ casa/~
scuola** to go home/to school

3 (*tempo*) at; (*epoca, stagione*) in; **alle
cinque** at five (o'clock); **~ mezzanotte/
Natale** at midnight/Christmas; **al mattino**
in the morning; **~ maggio/primavera** in
May/spring; **~ cinquant'anni** at fifty (years
of age); **~ domani!** see you tomorrow!

4 (*complemento di termine*) to; **dare qc ~
qn** to give sth to sb

5 (*mezzo, modo*) with, by; **~ piedi/cavallo**
on foot/horseback; **fatto ~ mano** made by
hand, handmade; **una barca ~ motore** a
motorboat; **~ uno ~ uno** one by one;
all'italiana the Italian way, in the Italian
fashion

6 (*rapporto*) a, per; (: *con prezzi*) at;
prendo 500.000 lire al mese I get
500,000 lire a *o* per month; **pagato ~ ore**
paid by the hour; **vendere qc ~ 2500 lire
il chilo** to sell sth at 2,500 lire a *o* per kilo

abbacchi'ato, a [abbak'kjato] *ag*
downhearted, in low spirits

abbagli'ante [abbaʎ'ʎante] *ag* dazzling; **~i**
smpl (*AUT*): **accendere gli ~i** to put one's
headlights on full (*BRIT*) *o* high (*US*) beam

abbagli'are [abbaʎ'ʎare] *vt* to dazzle;
(*illudere*) to delude; **ab'baglio** *sm*
blunder; **prendere un abbaglio** to

blunder, make a blunder

abbai'are *vi* to bark

abba'ino *sm* dormer window; (*soffitta*)
attic room

abbando'nare *vt* to leave, abandon,
desert; (*trascurare*) to neglect; (*rinunciare a*)
to abandon, give up; **~rsi** *vr* to let o.s. go;
~rsi a (*ricordi, vizio*) to give o.s. up to;
abban'dono *sm* abandonment; neglect;
(*SPORT*) withdrawal; (*fig*) abandon; **in
abbandono** (*edificio, giardino*) neglected

abbas'sare *vt* to lower; (*radio*) to turn
down; **~rsi** *vr* (*chinarsi*) to stoop, (*livello,
sole*) to go down; (*fig: umiliarsi*) to demean
o.s.; **~ i fari** (*AUT*) to dip *o* dim (*US*) one's
lights

ab'basso *escl*: **~ il re!** down with the king!

abbas'tanza [abbas'tantsa] *av* (*a
sufficienza*) enough; (*alquanto*) quite,
rather, fairly; **non è ~ furbo** he's not
shrewd enough; **un vino ~ dolce** quite a
sweet wine; **averne ~ di qn/qc** to have
had enough of sb/sth

ab'battere *vt* (*muro, casa*) to pull down;
(*ostacolo*) to knock down; (*albero*) to fell;
(: *sog: vento*) to bring down; (*bestie da
macello*) to slaughter; (*cane, cavallo*) to
destroy, put down; (*selvaggina, aereo*) to
shoot down; (*fig: sog: malattia, disgrazia*)
to lay low; **~rsi** *vr* (*avvilirsi*) to lose heart;
abbat'tuto, a *ag* (*fig*) depressed

abba'zia [abbat'tsia] *sf* abbey

abbece'dario [abbetʃe'darjo] *sm* primer

abbel'lire *vt* (*ornare*) to embellish

abbeve'rare *vt* to water; **~rsi** *vr* to drink

'abbia *etc vb vedi* **avere**

abbiccì [abbit'tʃi] *sm inv* alphabet;
(*sillabario*) primer; (*fig*) rudiments *pl*

abbi'enti *smpl*: **gli ~** the well-to-do

abbiglia'mento [abbiʎʎa'mento] *sm* dress

no pl; (indumenti) clothes pl; (industria) clothing industry

abbigli'are [abbiλ'λare] vt to dress up

abbi'nare vt: ~ **(a)** to combine (with)

abbindo'lare vt (fig) to cheat, trick

abbocca'mento sm talks pl, meeting

abboc'care vi (pesce) to bite; (tubi) to join; ~ **(all'amo)** (fig) to swallow the bait

abboc'cato, a ag (vino) sweetish

abbona'mento sm subscription; (alle ferrovie etc) season ticket; **fare l'~** to take out a subscription (o season ticket)

abbo'narsi vr: ~ **a un giornale** to take out a subscription to a newspaper; ~ **al teatro/alle ferrovie** to take out a season ticket for the theatre/the train; **abbo'nato, a** sm/f subscriber; season-ticket holder

abbon'dante ag abundant, plentiful; (giacca) roomy

abbon'danza [abbon'dantsa] sf abundance; plenty

abbon'dare vi to abound, be plentiful; ~ **in** o **di** to be full of, abound in

abbor'dabile ag (persona) approachable; (prezzo) reasonable

abbor'dare vt (nave) to board; (persona) to approach; (argomento) to tackle

abbotto'nare vt to button up, do up

abboz'zare [abbot'tsare] vt to sketch, outline; (SCULTURA) to rough-hew; ~ **un sorriso** to give a hint of a smile; **ab'bozzo** sm sketch, outline; (DIR) draft

abbracci'are [abbrat'tʃare] vt to embrace; (persona) to hug, embrace; (professione) to take up; (contenere) to include; **~rsi** vr to hug o embrace (one another); **ab'braccio** sm hug, embrace

abbrevi'are vt to shorten; (parola) to abbreviate

abbreviazi'one [abbrevjat'tsjone] sf abbreviation

abbron'zante [abbron'dzante] ag tanning, sun cpd

abbron'zare [abbron'dzare] vt (pelle) to tan; (metalli) to bronze; **~rsi** vr to tan, get a tan; **abbronza'tura** sf tan, suntan

abbrusto'lire vt (pane) to toast; (caffè) to roast

abbru'tire vt to exhaust; to degrade

abbu'ono sm (COMM) allowance, discount; (SPORT) handicap

abdi'care vi to abdicate; ~ **a** to give up, renounce

aberrazi'one [aberrat'tsjone] sf aberration

a'bete sm fir (tree); ~ **rosso** spruce

abi'etto, a ag despicable, abject

'abile ag (idoneo): ~ **(a qc/a fare qc)** fit (for sth/to do sth); (capace) able; (astuto) clever; (accorto) skilful; ~ **al servizio militare** fit for military service; **abilità** inv ability; cleverness; skill

abili'tato, a ag qualified; (TEL) which has an outside line; **abilitazi'one** sf qualification

a'bisso sm abyss, gulf

abi'tacolo sm (AER) cockpit; (AUT) inside; (: di camion) cab

abi'tante sm/f inhabitant

abi'tare vt to live in, dwell in ♦ vi: ~ **in campagna/a Roma** to live in the country/in Rome; **abi'tato, a** ag inhabited; lived in ♦ sm (anche: **centro abitato**) built-up area; **abitazi'one** sf residence; house

'abito sm dress no pl; (da uomo) suit; (da donna) dress; (abitudine, disposizione, REL) habit; **~i** smpl (vestiti) clothes; **in ~ da sera** in evening dress

abitu'ale ag usual, habitual; (cliente) regular

abitu'are vt: ~ **qn a** to get sb used o accustomed to; **~rsi a** to get used to, accustom o.s. to

abitudi'nario, a ag of fixed habits ♦ sm/f regular customer

abi'tudine sf habit; **aver l'~ di fare qc** to be in the habit of doing sth; **d'~** usually; **per ~** from o out of habit

abo'lire vt to abolish; (DIR) to repeal

abomi'nevole ag abominable

abo'rigeno [abo'ridʒeno] sm aborigine

abor'rire vt to abhor, detest

abor'tire vi (MED) to miscarry, have a

miscarriage; (: *deliberatamente*) to have an abortion; (*fig*) to miscarry, fail; **a'borto** *sm* miscarriage; abortion

abrasi'one *sf* abrasion; **abra'sivo, a** *ag*, *sm* abrasive

abro'gare *vt* to repeal, abrogate

A'bruzzo *sm*: **l'~, gli ~i** the Abruzzi

'abside *sf* apse

a'bulico, a, ci, che *ag* lacking in will power

abu'sare *vi*: **~ di** to abuse, misuse; (*alcool*) to take to excess; (*approfittare, violare*) to take advantage of; **a'buso** *sm* abuse, misuse; excessive use

a.C. *av abbr* (= *avanti Cristo*) B.C.

a'cacia, cie [a'katʃa] *sf* (*BOT*) acacia

'acca *sf* letter H; **non capire un'~** not to understand a thing

acca'demia *sf* (*società*) learned society; (*scuola: d'arte, militare*) academy; **acca'demico, a, ci, che** *ag* academic ♦ *sm* academician

acca'dere *vb impers* to happen, occur; **acca'duto** *sm*: **raccontare l'accaduto** to describe what has happened

accalap'piare *vt* to catch

accal'carsi *vr*: **~ (in)** to crowd (into)

accal'darsi *vr* to grow hot

accalo'rarsi *vr* (*fig*) to get excited

accampa'mento *sm* camp

accam'pare *vt* to encamp; (*fig*) to put forward, advance; **~rsi** *vr* to camp

accani'mento *sm* fury; (*tenacia*) tenacity, perseverance

acca'nirsi *vr* (*infierire*) to rage; (*ostinarsi*) to persist; **acca'nito, a** *ag* (*odio, gelosia*) fierce, bitter; (*lavoratore*) assiduous, dogged; (*fumatore*) inveterate

ac'canto *av* near, nearby; **~ a** *prep* near, beside, close to

accanto'nare *vt* (*problema*) to shelve; (*somma*) to set aside

accapar'rare *vt* (*COMM*) to corner, buy up; **~rsi qc** (*fig: simpatia, voti*) to secure sth (for o.s.)

accapigli'arsi [akkapiʎˈʎarsi] *vr* to come to blows; (*fig*) to quarrel

accappa'toio *sm* bathrobe

accappo'nare *vi*: **far ~ la pelle a qn** to bring sb out in goose pimples

accarez'zare [akkaretˈtsare] *vt* to caress, stroke, fondle; (*fig*) to toy with

acca'sarsi *vr* to set up house; to get married

accasci'arsi [akkaʃˈʃarsi] *vr* to collapse; (*fig*) to lose heart

accat'tone, a *sm/f* beggar

accaval'lare *vt* (*gambe*) to cross; **~rsi** *vr* (*sovrapporsi*) to overlap; (*addensarsi*) to gather

acce'care [attʃeˈkare] *vt* to blind ♦ *vi* to go blind

ac'cedere [•tˈtʃedere] *vi*: **~ a** to enter; (*richiesta*) to grant, accede to

accele'rare [attʃeleˈrare] *vt* to speed up ♦ *vi* (*AUT*) to accelerate; **~ il passo** to quicken one's pace; **accele'rato** *sm* (*FERR*) slow train; **accelera'tore** *sm* (*AUT*) accelerator; **accelerazi'one** *sf* acceleration

ac'cendere [atˈtʃendere] *vt* (*fuoco, sigaretta*) to light; (*luce, televisione*) to put on, switch on, turn on; (*AUT: motore*) to switch on; (*COMM: conto*) to open; (*fig: suscitare*) to inflame, stir up; **~rsi** *vr* (*luce*) to come o go on; (*legna*) to catch fire, ignite; **accen'dino** *sm*, **accendi'sigaro** *sm* (cigarette) lighter

accen'nare [attʃenˈnare] *vt* (*MUS*) to pick out the notes of; to hum ♦ *vi*: **~ a** (*fig: alludere a*) to hint at; (: *far atto di*) to make as if; **~ un saluto** (*con la mano*) to make as if to wave; (*col capo*) to half nod; **accenna a piovere** it looks as if it's going to rain

ac'cenno [atˈtʃenno] *sm* (*cenno*) sign; nod; (*allusione*) hint

accensi'one [attʃenˈsjone] *sf* (*vedi accendere*) lighting; switching on; opening; (*AUT*) ignition

accen'tare [attʃenˈtare] *vt* (*parlando*) to stress; (*scrivendo*) to accent

ac'cento [atˈtʃento] *sm* accent; (*FONETICA, fig*) stress; (*inflessione*) tone (of voice)

accen'trare [attʃenˈtrare] *vt* to centralize

accentu'are [attʃentu'are] vt to stress, emphasize; **~rsi** vr to become more noticeable

accerchi'are [attʃer'kjare] vt to surround, encircle

accerta'mento [attʃerta'mento] sm check; assessment

accer'tare [attʃer'tare] vt to ascertain; (*verificare*) to check; (*reddito*) to assess; **~rsi** vr: **~rsi (di)** to make sure (of)

ac'ceso, a [at'tʃeso] pp di **accendere ♦** ag lit; on; open; (*colore*) bright

acces'sibile [attʃes'sibile] ag (*luogo*) accessible; (*persona*) approachable; (*prezzo*) reasonable

ac'cesso [at'tʃesso] sm (*anche INFORM*) access; (*MED*) attack, fit; (*impulso violento*) fit, outburst

acces'sorio, a [attʃes'sɔrjo] ag secondary, of secondary importance; **~i** smpl accessories

ac'cetta [at'tʃetta] sf hatchet

accet'tabile [attʃet'tabile] ag acceptable

accet'tare [attʃet'tare] vt to accept; **~ di fare qc** to agree to do sth; **accettazi'one** sf acceptance; (*locale di servizio pubblico*) reception; **accettazione bagagli** (*AER*) check-in (desk)

ac'cetto, a [at'tʃetto] ag: **(ben) ~** welcome; (*persona*) well-liked

accezi'one [attʃet'tsjone] sf meaning

acchiap'pare [akkjap'pare] vt to catch

acci'acco, chi [at'tʃakko] sm ailment

acciaie'ria [attʃaje'ria] sf steelworks sg

acci'aio [at'tʃajo] sm steel

acciden'tale [attʃiden'tale] ag accidental

acciden'tato, a [attʃiden'tato] ag (*terreno etc*) uneven

acci'dente [attʃi'dente] sm (*caso imprevisto*) accident; (*disgrazia*) mishap; **non si capisce un ~** it's as clear as mud; **~i!** (*fam: per rabbia*) damn (it)!; (*: per meraviglia*) good heavens!

accigli'ato, a [attʃiʎ'ʎato] ag frowning

ac'cingersi [at'tʃindʒersi] vr: **~ a fare qc** to be about to do sth

acciuf'fare [attʃuf'fare] vt to seize, catch

acci'uga, ghe [at'tʃuga] sf anchovy

accla'mare vt (*applaudire*) to applaud; (*eleggere*) to acclaim; **acclamazi'one** sf applause; acclamation

acclima'tare vt to acclimatize; **~rsi** vr to become acclimatized

ac'cludere vt to enclose; **ac'cluso, a** pp di **accludere ♦** ag enclosed

accocco'larsi vr to crouch

accogli'ente [akkoʎ'ʎente] ag welcoming, friendly; **accogli'enza** sf reception; welcome

ac'cogliere [ak'kɔʎʎere] vt (*ricevere*) to receive; (*dare il benvenuto*) to welcome; (*approvare*) to agree to, accept; (*contenere*) to hold, accommodate

accol'lato, a ag (*vestito*) high-necked

accoltel'lare vt to knife, stab

ac'colto, a pp di **accogliere**

accoman'dita sf (*DIR*) limited partnership

accomia'tare vt to dismiss; **~rsi** vr: **~rsi (da)** to take one's leave (of)

accomoda'mento sm agreement, settlement

accomo'dante ag accommodating

accomo'dare vt (*aggiustare*) to repair, mend; (*riordinare*) to tidy; (*conciliare*) to settle; **~rsi** vr (*sedersi*) to sit down; **s'accomodi!** (*venga avanti*) come in!; (*si sieda*) take a seat!

accompagna'mento [akkompaɲɲa'mento] sm (*MUS*) accompaniment

accompa'gnare [akkompaɲ'ɲare] vt to accompany, come o go with; (*MUS*) to accompany; (*unire*) to couple; **~ la porta** to close the door gently

accompagna'tore, trice sm/f companion; **~ turistico** courier

accomu'nare vt to pool, share; (*avvicinare*) to unite

acconcia'tura [akkontʃa'tura] sf hairstyle

accondi'scendere [akkondiʃ'ʃendere] vi: **~ a** to agree o consent to; **accondi'sceso, a** pp di **accondiscendere**

acconsen'tire vi: **~ (a)** to agree o consent (to)

acconten'tare vt to satisfy; **~rsi di** to be satisfied with, content o.s. with

ac'conto sm part payment; **pagare una somma in ~** to pay a sum of money as a deposit

accoppi'are vt to couple, pair off; (BIOL) to mate; **~rsi** vr to pair off; to mate

acco'rato, a ag heartfelt

accorci'are [akkor'tʃare] vt to shorten; **~rsi** vr to become shorter

accor'dare vt to reconcile; (colori) to match; (MUS) to tune; (LING): **~ qc con qc** to make sth agree with sth; (DIR) to grant; **~rsi** vr to agree, come to an agreement; (colori) to match

ac'cordo sm agreement; (armonia) harmony; (MUS) chord; **essere d'~** to agree; **andare d'~** to get on well together; **d'~!** all right!, agreed!

ac'corgersi [ak'kordʒersi] vr: **~ di** to notice; (fig) to realize; **accorgi'mento** sm shrewdness no pl; (espediente) trick, device

ac'correre vi to run up

ac'corso, a pp di **accorrere**

ac'corto, a pp di **accorgersi ♦** ag shrewd; **stare ~** to be on one's guard

accos'tare vt (avvicinare): **~ qc a** to bring sth near to, put sth near to; (avvicinarsi a) to approach; (socchiudere: imposte) to half-close; (: porta) to leave ajar ♦ vi (NAUT) to come alongside; **~rsi a** to draw near, approach; (fig) to support

accovacci'arsi [akkovat'tʃarsi] vr to crouch

accoz'zaglia [akkot'tsaʎʎa] (peg) sf (di idee, oggetti) jumble, hotchpotch

accredi'tare vt (notizia) to confirm the truth of; (COMM) to credit; (diplomatico) to accredit; **~rsi** vr (fig) to gain credit

ac'crescere [ak'kreʃʃere] vt to increase; **~rsi** vr to increase, grow; **accresci'tivo, a** ag, sm (LING) augmentative; **accresci'uto, a** pp di **accrescere**

accucci'arsi [akkut'tʃarsi] vr (cane) to lie down

accu'dire vt (anche: vi: **~ a**) to attend to

accumu'lare vt to accumulate

accumula'tore sm (ELETTR) accumulator

accura'tezza [akkura'tettsa] sf care; accuracy

accu'rato, a ag (diligente) careful; (preciso) accurate

ac'cusa sf accusation; (DIR) charge; **la pubblica ~** the prosecution

accu'sare vt: **~ qn di qc** to accuse sb of sth; (DIR) to charge sb with sth; **~ ricevuta di** (COMM) to acknowledge receipt of

accu'sato, a sm/f accused; defendant

accusa'tore, 'trice sm/f accuser ♦ sm (DIR) prosecutor

a'cerbo, a [a'tʃerbo] ag bitter; (frutta) sour, unripe; (persona) immature

'acero [a'tʃero] sm maple

a'cerrimo, a [a'tʃerrimo] ag very fierce

a'ceto [a'tʃeto] sm vinegar

ace'tone [atʃe'tone] sm nail varnish remover

A.C.I. ['atʃi] sigla m = Automobile Club d'Italia

'acido, a ['atʃido] ag (sapore) acid, sour; (CHIM) acid ♦ sm (CHIM) acid

'acino ['atʃino] sm berry; **~ d'uva** grape

'acne sf acne

'acqua sf water; (pioggia) rain; **~e** sfpl (di mare, fiume etc) waters; **fare ~** (NAUT) to leak, take in water; **~ in bocca!** mum's the word!; **~ corrente** running water; **~ dolce** fresh water; **~ minerale** mineral water; **~ potabile** drinking water; **~ salata** salt water; **~ tonica** tonic water

acqua'forte (pl **acque'forti**) sf etching

a'cquaio sm sink

acqua'ragia [akkwa'radʒa] sf turpentine

a'cquario sm aquarium; (dello zodiaco): **A~** Aquarius

acqua'santa sf holy water

ac'quatico, a, ci, che ag aquatic; (SPORT, SCIENZA) water cpd

acqua'vite sf brandy

acquaz'zone [akkwat'tsone] sm cloudburst, heavy shower

acque'dotto sm aqueduct; waterworks pl, water system

'acqueo, a ag: **vapore ~** water vapour

acque'rello sm watercolour

acqui'rente *sm/f* purchaser, buyer

acqui'sire *vt* to acquire

acquis'tare *vt* to purchase, buy; *(fig)* to gain; **a'cquisto** *sm* purchase; **fare acquisti** to go shopping

acqui'trino *sm* bog, marsh

acquo'lina *sf*: **far venire l'~ in bocca a qn** to make sb's mouth water

a'cquoso, a *ag* watery

'acre *ag* acrid, pungent; *(fig)* harsh, biting

a'crobata, i, e *sm/f* acrobat

acu'ire *vt* to sharpen

a'culeo *sm* (ZOOL) sting; (BOT) prickle

a'cume *sm* acumen, perspicacity

a'custica *sf* (*scienza*) acoustics *sg*; (*di una sala*) acoustics *pl*

a'cuto, a *ag* (*appuntito*) sharp, pointed; (*suono, voce*) shrill, piercing; (MAT, LING, MED) acute; (*fig: dolore, desiderio*) intense; (: *perspicace*) acute, keen

ad (*before V*) *prep* = **a**

adagi'are [ada'dʒare] *vt* to lay *o* set down carefully; **~rsi** *vr* to lie down, stretch out

a'dagio [a'dadʒo] *av* slowly ♦ *sm* (MUS) adagio; (*proverbio*) adage, saying

adatta'mento *sm* adaptation

adat'tare *vt* to adapt; (*sistemare*) to fit; **~rsi (a)** (*ambiente, tempi*) to adapt (to); (*essere adatto*) to be suitable (for)

a'datto, a *ag*: **~ (a)** suitable (for), right (for)

addebi'tare *vt*: **~ qc a qn** to debit sb with sth

ad'debito *sm* (COMM) debit

adden'sare *vt* to thicken; **~rsi** *vr* to thicken; (*nuvole*) to gather

adden'tare *vt* to bite into

adden'trarsi *vr*: **~ in** to penetrate, go into

ad'dentro *av*: **essere molto ~ in qc** to be well-versed in sth

addestra'mento *sm* training

addes'trare *vt* to train; **~rsi** *vr* to train; **~rsi in qc** to practise (BRIT) *o* practice (US) sth

ad'detto, a *ag*: **~ a** (*persona*) assigned to; (*oggetto*) intended for ♦ *sm* employee; (*funzionario*) attaché; **~ commerciale/**

stampa commercial/press attaché; **gli ~i ai lavori** authorized personnel; *(fig)* those in the know

addì *av* (AMM): **~ 3 luglio 1999** on the 3rd of July 1999 (BRIT), on July 3rd 1999 (US)

addi'accio [ad'djattʃo] *sm* (MIL) bivouac; **dormire all'~** to sleep in the open

addi'etro *av* (*indietro*) behind; (*nel passato, prima*) before, ago

ad'dio *sm, escl* goodbye, farewell

addirit'tura *av* (*veramente*) really, absolutely; (*perfino*) even; (*direttamente*) directly, right away

ad'dirsi *vr*: **~ a** to suit, be suitable for

addi'tare *vt* to point out; *(fig)* to expose

addi'tivo *sm* additive

addizio'nare [addittsjo'nare] *vt* (MAT) to add (up); **addizi'one** *sf* addition

addob'bare *vt* to decorate; **ad'dobbo** *sm* decoration

addol'cire [addol'tʃire] *vt* (*caffè etc*) to sweeten; (*acqua, fig: carattere*) to soften; **~rsi** *vr* (*fig*) to mellow, soften

addolo'rare *vt* to pain, grieve; **~rsi (per)** to be distressed (by)

ad'dome *sm* abdomen

addomesti'care *vt* to tame

addormen'tare *vt* to put to sleep; **~rsi** *vr* to fall asleep, go to sleep

addos'sare *vt* (*appoggiare*): **~ qc a qc** to lean sth against sth; *(fig)*: **~ la colpa a qn** to lay the blame on sb; **~rsi qc** (*responsabilità etc*) to shoulder sth

ad'dosso *av* on; **mettersi ~ il cappotto** to put one's coat on; **~ a** (*sopra*) on; (*molto vicino*) right next to; **stare ~ a qn** (*fig*) to breathe down sb's neck; **dare ~ a qn** (*fig*) to attack sb

ad'dotto, a *pp di* **addurre**

ad'durre *vt* (DIR) to produce; (*citare*) to cite

adegu'are *vt*: **~ qc a** to adjust *o* relate sth to; **~rsi** *vr* to adapt; **adegu'ato, a** *ag* adequate; (*conveniente*) suitable; (*equo*) fair

a'dempiere *vt* to fulfil, carry out

adem'pire *vt* = **adempiere**

ade'rente *ag* adhesive; (*vestito*) close-fitting ♦ *sm/f* follower; **ade'renza** *sf* adhesion; **aderenze** *sfpl* connections, contacts

ade'rire *vi* (*stare attaccato*) to adhere, stick; ~ **a** to adhere to, stick to; (*fig: società, partito*) to join; (: *opinione*) to support; (*richiesta*) to agree to

ades'care *vt* to lure, entice

adesi'one *sf* adhesion; (*fig*) agreement, acceptance; **ade'sivo, a** *ag*, *sm* adhesive

a'desso *av* (*ora*) now; (*or ora, poco fa*) just now; (*tra poco*) any moment now

adia'cente [adja'tʃɛnte] *ag* adjacent

adi'bire *vt* (*usare*): ~ **qc a** to turn sth into

adi'rarsi *vr*: ~ (**con** *o* **contro qn per qc**) to get angry (with sb over sth)

a'dire *vt* (*DIR*): ~ **le vie legali** to take legal proceedings

'adito *sm*: **dare** ~ **a** to give rise to

adocchi'are [adok'kjare] *vt* (*scorgere*) to catch sight of; (*occhieggiare*) to eye

adole'scente [adoleʃ'ʃɛnte] *ag*, *sm/f* adolescent; **adole'scenza** *sf* adolescence

adope'rare *vt* to use; ~**rsi** *vr* to strive; ~**rsi per qn/qc** to do one's best for sb/sth

ado'rare *vt* to adore; (*REL*) to adore, worship

adot'tare *vt* to adopt; (*decisione, provvedimenti*) to pass; **adot'tivo, a** *ag* (*genitori*) adoptive; (*figlio, patria*) adopted; **adozi'one** *sf* adoption

adri'atico, a, ci, che *ag* Adriatic ♦ *sm*: **l'A~, il mare A~** the Adriatic, the Adriatic Sea

adu'lare *vt* to adulate, flatter

adulte'rare *vt* to adulterate

adul'terio *sm* adultery

a'dulto, a *ag* adult; (*fig*) mature ♦ *sm* adult, grown-up

adu'nanza [adu'nantsa] *sf* assembly, meeting

adu'nare *vt* to assemble, gather; ~**rsi** *vr* to assemble, gather; **adu'nata** *sf* (*MIL*) parade, muster

a'dunco, a, chi, che *ag* hooked

a'ereo, a *ag* air *cpd*; (*radice*) aerial ♦ *sm* aerial; (*aeroplano*) plane; ~ **a reazione** jet (plane); ~ **da caccia** fighter (plane); ~ **di**

linea airliner; **ae'robica** *sf* aerobics *sg*;
aerodi'namica *sf* aerodynamics *sg*;
aerodi'namico, a, ci, che *ag*
aerodynamic; (*affusolato*) streamlined;
aero'nautica *sf* (*scienza*) aeronautics *sg*;
aeronautica militare air force;
aero'plano *sm* (aero)plane (*BRIT*),
(air)plane (*US*)

aero'porto *sm* airport

aero'sol *sm inv* aerosol

'afa *sf* sultriness

af'fabile *ag* affable

affaccen'dato, a [affattʃen'dato] *ag*
(*persona*) busy

affacci'arsi [affat'tʃarsi] *vr*: ~ (**a**) to appear
(at)

affa'mato, a *ag* starving; (*fig*): ~ (**di**) eager
(for)

affan'nare *vt* to leave breathless; (*fig*) to
worry; ~**rsi** *vr*: ~**rsi per qn/qc** to worry
about sb/sth; **af'fanno** *sm* breathlessness;
(*fig*) anxiety, worry; **affan'noso, a** *ag*
(*respiro*) difficult; (*fig*) troubled, anxious

af'fare *sm* (*faccenda*) matter, affair; (*COMM*)
piece of business, (business) deal;
(*occasione*) bargain; (*DIR*) case; (*fam: cosa*)
thing; ~**i** *smpl* (*COMM*) business *sg*;
Ministro degli A~i esteri Foreign Secretary
(*BRIT*), Secretary of State (*US*); **affa'rista, i**
sm profiteer, unscrupulous businessman

affasci'nante [affaʃʃi'nante] *ag* fascinating

affasci'nare [affaʃʃi'nare] *vt* to bewitch;
(*fig*) to charm, fascinate

affati'care *vt* to tire; ~**rsi** *vr* (*durar fatica*)
to tire o.s. out

af'fatto *av* completely; **non ...** ~ not ... at
all; **niente** ~ not at all

affer'mare *vt* (*dichiarare*) to maintain,
affirm; ~**rsi** *vr* to assert o.s., make one's
name known; **affermazi'one** *sf*
affirmation, assertion; (*successo*)
achievement

affer'rare *vt* to seize, grasp; (*fig: idea*) to
grasp; ~**rsi** *vr*: ~**rsi a** to cling to

affet'tare *vt* (*tagliare a fette*) to slice;
(*ostentare*) to affect; **affet'tato, a** *ag*
sliced; affected ♦ *sm* sliced cold meat

affet'tivo, a *ag* emotional, affective

af'fetto *sm* affection; **affettu'oso, a** *ag* affectionate

affezio'narsi [affettsjo'narsi] *vr*: ~ **a** to grow fond of

affian'care *vt* to place side by side; (*MIL*) to flank; (*fig*) to support; ~ **a qc a qc** to place sth next to *o* beside sth; **~rsi a qn** to stand beside sb

affia'tato, a *ag*: **essere molto ~i** to get on very well

affibbi'are *vt* (*fig: dare*) to give

affi'dabile *ag* reliable

affida'mento *sm* (*DIR: di bambino*) custody; (*fiducia*): **fare ~ su qn** to rely on sb; **non dà nessun ~** he's not to be trusted

affi'dare *vt*: ~ **qc o qn a qn** to entrust sth *o* sb to sb; **~rsi** *vr*: **~rsi a** to place one's trust in

affievo'lirsi *vr* to grow weak

af'figgere [af'fiddʒere] *vt* to stick up, post up

affi'lare *vt* to sharpen

affili'arsi *vr*: ~ **a** to become affiliated to

affi'nare *vt* to sharpen

affinché [affin'ke] *cong* in order that, so that

af'fine *ag* similar; **affinità** *sf inv* affinity

affio'rare *vi* to emerge

affissi'one *sf* billposting

af'fisso, a *pp di* **affiggere** ♦ *sm* bill, poster; (*LING*) affix

affit'tare *vt* (*dare in affitto*) to let, rent (out); (*prendere in affitto*) to rent; **af'fitto** *sm* rent; (*contratto*) lease

af'fliggere [af'fliddʒere] *vt* to torment; **~rsi** *vr* to grieve; **af'flitto, a** *pp di* **affliggere**; **afflizi'one** *sf* distress, torment

afflosci'arsi [affloʃ'farsi] *vr* to go limp

afflu'ente *sm* tributary; **afflu'enza** *sf* flow; (*di persone*) crowd

afflu'ire *vi* to flow; (*fig: merci, persone*) to pour in; **af'flusso** *sm* influx

affo'gare *vt, vi* to drown; **~rsi** *vr* to drown; (*deliberatamente*) to drown o.s.

affol'lare *vt* to crowd; **~rsi** *vr* to crowd;

affol'lato, a *ag* crowded

affon'dare *vt* to sink

affran'care *vt* to free, liberate; (*AMM*) to redeem; (*lettera*) to stamp; (: *meccanicamente*) to frank (*BRIT*), meter (*US*); **~rsi** *vr* to free o.s.; **affranca'tura** *sf* (*di francobollo*) stamping; franking (*BRIT*), metering (*US*); (*tassa di spedizione*) postage

af'franto, a *ag* (*esausto*) worn out; (*abbattuto*) overcome

af'fresco, schi *sm* fresco

affret'tare *vt* to quicken, speed up; **~rsi** *vr* to hurry; **~rsi a fare qc** to hurry *o* hasten to do sth

affron'tare *vt* (*pericolo etc*) to face; (*nemico*) to confront; **~rsi** *vr* (*reciproco*) to come to blows

af'fronto *sm* affront, insult

affumi'care *vt* to fill with smoke; to blacken with smoke; (*alimenti*) to smoke

affuso'lato, a *ag* tapering

a'foso, a *ag* sultry, close

'Africa *sf*: **l'~** Africa; **afri'cano, a** *ag, sm/f* African

afrodi'siaco, a, ci, che *ag, sm* aphrodisiac

a'genda [a'dʒɛnda] *sf* diary

a'gente [a'dʒɛnte] *sm* agent; ~ **di cambio** stockbroker; ~ **di polizia** police officer; **agen'zia** *sf* agency; (*succursale*) branch; **agenzia di collocamento** employment agency; **agenzia immobiliare** estate agent's (office) (*BRIT*), real estate office (*US*); **agenzia pubblicitaria/viaggi** advertising/travel agency

agevo'lare [adʒevo'lare] *vt* to facilitate, make easy

a'gevole [a'dʒevole] *ag* easy; (*strada*) smooth

aggan'ciare [aggan'tʃare] *vt* to hook up; (*FERR*) to couple

ag'geggio [ad'dʒeddʒo] *sm* gadget, contraption

agget'tivo [addʒet'tivo] *sm* adjective

agghiacci'ante [aggjat'tʃante] *ag* chilling

agghin'darsi [aggin'darsi] *vr* to deck o.s. out

aggior'nare [addʒor'nare] *vt* (*opera, manuale*) to bring up-to-date; (*seduta etc*) to postpone; **~rsi** *vr* to bring (*o* keep) o.s. up-to-date; **aggior'nato, a** *ag* up-to-date

aggi'rare [addʒi'rare] *vt* to go round; (*fig: ingannare*) to trick; **~rsi** *vr* to wander about; **il prezzo s'aggira sul milione** the price is around the million mark

aggiudi'care [addʒudi'kare] *vt* to award; (*all'asta*) to knock down; **~rsi qc** to win sth

aggi'ungere [ad'dʒundʒere] *vt* to add; **aggi'unta** *sf* addition; **aggi'unto, a** *pp di* **aggiungere ♦** *ag* assistant *cpd* ♦ *sm* assistant

aggius'tare [addʒus'tare] *vt* (*accomodare*) to mend, repair; (*riassettare*) to adjust; (*fig: lite*) to settle; **~rsi** *vr* (*arrangiarsi*) to make do; (*con senso reciproco*) to come to an agreement

agglome'rato *sm* (*di rocce*) conglomerate; (*di legno*) chipboard; **~ urbano** built-up area

aggrap'parsi *vr*: **~ a** to cling to

aggra'vare *vt* (*aumentare*) to increase; (*appesantire: anche fig*) to weigh down, make heavy; (*pena*) to make worse; **~rsi** *vr* to worsen, become worse

aggrazi'ato, a [aggrat'tsjato] *ag* graceful

aggre'dire *vt* to attack, assault

aggre'gare *vt*: **~ qn a qc** to admit sb to sth; **~rsi** *vr* to join; **~rsi a** to join, become a member of

aggressi'one *sf* aggression; (*atto*) attack, assault

aggres'sivo, a *ag* aggressive

aggrot'tare *vt*: **~ le sopracciglia** to frown

aggrovigli'are [aggroviʎ'ʎare] *vt* to tangle; **~rsi** *vr* (*fig*) to become complicated

agguan'tare *vt* to catch, seize

aggu'ato *sm* trap; (*imboscata*) ambush; **tendere un ~ a qn** to set a trap for sb

agguer'rito, a *ag* fierce

agi'ato, a [a'dʒato] *ag* (*vita*) easy; (*persona*) well-off, well-to-do

'agile ['adʒile] *ag* agile, nimble; **agilità** *sf* agility, nimbleness

'agio ['adʒo] *sm* ease, comfort; **mettersi a proprio ~** to make o.s. at home *o* comfortable

a'gire [a'dʒire] *vi* to act; (*esercitare un'azione*) to take effect; (*TECN*) to work, function; **~ contro qn** (*DIR*) to take action against sb

agi'tare [adʒi'tare] *vt* (*bottiglia*) to shake; (*mano, fazzoletto*) to wave; (*fig: turbare*) to disturb; (: *incitare*) to stir (up); (: *dibattere*) to discuss; **~rsi** *vr* (*mare*) to be rough; (*malato, dormitore*) to toss and turn; (*bambino*) to fidget; (*emozionarsi*) to get upset; (*POL*) to agitate; **agi'tato, a** *ag* rough; restless; fidgety; upset, perturbed; **agitazi'one** *sf* agitation; (*POL*) unrest, agitation; **mettere in agitazione qn** to upset *o* distress sb

'agli ['aʎʎi] *prep + det vedi* **a**

'aglio ['aʎʎo] *sm* garlic

a'gnello [aɲ'ɲello] *sm* lamb

'ago (*pl* **'aghi**) *sm* needle

ago'nia *sf* agony

ago'nistico, a, ci, che *ag* athletic; (*fig*) competitive

agoniz'zare [agonid'dzare] *vi* to be dying

agopun'tura *sf* acupuncture

a'gosto *sm* August

a'graria *sf* agriculture

a'grario, a *ag* agrarian, agricultural; (*riforma*) land *cpd*

a'gricolo, a *ag* agricultural, farm *cpd*; **agricol'tore** *sm* farmer; **agricol'tura** *sf* agriculture, farming

agri'foglio [agri'fɔʎʎo] *sm* holly

agrimen'sore *sm* land surveyor

agritu'rismo *sm* farm holidays *pl*

'agro, a *ag* sour, sharp; **~dolce** *ag* bittersweet; (*salsa*) sweet and sour

a'grume *sm* (*spesso al pl: pianta*) citrus; (: *frutto*) citrus fruit

aguz'zare [agut'tsare] *vt* to sharpen; **~ gli orecchi** to prick up one's ears

a'guzzo, a [a'guttso] *ag* sharp

'ai *prep + det vedi* **a**

'Aia *sf*: **l'~** the Hague

'aia *sf* threshing floor

AIDS *sigla f o m* AIDS

ai'rone *sm* heron

aiu'ola *sf* flower bed

aiu'tante *sm/f* assistant ♦ *sm* (*MIL*) adjutant; (*NAUT*) master-at-arms; **~ di campo** aide-de-camp

aiu'tare *vt* to help; **~ qn (a fare)** to help sb (to do)

ai'uto *sm* help, assistance, aid; (*aiutante*) assistant; **venire in ~ di qn** to come to sb's aid; **~ chirurgo** assistant surgeon

aiz'zare [ait'tsare] *vt* to incite; **~ i cani contro qn** to set the dogs on sb

al *prep* + *det vedi* **a**

'ala (*pl* **'ali**) *sf* wing; **fare ~** to fall back, make way; **~ destra/sinistra** (*SPORT*) right/left wing

'alacre *ag* quick, brisk

a'lano *sm* Great Dane

a'lare *ag* wing *cpd*

'alba *sf* dawn

Alba'nia *sf*: **l'~** Albania

'albatro *sm* albatross

albeggi'are [albed'dʒare] *vi*, *vb impers* to dawn

alberghi'ero, a [alber'gjɛro] *ag* hotel *cpd*

al'bergo, ghi *sm* hotel; **~ della gioventù** youth hostel

'albero *sm* tree; (*NAUT*) mast; (*TECN*) shaft; **~ genealogico** family tree; **~ a gomiti** crankshaft; **~ di Natale** Christmas tree; **~ maestro** mainmast; **~ di trasmissione** transmission shaft

albi'cocca, che *sf* apricot; **albi'cocco, chi** *sm* apricot tree

'albo *sm* (*registro*) register, roll; (*AMM*) notice board

'album *sm* album; **~ da disegno** sketch book

al'bume *sm* albumen

'alce ['altʃe] *sm* elk

al'colico, a, ci, che *ag* alcoholic ♦ *sm* alcoholic drink

alcoliz'zato, a [alkolid'dzato] *sm/f* alcoholic

'alcool *sm* alcohol; **alco'olico** *etc* = **alcolico** *etc*

al'cuno, a (*det: dav sm:* **alcun** +*C*, *V*,

alcuno +*s impura, gn, pn, ps, x, z; dav sf:* **alcuna** +*C*, **alcun'** +*V*) *det* (*nessuno*): **non ... ~** no, not any; **~i, e** *det pl* some, a few; **non c'è ~a fretta** there's no hurry, there isn't any hurry; **senza alcun riguardo** without any consideration ♦ *pron pl:* **~i, e** some, a few

aldilà *sm*: **l'~** the after-life

alfa'beto *sm* alphabet

alfi'ere *sm* standard-bearer; (*MIL*) ensign; (*SCACCHI*) bishop

'alga, ghe *sf* seaweed *no pl*, alga

'algebra ['aldʒebra] *sf* algebra

Alge'ria [aldʒe'ria] *sf*: **l'~** Algeria

ali'ante *sm* (*AER*) glider

'alibi *sm inv* alibi

a'lice [a'litʃe] *sf* anchovy

alie'nare *vt* (*DIR*) to alienate, transfer; (*rendere ostile*) to alienate; **~rsi qn** to alienate sb; **alie'nato, a** *ag* alienated; transferred; (*fuor di senno*) insane ♦ *sm* lunatic, insane person; **alienazi'one** *sf* alienation; transfer; insanity

ali'eno, a *ag* (*avverso*): **~ (da)** opposed (to), averse (to) ♦ *sm/f* alien

alimen'tare *vt* to feed; (*TECN*) to feed; to supply; (*fig*) to sustain ♦ *ag* food *cpd*; **~i** *smpl* foodstuffs; (*anche:* **negozio di ~i**) grocer's shop; **alimentazi'one** *sf* feeding; supplying; sustaining; (*gli alimenti*) diet

ali'mento *sm* food; **~i** *smpl* (*cibo*) food *sg*; (*DIR*) alimony

a'liquota *sf* share; (*d'imposta*) rate

alis'cafo *sm* hydrofoil

'alito *sm* breath

all. *abbr* (= *allegato*) encl.

'alla *prep* + *det vedi* **a**

allacci'are [allat'tʃare] *vt* (*scarpe*) to tie, lace (up); (*cintura*) to do up, fasten; (*luce, gas*) to connect; (*amicizia*) to form

alla'gare *vt* to flood; **~rsi** *vr* to flood

allar'gare *vt* to widen; (*vestito*) to let out; (*aprire*) to open; (*fig: dilatare*) to extend

allar'mare *vt* to alarm

al'larme *sm* alarm; **~ aereo** air-raid warning

allar'mismo *sm* scaremongering

allat'tare *vt* to feed

'alle *prep + det vedi* **a**

alle'anza [alle'antsa] *sf* alliance

alle'arsi *vr* to form an alliance; **alle'ato, a** *ag* allied ♦ *sm/f* ally

alle'gare *vt* (*accludere*) to enclose; (*DIR: citare*) to cite, adduce; (*denti*) to set on edge; **alle'gato, a** *ag* enclosed ♦ *sm* enclosure; **in allegato** enclosed

allegge'rire [alledd3e'rire] *vt* to lighten, make lighter; (*fig: lavoro, tasse*) to reduce

alle'gria *sf* gaiety, cheerfulness

al'legro, a *ag* cheerful, merry; (*un po' brillo*) merry, tipsy; (*vivace: colore*) bright ♦ *sm* (*MUS*) allegro

allena'mento *sm* training

alle'nare *vt* to train; **~rsi** *vr* to train; **allena'tore** *sm* (*SPORT*) trainer, coach

allen'tare *vt* to slacken; (*disciplina*) to relax; **~rsi** *vr* to become slack; (*Ingranaggio*) to work loose

aller'gia, 'gie [aller'd3ia] *sf* allergy; **al'lergico, a, ci, che** *ag* allergic

alles'tire *vt* (*cena*) to prepare; (*esercito, nave*) to equip, fit out; (*spettacolo*) to stage

allet'tare *vt* to lure, entice

alleva'mento *sm* breeding, rearing; (*luogo*) stock farm

alle'vare *vt* (*animale*) to breed, rear; (*bambino*) to bring up

allevi'are *vt* to alleviate

alli'bito, a *ag* astounded

allibra'tore *sm* bookmaker

allie'tare *vt* to cheer up, gladden

alli'evo *sm* pupil; (*apprendista*) apprentice; (*MIL*) cadet

alliga'tore *sm* alligator

alline'are *vt* (*persone, cose*) to line up; (*TIP*) to align; (*fig: economia, salari*) to adjust, align; **~rsi** *vr* to line up; (*fig: a idee*): **~rsi a** to come into line with

'allo *prep + det vedi* **a**

al'locco, a, chi, che *sm* tawny owl ♦ *sm/f* oaf

allocuzi'one [allokut'tsjone] *sf* address, solemn speech

al'lodola *sf* (sky)lark

alloggi'are [allod'd3are] *vt* to accommodate ♦ *vi* to live; **al'loggio** *sm* lodging, accommodation (*BRIT*), accommodations (*US*)

allontana'mento *sm* removal; dismissal

allonta'nare *vt* to send away, send off; (*impiegato*) to dismiss; (*pericolo*) to avert, remove; (*estraniare*) to alienate; **~rsi** *vr*: **~rsi (da)** to go away (from); (*estraniarsi*) to become estranged (from)

al'lora *av* (*in quel momento*) then ♦ *cong* (*in questo caso*) well then; (*dunque*) well then, so; **la gente d'~** people then *o* in those days; **da ~ in poi** from then on

allor'ché [allor'ke] *cong* (*formale*) when, as soon as

al'loro *sm* laurel

'alluce ['allutʃe] *sm* big toe

alluci'nante [allutʃi'nante] *ag* awful; (*fam*) amazing

allucinazi'one [allutʃinat'tsjone] *sf* hallucination

al'ludere *vi*: **~ a** to allude to, hint at

allu'minio *sm* aluminium (*BRIT*), aluminum (*US*)

allun'gare *vt* to lengthen; (*distendere*) to prolong, extend; (*diluire*) to water down; **~rsi** *vr* to lengthen; (*ragazzo*) to stretch, grow taller; (*sdraiarsi*) to lie down, stretch out

allusi'one *sf* hint, allusion

al'luso, a *pp di* **alludere**

alluvi'one *sf* flood

al'meno *av* at least ♦ *cong*: **(se) ~** if only; **(se) ~ piovesse!** if only it would rain!

a'logeno, a [a'lɔdʒeno] *ag*: **lampada ~a** halogen lamp

a'lone *sm* halo

'Alpi *sfpl*: **le ~** the Alps

alpi'nismo *sm* mountaineering, climbing; **alpi'nista, i, e** *sm/f* mountaineer, climber

al'pino, a *ag* Alpine; mountain *cpd*

al'quanto *av* rather, a little; **~, a** *det* a certain amount of, some ♦ *pron* a certain amount, some; **~i, e** *det pl, pron pl* several, quite a few

alt *escl* halt!, stop!

alta'lena *sf* (*a funi*) swing; (*in bilico, anche fig*) seesaw

al'tare *sm* altar

alte'rare *vt* to alter, change; (*cibo*) to adulterate; (*registro*) to falsify; (*persona*) to irritate; **~rsi** *vr* (*cibo*) to go bad; (*persona*) to lose one's temper

al'terco, chi *sm* altercation, wrangle

alter'nare *vt* to alternate; **~rsi** *vr* to alternate; **alterna'tiva** *sf* alternative; **alterna'tivo, a** *ag* alternative; **alter'nato, a** *ag* alternate; (*ELETTR*) alternating; **alterna'tore** *sm* alternator

al'terno, a *ag* alternate; **a giorni ~i** on alternate days, every other day

al'tezza [al'tettsa] *sf* height; width, breadth; depth; pitch; (*GEO*) latitude; (*titolo*) highness; (*fig: nobiltà*) greatness; **essere all'~ di** to be on a level with; (*fig*) to be up to *o* equal to; **altez'zoso, a** *ag* haughty

al'ticcio, a, ci, ce [al'tittʃo] *ag* tipsy

altipi'ano *sm* = **altopiano**

alti'tudine *sf* altitude

'alto, a *ag* high; (*persona*) tall; (*tessuto*) wide, broad; (*sonno, acque*) deep; (*suono*) high(-pitched); (*GEO*) upper; (*: settentrionale*) northern ♦ *sm* top (part) ♦ *av* high; (*parlare*) aloud, loudly; **il palazzo è ~ 20 metri** the building is 20 metres high; **ad ~a voce** aloud; **a notte ~a** in the dead of night; **in ~** up, upwards; at the top; **dall'~ in** *o* **al basso** up and down; **degli ~i e bassi** (*fig*) ups and downs; **~a fedeltà** high fidelity, hi-fi; **~a finanza** high finance; **~a moda** haute couture; **~a società** high society

alto'forno *sm* blast furnace

altolo'cato, a *ag* of high rank

altopar'lante *sm* loudspeaker

altopi'ano (*pl* **altipi'ani**) *sm* plateau, upland plain

altret'tanto, a *ag, pron* as much; (*pl*) as many ♦ *av* equally; **tanti auguri! – grazie, ~** all the best! — thank you, the same to you

'altri *pron inv* (*qualcuno*) somebody; (*: in espressioni negative*) anybody; (*un'altra persona*) another (person)

altri'menti *av* otherwise

PAROLA CHIAVE

'altro, a *det* **1** (*diverso*) other, different; **questa è un'~a cosa** that's another *o* a different thing

2 (*supplementare*) other; **prendi un ~ cioccolatino** have another chocolate; **hai avuto ~e notizie?** have you had any more *o* any other news?

3 (*nel tempo*): **l'~ giorno** the other day; **l'altr'anno** last year; **l'~ ieri** the day before yesterday; **domani l'~** the day after tomorrow; **quest'~ mese** next month

4: **d'~a parte** on the other hand

♦ *pron* **1** (*persona, cosa diversa o supplementare*): **un ~, un'~a** another (one); **lo farà un ~** someone else will do it; **~i, e** others; **gli ~i** (*la gente*) others, other people; **l'uno e l'~** both (of them); **aiutarsi l'un l'~** to help one another; **da un giorno all'~** from day to day; (*nel giro di 24 ore*) from one day to the next; (*da un momento all'altro*) any day now

2 (*sostantivato: solo maschile*) something else; (*: in espressioni interrogative*) anything else; **non ho ~ da dire** I have nothing else *o* I don't have anything else to say; **più che ~** above all; **se non ~** at least; **tra l'~** among other things; **ci mancherebbe ~!** that's all we need!; **non faccio ~ che lavorare** I do nothing but work; **contento? – ~ che!** are you pleased? — and how!; *vedi* **senza; noialtri; voialtri; tutto**

---

al'tronde *av*: **d'~** on the other hand

al'trove *av* elsewhere, somewhere else

al'trui *ag inv* other people's ♦ *sm*: **l'~** other people's belongings *pl*

altru'ista, i, e *ag* altruistic

al'tura *sf* (*rialto*) height, high ground; (*alto mare*) open sea; **pesca d'~** deep-sea fishing

a'lunno, a *sm/f* pupil

alve'are *sm* hive

'alveo *sm* riverbed

al'zare [al'tsare] *vt* to raise, lift; (*issare*) to hoist; (*costruire*) to build, erect; **~rsi** *vr* to rise; (*dal letto*) to get up; (*crescere*) to grow tall (*o* taller); **~ le spalle** to shrug one's shoulders; **~rsi in piedi** to stand up, get to one's feet; **al'zata** *sf* lifting, raising; **un'alzata di spalle** a shrug

a'mabile *ag* lovable; (*vino*) sweet

a'maca, che *sf* hammock

amalga'mare *vt* to amalgamate

a'mante *ag*: **~ di** (*musica etc*) fond of ♦ *sm/f* lover/mistress

a'mare *vt* to love; (*amico, musica, sport*) to like

amareggi'ato, a [amared'dʒato] *ag* upset, saddened

ama'rena *sf* sour black cherry

ama'rezza [ama'rettsa] *sf* bitterness

a'maro, a *ag* bitter ♦ *sm* bitterness; (*liquore*) bitters *pl*

ambasci'ata [ambaʃ'ʃata] *sf* embassy; (*messaggio*) message; **ambascia'tore, 'trice** *sm/f* ambassador/ambassadress

ambe'due *ag inv*: **~ i ragazzi** both boys ♦ *pron inv* both

ambien'tare *vt* to acclimatize; (*romanzo, film*) to set; **~rsi** *vr* to get used to one's surroundings

ambi'ente *sm* environment; (*fig: insieme di persone*) milieu; (*stanza*) room

am'biguo, a *ag* ambiguous

am'bire *vt* (*anche: vi*: **~ a**) to aspire to

'ambito *sm* sphere, field

ambizi'one [ambit'tsjone] *sf* ambition; **ambizi'oso, a** *ag* ambitious

'ambo *ag inv* both ♦ (*al gioco*) double

'ambra *sf* amber; **~ grigia** ambergris

ambu'lante *ag* itinerant ♦ *sm* peddler

ambu'lanza [ambu'lantsa] *sf* ambulance

ambula'torio *sm* (*studio medico*) surgery

a'meno, a *ag* pleasant; (*strano*) funny

A'merica *sf*: **l'~** America; **l'~ latina** Latin America; **ameri'cano, a** *ag, sm/f* American

ami'anto *sm* asbestos

a'mica *sf vedi* **amico**

ami'chevole [ami'kevole] *ag* friendly

ami'cizia [ami'tʃittsja] *sf* friendship; **~e** *sfpl* (*amici*) friends

a'mico, a, ci, che *sm/f* friend; (*fidanzato*) boyfriend/girlfriend; **~ del cuore** *o* **intimo** bosom friend

'amido *sm* starch

ammac'care *vt* (*pentola*) to dent; (*persona*) to bruise; **~rsi** *vr* to bruise

ammaes'trare *vt* (*animale*) to train

ammai'nare *vt* to lower, haul down

amma'larsi *vr* to fall ill; **amma'lato, a** *ag* ill, sick ♦ *sm/f* sick person; (*paziente*) patient

ammali'are *vt* (*fig*) to enchant, charm

am'manco, chi *sm* deficit

ammanet'tare *vt* to handcuff

ammas'sare *vt* (*ammucchiare*) to amass; (*raccogliere*) to gather together; **~rsi** *vr* to pile up; to gather; **am'masso** *sm* mass; (*mucchio*) pile, heap; (*ECON*) stockpile

ammat'tire *vi* to go mad

ammaz'zare *vt* to kill; **~rsi** *vr* (*uccidersi*) to kill o.s.; (*rimanere ucciso*) to be killed; **~rsi di lavoro** to work o.s. to death

am'menda *sf* amends *pl*; (*DIR, SPORT*) fine

am'messo, a *pp di* **ammettere** ♦ *cong*: **~ che** supposing that

am'mettere *vt* to admit; (*riconoscere: fatto*) to acknowledge, admit; (*permettere*) to allow, accept; (*supporre*) to suppose

ammez'zato [ammed'dzato] *sm* (*anche: piano ~*) mezzanine, entresol

ammic'care *vi*: **~ (a)** to wink (at)

amminis'trare *vt* to run, manage; (*REL, DIR*) to administer; **amministra'tivo, a** *ag* administrative; **amministra'tore** *sm* administrator; (*di condominio*) flats manager; **amministratore delegato** managing director; **amministrazi'one** *sf* management; administration

ammiragli'ato [ammiraʎ'ʎato] *sm* admiralty

ammi'raglio [ammi'raʎʎo] *sm* admiral

ammi'rare *vt* to admire; **ammira'tore, 'trice** *sm/f* admirer; **ammirazi'one** *sf*

admiration
ammissi'one *sf* admission
ammobili'ato, a *ag* furnished
am'modo *av* properly ♦ *ag inv*
respectable, nice
am'mollo *sm*: **lasciare in ~** to leave to
soak
ammo'niaca *sf* ammonia
ammoni'mento *sm* warning;
admonishment
ammo'nire *vt* (*avvertire*) to warn;
(*rimproverare*) to admonish; (*DIR*) to caution
ammon'tare *vi*: **~ a** to amount to ♦ *sm*
(*total*) amount
ammorbi'dente *sm* fabric conditioner
ammorbi'dire *vt* to soften
ammortiz'zare [ammortid'dzare] *vt* (*ECON*)
to pay off, amortize; (*: spese d'impianto*) to
write off; (*AUT, TECN*) to absorb, deaden;
ammortizza'tore *sm* (*AUT, TECN*) shock-
absorber
ammucchi'are [ammuk'kjare] *vt* to pile
up, accumulate
ammuf'fire *vi* to go mouldy (*BRIT*) *o* moldy
(*US*)
ammutina'mento *sm* mutiny
ammuto'lire *vi* to be struck dumb
amnis'tia *sf* amnesty
'amo *sm* (*PESCA*) hook; (*fig*) bait
a'modo *av* = **ammodo**
a'more *sm* love; **~i** *smpl* love affairs; **il tuo
bambino è un ~** your baby's a darling;
fare l'~ *o* **all'~** to make love; **per ~ o per
forza** by hook or by crook; **amor proprio**
self-esteem, pride; **amo'revole** *ag* loving,
affectionate
a'morfo, a *ag* amorphous; (*fig: persona*)
lifeless
amo'roso, a *ag* (*affettuoso*) loving,
affectionate; (*d'amore: sguardo*) amorous;
(*: poesia, relazione*) love *cpd*
ampi'ezza [am'pjettsa] *sf* width, breadth;
spaciousness; (*fig: importanza*) scale, size
'ampio, a *ag* wide, broad; (*spazioso*)
spacious; (*abbondante: vestito*) loose;
(*: gonna*) full; (*: spiegazione*) ample, full
am'plesso *sm* intercourse

ampli'are *vt* (*ingrandire*) to enlarge;
(*allargare*) to widen
amplifi'care *vt* to amplify;
amplifica'tore *sm* (*TECN, MUS*) amplifier
am'polla *sf* (*vasetto*) cruet
ampu'tare *vt* (*MED*) to amputate
amu'leto *sm* lucky charm
anabbagli'ante [anabbaʎ'ʎante] *ag* (*AUT*)
dipped (*BRIT*), dimmed (*US*); **~i** *smpl*
dipped (*BRIT*) *o* dimmed (*US*) headlights
a'nagrafe *sf* (*registro*) register of births,
marriages and deaths; (*ufficio*) registry
office (*BRIT*), office of vital statistics (*US*)
anal'colico, a, ci, che *ag* non-alcoholic
♦ *sm* soft drink
analfa'beta, i, e *ag, sm/f* illiterate
anal'gesico, a, ci, che [anal'dʒeziko] *ag,
sm* analgesic
a'nalisi *sf inv* analysis; (*MED: esame*) test; **~
grammaticale** parsing; **ana'lista, i, e**
sm/f analyst; (*PSIC*) (psycho)analyst
analiz'zare [analid'dzare] *vt* to analyse;
(*MED*) to test
analo'gia, 'gie [analo'dʒia] *sf* analogy
a'nalogo, a, ghi, ghe *ag* analogous
'ananas *sm inv* pineapple
anar'chia [anar'kia] *sf* anarchy;
a'narchico, a, ci, che *ag* anarchic(al)
♦ *sm/f* anarchist
'ANAS *sigla f* (*= Azienda Nazionale
Autonoma delle Strade*) national roads
department
anato'mia *sf* anatomy; **ana'tomico, a,
ci, che** *ag* anatomical; (*sedile*) contoured
'anatra *sf* duck
'anca, che *sf* (*ANAT*) hip
'anche ['anke] *cong* (*inoltre, pure*) also, too;
(*perfino*) even; **vengo anch'io** I'm coming
too; **~ se** even if
an'cora¹ *av* still; (*di nuovo*) again; (*di più*)
some more; (*persino*): **~ più forte** even
stronger; **non ~** not yet; **~ una volta** once
more, once again; **~ un po'** a little more;
(*di tempo*) a little longer
'ancora² *sf* anchor; **gettare/levare l'~** to
cast/weigh anchor; **anco'raggio** *sm*
anchorage; **anco'rare** *vt* to anchor;

ancorarsi *vr* to anchor

anda'mento *sm* progress, movement; course; state

an'dante *ag (corrente)* current; *(di poco pregio)* cheap, second-rate ♦ *sm (MUS)* andante

an'dare *sm*: **a lungo ~** in the long run ♦ *vi* to go; *(essere adatto)*: **~ a** to suit; *(piacere)*: **il suo comportamento non mi va** I don't like the way he behaves; **ti va di andare al cinema?** do you feel like going to the cinema?; **andarsene** to go away; **questa camicia va lavata** this shirt needs a wash *o* should be washed; **~ a cavallo** to ride; **~ in macchina/aereo** to go by car/plane; **~ a fare qc** to go and do sth; **~ a pescare/ sciare** to go fishing/skiing; **~ a male** to go bad; **come va?** *(lavoro, progetto)* how are things?; **come va? — bene, grazie!** how are you? — fine, thanks!; **va fatto entro oggi** it's got to be done today; **ne va della nostra vita** our lives are at stake; **an'data** *sf* going; *(viaggio)* outward journey; **biglietto di sola andata** single *(BRIT) o* one-way ticket; **biglietto di andata e ritorno** return *(BRIT) o* round-trip *(US)* ticket; **anda'tura** *sf (modo di andare)* walk, gait; *(SPORT)* pace; *(NAUT)* tack

an'dazzo [an'dattso] *(peg) sm*: **prendere un brutto ~** to take a turn for the worse

andirivi'eni *sm inv* coming and going

'andito *sm* corridor, passage

an'drone *sm* entrance hall

a'neddoto *sm* anecdote

ane'lare *vi*: **~ a** to long for, yearn for

a'nelito *sm (fig)*: **~ di** longing *o* yearning for

a'nello *sm* ring; *(di catena)* link

a'nemico, a, ci, che *ag* anaemic

a'nemone *sm* anemone

aneste'sia *sf* anaesthesia; **anes'tetico, a, ci, che** *ag, sm* anaesthetic

anfite'atro *sm* amphitheatre

an'fratto *sm* ravine

an'gelico, a, ci, che [an'dʒeliko] *ag* angelic(al)

'angelo ['andʒelo] *sm* angel; **~ custode** guardian angel

anghe'ria [ange'ria] *sf* vexation

an'gina [an'dʒina] *sf* tonsillitis; **~ pectoris** angina

angli'cano, a *ag* Anglican

angli'cismo [angli'tʃizmo] *sm* anglicism

anglo'sassone *ag* Anglo-Saxon

ango'lare *ag* angular

angolazi'one [angolat'tsjone] *sf (FOT etc, fig)* angle

'angolo *sm* corner; *(MAT)* angle

an'goscia, sce [an'gɔʃʃa] *sf* deep anxiety, anguish *no pl*; **angosci'oso, a** *ag (d'angoscia)* anguished; *(che dà angoscia)* distressing, painful

angu'illa *sf* eel

an'guria *sf* watermelon

an'gustia *sf (ansia)* anguish, distress; *(povertà)* poverty, want

angusti'are *vt* to distress; **~rsi** *vr*: **~rsi (per)** to worry (about)

an'gusto, a *ag (stretto)* narrow

'anice ['anitʃe] *sm (CUC)* aniseed; *(BOT)* anise

a'nidride *sf (CHIM)*: **~ carbonica/solforosa** carbon/sulphur dioxide

'anima *sf* soul; *(abitante)* inhabitant; **non c'era ~ viva** there wasn't a living soul

ani'male *sm, ag* animal; **~ domestico** pet

ani'mare *vt* to give life to, liven up; *(incoraggiare)* to encourage; **~rsi** *vr* to become animated, come to life; **ani'mato, a** *ag* animate; *(vivace)* lively, animated; *(: strada)* busy; **anima'tore, 'trice** *sm/f* guiding spirit; *(CINEMA)* animator; *(di festa)* life and soul; **animazi'one** *sf* liveliness; *(di strada)* bustle; *(CINEMA)* animation; **animazione teatrale** amateur dramatics

'animo *sm (mente)* mind; *(cuore)* heart; *(coraggio)* courage; *(disposizione)* character, disposition; **avere in ~ di fare qc** to intend *o* have a mind to do sth; **perdersi d'~** to lose heart

'anitra *sf* = **anatra**

anna'cquare *vt* to water down, dilute

annaffi'are *vt* to water; **annaffia'toio** *sm* watering can an'nali *smpl* annals

annas'pare *vi* to flounder

an'nata *sf* year; (*importo annuo*) annual amount; **vino d'~** vintage wine

annebbi'are *vt* (*fig*) to cloud; **~rsi** *vr* to become foggy; (*vista*) to become dim

annega'mento *sm* drowning

anne'gare *vt*, *vi* to drown; **~rsi** *vr* (*accidentalmente*) to drown; (*deliberatamente*) to drown o.s.

anne'rire *vt* to blacken ♦ *vi* to become black

an'nesso, a *pp di* **annettere** ♦ *ag* attached; (*POL*) annexed; **... e tutti gli ~i e connessi** and so on and so forth

an'nettere *vt* (*POL*) to annex; (*accludere*) to attach

annichi'lire [anniki'lire] *vt* = **annichilare**

anni'darsi *vr* to nest

annien'tare *vt* to annihilate, destroy

anniver'sario *sm* anniversary

'anno *sm* year; **ha 8 ~i** he's 8 (years old)

anno'dare *vt* to knot, tie; (*fig: rapporto*) to form

annoi'are *vt* to bore; (*seccare*) to annoy; **~rsi** *vr* to be bored; to be annoyed

an'noso, a *ag* (*problema etc*) age-old

anno'tare *vt* (*registrare*) to note, note down; (*commentare*) to annotate; **annotazi'one** *sf* note; annotation

annove'rare *vt* to number

annu'ale *ag* annual

annu'ario *sm* yearbook

annu'ire *vi* to nod; (*acconsentire*) to agree

annul'lare *vt* to annihilate, destroy; (*contratto, francobollo*) to cancel; (*matrimonio*) to annul; (*sentenza*) to quash; (*risultati*) to declare void

annunci'are [annun'tʃare] *vt* to announce; (*dar segni rivelatori*) to herald; **annuncia'tore, 'trice** *sm/f* (*RADIO, TV*) announcer; **l'Annuncizi'one** *sf* the Annunciation

an'nuncio [an'nuntʃo] *sm* announcement; (*fig*) sign; **~ pubblicitario** advertisement; **~i economici** classified advertisements, small ads

'annuo, a *ag* annual, yearly

annu'sare *vt* to sniff, smell; **~ tabacco** to take snuff

'ano *sm* anus

anoma'lia *sf* anomaly

a'nomalo, a *ag* anomalous

a'nonimo, a *ag* anonymous ♦ *sm* (*autore*) anonymous writer (*o* painter *etc*); **società ~a** (*COMM*) joint stock company

anores'sia *sf* anorexia

anor'male *ag* abnormal ♦ *sm/f* subnormal person

ANSA *sigla f* (= *Agenzia Nazionale Stampa Associata*) press agency

'ansa *sf* (*manico*) handle; (*di fiume*) bend, loop

'ansia *sf* anxiety

ansi'età *sf* = **ansia**

ansi'mare *vi* to pant

ansi'oso, a *ag* anxious

'anta *sf* (*di finestra*) shutter; (*di armadio*) door

antago'nismo *sm* antagonism

an'tartico, a, ci, che *ag* Antarctic ♦ *sm*: **l'A~** the Antarctic

An'tartide *sf*: **l'~** Antarctica

antece'dente [antetʃe'dɛnte] *ag* preceding, previous

ante'fatto *sm* previous events *pl*; previous history

antegu'erra *sm* pre-war period

ante'nato *sm* ancestor, forefather

an'tenna *sf* (*RADIO, TV*) aerial; (*ZOOL*) antenna, feeler; (*NAUT*) yard; **~ parabolica** satellite dish

ante'prima *sf* preview

anteri'ore *ag* (*ruota, zampa*) front; (*fatti*) previous, preceding

antia'ereo, a *ag* anti-aircraft

antia'tomico, a, ci, che *ag* anti-nuclear; **rifugio ~** fallout shelter

antibi'otico, a, ci, che *ag, sm* antibiotic

anti'camera *sf* anteroom; **fare ~** to wait (for an audience)

antichità [antiki'ta] *sf inv* antiquity; (*oggetto*) antique

antici'pare [antitʃi'pare] *vt* (*consegna,*

visita) to bring forward, anticipate; (*somma di denaro*) to pay in advance; (*notizia*) to disclose ♦ *vi* to be ahead of time; **anticipazi'one** *sf* anticipation; (*di notizia*) advance information; (*somma di denaro*) advance; **an'ticipo** *sm* anticipation; (*di denaro*) advance; **in anticipo** early, in advance

an'tico, a, chi, che *ag* (*quadro, mobili*) antique; (*dell'antichità*) ancient; **all'~a** old-fashioned

anticoncezio'nale [antikontʃettsjo'nale] *sm* contraceptive

anticonfor'mista, i, e *ag, sm/f* nonconformist

anti'corpo *sm* antibody

an'tidoto *sm* antidote

anti'furto *sm* anti-theft device

anti'gelo [anti'dʒelo] *ag inv*: **(liquido) ~** (*per motore*) antifreeze; (*per cristalli*) de-icer

An'tille *sfpl*: **le ~** the West Indies

antin'cendio [antin'tʃendjo] *ag inv* fire *cpd*

antio'rario [antio'rarjo] *ag*: **in senso ~** anticlockwise

antl'pasto *sm* hors d'oeuvre

antipa'tia *sf* antipathy, dislike; **anti'patico, a, ci, che** *ag* unpleasant, disagreeable

antiquari'ato *sm* antique trade; **un oggetto d'~** an antique

anti'quario *sm* antique dealer

anti'quato, a *ag* antiquated, old-fashioned

antise'mita, i, e *ag* anti-Semitic

anti'settico, a, ci, che *ag, sm* antiseptic

antista'minico, a, ci, che *ag, sm* antihistamine

antolo'gia, 'gie [antolo'dʒia] *sf* anthology

anu'lare *ag* ring *cpd* ♦ *sm* third finger

'anzi ['antsi] *av* (*invece*) on the contrary; (*o meglio*) or rather, or better still

anzianità [antsjani'ta] *sf* old age; (*AMM*) seniority

anzi'ano, a [an'tsjano] *ag* old; (*AMM*) senior ♦ *sm/f* old person; senior member

anziché [antsi'ke] *cong* rather than

anzi'tutto [antsi'tutto] *av* first of all

apa'tia *sf* apathy, indifference

a'patico, a, ci, che *ag* apathetic

'ape *sf* bee

aperi'tivo *sm* apéritif

a'perto, a *pp di* aprire ♦ *ag* open; all'~ in the open (air)

aper'tura *sf* opening; (*ampiezza*) width; (*FOT*) aperture; ~ alare wing span

'apice ['apitʃe] *sm* apex; (*fig*) height

ap'nea *sf*: immergersi in ~ to dive without breathing apparatus

a'postolo *sm* apostle

a'postrofo *sm* apostrophe

appa'gare *vt* to satisfy

ap'palto *sm* (*COMM*) contract; dare/prendere in ~ un lavoro to let out/undertake a job on contract

appan'nare *vt* (*vetro*) to mist; (*vista*) to dim; ~rsi *vr* to mist over; to grow dim

appa'rato *sm* equipment, machinery; (*ANAT*) apparatus; ~ scenico (*TEATRO*) props *pl*

apparecchi'are [apparek'kjare] *vt* to prepare; (*tavola*) to set ♦ *vi* to set the table; apparecchia'tura *sf* equipment; (*macchina*) machine, device

appa'recchio [appa'rekkjo] *sm* piece of apparatus, device; (*aeroplano*) aircraft *inv*; ~ televisivo/telefonico television set/telephone

appa'rente *ag* apparent; appa'renza *sf* appearance; in *o* all'apparenza apparently

appa'rire *vi* to appear; (*sembrare*) to seem, appear; appari'scente *ag* (*colore*) garish, gaudy; (*bellezza*) striking

ap'parso, a *pp di* apparire

apparta'mento *sm* flat (*BRIT*), apartment (*US*)

appar'tarsi *vr* to withdraw; appar'tato, a *ag* (*luogo*) secluded

apparte'nere *vi*: ~ a to belong to

appassio'nare *vt* to thrill; (*commuovere*) to move; ~rsi a qc to take a great interest in sth; appassio'nato, a *ag* passionate, (*entusiasta*): appassionato (di) keen (on)

appas'sire *vi* to wither

appel'larsi *vr* (*ricorrere*): ~ a to appeal to; (*DIR*): ~ contro to appeal against; ap'pello *sm* roll-call; (*implorazione, DIR*) appeal; **fare appello a** to appeal to

ap'pena *av* (*a stento*) hardly, scarcely; (*solamente, da poco*) just ♦ *cong* as soon as; **(non) ~ furono arrivati ...** as soon as they had arrived ...; **~ ... che** *o* **quando** no sooner ... than

ap'pendere *vt* to hang (up)

appen'dice [appen'ditʃe] *sf* appendix; **romanzo d'~** popular serial

appendi'cite [appendi'tʃite] *sf* appendicitis

Appen'nini *smpl*: **gli ~** the Apennines

appesan'tire *vt* to make heavy; **~rsi** *vr* to grow stout

ap'peso, a *pp di* **appendere**

appe'tito *sm* appetite; **appeti'toso, a** *ag* appetising; (*fig*) attractive, desirable

appia'nare *vt* to level; (*fig*) to smooth away, iron out

appiat'tire *vt* to flatten; **~rsi** *vr* to become flatter; (*farsi piatto*) to flatten o.s.; **~rsi al suolo** to lie flat on the ground

appic'care *vt*: **~ il fuoco a** to set fire to, set on fire

appicci'care [appittʃi'kare] *vt* to stick; **~rsi** *vr* to stick; (*fig: persona*) to cling

appi'eno *av* fully

appigli'arsi [appiʎ'ʎarsi] *vr*: **~ a** (*afferrarsi*) to take hold of; (*fig*) to cling to; **ap'piglio** *sm* hold; (*fig*) pretext

appiso'larsi *vr* to doze off

applau'dire *vt, vi* to applaud; **ap'plauso** *sm* applause

appli'care *vt* to apply; (*regolamento*) to enforce; **~rsi** *vr* to apply o.s.; **applicazi'one** *sf* application; enforcement

appoggi'are [appod'dʒare] *vt* (*mettere contro*): **~ qc a qc** to lean *o* rest sth against sth; (*fig: sostenere*) to support; **~rsi** *vr*: **~rsi a** to lean against; (*fig*) to rely upon; **ap'poggio** *sm* support

appollai'arsi *vr* (*anche fig*) to perch

ap'porre *vt* to affix

appor'tare *vt* to bring

apposita'mente *av* specially; (*apposta*) on purpose

ap'posito, a *ag* appropriate

ap'posta *av* on purpose, deliberately

appos'tarsi *vr* to lie in wait

ap'prendere *vt* (*imparare*) to learn

appren'dista, i, e *sm/f* apprentice

apprensi'one *sf* apprehension; **appren'sivo, a** *ag* apprehensive

ap'presso *av* (*accanto, vicino*) close by, near; (*dietro*) behind; (*dopo, più tardi*) after, later ♦ *ag inv* (*dopo*): **il giorno ~** the next day; **~ a** (*vicino a*) near, close to

appres'tare *vt* to prepare, get ready; **~rsi** *vr*: **~rsi a fare qc** to prepare *o* get ready to do sth

ap'pretto *sm* starch

apprezza'mento [apprettsa'mento] *sm* appreciation; (*giudizio*) opinion

apprez'zare [appret'tsare] *vt* to appreciate

ap'proccio [ap'prɔttʃo] *sm* approach

appro'dare *vi* (*NAUT*) to land; (*fig*): **non ~ a nulla** to come to nothing; **ap'prodo** *sm* landing; (*luogo*) landing-place

approfit'tare *vi*: **~ di** to make the most of; (*peg*) to take advantage of

approfon'dire *vt* to deepen; (*fig*) to study in depth

appropri'ato, a *ag* appropriate

approssi'marsi *vr*: **~ a** to approach

approssima'tivo, a *ag* approximate, rough; (*impreciso*) inexact, imprecise

appro'vare *vt* (*condotta, azione*) to approve of; (*candidato*) to pass; (*progetto di legge*) to approve; **approvazi'one** *sf* approval

approvvigio'nare [approvvidʒo'nare] *vt* to supply

appunta'mento *sm* appointment; (*amoroso*) date; **darsi ~** to arrange to meet (one another)

appun'tato *sm* (*CARABINIERI*) corporal

ap'punto *sm* note; (*rimprovero*) reproach ♦ *av* (*proprio*) exactly, just; **per l'~!, ~!** exactly!

appu'rare *vt* to check, verify

apribot'tiglie [apribot'tiʎʎe] *sm inv* bottle opener

a'prile *sm* April

a'**prire** *vt* to open; (*via, cadavere*) to open up; (*gas, luce, acqua*) to turn on ♦ *vi* to open; ~**rsi** *vr* to open; ~**rsi a qn** to confide in sb, open one's heart to sb

apris'**catole** *sm inv* tin (*BRIT*) *o* can opener

a'**quario** *sm* = **acquario**

'**aquila** *sf* (*ZOOL*) eagle; (*fig*) genius

aqui'**lone** *sm* (*giocattolo*) kite; (*vento*) North wind

A'**rabia Sau'dita** *sf*: **l'~** Saudi Arabia

'**arabo, a** *ag, sm/f* Arab ♦ *sm* (*LING*) Arabic

a'**rachide** [a'rakide] *sf* peanut

ara'**gosta** *sf* crayfish; lobster

a'**rancia, ce** [a'rantʃa] *sf* orange; **aranci'ata** *sf* orangeade; **a'rancio** *sm* (*BOT*) orange tree; (*colore*) orange ♦ *ag inv* (*colore*) orange; **arancl'one** *ag inv*: (**color) arancione** bright orange

a'**rare** *vt* to plough (*BRIT*), plow (*US*)

a'**ratro** *sm* plough (*BRIT*), plow (*US*)

a'**razzo** [a'rattso] *sm* tapestry

arbi'**trare** *vt* (*SPORT*) to referee; to umpire; (*DIR*) to arbitrate

arbi'**trario, a** *ag* arbitrary

ar'**bitrio** *sm* will; (*abuso, sopruso*) arbitrary act

'**arbitro** *sm* arbiter, judge; (*DIR*) arbitrator; (*SPORT*) referee; (: *TENNIS, CRICKET*) umpire

ar'**busto** *sm* shrub

'**arca, che** *sf* (*sarcofago*) sarcophagus; **l'~ di Noè** Noah's ark

ar'**cangelo** [ar'kandʒelo] *sm* archangel

ar'**cata** *sf* (*ARCHIT, ANAT*) arch; (*ordine di archi*) arcade

archeolo'**gia** [arkeolo'dʒia] *sf* arch(a)eology; **arche'ologo, a, gi, ghe** *sm/f* arch(a)eologist

ar'**chetto** [ar'ketto] *sm* (*MUS*) bow

archi'**tettare** [arkitet'tare] *vt* (*fig: ideare*) to devise; (: *macchinare*) to plan, concoct

archi'**tetto** [arki'tetto] *sm* architect; **architet'tura** *sf* architecture

ar'**chivio** [ar'kivjo] *sm* archives *pl*; (*INFORM*) file

arci'**ere** [ar'tʃere] *sm* archer

ar'**cigno, a** [ar'tʃiɲɲo] *ag* grim, severe

arci'**vescovo** [artʃi'veskovo] *sm* archbishop

'**arco** *sm* (*arma, MUS*) bow; (*ARCHIT*) arch; (*MAT*) arc

arcoba'**leno** *sm* rainbow

arcu'**ato, a** *ag* curved, bent

ar'**dente** *ag* burning; (*fig*) burning, ardent

'**ardere** *vt, vi* to burn

ar'**desia** *sf* slate

ar'**dire** *vi* to dare ♦ *sm* daring; **ar'dito, a** *ag* brave, daring, bold; (*sfacciato*) bold

ar'**dore** *sm* blazing heat; (*fig*) ardour, fervour

'**arduo, a** *ag* arduous, difficult

'**area** *sf* area; (*EDIL*) land, ground

a'**rena** *sf* arena; (*per corride*) bullring; (*sabbia*) sand

are'**narsi** *vr* to run aground

areo'**plano** *sm* = **aeroplano**

'**argano** *sm* winch

argente'**ria** [ardʒente'ria] *sf* silverware, silver

Argen'**tina** [ardʒen'tina] *sf*: **l'~** Argentina; **argen'tino, a** *ag, sm/f* Argentinian

ar'**gento** [ar'dʒento] *sm* silver; **~ vivo** quicksilver

ar'**gilla** [ar'dʒilla] *sf* clay

'**argine** ['ardʒine] *sm* embankment, bank; (*diga*) dyke, dike

argo'**mento** *sm* argument; (*motivo*) motive; (*materia, tema*) subject

argu'**ire** *vt* to deduce

ar'**guto, a** *ag* sharp, quick-witted; **ar'guzia** *sf* wit; (*battuta*) witty remark

'**aria** *sf* air; (*espressione, aspetto*) air, look; (*MUS: melodia*) tune; (: *di opera*) aria; **mandare all'~ qc** to ruin *o* upset sth; **all'~ aperta** in the open (air)

'**arido, a** *ag* arid

arieggi'**are** [arjed'dʒare] *vt* (*cambiare aria*) to air; (*imitare*) to imitate

ari'**ete** *sm* ram; (*MIL*) battering ram; (*dello zodiaco*): **A~** Aries

a'**ringa, ghe** *sf* herring *inv*

a'**rista** *sf* (*CUC*) chine of pork

aristo'**cratico, a, ci, che** *ag* aristocratic

arit'**metica** *sf* arithmetic

arlec'**chino** [arlek'kino] *sm* harlequin

'**arma, i** *sf* weapon, arm; (*parte*

dell'esercito) arm; **chiamare alle ~i** to call up (*BRIT*), draft (*US*); **sotto le ~i** in the army (*o* forces); **alle ~i!** to arms!; **~ da fuoco** firearm

ar**'madio** *sm* cupboard; (*per abiti*) wardrobe; **~ a muro** built-in cupboard

armamen**'tario** *sm* equipment

arma**'mento** *sm* (*MIL*) armament; (*: materiale*) arms *pl*, weapons *pl*; (*NAUT*) fitting out; manning

ar**'mare** *vt* to arm; (*arma da fuoco*) to cock; (*NAUT: nave*) to rig, fit out; to man; (*EDIL: volta, galleria*) to prop up, shore up; **~rsi** *vr* to arm o.s.; (*MIL*) to take up arms; ar**'mata** *sf* (*MIL*) army; (*NAUT*) fleet; arma**'tore** *sm* shipowner; arma**'tura** *sf* (*struttura di sostegno*) framework; (*impalcatura*) scaffolding; (*STORIA*) armour *no pl*, suit of armour

armeggi**'are** [armed'dʒare] *vi*: **~ (intorno a qc)** to mess about (with sth)

armis**'tizio** [armis'tittsjo] *sm* armistice

armo**'nia** *sf* harmony; ar**'monica, che** *sf* (*MUS*) harmonica; **~ a bocca** mouth organ; ar**'monico, a, ci, che** *ag* harmonic; (*fig*) harmonious; armoni**'oso, a** *ag* harmonious

armoniz**'zare** [armonid'dzare] *vt* to harmonize; (*colori, abiti*) to match ♦ *vi* to be in harmony; to match

ar**'nese** *sm* tool, implement; (*oggetto indeterminato*) thing, contraption; **male in ~** (*malvestito*) badly dressed; (*di salute malferma*) in poor health; (*di condizioni economiche*) down-at-heel

'arnia *sf* hive

a**'roma, i** *sm* aroma; fragrance; **~i** *smpl* (*CUC*) herbs and spices; aromatera**'pia** *sf* aromatherapy; aro**'matico, a, ci, che** *ag* aromatic; (*cibo*) spicy

'arpa *sf* (*MUS*) harp

ar**'peggio** [ar'peddʒo] *sm* (*MUS*) arpeggio

ar**'pia** *sf* (*anche fig*) harpy

arpi**'one** *sm* (*gancio*) hook; (*cardine*) hinge; (*PESCA*) harpoon

arrabat**'tarsi** *vr* to do all one can, strive

arrabbi**'are** *vi* (*cane*) to be affected with

rabies; **~rsi** *vr* (*essere preso dall'ira*) to get angry, fly into a rage; arrabbi**'ato, a** *ag* rabid, with rabies; furious, angry

arraf**'fare** *vt* to snatch, seize; (*sottrarre*) to pinch

arrampi**'carsi** *vr* to climb (up)

arran**'care** *vi* to limp, hobble

arran**'giare** [arran'dʒare] *vt* to arrange; **~rsi** *vr* to manage, do the best one can

arre**'care** *vt* to bring; (*causare*) to cause

arreda**'mento** *sm* (*studio*) interior design; (*mobili etc*) furnishings *pl*

arre**'dare** *vt* to furnish; arreda**'tore, 'trice** *sm/f* interior designer; ar**'redo** *sm* fittings *pl*, furnishings *pl*

ar**'rendersi** *vr* to surrender

arres**'tare** *vt* (*fermare*) to stop, halt; (*catturare*) to arrest; **~rsi** *vr* (*fermarsi*) to stop; ar**'resto** *sm* (*cessazione*) stopping; (*fermata*) stop; (*cattura, MED*) arrest; **subire un arresto** to come to a stop *o* standstill; **mettere agli arresti** to place under arrest; **arresti domiciliari** house arrest *sg*

arre**'trare** *vt, vi* to withdraw; arre**'trato, a** *ag* (*lavoro*) behind schedule; (*paese, bambino*) backward; (*numero di giornale*) back *cpd*; **arretrati** *smpl* arrears

arric**'chire** [arrik'kire] *vt* to enrich; **~rsi** *vr* to become rich

arricci**'are** [arrit'tʃare] *vt* to curl

ar**'ringa, ghe** *sf* harangue; (*DIR*) address by counsel

arrischi**'are** [arris'kjare] *vt* to risk; **~rsi** *vr* to venture, dare; arrischi**'ato, a** *ag* risky; (*temerario*) reckless, rash

arri**'vare** *vi* to arrive; (*accadere*) to happen, occur; **~ a** (*livello, grado etc*) to reach; **lui arriva a Roma alle 7** he gets to *o* arrives at Rome at 7; **non ci arrivo** I can't reach it; (*fig: non capisco*) I can't understand it

arrive**'derci** [arrive'dertʃi] *escl* goodbye!

arrive**'derla** *escl* (*forma di cortesia*) goodbye!

arri**'vista, i, e** *sm/f* go-getter

ar**'rivo** *sm* arrival; (*SPORT*) finish, finishing line

arro**'gante** *ag* arrogant

arro'lare *vb* = **arruolare**

arros'sire *vi* (*per vergogna, timidezza*) to blush, flush; (*per gioia, rabbia*) to flush

arros'tire *vt* to roast; (*pane*) to toast; (*ai ferri*) to grill

ar'rosto *sm, ag inv* roast

arro'tare *vt* to sharpen; (*investire con un veicolo*) to run over

arroto'lare *vt* to roll up

arroton'dare *vt* (*forma, oggetto*) to round; (*stipendio*) to add to; (*somma*) to round off

arrovel'larsi *vr* to rack one's brains

arruf'fare *vt* to ruffle; (*fili*) to tangle; (*fig: questione*) to confuse

arruggi'nire [arruddʒi'nire] *vt* to rust; **~rsi** *vr* to rust; (*fig*) to become rusty

arruo'lare *vt* (MIL) to enlist; **~rsi** *vr* to enlist, join up

arse'nale *sm* (MIL) arsenal; (*cantiere navale*) dockyard

'arso, a *pp di* **ardere ♦** *ag* (*bruciato*) burnt; (*arido*) dry; **ar'sura** *sf* (*calore opprimente*) burning heat; (*siccità*) drought

'arte *sf* art; (*abilità*) skill

arte'fatto, a *ag* (*cibo*) adulterated; (*fig: modi*) artificial

ar'tefice [ar'tefitʃe] *sm/f* craftsman/woman; (*autore*) author

ar'teria *sf* artery

'artico, a, ci, che *ag* Arctic

artico'lare *ag* (ANAT) of the joints, articular **♦** *vt* to articulate; (*suddividere*) to divide, split up; **articolazi'one** *sf* articulation; (ANAT, TECN) joint

ar'ticolo *sm* article; **~ di fondo** (STAMPA) leader, leading article

'Artide *sm*: **l'~** the Arctic

artifici'ale [artifi'tʃale] *ag* artificial

arti'ficio [arti'fitʃo] *sm* (*espediente*) trick, artifice; (*ricerca di effetto*) artificiality

artigia'nato [artidʒa'nato] *sm* craftsmanship; craftsmen *pl*

artigi'ano, a [arti'dʒano] *sm/f* craftsman/woman

artiglie'ria [artiλλe'ria] *sf* artillery

ar'tiglio [ar'tiλλo] *sm* claw; (*di rapaci*) talon

ar'tista, i, e *sm/f* artist; **ar'tistico, a, ci, che** *ag* artistic

'arto *sm* (ANAT) limb

ar'trite *sf* (MED) arthritis

ar'trosi *sf* osteoarthritis

ar'zillo, a [ar'dzillo] *ag* lively, sprightly

a'scella [aʃ'ʃella] *sf* (ANAT) armpit

ascen'dente [aʃʃen'dente] *sm* ancestor; (*fig*) ascendancy; (ASTR) ascendant

ascensi'one [aʃʃen'sjone] *sf* (ALPINISMO) ascent; (REL): **l'A~** the Ascension

ascen'sore [aʃʃen'sore] *sm* lift

a'scesa [aʃ'ʃesa] *sf* ascent; (*al trono*) accession

a'scesso [aʃ'ʃesso] *sm* (MED) abscess

'ascia ['aʃʃa] (*pl* **'asce**) *sf* axe

asciugaca'pelli [aʃʃugaka'pelli] *sm* hair-dryer

asciuga'mano [aʃʃuga'mano] *sm* towel

asciu'gare [aʃʃu'gare] *vt* to dry; **~rsi** *vr* to dry o.s.; (*diventare asciutto*) to dry

asci'utto, a [aʃ'ʃutto] *ag* dry; (*fig: magro*) lean; (: *burbero*) curt; **restare a bocca ~a** (*fig*) to be disappointed

ascol'tare *vt* to listen to; **ascolta'tore, 'trice** *sm/f* listener; **as'colto** *sm*: **essere** *o* **stare in ascolto** to be listening; **dare** *o* **prestare ascolto (a)** to pay attention (to)

as'falto *sm* asphalt

asfissi'are *vt* to suffocate

'Asia *sf*: **l'~** Asia; **asi'atico, a, ci, che** *ag, sm/f* Asiatic, Asian

a'silo *sm* refuge, sanctuary; **~ (d'infanzia)** nursery(-school); **~ nido** crèche; **~ politico** political asylum

'asino *sm* donkey, ass

'asma *sf* asthma

'asola *sf* buttonhole

as'parago, gi *sm* asparagus *no pl*

aspet'tare *vt* to wait for; (*anche* COMM) to await; (*aspettarsi*) to expect **♦** *vi* to wait; **~rsi** *vr* to expect; **~ un bambino** to be expecting (a baby); **questo non me l'aspettavo** I wasn't expecting this; **aspetta'tiva** *sf* wait; expectation; **inferiore all'aspettativa** worse than expected; **essere in aspettativa** (AMM) to be on leave of absence

as'petto *sm* (*apparenza*) aspect, appearance, look; (*punto di vista*) point of view; **di bell'~** good-looking

aspi'rante *ag* (*attore etc*) aspiring ♦ *sm/f* candidate, applicant

aspira'polvere *sm inv* vacuum cleaner

aspi'rare *vt* (*respirare*) to breathe in, inhale; (*sog: apparecchi*) to suck (up) ♦ *vi*: **~ a** to aspire to; **aspira'tore** *sm* extractor fan

aspi'rina *sf* aspirin

aspor'tare *vt* (*anche MED*) to remove, take away

'aspro, a *ag* (*sapore*) sour, tart; (*odore*) acrid, pungent; (*voce, clima, fig*) harsh; (*superficie*) rough; (*paesaggio*) rugged

assaggi'are [assad'dʒare] *vt* to taste

assag'gini [assad'dʒini] *smpl* (*CUC*) selection of first courses

as'sai *av* (*molto*) a lot, much; (: *con ag*) very; (*a sufficienza*) enough ♦ *ag inv* (*quantità*) a lot of, much; (*numero*) a lot of, many; **~ contento** very pleased

assa'lire *vt* to attack, assail

as'salto *sm* attack, assault

assapo'rare *vt* to savour

assassi'nare *vt* to murder; to assassinate; (*fig*) to ruin; **assas'sinio** *sm* murder; assassination; **assas'sino, a** *ag* murderous ♦ *sm/f* murderer; assassin

'asse *sm* (*TECN*) axle; (*MAT*) axis ♦ *sf* board; **~ sf da stiro** ironing board

assedi'are *vt* to besiege; **as'sedio** *sm* siege

asse'gnare [assen'ɲare] *vt* to assign, allot; (*premio*) to award

as'segno [as'seɲɲo] *sm* allowance; (*anche*: **~ bancario**) cheque (*BRIT*), check (*US*); **contro ~** cash on delivery; **~ circolare** bank draft; **~ sbarrato** crossed cheque; **~ di viaggio** traveller's cheque; **~ a vuoto** dud cheque; **~i familiari** ≈ child benefit *no pl*

assem'blea *sf* assembly

assen'nato, a *ag* sensible

as'senso *sm* assent, consent

as'sente *ag* absent; (*fig*) faraway, vacant;

as'senza *sf* absence

asses'sore *sm* (*POL*) councillor

asses'tare *vt* (*mettere in ordine*) to put in order, arrange; **~rsi** *vr* to settle in; **~ un colpo a qn** to deal sb a blow

asse'tato, a *ag* thirsty, parched

as'setto *sm* order, arrangement; (*NAUT, AER*) trim; **in ~ di guerra** on a war footing

assicu'rare *vt* (*accertare*) to ensure; (*infondere certezza*) to assure; (*fermare, legare*) to make fast, secure; (*fare un contratto di assicurazione*) to insure; **~rsi** *vr* (*accertarsi*): **~rsi (di)** to make sure (of); (*contro il furto etc*): **~rsi (contro)** to insure o.s. (against); **assicu'rata** *sf* (*anche*: **lettera assicurata**) registered letter; **assicu'rato, a** *ag* insured; **assicurazi'one** *sf* assurance; insurance

assidera'mento *sm* exposure

as'siduo, a *ag* (*costante*) assiduous; (*frequentatore etc*) regular

assi'eme *av* (*insieme*) together; **~ a** (*together*) with

assil'lare *vt* to pester, torment

as'sillo *sm* (*fig*) worrying thought

as'sise *sfpl* (*DIR*) assizes; **Corte sf d'A~** Court of Assizes, ≈ Crown Court (*BRIT*)

assis'tente *sm/f* assistant; **~ sociale** social worker; **~ di volo** (*AER*) steward/stewardess

assis'tenza [assis'tɛntsa] *sf* assistance; **~ ospedaliera** free hospital treatment; **~ sanitaria** health service; **~ sociale** welfare services *pl*

as'sistere *vt* (*aiutare*) to assist, help; (*curare*) to treat ♦ *vi*: **~ (a qc)** (*essere presente*) to be present (at sth), to attend (sth)

'asso *sm* ace; **piantare qn in ~** to leave sb in the lurch

associ'are [asso'tʃare] *vt* to associate; **~rsi** *vr* to enter into partnership; **~rsi a** to become a member of, join; (*dolori, gioie*) to share in; **~ qn alle carceri** to take sb to prison

associazi'one [assotʃat'tsjone] *sf* association; (*COMM*) association, society; **~ a delinquere** (*DIR*) criminal association asso'dato, a *ag* well-founded

assogget'tare [assoddʒet'tare] *vt* to subject, subjugate

asso'lato, a *ag* sunny

assol'dare *vt* to recruit

as'solto, a *pp di* assolvere

assoluta'mente *av* absolutely

asso'luto, a *ag* absolute

assoluzi'one [assolut'tsjone] *sf* (DIR) acquittal; (REL) absolution

as'solvere *vt* (DIR) to acquit; (REL) to absolve; (adempiere) to carry out, perform

assomigli'are [assomiʎ'ʎare] *vi*: ~ a to resemble, look like

asson'nato, a *ag* sleepy

asso'pirsi *vr* to doze off

assor'bente *ag* absorbent ♦ *sm*: ~ igienico sanitary towel; ~ interno tampon

assor'bire *vt* to absorb

assor'dare *vt* to deafen

assorti'mento *sm* assortment

assor'tito, a *ag* assorted; matched, matching

as'sorto, a *ag* absorbed, engrossed

assottigli'are [assottiʎ'ʎare] *vt* to make thin, to thin; (aguzzare) to sharpen; (ridurre) to reduce; ~rsi *vr* to grow thin; (fig: ridursi) to be reduced

assue'fare *vt* to accustom; ~rsi a to get used to, accustom o.s. to

as'sumere *vt* (impiegato) to take on, engage; (responsabilità) to assume, take upon o.s.; (contegno, espressione) to assume, put on; (droga) to consume; as'sunto, a *pp di* assumere ♦ *sm* (tesi) proposition

assurdità *sf inv* absurdity; dire delle ~ to talk nonsense

as'surdo, a *ag* absurd

'asta *sf* pole; (vendita) auction

astan'teria *sf* casualty department

as'temio, a *ag* teetotal ♦ *sm/f* teetaller

aste'nersi *vr*: ~ (da) to abstain (from), refrain (from); (POL) to abstain (from)

aste'risco, schi *sm* asterisk

'astice ['astitʃe] *sm* lobster

asti'nenza [asti'nɛntsa] *sf* abstinence;

essere in crisi di ~ to suffer from withdrawal symptoms

'astio *sm* rancour, resentment

as'tratto, a *ag* abstract

'astro *sm* star

'astro... *prefisso*: astrolo'gia [astrolo'dʒia] *sf* astrology; as'trologo, a, ghi, ghe *sm/f* astrologer; astro'nauta, i, e *sm/f* astronaut; astro'nave *sf* space ship; astrono'mia *sf* astronomy; astro'nomico, a, ci, che *ag* astronomic(al)

as'tuccio [as'tuttʃo] *sm* case, box, holder

as'tuto, a *ag* astute, cunning, shrewd; as'tuzia *sf* astuteness, shrewdness; (azione) trick

A'tene *sf* Athens

ate'neo *sm* university

'ateo, a *ag*, *sm/f* atheist

at'lante *sm* atlas

at'lantico, a, ci, che *ag* Atlantic ♦ *sm*: l'A~, l'Oceano A~ the Atlantic, the Atlantic Ocean

at'leta, i, e *sm/f* athlete; at'letica *sf* athletics *sg*; atletica leggera track and field events *pl*; atletica pesante weightlifting and wrestling

atmos'fera *sf* atmosphere

a'tomico, a, ci, che *ag* atomic; (nucleare) atomic, atom *cpd*, nuclear

'atomo *sm* atom

'atrio *sm* entrance hall, lobby

a'troce [a'trotʃe] *ag* (che provoca orrore) dreadful; (terribile) atrocious

attacca'mento *sm* (fig) attachment, affection

attacca'panni *sm* hook, peg; (mobile) hall stand

attac'care *vt* (unire) to attach; (cucendo) to sew on; (far aderire) to stick (on); (appendere) to hang (up); (assalire: anche fig) to attack; (iniziare) to begin, start; (fig: contagiare) to pass on ♦ *vi* to stick, adhere; ~rsi *vr* to stick, adhere; (trasmettersi per contagio) to be contagious; (afferrarsi): ~rsi (a) to cling (to); (fig: affezionarsi): ~rsi (a) to become attached (to); ~ discorso to

start a conversation; **at'tacco, chi** sm
(azione offensiva: anche fig) attack; (MED)
attack, fit; (SCI) binding; (ELETTR) socket

atteggia'mento [atteddʒa'mento] sm
attitude

atteggi'arsi [atted'dʒarsi] vr: ~ **a** to pose as

attem'pato, a ag elderly

at'tendere vt to wait for, await ♦ vi: ~ **a**
to attend to

atten'dibile ag (storia) credible;
(testimone) reliable

atte'nersi vr: ~ **a** to keep o stick to

atten'tare vi: ~ **a** to make an attempt on;
atten'tato sm attack; **attentato alla vita
di qn** attempt on sb's life

at'tento, a ag attentive; (accurato) careful,
thorough; **stare ~ a qc** to pay attention to
sth; ~**!** be careful!

attenu'ante sf (DIR) extenuating
circumstance

attenu'are vt to attenuate; (dolore, rumore)
to lessen, deaden; (pena, tasse) to alleviate;
~**rsi** vr to ease, abate

attenzi'one [atten'tsjone] sf attention; ~**!**
watch out!, be careful!

atter'raggio [atter'raddʒo] sm landing

atter'rare vt to bring down ♦ vi to land

atter'rire vt to terrify

at'tesa sf waiting; (tempo trascorso
aspettando) wait; **essere in attesa di qc** to
be waiting for sth

at'teso, a pp di **attendere**

attes'tato sm certificate

'attico, ci sm attic

at'tiguo, a ag adjacent, adjoining

attil'lato, a ag (vestito) close-fitting

'attimo sm moment; **in un ~** in a moment

atti'nente ag: ~ **a** relating to, concerning

atti'rare vt to attract

atti'tudine sf (disposizione) aptitude;
(atteggiamento) attitude

atti'vare vt to activate; (far funzionare) to
set going, start

attività sf inv activity; (COMM) assets pl

at'tivo, a ag active; (COMM) profit-making,
credit cpd ♦ sm (COMM) assets pl; **in ~** in
credit

attiz'zare [attit'tsare] vt (fuoco) to poke

'atto sm act; (azione, gesto) action, act,
deed; (DIR: documento) deed, document; ~**i**
smpl (di congressi etc) proceedings;
mettere in ~ to put into action; **fare ~ di
fare qc** to make as if to do sth

at'tonito, a ag dumbfounded, astonished

attorcigli'are [attortʃiʎ'ʎare] vt to twist;
~**rsi** vr to twist

at'tore, 'trice sm/f actor/actress

at'torno av round, around, about; ~ **a**
round, around, about

at'tracco, chi sm (NAUT) docking no pl;
berth

attra'ente ag attractive

at'trarre vt to attract; **attrat'tiva** sf (fig:
fascino) attraction, charm; **at'tratto, a** pp
di **attrarre**

attraversa'mento sm: ~ **pedonale**
pedestrian crossing

attraver'sare vt to cross; (città, bosco, fig:
periodo) to go through; (sog: fiume) to run
through

attra'verso prep through; (da una parte
all'altra) across

attrazi'one [attrat'tsjone] sf attraction

attrez'zare [attret'tsare] vt to equip; (NAUT)
to rig; **attrezza'tura** sf equipment no pl;
rigging; **at'trezzo** sm tool, instrument;
(SPORT) piece of equipment

attribu'ire vt: ~ **qc a qn** (assegnare) to
give o award sth to sb; (quadro etc) to
attribute sth to sb; **attri'buto** sm attribute

at'trice [at'tritʃe] sf vedi **attore**

at'trito sm (anche fig) friction

attu'ale ag (presente) present; (di attualità)
topical; (che è in atto) actual; **attualità** sf
inv topicality; (avvenimento) current event;
attual'mente av at the moment, at
present

attu'are vt to carry out; ~**rsi** vr to be
realized

attu'tire vt to deaden, reduce

au'dace [au'datʃe] ag audacious, daring,
bold; (provocante) provocative; (sfacciato)
impudent, bold; **au'dacia** sf audacity,
daring; boldness; provocativeness;

impudence
audiovi'sivo, a *ag* audiovisual
audizi'one [audit'tsjone] *sf* hearing; (*MUS*) audition
'auge ['audʒe] *sf*: **in ~** popular
augu'rare *vt* to wish; **~rsi qc** to hope for sth
au'gurio *sm* (*presagio*) omen; (*voto di benessere etc*) (good) wish; **essere di buon/cattivo ~** to be of good omen/be ominous; **fare gli ~i a qn** to give sb one's best wishes; **tanti ~i!** all the best!
'aula *sf* (*scolastica*) classroom; (*universitaria*) lecture theatre; (*di edificio pubblico*) hall
aumen'tare *vt, vi* to increase; **au'mento** *sm* increase
au'reola *sf* halo
au'rora *sf* dawn
ausili'are *ag, sm, sm/f* auxiliary
aus'picio [aus'pitʃo] *sm* omen; (*protezione*) patronage; **sotto gli ~i di** under the auspices of
aus'tero, a *ag* austere
Aus'tralia *sf*: **l'~** Australia; **australi'ano, a** *ag, sm/f* Australian
'Austria *sf*: **l'~** Austria; **aus'triaco, a, ci, che** *ag, sm/f* Austrian
au'tentico, a, ci, che *ag* authentic, genuine
au'tista, i *sm* driver
'auto *sf inv* car
autoade'sivo, a *ag* self-adhesive ♦ *sm* sticker
autobiogra'fia *sf* autobiography
auto'botte *sf* tanker
'autobus *sm inv* bus
auto'carro *sm* lorry (*BRIT*), truck
autocorri'era *sf* coach, bus
au'tografo, a *ag, sm* autograph
auto'grill ® *sm inv* motorway restaurant
autogrù *sf inv* breakdown van
auto'linea *sf* bus company
au'toma, i *sm* automaton
auto'matico, a, ci, che *ag* automatic ♦ *sm* (*bottone*) snap fastener; (*fucile*) automatic
automazi'one [automat'tsjone] *sf* automation
auto'mezzo [auto'meddzo] *sm* motor vehicle
auto'mobile *sf* (motor) car
automobi'lista, i, e *sm/f* motorist
autono'leggio *sm* car hire
autono'mia *sf* autonomy; (*di volo*) range
au'tonomo, a *ag* autonomous, independent
autop'sia *sf* post-mortem, autopsy
auto'radio *sf inv* (*apparecchio*) car radio; (*autoveicolo*) radio car
au'tore, 'trice *sm/f* author
auto'revole *ag* authoritative; (*persona*) influential
autori'messa *sf* garage
autorità *sf inv* authority
autoriz'zare [autorid'dzare] *vt* (*permettere*) to authorize; (*giustificare*) to allow, sanction; **autorizzazi'one** *sf* authorization
autoscu'ola *sf* driving school
autos'top *sm* hitchhiking; **autostop'pista, i, e** *sm/f* hitchhiker
autos'trada *sf* motorway (*BRIT*), highway (*US*)
auto'treno *sm* articulated lorry (*BRIT*), semi (trailer) (*US*)
autove'icolo *sm* motor vehicle
auto'velox *sm inv* (police) speed camera
autovot'tura *sf* (motor) car
au'tunno *sm* autumn
avam'braccio [avam'brattʃo] (*pl* (*f*) **-cia**) *sm* forearm
avangu'ardia *sf* vanguard
a'vanti *av* (*stato in luogo*) in front; (*moto: andare, venire*) forward; (*tempo: prima*) before ♦ *prep* (*luogo*): **~ a** before, in front of; (*tempo*): **~ Cristo** before Christ ♦ *escl* (*entrate*) come (*o* go) in!; (*MIL*) forward!; (*coraggio*) come on! ♦ *sm inv* (*SPORT*) forward; **~ e indietro** backwards and forwards; **andare ~** to go forward; (*continuare*) to go on; (*precedere*) to go (on) ahead; (*orologio*) to be fast; **essere ~ negli studi** to be well advanced with one's studies

avanza'mento [avantsa'mento] *sm*
progress; promotion

avan'zare [avan'tsare] *vt* (*spostare in avanti*)
to move forward, advance; (*domanda*) to
put forward; (*promuovere*) to promote;
(*essere creditore*): **~ qc da qn** to be owed
sth by sb ♦ *vi* (*andare avanti*) to move
forward, advance; (*progredire*) to make
progress; (*essere d'avanzo*) to be left,
remain; **avan'zata** *sf* (*MIL*) advance;
a'vanzo *sm* (*residuo*) remains *pl*, left-overs
pl; (*MAT*) remainder; (*COMM*) surplus;
averne d'avanzo di qc to have more than
enough of sth; **avanzo di galera** jailbird

ava'ria *sf* (*guasto*) damage; (*: meccanico*)
breakdown

a'varo, a *ag* avaricious, miserly ♦ *sm* miser

a'vena *sf* oats *pl*

PAROLA CHIAVE

a'vere *sm* (*COMM*) credit; **gli ~i** (*ricchezze*)
wealth *sg*

♦ *vt* **1** (*possedere*) to have; **ha due
bambini/una bella casa** she has (got) two
children/a lovely house; **hai i capelli lunghi**
he has (got) long hair; **non ho da
mangiare/bere** I've (got) nothing to eat/
drink, I don't have anything to eat/drink
2 (*indossare*) to wear, have on; **aveva una
maglietta rossa** he was wearing *o* he had
on a red tee-shirt; **ha gli occhiali** he wears
o has glasses
3 (*ricevere*) to get; **hai avuto l'assegno?**
did you get *o* have you had the cheque?
4 (*età, dimensione*) to be; **ha 9 anni** he is 9
(years old); **la stanza ha 3 metri di
lunghezza** the room is 3 metres in length;
vedi **fame; paura** etc
5 (*tempo*): **quanti ne abbiamo oggi?**
what's the date today?; **ne hai per molto?**
will you be long?
6 (*fraseologia*): **avercela con qn** to be
angry with sb; **cos'hai?** what's wrong *o*
what's the matter (with you)?; **non ha
niente a che vedere** *o* **fare con me** it's
got nothing to do with me

♦ *vb aus* **1** to have; **aver bevuto/

mangiato** to have drunk/eaten
2 (*+da +infinito*): **~ da fare qc** to have to
do sth; **non hai che da chiederlo** you only
have to ask him

'avi *smpl* ancestors, forefathers

aviazi'one [avjat'tsjone] *sf* aviation; (*MIL*) air
force

avidità *sf* eagerness; greed

'avido, a *ag* eager; (*peg*) greedy

avo'cado *sm* avocado

a'vorio *sm* ivory

Avv. *abbr* = **avvocato**

avvalla'mento *sm* sinking *no pl*; (*effetto*)
depression

avvalo'rare *vt* to confirm

avvam'pare *vi* (*incendio*) to flare up

avvantaggi'are [avvantad'dʒare] *vt* to
favour; **~rsi** *vr*: **~rsi negli affari/sui
concorrenti** to get ahead in business/of
one's competitors

avvele'nare *vt* to poison

avve'nente *ag* attractive, charming

avveni'mento *sm* event

avve'nire *vi*, *vb impers* to happen, occur
♦ *sm* future

avven'tarsi *vr*: **~ su** *o* **contro qn/qc** to
hurl o.s. *o* rush at sb/sth

avven'tato, a *ag* rash, reckless

avven'tizio, a [avven'tittsjo] *ag* (*impiegato*)
temporary; (*guadagno*) casual

av'vento *sm* advent, coming; (*REL*): **l'A~**
Advent

avven'tore *sm* (*regular*) customer

avven'tura *sf* adventure; (*amorosa*) affair

avventu'rarsi *vr* to venture

avventu'roso, a *ag* adventurous

avve'rarsi *vr* to come true

av'verbio *sm* adverb

avver'sario, a *ag* opposing ♦ *sm*
opponent, adversary

av'verso, a *ag* (*contrario*) contrary;
(*sfavorevole*) unfavourable

avver'tenza [avver'tentsa] *sf*
(*ammonimento*) warning; (*cautela*) care;
(*premessa*) foreword; **~e** *sfpl* (*istruzioni per
l'uso*) instructions

avverti'mento *sm* warning
avver'tire *vt* (*avvisare*) to warn; (*rendere consapevole*) to inform, notify; (*percepire*) to feel
av'vezzo, a [av'vettso] *ag*: ~ **a** used to
avvia'mento *sm* (*atto*) starting; (*effetto*) start; (*AUT*) starting; (: *dispositivo*) starter; (*COMM*) goodwill
avvi'are *vt* (*mettere sul cammino*) to direct; (*impresa, trattative*) to begin, start; (*motore*) to start; ~**rsi** *vr* to set off, set out
avvicen'darsi [avvitʃen'darsi] *vr* to alternate
avvici'nare [avvitʃi'nare] *vt* to bring near; (*trattare con: persona*) to approach; ~**rsi** *vr*: ~**rsi (a qn/qc)** to approach (sb/sth), draw near (to sb/sth)
avvi'lire *vt* (*umiliare*) to humiliate; (*degradare*) to disgrace; (*scoraggiare*) to dishearten, discourage; ~**rsi** *vr* (*abbattersi*) to lose heart
avvilup'pare *vt* (*avvolgere*) to wrap up
avvinaz'zato, a [avvinat'tsato] *ag* drunk
avvin'cente *ag* captivating
av'vincere [av'vintʃere] *vt* to charm, enthral
avvinghi'are [avvin'gjare] *vt* to clasp; ~**rsi** *vr*: ~**rsi a** to cling to
avvi'sare *vt* (*far sapere*) to inform; (*mettere in guardia*) to warn; **av'viso** *sm* warning; (*annuncio*) announcement; (: *affisso*) notice; (*inserzione pubblicitaria*) advertisement; **a mio avviso** in my opinion; **avviso di chiamata** (*TEL*) call waiting service
avvis'tare *vt* to sight
avvi'tare *vt* to screw down (*o* in)
avviz'zire [avvit'tsire] *vi* to wither
avvo'cato, 'essa *sm/f* (*DIR*) barrister (*BRIT*), lawyer; (*fig*) defender, advocate
av'volgere [av'voldʒere] *vt* to roll up; (*avviluppare*) to wrap up; ~**rsi** *vr* (*avvilupparsi*) to wrap o.s. up;
avvol'gibile *sm* roller blind (*BRIT*), blind
avvol'toio *sm* vulture
azi'enda [ad'dzjenda] *sf* business, firm, concern; ~ **agricola** farm

azio'nare [attsjo'nare] *vt* to activate
azi'one [at'tsjone] *sf* action; (*COMM*) share; **azio'nista, i, e** *sm/f* (*COMM*) shareholder
a'zoto [ad'dzɔto] *sm* nitrogen
azzan'nare [attsan'nare] *vt* to sink one's teeth into
azzar'darsi [addzar'darsi] *vr*: ~ **a fare** to dare (to) do; **azzar'dato, a** *ag* (*impresa*) risky; (*risposta*) rash
az'zardo [ad'dzardo] *sm* risk
azzec'care [attsek'kare] *vt* (*risposta etc*) to get right
azzuf'farsi [attsuf'farsi] *vr* to come to blows
az'zurro, a [ad'dzurro] *ag* blue ♦ *sm* (*colore*) blue; **gli ~i** (*SPORT*) the Italian national team

B, b

bab'beo *sm* simpleton
'babbo *sm* (*fam*) dad, daddy; **B~ Natale** Father Christmas
bab'buccia, ce [bab'buttʃa] *sf* slipper; (*per neonati*) bootee
ba'bordo *sm* (*NAUT*) port side
ba'cato, a *ag* worm-eaten, rotten
'bacca, che *sf* berry
baccalà *sm* dried salted cod; (*fig: peg*) dummy
bac'cano *sm* din, clamour
bac'cello [bat'tʃɛllo] *sm* pod
bac'chetta [bak'ketta] *sf* (*verga*) stick, rod; (*di direttore d'orchestra*) baton; (*di tamburo*) drumstick; ~ **magica** magic wand
baci'are [ba'tʃare] *vt* to kiss; ~**rsi** *vr* to kiss (one another)
baci'nella [batʃi'nella] *sf* basin
ba'cino [ba'tʃino] *sm* basin; (*MINERALOGIA*) field, bed; (*ANAT*) pelvis; (*NAUT*) dock
'bacio ['batʃo] *sm* kiss
'baco, chi *sm* worm; ~ **da seta** silkworm
ba'dare *vi* (*fare attenzione*) to take care, be careful; (*occuparsi di*): ~ **a** to look after, take care of; (*dar ascolto*): ~ **a** to pay attention to; **bada ai fatti tuoi!** mind your

own business!
ba'dia *sf* abbey
ba'dile *sm* shovel
'**baffi** *smpl* moustache *sg*; (*di animale*) whiskers; **ridere sotto i ~** to laugh up one's sleeve; **leccarsi i ~** to lick one's lips
ba'gagli [ba'gaʎʎi] *smpl* luggage *sg*; **fare i ~** to pack
bagagli'aio [bagaʎ'ʎajo] *sm* luggage van (*BRIT*) *o* car (*US*); (*AUT*) boot (*BRIT*), trunk (*US*)
bagli'ore [baʎ'ʎore] *sm* flash, dazzling light; **un ~ di speranza** a ray of hope
ba'gnante [baɲ'ɲante] *sm/f* bather
ba'gnare [baɲ'ɲare] *vt* to wet; (*inzuppare*) to soak; (*innaffiare*) to water; (*sog: fiume*) to flow through; (*: mare*) to wash, bathe; **~rsi** *vr* to get wet; (*al mare*) to go swimming *o* bathing; (*in vasca*) to have a bath
ba'gnato, a [baɲ'ɲato] *ag* wet
ba'gnino [baɲ'ɲino] *sm* lifeguard
'**bagno** ['baɲɲo] *sm* bath; (*locale*) bathroom; **~i** *smpl* (*stabilimento*) baths; **fare il ~** to have a bath; (*nel mare*) to go swimming *o* bathing; **fare il ~ a qn** to give sb a bath; **mettere a ~** to soak; **~ schiuma** bubble bath
bagnoma'ria [baɲɲoma'ria] *sm*: **cuocere a ~** to cook in a double saucepan
'**baia** *sf* bay
baio'netta *sf* bayonet
balbet'tare *vi* to stutter, stammer; (*bimbo*) to babble ♦ *vt* to stammer out
balbuzi'ente [balbut'tsjɛnte] *ag* stuttering, stammering
bal'cone *sm* balcony
baldac'chino [baldak'kino] *sm* canopy
bal'danza [bal'dantsa] *sf* self-confidence
'**baldo, a** *ag* bold, daring
bal'doria *sf*: **fare ~** to have a riotous time
ba'lena *sf* whale
bale'nare *vb impers*: **balena** there's lightning ♦ *vi* to flash; **mi balenò un'idea** an idea flashed through my mind; **ba'leno** *sm* flash of lightning; **in un baleno** in a flash

ba'lestra *sf* crossbow
ba'lia *sf*: **in ~ di** at the mercy of
'**balla** *sf* (*di merci*) bale; (*fandonia*) (tall) story
bal'lare *vt*, *vi* to dance; **bal'lata** *sf* ballad
balle'rina *sf* dancer; ballet dancer; (*scarpa*) ballet shoe
balle'rino *sm* dancer; ballet dancer
bal'letto *sm* ballet
'**ballo** *sm* dance; (*azione*) dancing *no pl*; **essere in ~** (*fig: persona*) to be involved; (*: cosa*) to be at stake
ballot'taggio [ballot'taddʒo] *sm* (*POL*) second ballot
balne'are *ag* seaside *cpd*; (*stagione*) bathing
balneazi'one *sf* bathing; **è vietata la ~** bathing strictly prohibited
ba'locco, chi *sm* toy
ba'lordo, a *ag* stupid, senseless
'**balsamo** *sm* (*aroma*) balsam; (*lenimento, fig*) balm
balu'ardo *sm* bulwark
'**balza** ['baltsa] *sf* (*dirupo*) crag; (*di stoffa*) frill
bal'zare [bal'tsare] *vi* to bounce; (*lanciarsi*) to jump, leap; '**balzo** *sm* bounce; jump, leap; (*del terreno*) crag
bam'bagia [bam'badʒa] *sf* (*ovatta*) cotton wool (*BRIT*), absorbent cotton (*US*); (*cascame*) cotton waste
bam'bina *ag*, *sf vedi* **bambino**
bambi'naia *sf* nanny, nurse(maid)
bam'bino, a *sm/f* child
bam'boccio [bam'bɔttʃo] *sm* plump child; (*pupazzo*) rag doll
'**bambola** *sf* doll
bambù *sm* bamboo
ba'nale *ag* banal, commonplace
ba'nana *sf* banana; **ba'nano** *sm* banana tree
'**banca, che** *sf* bank; **~ dei dati** data bank
banca'rella *sf* stall
ban'cario, a *ag* banking, bank *cpd* ♦ *sm* bank clerk
banca'rotta *sf* bankruptcy; **fare ~** to go bankrupt

ban'chetto [ban'ketto] *sm* banquet
banchi'ere [ban'kjere] *sm* banker
ban'china [ban'kina] *sf (di porto)* quay; *(per pedoni, ciclisti)* path; *(di stazione)* platform; ~ **cedevole** *(AUT)* soft verge *(BRIT) o* shoulder *(US)*
'banco, chi *sm* bench; *(di negozio)* counter; *(di mercato)* stall; *(di officina)* (work-)bench; *(GEO, banca)* bank; ~ **di corallo** coral reef; ~ **degli imputati** dock; ~ **dei pegni** pawnshop; ~ **di nebbia** bank of fog; ~ **di prova** *(fig)* testing ground; ~ **dei testimoni** witness box
'Bancomat ® *sm inv* automated banking; *(tessera)* cash card
banco'nota *sf* banknote
'banda *sf* band; *(di stoffa)* band, stripe; *(lato, parte)* side; ~ **perforata** punch tape
banderu'ola *sf (METEOR)* weathercock
bandi'era *sf* flag, banner
ban'dire *vt* to proclaim; *(esiliare)* to exile; *(fig)* to dispense with
ban'dito *sm* outlaw, bandit
bandi'tore *sm (di aste)* auctioneer
'bando *sm* proclamation; *(esilio)* exile, banishment; ~ **alle chiacchiere!** that's enough talk!
'bandolo *sm*: **il ~ della matassa** *(fig)* the key to the problem
bar *sm inv* bar
'bara *sf* coffin
ba'racca, che *sf* shed, hut; *(peg)* hovel; **mandare avanti la ~** to keep things going
bara'onda *sf* hubbub, bustle
ba'rare *vi* to cheat
'baratro *sm* abyss
barat'tare *vt*: ~ **qc con** to barter sth for, swap sth for; ba'ratto *sm* barter
ba'rattolo *sm (di latta)* tin; *(di vetro)* jar; *(di coccio)* pot
'barba *sf* beard; **farsi la ~** to shave; **farla in ~ a qn** *(fig)* to do sth to sb's face; **che ~!** what a bore!
barbabi'etola *sf* beetroot *(BRIT)*, beet *(US)*; ~ **da zucchero** sugar beet
bar'barico, a, ci, che *ag* barbarian; barbaric

'barbaro, a *ag* barbarous; ~**i** *smpl* barbarians
barbi'ere *sm* barber
bar'bone *sm (cane)* poodle; *(vagabondo)* tramp
bar'buto, a *ag* bearded
'barca, che *sf* boat; ~ **a remi** rowing boat; ~ **a vela** sail(ing) boat; barcai'olo *sm* boatman
barcol'lare *vi* to stagger
bar'cone *sm (per ponti di barche)* pontoon
ba'rella *sf (lettiga)* stretcher
ba'rile *sm* barrel, cask
ba'rista, i, e *sm/f* barman/maid; *(proprietario)* bar owner
ba'ritono *sm* baritone
bar'lume *sm* glimmer, gleam
ba'rocco, a, chi, che *ag, sm* baroque
ba'rometro *sm* barometer
ba'rone *sm* baron; baro'nessa *sf* baroness
'barra *sf* bar; *(NAUT)* helm; *(linea grafica)* line, stroke
barri'care *vt* to barricade; barri'cata *sf* barricade
barri'era *sf* barrier; *(GEO)* reef
ba'ruffa *sf* scuffle
barzel'letta [bardzel'letta] *sf* joke, funny story
ba'sare *vt* to base, found; ~**rsi** *vr*: ~**rsi su** *(sog: fatti, prove)* to be based *o* founded on; *(: persona)* to base one's arguments on
'basco, a, schi, sche *ag* Basque ♦ *sm (copricapo)* beret
'base *sf* base; *(fig: fondamento)* basis; *(POL)* rank and file; **di ~** basic; **in ~ a** on the basis of, according to; **a ~ di caffè** coffee-based
ba'setta *sf* sideburn
ba'silica, che *sf* basilica
ba'silico *sm* basil
bassi'fondi *smpl*: **i ~** the slums
'basso, a *ag* low; *(di statura)* short; *(meridionale)* southern ♦ *sm* bottom, lower part; *(MUS)* bass; **la ~a Italia** southern Italy
bassorili'evo *sm* bas-relief
'basta *escl* (that's) enough!, that will do!
bas'tardo, a *ag (animale, pianta)* hybrid,

crossbreed; (*persona*) illegitimate, bastard (*peg*) ♦ *sm/f* illegitimate child, bastard (*peg*)

bas'tare *vi, vb impers* to be enough, be sufficient; **~ a qn** to be enough for sb; **basta chiedere** *o* **che chieda a un vigile** you have only to *o* need only ask a policeman

basti'mento *sm* ship, vessel

basto'nare *vt* to beat, thrash

baston'cino [baston'tʃino] *sm* (*SCI*) ski pole; **~i di pesce** fish fingers

bas'tone *sm* stick; **~ da passeggio** walking stick

bat'taglia [bat'taʎʎa] *sf* battle; fight

bat'taglio [bat'taʎʎo] *sm* (*di campana*) clapper; (*di porta*) knocker

battagli'one [battaʎ'ʎone] *sm* battalion

bat'tello *sm* boat

bat'tente *sm* (*imposta: di porta*) wing, flap; (*: di finestra*) shutter; (*batacchio: di porta*) knocker; (*: di orologio*) hammer; **chiudere i ~i** (*fig*) to shut up shop

'battere *vt* to beat; (*grano*) to thresh; (*percorrere*) to scour ♦ *vi* (*bussare*) to knock; (*urtare*): **~ contro** to hit *o* strike against; (*pioggia, sole*) to beat down; (*cuore*) to beat; (*TENNIS*) to serve; **~rsi** *vr* to fight; **~ le mani** to clap; **~ i piedi** to stamp one's feet; **~ a macchina** to type; **~ bandiera italiana** to fly the Italian flag; **~ in testa** (*AUT*) to knock; **in un batter d'occhio** in the twinkling of an eye

bat'teri *smpl* bacteria

batte'ria *sf* battery; (*MUS*) drums *pl*

bat'tesimo *sm* (*rito*) baptism; christening

battez'zare [batted'dzare] *vt* to baptize; to christen

batticu'ore *sm* palpitations *pl*

batti'mano *sm* applause

batti'panni *sm inv* carpet-beater

battis'tero *sm* baptistry

battis'trada *sm inv* (*di pneumatico*) tread; (*di gara*) pacemaker

battitap'peto *sm* vacuum cleaner

'battito *sm* beat, throb; **~ cardiaco** heartbeat

bat'tuta *sf* blow; (*di macchina da scrivere*) stroke; (*MUS*) bar; beat; (*TEATRO*) cue; (*frase spiritosa*) witty remark; (*di caccia*) beating; (*POLIZIA*) combing, scouring; (*TENNIS*) service

ba'ule *sm* trunk; (*AUT*) boot (*BRIT*), trunk (*US*)

'bava *sf* (*di animale*) slaver, slobber; (*di lumaca*) slime; (*di vento*) breath

bava'glino [bavaʎ'ʎino] *sm* bib

ba'vaglio [ba'vaʎʎo] *sm* gag

'bavero *sm* collar

Bavi'era *sf* Bavaria

ba'zar [bad'dzar] *sm inv* bazaar

baz'zecola [bad'dzekola] *sf* trifle

bazzi'care [battsi'kare] *vt* to frequent ♦ *vi*: **~ in/con** to frequent

be'ato, a *ag* blessed; (*fig*) happy; **~ te!** lucky you!

bebè *sm inv* baby

bec'caccia, ce [bek'kattʃa] *sf* woodcock

bec'care *vt* to peck; (*fig: raffreddore*) to catch; **~rsi qc** to catch sth

bec'cata *sf* peck

beccheggi'are [bekked'dʒare] *vi* to pitch

bec'chino [bek'kino] *sm* gravedigger

'becco, chi *sm* beak, bill; (*di caffettiera etc*) spout; lip

Be'fana *sf* old woman who, according to legend, brings children their presents at the Epiphany; (*Epifania*) Epiphany; (*donna brutta*): **b~** hag, witch

---
Befana

ⓘ The **Befana** *is a national holiday on the feast of the Epiphany. It takes its name from a legendary old woman,* **la Befana,** *who comes down the chimney during the night leaving gifts for children who have been good, and coal for those who have not.*

'beffa *sf* practical joke; **farsi ~e di qn** to make a fool of sb; **bef'fardo, a** *ag* scornful, mocking; **bef'fare** *vt* (*anche*: **beffarsi di**) to make a fool of, mock

'bega, ghe *sf* quarrel

'**begli** ['bɛʎʎi] *ag vedi* **bello**
'**bei** *ag vedi* **bello**
bel *ag vedi* **bello**
be'lare *vi* to bleat
'**belga, gi, ghe** *ag, sm/f* Belgian
'**Belgio** ['bɛldʒo] *sm*: **il ~** Belgium
bel'lezza [bel'lettsa] *sf* beauty
'**bella** *sf* (*SPORT*) decider; *vedi anche* **bello**

PAROLA CHIAVE

'**bello, a** (*ag*: *dav sm* **bel** +*C*, **bell'** +*V*, **bello** +*s impura, gn, pn, ps, x, z, pl* **bei** +*C*, **begli** +*s impura etc o V*) *ag* **1** (*oggetto, donna, paesaggio*) beautiful, lovely; (*uomo*) handsome; (*tempo*) beautiful, fine, lovely; **le belle arti** fine arts
2 (*quantità*): **una ~a cifra** a considerable sum of money; **un bel niente** absolutely nothing
3 (*rafforzativo*): **è una truffa ~a e buona!** it's a real fraud!; **è bell'e finito** it's already finished
♦ *sm* **1** (*bellezza*) beauty; (*tempo*) fine weather
2: **adesso viene il ~** now comes the best bit; **sul più ~** at the crucial point; **cosa fai di ~?** are you doing anything interesting?
♦ *av*: **fa ~** the weather is fine, it's fine

'**belva** *sf* wild animal
belve'dere *sm inv* panoramic viewpoint
benché [ben'ke] *cong* although
'**benda** *sf* bandage; (*per gli occhi*) blindfold; **ben'dare** *vt* to bandage; to blindfold
'**bene** *av* well; (*completamente, affatto*): **è ben difficile** it's very difficult ♦ *ag inv*: **gente ~** well-to-do people ♦ *sm* good; **~i** *smpl* (*averi*) property *sg*, estate *sg*; **io sto ~/poco ~** I'm well/not very well; **va ~** all right; **volere un ~ dell'anima a qn** to love sb very much; **un uomo per ~** a respectable man; **fare ~** to do the right thing; **fare ~ a** (*salute*) to be good for; **fare del ~ a qn** to do sb a good turn; **~i di consumo** consumer goods
bene'detto, a *pp di* **benedire** ♦ *ag* blessed, holy

bene'dire *vt* to bless; to consecrate; **benedizi'one** *sf* blessing
benedu'cato, a *ag* well-mannered
benefi'cenza [benefi'tʃɛntsa] *sf* charity
bene'ficio [bene'fitʃo] *sm* benefit; **con ~ d'inventario** (*fig*) with reservations
be'nefico, a, ci, che *ag* beneficial; charitable
beneme'renza [beneme'rentsa] *sf* merit
bene'merito, a *ag* meritorious
be'nessere *sm* well-being
benes'tante *ag* well-to-do
benes'tare *sm* consent, approval
be'nevolo, a *ag* benevolent
be'nigno, a [be'niɲɲo] *ag* kind, kindly; (*critica etc*) favourable; (*MED*) benign
benin'teso *av* of course
bensì *cong* but (rather)
benve'nuto, a *ag, sm* welcome; **dare il ~ a qn** to welcome sb
ben'zina [ben'dzina] *sf* petrol (*BRIT*), gas (*US*); **fare ~** to get petrol (*BRIT*) *o* gas (*US*); **~ verde** unleaded (petrol); **benzi'naio** *sm* petrol (*BRIT*) *o* gas (*US*) pump attendant
'**bere** *vt* to drink; **darla a ~ a qn** (*fig*) to fool sb
ber'lina *sf* (*AUT*) saloon (car) (*BRIT*), sedan (*US*)
Ber'lino *sf* Berlin
ber'noccolo *sm* bump; (*inclinazione*) flair
ber'retto *sm* cap
bersagli'are [bersaʎ'ʎare] *vt* to shoot at; (*colpire ripetutamente, fig*) to bombard
ber'saglio [ber'saʎʎo] *sm* target
bes'temmia *sf* curse; (*REL*) blasphemy
bestemmi'are *vi* to curse, swear; to blaspheme ♦ *vt* to curse, swear at; to blaspheme
'**bestia** *sf* animal; **andare in ~** (*fig*) to fly into a rage; **besti'ale** *ag* beastly; animal *cpd*; (*fam*): **fa un freddo bestiale** it's bitterly cold; **besti'ame** *sm* livestock; (*bovino*) cattle *pl*
'**bettola** (*peg*) *sf* dive
be'tulla *sf* birch
be'vanda *sf* drink, beverage
bevi'tore, 'trice *sm/f* drinker

be'vuta *sf* drink

be'vuto, a *pp di* **bere**

bi'ada *sf* fodder

bianche'ria [bjanke'ria] *sf* linen; **~ intima**
underwear; **~ da donna** ladies' underwear,
lingerie

bi'anco, a, chi, che *ag* white; (*non
scritto*) blank ♦ *sm* white; (*intonaco*)
whitewash ♦ *sm/f* white, white man/
woman; **in ~** (*foglio, assegno*) blank; (*notte*)
sleepless; **in ~ e nero** (*TV, FOT*) black and
white; **mangiare in ~** to follow a bland
diet; **pesce in ~** boiled fish; **andare in ~**
(*non riuscire*) to fail; **~ dell'uovo** egg-white

biasi'mare *vt* to disapprove of, censure;
bi'asimo *sm* disapproval, censure

'bibbia *sf* (*anche fig*) bible

bibe'ron *sm inv* feeding bottle

'bibita *sf* (soft) drink

biblio'teca, che *sf* library; (*mobile*)
bookcase; **bibliote'cario, a** *sm/f* librarian

bicarbo'nato *sm*: **~ (di sodio)**
bicarbonate (of soda)

bicchi'ere [bik'kjere] *sm* glass

bici'cletta [bitʃi'kletta] *sf* bicycle; **andare in
~** to cycle

bidé *sm inv* bidet

bi'dello, a *sm/f* (*INS*) janitor

bi'done *sm* drum, can; (*anche: ~
dell'immondizia*) (dust)bin; (*fam: truffa*)
swindle; **fare un ~ a qn** (*fam*) to let sb
down; to cheat sb

bien'nale *ag* biennial

Biennale di Venezia

ⓘ The **Biennale di Venezia** *is an
international contemporary art festival,
which takes place every two years at
Giardini. In its current form, it includes
exhibits from the countries taking part, a
thematic exhibition and a section for young
artists.*

---

bi'ennio *sm* period of two years

bi'etola *sf* beet

bifor'carsi *vr* to fork; **biforcazi'one** *sf*
fork

bighello'nare [bigello'nare] *vi* to loaf
(about)

bigiotte'ria [bidʒotte'ria] *sf* costume
jewellery; (*negozio*) jeweller's (*selling only
costume jewellery*)

bigli'ardo [biʎ'ʎardo] *sm* = **biliardo**

bigliet'taio, a *sm/f* (*in treno*) ticket
inspector; (*in autobus*) conductor

bigliette'ria [biʎʎette'ria] *sf* (*di stazione*)
ticket office; booking office; (*di teatro*) box
office

bigli'etto [biʎ'ʎetto] *sm* (*per viaggi,
spettacoli etc*) ticket; (*cartoncino*) card;
(*anche: ~ di banca*) (bank)note; **~
d'auguri/da visita** greetings/visiting card;
~ d'andata e ritorno return (ticket),
round-trip ticket (*US*)

bignè [biɲ'ɲe] *sm inv* cream puff

bigo'dino *sm* roller, curler

bi'gotto, a *ag* over-pious ♦ *sm/f* church
fiend

bi'lancia, ce [bi'lantʃa] *sf* (*pesa*) scales *pl*;
(*: di precisione*) balance; (*dello zodiaco*): **B~**
Libra; **~ commerciale/dei pagamenti**
balance of trade/payments; **bilanci'are** *vt*
(*pesare*) to weigh; (*: fig*) to weigh up;
(*pareggiare*) to balance

bi'lancio [bi'lantʃo] *sm* (*COMM*) balance
(-sheet); (*statale*) budget; **fare il ~ di** (*fig*)
to assess; **~ consuntivo** (final) balance; **~
preventivo** budget

'bile *sf* bile; (*fig*) rage, anger

bili'ardo *sm* billiards *sg*; billiard table

'bilico, chi *sm*: **essere in ~** to be
balanced; **tenere qn in ~** (*fig*) to keep sb in
suspense

bi'lingue *ag* bilingual

bili'one *sm* (*mille milioni*) thousand million;
(*milione di milioni*) billion (*BRIT*), trillion (*US*)

'bimbo, a *sm/f* little boy/girl

bimen'sile *ag* fortnightly

bimes'trale *ag* two-monthly, bimonthly

bi'nario, a *ag* (*sistema*) binary ♦ *sm*
(railway) track *o* line; (*piattaforma*)
platform; **~ morto** dead-end track

bi'nocolo *sm* binoculars *pl*

bio... *prefisso*: **bio'chimica** [bio'kimika] *sf*

biochemistry; **biodegra'dabile** *ag* biodegradable; **biogra'fia** *sf* biography; **biolo'gia** *sf* biology; **bio'logico, a, ci, che** *ag* biological

bi'ondo, a *ag* blond, fair

bir'bante *sm* rogue, rascal

biri'chino, a [biri'kino] *ag* mischievous ♦ *sm/f* scamp, little rascal

bi'rillo *sm* skittle (*BRIT*), pin (*US*); **~i** *smpl* (*gioco*) skittles *sg* (*BRIT*), bowling (*US*)

'biro ® *sf inv* biro ®

'birra *sf* beer; **a tutta ~** (*fig*) at top speed; **birra chiara** ≈ lager; **birra scura** ≈ stout; **birre'ria** *sf* ≈ bierkeller

bis *escl, sm inv* encore

bis'betico, a, ci, che *ag* ill-tempered, crabby

bisbigli'are [bizbiʎ'ʎare] *vt, vi* to whisper

'bisca, sche *sf* gambling-house

'biscia, sce ['biʃʃa] *sf* snake; **~ d'acqua** grass snake

bis'cotto *sm* biscuit

bises'tile *ag*: **anno ~** leap year

bis'lungo, a, ghi, ghe *ag* oblong

bis'nonno, a *sm/f* great grandfather/ grandmother

biso'gnare [bizoɲ'ɲare] *vb impers*: **bisogna che tu parta/lo faccia** you'll have to go/ do it; **bisogna parlargli** we'll (*o* I'll) have to talk to him

bi'sogno [bi'zoɲɲo] *sm* need; **~i** *smpl*: **fare i propri ~i** to relieve o.s.; **avere ~ di qc/di fare qc** to need sth/to do sth; **al ~, in caso di ~** if need be; **biso'gnoso, a** *ag* needy, poor; **bisognoso di** in need of, needing

bis'tecca, che *sf* steak, beefsteak

bisticci'are [bistit'tʃare] *vi* to quarrel, bicker; **~rsi** *vr* to quarrel, bicker; **bis'ticcio** *sm* quarrel, squabble; (*gioco di parole*) pun

'bisturi *sm* scalpel

bi'sunto, a *ag* very greasy

'bitter *sm inv* bitters *pl*

bi'vacco, chi *sm* bivouac

'bivio *sm* fork; (*fig*) dilemma

'bizza ['biddza] *sf* tantrum; **fare le ~e** (*bambino*) to be naughty

biz'zarro, a [bid'dzarro] *ag* bizarre, strange

biz'zeffe [bid'dzɛffe]: **a ~** *av* in plenty, galore

blan'dire *vt* to soothe; to flatter

'blando, a *ag* mild, gentle

bla'sone *sm* coat of arms

blate'rare *vi* to chatter

blin'dato, a *ag* armoured

bloc'care *vt* to block; (*isolare*) to isolate, cut off; (*porto*) to blockade; (*prezzi, beni*) to freeze; (*meccanismo*) to jam; **~rsi** *vr* (*motore*) to stall; (*freni, porta*) to jam, stick; (*ascensore*) to stop, get stuck

bloc'chetto [blok'ketto] *sm* notebook; (*di biglietti*) book

'blocco, chi *sm* block; (*MIL*) blockade; (*dei fitti*) restriction; (*quadernetto*) pad; (*fig: unione*) coalition; (*il bloccare*) blocking; isolating, cutting-off; blockading; freezing; jamming; **in ~** (*nell'insieme*) as a whole; (*COMM*) in bulk; **~ cardiaco** cardiac arrest

blu *ag inv, sm* dark blue

'blusa *sf* (*camiciotto*) smock; (*camicetta*) blouse

'boa *sm inv* (*ZOOL*) boa constrictor; (*sciarpa*) feather boa ♦ *sf* buoy

bo'ato *sm* rumble, roar

bo'bina *sf* reel, spool; (*di pellicola*) spool; (*di film*) reel, (*ELETTR*) coil

'bocca, che *sf* mouth; **in ~ al lupo!** good luck!

boc'caccia, ce [bok'kattʃa] *sf* (*malalingua*) gossip; **fare le ~ce** to pull faces

boc'cale *sm* jug; **~ da birra** tankard

boc'cetta [bot'tʃetta] *sf* small bottle

boccheggi'are [bokked'dʒare] *vi* to gasp

boc'chino [bok'kino] *sm* (*di sigaretta, sigaro: cannella*) cigarette-holder; cigar-holder; (*di pipa, strumenti musicali*) mouthpiece

'boccia, ce ['bottʃa] *sf* bottle; (*da vino*) decanter, carafe; (*palla*) bowl; **gioco delle ~ce** bowls *sg*

bocci'are [bot'tʃare] *vt* (*proposta, progetto*) to reject; (*INS*) to fail; (*BOCCE*) to hit; **boccia'tura** *sf* failure

bocci'olo [bot'tʃɔlo] *sm* bud
boc'cone *sm* mouthful, morsel
boc'coni *av* face downwards
'boia *sm inv* executioner; hangman
boi'ata *sf* botch
boicot'tare *vt* to boycott
'bolide *sm* meteor; **come un ~** like a flash, at top speed
'bolla *sf* bubble; (*MED*) blister; **~ papale** papal bull; **~ di consegna** (*COMM*) delivery note
bol'lare *vt* to stamp; (*fig*) to brand
bol'lente *ag* boiling; boiling hot
bol'letta *sf* bill; (*ricevuta*) receipt; **essere in ~** to be hard up
bollet'tino *sm* bulletin; (*COMM*) note; **~ meteorologico** weather report; **~ di spedizione** consignment note
bol'lire *vt, vi* to boil; **bol'lito** *sm* (*CUC*) boiled meat
bolli'tore *sm* (*CUC*) kettle; (*per riscaldamento*) boiler
'bollo *sm* stamp; **~ per patente** driving licence tax
'bomba *sf* bomb; **~ atomica** atom bomb
bombarda'mento *sm* bombardment; bombing
bombar'dare *vt* to bombard; (*da aereo*) to bomb
bombardi'ere *sm* bomber
bom'betta *sf* bowler (hat)
'bombola *sf* cylinder
bo'naccia, ce [bo'nattʃa] *sf* dead calm
bo'nario, a *ag* good-natured, kind
bo'nifica, che *sf* reclamation; reclaimed land
bo'nifico, ci *sm* (*riduzione, abbuono*) discount; (*versamento a terzi*) credit transfer
bontà *sf* goodness; (*cortesia*) kindness; **aver la ~ di fare qc** to be good *o* kind enough to do sth
borbot'tare *vi* to mumble
'borchia ['borkja] *sf* stud
borda'tura *sf* (*SARTORIA*) border, trim
bor'deaux [bor'dɔ] *ag inv, sm inv* maroon
'bordo *sm* (*NAUT*) ship's side; (*orlo*) edge; (*striscia di guarnizione*) border, trim; **a ~ di**

(*nave, aereo*) aboard, on board; (*macchina*) in
bor'gata *sf* (*in campagna*) hamlet
bor'ghese [bor'geze] *ag* (*spesso peg*) middle-class; bourgeois; **abito ~** civilian dress; **borghe'sia** *sf* middle classes *pl*; bourgeoisie
'borgo, ghi *sm* (*paesino*) village; (*quartiere*) district; (*sobborgo*) suburb
'boria *sf* self-conceit, arrogance
boro'talco *sm* talcum powder
bor'raccia, ce [bor'rattʃa] *sf* canteen, water-bottle
'borsa *sf* bag; (*anche:* **~ da signora**) handbag; (*ECON*): **la B~ (valori)** the Stock Exchange; **~ nera** black market; **~ della spesa** shopping bag; **~ di studio** grant; **borsai'olo** *sm* pickpocket; **borsel'lino** *sm* purse; **bor'setta** *sf* handbag; **bor'sista, i, e** *sm/f* (*ECON*) speculator; (*INS*) grant-holder
bos'caglia [bos'kaʎʎa] *sf* woodlands *pl*
boscai'olo *sm* woodcutter; forester
'bosco, schi *sm* wood; **bos'coso, a** *ag* wooded
'bossolo *sm* cartridge-case
bo'tanica *sf* botany
bo'tanico, a, ci, che *ag* botanical ♦ *sm* botanist
'botola *sf* trap door
'botta *sf* blow; (*rumore*) bang
'botte *sf* barrel, cask
bot'tega, ghe *sf* shop; (*officina*) workshop; **botte'gaio, a** *sm/f* shopkeeper; **botte'ghino** *sm* ticket office; (*del lotto*) public lottery office
bot'tiglia [bot'tiʎʎa] *sf* bottle; **bottiglie'ria** *sf* wine shop
bot'tino *sm* (*di guerra*) booty; (*di rapina, furto*) loot
'botto *sm* bang; crash; **di ~** suddenly
bot'tone *sm* button; **attaccare ~ a qn** (*fig*) to buttonhole sb
bo'vino, a *ag* bovine; **~i** *smpl* cattle
boxe [bɔks] *sf* boxing
'bozza ['bɔttsa] *sf* draft; sketch; (*TIP*) proof; **boz'zetto** *sm* sketch

'**bozzolo** ['bɔttsolo] *sm* cocoon
BR *sigla fpl* = **Brigate Rosse**
brac'care *vt* to hunt
brac'cetto [brat'tʃetto] *sm*: **a ~** arm in arm
bracci'ale [brat'tʃale] *sm* bracelet;
  (*distintivo*) armband; **braccia'letto** *sm*
  bracelet, bangle
bracci'ante [brat'tʃante] *sm* (*AGR*) day
  labourer
bracci'ata [brat'tʃata] *sf* (*nel nuoto*) stroke
'**braccio** ['brattʃo] (*pl(f)* **braccia**) *sm* (*ANAT*)
  arm; (*pl(m)* **bracci**: *di gru, fiume*) arm; (: *di*
  edificio) wing; **~ di mare** sound;
  bracci'olo *sm* (*appoggio*) arm
'**bracco, chi** *sm* hound
bracconi'ere *sm* poacher
'**brace** ['bratʃe] *sf* embers *pl*; **braci'ere** *sm*
  brazier
braci'ola [bra'tʃɔla] *sf* (*CUC*) chop
bra'mare *vt*: **~ qc/di fare** to long for sth/
  to do
'**branca, che** *sf* branch
'**branchia** ['brankja] *sf* (*ZOOL*) gill
'**branco, chi** *sm* (*di cani, lupi*) pack; (*di*
  pecore) flock; (*peg: di persone*) gang, pack
branco'lare *vi* to grope, feel one's way
'**branda** *sf* camp bed
bran'dello *sm* scrap, shred; **a ~i** in tatters,
  in rags
bran'dire *vt* to brandish
'**brano** *sm* piece; (*di libro*) passage
bra'sato *sm* braised beef
Bra'sile *sm*: **il ~** Brazil; **brasili'ano, a** *ag*,
  sm/f Brazilian
'**bravo, a** *ag* (*abile*) clever, capable, skilful;
  (*buono*) good, honest; (: *bambino*) good;
  (*coraggioso*) brave; **~!** well done!; (*a teatro*)
  bravo!
bra'vura *sf* cleverness, skill
'**breccia, ce** ['brettʃa] *sf* breach
bre'tella *sf* (*AUT*) link; **~e** *sfpl* (*di calzoni*)
  braces
'**breve** *ag* brief, short; **in ~** in short
brevet'tare *vt* to patent
bre'vetto *sm* patent; **~ di pilotaggio** pilot's
  licence (*BRIT*) *o* license (*US*)
'**brezza** ['breddza] *sf* breeze

'**bricco, chi** *sm* jug; **~ del caffè** coffeepot
bric'cone, a *sm/f* rogue, rascal
'**briciola** ['britʃola] *sf* crumb
'**briciolo** ['britʃolo] *sm* (*specie fig*) bit
'**briga, ghe** *sf* (*fastidio*) trouble, bother;
  pigliarsi la ~ di fare qc to take the trouble
  to do sth
brigadi'ere *sm* (*dei carabinieri etc*)
  ≈ sergeant
bri'gante *sm* bandit
bri'gata *sf* (*MIL*) brigade; (*gruppo*) group,
  party; **B~e Rosse** (*POL*) Red Brigades
'**briglia** ['briʎʎa] *sf* rein; **a ~ sciolta** at full
  gallop; (*fig*) at full speed
bril'lante *ag* bright; (*anche fig*) brilliant;
  (*che luccica*) shining ♦ *sm* diamond
bril'lare *vi* to shine; (*mina*) to blow up ♦ *vt*
  (*mina*) to set off
'**brillo, a** *ag* merry, tipsy
'**brina** *sf* hoarfrost
brin'dare *vi*: **~ a qn/qc** to drink to *o* toast
  sb/sth
'**brindisi** *sm inv* toast
'**brio** *sm* liveliness, go
bri'oche [bri'ɔʃ] *sf inv* brioche
bri'oso, a *ag* lively
bri'tannico, a, ci, che *ag* British
'**brivido** *sm* shiver; (*di ribrezzo*) shudder;
  (*fig*) thrill
brizzo'lato, a [brittso'lato] *ag* (*persona*)
  going grey; (*barba, capelli*) greying
'**brocca, che** *sf* jug
broc'cato *sm* brocade
'**broccolo** *sm* broccoli *sg*
'**brodo** *sm* broth; (*per cucinare*) stock; **~**
  ristretto consommé
brogli'accio [broʎ'ʎattʃo] *sm* scribbling pad
'**broglio** ['brɔʎʎo] *sm*: **~ elettorale**
  gerrymandering
bron'chite [bron'kite] *sf* (*MED*) bronchitis
'**broncio** ['brontʃo] *sm* sulky expression;
  tenere il ~ to sulk
'**bronco, chi** *sm* bronchial tube
bronto'lare *vi* to grumble; (*tuono,*
  stomaco) to rumble
'**bronzo** ['brondzo] *sm* bronze
bru'care *vt* to browse on, nibble at

brucia'pelo [brutʃa'pelo]: **a ~** *av* point-blank

bruci'are [bru'tʃare] *vt* to burn; (*scottare*) to scald ♦ *vi* to burn; **brucia'tore** *sm* burner; **brucia'tura** *sf* (*atto*) burning *no pl*; (*segno*) burn; (*scottatura*) scald; **bruci'ore** *sm* burning *o* smarting sensation; **bruciore di stomaco** heartburn

'bruco, chi *sm* caterpillar; grub

brughi'era [bru'gjɛra] *sf* heath, moor

bruli'care *vi* to swarm

'brullo, a *ag* bare, bleak

'bruma *sf* mist

'bruno, a *ag* brown, dark; (*persona*) dark(-haired)

'brusco, a, schi, sche *ag* (*sapore*) sharp; (*modi, persona*) brusque, abrupt; (*movimento*) abrupt, sudden

bru'sio *sm* buzz, buzzing

bru'tale *ag* brutal

'bruto, a *ag* (*forza*) brute *cpd* ♦ *sm* brute

brut'tezza [brut'tettsa] *sf* ugliness

'brutto, a *ag* ugly; (*cattivo*) bad; (*malattia, strada, affare*) nasty, bad; **~ tempo** bad weather; **brut'tura** *sf* (*cosa brutta*) ugly thing; (*sudiciume*) filth; (*azione meschina*) mean action

Bru'xelles [bry'sɛl] *sf* Brussels

bub'bone *sm* swelling

'buca, che *sf* hole; (*avvallamento*) hollow; **~ delle lettere** letterbox

buca'neve *sm inv* snowdrop

bu'care *vt* (*forare*) to make a hole (*o* holes) in; (*pungere*) to pierce; (*biglietto*) to punch; **~rsi** *vr* (*di eroina*) to mainline; **~ una gomma** to have a puncture

bu'cato *sm* (*operazione*) washing; (*panni*) wash, washing

'buccia, ce ['buttʃa] *sf* skin, peel

bucherel'lare [bukerel'lare] *vt* to riddle with holes

'buco, chi *sm* hole

bu'dello *sm* (*ANAT: pl(f)* **~a**) bowel, gut; (*fig: tubo*) tube; (*vicolo*) alley

bu'dino *sm* pudding

'bue *sm* ox; **carne di ~** beef

'bufalo *sm* buffalo

bu'fera *sf* storm

buf'fetto *sm*: **fare un ~ sulla guancia a qn** to give sb an affectionate pinch on the cheek

'buffo, a *ag* funny; (*TEATRO*) comic

buf'fone *sm* buffoon; (*peg*) clown

bu'gia, 'gie [bu'dʒia] *sf* lie; **dire una ~** to tell a lie; **bugi'ardo, a** *ag* lying, deceitful ♦ *sm/f* liar

bugi'gattolo [budʒi'gattolo] *sm* poky little room

'buio, a *ag* dark ♦ *sm* dark, darkness

'bulbo *sm* (*BOT*) bulb; **~ oculare** eyeball

Bulga'ria *sf*: **la ~** Bulgaria

bul'lone *sm* bolt

buona'notte *escl* good night! ♦ *sf*: **dare la ~ a** to say good night to

buona'sera *escl* good evening!

buongi'orno [bwon'dʒorno] *escl* good morning (*o* afternoon)!

buongus'taio, a *sm/f* gourmet

buon'gusto *sm* good taste

PAROLA CHIAVE
---

bu'ono, a (*ag: dav sm* **buon** +*C o V*, **buono** +*s impura, gn, pn, ps, x, z; dav sf* **buon'** +*V*) *ag* **1** (*gen*) good; **un buon pranzo/ristorante** a good lunch/restaurant; **(stai) ~!** behave!

2 (*benevolo*): **~ (con)** good (to), kind (to)

3 (*giusto, valido*) right; **al momento ~** at the right moment

4 (*adatto*): **~ a/da** fit for/to; **essere ~ a nulla** to be no good *o* use at anything

5 (*auguri*): **buon anno!** happy New Year!; **buon appetito!** enjoy your meal!; **buon compleanno!** happy birthday!; **buon divertimento!** have a nice time!; **~a fortuna!** good luck!; **buon riposo!** sleep well!; **buon viaggio!** bon voyage!, have a good trip!

6: **a buon mercato** cheap; **di buon'ora** early; **buon senso** common sense; **alla ~a** *ag* simple ♦ *av* in a simple way, without any fuss

♦ *sm* **1** (*bontà*) goodness, good

2 (*COMM*) voucher, coupon; **~ di cassa**

cash voucher; **~ di consegna** delivery note; **~ del Tesoro** Treasury bill

buontem'pone, a *sm/f* jovial person

burat'tino *sm* puppet

'burbero, a *ag* surly, gruff

'burla *sf* prank, trick; bur'lare *vt*: **burlare qc/qn, burlarsi di qc/qn** to make fun of sth/sb

burocra'zia [burokrat'tsia] *sf* bureaucracy

bur'rasca, sche *sf* storm

'burro *sm* butter

bur'rone *sm* ravine

bus'care *vt* (*anche:* **~rsi**: *raffreddore*) to get, catch; **buscarle** (*fam*) to get a hiding

bus'sare *vi* to knock

'bussola *sf* compass

'busta *sf* (*da lettera*) envelope; (*astuccio*) case; **in ~ aperta/chiusa** in an unsealed/sealed envelope; **~ paga** pay packet

busta'rella *sf* bribe, backhander

'busto *sm* bust; (*indumento*) corset, girdle; **a mezzo ~** (*foto*) half-length

buttafu'ori *sm inv* bouncer

but'tare *vt* to throw; (*anche:* **~ via**) to throw away; **~ giù** (*scritto*) to scribble down; (*cibo*) to gulp down; (*edificio*) to pull down, demolish; (*pasta, verdura*) to put into boiling water

C, c

ca'bina *sf* (*di nave*) cabin; (*da spiaggia*) beach hut; (*di autocarro, treno*) cab; (*di aereo*) cockpit; (*di ascensore*) cage; **~ telefonica** call *o* (tele)phone box; **cabi'nato** *sm* cabin cruiser

ca'cao *sm* cocoa

'caccia ['kattʃa] *sf* hunting; (*con fucile*) shooting; (*inseguimento*) chase; (*cacciagione*) game ♦ *sm inv* (*aereo*) fighter; (*nave*) destroyer; **~ grossa** big-game hunting; **~ all'uomo** manhunt

cacciabombardi'ere [kattʃabombar'djere] *sm* fighter-bomber

cacciagi'one [kattʃa'dʒone] *sf* game

cacci'are [kat'tʃare] *vt* to hunt; (*mandar via*) to chase away; (*ficcare*) to shove, stick ♦ *vi* to hunt; **~rsi** *vr*: **dove s'è cacciata la mia borsa?** where has my bag got to?; **~rsi nei guai** to get into trouble; **~ fuori qc** to whip *o* pull sth out; **~ un urlo** to let out a yell; **caccia'tore** *sm* hunter; **cacciatore di frodo** poacher

caccia'vite [kattʃa'vite] *sm inv* screwdriver

'cactus *sm inv* cactus

ca'davere *sm* (dead) body, corpse

ca'dente *ag* falling; (*casa*) tumbledown

ca'denza [ka'dentsa] *sf* cadence; (*ritmo*) rhythm; (*MUS*) cadenza

ca'dere *vi* to fall; (*denti, capelli*) to fall out; (*tetto*) to fall in; **questa gonna cade bene** this skirt hangs well; **lasciar ~** (*anche fig*) to drop; **~ dal sonno** to be falling asleep on one's feet; **~ dalle nuvole** (*fig*) to be taken aback

ca'detto, a *ag* younger; (*squadra*) junior *cpd* ♦ *sm* cadet

ca'duta *sf* fall; **la ~ dei capelli** hair loss

caffè *sm inv* coffee; (*locale*) café; **~ macchiato** coffee with a dash of milk; **~ macinato** ground coffee

caffel'latte *sm inv* white coffee

caffetti'era *sf* coffeepot

cagio'nare [kadʒo'nare] *vt* to cause

cagio'nevole [kadʒo'nevole] *ag* delicate, weak

cagli'are [kaʎ'ʎare] *vi* to curdle

'cagna ['kaɲɲa] *sf* (*ZOOL, peg*) bitch

ca'gnesco, a, schi, sche [kaɲ'ɲesko] *ag* (*fig*): **guardare qn in ~** to scowl at sb

cala'brone *sm* hornet

cala'maio *sm* inkpot; inkwell

cala'maro *sm* squid

cala'mita *sf* magnet

calamità *sf inv* calamity, disaster

ca'lare *vt* (*far discendere*) to lower; (*MAGLIA*) to decrease ♦ *vi* (*discendere*) to go (*o* come) down; (*tramontare*) to set, go down; **~ di peso** to lose weight

'calca *sf* throng, press

cal'cagno [kal'kaɲɲo] *sm* heel

cal'care *sm* limestone ♦ *vt* (*premere coi*

piedi) to tread, press down; (*premere con forza*) to press down; (*mettere in rilievo*) to stress; **~ la mano** to overdo it, exaggerate

'**calce** ['kaltʃe] *sm*: **in ~** at the foot of the page ♦ *sf* lime; **~ viva** quicklime

calces'truzzo [kaltʃes'truttso] *sm* concrete

calci'are [kal'tʃare] *vt, vi* to kick; **calcia'tore** *sm* footballer

'**calcio** ['kaltʃo] *sm* (*pedata*) kick; (*sport*) football, soccer; (*di pistola, fucile*) butt; (*CHIM*) calcium; **~ d'angolo** (*SPORT*) corner (kick); **~ di punizione** (*SPORT*) free kick

'**calco, chi** *sm* (*ARTE*) casting, moulding; cast, mould

calco'lare *vt* to calculate, work out, reckon; (*ponderare*) to weigh (up); **calcola'tore, 'trice** *ag* calculating ♦ *sm* calculator; (*fig*) calculating person; **calcolatore elettronico** computer; **calcola'trice** *sf* calculator

'**calcolo** *sm* (*anche MAT*) calculation; (*infinitesimale etc*) calculus; (*MED*) stone; **fare i propri ~i** (*fig*) to weigh the pros and cons; **per ~** out of self-interest

cal'daia *sf* boiler

caldeggi'are [kalded'dʒare] *vt* to support

'**caldo, a** *ag* warm; (*molto ~*) hot; (*fig: appassionato*) keen; hearty ♦ *sm* heat; **ho ~** I'm warm; I'm hot; **fa ~** it's warm; it's hot

calen'dario *sm* calendar

'**calibro** *sm* (*di arma*) calibre, bore; (*TECN*) callipers *pl*; (*fig*) calibre; **di grosso ~** (*fig*) prominent

'**calice** ['kalitʃe] *sm* goblet; (*REL*) chalice

ca'ligine [ka'lidʒine] *sf* fog; (*mista con fumo*) smog

'**callo** *sm* callus; (*ai piedi*) corn

'**calma** *sf* calm

cal'mante *sm* tranquillizer

cal'mare *vt* to calm; (*lenire*) to soothe; **~rsi** *vr* to grow calm, calm down; (*vento*) to abate; (*dolori*) to ease

calmi'ere *sm* controlled price

'**calmo, a** *ag* calm, quiet

'**calo** *sm* (*COMM: di prezzi*) fall; (*: di volume*) shrinkage; (*: di peso*) loss

ca'lore *sm* warmth; heat; **in ~** (*ZOOL*) on

heat

calo'ria *sf* calorie

calo'roso, a *ag* warm

calpes'tare *vt* to tread on, trample on; "**è vietato ~ l'erba**" "keep off the grass"

ca'lunnia *sf* slander; (*scritta*) libel

cal'vario *sm* (*fig*) affliction, cross

cal'vizie [kal'vittsje] *sf* baldness

'**calvo, a** *ag* bald

'**calza** ['kaltsa] *sf* (*da donna*) stocking; (*da uomo*) sock; **fare la ~** to knit; **~e di nailon** nylons, (nylon) stockings

cal'zare [kal'tsare] *vt* (*scarpe, guanti: mettersi*) to put on; (*: portare*) to wear ♦ *vi* to fit; **calza'tura** *sf* footwear

calzet'tone [kaltset'tone] *sm* heavy knee-length sock

cal'zino [kal'tsino] *sm* sock

calzo'laio [kaltso'lajo] *sm* shoemaker; (*che ripara scarpe*) cobbler; **calzole'ria** *sf* (*negozio*) shoe shop

calzon'cini [kaltson'tʃini] *smpl* shorts

cal'zone [kal'tsone] *sm* trouser leg; (*CUC*) savoury turnover made with pizza dough; **~i** *smpl* (*pantaloni*) trousers (*BRIT*), pants (*US*)

cambi'ale *sf* bill (of exchange); (*pagherò cambiario*) promissory note

cambia'mento *sm* change

cambi'are *vt* to change; (*modificare*) to alter, change; (*barattare*): **~ (qc con qn/ qc)** to exchange (sth with sb/for sth) ♦ *vi* to change, alter; **~rsi** *vr* (*d'abito*) to change; **~ casa** to move (house); **~ idea** to change one's mind; **~ treno** to change trains

'**cambio** *sm* change; (*modifica*) alteration, change; (*scambio, COMM*) exchange; (*corso dei cambi*) rate (of exchange); (*TECN, AUT*) gears *pl*; **in ~ di** in exchange for; **dare il ~ a qn** to take over from sb

'**camera** *sf* room; (*anche*: **~ da letto**) bedroom; (*POL*) chamber, house; **~ ardente** mortuary chapel; **~ d'aria** inner tube; (*di pallone*) bladder; **C~ di Commercio** Chamber of Commerce; **C~ dei Deputati** Chamber of Deputies, ≈ House of

Commons (*BRIT*), ≈ House of
Representatives (*US*); **~ a gas** gas chamber;
~ a un letto/a due letti/matrimoniale
single/twin-bedded/double room; **~ oscura**
(*FOT*) dark room
came'rata, i, e *sm/f* companion, mate
♦ *sf* dormitory
cameri'era *sf* (*domestica*) maid; (*che serve
a tavola*) waitress; (*che fa le camere*)
chambermaid
cameri'ere *sm* (man)servant; (*di ristorante*)
waiter
came'rino *sm* (*TEATRO*) dressing room
'camice ['kamitʃe] *sm* (*REL*) alb; (*per medici
etc*) white coat
cami'cetta [kami'tʃetta] *sf* blouse
ca'micia, cie [ka'mitʃa] *sf* (*da uomo*) shirt;
(*da donna*) blouse; **~ di forza** straitjacket
cami'netto *sm* hearth, fireplace
ca'mino *sm* chimney; (*focolare*) fireplace,
hearth
'camion *sm inv* lorry (*BRIT*), truck (*US*);
camion'cino *sm* van
cam'mello *sm* (*ZOOL*) camel; (*tessuto*)
camel hair
cammi'nare *vi* to walk; (*funzionare*) to
work, go; **cammi'nata** *sf* walk
cam'mino *sm* walk; (*sentiero*) path;
(*itinerario, direzione, tragitto*) way; **mettersi
in ~** to set *o* start off
camo'milla *sf* camomile; (*infuso*)
camomile tea
ca'morra *sf* camorra; racket
ca'moscio [ka'moʃʃo] *sm* chamois; **di ~**
(*scarpe, borsa*) suede *cpd*
cam'pagna [kam'paɲɲa] *sf* country,
countryside; (*POL, COMM, MIL*) campaign; **in
~** in the country; **andare in ~** to go to the
country; **fare una ~** to campaign;
campa'gnola *sf* (*AUT*) cross-country
vehicle; **campa'gnolo, a** *ag* country *cpd*
cam'pale *ag* field *cpd*; (*fig*): **una giornata
~** a hard day
cam'pana *sf* bell; (*anche: ~ di vetro*) bell
jar; **campa'nella** *sf* small bell; (*di tenda*)
curtain ring; **campa'nello** *sm* (*all'uscio,
da tavola*) bell

campa'nile *sm* bell tower, belfry;
campani'lismo *sm* parochialism
cam'pare *vi* to live; (*tirare avanti*) to get
by, manage
cam'pato, a *ag*: **~ in aria** unfounded
campeggi'are [kamped'dʒare] *vi* to camp;
(*risaltare*) to stand out; **campeggia'tore,
'trice** *sm/f* camper; **cam'peggio** *sm*
camping; (*terreno*) camp site; **fare (del)
campeggio** to go camping
cam'pestre *ag* country *cpd*, rural

| **Campidoglio** |

i The **Campidoglio**, one of the Seven
Hills of Rome, is the site of the **Comune
di Roma**.

---

campio'nario, a *ag*: **fiera ~a** trade fair
♦ *sm* collection of samples
campio'nato *sm* championship
campi'one, 'essa *sm/f* (*SPORT*) champion
♦ *sm* (*COMM*) sample
'campo *sm* field; (*MIL*) field; (*: accam-
pamento*) camp; (*spazio delimitato:
sportivo etc*) ground; field; (*di quadro*)
background; **i ~i** (*campagna*) the
countryside; **~ di aviazione** airfield; **~ di
battaglia** (*MIL, fig*) battlefield; **~ di golf** golf
course; **~ da tennis** tennis court; **~ visivo**
field of vision
campo'santo (*pl* **campisanti**) *sm*
cemetery
camuf'fare *vt* to disguise
'Canada *sm*: **il ~** Canada; **cana'dese** *ag,
sm/f* Canadian ♦ *sf* (*anche:* **tenda
canadese**) ridge tent
ca'naglia [ka'naʎʎa] *sf* rabble, mob;
(*persona*) scoundrel, rogue
ca'nale *sm* (*anche fig*) channel; (*artificiale*)
canal
'canapa *sf* hemp; **~ indiana** (*droga*)
cannabis
cana'rino *sm* canary
cancel'lare [kantʃel'lare] *vt* (*con la gomma*)
to rub out, erase; (*con la penna*) to strike
out; (*annullare*) to annul, cancel; (*disdire*) to
cancel

cancelle'ria [kantʃelleˈria] *sf* chancery; (*materiale per scrivere*) stationery

cancelli'ere [kantʃelˈljere] *sm* chancellor; (*di tribunale*) clerk of the court

can'cello [kanˈtʃello] *sm* gate

can'crena *sf* gangrene

'cancro *sm* (*MED*) cancer; (*dello zodiaco*): **C~** Cancer

candeg'gina [kandedˈdʒina] *sf* bleach

can'dela *sf* candle; **~ (di accensione)** (*AUT*) spark(ing) plug

cande'labro *sm* candelabra

candeli'ere *sm* candlestick

candi'dato, a *sm/f* candidate; (*aspirante a una carica*) applicant

'candido, a *ag* white as snow; (*puro*) pure; (*sincero*) sincere, candid

can'dito, a *ag* candied

can'dore *sm* brilliant white; purity; sincerity, candour

'cane *sm* dog; (*di pistola, fucile*) cock; **fa un freddo ~** it's bitterly cold; **non c'era un ~** there wasn't a soul; **~ da caccia/ uardia** hunting/guard dog; **~ lupo** alsatian

ca'nestro *sm* basket

'canfora *sf* camphor

cangi'ante [kanˈdʒante] *ag* iridescent

can'guro *sm* kangaroo

ca'nile *sm* kennel; (*di allevamento*) kennels *pl*; **~ municipale** dog pound

ca'nino, a *ag, sm* canine

'canna *sf* (*pianta*) reed; (*: indica, da zucchero*) cane; (*bastone*) stick, cane; (*di fucile*) barrel; (*di organo*) pipe; (*fam: droga*) joint; **~ da pesca** (fishing) rod; **~ da zucchero** sugar cane

can'nella *sf* (*CUC*) cinnamon

cannel'loni *smpl* pasta tubes stuffed with sauce and baked

cannocchi'ale [kannokˈkjale] *sm* telescope

can'none *sm* (*MIL*) gun; (*: STORIA*) cannon; (*tubo*) pipe, tube; (*piega*) box pleat; (*fig*) ace

can'nuccia, ce [kanˈnuttʃa] *sf* (drinking) straw

ca'noa *sf* canoe

'canone *sm* canon, criterion; (*mensile, annuo*) rent; fee

ca'nonico, ci *sm* (*REL*) canon

ca'noro, a *ag* (*uccello*) singing, song *cpd*

canot'taggio [kanotˈtaddʒo] *sm* rowing

canotti'era *sf* vest

ca'notto *sm* small boat, dinghy; canoe

cano'vaccio [kanoˈvattʃo] *sm* (*tela*) canvas; (*strofinaccio*) duster; (*trama*) plot

can'tante *sm/f* singer

can'tare *vt, vi* to sing; **cantau'tore, 'trice** *sm/f* singer-composer

canti'ere *sm* (*EDIL*) (building) site; (*anche:* **~ navale**) shipyard

canti'lena *sf* (*filastrocca*) lullaby; (*fig*) sing-song voice

can'tina *sf* cellar; (*bottega*) wine shop

'canto *sm* song; (*arte*) singing; (*REL*) chant; chanting; (*poesia*) poem, lyric; (*parte di una poesia*) canto; (*parte, lato*): **da un ~** on the one hand; **d'altro ~** on the other hand

canto'nata *sf* corner; **prendere una ~** (*fig*) to blunder

can'tone *sm* (*in Svizzera*) canton

can'tuccio [kanˈtuttʃo] *sm* corner, nook

canzo'nare [kantsoˈnare] *vt* to tease

can'zone [kanˈtsone] *sf* song; (*POESIA*) canzone; **canzoni'ere** *sm* (*MUS*) songbook; (*LETTERATURA*) collection of poems

'caos *sm inv* chaos; **ca'otico, a, ci, che** *ag* chaotic

C.A.P. *sigla m* = **codice di avviamento postale**

ca'pace [kaˈpatʃe] *ag* able, capable; (*ampio, vasto*) large, capacious; **sei ~ di farlo?** can you *o* are you able to do it?; **capacità** *sf inv* ability; (*DIR, di recipiente*) capacity; **capaci'tarsi** *vr* to understand

ca'panna *sf* hut

capan'none *sm* (*AGR*) barn; (*fabbricato industriale*) (factory) shed

ca'parbio, a *ag* stubborn

ca'parra *sf* deposit, down payment

ca'pello *sm* hair; **~i** *smpl* (*capigliatura*) hair *sg*

capez'zale [kapetˈtsale] *sm* bolster; (*fig*)

bedside

ca'pezzolo [ka'pettsolo] *sm* nipple

capi'enza [ka'pjentsa] *sf* capacity

capiglia'tura [kapiʎʎa'tura] *sf* hair

ca'pire *vt* to understand

capi'tale *ag* (*mortale*) capital; (*fondamentale*) main, chief ♦ *sf* (*città*) capital ♦ *sm* (*ECON*) capital; capita'lismo *sm* capitalism; capita'lista, i, e *ag*, *sm/f* capitalist

capitane'ria *sf*: ~ di porto port authorities *pl*

capi'tano *sm* captain

capi'tare *vi* (*giungere casualmente*) to happen to go, find o.s.; (*accadere*) to happen; (*presentarsi: cosa*) to turn up, present itself ♦ *vb impers* to happen; mi è capitato un guaio I've had a spot of trouble

capi'tello *sm* (*ARCHIT*) capital

ca'pitolo *sm* chapter

capi'tombolo *sm* headlong fall, tumble

'capo *sm* head; (*persona*) head, leader; (: *in ufficio*) head, boss; (: *in tribù*) chief; (*di oggetti*) head; top; end; (*GEO*) cape; andare a ~ to start a new paragraph; da ~ over again; ~ di bestiame head *inv* of cattle; ~ di vestiario item of clothing

'capo... *prefisso*: capocu'oco, chi *sm* head cook; Capo'danno *sm* New Year; capo'fitto: a capofitto *av* headfirst, headlong; capo'giro *sm* dizziness *no pl*; capola'voro, i *sm* masterpiece; capo'linea (*pl* capi'linea) *sm* terminus; capo'lino *sm*: fare capolino to peep out (*o in etc*); capolu'ogo (*pl* -ghi *o* capilu'oghi) *sm* chief town, administrative centre

capo'rale *sm* (*MIL*) lance corporal (*BRIT*), private first class (*US*)

'capo... *prefisso*: capostazi'one (*pl* capistazi'one) *sm* station master; capo'treno (*pl* capi'treno *o* capo'treni) *sm* guard

capo'volgere [kapo'voldʒere] *vt* to overturn; (*fig*) to reverse; ~rsi *vr* to overturn; (*barca*) to capsize; (*fig*) to be

reversed; capo'volto, a *pp di* capovolgere

'cappa *sf* (*mantello*) cape, cloak; (*del camino*) hood

cap'pella *sf* (*REL*) chapel; cappel'lano *sm* chaplain

cap'pello *sm* hat

'cappero *sm* caper

cap'pone *sm* capon

cap'potto *sm* (over)coat

cappuc'cino [kapput'tʃino] *sm* (*frate*) Capuchin monk; (*bevanda*) cappuccino, frothy white coffee

cap'puccio [kap'puttʃo] *sm* (*copricapo*) hood; (*della biro*) cap

'capra *sf* (she-)goat; ca'pretto *sm* kid

ca'priccio [ka'prittʃo] *sm* caprice, whim; (*bizza*) tantrum; fare i ~i to be very naughty; capricci'oso, a *ag* capricious, whimsical; naughty

Capri'corno *sm* Capricorn

capri'ola *sf* somersault

capri'olo *sm* roe deer

'capro *sm*: ~ espiatorio scapegoat

'capsula *sf* capsule; (*di arma, per bottiglie*) cap

cap'tare *vt* (*RADIO, TV*) to pick up; (*cattivarsi*) to gain, win

cara'bina *sf* rifle

carabini'ere *sm* member of Italian military police force

Originally part of the armed forces, the carabinieri *are police who now perform both military and civil duties and include paratroop units and mounted divisions.*

ca'raffa *sf* carafe

cara'mella *sf* sweet

ca'rattere *sm* character; (*caratteristica*) characteristic, trait; avere un buon ~ to be good-natured; caratte'ristica, che *sf* characteristic, trait, peculiarity; caratte'ristico, a, ci, che *ag* characteristic; caratteriz'zare *vt* to characterize

car'bone *sm* coal

carbu'rante *sm* (motor) fuel

carbura'tore *sm* carburettor

car'cassa *sf* carcass; (*fig: peg: macchina etc*) (old) wreck

carce'rato, a [kartʃe'rato] *sm/f* prisoner

'carcere ['kartʃere] *sm* prison; (*pena*) imprisonment

carci'ofo [kar'tʃɔfo] *sm* artichoke

car'diaco, a, ci, che *ag* cardiac, heart *cpd*

cardi'nale *ag, sm* cardinal

'cardine *sm* hinge

'cardo *sm* thistle

ca'renza [ka'rentsa] *sf* lack, scarcity; (*vitaminica*) deficiency

cares'tia *sf* famine; (*penuria*) scarcity, dearth

ca'rezza [ka'rettsa] *sf* caress; **carez'zare** *vt* to caress, stroke

'carica, che *sf* (*mansione ufficiale*) office, position; (*MIL, TECN, ELETTR*) charge; **ha una forte ~ di simpatia** he's very likeable; *vedi anche* **carico**

cari'care *vt* to load; (*orologio*) to wind up; (*batteria, MIL*) to charge

'carico, a, chi, che *ag* (*che porta un peso*): **~ di** loaded *o* laden with; (*fucile*) loaded; (*orologio*) wound up; (*batteria*) charged; (*colore*) deep; (*caffè, tè*) strong ♦ *sm* (*il caricare*) loading; (*ciò che si carica*) load; (*fig: peso*) burden, weight; **persona a ~** dependent; **essere a ~ di qn** (*spese etc*) to be charged to sb

'carie *sf* (*dentaria*) decay

ca'rino, a *ag* (*grazioso*) lovely, pretty, nice; (*riferito a uomo, anche simpatico*) nice

carità *sf* charity; **per ~!** (*escl di rifiuto*) good heavens, no!

carnagi'one [karna'dʒone] *sf* complexion

car'nale *ag* (*amore*) carnal

'carne *sf* flesh; (*bovina, ovina etc*) meat; **~ di manzo/maiale/pecora** beef/pork/mutton; **~ tritata** mince (*BRIT*), hamburger meat (*US*), minced (*BRIT*) *o* ground (*US*) meat

car'nefice [kar'nefitʃe] *sm* executioner; (*alla forca*) hangman

carne'vale *sm* carnival

---

i **Carnevale** *is the period between Epiphany (Jan. 6th) and the beginning of Lent. People wear fancy dress, and there are parties, processions of floats and bonfires. It culminates immediately before Lent in the festivities of* **martedì grasso** *(Shrove Tuesday).*

---

car'noso, a *ag* fleshy

'caro, a *ag* (*amato*) dear; (*costoso*) dear, expensive

ca'rogna [ka'roɲɲa] *sf* carrion; (*fig: fam*) swine

ca'rota *sf* carrot

caro'vana *sf* caravan

caro'vita *sm* high cost of living

carpenti'ere *sm* carpenter

car'pire *vt*: **~ qc a qn** (*segreto etc*) to get sth out of sb

car'poni *av* on all fours

car'rabile *ag* suitable for vehicles; **"passo ~"** "keep clear"

car'raio, a *ag*: **passo ~** driveway

carreggi'ata [karred'dʒata] *sf* carriageway (*BRIT*), (road)way

car'rello *sm* trolley; (*AER*) undercarriage; (*CINEMA*) dolly; (*di macchina da scrivere*) carriage

carri'era *sf* career; **fare ~** to get on; **a gran ~** at full speed

carri'ola *sf* wheelbarrow

'carro *sm* cart, wagon; **~ armato** tank; **~ attrezzi** breakdown van

car'rozza [kar'rottsa] *sf* carriage, coach

carrozze'ria [karrottse'ria] *sf* body, coachwork (*BRIT*); (*officina*) coachbuilder's workshop (*BRIT*), body shop

carroz'zina [karrot'tsina] *sf* pram (*BRIT*), baby carriage (*US*)

'carta *sf* paper; (*al ristorante*) menu; (*GEO*) map; plan; (*documento, da gioco*) card; (*costituzione*) charter; **~e** *sfpl* (*documenti*) papers, documents; **alla ~** (*al ristorante*) à la carte; **~ assegni** bank card; **~ assorbente** blotting paper; **~ bollata** o **da bollo** official stamped paper; **~ di credito** credit card; **~ (geografica)** map; **~ d'identità** identity card; **~ igienica** toilet paper; **~ d'imbarco** (*AER, NAUT*) boarding card; **~ da lettere** writing paper; **~ libera** (*AMM*) unstamped paper; **~ da parati** wallpaper; **~ stradale** road map; **~ verde** (*AUT*) green card; **~ vetrata** sandpaper; **~ da visita** visiting card

cartacar'bone (*pl* **cartecar'bone**) *sf* carbon paper

car'taccia, ce [kar'tattʃa] *sf* waste paper

carta'pecora *sf* parchment

carta'pesta *sf* papier-mâché

car'teggio [kar'teddʒo] *sm* correspondence

car'tella *sf* (*scheda*) card; (*custodia: di cartone*) folder; (*: di uomo d'affari etc*) briefcase; (*: di scolaro*) schoolbag, satchel; **~ clinica** (*MED*) case sheet

car'tello *sm* sign; (*pubblicitario*) poster; (*stradale*) sign, signpost; (*ECON*) cartel; (*in dimostrazioni*) placard; **cartel'lone** *sm* (*pubblicitario*) advertising poster; (*della tombola*) scoring frame; (*TEATRO*) playbill; **tenere il cartellone** (*spettacolo*) to have a long run

carti'era *sf* paper mill

car'tina *sf* (*AUT, GEO*) map

car'toccio [kar'tɔttʃo] *sm* paper bag

cartole'ria *sf* stationer's (shop)

carto'lina *sf* postcard; **~ postale** ready-stamped postcard

car'tone *sm* cardboard; (*ARTE*) cartoon; **~i animati** *smpl* (*CINEMA*) cartoons

car'tuccia, ce [kar'tuttʃa] *sf* cartridge

'casa *sf* house; (*in senso astratto*) home; (*COMM*) firm, house; **essere a ~** to be at home; **vado a ~ mia/tua** I'm going home/to your house; **~ di cura** nursing home; **~ dello studente** student hostel; **~e popolari** ≈ council houses (*o* flats) (*BRIT*), ≈ public housing units (*US*); **vino della ~** house wine

ca'sacca, che *sf* military coat; (*di fantino*) blouse

casa'linga, ghe *sf* housewife

casa'lingo, a, ghi, ghe *ag* household, domestic; (*fatto a casa*) home-made; (*semplice*) homely; (*amante della casa*) home-loving; **~ghi** *smpl* household articles; **cucina ~a** plain home cooking

cas'care *vi* to fall; **cas'cata** *sf* fall; (*d'acqua*) cascade, waterfall

ca'scina [kaʃ'ʃina] *sf* farmstead

'casco, schi *sm* helmet; (*del parrucchiere*) hair-dryer; (*di banane*) bunch

casei'ficio [kazei'fitʃo] *sm* creamery

ca'sella *sf* pigeon-hole; **~ postale** post office box

casel'lario *sm* filing cabinet; **~ giudiziale** court records *pl*

ca'sello *sm* (*di autostrada*) toll-house

ca'serma *sf* barracks *pl*

ca'sino (*fam*) *sm* brothel; (*confusione*) row, racket

casinò *sm inv* casino

'caso *sm* chance; (*fatto, vicenda*) event, incident; (*possibilità*) possibility; (*MED, LING*) case; **a ~** at random; **per ~** by chance, by accident; **in ogni ~, in tutti i ~i** in any case, at any rate; **al ~** should the opportunity arise; **nel ~ che** in case; **~ mai** if by chance; **~ limite** borderline case

caso'lare *sm* cottage

'cassa *sf* case, crate, box; (*bara*) coffin; (*mobile*) chest; (*involucro: di orologio etc*) case; (*macchina*) cash register, till; (*luogo di pagamento*) checkout (counter); (*fondo*) fund; (*istituto bancario*) bank; **~ automatica prelievi** cash dispenser; **~ continua** night safe; **~ integrazione: mettere in ~ integrazione** ≈ to lay off; **~ mutua** o **malattia** health insurance scheme; **~ di risparmio** savings bank; **~ toracica** (*ANAT*) chest

cassa'forte (*pl* **casse'forti**) *sf* safe

cassa'panca (*pl* **cassa'panche** *o* **casse'panche**) *sf* settle

casse'rola *sf* = **casseruola**

casseru'ola *sf* saucepan

cas'setta *sf* box; (*per registratore*) cassette; (*CINEMA, TEATRO*) box-office takings *pl*; **film**

di ~ box-office draw; **~ di sicurezza** strongbox; **~ delle lettere** letterbox

cas'setto *sm* drawer; **casset'tone** *sm* chest of drawers

cassi'ere, a *sm/f* cashier; *(di banca)* teller

casso'netto *sm* wheelie-bin

'casta *sf* caste

cas'tagna [kas'taɲɲa] *sf* chestnut

cas'tagno [kas'taɲɲo] *sm* chestnut (tree)

cas'tano, a *ag* chestnut (brown)

cas'tello *sm* castle; *(TECN)* scaffolding

casti'gare *vt* to punish; **cas'tigo, ghi** *sm* punishment

castità *sf* chastity

cas'toro *sm* beaver

cas'trare *vt* to castrate; to geld; to doctor *(BRIT)*, fix *(US)*

casu'ale *ag* chance *cpd*; *(INFORM)* random *cpd*

cata'comba *sf* catacomb

ca'talogo, ghi *sm* catalogue

catarifran'gente [katarifran'dʒɛnte] *sm* *(AUT)* reflector

ca'tarro *sm* catarrh

ca'tasta *sf* stack, pile

ca'tasto *sm* land register; land registry office

ca'tastrofe *sf* catastrophe, disaster

catego'ria *sf* category

ca'tena *sf* chain; **~ di montaggio** assembly line; **~e da neve** *(AUT)* snow chains; **cate'naccio** *sm* bolt

cate'ratta *sf* cataract; *(chiusa)* sluice-gate

cati'nella *sf*: **piovere a ~e** to pour

ca'tino *sm* basin

ca'trame *sm* tar

'cattedra *sf* teacher's desk; *(di docente)* chair

catte'drale *sf* cathedral

catti'veria *sf* malice, spite; naughtiness; *(atto)* spiteful act; *(parole)* malicious *o* spiteful remark

cattività *sf* captivity

cat'tivo, a *ag* bad; *(malvagio)* bad, wicked; *(turbolento: bambino)* bad, naughty; *(: mare)* rough; *(odore, sapore)* nasty, bad

cat'tolico, a, ci, che *ag, sm/f* (Roman) Catholic

cat'tura *sf* capture

cattu'rare *vt* to capture

cauc'ciù [kaut'tʃu] *sm* rubber

'causa *sf* cause; *(DIR)* lawsuit, case, action; **a ~ di, per ~ di** because of; **fare** *o* **muovere ~ a qn** to take legal action against sb

cau'sare *vt* to cause

cau'tela *sf* caution, prudence

caute'lare *vt* to protect; **~rsi** *vr*: **~rsi (da)** to take precautions (against)

'cauto, a *ag* cautious, prudent

cauzi'one [kaut'tsjone] *sf* security; *(DIR)* bail

cav. *abbr* = **cavaliere**

'cava *sf* quarry

caval'care *vt* *(cavallo)* to ride; *(muro)* to sit astride; *(sog: ponte)* to span; **caval'cata** *sf* ride; *(gruppo di persone)* riding party

cavalca'via *sm inv* flyover

cavalci'oni [kaval'tʃoni]: **a ~ di** *prep* astride

cavali'ere *sm* rider; *(feudale, titolo)* knight; *(soldato)* cavalryman; *(al ballo)* partner; **cavalle'resco, a, schi, sche** *ag* chivalrous; **cavalle'ria** *sf* *(di persona)* chivalry; *(milizia a cavallo)* cavalry

cavalle'rizzo, a [kavalle'rittso] *sm/f* riding instructor; circus rider

caval'letta *sf* grasshopper

caval'letto *sm* *(FOT)* tripod; *(da pittore)* easel

ca'vallo *sm* horse; *(SCACCHI)* knight; *(AUT: anche: ~ vapore)* horsepower; *(dei pantaloni)* crotch; **a ~** on horseback; **a ~ di** astride, straddling; **~ di battaglia** *(fig)* hobby-horse; **~ da corsa** racehorse

ca'vare *vt* *(togliere)* to draw out, extract, take out; *(: giacca, scarpe)* to take off; *(: fame, sete, voglia)* to satisfy; **cavarsela** to manage, get on all right; *(scamparla)* to get away with it

cava'tappi *sm inv* corkscrew

ca'verna *sf* cave

'cavia *sf* guinea pig

cavi'ale *sm* caviar

ca'viglia [ka'viʎʎa] *sf* ankle

ca'villo *sm* quibble

'cavo, a *ag* hollow ♦ *sm* (*ANAT*) cavity; (*corda, ELETTR, TEL*) cable

cavolfi'ore *sm* cauliflower

'cavolo *sm* cabbage; (*fam*): **non m'importa un ~** I don't give a damn; **~ di Bruxelles** Brussels sprout

cazzu'ola [kat'tswɔla] *sf* trowel

c/c *abbr* = **conto corrente**

CD *sm inv* CD

CD-ROM [tʃidi'rɔm] *sm inv* CD-ROM

C.E. [tʃe] *sigla f* (= *Comunità Europea*) EC

ce [tʃe] *pron, av vedi* ci

'cece ['tʃetʃe] *sm* chickpea

cecità [tʃetʃi'ta] *sf* blindness

'ceco, a ['tʃɛko] *ag, sm/f* Czech; **la Repubblica ~a** the Czech Republic

Cecoslo'vacchia [tʃekoslo'vakkja] *sf*: **la ~** Czechoslovakia

'cedere ['tʃɛdere] *vt* (*concedere: posto*) to give up; (*DIR*) to transfer, make over ♦ *vi* (*cadere*) to give way, subside; **~ (a)** to surrender (to), yield (to), give in (to); ce'devole *ag* (*terreno*) soft; (*fig*) yielding

'cedola ['tʃɛdola] *sf* (*COMM*) coupon; voucher

'cedro ['tʃɛdro] *sm* cedar; (*albero da frutto, frutto*) citron

'ceffo ['tʃeffo] (*peg*) *sm* ugly mug

cef'fone [tʃef'fone] *sm* slap, smack

ce'lare [tʃe'lare] *vt* to conceal; **~rsi** to hide

cele'brare [tʃele'brare] *vt* to celebrate; celebrazi'one *sf* celebration

'celebre ['tʃɛlebre] *ag* famous, celebrated; celebrità *sf inv* fame; (*persona*) celebrity

'celere ['tʃelere] *ag* fast, swift; (*corso*) crash *cpd*

ce'leste [tʃe'leste] *ag* celestial; heavenly; (*colore*) sky-blue

'celibe ['tʃelibe] *ag* single, unmarried

'cella ['tʃella] *sf* cell

'cellula ['tʃellula] *sf* (*BIOL, ELETTR, POL*) cell; cellu'lare *sm* cellphone

cellu'lite [tʃellu'lite] *sf* cellulite

cemen'tare [tʃemen'tare] *vt* (*anche fig*) to cement

ce'mento [tʃe'mento] *sm* cement; **~ armato** reinforced concrete

'cena ['tʃena] *sf* dinner; (*leggera*) supper

ce'nare [tʃe'nare] *vi* to dine, have dinner

'cencio ['tʃentʃo] *sm* piece of cloth, rag; (*per spolverare*) duster

'cenere ['tʃenere] *sf* ash

'cenno ['tʃenno] *sm* (*segno*) sign, signal; (*gesto*) gesture; (*col capo*) nod; (*con la mano*) wave; (*allusione*) hint, mention; (*breve esposizione*) short account; **far ~ di sì/no** to nod (one's head)/shake one's head

censi'mento [tʃensi'mento] *sm* census

cen'sura [tʃen'sura] *sf* censorship; censor's office; (*fig*) censure

cente'nario, a [tʃente'narjo] *ag* (*che ha cento anni*) hundred-year-old; (*che ricorre ogni cento anni*) centennial, centenary *cpd* ♦ *sm/f* centenarian ♦ *sm* centenary

cen'tesimo, a [tʃen'tezimo] *ag, sm* hundredth

cen'tigrado, a [tʃen'tigrado] *ag* centigrade; **20 gradi ~i** 20 degrees centigrade

cen'timetro [tʃen'timetro] *sm* centimetre

centi'naio [tʃenti'najo] (*pl(f)* **-aia**) *sm*: **un ~ (di)** a hundred; about a hundred

'cento ['tʃento] *num* a hundred, one hundred

cen'trale [tʃen'trale] *ag* central ♦ *sf*: **~ telefonica** (telephone) exchange; **~ elettrica** electric power station; centrali'nista *sm/f* operator; centra'lino *sm* (telephone) exchange; (*di albergo etc*) switchboard

cen'trare [tʃen'trare] *vt* to hit the centre of; (*TECN*) to centre

cen'trifuga [tʃen'trifuga] *sf* spin-dryer

'centro ['tʃentro] *sm* centre; **~ civico** civic centre; **~ commerciale** shopping centre; (*città*) commercial centre

'ceppo ['tʃeppo] *sm* (*di albero*) stump; (*pezzo di legno*) log

'cera ['tʃera] *sf* wax; (*aspetto*) appearance

ce'ramica, che [tʃe'ramika] *sf* ceramic; (*ARTE*) ceramics *sg*

cerbi'atto [tʃer'bjatto] *sm* (*ZOOL*) fawn

'cerca ['tʃerka] *sf*: **in o alla ~ di** in search of

cer'care [tʃer'kare] *vt* to look for, search for

♦ *vi*: **~ di fare qc** to try to do sth

'cerchia ['tʃerkja] *sf* circle

'cerchio ['tʃerkjo] *sm* circle; (*giocattolo, di botte*) hoop

cere'ale [tʃere'ale] *sm* cereal

ceri'monia [tʃeri'mɔnja] *sf* ceremony

ce'rino [tʃe'rino] *sm* wax match

'cernia ['tʃɛrnja] *sf* (*ZOOL*) stone bass

cerni'era [tʃer'njera] *sf* hinge; **~ lampo** zip (fastener) (*BRIT*), zipper (*US*)

'cernita ['tʃernita] *sf* selection

'cero ['tʃero] *sm* (church) candle

ce'rotto [tʃe'rɔtto] *sm* sticking plaster

certa'mente [tʃerta'mente] *av* certainly

cer'tezza [tʃer'tettsa] *sf* certainty

certifi'cato *sm* certificate; **~ medico/di nascita** medical/birth certificate

---
PAROLA CHIAVE

'certo, a ['tʃerto] *ag* (*sicuro*): **~ (di/che)** certain *o* sure (of/that)
♦ *det* 1 (*tale*) certain; **un ~ signor Smith** a (certain) Mr Smith
2 (*qualche; con valore intensivo*) some; **dopo un ~ tempo** after some time; **un fatto di una ~a importanza** a matter of some importance; **di una ~a età** past one's prime, not so young
♦ *pron*: **~i, e** *pl* some
♦ *av* (*certamente*) certainly; (*senz'altro*) of course; **di ~** certainly; **no (di) ~!, ~ che no!** certainly not!; **sì ~** yes indeed, certainly

---

cer'vello, i [tʃer'vello] (*ANAT*: *pl(f)* **-a**) *sm* brain

'cervo, a ['tʃervo] *sm/f* stag/doe ♦ *sm* deer; **~ volante** stag beetle

ce'sello [tʃe'zɛllo] *sm* chisel

ce'soie [tʃe'zoje] *sfpl* shears

ces'puglio [tʃes'puʎʎo] *sm* bush

ces'sare [tʃes'sare] *vi, vt* to stop, cease; **~ di fare qc** to stop doing sth

'cesso ['tʃesso] *sm* (*fam*) *sm* (*gabinetto*) bog

'cesta ['tʃesta] *sf* (large) basket

ces'tino [tʃes'tino] *sm* basket; (*per la carta straccia*) wastepaper basket; **~ da viaggio** (*FERR*) packed lunch (*o* dinner)

'cesto ['tʃesto] *sm* basket

'ceto ['tʃeto] *sm* (social) class

cetrio'lino [tʃetrio'lino] *sm* gherkin

cetri'olo [tʃetri'ɔlo] *sm* cucumber

CFC *sm inv* (= *clorofluorocarburo*) CFC

cfr. *abbr* (= *confronta*) cf

CGIL *sigla f* (= *Confederazione Generale Italiana del Lavoro*) *trades union organization*

PAROLA CHIAVE
---

che [ke] *pron* 1 (*relativo: persona: soggetto*) who; (*: oggetto*) whom, that; (*: cosa, animale*) which, that; **il ragazzo ~ è venuto** the boy who came; **l'uomo ~ io vedo** the man (whom) I see; **il libro ~ è sul tavolo** the book which *o* that is on the table; **il libro ~ vedi** the book (which *o* that) you see; **la sera ~ ti ho visto** the evening I saw you
2 (*interrogativo, esclamativo*) what; **~ (cosa) fai?** what are you doing?; **a ~ (cosa) pensi?** what are you thinking about?; **non sa ~ (cosa) fare** he doesn't know what to do; **ma ~ dici!** what are you saying!
3 (*indefinito*): **quell'uomo ha un ~ di losco** there's something suspicious about that man; **un certo non so ~** an indefinable something
♦ *det* 1 (*interrogativo: tra tanti*) what; (*: tra pochi*) which; **~ tipo di film preferisci?** what sort of film do you prefer?; **~ vestito ti vuoi mettere?** what (*o* which) dress do you want to put on?
2 (*esclamativo: seguito da aggettivo*) how; (*: seguito da sostantivo*) what; **~ buono!** how delicious!; **~ bel vestito!** what a lovely dress!
♦ *cong* 1 (*con proposizioni subordinate*) that; **credo ~ verrà** I think he'll come; **voglio ~ tu studi** I want you to study; **so ~ tu c'eri** I know (that) you were there; **non ~: non ~ sia sbagliato, ma ...** not that it's wrong, but ...
2 (*finale*) so that; **vieni qua, ~ ti veda** come here, so (that) I can see you

3 (*temporale*): **arrivai ~ eri già partito** you had already left when I arrived; **sono anni ~ non lo vedo** I haven't seen him for years
4 (*in frasi imperative, concessive*): **~ venga pure!** let him come by all means!; **~ tu sia benedetto!** may God bless you!
5 (*comparativo: con più, meno*) than; *vedi anche* **più; meno; così** *etc*

cheti'chella [keti'kɛlla]: **alla ~** *av* stealthily, unobtrusively

---

PAROLA CHIAVE

chi [ki] *pron* **1** (*interrogativo: soggetto*) who; (: *oggetto*) who, whom; **~ è?** who is it?; **di ~ è questo libro?** whose book is this?, whose is this book?; **con ~ parli?** who are you talking to?; **a ~ pensi?** who are you thinking about?; **~ di voi?** which of you?; **non so a ~ rivolgermi** I don't know who to ask
2 (*relativo*) whoever, anyone who; **dillo a ~ vuoi** tell whoever you like
3 (*indefinito*): **~ ... ~ ...** some ... others ...; **~ dice una cosa, ~ dice un'altra** some say one thing, others say another

---

chiacchie'rare [kjakkje'rare] *vi* to chat; (*discorrere futilmente*) to chatter; (*far pettegolezzi*) to gossip; **chiacchie'rata** *sf* chat; **chi'acchiere** *sfpl*: **fare due** *o* **quattro chiacchiere** to have a chat; **chiacchie'rone, a** *ag* talkative, chatty; gossipy ♦ *sm/f* chatterbox; gossip
chia'mare [kja'mare] *vt* to call; (*rivolgersi a qn*) to call (in), send for; **~rsi** *vr* (*aver nome*) to be called; **mi chiamo Paolo** my name is Paolo, I'm called Paolo; **~ alle armi** to call up; **~ in giudizio** to summon; **chia'mata** *sf* (*TEL*) call; (*MIL*) call-up
chia'rezza [kja'rettsa] *sf* clearness; clarity
chia'rire [kja'rire] *vt* to make clear; (*fig: spiegare*) to clear up, explain; **~rsi** *vr* to become clear
chi'aro, a ['kjaro] *ag* clear; (*luminoso*) clear, bright; (*colore*) pale, light
chiaroveg'gente [kjaroved'dʒɛnte] *sm/f*

clairvoyant
chi'asso ['kjasso] *sm* uproar, row; **chias'soso, a** *ag* noisy, rowdy; (*vistoso*) showy, gaudy
chi'ave ['kjave] *sf* key ♦ *ag inv* key *cpd*; **~ d'accensione** (*AUT*) ignition key; **~ inglese** monkey wrench; **~ di volta** keystone; **chiavis'tello** *sm* bolt
chi'azza ['kjattsa] *sf* stain; splash
'chicco, chi ['kikko] *sm* grain; (*di caffè*) bean; **~ d'uva** grape
chi'edere ['kjedere] *vt* (*per sapere*) to ask; (*per avere*) to ask for ♦ *vi*: **~ di qn** to ask after sb; (*al telefono*) to ask for *o* want sb; **~ qc a qn** to ask sb sth; to ask sb for sth
chi'erico, ci ['kjɛriko] *sm* cleric; altar boy
chi'esa ['kjɛza] *sf* church
chi'esto, a *pp di* **chiedere**
'chiglia ['kiʎʎa] *sf* keel
'chilo ['kilo] *sm* kilo; **chilo'grammo** *sm* kilogram(me); **chilome'traggio** *sm* ≈ mileage; **~metraggio illimitato** unlimited mileage; **chi'lometro** *sm* kilometre
'chimica ['kimika] *sf* chemistry
'chimico, a, ci, che ['kimiko] *ag* chemical ♦ *sm/f* chemist
'china ['kina] *sf* (*pendio*) slope, descent; (*inchiostro*) Indian ink
chi'nare [ki'nare] *vt* to lower, bend, ~rsi *vi* to stoop, bend
chi'nino [ki'nino] *sm* quinine
chi'occiola ['kjɔttʃola] *sf* snail; **scala a ~** spiral staircase
chi'odo ['kjɔdo] *sm* nail; (*fig*) obsession
chi'oma ['kjɔma] *sf* (*capelli*) head of hair
chi'osco, schi ['kjɔsko] *sm* kiosk, stall
chi'ostro ['kjɔstro] *sm* cloister
chiro'mante [kiro'mante] *sm/f* palmist
chirur'gia [kirur'dʒia] *sf* surgery; **~ estetica** cosmetic surgery; **chi'rurgo, ghi** *o* **gi** *sm* surgeon
chissà [kis'sa] *av* who knows, I wonder
chi'tarra [ki'tarra] *sf* guitar
chi'udere ['kjudere] *vt* to close, shut; (*luce, acqua*) to put off, turn off; (*definitivamente: fabbrica*) to close down, shut down;

(*strada*) to close; (*recingere*) to enclose; (*porre termine a*) to end ♦ *vi* to close, shut; to close down, shut down; to end; **~rsi** *vr* to shut, close; (*ritirarsi: anche fig*) to shut o.s. away; (*ferita*) to close up

chi'unque [ki'unkwe] *pron* (*relativo*) whoever; (*indefinito*) anyone, anybody; **~ sia** whoever it is

chi'uso, a ['kjuso] *pp di* **chiudere** ♦ *sf* (*di corso d'acqua*) sluice, lock; (*recinto*) enclosure; (*di discorso etc*) conclusion, ending; **chiu'sura** *sf* (*vedi* **chiudere**) closing; shutting; closing *o* shutting down; enclosing; putting *o* turning off; ending; (*dispositivo*) catch; fastening; fastener

---

PAROLA CHIAVE

---

ci [tʃi] (*dav lo, la, li, le, ne diventa* **ce**) *pron*
1 (*personale: complemento oggetto*) us; (*: a noi: complemento di termine*) (to) us; (*: riflessivo*) ourselves; (*: reciproco*) each other, one another; (*impersonale*): **~ si veste** we get dressed; **~ ha visti** he's seen us; **non ~ ha dato niente** he gave us nothing; **~ vestiamo** we get dressed; **~ amiamo** we love one another *o* each other
2 (*dimostrativo: di ciò, su ciò, in ciò etc*) about (*o* on *o* of) it; **non so cosa far~** I don't know what to do about it; **che c'entro io?** what have I got to do with it? ♦ *av* (*qui*) here; (*lì*) there; (*moto attraverso luogo*): **~ passa sopra un ponte** a bridge passes over it; **non ~ passa più nessuno** nobody comes this way any more; **esser~** *vedi* **essere**

---

cia'batta [tʃa'batta] *sf* slipper; (*pane*) ciabatta

ci'alda ['tʃalda] *sf* (*CUC*) wafer

ciam'bella [tʃam'bella] *sf* (*CUC*) ring-shaped cake; (*salvagente*) rubber ring

ci'ao ['tʃao] *escl* (*all'arrivo*) hello!; (*alla partenza*) cheerio! (*BRIT*), bye!

cias'cuno, a [tʃas'kuno] (*det: dav sm:* **ciascun** +*C, V,* **ciascuno** +*s impura, gn, pn, ps, x, z; dav sf:* **ciascuna** +*C,* **ciascun'** +*V*) *det* every, each; (*ogni*) every ♦ *pron* each

(one); (*tutti*) everyone, everybody

ci'barie [tʃi'barje] *sfpl* foodstuffs

'cibo ['tʃibo] *sm* food

ci'cala [tʃi'kala] *sf* cicada

cica'trice [tʃika'tritʃe] *sf* scar

'cicca ['tʃikka] *sf* cigarette end

'ciccia ['tʃittʃa] (*fam*) *sf* fat

cice'rone [tʃitʃe'rone] *sm* guide

ci'clismo [tʃi'klizmo] *sm* cycling; **ci'clista, i, e** *sm/f* cyclist

'ciclo ['tʃiklo] *sm* cycle; (*di malattia*) course

ciclomo'tore [tʃiklomo'tore] *sm* moped

ci'clone [tʃi'klone] *sm* cyclone

ci'cogna [tʃi'koɲɲa] *sf* stork

ci'coria [tʃi'korja] *sf* chicory

ci'eco, a, chi, che ['tʃeko] *ag* blind
♦ *sm/f* blind man/woman

ci'elo ['tʃelo] *sm* sky; (*REL*) heaven

'cifra ['tʃifra] *sf* (*numero*) figure; numeral; (*somma di denaro*) sum, figure; (*monogramma*) monogram, initials *pl*; (*codice*) code, cipher

'ciglio, i ['tʃiʎʎo] (*delle palpebre: pl(f)* **ciglia**) *sm* (*margine*) edge, verge; (eye)lash; (eye)lid; (*sopracciglio*) eyebrow

'cigno ['tʃiɲɲo] *sm* swan

cigo'lare [tʃiɡo'lare] *vi* to squeak, creak

'Cile ['tʃile] *sm*: **il ~** Chile

ci'lecca [tʃi'lekka] *sf*: **far ~** to fail

cili'egia, gie *o* **ge** [tʃi'ljedʒa] *sf* cherry; **cili'egio** *sm* cherry tree

cilin'drata [tʃilin'drata] *sf* (*AUT*) (cubic) capacity; **una macchina di grossa ~** a big-engined car

ci'lindro [tʃi'lindro] *sm* cylinder; (*cappello*) top hat

'cima ['tʃima] *sf* (*sommità*) top; (*di monte*) top, summit; (*estremità*) end; **in ~ a** at the top of; **da ~ a fondo** from top to bottom; (*fig*) from beginning to end

'cimice ['tʃimitʃe] *sf* (*ZOOL*) bug; (*puntina*) drawing pin (*BRIT*), thumbtack (*US*)

cimini'era [tʃimi'njera] *sf* chimney; (*di nave*) funnel

cimi'tero [tʃimi'tero] *sm* cemetery

'Cina ['tʃina] *sf*: **la ~** China

cin'cin [tʃin'tʃin] *escl* cheers!

cin cin [tʃin'tʃin] *escl* = **cincin**

'cinema ['tʃinema] *sm inv* cinema; **cine'presa** *sf* cine-camera

ci'nese [tʃi'nese] *ag, sm/f, sm* Chinese *inv*

'cingere ['tʃindʒere] *vt* (*attorniare*) to surround, encircle

'cinghia ['tʃingja] *sf* strap; (*cintura, TECN*) belt

cinghi'ale [tʃin'gjale] *sm* wild boar

cinguet'tare [tʃingwet'tare] *vi* to twitter

'cinico, a, ci, che ['tʃiniko] *ag* cynical ♦ *sm/f* cynic; **ci'nismo** *sm* cynicism

cin'quanta [tʃin'kwanta] *num* fifty; **cinquan'tesimo, a** *num* fiftieth

cinquan'tina [tʃiŋkwan'tina] *sf* (*serie*): **una ~ (di)** about fifty; (*età*): **essere sulla ~** to be about fifty

'cinque ['tʃinkwe] *num* five; **avere ~ anni** to be five (years old); **il ~ dicembre 1999** the fifth of December 1999; **alle ~** (*ora*) at five (o'clock)

cinque'cento [tʃinkwe'tʃento] *num* five hundred ♦ *sm*: **il C~** the sixteenth century

'cinto, a ['tʃinto] *pp di* **cingere**

cin'tura [tʃin'tura] *sf* belt; **~ di salvataggio** lifebelt (*BRIT*), life preserver (*US*); **~ di sicurezza** (*AUT, AER*) safety *o* seat belt

ciò [tʃɔ] *pron* this; that; **~ che** what; **~ nonostante** *o* **nondimeno** nevertheless, in spite of that

ci'occa, che ['tʃɔkka] *sf* (*di capelli*) lock

ciocco'lata [tʃokko'lata] *sf* chocolate; (*bevanda*) (hot) chocolate; **cioccola'tino** *sm* chocolate; **ciocco'lato** *sm* chocolate

cioè [tʃo'ɛ] *av* that is (to say)

ciondo'lare [tʃondo'lare] *vi* to dangle; (*fig*) to loaf (about); **ci'ondolo** *sm* pendant

ci'otola ['tʃɔtola] *sf* bowl

ci'ottolo ['tʃɔttolo] *sm* pebble; (*di strada*) cobble(stone)

ci'polla [tʃi'polla] *sf* onion; (*di tulipano etc*) bulb

ci'presso [tʃi'presso] *sm* cypress (tree)

'cipria ['tʃiprja] *sf* (face) powder

'Cipro ['tʃipro] *sm* Cyprus

'circa ['tʃirka] *av* about, roughly ♦ *prep* about, concerning; **a mezzogiorno ~** about midday

'circo, chi ['tʃirko] *sm* circus

circo'lare [tʃirko'lare] *vi* to circulate; (*AUT*) to drive (along), move (along) ♦ *ag* circular ♦ *sf* (*AMM*) circular; (*di autobus*) circle (line); **circolazi'one** *sf* circulation; (*AUT*): **la circolazione** (the) traffic

'circolo ['tʃirkolo] *sm* circle

circon'dare [tʃirkon'dare] *vt* to surround

circonfe'renza [tʃirkonfe'rentsa] *sf* circumference

circonvallazi'one [tʃirkonvallat'tsjone] *sf* ring road (*BRIT*), beltway (*US*); (*per evitare una città*) by-pass

circos'critto, a [tʃirkos'kritto] *pp di* **circoscrivere**

circos'crivere [tʃirkos'krivere] *vt* to circumscribe; (*fig*) to limit, restrict; **circoscrizi'one** *sf* (*AMM*) district, area; **circoscrizione elettorale** constituency

circos'petto, a [tʃirkos'petto] *ag* circumspect, cautious

circos'tante [tʃirkos'tante] *ag* surrounding, neighbouring

circos'tanza [tʃirkos'tantsa] *sf* circumstance; (*occasione*) occasion

cir'cuito [tʃir'kuito] *sm* circuit

CISL *sigla f* (= *Confederazione Italiana Sindacati Lavoratori*) *trades union organization*

'ciste ['tʃiste] *sf* = **cisti**

cis'terna [tʃis'terna] *sf* tank, cistern

'cisti ['tʃisti] *sf* cyst

C.I.T. [tʃit] *sigla f* = **Compagnia Italiana Turismo**

ci'tare [tʃi'tare] *vt* (*DIR*) to summon; (*autore*) to quote; (*a esempio, modello*) to cite; **citazi'one** *sf* summons *sg*; quotation; (*di persona*) mention

ci'tofono [tʃi'tɔfono] *sm* entry phone; (*in uffici*) intercom

città [tʃit'ta] *sf inv* town; (*importante*) city; **~ universitaria** university campus

cittadi'nanza [tʃittadi'nantsa] *sf* citizens *pl*; (*DIR*) citizenship

citta'dino, a [tʃitta'dino] *ag* town *cpd*; city *cpd* ♦ *sm/f* (*di uno Stato*) citizen; (*abitante*

di città) townsman, city dweller
ci'uco, a, chi, che ['tʃuko] *sm/f* ass,
donkey
ci'uffo ['tʃuffo] *sm* tuft
ci'vetta [tʃi'vetta] *sf* (*ZOOL*) owl; (*fig: donna*)
coquette, flirt ♦ *ag inv*: auto/nave ~
decoy car/ship
'civico, a, ci, che ['tʃiviko] *ag* civic;
(*museo*) municipal, town *cpd*; city *cpd*
ci'vile [tʃi'vile] *ag* civil; (*non militare*) civilian;
(*nazione*) civilized ♦ *sm* civilian
civilizzazi'one [tʃiviliddzat'tsjone] *sf*
civilization
civiltà [tʃivil'ta] *sf* civilization; (*cortesia*)
civility
'clacson *sm inv* (*AUT*) horn
cla'more *sm* (*frastuono*) din, uproar,
clamour; (*fig*) outcry; clamo'roso, a *ag*
noisy; (*fig*) sensational
clandes'tino, a *ag* clandestine; (*POL*)
underground, clandestine ♦ *sm/f* stowaway
clari'netto *sm* clarinet
'classe *sf* class; di ~ (*fig*) with class; of
excellent quality
'classico, a, ci, che *ag* classical;
(*tradizionale: moda*) classic(al) ♦ *sm* classic;
classical author
clas'sifica *sf* classification; (*SPORT*) placings
pl
classifi'care *vt* to classify; (*candidato,
compito*) to grade; ~rsi *vr* to be placed
'clausola *sf* (*DIR*) clause
'clava *sf* club
clavi'cembalo [klavi'tʃembalo] *sm*
harpsichord
cla'vicola *sf* (*ANAT*) collar bone
cle'mente *ag* merciful; (*clima*) mild;
cle'menza *sf* mercy, clemency; mildness
'clero *sm* clergy
cli'ente *sm/f* customer, client; clien'tela
sf customers *pl*, clientèle
'clima, i *sm* climate; cli'matico, a, ci,
che *ag* climatic; stazione climatica health
resort; climatizzatore *sm* air
conditioning system; climatizzazi'one *sf*
(*TECN*) air conditioning
'clinica, che *sf* (*scienza*) clinical medicine;

(*casa di cura*) clinic, nursing home; (*settore
d'ospedale*) clinic
'clinico, a, ci, che *ag* clinical ♦ *sm*
(*medico*) clinician
clo'aca, che *sf* sewer
'cloro *sm* chlorine
cloro'formio *sm* chloroform
club *sm inv* club
c.m. *abbr* = corrente mese
coabi'tare *vi* to live together
coagu'lare *vt* to coagulate ♦ *vi* to
coagulate; (*latte*) to curdle; ~rsi *vr* to
coagulate; to curdle
coalizi'one [koalit'tsjone] *sf* coalition
co'atto, a *ag* (*DIR*) compulsory, forced
'COBAS *sigla mpl* (= *Comitati di base*)
independent trades unions
Coca'Cola ® *sf* Coca-Cola ®
coca'ina *sf* cocaine
cocci'nella [kottʃi'nella] *sf* ladybird (*BRIT*),
ladybug (*US*)
'coccio ['kɔttʃo] *sm* earthenware; (*vaso*)
earthenware pot; ~i *smpl* (*frammenti*)
fragments (of pottery)
cocci'uto, a [kot'tʃuto] *ag* stubborn,
pigheaded
'cocco, chi *sm* (*pianta*) coconut palm;
(*frutto*): noce di ~ coconut ♦ *sm/f* (*fam*)
darling
cocco'drillo *sm* crocodile
cocco'lare *vt* to cuddle, fondle
co'cente [ko'tʃente] *ag* (*anche fig*) burning
co'comero *sm* watermelon
co'cuzzolo [ko'kuttsolo] *sm* top; (*di capo,
cappello*) crown
'coda *sf* tail; (*fila di persone, auto*) queue
(*BRIT*), line (*US*); (*di abiti*) train; con la ~
dell'occhio out of the corner of one's eye;
mettersi in ~ to queue (up) (*BRIT*), line up
(*US*); to join the queue (*BRIT*) *o* line (*US*); ~
di cavallo (*acconciatura*) ponytail
co'dardo, a *ag* cowardly ♦ *sm/f* coward
'codice ['koditʃe] *sm* code; ~ di
avviamento postale postcode (*BRIT*), zip
code (*US*); ~ fiscale tax code; ~ della
strada highway code
coe'rente *ag* coherent; coe'renza *sf*

coherence

coe'taneo, a *ag, sm/f* contemporary

'cofano *sm* (*AUT*) bonnet (*BRIT*), hood (*US*); (*forziere*) chest

'cogli ['kɔʎʎi] *prep* + *det* = **con** + **gli**; *vedi* **con**

'cogliere ['kɔʎʎere] *vt* (*fiore, frutto*) to pick, gather; (*sorprendere*) to catch, surprise; (*bersaglio*) to hit; (*fig: momento opportuno etc*) to grasp, seize, take; (*: capire*) to grasp; **~ qn in flagrante** *o* **in fallo** to catch sb red-handed

co'gnato, a [koɲ'ɲato] *sm/f* brother-/sister-in-law

co'gnome [koɲ'ɲome] *sm* surname

'coi *prep* + *det* = **con** + **i**; *vedi* **con**

coinci'denza [kointʃi'dɛntsa] *sf* coincidence; (*FERR, AER, di autobus*) connection

coin'cidere [koin'tʃidere] *vi* to coincide; **coin'ciso, a** *pp di* **coincidere**

coin'volgere [koin'vɔldʒere] *vt*: **~ in** to involve in; **coin'volto, a** *pp di* **coinvolgere**

col *prep* + *det* = **con** + **il**; *vedi* **con**

cola'brodo *sm inv* strainer

cola'pasta *sm inv* colander

co'lare *vt* (*liquido*) to strain; (*pasta*) to drain; (*oro fuso*) to pour ♦ *vi* (*sudore*) to drip; (*botte*) to leak; (*cera*) to melt; **~ a picco** *vt, vi* (*nave*) to sink

co'lata *sf* (*di lava*) flow; (*FONDERIA*) casting

colazi'one [kolat'tsjone] *sf* (*anche*: **prima ~**) breakfast; (*anche*: **seconda ~**) lunch; **fare ~** to have breakfast (*o* lunch)

co'lei *pron vedi* **colui**

co'lera *sm* (*MED*) cholera

'colica *sf* (*MED*) colic

'colla *sf* glue; (*di farina*) paste

collabo'rare *vi* to collaborate; **~ a** to collaborate on; (*giornale*) to contribute to; **collabora'tore, 'trice** *sm/f* collaborator; contributor

col'lana *sf* necklace; (*collezione*) collection, series

col'lant [kɔ'lã] *sm inv* tights *pl*

col'lare *sm* collar

col'lasso *sm* (*MED*) collapse

collau'dare *vt* to test, try out; **col'laudo** *sm* testing *no pl*; test

'colle *sm* hill

col'lega, ghi, ghe *sm/f* colleague

collega'mento *sm* connection; (*MIL*) liaison

colle'gare *vt* to connect, join, link; **~rsi** *vr* (*RADIO, TV*) to link up; **~rsi con** (*TEL*) to get through to

col'legio [kol'lɛdʒo] *sm* college; (*convitto*) boarding school; **~ elettorale** (*POL*) constituency

'collera *sf* anger

col'lerico, a, ci, che *ag* quick-tempered, irascible

col'letta *sf* collection

collettività *sf* community

collet'tivo, a *ag* collective; (*interesse*) general, everybody's; (*biglietto, visita etc*) group *cpd* ♦ *sm* (*POL*) (political) group

col'letto *sm* collar

collezio'nare [kollettsjo'nare] *vt* to collect

collezi'one [kollet'tsjone] *sf* collection

colli'mare *vi* to correspond, coincide

col'lina *sf* hill

col'lirio *sm* eyewash

collisi'one *sf* collision

'collo *sm* neck; (*di abito*) neck, collar; (*pacco*) parcel; **~ del piede** instep

colloca'mento *sm* (*impiego*) employment; (*disposizione*) placing, arrangement

collo'care *vt* (*libri, mobili*) to place; (*COMM: merce*) to find a market for

col'loquio *sm* conversation, talk; (*ufficiale, per un lavoro*) interview; (*INS*) preliminary oral exam

col'mare *vt*: **~ di** (*anche fig*) to fill with; (*dare in abbondanza*) to load *o* overwhelm with; **'colmo, a** *ag*: **colmo (di)** full (of) ♦ *sm* summit, top; (*fig*) height; **al colmo della disperazione** in the depths of despair; **è il colmo!** it's the last straw!

co'lombo, a *sm/f* dove; pigeon

co'lonia *sf* colony; (*per bambini*) holiday camp; (**acqua di**) **~** (eau de) cologne; **coloni'ale** *ag* colonial ♦ *sm/f* colonist, settler

co'lonna *sf* column; ~ **vertebrale** spine, spinal column

colon'nello *sm* colonel

co'lono *sm* (*coltivatore*) tenant farmer

colo'rante *sm* colouring

colo'rare *vt* to colour; (*disegno*) to colour in

co'lore *sm* colour; **a ~i** in colour, colour *cpd*; **farne di tutti i ~i** to get up to all sorts of mischief

colo'rito, a *ag* coloured; (*viso*) rosy, pink; (*linguaggio*) colourful ♦ *sm* (*tinta*) colour; (*carnagione*) complexion

co'loro *pron pl vedi* **colui**

co'losso *sm* colossus

'colpa *sf* fault; (*biasimo*) blame; (*colpevolezza*) guilt; (*azione colpevole*) offence; (*peccato*) sin; **di chi è la ~?** whose fault is it?; **è ~ sua** it's his fault; **per ~ di** through, owing to; **col'pevole** *ag* guilty

col'pire *vt* to hit, strike; (*fig*) to strike; **rimanere colpito da qc** to be amazed *o* struck by sth

'colpo *sm* (*urto*) knock; (: *affettivo*) blow, shock; (: *aggressivo*) blow; (*di pistola*) shot; (*MED*) stroke; (*rapina*) raid; **di ~** suddenly; **fare ~** to make a strong impression; **~ di grazia** coup de grâce; **~ di scena** (*TEATRO*) coup de théâtre; (*fig*) dramatic turn of events; **~ di sole** sunstroke; **~ di Stato** coup d'état; **~ di telefono** phone call; **~ di testa** (sudden) impulse *o* whim; **~ di vento** gust (of wind)

coltel'lata *sf* stab

col'tello *sm* knife; **~ a serramanico** clasp knife

colti'vare *vt* to cultivate; (*verdura*) to grow, cultivate; **coltiva'tore** *sm* farmer; **coltivazi'one** *sf* cultivation; growing

'colto, a *pp di* **cogliere** ♦ *ag* (*istruito*) cultured, educated

'coltre *sf* blanket

col'tura *sf* cultivation

co'lui (*f* **co'lei**, *pl* **co'loro**) *pron* the one; ~ **che parla** the one *o* the man *o* the person who is speaking; **colei che amo** the one *o* the woman *o* the person (whom) I love

'coma *sm inv* coma

comanda'mento *sm* (*REL*) commandment

coman'dante *sm* (*MIL*) commander, commandant; (*di reggimento*) commanding officer; (*NAUT, AER*) captain

coman'dare *vi* to be in command ♦ *vt* to command; (*imporre*) to order, command; ~ **a qn di fare** to order sb to do; **co'mando** *sm* (*ingiunzione*) order, command; (*autorità*) command; (*TECN*) control

co'mare *sf* (*madrina*) godmother

combaci'are [komba'tʃare] *vi* to meet; (*fig: coincidere*) to coincide

com'battere *vt, vi* to fight; **combatti'mento** *sm* fight; fighting *no pl*; (*di pugilato*) match

combi'nare *vt* to combine; (*organizzare*) to arrange; (*fam: fare*) to make, cause; **combinazi'one** *sf* combination; (*caso fortuito*) coincidence; **per combinazione** by chance

combus'tibile *ag* combustible ♦ *sm* fuel

com'butta (*peg*) *sf*: **in ~** in league

PAROLA CHIAVE

'come *av* **1** (*alla maniera di*) like; **ti comporti ~ lui** you behave like him *o* like he does; **bianco ~ la neve** (as) white as snow; **~ se** as if, as though

2 (*in qualità di*) as a; **lavora ~ autista** he works as a driver

3 (*interrogativo*) how; **~ ti chiami?** what's your name?; **~ sta?** how are you?; **com'è il tuo amico?** what is your friend like?; **~?** (*prego?*) pardon?, sorry?; **~ mai?** how come?; **~ mai non ci hai avvertiti?** why on earth didn't you warn us?

4 (*esclamativo*): **~ sei bravo!** how clever you are!; **~ mi dispiace!** I'm terribly sorry!

♦ *cong* **1** (*in che modo*) how; **mi ha spiegato ~ l'ha conosciuto** he told me how he met him

2 (*correlativo*) as; (*con comparativi di maggioranza*) than; **non è bravo ~ pensavo** he isn't as clever as I thought; **è meglio di ~ pensassi** it's better than I

thought
3 (*appena che, quando*) as soon as; ~
arrivò, iniziò a lavorare as soon as he
arrived, he set to work; *vedi* **così; tanto**

'**comico, a, ci, che** *ag* (*TEATRO*) comic;
(*buffo*) comical ♦ *sm* (*attore*) comedian,
comic actor

co'**mignolo** [ko'miɲɲolo] *sm* chimney top

cominci'**are** [komin'tʃare] *vt, vi* to begin,
start; ~ **a fare/col fare** to begin to do/by
doing

comi'**tato** *sm* committee

comi'**tiva** *sf* party, group

co'**mizio** [ko'mittsjo] *sm* (*POL*) meeting,
assembly

com'**mando** *sm inv* commando (squad)

com'**media** *sf* comedy; (*opera teatrale*)
play; (*: che fa ridere*) comedy; (*fig*)
playacting *no pl*; **commedi'ante** (*peg*)
sm/f third-rate actor/actress; (*fig*) sham

commemo'**rare** *vt* to commemorate

commenda'**tore** *sm official title awarded
for services to one's country*

commen'**tare** *vt* to comment on; (*testo*)
to annotate; (*RADIO, TV*) to give a
commentary on; **commenta'tore, 'trice**
sm/f commentator; **com'mento** *sm*
comment; (*a un testo, RADIO, TV*)
commentary

commerci'**ale** [kommer'tʃale] *ag*
commercial, trading; (*peg*) commercial

commerci'**ante** [kommer'tʃante] *sm/f*
trader, dealer; (*negoziante*) shopkeeper

commerci'**are** [kommer'tʃare] *vt, vi:* ~ **in**
to deal *o* trade in

com'**mercio** [kom'mertʃo] *sm* trade,
commerce; **essere in** ~ (*prodotto*) to be on
the market *o* on sale; **essere nel** ~
(*persona*) to be in business

com'**messa** *sf* (*COMM*) order

com'**messo, a** *pp di* **commettere** ♦ *sm/f*
shop assistant (*BRIT*), sales clerk (*US*) ♦ *sm*
(*impiegato*) clerk; ~ **viaggiatore**
commercial traveller

commes'**tibile** *ag* edible; ~**i** *smpl*
foodstuffs

com'**mettere** *vt* to commit

com'**miato** *sm* leave-taking

commi'**nare** *vt* (*DIR*) to threaten; to inflict

commissari'**ato** *sm* (*AMM*)
commissionership; (*: sede*) commissioner's
office; (*: di polizia*) police station

commis'**sario** *sm* commissioner; (*di
pubblica sicurezza*) ≈ (police)
superintendent (*BRIT*), (police) captain (*US*);
(*SPORT*) steward; (*membro di commissione*)
member of a committee *o* board

commissio'**nario** *sm* (*COMM*) agent,
broker

commissi'**one** *sf* (*incarico*) errand;
(*comitato, percentuale*) commission; (*COMM:
ordinazione*) order

commit'**tente** *sm/f* (*COMM*) purchaser,
customer

com'**mosso, a** *pp di* **commuovere**

commo'**vente** *ag* moving

commozi'**one** [kommot'tsjone] *sf* emotion,
deep feeling; ~ **cerebrale** (*MED*) concussion

commu'**overe** *vt* to move, affect; ~**rsi** *vr*
to be moved

commu'**tare** *vt* (*pena*) to commute;
(*ELETTR*) to change *o* switch over

co'**mò** *sm inv* chest of drawers

como'**dino** *sm* bedside table

comodità *sf inv* comfort; convenience

'**comodo, a** *ag* comfortable; (*facile*) easy;
(*conveniente*) convenient; (*utile*) useful,
handy ♦ *sm* comfort; convenience; **con** ~
at one's convenience *o* leisure; **fare il
proprio** ~ to do as one pleases; **far** ~ to be
useful *o* handy

compae'**sano, a** *sm/f* fellow
countryman; person from the same town

com'**pagine** [kom'padʒine] *sf* (*squadra*)
team

compa'**gnia** [kompaɲ'ɲia] *sf* company;
(*gruppo*) gathering

com'**pagno, a** [kom'paɲɲo] *sm/f* (*di classe,
gioco*) companion; (*POL*) comrade

compa'**rare** *vt* to compare

compara'**tivo, a** *ag, sm* comparative

compa'**rire** *vi* to appear; **com'parsa** *sf*
appearance; (*TEATRO*) walk-on; (*CINEMA*)

extra; **comparso, a** pp di **comparire**
compartecipazi'one [kompar-
tetʃipat'tsjone] sf sharing; (quota) share; ~
agli utili profit-sharing
comparti'mento sm compartment;
(AMM) district
compas'sato, a ag (persona) composed
compassi'one sf compassion, pity; **avere**
~ **di qn** to feel sorry for sb, to pity sb
com'passo sm (pair of) compasses pl;
callipers pl
compa'tibile ag (scusabile) excusable;
(conciliabile, INFORM) compatible
compa'tire vt (aver compassione di) to
sympathize with, feel sorry for; (scusare) to
make allowances for
com'patto, a ag compact; (roccia) solid;
(folla) dense; (fig: gruppo, partito) united
com'pendio sm summary; (libro)
compendium
compen'sare vt (equilibrare) to
compensate for, make up for; ~ **qn di**
(rimunerare) to pay o remunerate sb for;
(risarcire) to pay compensation to sb for;
(fig: fatiche, dolori) to reward sb for;
com'penso sm compensation; payment,
remuneration; reward; **in compenso**
(d'altra parte) on the other hand
'compera sf (acquisto) purchase; **fare le**
~e to do the shopping
compe'rare vt = **comprare**
compe'tente ag competent; (mancia) apt,
suitable; **compe'tenza** sf competence;
competenze sfpl (onorari) fees
com'petere vi to compete, vie; (DIR:
spettare): ~ **a** to lie within the competence
of; **competizi'one** sf competition
compia'cente [kompja'tʃente] ag
courteous, obliging; **compia'cenza** sf
courtesy
compia'cere [kompja'tʃere] vi: ~ **a** to
gratify, please ♦ vt to please; **~rsi** vr
(provare soddisfazione): **~rsi di** o **per qc** to
be delighted at sth; (rallegrarsi): **~rsi con**
qn to congratulate sb; (degnarsi): **~rsi di**
fare to be so good as to do;
compiaci'uto, a pp di **compiacere**

compi'angere [kom'pjandʒere] vt to
sympathize with, feel sorry for;
compi'anto, a pp di **compiangere**
'compiere vt (concludere) to finish,
complete; (adempiere) to carry out, fulfil;
~rsi vr (avverarsi) to be fulfilled, come true;
~ **gli anni** to have one's birthday
compi'lare vt (modulo) to fill in;
(dizionario, elenco) to compile
com'pire vt = **compiere**
compi'tare vt to spell out
'compito sm (incarico) task, duty; (dovere)
duty; (INS) exercise; (: a casa) piece of
homework; **fare i ~i** to do one's homework
com'pito, a ag well-mannered, polite
complemen'tare ag complementary;
(INS: materia) subsidiary
comple'mento sm complement; (MIL)
reserve (troops); ~ **oggetto** (LING) direct
object
complessità sf complexity
comples'sivo, a ag (globale)
comprehensive, overall; (totale: cifra) total
com'plesso, a ag complex ♦ sm (PSIC,
EDIL) complex; (MUS: corale) ensemble;
(: orchestrina) band; (: di musica pop)
group; **in** o **nel** ~ on the whole
comple'tare vt to complete
com'pleto, a ag complete; (teatro,
autobus) full ♦ sm suit; **al ~** full; (tutti
presenti) all present
compli'care vt to complicate; **~rsi** vr to
become complicated; **complicazi'one** sf
complication
'complice ['kɔmplitʃe] sm/f accomplice
complimen'tarsi vr: ~ **con** to
congratulate
compli'mento sm compliment; **~i** smpl
(cortesia eccessiva) ceremony sg; (ossequi)
regards, compliments; **~i!** congratulations!;
senza ~i! don't stand on ceremony!; make
yourself at home!; help yourself!
complot'tare vi to plot, conspire
com'plotto sm plot, conspiracy
compo'nente sm/f member ♦ sm
component

componi'mento *sm* (*DIR*) settlement; (*INS*) composition; (*poetico, teatrale*) work

com'porre *vt* (*musica, testo*) to compose; (*mettere in ordine*) to arrange; (*DIR: lite*) to settle; (*TIP*) to set; (*TEL*) to dial

comporta'mento *sm* behaviour

compor'tare *vt* (*implicare*) to involve; **~rsi** *vr* to behave

composi'tore, 'trice *sm/f* composer; (*TIP*) compositor, typesetter

composizi'one [komposit'tsjone] *sf* composition; (*DIR*) settlement

com'posta *sf* (*CUC*) stewed fruit *no pl*; (*AGR*) compost; *vedi anche* **composto**

compos'tezza [kompos'tettsa] *sf* composure; decorum

com'posto, a *pp di* **comporre** ♦ *ag* (*persona*) composed, self-possessed; (*: decoroso*) dignified; (*formato da più elementi*) compound *cpd* ♦ *sm* compound

com'prare *vt* to buy; **compra'tore, 'trice** *sm/f* buyer, purchaser

com'prendere *vt* (*contenere*) to comprise, consist of; (*capire*) to understand

comprensi'one *sf* understanding

compren'sivo, a *ag* (*prezzo*): **~ di** inclusive of; (*indulgente*) understanding

com'preso, a *pp di* **comprendere** ♦ *ag* (*incluso*) included

com'pressa *sf* (*MED: garza*) compress; (*: pastiglia*) tablet; *vedi anche* **compresso**

compressi'one *sf* compression

com'presso, a *pp di* **comprimere** ♦ *ag* (*vedi comprimere*) pressed; compressed; repressed

com'primere *vt* (*premere*) to press; (*FISICA*) to compress; (*fig*) to repress

compro'messo, a *pp di* **compromettere** ♦ *sm* compromise

compro'mettere *vt* to compromise

compro'vare *vt* to confirm

com'punto, a *ag* contrite

compu'tare *vt* to calculate

com'puter *sm inv* computer

computiste'ria *sf* accounting, book-keeping

'computo *sm* calculation

comu'nale *ag* municipal, town *cpd*, ≈ borough *cpd*

co'mune *ag* common; (*consueto*) common, everyday; (*di livello medio*) average; (*ordinario*) ordinary ♦ *sm* (*AMM*) town council; (*: sede*) town hall ♦ *sf* (*di persone*) commune; **fuori del ~** out of the ordinary; **avere in ~** to have in common, share; **mettere in ~** to share

comuni'care *vt* (*notizia*) to pass on, convey; (*malattia*) to pass on; (*ansia etc*) to communicate; (*trasmettere: calore etc*) to transmit, communicate; (*REL*) to administer communion to ♦ *vi* to communicate; **~rsi** *vr* (*propagarsi*): **~rsi a** to spread to; (*REL*) to receive communion

comuni'cato *sm* communiqué; **~ stampa** press release

comunicazi'one [komunikat'tsjone] *sf* communication; (*annuncio*) announcement; (*TEL*): **~ (telefonica)** (telephone) call; **dare la ~ a qn** to put sb through; **ottenere la ~** to get through

comuni'one *sf* communion; **~ di beni** (*DIR*) joint ownership of property

comu'nismo *sm* communism; **comu'nista, i, e** *ag, sm/f* communist

comunità *sf inv* community; **C~ Europea** European Community

co'munque *cong* however, no matter how ♦ *av* (*in ogni modo*) in any case; (*tuttavia*) however, nevertheless

con *prep* with; **partire col treno** to leave by train; **~ mio grande stupore** to my great astonishment; **~ tutto ciò** for all that

co'nato *sm*: **~ di vomito** retching

'conca, che *sf* (*GEO*) valley

con'cedere [kon'tʃedere] *vt* (*accordare*) to grant; (*ammettere*) to admit, concede; **~rsi qc** to treat o.s. to sth, to allow o.s. sth

concentra'mento [kontʃentra'mento] *sm* concentration

concen'trare [kontʃen'trare] *vt* to concentrate; **~rsi** *vr* to concentrate; **concentrazi'one** *sf* concentration

conce'pire [kontʃe'pire] *vt* (*bambino*) to conceive; (*progetto, idea*) to conceive (of);

(*metodo, piano*) to devise
con'cernere [kon'tʃɛrnere] *vt* to concern
concer'tare [kontʃer'tare] *vt* (*MUS*) to harmonize; (*ordire*) to devise, plan; **~rsi** *vr* to agree
con'certo [kon'tʃɛrto] *sm* (*MUS*) concert; (*: componimento*) concerto
concessio'nario [kontʃessjo'narjo] *sm* (*COMM*) agent, dealer
con'cesso, a [kon'tʃɛsso] *pp di* **concedere**
con'cetto [kon'tʃɛtto] *sm* (*pensiero, idea*) concept; (*opinione*) opinion
concezi'one [kontʃet'tsjone] *sf* conception
con'chiglia [kon'kiʎʎa] *sf* shell
'concia ['kɔntʃa] *sf* (*di pelle*) tanning; (*di tabacco*) curing; (*sostanza*) tannin
conci'are [kon'tʃare] *vt* (*pelli*) to tan; (*tabacco*) to cure; (*fig: ridurre in cattivo stato*) to beat up; **~rsi** *vr* (*sporcarsi*) to get in a mess; (*vestirsi male*) to dress badly
concili'are [kontʃi'ljare] *vt* to reconcile; (*contravvenzione*) to pay on the spot; (*sonno*) to be conducive to, induce; **~rsi qc** to gain *o* win sth (for o.s.); **~rsi qn** to win sb over; **~rsi con** to be reconciled with; **conciliazi'one** *sf* reconciliation; (*DIR*) settlement
con'cilio [kon'tʃiljo] *sm* (*REL*) council
con'cime [kon'tʃime] *sm* manure; (*chimico*) fertilizer
con'ciso, a [kon'tʃizo] *ag* concise, succinct
conci'tato, a [kontʃi'tato] *ag* excited, emotional
concitta'dino, a [kontʃitta'dino] *sm/f* fellow citizen
con'cludere *vt* to conclude; (*portare a compimento*) to conclude, finish, bring to an end; (*operare positivamente*) to achieve ♦ *vi* (*essere convincente*) to be conclusive; **~rsi** *vr* to come to an end, close; **conclusi'one** *sf* conclusion; (*risultato*) result; **conclu'sivo, a** *ag* conclusive; (*finale*) final; **con'cluso, a** *pp di* **concludere**
concor'danza [konkor'dantsa] *sf* (*anche LING*) agreement
concor'dare *vt* (*tregua, prezzo*) to agree

on; (*LING*) to make agree ♦ *vi* to agree; **concor'dato** *sm* agreement; (*REL*) concordat
con'corde *ag* (*d'accordo*) in agreement; (*simultaneo*) simultaneous
concor'rente *sm/f* competitor; (*INS*) candidate; **concor'renza** *sf* competition
con'correre *vi*: **~ (in)** (*MAT*) to converge *o* meet (in); **~ (a)** (*competere*) to compete (for); (*: INS: a una cattedra*) to apply (for); (*partecipare: a un'impresa*) to take part (in), contribute (to); **con'corso, a** *pp di* **concorrere** ♦ *sm* competition; (*INS*) competitive examination; **concorso di colpa** (*DIR*) contributory negligence
con'creto, a *ag* concrete
concussi'one *sf* (*DIR*) extortion
con'danna *sf* sentence; conviction; condemnation
condan'nare *vt* (*DIR*): **~ a** to sentence to; **~ per** to convict of; (*disapprovare*) to condemn; **condan'nato, a** *sm/f* convict
conden'sare *vt* to condense; **~rsi** *vr* to condense; **condensazi'one** *sf* condensation
condi'mento *sm* seasoning; dressing
con'dire *vt* to season; (*insalata*) to dress
condi'videre *vt* to share; **condi'viso, a** *pp di* **condividere**
condizio'nale [kondittsjo'nale] *ag* conditional ♦ *sm* (*LING*) conditional ♦ *sf* (*DIR*) suspended sentence
condizio'nare [kondittsjo'nare] *vt* to condition; **ad aria condizionata** air-conditioned; **condiziona'tore** *sm* air conditioner
condizi'one [kondit'tsjone] *sf* condition; **~i** *sfpl* (*di pagamento etc*) terms, conditions; **a ~ che** on condition that, provided that
condogli'anze [kondoʎ'ʎantse] *sfpl* condolences
condo'minio *sm* joint ownership; (*edificio*) jointly-owned building
condo'nare *vt* (*DIR*) to remit; **con'dono** *sm* remission; **condono fiscale** *conditional amnesty for people evading tax*
con'dotta *sf* (*modo di comportarsi*)

conduct, behaviour; (di un affare etc) handling; (di acqua) piping; (incarico sanitario) country medical practice controlled by a local authority

con'dotto, a pp di condurre ♦ ag: medico ~ local authority doctor (in country district) ♦ sm (canale, tubo) pipe, conduit; (ANAT) duct

condu'cente [kondu'tʃɛnte] sm driver

con'durre vt to conduct; (azienda) to manage; (accompagnare: bambino) to take; (automobile) to drive; (trasportare: acqua, gas) to convey, conduct; (fig) to lead ♦ vi to lead; condursi vr to behave, conduct o.s.

condut'tore ag: filo ~ (fig) thread ♦ sm (di mezzi pubblici) driver; (FISICA) conductor

con'farsi vr: ~ a to suit, agree with

confederazi'one [konfederat'tsjone] sf confederation

confe'renza [konfe'rɛntsa] sf (discorso) lecture; (riunione) conference; ~ stampa press conference; conferenzi'ere, a sm/f lecturer

confe'rire vt: ~ qc a qn to give sth to sb, bestow sth on sb ♦ vi to confer

con'ferma sf confirmation

confer'mare vt to confirm

confes'sare vt to confess; ~rsi vr to confess; andare a ~rsi (REL) to go to confession; confessio'nale ag, sm confessional; confessi'one sf confession; (setta religiosa) denomination; confes'sore sm confessor

con'fetto sm sugared almond; (MED) pill

confezio'nare [konfettsjo'nare] vt (vestito) to make (up); (merci, pacchi) to package

confezi'one [konfet'tsjone] sf (di abiti: da uomo) tailoring; (: da donna) dressmaking; (imballaggio) packaging; ~ regalo gift pack; ~i per signora ladies' wear; ~i da uomo menswear

confic'care vt: ~ qc in to hammer o drive sth into; ~rsi vr to stick

confi'dare vi: ~ in to confide in, rely on ♦ vt to confide; ~rsi con qn to confide in sb; confi'dente sm/f (persona amica)

confidant/confidante; (informatore) informer; confi'denza sf (familiarità) intimacy, familiarity; (fiducia) trust, confidence; (rivelazione) confidence; confidenzi'ale ag familiar, friendly; (segreto) confidential

configu'rarsi vr: ~ a to assume the shape o form of

confi'nare vi: ~ con to border on ♦ vt (POL) to intern; (fig) to confine; ~rsi vr (isolarsi): ~rsi in to shut o.s. up in

Confin'dustria sigla f (= Confederazione Generale dell'Industria Italiana) employers' association, ≈ CBI (BRIT)

con'fine sm boundary; (di paese) border, frontier

con'fino sm internment

confis'care vt to confiscate

con'flitto sm conflict

conflu'enza [konflu'ɛntsa] sf (di fiumi) confluence; (di strade) junction

conflu'ire vi (fiumi) to flow into each other, meet; (strade) to meet

con'fondere vt to mix up, confuse; (imbarazzare) to embarrass; ~rsi vr (mescolarsi) to mingle; (turbarsi) to be confused; (sbagliare) to get mixed up

confor'mare vt (adeguare): ~ a to adapt o conform to; ~rsi vr: ~rsi (a) to conform (to)

confor'tare vt to comfort, console; confor'tevole ag (consolante) comforting; (comodo) comfortable; con'forto sm comfort, consolation

confron'tare vt to compare

con'fronto sm comparison; in o a ~ di in comparison with, compared to; nei miei (o tuoi etc) ~i towards me (o you etc)

confusi'one sf confusion; (chiasso) racket, noise; (imbarazzo) embarrassment

con'fuso, a pp di confondere ♦ ag (vedi confondere) confused; embarrassed

confu'tare vt to refute

conge'dare [kondʒe'dare] vt to dismiss; (MIL) to demobilize; ~rsi vr to take one's leave; con'gedo sm (anche MIL) leave; prendere congedo da qn to take one's leave of sb; **congedo assoluto** (MIL) discharge

conge'gnare [kondʒeɲ'ɲare] *vt* to construct, put together; **con'gegno** *sm* device, mechanism

conge'lare [kondʒe'lare] *vt* to freeze; **~rsi** *vr* to freeze; **congela'tore** *sm* freezer

congestio'nare [kondʒestjo'nare] *vt* to congest

congesti'one [kondʒes'tjone] *sf* congestion

conget'tura [kondʒet'tura] *sf* conjecture

con'giungere [kon'dʒundʒere] *vt* to join (together); **~rsi** *vr* to join (together)

congiunti'vite [kondʒunti'vite] *sf* conjunctivitis

congiun'tivo [kondʒun'tivo] *sm* (LING) subjunctive

congi'unto, a [kon'dʒunto] *pp di* **congiungere** ♦ *ag* (*unito*) joined ♦ *sm/f* relative

congiun'tura [kondʒun'tura] *sf* (*giuntura*) junction, join; (ANAT) joint; (*circostanza*) juncture; (ECON) economic situation

congiunzi'one [kondʒun'tsjone] *sf* (LING) conjunction

congi'ura [kon'dʒura] *sf* conspiracy; **congiu'rare** *vi* to conspire

conglome'rato *sm* (GEO) conglomerate; (*fig*) conglomeration; (EDIL) concrete

congratu'larsi *vr*: **~ con qn per qc** to congratulate sb on sth

congratulazi'oni [kongratulat'tsjoni] *sfpl* congratulations

con'grega, ghe *sf* band, bunch

con'gresso *sm* congress

congu'aglio [kon'gwaʎʎo] *sm* balancing, adjusting; (*somma di denaro*) balance

coni'are *vt* to mint, coin; (*fig*) to coin

co'niglio [ko'niʎʎo] *sm* rabbit

coniu'gare *vt* (LING) to conjugate; **~rsi** *vr* to get married; **coniu'gato, a** *ag* (*sposato*) married; **coniugazi'one** *sf* (LING) conjugation

'coniuge ['kɔnjudʒe] *sm/f* spouse

connazio'nale [konnattsjo'nale] *sm/f* fellow-countryman/woman

connessi'one *sf* connection

con'nesso, a *pp di* **connettere**

con'nettere *vt* to connect, join ♦ *vi* (*fig*) to think straight

conni'vente *ag* conniving

conno'tati *smpl* distinguishing marks

'cono *sm* cone; **~ gelato** ice-cream cone

cono'scente [konoʃ'ʃente] *sm/f* acquaintance

cono'scenza [konoʃ'ʃentsa] *sf* (*il sapere*) knowledge *no pl*; (*persona*) acquaintance; (*facoltà sensoriale*) consciousness *no pl*; **perdere ~** to lose consciousness

co'noscere [ko'noʃʃere] *vt* to know; **ci siamo conosciuti a Firenze** we (first) met in Florence; **conosci'tore, 'trice** *sm/f* connoisseur; **conosci'uto, a** *pp di* **conoscere** ♦ *ag* well-known

con'quista *sf* conquest

conquis'tare *vt* to conquer; (*fig*) to gain, win

consa'crare *vt* (REL) to consecrate; (*: sacerdote*) to ordain; (*dedicare*) to dedicate; (*fig: uso etc*) to sanction; **~rsi a** to dedicate o.s. to

consangu'ineo, a *sm/f* blood relation

consa'pevole *ag*: **~ di** aware *o* conscious of; **consapevo'lezza** *sf* awareness, consciousness

'conscio, a, sci, sce ['kɔnʃo] *ag*: **~ di** aware *o* conscious of

consecu'tivo, a *ag* consecutive; (*successivo: giorno*) following, next

con'segna [kon'seɲɲa] *sf* delivery; (*merce consegnata*) consignment; (*custodia*) care, custody; (MIL: *ordine*) orders *pl*; (*: punizione*) confinement to barracks; **pagamento alla ~** cash on delivery; **dare qc in ~ a qn** to entrust sth to sb

conse'gnare [konseɲ'ɲare] *vt* to deliver; (*affidare*) to entrust, hand over; (MIL) to confine to barracks

consegu'enza [konse'gwentsa] *sf* consequence; **per *o* di ~** consequently

consegu'ire *vt* to achieve ♦ *vi* to follow

con'senso *sm* approval, consent

consen'tire *vi*: **~ a** to consent *o* agree to ♦ *vt* to allow, permit

con'serva *sf* (*CUC*) preserve; ~ **di frutta**
jam; ~ **di pomodoro** tomato purée

conser'vare *vt* (*CUC*) to preserve;
(*custodire*) to keep; (*: dalla distruzione etc*)
to preserve, conserve; ~rsi *vr* to keep

conserva'tore, 'trice *sm/f* (*POL*)
conservative

conservazi'one [konservat'tsjone] *sf*
preservation; conservation

conside'rare *vt* to consider; (*reputare*) to
consider, regard; **considerazi'one** *sf*
consideration; (*stima*) regard, esteem;
prendere in considerazione to take into
consideration; **conside'revole** *ag*
considerable

consigli'are [konsiʎ'ʎare] *vt* (*persona*) to
advise; (*metodo, azione*) to recommend,
advise, suggest; ~rsi *vr*: ~rsi **con qn** to ask
sb for advice; **consigli'ere, a** *sm/f*
adviser ♦ *sm*: **consigliere
d'amministrazione** board member;
consigliere comunale town councillor,
con'siglio *sm* (*suggerimento*) advice *no*
pl, piece of advice; (*assemblea*) council;
consiglio d'amministrazione board; **il
Consiglio dei Ministri** (*POL*) ≈ the
Cabinet; **Consiglio d'Europa** Council of
Europe

consis'tente *ag* thick; solid; (*fig*) sound,
valid; **consis'tenza** *sf* consistency,
thickness; solidity; validity

con'sistere *vi*: ~ **in** to consist of;
consis'tito, a *pp di* **consistere**

conso'lare *ag* consular ♦ *vt* (*confortare*) to
console, comfort; (*rallegrare*) to cheer up;
~rsi *vr* to be comforted; to cheer up

conso'lato *sm* consulate

consolazi'one [konsolat'tsjone] *sf*
consolation, comfort

'console¹ *sm* consul

con'sole² [kon'sɔl] *sf* (*quadro di comando*)
console

conso'nante *sf* consonant

'consono, a *ag*: ~ **a** consistent with,
consonant with

con'sorte *sm/f* consort

con'sorzio [kon'sɔrtsjo] *sm* consortium

con'stare *vi*: ~ **di** to consist of ♦ *vb*
impers: **mi consta che** it has come to my
knowledge that, it appears that

consta'tare *vt* to establish, verify;
constatazi'one *sf* observation;
constatazione amichevole *jointly-agreed
statement for insurance purposes*

consu'eto, a *ag* habitual, usual;
consue'tudine *sf* habit, custom;
(*usanza*) custom

consu'lente *sm/f* consultant;
consu'lenza *sf* consultancy

consul'tare *vt* to consult; ~rsi *vr*: ~rsi **con
qn** to seek the advice of sb;
consultazi'one *sf* consultation;
consultazioni *sfpl* (*POL*) talks, consultations

consul'torio *sm*: ~ **familiare** family
planning clinic

consu'mare *vt* (*logorare: abiti, scarpe*) to
wear out; (*usare*) to consume, use up;
(*mangiare, bere*) to consume, (*DIR*) to
consummate; ~rsi *vr* to wear out; to be
used up; (*anche fig*) to be consumed;
(*combustibile*) to burn out; **consuma'tore**
sm consumer; **consumazi'one** *sf* (*bibita*)
drink; (*spuntino*) snack; (*DIR*)
consummation; **consu'mismo** *sm*
consumerism; **con'sumo** *sm*
consumption; wear; use

consun'tivo *sm* (*ECON*) final balance

con'tabile *ag* accounts *cpd*, accounting
♦ *sm/f* accountant; **contabilità** *sf*
(*attività, tecnica*) accounting, accountancy;
(*insieme dei libri etc*) books *pl*, accounts *pl*;
(*ufficio*) accounts department

contachi'lometri [kontaki'lɔmetri] *sm inv*
≈ mileometer

conta'dino, a *sm/f* countryman/woman;
farm worker; (*peg*) peasant

contagi'are [konta'dʒare] *vt* to infect

con'tagio [kon'tadʒo] *sm* infection; (*per
contatto diretto*) contagion; (*epidemia*)
epidemic; **contagi'oso, a** *ag* infectious;
contagious

conta'gocce [konta'gottʃe] *sm inv* (*MED*)
dropper

contami'nare *vt* to contaminate

con'tante *sm* cash; **pagare in ~i** to pay cash

con'tare *vt* to count; (*considerare*) to consider ♦ *vi* to count, be of importance; **~ su qn** to count *o* rely on sb; **~ di fare qc** to intend to do sth; **conta'tore** *sm* meter

contat'tare *vt* to contact

con'tatto *sm* contact

'conte *sm* count

conteggi'are [konted'dʒare] *vt* to charge, put on the bill; **con'teggio** *sm* calculation

con'tegno [kon'teɲɲo] *sm* (*comportamento*) behaviour; (*atteggiamento*) attitude; **darsi un ~** to act nonchalant; to pull o.s. together

contem'plare *vt* to contemplate, gaze at; (*DIR*) to make provision for

contemporanea'mente *av* simultaneously; at the same time

contempo'raneo, a *ag, sm/f* contemporary

conten'dente *sm/f* opponent, adversary

con'tendere *vi* (*competere*) to compete; (*litigare*) to quarrel ♦ *vt*: **~ qc a qn** to contend with *o* be in competition with sb for sth

conte'nere *vt* to contain; **conteni'tore** *sm* container

conten'tare *vt* to please, satisfy; **~rsi di** to be satisfied with, content o.s. with

conten'tezza [konten'tettsa] *sf* contentment

con'tento, a *ag* pleased, glad; **~ di** pleased with

conte'nuto *sm* contents *pl*; (*argomento*) content

con'tesa *sf* dispute, argument

con'teso, a *pp di* **contendere**

con'tessa *sf* countess

contes'tare *vt* (*DIR*) to notify; (*fig*) to dispute; **contestazi'one** *sf* (*DIR*) notification; dispute; (*protesta*) protest

con'testo *sm* context

con'tiguo, a *ag*: **~ (a)** adjacent (to)

continen'tale *ag, sm/f* continental

conti'nente *ag* continent ♦ *sm* (*GEO*) continent; (*: terra ferma*) mainland

contin'gente [kontin'dʒente] *ag* contingent ♦ *sm* (*COMM*) quota; (*MIL*) contingent;

contin'genza *sf* circumstance; (*ECON*): **(indennità di) contingenza** cost-of-living allowance

continu'are *vt* to continue (with), go on with ♦ *vi* to continue, go on; **~ a fare qc** to go on *o* continue doing sth; **continuazi'one** *sf* continuation

continuità *sf* continuity

con'tinuo, a *ag* (*numerazione*) continuous; (*pioggia*) continual, constant; (*ELETTR*): **corrente ~a** direct current; **di ~** continually

'conto *sm* (*calcolo*) calculation; (*COMM, ECON*) account; (*di ristorante, albergo*) bill; (*fig: stima*) consideration, esteem; **fare i ~i con qn** to settle one's account with sb; **fare ~ su qn/qc** to count *o* rely on sb; **rendere ~ a qn di qc** to be accountable to sb for sth; **tener ~ di qn/qc** to take sb/sth into account; **per ~ di** on behalf of; **per ~ mio** as far as I'm concerned; **a ~i fatti, in fin dei ~i** all things considered; **~ corrente** current account; **~ alla rovescia** countdown

con'torcere [kon'tortʃere] *vt* to twist; **~rsi** *vr* to twist, writhe

contor'nare *vt* to surround

con'torno *sm* (*linea*) outline, contour; (*ornamento*) border; (*CUC*) vegetables *pl*

con'torto, a *pp di* **contorcere**

contrabbandi'ere, a *sm/f* smuggler

contrab'bando *sm* smuggling, contraband; **merce di ~** contraband, smuggled goods *pl*

contrab'basso *sm* (*MUS*) (double) bass

contraccambi'are *vt* (*favore etc*) to return

contraccet'tivo, a [kontrattʃet'tivo] *ag, sm* contraceptive

contrac'colpo *sm* rebound; (*di arma da fuoco*) recoil; (*fig*) repercussion

con'trada *sf* street; district

contrad'detto, a *pp di* **contraddire**

contrad'dire *vt* to contradict; **contraddit'torio, a** *ag* contradictory; (*sentimenti*) conflicting ♦ *sm* (*DIR*) cross-examination; **contraddizi'one** *sf* contradiction

contraf'fare *vt* (*persona*) to mimic; (*alterare: voce*) to disguise; (*firma*) to forge, counterfeit; **contraf'fatto, a** *pp di* **contraffare** ♦ *ag* counterfeit; **contraffazi'one** *sf* mimicking *no pl*; disguising *no pl*; forging *no pl*; (*cosa contraffatta*) forgery

contrap'peso *sm* counterbalance, counterweight

contrap'porre *vt*: ~ **qc a qc** to counter sth with sth; (*paragonare*) to compare sth with sth; **contrap'posto, a** *pp di* **contrapporre**

contraria'mente *av*: ~ **a** contrary to

contrari'are *vt* (*contrastare*) to thwart, oppose; (*irritare*) to annoy, bother; **~rsi** *vr* to get annoyed

contrarietà *sf* adversity; (*fig*) aversion

con'trario, a *ag* opposite; (*sfavorevole*) unfavourable ♦ *sm* opposite; **essere ~ a qc** (*persona*) to be against sth; **in caso ~** otherwise; **avere qc in ~** to have some objection; **al ~** on the contrary

con'trarre *vt* to contract; **contrarsi** *vr* to contract

contrasse'gnare [kontrassen'ɲare] *vt* to mark; **contras'segno** *sm* (*distintivo*) distinguishing mark; **spedire in contrassegno** to send C.O.D.

contras'tare *vt* (*avversare*) to oppose; (*impedire*) to bar; (*negare: diritto*) to contest, dispute ♦ *vi*: ~ **(con)** (*essere in disaccordo*) to contrast (with); (*lottare*) to struggle (with); **con'trasto** *sm* contrast; (*conflitto*) conflict; (*litigio*) dispute

contrat'tacco *sm* counterattack

contrat'tare *vt*, *vi* to negotiate

contrat'tempo *sm* hitch

con'tratto, a *pp di* **contrarre** ♦ *sm* contract; **contrattu'ale** *ag* contractual

contravvenzi'one [kontravven'tsjone] *sf* contravention; (*ammenda*) fine

contrazi'one [kontrat'tsjone] *sf* contraction; (*di prezzi etc*) reduction

contribu'ente *sm/f* taxpayer; ratepayer

(*BRIT*), property tax payer (*US*)

contribu'ire *vi* to contribute; **contri'buto** *sm* contribution; (*tassa*) tax

'contro *prep* against; ~ **di me/lui** against me/him; **pastiglie ~ la tosse** throat lozenges; ~ **pagamento** (*COMM*) on payment ♦ *prefisso*: **contro'battere** *vt* (*fig: a parole*) to answer back; (*: confutare*) to refute; **controfi'gura** *sf* (*CINEMA*) double; **controfir'mare** *vt* to countersign

control'lare *vt* (*accertare*) to check; (*sorvegliare*) to watch, control; (*tenere nel proprio potere, fig: dominare*) to control; **con'trollo** *sm* check; watch; control; **controllo delle nascite** birth control; **control'lore** *sm* (*FERR, AUTOBUS*) (ticket) inspector

controprodu'cente [kontroprodu'tʃente] *ag* counterproductive

contro'senso *sm* (*contraddizione*) contradiction in terms; (*assurdità*) nonsense

controspio'naggio [kontrospio'naddʒo] *sm* counterespionage

contro'versia *sf* controversy; (*DIR*) dispute

contro'verso, a *ag* controversial

contro'voglia [kontro'vɔʎʎa] *av* unwillingly

contu'macia [kontu'matʃa] *sf* (*DIR*) default

contusi'one *sf* (*MED*) bruise

convale'scente [konvaleʃ'ʃente] *ag, sm/f* convalescent; **convale'scenza** *sf* convalescence

convali'dare *vt* (*AMM*) to validate; (*fig: sospetto, dubbio*) to confirm

con'vegno [kon'veɲɲo] *sm* (*incontro*) meeting; (*congresso*) convention, congress; (*luogo*) meeting place

conve'nevoli *smpl* civilities

conveni'ente *ag* suitable; (*vantaggioso*) profitable; (*: prezzo*) cheap; **conveni'enza** *sf* suitability; advantage; cheapness; **le convenienze** *sfpl* social conventions

conve'nire *vi* (*riunirsi*) to gather, assemble; (*concordare*) to agree; (*tornare utile*) to be worthwhile ♦ *vb impers*: **conviene fare questo** it is advisable to do this; **conviene andarsene** we should go; **ne convengo** I agree

con'vento *sm* (*di frati*) monastery; (*di suore*) convent

convenzio'nale [konventsjo'nale] *ag* conventional

convenzi'one [konven'tsjone] *sf* (*DIR*) agreement; (*nella società*) convention; **le ~i** *sfpl* social conventions

conver'sare *vi* to have a conversation, converse

conversazi'one [konversat'tsjone] *sf* conversation; **fare ~** to chat, have a chat

conversi'one *sf* conversion; **~ ad U** (*AUT*) U-turn

conver'tire *vt* (*trasformare*) to change; (*POL, REL*) to convert; **~rsi** *vr*: **~rsi (a)** to be converted (to)

con'vesso, a *ag* convex

con'vincere [kon'vintʃere] *vt* to convince; **~ qn di qc** to convince sb of sth; **~ qn a fare qc** to persuade sb to do sth; **con'vinto, a** *pp di* **convincere**; **convinzi'one** *sf* conviction, firm belief

convis'suto, a *pp di* **convivere**

con'vivere *vi* to live together

convo'care *vt* to call, convene; (*DIR*) to summon; **convocazi'one** *sf* meeting; summons *sg*

convogli'are [konvoʎ'ʎare] *vt* to convey; (*dirigere*) to direct, send; **con'voglio** *sm* (*di veicoli*) convoy; (*FERR*) train

convulsi'one *sf* convulsion

con'vulso, a *ag* (*pianto*) violent, convulsive; (*attività*) feverish

coope'rare *vi*: **~ (a)** to cooperate (in); **coopera'tiva** *sf* cooperative; **cooperazi'one** *sf* cooperation

coordi'nare *vt* to coordinate; **coordi'nate** *sfpl* (*MAT, GEO*) coordinates; **coordi'nati** *smpl* (*MODA*) coordinates

co'perchio [ko'perkjo] *sm* cover; (*di pentola*) lid

co'perta *sf* cover; (*di lana*) blanket; (*da viaggio*) rug; (*NAUT*) deck

coper'tina *sf* (*STAMPA*) cover, jacket

co'perto, a *pp di* **coprire** ♦ *ag* covered; (*cielo*) overcast ♦ *sm* place setting; (*posto a*

tavola) place; (*al ristorante*) cover charge; **~ di** covered in *o* with

coper'tone *sm* (*AUT*) rubber tyre

coper'tura *sf* (*anche ECON, MIL*) cover; (*di edificio*) roofing

'copia *sf* copy; **brutta/bella ~** rough/final copy

copi'are *vt* to copy; **copia'trice** *sf* copier, copying machine

copi'one *sm* (*CINEMA, TEATRO*) script

'coppa *sf* (*bicchiere*) goblet; (*per frutta, gelato*) dish; (*trofeo*) cup, trophy; **~ dell'olio** oil sump (*BRIT*) *o* pan (*US*)

'coppia *sf* (*di persone*) couple; (*di animali, SPORT*) pair

coprifu'oco, chi *sm* curfew

copri'letto *sm* bedspread

co'prire *vt* to cover; (*occupare: carica, posto*) to hold; **~rsi** *vr* (*cielo*) to cloud over; (*vestirsi*) to wrap up, cover up; (*ECON*) to cover o.s.; **~rsi di** (*macchie, muffa*) to become covered in

co'raggio [ko'raddʒo] *sm* courage, bravery; **~!** (*forza!*) come on!; (*animo!*) cheer up!; **coraggi'oso, a** *ag* courageous, brave

co'rallo *sm* coral

co'rano *sm* (*REL*) Koran

co'razza [ko'rattsa] *sf* armour; (*di animali*) carapace, shell; (*MIL*) armour(-plating); **coraz'zata** *sf* battleship

corbelle'ria *sf* stupid remark; **~e** *sfpl* nonsense *no pl*

'corda *sf* cord; (*fune*) rope; (*spago, MUS*) string; **dare ~ a qn** to let sb have his (*o* her) way; **tenere sulla ~ qn** to keep sb on tenterhooks; **tagliare la ~** to slip away, sneak off; **~e vocali** vocal cords

cordi'ale *ag* cordial, warm ♦ *sm* (*bevanda*) cordial

cor'doglio [kor'dɔʎʎo] *sm* grief; (*lutto*) mourning

cor'done *sm* cord, string; (*linea: di polizia*) cordon; **~ ombelicale** umbilical cord

Co'rea *sf*: **la ~** Korea

coreogra'fia *sf* choreography

cori'andolo *sm* (*BOT*) coriander; **~i** *smpl* confetti *sg* cori'carsi *vr* to go to bed

'corna *sfpl vedi* **corno**

cor'nacchia [kor'nakkja] *sf* crow

corna'musa *sf* bagpipes *pl*

cor'netta *sf* (*MUS*) cornet; (*TEL*) receiver

cor'netto *sm* (*CUC*) croissant; (*gelato*) cone

cor'nice [kor'nitʃe] *sf* frame; (*fig*) setting, background

cornici'one [korni'tʃone] *sm* (*di edificio*) ledge; (*ARCHIT*) cornice

'corno (*pl(f)* **-a**) *sm* (*ZOOL*) horn; (*pl(m)* **-i**: *MUS*) horn; **fare le ~a a qn** to be unfaithful to sb

Corno'vaglia [korno'vaλλa] *sf*: **la ~** Cornwall

cor'nuto, a *ag* (*con corna*) horned; (*fam!: marito*) cuckolded ♦ *sm* (*fam!*) cuckold; (*: insulto*) bastard (!)

'coro *sm* chorus; (*REL*) choir

co'rona *sf* crown; (*di fiori*) wreath; coro'nare *vt* to crown

'corpo *sm* body; (*militare, diplomatico*) corps *inv*; **prendere ~** to take shape; **a ~ a ~** hand-to-hand; **~ di ballo** corps de ballet; **~ insegnante** teaching staff

corpo'rale *ag* bodily; (*punizione*) corporal

corpora'tura *sf* build, physique

corporazi'one [korporat'tsjone] *sf* corporation

corpu'lento, a *ag* stout

corre'dare *vt*: **~ di** to provide *o* furnish with; **cor'redo** *sm* equipment; (*di sposa*) trousseau

cor'reggere [kor'reddʒere] *vt* to correct; (*compiti*) to correct, mark

cor'rente *ag* (*acqua: di fiume*) flowing; (*: di rubinetto*) running; (*moneta, prezzo*) current; (*comune*) everyday ♦ *sm*: **essere al ~ (di)** to be well-informed (about); **mettere al ~ (di)** to inform (of) ♦ *sf* (*d'acqua*) current, stream; (*spiffero*) draught; (*ELETTR, METEOR*) current; (*fig*) trend, tendency; **la vostra lettera del 5 ~ mese** (*COMM*) your letter of the 5th of this month; **corrente'mente** *av* commonly; **parlare una lingua correntemente** to speak a language fluently

'correre *vi* to run; (*precipitarsi*) to rush; (*partecipare a una gara*) to race, run; (*fig: diffondersi*) to go round ♦ *vt* (*SPORT: gara*) to compete in; (*rischio*) to run; (*pericolo*) to face; **~ dietro a qn** to run after sb; **corre voce che ...** it is rumoured that ...

cor'retto, a *pp di* **correggere** ♦ *ag* (*comportamento*) correct, proper; **caffè ~ al cognac** coffee laced with brandy

correzi'one [korret'tsjone] *sf* correction; marking; **~ di bozze** proofreading

corri'doio *sm* corridor

corri'dore *sm* (*SPORT*) runner; (*: su veicolo*) racer

corri'era *sf* coach (*BRIT*), bus

corri'ere *sm* (*diplomatico, di guerra, postale*) courier; (*COMM*) carrier

corrispet'tivo *sm* (*somma*) amount due

corrispon'dente *ag* corresponding ♦ *sm/f* correspondent

corrispon'denza [korrispon'dentsa] *sf* correspondence

corris'pondere *vi* (*equivalere*): **~ (a)** to correspond (to) ♦ *vt* (*stipendio*) to pay; (*fig: amore*) to return; **corris'posto, a** *pp di* **corrispondere**

corrobo'rare *vt* to strengthen, fortify; (*fig*) to corroborate, bear out

cor'rodere *vt* to corrode; **~rsi** *vr* to corrode

cor'rompere *vt* to corrupt; (*comprare*) to bribe

corrosi'one *sf* corrosion

cor'roso, a *pp di* **corrodere**

cor'rotto, a *pp di* **corrompere** ♦ *ag* corrupt

corrucci'arsi [korrut'tʃarsi] *vr* to grow angry *o* vexed

corru'gare *vt* to wrinkle; **~ la fronte** to knit one's brows

corruzi'one [korrut'tsjone] *sf* corruption; bribery

'corsa *sf* running *no pl*; (*gara*) race; (*di autobus, taxi*) journey, trip; **fare una ~** to run, dash; (*SPORT*) to run a race

cor'sia *sf* (*AUT, SPORT*) lane; (*di ospedale*) ward

cor'sivo *sm* cursive (writing); (*TIP*) italics *pl*

'corso, a *pp di* **correre** ♦ *sm* course; (*strada cittadina*) main street; (*di unità monetaria*) circulation; (*di titoli, valori*) rate, price; **in ~** in progress, under way; (*annata*) current; **~ d'acqua** river, stream; (*artificiale*) waterway; **~ d'aggiornamento** refresher course; **~ serale** evening class

'corte *sf* (court)yard; (*DIR, regale*) court; **fare la ~ a qn** to court sb; **~ marziale** court-martial

cor'teccia, ce [kor'tettʃa] *sf* bark

corteggi'are [korted'dʒare] *vt* to court

cor'teo *sm* procession

cor'tese *ag* courteous; **corte'sia** *sf* courtesy; **per cortesia ...** excuse me, please ...

cortigi'ana [korti'dʒana] *sf* courtesan

cortigi'ano, a [korti'dʒano] *sm/f* courtier

cor'tile *sm* (court)yard

cor'tina *sf* curtain; (*anche fig*) screen

'corto, a *ag* short; **essere a ~ di qc** to be short of sth; **~ circuito** short-circuit

'corvo *sm* raven

'cosa *sf* thing; (*faccenda*) affair, matter, business *no pl*; (*che*) **~?** what?; (*che*) **cos'è?** what is it?; **a ~ pensi?** what are you thinking about?

'coscia, sce [ˈkɔʃʃa] *sf* thigh; **~ di pollo** (*CUC*) chicken leg

cosci'ente [koʃˈʃɛnte] *ag* conscious; **~ di** conscious *o* aware of; **cosci'enza** *sf* conscience; (*consapevolezza*) consciousness; **coscienzi'oso, a** *ag* conscientious

cosci'otto [koʃˈʃɔtto] *sm* (*CUC*) leg

cos'critto *sm* (*MIL*) conscript

PAROLA CHIAVE

così *av* **1** (*in questo modo*) like this, (in) this way; (*in tal modo*) so; **le cose stanno ~** this is the way things stand; **non ho detto ~!** I didn't say that!; **come stai? – (e) ~** how are you? — so-so; **e ~ via** and so on; **per ~ dire** so to speak

2 (*tanto*) so; **~ lontano** so far away; **un ragazzo ~ intelligente** such an intelligent boy

♦ *ag inv* (*tale*): **non ho mai visto un film ~** I've never seen such a film

♦ *cong* **1** (*perciò*) so, therefore

2: **~ ... come** as ... as; **non è ~ bravo come te** he's not as good as you; **~ ... che** so ... that

cosid'detto, a *ag* so-called

cos'metico, a, ci, che *ag, sm* cosmetic

cos'pargere [kos'pardʒere] *vt*: **~ di** to sprinkle with; **cos'parso, a** *pp di* **cospargere**

cos'petto *sm*: **al ~ di** in front of; in the presence of

cos'picuo, a *ag* considerable, large

cospi'rare *vi* to conspire; **cospirazi'one** *sf* conspiracy

'costa *sf* (*tra terra e mare*) coast(line); (*litorale*) shore; (*ANAT*) rib; **la C~ Azzurra** the French Riviera

cos'tante *ag* constant; (*persona*) steadfast ♦ *sf* constant

cos'tare *vi, vt* to cost; **~ caro** to be expensive, cost a lot

cos'tata *sf* (*CUC*) large chop

cos'tato *sm* (*ANAT*) ribs *pl*

costeggi'are [kosted'dʒare] *vt* to be close to; to run alongside

cos'tei *pron vedi* **costui**

costi'era *sf* stretch of coast

costi'ero, a *ag* coastal, coast *cpd*

costitu'ire *vt* (*comitato, gruppo*) to set up, form; (*sog: elementi, parti: comporre*) to make up, constitute; (*rappresentare*) to constitute; (*DIR*) to appoint; **~rsi alla polizia** to give o.s. up to the police

costituzio'nale [kostitutsjo'nale] *ag* constitutional

costituzi'one [kostitut'tsjone] *sf* setting up; building up; constitution

'costo *sm* cost; **a ogni** *o* **qualunque ~, a tutti i ~i** at all costs

'costola *sf* (*ANAT*) rib

cos'toro *pron pl vedi* **costui**

cos'toso, a *ag* expensive, costly

cos'tretto, a *pp di* **costringere**

cos'tringere [kos'trindʒere] *vt*: **~ qn a fare**

qc to force sb to do sth; **costrizi'one** sf coercion

costru'ire vt to construct, build; **costruzi'one** sf construction, building

cos'tui (f **cos'tei**, pl **cos'toro**) pron (soggetto) he/she; pl they; (complemento) him/her; pl them; **si può sapere chi è ~?** (peg) just who is that fellow?

cos'tume sm (uso) custom; (foggia di vestire, indumento) costume; **~i** smpl (condotta morale) morals, morality sg; **~ da bagno** bathing o swimming costume (BRIT), swimsuit; (da uomo) bathing o swimming trunks pl

co'tenna sf bacon rind

co'togna [ko'toɲɲa] sf quince

coto'letta sf (di maiale, montone) chop; (di vitello, agnello) cutlet

co'tone sm cotton; **~ idrofilo** cotton wool (BRIT), absorbent cotton (US)

'cotta sf (fam: innamoramento) crush

'cottimo sm: **lavorare a ~** to do piecework

'cotto, a pp di **cuocere ♦** ag cooked; (fam: innamorato) head-over-heels in love; **ben ~** (carne) well done

cot'tura sf cooking; (in forno) baking; (in umido) stewing

co'vare vt to hatch; (fig: malattia) to be sickening for; (: odio, rancore) to nurse ♦ vi (fuoco, fig) to smoulder

'covo sm den

co'vone sm sheaf

'cozza ['kɔttsa] sf mussel

coz'zare [kot'tsare] vi: **~ contro** to bang into, collide with

C.P. abbr (= casella postale) P.O. Box

crack [kræk] sm inv (droga) crack

'crampo sm cramp

'cranio sm skull

cra'tere sm crater

cra'vatta sf tie

cre'anza [kre'antsa] sf manners pl

cre'are vt to create; **cre'ato** sm creation; **crea'tore, 'trice** ag creative ♦ sm creator; **crea'tura** sf creature; (bimbo) baby, infant; **creazi'one** sf creation; (fondazione) foundation, establishment

cre'dente sm/f (REL) believer

cre'denza [kre'dentsa] sf belief; (armadio) sideboard

credenzi'ali [kreden'tsjali] sfpl credentials

'credere vt to believe ♦ vi: **~ in, ~ a** to believe in; **~ qn onesto** to believe sb (to be) honest; **~ che** to believe o think that; **~rsi furbo** to think one is clever

'credito sm (anche COMM) credit; (reputazione) esteem, repute; **comprare a ~** to buy on credit

'credo sm inv creed

'crema sf cream; (con uova, zucchero etc) custard; **~ solare** sun cream

cre'mare vt to cremate

Crem'lino sm: **il ~** the Kremlin

'crepa sf crack

cre'paccio [kre'pattʃo] sm large crack, fissure; (di ghiacciaio) crevasse

crepacu'ore sm broken heart

cre'pare vi (fam: morire) to snuff it, kick the bucket; **~ dalle risa** to split one's sides laughing

crepi'tare vi (fuoco) to crackle; (pioggia) to patter

cre'puscolo sm twilight, dusk

'crescere ['kreʃʃere] vi to grow ♦ vt (figli) to raise; **'crescita** sf growth; **cresci'uto, a** pp di **crescere**

'cresima sf (REL) confirmation

'crespo, a ag (capelli) frizzy; (tessuto) puckered ♦ sm crêpe

'cresta sf crest; (di polli, uccelli) crest, comb

'creta sf chalk; clay

cre'tino, a ag stupid ♦ sm/f idiot, fool

cric sm inv (TECN) jack

'cricca, che sf clique

cri'ceto [kri'tʃeto] sm hamster

crimi'nale ag, sm/f criminal

'crimine sm (DIR) crime

'crine sm horsehair; **crini'era** sf mane

crisan'temo sm chrysanthemum

'crisi sf inv crisis; (MED) attack, fit; **~ di nervi** attack o fit of nerves

cristalliz'zare [kristalid'dzare] vi to crystallize; (fig) to become fossilized; **~rsi**

vr to crystallize; to become fossilized

cris'tallo *sm* crystal

cristia'nesimo *sm* Christianity

cristi'ano, a *ag, sm/f* Christian

'Cristo *sm* Christ

cri'terio *sm* criterion; (*buon senso*) (common) sense

'critica, che *sf* criticism; **la ~** (*attività*) criticism; (*persone*) the critics *pl*; *vedi anche* **critico**

criti'care *vt* to criticize

'critico, a, ci, che *ag* critical ♦ *sm* critic

Croa'zia [kroa'ttsja] *sf* Croatia

croc'cante *ag* crisp, crunchy

'croce ['krotʃe] *sf* cross; **in ~** (*di traverso*) crosswise; (*fig*) on tenterhooks; **la C~ Rossa** the Red Cross

croce'figgere *etc* [krotʃe'fiddʒere] = **crocifiggere** *etc*

croce'via *sm inv* crossroads *sg*

croci'ata [kro'tʃata] *sf* crusade

cro'cicchio [kro'tʃikkjo] *sm* crossroads *sg*

croci'era [kro'tʃera] *sf* (*viaggio*) cruise; (*ARCHIT*) transept

croci'figgere [krotʃi'fiddʒere] *vt* to crucify; **crocifissi'one** *sf* crucifixion; **croci'fisso, a** *pp di* **crocifiggere**

crogi'olo [kro'dʒɔlo] *sm* (*fig*) melting pot

crol'lare *vi* to collapse; **'crollo** *sm* collapse; (*di prezzi*) slump, sudden fall

cro'mato, a *ag* chromium-plated

'cromo *sm* chrome, chromium

'cronaca, che *sf* (*STAMPA*) news *sg*; (*: rubrica*) column; (*TV, RADIO*) commentary; **fatto** *o* **episodio di ~** news item; **~ nera** crime news *sg*; crime column

'cronico, a, ci, che *ag* chronic

cro'nista, i *sm* (*STAMPA*) reporter

cronolo'gia [kronolo'dʒia] *sf* chronology

cro'nometro *sm* chronometer; (*a scatto*) stopwatch

'crosta *sf* crust

cros'tacei [kros'tatʃei] *smpl* shellfish

cros'tata *sf* (*CUC*) tart

cros'tino *sm* (*CUC*) croûton; (*: da antipasto*) canapé

'cruccio ['kruttʃo] *sm* worry, torment

cruci'verba *sm inv* crossword (puzzle)

cru'dele *ag* cruel; **crudeltà** *sf* cruelty

'crudo, a *ag* (*non cotto*) raw; (*aspro*) harsh, severe

cru'miro (*peg*) *sm* blackleg (*BRIT*), scab

'crusca *sf* bran

crus'cotto *sm* (*AUT*) dashboard

CSI *sigla f inv* (= *Comunità Stati Indipendenti*) CIS

'Cuba *sf* Cuba

cu'betto *sm*: **~ di ghiaccio** ice cube

'cubico, a, ci, che *ag* cubic

'cubo, a *ag* cubic ♦ *sm* cube; **elevare al ~** (*MAT*) to cube

cuc'cagna [kuk'kaɲɲa] *sf*: **paese della ~** land of plenty; **albero della ~** greasy pole (*fig*)

cuc'cetta [kut'tʃetta] *sf* (*FERR*) couchette; (*NAUT*) berth

cucchiai'ata [kukkja'jata] *sf* spoonful

cucchia'ino [kukkja'ino] *sm* teaspoon; coffee spoon

cucchi'aio [kuk'kjajo] *sm* spoon

'cuccia, ce ['kuttʃa] *sf* dog's bed; **a ~!** down!

'cucciolo ['kuttʃolo] *sm* cub; (*di cane*) puppy

cu'cina [ku'tʃina] *sf* (*locale*) kitchen; (*arte culinaria*) cooking, cookery; (*le vivande*) food, cooking; (*apparecchio*) cooker; **~ componibile** fitted kitchen; **cuci'nare** *vt* to cook

cu'cire [ku'tʃire] *vt* to sew, stitch; **cuci'trice** *sf* stapler; **cuci'tura** *sf* sewing, stitching; (*costura*) seam

cucù *sm inv* = **cuculo**

cu'culo *sm* cuckoo

'cuffia *sf* bonnet, cap; (*da infermiera*) cap; (*da bagno*) (bathing) cap; (*per ascoltare*) headphones *pl*, headset

cu'gino, a [ku'dʒino] *sm/f* cousin

| PAROLA CHIAVE |

'cui *pron* **1** (*nei complementi indiretti: persona*) whom; (*: oggetto, animale*) which; **la persona/le persone a ~ accennavi** the person/people you were referring to *o* to

whom you were referring; **i libri di ~ parlavo** the books I was talking about *o* about which I was talking; **il quartiere in ~ abito** the district where I live; **la ragione per** ~ the reason why
2 (*inserito tra articolo e sostantivo*) whose; **la donna i ~ figli sono scomparsi** the woman whose children have disappeared; **il signore, dal ~ figlio ho avuto il libro** the man from whose son I got the book

culi'naria *sf* cookery
'culla *sf* cradle
cul'lare *vt* to rock
culmi'nare *vi*: ~ **con** to culminate in
'culmine *sm* top, summit
'culo (*fam!*) *sm* arse (*Brit!*), ass (*US!*); (*fig: fortuna*): **aver** ~ to have the luck of the devil
'culto *sm* (*religione*) religion; (*adorazione*) worship, adoration; (*venerazione: anche fig*) cult
cul'tura *sf* culture; education, learning; cultu'rale *ag* cultural
cumula'tivo, a *ag* cumulative; (*prezzo*) inclusive; (*biglietto*) group *cpd*
'cumulo *sm* (*mucchio*) pile, heap; (*METEOR*) cumulus
'cuneo *sm* wedge
cu'netta *sf* (*avvallamento*) dip; (*di scolo*) gutter
cu'oca *sf vedi* cuoco
cu'ocere ['kwɔtʃere] *vt* (*alimenti*) to cook; (*mattoni etc*) to fire ♦ *vi* to cook; ~ **al forno** (*pane*) to bake; (*arrosto*) to roast; cu'oco, a, chi, che *sm/f* cook; (*di ristorante*) chef
cu'oio *sm* leather; ~ **capelluto** scalp
cu'ore *sm* heart; ~i *smpl* (*CARTE*) hearts; **avere buon** ~ to be kind-hearted; **stare a** ~ **a qn** to be important to sb
cupi'digia [kupi'didʒa] *sf* greed, covetousness
'cupo, a *ag* dark; (*suono*) dull; (*fig*) gloomy, dismal
'cupola *sf* dome; cupola
'cura *sf* care; (*MED: trattamento*) course of) treatment; **aver ~ di** (*occuparsi di*) to look

after; **a ~ di** (*libro*) edited by; ~ **dimagrante** diet
cu'rare *vt* (*malato, malattia*) to treat; (*: guarire*) to cure; (*aver cura di*) to take care of; (*testo*) to edit; ~**rsi** *vr* to take care of o.s.; (*MED*) to follow a course of treatment; ~**rsi di** to pay attention to
cu'rato *sm* parish priest; (*protestante*) vicar, minister
cura'tore, 'trice *sm/f* (*DIR*) trustee; (*di antologia etc*) editor
curio'sare *vi* to look round, wander round; (*tra libri*) to browse; ~ **nei negozi** to look *o* wander round the shops
curiosità *sf inv* curiosity; (*cosa rara*) curio, curiosity
curi'oso, a *ag* curious; **essere ~ di** to be curious about
cur'sore *sm* (*INFORM*) cursor
'curva *sf* curve; (*stradale*) bend, curve
cur'vare *vt* to bend ♦ *vi* (*veicolo*) to take a bend; (*strada*) to bend, curve; ~**rsi** *vr* to bend; (*legno*) to warp
'curvo, a *ag* curved; (*piegato*) bent
cusci'netto [kuʃʃi'netto] *sm* pad; (*TECN*) bearing ♦ *ag inv*: **stato** ~ buffer state; ~ **a sfere** ball bearing
cu'scino [kuʃ'ʃino] *sm* cushion; (*guanciale*) pillow
'cuspide *sf* (*ARCHIT*) spire
cus'tode *sm/f* keeper, custodian
cus'todia *sf* care; (*DIR*) custody; (*astuccio*) case, holder
custo'dire *vt* (*conservare*) to keep; (*assistere*) to look after, take care of; (*fare la guardia*) to guard
'cute *sf* (*ANAT*) skin
C.V. *abbr* (= *cavallo vapore*) h.p.

D, d

da (*da+il = dal, da+lo = dallo, da+l'* = dall', *da+la = dalla, da+i = dai, da+gli* = dagli, *da+le = dalle*) *prep* **1** (*agente*) by;

dipinto ~ un grande artista painted by a great artist
2 (*causa*) with; **tremare dalla paura** to tremble with fear
3 (*stato in luogo*) at; **abito ~ lui** I'm living at his house *o* with him; **sono dal giornalaio/~ Francesco** I'm at the newsagent's/Francesco's (house)
4 (*moto a luogo*) to; (*moto per luogo*) through; **vado ~ Pietro/dal giornalaio** I'm going to Pietro's/to the newsagent's; **sono passati dalla finestra** they came in through the window
5 (*provenienza, allontanamento*) from; **arrivare/partire ~ Milano** to arrive/depart from Milan; **scendere dal treno/dalla macchina** to get off the train/out of the car; **si trova a 5 km ~ qui** it's 5 km from here
6 (*tempo: durata*) for; (: *a partire da: nel passato*) since; (: *nel futuro*) from; **vivo qui ~ un anno** I've been living here for a year; **è dalle 3 che ti aspetto** I've been waiting for you since 3 (o'clock); **~ oggi in poi** from today onwards; **~ bambino** as a child, when I (*o* he *etc*) was a child
7 (*modo, maniera*) like; **comportarsi ~ uomo** to behave like a man; **l'ho fatto ~ me** I did it (by) myself
8 (*descrittivo*): **una macchina ~ corsa** a racing car; **una ragazza dai capelli biondi** a girl with blonde hair; **un vestito ~ 100.000 lire** a 100,000 lire dress

---

da 'capo *av* = **daccapo**
dac'capo *av* (*di nuovo*) (once) again; (*dal principio*) all over again, from the beginning
'dado *sm* (*da gioco*) dice *o* die; (*CUC*) stock (*BRIT*) *o* bouillon (*US*) cube; (*TECN*) (screw)nut; **giocare a ~i** to play dice
daf'fare *sm* work, toil
'dagli ['daʎʎi] *prep + det vedi* **da**
'dai *prep + det vedi* **da**
'daino *sm* (*fallow*) deer *inv*; (*pelle*) buckskin
dal *prep + det vedi* **da**
dall' *prep + det vedi* **da**
'dalla *prep + det vedi* **da**
'dalle *prep + det vedi* **da**
'dallo *prep + det vedi* **da**
dal'tonico, a, ci, che *ag* colour-blind
'dama *sf* lady; (*nei balli*) partner; (*gioco*) draughts *sg* (*BRIT*), checkers *sg* (*US*)
damigi'ana [dami'dʒana] *sf* demijohn
da'naro *sm* = **denaro**
da'nese *ag* Danish ♦ *sm/f* Dane ♦ *sm* (*LING*) Danish
Dani'marca *sf*: **la ~** Denmark
dan'nare *vt* (*REL*) to damn; **~rsi** *vr* (*fig: tormentarsi*) to be worried to death; **far ~ qn** to drive sb mad; **dannazi'one** *sf* damnation
danneggi'are [danned'dʒare] *vt* to damage; (*rovinare*) to spoil; (*nuocere*) to harm
'danno *sm* damage; (*a persona*) harm, injury; **~i** *smpl* (*DIR*) damages; **dan'noso, a** *ag*: **dannoso (a, per)** harmful (to), bad (for)
Da'nubio *sm*: **il ~** the Danube
'danza ['dantsa] *sf*: **la ~** dancing; **una ~** a dance
dan'zare [dan'tsare] *vt, vi* to dance
dapper'tutto *av* everywhere
dap'poco *ag inv* inept, worthless
dap'prima *av* at first
'dare *sm* (*COMM*) debit ♦ *vt* to give; (*produrre: frutti, suono*) to produce ♦ *vi* (*guardare*): **~ su** to look (out) onto; **~rsi** *vr*: **~rsi a** to dedicate o.s. to; **~rsi al commercio** to go into business; **~rsi al bere** to take to drink; **~ da mangiare a qn** to give sb sth to eat; **~ per certo qc** to consider sth certain; **~ per morto qn** to give sb up for dead; **~rsi per vinto** to give in
'darsena *sf* dock; dockyard
'data *sf* date; **~ di nascita** date of birth
da'tare *vt* to date ♦ *vi*: **~ da** to date from
'dato, a *ag* (*stabilito*) given ♦ *sm* datum; **~i** *smpl* data *pl*; **~ che** given that; **un ~ di fatto** a fact
da'tore, trice *sm/f*: **~ di lavoro** employer
'dattero *sm* date

dattilogra'fare *vt* to type; **dattilogra'fia** *sf* typing; **datti'lografo, a** *sm/f* typist

da'vanti *av* in front; (*dirimpetto*) opposite ♦ *ag inv* front ♦ *sm* front; **~ a** in front of; facing, opposite; (*in presenza di*) before, in front of

davan'zale [davan'tsale] *sm* windowsill

d'a'vanzo [da'vantso] *av* more than enough

dav'vero *av* really, indeed

'dazio ['dattsjo] *sm* (*somma*) duty; (*luogo*) customs *pl*

DC *sigla f* = **Democrazia Cristiana**

d. C. *ad abbr* (= *dopo Cristo*) A.D.

'dea *sf* goddess

'debito, a *ag* due, proper ♦ *sm* debt; (*COMM: dare*) debit; **a tempo ~** at the right time; **debi'tore, 'trice** *sm/f* debtor

'debole *ag* weak, feeble; (*suono*) faint; (*luce*) dim ♦ *sm* weakness; **debo'lezza** *sf* weakness

debut'tare *vi* to make one's début; **de'butto** *sm* début

deca'denza [deka'dɛntsa] *sf* decline; (*DIR*) loss, forfeiture

decaffei'nato, a *ag* decaffeinated

decan'tare *vt* to praise, sing the praises of

decapi'tare *vt* to decapitate

decappot'tabile *ag, sf* convertible

dece'duto, a [detʃe'duto] *ag* deceased

de'cennio [de'tʃɛnnjo] *sm* decade

de'cente [de'tʃɛnte] *ag* decent, respectable, proper; (*accettabile*) satisfactory, decent

de'cesso [de'tʃɛsso] *sm* death

de'cidere [de'tʃidere] *vt*: **~ qc** to decide on sth; (*questione, lite*) to settle sth; **~ di fare/che** to decide to do/that; **~ di qc** (*sog: cosa*) to determine sth; **~rsi (a fare)** to decide (to do), make up one's mind (to do)

deci'frare [detʃi'frare] *vt* to decode; (*fig*) to decipher, make out

deci'male [detʃi'male] *ag* decimal

'decimo, a ['dɛtʃimo] *num* tenth

de'cina [de'tʃina] *sf* ten; (*circa dieci*): **una ~ (di)** about ten

decisi'one [detʃi'zjone] *sf* decision;

prendere una ~ to make a decision

de'ciso, a [de'tʃizo] *pp di* **decidere**

declas'sare *vt* to downgrade; to lower in status

decli'nare *vi* (*pendio*) to slope down; (*fig: diminuire*) to decline ♦ *vt* to decline; **declinazi'one** *sf* (*LING*) declension; **de'clino** *sm* decline

decodifica'tore *sm* (*TEL*) decoder

decol'lare *vi* (*AER*) to take off; **de'collo** *sm* take-off

decolo'rare *vt* to bleach

decom'porre *vt* to decompose; **decomporsi** *vr* to decompose; **decom'posto, a** *pp di* **decomporre**

deconge'lare [dekondʒe'lare] *vt* to defrost

deco'rare *vt* to decorate; **decora'tore, 'trice** *sm/f* (*interior*) decorator; **decorazi'one** *sf* decoration

de'coro *sm* decorum; **deco'roso, a** *ag* decorous, dignified

de'correre *vi* to pass, elapse; (*avere effetto*) to run, have effect; **de'corso, a** *pp di* **decorrere** ♦ *sm* (*evoluzione: anche MED*) course

de'crepito, a *ag* decrepit

de'crescere [de'kreʃʃere] *vi* (*diminuire*) to decrease, diminish; (*acque*) to subside, go down; (*prezzi*) to go down; **decresci'uto, a** *pp di* **decrescere**

de'creto *sm* decree; **~ legge** *decree with the force of law*

'dedalo *sm* maze, labyrinth

'dedica, che *sf* dedication

dedi'care *vt* to dedicate

'dedito, a *ag*: **~ a** (*studio etc*) dedicated *o* devoted to; (*vizio*) addicted to

de'dotto, a *pp di* **dedurre**

de'durre *vt* (*concludere*) to deduce; (*defalcare*) to deduct; **deduzi'one** *sf* deduction

defal'care *vt* to deduct

defe'rente *ag* respectful, deferential

defe'rire *vt*: **~ a** (*DIR*) to refer to

defezi'one [defet'tsjone] *sf* defection, desertion

defici'ente [defi'tʃɛnte] *ag* (*mancante*): **~ di**

deficient in; *(insufficiente)* insufficient
♦ *sm/f* mental defective; *(peg: cretino)* idiot

'deficit ['dɛfitʃit] *sm inv (ECON)* deficit

defi'nire *vt* to define; *(risolvere)* to settle;
defini'tivo, a *ag* definitive, final;
definizi'one *sf* definition; settlement

deflet'tore *sm (AUT)* quarter-light

de'flusso *sm (della marea)* ebb

defor'mare *vt (alterare)* to put out of
shape; *(corpo)* to deform; *(pensiero, fatto)*
to distort; **~rsi** *vr* to lose its shape

de'forme *ag* deformed; disfigured;
deformità *sf inv* deformity

defrau'dare *vt*: **~ qn di qc** to defraud sb
of sth, cheat sb out of sth

de'funto, a *ag* late *cpd* ♦ *sm/f* deceased

degene'rare [dedʒene'rare] *vi* to
degenerate; **de'genere** *ag* degenerate

de'gente [de'dʒɛnte] *sm/f (in ospedale)* in-
patient

'degli ['deʎʎi] *prep + det vedi* **di**

de'gnarsi [deɲ'ɲarsi] *vr*: **~ di fare** to deign
o condescend to do

'degno, a *ag* dignified; **~ di** worthy of; **~
di lode** praiseworthy

degra'dare *vt (MIL)* to demote; *(privare
della dignità)* to degrade; **~rsi** *vr* to
demean o.s.

degustazi'one [degustat'tsjone] *sf*
sampling, tasting

'dei *prep + det vedi* **di**

del *prep + det vedi* **di**

dela'tore, 'trice *sm/f* police informer

'delega, ghe *sf (procura)* proxy

dele'gare *vt* to delegate; **dele'gato** *sm*
delegate

dele'terio, a *ag* damaging; *(per salute etc)*
harmful

del'fino *sm (ZOOL)* dolphin; *(STORIA)*
dauphin; *(fig)* probable successor

delibe'rare *vt* to come to a decision on
♦ *vi (DIR)*: **~ (su qc)** to rule (on sth)

delica'tezza [delika'tettsa] *sf* delicacy;
frailty; thoughtfulness; tactfulness

deli'cato, a *ag* delicate; *(salute)* delicate,
frail; *(fig: gentile)* thoughtful, considerate;
(: che dimostra tatto) tactful

deline'are *vt* to outline; **~rsi** *vr* to be
outlined; *(fig)* to emerge

delin'quente *sm/f* criminal, delinquent; **~
abituale** regular offender, habitual
offender; **delin'quenza** *sf* criminality,
delinquency; **delinquenza minorile**
juvenile delinquency

deli'rare *vi* to be delirious, rave; *(fig)* to
rave

de'lirio *sm* delirium; *(ragionamento
insensato)* raving; *(fig)*: **andare/mandare
in ~** to go/send into a frenzy

de'litto *sm* crime

de'lizia [de'littsja] *sf* delight; **delizi'oso, a**
ag delightful; *(cibi)* delicious

dell' *prep + det vedi* **di**

'della *prep + det vedi* **di**

'delle *prep + det vedi* **di**

'dello *prep + det vedi* **di**

delta'plano *sm* hang-glider; **volo col ~**
hang-gliding

de'ludere *vt* to disappoint; **delusi'one** *sf*
disappointment; **de'luso, a** *pp di*
deludere

de'manio *sm* state property

de'menza [de'mɛntsa] *sf* dementia;
(stupidità) foolishness

demo'cratico, a, ci, che *ag* democratic

democra'zia [demokrat'tsia] *sf* democracy

democristi'ano, a *ag, sm/f* Christian
Democrat

demo'lire *vt* to demolish

'demone *sm* demon

de'monio *sm* demon, devil; **il D~** the Devil

de'naro *sm* money

denomi'nare *vt* to name;
denominazi'one *sf* name;
denomination; **denominazione d'origine
controllata** *label guaranteeing the quality
and origin of a wine*

densità *sf inv* density

'denso, a *ag* thick, dense

den'tale *ag* dental

'dente *sm* tooth; *(di forchetta)* prong; **al ~**
(CUC: pasta) al dente; **~i del giudizio**
wisdom teeth; **denti'era** *sf* (set of) false
teeth *pl*

denti'fricio [denti'fritʃo] *sm* toothpaste
den'tista, i, e *sm/f* dentist
'dentro *av* inside; (*in casa*) indoors; (*fig: nell'intimo*) inwardly ♦ *prep*: ~ **(a)** in; **piegato in** ~ folded over; **qui/là** ~ in here/there; ~ **di sé** (*pensare, brontolare*) to oneself
de'nuncia, ce *o* **cie** [de'nuntʃa] *sf* denunciation; declaration; ~ **dei redditi** (income) tax return
denunci'are [denun'tʃare] *vt* to denounce; (*dichiarare*) to declare
de'nunzia *etc* [de'nuntsja] = **denuncia** *etc*
denutrizi'one [denutrit'tsjone] *sf* malnutrition
deodo'rante *sm* deodorant
depe'rire *vi* to waste away
depila'torio, a *ag* hair-removing *cpd*, depilatory
dépli'ant [depli'ɑ̃] *sm inv* leaflet; (*opuscolo*) brochure
deplo'revole *ag* deplorable
de'porre *vt* (*depositare*) to put down; (*rimuovere: da una carica*) to remove; (: *re*) to depose; (*DIR*) to testify
depor'tare *vt* to deport
deposi'tare *vt* (*gen, GEO, ECON*) to deposit; (*lasciare*) to leave; (*merci*) to store
de'posito *sm* deposit; (*luogo*) warehouse; depot; (: *MIL*) depot; ~ **bagagli** left-luggage office
deposizi'one [depozit'tsjone] *sf* deposition, (*da una carica*) removal
de'posto, a *pp di* **deporre**
depra'vato, a *ag* depraved ♦ *sm/f* degenerate
depre'dare *vt* to rob, plunder
depressi'one *sf* depression
de'presso, a *pp di* **deprimere** ♦ *ag* depressed
deprez'zare [depret'tsare] *vt* (*ECON*) to depreciate
de'primere *vt* to depress
depu'rare *vt* to purify
depu'tato *sm* (*POL*) deputy, ≈ Member of Parliament (*BRIT*), ≈ Member of Congress (*US*)

deragli'are [deraʎ'ʎare] *vi* to be derailed; **far** ~ to derail
dere'litto, a *ag* derelict
dere'tano (*fam*) *sm* bottom, buttocks *pl*
de'ridere *vt* to mock, deride; **de'riso, a** *pp di* **deridere**
de'riva *sf* (*NAUT, AER*) drift; **andare alla** ~ (*anche fig*) to drift
deri'vare *vi*: ~ **da** to derive from ♦ *vt* to derive; (*corso d'acqua*) to divert; **derivazi'one** *sf* derivation; diversion
derma'tologo, a, gi, ghe *sm/f* dermatologist
der'rate *sfpl*: ~ **alimentari** foodstuffs
deru'bare *vt* to rob
des'critto, a *pp di* **descrivere**
des'crivere *vt* to describe; **descrizi'one** *sf* description
de'serto, a *ag* deserted ♦ *sm* (*GEO*) desert; **isola** ~**a** desert island
deside'rare *vt* to want, wish for; (*sessualmente*) to desire; ~ **fare/che qn faccia** to want o wish to do/sb to do; **desidera fare una passeggiata?** would you like to go for a walk?
desi'derio *sm* wish; (*più intenso, carnale*) desire
deside'roso, a *ag*: ~ **di** longing *o* eager for
desi'nenza [dezi'nentsa] *sf* (*LING*) ending, inflexion
de'sistere *vi*: ~ **da** to give up, desist from; **desis'tito, a** *pp di* **desistere**
deso'lato, a *ag* (*paesaggio*) desolate; (*persona: spiacente*) sorry
des'tare *vt* to wake (up); (*fig*) to awaken, arouse; ~**rsi** *vr* to wake (up)
desti'nare *vt* to destine; (*assegnare*) to appoint, assign; (*indirizzare*) to address; ~ **qc a qn** to intend to give sth to sb, intend sb to have sth; **destina'tario, a** *sm/f* (*di lettera*) addressee
destinazi'one [destinat'tsjone] *sf* destination; (*uso*) purpose
des'tino *sm* destiny, fate
destitu'ire *vt* to dismiss, remove
'desto, a *ag* (wide) awake

'destra *sf* (*mano*) right hand; (*parte*) right (side); (*POL*): **la ~** the Right; **a ~** (*essere*) on the right; (*andare*) to the right

destreggi'arsi [destred'dʒarsi] *vr* to manoeuvre (*BRIT*), maneuver (*US*)

des'trezza [des'trettsa] *sf* skill, dexterity

'destro, a *ag* right, right-hand

dete'nere *vt* (*incarico, primato*) to hold; (*proprietà*) to have, possess; (*in prigione*) to detain, hold; **dete'nuto, a** *sm/f* prisoner; **detenzi'one** *sf* holding; possession; detention

deter'gente [deter'dʒɛnte] *ag* detergent; (*crema, latte*) cleansing ♦ *sm* detergent

deterio'rare *vt* to damage; **~rsi** *vr* to deteriorate

determi'nare *vt* to determine; **determinazi'one** *sf* determination; (*decisione*) decision

deter'sivo *sm* detergent

detes'tare *vt* to detest, hate

de'trarre *vt*: **~ (da)** to deduct (from), take away (from); **de'tratto, a** *pp di* **detrarre**; **detrazi'one** *sf* deduction; **detrazione d'imposta** tax allowance

de'trito *sm* (*GEO*) detritus

'detta *sf*: **a ~ di** according to

dettagli'are [dettaʎ'ʎare] *vt* to detail, give full details of

det'taglio [det'taʎʎo] *sm* detail; (*COMM*): **il ~** retail; **al ~** (*COMM*) retail; separately

det'tare *vt* to dictate; **~ legge** (*fig*) to lay down the law; **det'tato** *sm* dictation; **detta'tura** *sf* dictation

'detto, a *pp di* **dire** ♦ *ag* (*soprannominato*) called, known as; (*già nominato*) above-mentioned ♦ *sm* saying; **~ fatto** no sooner said than done

detur'pare *vt* to disfigure; (*moralmente*) to sully

devas'tare *vt* to devastate; (*fig*) to ravage

devi'are *vi*: **~ (da)** to turn off (from) ♦ *vt* to divert; **deviazi'one** *sf* (*anche AUT*) diversion

devo'luto, a *pp di* **devolvere**

devoluzi'one [devolut'tsjone] *sf* (*DIR*) devolution, transfer

de'volvere *vt* (*DIR*) to transfer, devolve

de'voto, a *ag* (*REL*) devout, pious; (*affezionato*) devoted

devozi'one [devot'tsjone] *sf* devoutness; (*anche REL*) devotion

---

PAROLA CHIAVE

di (*di+il* = **del**, *di+lo* = **dello**, *di+l'* = **dell'**, *di+la* = **della**, *di+i* = **dei**, *di+gli* = **degli**, *di+le* = **delle**) *prep* **1** (*possesso, specificazione*) of; (*composto da, scritto da*) by; **la macchina ~ Paolo/mio fratello** Paolo's/my brother's car; **un amico ~ mio fratello** a friend of my brother's, one of my brother's friends; **un quadro ~ Botticelli** a painting by Botticelli

2 (*caratterizzazione, misura*) of; **una casa ~ mattoni** a brick house, a house made of bricks; **un orologio d'oro** a gold watch; **un bimbo ~ 3 anni** a child of 3, a 3-year-old child

3 (*causa, mezzo, modo*) with; **tremare ~ paura** to tremble with fear; **morire ~ cancro** to die of cancer; **spalmare ~ burro** to spread with butter

4 (*argomento*) about, of; **discutere ~ sport** to talk about sport

5 (*luogo: provenienza*) from; out of; **essere ~ Roma** to be from Rome; **uscire ~ casa** to come out of *o* leave the house

6 (*tempo*) in; **d'estate/d'inverno** in (the) summer/winter; **~ notte** by night, at night; **~ mattina/sera** in the morning/evening; **~ lunedì** on Mondays

♦ *det* (*una certa quantità di*) some; (: *negativo*) any; (: *interrogativo*) any, some; **del pane** (some) bread; **delle caramelle** (some) sweets; **degli amici miei** some friends of mine; **vuoi del vino?** do you want some *o* any wine?

---

dia'bete *sm* diabetes *sg*

di'acono *sm* (*REL*) deacon

dia'dema, i *sm* diadem; (*di donna*) tiara

dia'framma, i *sm* (*divisione*) screen; (*ANAT, FOT, contraccettivo*) diaphragm

di'agnosi [di'aɲɲozi] *sf* diagnosis *sg*

diago'nale *ag, sf* diagonal
dia'gramma, i *sm* diagram
dia'letto *sm* dialect
di'alisi *sf* dialysis *sg*
di'alogo, ghi *sm* dialogue
dia'mante *sm* diamond
di'ametro *sm* diameter
di'amine *escl*: **che ~ ...?** what on earth ...?
diaposi'tiva *sf* transparency, slide
di'ario *sm* diary
diar'rea *sf* diarrhoea
di'avolo *sm* devil
di'battere *vt* to debate, discuss; **~rsi** *vr* to struggle; **di'battito** *sm* debate, discussion
dicas'tero *sm* ministry
di'cembre [di'tʃɛmbre] *sm* December
dice'ria [ditʃe'ria] *sf* rumour, piece of gossip
dichia'rare [dikja'rare] *vt* to declare; **dichiarazi'one** *sf* declaration
dician'nove [ditʃan'nɔve] *num* nineteen
dicias'sette [ditʃas'sette] *num* seventeen
dici'otto [di'tʃɔtto] *num* eighteen
dici'tura [ditʃi'tura] *sf* words *pl*, wording
di'eci ['djɛtʃi] *num* ten; **die'cina** *sf* = **decina**
'diesel ['dizəl] *sm inv* diesel engine
di'eta *sf* diet; **essere a ~** to be on a diet
di'etro *av* behind; (*in fondo*) at the back ♦ *prep* behind; (*tempo: dopo*) after ♦ *sm* back, rear ♦ *ag inv* back *cpd*; **le zampe di ~** the hind legs; **~ richiesta** on demand; (*scritta*) on application
di'fatti *cong* in fact, as a matter of fact
di'fendere *vt* to defend; **difen'sivo, a** *ag* defensive ♦ *sf*: **stare sulla difensiva** (*anche fig*) to be on the defensive; **difen'sore, a** *sm/f* defender; **avvocato difensore** counsel for the defence; **di'fesa** *sf* defence; **di'feso, a** *pp di* **difendere**
difet'tare *vi* to be defective; **~ di** to be lacking in, lack; **difet'tivo, a** *ag* defective
di'fetto *sm* (*mancanza*): **~ di** lack of, shortage of; (*di fabbricazione*) fault, flaw, defect; (*morale*) fault, failing, defect; (*fisico*) defect; **far ~** to be lacking; **in ~** at fault; in the wrong; **difet'toso, a** *ag* defective, faulty

diffa'mare *vt* to slander; to libel
diffe'rente *ag* different
diffe'renza [diffe'rɛntsa] *sf* difference; **a ~ di** unlike
differenzi'are [differen'tsjare] *vt* to differentiate; **~rsi da** to differentiate o.s. from; to differ from
diffe'rire *vt* to postpone, defer ♦ *vi* to be different
dif'ficile [dif'fitʃile] *ag* difficult; (*persona*) hard to please, difficult (to please); (*poco probabile*): **è ~ che sia libero** it is unlikely that he'll be free ♦ *sm* difficult part; difficulty; **difficoltà** *sf inv* difficulty
dif'fida *sf* (*DIR*) warning, notice
diffi'dare *vi*: **~ di** to be suspicious o distrustful of ♦ *vt* (*DIR*) to warn; **~ qn dal fare qc** to warn sb not to do sth, caution sb against doing sth; **diffi'dente** *ag* suspicious, distrustful; **diffi'denza** *sf* suspicion, distrust
dif'fondere *vt* (*luce, calore*) to diffuse; (*notizie*) to spread, circulate; **~rsi** *vr* to spread; **diffusi'one** *sf* diffusion; spread; (*anche di giornale*) circulation; (*FISICA*) scattering; **dif'fuso, a** *pp di* **diffondere** ♦ *ag* (*malattia, fenomeno*) widespread
difi'lato *av* (*direttamente*) straight, directly; (*subito*) straight away
dif'terite *sf* (*MED*) diphtheria
'diga, ghe *sf* dam; (*portuale*) breakwater
dige'rente [didʒe'rɛnte] *ag* (*apparato*) digestive
dige'rire [didʒe'rire] *vt* to digest; **digesti'one** *sf* digestion; **diges'tivo, a** *ag* digestive ♦ *sm* (after-dinner) liqueur
digi'tale [didʒi'tale] *ag* digital; (*delle dita*) finger *cpd*, digital ♦ *sf* (*BOT*) foxglove
digi'tare [didʒi'tare] *vt, vi* (*INFORM*) to key (in)
digiu'nare [didʒu'nare] *vi* to starve o.s.; (*REL*) to fast; **digi'uno, a** *ag*: **essere digiuno** not to have eaten ♦ *sm* fast; **a digiuno** on an empty stomach
dignità [diɲɲi'ta] *sf inv* dignity; **digni'toso, a** *ag* dignified
'DIGOS ['digɔs] *sigla f* (= *Divisione*

Investigazioni Generali e Operazioni Speciali) police department dealing with political security

digri'gnare [digriɲ'ɲare] *vt*: **~ i denti** to grind one's teeth

dila'gare *vi* to flood; *(fig)* to spread

dilani'are *vt (preda)* to tear to pieces

dilapi'dare *vt* to squander, waste

dila'tare *vt* to dilate; *(gas)* to cause to expand; *(passaggio, cavità)* to open (up); **~rsi** *vr* to dilate; *(FISICA)* to expand

dilazio'nare [dilattsjo'nare] *vt* to delay, defer; **dilazi'one** *sf* delay; *(COMM: di pagamento etc)* extension; *(rinvio)* postponement

dilegu'are *vi* to vanish, disappear; **~rsi** *vr* to vanish, disappear

di'lemma, i *sm* dilemma

dilet'tante *sm/f* dilettante; *(anche SPORT)* amateur

dilet'tare *vt* to give pleasure to, delight; **~rsi** *vr*: **~rsi di** to take pleasure in, enjoy

di'letto, a *ag* dear, beloved ♦ *sm* pleasure, delight

dili'gente [dili'dʒɛnte] *ag (scrupoloso)* diligent; *(accurato)* careful, accurate; **dili'genza** *sf* diligence; care; *(carrozza)* stagecoach

dilu'ire *vt* to dilute

dilun'garsi *vr (fig)*: **~ su** to talk at length on *o* about

diluvi'are *vb impers* to pour (down)

di'luvio *sm* downpour; *(inondazione, fig)* flood

dima'grire *vi* to get thinner, lose weight

dime'nare *vt* to wave, shake; **~rsi** *vr* to toss and turn; *(fig)* to struggle; **~ la coda** *(sog: cane)* to wag its tail

dimensi'one *sf* dimension; *(grandezza)* size

dimenti'canza [dimenti'kantsa] *sf* forgetfulness; *(errore)* oversight, slip; **per ~** inadvertently

dimenti'care *vt* to forget; **~rsi di qc** to forget sth

di'messo, a *pp di* **dimettere** ♦ *ag (voce)* subdued; *(uomo, abito)* modest, humble

dimesti'chezza [dimesti'kettsa] *sf* familiarity

di'mettere *vt*: **~ qn da** to dismiss sb from; *(dall'ospedale)* to discharge sb from; **~rsi (da)** to resign (from)

dimez'zare [dimed'dzare] *vt* to halve

diminu'ire *vt* to reduce, diminish; *(prezzi)* to bring down, reduce ♦ *vi* to decrease, diminish; *(rumore)* to die down, die away; *(prezzi)* to fall, go down; **diminuzi'one** *sf* decreasing, diminishing

dimissi'oni *sfpl* resignation *sg*; **dare** *o* **presentare le ~** to resign, hand in one's resignation

di'mora *sf* residence

dimo'rare *vi* to reside

dimos'trare *vt* to demonstrate, show; *(provare)* to prove, demonstrate; **~rsi** *vr*: **~rsi molto abile** to show o.s. *o* prove to be very clever; **dimostra 30 anni** he looks about 30 (years old); **dimostrazi'one** *sf* demonstration; proof

di'namica *sf* dynamics *sg*

di'namico, a, ci, che *ag* dynamic

dina'mite *sf* dynamite

'dinamo *sf inv* dynamo

di'nanzi [di'nantsi]: **~ a** *prep* in front of

dini'ego, ghi *sm* refusal; denial

dinocco'lato, a *ag* lanky

din'torno *av* round, (round) about; **~i** *smpl* outskirts; **nei ~i di** in the vicinity *o* neighbourhood of

'dio *(pl* **'dei)** *sm* god; **D~** God; **gli dei** the gods; **D~ mio!** my goodness!, my God!

di'ocesi [di'ɔtʃezi] *sf inv* diocese

dipa'nare *vt (lana)* to wind into a ball; *(fig)* to disentangle, sort out

diparti'mento *sm* department

dipen'dente *ag* dependent ♦ *sm/f* employee; **dipen'denza** *sf* dependence; **essere alle dipendenze di qn** to be employed by sb *o* in sb's employ

di'pendere *vi*: **~ da** to depend on; *(finanziariamente)* to be dependent on; *(derivare)* to come from, be due to; **di'peso, a** *pp di* **dipendere**

di'pingere [di'pindʒere] *vt* to paint;

di'pinto, a *pp di* dipingere ♦ *sm* painting

di'ploma, i *sm* diploma

diplo'mare *vt* to award a diploma to, graduate (*US*); **~rsi** *vr* to obtain a diploma, graduate (*US*)

diplo'matico, a, ci, che *ag* diplomatic ♦ *sm* diplomat

diploma'zia [diplomat'tsia] *sf* diplomacy

di'porto: imbarcazione da ~ *sf* pleasure craft

dira'dare *vt* to thin (out); (*visite*) to reduce, make less frequent; **~rsi** *vr* to disperse; (*nebbia*) to clear (up)

dira'mare *vt* to issue ♦ *vi* (*strade*) to branch; **~rsi** *vr* to branch

'dire *vt* to say; (*segreto, fatto*) to tell; ~ qc a qn to tell sb sth; ~ a qn di fare qc to tell sb to do sth; ~ di sì/no to say yes/no; si dice che ... they say that ...; si direbbe che ... it looks (*o* sounds) as though ...; dica, signora? (*in un negozio*) yes, Madam, can I help you?

di'retto, a *ag di* dirigere ♦ *ag* direct ♦ *sm* (*FERR*) through train

diret'tore, 'trice *sm/f* (*di azienda*) director; manager/ess; (*di scuola elementare*) head (teacher) (*BRIT*), principal (*US*); ~ d'orchestra conductor; ~ vendite sales director *o* manager

direzi'one [diret'tsjone] *sf* board of directors; management; (*senso di movimento*) direction; in ~ di in the direction of, towards

diri'gente [diri'dʒɛnte] *sm/f* executive; (*POL*) leader ♦ *ag*: classe ~ ruling class

di'rigere [di'ridʒere] *vt* to direct; (*impresa*) to run, manage; (*MUS*) to conduct; **~rsi** *vr*: ~rsi verso *o* a to make *o* head for

dirim'petto *av* opposite; ~ a opposite, facing

di'ritto, a *ag* straight; (*onesto*) straight, upright *o av* straight, directly; andare ~ to go straight on ♦ *sm* right side; (*TENNIS*) forehand; (*MAGLIA*) plain stitch; (*prerogativa*) right; (*leggi, scienza*): il ~ law; ~i *smpl* (*tasse*) duty *sg*; stare ~ to stand up straight; aver ~ a qc to be entitled to sth;

~i d'autore royalties

dirit'tura *sf* (*SPORT*) straight; (*fig*) rectitude

diroc'cato, a *ag* tumbledown, in ruins

dirot'tare *vt* (*nave, aereo*) to change the course of; (*aereo: sotto minaccia*) to hijack; (*traffico*) to divert ♦ *vi* (*nave, aereo*) to change course; dirotta'tore, 'trice *sm/f* hijacker

di'rotto, a *ag* (*pioggia*) torrential; (*pianto*) unrestrained; piovere a ~ to pour; piangere a ~ to cry one's heart out

di'rupo *sm* crag, precipice

disabi'tato, a *ag* uninhabited

disabitu'arsi *vr*: ~ a to get out of the habit of

disac'cordo *sm* disagreement

disadat'tato, a *ag* (*PSIC*) maladjusted

disa'dorno, a *ag* plain, unadorned

disagi'ato, a [diza'dʒato] *ag* poor, needy; (*vita*) hard

di'sagio [di'zadʒo] *sm* discomfort; (*disturbo*) inconvenience; (*fig: imbarazzo*) embarrassment; essere a ~ to be ill at ease

disappro'vare *vt* to disapprove of; disapprovazi'one *sf* disapproval

disap'punto *sm* disappointment

disar'mare *vt, vi* to disarm; di'sarmo *sm* (*MIL*) disarmament

di'sastro *sm* disaster

disat'tento, a *ag* inattentive; disattenzi'one *sf* carelessness, lack of attention

disa'vanzo [diza'vantso] *sm* (*ECON*) deficit

disavven'tura *sf* misadventure, mishap

dis'brigo, ghi *sm* (*prompt*) clearing up *o* settlement

dis'capito *sm*: a ~ di to the detriment of

dis'carica, che *sf* (*di rifiuti*) rubbish tip *o* dump

discen'dente [diʃʃen'dɛnte] *ag* descending ♦ *sm/f* descendant

di'scendere [diʃ'ʃɛndere] *vt* to go (*o* come) down ♦ *vi* to go (*o* come) down; (*strada*) to go down; (*smontare*) to get off; ~ da (*famiglia*) to be descended from; ~ dalla macchina/dal treno to get out of the car/out of *o* off the train; ~ da cavallo to dismount, get off one's horse

di'scepolo, a [diʃʃepolo] _sm/f_ disciple

di'scernere [diʃʃernere] _vt_ to discern

di'scesa [diʃʃesa] _sf_ descent; (_pendio_) slope; **in ~** (_strada_) downhill _cpd_, sloping; **~ libera** (_SCI_) downhill (race)

di'sceso, a [diʃʃeso] _pp di_ **discendere**

disci'ogliere [diʃʃɔʎʎere] _vt_ to dissolve; (_fondere_) to melt; **~rsi** _vr_ to dissolve; to melt; **disci'olto, a** _pp di_ **disciogliere**

disci'plina [diʃʃi'plina] _sf_ discipline; **discipli'nare** _ag_ disciplinary ♦ _vt_ to discipline

'disco, schi _sm_ disc; (_SPORT_) discus; (_fonografico_) record; (_INFORM_) disk; **~ orario** (_AUT_) parking disc; **~ rigido** (_INFORM_) hard disk; **~ volante** flying saucer

discol'pare _vt_ to clear of blame

disco'noscere [disko'noʃʃere] _vt_ (_figlio_) to disown; (_meriti_) to ignore, disregard; **disconosci'uto, a** _pp di_ **disconoscere**

dis'corde _ag_ conflicting, clashing; **dis'cordia** _sf_ discord; (_dissidio_) disagreement, clash

dis'correre _vi_: **~ (di)** to talk (about)

dis'corso, a _pp di_ **discorrere** ♦ _sm_ speech; (_conversazione_) conversation, talk

dis'costo, a _ag_ faraway, distant ♦ _av_ far away; **~ da** far from

disco'teca, che _sf_ (_raccolta_) record library; (_locale_) disco

discre'panza [diskre'pantsa] _sf_ disagreement

dis'creto, a _ag_ discreet; (_abbastanza buono_) reasonable, fair; **discrezi'one** _sf_ discretion; (_giudizio_) judgment, discernment; **a discrezione di** at the discretion of

discriminazi'one [diskriminat'tsjone] _sf_ discrimination

discussi'one _sf_ discussion; (_litigio_) argument; **fuori ~** out of the question

dis'cusso, a _pp di_ **discutere**

dis'cutere _vt_ to discuss, debate; (_contestare_) to question ♦ _vi_ (_conversare_): **~ (di)** to discuss; (_litigare_) to argue

disde'gnare [disdeɲ'ɲare] _vt_ to scorn

dis'detta _sf_ (_di prenotazione etc_) cancellation; (_sfortuna_) bad luck

dis'detto, a _pp di_ **disdire**

dis'dire _vt_ (_prenotazione_) to cancel; (_DIR_): **~ un contratto d'affitto** to give notice (to quit)

dise'gnare [disen'ɲare] _vt_ to draw; (_progettare_) to design; (_fig_) to outline

disegna'tore, 'trice _sm/f_ designer

di'segno [di'seɲɲo] _sm_ drawing; design; outline; **~ di legge** (_DIR_) bill

diser'bante _sm_ weed-killer

diser'tare _vt, vi_ to desert; **diser'tore** _sm_ (_MIL_) deserter

dis'fare _vt_ to undo; (_valigie_) to unpack; (_meccanismo_) to take to pieces; (_neve_) to melt; **~rsi** _vr_ to come undone; (_neve_) to melt; **~ il letto** to strip the bed; **~rsi di qn** (_liberarsi_) to get rid of sb; **dis'fatta** _sf_ (_sconfitta_) rout; **dis'fatto, a** _pp di_ **disfare**

dis'gelo [diz'dʒelo] _sm_ thaw

dis'grazia [diz'grattsja] _sf_ (_sventura_) misfortune; (_incidente_) accident, mishap; **disgrazi'ato, a** _ag_ unfortunate ♦ _sm/f_ wretch

disgre'gare _vt_ to break up; **~rsi** _vr_ to break up

disgu'ido _sm_ hitch; **~ postale** error in postal delivery

disgus'tare _vt_ to disgust; **~rsi** _vr_: **~rsi di** to be disgusted by

dis'gusto _sm_ disgust; **disgus'toso, a** _ag_ disgusting

disidra'tare _vt_ to dehydrate

disil'ludere _vt_ to disillusion, disenchant

disimpa'rare _vt_ to forget

disinfet'tante _ag, sm_ disinfectant

disinfet'tare _vt_ to disinfect

disini'bito, a _ag_ uninhibited

disinte'grare _vt, vi_ to disintegrate

disinteres'sarsi _vr_: **~ di** to take no interest in

disinte'resse _sm_ indifference; (_generosità_) unselfishness

disintossi'care _vt_ (_alcolizzato, drogato_) to treat for alcoholism (_o drug addiction_); **~ l'organismo** to clear out one's system

disin'volto, a *ag* casual, free and easy; **disinvol'tura** *sf* casualness, ease

disles'sia *sf* dyslexia

dislo'care *vt* to station, position

dismi'sura *sf* excess; **a ~ to** excess, excessively

disobbe'dire *etc* = **disubbidire** *etc*

disoccu'pato, a *ag* unemployed ♦ *sm/f* unemployed person; **disoccupazi'one** *sf* unemployment

diso'nesto, a *ag* dishonest

diso'nore *sm* dishonour, disgrace

di'sopra *av* (*con contatto*) on top; (*senza contatto*) above; (*al piano superiore*) upstairs ♦ *ag inv* (*superiore*) upper ♦ *sm inv* top, upper part

disordi'nato, a *ag* untidy; (*privo di misura*) irregular, wild

di'sordine *sm* (*confusione*) disorder, confusion; (*sregolatezza*) debauchery

disorien'tare *vt* to disorientate; **~rsi** *vr* (*fig*) to get confused, lose one's bearings

di'sotto *av* below, underneath; (*in fondo*) at the bottom; (*al piano inferiore*) downstairs ♦ *ag inv* (*inferiore*) lower; bottom *cpd* ♦ *sm inv* (*parte inferiore*) lower part; bottom

dis'paccio [dis'pattʃo] *sm* dispatch

'dispari *ag inv* odd, uneven

dis'parte: in ~ *av* (*da lato*) aside, apart; **tenersi** *o* **starsene in ~** to keep o.s., hold o.s. aloof

dispendi'oso, a *ag* expensive

dis'pensa *sf* pantry, larder; (*mobile*) sideboard; (*DIR*) exemption; (*REL*) dispensation; (*fascicolo*) number, issue

dispen'sare *vt* (*elemosine, favori*) to distribute; (*esonerare*) to exempt

dispe'rare *vi*: **~ (di)** to despair (of); **~rsi** *vr* to despair; **dispe'rato, a** *ag* (*persona*) in despair; (*caso, tentativo*) desperate; **disperazi'one** *sf* despair

dis'perdere *vt* (*disseminare*) to disperse; (*MIL*) to scatter, rout; (*fig: consumare*) to waste, squander; **~rsi** *vr* to disperse; to scatter; **dis'perso, a** *pp di* **disperdere** ♦ *sm/f* missing person

dis'petto *sm* spite *no pl*, spitefulness *no pl*; **fare un ~ a qn** to play a (nasty) trick on sb; **a ~ di** in spite of; **dispet'toso, a** *ag* spiteful

dispia'cere [dispja'tʃere] *sm* (*rammarico*) regret, sorrow; (*dolore*) grief; **~i** *smpl* (*preoccupazioni*) troubles, worries ♦ *vi*: **~ a** to displease ♦ *vb impers*: **mi dispiace (che)** I am sorry (that); **se non le dispiace, me ne vado adesso** if you don't mind, I'll go now; **dispiaci'uto, a** *pp di* **dispiacere** ♦ *ag* sorry

dispo'nibile *ag* available; **disponibilità** *sf inv* (*di biglietti, camere*) availability; (*gentilezza*) helpfulness; (*spec pl: FIN*) liquid assets *pl*

dis'porre *vt* (*sistemare*) to arrange; (*preparare*) to prepare; (*DIR*) to order; (*persuadere*): **~ qn a** to incline *o* dispose sb towards ♦ *vi* (*decidere*) to decide; (*usufruire*): **~ di** to use, have at one's disposal; (*essere dotato*): **~ di** to have; **disporsi** *vr* (*ordinarsi*) to place o.s., arrange o.s.

disposi'tivo *sm* (*meccanismo*) device

disposizi'one [dispozit'tsjone] *sf* arrangement, layout; (*stato d'animo*) mood; (*tendenza*) bent, inclination; (*comando*) order; (*DIR*) provision, regulation; **a ~ di qn** at sb's disposal

dis'posto, a *pp di* **disporre**

disprez'zare [dispret'tsare] *vt* to despise

dis'prezzo [dis'prettso] *sm* contempt

'disputa *sf* dispute, quarrel

dispu'tare *vt* (*contendere*) to dispute, contest; (*gara*) to take part in ♦ *vi* to quarrel; **~ di** to discuss; **~rsi qc** to fight for sth

dissan'guare *vt* (*fig: persona*) to bleed white; (*: patrimonio*) to suck dry; **~rsi** *vr* (*MED*) to lose blood; (*fig: rovinarsi*) to ruin o.s.

dissec'care *vt* to dry up; **~rsi** *vr* to dry up

dissemi'nare *vt* to scatter; (*fig: notizie*) to spread

dis'senso *sm* dissent; (*disapprovazione*) disapproval

dissente'ria *sf* dysentery

dissen'tire *vi*: ~ **(da)** to disagree (with)

dissertazi'one [dissertat'tsjone] *sf* dissertation

disser'vizio [disser'vittsjo] *sm* inefficiency

disses'tare *vt* (*ECON*) to ruin; **dis'sesto** *sm* (financial) ruin

disse'tante *ag* refreshing

dis'sidio *sm* disagreement

dis'simile *ag* different, dissimilar

dissimu'lare *vt* (*fingere*) to dissemble; (*nascondere*) to conceal

dissi'pare *vt* to dissipate; (*scialacquare*) to squander, waste

dis'solto, a *pp di* **dissolvere**

disso'luto, a *pp di* **dissolvere** ♦ *ag* dissolute, licentious

dis'solvere *vt* to dissolve; (*neve*) to melt; (*fumo*) to disperse; **~rsi** *vr* to dissolve; to melt; to disperse

dissu'adere *vt*: ~ **qn da** to dissuade sb from; **dissu'aso, a** *pp di* **dissuadere**

distac'care *vt* to detach, separate; (*SPORT*) to leave behind; **~rsi** *vr* to be detached; (*fig*) to stand out; **~rsi da** (*fig: allontanarsi*) to grow away from

dis'tacco, chi *sm* (*separazione*) separation; (*fig: indifferenza*) detachment; (*SPORT*): **vincere con un ~ di ...** to win by a distance of ...

dis'tante *av* far away ♦ *ag*: ~ **(da)** distant (from), far away (from)

dis'tanza [dis'tantsa] *sf* distance

distanzi'are [distan'tsjare] *vt* to space out, place at intervals; (*SPORT*) to outdistance; (*fig: superare*) to outstrip, surpass

dis'tare *vi*: **distiamo pochi chilometri da Roma** we are only a few kilometres (away) from Rome

dis'tendere *vt* (*coperta*) to spread out; (*gambe*) to stretch (out); (*mettere a giacere*) to lay; (*rilassare: muscoli, nervi*) to relax; **~rsi** *vr* (*rilassarsi*) to relax; (*sdraiarsi*) to lie down; **distensi'one** *sf* stretching; relaxation; (*POL*) détente

dis'tesa *sf* expanse, stretch

dis'teso, a *pp di* **distendere**

distil'lare *vt* to distil

distille'ria *sf* distillery

dis'tinguere *vt* to distinguish

dis'tinta *sf* (*nota*) note; (*elenco*) list

distin'tivo, a *ag* distinctive; distinguishing ♦ *sm* badge

dis'tinto, a *pp di* **distinguere** ♦ *ag* (*dignitoso ed elegante*) distinguished; **~i saluti** (*in lettera*) yours faithfully

distinzi'one [distin'tsjone] *sf* distinction

dis'togliere [dis'tɔʎʎere] *vt*: ~ **da** to take away from; (*fig*) to dissuade from; **dis'tolto, a** *pp di* **distogliere**

distorsi'one *sf* (*MED*) sprain; (*FISICA, OTTICA*) distortion

dis'trarre *vt* to distract; (*divertire*) to entertain, amuse; **distrarsi** *vr* (*non fare attenzione*) to be distracted, let one's mind wander; (*svagarsi*) to amuse *o* enjoy o.s.; **dis'tratto, a** *pp di* **distrarre** ♦ *ag* absent-minded; (*disattento*) inattentive; **distrazi'one** *sf* absent-mindedness; inattention; (*svago*) distraction, entertainment

dis'tretto *sm* district

distribu'ire *vt* to distribute; (*CARTE*) to deal (out); (*posta*) to deliver; (*lavoro*) to allocate, assign; (*ripartire*) to share out; **distribu'tore** *sm* (*di benzina*) petrol (*BRIT*) *o* gas (*US*) pump; (*AUT, ELETTR*) distributor; (*automatico*) vending machine; **distribuzi'one** *sf* distribution; delivery

distri'care *vt* to disentangle, unravel

dis'truggere [dis'truddʒere] *vt* to destroy; **dis'trutto, a** *pp di* **distruggere**; **distruzi'one** *sf* destruction

distur'bare *vt* to disturb, trouble; (*sonno, lezioni*) to disturb, interrupt; **~rsi** *vr* to put o.s. out

dis'turbo *sm* trouble, bother, inconvenience; (*indisposizione*) (slight) disorder, ailment; **~i** *smpl* (*RADIO, TV*) static *sg*

disubbidi'ente *ag* disobedient; **disubbidi'enza** *sf* disobedience

disubbi'dire *vi*: ~ **(a qn)** to disobey (sb)

disugu'ale *ag* unequal; (*diverso*) different;

(*irregolare*) uneven
disu'mano, a *ag* inhuman
di'suso *sm*: andare *o* cadere in ~ to fall
into disuse
'dita *fpl di* dito
di'tale *sm* thimble
'dito (*pl(f)* 'dita) *sm* finger; (*misura*) finger,
finger's breadth; ~ (del piede) toe
'ditta *sf* firm, business
ditta'tore *sm* dictator
ditta'tura *sf* dictatorship
dit'tongo, ghi *sm* diphthong
di'urno, a *ag* day *cpd*, daytime *cpd*
'diva *sf vedi* divo
diva'gare *vi* to digress
divam'pare *vi* to flare up, blaze up
di'vano *sm* sofa; divan
divari'care *vt* to open wide
di'vario *sm* difference
dive'nire *vi* = diventare
diven'tare *vi* to become; ~ famoso/
professore to become famous/a teacher
dive'nuto, a *pp di* divenire
di'verbio *sm* altercation
di'vergere [di'vɛrdʒere] *vi* to diverge
diversifi'care *vt* to diversify, vary; to
differentiate
diversi'one *sf* diversion
diversità *sf inv* difference, diversity;
(*varietà*) variety
diver'sivo *sm* diversion, distraction
di'verso, a *ag* (*differente*) ~ (da) different
(from); ~i, e *det pl* several, various; (*COMM*)
sundry ♦ *pron pl* several (people), many
(people)
diver'tente *ag* amusing
diverti'mento *sm* amusement, pleasure;
(*passatempo*) pastime, recreation
diver'tire *vt* to amuse, entertain; ~rsi *vr* to
amuse *o* enjoy o.s.
divi'dendo *sm* dividend
di'videre *vt* (*anche MAT*) to divide;
(*distribuire, ripartire*) to divide (up), split
(up); ~rsi *vr* (*separarsi*) to separate; (*strade*)
to fork
divi'eto *sm* prohibition; "~ di sosta" (*AUT*)
"no parking"

divinco'larsi *vr* to wriggle, writhe
divinità *sf inv* divinity
di'vino, a *ag* divine
di'visa *sf* (*MIL etc*) uniform; (*COMM*) foreign
currency
divisi'one *sf* division
di'viso, a *pp di* dividere
'divo, a *sm/f* star
divo'rare *vt* to devour
divorzi'are [divor'tsjare] *vi*: ~ (da qn) to
divorce (sb); divorzi'ato, a *sm/f* divorcee
di'vorzio [di'vɔrtsjo] *sm* divorce
divul'gare *vt* to divulge, disclose; (*rendere
comprensibile*) to popularize; ~rsi *vr* to
spread
dizio'nario [ditsjo'narjo] *sm* dictionary
dizi'one [dit'tsjone] *sf* diction;
pronunciation
do *sm* (*MUS*) C; (: *solfeggiando*) do(h)
DOC [dɔk] *abbr* (= *denominazione di origine
controllata*) *label guaranteeing the quality
of wine*
'doccia, ce [dottʃa] *sf* (*bagno*) shower;
fare la ~ to have a shower
do'cente [do'tʃɛnte] *ag* teaching ♦ *sm/f*
teacher; (*di università*) lecturer
'docile [dɔtʃile] *ag* docile
documen'tare *vt* to document; ~rsi *vr*:
~rsi (su) to gather information *o* material
(about)
documen'tario *sm* documentary
docu'mento *sm* document; ~i *smpl*
(*d'identità etc*) papers
'dodici ['doditʃi] *num* twelve
do'gana *sf* (*ufficio*) customs *pl*; (*tassa*)
(customs) duty; passare la ~ to go
through customs; doga'nale *ag* customs
cpd; dogani'ere *sm* customs officer
'doglie ['dɔʎʎe] *sfpl* (*MED*) labour *sg*, labour
pains
'dolce ['doltʃe] *ag* sweet; (*carattere, persona*)
gentle, mild; (*fig: mite: clima*) mild; (*non
ripido: pendio*) gentle ♦ *sm* (*sapore dolce*)
sweetness, sweet taste; (*CUC: portata*)
sweet, dessert; (: *torta*) cake; dol'cezza *sf*
sweetness; softness; mildness; gentleness;
dolcifi'cante *sm* sweetener; dolci'umi

smpl sweets

do'lente *ag* sorrowful, sad

do'lere *vi* to be sore, hurt, ache; **~rsi** *vr* to complain; (*essere spiacente*): **~rsi di** to be sorry for; **mi duole la testa** my head aches, I've got a headache

'dollaro *sm* dollar

'dolo *sm* (*DIR*) malice

Dolo'miti *sfpl*: **le ~** the Dolomites

do'lore *sm* (*fisico*) pain; (*morale*) sorrow, grief; **dolo'roso, a** *ag* painful; sorrowful, sad

do'loso, a *ag* (*DIR*) malicious

do'manda *sf* (*interrogazione*) question; (*richiesta*) demand; (*: cortese*) request; (*DIR: richiesta scritta*) application; (*ECON*): **la ~** demand; **fare una ~ a qn** to ask sb a question; **fare ~ (per un lavoro)** to apply (for a job)

doman'dare *vt* (*per avere*) to ask for; (*per sapere*) to ask; (*esigere*) to demand; **~rsi** *vr* to wonder; to ask o.s.; **~ qc a qn** to ask sb for sth; to ask sb sth

do'mani *av* tomorrow ♦ *sm*: **il ~** (*il futuro*) the future; (*il giorno successivo*) the next day; **~ l'altro** the day after tomorrow

do'mare *vt* to tame

domat'tina *av* tomorrow morning

do'menica, che *sf* Sunday; **di** *o* **la ~** on Sundays; **domeni'cale** *ag* Sunday *cpd*

do'mestica, che *sf vedi* **domestico**

do'mestico, a, ci, che *ag* domestic ♦ *sm/f* servant, domestic

domi'cilio [domi'tʃiljo] *sm* (*DIR*) domicile, place of residence

domi'nare *vt* to dominate; (*fig: sentimenti*) to control, master ♦ *vi* to be in the dominant position; **~rsi** *vr* (*controllarsi*) to control o.s.; **~ su** (*fig*) to surpass, outclass; **dominazi'one** *sf* domination

do'minio *sm* dominion; (*fig: campo*) field, domain

do'nare *vt* to give, present; (*per beneficenza etc*) to donate ♦ *vi* (*fig*): **~ a** to suit, become; **~ sangue** to give blood; **dona'tore, 'trice** *sm/f* donor; **donatore di sangue/di organi** blood/organ donor

dondo'lare *vt* (*cullare*) to rock; **~rsi** *vr* to swing, sway; **'dondolo** *sm*: **sedia/cavallo a dondolo** rocking chair/horse

'donna *sf* woman; **~ di casa** housewife; home-loving woman; **~ di servizio** maid

donnai'olo *sm* ladykiller

'donnola *sf* weasel

'dono *sm* gift

'dopo *av* (*tempo*) afterwards; (*: più tardi*) later; (*luogo*) after, next ♦ *prep* after ♦ *cong* (*temporale*): **~ aver studiato** after having studied; **~ mangiato va a dormire** after having eaten *o* after a meal he goes for a sleep ♦ *ag inv*: **il giorno ~** the following day; **un anno ~** a year later; **~ di me/lui** after me/him

dopo'barba *sm inv* after-shave

dopodo'mani *av* the day after tomorrow

dopogu'erra *sm* postwar years *pl*

dopo'pranzo [dopo'prandzo] *av* after lunch (*o* dinner)

doposcì [dopoʃ'ʃi] *sm inv* après-ski outfit

doposcu'ola *sm inv* school club offering extra tuition and recreational facilities

dopo'sole *sm inv* aftersun (lotion)

dopo'tutto *av* (*tutto considerato*) after all

doppi'aggio [dop'pjaddʒo] *sm* (*CINEMA*) dubbing

doppi'are *vt* (*NAUT*) to round; (*SPORT*) to lap; (*CINEMA*) to dub

'doppio, a *ag* double; (*fig: falso*) double-dealing, deceitful ♦ *sm* (*quantità*): **il ~ (di)** twice as much (*o* many), double the amount (*o* number) of; (*SPORT*) doubles *pl* ♦ *av* double

doppi'one *sm* duplicate (copy)

doppio'petto *sm* double-breasted jacket

do'rare *vt* to gild; (*CUC*) to brown; **do'rato, a** *ag* golden; (*ricoperto d'oro*) gilt, gilded; **dora'tura** *sf* gilding

dormicchi'are [dormik'kjare] *vi* to doze

dormigli'one, a [dormiʎ'ʎone] *sm/f* sleepyhead

dor'mire *vt, vi* to sleep; **andare a ~** to go to bed; **dor'mita** *sf*: **farsi una dormita** to have a good sleep

dormi'torio *sm* dormitory

dormi'veglia [dormi'veʎʎa] *sm* drowsiness

'**dorso** *sm* back; (*di montagna*) ridge, crest; (*di libro*) spine; **a ~ di cavallo** on horseback

do'sare *vt* to measure out; (*MED*) to dose

'**dose** *sf* quantity, amount; (*MED*) dose

'**dosso** *sm* (*rilievo*) rise; (*di strada*) bump; (*dorso*): **levarsi di ~ i vestiti** to take one's clothes off

do'tare *vt*: **~ di** to provide *o* supply with; **dotazi'one** *sf* (*insieme di beni*) endowment; (*di macchine etc*) equipment

'**dote** *sf* (*di sposa*) dowry; (*assegnata a un ente*) endowment; (*fig*) gift, talent

Dott. *abbr* (= *dottore*) Di.

'**dotto, a** *ag* (*colto*) learned ♦ *sm* (*sapiente*) scholar; (*ANAT*) duct

dotto'rato *sm* degree; **~ di ricerca** doctorate, doctor's degree

dot'tore, essa *sm/f* doctor

dot'trina *sf* doctrine

Dott.ssa *abbr* (= *dottoressa*) Dr.

'**dove** *av* (*gen*) where; (*in cui*) where, in which; (*dovunque*) wherever ♦ *cong* (*mentre, laddove*) whereas; **~ sei?/vai?** where are you?/are you going?; **dimmi dov'è** tell me where it is; **di ~ sei?** where are you from?; **per ~ si passa?** which way should we go?; **la città ~ abito** the town where *o* in which I live; **siediti ~ vuoi** sit wherever you like

do'vere *sm* (*obbligo*) duty ♦ *vt* (*essere debitore*): **~ qc (a qn)** to owe (sb) sth ♦ *vi* (*seguito dall'infinito: obbligo*) to have to; **rivolgersi a chi di ~** to apply to the appropriate authority *o* person; **lui deve farlo** he has to do it, he must do it; **è dovuto partire** he had to leave; **ha dovuto pagare** he had to pay; (: *intenzione*): **devo partire domani** I'm (due) to leave tomorrow; (: *probabilità*): **dev'essere tardi** it must be late; **come si deve** (*lavorare, comportarsi*) properly; **una persona come si deve** a respectable person

dove'roso, a *ag* (right and) proper

do'vunque *av* (*in qualunque luogo*) wherever; (*dappertutto*) everywhere; **~ io vada** wherever I go

do'vuto, a *ag* (*causato*): **~ a** due to

doz'zina [dod'dzina] *sf* dozen; **una ~ di uova** a dozen eggs

dozzi'nale [doddzi'nale] *ag* cheap, second-rate

dra'gare *vt* to dredge

'**drago, ghi** *sm* dragon

'**dramma, i** *sm* drama; **dram'matico, a, ci, che** *ag* dramatic; **drammatiz'zare** *vt* to dramatize; **dramma'turgo, ghi** *sm* playwright, dramatist

drappeggi'are [drapedd'dʒare] *vt* to drape

drap'pello *sm* (*MIL*) squad; (*gruppo*) band, group

'**drastico, a, ci, che** *ag* drastic

dre'naggio [dre'naddʒo] *sm* drainage

dre'nare *vt* to drain

'**dritto, a** *ag, av* = **diritto**

driz'zare [drit'tsare] *vt* (*far tornare dritto*) to straighten; (*innalzare: antenna, muro*) to erect; **~rsi** *vr*: **~rsi (in piedi)** to stand up; **~ le orecchie** to prick up one's ears

'**droga, ghe** *sf* (*sostanza aromatica*) spice; (*stupefacente*) drug; **dro'gare** *vt* to season, spice; to drug, dope; **drogarsi** *vr* to take drugs; **dro'gato, a** *sm/f* drug addict

droghe'ria [droge'ria] *sf* grocer's shop (*BRIT*), grocery (store) (*US*)

'**dubbio, a** *ag* (*incerto*) doubtful, dubious; (*ambiguo*) dubious ♦ *sm* (*incertezza*) doubt; **avere il ~ che** to be afraid that, suspect that; **mettere in ~ qc** to question sth; **dubbi'oso, a** *ag* doubtful, dubious

dubi'tare *vi*: **~ di** to doubt; (*risultato*) to be doubtful of

Dub'lino *sf* Dublin

'**duca, chi** *sm* duke

du'chessa [du'kessa] *sf* duchess

'**due** *num* two

due'cento [due'tʃento] *num* two hundred ♦ *sm*: **il D~** the thirteenth century

due'pezzi [due'pettsi] *sm* (*costume da bagno*) two-piece swimsuit; (*abito femminile*) two-piece suit

du'etto *sm* duet

'dunque *cong (perciò)* so, therefore; *(riprendendo il discorso)* well (then) ♦ *sm inv*: **venire al ~** to come to the point

du'omo *sm* cathedral

'duplex *sm inv (TEL)* party line

dupli'cato *sm* duplicate

'duplice ['duplitʃe] *ag* double, twofold; **in ~ copia** in duplicate

du'rante *prep* during

du'rare *vi* to last; **~ fatica a** to have difficulty in; **du'rata** *sf* length (of time); duration; **dura'turo, a** *ag* lasting

du'rezza [du'rettsa] *sf* hardness; stubbornness; harshness; toughness

'duro, a *ag (pietra, lavoro, materasso, problema)* hard; *(persona: ostinato)* stubborn, obstinate; *(: severo)* harsh, hard; *(voce)* harsh; *(carne)* tough ♦ *sm* hardness; *(difficoltà)* hard part; *(persona)* tough guy; **tener ~** to stand firm, hold out; **~ d'orecchi** hard of hearing

du'rone *sm* hard skin

E, e

e *(dav V spesso* **ed**) *cong* and; **~ lui?** what about him?; **~ compralo!** well buy it then!

E. *abbr (= est)* E

è *vb vedi* **essere**

'ebano *sm* ebony

eb'bene *cong* well (then)

eb'brezza [eb'brettsa] *sf* intoxication

'ebbro, a *ag* drunk; **~ di** *(gioia etc)* beside o.s. with

'ebete *ag* stupid, idiotic

ebollizi'one [ebollit'tsjone] *sf* boiling; **punto di ~** boiling point

e'braico, a, ci, che *ag* Hebrew, Hebraic ♦ *sm (LING)* Hebrew

e'breo, a *ag* Jewish ♦ *sm/f* Jew/Jewess

'Ebridi *sfpl*: **le (isole) ~** the Hebrides

ecc *av abbr (= eccetera)* etc

ecce'denza [ettʃe'dentsa] *sf* excess, surplus

ec'cedere [et'tʃɛdere] *vt* to exceed ♦ *vi* to go too far; **~ nel bere/mangiare** to indulge in drink/food to excess

eccel'lente [ettʃel'lente] *ag* excellent; **eccel'lenza** *sf* excellence; *(titolo)* Excellency

ec'cellere [et'tʃellere] *vi*: **~ (in)** to excel (at); **ec'celso, a** *pp di* **eccellere**

ec'centrico, a, ci, che [et'tʃentriko] *ag* eccentric

ecces'sivo, a [ettʃes'sivo] *ag* excessive

ec'cesso [et'tʃɛsso] *sm* excess; **all'~** *(gentile, generoso)* to excess, excessively; **~ di velocità** *(AUT)* speeding

ec'cetera [et'tʃetera] *av* et cetera, and so on

ec'cetto [et'tʃetto] *prep* except, with the exception of; **~ che** except, other than; **~ che (non)** unless

eccettu'are [ettʃettu'are] *vt* to except

eccezio'nale [ettʃetsjo'nale] *ag* exceptional

eccezi'one [ettʃet'tsjone] *sf* exception; *(DIR)* objection; **a ~ di** with the exception of, except for; **d'~** exceptional

ec'cidio [et'tʃidio] *sm* massacre

ecci'tare [ettʃi'tare] *vt (curiosità, interesse)* to excite, arouse; *(folla)* to incite; **~rsi** *vr* to get excited; *(sessualmente)* to become aroused; **eccitazi'one** *sf* excitement

'ecco *av (per dimostrare)*: **~ il treno!** here's *o* here comes the train!; *(dav pron)*: **~mi!** here I am!; **~ne uno!** here's one (of them)!; *(dav pp)*: **~ fatto!** there, that's it done!

echeggi'are [eked'dʒare] *vi* to echo

e'clissi *sf* eclipse

'eco *(pl(m)* **'echi)** *sm o f* echo

ecogra'fia *sf (MED)* scan

ecolo'gia [ekolo'dʒia] *sf* ecology

econo'mia *sf* economy; *(scienza)* economics *sg*; *(risparmio: azione)* saving; **fare ~** to economize, make economies; **eco'nomico, a, ci, che** *ag* economic; *(poco costoso)* economical; **econo'mista, i** *sm* economist; **economiz'zare** *vt, vi* to save; **e'conomo, a** *ag* thrifty ♦ *sm/f (INS)* bursar

E'CU [e'ku] *sm inv (= Unità monetaria europea)* ECU *n*

ed *cong vedi* **e**

'edera *sf* ivy

e'dicola *sf* newspaper kiosk *o* stand (*US*)
edifi'care *vt* to build; (*fig: teoria, azienda*)
  to establish; (*indurre al bene*) to edify
edi'ficio [edi'fitʃo] *sm* building
e'dile *ag* building *cpd*; edi'lizia *sf* building,
  building trade; edi'lizio, a *ag* building
  cpd
Edim'burgo *sf* Edinburgh
edi'tore, 'trice *ag* publishing *cpd* ♦ *sm/f*
  publisher; (*curatore*) editor; edito'ria *sf*
  publishing; editori'ale *ag* publishing *cpd*
  ♦ *sm* editorial, leader
edizi'one [edit'tsjone] *sf* edition; (*tiratura*)
  printing
edu'care *vt* to educate; (*gusto, mente*) to
  train; ~ qn a fare to train sb to do;
  edu'cato, a *ag* polite, well-mannered;
  educazi'one *sf* education; (*familiare*)
  upbringing; (*comportamento*) (good)
  manners *pl*; educazione fisica (*INS*)
  physical training *o* education
effemi'nato, a *ag* effeminate
effet'tivo, a *ag* (*reale*) real, actual;
  (*impiegato, professore*) (*MIL*)
  regular ♦ *sm* (*MIL*) strength; (*di patrimonio*
  etc) sum total
ef'fetto *sm* effect; (*COMM: cambiale*) bill;
  (*fig: impressione*) impression; in ~i in fact,
  actually; ~ serra greenhouse effect;
  effettu'are *vt* to effect, carry out
effi'cace [effi'katʃe] *ag* effective
effici'ente [effi'ʃɛnte] *ag* efficient;
  effici'enza *sf* efficiency
ef'fimero, a *ag* ephemeral
E'geo [e'dʒɛo] *sm*: l'~, il mare ~ the Aegean
  (Sea)
E'gitto [e'dʒitto] *sm*: l'~ Egypt
egizi'ano, a [edʒit'tsjano] *ag, sm/f*
  Egyptian
'egli ['eʎʎi] *pron* he; ~ stesso he himself
ego'ismo *sm* selfishness, egoism;
  ego'ista, i, e *ag* selfish, egoistic ♦ *sm/f*
  egoist
egr. *abbr* = egregio
e'gregio, a, gi, gie [e'grɛdʒo] *ag* (*nelle*
  lettere): E~ Signore Dear Sir
eguagli'anza *etc* [egwaʎ'ʎantsa]

= uguaglianza *etc*
E.I. *abbr* = Esercito Italiano
elabo'rare *vt* (*progetto*) to work out,
  elaborate; (*dati*) to process; elabora'tore
  sm (*INFORM*): elaboratore elettronico
  computer; elaborazi'one *sf* elaboration;
  elaborazione dei dati data processing
elasticiz'zato, a [elastitʃid'dzato] *ag*
  stretch *cpd*
e'lastico, a, ci, che *ag* elastic; (*fig:*
  andatura) springy; (*: decisione, vedute*)
  flexible ♦ *sm* (*di gomma*) rubber band; (*per*
  il cucito) elastic *no pl*
ele'fante *sm* elephant
ele'gante *ag* elegant
e'leggere [e'lɛddʒere] *vt* to elect
elemen'tare *ag* elementary; le (scuole) ~i
  sfpl primary (*BRIT*) *o* grade (*US*) school
ele'mento *sm* element; (*parte componente*)
  element, component, part; ~i *smpl* (*della*
  scienza etc) elements, rudiments
ele'mosina *sf* charity, alms *pl*; chiedere
  l'~ to beg
elen'care *vt* to list
e'lenco, chi *sm* list; ~ telefonico
  telephone directory
e'letto, a *pp di* eleggere ♦ *sm/f*
  (*nominato*) elected member; eletto'rale
  ag electoral, election *cpd*; eletto'rato *sm*
  electorate; elet'tore, 'trice *sm/f* voter,
  elector
elet'trauto *sm inv* workshop for car
  electrical repairs; (*tecnico*) car electrician
elettri'cista, i [elettri'tʃista] *sm* electrician
elettricità [elettritʃi'ta] *sf* electricity
e'lettrico, a, ci, che *ag* electric(al)
elettriz'zare [elettrid'dzare] *vt* to electrify
e'lettro... *prefisso*: elettrocar-
  dio'gramma, i *sm* electrocardiogram;
  elettrodo'mestico, a, ci, che *ag*:
  apparecchi elettrodomestici domestic
  (electrical) appliances; elet'trone *sm*
  electron; elet'tronica *sf* electronics
  sg; elet'tronico, a, ci, che *ag*
  electronic
ele'vare *vt* to raise; (*edificio*) to erect;
  (*multa*) to impose

elezi'one [elet'tsjone] *sf* election; **~i** *sfpl* (POL) election(s)

'elica, che *sf* propeller

eli'cottero *sm* helicopter

elimi'nare *vt* to eliminate; **elimina'toria** *sf* eliminating round

'elio *sm* helium

'ella *pron* she; (*forma di cortesia*) you; ~ **stessa** she herself; you yourself

el'metto *sm* helmet

e'logio [e'lɔdʒo] *sm* (*discorso, scritto*) eulogy; (*lode*) praise (*di solito no pl*)

elo'quente *ag* eloquent

e'ludere *vt* to evade; **elu'sivo, a** *ag* evasive

ema'nare *vt* to send out, give off; (*fig: leggi, decreti*) to issue ♦ *vi*: ~ **da** to come from

emanci'pare [emantʃi'pare] *vt* to emancipate; **~rsi** *vr* (*fig*) to become liberated *o* emancipated

embri'one *sm* embryo

emenda'mento *sm* amendment

emen'dare *vt* to amend

emer'genza [emer'dʒentsa] *sf* emergency; **in caso di** ~ in an emergency

e'mergere [e'mɛrdʒere] *vi* to emerge; (*sommergibile*) to surface; (*fig: distinguersi*) to stand out; **e'merso, a** *pp di* **emergere**

e'messo, a *pp di* **emettere**

e'mettere *vt* (*suono, luce*) to give out, emit; (*onde radio*) to send out; (*assegno, francobollo, ordine*) to issue

emi'crania *sf* migraine

emi'grare *vi* to emigrate; **emigrazi'one** *sf* emigration

emi'nente *ag* eminent, distinguished

emis'fero *sm* hemisphere; ~ **boreale/ australe** northern/southern hemisphere

emissi'one *sf* (*vedi* emettere) emission; sending out; issue; (RADIO) broadcast

emit'tente *ag* (*banca*) issuing; (RADIO) broadcasting, transmitting ♦ *sf* (RADIO) transmitter

emorra'gia, 'gie [emorra'dʒia] *sf* haemorrhage

emor'roidi *sfpl* haemorrhoids *pl* (BRIT),

hemorrhoids *pl* (US)

emo'tivo, a *ag* emotional

emozio'nante [emottsjo'nante] *ag* exciting, thrilling

emozio'nare [emottsjo'nare] *vt* (*appassionare*) to thrill, excite; (*commuovere*) to move; (*innervosire*) to upset; **~rsi** *vr* to be excited; to be moved; to be upset

emozi'one [emot'tsjone] *sf* emotion; (*agitazione*) excitement

'empio, a *ag* (*sacrilego*) impious; (*spietato*) cruel, pitiless; (*malvagio*) wicked, evil

emulsi'one *sf* emulsion

enciclope'dia [entʃiklope'dia] *sf* encyclopaedia

endove'noso, a *ag* (MED) intravenous

'ENEL ['enel] *sigla m* (= *Ente Nazionale per l'Energia Elettrica*) *national electricity company*

ener'gia, 'gie [ener'dʒia] *sf* (FISICA) energy; (*fig*) energy, strength, vigour; ~ **eolica** wind power; ~ **solare** solar energy, solar power; **e'nergico, a, ci, che** *ag* energetic, vigorous

'enfasi *sf* emphasis; (*peg*) bombast, pomposity; **en'fatico, a, ci, che** *ag* emphatic; pompous

en'nesimo, a *ag* (MAT, *fig*) nth; **per l'~a volta** for the umpteenth time

e'norme *ag* enormous, huge; **enormità** *sf inv* enormity, huge size; (*assurdità*) absurdity; **non dire enormità!** don't talk nonsense!

'ente *sm* (*istituzione*) body, board, corporation; (FILOSOFIA) being

en'trambi, e *pron pl* both (of them) ♦ *ag pl*: ~ **i ragazzi** both boys, both of the boys

en'trare *vi* to go (*o* come) in; ~ **in** (*luogo*) to enter, go (*o* come) into; (*trovar posto, poter stare*) to fit into; (*essere ammesso a: club etc*) to join, become a member of; ~ **in automobile** to get into the car; **far** ~ **qn** (*visitatore etc*) to show sb in; **questo non c'entra** (*fig*) that's got nothing to do with it; **en'trata** *sf* entrance, entry; **entrate** *sfpl* (COMM) receipts, takings; (ECON) income *sg* '**entro** *prep* (*temporale*) within

entusias'mare *vt* to excite, fill with enthusiasm; **~rsi (per qc/qn)** to become enthusiastic (about sth/sb); **entusi'asmo** *sm* enthusiasm; **entusi'asta, i, e** *ag* enthusiastic ♦ *sm/f* enthusiast; **entusi'astico, a, ci, che** *ag* enthusiastic

enunci'are [enun'tʃare] *vt* (*teoria*) to set out

epa'tite *sf* hepatitis

'**epico, a, ci, che** *ag* epic

epide'mia *sf* epidemic

epi'dermide *sf* skin, epidermis

Epifa'nia *sf* Epiphany

epiles'sia *sf* epilepsy

e'pilogo, ghi *sm* conclusion

epi'sodio *sm* episode

e'piteto *sm* epithet

'**epoca, che** *sf* (*periodo storico*) age, era; (*tempo*) time, (*GEO*) period

ep'pure *cong* and yet, nevertheless

equa'tore *sm* equator

equazi'one [ekwat'tsjone] *sf* (*MAT*) equation

e'questre *ag* equestrian

equi'latero, a *ag* equilateral

equili'brare *vt* to balance; **equi'librio** *sm* balance, equilibrium; **perdere l'~** to lose one's balance

e'quino, a *ag* horse *cpd*, equine

equipaggi'are [ekwipad'dʒare] *vt* (*di persone*) to man; (*di mezzi*) to equip; **equi'paggio** *sm* crew

equipa'rare *vt* to make equal

equità *sf* equity, fairness

equitazi'one [ekwitat'tsjone] *sf* (*horse-*)riding

equiva'lente *ag, sm* equivalent; **equiva'lenza** *sf* equivalence

equivo'care *vi* to misunderstand; **e'quivoco, a, ci, che** *ag* equivocal, ambiguous; (*sospetto*) dubious ♦ *sm* misunderstanding; **a scanso di equivoci** to avoid any misunderstanding; **giocare sull'equivoco** to equivocate

'**equo, a** *ag* fair, just

'**era** *sf* era

'**erba** *sf* grass; (*aromatica, medicinale*) herb;

in ~ (*fig*) budding; **er'baccia, ce** *sf* weed

e'rede *sm/f* heir; **eredità** *sf* (*DIR*) inheritance; (*BIOL*) heredity; **lasciare qc in eredità a qn** to leave *o* bequeath sth to sb; **eredi'tare** *vt* to inherit; **eredi'tario, a** *ag* hereditary

ere'mita, i *sm* hermit

ere'sia *sf* heresy; **e'retico, a, ci, che** *ag* heretical ♦ *sm/f* heretic

e'retto, a *pp di* **erigere** ♦ *ag* erect, upright; **erezi'one** *sf* (*FISIOL*) erection

er'gastolo *sm* (*DIR: pena*) life imprisonment

'**erica** *sf* heather

e'rigere [e'ridʒere] *vt* to erect, raise; (*fig: fondare*) to found

ERM *sigla* (= *Meccanismo dei tassi di cambio*) ERM *n*

ermel'lino *sm* ermine

er'metico, a, ci, che *ag* hermetic

'**ernia** *sf* (*MED*) hernia

e'roe *sm* hero

ero'gare *vt* (*somme*) to distribute; (*gas, servizi*) to supply

e'roico, a, ci, che *ag* heroic

ero'ina *sf* heroine; (*droga*) heroin

ero'ismo *sm* heroism

erosi'one *sf* erosion

e'rotico, a, ci, che *ag* erotic

er'rare *vi* (*vagare*) to wander, roam; (*sbagliare*) to be mistaken

er'rore *sm* error, mistake; (*morale*) error; **per ~** by mistake

'**erta** *sf* steep slope; **stare all'~** to be on the alert

erut'tare *vt* (*sog: vulcano*) to throw out, belch

eruzi'one [erut'tsjone] *sf* eruption

esacer'bare [ezatʃer'bare] *vt* to exacerbate

esage'rare [ezadʒe'rare] *vt* to exaggerate ♦ *vi* to exaggerate; (*eccedere*) to go too far; **esagerazi'one** *sf* exaggeration

e'sagono *sm* hexagon

esal'tare *vt* to exalt; (*entusiasmare*) to excite, stir; **esal'tato, a** *sm/f* fanatic

e'same *sm* examination; (*INS*) exam, examination; **fare** *o* **dare un ~** to sit *o* take an exam; **~ del sangue** blood test

esami'nare *vt* to examine

e'sanime *ag* lifeless

esaspe'rare *vt* to exasperate; to exacerbate; **~rsi** *vr* to become annoyed *o* exasperated; **esasperazi'one** *sf* exasperation

esatta'mente *av* exactly; accurately, precisely

esat'tezza [ezat'tettsa] *sf* exactitude, accuracy, precision

e'satto, a *pp di* **esigere ♦** *ag* (*calcolo, ora*) correct, right, exact; (*preciso*) accurate, precise; (*puntuale*) punctual

esat'tore *sm* (*di imposte etc*) collector

esau'dire *vt* to grant, fulfil

esauri'ente *ag* exhaustive

esauri'mento *sm* exhaustion; **~ nervoso** nervous breakdown

esau'rire *vt* (*stancare*) to exhaust, wear out; (*provviste, miniera*) to exhaust; **~rsi** *vr* to exhaust o.s., wear o.s. out; (*provviste*) to run out; **esau'rito, a** *ag* exhausted; (*merci*) sold out; **registrare il tutto esaurito** (*TEATRO*) to have a full house; **e'sausto, a** *ag* exhausted

'esca (*pl* **'esche**) *sf* bait

escande'scenza [eskandeʃʃentsa] *sf*: **dare in ~e** to lose one's temper, fly into a rage

'esce *etc vb vedi* **uscire**

eschi'mese [eski'mese] *ag, sm/f* Eskimo

escla'mare *vi* to exclaim, cry out; **esclamazi'one** *sf* exclamation

es'cludere *vt* to exclude

esclu'siva *sf* (*DIR, COMM*) exclusive *o* sole rights *pl*

esclu'sivo, a *ag* exclusive

es'cluso, a *pp di* **escludere**

'esco *etc vb vedi* **uscire**

escogi'tare [eskodʒi'tare] *vt* to devise, think up

escursi'one *sf* (*gita*) excursion, trip; (*: a piedi*) hike, walk; (*METEOR*) range

ese'crare *vt* to loathe, abhor

esecu'tivo, a *ag, sm* executive

esecu'tore, 'trice *sm/f* (*MUS*) performer; (*DIR*) executor

esecuzi'one [ezekut'tsjone] *sf* execution, carrying out; (*MUS*) performance; **~ capitale** execution

esegu'ire *vt* to carry out, execute; (*MUS*) to perform, execute

e'sempio *sm* example; **per ~** for example, for instance; **fare un ~** to give an example; **esem'plare** *ag* exemplary **♦** *sm* example; (*copia*) copy; **esemplifi'care** *vt* to exemplify

esen'tare *vt*: **~ qn/qc da** to exempt sb/sth from

e'sente *ag*: **~ da** (*dispensato da*) exempt from; (*privo di*) free from; **esenzi'one** *sf* exemption

e'sequie *sfpl* funeral rites; funeral service *sg*

eser'cente [ezer'tʃente] *sm/f* trader, dealer; shopkeeper

eserci'tare [ezertʃi'tare] *vt* (*professione*) to practise (*BRIT*), practice (*US*); (*allenare: corpo, mente*) to exercise, train; (*diritto*) to exercise; (*influenza, pressione*) to exert; **~rsi** *vr* to practise; **~rsi alla lotta** to practise fighting; **esercitazi'one** *sf* (*scolastica, militare*) exercise

e'sercito [e'zɛrtʃito] *sm* army

eser'cizio [ezer'tʃittsjo] *sm* practice; exercising; (*fisico, di matematica*) exercise; (*ECON*) financial year; (*azienda*) business, concern; **in ~** (*medico etc*) practising

esi'bire *vt* to exhibit, display; (*documenti*) to produce, present; **~rsi** *vr* (*attore*) to perform; (*fig*) to show off; **esibizi'one** *sf* exhibition; (*di documento*) presentation; (*spettacolo*) show, performance

esi'gente [ezi'dʒente] *ag* demanding; **esi'genza** *sf* demand, requirement

e'sigere [e'zidʒere] *vt* (*pretendere*) to demand; (*richiedere*) to demand, require; (*imposte*) to collect

e'siguo, a *ag* small, slight

'esile *ag* (*persona*) slender, slim; (*stelo*) thin; (*voce*) faint

esili'are *vt* to exile; **e'silio** *sm* exile

e'simere *vt*: **~ qn/qc da** to exempt sb/sth from; **~rsi** *vr*: **~rsi da** to get out of

esis'tenza [ezis'tentsa] *sf* existence

e'sistere *vi* to exist

esis'tito, a *pp di* esistere

esi'tare *vi* to hesitate; esitazi'one *sf* hesitation

'esito *sm* result, outcome

'esodo *sm* exodus

esone'rare *vt* to exempt

e'sordio *sm* début

esor'tare *vt*: ~ qn a fare to urge sb to do

e'sotico, a, ci, che *ag* exotic

es'pandere *vt* to expand; (*confini*) to extend; (*influenza*) to extend, spread; ~rsi *vr* to expand; espansi'one *sf* expansion; espan'sivo, a *ag* expansive, communicative

espatri'are *vi* to leave one's country

espedi'ente *sm* expedient

es'pellere *vt* to expel

esperi'enza [espe'rjɛntsa] *sf* experience

esperi'mento *sm* experiment

es'perto, a *ag, sm* expert

espi'are *vt* to atone for

espi'rare *vt, vi* to breathe out

espli'care *vt* (*attività*) to carry out, perform

es'plicito, a [es'plitʃito] *ag* explicit

es'plodere *vi* (*anche fig*) to explode ♦ *vt* to fire

esplo'rare *vt* to explore; esplora'tore *sm* explorer; giovane esploratore (boy) scout

esplosi'one *sf* explosion; esplo'sivo, a *ag, sm* explosive; es'ploso, a *pp di* esplodere

espo'nente *sm/f* (*rappresentante*) representative

es'porre *vt* (*merci*) to display; (*quadro*) to exhibit, show; (*fatti, idee*) to explain, set out; (*porre in pericolo, FOT*) to expose

espor'tare *vt* to export; esportazi'one *sf* exportation; export

esposizi'one [espozit'tsjone] *sf* displaying; exhibiting; setting out; (*anche FOT*) exposure; (*mostra*) exhibition; (*narrazione*) explanation, exposition

es'posto, a *pp di* esporre ♦ *ag*: ~ a nord facing north ♦ *sm* (AMM) statement, account; (: *petizione*) petition

espressi'one *sf* expression

espres'sivo, a *ag* expressive

es'presso, a *pp di* esprimere ♦ *ag* express ♦ *sm* (*lettera*) express letter; (*anche*: treno ~) express train; (*anche*: caffè ~) espresso

es'primere *vt* to express

espulsi'one *sf* expulsion; es'pulso, a *pp di* espellere

'essa (*pl* 'esse) *pron f vedi* esso

es'senza [es'sentsa] *sf* essence; essenzi'ale *ag* essential; l'essenziale the main *o* most important thing

---

PAROLA CHIAVE

'essere *sm* being; ~ umano human being ♦ *vb copulativo* 1 (*con attributo, sostantivo*) to be; sei giovane/simpatico you are *o* you're young/nice; è medico he is *o* he's a doctor

2 (+*di*: *appartenere*) to be; di chi è la penna? whose pen is it?; è di Carla it is *o* it's Carla's, it belongs to Carla

3 (+*di*: *provenire*) to be; è di Venezia he is *o* he's from Venice

4 (*data, ora*): è il 15 agosto/lunedì it is *o* it's the 15th of August/Monday; che ora è?, che ore sono? what time is it?; è l'una it is *o* it's one o'clock; sono le due it is *o* it's two o'clock

5 (*costare*): quant'è? how much is it?; sono 20.000 lire it's 20,000 lire

♦ *vb aus* 1 (*attivo*): ~ arrivato/venuto to have arrived/come; è già partita she has already left

2 (*passivo*) to be; ~ fatto da to be made by; è stata uccisa she has been killed

3 (*riflessivo*): si sono lavati they washed, they got washed

4 (+*da* +*infinito*): è da farsi subito it must be *o* is to be done immediately

♦ *vi* 1 (*esistere, trovarsi*) to be; sono a casa I'm at home; ~ in piedi/seduto to be standing/sitting

2 esserci: c'è there is; ci sono there are;

che c'è? what's the matter?, what is it?; **ci sono!** (*fig: ho capito*) I get it!; *vedi anche* **ci** ♦ *vb impers:* **è tardi/Pasqua** it's late/Easter; **è possibile che venga** he may come; **è così** that's the way it is

'**esso, a** *pron* it; (*riferito a persona: soggetto*) he/she; (: *complemento*) him/her; **~i, e** *pron pl* they; (*complemento*) them

est *sm* east

'**estasi** *sf* ecstasy

es'tate *sf* summer

es'tendere *vt* to extend; **~rsi** *vr* (*diffondersi*) to spread; (*territorio, confini*) to extend; **estensi'one** *sf* extension; (*di superficie*) expanse; (*di voce*) range

esteri'ore *ag* outward, external

ester'nare *vt* to express

es'terno, a *ag* (*porta, muro*) outer, outside; (*scala*) outside; (*alunno, impressione*) external ♦ *sm* outside, exterior ♦ *sm/f* (*allievo*) day pupil; **per uso ~** for external use only

'**estero, a** *ag* foreign ♦ *sm:* **all'~** abroad

es'teso, a *pp di* **estendere** ♦ *ag* extensive, large; **scrivere per ~** to write in full

es'tetico, a, ci, che *ag* aesthetic ♦ *sf* (*disciplina*) aesthetics *sg*; (*bellezza*) attractiveness; **este'tista, i, e** *sm/f* beautician

'**estimo** *sm* valuation; (*disciplina*) surveying

es'tinguere *vt* to extinguish, put out; (*debito*) to pay off; **~rsi** *vr* to go out; (*specie*) to become extinct; **es'tinto, a** *pp di* **estinguere; estin'tore** *sm* (fire) extinguisher; **estinzi'one** *sf* putting out; (*di specie*) extinction

estir'pare *vt* (*pianta*) to uproot, pull up; (*fig: vizio*) to eradicate

es'tivo, a *ag* summer *cpd*

es'torcere [es'tɔrtʃere] *vt:* **~ qc (a qn)** to extort sth (from sb); **es'torto, a** *pp di* **estorcere**

estradizi'one [estradit'tsjone] *sf* extradition

es'traneo, a *ag* foreign ♦ *sm/f* stranger; **rimanere ~ a qc** to take no part in sth

es'trarre *vt* to extract; (*minerali*) to mine; (*sorteggiare*) to draw; **es'tratto, a** *pp di* **estrarre** ♦ *sm* extract; (*di documento*) abstract; **estratto conto** statement of account; **estratto di carne** (*CUC*) meat extract; **estratto di nascita** birth certificate; **estrazi'one** *sf* extraction; mining; drawing *no pl*; draw

estremità *sf inv* extremity, end ♦ *sfpl* (*ANAT*) extremities

es'tremo, a *ag* extreme; (*ultimo: ora, tentativo*) final, last ♦ *sm* extreme; (*di pazienza, forze*) limit, end; **~i** *smpl* (*AMM: dati essenziali*) details, particulars; **l'~ Oriente** the Far East

'**estro** *sm* (*capriccio*) whim, fancy; (*ispirazione creativa*) inspiration; **es'troso, a** *ag* whimsical, capricious; inspired

estro'verso, a *ag, sm* extrovert

'**esule** *sm/f* exile

età *sf inv* age; **all'~ di 8 anni** at the age of 8, at 8 years of age; **ha la mia ~** he (*o* she) is the same age as me *o* as I am; **raggiungere la maggiore ~** to come of age; **essere in ~ minore** to be under age

'**etere** *sm* ether; **et'tereo, a** *ag* ethereal

eternità *sf* eternity

e'terno, a *ag* eternal

etero'geneo, a [etero'dʒɛneo] *ag* heterogeneous

'**etica** *sf* ethics *sg*; *vedi anche* **etico**

eti'chetta [eti'ketta] *sf* label; (*cerimoniale*): **l'~** etiquette

'**etico, a, ci, che** *ag* ethical

etimolo'gia, 'gie [etimolo'dʒia] *sf* etymology

Eti'opia *sf:* **l'~** Ethiopia

'**Etna** *sm:* **l'~** Etna

'**etnico, a, ci, che** *ag* ethnic

e'trusco, a, schi, sche *ag, sm/f* Etruscan

'**ettaro** *sm* hectare (= *10,000 m²*)

'**etto** *sm abbr* = **ettogrammo**

etto'grammo *sm* hectogram(me) (= *100 grams*)

Eucaris'tia *sf:* **l'~** the Eucharist

eurocity [euro'siti] *sm* international express

train
Eu'ropa *sf*: **l'~** Europe; **euro'peo, a** *ag*,
sm/f European
evacu'are *vt* to evacuate
e'vadere *vi* (*fuggire*): **~ da** to escape from
♦ *vt* (*sbrigare*) to deal with, dispatch;
(*tasse*) to evade
evan'gelico, a, ci, che [evan'dʒeliko] *ag*
evangelical
evapo'rare *vi* to evaporate;
evaporazi'one *sf* evaporation
evasi'one *sf* (*vedi evadere*) escape;
dispatch; **~ fiscale** tax evasion
eva'sivo, a *ag* evasive
e'vaso, a *pp di* evadere ♦ *sm* escapee
eveni'enza [eve'njentsa] *sf*: **pronto(a) per
ogni ~** ready for any eventuality
e'vento *sm* event
eventu'ale *ag* possible
eventual'mente *av* if necessary
evi'dente *ag* evident, obvious; **evi'denza**
sf obviousness; **mettere in evidenza** to
point out, highlight; **evidenzi'are** *vt* to
emphasize; (*con evidenziatore*) to highlight;
evidenzia'tore *sm* highlighter
evi'tare *vt* to avoid; **~ di fare** to avoid
doing; **~ qc a qn** to spare sb sth
'evo *sm* age, epoch
evo'care *vt* to evoke
evo'luto, a *pp di* evolvere ♦ *ag* (*civiltà*)
(highly) developed, advanced; (*persona*)
independent
evoluzi'one [evolut'tsjone] *sf* evolution
e'volversi *vr* to evolve
ev'viva *escl* hurrah!; **~ il re!** long live the
king!, hurrah for the king!
ex *prefisso* ex, former
'extra *ag inv* first-rate; top-quality ♦ *sm inv*
extra; **extracomuni'tario, a** *ag* from
outside the EC ♦ *sm/f* non-EC citizen;
extraconiu'gale *ag* extramarital

F, f

fa *vb vedi* fare ♦ *sm inv* (*MUS*) F;
(: *solfeggiando la scala*) fa ♦ *av*: **10 anni ~**
10 years ago
fabbi'sogno [fabbi'zoɲɲo] *sm* needs *pl*,
requirements *pl*
'fabbrica *sf* factory; **fabbri'cante** *sm*
manufacturer, maker; **fabbri'care** *vt* to
build; (*produrre*) to manufacture, make;
(*fig*) to fabricate, invent
'fabbro *sm* (black)smith
fac'cenda [fat'tʃɛnda] *sf* matter, affair; (*cosa
da fare*) task, chore
fac'chino [fak'kino] *sm* porter
'faccia, ce ['fattʃa] *sf* face; (*di moneta,
medaglia*) side; **~ a ~** face to face
facci'ata [fat'tʃata] *sf* façade; (*di pagina*)
side
'faccio ['fattʃo] *vb vedi* fare
'facile ['fatʃile] *ag* easy; (*disposto*): **~ a**
inclined to, prone to; (*probabile*): **è ~ che
piova** it's likely to rain; **facilità** *sf* easiness;
(*disposizione, dono*) aptitude; **facili'tare** *vt*
to make easier
facino'roso, a [fatʃino'roso] *ag* violent
facoltà *sf inv* faculty; (*autorità*) power
facolta'tivo, a *ag* optional; (*fermata
d'autobus*) request *cpd*
fac'simile *sm* facsimile
'faggio ['faddʒo] *sm* beech
fagi'ano [fa'dʒano] *sm* pheasant
fagio'lino [fadʒo'lino] *sm* French (*BRIT*) *o*
string bean
fagi'olo [fa'dʒɔlo] *sm* bean
fa'gotto *sm* bundle; (*MUS*) bassoon; **far ~**
(*fig*) to pack up and go
'fai *vb vedi* fare
'falce ['faltʃe] *sf* scythe; **falci'are** *vt* to cut;
(*fig*) to mow down
'falco, chi *sm* hawk
fal'cone *sm* falcon
'falda *sf* layer, stratum; (*di cappello*) brim;
(*di cappotto*) tails *pl*; (*di monte*) lower
slope; (*di tetto*) pitch

fale'gname [faleɲ'ɲame] *sm* joiner

fal'lace [fal'latʃe] *ag* misleading

falli'mento *sm* failure; bankruptcy

fal'lire *vi* (*non riuscire*): ~ **(in)** to fail (in); (*DIR*) to go bankrupt ♦ *vt* (*colpo, bersaglio*) to miss; **fal'lito, a** *ag* unsuccessful; bankrupt ♦ *sm/f* bankrupt

'fallo *sm* error, mistake; (*imperfezione*) defect, flaw; (*SPORT*) foul; fault; **senza ~** without fail

falò *sm inv* bonfire

fal'sare *vt* to distort, misrepresent; **fal'sario** *sm* forger; counterfeiter; **falsifi'care** *vt* to forge; (*monete*) to forge, counterfeit

'falso, a *ag* false; (*errato*) wrong; (*falsificato*) forged; fake; (*: oro, gioielli*) imitation *cpd* ♦ *sm* forgery; **giurare il ~** to commit perjury

'fama *sf* fame; (*reputazione*) reputation, name

'fame *sf* hunger; **aver ~** to be hungry; **fa'melico, a, ci, che** *ag* ravenous

fa'miglia [fa'miʎʎa] *sf* family

famili'are *ag* (*della famiglia*) family *cpd*; (*ben noto*) familiar; (*rapporti, atmosfera*) friendly; (*LING*) informal, colloquial ♦ *sm/f* relative, relation; **familiarità** *sf* familiarity; friendliness; informality

fa'moso, a *ag* famous, well-known

fa'nale *sm* (*AUT*) light, lamp (*BRIT*); (*luce stradale, NAUT*) light; (*di faro*) beacon

fa'natico, a, ci, che *ag* fanatical; (*del teatro, calcio etc*): ~ **di** *o* **per** mad *o* crazy about ♦ *sm/f* fanatic; (*tifoso*) fan

fanci'ullo, a [fan'tʃullo] *sm/f* child

fan'donia *sf* tall story; **~e** *sfpl* (*assurdità*) nonsense *sg*

fan'fara *sf* (*musica*) fanfare

'fango, ghi *sm* mud; **fan'goso, a** *ag* muddy

'fanno *vb vedi* **fare**

fannul'lone, a *sm/f* idler, loafer

fantasci'enza [fantaʃ'ʃɛntsa] *sf* science fiction

fanta'sia *sf* fantasy, imagination; (*capriccio*) whim, caprice ♦ *ag inv*: **vestito ~**

patterned dress

fan'tasma, i *sm* ghost, phantom

fan'tastico, a, ci, che *ag* fantastic; (*potenza, ingegno*) imaginative

'fante *sm* infantryman; (*CARTE*) jack, knave (*BRIT*); **fante'ria** *sf* infantry

fan'toccio [fan'tɔttʃo] *sm* puppet

fara'butto *sm* crook

fard *sm inv* blusher

far'dello *sm* bundle; (*fig*) burden

PAROLA CHIAVE

'fare *sm* **1** (*modo di fare*): **con ~ distratto** absent-mindedly; **ha un ~ simpatico** he has a pleasant manner
2: **sul far del giorno/della notte** at daybreak/nightfall
♦ *vt* **1** (*fabbricare, creare*) to make; (*: casa*) to build; (*: assegno*) to make out; **~ un pasto/una promessa/un film** to make a meal/a promise/a film; **~ rumore** to make a noise
2 (*effettuare: lavoro, attività, studi*) to do; (*: sport*) to play; **cosa fa?** (*adesso*) what are you doing?; (*di professione*) what do you do?; **~ psicologia/italiano** (*INS*) to do psychology/Italian; **~ un viaggio** to go on a trip *o* journey; **~ una passeggiata** to go for a walk; **~ la spesa** to do the shopping
3 (*funzione*) to be; (*TEATRO*) to play, be; **~ il medico** to be a doctor; **~ il malato** (*fingere*) to act the invalid
4 (*suscitare: sentimenti*): **~ paura a qn** to frighten sb; **(non) fa niente** (*non importa*) it doesn't matter
5 (*ammontare*): **3 più 3 fa 6** 3 and 3 are *o* make 6; **fanno 6.000 lire** that's 6,000 lire; **Roma fa 2.000.000 di abitanti** Rome has 2,000,000 inhabitants; **che ora fai?** what time do you make it?
6 (+*infinito*): **far ~ qc a qn** (*obbligare*) to make sb do sth; (*permettere*) to let sb do sth; **fammi vedere** let me see; **far partire il motore** to start (up) the engine; **far riparare la macchina/costruire una casa** to get *o* have the car repaired/a house built
7: **~rsi**: **~rsi una gonna** to make o.s. a

skirt; **~rsi un nome** to make a name for o.s.; **~rsi la permanente** to get a perm; **~rsi tagliare i capelli** to get one's hair cut; **~rsi operare** to have an operation
8 (*fraseologia*): **farcela** to succeed, manage; **non ce la faccio più** I can't go on; **ce la faremo** we'll make it; **me l'hanno fatta!** (*imbrogliare*) I've been done!; **lo facevo più giovane** I thought he was younger; **fare sì/no con la testa** to nod/shake one's head

♦ *vi* **1** (*agire*) to act, do; **fate come volete** do as you like; **~ presto** to be quick; **~ da** to act as; **non c'è niente da ~** it's no use; **saperci ~ con qn/qc** to know how to deal with sb/sth; **faccia pure!** go ahead!
2 (*dire*) to say; **"davvero?" fece** "really?" he said
3: **~ per** (*essere adatto*) to be suitable for; **~ per ~ qc** to be about to do sth; **fece per andarsene** he made as if to leave
4: **~rsi: si fa così** you do it like this, this is the way it's done; **non si fa così!** (*rimprovero*) that's no way to behave!; **la festa non si fa** the party is off
5: **~ a gara con qn** to compete o vie with sb; **~ a pugni** to come to blows; **~ in tempo a ~** to be in time to do

♦ *vb impers*: **fa bel tempo** the weather is fine; **fa caldo/freddo** it's hot/cold; **fa notte** it's getting dark

♦ *vr*: **~rsi 1** (*diventare*) to become; **~rsi prete** to become a priest; **~rsi grande/vecchio** to grow tall/old
2 (*spostarsi*): **~rsi avanti/indietro** to move forward/back
3 (*fam: drogarsi*) to be a junkie

far'falla *sf* butterfly
fa'rina *sf* flour
farma'cia, 'cie [farma'tʃia] *sf* pharmacy; (*negozio*) chemist's (shop) (*BRIT*), pharmacy; **farma'cista, i, e** *sm/f* chemist (*BRIT*), pharmacist
'farmaco, ci *o* **chi** *sm* drug, medicine
'faro *sm* (*NAUT*) lighthouse; (*AER*) beacon; (*AUT*) headlight

'farsa *sf* farce
'fascia, sce ['faʃʃa] *sf* band, strip; (*MED*) bandage; (*di sindaco, ufficiale*) sash; (*parte di territorio*) strip, belt; (*di contribuenti etc*) group, band; **essere in ~sce** (*anche fig*) to be in one's infancy; **~ oraria** time band
fasci'are [faʃ'ʃare] *vt* to bind; (*MED*) to bandage
fa'scicolo [faʃ'ʃikolo] *sm* (*di documenti*) file, dossier; (*di rivista*) issue, number; (*opuscolo*) booklet, pamphlet
'fascino ['faʃʃino] *sm* charm, fascination
'fascio ['faʃʃo] *sm* bundle, sheaf; (*di fiori*) bunch; (*di luce*) beam; (*POL*): **il F~** the Fascist Party
fa'scismo [faʃ'ʃizmo] *sm* fascism
'fase *sf* phase; (*TECN*) stroke; **fuori ~** (*motore*) rough
fas'tidio *sm* bother, trouble; **dare ~ a qn** to bother o annoy sb; **sento ~ allo stomaco** my stomach's upset; **avere ~i con la polizia** to have trouble o bother with the police; **fastidi'oso, a** *ag* annoying, tiresome
'fasto *sm* pomp, splendour
'fata *sf* fairy
fa'tale *ag* fatal; (*inevitabile*) inevitable; (*fig*) irresistible; **fatalità** *sf inv* inevitability; (*avversità*) misfortune; (*fato*) fate, destiny
fa'tica, che *sf* hard work, toil; (*sforzo*) effort; (*di metalli*) fatigue; **a ~** with difficulty; **fare ~ a fare qc** to have a job doing sth; **fati'care** *vi* to toil; **faticare a fare qc** to have difficulty doing sth; **fati'coso, a** *ag* tiring, exhausting; (*lavoro*) laborious
'fato *sm* fate, destiny
'fatto, a *pp di* **fare** ♦ *ag*: **un uomo ~** a grown man; **a mano/in casa** hand-/home-made ♦ *sm* fact; (*azione*) deed; (*avvenimento*) event, occurrence; (*di romanzo, film*) action, story; **cogliere qn sul ~** to catch sb red-handed; **il ~ sta o è che** the fact remains o is that; **in ~ di** as for, as far as ... is concerned
fat'tore *sm* (*AGR*) farm manager; (*MAT, elemento costitutivo*) factor

fatto'ria *sf* farm; farmhouse

fatto'rino *sm* errand-boy; (*di ufficio*) office-boy; (*d'albergo*) porter

fat'tura *sf* (*COMM*) invoice; (*di abito*) tailoring; (*malia*) spell

fattu'rare *vt* (*COMM*) to invoice

fattu'rato *sm* (*COMM*) turnover

'fatuo, a *ag* vain, fatuous

'fauna *sf* fauna

fau'tore, trice *sm/f* advocate, supporter

fa'villa *sf* spark

'favola *sf* (*fiaba*) fairy tale; (*d'intento morale*) fable; (*fandonia*) yarn; **favo'loso, a** *ag* fabulous; (*incredibile*) incredible

fa'vore *sm* favour; **per ~** please; **fare un ~ a qn** to do sb a favour; **favo'revole** *ag* favourable

favo'rire *vt* to favour; (*il commercio, l'industria, le arti*) to promote, encourage; **vuole ~?** won't you help yourself?; **favorisca in salotto** please come into the sitting room; **favo'rito, a** *ag, sm/f* favourite

fazzo'letto [fattso'letto] *sm* handkerchief; (*per la testa*) (head)scarf; **~ di carta** tissue

feb'braio *sm* February

'febbre *sf* fever; **aver la ~** to have a high temperature; **~ da fieno** hay fever; **feb'brile** *ag* (*anche fig*) feverish

'feccia, ce ['fettʃa] *sf* dregs *pl*

'fecola *sf* potato flour

fecondazi'one [fekondat'tsjone] *sf* fertilization; **~ artificiale** artificial insemination

fe'condo, a *ag* fertile

'fede *sf* (*credenza*) belief, faith; (*REL*) faith; (*fiducia*) faith, trust; (*fedeltà*) loyalty; (*anello*) wedding ring; (*attestato*) certificate; **aver ~ in qn** to have faith in sb; **in buona/cattiva ~** in good/bad faith; **"in ~"** (*DIR*) "in witness whereof"; **fe'dele** *ag*: **fedele (a)** faithful (to) ♦ *sm/f* follower; **i fedeli** (*REL*) the faithful; **fedeltà** *sf* faithfulness; (*coniugale*) fidelity; **alta fedeltà** (*RADIO*) high fidelity

'federa *sf* pillowslip, pillowcase

fede'rale *ag* federal

'fegato *sm* liver; (*fig*) guts *pl*, nerve

'felce ['feltʃe] *sf* fern

fe'lice [fe'litʃe] *ag* happy; (*fortunato*) lucky; **felicità** *sf* happiness

felici'tarsi [felitʃi'tarsi] *vr* (*congratularsi*): **~ con qn per qc** to congratulate sb on sth

fe'lino, a *ag, sm* feline

'felpa *sf* sweatshirt

'feltro *sm* felt

'femmina *sf* (*ZOOL, TECN*) female; (*figlia*) girl, daughter; (*spesso peg*) woman; **femmi'nile** *ag* feminine; (*sesso*) female; (*lavoro, giornale, moda*) woman's ♦ *sm* (*LING*) feminine; **femmi'nismo** *sm* feminism

'fendere *vt* to cut through; **fendi'nebbia** *sm inv* (*AUT*) fog lamp

fe'nomeno *sm* phenomenon

'feretro *sm* coffin

feri'ale *ag*: **giorno ~** weekday

'ferie *sfpl* holidays (*BRIT*), vacation *sg* (*US*); **andare in ~** to go on holiday *o* vacation

fe'rire *vt* to injure; (*deliberatamente: MIL etc*) to wound; (*colpire*) to hurt; **fe'rita** *sf* injury, wound; **fe'rito, a** *sm/f* wounded *o* injured man/woman

'ferma *sf* (*MIL*) (period of) service; (*CACCIA*): **cane da ~** pointer

fer'maglio [fer'maʎʎo] *sm* clasp; (*per documenti*) clip

fer'mare *vt* to stop, halt; (*POLIZIA*) to detain, hold ♦ *vi* to stop; **~rsi** *vr* to stop, halt; **~rsi a fare qc** to stop to do sth

fer'mata *sf* stop; **~ dell'autobus** bus stop

fer'mento *sm* (*anche fig*) ferment; (*lievito*) yeast

fer'mezza [fer'mettsa] *sf* (*fig*) firmness, steadfastness

'fermo, a *ag* still, motionless; (*veicolo*) stationary; (*orologio*) not working; (*saldo: anche fig*) firm; (*voce, mano*) steady ♦ *escl* stop!; keep still! ♦ *sm* (*chiusura*) catch, lock; (*DIR*): **~ di polizia** police detention

'fermo 'posta *av, sm inv* poste restante (*BRIT*), general delivery (*US*)

fe'roce [fe'rɔtʃe] *ag* (*animale*) fierce, ferocious; (*persona*) cruel, fierce; (*fame,* *dolore*) raging; **le bestie ~i** wild animals

ferra'gosto *sm* (*festa*) feast of the Assumption; (*periodo*) August holidays *pl*

---
ferragosto
---

i **Ferragosto** *is a national holiday which falls on 15 August and is the most important holiday of the summer season. Most people extend it by taking the days around the 15th off too. Consequently during this period, most of industry and commerce is at a standstill.*

---

ferra'menta *sfpl:* **negozio di ~** ironmonger's (*BRIT*), hardware shop *o* store (*US*)

fer'rato, a *ag* (*FERR*): **strada ~a** railway (*BRIT*) *o* railroad (*US*) line; (*fig*): **essere ~ in** to be well up in

'ferro *sm* iron; **una bistecca ai ~i** a grilled steak; **~ battuto** wrought iron; **~ da calza** knitting needle; **~ di cavallo** horseshoe; **~ da stiro** iron

ferro'via *sf* railway (*BRIT*), railroad (*US*); **ferrovi'ario, a** *ag* railway *cpd* (*BRIT*), railroad *cpd* (*US*); **ferrovi'ere** *sm* railwayman (*BRIT*), railroad man (*US*)

'fertile *ag* fertile; **fertiliz'zante** *sm* fertilizer

'fervido, a *ag* fervent

'fervore *sm* fervour, ardour

'fesso, a *pp di* **fendere** ♦ *ag* (*fam: sciocco*) crazy, cracked

fes'sura *sf* crack, split; (*per gettone, moneta*) slot

'festa *sf* (*religiosa*) feast; (*pubblica*) holiday; (*compleanno*) birthday; (*onomastico*) name day; (*ricevimento*) celebration, party; **far ~** to have a holiday; to live it up; **far ~ a qn** to give sb a warm welcome

---
festa della Repubblica
---

i *The* **festa della Repubblica**, *which takes place on 2 June, celebrates the founding of the Italian Republic after the fall of the monarchy and the subsequent referendum in 1946. It is marked by*

military parades and political speeches.

---

festeggi'are [fested'dʒare] *vt* to celebrate; (*persona*) to have a celebration for

fes'tino *sm* party; (*con balli*) ball

fes'tivo, a *ag* (*atmosfera*) festive; **giorno ~** holiday

fes'toso, a *ag* merry, joyful

fe'ticcio [fe'tittʃo] *sm* fetish

'feto *sm* foetus (*BRIT*), fetus (*US*)

'fetta *sf* slice

fettuc'cine [fettut'tʃine] *sfpl* (*CUC*) ribbon-shaped pasta

FF.SS. *abbr* = **Ferrovie dello Stato**

fi'aba *sf* fairy tale

fi'acca *sf* weariness; (*svogliatezza*) listlessness

fiac'care *vt* to weaken

fi'acco, a, chi, che *ag* (*stanco*) tired, weary; (*svogliato*) listless; (*debole*) weak; (*mercato*) slack

fi'accola *sf* torch

fi'ala *sf* phial

fi'amma *sf* flame

fiam'mante *ag* (*colore*) flaming; **nuovo ~** brand new

fiam'mifero *sm* match

fiam'mingo, a, ghi, ghe *ag* Flemish ♦ *sm/f* Fleming ♦ *sm* (*LING*) Flemish; **i F~ghi** the Flemish

fiancheggi'are [fjanked'dʒare] *vt* to border; (*fig*) to support, back (up); (*MIL*) to flank

fi'anco, chi *sm* side; (*MIL*) flank; **di ~** sideways, from the side; **a ~ a ~** side by side

fi'asco, schi *sm* flask; (*fig*) fiasco; **fare ~** to fail

fi'ato *sm* breath; (*resistenza*) stamina; **avere il ~ grosso** to be out of breath; **prendere ~** to catch one's breath; **~i** *smpl* (*MUS*) wind instruments; **strumento a ~** wind instrument

'fibbia *sf* buckle

'fibra *sf* fibre; (*fig*) constitution

fic'care *vt* to push, thrust, drive; **~rsi** *vr* (*andare a finire*) to get to 'fico, chi sm (pianta) fig tree; (frutto) fig; ~ d'India prickly pear; ~ secco dried fig

fidanza'mento [fidantsa'mento] sm engagement

fidan'zarsi [fidan'tsarsi] vr to get engaged; fidan'zato, a sm/f fiancé/fiancée

fi'darsi vr: ~ di to trust; fi'dato, a ag reliable, trustworthy

'fido, a ag faithful, loyal ♦ sm (COMM) credit

fi'ducia [fi'dutʃa] sf confidence, trust; incarico di ~ position of trust, responsible position; persona di ~ reliable person

fi'ele sm (fig) bitterness

fie'nile sm barn; hayloft

fi'eno sm hay

fi'era sf fair

fie'rezza [fje'rettsa] sf pride

fi'ero, a ag proud; (audace) bold

'fifa (fam) sf: aver ~ to have the jitters

'figlia ['fiʎʎa] sf daughter

figli'astro, a [fiʎ'ʎastro] sm/f stepson/daughter

'figlio ['fiʎʎo] sm son; (senza distinzione di sesso) child; ~ di papà spoilt, wealthy young man; ~ unico only child; figli'occio, a, ci, ce sm/f godchild, godson/daughter

fi'gura sf figure; (forma, aspetto esterno) form, shape; (illustrazione) picture, illustration; far ~ to look smart; fare una brutta ~ to make a bad impression

figu'rare vi to appear ♦ vt: ~rsi qc to imagine sth; ~rsi vr: figurati! imagine that!; ti do noia? — ma figurati! am I disturbing you? — not at all!

figura'tivo, a ag figurative

figu'rina sf figurine; (cartoncino) picture card

'fila sf row, line; (coda) queue; (serie) series, string; di ~ in succession; fare la ~ to queue; in ~ indiana in single file

filantro'pia sf philanthropy

fi'lare vt to spin ♦ vi (baco, ragno) to spin; (formaggio fuso) to go stringy; (discorso) to hang together; (fam: amoreggiare) to go steady; (muoversi a forte velocità) to go at full speed; ~ diritto (fig) to toe the line; ~ via to dash off

filas'trocca, che sf nursery rhyme

filate'lia sf philately, stamp collecting

fi'lato, a ag spun ♦ sm yarn; 3 giorni ~i 3 days running o on end

fi'letto sm (di vite) thread; (di carne) fillet

fili'ale ag filial ♦ sf (di impresa) branch

fili'grana sf (in oreficeria) filigree; (su carta) watermark

film sm inv film; fil'mare vt to film

'filo sm (anche fig) thread; (filato) yarn; (metallico) wire; (di lama, rasoio) edge; per ~ e per segno in detail; ~ d'erba blade of grass; ~ interdentale dental floss; ~ di perle string of pearls; ~ spinato barbed wire; con un ~ di voce in a whisper

'filobus sm inv trolley bus

filon'cino [filon'tʃino] sm ≈ French stick

fi'lone sm (di minerali) seam, vein; (pane) ≈ Vienna loaf; (fig) trend

filoso'fia sf philosophy; fi'losofo, a sm/f philosopher

fil'trare vt, vi to filter

'filtro sm filter; ~ dell'olio (AUT) oil filter

fin av, prep = fino

fi'nale ag final ♦ sm (di opera) end, ending; (: MUS) finale ♦ sf (SPORT) final; finalità sf (scopo) aim, purpose; final'mente av finally, at last

fi'nanza [fi'nantsa] sf finance; ~e sfpl (di individuo, Stato) finances; finanzi'ario, a ag financial; finanzi'ere sm financier; (doganale) customs officer; (della tributaria) inland revenue officer

finché [fin'ke] cong (per tutto il tempo che) as long as; (fino al momento in cui) until; aspetta ~ io (non) sia ritornato wait until I get back

'fine ag (lamina, carta) thin; (capelli, polvere) fine; (vista, udito) keen, sharp; (persona: raffinato) refined, distinguished; (osservazione) subtle ♦ sf end ♦ sm aim, purpose; (esito) result, outcome; secondo ~ ulterior motive; in o alla ~ in the end, finally; ~ settimana sm o f inv weekend

fi'nestra sf window; fines'trino sm (di

treno, auto) window

'**fingere** ['findʒere] *vt* to feign; (*supporre*) to imagine, suppose; ~**rsi** *vr*: ~**rsi ubriaco/pazzo** to pretend to be drunk/mad; ~ **di fare** to pretend to do

fini'mondo *sm* pandemonium

fi'nire *vt* to finish ♦ *vi* to finish, end; ~ **di fare** (*compiere*) to finish doing; (*smettere*) to stop doing; ~ **in galera** to end up *o* finish up in prison; **fini'tura** *sf* finish

finlan'dese *ag, sm* (LING) Finnish ♦ *sm/f* Finn

Fin'landia *sf*: **la** ~ Finland

'**fino, a** *ag* (*capelli, seta*) fine; (*oro*) pure; (*fig: acuto*) shrewd ♦ *av* (*spesso troncato in* **fin**: *pure, anche*) even ♦ *prep* (*spesso troncato in* **fin**: *tempo*): **fin quando?** till when?; (: *luogo*): **fin qui** as far as here; ~ **a** (*tempo*) until, till; (*luogo*) as far as, (up) to); **fin da domani** from tomorrow onwards; **fin da ieri** since yesterday; **fin dalla nascita** from *o* since birth

fi'nocchio [fi'nɔkkjo] *sm* fennel; (*fam: peg: omosessuale*) queer

fi'nora *av* up till now

'**finta** *sf* pretence, sham; (SPORT) feint; **far ~a (di fare)** to pretend (to do)

'**finto, a** *pp di* **fingere** ♦ *ag* false; artificial

finzi'one [fin'tsjone] *sf* pretence, sham

fi'occo, chi *sm* (*di nastro*) bow; (*di stoffa, lana*) flock; (*di neve*) flake; (NAUT) jib; **coi ~chi** (*fig*) first-rate; ~**chi di granoturco** cornflakes

fi'ocina ['fjɔtʃina] *sf* harpoon

fi'oco, a, chi, che *ag* faint, dim

fi'onda *sf* catapult

fio'raio, a *sm/f* florist

fi'ore *sm* flower; ~**i** *smpl* (CARTE) clubs; **a fior d'acqua** on the surface of the water; **avere i nervi a fior di pelle** to be on edge

fioren'tino, a *ag* Florentine

fio'retto *sm* (SCHERMA) foil

fio'rire *vi* (*rosa*) to flower; (*albero*) to blossom; (*fig*) to flourish

Fi'renze [fi'rɛntse] *sf* Florence

'**firma** *sf* signature

fir'mare *vt* to sign; **un abito firmato** a designer suit

fisar'monica, che *sf* accordion

fis'cale *ag* fiscal, tax *cpd*; **medico** ~ doctor *employed by Social Security to verify cases of sick leave*

fischi'are [fis'kjare] *vi* to whistle ♦ *vt* to whistle; (*attore*) to boo, hiss

'**fischio** ['fiskjo] *sm* whistle

'**fisco** *sm* tax authorities *pl*, ≈ Inland Revenue (BRIT), ≈ Internal Revenue Service (US)

'**fisica** *sf* physics *sg*

'**fisico, a, ci, che** *ag* physical ♦ *sm/f* physicist ♦ *sm* physique

fisiolo'gia [fizjolo'dʒia] *sf* physiology

fisiono'mia *sf* face, physiognomy

fisotera'pia *sf* physiotherapy

fis'sare *vt* to fix, fasten; (*guardare intensamente*) to stare at; (*data, condizioni*) to fix, establish, set; (*prenotare*) to book; ~**rsi su** (*sog: sguardo, attenzione*) to focus on; (*fig: idea*) to become obsessed with; **fissazi'one** *sf* (PSIC) fixation

'**fisso, a** *ag* fixed; (*stipendio, impiego*) regular ♦ *av*: **guardare ~ qc/qn** to stare at sth/sb

'**fitta** *sf* sharp pain; *vedi anche* **fitto**

fit'tizio, a *ag* fictitious, imaginary

'**fitto, a** *ag* thick, dense; (*pioggia*) heavy ♦ *sm* depths *pl*, middle; (*affitto, pigione*) rent

fi'ume *sm* river

fiu'tare *vt* to smell, sniff; (*sog: animale*) to scent; (*fig: inganno*) to get wind of, smell; ~ **tabacco/cocaina** to take snuff/cocaine; **fi'uto** *sm* (sense of) smell; (*fig*) nose

fla'gello [fla'dʒello] *sm* scourge

fla'grante *ag*: **cogliere qn in** ~ to catch sb red-handed

fla'nella *sf* flannel

flash [flaʃ] *sm inv* (FOT) flash; (*giornalistico*) newsflash

'**flauto** *sm* flute

'**flebile** *ag* faint, feeble

'**flemma** *sf* (*calma*) coolness, phlegm

fles'sibile *ag* pliable; (*fig: che si adatta*) flexible

'flesso, a *pp di* **flettere**

flessu'oso, a *ag* supple, lithe

'flettere *vt* to bend

'flipper *sm inv* pinball machine

F.lli *abbr* (= *fratelli*) Bros.

'flora *sf* flora

'florido, a *ag* flourishing; (*fig*) glowing with health

'floscio, a, sci, sce ['flɔʃʃo] *ag* (*cappello*) floppy, soft; (*muscoli*) flabby

'flotta *sf* fleet

'fluido, a *ag, sm* fluid

flu'ire *vi* to flow

flu'oro *sm* fluorine

fluo'ruro *sm* fluoride

'flusso *sm* flow; (*FISICA, MED*) flux; **~ e riflusso** ebb and flow

fluttu'are *vi* (*mare*) to rise and fall; (*ECON*) to fluctuate

fluvi'ale *ag* river *cpd*, fluvial

'foca, che *sf* (*ZOOL*) seal

fo'caccia, ce [fo'kattʃa] *sf* kind of pizza; (*dolce*) bun

'foce ['fotʃe] *sf* (*GEO*) mouth

foco'laio *sm* (*MED*) centre of infection; (*fig*) hotbed

foco'lare *sm* hearth, fireside; (*TECN*) furnace

'fodera *sf* (*di vestito*) lining; (*di libro, poltrona*) cover; **fode'rare** *vt* to line; to cover

'fodero *sm* (*di spada*) scabbard; (*di pugnale*) sheath; (*di pistola*) holster

'foga *sf* enthusiasm, ardour

'foggia, ge ['fɔddʒa] *sf* (*maniera*) style; (*aspetto*) form, shape

'foglia ['fɔʎʎa] *sf* leaf; **~ d'argento/d'oro** silver/gold leaf; **fogli'ame** *sm* foliage, leaves *pl*

'foglio ['fɔʎʎo] *sm* (*di carta*) sheet (of paper); (*di metallo*) sheet; **~ rosa** (*AUT*) provisional licence; **~ di via** (*DIR*) expulsion order; **~ volante** pamphlet

'fogna ['foɲɲa] *sf* drain, sewer; **fogna'tura** *sf* drainage, sewerage

föhn [føːn] *sm inv* hair dryer

folgo'rare *vt* (*sog: fulmine*) to strike down;

(*: alta tensione*) to electrocute

'folla *sf* crowd, throng

'folle *ag* mad, insane; (*TECN*) idle; **in ~** (*AUT*) in neutral

fol'lia *sf* folly, foolishness; foolish act; (*pazzia*) madness, lunacy

'folto, a *ag* thick

fomen'tare *vt* to stir up, foment

fon *sm inv* hair dryer

fondamen'tale *ag* fundamental, basic

fonda'mento *sm* foundation; **~a** *sfpl* (*EDIL*) foundations

fon'dare *vt* to found; (*fig: dar base*): **~ qc su** to base sth on; **fondazi'one** *sf* foundation

'fondere *vt* (*neve*) to melt; (*metallo*) to fuse, melt; (*fig: colori*) to merge, blend; (*: imprese, gruppi*) to merge ♦ *vi* to melt; **~rsi** *vr* to melt; (*fig: partiti, correnti*) to unite, merge; **fonde'ria** *sf* foundry

'fondo, a *ag* deep ♦ *sm* (*di recipiente, pozzo*) bottom; (*di stanza*) back; (*quantità di liquido che resta, deposito*) dregs *pl*; (*sfondo*) background; (*unità immobiliare*) property, estate; (*somma di denaro*) fund; (*SPORT*) long-distance race; **~i** *smpl* (*denaro*) funds; **a notte ~a** at dead of night; **in ~ a** at the bottom of; at the back of; (*strada*) at the end of; **andare a ~** (*nave*) to sink; **conoscere a ~** to know inside out; **dar ~ a** (*fig: provviste, soldi*) to use up; **in ~** (*fig*) after all, all things considered; **andare fino in ~ a** (*fig*) to examine thoroughly; **a ~ perduto** (*COMM*) without security; **~i di caffè** coffee grounds; **~i di magazzino** old *o* unsold stock *sg*

fo'netica *sf* phonetics *sg*

fon'tana *sf* fountain

'fonte *sf* spring, source; (*fig*) source ♦ *sm*: **~ battesimale** (*REL*) font

fon'tina *sm* sweet full-fat hard cheese from Val d'Aosta

fo'raggio [fo'raddʒo] *sm* fodder, forage

fo'rare *vt* to pierce, make a hole in; (*pallone*) to burst; (*biglietto*) to punch; **~ una gomma** to burst a tyre (*BRIT*) *o* tire (*US*) '**forbici** ['fɔrbitʃi] *sfpl* scissors

'**forca, che** *sf* (*AGR*) fork, pitchfork; (*patibolo*) gallows *sg*

for'**cella** [for'tʃella] *sf* (*TECN*) fork; (*di monte*) pass

for'**chetta** [for'ketta] *sf* fork

for'**cina** [for'tʃina] *sf* hairpin

'**forcipe** ['fɔrtʃipe] *sm* forceps *pl*

fo'**resta** *sf* forest

foresti'**ero, a** *ag* foreign ♦ *sm/f* foreigner

'**forfora** *sf* dandruff

forgi'**are** *vt* to forge

'**forma** *sf* form; (*aspetto esteriore*) form, shape; (*DIR: procedura*) procedure; (*per calzature*) last; (*stampo da cucina*) mould; ~**e** *sfpl* (*del corpo*) figure, shape; **le ~e** (*convenzioni*) appearances; **essere in** ~ to be in good shape

formag'**gino** [formad'dʒino] *sm* processed cheese

for'**maggio** [for'maddʒo] *sm* cheese

for'**male** *ag* formal; **formalità** *sf inv* formality

for'**mare** *vt* to form, shape, make; (*numero di telefono*) to dial; (*fig: carattere*) to form, mould; ~**rsi** *vr* to form, take shape; for'**mato** *sm* format, size; formazi'**one** *sf* formation; (*fig: educazione*) training

for'**mica, che** *sf* ant; formi'**caio** *sm* anthill

formico'**lare** *vi* (*anche fig*): ~ **di** to be swarming with; **mi formicola la gamba** I've got pins and needles in my leg; formico'**lio** *sm* pins and needles *pl*; swarming

formi'**dabile** *ag* powerful, formidable; (*straordinario*) remarkable

'**formula** *sf* formula; ~ **di cortesia** courtesy form

formu'**lare** *vt* to formulate; to express

for'**nace** [for'natʃe] *sf* (*per laterizi etc*) kiln; (*per metalli*) furnace; ~ **a microonde** microwave oven

for'**naio** *sm* baker

for'**nello** *sm* (*elettrico, a gas*) ring; (*di pipa*) bowl

for'**nire** *vt*: ~ **qn di qc**, ~ **qc a qn** to provide *o* supply sb with sth, to supply sth to sb

'**forno** *sm* (*di cucina*) oven; (*panetteria*) bakery; (*TECN: per calce etc*) kiln; (: *per metalli*) furnace; ~ **a microonde** microwave oven

'**foro** *sm* (*buco*) hole; (*STORIA*) forum; (*tribunale*) (law) court

'**forse** *av* perhaps, maybe; (*circa*) about; **essere in** ~ to be in doubt

forsen'**nato, a** *ag* mad, insane

'**forte** *ag* strong; (*suono*) loud; (*spesa*) considerable, great; (*passione, dolore*) great, deep ♦ *av* strongly; (*velocemente*) fast; (*a voce alta*) loud(ly); (*violentemente*) hard ♦ *sm* (*edificio*) fort; (*specialità*) forte, strong point; **essere** ~ **in qc** to be good at sth

for'**tezza** [for'tettsa] *sf* (*morale*) strength; (*luogo fortificato*) fortress

for'**tuito, a** *ag* fortuitous, chance

for'**tuna** *sf* (*destino*) fortune, luck; (*buona sorte*) success, fortune; (*eredità, averi*) fortune; **per** ~ luckily, fortunately; **di** ~ makeshift, improvised; **atterraggio di** ~ emergency landing; fortu'**nato, a** *ag* lucky, fortunate; (*coronato da successo*) successful

'**forza** ['fɔrtsa] *sf* strength; (*potere*) power; (*FISICA*) force; ~**e** *sfpl* (*fisiche*) strength *sg*; (*MIL*) forces ♦ *escl* come on!, per ~ against one's will; (*naturalmente*) of course; **a viva** ~ by force; **a** ~ **di** by dint of; ~ **maggiore** circumstances beyond one's control; **la** ~ **pubblica** the police *pl*; **le** ~**e armate** the armed forces; ~**e dell'ordine** the forces of law and order

for'**zare** [for'tsare] *vt* to force; ~ **qn a fare** to force sb to do; for'**zato, a** *ag* forced ♦ *sm* (*DIR*) prisoner sentenced to hard labour

fos'**chia** [fos'kia] *sf* mist, haze

'**fosco, a, schi, sche** *ag* dark, gloomy

'**fosforo** *sm* phosphorous

'**fossa** *sf* pit; (*di cimitero*) grave; ~ **biologica** septic tank

fos'**sato** *sm* ditch; (*di fortezza*) moat

fos'**setta** *sf* dimple

'**fossile** *ag, sm* fossil

'**fosso** *sm* ditch; (*MIL*) trench

'**foto** *sf* photo ♦ *prefisso*: **foto'copia** *sf* photocopy; **fotocopi'are** *vt* to photocopy; **fotogra'fare** *vt* to photograph; **fotogra'fia** *sf* (*procedimento*) photography; (*immagine*) photograph; **fare una fotografia** to take a photograph; **una fotografia a colori/in bianco e nero** a colour/black and white photograph; **fo'tografo, a** *sm/f* photographer; **fotoro'manzo** *sm* romantic picture story; **foto'tessera** *sf* passport-size photo

fra *prep* = **tra**

fracas'sare *vt* to shatter, smash; **~rsi** *vr* to shatter, smash; (*veicolo*) to crash; **fra'casso** *sm* smash; crash; (*baccano*) din, racket

'**fradicio, a, ci, ce** ['fraditʃo] *ag* (*molto bagnato*) soaking (wet); **ubriaco ~** blind drunk

'**fragile** ['fradʒile] *ag* fragile; (*fig: salute*) delicate

'**fragola** *sf* strawberry

fra'gore *sm* roar; (*di tuono*) rumble

frago'roso, a *ag* deafening

fra'grante *ag* fragrant

frain'tendere *vt* to misunderstand; **frain'teso, a** *pp di* **fraintendere**

fram'mento *sm* fragment

'**frana** *sf* landslide; (*fig: persona*): **essere una ~** to be useless; **fra'nare** *vi* to slip, slide down

fran'cese [fran'tʃeze] *ag* French ♦ *sm/f* Frenchman/woman ♦ *sm* (*LING*) French; **i F~i** the French

fran'chezza [fran'kettsa] *sf* frankness, openness

'**Francia** ['frantʃa] *sf*: **la ~** France

'**franco, a, chi, che** *ag* (*COMM*) free; (*sincero*) frank, open, sincere ♦ *sm* (*moneta*) franc; **farla ~a** (*fig*) to get off scot-free; **~ di dogana** duty-free; **prezzo ~ fabbrica** ex-works price; **~ tiratore** *sm* sniper

franco'bollo *sm* (*postage*) stamp

fran'gente [fran'dʒɛnte] *sm* (*onda*) breaker; (*scoglio emergente*) reef; (*circostanza*) situation, circumstance

'**frangia, ge** ['frandʒa] *sf* fringe

frantu'mare *vt* to break into pieces, shatter; **~rsi** *vr* to break into pieces, shatter

frap'pé *sm* milk shake

'**frasca, sche** *sf* (leafy) branch

'**frase** *sf* (*LING*) sentence; (*locuzione, espressione, MUS*) phrase; **~ fatta** set phrase

'**frassino** *sm* ash (tree)

frastagli'ato, a [frastaʎ'ʎato] *ag* (*costa*) indented, jagged

frastor'nare *vt* to daze; to befuddle

frastu'ono *sm* hubbub, din

'**frate** *sm* friar, monk

fratel'lanza [fratel'lantsa] *sf* brotherhood; (*associazione*) fraternity

fratel'lastro *sm* stepbrother

fra'tello *sm* brother; **~i** *smpl* brothers; (*nel senso di fratelli e sorelle*) brothers and sisters

fra'terno, a *ag* fraternal, brotherly

frat'tanto *av* in the meantime, meanwhile

frat'tempo *sm*: **nel ~** in the meantime, meanwhile

frat'tura *sf* fracture; (*fig*) split, break

frazi'one [frat'tsjone] *sf* fraction; (*di comune*) small town

'**freccia, ce** ['frettʃa] *sf* arrow; **~ di direzione** (*AUT*) indicator

fred'dare *vt* to shoot dead

fred'dezza [fred'dettsa] *sf* coldness

'**freddo, a** *ag, sm* cold; **fa ~** it's cold; **aver ~** to be cold; **a ~** (*fig*) deliberately; **freddo'loso, a** *ag* sensitive to the cold

fred'dura *sf* pun

fre'gare *vt* to rub; (*fam: truffare*) to take in, cheat; (: *rubare*) to swipe, pinch; **fregarsene** (*fam!*): **chi se ne frega?** who gives a damn (about it)?

fre'gata *sf* rub; (*fam*) swindle; (*NAUT*) frigate

'**fregio** ['fredʒo] *sm* (*ARCHIT*) frieze; (*ornamento*) decoration

'**fremere** *vi*: **~ di** to tremble *o* quiver with; '**fremito** *sm* tremor, quiver

fre'nare *vt* (*veicolo*) to slow down; (*cavallo*) to rein in; (*lacrime*) to restrain, hold back

♦ *vi* to brake; **~rsi** *vr* (*fig*) to restrain o.s., control o.s.; **fre'nata** *sf*: **fare una frenata** to brake

frene'sia *sf* frenzy

'freno *sm* brake; (*morso*) bit; **~ a disco** disc brake; **~ a mano** handbrake; **tenere a ~** to restrain

frequen'tare *vt* (*scuola, corso*) to attend; (*locale, bar*) to go to, frequent; (*persone*) to see (often)

fre'quente *ag* frequent; **di ~** frequently; **fre'quenza** *sf* frequency; (*INS*) attendance

fres'chezza [fres'kettsa] *sf* freshness

'fresco, a, schi, sche *ag* fresh; (*temperatura*) cool; (*notizia*) recent, fresh ♦ *sm*: **stare ~** (*fig*) to be in for it; **mettere al ~** to put in a cool place

'fretta *sf* hurry, haste; **in ~** in a hurry; **in ~ e furia** in a mad rush; **aver ~** to be in a hurry; **fretto'loso, a** *ag* (*persona*) in a hurry; (*lavoro etc*) hurried, rushed

fri'abile *ag* (*terreno*) friable; (*pasta*) crumbly

'friggere ['friddʒere] *vt* to fry ♦ *vi* (*olio etc*) to sizzle

'frigido, a ['fridʒido] *ag* (*MED*) frigid

'frigo *sm* fridge

frigo'rifero, a *ag* refrigerating ♦ *sm* refrigerator

fringu'ello *sm* chaffinch

frit'tata [frit'tsjone] *sf* omelette; **fare una ~** (*fig*) to make a mess of things

frit'tella *sf* (*CUC*) fritter

'fritto, a *pp di* **friggere** ♦ *ag* fried ♦ *sm* fried food; **~ misto** mixed fry

frit'tura *sf* (*CUC*): **~ di pesce** mixed fried fish

'frivolo, a *ag* frivolous

frizi'one [frit'tsjone] *sf* friction; (*di pelle*) rub, rub-down; (*AUT*) clutch

friz'zante [frid'dzante] *ag* (*anche fig*) sparkling

fro'dare *vt* to defraud, cheat

'frode *sf* fraud; **~ fiscale** tax evasion

'frollo, a *ag* (*carne*) tender; (*: di selvaggina*) high; **pasta ~a** short(crust) pastry

'fronda *sf* (leafy) branch; (*di partito politico*) internal opposition

fron'tale *ag* frontal; (*scontro*) head-on

'fronte *sf* (*ANAT*) forehead; (*di edificio*) front, façade ♦ *sm* (*MIL, POL, METEOR*) front; **a ~, di ~** facing, opposite; **di ~ a** (*posizione*) opposite, facing, in front of; (*a paragone di*) compared with

fronteggi'are [fronted'dʒare] *vt* (*avversari, difficoltà*) to face, stand up to; (*spese*) to cope with

fronti'era *sf* border, frontier

'fronzolo ['frondzolo] *sm* frill

'frottola *sf* fib; **~e** *sfpl* (*assurdità*) nonsense *sg*

fru'gare *vi* to rummage ♦ *vt* to search

frul'lare *vt* (*CUC*) to whisk ♦ *vi* (*uccelli*) to flutter; **frul'lato** *sm* milk shake; fruit drink; **frulla'tore** *sm* electric mixer; **frul'lino** *sm* whisk

fru'mento *sm* wheat

fru'scio [fruʃ'ʃio] *sm* rustle; rustling; (*di acque*) murmur

'frusta *sf* whip; (*CUC*) whisk

frus'tare *vt* to whip

frus'tino *sm* riding crop

frus'trare *vt* to frustrate

'frutta *sf* fruit; (*portata*) dessert; **~ candita / secca** candied/dried fruit

frut'tare *vi* to bear dividends, give a return

frut'teto *sm* orchard

frutti'vendolo, a *sm/f* greengrocer (*BRIT*), produce dealer (*US*)

'frutto *sm* fruit; (*fig: risultato*) result(s); (*ECON: interesse*) interest; (*: reddito*) income; **~i di mare** seafood *sg*

FS *abbr* = **Ferrovie dello Stato**

fu *vb vedi* **essere** ♦ *ag inv*: **il ~ Paolo Bianchi** the late Paolo Bianchi

fuci'lare [futʃi'lare] *vt* to shoot; **fuci'lata** *sf* rifle shot

fu'cile [fu'tʃile] *sm* rifle, gun; (*da caccia*) shotgun, gun

fu'cina [fu'tʃina] *sf* forge

'fuga *sf* escape, flight; (*di gas, liquidi*) leak; (*MUS*) fugue; **~ di cervelli** brain drain

fu'gace [fu'gatʃe] *ag* fleeting, transient

fug'gevole [fud'dʒevole] *ag* fleeting

fuggi'asco, a, schi, sche [fud'dʒasko] *ag, sm/f* fugitive

fuggi'fuggi [fuddʒi'fuddʒi] *sm* scramble, stampede

fug'gire [fud'dʒire] *vi* to flee, run away; (*fig: passar veloce*) to fly ♦ *vt* to avoid; **fuggi'tivo, a** *sm/f* fugitive, runaway

ful'gore *sm* brilliance, splendour

fu'liggine [fu'liddʒine] *sf* soot

fulmi'nare *vt* (*sog: fulmine*) to strike; (*: elettricità*) to electrocute; (*con arma da fuoco*) to shoot dead; (*fig: con lo sguardo*) to look daggers at

'fulmine *sm* thunderbolt; lightning *no pl*

fu'mare *vi* to smoke; (*emettere vapore*) to steam ♦ *vt* to smoke; **fu'mata** *sf* (*segnale*) smoke signal; **farsi una fumata** to have a smoke; **fuma'tore, 'trice** *sm/f* smoker

fu'metto *sm* comic strip; **giornale** *sm* a ~**i** comic

'fumo *sm* smoke; (*vapore*) steam; (*il fumare tabacco*) smoking; **~i** *smpl* (*industriali etc*) fumes; **i ~i dell'alcool** the after-effects of drink; **vendere ~** to deceive, cheat; **~ passivo** passive smoking; **fu'moso, a** *ag* smoky; (*fig*) muddled

fu'nambolo, a *sm/f* tightrope walker

'fune *sf* rope, cord; (*più grossa*) cable

'funebre *ag* (*rito*) funeral; (*aspetto*) gloomy, funereal

fune'rale *sm* funeral

'fungere ['fundʒere] *vi*: **~ da** to act as

'fungo, ghi *sm* fungus; (*commestibile*) mushroom; **~ velenoso** toadstool

funico'lare *sf* funicular railway

funi'via *sf* cable railway

funzio'nare [funtsjo'nare] *vi* to work, function; (*fungere*): **~ da** to act as

funzio'nario [funtsjo'narjo] *sm* official

funzi'one [fun'tsjone] *sf* function; (*carica*) post, position; (*REL*) service; **in ~** (*meccanismo*) in operation; **in ~ di** (*come*) as; **fare la ~ di qn** (*farne le veci*) to take sb's place

fu'oco, chi *sm* fire; (*fornello*) ring; (*FOT, FISICA*) focus; **dare ~ a qc** to set fire to sth;

far ~ (*sparare*) to fire; **~ d'artificio** firework

fuorché [fwor'ke] *cong, prep* except

fu'ori *av* outside; (*all'aperto*) outdoors, outside; (*fuori di casa, SPORT*) out; (*esclamativo*) get out! ♦ *prep*: **~ (di)** out of, outside ♦ *sm* outside; **lasciar ~ qc/qn** to leave sth/sb out; **far ~ qn** (*fam*) to kill sb, do sb in; **essere ~ di sé** to be beside o.s.; **~ luogo** (*inopportuno*) out of place, uncalled for; **~ mano** out of the way, remote; **~ pericolo** out of danger; **~ uso** old-fashioned; obsolete

fu'ori... *prefisso*: **fuori'bordo** *sm inv* speedboat (with outboard motor); outboard motor; **fuori'classe** *sm/f* (*undisputed*) champion; **fuorigi'oco** *sm* offside; **fuori'legge** *sm/f inv* outlaw; **fuori'serie** *ag inv* (*auto etc*) custom-built ♦ *sf* custom-built car; **fuori'strada** *sm* (*AUT*) cross-country vehicle;

fuor(i)u'scito, a *sm/f* exile; **fuorvi'are** *vt* to mislead; (*fig*) to lead astray ♦ *vi* to go astray

'furbo, a *ag* clever, smart; (*peg*) cunning

fu'rente *ag*: **~ (contro)** furious (with)

fur'fante *sm* rascal, scoundrel

fur'gone *sm* van

'furia *sf* (*ira*) fury, rage; (*fig: impeto*) fury, violence; (*fretta*) rush; **a ~ di** by dint of; **andare su tutte le ~e** to get into a towering rage; **furi'bondo, a** *ag* furious

furi'oso, a *ag* furious

fu'rore *sm* fury; (*esaltazione*) frenzy; **far ~** to be all the rage

fur'tivo, a *ag* furtive

'furto *sm* theft; **~ con scasso** burglary

'fusa *sfpl*: **fare le ~** to purr

fu'sibile *sm* (*ELETTR*) fuse

fusi'one *sf* (*di metalli*) fusion, melting; (*colata*) casting; (*COMM*) merger; (*fig*) merging

'fuso, a *pp di* **fondere** ♦ *sm* (*FILATURA*) spindle; **~ orario** time zone

fus'tagno [fus'tanno] *sm* corduroy

fus'tino *sm* (*di detersivo*) tub

'fusto *sm* stem; (*ANAT, di albero*) trunk; (*recipiente*) drum, can

fu'turo, a *ag, sm* future

G, g

gab'bare *vt* to take in, dupe; **~rsi** *vr*: **~rsi di qn** to make fun of sb
'gabbia *sf* cage; (*da imballaggio*) crate; **~ dell'ascensore** lift (*BRIT*) *o* elevator (*US*) shaft; **~ toracica** (*ANAT*) rib cage
gabbi'ano *sm* (sea)gull
gabi'netto *sm* (*MED etc*) consulting room; (*POL*) ministry; (*WC*) toilet, lavatory; (*INS: di fisica etc*) laboratory
'gaffe [gaf] *sf inv* blunder
gagli'ardo, a [gaʎˈʎardo] *ag* strong, vigorous
'gaio, a *ag* cheerful, gay
'gala *sf* (*sfarzo*) pomp; (*festa*) gala
ga'lante *ag* gallant, courteous; (*avventura*) amorous; **galante'ria** *sf* gallantry
galantu'omo (*pl* **galantu'omini**) *sm* gentleman
ga'lassia *sf* galaxy
gala'teo *sm* (good) manners *pl*
gale'otto *sm* (*rematore*) galley slave; (*carcerato*) convict
ga'lera *sf* (*NAUT*) galley; (*prigione*) prison
'galla *sf*: **a ~** afloat; **venire a ~** to surface, come to the surface; (*fig: verità*) to come out
galleggi'ante [galledˈdʒante] *ag* floating ♦ *sm* (*di pescatore, lenza, TECN*) float
galleggi'are [galledˈdʒare] *vi* to float
galle'ria *sf* (*traforo*) tunnel; (*ARCHIT, d'arte*) gallery; (*TEATRO*) circle; (*strada coperta con negozi*) arcade
'Galles *sm*: **il ~** Wales; **gal'lese** *ag, sm* (*LING*) Welsh ♦ *sm/f* Welshman/woman
gal'letta *sf* cracker
gal'lina *sf* hen
'gallo *sm* cock
gal'lone *sm* piece of braid; (*MIL*) stripe; (*unità di misura*) gallon
galop'pare *vi* to gallop
ga'loppo *sm* gallop; **al** *o* **di ~** at a gallop
'gamba *sf* leg; (*asta: di lettera*) stem; **in ~**

(*in buona salute*) well; (*bravo, sveglio*) bright, smart; **prendere qc sotto ~** (*fig*) to treat sth too lightly
gambe'retto *sm* shrimp
'gambero *sm* (*di acqua dolce*) crayfish; (*di mare*) prawn
'gambo *sm* stem; (*di frutta*) stalk
'gamma *sf* (*MUS*) scale; (*di colori, fig*) range
ga'nascia, sce [gaˈnaʃʃa] *sf* jaw; **~sce del freno** (*AUT*) brake shoes
'gancio [ˈgantʃo] *sm* hook
'gangheri [ˈgangeri] *smpl*: **uscire dai ~** (*fig*) to fly into a temper
'gara *sf* competition; (*SPORT*) competition; contest; match; (*: corsa*) race; **fare a ~** to compete, vie
ga'rage [gaˈraʒ] *sm inv* garage
garan'tire *vt* to guarantee; (*debito*) to stand surety for; (*dare per certo*) to assure
garan'zia [garanˈtsia] *sf* guarantee; (*pegno*) security
gar'bato, a *ag* courteous, polite
'garbo *sm* (*buone maniere*) politeness, courtesy; (*di vestito etc*) grace, style
gareggi'are [garedˈdʒare] *vi* to compete
garga'rismo *sm* gargle; **fare i ~i** to gargle
ga'rofano *sm* carnation; **chiodo di ~** clove
'garza [ˈgardza] *sf* (*per bende*) gauze
gar'zone [garˈdzone] *sm* (*di negozio*) boy
gas *sm inv* gas; **a tutto ~** at full speed; **dare ~** (*AUT*) to accelerate
ga'solio *sm* diesel (oil)
ga's(s)ato, a *ag* (*bibita*) aerated, fizzy
gas'sosa *sf* fizzy drink
gas'soso, a *ag* gaseous, gassy
gastrono'mia *sf* gastronomy
gat'tino *sm* kitten
'gatto, a *sm/f* cat, tomcat/she-cat; **~ selvatico** wildcat; **~ delle nevi** (*AUT, SCI*) snowcat
gatto'pardo *sm*: **~ africano** serval; **~ americano** ocelot
'gaudio *sm* joy, happiness
ga'vetta *sf* (*MIL*) mess tin; **venire dalla ~** (*MIL, fig*) to rise from the ranks
'gazza [ˈgaddza] *sf* magpie

gaz'zella [gad'dzɛlla] *sf* gazelle

gaz'zetta [gad'dzetta] *sf* news sheet; **G~ Ufficiale** *official publication containing details of new laws*

gel [dʒɛl] *sm inv* gel

ge'lare [dʒe'lare] *vt, vi, vb impers* to freeze; **ge'lata** *sf* frost

gelate'ria [dʒelate'ria] *sf* ice-cream shop

gela'tina [dʒela'tina] *sf* gelatine; **~ esplosiva** dynamite; **~ di frutta** fruit jelly

ge'lato, a [dʒe'lato] *ag* frozen ♦ *sm* ice cream

'gelido, a ['dʒɛlido] *ag* icy, ice-cold

'gelo ['dʒɛlo] *sm* (*temperatura*) intense cold; (*brina*) frost; (*fig*) chill; **ge'lone** *sm* chilblain

gelo'sia [dʒelo'sia] *sf* jealousy

ge'loso, a [dʒe'loso] *ag* jealous

'gelso ['dʒɛlso] *sm* mulberry (tree)

gelso'mino [dʒelso'mino] *sm* jasmine

ge'mello, a [dʒe'mɛllo] *ag, sm/f* twin; **~i** *smpl* (*di camicia*) cufflinks; (*dello zodiaco*): **G~i** Gemini *sg*

'gemere ['dʒɛmere] *vi* to moan, groan; (*cigolare*) to creak; **'gemito** *sm* moan, groan

'gemma ['dʒɛmma] *sf* (*BOT*) bud; (*pietra preziosa*) gem

gene'rale [dʒene'rale] *ag, sm* general; **in ~** (*per sommi capi*) in general terms; (*di solito*) usually, in general; **generalità** *sfpl* (*dati d'identità*) particulars; **generaliz'zare** *vt, vi* to generalize; **general'mente** *av* generally

gene'rare [dʒene'rare] *vt* (*dar vita*) to give birth to; (*produrre*) to produce; (*causare*) to arouse; (*TECN*) to produce, generate; **genera'tore** *sm* (*TECN*) generator; **generazi'one** *sf* generation

'genere ['dʒɛnere] *sm* kind, type, sort; (*BIOL*) genus; (*merce*) article, product; (*LING*) gender; (*ARTE, LETTERATURA*) genre; **in ~** generally, as a rule; **il ~ umano** mankind; **~i alimentari** foodstuffs

ge'nerico, a, ci, che [dʒe'nɛriko] *ag* generic; (*vago*) vague, imprecise

'genero ['dʒɛnero] *sm* son-in-law

generosità [dʒenerosi'ta] *sf* generosity

gene'roso, a [dʒene'roso] *ag* generous

ge'netica [dʒe'nɛtika] *sf* genetics *sg*

ge'netico, a, ci, che [dʒe'nɛtiko] *ag* genetic

gen'giva [dʒen'dʒiva] *sf* (*ANAT*) gum

geni'ale [dʒen'jale] *ag* (*persona*) of genius; (*idea*) ingenious, brilliant

'genio ['dʒɛnjo] *sm* genius; **andare a ~ a qn** to be to sb's liking, appeal to sb

geni'tale [dʒeni'tale] *ag* genital; **~i** *smpl* genitals

geni'tore [dʒeni'tore] *sm* parent, father *o* mother; **i miei ~i** my parents, my father and mother

gen'naio [dʒen'najo] *sm* January

'Genova ['dʒɛnova] *sf* Genoa

gen'taglia [dʒen'taʎʎa] (*peg*) *sf* rabble

'gente ['dʒɛnte] *sf* people *pl*

gen'tile [dʒen'tile] *ag* (*persona, atto*) kind; (*: garbato*) courteous, polite; (*nelle lettere*): **G~ Signore** Dear Sir; (*: sulla busta*): **G~ Signor Fernando Villa** Mr Fernando Villa; **genti'lezza** *sf* kindness; courtesy, politeness; **per gentilezza** (*per favore*) please

gentilu'omo [dʒentil'wɔmo] (*pl* **gentilu'omini**) *sm* gentleman

genu'ino, a [dʒenu'ino] *ag* (*prodotto*) natural; (*persona, sentimento*) genuine, sincere

geogra'fia [dʒeogra'fia] *sf* geography

geolo'gia [dʒeolo'dʒia] *sf* geology

ge'ometra, i, e [dʒe'ɔmetra] *sm/f* (*professionista*) surveyor

geome'tria [dʒeome'tria] *sf* geometry; **geo'metrico, a, ci, che** *ag* geometric(al)

gerar'chia [dʒerar'kia] *sf* hierarchy

ge'rente [dʒe'rɛnte] *sm/f* manager/ manageress

'gergo, ghi ['dʒɛrgo] *sm* jargon; slang

geria'tria [dʒerja'tria] *sf* geriatrics *sg*

Ger'mania [dʒer'manja] *sf*: **la ~** Germany; **la ~ occidentale/orientale** West/East Germany

'germe ['dʒɛrme] *sm* germ; (*fig*) seed

germogli'are [dʒermoʎ'ʎare] *vi* to sprout; to germinate; **ger'moglio** *sm* shoot; bud

gero'glifico, ci [dʒero'glifiko] *sm* hieroglyphic

'gesso ['dʒɛsso] *sm* chalk; (*SCULTURA, MED, EDIL*) plaster; (*statua*) plaster figure; (*minerale*) gypsum

gesti'one [dʒes'tjone] *sf* management

ges'tire [dʒes'tire] *vt* to run, manage

'gesto ['dʒɛsto] *sm* gesture

ges'tore [dʒes'tore] *sm* manager

Gesù [dʒe'zu] *sm* Jesus

gesu'ita, i [dʒezu'ita] *sm* Jesuit

get'tare [dʒet'tare] *vt* to throw; (*anche*: ~ **via**) to throw away *o* out; (*SCULTURA*) to cast; (*EDIL*) to lay; (*acqua*) to spout; (*grido*) to utter; **~rsi** *vr*: **~rsi in** (*sog: fiume*) to flow into; **~ uno sguardo su** to take a quick look at; **get'tata** *sf* (*di cemento, gesso, metalli*) cast; (*diga*) jetty

'getto ['dʒetto] *sm* (*di gas, liquido, AER*) jet; **a ~ continuo** uninterruptedly; **di ~** (*fig*) straight off, in one go

get'tone [dʒet'tone] *sm* token; (*per giochi*) counter; (: *roulette etc*) chip; **~ telefonico** telephone token

ghiacci'aio [gjat'tʃajo] *sm* glacier

ghiacci'are [gjat'tʃare] *vt* to freeze; (*fig*): **~ qn** to make sb's blood run cold ♦ *vi* to freeze, ice over; **ghiacci'ato, a** *ag* frozen; (*bevanda*) ice-cold

ghi'accio ['gjattʃo] *sm* ice

ghiacci'olo [gjat'tʃɔlo] *sm* icicle; (*tipo di gelato*) ice lolly (*BRIT*), popsicle (*US*)

ghi'aia ['gjaja] *sf* gravel

ghi'anda ['gjanda] *sf* (*BOT*) acorn

ghi'andola ['gjandola] *sf* gland

ghigliot'tina [giʎʎot'tina] *sf* guillotine

ghi'gnare [gin'ɲare] *vi* to sneer

ghi'otto, a ['gjotto] *ag* greedy; (*cibo*) delicious, appetizing; **ghiot'tone, a** *sm/f* glutton

ghiri'goro [giri'gɔro] *sm* scribble, squiggle

ghir'landa [gir'landa] *sf* garland, wreath

'ghiro ['giro] *sm* dormouse

'ghisa ['giza] *sf* cast iron

già [dʒa] *av* already; (*ex, in precedenza*)

formerly ♦ *escl* of course!, yes indeed!

gi'acca, che ['dʒakka] *sf* jacket; **~ a vento** windcheater (*BRIT*), windbreaker (*US*)

giacché [dʒak'ke] *cong* since, as

giac'chetta [dʒak'ketta] *sf* (light) jacket

gia'cenza [dʒa'tʃɛntsa] *sf*: **merce in ~** goods in stock; **~e di magazzino** unsold stock

gia'cere [dʒa'tʃere] *vi* to lie; **giaci'mento** *sm* deposit

gia'cinto [dʒa'tʃinto] *sm* hyacinth

gi'ada ['dʒada] *sf* jade

giaggi'olo [dʒad'dʒɔlo] *sm* iris

giagu'aro [dʒa'gwaro] *sm* jaguar

gi'allo ['dʒallo] *ag* yellow; (*carnagione*) sallow ♦ *sm* yellow; (*anche*: **romanzo ~**) detective novel; (*anche*: **film ~**) detective film; **~ dell'uovo** yolk

giam'mai [dʒam'mai] *av* never

Giap'pone [dʒap'pone] *sm* Japan; **giappo'nese** *ag, sm/f, sm* Japanese *inv*

gi'ara ['dʒara] *sf* jar

giardi'naggio [dʒardi'nadddʒo] *sm* gardening

giardini'era [dʒardi'njera] *sf* (*misto di sottaceti*) mixed pickles *pl*

giardini'ere, a [dʒardi'njere] *sm/f* gardener

giar'dino [dʒar'dino] *sm* garden; **~ d'infanzia** nursery school; **~ pubblico** public gardens *pl*, (public) park; **~ zoologico** zoo

giarretti'era [dʒarret'tjera] *sf* garter

giavel'lotto [dʒavel'lɔtto] *sm* javelin

gi'gante, 'essa [dʒi'gante] *sm/f* giant ♦ *ag* giant, gigantic; (*COMM*) giant-size; **gigan'tesco, a, schi, sche** *ag* gigantic

'giglio ['dʒiʎʎo] *sm* lily

gilè [dʒi'le] *sm inv* waistcoat

gin [dʒin] *sm inv* gin

gine'cologo, a, gi, ghe [dʒine'kɔlogo] *sm/f* gynaecologist

gi'nepro [dʒi'nepro] *sm* juniper

gi'nestra [dʒi'nestra] *sf* (*BOT*) broom

Gi'nevra [dʒi'nevra] *sf* Geneva

gingil'larsi [dʒindʒil'larsi] *vr* to fritter away one's time; (*giocare*): **~ con** to fiddle with

gin'gillo [dʒin'dʒillo] *sm* plaything

gin'nasio [dʒin'nazjo] *sm* the 4th and 5th year of secondary school in Italy

gin'nasta, i, e [dʒin'nasta] *sm/f* gymnast; **gin'nastica** *sf* gymnastics *sg*; (*esercizio fisico*) keep-fit exercises; (*INS*) physical education

gi'nocchio [dʒi'nɔkkjo] (*pl(m)* **gi'nocchi** *o pl(f)* **gi'nocchia**) *sm* knee; **stare in ~** to kneel, be on one's knees; **mettersi in ~** to kneel (down); **ginocchi'oni** *av* on one's knees

gio'care [dʒo'kare] *vt* to play; (*scommettere*) to stake, wager, bet; (*ingannare*) to take in ♦ *vi* to play; (*a roulette etc*) to gamble; (*fig*) to play a part, be important; **~ a** (*gioco, sport*) to play; (*cavalli*) to bet on; **~rsi la carriera** to put one's career at risk; **gioca'tore, 'trice** *sm/f* player; gambler

gio'cattolo [dʒo'kattolo] *sm* toy

gio'chetto [dʒo'ketto] *sm* (*tranello*) trick; (*fig*): **è un ~** it's child's play

gi'oco, chi ['dʒɔko] *sm* game; (*divertimento, TECN*) play; (*al casinò*) gambling; (*CARTE*) hand; (*insieme di pezzi etc necessari per un gioco*) set; **per ~** for fun; **fare il doppio ~ con qn** to double-cross sb; **~ d'azzardo** game of chance; **~ degli scacchi** chess set; **i Giochi Olimpici** the Olympic Games

giocoli'ere [dʒoko'ljere] *sm* juggler

gio'coso, a [dʒo'koso] *ag* playful, jesting

gi'ogo, ghi ['dʒɔgo] *sm* yoke

gi'oia ['dʒɔja] *sf* joy, delight; (*pietra preziosa*) jewel, precious stone

gioielle'ria [dʒojelle'ria] *sf* jeweller's craft; jeweller's (shop)

gioiel'liere, a [dʒojel'ljere] *sm/f* jeweller

gioi'ello [dʒo'jello] *sm* jewel, piece of jewellery; **i miei ~i** my jewels *o* jewellery

gioi'oso, a [dʒo'joso] *ag* joyful

Gior'dania [dʒor'danja] *sf*: **la ~** Jordan

giorna'laio, a [dʒorna'lajo] *sm/f* newsagent (*BRIT*), newsdealer (*US*)

gior'nale [dʒor'nale] *sm* newspaper; (*diario*) journal, diary; (*COMM*) journal; **~ di bordo** log; **~ radio** radio news *sg*

giornali'ero, a [dʒorna'ljero] *ag* daily; (*che varia: umore*) changeable ♦ *sm* day labourer

giorna'lismo [dʒorna'lizmo] *sm* journalism

giorna'lista, i, e [dʒorna'lista] *sm/f* journalist

gior'nata [dʒor'nata] *sf* day; **~ lavorativa** working day

gi'orno ['dʒorno] *sm* day; (*opposto alla notte*) day, daytime; (*luce del ~*) daylight; **al ~** per day; **di ~** by day; **al ~ d'oggi** nowadays

---

giorno dei morti

ⓘ **Il giorno dei Morti**, *All Souls' Day*, *falls on 2 November. On that day, relatives make a special visit to the graves of loved ones, to lay flowers.*

---

gi'ostra ['dʒɔstra] *sf* (*per bimbi*) merry-go-round; (*torneo storico*) joust

gi'ovane ['dʒovane] *ag* young; (*aspetto*) youthful ♦ *sm/f* youth/girl, young man/woman; **i ~i** young people; **giova'nile** *ag* youthful; (*scritti*) early; (*errore*) of youth; **giova'notto** *sm* young man

gio'vare [dʒo'vare] *vi*: **~ a** (*essere utile*) to be useful to; (*far bene*) to be good for ♦ *vb impers* (*essere bene, utile*) to be useful; **~rsi di qc** to make use of sth

giovedì [dʒove'di] *sm inv* Thursday; **di** *o* **il ~** on Thursdays

gioventù [dʒoven'tu] *sf* (*periodo*) youth; (*i giovani*) young people *pl*, youth

giovi'ale [dʒo'vjale] *ag* jovial, jolly

giovi'nezza [dʒovi'nettsa] *sf* youth

gira'dischi [dʒira'diski] *sm inv* record player

gi'raffa [dʒi'raffa] *sf* giraffe

gi'randola [dʒi'randola] *sf* (*fuoco d'artificio*) Catherine wheel; (*giocattolo*) toy windmill; (*banderuola*) weather vane, weathercock

gi'rare [dʒi'rare] *vt* (*far ruotare*) to turn; (*percorrere, visitare*) to go round; (*CINEMA*) to shoot; to make; (*COMM*) to endorse ♦ *vi* to turn; (*più veloce*) to spin; (*andare in giro*) to wander, go around; **~rsi** *vr* to turn; **~**

attorno a to go round; to revolve round; **far ~ la testa a qn** to make sb dizzy; (*fig*) to turn sb's head

girar'rosto [dʒirar'rɔsto] *sm* (*CUC*) spit

gira'sole [dʒira'sole] *sm* sunflower

gi'rata [dʒi'rata] *sf* (*passeggiata*) stroll; (*con veicolo*) drive; (*COMM*) endorsement

gira'volta [dʒira'vɔlta] *sf* twirl, turn; (*curva*) sharp bend; (*fig*) about-turn

gi'revole [dʒi'revole] *ag* revolving, turning

gi'rino [dʒi'rino] *sm* tadpole

'giro ['dʒiro] *sm* (*circuito, cerchio*) circle; (*di chiave, manovella*) turn; (*viaggio*) tour, excursion; (*passeggiata*) stroll, walk; (*in macchina*) drive; (*in bicicletta*) ride; (*SPORT: della pista*) lap; (*di denaro*) circulation; (*CARTE*) hand; (*TECN*) revolution; **prendere in ~ qn** (*fig*) to pull sb's leg; **fare un ~** to go for a walk (*o* a drive *o* a ride); **andare in ~** to go about, walk around; **a stretto ~ di posta** by return of post; **nel ~ di un mese** in a month's time; **essere nel ~** (*fig*) to belong to a circle (of friends); **~ d'affari** (*COMM*) turnover; **~ di parole** circumlocution; **~ di prova** (*AUT*) test drive; **~ turistico** sightseeing tour; **giro'collo** *sm*: **a girocollo** crew-neck *cpd*

gironzo'lare [dʒirondzo'lare] *vi* to stroll about

'gita ['dʒita] *sf* excursion, trip; **fare una ~** to go for a trip, go on an outing

gi'tano, a [dʒi'tano] *sm/f* gipsy

giù [dʒu] *av* down; (*dabbasso*) downstairs; **in ~** downwards, down; **~ di lì** (*pressappoco*) thereabouts; **bambini da 6 anni in ~** children aged 6 and under; **~ per: cadere ~ per le scale** to fall down the stairs; **essere ~** (*fig: di salute*) to be run down; (*: di spirito*) to be depressed

giub'botto [dʒub'bɔtto] *sm* jerkin; **~ antiproiettile** bulletproof vest

gi'ubilo ['dʒubilo] *sm* rejoicing

giudi'care [dʒudi'kare] *vt* to judge; (*accusato*) to try; (*lite*) to arbitrate in; **~ qn/qc bello** to consider sb/sth (to be) beautiful

gi'udice ['dʒuditʃe] *sm* judge; **~**

conciliatore justice of the peace; **~ istruttore** examining (*BRIT*) *o* committing (*US*) magistrate; **~ popolare** member of a jury

giu'dizio [dʒu'dittsjo] *sm* judgment; (*opinione*) opinion; (*DIR*) judgment, sentence; (*: processo*) trial; (*: verdetto*) verdict; **aver ~** to be wise *o* prudent; **citare in ~** to summons; **giudizi'oso, a** *ag* prudent, judicious

gi'ugno ['dʒuɲɲo] *sm* June

giul'lare [dʒul'lare] *sm* jester

giu'menta [dʒu'menta] *sf* mare

gi'unco, chi ['dʒunko] *sm* rush

gi'ungere ['dʒundʒere] *vi* to arrive ♦ *vt* (*mani etc*) to join; **~ a** to arrive at, reach

gi'ungla ['dʒungla] *sf* jungle

gi'unta ['dʒunta] *sf* addition; (*organo esecutivo, amministrativo*) council, board; **per ~** into the bargain, in addition; **~a militare** military junta

gi'unto, a ['dʒunto] *pp di* **giungere** ♦ *sm* (*TECN*) coupling, joint; **giun'tura** *sf* joint

giuo'care [dʒwo'kare] *etc* = **giocare** *etc*

giura'mento [dʒura'mento] *sm* oath; **~ falso** perjury

giu'rare [dʒu'rare] *vt* to swear ♦ *vi* to swear, take an oath; **giu'rato, a** *ag*: **nemico giurato** sworn enemy ♦ *sm/f* juror, juryman/woman

giu'ria [dʒu'ria] *sf* jury

giu'ridico, a, ci, che [dʒu'ridiko] *ag* legal

giustifi'care [dʒustifi'kare] *vt* to justify; **giustificazi'one** *sf* justification; (*INS*) (note of) excuse

gius'tizia [dʒus'tittsja] *sf* justice; **giustizi'are** *vt* to execute, put to death; **giustizi'ere** *sm* executioner

gi'usto, a ['dʒusto] *ag* (*equo*) fair, just; (*vero*) true, correct; (*adatto*) right, suitable; (*preciso*) exact, correct ♦ *av* (*esattamente*) exactly, precisely; (*per l'appunto, appena*) just; **arrivare ~** to arrive just in time; **ho ~ bisogno di te** you're just the person I need

glaci'ale [gla'tʃale] *ag* glacial

gli [ʎi] (*dav V, s impura, gn, pn, ps, x, z*) *det mpl* the ♦ *pron* (*a lui*) to him; (*a esso*) to it; (*in coppia con lo, la, li, le, ne: a lui, a lei, a loro etc*): **gliele do** I'm giving them to him (*o her o them*); *vedi anche* **il**

gli'ela ['ʎela] *etc vedi* **gli**

glo'bale *ag* overall

'globo *sm* globe

'globulo *sm* (ANAT): ~ **rosso/bianco** red/white corpuscle

'gloria *sf* glory; **glori'oso, a** *ag* glorious

glos'sario *sm* glossary

'gnocchi ['ɲɔkki] *smpl* (CUC) small dumplings made of semolina pasta or potato

'gobba *sf* (ANAT) hump; (*protuberanza*) bump

'gobbo, a *ag* hunchbacked; (*ricurvo*) round-shouldered ♦ *sm/f* hunchback

'goccia, ce ['gɔttʃa] *sf* drop; **goccio'lare** *vi*, *vt* to drip

go'dere *vi* (*compiacersi*): ~ (**di**) to be delighted (at), rejoice (at); (*trarre vantaggio*): ~ **di** to enjoy, benefit from ♦ *vt* to enjoy; **~rsi la vita** to enjoy life; **~sela** to have a good time, enjoy o.s.; **godi'mento** *sm* enjoyment

'goffo, a *ag* clumsy, awkward

'gola *sf* (ANAT) throat; (*golosità*) gluttony, greed; (*di camino*) flue; (*di monte*) gorge; **fare ~** (*anche fig*) to tempt

golf *sm inv* (SPORT) golf; (*maglia*) cardigan

'golfo *sm* gulf

go'loso, a *ag* greedy

'gomito *sm* elbow; (*di strada etc*) sharp bend

go'mitolo *sm* ball

'gomma *sf* rubber; (*per cancellare*) rubber, eraser; (*di veicolo*) tyre (BRIT), tire (US); ~ **americana** *o* **da masticare** chewing gum; ~ **a terra** flat tyre (BRIT) *o* tire (US); **gommapi'uma** ® *sf* foam rubber; **gom'mone** *sm* rubber dinghy

'gondola *sf* gondola; **gondoli'ere** *sm* gondolier

gonfa'lone *sm* banner

gonfi'are *vt* (*pallone*) to blow up, inflate; (*dilatare, ingrossare*) to swell; (*fig: notizia*) to exaggerate; **~rsi** *vr* to swell; (*fiume*) to rise; **'gonfio, a** *ag* swollen; (*stomaco*) bloated; (*vela*) full; **gonfi'ore** *sm* swelling

gongo'lare *vi* to look pleased with o.s.; ~ **di gioia** to be overjoyed

'gonna *sf* skirt; ~ **pantalone** culottes *pl*

'gonzo ['gondzo] *sm* simpleton, fool

gorgheggi'are [gorged'dʒare] *vi* to warble; to trill

'gorgo, ghi *sm* whirlpool

gorgogli'are [gorgoʎ'ʎare] *vi* to gurgle

go'rilla *sm inv* gorilla; (*guardia del corpo*) bodyguard

'gotta *sf* gout

gover'nante *sm/f* ruler ♦ *sf* (*di bambini*) governess; (*donna di servizio*) housekeeper

gover'nare *vt* (*stato*) to govern, rule; (*pilotare, guidare*) to steer; (*bestiame*) to tend, look after; **governa'tivo, a** *ag* government *cpd*; **governa'tore** *sm* governor

go'verno *sm* government

gozzovigli'are [gottsoviʎ'ʎare] *vi* to make merry, carouse

gracchi'are [grak'kjare] *vi* to caw

graci'dare [gratʃi'dare] *vi* to croak

'gracile ['gratʃile] *ag* frail, delicate

gra'dasso *sm* boaster

gradazi'one [gradat'tsjone] *sf* (*sfumatura*) gradation; ~ **alcolica** alcoholic content, strength

gra'devole *ag* pleasant, agreeable

gradi'mento *sm* pleasure, satisfaction; **è di suo ~?** is it to your liking?

gradi'nata *sf* flight of steps; (*in teatro, stadio*) tiers *pl*

gra'dino *sm* step; (ALPINISMO) foothold

gra'dire *vt* (*accettare con piacere*) to accept; (*desiderare*) to wish, like; **gradisce una tazza di tè?** would you like a cup of tea?; **gra'dito, a** *ag* pleasing; welcome

'grado *sm* (MAT, FISICA *etc*) degree; (*stadio*) degree, level; (MIL, *sociale*) rank; **essere in ~ di fare** to be in a position to do

gradu'ale *ag* gradual

gradu'are *vt* to grade; **gradu'ato, a** *ag* (*esercizi*) graded; (*scala, termometro*) graduated ♦ *sm* (MIL) non-commissioned officer

'graffa *sf* (*gancio*) clip; (*segno grafico*) brace

graffi'are *vt* to scratch

'graffio *sm* scratch

gra'fia *sf* spelling; (*scrittura*) handwriting

'grafica *sf* graphic arts *pl*

'grafico, a, ci, che *ag* graphic ♦ *sm* graph; (*persona*) graphic designer

gra'migna [gra'miɲɲa] *sf* weed; couch grass

gram'matica, che *sf* grammar; **grammati'cale** *ag* grammatical

'grammo *sm* gram(me)

gran *ag vedi* **grande**

'grana *sf* (*granello, di minerali, corpi spezzati*) grain; (*fam: seccatura*) trouble; (*: soldi*) cash ♦ *sm inv* Parmesan (cheese)

gra'naio *sm* granary, barn

gra'nata *sf* (*proiettile*) grenade

Gran Bre'tagna [-bre'taɲɲa] *sf*: **la ~** Great Britain

'granchio ['grankjo] *sm* crab; (*fig*) blunder; **prendere un ~** (*fig*) to blunder

grandango'lare *sm* wide-angle lens *sg*

'grande (*qualche volta* **gran** +*C*, **grand'** +*V*) *ag* (*grosso, largo, vasto*) big, large; (*alto*) tall; (*lungo*) long; (*in sensi astratti*) great ♦ *sm/f* (*persona adulta*) adult, grown-up; (*chi ha ingegno e potenza*) great man/ woman; **fare le cose in ~** to do things in style; **una gran bella donna** a very beautiful woman; **non è una gran cosa** *o* **un gran che** it's nothing special; **non ne so gran che** I don't know very much about it

grandeggi'are [grandeds'dʒare] *vi* (*emergere per grandezza*): **~ su** to tower over; (*darsi arie*) to put on airs

gran'dezza [gran'dettsa] *sf* (*dimensione*) size; magnitude; (*fig*) greatness; **in ~ naturale** lifesize

grandi'nare *vb impers* to hail

'grandine *sf* hail

gran'duca, chi *sm* grand duke

gra'nello *sm* (*di cereali, uva*) seed; (*di frutta*) pip; (*di sabbia, sale etc*) grain

gra'nita *sf* kind of water ice

gra'nito *sm* granite

'grano *sm* (*in quasi tutti i sensi*) grain; (*frumento*) wheat; (*di rosario, collana*) bead; **~ di pepe** peppercorn

gran'turco *sm* maize

'grappa *sf* rough, strong brandy

'grappolo *sm* bunch, cluster

gras'setto, che *sm* (*TIP*) bold (type)

'grasso, a *ag* fat; (*cibo*) fatty; (*pelle*) greasy; (*terreno*) rich; (*fig: guadagno, annata*) plentiful ♦ *sm* (*di persona, animale*) fat; (*sostanza che unge*) grease; **gras'soccio, a, ci, ce** *ag* plump

'grata *sf* grating

gra'ticola *sf* grill

gra'tifica, che *sf* bonus

'gratis *av* free, for nothing

grati'tudine *sf* gratitude

'grato, a *ag* grateful; (*gradito*) pleasant, agreeable

gratta'capo *sm* worry, headache

grattaci'elo [gratta'tʃɛlo] *sm* skyscraper

grat'tare *vt* (*pelle*) to scratch; (*raschiare*) to scrape; (*pane, formaggio, carote*) to grate; (*fam: rubare*) to pinch ♦ *vi* (*stridere*) to grate; (*AUT*) to grind; **~rsi** *vr* to scratch o.s.; **gratta e vinci** ≈ scratch card

grat'tugia, gie [grat'tudʒa] *sf* grater; **grattugi'are** *vt* to grate; **pane grattugiato** breadcrumbs *pl*

gra'tuito, a *ag* free; (*fig*) gratuitous

gra'vare *vt* to burden ♦ *vi*: **~ su** to weigh on

'grave *ag* (*danno, pericolo, peccato etc*) grave, serious; (*responsabilità*) heavy, grave; (*contegno*) grave, solemn; (*voce, suono*) deep, low-pitched; (*LING*): **accento ~** grave accent; **un malato ~** a person who is seriously ill

gravi'danza [gravi'dantsa] *sf* pregnancy

'gravido, a *ag* pregnant

gravità *sf* seriousness; (*anche FISICA*) gravity

gra'voso, a *ag* heavy, onerous

'grazia ['grattsja] *sf* grace; (*favore*) favour; (*DIR*) pardon; **grazi'are** *vt* (*DIR*) to pardon

'grazie ['grattsje] *escl* thank you!; **~ mille!** *o* **tante!** *o* **infinite!** thank you very much!; **~**

a thanks to

grazi'oso, a [grat'tsjoso] *ag* charming, delightful; (*gentile*) gracious

'Grecia ['grɛtʃa] *sf*: **la ~** Greece; **'greco, a, ci, che** *ag, sm/f, sm* Greek

'gregge ['greddʒe] (*pl(f)* **-i**) *sm* flock

'greggio, gi ['greddʒo] *sm* (*anche*: **petrolio ~**) crude (oil)

grembi'ule *sm* apron; (*sopravveste*) overall

'grembo *sm* lap; (*ventre della madre*) womb

gre'mito, a *ag*: **~ (di)** packed *o* crowded (with)

'gretto, a *ag* mean, stingy; (*fig*) narrow-minded

'greve *ag* heavy

'grezzo, a ['greddzo] *ag* raw, unrefined; (*diamante*) rough, uncut; (*tessuto*) unbleached

gri'dare *vi* (*per chiamare*) to shout, cry (out); (*strillare*) to scream, yell ♦ *vt* to shout (out), yell (out); **~ aiuto** to cry *o* shout for help

'grido (*pl(m)* **-i** *o pl(f)* **-a**) *sm* shout, cry; scream, yell; (*di animale*) cry; **di ~** famous

'grigio, a, gi, gie ['gridʒo] *ag, sm* grey

'griglia ['griʎʎa] *sf* (*per arrostire*) grill; (*ELETTR*) grid; (*inferriata*) grating; **alla ~** (*CUC*) grilled; **grigli'ata** *sf* (*CUC*) grill

gril'letto *sm* trigger

'grillo *sm* (*ZOOL*) cricket; (*fig*) whim

grimal'dello *sm* picklock

'grinta *sf* grim expression; (*SPORT*) fighting spirit

'grinza ['grintsa] *sf* crease, wrinkle; (*ruga*) wrinkle; **non fare una ~** (*fig: ragionamento*) to be faultless; **grin'zoso, a** *ag* creased; wrinkled

gris'sino *sm* bread-stick

'gronda *sf* eaves *pl*

gron'daia *sf* gutter

gron'dare *vi* to pour; (*essere bagnato*): **~ di** to be dripping with ♦ *vt* to drip with

'groppa *sf* (*di animale*) back, rump; (*fam: dell'uomo*) back, shoulders *pl*

'groppo *sm* tangle; **avere un ~ alla gola** (*fig*) to have a lump in one's throat

gros'sezza [gros'settsa] *sf* size; thickness

gros'sista, i, e *sm/f* (*COMM*) wholesaler

'grosso, a *ag* big, large; (*di spessore*) thick; (*grossolano: anche fig*) coarse; (*grave, insopportabile*) serious, great; (*tempo, mare*) rough ♦ *sm*: **il ~ di** the bulk of; **un pezzo ~** (*fig*) a VIP, a bigwig; **farla ~a** to do something very stupid; **dirle ~e** to tell tall stories; **sbagliarsi di ~** to be completely wrong

grosso'lano, a *ag* rough, coarse; (*fig*) coarse, crude; (*: errore*) stupid

grosso'modo *av* roughly

'grotta *sf* cave; grotto

grot'tesco, a, schi, sche *ag* grotesque

grovi'era *sm o f* gruyère (cheese)

gro'viglio [gro'viʎʎo] *sm* tangle; (*fig*) muddle

gru *sf inv* crane

'gruccia, ce ['gruttʃa] *sf* (*per camminare*) crutch; (*per abiti*) coat-hanger

gru'gnire [gruɲ'ɲire] *vi* to grunt; **gru'gnito** *sm* grunt

'grugno ['gruɲɲo] *sm* snout; (*fam: faccia*) mug

'grullo, a *ag* silly, stupid

'grumo *sm* (*di sangue*) clot; (*di farina etc*) lump

'gruppo *sm* group; **~ sanguigno** blood group

gruvi'era *sm o f* = **groviera**

guada'gnare [gwadaɲ'ɲare] *vt* (*ottenere*) to gain; (*soldi, stipendio*) to earn; (*vincere*) to win; (*raggiungere*) to reach

gua'dagno [gwa'daɲɲo] *sm* earnings *pl*; (*COMM*) profit; (*vantaggio, utile*) advantage, gain; **~ lordo/netto** gross/net earnings *pl*

'guado *sm* ford; **passare a ~** to ford

gu'ai *escl*: **~ a te** (*o lui etc*)**!** woe betide you (*o him etc*)!

gua'ina *sf* (*fodero*) sheath; (*indumento per donna*) girdle

gu'aio *sm* trouble, mishap; (*inconveniente*) trouble, snag

gua'ire *vi* to whine, yelp

gu'ancia, ce ['gwantʃa] *sf* cheek

guanci'ale [gwan'tʃale] *sm* pillow

gu'anto *sm* glove

gu'arda... *prefisso*: ~'**boschi** *sm inv*
forester; ~'**caccia** *sm inv* gamekeeper;
~'**coste** *sm inv* coastguard; *(nave)*
coastguard patrol vessel; ~'**linee** *sm inv*
(SPORT) linesman

guar'dare *vt (con lo sguardo: osservare)* to
look at; *(film, televisione)* to watch;
(custodire) to look after, take care of ♦ *vi* to
look; *(badare)*: ~ **a** to pay attention to;
(luoghi: esser orientato): ~ **a** to face; ~**rsi** *vr*
to look at o.s.; ~**rsi da** *(astenersi)* to refrain
from; *(stare in guardia)* to beware of; ~**rsi
dal fare** to take care not to do; **guarda di
non sbagliare** try not to make a mistake; ~
a vista qn to keep a close watch on sb

guarda'roba *sm inv* wardrobe; *(locale)*
cloakroom; **guardarobi'ere, a** *sm/f*
cloakroom attendant

gu'ardia *sf (individuo, corpo)* guard;
(sorveglianza) watch; **fare la ~ a qc/qn** to
guard sth/sb; **stare in ~** *(fig)* to be on
one's guard; **di ~** *(medico)* on call; ~
carceraria *(prison)* warder; ~ **del corpo**
bodyguard; ~ **di finanza** *(corpo)* customs
pl; *(persona)* customs officer; ~ **medica**
emergency doctor service

Guardia di finanza

ⓘ The **Guardia di finanza** *is a military
body which deals with infringements of
the laws relating to income tax and
monopolies. It reports to the Ministers of
Finance, Justice or Agriculture.*

---

guardi'ano, a *sm/f (di carcere)* warder;
(di villa etc) caretaker; *(di museo)*
custodian; *(di zoo)* keeper; ~ **notturno**
night watchman

guar'dingo, a, ghi, ghe *ag* wary,
cautious

guardi'ola *sf* porter's lodge; *(MIL)* look-out
tower

guard'rail ['ga:dreil] *sm inv* crash barrier

guarigi'one [gwari'dʒone] *sf* recovery

gua'rire *vt (persona, malattia)* to cure;
(ferita) to heal ♦ *vi* to recover, be cured; to

heal (up)

guarnigi'one [gwarni'dʒone] *sf* garrison

guar'nire *vt (ornare: abiti)* to trim; *(CUC)* to
garnish; **guarnizi'one** *sf* trimming;
garnish; *(TECN)* gasket

guasta'feste *sm/f inv* spoilsport

guas'tare *vt* to spoil, ruin; *(meccanismo)* to
break; ~**rsi** *vr (cibo)* to go bad;
(meccanismo) to break down; *(tempo)* to
change for the worse

gu'asto, a *ag (non funzionante)* broken;
(: telefono etc) out of order; *(andato a
male)* bad, rotten; *(: dente)* decayed, bad;
(fig: corrotto) depraved ♦ *sm* breakdown;
(avaria) failure; ~ **al motore** engine failure

gu'ercio, a, ci, ce ['gwertʃo] *ag* cross-
eyed

gu'erra *sf* war; *(tecnica: atomica, chimica
etc)* warfare; **fare la ~ (a)** to wage war
(against); ~ **mondiale** world war;
guerri'ero, a *ag* warlike ♦ *sm* warrior;
guer'riglia *sf* guerrilla warfare;
guerrigli'ero *sm* guerrilla

'gufo *sm* owl

gu'ida *sf* guidebook; *(comando, direzione)*
guidance, direction; *(AUT)* driving; *(tappeto,
di tenda, cassetto)* runner; ~ **a destra/
sinistra** *(AUT)* right-/left-hand drive; ~
telefonica telephone directory; ~ **turistica**
tourist guide

gui'dare *vt* to guide; *(squadra, rivolta)* to
lead; *(auto)* to drive; *(aereo, nave)* to pilot;
sai ~? can you drive?; **guida'tore, trice**
sm/f (conducente) driver

guin'zaglio [gwin'tsaʎʎo] *sm* leash, lead

gu'isa *sf*: **a ~ di** like, in the manner of

guiz'zare [gwit'tsare] *vi* to dart; to flicker;
to leap

'guscio ['guʃʃo] *sm* shell

gus'tare *vt (cibi)* to taste; *(: assaporare con
piacere)* to enjoy, savour; *(fig)* to enjoy,
appreciate ♦ *vi*: ~ **a** to please; **non mi
gusta affatto** I don't like it at all

'gusto *sm* taste; *(sapore)* flavour;
(godimento) enjoyment; **al ~ di fragola**
strawberry-flavoured; **mangiare di ~** to eat
heartily; **prenderci ~: ci ha preso ~** he's

acquired a taste for it, he's got to like it;
gus'toso, a *ag* tasty; *(fig)* agreeable

H, h

h *abbr* = **ora; altezza**
ha *etc* [a] *vb vedi* **avere**
ha'cker [hæ'kə*] *sm inv* hacker
hall [hɔl] *sf inv* hall, foyer
'handicap ['handikap] *sm inv* handicap;
handicap'pato, a *ag* handicapped
◆ *sm/f* handicapped person, disabled
person
'hanno ['anno] *vb vedi* **avere**
'hascisc ['haʃiʃ] *sm* hashish
'herpes ['ɛrpes] *sm* (*MED*) herpes *sg*; ~
zoster shingles *sg*
ho [ɔ] *vb vedi* **avere**
'hobby ['hɔbi] *sm inv* hobby
'hockey ['hɔki] *sm* hockey; ~ **su ghiaccio**
ice hockey
'hostess ['houstis] *sf inv* air hostess (*BRIT*) o
stewardess
ho'tel *sm inv* hotel

I, i

i *det mpl* the
i'ato *sm* hiatus
ibernazi'one [ibernat'tsjone] *sf* hibernation
'ibrido, a *ag, sm* hybrid
Id'dio *sm* God
i'dea *sf* idea; (*opinione*) opinion, view;
(*ideale*) ideal; **dare l'~ di** to seem, look like;
~ **fissa** obsession; **neanche** o **neppure per**
~! certainly not!
ide'ale *ag, sm* ideal
ide'are *vt* (*immaginare*) to think up,
conceive; (*progettare*) to plan
i'dentico, a, ci, che *ag* identical
identifi'care *vt* to identify;
identificazi'one *sf* identification
identità *sf inv* identity
ideolo'gia, 'gie [ideolo'dʒia] *sf* ideology
idi'oma, i *sm* idiom, language;

idio'matico, a, ci, che *ag* idiomatic;
frase idiomatica idiom
idi'ota, i, e *ag* idiotic ◆ *sm/f* idiot
idola'trare *vt* to worship; (*fig*) to idolize
'idolo *sm* idol
idoneità *sf* suitability
i'doneo, a *ag*: ~ **a** suitable for, fit for; (*MIL*)
fit for; (*qualificato*) qualified for
i'drante *sm* hydrant
idra'tante *ag* moisturizing ◆ *sm*
moisturizer
i'draulica *sf* hydraulics *sg*
i'draulico, a, ci, che *ag* hydraulic ◆ *sm*
plumber
idroe'lettrico, a, ci, che *ag*
hydroelectric
i'drofilo, a *ag vedi* **cotone**
i'drogeno [i'drɔdʒeno] *sm* hydrogen
idros'calo *sm* seaplane base
idrovo'lante *sm* seaplane
i'ena *sf* hyena
i'eri *av, sm* yesterday; **il giornale di** ~
yesterday's paper; ~ **l'altro** the day before
yesterday; ~ **sera** yesterday evening
igi'ene [i'dʒene] *sf* hygiene; ~ **pubblica**
public health; **igi'enico, a, ci, che** *ag*
hygienic; (*salubre*) healthy
i'gnaro, a [iɲ'ɲaro] *ag*: ~ **di** unaware of,
ignorant of
i'gnobile [iɲ'ɲɔbile] *ag* despicable, vile
igno'rante [iɲɲo'rante] *ag* ignorant
igno'rare [iɲɲo'rare] *vt* (*non sapere,
conoscere*) to be ignorant o unaware of, not
to know; (*fingere di non vedere, sentire*) to
ignore
i'gnoto, a [iɲ'ɲɔto] *ag* unknown

PAROLA CHIAVE
---

il (*pl (m)* **i**; *diventa* **lo** (*pl* **gli**) *davanti a s
impura, gn, pn, ps, x, z;* f **la** (*pl* **le**) *det m*
1 the; ~ **libro/lo studente/l'acqua** the
book/the student/the water; **gli scolari** the
pupils
2 (*astrazione*): ~ **coraggio/l'amore/la
giovinezza** courage/love/youth
3 (*tempo*): ~ **mattino/la sera** in the
morning/evening; ~ **venerdì** *etc*

(*abitualmente*) on Fridays *etc*; (*quel giorno*) on (the) Friday *etc*; **la settimana prossima** next week

4 (*distributivo*) a, an; **2.500 lire ~ chilo/ paio** 2,500 lire a *o* per kilo/pair

5 (*partitivo*) some, any; **hai messo lo zucchero?** have you added sugar?; **hai comprato ~ latte?** did you buy (some *o* any) milk?

6 (*possesso*): **aprire gli occhi** to open one's eyes; **rompersi la gamba** to break one's leg; **avere i capelli neri/~ naso rosso** to have dark hair/a red nose

7 (*con nomi propri*): **~ Petrarca** Petrarch; **~ Presidente Clinton** President Clinton; **dov'è la Francesca?** where's Francesca?

8 (*con nomi geografici*): **~ Tevere** the Tiber; **l'Italia** Italy; **~ Regno Unito** the United Kingdom; **l'Everest** Everest

'ilare *ag* cheerful; **ilarità** *sf* hilarity, mirth

illazi'one [illat'tsjone] *sf* inference, deduction

ille'gale *ag* illegal

illeg'gibile [illed'dʒibile] *ag* illegible

ille'gittimo, a [ille'dʒittimo] *ag* illegitimate

il'leso, a *ag* unhurt, unharmed

illi'bato, a *ag*: **donna ~a** virgin

illimi'tato, a *ag* boundless; unlimited

ill.mo *abbr* = **illustrissimo**

il'ludere *vt* to deceive, delude; **~rsi** *vr* to deceive o.s., delude o.s.

illumi'nare *vt* to light up, illuminate; (*fig*) to enlighten; **~rsi** *vr* to light up; **~ a giorno** to floodlight; **illuminazi'one** *sf* lighting; illumination; floodlighting; (*fig*) flash of inspiration

illusi'one *sf* illusion; **farsi delle ~i** to delude o.s.

illusio'nismo *sm* conjuring

il'luso, a *pp di* **illudere**

illus'trare *vt* to illustrate; **illustra'tivo, a** *ag* illustrative; **illustrazi'one** *sf* illustration

il'lustre *ag* eminent, renowned; **illus'trissimo, a** *ag* (*negli indirizzi*) very revered

imbacuc'care *vt* to wrap up; **~rsi** *vr* to

wrap up

imbal'laggio [imbal'laddʒo] *sm* packing *no pl*

imbal'lare *vt* to pack; (*AUT*) to race; **~rsi** *vr* (*AUT*) to race

imbalsa'mare *vt* to embalm

imbambo'lato, a *ag* (*sguardo*) vacant, blank

imban'dire *vt*: **~ un pranzo** to prepare a lavish meal

imbaraz'zare [imbarat'tsare] *vt* (*mettere a disagio*) to embarrass; (*ostacolare: movimenti*) to hamper

imba'razzo [imba'rattso] *sm* (*disagio*) embarrassment; (*perplessità*) puzzlement, bewilderment; **~ di stomaco** indigestion

imbarca'dero *sm* landing stage

imbar'care *vt* (*passeggeri*) to embark; (*merci*) to load; **~rsi** *vr*: **~rsi su** to board; **~rsi per l'America** to sail for America; **~rsi in** (*fig: affare etc*) to embark on

imbaroazi'one [imbarkat'tsjone] *sf* (*small*) boat, (small) craft *inv*; **~ di salvataggio** lifeboat

im'barco, chi *sm* embarkation; loading; boarding; (*banchina*) landing stage

imbas'tire *vt* (*cucire*) to tack; (*fig: abbozzare*) to sketch, outline

im'battersi *vr*: **~ in** (*incontrare*) to bump *o* run into

imbat'tibile *ag* unbeatable, invincible

imbavagli'are [imbavaʎ'ʎare] *vt* to gag

imbec'cata *sf* (*TEATRO*) prompt

imbe'cille [imbe'tʃille] *ag* idiotic ♦ *sm/f* idiot; (*MED*) imbecile

imbel'lire *vt* to adorn, embellish ♦ *vi* to grow more beautiful

im'berbe *ag* beardless

im'bevere *vt* to soak; **~rsi** *vr*: **~rsi di** to soak up, absorb

imbian'care *vt* to whiten; (*muro*) to whitewash ♦ *vi* to become *o* turn white

imbian'chino [imbjan'kino] *sm* (house) painter, painter and decorator

imboc'care *vt* (*bambino*) to feed; (*entrare: strada*) to enter, turn into

imbocca'tura *sf* mouth; (*di strada, porto*)

entrance; (MUS, del morso) mouthpiece
im'bocco, chi sm entrance
imbos'care vt to hide; ~rsi vr (MIL) to evade military service
imbos'cata sf ambush
imbottigli'are [imbottiʎ'ʎare] vt to bottle; (NAUT) to blockade; (MIL) to hem in; ~rsi vr to be stuck in a traffic jam
imbot'tire vt to stuff; (giacca) to pad; imbot'tita sf quilt; imbot'tito, a ag stuffed; (giacca) padded; panino imbottito filled roll; imbotti'tura sf stuffing; padding
imbrat'tare vt to dirty, smear, daub
imbrigli'are [imbriʎ'ʎare] vt to bridle
imbroc'care vt (fig) to guess correctly
imbrogli'are [imbroʎ'ʎare] vt to mix up; (fig: raggirare) to deceive, cheat; (: confondere) to confuse, mix up; ~rsi vr to get tangled; (fig) to become confused; im'broglio sm (groviglio) tangle; (situazione confusa) mess; (truffa) swindle, trick; imbrogli'one, a sm/f cheat, swindler
imbronci'ato, a ag sulky
imbru'nire vi, vb impers to grow dark; all'~ at dusk
imbrut'tire vt to make ugly ♦ vi to become ugly
imbu'care vt to post
imbur'rare vt to butter
im'buto sm funnel
imi'tare vt to imitate; (riprodurre) to copy; (assomigliare) to look like; imitazi'one sf imitation
immaco'lato, a ag spotless; immaculate
immagazzi'nare [immagaddzi'nare] vt to store
immagi'nare [immadʒi'nare] vt to imagine; (supporre) to suppose; (inventare) to invent; s'immagini! don't mention it!, not at all!; immagi'nario, a ag imaginary; immaginazi'one sf imagination; (cosa immaginata) fancy
im'magine [im'madʒine] sf image; (rappresentazione grafica, mentale) picture
imman'cabile ag certain; unfailing

im'mane ag (smisurato) enormous; (spaventoso) terrible
immangi'abile [imman'dʒabile] ag inedible
immatrico'lare vt to register; ~rsi vr (INS) to matriculate, enrol; immatricolazi'one sf registration; matriculation, enrolment
imma'turo, a ag (frutto) unripe; (persona) immature; (prematuro) premature
immedesi'marsi vr: ~ in to identify with
immedi'ato, a ag immediate
immediata'mente av immediately, at once
im'memore ag: ~ di forgetful of
im'menso, a ag immense
im'mergere [im'merdʒere] vt to immerse, plunge; ~rsi vr to plunge; (sommergibile) to dive, submerge; (dedicarsi a): ~rsi in to immerse o.s. in
immeri'tato, a ag undeserved
immeri'tevole ag undeserving, unworthy
immersi'one sf immersion; (di sommergibile) submersion, dive; (di palombaro) dive
im'merso, a pp di immergere
im'mettere vt: ~ (in) to introduce (into); ~ dati in un computer to enter data on a computer
immi'grato, a sm/f immigrant; immigrazi'one sf immigration
immi'nente ag imminent
immischi'are [immis'kjare] vt: ~ qn in to involve sb in; ~rsi in to interfere o meddle in
immissi'one sf (di aria, gas) intake; ~ di dati (INFORM) data entry
im'mobile ag motionless, still; ~i smpl (anche: beni ~i) real estate sg; immobili'are ag (DIR) property cpd; immobilità sf stillness; immobility
immo'desto, a ag immodest
immo'lare vt to sacrifice, immolate
immon'dizia [immon'dittsja] sf dirt, filth; (spesso al pl: spazzatura, rifiuti) rubbish no pl, refuse no pl
im'mondo, a ag filthy, foul
immo'rale ag immoral
immor'tale ag immortal

im'mune *ag* (*esente*) exempt; (*MED, DIR*) immune; **immunità** *sf* immunity; **immunità parlamentare** parliamentary privilege

immu'tabile *ag* immutable; unchanging

impacchet'tare [impakket'tare] *vt* to pack up

impacci'are [impat'tʃare] *vt* to hinder, hamper; **impacci'ato, a** *ag* awkward, clumsy; (*imbarazzato*) embarrassed; **im'paccio** *sm* obstacle; (*imbarazzo*) embarrassment; (*situazione imbarazzante*) awkward situation

im'pacco, chi *sm* (*MED*) compress

impadro'nirsi *vr*: ~ **di** to seize, take possession of; (*fig: apprendere a fondo*) to master

impa'gabile *ag* priceless

impagi'nare [impadʒi'nare] *vt* (*TIP*) to paginate, page (up)

impagli'are [impaʎ'ʎare] *vt* to stuff (with straw)

impa'lato, a *ag* (*fig*) stiff as a board

impalca'tura *sf* scaffolding

impalli'dire *vi* to turn pale; (*fig*) to fade

impa'nare *vt* (*CUC*) to dip in breadcrumbs

impanta'narsi *vr* to sink (in the mud); (*fig*) to get bogged down

impappi'narsi *vr* to stammer, falter

impa'rare *vt* to learn

imparen'tarsi *vr*: ~ **con** to marry into

'impari *ag* *inv* (*disuguale*) unequal; (*dispari*) odd

impar'tire *vt* to bestow, give

imparzi'ale [impar'tsjale] *ag* impartial, unbiased

impas'sibile *ag* impassive

impas'tare *vt* (*pasta*) to knead

im'pasto *sm* (*l'impastare: di pane*) kneading; (: *di cemento*) mixing; (*pasta*) dough; (*anche fig*) mixture

im'patto *sm* impact

impau'rire *vt* to scare, frighten ♦ *vi* (*anche: ~rsi*) to become scared *o* frightened

im'pavido, a *ag* intrepid, fearless

impazi'ente [impat'tsjente] *ag* impatient; **impazi'enza** *sf* impatience

impaz'zata [impat'tsata] *sf*: **all'~** (*precipitosamente*) at breakneck speed

impaz'zire [impat'tsire] *vi* to go mad; ~ **per qn/qc** to be crazy about sb/sth

impec'cabile *ag* impeccable

impedi'mento *sm* obstacle, hindrance

impe'dire *vt* (*vietare*): ~ **a qn di fare** to prevent sb from doing; (*ostruire*) to obstruct; (*impacciare*) to hamper, hinder

impe'gnare [impeɲ'ɲare] *vt* (*dare in pegno*) to pawn; (*onore etc*) to pledge; (*prenotare*) to book, reserve; (*obbligare*) to oblige; (*occupare*) to keep busy; (*MIL: nemico*) to engage; ~**rsi** *vr* (*vincolarsi*): ~**rsi a fare** to undertake to do; (*mettersi risolutamente*): ~**rsi in qc** to devote o.s. to sth; ~**rsi con qn** (*accordarsi*) to come to an agreement with sb; **impe'gnativo, a** *ag* binding; (*lavoro*) demanding, exacting; **impe'gnato, a** *ag* (*occupato*) busy; (*fig: romanzo, autore*) committed, engagé

im'pegno *sm* (*obbligo*) obligation; (*promessa*) promise, pledge; (*zelo*) diligence, zeal; (*compito, d'autore*) commitment

impel'lente *ag* pressing, urgent

impene'trabile *ag* impenetrable

impen'narsi *vr* (*cavallo*) to rear up; (*AER*) to nose up; (*fig*) to bridle

impen'sato, a *ag* unforeseen, unexpected

impensie'rire *vt* to worry; ~**rsi** *vi* to worry

impe'rare *vi* (*anche fig*) to reign, rule

impera'tivo, a *ag*, *sm* imperative

impera'tore, 'trice *sm/f* emperor/ empress

imperdo'nabile *ag* unforgivable, unpardonable

imper'fetto, a *ag* imperfect ♦ *sm* (*LING*) imperfect (tense); **imperfezi'one** *sf* imperfection

imperi'ale *ag* imperial

imperi'oso, a *ag* (*persona*) imperious; (*motivo, esigenza*) urgent, pressing

impe'rizia [impe'rittsja] *sf* lack of experience

imperma'lirsi *vr* to take offence

imperme'abile *ag* waterproof ♦ *sm* raincoat

imperni'are *vt*: ~ qc su to hinge sth on; *(fig)* to base sth on; ~**rsi** *vr (fig)*: ~**rsi su** to be based on

im'pero *sm* empire; *(forza, autorità)* rule, control

imperscru'tabile *ag* inscrutable

imperso'nale *ag* impersonal

imperso'nare *vt* to personify; *(TEATRO)* to play, act (the part of)

imperter'rito, a *ag* fearless, undaunted; impassive

imperti'nente *ag* impertinent

imperver'sare *vi* to rage

'impeto *sm (moto, forza)* force, impetus; *(assalto)* onslaught; *(fig: impulso)* impulse; *(: slancio)* transport; **con ~** energetically, vehemently

impet'tito, a *ag* stiff, erect

impetu'oso, a *ag (vento)* strong, raging; *(persona)* impetuous

impian'tare *vt (motore)* to install; *(azienda, discussione)* to establish, start

impi'anto *sm (installazione)* installation; *(apparecchiature)* plant; *(sistema)* system; ~ **elettrico** wiring; ~ **sportivo** sports complex; ~**i di risalita** *(SCI)* ski lifts

impiastricci'are [impjastrit'tʃare] *vt* = **impiastrare**

impi'astro *sm* poultice

impic'care *vt* to hang; ~**rsi** *vr* to hang o.s.

impicci'are [impit'tʃare] *vt* to hinder, hamper; ~**rsi** *vr* to meddle, interfere; **im'piccio** *sm (ostacolo)* hindrance; *(seccatura)* trouble, bother; *(affare imbrogliato)* mess; **essere d'impiccio** to be in the way

impie'gare *vt (usare)* to use, employ; *(spendere: denaro, tempo)* to spend; *(investire)* to invest; **impie'gato, a** *sm/f* employee

impi'ego, ghi *sm (uso)* use; *(occupazione)* employment; *(posto di lavoro)* (regular) job, post; *(ECON)* investment

impieto'sire *vt* to move to pity; ~**rsi** *vr* to be moved to pity

impie'trire *vt (fig)* to petrify

impigli'are [impiʎ'ʎare] *vt* to catch, entangle; ~**rsi** *vr* to get caught up *o* entangled

impi'grire *vt* to make lazy ♦ *vi (anche:* ~**rsi)** to grow lazy

impli'care *vt* to imply; *(coinvolgere)* to involve; **implicazi'one** *sf* implication

im'plicito, a [im'plitʃito] *ag* implicit

implo'rare *vt* to implore; *(pietà etc)* to beg for

impolve'rare *vt* to cover with dust; ~**rsi** *vr* to get dusty

impo'nente *ag* imposing, impressive

impo'nibile *ag* taxable ♦ *sm* taxable income

impopo'lare *ag* unpopular

im'porre *vt* to impose; *(costringere)* to force, make; *(far valere)* to impose, enforce; **imporsi** *vr (persona)* to assert o.s.; *(cosa: rendersi necessario)* to become necessary; *(aver successo: moda, attore)* to become popular; ~ **a qn di fare** to force sb to do, make sb do

impor'tante *ag* important; **impor'tanza** *sf* importance; **dare importanza a qc** to attach importance to sth; **darsi importanza** to give o.s. airs

impor'tare *vt (introdurre dall'estero)* to import ♦ *vi* to matter, be important ♦ *vb impers (essere necessario)* to be necessary; *(interessare)* to matter; **non importa!** it doesn't matter!; **non me ne importa!** I don't care!; **importazi'one** *sf* importation; *(merci importate)* imports *pl*

im'porto *sm (total)* amount

importu'nare *vt* to bother

impor'tuno, a *ag* irksome, annoying

imposizi'one [impozit'tsjone] *sf* imposition; order, command; *(onere, imposta)* tax

imposses'sarsi *vr*: ~ **di** to seize, take possession of

impos'sibile *ag* impossible; **fare l'~** to do one's utmost, do all one can; **impossibilità** *sf* impossibility; **essere nell'impossibilità di fare qc** to be unable to do sth

im'posta *sf (di finestra)* shutter; *(tassa)* tax; **~ sul reddito** income tax; **~ sul valore aggiunto** value added tax *(BRIT)*, sales tax *(US)*

impos'tare *vt (imbucare)* to post; *(preparare)* to plan, set out; *(avviare)* to begin, start off; *(voce)* to pitch

im'posto, a *pp di* **imporre**

impo'tente *ag* weak, powerless; *(anche MED)* impotent

impove'rire *vt* to impoverish ♦ *vi (anche:* **~rsi**) to become poor

imprati'cabile *ag (strada)* impassable; *(campo da gioco)* unplayable

Imprati'chirsi [imprati'kirsi] *vr:* **~rsi in qc** to practise *(BRIT)* o practice *(US)* sth

impre'gnare [impren'nare] *vt:* **~ (di)** *(imbevere)* to soak o impregnate (with); *(riempire: anche fig)* to fill (with)

imprendi'tore *sm (industriale)* entrepreneur; *(appaltatore)* contractor; **piccolo ~** small businessman

im'presa *sf (iniziativa)* enterprise; *(azione)* exploit; *(azienda)* firm, concern

impre'sario *sm (TEATRO)* manager, impresario; **~ di pompe funebri** funeral director

imprescin'dibile [impreʃʃin'dibile] *ag* not to be ignored

impressio'nante *ag* impressive; upsetting

impressio'nare *vt* to impress; *(turbare)* to upset; *(FOT)* to expose; **~rsi** *vi* to be easily upset

impressi'one *sf* impression; *(fig: sensazione)* sensation, feeling; *(stampa)* printing; **fare ~** *(colpire)* to impress; *(turbare)* to frighten, upset; **fare buona/cattiva ~ a** to make a good/bad impression on

im'presso, a *pp di* **imprimere**

impres'tare *vt:* **~ qc a qn** to lend sth to sb

impreve'dibile *ag* unforeseeable; *(persona)* unpredictable

imprevi'dente *ag* lacking in foresight

impre'visto, a *ag* unexpected, unforeseen

♦ *sm* unforeseen event; **salvo ~i** unless anything unexpected happens

imprigio'nare [impridʒo'nare] *vt* to imprison

im'primere *vt (anche fig)* to impress, stamp; *(comunicare: movimento)* to transmit, give

impro'babile *ag* improbable, unlikely

im'pronta *sf* imprint, impression, sign; *(di piede, mano)* print; *(fig)* mark, stamp; **~ digitale** fingerprint

impro'perio *sm* insult

im'proprio, a *ag* improper; **arma ~a** offensive weapon

improvvisa'mente *av* suddenly; unexpectedly

improvvi'sare *vt* to improvise; **~rsi** *vr:* **~rsi cuoco** (to decide to) act as cook; **improvvi'sata** *sf (pleasant)* surprise

improv'viso, a *ag (imprevisto)* unexpected; *(subitaneo)* sudden; **all'~** unexpectedly; suddenly

impru'dente *ag* unwise, rash

impu'dente *ag* impudent

impu'dico, a, chi, che *ag* immodest

impu'gnare [impun'nare] *vt* to grasp, grip; *(DIR)* to contest

impul'sivo, a *ag* impulsive

im'pulso *sm* impulse

impun'tarsi *vr* to stop dead, refuse to budge; *(fig)* to be obstinate

impu'tare *vt (ascrivere):* **~ qc a** to attribute sth to; *(DIR: accusare):* **~ qn di** to charge sb with, accuse sb of; **impu'tato, a** *sm/f (DIR)* accused, defendant; **imputazi'one** *sf (DIR)* charge

imputri'dire *vi* to rot

PAROLA CHIAVE

in *(in+il =* **nel**, *in+lo =* **nello**, *in+l' =* **nell'**, *in+la =* **nella**, *in+i =* **nei**, *in+gli =* **negli**, *in+le =* **nelle**) *prep* **1** *(stato in luogo)* in; **vivere ~ Italia/città** to live in Italy/town; **essere ~ casa/ufficio** to be at home/the office; **se fossi ~ te** if I were you

2 *(moto a luogo)* to; *(: dentro)* into; **andare ~ Germania/città** to go to Germany/

town; **andare ~ ufficio** to go to the office; **entrare ~ macchina/casa** to get into the car/go into the house

3 (*tempo*) in; **nel 1999** in 1999; **~ giugno/estate** in June/summer

4 (*modo, maniera*) in; **~ silenzio** in silence; **~ abito da sera** in evening dress; **~ guerra** at war; **~ vacanza** on holiday; **Maria Bianchi ~ Rossi** Maria Rossi née Bianchi

5 (*mezzo*) by; **viaggiare ~ autobus/treno** to travel by bus/train

6 (*materia*) made of; **~ marmo** made of marble, marble *cpd*; **una collana ~ oro** a gold necklace

7 (*misura*) in; **siamo ~ quattro** there are four of us; **~ tutto** in all

8 (*fine*): **dare ~ dono** to give as a gift; **spende tutto ~ alcool** he spends all his money on drink; **~ onore di** in honour of

inabi'tabile *ag* uninhabitable
inacces'sibile [inattʃes'sibile] *ag* (*luogo*) inaccessible; (*persona*) unapproachable
inaccet'tabile [inattʃet'tabile] *ag* unacceptable
ina'datto, a *ag*: **~ (a)** unsuitable *o* unfit (for)
inadegu'ato, a *ag* inadequate
inadempi'enza [inadem'pjentsa] *sf*: **~ (a)** non-fulfilment (of)
inaffer'rabile *ag* elusive; (*concetto, senso*) difficult to grasp
inalbe'rarsi *vr* (*fig*) to flare up, fly off the handle
inalte'rabile *ag* unchangeable; (*colore*) fast, permanent; (*affetto*) constant
inalte'rato, a *ag* unchanged
inami'dato, a *ag* starched
inani'mato, a *ag* inanimate; (*senza vita: corpo*) lifeless
inappa'gabile *ag* insatiable
inappel'labile *ag* (*decisione*) final, irrevocable; (*DIR*) final, not open to appeal
inappe'tenza [inappe'tentsa] *sf* (*MED*) lack of appetite
inappun'tabile *ag* irreproachable

inar'care *vt* (*schiena*) to arch; (*sopracciglia*) to raise; **~rsi** *vr* to arch
inari'dire *vt* to make arid, dry up ♦ *vi* (*anche*: **~rsi**) to dry up, become arid
inaspet'tato, a *ag* unexpected
inas'prire *vt* (*disciplina*) to tighten up, make harsher; (*carattere*) to embitter; **~rsi** *vr* to become harsher; to become bitter; to become worse
inattac'cabile *ag* (*anche fig*) unassailable; (*alibi*) cast-iron
inatten'dibile *ag* unreliable
inat'teso, a *ag* unexpected
inattu'abile *ag* impracticable
inau'dito, a *ag* unheard of
inaugu'rare *vt* to inaugurate, open; (*monumento*) to unveil
inavver'tenza [inavver'tentsa] *sf* carelessness, inadvertence
incagli'are [inkaʎ'ʎare] *vi* (*NAUT: anche*: **~rsi**) to run aground
incal'lito, a *ag* calloused; (*fig*) hardened, inveterate; (*: insensibile*) hard
incal'zare [inkal'tsare] *vt* to follow *o* pursue closely; (*fig*) to press ♦ *vi* (*urgere*) to be pressing; (*essere imminente*) to be imminent
incammi'nare *vt* (*fig: avviare*) to start up; **~rsi** *vr* to set off
incande'scente [inkandeʃ'ʃente] *ag* incandescent, white-hot
incan'tare *vt* to enchant, bewitch; **~rsi** *vr* (*rimanere intontito*) to be spellbound; to be in a daze; (*meccanismo: bloccarsi*) to jam; **incanta'tore, 'trice** *ag* enchanting, bewitching ♦ *sm/f* enchanter/enchantress; **incan'tesimo** *sm* spell, charm; **incan'tevole** *ag* charming, enchanting
in'canto *sm* spell, charm, enchantment; (*asta*) auction; **come per ~** as if by magic; **mettere all'~** to put up for auction
inca'pace [inka'patʃe] *ag* incapable; **incapacità** *sf* inability; (*DIR*) incapacity
incapo'nirsi *vr* to be stubborn, be determined
incap'pare *vi*: **~ in qc/qn** (*anche fig*) to run into sth/sb

incapricci'arsi [inkaprit'tʃarsi] *vr:* ~ **di** to take a fancy to *o* for

incapsu'lare *vt* (*dente*) to crown

incarce'rare [inkartʃe'rare] *vt* to imprison

incari'care *vt:* ~ **qn di fare** to give sb the responsibility of doing; ~**rsi di** to take care *o* charge of; **incari'cato, a** *ag:* **incaricato (di)** in charge (of), responsible (for) ♦ *sm/f* delegate, representative; **professore incaricato** teacher with a temporary appointment

in'carico, chi *sm* task, job

incar'nare *vt* to embody; ~**rsi** *vr* to be embodied; (*REL*) to become incarnate

incarta'mento *sm* dossier, file

incar'tare *vt* to wrap (in paper)

incas'sare *vt* (*merce*) to pack (in cases); (*gemma: incastonare*) to set; (*ECON: riscuotere*) to collect; (*PUGILATO: colpi*) to take, stand up to; **in'casso** *sm* cashing, encashment; (*introito*) takings *pl*

incasto'nare *vt* to set; **incastona'tura** *sf* setting

incas'trare *vt* to fit in, insert; (*fig: intrappolare*) to catch; ~**rsi** *vr* (*combaciare*) to fit together; (*restare bloccato*) to become stuck; **in'castro** *sm* slot, groove; (*punto di unione*) joint

incate'nare *vt* to chain up

incatra'mare *vt* to tar

incatti'vire *vt* to make wicked; ~**rsi** *vr* to turn nasty

in'cauto, a *ag* imprudent, rash

inca'vare *vt* to hollow out; **in'cavo** *sm* hollow; (*solco*) groove

incendi'are [intʃen'djare] *vt* to set fire to; ~**rsi** *vr* to catch fire, burst into flames

incendi'ario, a [intʃen'djarjo] *ag* incendiary ♦ *sm/f* arsonist

in'cendio [in'tʃendjo] *sm* fire

incene'rire [intʃene'rire] *vt* to burn to ashes, incinerate; (*cadavere*) to cremate; ~**rsi** *vr* to be burnt to ashes

in'censo [in'tʃenso] *sm* incense

incensu'rato, a [intʃensu'rato] *ag* (*DIR*): **essere ~** to have a clean record

incen'tivo [intʃen'tivo] *sm* incentive

incep'pare [intʃep'pare] *vt* to obstruct, hamper; ~**rsi** *vr* to jam

ince'rata [intʃe'rata] *sf* (*tela*) tarpaulin; (*impermeabile*) oilskins *pl*

incer'tezza [intʃer'tettsa] *sf* uncertainty

in'certo, a [in'tʃerto] *ag* uncertain; (*irresoluto*) undecided, hesitating ♦ *sm* uncertainty

in'cetta [in'tʃetta] *sf* buying up; **fare ~ di qc** to buy up sth

inchi'esta [in'kjesta] *sf* investigation, inquiry

inchi'nare [inki'nare] *vt* to bow; ~**rsi** *vr* to bend down; (*per riverenza*) to bow; (*i don na*) to curtsy; **in'chino** *sm* bow; curtsy

inchio'dare [inkjo'dare] *vt* to nail (down); ~ **la macchina** (*AUT*) to jam on the brakes

inchi'ostro [in'kjɔstro] *sm* ink; ~ **simpatico** invisible ink

inciam'pare [intʃam'pare] *vi* to trip, stumble

inci'ampo [in'tʃampo] *sm* obstacle; **essere d'~ a qn** (*fig*) to be in sb's way

inci'dente [intʃi'dente] *sm* accident; ~ **d'auto** car accident

inci'denza [intʃi'dentsa] *sf* incidence; **avere una forte ~ su qc** to affect sth greatly

in'cidere [in'tʃidere] *vi:* ~ **su** to bear upon, affect ♦ *vt* (*tagliare incavando*) to cut into; (*ARTE*) to engrave; to etch; (*canzone*) to record

in'cinta [in'tʃinta] *ag f* pregnant

incipri'are [intʃi'prjare] *vt* to powder

in'circa [in'tʃirka] *av:* **all'~** more or less, very nearly

incisi'one [intʃi'zjone] *sf* cut; (*disegno*) engraving; etching; (*registrazione*) recording; (*MED*) incision

in'ciso, a [in'tʃizo] *pp di* **incidere** ♦ *sm:* **per ~** incidentally, by the way

inci'tare [intʃi'tare] *vt* to incite

inci'vile [intʃi'vile] *ag* uncivilized; (*villano*) impolite

incl. *abbr* (= *incluso*) encl.

incli'nare *vt* to tilt; ~**rsi** *vr* (*barca*) to list; (*aereo*) to bank; **incli'nato, a** *ag* sloping; **inclinazi'one** *sf* slope; (*fig*) inclination, tendency; **in'cline** *ag*: **incline a** inclined to

in'cludere *vt* to include; (*accludere*) to enclose; **in'cluso, a** *pp di* **includere** ♦ *ag* included; enclosed

incoe'rente *ag* incoherent; (*contraddittorio*) inconsistent

in'cognita [in'kɔɲɲita] *sf* (*MAT, fig*) unknown quantity

in'cognito, a [in'kɔɲɲito] *ag* unknown ♦ *sm*: **in ~** incognito

incol'lare *vt* to glue, gum; (*unire con colla*) to stick together

incolon'nare *vt* to draw up in columns

inco'lore *ag* colourless

incol'pare *vt*: **~ qn di** to charge sb with

in'colto, a *ag* (*terreno*) uncultivated; (*trascurato: capelli*) neglected; (*persona*) uneducated

in'columе *ag* safe and sound, unhurt

incom'benza [inkom'bentsa] *sf* duty, task

in'combere *vi* (*sovrastare minacciando*): **~ su** to threaten, hang over

incominci'are [inkomin'tʃare] *vi, vt* to begin, start

in'comodo *sm* inconvenience

incompe'tente *ag* incompetent

incompi'uto, a *ag* unfinished, incomplete

incom'pleto, a *ag* incomplete

incompren'sibile *ag* incomprehensible

incom'preso, a *ag* not understood; misunderstood

inconce'pibile [inkontʃe'pibile] *ag* inconceivable

inconcili'abile [inkontʃi'ljabile] *ag* irreconcilable

inconclu'dente *ag* inconclusive; (*persona*) ineffectual

incondizio'nato, a [inkondittsjo'nato] *ag* unconditional

inconfu'tabile *ag* irrefutable

incongru'ente *ag* inconsistent

inconsa'pevole *ag*: **~ di** unaware of, ignorant of

in'conscio, a, sci, sce [in'kɔnʃo] *ag* unconscious ♦ *sm* (*PSIC*): **l'~** the unconscious

inconsis'tente *ag* insubstantial; unfounded

inconsu'eto, a *ag* unusual

incon'sulto, a *ag* rash

incon'trare *vt* to meet; (*difficoltà*) to meet with; **~rsi** *vr* to meet

incontras'tabile *ag* incontrovertible, indisputable

in'contro *av*: **~ a** (*verso*) towards ♦ *sm* meeting; (*SPORT*) match; meeting; **~ di calcio** football match

inconveni'ente *sm* drawback, snag

incoraggia'mento [inkoraddʒa'mento] *sm* encouragement

incoraggi'are [inkorad'dʒare] *vt* to encourage

incornici'are [inkorni'tʃare] *vt* to frame

incoro'nare *vt* to crown; **incoronazi'one** *sf* coronation

incorpo'rare *vt* to incorporate; (*fig: annettere*) to annex

in'correre *vi*: **~ in** to meet with, run into

incosci'ente [inkoʃ'ʃente] *ag* (*inconscio*) unconscious; (*irresponsabile*) reckless, thoughtless; **incosci'enza** *sf* unconsciousness; recklessness, thoughtlessness

incre'dibile *ag* incredible, unbelievable

in'credulo, a *ag* incredulous, disbelieving

incremen'tare *vt* to increase; (*dar sviluppo a*) to promote

incre'mento *sm* (*sviluppo*) development; (*aumento numerico*) increase, growth

incresci'oso, a [inkreʃ'ʃoso] *ag* (*incidente etc*) regrettable

incres'parsi *vr* (*acqua*) to ripple; (*capelli*) to go frizzy; (*pelle, tessuto*) to wrinkle

incrimi'nare *vt* (*DIR*) to charge

incri'nare *vt* to crack; (*fig: rapporti, amicizia*) to cause to deteriorate; **~rsi** *vr* to crack; to deteriorate; **incrina'tura** *sf* crack; (*fig*) rift

incroci'are [inkro'tʃare] *vt* to cross; (*incontrare*) to meet ♦ *vi* (*NAUT, AER*) to cruise; **~rsi** *vr* (*strade*) to cross, intersect; (*persone, veicoli*) to pass each other; **~ le braccia/le gambe** to fold one's arms/cross

one's legs; **incrocia'tore** *sm* cruiser
in'crocio [in'krotʃo] *sm* (*anche FERR*)
crossing; (*di strade*) crossroads
incros'tare *vt* to encrust
incuba'trice [inkuba'tritʃe] *sf* incubator
'incubo *sm* nightmare
in'cudine *sf* anvil
incu'rante *ag*: ~ **(di)** heedless (of), careless
(of)
incurio'sire *vt* to make curious; **~rsi** *vr* to
become curious
incursi'one *sf* raid
incur'vare *vt* to bend, curve; **~rsi** *vr* to
bend, curve
in'cusso, a *pp di* **incutere**
incusto'dito, a *ag* unguarded,
unattended
in'cutere *vt*: ~ **timore / rispetto a qn** to
strike fear into sb/command sb's respect
'indaco *sm* indigo
indaffa'rato, a *ag* busy
inda'gare *vt* to investigate
in'dagine [in'dadʒine] *sf* investigation,
inquiry; (*ricerca*) research, study
indebi'tarsi *vr* to run *o* get into debt
in'debito, a *ag* undue; undeserved
indebo'lire *vt, vi* (*anche*: **~rsi**) to weaken
inde'cente [inde'tʃɛnte] *ag* indecent;
inde'cenza *sf* indecency
inde'ciso, a [inde'tʃizo] *ag* indecisive;
(*irresoluto*) undecided
inde'fesso, a *ag* untiring, indefatigable
indefi'nito, a *ag* (*anche LING*) indefinite;
(*impreciso, non determinato*) undefined
in'degno, a [in'deɲɲo] *ag* (*atto*) shameful;
(*persona*) unworthy
indelica'tezza [indelika'tettsa] *sf*
tactlessness
indemoni'ato, a *ag* possessed (by the
devil)
in'denne *ag* unhurt, uninjured; **indennità**
sf inv (*rimborso: di spese*) allowance; (*: di
perdita*) compensation, indemnity;
indennità di contingenza cost-of-living
allowance; **indennità di trasferta** travel
expenses *pl*
indenniz'zare [indennid'dzare] *vt* to

compensate; **inden'nizzo** *sm* (*somma*)
compensation, indemnity
indero'gabile *ag* binding
'India *sf*: **l'~** India; **indi'ano, a** *ag* Indian
♦ *sm/f* (*d'India*) Indian; (*d'America*) Native
American, (American) Indian
indiavo'lato, a *ag* possessed (by the
devil); (*vivace, violento*) wild
indi'care *vt* (*mostrare*) to show, indicate;
(*: col dito*) to point to, point out; (*consigliare*) to suggest, recommend; **indica'tivo,
a** *ag* indicative ♦ *sm* (*LING*) indicative
(mood); **indica'tore** *sm* (*elenco*) guide;
directory; (*TECN*) gauge; indicator;
indicatore di velocità (*AUT*) speedometer;
indicatore della benzina fuel gauge;
indicazi'one *sf* indication; (*informazione*)
piece of information
'indice ['inditʃe] *sm* index; (*fig*) sign; (*dito*)
index finger, forefinger; ~ **di gradimento**
(*RADIO, TV*) popularity rating
indi'cibile [indi'tʃibile] *ag* inexpressible
indietreggi'are [indietred'dʒare] *vi* to draw
back, retreat
indi'etro *av* back; (*guardare*) behind, back;
(*andare, cadere: anche*: **all'~**) backwards;
rimanere ~ to be left behind; **essere ~**
(*col lavoro*) to be behind; (*orologio*) to be
slow; **rimandare qc ~** to send sth back
indi'feso, a *ag* (*città etc*) undefended;
(*persona*) defenceless
indiffe'rente *ag* indifferent; **indiffe'renza**
sf indifference
in'digeno, a [in'didʒeno] *ag* indigenous,
native ♦ *sm/f* native
indi'gente [indi'dʒɛnte] *ag* poverty-stricken,
destitute; **indi'genza** *sf* extreme poverty
indigesti'one [indidʒes'tjone] *sf*
indigestion
indi'gesto, a [indi'dʒɛsto] *ag* indigestible
indi'gnare [indiɲ'ɲare] *vt* to fill with
indignation; **~rsi** *vr* to get indignant
indimenti'cabile *ag* unforgettable
indipen'dente *ag* independent;
indipen'denza *sf* independence
in'dire *vt* (*concorso*) to announce; (*elezioni*)
to call

indi'retto, a *ag* indirect
indiriz'zare [indirit'tsare] *vt (dirigere)* to direct; *(mandare)* to send; *(lettera)* to address
indi'rizzo [indi'rittso] *sm* address; *(direzione)* direction; *(avvio)* trend, course
indis'creto, a *ag* indiscreet
indis'cusso, a *ag* unquestioned
indispen'sabile *ag* indispensable, essential
indispet'tire *vt* to irritate, annoy ♦ *vi (anche: ~rsi)* to get irritated *o* annoyed
in'divia *sf* endive
individu'ale *ag* individual; **individualità** *sf* individuality
individu'are *vt (dar forma distinta a)* to characterize; *(determinare)* to locate; *(riconoscere)* to single out
indi'viduo *sm* individual
indizi'ato, a *ag* suspected ♦ *sm/f* suspect
in'dizio [in'dittsjo] *sm (segno)* sign, indication; *(POLIZIA)* clue; *(DIR)* piece of evidence
'indole *sf* nature, character
indolen'zito, a [indolen'tsito] *ag* stiff, aching; *(intorpidito)* numb
indo'lore *ag* painless
indo'mani *sm:* **l'~** the next day, the following day
Indo'nesia *sf:* **l'~** Indonesia
indos'sare *vt (mettere indosso)* to put on; *(avere indosso)* to have on; **indossa'tore, 'trice** *sm/f* model
in'dotto, a *pp di* **indurre**
indottri'nare *vt* to indoctrinate
indovi'nare *vt (scoprire)* to guess; *(immaginare)* to imagine, guess; *(il futuro)* to foretell; **indovi'nato, a** *ag* successful; *(scelta)* inspired; **indovi'nello** *sm* riddle; **indo'vino, a** *sm/f* fortuneteller
indubbia'mente *av* undoubtedly
in'dubbio, a *ag* certain, undoubted
indugi'are [indu'dʒare] *vi* to take one's time, delay
in'dugio [in'dudʒo] *sm (ritardo)* delay; **senza ~** without delay
indul'gente [indul'dʒɛnte] *ag* indulgent;

(giudice) lenient; **indul'genza** *sf* indulgence; leniency
in'dulgere [in'duldʒere] *vi:* **~ a** *(accondiscendere)* to comply with; *(abbandonarsi)* to indulge in; **in'dulto, a** *pp di* **indulgere** ♦ *sm (DIR)* pardon
indu'mento *sm* article of clothing, garment; **~i** *smpl (vestiti)* clothes
indu'rire *vt* to harden ♦ *vi (anche: ~rsi)* to harden, become hard
in'durre *vt:* **~ qn a fare qc** to induce *o* persuade sb to do sth; **~ qn in errore** to mislead sb
in'dustria *sf* industry; **industri'ale** *ag* industrial ♦ *sm* industrialist
industri'arsi *vr* to do one's best, try hard
industri'oso, a *ag* industrious, hard-working
induzi'one [indut'tsjone] *sf* induction
inebe'tito, a *ag* dazed, stunned
inebri'are *vt (anche fig)* to intoxicate; **~rsi** *vr* to become intoxicated
inecce'pibile [inettʃe'pibile] *ag* unexceptionable
i'nedia *sf* starvation
i'nedito, a *ag* unpublished
ineffi'cace [ineffi'katʃe] *ag* ineffective
ineffici'ente [ineffi'tʃɛnte] *ag* inefficient
inegu'ale *ag* unequal; *(irregolare)* uneven
ine'rente *ag:* **~ a** concerning, regarding
i'nerme *ag* unarmed; defenceless
inerpi'carsi *vr:* **~ (su)** to clamber (up)
i'nerte *ag* inert; *(inattivo)* indolent, sluggish; **i'nerzia** *sf* inertia; indolence, sluggishness
ine'satto, a *ag (impreciso)* inexact; *(erroneo)* incorrect; *(AMM: non riscosso)* uncollected
inesis'tente *ag* non-existent
inesperi'enza [inespe'rjentsa] *sf* inexperience
ines'perto, a *ag* inexperienced
i'netto, a *ag (incapace)* inept; *(che non ha attitudine):* **~ (a)** unsuited (to)
ine'vaso, a *ag (ordine, corrispondenza)* outstanding
inevi'tabile *ag* inevitable
i'nezia [i'nettsja] *sf* trifle, thing of no

importance

infagot'tare *vt* to bundle up, wrap up; **~rsi** *vr* to wrap up

infal'libile *ag* infallible

infa'mante *ag* defamatory

in'fame *ag* infamous; (*fig: cosa, compito*) awful, dreadful

infan'gare *vt* to cover with mud; (*fig: reputazione*) to sully

infan'tile *ag* child *cpd*; childlike; (*adulto, azione*) childish; **letteratura ~** children's books *pl*

in'fanzia [in'fantsja] *sf* childhood; (*bambini*) children *pl*; **prima ~** babyhood, infancy

infari'nare *vt* to cover with (*o* sprinkle with *o* dip in) flour; **infarina'tura** *sf* (*fig*) smattering

in'farto *sm* (*MED*) heart attack

infasti'dire *vt* to annoy, irritate; **~rsi** *vr* to get annoyed *o* irritated

infati'cabile *ag* tireless, untiring

in'fatti *cong* as a matter of fact, in fact, actually

infatu'arsi *vr*: **~ di** to become infatuated with, fall for; **infatuazi'one** *sf* infatuation

in'fausto, a *ag* unpropitious, unfavourable

infe'condo, a *ag* infertile

infe'dele *ag* unfaithful; **infedeltà** *sf* infidelity

infe'lice [infe'litʃe] *ag* unhappy; (*sfortunato*) unlucky, unfortunate; (*inopportuno*) inopportune, ill-timed; (*mal riuscito: lavoro*) bad, poor; **infelicità** *sf* unhappiness

inferi'ore *ag* lower; (*per intelligenza, qualità*) inferior ♦ *sm/f* inferior; **~ a** (*numero, quantità*) less *o* smaller than; (*meno buono*) inferior to; **~ alla media** below average; **inferiorità** *sf* inferiority

inferme'ria *sf* infirmary; (*di scuola, nave*) sick bay

infermi'ere, a *sm/f* nurse

infermità *sf inv* illness; infirmity

in'fermo, a *ag* (*ammalato*) ill; (*debole*) infirm

infer'nale *ag* infernal; (*proposito, complotto*) diabolical

in'ferno *sm* hell

inferri'ata *sf* grating

infervo'rarsi *vr* to get excited, get carried away

infes'tare *vt* to infest

infet'tare *vt* to infect; **~rsi** *vr* to become infected; **infet'tivo, a** *ag* infectious; **in'fetto, a** *ag* infected; (*acque*) polluted, contaminated; **infezi'one** *sf* infection

infiac'chire [infjak'kire] *vt* to weaken ♦ *vi* (*anche*: **~rsi**) to grow weak

infiam'mabile *ag* inflammable

infiam'mare *vt* to set alight; (*fig, MED*) to inflame; **~rsi** *vr* to catch fire; (*MED*) to become inflamed; **infiammazi'one** *sf* (*MED*) inflammation

in'fido, a *ag* unreliable, treacherous

infie'rire *vi*: **~ su** (*fisicamente*) to attack furiously; (*verbalmente*) to rage at

in'figgere [in'fiddʒere] *vt*: **~ qc in** to thrust *o* drive sth into

infi'lare *vt* (*ago*) to thread; (*mettere: chiave*) to insert; (*: anello, vestito*) to slip *o* put on; (*strada*) to turn into, take; **~rsi** *vr*: **~rsi in** to slip into; (*indossare*) to slip on; **~ l'uscio** to slip in; to slip out

infil'trarsi *vr* to penetrate, seep through; (*MIL*) to infiltrate; **infiltrazi'one** *sf* infiltration

infil'zare [infil'tsare] *vt* (*infilare*) to string together; (*trafiggere*) to pierce

'infimo, a *ag* lowest

in'fine *av* finally; (*insomma*) in short

infinità *sf* infinity; (*in quantità*): **un'~ di** an infinite number of

infi'nito, a *ag* infinite; (*LING*) infinitive ♦ *sm* infinity; (*LING*) infinitive; **all'~** (*senza fine*) endlessly

infinocchi'are [infinok'kjare] (*fam*) *vt* to hoodwink

infischi'arsi [infis'kjarsi] *vr*: **~ di** not to care about

in'fisso, a *pp di* **infiggere** ♦ *sm* fixture; (*di porta, finestra*) frame

infit'tire *vt, vi* (*anche*: **~rsi**) to thicken

inflazi'one [inflat'tsjone] *sf* inflation

in'fliggere [in'fliddʒere] *vt* to inflict; **in'flitto, a** *pp di* **infliggere**

influ'ente *ag* influential; **influ'enza** *sf* influence; (*MED*) influenza, flu

influ'ire *vi*: ~ **su** to influence

in'flusso *sm* influence

infol'tire *vt, vi* to thicken

infon'dato, a *ag* unfounded, groundless

in'fondere *vt*: ~ **qc in qn** to instill sth in sb

infor'care *vt* to fork (up); (*bicicletta, cavallo*) to get on; (*occhiali*) to put on

infor'mare *vt* to inform, tell; **~rsi** *vr*: **~rsi (di** *o* **su)** to inquire (about)

infor'matica *sf* computer science

informa'tivo, a *ag* informative

informa'tore *sm* informer

informazi'one [informat'tsjone] *sf* piece of information; **prendere ~i sul conto di qn** to get information about sb; **chiedere un'~** to ask for (some) information

in'forme *ag* shapeless

informico'larsi *vr* = **informicolirsi**

informico'lirsi *vr* to have pins and needles

infor'tunio *sm* accident; ~ **sul lavoro** industrial accident, accident at work

infos'sarsi *vr* (*terreno*) to sink; (*guance*) to become hollow; **infos'sato, a** *ag* hollow; (*occhi*) deep-set; (*: per malattia*) sunken

in'frangere [in'frandʒere] *vt* to smash; (*fig: legge, patti*) to break; **~rsi** *vr* to smash, break; **infran'gibile** *ag* unbreakable; **in'franto, a** *pp di* **infrangere ♦** *ag* broken

infrazi'one [infrat'tsjone] *sf*: ~ **a** breaking of, violation of

infredda'tura *sf* slight cold

infreddo'lito, a *ag* cold, chilled

infruttu'oso, a *ag* fruitless

infu'ori *av* out; **all'~** outwards; **all'~ di** (*eccetto*) except, with the exception of

infuri'are *vi* to rage; **~rsi** *vr* to fly into a rage

infusi'one *sf* infusion

in'fuso, a *pp di* **infondere ♦** *sm* infusion

Ing. *abbr* = **ingegnere**

ingabbi'are *vt* to cage

ingaggi'are [ingad'dʒare] *vt* (*assumere con compenso*) to take on, hire; (*SPORT*) to sign on; (*MIL*) to engage; **in'gaggio** *sm* hiring;

signing on

ingan'nare *vt* to deceive; (*fisco*) to cheat; (*eludere*) to dodge, elude; (*fig: tempo*) to while away ♦ *vi* (*apparenza*) to be deceptive; **~rsi** *vr* to be mistaken, be wrong; **ingan'nevole** *ag* deceptive

in'ganno *sm* deceit, deception; (*azione*) trick; (*menzogna, frode*) cheat, swindle; (*illusione*) illusion

ingarbugli'are [ingarbuʎ'ʎare] *vt* to tangle; (*fig*) to confuse, muddle; **~rsi** *vr* to become confused *o* muddled

inge'gnarsi [indʒeɲ'ɲarsi] *vr* to do one's best, try hard; ~ **per vivere** to live by one's wits

inge'gnere [indʒeɲ'ɲere] *sm* engineer; ~ **civile/navale** civil/naval engineer; **ingegne'ria** *sf* engineering; ~ **genetica** genetic engineering

in'gegno [in'dʒeɲɲo] *sm* (*intelligenza*) intelligence, brains *pl*; (*capacità creativa*) ingenuity; (*disposizione*) talent; **inge'gnoso, a** *ag* ingenious, clever

ingelo'sire [indʒelo'zire] *vt* to make jealous ♦ *vi* (*anche*: **~rsi**) to become jealous

in'gente [in'dʒɛnte] *ag* huge, enormous

ingenuità [indʒenui'ta] *sf* ingenuousness

in'genuo, a [in'dʒɛnuo] *ag* ingenuous, naïve

inge'rire [indʒe'rire] *vt* to ingest

inges'sare [indʒes'sare] *vt* (*MED*) to put in plaster; **ingessa'tura** *sf* plaster

Inghil'terra [ingil'terra] *sf*: **l'~** England

inghiot'tire [ingjot'tire] *vt* to swallow

ingial'lire [indʒal'lire] *vi* to go yellow

ingigan'tire [indʒigan'tire] *vt* to enlarge, magnify ♦ *vi* to become gigantic *o* enormous

inginocchi'arsi [indʒinok'kjarsi] *vr* to kneel (down)

ingiù [in'dʒu] *av* down, downwards

ingiunzi'one [indʒun'tsjone] *sf* injunction

ingi'uria [in'dʒurja] *sf* insult; (*fig: danno*) damage; **ingiuri'are** *vt* to insult, abuse; **ingiuri'oso, a** *ag* insulting, abusive

ingius'tizia [indʒus'tittsja] *sf* injustice

ingi'usto, a [in'dʒusto] *ag* unjust, unfair

in'glese *ag* English ♦ *sm/f* Englishman/woman ♦ *sm* (*LING*) English; **gli ~i** the English; **andarsene** *o* **filare all'~** to take French leave

ingoi'are *vt* to gulp (down); (*fig*) to swallow (up)

ingol'fare *vt* (*motore*) to flood; **~rsi** *vr* to flood

ingom'brante *ag* cumbersome

ingom'brare *vt* (*strada*) to block; (*stanza*) to clutter up; **in'gombro, a** *ag* (*strada, passaggio*) blocked ♦ *sm* obstacle; **essere d'ingombro** to be in the way

in'gordo, a *ag*: **~ di** greedy for

in'gorgo, ghi *sm* blockage, obstruction; (*anche*: **~ stradale**) traffic jam

ingoz'zare [ingot'tsare] *vt* (*animali*) to fatten; (*fig: persona*) to stuff; **~rsi** *vr*: **~rsi (di)** to stuff o.s. (with)

ingra'naggio [ingra'naddʒo] *sm* (*TECN*) gear; (*di orologio*) mechanism; **gli ~i della burocrazia** the bureaucratic machinery

ingra'nare *vi* to mesh, engage ♦ *vt* to engage; **~ la marcia** to get into gear

ingrandi'mento *sm* enlargement; extension

ingran'dire *vt* (*anche FOT*) to enlarge; (*estendere*) to extend; (*OTTICA, fig*) to magnify ♦ *vi* (*anche*: **~rsi**) to become larger *o* bigger; (*aumentare*) to grow, increase; (*espandersi*) to expand

ingras'sare *vt* to make fat; (*animali*) to fatten; (*lubrificare*) to oil, lubricate ♦ *vi* (*anche*: **~rsi**) to get fat, put on weight

in'grato, a *ag* ungrateful; (*lavoro*) thankless, unrewarding

ingredi'ente *sm* ingredient

in'gresso *sm* (*porta*) entrance; (*atrio*) hall; (*l'entrare*) entrance, entry; (*facoltà di entrare*) admission; **"~ libero"** "admission free"

ingros'sare *vt* to increase; (*folla, livello*) to swell ♦ *vi* (*anche*: **~rsi**) to increase; to swell

in'grosso *av*: **all'~** (*COMM*) wholesale; (*all'incirca*) roughly, about

ingua'ribile *ag* incurable

'inguine *sm* (*ANAT*) groin

ini'bire *vt* to forbid, prohibit; (*PSIC*) to inhibit; **inibizi'one** *sf* prohibition; inhibition

iniet'tare *vt* to inject; **~rsi** *vr*: **~rsi di sangue** (*occhi*) to become bloodshot; **iniezi'one** *sf* injection

inimi'carsi *vr*: **~ con qn** to fall out with sb

ininter'rotto, a *ag* unbroken; uninterrupted

iniquità *sf inv* iniquity; (*atto*) wicked action

inizi'ale [init'tsjale] *ag, sf* initial

inizi'are [init'tsjare] *vi, vt* to begin, start; **~ qn a** to initiate sb into; (*pittura etc*) to introduce sb to; **~ a fare qc** to start doing sth

inizia'tiva [inittsja'tiva] *sf* initiative; **~ privata** private enterprise

i'nizio [i'nittsjo] *sm* beginning; **all'~** at the beginning, at the start; **dare ~ a qc** to start sth, get sth going

innaffi'are *etc* = **annaffiare** *etc*

innal'zare [innal'tsare] *vt* (*sollevare, alzare*) to raise; (*rizzare*) to erect; **~rsi** *vr* to rise

innamo'rarsi *vr*: **~ (di qn)** to fall in love (with sb); **innamo'rato, a** *ag* (*che nutre amore*): **innamorato (di)** in love (with); (*appassionato*): **innamorato di** very fond of ♦ *sm/f* lover; sweetheart

in'nanzi [in'nantsi] *av* (*stato in luogo*) in front, ahead; (*moto a luogo*) forward, on; (*tempo: prima*) before ♦ *prep* (*prima*) before; **~ a** in front of; **innanzi'tutto** *av* first of all

in'nato, a *ag* innate

innatu'rale *ag* unnatural

inne'gabile *ag* undeniable

innervo'sire *vt*: **~ qn** to get on sb's nerves; **~rsi** *vr* to get irritated *o* upset

innes'care *vt* to prime

innes'tare *vt* (*BOT, MED*) to graft; (*TECN*) to engage; (*inserire: presa*) to insert; **in'nesto** *sm* graft; grafting *no pl*; (*TECN*) clutch; (*ELETTR*) connection

'inno *sm* hymn; **~ nazionale** national anthem

inno'cente [inno'tʃente] *ag* innocent;

inno'cenza *sf* innocence

in'nocuo, a *ag* innocuous, harmless

innova'tivo, a *ag* innovative

innume'revole *ag* innumerable

ino'doro, a *ag* odourless

inol'trare *vt* (*AMM*) to pass on, forward; ~rsi *vr* (*addentrarsi*) to advance, go forward

i'noltre *av* besides, moreover

inon'dare *vt* to flood; inondazi'one *sf* flooding *no pl*; flood

inope'roso, a *ag* inactive, idle

inoppor'tuno, a *ag* untimely, ill-timed; inappropriate; (*momento*) inopportune

inorgo'glire [inorgoʎˈʎire] *vt* to make proud ♦ *vi* (*anche*: ~rsi) to become proud; ~rsi di qc to pride o.s. on sth

inorri'dire *vt* to horrify ♦ *vi* to be horrified

inospi'tale *ag* inhospitable

inosser'vato, a *ag* (*non notato*) unobserved; (*non rispettato*) not observed, not kept

inossi'dabile *ag* stainless

inqua'drare *vt* (*foto, immagine*) to frame; (*fig*) to situate, set

inquie'tare *vt* (*turbare*) to disturb, worry; ~rsi *vr* to worry, become anxious; (*impazientirsi*) to get upset

inqui'eto, a *ag* restless; (*preoccupato*) worried, anxious; inquie'tudine *sf* anxiety, worry

inqui'lino, a *sm/f* tenant

inquina'mento *sm* pollution

inqui'nare *vt* to pollute

inqui'sire *vt*, *vi* to investigate; inquisi'tore, 'trice *ag* (*sguardo*) inquiring; inquisizi'one *sf* (*STORIA*) inquisition

insabbi'are *vt* (*fig: pratica*) to shelve; ~rsi *vr* (*arenarsi: barca*) to run aground; (*fig: pratica*) to be shelved

insac'cati *smpl* (*CUC*) sausages

insa'lata *sf* salad; ~ mista mixed salad; insalati'era *sf* salad bowl

insa'lubre *ag* unhealthy

insa'nabile *ag* (*piaga*) which cannot be healed; (*situazione*) irremediable; (*odio*) implacable

insangui'nare *vt* to stain with blood

insa'puta *sf*: all'~ di qn without sb knowing

insce'nare [inʃeˈnare] *vt* (*TEATRO*) to stage, put on; (*fig*) to stage

insedi'are *vt* to install; ~rsi *vr* to take up office; (*popolo, colonia*) to settle

in'segna [inˈseɲɲa] *sf* sign; (*emblema*) sign, emblem; (*bandiera*) flag, banner; ~e *sfpl* (*decorazioni*) insignia *pl*

insegna'mento [inseɲɲaˈmento] *sm* teaching

inse'gnante [inseɲˈɲante] *ag* teaching ♦ *sm/f* teacher

inse'gnare [inseɲˈɲare] *vt*, *vi* to teach; ~ a qn qc to teach sb sth; ~ a qn a fare qc to teach sb (how) to do sth

insegui'mento *sm* pursuit, chase

insegu'ire *vt* to pursue, chase

inselvati'chire [inselvatiˈkire] *vi* (*anche*: ~rsi) to grow wild

insena'tura *sf* inlet, creek

insen'sato, a *ag* senseless, stupid

insen'sibile *ag* (*nervo*) insensible; (*persona*) indifferent

inse'rire *vt* to insert; (*ELETTR*) to connect; (*allegare*) to enclose; (*annuncio*) to put in, place; ~rsi *vr* (*fig*): ~rsi in to become part of; in'serto *sm* (*pubblicazione*) insert

inservi'ente *sm/f* attendant

inserzi'one [inserˈtsjone] *sf* insertion; (*avviso*) advertisement; fare un'~ sul giornale to put an advertisement in the paper

insetti'cida, i [insettiˈtʃida] *sm* insecticide

in'setto *sm* insect

insi'curo, a *ag* insecure

in'sidia *sf* snare, trap; (*pericolo*) hidden danger; insidi'are *vt*: ~ la vita di qn to make an attempt on sb's life

insi'eme *av* together ♦ *prep*: ~ a *o* con together with ♦ *sm* whole; (*MAT, servizio, assortimento*) set; (*MODA*) ensemble, outfit; tutti ~ all together; tutto ~ all together; (*in una volta*) at one go; nell'~ on the whole; d'~ (*veduta etc*) overall in'signe [in'sinɲe] ag (persona) famous, distinguished; (città, monumento) notable

insignifi'cante [insiɲɲifi'kante] ag insignificant

insi'gnire [insiɲ'ɲire] vt: ~ qn di to honour o decorate sb with

insin'cero, a [insin'tʃero] ag insincere

insinda'cabile ag unquestionable

insinu'are vt (introdurre): ~ qc in to slip o slide sth into; (fig) to insinuate, imply; ~rsi vr: ~rsi in to seep into; (fig) to creep into; to worm one's way into

in'sipido, a ag insipid

insis'tente ag insistent; persistent

insis'tere vi: ~ su qc to insist on sth; ~ in qc/a fare (perseverare) to persist in sth/in doing; insis'tito, a pp di insistere

insoddis'fatto, a ag dissatisfied

insoffe'rente ag intolerant

insolazi'one [insolat'tsjone] sf (MED) sunstroke

inso'lente ag insolent; insolen'tire vi to grow insolent ♦ vt to insult, be rude to

in'solito, a ag unusual, out of the ordinary

inso'luto, a ag (non risolto) unsolved

in'somma av (in conclusione) in short; (dunque) well ♦ escl for heaven's sake!

in'sonne ag sleepless; in'sonnia sf insomnia, sleeplessness

inson'nolito, a ag sleepy, drowsy

insoppor'tabile ag unbearable

in'sorgere [in'sordʒere] vi (ribellarsi) to rise up, rebel; (apparire) to come up, arise

in'sorto, a pp di insorgere ♦ sm/f rebel, insurgent

insospet'tire vt to make suspicious ♦ vi (anche: ~rsi) to become suspicious

inspi'rare vt to breathe in, inhale

in'stabile ag (carico, indole) unstable; (tempo) unsettled; (equilibrio) unsteady

instal'lare vt to install; ~rsi vr (sistemarsi): ~rsi in to settle in; installazi'one sf installation

instan'cabile ag untiring, indefatigable

instau'rare vt to introduce, institute

instra'dare vt: ~ (verso) to direct (towards)

insuc'cesso [insut'tʃesso] sm failure, flop

insudici'are [insudi'tʃare] vt to dirty; ~rsi vr to get dirty

insuffici'ente [insuffi'tʃente] ag insufficient; (compito, allievo) inadequate; insuffici'enza sf insufficiency; inadequacy; (INS) fail

insu'lare ag insular

insu'lina sf insulin

in'sulso, a ag (sciocco) inane, silly; (persona) dull, insipid

insul'tare vt to insult, affront

in'sulto sm insult, affront

insussis'tente ag non-existent

intac'care vt (fare tacche) to cut into; (corrodere) to corrode; (fig: cominciare ad usare: risparmi) to break into; (: ledere) to damage

intagli'are [intaʎ'ʎare] vt to carve; in'taglio sm carving

intan'gibile [intan'dʒibile] ag untouchable; inviolable

in'tanto av (nel frattempo) meanwhile, in the meantime; (per cominciare) just to begin with; ~ che while

in'tarsio sm inlaying no pl, marquetry no pl; inlay

inta'sare vt to choke (up), block (up); (AUT) to obstruct, block; ~rsi vr to become choked o blocked

intas'care vt to pocket

in'tatto, a ag intact; (puro) unsullied

intavo'lare vt to start, enter into

inte'grale ag complete; (pane, farina) wholemeal (BRIT), whole-wheat (US); (MAT): calcolo ~ integral calculus

inte'grante ag: parte ~ integral part

inte'grare vt to complete; (MAT) to integrate; ~rsi vr (persona) to become integrated

integrità sf integrity

'integro, a ag (intatto, intero) complete, whole; (retto) upright

intelaia'tura sf frame; (fig) structure, framework

intel'letto sm intellect; intellettu'ale ag, sm/f intellectual

intelli'gente [intelli'dʒɛnte] *ag* intelligent; **intelli'genza** *sf* intelligence

intem'perie *sfpl* bad weather *sg*

intempes'tivo, a *ag* untimely

inten'dente *sm*: ~ **di Finanza** inland (*BRIT*) *o* internal (*US*) revenue officer; **inten'denza** *sf*: **intendenza di Finanza** inland (*BRIT*) *o* internal (*US*) revenue office

in'tendere *vt* (*avere intenzione*): ~ **fare qc** to intend *o* mean to do sth; (*comprendere*) to understand; (*udire*) to hear; (*significare*) to mean; ~**rsi** *vr* (*conoscere*): ~**rsi di** to know a lot about, be a connoisseur of; (*accordarsi*) to get on (well); **intendersela con qn** (*avere una relazione amorosa*) to have an affair with sb; **intendi'mento** *sm* (*intelligenza*) understanding; (*proposito*) intention; **intendi'tore, 'trice** *sm/f* connoisseur, expert

intene'rire *vt* (*fig*) to move (to pity); ~**rsi** *vr* (*fig*) to be moved

inten'sivo, a *ag* intensive

in'tenso, a *ag* intense

in'tento, a *ag* (*teso, assorto*): ~ **(a)** intent (on), absorbed (in) ♦ *sm* aim, purpose

intenzio'nale [intentsjo'nale] *ag* intentional

intenzi'one [inten'tsjone] *sf* intention; (*DIR*) intent; **avere** ~ **di fare qc** to intend to do sth, have the intention of doing sth

interat'tivo, a *ag* interactive

interca'lare *sm* pet phrase, stock phrase ♦ *vt* to insert

interca'pedine *sf* gap, cavity

intercet'tare [intertʃet'tare] *vt* to intercept

intercity [intası'ti] *sm inv* (*FERR*) ≈ intercity (train)

inter'detto, a *pp di* **interdire** ♦ *ag* forbidden, prohibited; (*sconcertato*) dumbfounded ♦ *sm* (*REL*) interdict

inter'dire *vt* to forbid, prohibit, ban; (*REL*) to interdict; (*DIR*) to deprive of civil rights; **interdizi'one** *sf* prohibition, ban

interessa'mento *sm* interest

interes'sante *ag* interesting; **essere in stato** ~ to be expecting (a baby)

interes'sare *vt* to interest; (*concernere*) to concern, be of interest to; (*far intervenire*): ~ **qn a** to draw sb's attention to ♦ *vi*: ~ **a** to interest, matter to; ~**rsi** *vr* (*mostrare interesse*): ~**rsi a** to take an interest in, be interested in; (*occuparsi*): ~**rsi di** to take care of

inte'resse *sm* (*anche COMM*) interest

inter'faccia, ce [inter'fattʃa] *sf* (*INFORM*) interface

interfe'renza [interfe'rɛntsa] *sf* interference

interfe'rire *vi* to interfere

interiezi'one [interjet'tsjone] *sf* exclamation, interjection

interi'ora *sfpl* entrails

interi'ore *ag* interior, inner, inside, internal; (*fig*) inner

inter'ludio *sm* (*MUS*) interlude

inter'medio, a *ag* intermediate

inter'mezzo [inter'mɛddzo] *sm* (*intervallo*) interval; (*breve spettacolo*) intermezzo

inter'nare *vt* (*arrestare*) to intern; (*MED*) to commit (to a mental institution)

internazio'nale [internattsjo'nale] *ag* international

in'terno, a *ag* (*di dentro*) internal, interior, inner; (*: mare*) inland; (*nazionale*) domestic; (*allievo*) boarding ♦ *sm* inside, interior; (*di paese*) interior; (*fodera*) lining; (*di appartamento*) flat (number); (*TEL*) extension ♦ *sm/f* (*INS*) boarder; ~**i** *smpl* (*CINEMA*) interior shots; **all'**~ inside; **Ministero degli I~i** Ministry of the Interior, ≈ Home Office (*BRIT*), Department of the Interior (*US*)

in'tero, a *ag* (*integro, intatto*) whole, entire; (*completo, totale*) complete; (*numero*) whole; (*non ridotto: biglietto*) full; (*latte*) full-cream

interpel'lare *vt* to consult

inter'porre *vt* (*ostacolo*): ~ **qc a qc** to put sth in the way of sth; (*influenza*) to use; **interporsi** *vr* to intervene; **interporsi fra** (*mettersi in mezzo*) to come between; **inter'posto, a** *pp di* **interporre**

interpre'tare *vt* to interpret; **in'terprete** *sm/f* interpreter; (*TEATRO*) actor/actress, performer; (*MUS*) performer

interregio'nale [interredʒo'nale] *sm* long

distance train (*stopping frequently*)

interro'gare *vt* to question; (*INS*) to test; interroga'tivo, a *ag* (*occhi, sguardo*) questioning, inquiring; (*LING*) interrogative ♦ *sm* question; (*fig*) mystery; interroga'torio, a *ag* interrogatory, questioning ♦ *sm* (*DIR*) questioning *no pl*; interrogazi'one *sf* questioning *no pl*; (*INS*) oral test

inter'rompere *vt* to interrupt; (*studi, trattative*) to break off, interrupt; ~rsi *vr* to break off, stop; inter'rotto, a *pp di* interrompere

interrut'tore *sm* switch

interruzi'one [interrut'tsjone] *sf* interruption; break

interse'care *vt* to intersect; ~rsi *vr* to intersect

inter'stizio [inter'stittsjo] *sm* interstice, crack

interur'bana *sf* trunk *o* long-distance call

interur'bano, a *ag* inter-city; (*TEL: chiamata*) trunk *cpd*, long-distance; (*: telefono*) long-distance

inter'vallo *sm* interval; (*spazio*) space, gap

interve'nire *vi* (*partecipare*): ~ a to take part in; (*intromettersi: anche POL*) to intervene; (*MED: operare*) to operate; inter'vento *sm* participation; (*intromissione*) intervention; (*MED*) operation; fare un intervento nel corso di (*dibattito, programma*) to take part in

inter'vista *sf* interview; intervis'tare *vt* to interview

in'tesa *sf* understanding; (*accordo*) agreement, understanding

in'teso, a *pp di* intendere ♦ *ag* agreed; siamo ~i? OK?

intes'tare *vt* (*lettera*) to address; (*proprietà*): ~ a to register in the name of; ~ un assegno a qn to make out a cheque to sb; intestazi'one *sf* heading; (*su carta da lettere*) letterhead

intes'tino, a *ag* (*lotte*) internal, civil ♦ *sm* (*ANAT*) intestine

inti'mare *vt* to order, command; intimazi'one *sf* order, command

intimidazi'one [intimidat'tsjone] *sf* intimidation

intimi'dire *vt* to intimidate ♦ *vi* (*anche: ~rsi*) to grow shy

intimità *sf* intimacy; privacy; (*familiarità*) familiarity

'intimo, a *ag* intimate; (*affetti, vita*) private; (*fig: profondo*) inmost ♦ *sm* (*persona*) intimate *o* close friend; (*dell'animo*) bottom, depths *pl*; parti ~e (*ANAT*) private parts

intimo'rire *vt* to frighten; ~rsi *vr* to become frightened

in'tingolo *sm* sauce; (*pietanza*) stew

intiriz'zire [intirid'dzire] *vt* to numb ♦ *vi* (*anche: ~rsi*) to go numb

intito'lare *vt* to give a title to; (*dedicare*) to dedicate

intolle'rabile *ag* intolerable

intolle'rante *ag* intolerant

in'tonaco, ci *o* chi *sm* plaster

into'nare *vt* (*canto*) to start to sing; (*armonizzare*) to match; ~rsi *vr* (*colori*) to go together; ~rsi a (*carnagione*) to suit; (*abito*) to go with, match

inton'tire *vt* to stun, daze ♦ *vi* (*anche: ~rsi*) to be stunned *o* dazed

in'toppo *sm* stumbling block, obstacle

in'torno *av* around; ~ a (*attorno a*) around; (*riguardo, circa*) about

intorpi'dire *vt* to numb; (*fig*) to make sluggish ♦ *vi* (*anche: ~rsi*) to grow numb; (*fig*) to become sluggish

intossi'care *vt* to poison; intossicazi'one *sf* poisoning

intralci'are [intral'tʃare] *vt* to hamper, hold up

intransi'tivo, a *ag, sm* intransitive

intrapren'dente *ag* enterprising, go-ahead

intra'prendere *vt* to undertake

intrat'tabile *ag* intractable

intratte'nere *vt* to entertain; to engage in conversation; ~rsi *vr* to linger; ~rsi su qc to dwell on sth

intrave'dere *vt* to catch a glimpse of; (*fig*) to foresee

intrecci'are [intret'tʃare] *vt* (*capelli*) to plait, braid; (*intessere: anche fig*) to interweave, intertwine; **~rsi** *vr* to intertwine, become interwoven; **~ le mani** to clasp one's hands; **in'treccio** *sm* (*fig: trama*) plot, story

intri'gare *vi* to manoeuvre (BRIT), maneuver (US), scheme; **in'trigo, ghi** *sm* plot, intrigue

in'trinseco, a, ci, che *ag* intrinsic

in'triso, a *ag*: **~ (di)** soaked (in)

intro'durre *vt* to introduce; (*chiave etc*): **~ qc in** to insert sth into; (*persone: far entrare*) to show in; **introdursi** *vr* (*moda, tecniche*) to be introduced; **introdursi in** (*persona: penetrare*) to enter; (*: entrare furtivamente*) to steal *o* slip into; **introduzi'one** *sf* introduction

in'troito *sm* income, revenue

intro'mettersi *vr* to interfere, meddle; (*interporsi*) to interpose

in'truglio [in'truʎʎo] *sm* concoction

intrusi'one *sf* intrusion; interference

in'truso, a *sm/f* intruder

intu'ire *vt* to perceive by intuition; (*rendersi conto*) to realize; **in'tuito** *sm* intuition; (*perspicacia*) perspicacity; **intuizi'one** *sf* intuition

inu'mano, a *ag* inhuman

inumi'dire *vt* to dampen, moisten; **~rsi** *vr* to become damp *o* wet

i'nutile *ag* useless; (*superfluo*) pointless, unnecessary; **inutilità** *sf* uselessness; pointlessness

inutil'mente *av* unnecessarily; (*senza risultato*) in vain

inva'dente *ag* (*fig*) interfering, nosey

in'vadere *vt* to invade; (*affollare*) to swarm into, overrun; (*sog: acque*) to flood

inva'ghirsi [inva'girsi] *vr*: **~ di** to take a fancy to

invalidità *sf* infirmity; disability; (DIR) invalidity

in'valido, a *ag* (*infermo*) infirm, invalid; (*al lavoro*) disabled; (DIR: *nullo*) invalid ♦ *sm/f* invalid; disabled person

in'vano *av* in vain

invasi'one *sf* invasion

in'vaso, a *pp di* **invadere**

inva'sore, invadi'trice [invadi'tritʃe] *ag* invading ♦ *sm* invader

invecchi'are [invek'kjare] *vi* (*persona*) to grow old; (*vino, popolazione*) to age; (*moda*) to become dated ♦ *vt* to age; (*far apparire più vecchio*) to make look older

in'vece [in'vetʃe] *av* instead; (*al contrario*) on the contrary; **~ di** instead of

inve'ire *vi*: **~ contro** to rail against

inven'tare *vt* to invent; (*pericoli, pettegolezzi*) to make up, invent

inven'tario *sm* inventory; (COMM) stocktaking *no pl*

inven'tivo, a *ag* inventive ♦ *sf* inventiveness

inven'tore *sm* inventor

invenzi'one [inven'tsjone] *sf* invention; (*bugia*) lie, story

inver'nale *ag* winter *cpd*; (*simile all'inverno*) wintry

in'verno *sm* winter

invero'simile *ag* unlikely

inversi'one *sf* inversion; reversal; **"divieto d'~"** (AUT) "no U-turns"

in'verso, a *ag* opposite; (MAT) inverse ♦ *sm* contrary, opposite; **in senso ~** in the opposite direction; **in ordine ~** in reverse order

inver'tire *vt* to invert, reverse; **~ la marcia** (AUT) to do a U-turn; **inver'tito, a** *sm/f* homosexual

investi'gare *vt, vi* to investigate; **investiga'tore, trice** *sm/f* investigator, detective; **investigazi'one** *sf* investigation, inquiry

investi'mento *sm* (ECON) investment

inves'tire *vt* (*denaro*) to invest; (*sog: veicolo: pedone*) to knock down; (*: altro veicolo*) to crash into; (*apostrofare*) to assail; (*incaricare*): **~ qn di** to invest sb with

invi'are *vt* to send; **invi'ato, a** *sm/f* envoy; (STAMPA) correspondent

in'vidia *sf* envy; **invidi'are** *vt*: **invidiare qn (per qc)** to envy sb for sth; **invidiare qc a qn** to envy sb sth; **invidi'oso, a** *ag* envious

in'vio, 'vii *sm* sending; *(insieme di merci)* consignment

invipe'rito, a *ag* furious

invischi'are [invis'kjare] *vt (fig)*: **~ qn in** to involve sb in; **~rsi** *vr*: **~rsi (con qn/in qc)** to get mixed up *o* involved (with sb/in sth)

invi'sibile *ag* invisible

invi'tare *vt* to invite; **~ qn a fare** to invite sb to do; **invi'tato, a** *sm/f* guest; **in'vito** *sm* invitation

invo'care *vt (chiedere: aiuto, pace)* to cry out for; *(appellarsi: la legge, Dio)* to appeal to, invoke

invogli'are [invoʎ'ʎare] *vt*: **~ qn a fare** to tempt sb to do, induce sb to do

involon'tario, a *ag (errore)* unintentional; *(gesto)* involuntary

invol'tino *sm (CUC)* roulade

in'volto *sm (pacco)* parcel; *(fagotto)* bundle

in'volucro *sm* cover, wrapping

involuzi'one [involut'tsjone] *sf (di stile)* convolutedness; *(regresso)*: **subire un'~** to regress

inzacche'rare [intsakke'rare] *vt* to spatter with mud

inzup'pare [intsup'pare] *vt* to soak; **~rsi** *vr* to get soaked

'io *pron* I ♦ *sm inv*: **l'~** the ego, the self; **~ stesso(a)** I myself

l'odio *sm* iodine

l'onio *sm*: **lo ~, il mar ~** the Ionian (Sea)

Iper'mercato *sm* hypermarket

ipertensi'one *sf* high blood pressure, hypertension

ip'nosi *sf* hypnosis; **ipno'tismo** *sm* hypnotism; **ipnotiz'zare** *vt* to hypnotize

ipocri'sia *sf* hypocrisy

i'pocrita, i, e *ag* hypocritical ♦ *sm/f* hypocrite

ipo'teca, che *sf* mortgage; **ipote'care** *vt* to mortgage

i'potesi *sf inv* hypothesis; **ipo'tetico, a, ci, che** *ag* hypothetical

'ippica *sf* horseracing

'ippico, a, ci, che *ag* horse *cpd*

ippocas'tano *sm* horse chestnut

ip'podromo *sm* racecourse

ippo'potamo *sm* hippopotamus

'ira *sf* anger, wrath

I'ran *sm*: **l'~** Iran

I'raq *sm*: **l'~** Iraq

'iride *sf (arcobaleno)* rainbow; *(ANAT, BOT)* iris

Ir'landa *sf*: **l'~** Ireland; **l'~ del Nord** Northern Ireland, Ulster; **la Repubblica d'~** Eire, the Republic of Ireland; **irlan'dese** *ag* Irish ♦ *sm/f* Irishman/woman; **gli Irlandesi** the Irish

iro'nia *sf* irony; **i'ronico, a, ci, che** *ag* ironic(al)

irradi'are *vt* to radiate; *(sog: raggi di luce: illuminare)* to shine on ♦ *vi (diffondersi: anche: ~rsi)* to radiate

irragio'nevole [irradʒo'nevole] *ag* irrational; unreasonable

irrazio'nale [irrattsjo'nale] *ag* irrational

irre'ale *ag* unreal

irrecupe'rabile *ag* irretrievable; *(fig: persona)* irredeemable

irrecu'sabile *ag (offerta)* not to be refused; *(prova)* irrefutable

irrego'lare *ag* irregular; *(terreno)* uneven

irremo'vibile *ag (fig)* unshakeable, unyielding

irrepa'rabile *ag* irreparable; *(fig)* inevitable

irrepe'ribile *ag* nowhere to be found

irrequi'eto, a *ag* restless

irresis'tibile *ag* irresistible

irrespon'sabile *ag* irresponsible

irridu'cibile [irridu'tʃibile] *ag* irreducible; *(fig)* indomitable

irri'gare *vt (annaffiare)* to irrigate; *(sog: fiume etc)* to flow through; **irrigazi'one** *sf* irrigation

irrigi'dire [irridʒi'dire] *vt* to stiffen; **~rsi** *vr* to stiffen

irri'sorio, a *ag* derisory

irri'tare *vt (mettere di malumore)* to irritate, annoy; *(MED)* to irritate; **~rsi** *vr (stizzirsi)* to become irritated *o* annoyed; *(MED)* to become irritated; **irritazi'one** *sf* irritation; annoyance

ir'rompere *vi*: **~ in** to burst into

irro'rare *vt* to sprinkle; (*AGR*) to spray

irru'ente *ag* (*fig*) impetuous, violent

irruzi'one [irrut'tsjone] *sf*: **fare ~ in** to burst into; (*sog: polizia*) to raid

'irto, a *ag* bristly; **~ di** bristling with

is'critto, a *pp di* **iscrivere ♦** *sm/f* member; **per** *o* **in ~** in writing

is'crivere *vt* to register, enter; (*persona*): ~ **(a)** to register (in), enrol (in); **~rsi** *vr*: **~rsi (a)** (*club, partito*) to join; (*università*) to register *o* enrol (at); (*esame, concorso*) to register *o* enter (for); **iscrizi'one** *sf* (*epigrafe etc*) inscription; (*a scuola, società*) enrolment, registration; (*registrazione*) registration

Is'lam *sm*: **l'~** Islam

Is'landa *sf*: **l'~** Iceland

'isola *sf* island; **~ pedonale** (*AUT*) pedestrian precinct

isola'mento *sm* isolation; (*TECN*) insulation

iso'lante *ag* insulating ♦ *sm* insulator

iso'lare *vt* to isolate; (*TECN*) to insulate; (*: acusticamente*) to soundproof; **iso'lato, a** *ag* isolated; insulated ♦ *sm* (*gruppo di edifici*) block

ispetto'rato *sm* inspectorate

ispet'tore *sm* inspector

ispezio'nare [ispettsjo'nare] *vt* to inspect; **ispezi'one** *sf* inspection

'ispido, a *ag* bristly, shaggy

ispi'rare *vt* to inspire; **~rsi** *vr*: **~rsi a** to draw one's inspiration from

Isra'ele *sm*: **l'~** Israel; **israeli'ano, a** *ag, sm/f* Israeli

is'sare *vt* to hoist

istan'taneo, a *ag* instantaneous ♦ *sf* (*FOT*) snapshot

is'tante *sm* instant, moment; **all'~, sull'~** instantly, immediately

is'tanza [is'tantsa] *sf* petition, request

is'terico, a, ci, che *ag* hysterical

iste'rismo *sm* hysteria

isti'gare *vt* to incite; **istigazi'one** *sf* incitement; **istigazione a delinquere** (*DIR*) incitement to crime

is'tinto *sm* instinct

istitu'ire *vt* (*fondare*) to institute, found; (*porre: confronto*) to establish; (*intraprendere: inchiesta*) to set up

isti'tuto *sm* institute; (*di università*) department; (*ente, DIR*) institution; **~ di bellezza** beauty salon

istituzi'one [istitut'tsjone] *sf* institution

'istmo *sm* (*GEO*) isthmus

'istrice ['istritʃe] *sm* porcupine

istri'one (*peg*) *sm* ham actor

istru'ire *vt* (*insegnare*) to teach; (*ammaestrare*) to train; (*informare*) to instruct, inform; (*DIR*) to prepare; **istrut'tore, 'trice** *sm/f* instructor ♦ *ag*: **giudice istruttore** *vedi* **giudice**; **istrut'toria** *sf* (*DIR*) (preliminary) investigation and hearing; **istruzi'one** *sf* education; training; (*direttiva*) instruction

I'talia *sf*: **l'~** Italy

itali'ano, a *ag* Italian ♦ *sm/f* Italian ♦ *sm* (*LING*) Italian; **gli i~i** the Italians

itine'rario *sm* itinerary

itte'rizia [itte'rittsja] *sf* (*MED*) jaundice

'ittico, a, ci, che *ag* fish *cpd*; fishing *cpd*

Iugos'lavia *etc* = **Jugoslavia** *etc*

i'uta *sf* jute

I.V.A. ['iva] *sigla f* (= *imposta sul valore aggiunto*) VAT

J, j

jazz [dʒaz] *sm* jazz

jeans [dʒinz] *smpl* jeans

Jugos'lavia [jugoz'lavja] *sf*: **la ~** Yugoslavia; **la ex-~** former Yugoslavia; **jugos'lavo, a** *ag, sm/f* Yugoslav(ian)

'juta ['juta] *sf* = **iuta**

K, k

K *abbr* (*INFORM*) K

k *abbr* (= *kilo*) k

karatè *sm* karate

Kg *abbr* (= *chilogrammo*) kg

'killer *sm inv* gunman, hired gun

'kiwi ['kiwi] *sm inv* kiwi fruit

km *abbr* (= *chilometro*) km
'krapfen *sm inv* (CUC) doughnut

L, l

l' *det vedi* **la; lo; il**
la¹ (*dav V* **l'**) *det f the* ♦ *pron* (*oggetto: persona*) her; (: *cosa*) it; (: *forma di cortesia*) you; *vedi anche* **il**
la² *sm inv* (MUS) A; (: *solfeggiando*) la
là *av* there; **di ~** (*da quel luogo*) from there; (*in quel luogo*) in there; (*dall'altra parte*) over there; **di ~ di** beyond; **per di ~** that way; **più in ~** further on; (*tempo*) later on; **fatti in ~** move up; **~ dentro/sopra/sotto** in/up (*o* on)/under there; *vedi anche* **quello**
'labbro (*pl(f):* **labbra**: *solo nel senso* ANAT) *sm* lip
labi'rinto *sm* labyrinth, maze
labora'torio *sm* (*di ricerca*) laboratory; (*di arti, mestieri*) workshop; **~ linguistico** language laboratory
labori'oso, a *ag* (*faticoso*) laborious; (*attivo*) hard-working
labu'rista, i, e *ag* Labour (BRIT) *cpd* ♦ *sm/f* Labour Party member (BRIT)
'lacca, che *sf* lacquer
'laccio [ˈlattʃo] *sm* noose; (*legaccio, stringa*) lasso; (*di scarpa*) lace, **~ emostatico** tourniquet
lace'rare [latʃeˈrare] *vt* to tear to shreds, lacerate; **~rsi** *vr* to tear; **'lacero, a** *ag* (*logoro*) torn, tattered; (MED) lacerated
'lacrima *sf* tear; **in ~e** in tears; **lacri'mare** *vi* to water; **lacri'mogeno, a** *ag:* **gas lacrimogeno** tear gas
la'cuna *sf* (*fig*) gap
'ladro *sm* thief; **ladro'cinio** *sm* theft, larceny
laggiù [ladˈdʒu] *av* down there; (*di là*) over there
la'gnarsi [laɲˈɲarsi] *vr:* **~ (di)** to complain (about)
'lago, ghi *sm* lake
la'guna *sf* lagoon

'laico, a, ci, che *ag* (*apostolato*) lay; (*vita*) secular; (*scuola*) non-denominational ♦ *sm/f* layman/woman
'lama *sm inv* (ZOOL) llama; (REL) lama ♦ *sf* blade
lam'bire *vt* to lick; to lap
lamen'tare *vt* to lament; **~rsi** *vr* (*emettere lamenti*) to moan, groan; (*rammaricarsi*): **~rsi (di)** to complain (about); **lamen'tela** *sf* complaining *no pl;* **lamen'tevole** *ag* (*voce*) complaining, plaintive; (*destino*) pitiful; **la'mento** *sm* moan, groan; wail; **lamen'toso, a** *ag* plaintive
la'metta *sf* razor blade
lami'era *sf* sheet metal
'lamina *sf* (*lastra sottile*) thin sheet (*o* layer *o* plate); **~ d'oro** gold leaf; gold foil; **lami'nare** *vt* to laminate; **lami'nato, a** *ag* laminated; (*tessuto*) lamé ♦ *sm* laminate
'lampada *sf* lamp; **~ a gas** gas lamp; **~ da tavolo** table lamp
lampa'dario *sm* chandelier
lampa'dina *sf* light bulb; **~ tascabile** pocket torch (BRIT) *o* flashlight (US)
lam'pante *ag* (*fig: evidente*) crystal clear, evident
lampeggi'are [lampedˈdʒare] *vi* (*luce, fari*) to flash ♦ *vb impers:* **lampeggia** there's lightning; **lampeggia'tore** *sm* (AUT) indicator
lampi'one *sm* street light *o* lamp (BRIT)
'lampo *sm* (METEOR) flash of lightning; (*di luce, fig*) flash; **~i** *smpl* lightning *no pl* ♦ *ag inv:* **cerniera ~** zip (*fastener*) (BRIT), zipper (US); **guerra ~** blitzkrieg
lam'pone *sm* raspberry
'lana *sf* wool; **~ d'acciaio** steel wool; **pura ~ vergine** pure new wool; **~ di vetro** glass wool
lan'cetta [lanˈtʃetta] *sf* (*indice*) pointer, needle; (*di orologio*) hand
'lancia [ˈlantʃa] *sf* (*arma*) lance; (: *picca*) spear; (*di pompa antincendio*) nozzle; (*imbarcazione*) launch
lanciafi'amme [lantʃaˈfjamme] *sm inv* flamethrower
lanci'are [lanˈtʃare] *vt* to throw, hurl, fling;

(*SPORT*) to throw; (*far partire: automobile*) to get up to full speed; (*bombe*) to drop; (*razzo, prodotto, moda*) to launch; **~rsi** *vr*: **~rsi contro/su** to throw *o* hurl *o* fling o.s. against/on; **~rsi in** (*fig*) to embark on

lanci'nante [lantʃi'nante] *ag* (*dolore*) shooting, throbbing; (*grido*) piercing

'lancio ['lantʃo] *sm* throwing *no pl*; throw; dropping *no pl*; drop; launching *no pl*; launch; **~ del peso** putting the shot

'landa *sf* (*GEO*) moor

'languido, a *ag* (*fiacco*) languid, weak; (*tenero, malinconico*) languishing

langu'ore *sm* weakness, languor

lani'ficio [lani'fitʃo] *sm* woollen mill

la'noso, a *ag* woolly

lan'terna *sf* lantern; (*faro*) lighthouse

la'nugine [la'nudʒine] *sf* down

lapi'dario, a *ag* (*fig*) terse

'lapide *sf* (*di sepolcro*) tombstone; (*commemorativa*) plaque

'lapis *sm inv* pencil

Lap'ponia *sf* Lapland

'lapsus *sm inv* slip

'laptop ['læptɔp] *sm inv* laptop (computer)

'lardo *sm* bacon fat, lard

lar'ghezza [lar'gettsa] *sf* width; breadth; looseness; generosity; **~ di vedute** broad-mindedness

'largo, a, ghi, ghe *ag* wide; broad; (*maniche*) wide; (*abito: troppo ampio*) loose; (*fig*) generous ♦ *sm* width; breadth; (*mare aperto*): **il ~** the open sea ♦ *sf*: **stare** *o* **tenersi alla ~a (da qn/qc)** to keep one's distance (from sb/sth), keep away (from sb/sth); **~ due metri** two metres wide; **~ di spalle** broad-shouldered; **di ~ghe vedute** broad-minded; **su ~a scala** on a large scale; **di manica ~a** generous, open-handed; **al ~ di Genova** off (the coast of) Genoa; **farsi ~ tra la folla** to push one's way through the crowd

'larice ['laritʃe] *sm* (*BOT*) larch

larin'gite [larin'dʒite] *sf* laryngitis

'larva *sf* larva; (*fig*) shadow

la'sagne [la'zaɲɲe] *sfpl* lasagna *sg*

lasci'are [laʃ'ʃare] *vt* to leave;

(*abbandonare*) to leave, abandon, give up; (*cessare di tenere*) to let go of ♦ *vb aus*: **~ fare qn** to let sb do; **~ andare** *o* **correre** *o* **perdere** to let things go their own way; **~ stare qc/qn** to leave sth/sb alone; **~rsi** *vr* (*persone*) to part; (*coppia*) to split up; **~rsi andare** to let o.s. go

'lascito ['laʃʃito] *sm* (*DIR*) legacy

'laser ['lazer] *ag, sm inv*: **(raggio) ~** laser (beam)

lassa'tivo, a *ag, sm* laxative

'lasso *sm*: **~ di tempo** interval, lapse of time

lassù *av* up there

'lastra *sf* (*di pietra*) slab; (*di metallo, FOT*) plate; (*di ghiaccio, vetro*) sheet; (*radiografica*) X-ray (plate)

lastri'cato *sm* paving

late'rale *ag* lateral, side *cpd*; (*uscita, ingresso etc*) side *cpd* ♦ *sm* (*CALCIO*) half-back

late'rizio [late'rittsjo] *sm* (*perforated*) brick

lati'fondo *sm* large estate

la'tino, a *ag, sm* Latin; **~-ameri'cano, a** *ag* Latin-American

lati'tante *sm/f* fugitive (from justice)

lati'tudine *sf* latitude

'lato, a *ag* (*fig*) wide, broad ♦ *sm* side; (*fig*) aspect, point of view; **in senso ~** broadly speaking

la'trare *vi* to bark

la'trina *sf* public lavatory

'latta *sf* tin (plate); (*recipiente*) tin, can

lat'taio, a *sm/f* milkman/woman; dairyman/woman

lat'tante *ag* unweaned

'latte *sm* milk; **~ detergente** cleansing milk *o* lotion; **~ in polvere** dried *o* powdered milk; **~ scremato** skimmed milk; **latte'ria** *sf* dairy; **latti'cini** *smpl* dairy products

lat'tina *sf* (*di birra etc*) can

lat'tuga, ghe *sf* lettuce

'laurea *sf* degree; **laurearsi** *vr* to graduate; **laure'ato, a** *ag, sm/f* graduate

'lauro *sm* laurel

'lauto, a *ag* (*pranzo, mancia*) lavish

'lava *sf* lava

la'vabo *sm* washbasin

la'vaggio [la'vaddʒo] *sm* washing *no pl*; ~ **del cervello** brainwashing *no pl*

la'vagna [la'vaɲɲa] *sf* (GEO) slate; (*di scuola*) blackboard

la'vanda *sf* (*anche* MED) wash; (BOT) lavender; **lavan'daia** *sf* washerwoman; **lavande'ria** *sf* laundry; **lavanderia automatica** launderette; **lavanderia a secco** dry-cleaner's; **lavan'dino** *sm* sink

lavapi'atti *sm/f* dishwasher

la'vare *vt* to wash; ~**rsi** *vr* to wash, have a wash; ~ **a secco** to dry-clean; ~**rsi le mani/i denti** to wash one's hands/clean one's teeth

lava'secco *sm o f inv* drycleaner's

lavasto'viglie [lavasto'viʎʎe] *sm o f inv* (*macchina*) dishwasher

lava'trice [lava'tritʃe] *sf* washing machine

lava'tura *sf* washing *no pl*; ~ **di piatti** dishwater

lavo'rante *sm/f* worker

lavo'rare *vi* to work; (*fig: bar, studio etc*) to do good business ♦ *vt* to work; ~**rsi qn** (*persuaderlo*) to work on sb; ~ **a** to work on; ~ **a maglia** to knit; **lavora'tivo, a** *ag* working; **lavora'tore, 'trice** *sm/f* worker ♦ *ag* working; **lavorazi'one** *sf* (*gen*) working; (*di legno, pietra*) carving; (*di film*) making; (*di prodotto*) manufacture; (*modo di esecuzione*) workmanship; **lavo'rio** *sm* intense activity

la'voro *sm* work; (*occupazione*) job, work *no pl*; (*opera*) piece of work, job; (ECON) labour; ~**i forzati** hard labour *sg*; ~**i pubblici** public works

le *det fpl* the ♦ *pron* (*oggetto*) them; (: *a lei, a essa*) (to) her; (: *forma di cortesia*) (to) you; *vedi anche* **il**

le'ale *ag* loyal; (*sincero*) sincere; (*onesto*) fair; **lealtà** *sf* loyalty; sincerity; fairness

'lebbra *sf* leprosy

'lecca 'lecca *sm inv* lollipop

leccapi'edi (*peg*) *sm/f inv* toady, bootlicker

lec'care *vt* to lick; (*sog: gatto: latte etc*) to lick *o* lap up; (*fig*) to flatter; ~**rsi i baffi** to lick one's lips

'leccio ['lettʃo] *sm* holm oak, ilex

leccor'nia *sf* titbit, delicacy

'lecito, a ['letʃito] *ag* permitted, allowed

'ledere *vt* to damage, injure

'lega, ghe *sf* league; (*di metalli*) alloy

le'gaccio [le'gattʃo] *sm* string, lace

le'gale *ag* legal ♦ *sm* lawyer; **legaliz'zare** *vt* to authenticate; (*regolarizzare*) to legalize

le'game *sm* (*corda, fig: affettivo*) tie, bond; (*nesso logico*) link, connection

le'gare *vt* (*prigioniero, capelli, cane*) to tie (up); (*libro*) to bind; (CHIM) to alloy; (*fig: collegare*) to bind, join ♦ *vi* (*far lega*) to unite, (*fig*) to get on well

le'gato *sm* (REL) legate; (DIR) legacy, bequest

lega'tura *sf* (*di libro*) binding; (MUS) ligature

le'genda [le'dʒɛnda] *sf* (*di carta geografica etc*) = **leggenda**

'legge ['leddʒe] *sf* law

leg'genda [led'dʒɛnda] *sf* (*narrazione*) legend; (*di carta geografica etc*) key, legend

'leggere ['leddʒere] *vt, vi* to read

legge'rezza [leddʒe'rettsa] *sf* lightness; thoughtlessness; fickleness

leg'gero, a [led'dʒɛro] *ag* light; (*agile, snello*) nimble, agile, light; (*tè, caffè*) weak; (*fig: non grave, piccolo*) slight; (: *spensierato*) thoughtless; (: *incostante*) fickle; free and easy; **alla ~a** thoughtlessly

leggi'adro, a [led'dʒadro] *ag* pretty, lovely; (*movimenti*) graceful

leg'gio, 'gii [led'dʒio] *sm* lectern; (MUS) music stand

legisla'tura [ledʒizla'tura] *sf* legislature

legislazi'one [ledʒizlat'tsjone] *sf* legislation

le'gittimo, a [le'dʒittimo] *ag* legitimate; (*fig: giustificato, lecito*) justified, legitimate; ~**a difesa** (DIR) self-defence

'legna ['leɲɲa] *sf* firewood; **le'gname** *sm* wood, timber

'legno ['leɲɲo] *sm* wood; (*pezzo di ~*) piece of wood; **di ~** wooden; ~ **compensato** plywood; **le'gnoso, a** *ag* wooden; woody; (*carne*) tough

le'gumi *smpl* (*BOT*) pulses

'lei *pron* (*soggetto*) she; (*oggetto: per dare rilievo, con preposizione*) her; (*forma di cortesia: anche:* **L~**) you ♦ *sm*: **dare del ~ a qn** to address sb as "lei"; **~ stessa** she herself; you yourself

'lembo *sm* (*di abito, strada*) edge; (*striscia sottile: di terra*) strip

'lemma, i *sm* headword

'lemme 'lemme *av* (*very*) very slowly

'lena *sf* (*fig*) energy, stamina

le'nire *vt* to soothe

lenta'mente *av* slowly

'lente *sf* (*OTTICA*) lens *sg*; **~ d'ingrandimento** magnifying glass; **~i a contatto** *o* **corneali** contact lenses

len'tezza [len'tettsa] *sf* slowness

len'ticchia [len'tikkja] *sf* (*BOT*) lentil

len'tiggine [len'tiddʒine] *sf* freckle

'lento, a *ag* slow; (*molle: fune*) slack; (*non stretto: vite, abito*) loose ♦ *sm* (*ballo*) slow dance

'lenza ['lentsa] *sf* fishing-line

lenzu'olo [len'tswɔlo] *sm* sheet; **~a** *sfpl* pair of sheets

le'one *sm* lion; (*dello zodiaco*): **L~** Leo

lepo'rino, a *ag*: **labbro ~** harelip

'lepre *sf* hare

'lercio, a, ci, cie ['lertʃo] *ag* filthy

'lesbica, che *sf* lesbian

lesi'nare *vt* to be stingy with ♦ *vi*: **~ (su)** to skimp (on), be stingy (with)

lesi'one *sf* (*MED*) lesion; (*DIR*) injury, damage; (*EDIL*) crack

'leso, a *pp di* **ledere** ♦ *ag* (*offeso*) injured; **parte ~a** (*DIR*) injured party

les'sare *vt* (*CUC*) to boil

'lessico, ci *sm* vocabulary; lexicon

'lesso, a *ag* boiled ♦ *sm* boiled meat

'lesto, a *ag* quick; (*agile*) nimble; **~ di mano** (*per rubare*) light-fingered; (*per picchiare*) free with one's fists

le'tale *ag* lethal; fatal

leta'maio *sm* dunghill

le'tame *sm* manure, dung

le'targo, ghi *sm* lethargy; (*ZOOL*) hibernation

le'tizia [le'tittsja] *sf* joy, happiness

'lettera *sf* letter; **~e** *sfpl* (*letteratura*) literature *sg*; (*studi umanistici*) arts (subjects); **alla ~** literally; **in ~e** in words, in full; **lette'rale** *ag* literal

lette'rario, a *ag* literary

lette'rato, a *ag* well-read, scholarly

lettera'tura *sf* literature

let'tiga, ghe *sf* (*barella*) stretcher

let'tino *sm* cot (*BRIT*), crib (*US*)

'letto, a *pp di* **leggere** ♦ *sm* bed; **andare a ~** to go to bed; **~ a castello** bunk beds *pl*; **~ a una piazza/a due piazze** *o* **matrimoniale** single/double bed

let'tore, 'trice *sm/f* reader; (*INS*) (foreign language) assistant (*BRIT*), (foreign) teaching assistant (*US*) ♦ *sm* (*TECN*): **~ ottico** optical character reader

let'tura *sf* reading

leuce'mia [leutʃe'mia] *sf* leukaemia

'leva *sf* lever; (*MIL*) conscription; **far ~ su qn** to work on sb; **~ del cambio** (*AUT*) gear lever

le'vante *sm* east; (*vento*) East wind; **il L~** the Levant

le'vare *vt* (*occhi, braccio*) to raise; (*sollevare, togliere: tassa, divieto*) to lift; (*indumenti*) to take off, remove; (*rimuovere*) to take away; (: *dal di sopra*) to take off; (: *dal di dentro*) to take out; **~rsi** *vr* to get up; (*sole*) to rise; **le'vata** *sf* (*di posta*) collection

leva'toio, a *ag*: **ponte ~** drawbridge

leva'tura *sf* intelligence, mental capacity

levi'gare *vt* to smooth; (*con carta vetrata*) to sand

levri'ere *sm* greyhound

lezi'one [let'tsjone] *sf* lesson; (*UNIV*) lecture; **fare ~** to teach; to lecture; **dare una ~ a qn** to teach sb a lesson

lezi'oso, a [let'tsjoso] *ag* affected; simpering

'lezzo ['leddzo] *sm* stench, stink

li *pron pl* (*oggetto*) them

lì *av* there; **di** *o* **da ~** from there; **per di ~** that way; **di ~ a pochi giorni** a few days later; **~ per ~** there and then; at first; **essere ~ (~) per fare** to be on the point of doing, be about to do; **~ dentro** in there; **~ sotto** under there; **~ sopra** on there; up there; *vedi anche* **quello**

liba'nese *ag, sm/f* Lebanese *inv*

Li'bano *sm:* **il ~** the Lebanon

'libbra *sf (peso)* pound

li'beccio [li'bettʃo] *sm* south-west wind

li'bello *sm* libel

li'bellula *sf* dragonfly

libe'rale *ag, sm/f* liberal

liberaliz'zare [liberalid'dzare] *vt* to liberalize

libe'rare *vt (rendere libero: prigioniero)* to release; *(: popolo)* to free, liberate; *(sgombrare: passaggio)* to clear; *(: stanza)* to vacate; *(produrre: energia)* to release; **~rsi** *vr:* **~rsi di qc/qn** to get rid of sth/sb; **libera'tore, 'trice** *ag* liberating ♦ *sm/f* liberator; **liberazi'one** *sf* liberation, freeing; release; rescuing

---
Liberazione

> *The* **Liberazione** *is a national holiday which falls on 25 April. It commemorates the liberation of Italy at the end of the Second World War.*

'libero, a *ag* free; *(strada)* clear; *(non occupato: posto etc)* vacant; not taken; empty; not engaged; **~ da** free from; **~ arbitrio** free will; **~ professionista** self-employed professional person; **~ scambio** free trade; **libertà** *sf inv* freedom; *(tempo disponibile)* free time ♦ *sfpl (licenza)* liberties; **in libertà provvisoria/vigilata** released without bail/on probation

'Libia *sf:* **la ~** Libya; **'libico, a, ci, che** *ag, sm/f* Libyan

li'bidine *sf* lust

li'braio *sm* bookseller

li'brarsi *vr* to hover

libre'ria *sf (bottega)* bookshop; *(stanza)* library; *(mobile)* bookcase

li'bretto *sm* booklet; *(taccuino)* notebook;

(MUS) libretto; **~ degli assegni** cheque book; **~ di circolazione** *(AUT)* logbook; **~ di risparmio** (savings) bank-book, passbook; **~ universitario** student's report book

'libro *sm* book; **~ di cassa** cash book; **~ mastro** ledger; **~ paga** payroll; **~ di testo** textbook

li'cenza [li'tʃentsa] *sf (permesso)* permission, leave; *(di pesca, caccia, circolazione)* permit, licence; *(MIL)* leave; *(INS)* school leaving certificate; *(libertà)* liberty; licence; licentiousness; **andare in ~** *(MIL)* to go on leave

licenzia'mento [litʃentsja'mento] *sm* dismissal

licenzi'are [litʃen'tsjare] *vt (impiegato)* to dismiss; *(COMM: per eccesso di personale)* to make redundant; *(INS)* to award a certificate to; **~rsi** *vr (impiegato)* to resign, hand in one's notice; *(INS)* to obtain one's school-leaving certificate

li'ceo [li'tʃeo] *sm (INS)* secondary *(BRIT) o* high *(US)* school *(for 14- to 19-year-olds)*

'lido *sm* beach, shore

li'eto, a *ag* happy, glad; **"molto ~"** *(nelle presentazioni)* "pleased to meet you"

li'eve *ag* light; *(di poco conto)* slight; *(sommesso: voce)* faint, soft

lievi'tare *vi (anche fig)* to rise ♦ *vt* to leaven

li'evito *sm* yeast; **~ di birra** brewer's yeast

'ligio, a, gi, gie ['lidʒo] *ag* faithful, loyal

'lilla *sm inv* lilac

'lillà *sm inv* lilac

'lima *sf* file

limacci'oso, a [limat'tʃoso] *ag* slimy; muddy

li'mare *vt* to file (down); *(fig)* to polish

'limbo *sm (REL)* limbo

li'metta *sf* nail file

limi'tare *vt* to limit, restrict; *(circoscrivere)* to bound, surround; **limita'tivo, a** *ag* limiting, restricting; **limi'tato, a** *ag* limited, restricted

'limite *sm* limit; *(confine)* border, boundary; **~ di velocità** speed limit

li'mitrofo, a *ag* neighbouring

limo'nata *sf* lemonade (*BRIT*), (lemon) soda (*US*); lemon squash (*BRIT*), lemonade (*US*)

li'mone *sm* (*pianta*) lemon tree; (*frutto*) lemon

'limpido, a *ag* clear; (*acqua*) limpid, clear

'lince [ˈlintʃe] *sf* lynx

linci'are *vt* to lynch

'lindo, a *ag* tidy, spick and span; (*biancheria*) clean

'linea *sf* line; (*di mezzi pubblici di trasporto: itinerario*) route; (*: servizio*) service; **a grandi ~e** in outline; **mantenere la ~** to look after one's figure; **aereo di ~** airliner; **nave di ~** liner; **volo di ~** scheduled flight; **~ aerea** airline; **~ di partenza/d'arrivo** (*SPORT*) starting/finishing line; **~ di tiro** line of fire

linea'menti *smpl* features; (*fig*) outlines

line'are *ag* linear; (*fig*) coherent, logical

line'etta *sf* (*trattino*) dash; (*d'unione*) hyphen

lin'gotto *sm* ingot, bar

'lingua *sf* (*ANAT, CUC*) tongue; (*idioma*) language; **mostrare la ~** to stick out one's tongue; **di ~ italiana** Italian-speaking; **~ madre** mother tongue; **una ~ di terra** a spit of land

lingu'aggio [linˈgwaddʒo] *sm* language

lingu'etta *sf* (*di strumento*) reed; (*di scarpa, TECN*) tongue; (*di busta*) flap

lingu'istica *sf* linguistics *sg*

'lino *sm* (*pianta*) flax; (*tessuto*) linen

li'noleum *sm inv* linoleum, lino

liposuzi'one [liposutˈtsjone] *sf* liposuction

lique'fare *vt* (*render liquido*) to liquefy; (*fondere*) to melt; **~rsi** *vr* to liquefy; to melt

liqui'dare *vt* (*società, beni, persona: uccidere*) to liquidate; (*persona: sbarazzarsene*) to get rid of; (*conto, problema*) to settle; (*COMM: merce*) to sell off, clear; **liquidazi'one** *sf* liquidation; settlement; clearance sale

liquidità *sf* liquidity

'liquido, a *ag, sm* liquid; **~ per freni** brake fluid

liqui'rizia [likwiˈrittsja] *sf* liquorice

li'quore *sm* liqueur

'lira *sf* (*unità monetaria*) lira; (*MUS*) lyre; **~ sterlina** pound sterling

'lirica, che *sf* (*poesia*) lyric poetry; (*componimento poetico*) lyric; (*MUS*) opera

'lirico, a, ci, che *ag* lyric(al); (*MUS*) lyric; **cantante/teatro ~** opera singer/house

'lisca, sche *sf* (*di pesce*) fishbone

lisci'are [liʃˈʃare] *vt* to smooth; (*fig*) to flatter

'liscio, a, sci, sce [ˈliʃʃo] *ag* smooth; (*capelli*) straight; (*mobile*) plain; (*bevanda alcolica*) neat; (*fig*) straightforward, simple ♦ *av*: **andare ~** to go smoothly; **passarla ~a** to get away with it

'liso, a *ag* worn out, threadbare

'lista *sf* (*elenco*) list; **~ elettorale** electoral roll; **~ delle vivande** menu; **~ delle spese** shopping list

lis'tino *sm* list; **~ dei cambi** (foreign) exchange rate; **~ dei prezzi** price list

Lit. *abbr* = **lire italiane**

'lite *sf* quarrel, argument; (*DIR*) lawsuit

liti'gare *vi* to quarrel; (*DIR*) to litigate

li'tigio [liˈtidʒo] *sm* quarrel; **litigi'oso, a** *ag* quarrelsome; (*DIR*) litigious

litogra'fia *sf* (*sistema*) lithography; (*stampa*) lithograph

lito'rale *ag* coastal, coast *cpd* ♦ *sm* coast

'litro *sm* litre

livel'lare *vt* to level, make level; **~rsi** *vr* to become level; (*fig*) to level out, balance out

li'vello *sm* level; (*fig*) level, standard; **ad alto ~** (*fig*) high-level; **~ del mare** sea level

'livido, a *ag* livid; (*per percosse*) bruised, black and blue; (*cielo*) leaden ♦ *sm* bruise

li'vore *sm* malice, spite

Li'vorno *sf* Livorno, Leghorn

li'vrea *sf* livery

'lizza [ˈlittsa] *sf* lists *pl*; **scendere in ~** (*anche fig*) to enter the lists

lo (*dav s impura, gn, pn, ps, x, z; dav V* **l'**) *det m* the ♦ *pron* (*oggetto: persona*) him; (*: cosa*) it; **~ sapevo** I knew it; **~ so** I know; **sii buono, anche se lui non ~ è** be good, even if he isn't; *vedi anche* **il**

lo'cale *ag* local ♦ *sm* room; (*luogo pubblico*) premises *pl*; **~ notturno** nightclub;

località *sf inv* locality; **localiz'zare** *vt* (*circoscrivere*) to confine, localize; (*accertare*) to locate, place

lo'canda *sf* inn; **locandi'ere, a** *sm/f* innkeeper

loca'tario, a *sm/f* tenant

loca'tore, 'trice *sm/f* landlord/lady

locazi'one [lokat'tsjone] *sf* (*da parte del locatario*) renting *no pl*; (*da parte del locatore*) renting out *no pl*, letting *no pl*; (**contratto di**) ~ lease; (**canone di**) ~ rent; **dare in** ~ to rent out, let

locomo'tiva *sf* locomotive

locomo'tore *sm* electric locomotive

locomozi'one [lokomot'tsjone] *sf* locomotion, **mezzi di** ~ vehicles, means of transport

lo'custa *sf* locust

locuzi'one [lokut'tsjone] *sf* phrase, expression

lo'dare *vt* to praise

'lode *sf* praise; (*INS*): **laurearsi con 110 e** ~ ≈ to graduate with a first-class honours degree (*BRIT*), graduate summa cum laude (*US*)

'loden *sm inv* (*stoffa*) loden; (*cappotto*) loden overcoat

lo'devole *ag* praiseworthy

loga'ritmo *sm* logarithm

'loggia, ge ['lɔddʒa] *sf* (*ARCHIT*) loggia; (*circolo massonico*) lodge; **loggi'one** *sm* (*di teatro*): **il loggione** the Gods *sg*

'logica *sf* logic

'logico, a, ci, che ['lɔdʒiko] *ag* logical

logo'rare *vt* to wear out; (*sciupare*) to waste; **~rsi** *vr* to wear out; (*fig*) to wear o.s. out

logo'rio *sm* wear and tear; (*fig*) strain

'logoro, a *ag* (*stoffa*) worn out, threadbare; (*persona*) worn out

lom'baggine [lom'baddʒine] *sf* lumbago

Lombar'dia *sf*: **la** ~ Lombardy

lom'bata *sf* (*taglio di carne*) loin

'lombo *sm* (*ANAT*) loin

lom'brico, chi *sm* earthworm

londi'nese *ag* London *cpd* ♦ *sm/f* Londoner

'Londra *sf* London

lon'gevo, a ['lonˈdʒevo] *ag* long-lived

longi'tudine [londʒi'tudine] *sf* longitude

lonta'nanza [lonta'nantsa] *sf* distance; absence

lon'tano, a *ag* (*distante*) distant, faraway; (*assente*) absent; (*vago: sospetto*) slight, remote; (*tempo: remoto*) far-off, distant; (*parente*) distant, remote ♦ *av* far; **è ~ a la casa?** is it far to the house?, is the house far from here?; **è ~ un chilometro** it's a kilometre away *o* a kilometre from here; **più** ~ farther; **da** *o* **di** ~ from a distance; ~ **da** a long way from; **alla ~a** slightly, vaguely

'lontra *sf* otter

lo'quace [lo'kwatʃe] *ag* talkative, loquacious; (*fig: gesto etc*) eloquent

'lordo, a *ag* dirty, filthy; (*peso, stipendio*) gross

'loro *pron pl* (*oggetto, con preposizione*) them; (*complemento di termine*) to them; (*soggetto*) they; (*forma di cortesia: anche:* **L~**) you; to you; **il(la)** ~, **i(le)** ~ *det* their; (*forma di cortesia: anche:* **L~**) your ♦ *pron* theirs; (*forma di cortesia: anche:* **L~**) yours; ~ **stessi(e)** they themselves; you yourselves

'losco, a, schi, sche *ag* (*fig*) shady, suspicious

'lotta *sf* struggle, fight; (*SPORT*) wrestling; ~ **libera** all-in wrestling; **lot'tare** *vi* to fight, struggle; to wrestle; **lotta'tore, trice** *sm/f* wrestler

lotte'ria *sf* lottery; (*di gara ippica*) sweepstake

'lotto *sm* (*gioco*) (state) lottery; (*parte*) lot; (*EDIL*) site

lozi'one [lot'tsjone] *sf* lotion

lubrifi'cante *sm* lubricant

lubrifi'care *vt* to lubricate

luc'chetto [luk'ketto] *sm* padlock

lucci'care [luttʃi'kare] *vi* to sparkle, glitter, twinkle

'luccio ['luttʃo] *sm* (*ZOOL*) pike

'lucciola ['luttʃola] *sf* (*ZOOL*) firefly; glowworm

'luce ['lutʃe] *sf* light; (*finestra*) window; **alla**

~ **di** by the light of; **fare** ~ **su qc** (*fig*) to shed *o* throw light on sth; ~ **del sole/della luna** sun/moonlight; **lu'cente** *ag* shining

lucer'nario [lutʃer'narjo] *sm* skylight

lu'certola [lu'tʃertola] *sf* lizard

luci'dare [lutʃi'dare] *vt* to polish

lucida'trice [lutʃida'tritʃe] *sf* floor polisher

'**lucido, a** ['lutʃido] *ag* shining, bright; (*lucidato*) polished; (*fig*) lucid ♦ *sm* shine, lustre; (*per scarpe etc*) polish; (*disegno*) tracing

'**lucro** *sm* profit, gain; **lu'croso, a** *ag* lucrative, profitable

'**luglio** ['luʎʎo] *sm* July

'**lugubre** *ag* gloomy

'**lui** *pronome* (*soggetto*) he; (*oggetto: per dare rilievo, con preposizione*) him; ~ **stesso** he himself

lu'maca, che *sf* slug; (*chiocciola*) snail

'**lume** *sm* light; (*lampada*) lamp; (*fig*): **chiedere ~i a qn** to ask sb for advice; **a ~ di naso** (*fig*) by rule of thumb

lumi'naria *sf* (*per feste*) illuminations *pl*

lumi'noso, a *ag* (*che emette luce*) luminous; (*cielo, colore, stanza*) bright; (*sorgente*) of light, light *cpd*; (*fig: sorriso*) bright, radiant

'**luna** *sf* moon; ~ **nuova/piena** new/full moon; ~ **di miele** honeymoon

'**luna park** *sm inv* amusement park, funfair

lu'nare *ag* lunar, moon *cpd*

lu'nario *sm* almanac; **sbarcare il** ~ to make ends meet

lu'natico, a, ci, che *ag* whimsical, temperamental

lunedì *sm inv* Monday; **di** *o* **il** ~ on Mondays

lun'gaggine [lun'gaddʒine] *sf* slowness; **~i della burocrazia** red tape

lun'ghezza [lun'gettsa] *sf* length; ~ **d'onda** (*FISICA*) wavelength

'**lungi** ['lundʒi]: ~ **da** *prep* far from

'**lungo, a, ghi, ghe** *ag* long; (*lento: persona*) slow; (*diluito: caffè, brodo*) weak, watery, thin ♦ *sm* length ♦ *prep* along; ~ **3 metri** 3 metres long; **a** ~ for a long time; **a ~ andare** in the long run; **di gran ~a**

(*molto*) by far; **andare in** ~ *o* **per le lunghe** to drag on; **saperla ~a** to know what's what; **in** ~ **e in largo** far and wide, all over; ~ **il corso dei secoli** throughout the centuries

lungo'mare *sm* promenade

lu'notto *sm* (*AUT*) rear *o* back window; ~ **termico** heated rear window

lu'ogo, ghi *sm* place; (*posto: di incidente etc*) scene, site; (*punto, passo di libro*) passage; **in ~ di** instead of; **in primo ~** in the first place; **aver** ~ to take place; **dar ~ a** to give rise to; ~ **comune** commonplace; ~ **di nascita** birthplace; (*AMM*) place of birth; ~ **di provenienza** place of origin

luogote'nente *sm* (*MIL*) lieutenant

lu'para *sf* sawn-off shotgun

'**lupo, a** *sm/f* wolf

'**luppolo** *sm* (*BOT*) hop

'**lurido, a** *ag* filthy

lu'singa, ghe *sf* (*spesso al pl*) flattery *no pl*

lusin'gare *vt* to flatter; **lusinghi'ero, a** *ag* flattering, gratifying

lus'sare *vt* (*MED*) to dislocate

Lussem'burgo *sm* (*stato*): **il** ~ Luxembourg ♦ *sf* (*città*) Luxembourg

'**lusso** *sm* luxury; **di** ~ luxury *cpd*; **lussu'oso, a** *ag* luxurious

lussureggi'ante [lussured'dʒante] *ag* luxuriant

lus'suria *sf* lust

lus'trare *vt* to polish, shine

lustras'carpe *sm/f inv* shoeshine

lus'trino *sm* sequin

'**lustro, a** *ag* shiny; (*pelo*) glossy ♦ *sm* shine, gloss; (*fig*) prestige, glory; (*quinquennio*) five-year period

'**lutto** *sm* mourning; **essere in/portare il** ~ to be in/wear mourning; **luttu'oso, a** *ag* mournful, sad

M, m

ma *cong* but; **~ insomma!** for goodness sake!; **~ no!** of course not!

'**macabro, a** *ag* gruesome, macabre

macché [mak'ke] *escl* not at all!, certainly not!

macche'roni [makke'roni] *smpl* macaroni *sg*

'**macchia** ['makkja] *sf* stain, spot; (*chiazza di diverso colore*) spot; splash, patch; (*tipo di boscaglia*) scrub; **alla ~** (*fig*) in hiding;

macchi'are *vt* (*sporcare*) to stain, mark; **macchiarsi** *vr* (*persona*) to get o.s. dirty; (*stoffa*) to stain; to get stained o marked

'**macchina** ['makkina] *sf* machine; (*motore, locomotiva*) engine; (*automobile*) car; (*fig: meccanismo*) machinery; **andare in ~** (*AUT*) to go by car; (*STAMPA*) to go to press; **~ da cucire** sewing machine; **~ fotografica** camera; **~ da presa** cine o movie camera; **~ da scrivere** typewriter; **~ a vapore** steam engine

macchi'nare [makki'nare] *vt* to plot

macchi'nario [makki'narjo] *sm* machinery

macchi'netta [makki'netta] (*fam*) *sf* (*caffettiera*) percolator; (*accendino*) lighter

macchi'nista, i [makki'nista] *sm* (*di treno*) engine-driver; (*di nave*) engineer

macchi'noso, a [makki'noso] *ag* complex, complicated

mace'donia [matʃe'dɔnja] *sf* fruit salad

macel'laio [matʃel'lajo] *sm* butcher

macel'lare [matʃel'lare] *vt* to slaughter, butcher; **macelle'ria** *sf* butcher's (shop); **ma'cello** *sm* (*mattatoio*) slaughterhouse, abattoir (*BRIT*); (*fig*) slaughter, massacre; (*: disastro*) shambles *sg*

mace'rare [matʃe'rare] *vt* to macerate; (*CUC*) to marinate; **~rsi** *vr* (*fig*): **~rsi in** to be consumed with

ma'cerie [ma'tʃɛrje] *sfpl* rubble *sg*, debris *sg*

ma'cigno [ma'tʃiɲɲo] *sm* (*masso*) rock, boulder

'**macina** ['matʃina] *sf* (*pietra*) millstone;

(*macchina*) grinder; **macinacaffè** *sm inv* coffee grinder; **macina'pepe** *sm inv* peppermill

maci'nare [matʃi'nare] *vt* to grind; (*carne*) to mince (*BRIT*), grind (*US*); **maci'nato** *sm* meal, flour; (*carne*) minced (*BRIT*) o ground (*US*) meat

maci'nino [matʃi'nino] *sm* coffee grinder; peppermill

'**madido, a** *ag*: **~ (di)** wet o moist (with)

Ma'donna *sf* (*REL*) Our Lady

mador'nale *ag* enormous, huge

'**madre** *sf* mother; (*matrice di bolletta*) counterfoil ♦ *ag inv* mother *cpd*; **ragazza ~** unmarried mother; **scena ~** (*TEATRO*) principal scene; (*fig*) terrible scene

madre'lingua *sf* mother tongue, native language

madre'perla *sf* mother-of-pearl

ma'drina *sf* godmother

maestà *sf inv* majesty; **maes'toso, a** *ag* majestic

ma'estra *sf vedi* **maestro**

maes'trale *sm* north-west wind, mistral

maes'tranze [maes'trantse] *sfpl* workforce *sg*

maes'tria *sf* mastery, skill

ma'estro, a *sm/f* (*INS: anche:* **~ di scuola** o **elementare**) primary (*BRIT*) o grade school (*US*) teacher; (*esperto*) expert ♦ *sm* (*artigiano, fig: guida*) master; (*MUS*) maestro ♦ *ag* (*principale*) main; (*di grande abilità*) masterly, skilful; **~a d'asilo** nursery teacher; **~ di cerimonie** master of ceremonies

'**mafia** *sf* Mafia; **mafi'oso** *sm* member of the Mafia

'**maga** *sf* sorceress

ma'gagna [ma'gaɲɲa] *sf* defect, flaw, blemish; (*noia, guaio*) problem

ma'gari *escl* (*esprime desiderio*): **~ fosse vero!** if only it were true!; **ti piacerebbe andare in Scozia? — ~!** would you like to go to Scotland? — and how! ♦ *av* (*anche*) even; (*forse*) perhaps

magaz'zino [magad'dzino] *sm* warehouse; **grande ~** department store

'**maggio** ['maddʒo] *sm* May

maggio'rana [maddʒo'rana] *sf* (*BOT*) (sweet) marjoram

maggio'ranza [maddʒo'rantsa] *sf* majority

maggio'rare [maddʒo'rare] *vt* to increase, raise

maggior'domo [maddʒor'dɔmo] *sm* butler

maggi'ore [mad'dʒore] *ag* (*comparativo: più grande*) bigger, larger; taller; greater; (*: più vecchio: sorella, fratello*) older, elder; (*: di grado superiore*) senior; (*: più importante, MIL, MUS*) major; (*superlativo*) biggest, largest; tallest; greatest; oldest, eldest ♦ *sm/f* (*di grado*) superior; (*di età*) elder; (*MIL*) major; (*: AER*) squadron leader; **la maggior parte** the majority; **andare per la ~** (*cantante etc*) to be very popular; **maggio'renne** *ag* of age ♦ *sm/f* person who has come of age; **maggior'mente** *av* much more; (*con senso superlativo*) most

ma'gia [ma'dʒia] *sf* magic; **'magico, a, ci, che** *ag* magic; (*fig*) fascinating, charming, magical

'magio ['madʒo] *sm* (*REL*): **i re Magi** the Magi, the Three Wise Men

magis'tero [madʒis'tero] *sm*: **facoltà di M~** ≈ teachers' training college; **magis'trale** *ag* primary (*BRIT*) o grade school (*US*) teachers', primary (*BRIT*) o grade school (*US*) teaching *cpd*; skilful

magis'trato [madʒis'trato] *sm* magistrate; **magistra'tura** *sf* magistrature; (*magistrati*): **la magistratura** the Bench

'maglia ['maʎʎa] *sf* stitch; (*lavoro ai ferri*) knitting *no pl*; (*tessuto, SPORT*) jersey; (*maglione*) jersey, sweater; (*di catena*) link; (*di rete*) mesh; **~ diritta/rovescia** plain/purl; **maglie'ria** *sf* knitwear; (*negozio*) knitwear shop; **magli'etta** *sf* (*canottiera*) vest; (*tipo camicia*) T-shirt; **magli'ficio** *sm* knitwear factory

'maglio ['maʎʎo] *sm* mallet; (*macchina*) power hammer

magli'one *sm* sweater, jumper

ma'gnanimo, a [maɲ'ɲanimo, a] *ag* magnanimous

ma'gnete [maɲ'ɲete] *sm* magnet; **ma'gnetico, a, ci, che** *ag* magnetic

magne'tofono [maɲɲe'tɔfono] *sm* tape recorder

ma'gnifico, a, ci, che [maɲ'ɲifiko] *ag* magnificent, splendid; (*ospite*) generous

'magno, a ['maɲɲo] *ag*: **aula ~a** main hall

ma'gnolia [maɲ'ɲɔlja] *sf* magnolia

'mago, ghi *sm* (*stregone*) magician, wizard; (*illusionista*) magician

ma'grezza [ma'grettsa] *sf* thinness

'magro, a *ag* (*very*) thin, skinny; (*carne*) lean; (*formaggio*) low-fat; (*fig: scarso, misero*) meagre, poor; (*: meschino: scusa*) poor, lame; **mangiare di ~** not to eat meat

'mai *av* (*nessuna volta*) never; (*talvolta*) ever; **non ... ~** never; **~ più** never again; **come ~?** why (o how) on earth?; **chi/dove/quando ~?** whoever/wherever/whenever?

mai'ale *sm* (*ZOOL*) pig; (*carne*) pork

maio'nese *sf* mayonnaise

'mais *sm inv* maize

mai'uscola *sf* capital letter

mai'uscolo, a *ag* (*lettera*) capital; (*fig*) enormous, huge

mal *av, sm vedi* **male**

malac'corto, a *ag* rash, careless

mala'fede *sf* bad faith

mala'lingua (*pl* **male'lingue**) *sf* gossip(monger)

mala'mente *av* badly; dangerously

malan'dato, a *ag* (*persona: di salute*) in poor health; (*: di condizioni finanziarie*) badly off; (*trascurato*) shabby

ma'lanno *sm* (*disgrazia*) misfortune; (*malattia*) ailment

mala'pena *sf*: **a ~** hardly, scarcely

ma'laria *sf* (*MED*) malaria

mala'sorte *sf* bad luck

mala'ticcio, a [mala'tittʃo] *ag* sickly

ma'lato, a *ag* ill, sick; (*gamba*) bad; (*pianta*) diseased ♦ *sm/f* sick person; (*in ospedale*) patient; **malat'tia** *sf* (*infettiva etc*) illness, disease; (*cattiva salute*) illness, sickness; (*di pianta*) disease

malau'gurio *sm* bad o ill omen

mala'vita *sf* underworld

mala'voglia [mala'vɔʎʎa] *sf*: **di ~** unwillingly, reluctantly

mal'concio, a, ci, ce [mal'kontʃo] ag in a sorry state

malcon'tento sm discontent

malcos'tume sm immorality

mal'destro, a ag (inabile) inexpert, inexperienced; (goffo) awkward

maldi'cenza [maldi'tʃentsa] sf malicious gossip

maldis'posto, a ag: ~ (verso) ill-disposed (towards)

'male av badly ♦ sm (ciò che è ingiusto, disonesto) evil; (danno, svantaggio) harm; (sventura) misfortune; (dolore fisico, morale) pain, ache; di ~ in peggio from bad to worse; sentirsi ~ to feel ill; far ~ (dolere) to hurt; far ~ alla salute to be bad for one's health; far del ~ a qn to hurt o harm sb; restare o rimanere ~ to be sorry; to be disappointed; to be hurt; andare a ~ to go bad; come va? — non c'è ~ how are you? — not bad; mal di cuore heart trouble; ~ di dente toothache; mal di mare seasickness; avere mal di gola/testa to have a sore throat/a headache; aver ~ ai piedi to have sore feet

male'detto, a pp di maledire ♦ ag cursed, damned; (fig: fam) damned, blasted

male'dire vt to curse; maledizi'one sf curse; maledizione! damn it!

maledu'cato, a ag rude, ill-mannered

male'fatta sf misdeed

male'ficio [male'fitʃo] sm witchcraft

ma'lefico, a, ci, che ag (influsso, azione) evil

ma'lessere sm indisposition, slight illness; (fig) uneasiness

ma'levolo, a ag malevolent

malfa'mato, a ag notorious

mal'fatto, a ag (persona) deformed; (oggetto) badly made; (lavoro) badly done

malfat'tore, 'trice sm/f wrongdoer

mal'fermo, a ag unsteady, shaky; (salute) poor, delicate

malformazi'one [malformat'tsjone] sf malformation

malgo'verno sm maladministration

mal'grado prep in spite of, despite ♦ cong although; mio (o tuo etc) ~ against my (o your etc) will

mali'gnare [malin'nare] vi: ~ su to malign, speak ill of

ma'ligno, a [ma'linno] ag (malvagio) malicious, malignant; (MED) malignant

malinco'nia sf melancholy, gloom;

malin'conico, a, ci, che ag melancholy

malincu'ore: a ~ av reluctantly, unwillingly

malintenzio'nato, a [malintentsjo'nato] ag ill-intentioned

malin'teso, a ag misunderstood; (riguardo, senso del dovere) mistaken, wrong ♦ sm misunderstanding

ma'lizia [ma'littsja] sf (malignità) malice; (furbizia) cunning; (espediente) trick; malizi'oso, a ag malicious; cunning; (vivace, birichino) mischievous

mal'loppo sm (involto) bundle; (fam: refurtiva) loot

malme'nare vt to beat up

mal'messo, a ag shabby

malnu'trito, a ag undernourished

ma'locchio [ma'lɔkkjo] sm evil eye

ma'lora sf: andare in ~ to go to the dogs

ma'lore sm (sudden) illness

mal'sano, a ag unhealthy

malsi'curo, a ag unsafe

'Malta sf Malta

'malta sf (EDIL) mortar

mal'tempo sm bad weather

'malto sm malt

maltrat'tare vt to ill-treat

malu'more sm bad mood; (irritabilità) bad temper; (discordia) ill feeling; di ~ in a bad mood

mal'vagio, a, gi, gie [mal'vadʒo] ag wicked, evil

malversazi'one [malversat'tsjone] sf (DIR) embezzlement

mal'visto, a ag: ~ (da) disliked (by), unpopular (with)

malvi'vente sm criminal

malvolenti'eri av unwillingly, reluctantly

'mamma sf mummy, mum; ~ mia! my

goodness!

mam'mella *sf* (ANAT) breast; (*di vacca, capra etc*) udder

mam'mifero *sm* mammal

'mammola *sf* (BOT) violet

ma'nata *sf* (*colpo*) slap; (*quantità*) handful

'manca *sf* left (hand); **a destra e a ~** left, right and centre, on all sides

man'canza [man'kantsa] *sf* lack; (*carenza*) shortage, scarcity; (*fallo*) fault; (*imperfezione*) failing, shortcoming; **per ~ di tempo** through lack of time; **in ~ di meglio** for lack of anything better

man'care *vi* (*essere insufficiente*) to be lacking; (*venir meno*) to fail; (*sbagliare*) to be wrong, make a mistake; (*non esserci*) to be missing, not to be there; (*essere lontano*): **~ (da)** to be away (from) ♦ *vt* to miss; **~ di** to lack; **~ a** (*promessa*) to fail to keep; **tu mi manchi** I miss you; **mancò poco che morisse** he very nearly died; **mancano ancora 10 sterline** we're still £10 short; **manca un quarto alle 6** it's a quarter to 6; **man'cato, a** *ag* (*tentativo*) unsuccessful; (*artista*) failed

'mancia, ce ['mantʃa] *sf* tip; **~ competente** reward

manci'ata [man'tʃata] *sf* handful

man'cino, a [man'tʃino] *ag* (*braccio*) left; (*persona*) left-handed; (*fig*) underhand

'manco *av* (*nemmeno*): **~ per sogno** *o* **per idea!** not on your life!

man'dante *sm/f* (*di delitto*) instigator

manda'rancio [manda'rantʃo] *sm* clementine

man'dare *vt* to send; (*far funzionare: macchina*) to drive; (*emettere*) to send out; (*: grido*) to give, utter, let out; **~ a chiamare qn** to send for sb; **~ avanti** (*fig: famiglia*) to provide for; (*: fabbrica*) to run, look after; **~ giù** to send down; (*anche fig*) to swallow; **~ via** to send away; (*licenziare*) to fire

manda'rino *sm* mandarin (orange); (*cinese*) mandarin

man'data *sf* (*quantità*) lot, batch; (*di chiave*) turn; **chiudere a doppia ~** to

double-lock

man'dato *sm* (*incarico*) commission; (DIR: *provvedimento*) warrant; (*di deputato etc*) mandate; (*ordine di pagamento*) postal *o* money order; **~ d'arresto** warrant for arrest

man'dibola *sf* mandible, jaw

'mandorla *sf* almond; **'mandorlo** *sm* almond tree

'mandria *sf* herd

maneggi'are [maned'dʒare] *vt* (*creta, cera*) to mould, work, fashion; (*arnesi, utensili*) to handle; (: *adoperare*) to use; (*fig: persone, denaro*) to handle, deal with; **ma'neggio** *sm* moulding; handling; use; (*intrigo*) plot, scheme; (*per cavalli*) riding school

ma'nesco, a, schi, sche *ag* free with one's fists

ma'nette *sfpl* handcuffs

manga'nello *sm* club

manga'nese *sm* manganese

mange'reccio, a, ci, ce [mandʒe'rettʃo] *ag* edible

mangi'are [man'dʒare] *vt* to eat; (*intaccare*) to eat into *o* away; (CARTE, SCACCHI *etc*) to take ♦ *vi* to eat ♦ *sm* eating; (*cibo*) food; (*cucina*) cooking; **~rsi le parole** to mumble; **~rsi le unghie** to bite one's nails; **mangia'toia** *sf* feeding-trough

man'gime [man'dʒime] *sm* fodder

'mango, ghi *sm* mango

ma'nia *sf* (PSIC) mania; (*fig*) obsession, craze; **ma'niaco, a, ci, che** *ag* suffering from a mania; **maniaco (di)** obsessed (by), crazy (about)

'manica *sf* sleeve; (*fig: gruppo*) gang, bunch; (GEO): **la M~, il Canale della M~** the (English) Channel; **essere di ~ larga/ stretta** to be easy-going/strict; **~ a vento** (AER) wind sock

mani'chino [mani'kino] *sm* (*di sarto, vetrina*) dummy

'manico, ci *sm* handle; (MUS) neck

mani'comio *sm* mental hospital; (*fig*) madhouse

mani'cotto *sm* muff; (TECN) coupling; sleeve

mani'cure *sm o f inv* manicure ♦ *sf inv* manicurist

mani'era *sf* way, manner; (*stile*) style, manner; **~e** *sfpl* (*comportamento*) manners; **in ~ che** so that; **in ~ da** so as to; **in tutte le ~e** at all costs

manie'rato, a *ag* affected

manifat'tura *sf* (*lavorazione*) manufacture; (*stabilimento*) factory

manifes'tare *vt* to show, display; (*esprimere*) to express; (*rivelare*) to reveal, disclose ♦ *vi* to demonstrate; **~rsi** *vr*: to show o.s.; **~rsi amico** to prove o.s. (to be) a friend; **manifestazi'one** *sf* show, display; expression; (*sintomo*) sign, symptom; (*dimostrazione pubblica*) demonstration; (*cerimonia*) event

mani'festo, a *ag* obvious, evident ♦ *sm* poster, bill; (*scritto ideologico*) manifesto

ma'niglia [ma'niʎʎa] *sf* handle; (*sostegno: negli autobus etc*) strap

manipo'lare *vt* to manipulate; (*alterare: vino*) to adulterate; **manipolazi'one** *sf* manipulation; adulteration

---

mani pulite

Mani pulite is a term used to describe the judicial operation which identified, gathered evidence against, and brought to trial a number of politicians and industrialists implicated in bribery and corruption scandals. See also **Tangentopoli.**

'**manna** *sf* (*REL*) manna; (*fig*) godsend

man'naia *sf* (*del boia*) (executioner's) axe; (*per carni*) cleaver

man'naro: lupo ~ *sm* werewolf

'**mano, i** *sf* hand; (*strato: di vernice etc*) coat; (*fig: di notizia*) hand; **di prima ~** (*notizia*) first-hand; **di seconda ~** second-hand; **man ~** little by little, gradually; **man ~ che** as; **darsi o stringersi la ~** to shake hands; **mettere le ~i avanti** (*fig*) to safeguard o.s.; **restare a ~i vuote** to be left empty-handed; **venire alle ~i** to come to blows; **a ~** by hand; **~i in alto!** hands up!

mano'dopera *sf* labour

mano'messo, a *pp di* **manomettere**

ma'nometro *sm* gauge, manometer

mano'mettere *vt* (*alterare*) to tamper with; (*aprire indebitamente*) to break open illegally

ma'nopola *sf* (*dell'armatura*) gauntlet; (*guanto*) mitt; (*di impugnatura*) hand-grip; (*pomello*) knob

manos'critto, a *ag* handwritten ♦ *sm* manuscript

mano'vale *sm* labourer

mano'vella *sf* handle; (*TECN*) crank

ma'novra *sf* manoeuvre (*BRIT*), maneuver (*US*); (*FERR*) shunting; **mano'vrare** *vt* (*veicolo*) to manoeuvre (*BRIT*), maneuver (*US*); (*macchina, congegno*) to operate; (*fig: persona*) to manipulate ♦ *vi* to manoeuvre

manro'vescio [manro'veʃʃo] *sm* slap (*with back of hand*)

man'sarda *sf* attic

mansi'one *sf* task, duty, job

mansu'eto, a *ag* gentle, docile

man'tello *sm* cloak; (*fig: di neve etc*) blanket, mantle; (*ZOOL*) coat

mante'nere *vt* to maintain; (*adempiere: promesse*) to keep, abide by; (*provvedere a*) to support, maintain; **~rsi** *vr*: **~rsi calmo/ giovane** to stay calm/young; **manteni'mento** *sm* maintenance

'**mantice** ['mantitʃe] *sm* bellows *pl*

'**manto** *sm* cloak; **~ stradale** road surface

manu'ale *ag* manual ♦ *sm* (*testo*) manual, handbook

ma'nubrio *sm* handle; (*di bicicletta etc*) handlebars *pl*; (*SPORT*) dumbbell

manu'fatto *sm* manufactured article

manutenzi'one [manuten'tsjone] *sf* maintenance, upkeep; (*d'impianti*) maintenance, servicing

'**manzo** ['mandzo] *sm* (*ZOOL*) steer; (*carne*) beef

'**mappa** *sf* (*GEO*) map; **mappa'mondo** *sm* map of the world; (*globo girevole*) globe

mara'tona *sf* marathon

'**marca, che** *sf* (*COMM: di prodotti*) brand; (*contrassegno, scontrino*) ticket, check;

prodotto di ~ (*di buona qualità*) high-class product; **~ da bollo** official stamp

mar'care *vt* (*munire di contrassegno*) to mark; (*a fuoco*) to brand; (*SPORT: gol*) to score; (*: avversario*) to mark; (*accentuare*) to stress; **~ visita** (*MIL*) to report sick

'**Marche** ['marke] *sfpl*: **le ~** the Marches (*region of central Italy*)

mar'chese, a [mar'keze] *sm/f* marquis *o* marquess/marchioness

marchi'are [mar'kjare] *vt* to brand; '**marchio** *sm* (*di bestiame*, COMM, *fig*) brand; **marchio depositato** registered trademark; **marchio di fabbrica** trademark

'**marcia, ce** ['martʃa] *sf* (*anche* MUS, MIL) march; (*funzionamento*) running; (*il camminare*) walking; (*AUT*) gear; **mettere in ~** to start; **mettersi in ~** to get moving; **far ~ indietro** (*AUT*) to reverse; (*fig*) to back-pedal

marciapi'ede [martʃa'pjɛde] *sm* (*di strada*) pavement (*BRIT*), sidewalk (*US*); (*FERR*) platform

marci'are [mar'tʃare] *vi* to march; (*andare: treno, macchina*) to go; (*funzionare*) to run, work

'**marcio, a, ci, ce** ['martʃo] *ag* (*frutta, legno*) rotten, bad; (*MED*) festering; (*fig*) corrupt, rotten

mar'cire [mar'tʃire] *vi* (*andare a male*) to go bad, rot; (*suppurare*) to fester; (*fig*) to rot, waste away

'**marco, chi** *sm* (*unità monetaria*) mark

'**mare** *sm* sea; **in ~** at sea; **andare al ~** (*in vacanza etc*) to go to the seaside; **il M~ del Nord** the North Sea

ma'rea *sf* tide; **alta/bassa ~** high/low tide

mareggi'ata [mared'dʒata] *sf* heavy sea

mare'moto *sm* seaquake

maresci'allo [mareʃ'ʃallo] *sm* (*MIL*) marshal; (*: sottufficiale*) warrant officer

marga'rina *sf* margarine

marghe'rita [marge'rita] *sf* (ox-eye) daisy, marguerite; (*di stampante*) daisy wheel

'**margine** ['mardʒine] *sm* margin; (*di bosco, via*) edge, border

ma'rina *sf* navy; (*costa*) coast; (*quadro*)

seascape; **~ militare/mercantile** navy/merchant navy (*BRIT*) *o* marine (*US*)

mari'naio *sm* sailor

mari'nare *vt* (*CUC*) to marinate; **~ la scuola** to play truant; **mari'nata** *sf* marinade

ma'rino, a *ag* sea *cpd*, marine

mario'netta *sf* puppet

mari'tare *vt* to marry; **~rsi** *vr*: **~rsi a** *o* **con qn** to marry sb, get married to sb

ma'rito *sm* husband

ma'rittimo, a *ag* maritime, sea *cpd*

mar'maglia [mar'maʎʎa] *sf* mob, riff-raff

marmel'lata *sf* jam; (*di agrumi*) marmalade

'**marmo** *sm* marble

mar'mocchio [mar'mɔkkjo] *sm* (*fam*) tot, kid

mar'motta *sf* (*ZOOL*) marmot

Ma'rocco *sm*: **il ~** Morocco

mar'rone *ag inv* brown ♦ *sm* (*BOT*) chestnut

mar'sala *sm inv* (*vino*) Marsala

mar'sina *sf* tails *pl*, tail coat

mar'supio *sm* pouch; (*per denaro*) bum bag; (*per neonato*) sling

marte'dì *sm inv* Tuesday; **di** *o* **il ~** on Tuesdays; **~ grasso** Shrove Tuesday

martel'lare *vt* to hammer ♦ *vi* (*pulsare*) to throb; (*: cuore*) to thump

mar'tello *sm* hammer; (*di uscio*) knocker

marti'netto *sm* (*TECN*) jack

'**martire** *sm/f* martyr; **mar'tirio** *sm* martyrdom; (*fig*) agony, torture

'**martora** *sf* marten

martori'are *vt* to torment, torture

mar'xista, i, e *ag, sm/f* Marxist

marza'pane [martsa'pane] *sm* marzipan

'**marzo** ['martso] *sm* March

mascal'zone [maskal'tsone] *sm* rascal, scoundrel

ma'scella [maʃ'ʃella] *sf* (*ANAT*) jaw

'**maschera** ['maskera] *sf* mask; (*travestimento*) disguise; (*: per un ballo etc*) fancy dress; (*TEATRO, CINEMA*) usher/

usherette; (*personaggio del teatro*) stock character; **masche'rare** *vt* to mask; (*travestire*) to disguise; to dress up; (*fig: celare*) to hide, conceal; (*MIL*) to camouflage; **~rsi da** to disguise o.s. as; to dress up as; (*fig*) to masquerade as

mas'chile [mas'kile] *ag* masculine; (*sesso, popolazione*) male; (*abiti*) men's; (*per ragazzi: scuola*) boys'

'maschio, a ['maskjo] *ag* (*BIOL*) male; (*virile*) manly ♦ *sm* (*anche ZOOL, TECN*) male; (*uomo*) man; (*ragazzo*) boy; (*figlio*) son

masco'lino, a *ag* masculine

'massa *sf* mass; (*di errori etc*): **una ~ di** heaps of, masses of; (*di gente*) mass, multitude; (*ELETTR*) earth; **in ~** (*COMM*) in bulk; (*tutti insieme*) en masse; **adunata in ~** mass meeting; **di ~** (*cultura, manifestazione*) mass

mas'sacro *sm* massacre, slaughter; (*fig*) mess, disaster

mas'saggio [mas'saddʒo] *sm* massage

mas'saia *sf* housewife

masse'rizie [masse'rittsje] *sfpl* (household) furnishings

mas'siccio, a, ci, ce [mas'sittʃo] *ag* (*oro, legno*) solid; (*palazzo*) massive; (*corporatura*) stout ♦ *sm* (*GEO*) massif

'massima *sf* (*sentenza, regola*) maxim; (*METEOR*) maximum temperature; **in linea di ~** generally speaking; *vedi anche* **massimo**

massi'male *sm* maximum

'massimo, a *ag, sm* maximum; **al ~** at (the) most

'masso *sm* rock, boulder

mas'sone *sm* freemason; **massone'ria** *sf* freemasonry

mas'tello *sm* tub

masti'care *vt* to chew

'mastice ['mastitʃe] *sm* mastic; (*per vetri*) putty

mas'tino *sm* mastiff

ma'tassa *sf* skein

mate'matica *sf* mathematics *sg*

mate'matico, a, ci, che *ag*

mathematical ♦ *sm/f* mathematician

materas'sino *sm* mat; (*gonfiabile*) air bed

mate'rasso *sm* mattress; **~ a molle** spring *o* interior-sprung mattress

ma'teria *sf* (*FISICA*) matter; (*TECN, COMM*) material, matter *no pl*; (*disciplina*) subject; (*argomento*) subject matter, material; **~e prime** raw materials; **in ~ di** (*per quanto concerne*) on the subject of

materi'ale *ag* material; (*fig: grossolano*) rough, rude ♦ *sm* material; (*insieme di strumenti etc*) equipment *no pl*, materials *pl*

maternità *sf* motherhood, maternity; (*reparto*) maternity ward

ma'terno, a *ag* (*amore, cura etc*) maternal, motherly; (*nonno*) maternal; (*lingua, terra*) mother *cpd*

ma'tita *sf* pencil

ma'trice [ma'tritʃe] *sf* matrix; (*COMM*) counterfoil; (*fig: origine*) background

ma'tricola *sf* (*registro*) register; (*numero*) registration number; (*nell'università*) freshman, fresher

ma'trigna [ma'triɲɲa] *sf* stepmother

matrimoni'ale *ag* matrimonial, marriage *cpd*

matri'monio *sm* marriage, matrimony; (*durata*) marriage, married life; (*cerimonia*) wedding

ma'trona *sf* (*fig*) matronly woman

mat'tina *sf* morning; **matti'nata** *sf* morning; (*spettacolo*) matinée, afternoon performance; **mattini'ero, a** *ag*: **essere mattiniero** to be an early riser

mat'tino *sm* morning

'matto, a *ag* mad, crazy; (*fig: falso*) false, imitation ♦ *sm/f* madman/woman; **avere una voglia ~a di qc** to be dying for sth

mat'tone *sm* brick; (*fig*): **questo libro/film è un ~** this book/film is heavy going

matto'nella *sf* tile

matu'rare *vi* (*anche: ~rsi*) (*frutta, grano*) to ripen; (*ascesso*) to come to a head; (*fig: persona, idea, ECON*) to mature ♦ *vt* to ripen; to (make) mature

maturità *sf* maturity; (*di frutta*) ripeness, maturity; (*INS*) school-leaving examination,

≈ GCE A-levels (*BRIT*)

ma'turo, a *ag* mature; (*frutto*) ripe, mature

maxiprocesso *n* criminal trial involving large numbers of co-accused

'mazza ['mattsa] *sf* (*bastone*) club; (*martello*) sledge-hammer; (*SPORT: da golf*) club; (: *da baseball, cricket*) bat

maz'zata [mat'tsata] *sf* (*anche fig*) heavy blow

'mazzo ['mattso] *sm* (*di fiori, chiavi etc*) bunch; (*di carte da gioco*) pack

me *pron* me; ~ **stesso(a)** myself; **sei bravo quanto ~** you are as clever as I (am) *o* as me

me'andro *sm* meander

mec'canica, che *sf* mechanics *sg*; (*attività tecnologica*) mechanical engineering; (*meccanismo*) mechanism

mec'canico, a, ci, che *ag* mechanical ♦ *sm* mechanic

mecca'nismo *sm* mechanism

me'daglia [me'daʎʎa] *sf* medal; **medagli'one** *sm* (*ARCHIT*) medallion; (*gioiello*) locket

me'desimo, a *ag* same; (*in persona*): **io ~** I myself

'media *sf* average; (*MAT*) mean; (*INS: voto*) end-of-term average; **in ~** on average; *vedi anche* **medio**

medi'ano, a *ag* median; (*valore*) mean ♦ *sm* (*CALCIO*) half-back

medi'ante *prep* by means of

medi'are *vt* (*fare da mediatore*) to act as mediator in; (*MAT*) to average

media'tore, 'trice *sm/f* mediator; (*COMM*) middle man, agent

medica'mento *sm* medicine, drug

medi'care *vt* to treat; (*ferita*) to dress; **medicazi'one** *sf* treatment, medication; dressing

medi'cina [medi'tʃina] *sf* medicine; ~ **legale** forensic medicine; **medici'nale** *ag* medicinal ♦ *sm* drug, medicine

'medico, a, ci, che *ag* medical ♦ *sm* doctor; ~ **generico** general practitioner, GP

medie'vale *ag* medieval

'medio, a *ag* average; (*punto, ceto*) middle; (*altezza, statura*) medium ♦ *sm* (*dito*) middle finger; **licenza ~a** *leaving certificate awarded at the end of 3 years of secondary education;* **scuola ~a** *first 3 years of secondary school*

medi'ocre *ag* mediocre, poor

medioe'vale *ag* = **medievale**

medio'evo *sm* Middle Ages *pl*

medi'tare *vt* to ponder over, meditate on; (*progettare*) to plan, think out ♦ *vi* to meditate

mediter'raneo, a *ag* Mediterranean; **il (mare) M~** the Mediterranean (Sea)

me'dusa *sf* (*ZOOL*) jellyfish

me'gafono *sm* megaphone

'meglio ['mɛʎʎo] *av, ag inv* better; (*con senso superlativo*) best ♦ *sm* (*la cosa migliore*): **il ~** the best (thing); **faresti ~ ad andartene** you had better leave; **alla ~** at best one can; **andar di bene in ~** to get better and better; **fare del proprio ~** to do one's best; **per il ~** for the best; **aver la ~ su qn** to get the better of sb

'mela *sf* apple; ~ **cotogna** quince

mela'grana *sf* pomegranate

melan'zana [melan'dzana] *sf* aubergine (*BRIT*), eggplant (*US*)

me'lenso, a *ag* dull, stupid

mel'lifluo, a (*peg*) *ag* sugary, honeyed

'melma *sf* mud, mire

'melo *sm* apple tree

melo'dia *sf* melody

me'lone *sm* (musk)melon

'membro *sm* member; (*pl(f)*~a: *arto*) limb

memo'randum *sm inv* memorandum

me'moria *sf* memory; ~**e** *sfpl* (*opera autobiografica*) memoirs; **a ~** (*imparare, sapere*) by heart; **a ~ d'uomo** within living memory; **memori'ale** *sm* (*raccolta di memorie*) memoirs *pl*; (*DIR*) memorial

mena'dito: **a ~** *av* perfectly, thoroughly; **sapere qc a ~** to have sth at one's fingertips

me'nare *vt* to lead; (*picchiare*) to hit, beat; (*dare: colpi*) to deal; ~ **la coda** (*cane*) to wag its tail

mendi'cante *sm/f* beggar

mendi'care *vt* to beg for ♦ *vi* to beg

┌─────────────────────┐
│ **PAROLA CHIAVE** │
└─────────────────────┘

'**meno** *av* 1 (*in minore misura*) less;
dovresti mangiare ~ you should eat less,
you shouldn't eat so much
2 (*comparativo*): **~ ... di** not as ... as, less ...
than; **sono ~ alto di te** I'm not as tall as
you (are), I'm less tall than you (are); **~ ...
che** not as ... as, less ... than; **~ che mai**
less than ever; **è ~ intelligente che ricco**
he's more rich than intelligent; **~ fumo più
mangio** the less I smoke the more I eat
3 (*superlativo*) least; **il ~ dotato degli
studenti** the least gifted of the students; **è
quello che compro ~ spesso** it's the one
I buy least often
4 (*MAT*) minus; **8 ~ 5** 8 minus 5, 8 take
away 5; **sono le 8 ~ un quarto** it's a
quarter to 8; **~ 5 gradi** 5 degrees below
zero, minus 5 degrees; **mille lire in ~** a
thousand lire less
5 (*fraseologia*): **quanto ~ poteva
telefonare** he could at least have phoned;
non so se accettare o ~ I don't know
whether to accept or not; **fare a ~ di qc/
qn** to do without sth/sb; **non potevo fare
a ~ di ridere** I couldn't help laughing; **~
male!** thank goodness!; **~ male che sei
arrivato** it's a good job that you've come
♦ *ag inv* (*tempo, denaro*) less; (*errori,
persone*) fewer; **ha fatto ~ errori di tutti** he
made fewer mistakes than anyone, he
made the fewest mistakes of all
♦ *sm inv* 1: **il ~** (*il minimo*) the least;
parlare del più e del ~ to talk about this
and that
2 (*MAT*) minus
♦ *prep* (*eccetto*) except (for), apart from; **a
~ che, a ~ di** unless; **a ~ che non piova**
unless it rains; **non posso, a ~ di
prendere ferie** I can't, unless I take some
leave

meno'mare *vt* (*danneggiare*) to maim,
disable
meno'pausa *sf* menopause

'**mensa** *sf* (*locale*) canteen; (*: MIL*) mess;
(*: nelle università*) refectory
men'sile *ag* monthly ♦ *sm* (*periodico*)
monthly (magazine); (*stipendio*) monthly
salary
'**mensola** *sf* bracket; (*ripiano*) shelf;
(*ARCHIT*) corbel
'**menta** *sf* mint; (*anche*: **~ piperita**)
peppermint; (*bibita*) peppermint cordial;
(*caramella*) mint, peppermint
men'tale *ag* mental; **mentalità** *sf inv*
mentality
'**mente** *sf* mind; **imparare/sapere qc a ~**
to learn/know sth by heart; **avere in ~ qc**
to have sth in mind; **passare di ~ a qn** to
slip sb's mind
men'tire *vi* to lie
'**mento** *sm* chin
men'tolo *sm* menthol
'**mentre** *cong* (*temporale*) while;
(*avversativo*) whereas
menù *sm inv* menu; **~ turistico** set menu
menzio'nare [mentsjo'nare] *vt* to mention
menzi'one [men'tsjone] *sf* mention; **fare ~
di** to mention
men'zogna [men'tsɔɲɲa] *sf* lie
mera'viglia [mera'viʎʎa] *sf* amazement,
wonder; (*persona, cosa*) marvel, wonder; **a
~** perfectly, wonderfully; **meravigli'are** *vt*
to amaze, astonish; **meravigliarsi (di)** to
marvel (at); (*stupirsi*) to be amazed (at), be
astonished (at); **meravigli'oso, a** *ag*
wonderful, marvellous
mer'cante *sm* merchant; **~ d'arte** art
dealer; **mercanteggi'are** *vt* (*onore, voto*)
to sell ♦ *vi* to bargain, haggle;
mercan'tile *ag* commercial, mercantile;
(*nave, marina*) merchant *cpd* ♦ *sm* (*nave*)
merchantman; **mercan'zia** *sf*
merchandise, goods *pl*
mer'cato *sm* market; **~ dei cambi**
exchange market; **~ nero** black market
'**merce** ['mertʃe] *sf* goods *pl*, merchandise;
~ deperibile perishable goods *pl*
mercé [mer'tʃe] *sf* mercy
merce'nario, a [mertʃe'narjo] *ag, sm*
mercenary

merce'ria [mertʃe'ria] *sf (articoli)*
haberdashery (*BRIT*), notions *pl* (*US*);
(*bottega*) haberdasher's shop (*BRIT*), notions
store (*US*)

mercoledì *sm inv* Wednesday; **di** *o* **il ~** on
Wednesdays; **~ delle Ceneri** Ash
Wednesday

---
mercoledì delle ceneri
---

i Mercoledì delle ceneri, *in the
Catholic Church, marks the beginning of
Lent. On that day, people go to church and
are marked on the forehead with ash from
the burning of the blessed olive branch. Ash
Wednesday is a day of fasting, abstinence
and penitence.*

---

mer'curio *sm* mercury

'merda (*fam!*) *sf* shit (*!*)

me'renda *sf* afternoon snack

meridi'ana *sf (orologio)* sundial

meridi'ano, a *ag* meridian; midday *cpd*,
noonday ♦ *sm* meridian

meridio'nale *ag* southern ♦ *sm/f*
southerner

meridi'one *sm* south

me'ringa, ghe *sf (CUC)* meringue

meri'tare *vt* to deserve, merit ♦ *vb impers*:
merita andare it's worth going

meri'tevole *ag* worthy

'merito *sm* merit; (*valore*) worth; **in ~ a** as
regards, with regard to; **dare ~ a qn di** to
give sb credit for; **finire a pari ~** to finish
joint first (*o* second *etc*); to tie;
meri'torio, a *ag* praiseworthy

mer'letto *sm* lace

'merlo *sm (ZOOL)* blackbird; (*ARCHIT*)
battlement

mer'luzzo [mer'luttso] *sm (ZOOL)* cod

mes'chino, a [mes'kino] *ag* wretched;
(*scarso*) scanty, poor; (*persona: gretta*)
mean; (*: limitata*) narrow-minded, petty

mesco'lanza [mesko'lantsa] *sf* mixture

mesco'lare *vt* to mix; (*vini, colori*) to
blend; (*mettere in disordine*) to mix up,
muddle up; (*carte*) to shuffle; **~rsi** *vr* to
mix; to blend; to get mixed up; (*fig*): **~rsi**

in to get mixed up in, meddle in

'mese *sm* month

'messa *sf (REL)* mass; (*il mettere*): **~ in moto**
starting; **~ in piega** set; **~ a punto** (*TECN*)
adjustment; (*AUT*) tuning; (*fig*) clarification;
~ in scena = messinscena

messag'gero [messad'dʒero] *sm*
messenger

mes'saggio [mes'saddʒo] *sm* message

mes'sale *sm (REL)* missal

'messe *sf* harvest

Mes'sia *sm inv (REL)*: **il ~** the Messiah

'Messico *sm*: **il ~** Mexico

messin'scena [messin'ʃena] *sf (TEATRO)*
production

'messo, a *pp di* **mettere** ♦ *sm* messenger

mesti'ere *sm (professione)* job; (*: manuale*)
trade; (*: artigianale*) craft; (*fig: abilità nel
lavoro*) skill, technique; **essere del ~** to
know the tricks of the trade

'mesto, a *ag* sad, melancholy

'mestolo *sm (CUC)* ladle

mestruazi'one [mestruat'tsjone] *sf*
menstruation

'meta *sf* destination; (*fig*) aim, goal

metà *sf inv (punto di mezzo)* middle;
dividere qc a *o* **per ~** to divide sth in half,
halve sth; **fare a ~ (di qc con qn)** to go
halves (with sb in sth); **a ~ prezzo** at half
price; **a ~ strada** halfway

me'tafora *sf* metaphor

me'tallico, a, ci, che *ag (di metallo)*
metal *cpd*; (*splendore, rumore etc*) metallic

me'tallo *sm* metal

metalmec'canico, a, ci, che *ag*
engineering *cpd* ♦ *sm* engineering worker

me'tano *sm* methane

meteorolo'gia [meteorolo'dʒia] *sf*
meteorology; **meteoro'logico, a, ci,
che** *ag* meteorological, weather *cpd*

me'ticcio, a, ci, ce [me'tittʃo] *sm/f* half-
caste, half-breed

me'todico, a, ci, che *ag* methodical

'metodo *sm* method

'metrica *sf* metrics *sg*; **'metrico, a, ci,
che** *ag* metric; (*POESIA*) metrical

'metro *sm* metre; (*nastro*) tape measure;

(asta) (metre) rule

metropoli'tana *sf* underground, subway

metropoli'tano, a *ag* metropolitan

'**mettere** *vt* to put; *(abito)* to put on; *(: portare)* to wear; *(installare: telefono)* to put in; *(fig: provocare)*: ~ **fame/allegria a qn** to make sb hungry/happy; *(supporre)*: **mettiamo che ...** let's suppose *o* say that ... ; ~**rsi** *vr (persona)* to put o.s.; *(oggetto)* to go; *(disporsi: faccenda)* to turn out; ~**rsi a sedere** to sit down; ~**rsi a letto** to get into bed; *(per malattia)* to take to one's bed; ~**rsi il cappello** to put on one's hat; ~**rsi a** *(cominciare)* to begin to, start to; ~**rsi al lavoro** to set to work; ~**rsi con qn** *(in società)* to team up with sb; *(in coppia)* to start going out with sb; ~**rci**: ~**rci molta cura/molto tempo** to take a lot of care/a lot of time; **ci ho messo 3 ore per venire** it's taken me 3 hours to get here; ~**rcela tutta** to do one's best; ~ **a tacere qn/qc** to keep sb/sth quiet; ~ **su casa** to set up house; ~ **su un negozio** to start a shop; ~ **via** to put away

'**mezza** ['meddza] *sf*: **la** ~ half-past twelve *(in the afternoon); vedi anche* **mezzo**

mez'zadro [med'dzadro] *sm (AGR)* sharecropper

mezza'luna [meddza'luna] *sf* half-moon; *(dell'islamismo)* crescent; *(coltello)* (semicircular) chopping knife

mezza'nino [meddza'nino] *sm* mezzanine (floor)

mez'zano, a [med'dzano] *ag (medio)* average, medium; *(figlio)* middle *cpd* ♦ *sm/f (ruffiano)* pimp

mezza'notte [meddza'nɔtte] *sf* midnight

'**mezzo, a** ['meddzo] *ag* half; **un ~ litro/panino** half a litre/roll ♦ *av* half-; ~ **morto** half-dead ♦ *sm (metà)* half; *(parte centrale: di strada etc)* middle; *(per raggiungere un fine)* means *sg*; *(veicolo)* vehicle; *(nell'indicare l'ora)*: **le nove e** ~ half past nine; **mezzogiorno e** ~ half past twelve; ~**i** *smpl (possibilità economiche)* means; **di** ~**a età** middle-aged; **un soprabito di** ~**a stagione** a spring *(o* autumn) coat; **di** ~

middle, in the middle; **andarci di** ~ *(patir danno)* to suffer; **levarsi** *o* **togliersi di** ~ to get out of the way; **in** ~ **a** in the middle of; **per** *o* **a** ~ **di** by means of; ~**i di comunicazione di massa** mass media *pl*; ~**i pubblici** public transport *sg*; ~**i di trasporto** means of transport

mezzogi'orno [meddzo'dʒorno] *sm* midday, noon; **a** ~ at 12 (o'clock) *o* midday *o* noon; **il** ~ **d'Italia** southern Italy

mez'z'ora [med'dzora] *sf* half-hour, half an hour

mi *(dav lo, la, li, le, ne diventa* **me**) *pron (oggetto)* me; *(complemento di termine)* to me; *(riflessivo)* myself ♦ *sm (MUS)* E; *(: solfeggiando la scala)* mi

'**mia** *vedi* **mio**

miago'lare *vi* to miaow, mew

'**mica** *av (fam)*: **non ...** ~ not ... at all; **non sono** ~ **stanco** I'm not a bit tired; **non sarà** ~ **partito?** he wouldn't have left, would he?; ~ **male** not bad

'**miccia, ce** ['mittʃa] *sf* fuse

micidi'ale [mitʃi'djale] *ag* fatal; *(dannosissimo)* deadly

mi'crofono *sm* microphone

micros'copio *sm* microscope

mi'dollo *(pl(f)* ~**a**) *sm (ANAT)* marrow; ~ **osseo** bone marrow

'**mie** *vedi* **mio**

mi'ei *vedi* **mio**

mi'ele *sm* honey

mi'etere *vt (AGR)* to reap, harvest; *(fig: vite)* to take, claim

'**miglia** ['miʎʎa] *sfpl di* **miglio**

migli'aio [miʎ'ʎajo] *(pl(f)* ~**a**) *sm* thousand; **un** ~ **(di)** about a thousand; **a** ~**a** by the thousand, in thousands

'**miglio** ['miʎʎo] *sm (BOT)* millet; *(pl(f)* ~**a**: *unità di misura)* mile; ~ **marino** *o* **nautico** nautical mile

migliora'mento [miʎʎora'mento] *sm* improvement

miglio'rare [miʎʎo'rare] *vt, vi* to improve

migli'ore [miʎ'ʎore] *ag (comparativo)* better; *(superlativo)* best ♦ *sm*: **il** ~ the best (thing) ♦ *sm/f*: **il(la)** ~ the best (person); **il**

miglior vino di questa regione the best wine in this area

'**mignolo** ['miɲɲolo] *sm* (*ANAT*) little finger, pinkie; (*: dito del piede*) little toe

mi'**grare** *vi* to migrate

'**mila** *pl di* mille

Mi'lano *sf* Milan

miliar'dario, a *sm/f* millionaire

mili'ardo *sm* thousand million, billion (*US*)

mili'are *ag*: **pietra** ~ milestone

mili'one *sm* million; **due ~i di lire** two million lire

mili'tante *ag, sm/f* militant

mili'tare *vi* (*MIL*) to be a soldier, serve; (*fig: in un partito*) to be a militant ♦ *ag* military ♦ *sm* serviceman; **fare il** ~ to do one's military service

'**milite** *sm* soldier

millanta'tore, 'trice *sm/f* boaster

'**mille** (*pl* **mila**) *num* a *o* one thousand; **dieci mila** ten thousand

mille'foglie [mille'fɔλλe] *sm inv* (*CUC*) cream *o* vanilla slice

mil'lennio *sm* millennium

millepi'edi *sm inv* centipede

mil'lesimo, a *ag, sm* thousandth

milli'grammo *sm* milligram(me)

mil'limetro *sm* millimetre

'**milza** ['miltsa] *sf* (*ANAT*) spleen

mimetiz'zare [mimetid'dzare] *vt* to camouflage; ~**rsi** *vr* to camouflage o.s.

'**mimica** *sf* (*arte*) mime

'**mimo** *sm* (*attore, componimento*) mime

mi'mosa *sf* mimosa

'**mina** *sf* (*esplosiva*) mine; (*di matita*) lead

mi'naccia, ce [mi'nattʃa] *sf* threat; **minacci'are** *vt* to threaten; **minacciare qn di morte** to threaten to kill sb; **minacciare di fare qc** to threaten to do sth; **minacci'oso, a** *ag* threatening

mi'nare *vt* (*MIL*) to mine; (*fig*) to undermine

mina'tore *sm* miner

mina'torio, a *ag* threatening

mine'rale *ag, sm* mineral

mine'rario, a *ag* (*delle miniere*) mining; (*dei minerali*) ore *cpd*

mi'nestra *sf* soup; ~ **in brodo/di verdure** noodle/vegetable soup; **mines'trone** *sm* thick vegetable and pasta soup

mingher'lino, a [minger'lino] *ag* thin, slender

'**mini** *ag inv* mini ♦ *sf inv* miniskirt

minia'tura *sf* miniature

mini'era *sf* mine

mini'gonna *sf* miniskirt

'**minimo, a** *ag* minimum, least, slightest; (*piccolissimo*) very small, slight; (*il più basso*) lowest, minimum ♦ *sm* minimum; **al** ~ at least; **girare al** ~ (*AUT*) to idle

minis'tero *sm* (*POL, REL*) ministry; (*governo*) government; **M~ delle Finanze** Ministry of Finance, ≈ Treasury

mi'nistro *sm* (*POL, REL*) minister

mino'ranza [mino'rantsa] *sf* minority

mino'rato, a *ag* handicapped ♦ *sm/f* physically (*o* mentally) handicapped person

mi'nore *ag* (*comparativo*) less; (*più piccolo*) smaller; (*numero*) lower; (*inferiore*) lower, inferior; (*meno importante*) minor; (*più giovane*) younger; (*superlativo*) least; smallest; lowest; youngest ♦ *sm/f* = **minorenne**

mino'renne *ag* under age ♦ *sm/f* minor, person under age

mi'nuscolo, a *ag* (*scrittura, carattere*) small; (*piccolissimo*) tiny ♦ *sf* small letter

mi'nuta *sf* rough copy, draft

mi'nuto, a *ag* tiny, minute; (*pioggia*) fine; (*corporatura*) delicate, fine ♦ *sm* (*unità di misura*) minute; **al** ~ (*COMM*) retail

'**mio** (*f* '**mia**, *pl* **mi'ei, 'mie**) *det*: **il** ~, **la mia** *etc* my ♦ *pron*: **il** ~, **la mia** *etc* mine; **i miei** my family; **un** ~ **amico** a friend of mine

'**miope** *ag* short-sighted

'**mira** *sf* (*anche fig*) aim; **prendere la** ~ to take aim; **prendere di** ~ **qn** (*fig*) to pick on sb

mi'rabile *ag* admirable, wonderful

mi'racolo *sm* miracle

mi'raggio [mi'raddʒo] *sm* mirage

mi'rare *vi*: ~ **a** to aim at

mi'rino *sm* (*TECN*) sight; (*FOT*) viewer, viewfinder

mir'tillo *sm* bilberry (*BRIT*), blueberry (*US*), whortleberry

mi'scela [miʃʃela] *sf* mixture; (*di caffè*) blend

miscel'lanea [miʃʃelˈlanea] *sf* miscellany

'mischia ['miskja] *sf* scuffle; (*RUGBY*) scrum, scrummage

mischi'are [misˈkjare] *vt* to mix, blend; **~rsi** *vr* to mix, blend

mis'cuglio [misˈkuʎʎo] *sm* mixture, hotchpotch, jumble

mise'rabile *ag* (*infelice*) miserable, wretched; (*povero*) poverty-stricken; (*di scarso valore*) miserable

mi'seria *sf* extreme poverty; (*infelicità*) misery; **~e** *sfpl* (*del mondo etc*) misfortunes, troubles; **porca ~!** (*fam*) blast!, damn!

miseri'cordia *sf* mercy, pity

'misero, a *ag* miserable, wretched; (*povero*) poverty-stricken; (*insufficiente*) miserable

mis'fatto *sm* misdeed, crime

mi'sogino [miˈzɔdʒino] *sm* misogynist

'missile *sm* missile

missio'nario, a *ag, sm/f* missionary

missi'one *sf* mission

misteri'oso, a *ag* mysterious

mis'tero *sm* mystery

'misto, a *ag* mixed; (*scuola*) mixed, coeducational ♦ *sm* mixture

mis'tura *sf* mixture

mi'sura *sf* measure; (*misurazione, dimensione*) measurement; (*taglia*) size; (*provvedimento*) measure, step; (*moderazione*) moderation; (*MUS*) time; (*: divisione*) bar; (*fig: limite*) bounds *pl*, limit; **nella ~ in cui** inasmuch as, insofar as; **(fatto) su ~** made to measure

misu'rare *vt* (*ambiente, stoffa*) to measure; (*terreno*) to survey; (*abito*) to try on; (*pesare*) to weigh; (*fig: parole etc*) to weigh up; (*: spese, cibo*) to limit ♦ *vi* to measure; **~rsi** *vr*: **~rsi con qn** to have a confrontation with sb; to compete with sb; **misu'rato, a** *ag* (*ponderato*) measured; (*moderato*) moderate

'mite *ag* mild

miti'gare *vt* to mitigate, lessen; (*lenire*) to soothe, relieve; **~rsi** *vr* (*odio*) to subside; (*tempo*) to become milder

'mito *sm* myth; **mitolo'gia, 'gie** *sf* mythology

'mitra *sf* (*REL*) mitre ♦ *sm inv* (*arma*) sub-machine gun

mitraglia'trice [mitraʎʎatritʃe] *sf* machine gun

mit'tente *sm/f* sender

'mobile *ag* mobile; (*parte di macchina*) moving; (*DIR: bene*) movable, personal ♦ *sm* (*arredamento*) piece of furniture; **~i** *smpl* (*mobilia*) furniture *sg*

mo'bilia *sf* furniture

mobili'are *ag* (*DIR*) personal, movable

mo'bilio *sm* = **mobilia**

mobili'tare *vt* to mobilize

mocas'sino *sm* moccasin

mocci'oso, a [mottˈʃoso, a] *sm/f* (*peg*) snotty(-nosed) kid

'moccolo *sm* (*di candela*) candle-end; (*fam: bestemmia*) oath; (*: moccio*) snot; **reggere il ~** to play gooseberry (*BRIT*), act as chaperon

'moda *sf* fashion; **alla ~, di ~** fashionable, in fashion

modalità *sf inv* formality

mo'della *sf* model

model'lare *vt* (*creta*) to model, shape; **~rsi** *vr*: **~rsi su** to model o.s. on

mo'dello *sm* model; (*stampo*) mould ♦ *ag inv* model *cpd*

'modem *sm inv* modem

mode'rare *vt* to moderate; **~rsi** *vr* to restrain o.s.; **mode'rato, a** *ag* moderate

modera'tore, 'trice *sm/f* moderator

mo'derno, a *ag* modern

mo'destia *sf* modesty

mo'desto, a *ag* modest

'modico, a, ci, che *ag* reasonable, moderate

mo'difica, che *sf* modification

modifi'care *vt* to modify, alter; **~rsi** *vr* to alter, change

mo'dista *sf* milliner

'modo *sm* way, manner; (*mezzo*) means,

way; (*occasione*) opportunity; (*LING*) mood; (*MUS*) mode; **~i** *smpl* (*comportamento*) manners; **a suo ~, a ~ suo** in his own way; **ad** *o* **in ogni ~** anyway; **di** *o* **in ~ che** so that; **in ~ da** so as to; **in tutti i ~i** at all costs; (*comunque sia*) anyway; (*in ogni caso*) in any case; **in qualche ~** somehow or other; **~ di dire** turn of phrase; **per ~ di dire** so to speak

modu'lare *vt* to modulate; **modulazi'one** *sf* modulation; **modulazione di frequenza** frequency modulation

'modulo *sm* (*modello*) form; (*ARCHIT, lunare, di comando*) module

'mogano *sm* mahogany

'mogio, a, gi, gie ['mɔdʒo] *ag* down in the dumps, dejected

'moglie ['moʎʎe] *sf* wife

mo'ine *sfpl* cajolery *sg*; (*leziosità*) affectation *sg*

'mola *sf* millstone; (*utensile abrasivo*) grindstone

mo'lare *sm* (*dente*) molar

'mole *sf* mass; (*dimensioni*) size; (*edificio grandioso*) massive structure

moles'tare *vt* to bother, annoy; **mo'lestia** *sf* annoyance, bother; **recar molestia a qn** to bother sb; **mo'lesto, a** *ag* annoying

'molla *sf* spring; **~e** *sfpl* (*per camino*) tongs

mol'lare *vt* to release, let go; (*NAUT*) to ease; (*fig: ceffone*) to give ♦ *vi* (*cedere*) to give in

'molle *ag* soft; (*muscoli*) flabby

mol'letta *sf* (*per capelli*) hairgrip; (*per panni stesi*) clothes peg

mol'lica, che *sf* crumb, soft part

mol'lusco, schi *sm* mollusc

'molo *sm* mole, breakwater; jetty

mol'teplice [mol'teplitʃe] *ag* (*formato di più elementi*) complex; **~i** *pl* (*svariati: interessi, attività*) numerous, various

moltipli'care *vt* to multiply; **~rsi** *vr* to multiply; to increase in number; **moltiplicazi'one** *sf* multiplication

---

PAROLA CHIAVE

'molto, a *det* (*quantità*) a lot of, much; (*numero*) a lot of, many; **~ pane / carbone** a lot of bread/coal; **~a gente** a lot of people, many people; **~i libri** a lot of books, many books; **non ho ~ tempo** I haven't got much time; **per ~ (tempo)** for a long time

♦ *av* **1** a lot, (very) much; **viaggia ~** he travels a lot; **non viaggia ~** he doesn't travel much *o* a lot

2 (*intensivo: con aggettivi, avverbi*) very; (: *con participio passato*) (very) much; **~ buono** very good; **~ migliore, ~ meglio** much *o* a lot better

♦ *pron* much, a lot; **~i, e** *pron pl* many, a lot; **~i pensano che ...** many (people) think ...

---

momen'taneo, a *ag* momentary, fleeting

mo'mento *sm* moment; **da un ~ all'altro** at any moment; (*all'improvviso*) suddenly; **al ~ di fare** just as I was (*o* you were *o* he was *etc*) doing; **per il ~** for the time being; **dal ~ che** ever since; (*dato che*) since; **a ~i** (*da un ~ all'altro*) any time *o* moment now; (*quasi*) nearly

'monaca, che *sf* nun

'Monaco *sf* Monaco; **~ (di Baviera)** Munich

'monaco, ci *sm* monk

mo'narca, chi *sm* monarch; **monar'chia** *sf* monarchy

monas'tero *sm* (*di monaci*) monastery; (*di monache*) convent; **mo'nastico, a, ci, che** *ag* monastic

'monco, a, chi, che *ag* maimed; (*fig*) incomplete

mon'dano, a *ag* (*anche fig*) worldly; (*dell'alta società*) society *cpd*; fashionable

mon'dare *vt* (*frutta, patate*) to peel; (*piselli*) to shell; (*pulire*) to clean

mondi'ale *ag* (*campionato, popolazione*) world *cpd*; (*influenza*) world-wide

'mondo *sm* world; (*grande quantità*): **un ~ di** lots of, a host of; **il bel ~** high society mo'nello, a *sm/f* street urchin; (*ragazzo vivace*) scamp, imp

mo'neta *sf* coin; (*ECON: valuta*) currency; (*denaro spicciolo*) (small) change; ~ **estera** foreign currency; ~ **legale** legal tender; mone'tario, a *ag* monetary

mongo'loide *ag, sm/f* (*MED*) mongol

'monito *sm* warning

'monitor *sm inv* (*TECN, TV*) monitor

monolo'cale *sm* studio flat

mono'polio *sm* monopoly

mo'notono, a *ag* monotonous

monsi'gnore [monsin'nore] *sm* (*REL: titolo*) Your (*o* His) Grace

mon'sone *sm* monsoon

monta'carichi [monta'kariki] *sm inv* hoist, goods lift

mon'taggio [mon'taddʒo] *sm* (*TECN*) assembly; (*CINEMA*) editing

mon'tagna [mon'tanna] *sf* mountain; (*zona montuosa*): **la ~** the mountains *pl*; **andare in ~** to go to the mountains; ~**e russe** roller coaster *sg*, big dipper *sg* (*BRIT*); monta'gnoso, a *ag* mountainous

monta'naro, a *ag* mountain *cpd* ♦ *sm/f* mountain dweller

mon'tano, a *ag* mountain *cpd*; alpine

mon'tare *vt* to go (*o* come) up; (*cavallo*) to ride; (*apparecchiatura*) to set up, assemble; (*CUC*) to whip; (*ZOOL*) to cover; (*incastonare*) to mount, set; (*CINEMA*) to edit; (*FOT*) to mount ♦ *vi* to go (*o* come) up; (*a cavallo*): ~ **bene/male** to ride well/ badly; (*aumentare di livello, volume*) to rise; ~**rsi** *vr* to become big-headed; ~ **qc** to exaggerate sth; ~ **qn** *o* **la testa a qn** to turn sb's head; ~ **in bicicletta/macchina/ treno** to get on a bicycle/into a car/on a train; ~ **a cavallo** to get on *o* mount a horse

monta'tura *sf* assembling *no pl*; (*di occhiali*) frames *pl*; (*di gioiello*) mounting, setting; (*fig*): ~ **pubblicitaria** publicity stunt

'monte *sm* mountain; **a ~** upstream; **mandare a ~ qc** to upset sth, cause sth to fail; **il M~ Bianco** Mont Blanc; ~ **di pietà** pawnshop

mon'tone *sm* (*ZOOL*) ram; **carne di ~** mutton

montu'oso, a *ag* mountainous

monu'mento *sm* monument

mo'quette [mɔ'kɛt] *sf inv* fitted carpet

'mora *sf* (*del rovo*) blackberry; (*del gelso*) mulberry; (*DIR*) delay; (*: somma*) arrears *pl*

mo'rale *ag* moral ♦ *sf* (*scienza*) ethics *sg*, moral philosophy; (*complesso di norme*) moral standards *pl*, morality; (*condotta*) morals *pl*; (*insegnamento morale*) moral ♦ *sm* morale; **essere giù di ~** to be feeling down; **moralità** *sf* morality; (*condotta*) morals *pl*

'morbido, a *ag* soft; (*pelle*) soft, smooth

mor'billo *sm* (*MED*) measles *sg*

'morbo *sm* disease

mor'boso, a *ag* (*fig*) morbid

mor'dace [mor'datʃe] *ag* biting, cutting

mor'dente *sm* (*fig: di satira, critica*) bite; (*: di persona*) drive

'mordere *vt* to bite; (*addentare*) to bite into

mori'bondo, a *ag* dying, moribund

morige'rato, a [moridʒe'rato] *ag* of good morals

mo'rire *vi* to die; (*abitudine, civiltà*) to die out; ~ **di fame** to die of hunger; (*fig*) to be starving; ~ **di noia/paura** to be bored/ scared to death; **fa un caldo da ~** it's terribly hot

mormo'rare *vi* to murmur; (*brontolare*) to grumble

'moro, a *ag* dark(-haired); dark(-complexioned); **i M~i** *smpl* (*STORIA*) the Moors

mo'roso, a *ag* in arrears ♦ *sm/f* (*fam: innamorato*) sweetheart

'morsa *sf* (*TECN*) vice; (*fig: stretta*) grip

morsi'care *vt* to nibble (at), gnaw (at); (*sog: insetto*) to bite

'morso, a *pp di* **mordere** ♦ *sm* bite; (*di insetto*) sting; (*parte della briglia*) bit; ~**i della fame** pangs of hunger

mor'taio *sm* mortar

mor'tale *ag, sm* mortal; **mortalità** *sf* mortality, death rate

'**morte** *sf* death
mortifi'care *vt* to mortify
'**morto, a** *pp di* **morire** ♦ *ag* dead ♦ *sm/f*
  dead man/woman; **i ~i** the dead; **fare il ~**
  (*nell'acqua*) to float on one's back; **il Mar**
  M~ the Dead Sea
mor'torio *sm* (*anche fig*) funeral
mo'saico, ci *sm* mosaic
'**Mosca** *sf* Moscow
'**mosca, sche** *sf* fly; **~ cieca** blind-man's-
  buff
mos'cato *sm* muscatel (wine)
mosce'rino [moʃʃe'rino] *sm* midge, gnat
mos'chea [mos'kea] *sf* mosque
mos'chetto [mos'ketto] *sm* musket
'**moscio, a, sci, sce** ['mɔʃʃo] *ag* (*fig*)
  lifeless
mos'cone *sm* (*ZOOL*) bluebottle; (*barca*)
  pedalo; (: *a remi*) kind of pedalo with oars
'**mossa** *sf* movement; (*nel gioco*) move
'**mosso, a** *pp di* **muovere** ♦ *ag* (*mare*)
  rough; (*capelli*) wavy; (*FOT*) blurred
mos'tarda *sf* mustard
'**mostra** *sf* exhibition, show; (*ostentazione*)
  show; **in ~** on show; **far ~ di** (*fingere*) to
  pretend; **far ~ di sé** to show off
mos'trare *vt* to show; **~rsi** *vr* to appear
'**mostro** *sm* monster; **mostru'oso, a** *ag*
  monstrous
mo'tel *sm inv* motel
moti'vare *vt* (*causare*) to cause;
  (*giustificare*) to justify, account for;
  motivazi'one *sf* justification; motive;
  (*PSIC*) motivation
mo'tivo *sm* (*causa*) reason, cause;
  (*movente*) motive; (*letterario*) (central)
  theme; (*disegno*) motif, design, pattern;
  (*MUS*) motif; **per quale ~?** why?, for what
  reason?
'**moto** *sm* (*anche FISICA*) motion;
  (*movimento, gesto*) movement; (*esercizio
  fisico*) exercise; (*sommossa*) rising, revolt;
  (*commozione*) feeling, impulse ♦ *sf inv*
  (*motocicletta*) motorbike; **mettere in ~** to
  set in motion; (*AUT*) to start up
motoci'cletta [mototʃi'kletta] *sf*
  motorcycle; **motoci'clismo** *sm*

  motorcycling, motorcycle racing;
  motoci'clista, i, e *sm/f* motorcyclist
mo'tore, 'trice *ag* motor; (*TECN*) driving
  ♦ *sm* engine, motor; **a ~** motor *cpd*,
  power-driven; **~ a combustione interna/a
  reazione** internal combustion/jet engine;
  moto'rino *sm* moped; **motorino di
  avviamento** (*AUT*) starter; **motoriz'zato,
  a** *ag* (*truppe*) motorized; (*persona*) having a
  car *o* transport
motos'cafo *sm* motorboat
'**motto** *sm* (*battuta scherzosa*) witty remark;
  (*frase emblematica*) motto, maxim
mo'vente *sm* motive
movimen'tare *vt* to liven up
movi'mento *sm* movement; (*fig*) activity,
  hustle and bustle; (*MUS*) tempo, movement
mozi'one [mot'tsjone] *sf* (*POL*) motion
moz'zare [mot'tsare] *vt* to cut off; (*coda*) to
  dock; **~ il fiato *o* il respiro a qn** (*fig*) to
  take sb's breath away
mozza'rella [mottsa'rɛlla] *sf* mozzarella (*a
  moist Neapolitan curd cheese*)
mozzi'cone [mottsi'kone] *sm* stub, butt,
  end; (*anche*: **~ di sigaretta**) cigarette end
'**mozzo** ['mottso] *sm* (*NAUT*) ship's boy
'**mucca, che** *sf* cow
'**mucchio** ['mukkjo] *sm* pile, heap; (*fig*): **un
  ~ di** lots of, heaps of
'**muco, chi** *sm* mucus
'**muffa** *sf* mould, mildew
mug'gire [mud'dʒire] *vi* (*vacca*) to low,
  moo; (*toro*) to bellow; (*fig*) to roar;
  mug'gito *sm* low, moo; bellow; roar
mu'ghetto [mu'getto] *sm* lily of the valley
mu'gnaio, a [muɲ'ɲajo] *sm/f* miller
mugo'lare *vi* (*cane*) to whimper, whine;
  (*fig: persona*) to moan
muli'nare *vi* to whirl, spin (round and
  round)
muli'nello *sm* (*moto vorticoso*) eddy, whirl;
  (*di canna da pesca*) reel
mu'lino *sm* mill; **~ a vento** windmill
'**mulo** *sm* mule
'**multa** *sf* fine; **mul'tare** *vt* to fine
'**multiplo, a** *ag, sm* multiple
multiproprietà *sf inv* time-share

'**mummia** *sf* mummy

'**mungere** ['mundʒere] *vt* (*anche fig*) to milk

munici'pale [munitʃi'pale] *ag* municipal; town *cpd*

muni'cipio [muni'tʃipjo] *sm* town council, corporation; (*edificio*) town hall

mu'nire *vt*: ~ **qc/qn di** to equip sth/sb with

munizi'oni [munit'tsjoni] *sfpl* (*MIL*) ammunition *sg*

'**munto, a** *pp di* **mungere**

mu'overe *vt* to move; (*ruota, macchina*) to drive; (*sollevare: questione, obiezione*) to raise, bring up; (: *accusa*) to make, bring forward; ~**rsi** *vr* to move; **muoviti!** hurry up!, get a move on!

'**mura** *sfpl vedi* **muro**

mu'raglia [mu'raʎʎa] *sf* (high) wall

mu'rale *ag* wall *cpd*; mural

mu'rare *vt* (*persona, porta*) to wall up

mura'tore *sm* mason; bricklayer

'**muro** *sm* wall; ~**a** *sfpl* (*cinta cittadina*) walls; **a** ~ wall *cpd*; (*armadio etc*) built-in; ~ **del suono** sound barrier; **mettere al** ~ (*fucilare*) to shoot *o* execute (by firing squad)

'**muschio** ['muskjo] *sm* (*ZOOL*) musk; (*BOT*) moss

musco'lare *ag* muscular, muscle *cpd*

'**muscolo** *sm* (*ANAT*) muscle

mu'seo *sm* museum

museru'ola *sf* muzzle

'**musica** *sf* music; ~ **da ballo/camera** dance/chamber music; **musi'cale** *ag* musical; **musi'cista, i, e** *sm/f* musician

'**muso** *sm* muzzle; (*di auto, aereo*) nose; **tenere il** ~ to sulk; **mu'sone, a** *sm/f* sulky person

'**muta** *sf* (*di animali*) moulting; (*di serpenti*) sloughing; (*per immersioni subacquee*) diving suit; (*gruppo di cani*) pack

muta'mento *sm* change

mu'tande *sfpl* (*da uomo*) (under)pants; **mutan'dine** *sfpl* (*da donna, bambino*) pants (*BRIT*), briefs

mu'tare *vt, vi* to change, alter; **mutazi'one** *sf* change, alteration; (*BIOL*)

mutation; **mu'tevole** *ag* changeable

muti'lare *vt* to mutilate, maim; (*fig*) to mutilate, deface; **muti'lato, a** *sm/f* disabled person (*through loss of limbs*)

mu'tismo *sm* (*MED*) mutism; (*atteggiamento*) (stubborn) silence

'**muto, a** *ag* (*MED*) dumb; (*emozione, dolore, CINEMA*) silent; (*LING*) silent, mute; (*carta geografica*) blank; ~ **per lo stupore** *etc* speechless with amazement *etc*

'**mutua** *sf* (*anche*: **cassa ~**) health insurance scheme

mutu'are *vt* (*fig*) to borrow

mutu'ato, a *sm/f* member of a health insurance scheme

'**mutuo, a** *ag* (*reciproco*) mutual ♦ *sm* (*ECON*) (long-term) loan

N, n

N. *abbr* (= *nord*) N

'**nacchere** ['nakkere] *sfpl* castanets

'**nafta** *sf* naphtha; (*per motori diesel*) diesel oil

nafta'lina *sf* (*CHIM*) naphthalene; (*tarmicida*) mothballs *pl*

'**naia** *sf* (*MIL*) slang term for national service

'**nailon** *sm* nylon

'**nanna** *sf* (*linguaggio infantile*): **andare a** ~ to go to beddy-byes

'**nano, a** *ag, sm/f* dwarf

napole'tano, a *ag, sm/f* Neapolitan

'**Napoli** *sf* Naples

'**nappa** *sf* tassel

nar'ciso [nar'tʃizo] *sm* narcissus

nar'cosi *sf* narcosis

nar'cotico, ci *sm* narcotic

na'rice [na'ritʃe] *sf* nostril

nar'rare *vt* to tell the story of, recount; **narra'tiva** *sf* (*branca letteraria*) fiction; **narra'tivo, a** *ag* narrative; **narra'tore, 'trice** *sm/f* narrator; **narrazi'one** *sf* narration; (*racconto*) story, tale

na'sale *ag* nasal

'**nascere** ['naʃʃere] *vi* (*bambino*) to be born; (*pianta*) to come *o* spring up; (*fiume*) to

rise, have its source; (*sole*) to rise; (*dente*)
to come through; (*fig: derivare, conseguire*):
~ da to arise from, be born out of; **è nata
nel 1952** she was born in 1952; **'nascita**
sf birth

nas'condere *vt* to hide, conceal; **~rsi** *vr*
to hide; **nascon'diglio** *sm* hiding place;
nascon'dino *sm* (*gioco*) hide-and-seek;
nas'costo, a *pp di* **nascondere ♦** *ag*
hidden; **di nascosto** secretly

na'sello *sm* (*ZOOL*) hake

'naso *sm* nose

'nastro *sm* ribbon; (*magnetico, isolante,
SPORT*) tape; **~ adesivo** adhesive tape; **~
trasportatore** conveyor belt

nas'turzio [nas'turtsjo] *sm* nasturtium

na'tale *ag* of one's birth ♦ *sm* (*REL*): **N~**
Christmas; (*giorno della nascita*) birthday;
natalità *sf* birth rate; **nata'lizio, a** *ag*
(*del Natale*) Christmas *cpd*

na'tante *sm* craft *inv*, boat

'natica, che *sf* (*ANAT*) buttock

na'tio, a, 'tii, 'tie *ag* native

Nativ'ità *sf* (*REL*) Nativity

na'tivo, a *ag*, *sm/f* native

'nato, a *pp di* **nascere** ♦ *ag*: **un attore ~** a
born actor; **~a Pieri** née Pieri

na'tura *sf* nature; **pagare in ~** to pay in
kind; **~ morta** still life

natu'rale *ag* natural; **natura'lezza** *sf*
naturalness; **natura'lista, i, e** *sm/f*
naturalist

naturaliz'zare [naturalid'dzare] *vt* to
naturalize

natural'mente *av* naturally; (*certamente,
sì*) of course

naufra'gare *vi* (*nave*) to be wrecked;
(*persona*) to be shipwrecked; (*fig*) to fall
through; **nau'fragio** *sm* shipwreck; (*fig*)
ruin, failure; **'naufrago, ghi** *sm* castaway,
shipwreck victim

'nausea *sf* nausea; **nausea'bondo, a** *ag*
nauseating, sickening; **nause'are** *vt* to
nauseate, make (feel) sick

'nautica *sf* (art of) navigation

'nautico, a, ci, che *ag* nautical

na'vale *ag* naval

na'vata *sf* (*anche: ~ **centrale***) nave; (*anche:
~ **laterale***) aisle

'nave *sf* ship, vessel; **~ cisterna** tanker; **~
da guerra** warship; **~ passeggeri**
passenger ship

na'vetta *sf* shuttle; (*servizio di
collegamento*) shuttle (service)

navi'cella [navi'tʃɛlla] *sf* (*di aerostato*)
gondola; **~ spaziale** spaceship

navi'gare *vi* to sail; **~ in Internet** to surf
the Net; **navigazi'one** *sf* navigation

na'viglio [na'viʎʎo] *sm* (*canale artificiale*)
canal; **~ da pesca** fishing fleet

nazio'nale [nattsjo'nale] *ag* national ♦ *sf*
(*SPORT*) national team; **nazio'nalismo** *sm*
nationalism; **nazionalità** *sf inv* nationality

nazi'one [nat'tsjone] *sf* nation

PAROLA CHIAVE

ne *pron* 1 (*di lui, lei, loro*) of him/her/them;
about him/her/them; **~ riconosco la voce**
I recognize his (*o* her) voice
2 (*di questa, quella cosa*) of it; about it; **~
voglio ancora** I want some more (of it *o*
them); **non parliamone più!** let's not talk
about it any more!
3 (*con valore partitivo*): **hai dei libri? – sì,
~ ho** have you any books? — yes, I have
(some); **hai del pane? – no, non ~ ho**
have you any bread? — no, I haven't any;
quanti anni hai? – ~ ho 17 how old are
you? — I'm 17
♦ *av* (*moto da luogo: da lì*) from there; **~
vengo ora** I've just come from there

---

né *cong*: **~ ... ~** neither ... nor; **~ l'uno ~
l'altro lo vuole** neither of them wants it;
non parla ~ l'italiano ~ il tedesco he
speaks neither Italian nor German, he
doesn't speak either Italian or German; **non
piove ~ nevica** it isn't raining or snowing

ne'anche [ne'anke] *av, cong* not even; **non
... ~** not even; **~ se volesse potrebbe
venire** he couldn't come even if he wanted
to; **non l'ho visto — ~ io** I didn't see him
— neither did I *o* I didn't either; **~ per idea
o sogno!** not on your life!

'**nebbia** *sf* fog; *(foschia)* mist; **nebbi'oso, a** *ag* foggy; misty

nebu'loso, a *ag (atmosfera)* hazy; *(fig)* hazy, vague

necessaria'mente [netʃessarja'mente] *av* necessarily

neces'sario, a [netʃes'sarjo] *ag* necessary

necessità [netʃessi'ta] *sf inv* necessity; *(povertà)* need, poverty; **necessi'tare** *vt* to require ♦ *vi (aver bisogno)*: **necessitare di** to need

necro'logio [nekro'lɔdʒo] *sm* obituary notice

ne'**fando, a** *ag* infamous, wicked

ne'**fasto, a** *ag* inauspicious, ill-omened

ne'**gare** *vt* to deny; *(rifiutare)* to deny, refuse; ~ **di aver fatto/che** to deny having done/that; **nega'tivo, a** *ag, sf, sm* negative; **negazi'one** *sf* negation

ne'**gletto, a** *ag (trascurato)* neglected

'**negli** ['neʎʎi] *prep +det vedi* **in**

negli'**gente** [negli'dʒɛnte] *ag* negligent, careless; **negli'genza** *sf* negligence, carelessness

negozi'**ante** [negot'tsjante] *sm/f* trader, dealer; *(bottegaio)* shopkeeper *(BRIT)*, storekeeper *(US)*

negozi'**are** [negot'tsjare] *vt* to negotiate ♦ *vi*: ~ **in** to trade *o* deal in; **negozi'ato** *sm* negotiation

ne'**gozio** [ne'gɔttsjo] *sm (locale)* shop *(BRIT)*, store *(US)*

'**negro, a** *ag, sm/f* Negro

'**nei** *prep +det vedi* **in**

nel *prep +det vedi* **in**

nell' *prep +det vedi* **in**

'**nella** *prep +det vedi* **in**

'**nelle** *prep +det vedi* **in**

'**nello** *prep +det vedi* **in**

'**nembo** *sm (METEOR)* nimbus

ne'**mico, a, ci, che** *ag* hostile; *(MIL)* enemy *cpd* ♦ *sm/f* enemy; **essere ~ di** to be strongly averse *o* opposed to

nem'**meno** *av, cong* = **neanche**

'**nenia** *sf* dirge; *(motivo monotono)* monotonous tune

'**neo** *sm* mole; *(fig)* slight flaw

'**neo...** *prefisso* neo...

'**neon** *sm (CHIM)* neon

neo'**nato, a** *ag* newborn ♦ *sm/f* newborn baby

neozelan'**dese** [neoddzelan'dese] *ag* New Zealand *cpd* ♦ *sm/f* New Zealander

nep'**pure** *av, cong* = **neanche**

'**nerbo** *sm* lash; *(fig)* strength, backbone; **nerbo'ruto, a** *ag* muscular; robust

ne'**retto** *sm (TIP)* bold type

'**nero, a** *ag* black; *(scuro)* dark ♦ *sm* black; **il Mar N~** the Black Sea

nerva'**tura** *sf (ANAT)* nervous system; *(BOT)* veining; *(ARCHIT, TECN)* rib

'**nervo** *sm (ANAT)* nerve; *(BOT)* vein; **avere i ~i** to be on edge; **dare sui ~i a qn** to get on sb's nerves; **ner'voso, a** *ag* nervous; *(irritabile)* irritable ♦ *sm (fam)*: **far venire il nervoso a qn** to get on sb's nerves

'**nespola** *sf (BOT)* medlar; *(fig)* blow, punch; '**nespolo** *sm* medlar tree

'**nesso** *sm* connection, link

PAROLA CHIAVE
---

nes'**suno, a** *(det: dav sm* **nessun** +C, V, **nessuno** +*s impura, gn, pn, ps, x, z; dav sf* **nessuna** +C, **nessun'** +*V)* **det 1** *(non uno)* no, *espressione negativa* +any; **non c'è nessun libro** there isn't any book, there is no book; **nessun altro** no one else, nobody else; **nessun'altra cosa** nothing else; **in nessun luogo** nowhere

2 *(qualche)* any; **hai ~a obiezione?** do you have any objections?

♦ *pron* **1** *(non uno)* no one, nobody, *espressione negativa* +any(one); *(: cosa)* none, *espressione negativa* +any; ~ **è venuto, non è venuto ~** nobody came

2 *(qualcuno)* anyone, anybody; **ha telefonato ~?** did anyone phone?

---

net'**tare**[1] *vt* to clean

'**nettare**[2] *sm* nectar

net'**tezza** [net'tettsa] *sf* cleanness, cleanliness; ~ **urbana** cleansing department

'**netto, a** *ag (pulito)* clean; *(chiaro)* clear, clear-cut; *(deciso)* definite; *(ECON)* net

nettur'bino *sm* dustman (*BRIT*), garbage collector (*US*)

neu'rosi *sf* = **nevrosi**

neu'trale *ag* neutral; **neutralità** *sf* neutrality; **neutraliz'zare** *vt* to neutralize

'neutro, a *ag* neutral; (*LING*) neuter ♦ *sm* (*LING*) neuter

'neve *sf* snow; **nevi'care** *vb impers* to snow; **nevi'cata** *sf* snowfall

ne'vischio [ne'viskjo] *sm* sleet

ne'voso, a *ag* snowy; snow-covered

nevral'gia [nevral'dʒia] *sf* neuralgia

nevras'tenico, a, ci, che *ag* (*MED*) neurasthenic; (*fig*) hot-tempered

ne'vrosi *sf* neurosis

'nibbio *sm* (*ZOOL*) kite

'nicchia ['nikkja] *sf* niche; (*naturale*) cavity, hollow

nicchi'are [nik'kjare] *vi* to shilly-shally, hesitate

'nichel ['nikel] *sm* nickel

nico'tina *sf* nicotine

'nido *sm* nest; **a ~ d'ape** (*tessuto etc*) honeycomb *cpd*

PAROLA CHIAVE
---

ni'ente *pron* 1 (*nessuna cosa*) nothing; **~ può fermarlo** nothing can stop him; **~ di ~** absolutely nothing; **nient'altro** nothing else; **nient'altro che** nothing but, just, only; **~ affatto** not at all, not in the least; **come se ~ fosse** as if nothing had happened; **cose da ~** trivial matters; **per ~** (*gratis, invano*) for nothing
2 (*qualcosa*): **hai bisogno di ~?** do you need anything?
3: **non ... ~** nothing, *espressione negativa* +anything; **non ho visto ~** I saw nothing, I didn't see anything; **non ho ~ da dire** I have nothing *o* haven't anything to say ♦ *sm* nothing; **un bel ~** absolutely nothing; **basta un ~ per farla piangere** the slightest thing is enough to make her cry ♦ *av* (*in nessuna misura*): **non ... ~** not ... at all; **non è (per) ~ buono** it isn't good at all

---

nientedi'meno *av* actually, even ♦ *escl* really!, I say!

niente'meno *av, escl* = **nientedimeno**

'Nilo *sm*: **il ~** the Nile

'ninfa *sf* nymph

nin'fea *sf* water lily

ninna-'nanna *sf* lullaby

'ninnolo *sm* (*gingillo*) knick-knack

ni'pote *sm/f* (*di zii*) nephew/niece; (*di nonni*) grandson/daughter, grand-child

'nitido, a *ag* clear; (*specchio*) bright

ni'trato *sm* nitrate

'nitrico, a, ci, che *ag* nitric

ni'trire *vi* to neigh

ni'trito *sm* (*di cavallo*) neighing *no pl*; neigh; (*CHIM*) nitrite

nitroglice'rina [nitrogliʧe'rina] *sf* nitroglycerine

no *av* (*risposta*) no; **vieni o ~?** are you coming or not?; **perché ~?** why not?; **lo conosciamo? – tu ~ ma io sì** do we know him? — you don't but I do; **verrai, ~?** you'll come, won't you?

'nobile *ag* noble ♦ *sm/f* noble, nobleman/woman; **nobili'are** *ag* noble; **nobiltà** *sf* nobility; (*di azione*) nobleness

'nocca, che *sf* (*ANAT*) knuckle

nocci'ola [not'ʧola] *ag inv* (*colore*) hazel, light brown ♦ *sf* hazelnut

noccio'lina [notʧo'lina] *sf*: **~ americana** peanut

'nocciolo[1] ['nɔtʧolo] *sm* (*di frutto*) stone; (*fig*) heart, core

noc'ciolo[2] [not'ʧɔlo] *sm* (*albero*) hazel

'noce ['noʧe] *sm* (*albero*) walnut tree ♦ *sf* (*frutto*) walnut; **~ moscata** nutmeg

no'civo, a [no'ʧivo] *ag* harmful, noxious

'nodo *sm* (*di cravatta, legname, NAUT*) knot; (*AUT, FERR*) junction; (*MED, ASTR, BOT*) node; (*fig: legame*) bond, tie; (*: punto centrale*) heart, crux; **avere un ~ alla gola** to have a lump in one's throat; **no'doso, a** *ag* (*tronco*) gnarled

'noi *pron* (*soggetto*) we; (*oggetto: per dare rilievo, con preposizione*) us; **~ stessi(e)** we ourselves; (*oggetto*) ourselves

'**noia** *sf* boredom; (*disturbo, impaccio*) bother *no pl*, trouble *no pl*; **avere qn/qc a ~** not to like sb/sth; **mi è venuto a ~** I'm tired of it; **dare ~ a** to annoy; **avere delle ~e con qn** to have trouble with sb

noi'altri *pron* we

noi'oso, a *ag* boring; (*fastidioso*) annoying, troublesome

noleggi'are [noled'dʒare] *vt* (*prendere a noleggio*) to hire (*BRIT*), rent; (*dare a noleggio*) to hire out (*BRIT*), rent (out); (*aereo, nave*) to charter; **no'leggio** *sm* hire (*BRIT*), rental; charter

'**nolo** *sm* hire (*BRIT*); rental; charter; (*per trasporto merci*) freight; **prendere/dare a ~ qc** to hire/hire out sth

'**nomade** *ag* nomadic ♦ *sm/f* nomad

'**nome** *sm* name; (*LING*) noun; **in/a ~ di** in the name of; **di o per ~** (*chiamato*) called, named; **conoscere qn di ~** to know sb by name; **~ d'arte** stage name; **~ di battesimo** Christian name; **~ di famiglia** surname

no'mea *sf* notoriety

no'mignolo [no'miɲɲolo] *sm* nickname

nomina *sf* appointment

nomi'nale *ag* nominal; (*LING*) noun *cpd*

nomi'nare *vt* to name; (*eleggere*) to appoint; (*citare*) to mention

nomina'tivo, a *ag* (*LING*) nominative; (*ECON*) registered ♦ *sm* (*LING*) anche: **caso ~**) nominative (case); (*AMM*) name

non *av* not ♦ *prefisso* non-; *vedi* **affatto; appena** *etc*

nonché [non'ke] *cong* (*tanto più, tanto meno*) let alone; (*e inoltre*) as well as

noncu'rante *ag*: **~ (di)** careless (of), indifferent (to); **noncu'ranza** *sf* carelessness, indifference

nondi'meno *cong* (*tuttavia*) however; (*nonostante*) nevertheless

'**nonno, a** *sm/f* grandfather/mother; (*in senso più familiare*) grandma/grandpa; **~i** *smpl* grandparents

non'nulla *sm inv*: **un ~** nothing, a trifle

'**nono, a** *ag, sm* ninth

nonos'tante *prep* in spite of,

notwithstanding ♦ *cong* although, even though

nontiscordardimé *sm inv* (*BOT*) forget-me-not

nord *sm* North ♦ *ag inv* north; northern; **il Mare del N~** the North Sea; **nor'dest** *sm* north-east; '**nordico, a, ci, che** *ag* nordic, northern European; **nor'dovest** *sm* north-west

'**norma** *sf* (*principio*) norm; (*regola*) regulation, rule; (*consuetudine*) custom, rule; **a ~ di legge** according to law, as laid down by law

nor'male *ag* normal; standard *cpd*; **normalità** *sf* normality; **normaliz'zare** *vt* to normalize, bring back to normal

normal'mente *av* normally

norve'gese [norve'dʒese] *ag, sm/f, sm* Norwegian

Nor'vegia [nor'vedʒa] *sf*: **la ~** Norway

nostal'gia [nostal'dʒia] *sf* (*di casa, paese*) homesickness; (*del passato*) nostalgia; **nos'talgico, a, ci, che** *ag* homesick; nostalgic

nos'trano, a *ag* local; national; home-produced

'**nostro, a** *det*: **il(la) ~(a)** *etc* our ♦ *pron*: **il(la) ~(a)** *etc* ours ♦ *sm*: **il ~** our money; our belongings; **i ~i** our family; our own people, è dei ~i he's one of us

'**nota** *sf* (*segno*) mark; (*comunicazione scritta, MUS*) note; (*fattura*) bill; (*elenco*) list; **degno di ~** noteworthy, worthy of note

no'tabile *ag* notable ♦ *sm* prominent citizen

no'taio *sm* notary

no'tare *vt* (*segnare: errori*) to mark; (*registrare*) to note (down), write down; (*rilevare, osservare*) to note, notice; **farsi ~** to get o.s. noticed

no'tevole *ag* (*talento*) notable, remarkable; (*peso*) considerable

no'tifica, che *sf* notification

notifi'care *vt* (*DIR*): **~ qc a qn** to notify sb of sth, give sb notice of sth

no'tizia [no'tittsja] *sf* (piece of) news *sg*; (*informazione*) piece of information; **~e** *sfpl*

(*informazioni*) news *sg*; information *sg*;
notizi'ario *sm* (RADIO, TV, STAMPA) news *sg*
'noto, a *ag* (well-)known
notorietà *sf* fame; notoriety
no'torio, a *ag* well-known; (*peg*) notorious
nott'ambulo, a *sm/f* night-bird (*fig*)
nott'tata *sf* night
'notte *sf* night; di ~ at night; (*durante la
notte*) in the night, during the night; ~
bianca sleepless night; notte'tempo *av*
at night; during the night
not'turno, a *ag* nocturnal; (*servizio,
guardiano*) night *cpd*
no'vanta *num* ninety; novan'tesimo, a
num ninetieth; novan'tina *sf*: **una
novantina (di)** about ninety
'nove *num* nine
nove'cento [nove'tʃento] *num* nine
hundred ♦ *sm*: **il N~** the twentieth century
no'vella *sf* (LETTERATURA) short story
novel'lino, a *ag* (*pivello*) green,
inexperienced
no'vello, a *ag* (*piante, patate*) new;
(*insalata, verdura*) early; (*sposo*) newly-
married
no'vembre *sm* November
novi'lunio *sm* (ASTR) new moon
novità *sf inv* novelty; (*innovazione*)
innovation; (*cosa originale, insolita*)
something new; (*notizia*) (piece of) news
sg; **le ~ della moda** the latest fashions
no'vizio, a [no'vittsjo] *sm/f* (REL) novice;
(*tirocinante*) beginner, apprentice
nozi'one [not'tsjone] *sf* notion, idea; **~i** *sfpl*
(*rudimenti*) basic knowledge *sg*, rudiments
'nozze ['nɔttse] *sfpl* wedding *sg*, marriage
sg; ~ **d'argento/d'oro** silver/golden
wedding *sg*
ns. *abbr* (COMM) = **nostro**
'nube *sf* cloud; nubi'fragio *sm* cloudburst
'nubile *ag* (*donna*) unmarried, single
'nuca *sf* nape of the neck
nucle'are *ag* nuclear
'nucleo *sm* nucleus; (*gruppo*) team, unit,
group; (MIL, POLIZIA) squad; **il ~ familiare**
the family unit
nu'dista, i, e *sm/f* nudist

'nudo, a *ag* (*persona*) bare, naked, nude;
(*membra*) bare, naked; (*montagna*) bare
♦ *sm* (ARTE) nude
'nugolo *sm*: **un ~ di** a whole host of
'nulla *pron, av* = **niente** ♦ *sm*: **il ~** nothing
nulla'osta *sm inv* authorization
nullità *sf inv* nullity; (*persona*) nonentity
'nullo, a *ag* useless, worthless; (DIR) null
(and void); (SPORT): **incontro ~** draw
nume'rale *ag, sm* numeral
nume'rare *vt* to number; numerazi'one
sf numbering; (*araba, decimale*) notation
nu'merico, a, ci, che *ag* numerical
'numero *sm* number; (*romano, arabo*)
numeral; (*di spettacolo*) act, turn; ~ **civico**
house number; ~ **di telefono** telephone
number; nume'roso, a *ag* numerous,
many; (*con sostantivo sg*) large
'nunzio ['nuntsjo] *sm* (REL) nuncio
nu'ocere ['nwɔtʃere] *vi*: ~ **a** to harm,
damage; nuoci'uto, a *pp di* nuocere
nu'ora *sf* daughter-in-law
nuo'tare *vi* to swim; (*galleggiare: oggetti*)
to float; nuota'tore, 'trice *sm/f*
swimmer; nu'oto *sm* swimming
nu'ova *sf* (*notizia*) (piece of) news *sg*; *vedi
anche* **nuovo**
nuova'mente *av* again
Nu'ova Ze'landa [-dze'landa] *sf*: **la ~**
New Zealand
nu'ovo, a *ag* new; di ~ again; ~
fiammante *o* **di zecca** brand-new
nutri'ente *ag* nutritious, nourishing
nutri'mento *sm* food, nourishment
nu'trire *vt* to feed; (*fig: sentimenti*) to
harbour, nurse; nutri'tivo, a *ag*
nutritional; (*alimento*) nutritious;
nutrizi'one *sf* nutrition
'nuvola *sf* cloud; nuvo'loso, a *ag* cloudy
nuzi'ale [nut'tsjale] *ag* nuptial; wedding *cpd*

O, o

o (*dav V spesso* **od**) *cong* or; ~ **...** ~ either ... or; ~ **l'uno** ~ **l'altro** either (of them)

O. *abbr* (= *ovest*) W

'oasi *sf inv* oasis

obbedi'ente *etc* = **ubbidiente** *etc*

obbli'gare *vt* (*costringere*): ~ **qn a fare** to force *o* oblige sb to do; (*DIR*) to bind; **~rsi** *vr*: **~rsi a fare** to undertake to do; **obbli'gato, a** *ag* (*costretto, grato*) obliged; (*percorso, tappa*) set, fixed; **obbliga'torio, a** *ag* compulsory, obligatory; **obbligazi'one** *sf* (*COMM*) bond, debenture; **'obbligo, ghi** *sm* obligation; (*dovere*) duty; **avere l'obbligo di fare** to be obliged to do; **essere d'obbligo** (*discorso, applauso*) to be called for

ob'brobrio *sm* disgrace; (*fig*) eyesore

o'beso, a *ag* obese

obiet'tare *vt*: ~ **che** to object that; ~ **su qc** to object to sth, raise objections concerning sth

obiet'tivo, a *ag* objective ♦ *sm* (*OTTICA, FOT*) lens *sg*, objective; (*MIL, fig*) objective

obiet'tore *sm* objector; ~ **di coscienza** conscientious objector

obiezi'one [objet'tsjone] *sf* objection

obi'torio *sm* morgue, mortuary

o'bliquo, a *ag* oblique; (*inclinato*) slanting; (*fig*) devious, underhand

oblite'rare *vt* (*biglietto*) to stamp; (*francobollo*) to cancel

oblò *sm inv* porthole

o'blungo, a, ghi, ghe *ag* oblong

'oboe *sm* (*MUS*) oboe

'oca (*pl* **'oche**) *sf* goose

occasi'one *sf* (*caso favorevole*) opportunity; (*causa, motivo, circostanza*) occasion; (*COMM*) bargain; **d'~** (*a buon prezzo*) bargain *cpd*; (*usato*) secondhand

occhi'aia [ok'kjaja] *sf* eye socket; **avere le ~e** to have shadows under one's eyes

occhi'ali [ok'kjali] *smpl* glasses, spectacles; ~ **da sole** sunglasses; ~ **da vista** (prescription) glasses

occhi'ata [ok'kjata] *sf* look, glance; **dare un'~** to have a look at

occhi'ello [ok'kjello] *sm* buttonhole; (*asola*) eyelet

'occhio ['okkjo] *sm* eye; ~! careful!, watch out!; **a ~ nudo** with the naked eye; **a quattr'~i** privately, tête-à-tête; **dare all'~ o nell'~ a qn** to catch sb's eye; **fare l'~ a qc** to get used to sth; **tenere d'~ qn** to keep an eye on sb; **vedere di buon/mal ~ qc** to look favourably/unfavourably on sth

occhio'lino [okkjo'lino] *sm*: **fare l'~ a qn** to wink at sb

occiden'tale [ottʃiden'tale] *ag* western ♦ *sm/f* Westerner

occi'dente [ottʃi'dɛnte] *sm* west; (*POL*): **l'O~** the West; **a ~** in the west

oc'cipite [ot'tʃipite] *sm* back of the head, occiput

oc'cludere *vt* to block; **occlusi'one** *sf* blockage, obstruction; **oc'cluso, a** *pp di* **occludere**

occor'rente *ag* necessary ♦ *sm* all that is necessary

occor'renza [okkor'rɛntsa] *sf* necessity, need; **all'~** in case of need

oc'correre *vi* to be needed, be required ♦ *vb impers*: **occorre farlo** it must be done; **occorre che tu parta** you must leave, you'll have to leave; **mi occorrono i soldi** I need the money; **oc'corso, a** *pp di* **occorrere**

occul'tare *vt* to hide, conceal

oc'culto, a *ag* hidden, concealed; (*scienze, forze*) occult

occu'pare *vt* to occupy; (*manodopera*) to employ; (*ingombrare*) to occupy, take up; **~rsi** *vr* to occupy o.s., keep o.s. busy; (*impiegarsi*) to get a job; **~rsi di** (*interessarsi*) to take an interest in; (*prendersi cura di*) to look after, take care of; **occu'pato, a** *ag* (*MIL, POL*) occupied; (*persona: affaccendato*) busy; (*posto, sedia*) taken; (*toilette, TEL*) engaged; **occupazi'one** *sf* occupation; (*impiego,*

lavoro) job; (*ECON*) employment
o'**ceano** [o'tʃeano] *sm* ocean
'**ocra** *sf* ochre
ocu'**lare** *ag* ocular, eye *cpd*; **testimone ~** eye witness
ocu'**lato, a** *ag* (*attento*) cautious, prudent; (*accorto*) shrewd
ocu'**lista, i, e** *sm/f* eye specialist, oculist
'**ode** *sf* ode
odi'**are** *vt* to hate, detest
odi'**erno, a** *ag* today's, of today; (*attuale*) present
'**odio** *sm* hatred; **avere in ~ qc/qn** to hate *o* detest sth/sb; **odi'oso, a** *ag* hateful, odious
odo'**rare** *vt* (*annusare*) to smell; (*profumare*) to perfume, scent ♦ *vi*: **~ (di)** to smell (of); **odo'rato** *sm* sense of smell
o'**dore** *sm* smell; **gli ~i** *smpl* (*CUC*) (aromatic) herbs; **odo'roso, a** *ag* sweet-smelling
of'**fendere** *vt* to offend; (*violare*) to break, violate; (*insultare*) to insult; (*ferire*) to hurt; **~rsi** *vr* (*con senso reciproco*) to insult one another; (*risentirsi*): **~rsi (di)** to take offence (at), be offended (by); **offen'sivo, a** *ag*, *sf* offensive
offe'**rente** *sm* (*in aste*): **al maggior ~** to the highest bidder
of'**ferta** *sf* offer; (*donazione, anche REL*) offering; (*in gara d'appalto*) tender; (*in aste*) bid; (*ECON*) supply; **''~e d'impiego''** ''situations vacant''; **fare un'~a** to make an offer; to tender; to bid
of'**ferto, a** *pp di* **offrire**
of'**fesa** *sf* insult, affront; (*MIL*) attack; (*DIR*) offence; *vedi anche* **offeso**
of'**feso, a** *pp di* **offendere** ♦ *ag* offended; (*fisicamente*) hurt, injured ♦ *sm/f* offended party; **essere ~ con qn** to be annoyed with sb; **parte ~a** (*DIR*) plaintiff
offi'**cina** [offi'tʃina] *sf* workshop
of'**frire** *vt* to offer; **~rsi** *vr* (*proporsi*) to offer (o.s.), volunteer; (*occasione*) to present itself; (*esporsi*): **~rsi a** to expose o.s. to; **ti offro da bere** I'll buy you a drink
offus'**care** *vt* to obscure, darken; (*fig*:

intelletto) to dim, cloud; (: *fama*) to obscure, overshadow; **~rsi** *vr* to grow dark; to cloud, grow dim; to be obscured
ogget'**tivo, a** [oddʒet'tivo] *ag* objective
og'**getto** [od'dʒetto] *sm* object; (*materia, argomento*) subject (matter); **~i smarriti** lost property *sg*
'**oggi** ['ɔddʒi] *av, sm* today; **~ a otto** a week today; **oggigi'orno** *av* nowadays
'**ogni** ['oɲɲi] *det* every, each; (*tutti*) all; (*con valore distributivo*) every; **~ uomo è mortale** all men are mortal; **viene ~ due giorni** he comes every two days; **~ cosa** everything; **ad ~ costo** at all costs, at any price; **in ~ luogo** everywhere; **~ tanto** every so often; **~ volta che** every time that
Ognis'**santi** [oɲɲis'santi] *sm* All Saints' Day
o'**gnuno** [oɲ'ɲuno] *pron* everyone, everybody
'**ohi** *escl* oh!; (*esprimendo dolore*) ow!
ohi**mè** *escl* oh dear!
O'**landa** *sf*: **l'~** Holland; **olan'dese** *ag* Dutch ♦ *sm* (*LING*) Dutch ♦ *sm/f* Dutchman/woman; **gli Olandesi** the Dutch
oleo'**dotto** *sm* oil pipeline
ole'**oso, a** *ag* oily; (*che contiene olio*) oil-yielding
ol'**fatto** *sm* sense of smell
oli'**are** *vt* to oil
oli'**era** *sf* oil cruet
olim'**piadi** *sfpl* Olympic games; o'**limpico, a, ci, che** *ag* Olympic
'**olio** *sm* oil; **sott'~** (*CUC*) in oil; **~ di fegato di merluzzo** cod liver oil; **~ d'oliva** olive oil; **~ di semi** vegetable oil
o'**liva** *sf* olive; **oli'vastro, a** *ag* olive(-coloured); (*carnagione*) sallow; **oli'veto** *sm* olive grove; o'**livo** *sm* olive tree
'**olmo** *sm* elm
oltraggi'**are** [oltrad'dʒare] *vt* to outrage; to offend gravely
ol'**traggio** [ol'traddʒo] *sm* outrage; offence, insult; **~ a pubblico ufficiale** (*DIR*) insulting a public official; **~ al pudore** (*DIR*) indecent behaviour; **oltraggi'oso, a** *ag* offensive
ol'**tralpe** *av* beyond the Alps
ol'**tranza** [ol'trantsa] *sf*: **a ~** to the last, to

the bitter end

'oltre *av* (*più in là*) further; (*di più: aspettare*) longer, more ♦ *prep* (*di là da*) beyond, over, on the other side of; (*più di*) more than, over; (*in aggiunta a*) besides; (*eccetto*): **~ a** except, apart from; **oltre'mare** *av* overseas; **oltre'modo** *av* extremely; **oltrepas'sare** *vt* to go beyond, exceed

o'maggio [o'maddʒo] *sm* (*dono*) gift; (*segno di rispetto*) homage, tribute; **~i** *smpl* (*complimenti*) respects; **rendere ~ a** to pay homage *o* tribute to; **in ~** (*copia, biglietto*) complimentary

ombe'lico, chi *sm* navel

'ombra *sf* (*zona non assolata, fantasma*) shade; (*sagoma scura*) shadow; **sedere all'~** to sit in the shade; **restare nell'~** (*fig*) to remain in obscurity

om'brello *sm* umbrella; **ombrel'lone** *sm* beach umbrella

om'bretto *sm* eyeshadow

om'broso, a *ag* shady, shaded; (*cavallo*) nervous, skittish; (*persona*) touchy, easily offended

ome'lia *sf* (REL) homily, sermon

omeopa'tia *sf* homoeopathy

omertà *sf* conspiracy of silence

o'messo, a *pp di* **omettere**

o'mettere *vt* to omit, leave out; **~ di fare** to omit *o* fail to do

omi'cida, i, e [omi'tʃida] *ag* homicidal, murderous ♦ *sm/f* murderer/eress

omi'cidio [omi'tʃidjo] *sm* murder; **~ colposo** culpable homicide

omissi'one *sf* omission; **~ di soccorso** (DIR) failure to stop and give assistance

omogeneiz'zato [omodʒeneid'dzato] *sm* baby food

omo'geneo, a [omo'dʒɛneo] *ag* homogeneous

omolo'gare *vt* to approve, recognize; to ratify

o'monimo, a *sm/f* namesake ♦ *sm* (LING) homonym

omosessu'ale *ag, sm/f* homosexual

'oncia, ce ['ontʃa] *sf* ounce

'onda *sf* wave; **mettere *o* mandare in ~** (RADIO, TV) to broadcast; **andare in ~** (RADIO, TV) to go on the air; **~e corte/ medie/lunghe** short/medium/long wave;

on'data *sf* wave, billow; (*fig*) wave, surge; **a ondate** in waves; **ondata di caldo** heatwave

ondeggi'are [onded'dʒare] *vi* (*acqua*) to ripple; (*muoversi sulle onde: barca*) to rock, roll; (*fig: muoversi come le onde, barcollare*) to sway; (: *essere incerto*) to waver

'onere *sm* burden; **~i fiscali** taxes; **one'roso, a** *ag* (*fig*) heavy, onerous

onestà *sf* honesty

o'nesto, a *ag* (*probo, retto*) honest; (*giusto*) fair; (*casto*) chaste, virtuous

'onice ['ɔnitʃe] *sf* onyx

onnipo'tente *ag* omnipotent

ono'mastico, ci *sm* name-day

ono'ranze [ono'rantse] *sfpl* honours; **~ funebri** funeral (service)

ono'rare *vt* to honour; (*far onore a*) to do credit to; **~rsi** *vr*: **~rsi di** to feel honoured at, be proud of

ono'rario, a *ag* honorary ♦ *sm* fee

o'nore *sm* honour; **in ~ di** in honour of; **fare gli ~i di casa** to play host (*o* hostess); **fare ~ a** to honour; (*pranzo*) to do justice to; (*famiglia*) to be a credit to; **farsi ~** to distinguish o.s.; **ono'revole** *ag* honourable ♦ *sm/f* (POL) ≈ Member of Parliament (BRIT), ≈ Congressman/woman (US); **onorifi'cenza** *sf* honour; decoration; **ono'rifico, a, ci, che** *ag* honorary

'onta *sf* shame, disgrace

on'tano *sm* (BOT) alder

'O.N.U. ['ɔnu] *sigla f* (= *Organizzazione delle Nazioni Unite*) UN, UNO

o'paco, a, chi, che *ag* (*vetro*) opaque; (*metallo*) dull, matt

o'pale *sm o f* opal

'opera *sf* work; (*azione rilevante*) action, deed, work; (MUS) work; opus; (: *melodramma*) opera; (: *teatro*) opera house; (*ente*) institution, organization; **~ d'arte** work of art; **~ lirica** (grand) opera;

~e pubbliche public works
ope'raio, a *ag* working-class; workers'
♦ *sm/f* worker; **classe ~a** working class
ope'rare *vt* to carry out, make; (*MED*) to
operate on ♦ *vi* to operate, work; (*rimedio*)
to act, work; (*MED*) to operate; **~rsi** *vr*
(*MED*) to have an operation; **~rsi**
d'appendicite to have one's appendix out;
opera'tivo, a *ag* operative, operating;
opera'tore, 'trice *sm/f* operator; (*TV*,
CINEMA) cameraman; **operatore**
economico agent, broker; **operatore**
turistico tour operator; **opera'torio, a** *ag*
(*MED*) operating; **operazi'one** *sf*
operation
ope'retta *sf* (*MUS*) operetta, light opera
ope'roso, a *ag* busy, active, hard-working
opini'one *sf* opinion; **~ pubblica** public
opinion
'oppio *sm* opium
oppo'nente *ag* opposing ♦ *sm/f* opponent
op'porre *vt* to oppose; **opporsi** *vr*:
opporsi (a qc) to oppose (sth); to object
(to sth); **~ resistenza / un rifiuto** to offer
resistance/refuse
opportu'nista, i, e *sm/f* opportunist
opportunità *sf inv* opportunity;
(*convenienza*) opportuneness, timeliness
oppor'tuno, a *ag* timely, opportune
opposi'tore, 'trice *sm/f* opposer,
opponent
opposizi'one [oppozit'tsjone] *sf*
opposition; (*DIR*) objection
op'posto, a *pp di* **opporre** ♦ *ag* opposite;
(*opinioni*) conflicting ♦ *sm* opposite,
contrary; **all'~** on the contrary
oppressi'one *sf* oppression
oppres'sivo, a *ag* oppressive
op'presso, a *pp di* **opprimere**
oppres'sore *sm* oppressor
op'primere *vt* (*premere, gravare*) to weigh
down; (*estenuare: sog: caldo*) to suffocate,
oppress; (*tiranneggiare: popolo*) to oppress
op'pure *cong* or (else)
op'tare *vi*: **~ per** to opt for
o'puscolo *sm* booklet, pamphlet
opzi'one [op'tsjone] *sf* option

'ora¹ *sf* (*60 minuti*) hour; (*momento*) time;
che ~ è?, che ~e sono? what time is it?;
non veder l'~ di fare to long to do, look
forward to doing; **di buon'~** early; **alla**
buon'~! at last!; **~ di cena** dinner time; **~**
legale *o* **estiva** summer time (*BRIT*),
daylight saving time (*US*); **~ locale** local
time; **~ di pranzo** lunchtime; **~ di punta**
(*AUT*) rush hour
ora² *av* (*adesso*) now; (*poco fa*): **è uscito**
proprio ~ he's just gone out; (*tra poco*)
presently, in a minute; (*correlativo*): **~ ... ~**
now ... now; **d'~ in avanti** *o* **poi** from now
on; **or ~** just now, a moment ago; **5 anni**
or sono 5 years ago; **~ come ~** right now,
at present
o'racolo *sm* oracle
'orafo *sm* goldsmith
o'rale *ag, sm* oral
ora'mai *av* = **ormai**
o'rario, a *ag* hourly; (*fuso, segnale*) time
cpd; (*velocità*) per hour ♦ *sm* timetable,
schedule; (*di ufficio, visite etc*) hours *pl*,
time(s *pl*); **in ~** on time
o'rata *sf* (*ZOOL*) sea bream
ora'tore, 'trice *sm/f* speaker; orator
ora'toria *sf* (*arte*) oratory
ora'torio, a *ag* oratorical ♦ *sm* (*REL*)
oratory; (*MUS*) oratorio
ora'zione [orat'tsjone] *sf* (*REL*) prayer;
(*discorso*) speech, oration
or'bene *cong* so, well (then)
'orbita *sf* (*ASTR, FISICA*) orbit; (*ANAT*)
(eye-)socket
or'chestra [or'kɛstra] *sf* orchestra;
orches'trare *vt* to orchestrate; (*fig*) to
mount, stage-manage
orchi'dea [orki'dɛa] *sf* orchid
'orco, chi *sm* ogre
'orda *sf* horde
or'digno [or'diɲɲo] *sm* (*esplosivo*) explosive
device
ordi'nale *ag, sm* ordinal
ordina'mento *sm* order, arrangement;
(*regolamento*) regulations *pl*, rules *pl*; **~**
scolastico / giuridico education/legal
system

ordi'nanza [ordi'nantsa] sf (DIR, MIL) order; (persona: MIL) orderly, batman; d'~ (MIL) regulation cpd

ordi'nare vt (mettere in ordine) to arrange, organize; (COMM) to order; (prescrivere: medicina) to prescribe; (comandare): ~ a qn di fare qc to order o command sb to do sth; (REL) to ordain

ordi'nario, a ag (comune) ordinary; everyday; standard; (grossolano) coarse, common ♦ sm ordinary; (INS: di università) full professor

ordi'nato, a ag tidy, orderly

ordinazi'one [ordinat'tsjone] sf (COMM) order; (REL) ordination; eseguire qc su ~ to make sth to order

'ordine sm order; (carattere): d'~ pratico of a practical nature; all'~ (COMM: assegno) to order; di prim'~ first-class; fino a nuovo ~ until further notice; essere in ~ (documenti) to be in order; (stanza, persona) to be tidy; mettere in ~ to put in order, tidy (up); ~ del giorno (di seduta) agenda; (MIL) order of the day; ~ di pagamento (COMM) order for payment; l'~ pubblico law and order; ~i (sacri) (REL) holy orders

or'dire vt (fig) to plot, scheme; or'dito sm (di tessuto) warp

orec'chino [orek'kino] sm earring

o'recchio [o'rekkjo] (pl(f) o'recchie) sm (ANAT) ear

orecchi'oni [orek'kjoni] smpl (MED) mumps sg

o'refice [o'refitʃe] sm goldsmith; jeweller; orefice'ria sf (arte) goldsmith's art; (negozio) jeweller's (shop)

'orfano, a ag orphan(ed) ♦ sm/f orphan; ~ di padre/madre fatherless/motherless; orfano'trofio sm orphanage

orga'netto sm barrel organ; (fam: armonica a bocca) mouth organ; (: fisarmonica) accordion

or'ganico, a, ci, che ag organic ♦ sm personnel, staff

organi'gramma, i sm organization chart

orga'nismo sm (BIOL) organism; (corpo umano) body; (AMM) body, organism

organiz'zare [organid'dzare] vt to organize; ~rsi vr to get organized; organizza'tore, 'trice ag organizing ♦ sm/f organizer; organizzazi'one sf organization

'organo sm organ; (di congegno) part; (portavoce) spokesman, mouthpiece

or'gasmo sm (FISIOL) orgasm; (fig) agitation, anxiety

'orgia, ge ['ɔrdʒa] sf orgy

or'goglio [or'gɔʎʎo] sm pride; orgogli'oso, a ag proud

orien'tale ag oriental; eastern; east

orienta'mento sm positioning; orientation; direction; senso di ~ sense of direction; perdere l'~ to lose one's bearings; ~ professionale careers guidance

orien'tare vt (situare) to position; (fig) to direct, orientate; ~rsi vr to find one's bearings; (fig: tendere) to tend, lean; (: indirizzarsi): ~rsi verso to take up, go in for

ori'ente sm east; l'O~ the East, the Orient; a ~ in the east

o'rigano sm oregano

origi'nale [oridʒi'nale] ag original; (bizzarro) eccentric ♦ sm original; originalità sf originality; eccentricity

origi'nare [oridʒi'nare] vt to bring about, produce ♦ vi: ~ da to arise o spring from

origi'nario, a [oridʒi'narjo] ag original; essere ~ di to be a native of; (provenire da) to originate from; to be native to

o'rigine [o'ridʒine] sf origin; all'~ originally; d'~ inglese of English origin; dare ~ a to give rise to

origli'are [oriʎ'ʎare] vi: ~ (a) to eavesdrop (on)

o'rina sf urine

ori'nare vi to urinate ♦ vt to pass; orina'toio sm (public) urinal

ori'undo, a ag: essere ~ di Milano etc to be of Milanese etc extraction o origin ♦ sm/f person of foreign extraction o origin

orizzon'tale [oriddzon'tale] ag horizontal

oriz'zonte [orid'dzonte] sm horizon

or'lare vt to hem

'**orlo** *sm* edge, border; (*di recipiente*) rim, brim; (*di vestito etc*) hem

'**orma** *sf* (*di persona*) footprint; (*di animale*) track; (*impronta, traccia*) mark, trace

or'**mai** *av* by now, by this time; (*adesso*) now; (*quasi*) almost, nearly

ormeggi'**are** [ormed'dʒare] *vt* (*NAUT*) to moor; or'**meggio** *sm* (*atto*) mooring *no pl*; (*luogo*) moorings *pl*

or'**mone** *sm* hormone

ornamen'**tale** *ag* ornamental, decorative

orna'**mento** *sm* ornament, decoration

or'**nare** *vt* to adorn, decorate; ~**rsi** *vr*: ~**rsi (di)** to deck o.s. (out) (with); or'**nato, a** *ag* ornate

ornitolo'**gia** [ornitolo'dʒia] *sf* ornithology

'**oro** *sm* gold; **d'~, in ~** gold *cpd*; **d'~** (*colore, occasione*) golden; (*persona*) marvellous

orologe'**ria** [orolodʒe'ria] *sf* watchmaking *no pl*; watchmaker's (shop); clockmaker's (shop); **bomba a ~** time bomb

orologi'**aio** [orolo'dʒajo] *sm* watchmaker; clockmaker

oro'**logio** [oro'lɔdʒo] *sm* clock; (*da tasca, da polso*) watch; ~ **da polso** wristwatch; ~ **al quarzo** quartz watch

o'**roscopo** *sm* horoscope

or'**rendo, a** *ag* (*spaventoso*) horrible, awful; (*bruttissimo*) hideous

or'**ribile** *ag* horrible

'**orrido, a** *ag* fearful, horrid

orripi'**lante** *ag* hair-raising, horrifying

or'**rore** *sm* horror; **avere in ~ qn/qc** to loathe *o* detest sb/sth; **mi fanno ~** I loathe *o* detest them

orsacchi'**otto** [orsak'kjɔtto] *sm* teddy bear

'**orso** *sm* bear; ~ **bruno/bianco** brown/polar bear

or'**taggio** [or'taddʒo] *sm* vegetable

or'**tensia** *sf* hydrangea

or'**tica, che** *sf* (stinging) nettle

orti'**caria** *sf* nettle rash

'**orto** *sm* vegetable garden, kitchen garden; (*AGR*) market garden (*BRIT*), truck farm (*US*)

orto'**dosso, a** *ag* orthodox

ortogra'**fia** *sf* spelling

orto'**lano, a** *sm/f* (*venditore*) greengrocer (*BRIT*), produce dealer (*US*)

orto'**pedia** *sf* orthopaedics *sg*; orto'**pedico, a, ci, che** *ag* orthopaedic ♦ *sm* orthopaedic specialist

orzai'**olo** [ordza'jɔlo] *sm* (*MED*) stye

or'**zata** [or'dzata] *sf* barley water

'**orzo** ['ordzo] *sm* barley

o'**sare** *vt, vi* to dare; ~ **fare** to dare (to) do

osceni'**tà** [oʃʃeni'ta] *sf inv* obscenity

o'**sceno, a** [oʃ'ʃɛno] *ag* obscene; (*ripugnante*) ghastly

oscil'**lare** [oʃʃil'lare] *vi* (*pendolo*) to swing; (*dondolare: al vento etc*) to rock; (*variare*) to fluctuate; (*TECN*) to oscillate; (*fig*): ~ **fra** to waver *o* hesitate between; oscillazi'**one** *sf* oscillation; (*di prezzi, temperatura*) fluctuation

oscura'**mento** *sm* darkening; obscuring; (*in tempo di guerra*) blackout

oscu'**rare** *vt* to darken, obscure; (*fig*) to obscure; ~**rsi** *vr* (*cielo*) to darken, cloud over; (*persona*): **si oscurò in volto** his face clouded over

os'**curo, a** *ag* dark; (*fig*) obscure; humble, lowly ♦ *sm*: **all'~** in the dark; **tenere qn all'~ di qc** to keep sb in the dark about sth

ospe'**dale** *sm* hospital; ospedali'**ero, a** *ag* hospital *cpd*

ospi'**tale** *ag* hospitable; ospitali'**tà** *sf* hospitality

ospi'**tare** *vt* to give hospitality to; (*sog: albergo*) to accommodate

'**ospite** *sm/f* (*persona che ospita*) host/hostess; (*persona ospitata*) guest

os'**pizio** [os'pittsjo] *sm* (*per vecchi etc*) home

'**ossa** *sfpl vedi* **osso**

ossa'**tura** *sf* (*ANAT*) skeletal structure, frame; (*TECN, fig*) framework

'**osseo, a** *ag* bony; (*tessuto etc*) bone *cpd*

os'**sequio** *sm* deference, respect; ~**i** *smpl* (*saluto*) respects, regards; ossequi'**oso, a** *ag* obsequious

osser'**vanza** [osser'vantsa] *sf* observance

osser'**vare** *vt* to observe, watch; (*esaminare*) to examine; (*notare, rilevare*) to

notice, observe; (*DIR: la legge*) to observe, respect; (*mantenere: silenzio*) to keep, observe; **far ~ qc a qn** to point sth out to sb; **osserva'tore, 'trice** *ag* observant, perceptive ♦ *sm/f* observer;
osserva'torio *sm* (*ASTR*) observatory; (*MIL*) observation post; **osservazi'one** *sf* observation; (*di legge etc*) observance; (*considerazione critica*) observation, remark; (*rimprovero*) reproof; **in osservazione** under observation

ossessio'nare *vt* to obsess, haunt; (*tormentare*) to torment, harass

ossessi'one *sf* obsession

os'sesso, a *ag* (*spiritato*) possessed

os'sia *cong* that is, to be precise

ossi'buchi [ossi'buki] *smpl di* **ossobuco**

ossi'dare *vt* to oxidize; **~rsi** *vr* to oxidize

'ossido *sm* oxide; **~ di carbonio** carbon monoxide

ossige'nare [ossidʒe'nare] *vt* to oxygenate; (*decolorare*) to bleach; **acqua ossigenata** hydrogen peroxide

os'sigeno *sm* oxygen

'osso (*pl(f)* **ossa** *nel senso ANAT*) *sm* bone; **d'~** (*bottone etc*) of bone, bone *cpd*

osso'buco (*pl* **ossi'buchi**) *sm* (*CUC*) marrowbone; (*: piatto*) stew made with knuckle of veal in tomato sauce

os'suto, a *ag* bony

ostaco'lare *vt* to block, obstruct

os'tacolo *sm* obstacle; (*EQUITAZIONE*) hurdle, jump

os'taggio [os'taddʒo] *sm* hostage

'oste, os'tessa *sm/f* innkeeper

osteggi'are [osted'dʒare] *vt* to oppose, be opposed to

os'tello *sm*: **~ della gioventù** youth hostel

osten'tare *vt* to make a show of, flaunt; **ostentazi'one** *sf* ostentation, show

oste'ria *sf* inn

os'tessa *sf vedi* **oste**

os'tetrica *sf* midwife; **os'tetrico, a, ci, che** *ag* obstetric ♦ *sm* obstetrician

'ostia *sf* (*REL*) host; (*per medicinali*) wafer

'ostico, a, ci, che *ag* (*fig*) harsh; hard, difficult; unpleasant

os'tile *ag* hostile; **ostilità** *sf inv* hostility ♦ *sfpl* (*MIL*) hostilities

osti'narsi *vr* to insist, dig one's heels in; **~ a fare** to persist (obstinately) in doing; **osti'nato, a** *ag* (*caparbio*) obstinate; (*tenace*) persistent, determined; **ostinazi'one** *sf* obstinacy; persistence

'ostrica, che *sf* oyster

ostru'ire *vt* to obstruct, block; **ostruzi'one** *sf* obstruction, blockage

'otre *sm* (*recipiente*) goatskin

ottago'nale *ag* octagonal

ot'tagono *sm* octagon

ot'tanta *num* eighty; **ottan'tesimo, a** *num* eightieth; **ottan'tina** *sf*: **una ottantina (di)** about eighty

ot'tava *sf* octave

ot'tavo, a *num* eighth

ottempe'rare *vi*: **~ a** to comply with, obey

otte'nere *vt* to obtain, get; (*risultato*) to achieve, obtain

'ottica *sf* (*scienza*) optics *sg*; (*FOT: lenti, prismi etc*) optics *pl*

'ottico, a, ci, che *ag* (*della vista: nervo*) optic; (*dell'ottica*) optical ♦ *sm* optician

ottima'mente *av* excellently, very well

otti'mismo *sm* optimism; **otti'mista, i, e** *sm/f* optimist

'ottimo, a *ag* excellent, very good

'otto *num* eight

ot'tobre *sm* October

otto'cento [otto'tʃento] *num* eight hundred ♦ *sm*: **l'O~** the nineteenth century

ot'tone *sm* brass; **gli ~i** (*MUS*) the brass

ottu'rare *vt* to close (up); (*dente*) to fill; **ottura'tore** *sm* (*FOT*) shutter; (*nelle armi*) breechblock; **otturazi'one** *sf* closing (up); (*dentaria*) filling

ot'tuso, a *ag* (*MAT, fig*) obtuse; (*suono*) dull

o'vaia *sf* (*ANAT*) ovary

o'vale *ag, sm* oval

o'vatta *sf* cotton wool; (*per imbottire*) padding, wadding; **ovat'tare** *vt* (*fig: smorzare*) to muffle

ovazi'one [ovat'tsjone] *sf* ovation

over'dose ['ouvədous] *sf inv* overdose

'**ovest** *sm* west
o'**vile** *sm* pen, enclosure
o'**vino, a** *ag* sheep *cpd*, ovine
ovulazi'**one** [ovulat'tsjone] *sf* ovulation
'**ovulo** *sm* (FISIOL) ovum
o'**vunque** *av* = **dovunque**
ov'**vero** *cong* (ossia) that is, to be precise; (oppure) or (else)
ovvi'**are** *vi*: ~ **a** to obviate
'**ovvio, a** *ag* obvious
ozi'**are** [ot'tsjare] *vi* to laze, idle
'**ozio** ['ɔttsjo] *sm* idleness; (tempo libero) leisure; **ore d'~** leisure time; **stare in ~** to be idle; **ozi'oso, a** *ag* idle
o'**zono** [o'dzɔno] *sm* ozone

P, p

P *abbr* (= parcheggio) P; (AUT: = principiante) L
pa'**cato, a** *ag* quiet, calm
'**pacca** *sf* pat
pac'**chetto** [pak'ketto] *sm* packet; ~ **azionario** (COMM) shareholding
pacchi'**ano, a** [pak'kjano] *ag* vulgar
'**pacco, chi** *sm* parcel; (involto) bundle
'**pace** ['patʃe] *sf* peace; **darsi ~** to resign o.s.; **fare la ~ con** to make it up with
pacifi'**care** [patʃifi'kare] *vt* (riconciliare) to reconcile, make peace between; (mettere in pace) to pacify
pa'**cifico, a, ci, che** [pa'tʃi:fiko] *ag* (persona) peaceable; (vita) peaceful; (fig: indiscusso) indisputable; (: ovvio) obvious, clear ♦ *sm*: **il P~, l'Oceano P~** the Pacific (Ocean)
paci'**fista, i, e** [patʃi'fista] *sm/f* pacifist
pa'**della** *sf* frying pan; (per infermi) bedpan
padigli'**one** [padiʎ'ʎone] *sm* pavilion
'**Padova** *sf* Padua
'**padre** *sm* father; **~i** *smpl* (antenati) forefathers
pa'**drino** *sm* godfather
padro'**nanza** [padro'nantsa] *sf* command, mastery
pa'**drone, a** *sm/f* master/mistress;

(proprietario) owner; (datore di lavoro) employer; **essere ~ di sé** to be in control of o.s.; ~ **di casa** (ospite) host/hostess; (per gli inquilini) landlord/lady;
padroneggi'**are** *vt* (fig: sentimenti) to master, control; (: materia) to master, know thoroughly; **padroneggiarsi** *vr* to control o.s.
pae'**saggio** [pae'zaddʒo] *sm* landscape
pae'**sano, a** *ag* country *cpd* ♦ *sm/f* villager; countryman/woman
pa'**ese** *sm* (nazione) country, nation; (terra) country, land; (villaggio) village; (small) town; ~ **di provenienza** country of origin; **i P~i Bassi** the Netherlands
paf'**futo, a** *ag* chubby, plump
'**paga, ghe** *sf* pay, wages *pl*
paga'**mento** *sm* payment
pa'**gano, a** *ag, sm/f* pagan
pa'**gare** *vt* to pay; (acquisto, fig: colpa) to pay for; (contraccambiare) to repay, pay back ♦ *vi* to pay; **quanto l'hai pagato?** how much did you pay for it?; ~ **con carta di credito** to pay by credit card; ~ **in contanti** to pay cash
pa'**gella** [pa'dʒella] *sf* (INS) report card
'**paggio** ['paddʒo] *sm* page(boy)
paghe'**rò** [page'rɔ] *sm inv* acknowledgement of a debt, IOU
'**pagina** ['padʒina] *sf* page; **~e gialle** Yellow Pages
'**paglia** ['paʎʎa] *sf* straw
pagliac'**cetto** [paʎʎat'tʃetto] *sm* (per bambini) rompers *pl*
pagli'**accio** [paʎ'ʎattʃo] *sm* clown
pagli'**etta** [paʎ'ʎetta] *sf* (cappello per uomo) (straw) boater; (per tegami etc) steel wool
pa'**gnotta** [paɲ'ɲɔtta] *sf* round loaf
'**paio** (pl(f) '**paia**) *sm* pair; **un ~ di** (alcuni) a couple of
pai'**olo** *sm* (copper) pot
'**pala** *sf* shovel; (di remo, ventilatore, elica) blade; (di ruota) paddle
pa'**lato** *sm* palate
pa'**lazzo** [pa'lattso] *sm* (reggia) palace; (edificio) building; ~ **di giustizia** courthouse; ~ **dello sport** sports stadium

---

palazzi

Rome has a number of palazzi, *which are now associated with various government departments and political figures or groups.* Palazzo Chigi, *in Piazza Colonna, dates from the 16th century and has, since 1961, been the Prime Minister's office and the place where the cabinet meets.* Palazzo Madama, *also built in the 16th century, has been the seat of the Senate since 1871.* Palazzo di Montecitorio, *which was completed in 1694, has housed the* Camera dei deputati *since 1870.* Palazzo Viminale, *which takes its name from the hill in Rome on which it stands, is the home of the Ministry of the Interior.*

'**palco, chi** *sm* (*TEATRO*) box; (*tavolato*) platform, stand; (*ripiano*) layer

palco'scenico, ci [palkoʃʃɛniko] *sm* (*TEATRO*) stage

pale'sare *vt* to reveal, disclose; **~rsi** *vr* to reveal *o* show o.s.

pa'lese *ag* clear, evident

Pales'tina *sf*: **la ~** Palestine

pa'lestra *sf* gymnasium; (*esercizio atletico*) exercise; (*fig*) training ground, school

pa'letta *sf* spade; (*per il focolare*) shovel; (*del capostazione*) signalling disc

pa'letto *sm* stake, peg; (*spranga*) bolt

'**palio** *sm* (*gara*): **il P~** horse race run at *Siena*; **mettere qc in ~** to offer sth as a prize

---

palio

The palio *is a horse race which takes place in a number of Italian towns, the most famous being the one in Siena. This is usually held twice a year on 2 July and 16 August in the Piazza del Campo, Siena. 10 of the 17* contrade *or districts take part, each represented by a horse and rider. The winner is the first horse to complete the course, whether it has a rider or not.*

'**palla** *sf* ball; (*pallottola*) bullet; **~ canestro** *sm* basketball; **~ nuoto** *sm* water polo; **~ ovale** rugby ball; **~ volo** *sm* volleyball

palleggi'are [palled'dʒare] *vi* (*CALCIO*) to practise with the ball; (*TENNIS*) to knock up

pallia'tivo *sm* palliative; (*fig*) stopgap measure

'**pallido, a** *ag* pale

pal'lina *sf* (*biglia*) marble

pallon'cino [pallon'tʃino] *sm* balloon; (*lampioncino*) Chinese lantern

pal'lone *sm* (*palla*) ball; (*CALCIO*) football; (*aerostato*) balloon; **gioco del ~** football

pal'lore *sm* pallor, paleness

pal'lottola *sf* pellet; (*proiettile*) bullet

'**palma** *sf* (*ANAT*) = **palmo**; (*BOT, simbolo*) palm; **~ da datteri** date palm

'**palmo** *sm* (*ANAT*) palm; **restare con un ~ di naso** to be badly disappointed

'**palo** *sm* (*legno appuntito*) stake; (*sostegno*) pole; **fare da** *o* **il ~** (*fig*) to act as look-out

palom'baro *sm* diver

pa'lombo *sm* (*pesce*) dogfish

pal'pare *vt* to feel, finger

'**palpebra** *sf* eyelid

palpi'tare *vi* (*cuore, polso*) to beat; (: *più forte*) to pound, throb; (*fremere*) to quiver; '**palpito** *sm* (*del cuore*) beat; (*fig: d'amore etc*) throb

paltò *sm inv* overcoat

pa'lude *sf* marsh, swamp; **palu'doso, a** *ag* marshy, swampy

pa'lustre *ag* marsh *cpd*, swamp *cpd*

'**pampino** *sm* vine leaf

'**panca, che** *sf* bench

pancarrè *sm* sliced square bread

pan'cetta [pan'tʃetta] *sf* (*CUC*) bacon

pan'chetto [pan'ketto] *sm* stool; footstool

pan'china [pan'kina] *sf* garden seat; (*di giardino pubblico*) (park) bench

'**pancia, ce** ['pantʃa] *sf* belly, stomach; **mettere** *o* **fare ~** to be getting a paunch; **avere mal di ~** to have stomachache *o* a sore stomach

panci'otto [pan'tʃɔtto] *sm* waistcoat

'pancreas *sm inv* pancreas

'panda *sm inv* panda

pande'monio *sm* pandemonium

'pane *sm* bread; (*pagnotta*) loaf (of bread); (*forma*): **un ~ di burro** a pat of butter; **guadagnarsi il ~** to earn one's living; **~ a cassetta** sliced bread; **~ di Spagna** sponge cake; **~ integrale** wholemeal bread; **~ tostato** toast

panette'ria *sf* (*forno*) bakery; (*negozio*) baker's (shop), bakery

panetti'ere, a *sm/f* baker

panet'tone *sm* a kind of spiced brioche with sultanas, eaten at Christmas

'panfilo *sm* yacht

pangrat'tato *sm* breadcrumbs *pl*

'panico, a, ci, che *ag*, *sm* panic

pani'ere *sm* basket

pani'ficio [pani'fitʃo] *sm* (*forno*) bakery; (*negozio*) baker's (shop), bakery

pa'nino *sm* roll; **~ caldo** toasted sandwich; **~ imbottito** filled roll; sandwich; **panino'teca** *sf* sandwich bar

'panna *sf* (*CUC*) cream; (*TECN*) = **panne**; **~ da cucina** cooking cream; **~ montata** whipped cream

'panne *sf inv*: **essere in ~** (*AUT*) to have broken down

pan'nello *sm* panel; **~ solare** solar panel

'panno *sm* cloth; **~i** *smpl* (*abiti*) clothes; **mettiti nei miei ~i** (*fig*) put yourself in my shoes

pan'nocchia [pan'nɔkkja] *sf* (*di mais etc*) ear

panno'lino *sm* (*per bambini*) nappy (*BRIT*), diaper (*US*)

pano'rama, i *sm* panorama; **pano'ramico, a, ci, che** *ag* panoramic; **strada panoramica** scenic route

panta'loni *smpl* trousers (*BRIT*), pants (*US*), pair *sg* of trousers *o* pants

pan'tano *sm* bog

pan'tera *sf* panther

pan'tofola *sf* slipper

panto'mima *sf* pantomime

pan'zana [pan'tsana] *sf* fib, tall story

pao'nazzo, a [pao'nattso] *ag* purple

'papa, i *sm* pope

papà *sm inv* dad(dy)

pa'pale *ag* papal

pa'pato *sm* papacy

pa'pavero *sm* poppy

'papera *sf* (*fig*) slip of the tongue, blunder; *vedi anche* **papero**

'papero, a *sm/f* (*ZOOL*) gosling

pa'piro *sm* papyrus

'pappa *sf* baby cereal

pappa'gallo *sm* parrot; (*fig: uomo*) Romeo, wolf

pappa'gorgia, ge [pappa'gɔrdʒa] *sf* double chin

pap'pare *vt* (*fam: anche:* **~rsi**) to gobble up

'para *sf*: **suole di ~** crepe soles

pa'rabola *sf* (*MAT*) parabola; (*REL*) parable

para'brezza [para'breddza] *sm inv* (*AUT*) windscreen (*BRIT*), windshield (*US*)

paraca'dute *sm inv* parachute

para'carro *sm* kerbstone (*BRIT*), curbstone (*US*)

para'diso *sm* paradise

parados'sale *ag* paradoxical

para'dosso *sm* paradox

para'fango, ghi *sm* mudguard

paraf'fina *sf* paraffin, paraffin wax

para'fulmine *sm* lightning conductor

pa'raggi [pa'raddʒi] *smpl*: **nei ~** in the vicinity, in the neighbourhood

parago'nare *vt*: **~ con/a** to compare with/to

para'gone *sm* comparison; (*esempio analogo*) analogy, parallel; **reggere al ~** to stand comparison

pa'ragrafo *sm* paragraph

pa'ralisi *sf* paralysis; **para'litico, a, ci, che** *ag*, *sm/f* paralytic

paraliz'zare [paralid'dzare] *vt* to paralyze

paral'lela *sf* parallel (line); **~e** *sfpl* (*attrezzo ginnico*) parallel bars

paral'lelo, a *ag* parallel ♦ *sm* (*GEO*) parallel; (*comparazione*): **fare un ~ tra** to draw a parallel between

para'lume *sm* lampshade

pa'rametro *sm* parameter

para'noia *sf* paranoia; **para'noico, a, ci, che** *ag, sm/f* paranoid

para'occhi [para'ɔkki] *smpl* blinkers

para'petto *sm* balustrade

para'piglia [para'piʎʎa] *sm* commotion, uproar

pa'rare *vt* (*addobbare*) to adorn, deck; (*proteggere*) to shield, protect; (*scansare: colpo*) to parry; (*CALCIO*) to save ♦ *vi*: **dove vuole andare a ~?** what are you driving at?; **~rsi** *vr* (*presentarsi*) to appear, present o.s.

para'sole *sm inv* parasol, sunshade

paras'sita, i *sm* parasite

pa'rata *sf* (*SPORT*) save; (*MIL*) review, parade

para'tia *sf* (*di nave*) bulkhead

para'urti *sm inv* (*AUT*) bumper

para'vento *sm* folding screen; **fare da ~ a qn** (*fig*) to shield sb

par'cella [par'tʃella] *sf* account, fee (of *lawyer etc*)

parcheggi'are [parked'dʒare] *vt* to park; **par'cheggio** *no pl; (luogo)* car park; (*singolo posto*) parking space

par'chimetro [par'kimetro] *sm* parking meter

'parco¹, chi *sm* park; (*spazio per deposito*) depot; (*complesso di veicoli*) fleet

'parco², a, chi, che *ag*: ~ **(in)** (*sobrio*) moderate (in); (*avaro*) sparing (with)

pa'recchio, a [pa'rekkjo] *det* quite a lot of; (*tempo*) quite a lot of, a long; **~i, e** *det pl* quite a lot of, several ♦ *pron* quite a lot, quite a bit; (*tempo*) quite a while, a long time; **~i, e** *pron pl* quite a lot, several ♦ *av* (*con ag*) quite, rather; (*con vb*) quite a lot, quite a bit

pareggi'are [pared'dʒare] *vt* to make equal; (*terreno*) to level, make level; (*bilancio, conti*) to balance ♦ *vi* (*SPORT*) to draw; **pa'reggio** *sm* (*ECON*) balance; (*SPORT*) draw

pa'rente *sm/f* relative, relation

paren'tela *sf* (*vincolo di sangue, fig*) relationship

pa'rentesi *sf* (*segno grafico*) bracket, parenthesis; (*frase incisa*) parenthesis; (*digressione*) parenthesis, digression

pa'rere *sm* (*opinione*) opinion; (*consiglio*) advice, opinion; **a mio ~** in my opinion ♦ *vi* to seem, appear ♦ *vb impers*: **pare che** it seems *o* appears that, they say that; **mi pare che** it seems to me that; **mi pare di sì** I think so; **fai come ti pare** do as you like; **che ti pare del mio libro?** what do you think of my book?

pa'rete *sf* wall

'pari *ag inv* (*uguale*) equal, same; (*in giochi*) equal; drawn, tied; (*MAT*) even ♦ *sm inv* (*POL: di Gran Bretagna*) peer ♦ *sm/f inv* peer, equal; **copiato ~ ~** copied word for word; **alla ~** on the same level; **ragazza alla ~** au pair girl; **mettersi alla ~ con** to place o.s. on the same level as; **mettersi in ~ con** to catch up with; **andare di ~ passo con qn** to keep pace with sb

Pa'rigi [pa'ridʒi] *sf* Paris

pa'riglia [pa'riʎʎa] *sf* pair; **rendere la ~** to give tit for tat

parità *sf* parity, equality; (*SPORT*) draw, tie

parlamen'tare *ag* parliamentary ♦ *sm/f* ≈ Member of Parliament (*BRIT*), ≈ Congressman/woman (*US*) ♦ *vi* to negotiate, parley

parla'mento *sm* parliament

parlan'tina (*fam*) *sf* talkativeness; **avere ~** to have the gift of the gab

par'lare *vi* to speak, talk; (*confidare cose segrete*) to talk ♦ *vt* to speak; **~ (a qn) di** to speak *o* talk (to sb) about; **parla'torio** *sm* (*di carcere etc*) visiting room; (*REL*) parlour

parmigi'ano [parmi'dʒano] *sm* (*grana*) Parmesan (cheese)

paro'dia *sf* parody

pa'rola *sf* word; (*facoltà*) speech; **~e** *sfpl* (*chiacchiere*) talk *sg*; **chiedere la ~** to ask permission to speak; **prendere la ~** to take the floor; **~ d'onore** word of honour; **~ d'ordine** (*MIL*) password; **~e incrociate** crossword (puzzle) *sg*; **paro'laccia, ce** *sf* bad word, swearword

par'rocchia [par'rɔkkja] *sf* parish; parish church

'parroco, ci *sm* parish priest

par'rucca, che *sf* wig
parrucchi'ere, a [parruk'kjɛre] *sm/f*
hairdresser ♦ *sm* barber
parsi'monia *sf* frugality, thrift
'parso, a *pp di* **parere**
'parte *sf* part; (*lato*) side; (*quota spettante a ciascuno*) share; (*direzione*) direction; (*POL*) party; faction; (*DIR*) party; **a ~** *ag* separate ♦ *av* separately; **scherzi a ~** joking aside; **a ~ ciò** apart from that; **da ~** (*in disparte*) to one side, aside; **d'altra ~** on the other hand; **da ~ di** (*per conto di*) on behalf of; **da ~ mia** as far as I'm concerned, as for me; **da ~ a ~** right through; **da ogni ~** on all sides, everywhere; (*moto da luogo*) from all sides; **da nessuna ~** nowhere; **da questa ~** (*in questa direzione*) this way; **prendere ~ a qc** to take part in sth; **mettere da ~** to put aside; **mettere qn a ~ di** to inform sb of
parteci'pare [partetʃi'pare] *vi*: **~ a** to take part in, participate in; (*utili etc*) to share in; (*spese etc*) to contribute to; (*dolore, successo di qn*) to share (in);
partecipazi'one *sf* participation; sharing; (*ECON*) interest; **partecipazione agli utili** profit-sharing; **partecipazioni di nozze** *wedding announcement card*; **par'tecipe** *ag* participating; **essere partecipe di** to take part in, participate in; to share (in); (*consapevole*) to be aware of
parteggi'are [parted'dʒare] *vi*: **~ per** to side with, be on the side of
par'tenza [par'tɛntsa] *sf* departure; (*SPORT*) start; **essere in ~** to be about to leave, be leaving
parti'cella [parti'tʃɛlla] *sf* particle
parti'cipio [parti'tʃipjo] *sm* participle
partico'lare *ag* (*specifico*) particular; (*proprio*) personal, private; (*speciale*) special, particular; (*caratteristico*) distinctive, characteristic; (*fuori dal comune*) peculiar ♦ *sm* detail, particular; **in ~** in particular, particularly; **particolarità** *sf inv* particularity; detail; characteristic, feature
partigi'ano, a [parti'dʒano] *ag* partisan ♦ *sm* (*MIL*) partisan

par'tire *vi* to go, leave; (*allontanarsi*) to go (*o drive etc*) away *o* off; (*petardo, colpo*) to go off; (*fig: avere inizio, SPORT*) to start; **sono partita da Roma alle 7** I left Rome at 7; **il volo parte da Ciampino** the flight leaves from Ciampino; **a ~ da** from
par'tita *sf* (*COMM*) lot, consignment; (*ECON: registrazione*) entry, item; (*CARTE, SPORT: gioco*) game; (*: competizione*) match, game; **~ di caccia** hunting party; **~ IVA** VAT registration number
par'tito *sm* (*POL*) party; (*decisione*) decision, resolution; (*persona da maritare*) match
parti'tura *sf* (*MUS*) score
'parto *sm* (*MED*) delivery, (child)birth; labour; **parto'rire** *vt* to give birth to; (*fig*) to produce
parzi'ale [par'tsjale] *ag* (*limitato*) partial; (*non obiettivo*) biased, partial
'pascere ['paʃʃere] *vt* (*brucare*) to graze on; (*far pascolare*) to graze, pasture; **pasci'uto, a** *pp di* **pascere**
pasco'lare *vt, vi* to graze
'pascolo *sm* pasture
'Pasqua *sf* Easter; **pas'quale** *ag* Easter *cpd*; **Pas'quetta** *sf* Easter Monday
pas'sabile *ag* fairly good, passable
pas'saggio [pas'saddʒo] *sm* passing *no pl*, passage; (*traversata*) crossing *no pl*, passage; (*luogo, prezzo della traversata, brano di libro etc*) passage; (*su veicolo altrui*) lift (*BRIT*), ride; (*SPORT*) pass; **di ~** (*persona*) passing through; **~ pedonale/a livello** pedestrian/level (*BRIT*) *o* grade (*US*) crossing
passamon'tagna [passamon'taɲɲa] *sm inv* balaclava
pas'sante *sm/f* passer-by ♦ *sm* loop
passa'porto *sm* passport
pas'sare *vi* (*andare*) to go; (*veicolo, pedone*) to pass (by), go by; (*fare una breve sosta: postino etc*) to come, call; (*: amico: per fare una visita*) to call *o* drop in; (*sole, aria, luce*) to get through; (*trascorrere: giorni, tempo*) to pass, go by; (*fig: proposta di legge*) to be passed; (*: dolore*) to pass, go away; (*CARTE*) to pass ♦ *vt* (*attraversare*) to cross; (*trasmettere: messaggio*): **~ qc a qn**

to pass sth on to sb; (*dare*): **~ qc a qn** to pass sth to sb, give sb sth; (*trascorrere: tempo*) to spend; (*superare: esame*) to pass; (*triturare: verdura*) to strain; (*approvare*) to pass, approve; (*oltrepassare, sorpassare: anche fig*) to go beyond, pass; (*fig: subire*) to go through; **~ da ... a** to pass from ... to; **~ di padre in figlio** to be handed down *o* to pass from father to son; **~ per** (*anche fig*) to go through; **~ per stupido/un genio** to be taken for a fool/a genius; **~ sopra** (*anche fig*) to pass over; **~ attraverso** (*anche fig*) to go through; **~ alla storia** to pass into history; **~ a un esame** to go up (to the next class) after an exam; **~ inosservato** to go unnoticed; **~ di moda** to go out of fashion; **le passo il Signor X** (*al telefono*) here is Mr X; I'm putting you through to Mr X; **lasciar ~ qn/qc** to let sb/sth through; **come te la passi?** how are you getting on *o* along?

pas'sata *sf*: **dare una ~ di vernice a qc** to give sth a coat of paint; **dare una ~ al giornale** to have a look at the paper, skim through the paper

passa'tempo *sm* pastime, hobby

pas'sato, a *ag* past; (*sfiorito*) faded ♦ *sm* past; (*LING*) past (tense); **~ prossimo** (*LING*) present perfect; **~ remoto** (*LING*) past historic; **~ di verdura** (*CUC*) vegetable purée

passaver'dura *sm inv* vegetable mill

passeg'gero, a [passed'dʒero] *ag* passing ♦ *sm/f* passenger

passeggi'are [passed'dʒare] *vi* to go for a walk; (*in veicolo*) to go for a drive; **passeggi'ata** *sf* walk; drive; (*luogo*) promenade; **fare una passeggiata** to go for a walk (*o* drive); **passeg'gino** *sm* pushchair (*BRIT*), stroller (*US*); **pas'seggio** *sm* walk, stroll; (*luogo*) promenade

passe'rella *sf* footbridge; (*di nave, aereo*) gangway; (*pedana*) catwalk

'passero *sm* sparrow

pas'sibile *ag*: **~ di** liable to

passi'one *sf* passion

pas'sivo, a *ag* passive ♦ *sm* (*LING*) passive; (*ECON*) debit; (: *complesso dei debiti*) liabilities *pl*

'passo *sm* step; (*andatura*) pace; (*rumore*) (foot)step; (*orma*) footprint; (*passaggio, fig: brano*) passage; (*valico*) pass; **a ~ d'uomo** at walking pace; **~ (a) ~** step by step; **fare due** *o* **quattro ~i** to go for a walk *o* a stroll; **di questo ~** at this rate; **"~ carraio"** "vehicle entrance — keep clear"

'pasta *sf* (*CUC*) dough; (: *impasto per dolce*) pastry; (: *anche*: **~ alimentare**) pasta; (*massa molle di materia*) paste; (*fig: indole*) nature; **~e** *sfpl* (*pasticcini*) pastries; **~ in brodo** noodle soup

pastasci'utta [pastaʃ'ʃutta] *sf* pasta

pas'tella *sf* batter

pas'tello *sm* pastel

pas'ticca, che *sf* = **pastiglia**

pasticce'ria [pastittʃe'ria] *sf* (*pasticcini*) pastries *pl*, cakes *pl*; (*negozio*) cake shop; (*arte*) confectionery

pasticci'are [pastit'tʃare] *vt* to mess up, make a mess of ♦ *vi* to make a mess

pasticci'ere, a [pastit'tʃere] *sm/f* pastrycook; confectioner

pas'ticcio [pas'tittʃo] *sm* (*CUC*) pie; (*lavoro disordinato, imbroglio*) mess; **trovarsi nei ~i** to get into trouble

pasti'ficio [pasti'fitʃo] *sm* pasta factory

pas'tiglia [pas'tiʎʎa] *sf* pastille, lozenge

pas'tina *sf* small pasta shapes used in soup

'pasto *sm* meal

pas'tore *sm* shepherd; (*REL*) pastor, minister; (*anche*: **cane ~**) sheepdog; **~ tedesco** (*ZOOL*) Alsatian, German shepherd

pastoriz'zare [pastorid'dzare] *vt* to pasteurize

pas'toso, a *ag* doughy; pasty; (*fig: voce, colore*) mellow, soft

pas'trano *sm* greatcoat

pa'tata *sf* potato; **~e fritte** chips (*BRIT*), French fries; **pata'tine** *sfpl* (*patato*) crisps; **~ fritte** chips

pata'trac *sm* (*crollo: anche fig*) crash

paté *sm inv* pâté

pa'tella *sf* (*ZOOL*) limpet

pa'tema, i *sm* anxiety, worry

pa'tente *sf* licence; (*anche:* ~ **di guida**) driving licence (*BRIT*), driver's license (*US*)

paternità *sf* paternity, fatherhood

pa'terno, a *ag* (*affetto, consigli*) fatherly; (*casa, autorità*) paternal

pa'tetico, a, ci, che *ag* pathetic; (*commovente*) moving, touching

pa'tibolo *sm* gallows *sg*, scaffold

'patina *sf* (*su rame etc*) patina; (*sulla lingua*) fur, coating

pa'tire *vt, vi* to suffer

pa'tito, a *sm/f* enthusiast, fan, lover

patolo'gia [patolo'dʒia] *sf* pathology; **pato'logico, a, ci, che** *ag* pathological

'patria *sf* homeland

patri'arca, chi *sm* patriarch

pa'trigno [pa'triɲɲo] *sm* stepfather

patri'monio *sm* estate, property; (*fig*) heritage

patri'ota, i, e *sm/f* patriot; **patri'ottico, a, ci, che** *ag* patriotic; **patriot'tismo** *sm* patriotism

patroci'nare [patrotʃi'nare] *vt* (*DIR: difendere*) to defend; (*sostenere*) to sponsor, support; **patro'cinio** *sm* defence; support, sponsorship

patro'nato *sm* patronage; (*istituzione benefica*) charitable institution *o* society

pa'trono *sm* (*REL*) patron saint; (*socio di patronato*) patron; (*DIR*) counsel

'patta *sf* flap; (*dei pantaloni*) fly

patteggia'mento [patteddʒa'mento] *sm* (*DIR*) plea bargaining

patteggi'are [patted'dʒare] *vt, vi* to negotiate; (*DIR*) to plea-bargain

patti'naggio [patti'naddʒo] *sm* skating

patti'nare *vi* to skate; ~ **sul ghiaccio** to ice-skate; **pattina'tore, 'trice** *sm/f* skater; **'pattino¹** *sm* skate; (*di slitta*) runner; (*AER*) skid; (*TECN*) sliding block; **pattini (da ghiaccio)** (ice) skates; **pattini a rotelle** roller skates; **pat'tino²** *sm* (*barca*) *kind of pedalo with oars*

'patto *sm* (*accordo*) pact, agreement; (*condizione*) term, condition; **a ~ che** on condition that

pat'tuglia [pat'tuʎʎa] *sf* (*MIL*) patrol

pattu'ire *vt* to reach an agreement on

pattumi'era *sf* (dust)bin (*BRIT*), ashcan (*US*)

pa'ura *sf* fear; **aver ~ di/di fare/che** to be frightened *o* afraid of/of doing/that; **far ~ a** to frighten; **per ~ di/che** for fear of/that; **pau'roso, a** *ag* (*che fa paura*) frightening; (*che ha paura*) fearful, timorous

'pausa *sf* (*sosta*) break; (*nel parlare, MUS*) pause

pavi'mento *sm* floor

pa'vone *sm* peacock; **pavoneggi'arsi** *vr* to strut about, show off

pazien'tare [pattsjen'tare] *vi* to be patient

pazi'ente [pat'tsjɛnte] *ag, sm/f* patient; **pazi'enza** *sf* patience

paz'zesco, a, schi, sche [pat'tsesko] *ag* mad, crazy

paz'zia [pat'tsia] *sf* (*MED*) madness, insanity; (*azione*) folly; (*di azione, decisione*) madness, folly

'pazzo, a ['pattso] *ag* (*MED*) mad, insane; (*strano*) wild, mad ♦ *sm/f* madman/woman; ~ **di** (*gioia, amore etc*) mad *o* crazy with; ~ **per qc/qn** mad *o* crazy about sth/sb

PCI *sigla m* = **Partito Comunista Italiano**

'pecca, che *sf* defect, flaw, fault

peccami'noso, a *ag* sinful

pec'care *vi* to sin; (*fig*) to err

pec'cato *sm* sin; **è un ~ che** it's a pity that; **che ~!** what a shame *o* pity!

pecca'tore, 'trice *sm/f* sinner

'pece ['petʃe] *sf* pitch

Pe'chino [pe'kino] *sf* Beijing

'pecora *sf* sheep; **peco'raio** *sm* shepherd; **peco'rino** *sm* sheep's milk cheese

peculi'are *ag:* ~ **di** peculiar to

pe'daggio [pe'daddʒo] *sm* toll

pedago'gia [pedago'dʒia] *sf* pedagogy, educational methods *pl*

peda'lare *vi* to pedal; (*andare in bicicletta*) to cycle

pe'dale *sm* pedal

pe'dana *sf* footboard; (*SPORT: nel salto*) springboard; (: *nella scherma*) piste

pe'dante *ag* pedantic ♦ *sm/f* pedant

pe'data *sf* (*impronta*) footprint; (*colpo*) kick; **prendere a ~e qn/qc** to kick sb/sth

pede'rasta, i *sm* pederast; homosexual

pedi'atra, i, e *sm/f* paediatrician; **pedia'tria** *sf* paediatrics *sg*

pedi'cure *sm/f inv* chiropodist

pe'dina *sf* (*della dama*) draughtsman (*BRIT*), draftsman (*US*); (*fig*) pawn

pedi'nare *vt* to shadow, tail

pedo'nale *ag* pedestrian

pe'done, a *sm/f* pedestrian ♦ *sm* (*SCACCHI*) pawn

'peggio ['pɛddʒo] *av*, *ag inv* worse ♦ *sm o f*: **il o la ~** the worst; **alla ~** at worst, if the worst comes to the worst; **peggiora'mento** *sm* worsening; **peggio'rare** *vt* to make worse, worsen ♦ *vi* to grow worse, worsen; **peggiora'tivo, a** *ag* pejorative; **peggi'ore** *ag* (*comparativo*) worse; (*superlativo*) worst ♦ *sm/f*: **il(la) peggiore** the worst (person)

'pegno ['peɲɲo] *sm* (*DIR*) security, pledge; (*nei giochi di società*) forfeit; (*fig*) pledge, token; **dare in ~ qc** to pawn sth

pe'lare *vt* (*spennare*) to pluck; (*spellare*) to skin; (*sbucciare*) to peel; (*fig*) to make pay through the nose; **~rsi** *vr* to go bald

pe'lato, a *ag*: **pomodori ~i** tinned tomatoes

pel'lame *sm* skins *pl*, hides *pl*

'pollo *sf* skin; (*di animale*) skin, hide; (*cuoio*) leather; **avere la ~ d'oca** to have goose pimples *o* gooseflesh

pellegri'naggio [pellegri'naddʒo] *sm* pilgrimage

pelle'grino, a *sm/f* pilgrim

pelle'rossa (*pl* pelli'rosse) *sm/f* Red Indian

pellette'ria *sf* leather goods *pl*; (*negozio*) leather goods shop

pelli'cano *sm* pelican

pellicce'ria [pellittʃe'ria] *sf* (*negozio*) furrier's (shop)

pel'liccia, ce [pel'littʃa] *sf* (*mantello di animale*) coat, fur; (*indumento*) fur coat

pel'licola *sf* (*membrana sottile*) film, layer; (*FOT, CINEMA*) film

'pelo *sm* hair; (*pelame*) coat, hair; (*pelliccia*) fur; (*di tappeto*) pile; (*di liquido*) surface; **per un ~: per un ~ non ho perduto il treno** I very nearly missed the train; **c'è mancato un ~ che affogasse** he escaped drowning by the skin of his teeth; **pe'loso, a** *ag* hairy

'peltro *sm* pewter

pe'luria *sf* down

'pena *sf* (*DIR*) sentence; (*punizione*) punishment; (*sofferenza*) sadness *no pl*, sorrow; (*fatica*) trouble *no pl*, effort; (*difficoltà*) difficulty; **far ~** to be pitiful; **mi fai ~** I feel sorry for you; **prendersi o darsi la ~ di fare** to go to the trouble of doing; **~ di morte** death sentence; **~ pecuniaria** fine; **pe'nale** *ag* penal; **penalità** *sf inv* penalty; **penaliz'zare** *vt* (*SPORT*) to penalize

pe'nare *vi* (*patire*) to suffer; (*faticare*) to struggle

pen'dente *ag* hanging; leaning ♦ *sm* (*ciondolo*) pendant; (*orecchino*) drop earring; **pen'denza** *sf* slope, slant; (*grado d'inclinazione*) gradient; (*ECON*) outstanding account

'pendere *vi* (*essere appeso*): **~ da** to hang from; (*essere inclinato*) to lean; (*fig: incombere*): **~ su** to hang over

pen'dice [pen'ditʃe] *sf*. **alle ~i del monte** at the foot of the mountain

pen'dio, 'dii *sm* slope, slant; (*luogo in pendenza*) slope

'pendola *sf* pendulum clock

pendo'lare *sm/f* commuter

pendo'lino *sm* high-speed train

'pendolo *sm* (*peso*) pendulum; (*anche*: **orologio a ~**) pendulum clock

'pene *sm* penis

pene'trante *ag* piercing, penetrating

pene'trare *vi* to come *o* get in ♦ *vt* to penetrate; **~ in** to enter; (*sog: proiettile*) to penetrate; (: *acqua, aria*) to go *o* come into

penicil'lina [penitʃil'lina] *sf* penicillin

pe'nisola *sf* peninsula

peni'tenza [peni'tɛntsa] *sf* penitence;

(*punizione*) penance

penitenzi'ario [peniten'tsjarjo] *sm* prison

'penna *sf* (*di uccello*) feather; (*per scrivere*) pen; **~e** *sfpl* (*CUC*) quills (*type of pasta*); **~ stilografica/a sfera** fountain/ballpoint pen

penna'rello *sm* felt(-tip) pen

pennel'lare *vi* to paint

pen'nello *sm* brush; (*per dipingere*) (paint)brush; **a ~** (*perfettamente*) to perfection, perfectly; **~ per la barba** shaving brush

pen'nino *sm* nib

pen'none *sm* (*NAUT*) yard; (*stendardo*) banner, standard

pe'nombra *sf* half-light, dim light

pe'noso, a *ag* painful, distressing; (*faticoso*) tiring, laborious

pen'sare *vi* to think ♦ *vt* to think; (*inventare, escogitare*) to think out; **~ a** to think of; (*amico, vacanze*) to think of *o* about; (*problema*) to think about; **~ di fare qc** to think of doing sth; **ci penso io** I'll see to *o* take care of it

pensi'ero *sm* thought; (*modo di pensare, dottrina*) thinking *no pl*; (*preoccupazione*) worry, care, trouble; **stare in ~ per qn** to be worried about sb; **pensie'roso, a** *ag* thoughtful

'pensile *ag* hanging

pensi'lina *sf* (*per autobus*) bus shelter

pensio'nante *sm/f* (*presso una famiglia*) lodger; (*di albergo*) guest

pensio'nato, a *sm/f* pensioner

pensi'one *sf* (*al prestatore di lavoro*) pension; (*vitto e alloggio*) board and lodging; (*albergo*) boarding house; **andare in ~** to retire; **mezza ~** half board; **~ completa** full board

pen'soso, a *ag* thoughtful, pensive, lost in thought

pentapar'tito *sm* five-party government

Pente'coste *sf* Pentecost, Whit Sunday (*BRIT*)

penti'mento *sm* repentance, contrition

pen'tirsi *vr:* **~ di** to repent of; (*rammaricarsi*) to regret, be sorry for

'pentola *sf* pot; **~ a pressione** pressure

cooker

pe'nultimo, a *ag* last but one (*BRIT*), next to last, penultimate

pe'nuria *sf* shortage

penzo'lare [pendzo'lare] *vi* to dangle, hang loosely; **penzo'loni** *av* dangling, hanging down; **stare penzoloni** to dangle, hang down

'pepe *sm* pepper; **~ macinato/in grani** ground/whole pepper

pepero'nata *sf* (*CUC*) stewed peppers, tomatoes and onions

pepe'rone *sm* pepper, capsicum; (*piccante*) chili

pe'pita *sf* nugget

PAROLA CHIAVE

---

per *prep* **1** (*moto attraverso luogo*) through; **i ladri sono passati ~ la finestra** the thieves got in (*o* out) through the window; **l'ho cercato ~ tutta la casa** I've searched the whole house *o* all over the house for it

2 (*moto a luogo*) for, to; **partire ~ la Germania/il mare** to leave for Germany/ the sea; **il treno ~ Roma** the Rome train, the train for *o* to Rome

3 (*stato in luogo*): **seduto/sdraiato ~ terra** sitting/lying on the ground

4 (*tempo*) for; **~ anni/lungo tempo** for years/a long time; **~ tutta l'estate** throughout the summer, all summer long; **lo rividi ~ Natale** I saw him again at Christmas; **lo faccio ~ lunedì** I'll do it for Monday

5 (*mezzo, maniera*) by; **~ lettera/via aerea/ferrovia** by letter/airmail/rail; **prendere qn ~ un braccio** to take sb by the arm

6 (*causa, scopo*) for; **assente ~ malattia** absent because of *o* through *o* owing to illness; **ottimo ~ il mal di gola** excellent for sore throats

7 (*limitazione*) for; **è troppo difficile ~ lui** it's too difficult for him; **~ quel che mi riguarda** as far as I'm concerned; **~ poco che sia** however little it may be; **~ questa volta ti perdono** I'll forgive you this time

8 (*prezzo, misura*) for; (*distributivo*) a, per; **venduto ~ 3 milioni** sold for 3 million; **1000 lire ~ persona** 1000 lire a *o* per person; **uno ~ volta** one at a time; **uno ~ uno** one by one; **5 ~ cento** 5 per cent; **3 ~ 4 fa 12** 3 times 4 equals 12; **dividere/moltiplicare 12 ~ 4** to divide/multiply 12 by 4

9 (*in qualità di*) as; (*al posto di*) for; **avere qn ~ professore** to have sb as a teacher; **ti ho preso ~ Mario** I mistook you for Mario, I thought you were Mario; **dare ~ morto qn** to give sb up for dead

10 (*seguito da vb: finale*): **~ fare qc** (so as) to do sth, in order to do sth; (: *causale*): **~ aver fatto qc** for having done sth; (: *consecutivo*): **è abbastanza grande ~ andarci da solo** he's big enough to go on his own

'**pera** *sf* pear
pe'raltro *av* moreover, what's more
per'bene *ag inv* respectable, decent ♦ *av* (*con cura*) properly, well
percentu'ale [pertʃentu'ale] *sf* percentage
perce'pire [pertʃe'pire] *vt* (*sentire*) to perceive; (*ricevere*) to receive; **percezi'one** *sf* perception

---

PAROLA CHIAVE

---

perché [per'ke] *av* why; **~ no?** why not?; **non vuoi andarci?** why don't you want to go?; **spiegami ~ l'hai fatto** tell me why you did it
♦ *cong* **1** (*causale*) because; **non posso uscire ~ ho da fare** I can't go out because *o* as I've a lot to do
2 (*finale*) in order that, so that; **te lo do ~ tu lo legga** I'm giving it to you so (that) you can read it
3 (*consecutivo*): **è troppo forte ~ si possa batterlo** he's too strong to be beaten
♦ *sm inv* reason; **il ~ di** the reason for

---

perciò [per'tʃɔ] *cong* so, for this (*o* that) reason
per'correre *vt* (*luogo*) to go all over;
(: *paese*) to travel up and down, go all over; (*distanza*) to cover
per'corso, a *pp di* **percorrere** ♦ *sm* (*tragitto*) journey; (*tratto*) route
per'cossa *sf* blow
per'cosso, a *pp di* **percuotere**
percu'otere *vt* to hit, strike
percussi'one *sf* percussion; **strumenti a ~** (*MUS*) percussion instruments
'**perdere** *vt* to lose; (*lasciarsi sfuggire*) to miss; (*sprecare: tempo, denaro*) to waste ♦ *vi* to lose; (*serbatoio etc*) to leak; **~rsi** *vr* (*smarrirsi*) to get lost; (*svanire*) to disappear, vanish; **saper ~** to be a good loser; **lascia ~!** forget it!, never mind!
perdigi'orno [perdi'dʒorno] *sm/f inv* idler, waster
'**perdita** *sf* loss; (*spreco*) waste; (*fuoriuscita*) leak; **siamo in ~** (*COMM*) we are running at a loss; **a ~ d'occhio** as far as the eye can see
perdo'nare *vt* to pardon, forgive; (*scusare*) to excuse, pardon
per'dono *sm* forgiveness; (*DIR*) pardon
perdu'rare *vi* to go on, last
perduta'mente *av* desperately, passionately
per'duto, a *pp di* **perdere**
peregri'nare *vi* to wander, roam
pe'renne *ag* eternal, perpetual, perennial; (*BOT*) perennial
peren'torio, a *ag* peremptory; (*definitivo*) final
per'fetto, a *ag* perfect ♦ *sm* (*LING*) perfect (tense)
perfezio'nare [perfettsjo'nare] *vt* to improve, perfect; **~rsi** *vr* to improve
perfezi'one [perfet'tsjone] *sf* perfection
'**perfido, a** *ag* perfidious, treacherous
per'fino *av* even
perfo'rare *vt* to perforate; to punch a hole (*o* holes) in; (*banda, schede*) to punch; (*trivellare*) to drill; **perfora'trice** *sf* (*TECN*) boring *o* drilling machine; (*INFORM*) card punch; **perforazi'one** *sf* perforation; punching; drilling; (*INFORM*) punch; (*MED*) perforation

perga'mena *sf* parchment

'pergola *sf* (*per rampicanti*) pergola

perico'lante *ag* precarious

pe'ricolo *sm* danger; **mettere in ~** to endanger, put in danger; **perico'loso, a** *ag* dangerous

perife'ria *sf* (*di città*) outskirts *pl*

pe'rifrasi *sf* circumlocution

pe'rimetro *sm* perimeter

peri'odico, a, ci, che *ag* periodic(al); (*MAT*) recurring ♦ *sm* periodical

pe'riodo *sm* period

peripe'zie [peripet'tsie] *sfpl* ups and downs, vicissitudes

pe'rire *vi* to perish, die

pe'rito, a *ag* expert, skilled ♦ *sm/f* expert; (*agronomo, navale*) surveyor; **un ~ chimico** a qualified chemist

pe'rizia [pe'rittsja] *sf* (*abilità*) ability; (*giudizio tecnico*) expert opinion; expert's report

'perla *sf* pearl; **per'lina** *sf* bead

perlus'trare *vt* to patrol

perma'loso, a *ag* touchy

perma'nente *ag* permanent ♦ *sf* permanent wave, perm; **perma'nenza** *sf* permanence; (*soggiorno*) stay

perma'nere *vi* to remain

perme'are *vt* to permeate

per'messo, a *pp di* **permettere** ♦ *sm* (*autorizzazione*) permission, leave; (*dato a militare, impiegato*) leave; (*licenza*) licence, permit; (*MIL: foglio*) pass; **~?, è ~?** (*posso entrare?*) may I come in?; (*posso passare?*) excuse me; **~ di lavoro/pesca** work/fishing permit; **~ di soggiorno** residence permit

per'mettere *vt* to allow, permit; **~ a qn qc/di fare** to allow sb sth/to do; **~rsi qc/di fare** to allow o.s. sth/to do; (*avere la possibilità*) to afford sth/to do

per'nacchia [per'nakkja] (*fam*) *sf*: **fare una ~** to blow a raspberry

per'nice [per'nitʃe] *sf* partridge

'perno *sm* pivot

pernot'tare *vi* to spend the night, stay overnight

'pero *sm* pear tree

però *cong* (*ma*) but; (*tuttavia*) however, nevertheless

pero'rare *vt* (*DIR, fig*): **~ la causa di qn** to plead sb's case

perpendico'lare *ag, sf* perpendicular

perpe'trare *vt* to perpetrate

perpetu'are *vt* to perpetuate

per'petuo, a *ag* perpetual

per'plesso, a *ag* perplexed; uncertain, undecided

perqui'sire *vt* to search; **perquisizi'one** *sf* (police) search

persecu'tore *sm* persecutor

persecuzi'one [persekut'tsjone] *sf* persecution

persegu'ire *vt* to pursue

persegui'tare *vt* to persecute

perseve'rante *ag* persevering

perseve'rare *vi* to persevere

'Persia *sf*: **la ~** Persia

persi'ana *sf* shutter; **~ avvolgibile** roller shutter

persi'ano, a *ag, sm/f* Persian

'persico, a, ci, che *ag*: **il golfo P~** the Persian Gulf

per'sino *av* = **perfino**

persis'tente *ag* persistent

per'sistere *vi* to persist; **~ a fare** to persist in doing; **persis'tito, a** *pp di* **persistere**

'perso, a *pp di* **perdere**

per'sona *sf* person; (*qualcuno*): **una ~** someone, somebody; *espressione interrogativa* +anyone *o* anybody; **~e** *sfpl* people; **non c'è ~ che ...** there's nobody who ..., there isn't anybody who ...

perso'naggio [perso'naddʒo] *sm* (*persona ragguardevole*) personality, figure; (*tipo*) character, individual; (*LETTERATURA*) character

perso'nale *ag* personal ♦ *sm* staff; personnel; (*figura fisica*) build

personalità *sf inv* personality

personifi'care *vt* to personify; to embody

perspi'cace [perspi'katʃe] *ag* shrewd, discerning

persu'adere *vt*: **~ qn (di qc/a fare)** to

persuade sb (of sth/to do); **persuasi'one** *sf* persuasion; **persua'sivo, a** *ag* persuasive; **persu'aso, a** *pp di* **persuadere**

per'tanto *cong* (*quindi*) so, therefore

'pertica, che *sf* pole

perti'nente *ag:* ~ (a) relevant (to), pertinent (to)

per'tosse *sf* whooping cough

per'tugio [per'tudʒo] *sm* hole, opening

perturbazi'one [perturbat'tsjone] *sf* disruption; perturbation; ~ **atmosferica** atmospheric disturbance

per'vadere *vt* to pervade; **per'vaso, a** *pp di* **pervadere**

perve'nire *vi:* ~ **a** to reach, arrive at, come to; (*venire in possesso*): **gli pervenne una fortuna** he inherited a fortune; **far ~ qc a** to have sth sent to; **perve'nuto, a** *pp di* **pervenire**

per'verso, a *ag* depraved; perverse

p. es. *abbr* (= *per esempio*) e.g.

'pesa *sf* weighing *no pl*; weighbridge

pe'sante *ag* heavy

pe'sare *vt* to weigh ♦ *vi* (*avere un peso*) to weigh; (*essere pesante*) to be heavy; (*fig*) to carry weight; ~ **su** (*fig*) to lie heavy on; to influence; to hang over

'pesca (*pl* **pesche:** *frutto*) *sf* peach; (*il pescare*) fishing; **andare a** ~ to go fishing; ~ **di beneficenza** (*lotteria*) lucky dip; ~ **con la lenza** angling

pes'care *vt* (*pesce*) to fish for; to catch; (*qc nell'acqua*) to fish out; (*fig: trovare*) to get hold of, find; **andare a** ~ to go fishing

pesca'tore *sm* fisherman; angler

'pesce ['peʃʃe] *sm* fish *gen inv*; **P~i** (*dello zodiaco*) Pisces; ~ **d'aprile!** April Fool!; ~ **spada** swordfish; **pesce'cane** *sm* shark

---
pesce d'aprile

ⓘ **Il pesce d'aprile** *is a practical joke played on 1 April. It takes its name from the traditional prank of surreptitiously sticking a paper fish on someone's back.*

---

pesche'reccio [peske'rettʃo] *sm* fishing

boat

pesche'ria [peske'ria] *sf* fishmonger's (shop) (*BRIT*), fish store (*US*)

pesci'vendolo, a [peʃʃi'vendolo] *sm/f* fishmonger (*BRIT*), fish merchant (*US*)

'pesco, schi *sm* peach tree

pes'coso, a *ag* abounding in fish

'peso *sm* weight; (*SPORT*) shot; **rubare sul** ~ to give short weight; **essere di** ~ **a qn** (*fig*) to be a burden to sb; ~ **lordo/netto** gross/net weight; ~ **piuma/mosca/gallo/medio/massimo** (*PUGILATO*) feather/fly/bantam/middle/heavyweight

pessi'mismo *sm* pessimism; **pessi'mista, i, e** *ag* pessimistic ♦ *sm/f* pessimist

'pessimo, a *ag* very bad, awful

pes'tare *vt* to tread on, trample on; (*sale, pepe*) to grind; (*uva, aglio*) to crush; (*fig: picchiare*): ~ **qn** to beat sb up

'peste *sf* plague; (*persona*) nuisance, pest

pes'tello *sm* pestle

pesti'lenza [pesti'lentsa] *sf* pestilence; (*fetore*) stench

'pesto, a *ag:* **c'è buio** ~ it's pitch-dark; **occhio** ~ black eye ♦ *sm* (*CUC*) sauce made with basil, garlic, cheese and oil

'petalo *sm* (*BOT*) petal

pe'tardo *sm* firecracker, banger (*BRIT*)

petizi'one [petit'tsjone] *sf* petition

'peto (*fam!*) *sm* fart (!)

petrol'chimica [petrol'kimika] *sf* petrochemical industry

petroli'era *sf* (*nave*) oil tanker

petro'lifero, a *ag* oil-bearing; oil *cpd*

pe'trolio *sm* oil, petroleum; (*per lampada, fornello*) paraffin

pettego'lare *vi* to gossip

pettego'lezzo [pettego'leddzo] *sm* gossip *no pl*; **fare ~i** to gossip

pet'tegolo, a *ag* gossipy ♦ *sm/f* gossip

petti'nare *vt* to comb (the hair of); ~**rsi** *vr* to comb one's hair; **pettina'tura** *sf* (*acconciatura*) hairstyle

'pettine *sm* comb; (*ZOOL*) scallop

petti'rosso *sm* robin

'petto *sm* chest; (*seno*) breast, bust; (*CUC: di*

carne bovina) brisket; (: *di pollo etc*) breast;
a doppio ~ (*abito*) double-breasted;
petto'ruto, a *ag* broad-chested; full-
breasted
petu'lante *ag* insolent
pe'tunia *sf* (BOT) petunia
'pezza ['pettsa] *sf* piece of cloth; (*toppa*)
patch; (*cencio*) rag, cloth
pez'zato, a [pet'tsato] *ag* piebald
pez'zente [pet'tsɛnte] *sm/f* beggar
'pezzo ['pettso] *sm* (*gen*) piece; (*brandello,
frammento*) piece, bit; (*di macchina, arnese
etc*) part; (STAMPA) article; (*di tempo*):
aspettare un ~ to wait quite a while *o*
some time; **in** *o* **a ~i** in pieces; **andare in
~i** to break into pieces; **un bel ~ d'uomo** a
fine figure of a man; **abito a due ~i** two-
piece suit; **~ di cronaca** (STAMPA) report; **~
grosso** (*fig*) bigwig; **~ di ricambio** spare
part
pia'cente [pja'tʃɛnte] *ag* attractive
pia'cere [pja'tʃere] *vi* to please; **una
ragazza che piace** a likeable girl; an
attractive girl; **~ a: mi piace** I like it; **quei
ragazzi non mi piacciono** I don't like
those boys; **gli piacerebbe andare al
cinema** he would like to go to the cinema
♦ *sm* pleasure; (*favore*) favour; "**~!**" (*nelle
presentazioni*) "pleased to meet you!"; **con
~** certainly, with pleasure; **per ~!** please;
fare un ~ a qn to do sb a favour;
pia'cevole *ag* pleasant, agreeable;
piaci'uto, a *pp di* **piacere**
pi'aga, ghe *sf* (*lesione*) sore; (*ferita: anche
fig*) wound; (*fig: flagello*) scourge, curse;
(: *persona*) pest, nuisance
piagnis'teo [pjaɲɲis'teo] *sm* whining,
whimpering
piagnuco'lare [pjaɲɲuko'lare] *vi* to
whimper
pi'alla *sf* (*arnese*) plane; **pial'lare** *vt* to
plane
pi'ana *sf* stretch of level ground; (*più
estesa*) plain
pianeggi'ante [pjaned'dʒante] *ag* flat, level
piane'rottolo *sm* landing
pia'neta *sm* (ASTR) planet

pi'angere ['pjandʒere] *vi* to cry, weep;
(*occhi*) to water ♦ *vt* to cry, weep;
(*lamentare*) to bewail, lament; **~ la morte
di qn** to mourn sb's death
pianifi'care *vt* to plan; **pianificazi'one**
sf planning
pia'nista, i, e *sm/f* pianist
pi'ano, a *ag* (*piatto*) flat, level; (MAT) plane;
(*chiaro*) clear, plain ♦ *av* (*adagio*) slowly; (*a
bassa voce*) softly; (*con cautela*) slowly,
carefully ♦ *sm* (MAT) plane; (GEO) plain;
(*livello*) level, plane; (*di edificio*) floor;
(*programma*) plan; (MUS) piano; **pian ~** very
slowly; (*poco a poco*) little by little; **in
primo/secondo ~** in the foreground/
background; **di primo ~** (*fig*) prominent,
high-ranking
piano'forte *sm* piano, pianoforte
pi'anta *sf* (BOT) plant; (ANAT: *anche*: **~ del
piede**) sole (of the foot); (*grafico*) plan;
(*topografica*) map; **in ~ stabile** on the
permanent staff; **piantagi'one** *sf*
plantation; **pian'tare** *vt* to plant;
(*conficcare*) to drive *o* hammer in; (*tenda*)
to put up, pitch; (*fig: lasciare*) to leave,
desert; **~rsi** *vr*: **~rsi davanti a qn** to plant
o.s. in front of sb; **piantala!** (*fam*) cut it
out!
pianter'reno *sm* ground floor
pian'tina *sf* (*carta*) map
pi'anto, a *pp di* **piangere** ♦ *sm* tears *pl*,
crying
pian'tone *sm* (*vigilante*) sentry, guard;
(*soldato*) orderly; (AUT) steering column
pia'nura *sf* plain
pi'astra *sf* plate; (*di pietra*) slab; (*di fornello*)
hotplate; **~ di registrazione** tape deck;
panino alla ~ ≈ toasted sandwich
pias'trella *sf* tile
pias'trina *sf* (MIL) identity disc
piatta'forma *sf* (*anche fig*) platform
piat'tino *sm* saucer
pi'atto, a *ag* flat; (*fig: scialbo*) dull ♦ *sm*
(*recipiente, vivanda*) dish; (*portata*) course;
(*parte piana*) flat (part); **~i** *smpl* (MUS)
cymbals; **~ fondo** soup dish; **~ forte** main
course; **~ del giorno** dish of the day, plat

du jour; ~ **del giradischi** turntable

pi'azza ['pjattsa] *sf* square; (*COMM*) market; **far ~ pulita** to make a clean sweep; ~ **d'armi** (*MIL*) parade ground; **piaz'zale** *sm* (large) square

piaz'zare [pjat'tsare] *vt* to place; (*COMM*) to market, sell; **~rsi** *vr* (*SPORT*) to be placed

piaz'zista, i [pjat'tsista] *sm* (*COMM*) commercial traveller

piaz'zola [pjat'tsɔla] *sf* (*AUT*) lay-by

'picca, che *sf* pike; **~che** *sfpl* (*CARTE*) spades

pic'cante *ag* hot, pungent; (*fig*) racy; biting

pic'carsi *vr*: ~ **di fare** to pride o.s. on one's ability to do; ~ **per qc** to take offence at sth

pic'chetto [pik'ketto] *sm* (*MIL, di scioperanti*) picket; (*di tenda*) peg

picchi'are [pik'kjare] *vt* (*persona: colpire*) to hit, strike; (*: prendere a botte*) to beat (up); (*battere*) to beat; (*sbattere*) to bang ♦ *vi* (*bussare*) to knock; (*: con forza*) to bang; (*colpire*) to hit, strike; (*sole*) to beat down; **picchi'ata** *sf* (*AER*) dive

picchiet'tare [pikkjet'tare] *vt* (*punteggiare*) to spot, dot; (*colpire*) to tap

'picchio ['pikkjo] *sm* woodpecker

pic'cino, a [pit'tʃino] *ag* tiny, very small

piccio'naia [pittʃo'naja] *sf* pigeon-loft; (*TEATRO*): **la ~** the gods *sg*

picci'one [pit'tʃone] *sm* pigeon

'picco, chi *sm* peak; **a ~** vertically

'piccolo, a *ag* small; (*oggetto, mano, di età: bambino*) small, little (*dav sostantivo*); (*di breve durata: viaggio*) short; (*fig*) mean, petty ♦ *sm/f* child, little one; **~i** *smpl* (*di animale*) young *pl*; **in ~** in miniature

pic'cone *sm* pick(-axe)

pic'cozza [pik'kɔttsa] *sf* ice-axe

pic'nic *sm inv* picnic

pi'docchio [pi'dɔkkjo] *sm* louse

pi'ede *sm* foot; (*di mobile*) leg; **in ~i** standing; **a ~i** on foot; **a ~i nudi** barefoot; **su due ~i** (*fig*) at once; **prendere ~** (*fig*) to gain ground, catch on; **sul ~ di guerra** (*MIL*) ready for action; ~ **di porco** crowbar

piedes'tallo *sm* pedestal

piedipi'atti *sm inv* (*peg*) cop

pi'ega, ghe *sf* (*piegatura, GEO*) fold; (*di gonna*) pleat; (*di pantaloni*) crease; (*grinza*) wrinkle, crease; **prendere una brutta ~** (*fig*) to take a turn for the worse

pie'gare *vt* to fold; (*braccia, gambe, testa*) to bend ♦ *vi* to bend; **~rsi** *vr* to bend; (*fig*): **~rsi (a)** to yield (to), submit (to); **pieghet'tare** *vt* to pleat; **pie'ghevole** *ag* pliable, flexible; (*porta*) folding

Pie'monte *sm*: **il ~** Piedmont

pi'ena *sf* (*di fiume*) flood, spate

pi'eno, a *ag* full; (*muro, mattone*) solid ♦ *sm* (*colmo*) height, peak; (*carico*) full load; ~ **di** full of; **in ~ giorno** in broad daylight; **fare il ~ (di benzina)** to fill up (with petrol)

pietà *sf* pity; (*REL*) piety; **senza ~** pitiless, merciless; **avere ~ di** (*compassione*) to pity, feel sorry for; (*misericordia*) to have pity *o* mercy on

pie'tanza [pje'tantsa] *sf* dish, course

pie'toso, a *ag* (*compassionevole*) pitying, compassionate; (*che desta pietà*) pitiful

pi'etra *sf* stone; ~ **preziosa** precious stone, gem; **pie'traia** *sf* (*terreno*) stony ground; **pietrifi'care** *vt* to petrify; (*fig*) to transfix, paralyze

'piffero *sm* (*MUS*) pipe

pig'iama, i [pi'dʒama] *sm* pyjamas *pl*

'pigia 'pigia ['pidʒa'pidʒa] *sm* crowd, press

pigi'are [pi'dʒare] *vt* to press

pigi'one [pi'dʒone] *sf* rent

pigli'are [piʎ'ʎare] *vt* to take, grab; (*afferrare*) to catch

'piglio ['piʎʎo] *sm* look, expression

pig'meo, a *sm/f* pygmy

'pigna ['piɲɲa] *sf* pine cone

pi'gnolo, a [piɲ'ɲɔlo] *ag* pernickety

pigno'rare [piɲɲo'rare] *vt* to distrain

pigo'lare *vi* to cheep, chirp

pi'grizia [pi'grittsja] *sf* laziness

'pigro, a *ag* lazy

'pila *sf* (*catasta, di ponte*) pile; (*ELETTR*) battery; (*torcia*) torch (*BRIT*), flashlight

pi'lastro *sm* pillar

'pillola sf pill; prendere la ~ to be on the pill

pi'lone sm (di ponte) pier; (di linea elettrica) pylon

pi'lota, i, e sm/f pilot; (AUT) driver ♦ ag inv pilot cpd; ~ automatico automatic pilot; pilo'tare vt to pilot; to drive

pinaco'teca, che sf art gallery

pi'neta sf pinewood

ping-'pong [piŋ'pɔŋ] sm table tennis

'pingue ag fat, corpulent

pingu'ino sm (ZOOL) penguin

'pinna sf (di pesce) fin; (di cetaceo, per nuotare) flipper

'pino sm pine (tree); pi'nolo sm pine kernel

'pinza ['pintsa] sf pliers pl; (MED) forceps pl; (ZOOL) pincer

pinzette [pin'tsette] sfpl tweezers

'pio, a, 'pii, 'pie ag pious; (opere, istituzione) charitable, charity cpd

pi'oggia, ge ['pjɔddʒa] sf rain; ~ acida acid rain

pi'olo sm peg; (di scala) rung

piom'bare vi to fall heavily; (gettarsi con impeto): ~ su to fall upon, assail ♦ vt (dente) to fill; piomba'tura sf (di dente) filling

piom'bino sm (sigillo) (lead) seal; (del filo a piombo) plummet; (PESCA) sinker

pi'ombo sm (CHIM) lead; a ~ (cadere) straight down; senza ~ (benzina) unleaded

pioni'ere, a sm/f pioneer

pi'oppo sm poplar

pi'overe vb impers to rain ♦ vi (fig: scendere dall'alto) to rain down; (lettere, regali) to pour into; piovigginare vb impers to drizzle; pio'voso, a ag rainy

pi'ovra sf octopus

'pipa sf pipe

pipì (fam) sf: fare ~ to have a wee (wee)

pipis'trello sm (ZOOL) bat

pi'ramide sf pyramid

pi'rata, i sm pirate; ~ della strada hit-and-run driver

Pire'nei smpl: i ~ the Pyrenees

'pirico, a, ci, che ag: polvere ~a

gunpowder

pi'rite sf pyrite

pi'rofilo, a ag heat-resistant; pi'rofila sf heat-resistant dish

pi'roga, ghe sf dug-out canoe

pi'romane sm/f pyromaniac; arsonist

pi'roscafo sm steamer, steamship

pisci'are [piʃ'ʃare] (fam!) vi to piss (!), pee (!)

pi'scina [piʃ'ʃina] sf (swimming) pool; (stabilimento) (swimming) baths pl

pi'sello sm pea

piso'lino sm nap

'pista sf (traccia) track, trail; (di stadio) track; (di pattinaggio) rink; (da sci) run; (AER) runway; (di circo) ring; ~ da ballo dance floor

pis'tacchio [pis'takkjo] sm pistachio (tree); pistachio (nut)

pis'tola sf pistol, gun

pis'tone sm piston

pi'tone sm python

pit'tore, 'trice sm/f painter; pitto'resco, a, schi, sche ag picturesque

pit'tura sf painting; pittu'rare vt to paint

PAROLA CHIAVE

più av 1 (in maggiore quantità) more; ~ del solito more than usual; in ~, di ~ more; ne voglio di ~ I want some more; ci sono 3 persone in o di ~ there are 3 more o extra people; ~ o meno more or less; per di ~ (inoltre) what's more, moreover

2 (comparativo) more, aggettivo corto +...er; ~ ... di/che more ... than; lavoro ~ di te/Paola I work harder than you/Paola; è ~ intelligente che ricco he's more intelligent than rich

3 (superlativo) most, aggettivo corto +...est; il ~ grande/intelligente the biggest/most intelligent; è quello che compro ~ spesso that's the one I buy most often; al ~ presto as soon as possible; al ~ tardi at the latest

4 (negazione): non ... ~ no more, no longer; non ho ~ soldi I've got no more money, I don't have any more money; non

lavoro ~ I'm no longer working, I don't work any more; **a ~ non posso** (*gridare*) at the top of one's voice; (*correre*) as fast as one can

5 (*MAT*) plus; **4 ~ 5 fa 9** 4 plus 5 equals 9; **~ 5 gradi** 5 degrees above freezing, plus 5

♦ *prep* plus

♦ *ag inv* **1**: **~ ... (di)** more ... (than); **~ denaro/tempo** more money/time; **~ persone di quante ci aspettassimo** more people than we expected

2 (*numerosi, diversi*) several; **l'aspettai per ~ giorni** I waited for it for several days

♦ *sm* **1** (*la maggior parte*): **il ~ è fatto** most of it is done

2 (*MAT*) plus (sign)

3 i ~ the majority

piucchepper'fetto [pjukkepper'fetto] *sm* (*LING*) pluperfect, past perfect

pi'uma *sf* feather; **piu'maggio** *sm* plumage, feathers *pl*; **piu'mino** *sm* (eider)down; (*per letto*) eiderdown; (: *tipo danese*) duvet, continental quilt; (*giacca*) quilted jacket (*with goose-feather padding*); (*per cipria*) powder puff; (*per spolverare*) feather duster

piut'tosto *av* rather; **~ che** (*anziché*) rather than

pi'vollo, a *sm/f* greenhorn

'pizza ['pittsa] *sf* pizza; **pizze'ria** *sf* place where pizzas are made, sold or eaten

pizzi'cagnolo, a [pittsi'kaɲɲolo] *sm/f* specialist grocer

pizzi'care [pittsi'kare] *vt* (*stringere*) to nip, pinch; (*pungere*) to sting; to bite; (*MUS*) to pluck ♦ *vi* (*prudere*) to itch, be itchy; (*cibo*) to be hot *o* spicy

pizziche'ria [pittsike'ria] *sf* delicatessen (shop)

'pizzico, chi ['pittsiko] *sm* (*pizzicotto*) pinch, nip; (*piccola quantità*) pinch, dash; (*d'insetto*) sting; bite

pizzi'cotto [pittsi'kɔtto] *sm* pinch, nip

'pizzo ['pittso] *sm* (*merletto*) lace; (*barbetta*) goatee beard

pla'care *vt* to placate, soothe; **~rsi** *vr* to

calm down

'placca, che *sf* plate; (*con iscrizione*) plaque; (*anche*: **~ dentaria**) (dental) plaque; **plac'care** *vt* to plate; **placcato in oro/argento** gold-/silver-plated

'placido, a ['platʃido] *ag* placid, calm

plagi'are [pla'dʒare] *vt* (*copiare*) to plagiarize; **'plagio** *sm* plagiarism

pla'nare *vi* (*AER*) to glide

'plancia, ce ['plantʃa] *sf* (*NAUT*) bridge

plane'tario, a *ag* planetary ♦ *sm* (*locale*) planetarium

'plasma *sm* plasma

plas'mare *vt* to mould, shape

'plastica, che *sf* (*arte*) plastic arts *pl*; (*MED*) plastic surgery; (*sostanza*) plastic

'plastico, a, ci, che *ag* plastic ♦ *sm* (*rappresentazione*) relief model; (*esplosivo*): **bomba al ~** plastic bomb

plasti'lina ® *sf* plasticine ®

'platano *sm* plane tree

pla'tea *sf* (*TEATRO*) stalls *pl*

'platino *sm* platinum

pla'tonico, a, ci, che *ag* platonic

plau'sibile *ag* plausible

'plauso *sm* (*fig*) approval

ple'baglia [ple'baʎʎa] (*peg*) *sf* rabble, mob

'plebe *sf* common people; **ple'beo, a** *ag* plebeian; (*volgare*) coarse, common

ple'nario, a *ag* plenary

pleni'lunio *sm* full moon

'plettro *sm* plectrum

pleu'rite *sf* pleurisy

'plico, chi *sm* (*pacco*) parcel; **in ~ a parte** (*COMM*) under separate cover

plo'tone *sm* (*MIL*) platoon; **~ d'esecuzione** firing squad

'plumbeo, a *ag* leaden

plu'rale *ag, sm* plural; **pluralità** *sf* plurality; (*maggioranza*) majority

plusva'lore *sm* (*ECON*) surplus

pneu'matico, a, ci, che *ag* inflatable; pneumatic ♦ *sm* (*AUT*) tyre (*BRIT*), tire (*US*)

po' *av, sm vedi* **poco**

PAROLA CHIAVE

'poco, a, chi, che *ag* (*quantità*) little, not

much; (*numero*) few, not many; **~ pane/ denaro/spazio** little *o* not much bread/ money/space; **~che persone/idee** few *o* not many people/ideas; **ci vediamo tra ~** (*sottinteso: tempo*) see you soon
♦ *av* **1** (*in piccola quantità*) little, not much; (*numero limitato*) few, not many; **guadagna ~** he doesn't earn much, he earns little
2 (*con ag, av*) (a) little, not very; **sta ~ bene** he isn't very well; **è ~ più vecchia di lui** she's a little *o* slightly older than him
3 (*tempo*): **~ dopo/prima** shortly afterwards/before; **il film dura ~** the film doesn't last very long; **ci vediamo molto ~** we don't see each other very often, we hardly ever see each other
4: un po' a little, a bit; **è un po' corto** it's a little *o* a bit short; **arriverà fra un po'** he'll arrive shortly *o* in a little while
5: a dir ~ to say the least; **a ~ a ~** little by little; **per ~ non cadevo** I nearly fell; **è una cosa da ~** it's nothing, it's of no importance; **una persona da ~** a worthless person
♦ *pron* (a) little; **~chi, che** *pron pl* (*persone*) few (people); (*cose*) few
♦ *sm* **1** little; **vive del ~ che ha** he lives on the little he has
2: un po' a little; **un po' di zucchero** a little sugar; **un bel po' di denaro** quite a lot of money; **un po' per ciascuno** a bit each

po'**dere** *sm* (*AGR*) farm
pode'**roso, a** *ag* powerful
podes'**tà** *sm inv* (*nel fascismo*) podesta, mayor
'**podio** *sm* dais, platform; (*MUS*) podium
po'**dismo** *sm* (*SPORT*) track events *pl*
po'**ema, i** *sm* poem
poe'**sia** *sf* (*arte*) poetry; (*componimento*) poem
po'**eta, 'essa** *sm/f* poet/poetess; po'**etico, a, ci, che** *ag* poetic(al)
poggi'**are** [pod'dʒare] *vt* to lean, rest; (*posare*) to lay, place; **poggia'testa** *sm*

inv (*AUT*) headrest
'**poggio** ['pɔddʒo] *sm* hillock, knoll
poggi'**olo** [pod'dʒɔlo] *sm* balcony
'**poi** *av* then; (*alla fine*) finally, at last; **e ~** (*inoltre*) and besides; **questa ~ (è bella)!** (*ironico*) that's a good one!
poi'**ché** [poi'ke] *cong* since, as
'**poker** *sm* poker
po'**lacco, a, chi, che** *ag* Polish ♦ *sm/f* Pole
po'**lare** *ag* polar
po'**lemica, che** *sf* controversy
po'**lemico, a, ci, che** *ag* polemic(al), controversial
po'**lenta** *sf* (*CUC*) sort of thick porridge *made with maize flour*
poliambula'**torio** *sm* health centre
poli'**clinico, ci** *sm* general hospital, polyclinic
poli'**estere** *sm* polyester
'**polio(mie'lite)** *sf* polio(myelitis)
'**polipo** *sm* polyp
polisti'**rolo** *sm* polystyrene
poli'**tecnico, ci** *sm* postgraduate technical college
po'**litica, che** *sf* politics *sg*; (*linea di condotta*) policy; *vedi anche* **politico**
politiciz'**zare** [polititʃid'dzare] *vt* to politicize
po'**litico, a, ci, che** *ag* political ♦ *sm/f* politician
poli'**zia** [polit'tsia] *sf* police; **~ giudiziaria** ≈ Criminal Investigation Department (*BRIT*), ≈ Federal Bureau of Investigation (*US*); **~ stradale** traffic police; **polizi'esco, a, schi, sche** *ag* police *cpd*; (*film, romanzo*) detective *cpd*; **polizi'otto** *sm* policeman; **cane poliziotto** police dog; **donna poliziotto** policewoman

---

polizia di stato

i The function of the **polizia di stato** is to maintain public order, to uphold the law and prevent and investigate crime. They are a civil body, reporting to the Minister of the Interior.

'polizza ['pɔlittsa] sf (COMM) bill; ~ di assicurazione insurance policy; ~ di carico bill of lading

pol'laio sm henhouse

pol'lame sm poultry

pol'lastro sm (ZOOL) cockerel

'pollice ['pɔllitʃe] sm thumb

'polline sm pollen

'pollo sm chicken

pol'mone sm lung; ~ d'acciaio (MED) iron lung; polmo'nite sf pneumonia

'polo sm (GEO, FISICA) pole; (gioco) polo; il ~ sud/nord the South/North Pole

Po'lonia sf: la ~ Poland

'polpa sf flesh, pulp; (carne) lean meat

pol'paccio [pol'pattʃo] sm (ANAT) calf

polpas'trello sm fingertip

pol'petta sf (CUC) meatball; polpet'tone sm (CUC) meatloaf

'polpo sm octopus

pol'poso, a ag fleshy

pol'sino sm cuff

'polso sm (ANAT) wrist; (pulsazione) pulse; (fig: forza) drive, vigour

pol'tiglia [pol'tiʎʎa] sf (composto) mash, mush; (di fango e neve) slush

pol'trire vi to laze about

pol'trona sf armchair; (TEATRO: posto) seat in the front stalls (BRIT) o orchestra (US)

pol'trone ag lazy, slothful

'polvere sf dust; (anche: ~ da sparo) (gun)powder; (sostanza ridotta minutissima) powder, dust; latte in ~ dried o powdered milk; caffè in ~ instant coffee; sapone in ~ soap powder; polveri'era sf (MIL) (gun)-powder magazine; polveriz'zare vt to pulverize; (nebulizzare) to atomize; (fig) to crush, pulverize; to smash; polve'rone sm thick cloud of dust; polve'roso, a ag dusty

po'mata sf ointment, cream

po'mello sm knob

pomeridi'ano, a ag afternoon cpd; nelle ore ~e in the afternoon

pome'riggio [pome'riddʒo] sm afternoon

'pomice ['pɔmitʃe] sf pumice

'pomo sm (mela) apple; (ornamentale) knob; (di sella) pommel; ~ d'Adamo (ANAT) Adam's apple

pomo'doro sm tomato

'pompa sf pump; (sfarzo) pomp (and ceremony); ~e funebri funeral parlour sg (BRIT), undertaker's sg; pom'pare vt to pump; (trarre) to pump out; (gonfiare d'aria) to pump up

pom'pelmo sm grapefruit

pompi'ere sm fireman

pom'poso, a ag pompous

ponde'rare vt to ponder over, consider carefully

ponde'roso, a ag (anche fig) weighty

po'nente sm west

'ponte sm bridge; (di nave) deck; (: anche: ~ di comando) bridge; (impalcatura) scaffold; fare il ~ (fig) to take the extra day off (between 2 public holidays); governo ~ interim government; ~ aereo airlift; ~ sospeso suspension bridge

pon'tefice [pon'tefitʃe] sm (REL) pontiff

pontifi'care vi (anche fig) to pontificate

ponti'ficio, a, ci, cie [ponti'fitʃo] ag papal

popo'lano, a ag popular, of the people

popo'lare ag popular; (quartiere, clientela) working-class ♦ vt (rendere abitato) to populate; ~rsi vr to fill with people, get crowded; popolarità sf popularity; popolazione sf population

'popolo sm people; popo'loso, a ag densely populated

'poppa sf (di nave) stern; (seno) breast

pop'pare vt to suck

poppa'toio sm (feeding) bottle

porcel'lana [portʃel'lana] sf porcelain, china; piece of china

porcel'lino, a [portʃel'lino] sm/f piglet

porche'ria [porke'ria] sf filth, muck; (fig: oscenità) obscenity; (: azione disonesta) dirty trick; (: cosa mal fatta) rubbish

por'cile [por'tʃile] sm pigsty

por'cino, a [por'tʃino] ag of pigs, pork cpd ♦ sm (fungo) type of edible mushroom

'porco, ci sm pig; (carne) pork

porcos'pino sm porcupine

'porgere ['pɔrdʒere] *vt* to hand, give; (*tendere*) to hold out

pornogra'fia *sf* pornography; **porno'grafico, a, ci, che** *ag* pornographic

'poro *sm* pore; **po'roso, a** *ag* porous

'porpora *sf* purple

'porre *vt* (*mettere*) to put; (*collocare*) to place; (*posare*) to lay (down), put (down); (*fig: supporre*): **poniamo (il caso) che ...** let's suppose that ...; **porsi** *vr* (*mettersi*): **porsi a sedere/in cammino** to sit down/set off; **~ una domanda a qn** to ask sb a question, put a question to sb

'porro *sm* (*BOT*) leek; (*MED*) wart

'porta *sf* door; (*SPORT*) goal; **~e** *sfpl* (*di città*) gates; **a ~e chiuse** (*DIR*) in camera

'porta... *prefisso*: **portaba'gagli** *sm inv* (*facchino*) porter; (*AUT, FERR*) luggage rack; **porta'cenere** *sm inv* ashtray; **portachi'avi** *sm inv* keyring; **porta'cipria** *sm inv* powder compact; **porta'erei** *sf inv* (*nave*) aircraft carrier; **portafi'nestra** (*pl* **portefi'nestre**) *sf* French window; **porta'foglio** *sm* wallet; (*POL, BORSA*) portfolio; **portafor'tuna** *sm inv* lucky charm; mascot; **portagi'oie** *sm inv* jewellery box

porta'lettere *sm/f inv* postman/woman (*BRIT*), mailman/woman (*US*)

porta'mento *sm* carriage, bearing

portamo'nete *sm inv* purse

por'tante *ag* (*muro etc*) supporting, load-bearing

portan'tina *sf* sedan chair; (*per ammalati*) stretcher

por'tare *vt* (*sostenere, sorreggere: peso, bambino, pacco*) to carry; (*indossare: abito, occhiali*) to wear; (: *capelli lunghi*) to have; (*avere: nome, titolo*) to have, bear; (*recare*): **~ qc a qn** to take (*o* bring) sth to sb; (*fig: sentimenti*) to bear; **~rsi** *vr* (*recarsi*) to go; **~ avanti** (*discorso, idea*) to pursue; **~ via** to take away; (*rubare*) to take; **~ i bambini a spasso** to take the children for a walk; **~ fortuna** to bring good luck

portasiga'rette *sm inv* cigarette case

por'tata *sf* (*vivanda*) course; (*AUT*) carrying (*o* loading) capacity; (*di arma*) range; (*volume d'acqua*) rate of flow; (*fig: limite*) scope, capability; (: *importanza*) impact, import; **alla ~ di tutti** (*conoscenza*) within everybody's capabilities; (*prezzo*) within everybody's means; **a/fuori ~ (di)** within/out of reach (of); **a ~ di mano** within (arm's) reach

por'tatile *ag* portable

por'tato, a *ag* (*incline*): **~ a** inclined *o* apt to

porta'tore, 'trice *sm/f* (*anche COMM*) bearer; (*MED*) carrier

portau'ovo *sm inv* eggcup

porta'voce ['porta'votʃe] *sm/f inv* spokesman/woman

por'tento *sm* wonder, marvel

porticci'olo [portit'tʃɔlo] *sm* marina

'portico, ci *sm* portico

porti'era *sf* (*AUT*) door

porti'ere *sm* (*portinaio*) concierge, caretaker; (*di hotel*) porter; (*nel calcio*) goalkeeper

porti'naio, a *sm/f* concierge, caretaker

portine'ria *sf* caretaker's lodge

'porto, a *pp di* **porgere** ♦ *sm* (*NAUT*) harbour, port ♦ *sm inv* port (wine); **~ d'armi** (*documento*) gun licence

Porto'gallo *sm*: **il ~** Portugal; **porto'ghese** *ag, sm/f, sm* Portuguese *inv*

por'tone *sm* main entrance, main door

portu'ale *ag* harbour *cpd*, port *cpd* ♦ *sm* dock worker

porzi'one [por'tsjone] *sf* portion, share; (*di cibo*) portion, helping

'posa *sf* (*FOT*) exposure; (*atteggiamento, di modello*) pose

posa'cenere [posa'tʃenere] *sm inv* ashtray

po'sare *vt* to put (down), lay (down) ♦ *vi* (*ponte, edificio, teoria*): **~ su** to rest on; (*FOT, atteggiarsi*) to pose; **~rsi** *vr* (*aereo*) to land; (*uccello*) to alight; (*sguardo*) to settle

po'sata *sf* piece of cutlery; **~e** *sfpl* (*servizio*) cutlery *sg*

po'sato, a *ag* serious

pos'critto *sm* postscript

posi'tivo, a *ag* positive
posizi'one [pozit'tsjone] *sf* position; **prendere ~** (*fig*) to take a stand; **luci di ~** (*AUT*) sidelights
posolo'gia, 'gie [pozolo'dʒia] *sf* dosage, directions *pl* for use
pos'porre *vt* to place after; (*differire*) to postpone, defer; **pos'posto, a** *pp di* **posporre**
posse'dere *vt* to own, possess; (*qualità, virtù*) to have, possess; **possedi'mento** *sm* possession
posses'sivo, a *ag* possessive
pos'sesso *sm* ownership *no pl*; possession
posses'sore *sm* owner
pos'sibile *ag* possible ♦ *sm*: **fare tutto il ~** to do everything possible; **nei limiti del ~** as far as possible; **al più tardi ~** as late as possible; **possibilità** *sf inv* possibility ♦ *sfpl* (*mezzi*) means; **aver la possibilità di fare** to be in a position to do; to have the opportunity to do
possi'dente *sm/f* landowner
'posta *sf* (*servizio*) post, postal service; (*corrispondenza*) post, mail; (*ufficio postale*) post office; (*nei giochi d'azzardo*) stake; **~e** *sfpl* (*amministrazione*) post office; **~ aerea** airmail; **~ elettronica** E-mail, e-mail, electronic mail; **ministro delle P~e e Telecomunicazioni** Postmaster General; **posta'giro** *sm* post office cheque, postal giro (*BRIT*); **pos'tale** *ag* postal, post office *cpd*
post'bellico, a, ci, che *ag* postwar
posteggi'are [posted'dʒare] *vt, vi* to park; **posteggia'tore, trice** *sm/f* car park attendant; **pos'teggio** *sm* car park (*BRIT*), parking lot (*US*); (*di taxi*) rank (*BRIT*), stand (*US*)
postelegra'fonico, a, ci, che *ag* postal and telecommunications *cpd*
'poster *sm inv* poster
posteri'ore *ag* (*dietro*) back; (*dopo*) later ♦ *sm* (*fam: sedere*) behind
pos'ticcio, a, ci, ce [pos'tittʃo] *ag* false ♦ *sm* hairpiece
postici'pare [postitʃi'pare] *vt* to defer, postpone
pos'tilla *sf* marginal note
pos'tino *sm* postman (*BRIT*), mailman (*US*)
'posto, a *pp di* **porre** ♦ *sm* (*sito, posizione*) place; (*impiego*) job; (*spazio libero*) room, space; (*di parcheggio*) space; (*sedile: al teatro, in treno etc*) seat; (*MIL*) post; **a ~** (*in ordine*) in place, tidy; (*fig*) settled; (*: persona*) reliable; **al ~ di** in place of; **sul ~** on the spot; **mettere a ~** to tidy (up), put in order; (*faccende*) to straighten out; **~ di blocco** roadblock; **~ di polizia** police station
pos'tribolo *sm* brothel
'postumo, a *ag* posthumous; (*tardivo*) belated; **~i** *smpl* (*conseguenze*) after-effects, consequences
po'tabile *ag* drinkable; **acqua ~** drinking water
po'tare *vt* to prune
po'tassio *sm* potassium
po'tente *ag* (*nazione*) strong, powerful; (*veleno, farmaco*) potent, strong; **po'tenza** *sf* power; (*forza*) strength
potenzi'ale [poten'tsjale] *ag, sm* potential

| PAROLA CHIAVE |

po'tere *sm* power; **al ~** (*partito etc*) in power; **~ d'acquisto** purchasing power ♦ *vb aus* **1** (*essere in grado di*) can, be able to; **non ha potuto ripararlo** he couldn't o he wasn't able to repair it; **non è potuto venire** he couldn't o he wasn't able to come; **spiacente di non poter aiutare** sorry not to be able to help
2 (*avere il permesso*) can, may, be allowed to; **posso entrare?** can o may I come in?; **si può sapere dove sei stato?** where on earth have you been?
3 (*eventualità*) may, might, could; **potrebbe essere vero** it might o could be true; **può aver avuto un incidente** he may o might o could have had an accident; **può darsi** perhaps; **può darsi** o **essere che non venga** he may o might not come
4 (*augurio*): **potessi almeno parlargli!** if only I could speak to him!

5 (*suggerimento*): **potresti almeno scusarti!** you could at least apologize! ♦ *vt* can, be able to; **può molto per noi** he can do a lot for us; **non ne posso più** (*per stanchezza*) I'm exhausted; (*per rabbia*) I can't take any more

potestà *sf* (*potere*) power; (*DIR*) authority

'povero, a *ag* poor; (*disadorno*) plain, bare ♦ *sm/f* poor man/woman; **i ~i** the poor; **~ di** lacking in, having little; **povertà** *sf* poverty

'pozza ['pottsa] *sf* pool

poz'zanghera [pot'tsangera] *sf* puddle

'pozzo ['pottso] *sm* well; (*cava: di carbone*) pit; (*di miniera*) shaft; **~ petrolifero** oil well

pran'zare [pran'dzare] *vi* to dine, have dinner; to lunch, have lunch

'pranzo ['prandzo] *sm* dinner; (*a mezzogiorno*) lunch

'prassi *sf* usual procedure

'pratica, che *sf* practice; (*esperienza*) experience; (*conoscenza*) knowledge, familiarity; (*tirocinio*) training, practice; (*AMM: affare*) matter, case; (: *incartamento*) file, dossier; **in ~** (*praticamente*) in practice; **mettere in ~** to put into practice

prati'cabile *ag* (*progetto*) practicable, feasible; (*luogo*) passable, practicable

prati'cante *sm/f* apprentice, trainee; (*REL*) (regular) churchgoer

prati'care *vt* to practise; (*SPORT: tennis etc*) to play; (: *nuoto, scherma etc*) to go in for; (*eseguire: apertura, buco*) to make; **~ uno sconto** to give a discount

'pratico, a, ci, che *ag* practical; **~ di** (*esperto*) experienced *o* skilled in; (*familiare*) familiar with

'prato *sm* meadow; (*di giardino*) lawn

preav'viso *sm* notice; **telefonata con ~** personal *o* person to person call

pre'cario, a *ag* precarious; (*INS*) temporary

precauzi'one [prekaut'tsjone] *sf* caution, care; (*misura*) precaution

prece'dente [pretʃe'dɛnte] *ag* previous ♦ *sm* precedent; **il discorso/film ~** the previous *o* preceding speech/film; **senza ~i**

unprecedented; **~i penali** criminal record *sg*; **prece'denza** *sf* priority, precedence; (*AUT*) right of way

pre'cedere [pre'tʃedere] *vt* to precede, go (*o come*) before

pre'cetto [pre'tʃetto] *sm* precept; (*MIL*) call-up notice

precet'tore [pretʃet'tore] *sm* (*private*) tutor

precipi'tare [pretʃipi'tare] *vi* (*cadere*) to fall headlong; (*fig: situazione*) to get out of control ♦ *vt* (*gettare dall'alto in basso*) to hurl, fling; (*fig: affrettare*) to rush; **~rsi** *vr* (*gettarsi*) to hurl *o* fling o.s.; (*affrettarsi*) to rush; **precipitazi'one** *sf* (*METEOR*) precipitation; (*fig*) haste; **precipi'toso, a** *ag* (*caduta, fuga*) headlong; (*fig: avventato*) rash, reckless; (: *affrettato*) hasty, rushed

preci'pizio [pretʃi'pittsjo] *sm* precipice; **a ~** (*fig: correre*) headlong

preci'sare [pretʃi'zare] *vt* to state, specify; (*spiegare*) to explain (in detail)

precisi'one [pretʃi'zjone] *sf* precision; accuracy

pre'ciso, a [pre'tʃizo] *ag* (*esatto*) precise; (*accurato*) accurate, precise; (*deciso: idee*) precise, definite; (*uguale*): **2 vestiti ~i** 2 dresses exactly the same; **sono le 9 ~e** it's exactly 9 o'clock

pre'cludere *vt* to block, obstruct; **pre'cluso, a** *pp di* **precludere**

pre'coce [pre'kɔtʃe] *ag* early; (*bambino*) precocious; (*vecchiaia*) premature

precon'cetto [prekon'tʃetto] *sm* preconceived idea, prejudice

precur'sore *sm* forerunner, precursor

'preda *sf* (*bottino*) booty; (*animale, fig*) prey; **essere ~ di** to fall prey to; **essere in ~ a** to be prey to; **preda'tore** *sm* predator

predeces'sore, a [predetʃes'sore] *sm/f* predecessor

predesti'nare *vt* to predestine

pre'detto, a *pp di* **predire**

'predica, che *sf* sermon; (*fig*) lecture, talking-to

predi'care *vt, vi* to preach

predi'cato *sm* (*LING*) predicate

predi'letto, a *pp di* **prediligere** ♦ *ag, sm/f* favourite

predilezi'one [predilet'tsjone] *sf* fondness, partiality; **avere una ~ per qc/qn** to be partial to sth/fond of sb

predi'ligere [predi'lidʒere] *vt* to prefer, have a preference for

pre'dire *vt* to foretell, predict

predis'porre *vt* to get ready, prepare; **~ qn a qc** to predispose sb to sth; **predis'posto, a** *pp di* **predisporre**

predizi'one [predit'tsjone] *sf* prediction

predomi'nare *vi* to predominate; **predo'minio** *sm* predominance; supremacy

prefabbri'cato, a *ag* (*EDIL*) prefabricated

prefazi'one [prefat'tsjone] *sf* preface, foreword

prefe'renza [prefe'rɛntsa] *sf* preference; **preferenzi'ale** *ag* preferential; **corsia ~** bus and taxi lane

prefe'rire *vt* to prefer, like better; **~ il caffè al tè** to prefer coffee to tea, like coffee better than tea; **prefe'rito, a** *ag* favourite

pre'fetto *sm* prefect; **prefet'tura** *sf* prefecture

pre'figgersi [pre'fiddʒersi] *vr*: **~ uno scopo** to set o.s. a goal

pre'fisso, a *pp di* **prefiggere** ♦ *sm* (*LING*) prefix; (*TEL*) dialling (*BRIT*) o dial (*US*) code

pre'gare *vi* to pray ♦ *vt* (*REL*) to pray to; (*implorare*) to beg; (*chiedere*): **~ qn di fare** to ask sb to do; **farsi ~** to need coaxing o persuading

pre'gevole [pre'dʒevole] *ag* valuable

preghi'era [pre'gjera] *sf* (*REL*) prayer; (*domanda*) request

pregi'ato, a [pre'dʒato] *ag* (*di valore*) valuable; **vino ~** vintage wine

'pregio ['predʒo] *sm* (*stima*) esteem, regard; (*qualità*) (good) quality, merit; (*valore*) value, worth

pregiudi'care [predʒudi'kare] *vt* to prejudice, harm, be detrimental to; **pregiudi'cato, a** *sm/f* (*DIR*) previous offender

pregiu'dizio [predʒu'dittsjo] *sm* (*idea errata*) prejudice; (*danno*) harm *no pl*

'pregno, a ['preɲɲo] *ag* (*saturo*): **~ di** full of, saturated with

'prego *escl* (*a chi ringrazia*) don't mention it!; (*invitando qn ad accomodarsi*) please sit down!; (*invitando qn ad andare prima*) after you!

pregus'tare *vt* to look forward to

preis'torico, a, ci, che *ag* prehistoric

pre'lato *sm* prelate

prele'vare *vt* (*denaro*) to withdraw; (*campione*) to take; (*sog: polizia*) to take, capture

preli'evo *sm* (*di denaro*) withdrawal; (*MED*): **fare un ~ (di)** to take a sample (of)

prelimi'nare *ag* preliminary; **~i** *smpl* preliminary talks; preliminaries

pre'ludio *sm* prelude

pré-ma'man [prema'ma] *sm inv* maternity dress

prema'turo, a *ag* premature

premeditazi'one [premeditat'tsjone] *sf* (*DIR*) premeditation; **con ~** *ag* premeditated ♦ *av* with intent

premere *vt* to press ♦ *vi*: **~ su** to press down on; (*fig*) to put pressure on; **~ a** (*fig: importare*) to matter to

pre'messa *sf* introductory statement, introduction

pro'messo, a *pp di* **premettere**

pre'mettere *vt* to put before; (*dire prima*) to start by saying, state first

premi'are *vt* to give a prize to; (*fig: merito, onestà*) to reward

'premio *sm* prize; (*ricompensa*) reward; (*COMM*) premium; (*AMM: indennità*) bonus

premu'nirsi *vr*: **~ di** to provide o.s. with; **~ contro** to protect o.s. from, guard o.s. against

pre'mura *sf* (*fretta*) haste, hurry; (*riguardo*) attention, care; **premu'roso, a** *ag* thoughtful, considerate

prena'tale *ag* antenatal

'prendere *vt* to take; (*andare a prendere*) to get, fetch; (*ottenere*) to get; (*guadagnare*) to get, earn; (*catturare: ladro,* *pesce*) to catch; (*collaboratore, dipendente*) to take on; (*passeggero*) to pick up; (*chiedere: somma, prezzo*) to charge, ask; (*trattare: persona*) to handle ♦ *vi* (*colla, cemento*) to set; (*pianta*) to take; (*fuoco: nel camino*) to catch; (*voltare*): ~ **a destra** to turn (to the) right; **~rsi** *vr* (*azzuffarsi*): **~rsi a pugni** to come to blows; **prendi qualcosa?** (*da bere, da mangiare*) would you like something to eat (*o* drink)?; **prendo un caffè** I'll have a coffee; **~ qn/ qc per** (*scambiare*) to take sb/sth for; **~ fuoco** to catch fire; **~ parte a** to take part in; **~rsi cura di qn/qc** to look after sb/sth; **prendersela** (*adirarsi*) to get annoyed; (*preoccuparsi*) to get upset, worry

prendi'sole *sm inv* sundress

preno'tare *vt* to book, reserve; **prenotazi'one** *sf* booking, reservation

preoccu'pare *vt* to worry; to preoccupy; **~rsi** *vr*: **~rsi di qn/qc** to worry about sb/ sth; **~rsi per qn** to be anxious for sb; **preoccupazi'one** *sf* worry, anxiety

prepa'rare *vt* to prepare; (*esame, concorso*) to prepare for; **~rsi** *vr* (*vestirsi*) to get ready; **~rsi a qc/a fare** to get ready *o* prepare (o.s.) for sth/to do; **~ da mangiare** to prepare a meal; **prepara'tivi** *smpl* preparations; **prepa'rato** *sm* (*prodotto*) preparation; **preparazi'one** *sf* preparation

preposizi'one [prepozit'tsjone] *sf* (*LING*) preposition

prepo'tente *ag* (*persona*) domineering, arrogant; (*bisogno, desiderio*) overwhelming, pressing ♦ *sm/f* bully; **prepo'tenza** *sf* arrogance; arrogant behaviour

'presa *sf* taking *no pl*; catching *no pl*; (*di città*) capture; (*indurimento: di cemento*) setting; (*appiglio, SPORT*) hold; (*di acqua, gas*) (supply) point; (*ELETTR*): **~ di corrente** socket; (: *al muro*) point; (*piccola quantità: di sale etc*) pinch; (*CARTE*) trick; **far ~** (*colla*) to set; **far ~ sul pubblico** to catch the public's imagination; **~ d'aria** air inlet; **essere alle ~e con** (*fig*) to be struggling

with

pre'sagio [pre'zadʒo] *sm* omen

presa'gire [preza'dʒire] *vt* to foresee

'presbite *ag* long-sighted

presbi'terio *sm* presbytery

pre'scindere [preʃ'ʃindere] *vi*: **~ da** to leave out of consideration; **a ~ da** apart from

pres'critto, a *pp di* **prescrivere**

pres'crivere *vt* to prescribe; **prescrizi'one** *sf* (*MED, DIR*) prescription; (*norma*) rule, regulation

presen'tare *vt* to present; (*far conoscere*): **~ qn (a)** to introduce sb (to); (*AMM: inoltrare*) to submit; **~rsi** *vr* (*recarsi, farsi vedere*) to present o.s., appear; (*farsi conoscere*) to introduce o.s.; (*occasione*) to arise; **~rsi come candidato** (*POL*) to stand as a candidate; **~rsi bene/male** to have a good/poor appearance; **presentazi'one** *sf* presentation; introduction

pre'sente *ag* present; (*questo*) this ♦ *sm* present; **i ~i** those present; **aver ~ qc/qn** to remember sth/sb

presenti'mento *sm* premonition

pre'senza [pre'zɛntsa] *sf* presence; (*aspetto esteriore*) appearance; **~ di spirito** presence of mind

pre'sepe, pre'sepio *sm* crib

preser'vare *vt* to protect; to save; **preserva'tivo** *sm* sheath, condom

'preside *sm/f* (*INS*) head (teacher) (*BRIT*), principal (*US*); (*di facoltà universitaria*) dean

presi'dente *sm* (*POL*) president; (*di assemblea, COMM*) chairman; **~ del consiglio** prime minister; **presiden'tessa** *sf* president; president's wife; chairwoman; **presi'denza** *sf* presidency; office of president; chairmanship

presidi'are *vt* to garrison; **pre'sidio** *sm* garrison

presi'edere *vt* to preside over ♦ *vi*: **~ a** to direct, be in charge of

'preso, a *pp di* **prendere**

'pressa *sf* (*TECN*) press

pressap'poco *av* about, roughly

pres'sare *vt* to press

pressi'one *sf* pressure; **far ~ su qn** to put pressure on sb; **~ sanguigna** blood pressure

'presso *av (vicino)* nearby, close at hand ♦ *prep (vicino a)* near; *(accanto a)* beside, next to; *(in casa di)*: **~ qn** at sb's home; *(nelle lettere)* care of, c/o; *(alle dipendenze di)*: **lavora ~ di noi** he works for *o* with us ♦ *smpl*: **nei ~i di** near, in the vicinity of

pressuriz'zare [pressurid'dzare] *vt* to pressurize

presta'nome *(peg) sm/f inv* figurehead

pres'tante *ag* good-looking

pres'tare *vt*: **~ (qc a qn)** to lend (sb sth *o* sth to sb); **~rsi** *vr (offrirsi)*: **~rsi a fare** to offer to do; *(essere adatto)*: **~rsi a** to lend itself to, be suitable for; **~ aiuto** to lend a hand; **~ attenzione** to pay attention; **~ fede a qc/qn** to give credence to sth/sb; **~ orecchio** to listen; **prestazi'one** *sf (TECN, SPORT)* performance; **prestazioni** *sfpl (di persona: servizi)* services

prestigia'tore, 'trice [prestidʒa'tore] *sm/f* conjurer

pres'tigio [pres'tidʒo] *sm (fama)* prestige; *(illusione)*: **gioco di ~** conjuring trick

'prestito *sm* lending *no pl*; loan; **dar in ~** to lend; **prendere in ~** to borrow

'presto *av (tra poco)* soon; *(in fretta)* quickly; *(di buon'ora)* early; **a ~** see you soon; **fare ~ a fare qc** to hurry up and do sth; *(non costare fatica)* to have no trouble doing sth; **si fa ~ a criticare** it's easy to criticize

pre'sumere *vt* to presume, assume; **pre'sunto, a** *pp di* **presumere**

presuntu'oso, a *ag* presumptuous

presunzi'one [prezun'tsjone] *sf* presumption

presup'porre *vt* to suppose; to presuppose

'prete *sm* priest

preten'dente *sm/f* pretender ♦ *sm (corteggiatore)* suitor

pre'tendere *vt (esigere)* to demand,

require; *(sostenere)*: **~ che** to claim that; **pretende di aver sempre ragione** he thinks he's always right

pretenzi'oso, a [preten'tsjoso] *ag* pretentious

pre'tesa *sf (esigenza)* claim, demand; *(presunzione, sfarzo)* pretentiousness; **senza ~e** unpretentious

pre'teso, a *pp di* **pretendere**

pre'testo *sm* pretext, excuse

pre'tore *sm* magistrate; **pre'tura** *sf* magistracy; *(sede)* magistrate's court

preva'lente *ag* prevailing; **preva'lenza** *sf* predominance

preva'lere *vi* to prevail; **pre'valso, a** *pp di* **prevalere**

preve'dere *vt (indovinare)* to foresee; *(presagire)* to foretell; *(considerare)* to make provision for

pre'vendita *sf* advance booking

preve'nire *vt (anticipare)* to forestall; to anticipate; *(evitare)* to avoid, prevent

preven'tivo, a *ag* preventive ♦ *sm (COMM)* estimate

prevenzi'one [preven'tsjone] *sf* prevention; *(preconcetto)* prejudice

previ'dente *ag* showing foresight; prudent; **previ'denza** *sf* foresight; **istituto di previdenza** provident institution; **previdenza sociale** social security *(BRIT)*, welfare *(US)*

previsi'one *sf* forecast, prediction; **i meteorologiche** *o* **del tempo** weather forecast *sg*

pre'visto, a *pp di* **prevedere** ♦ *sm*: **più/meno del ~** more/less than expected

prezi'oso, a [pret'tsjoso] *ag* precious; invaluable ♦ *sm* jewel; valuable

prez'zemolo [pret'tsemolo] *sm* parsley

'prezzo ['prettso] *sm* price; **~ d'acquisto/di vendita** buying/selling price

prigi'one [pri'dʒone] *sf* prison; **prigio'nia** *sf* imprisonment; **prigioni'ero, a** *ag* captive ♦ *sm/f* prisoner

'prima *sf (TEATRO)* first night; *(CINEMA)* première; *(AUT)* first gear; *vedi anche* **primo** ♦ *av* before; *(in anticipo)* in advance, beforehand; (*per l'addietro*) at one time, formerly; (*più presto*) sooner, earlier; (*in primo luogo*) first ♦ *cong:* ~ **di fare/che parta** before doing/he leaves; ~ **di** before; ~ **o poi** sooner or later

pri'mario, a *ag* primary; (*principale*) chief, leading, primary ♦ *sm* (MED) chief physician

pri'mato *sm* supremacy; (SPORT) record

prima'vera *sf* spring; **primave'rile** *ag* spring *cpd*

primeggi'are [primed'dʒare] *vi* to excel, be one of the best

primi'tivo, a *ag* primitive; original

pri'mizie [pri'mittsje] *sfpl* early produce *sg*

'primo, a *ag* first; (*fig*) initial; basic; prime ♦ *sm/f* first (one) ♦ *sm* (CUC) first course; (*in date*): **il ~ luglio** the first of July; **le ~e ore del mattino** the early hours of the morning; **ai ~i di maggio** at the beginning of May; **viaggiare in ~a** to travel first-class; **in ~ luogo** first of all, in the first place; **di prim'ordine** *o* **~a qualità** first-class, first-rate; **in un ~ tempo** at first; **~a donna** leading lady; (*di opera lirica*) prima donna

primo'genito, a [primo'dʒenito] *ag, sm/f* firstborn

primordi'ale *ag* primordial

'primula *sf* primrose

princi'pale [printʃi'pale] *ag* main, principal ♦ *sm* manager, boss

princi'pato [printʃi'pato] *sm* principality

'principe ['printʃipe] *sm* prince; ~ **ereditario** crown prince; **princi'pessa** *sf* princess

principi'ante [printʃi'pjante] *sm/f* beginner

prin'cipio [prin'tʃipjo] *sm* (*inizio*) beginning, start; (*origine*) origin, cause; (*concetto, norma*) principle; **al** *o* **in** ~ at first; **per** ~ on principle

pri'ore *sm* (REL) prior

priorità *sf* priority

'prisma, i *sm* prism

pri'vare *vt:* ~ **qn di** to deprive sb of; **~rsi di** to go *o* do without

pri'vato, a *ag* private ♦ *sm/f* private citizen; **in** ~ in private

privazi'one [privat'tsjone] *sf* privation,

hardship

privilegi'are [privile'dʒare] *vt* to grant a privilege to

privi'legio [privi'ledʒo] *sm* privilege

'privo, a *ag:* ~ **di** without, lacking

pro *prep* for, on behalf of ♦ *sm inv* (*utilità*) advantage, benefit; **a che ~?** what's the use?; **il ~ e il contro** the pros and cons

pro'babile *ag* probable, likely; **probabilità** *sf inv* probability

pro'blema, i *sm* problem

pro'boscide [pro'bɔʃʃide] *sf* (*di elefante*) trunk

procacci'are [prokat'tʃare] *vt* to get, obtain

pro'cedere [pro'tʃedere] *vi* to proceed; (*comportarsi*) to behave; (*iniziare*): ~ **a** to start; ~ **contro** (DIR) to start legal proceedings against; **procedi'mento** *sm* (*modo di condurre*) procedure; (*di avvenimenti*) course; (TECN) process; **procedimento penale** (DIR) criminal proceedings; **proce'dura** *sf* (DIR) procedure

proces'sare [protʃes'sare] *vt* (DIR) to try

processi'one [protʃes'sjone] *sf* procession

pro'cesso [pro'tʃesso] *sm* (DIR) trial; proceedings *pl*; (*metodo*) process

pro'cinto [pro'tʃinto] *sm:* **in** ~ **di fare** about to do, on the point of doing

pro'clama, i *sm* proclamation

procla'mare *vt* to proclaim

procre'are *vt* to procreate

pro'cura *sf* (DIR) proxy; power of attorney; (*ufficio*) attorney's office

procu'rare *vt:* ~ **qc a qn** (*fornire*) to get *o* obtain sth for sb; (*causare: noie etc*) to bring *o* give sb sth

procura'tore, 'trice *sm/f* (DIR) ≈ solicitor; (*: chi ha la procura*) attorney; proxy; ~ **generale** (*in corte d'appello*) public prosecutor; (*in corte di cassazione*) Attorney General; ~ **della Repubblica** (*in corte d'assise, tribunale*) public prosecutor

prodi'gare *vt* to be lavish with; **~rsi per qn** to do all one can for sb

pro'digio [pro'didʒo] *sm* marvel, wonder; (*persona*) prodigy; **prodigi'oso, a** *ag* prodigious; phenomenal

'**prodigo, a, ghi, ghe** *ag* lavish, extravagant

pro'**dotto, a** *pp di* **produrre** ♦ *sm* product; **~i agricoli** farm produce *sg*

pro'**durre** *vt* to produce; **produttività** *sf* productivity; **produt'tivo, a** *ag* productive; **produt'tore, 'trice** *sm/f* producer; **produzi'one** *sf* production; (*rendimento*) output

pro'**emio** *sm* introduction, preface

Prof. *abbr* (= *professore*) Prof

profa'**nare** *vt* to desecrate

pro'**fano, a** *ag* (*mondano*) secular; profane; (*sacrilego*) profane

profe'**rire** *vt* to utter

profes'**sare** *vt* to profess; (*medicina etc*) to practise

professio'**nale** *ag* professional

professi'**one** *sf* profession; **professio'nista, i, e** *sm/f* professional

profes'**sore, 'essa** *sm/f* (*INS*) teacher; (: *di università*) lecturer; (: *titolare di cattedra*) professor

pro'**feta, i** *sm* prophet; **profe'zia** *sf* prophecy

pro'**ficuo, a** *ag* useful, profitable

profi'**larsi** *vr* to stand out, be silhouetted; to loom up

profi'**lattico** *sm* condom

pro'**filo** *sm* profile; (*breve descrizione*) sketch, outline; **di ~** in profile

pro'**fitto** *sm* advantage, profit, benefit; (*fig: progresso*) progress; (*COMM*) profit

profondi'**tà** *sf inv* depth

pro'**fondo, a** *ag* deep; (*rancore, meditazione*) profound ♦ *sm* depth(s *pl*), bottom; **~ 8 metri** 8 metres deep

'**profugo, a, ghi, ghe** *sm/f* refugee

profu'**mare** *vt* to perfume ♦ *vi* to be fragrant; **~rsi** *vr* to put on perfume *o* scent

profume'**ria** *sf* perfumery; (*negozio*) perfume shop

pro'**fumo** *sm* (*prodotto*) perfume, scent; (*fragranza*) scent, fragrance

profusi'**one** *sf* profusion; **a ~** in plenty

proget'**tare** [prodʒet'tare] *vt* to plan;

(*edificio*) to plan, design; pro'**getto** *sm* plan; (*idea*) plan, project; **progetto di legge** bill

pro'**gramma, i** *sm* programme; (*TV, RADIO*) programmes *pl*; (*INS*) syllabus, curriculum; (*INFORM*) program; **program'mare** *vt* (*TV, RADIO*) to put on; (*INFORM*) to program; (*ECON*) to plan; **programma'tore, 'trice** *sm/f* (*INFORM*) computer programmer

progre'**dire** *vi* to progress, make progress

progres'**sivo, a** *ag* progressive

pro'**gresso** *sm* progress *no pl*; **fare ~i** to make progress

proi'**bire** *vt* to forbid, prohibit; **proibi'tivo, a** *ag* prohibitive; **proibizi'one** *sf* prohibition

proiet'**tare** *vt* (*gen, GEOM, CINEMA*) to project; (: *presentare*) to show, screen; (*luce, ombra*) to throw, cast, project; **proi'ettile** *sm* projectile, bullet (*o* shell etc); **proiet'tore** *sm* (*CINEMA*) projector; (*AUT*) headlamp; (*MIL*) searchlight; **proiezi'one** *sf* (*CINEMA*) projection; showing

'**prole** *sf* children *pl*, offspring

prole'**tario, a** *ag, sm* proletarian

prolife'**rare** *vi* (*fig*) to proliferate

pro'**lisso, a** *ag* verbose

'**prologo, ghi** *sm* prologue

prolun'**ga, ghe** *sf* (*di cavo etc*) extension

prolun'**gare** *vt* (*discorso, attesa*) to prolong; (*linea, termine*) to extend

prome'**moria** *sm inv* memorandum

pro'**messa** *sf* promise

pro'**messo, a** *pp di* **promettere**

pro'**mettere** *vt* to promise ♦ *vi* to be *o* look promising; **~ a qn di fare** to promise sb that one will do

promi'**nente** *ag* prominent

promiscui'**tà** *sf* promiscuousness

promon'**torio** *sm* promontory, headland

pro'**mosso, a** *pp di* **promuovere**

promo'**tore, trice** *sm/f* promoter, organizer

promozi'**one** [promot'tsjone] *sf* promotion

promul'**gare** *vt* to promulgate

promu'overe *vt* to promote
proni'pote *sm/f* (*di nonni*) great-grandchild, great-grandson/granddaughter; (*di zii*) great-nephew/niece; **~i** *smpl* (*discendenti*) descendants
pro'nome *sm* (*LING*) pronoun
pro'nostico, ci *sm* forecast, prediction
pron'tezza [pron'tettsa] *sf* readiness; quickness, promptness
'**pronto, a** *ag* ready; (*rapido*) fast, quick, prompt; **~!** (*TEL*) hello!; **~ all'ira** quick-tempered; **~ soccorso** first aid
prontu'ario *sm* manual, handbook
pro'nuncia [pro'nuntʃa] *sf* pronunciation
pronunci'are [pronun'tʃare] *vt* (*parola, sentenza*) to pronounce; (*dire*) to utter; (*discorso*) to deliver; **~rsi** *vr* to declare one's opinion; **pronunci'ato, a** *ag* (*spiccato*) pronounced, marked; (*sporgente*) prominent
pro'nunzia *etc* [pro'nuntsja] = **pronuncia** *etc*
propa'ganda *sf* propaganda
propa'gare *vt* (*notizia, malattia*) to spread; (*REL, BIOL*) to propagate; **~rsi** *vr* to spread; (*BIOL*) to propagate; (*FISICA*) to be propagated
pro'pendere *vi*: **~ per** to favour, lean towards; **propensi'one** *sf* inclination, propensity; **pro'penso, a** *pp di* **propendere**
propi'nare *vt* to administer
pro'pizio, a [pro'pittsjo] *ag* favourable
pro'porre *vt* (*suggerire*): **~ qc (a qn)** to suggest sth (to sb); (*candidato*) to put forward; (*legge, brindisi*) to propose; **~ di fare** to suggest *o* propose doing; **proporsi di fare** to propose *o* intend to do; **proporsi una meta** to set o.s. a goal
proporzio'nale [proportsjo'nale] *ag* proportional
proporzio'nare [proportsjo'nare] *vt*: **~ qc a** to proportion *o* adjust sth to
proporzi'one [propor'tsjone] *sf* proportion; **in ~ a** in proportion to
pro'posito *sm* (*intenzione*) intention, aim; (*argomento*) subject, matter; **a ~ di**

regarding, with regard to; **di ~** (*apposta*) deliberately, on purpose; **a ~** by the way; **capitare a ~** (*cosa, persona*) to turn up at the right time
proposizi'one [propozit'tsjone] *sf* (*LING*) clause; (: *periodo*) sentence
pro'posta *sf* proposal; (*suggerimento*) suggestion; **~a di legge** bill
pro'posto, a *pp di* **proporre**
proprietà *sf inv* (*ciò che si possiede*) property *gen no pl*, estate; (*caratteristica*) property; (*correttezza*) correctness; **proprie'tario, a** *sm/f* owner; (*di albergo etc*) proprietor, owner; (*per l'inquilino*) landlord/lady
'**proprio, a** *ag* (*possessivo*) own; (: *impersonale*) one's; (*esatto*) exact, correct, proper; (*senso, significato*) literal; (*LING: nome*) proper; (*particolare*): **~ di** characteristic of, peculiar to ♦ *av* (*precisamente*) just, exactly; (*davvero*) really; (*affatto*): **non ... ~** not ... at all; **l'ha visto con i (suoi) ~i occhi** he saw it with his own eyes
'**prora** *sf* (*NAUT*) bow(s *pl*), prow
'**proroga, ghe** *sf* extension; postponement; **proro'gare** *vt* to extend; (*differire*) to postpone, defer
pro'rompere *vi* to burst out; **pro'rotto, a** *pp di* **prorompere**
'**prosa** *sf* prose; **pro'saico, a, ci, che** *ag* (*fig*) prosaic, mundane
pro'sciogliere [proʃ'ʃɔʎʎere] *vt* to release; (*DIR*) to acquit; **prosci'olto, a** *pp di* **prosciogliere**
prosciu'gare [proʃʃu'gare] *vt* (*terreni*) to drain, reclaim; **~rsi** *vr* to dry up
prosci'utto [proʃ'ʃutto] *sm* ham; **~ cotto/ crudo** cooked/cured ham
prosegui'mento *sm* continuation; **buon ~!** all the best!; (*a chi viaggia*) enjoy the rest of your journey!
prosegu'ire *vt* to carry on with, continue ♦ *vi* to carry on, go on
prospe'rare *vi* to thrive; **prosperità** *sf* prosperity; '**prospero, a** *ag* (*fiorente*) flourishing, thriving, prosperous;

prospe'roso, a *ag* (*robusto*) hale and hearty; (: *ragazza*) buxom

prospet'tare *vt* (*esporre*) to point out, show; **~rsi** *vr* to look, appear

prospet'tiva *sf* (*ARTE*) perspective; (*veduta*) view; (*fig: previsione, possibilità*) prospect

pros'petto *sm* (*DISEGNO*) elevation; (*veduta*) view, prospect; (*facciata*) façade, front; (*tabella*) table; (*sommario*) summary

prospici'ente [prospi'tʃɛnte] *ag*: **~ qc** facing *o* overlooking sth

prossimità *sf* nearness, proximity; **in ~ di** near (to), close to

'prossimo, a *ag* (*vicino*): **~ a** near (to), close to; (*che viene subito dopo*) next; (*parente*) close ♦ *sm* neighbour, fellow man

prosti'tuta *sf* prostitute; **prostituzi'one** *sf* prostitution

pros'trare *vt* (*fig*) to exhaust, wear out; **~rsi** *vr* (*fig*) to humble o.s.

protago'nista, i, e *sm/f* protagonist

pro'teggere [pro'tɛddʒere] *vt* to protect

proteggi'slip [proteddʒi'zlip] *sm inv* panty liner

prote'ina *sf* protein

pro'tendere *vt* to stretch out; **pro'teso, a** *pp di* **protendere**

pro'testa *sf* protest

protes'tante *ag*, *sm/f* Protestant

protes'tare *vt, vi* to protest; **~rsi** *vr*: **~rsi innocente** *etc* to protest one's innocence *o* that one is innocent *etc*

protet'tivo, a *ag* protective

pro'tetto, a *pp di* **proteggere**

protet'tore, 'trice *sm/f* protector; (*sostenitore*) patron

protezi'one [protet'tsjone] *sf* protection; (*patrocinio*) patronage

protocol'lare *vt* to register ♦ *ag* formal; of protocol; **proto'collo** *sm* protocol; (*registro*) register of documents

pro'totipo *sm* prototype

pro'trarre *vt* (*prolungare*) to prolong; **pro'tratto, a** *pp di* **protrarre**

protube'ranza [protube'rantsa] *sf* protuberance, bulge

'prova *sf* (*esperimento, cimento*) test, trial; (*tentativo*) attempt, try; (*MAT, testimonianza, documento etc*) proof; (*DIR*) evidence *no pl*, proof; (*INS*) exam, test; (*TEATRO*) rehearsal; (*di abito*) fitting; **a ~ di** (*in testimonianza di*) as proof of; **a ~ di fuoco** fireproof; **fino a ~ contraria** until it is proved otherwise; **mettere alla ~** to put to the test; **giro di ~** test *o* trial run; **~ generale** (*TEATRO*) dress rehearsal

pro'vare *vt* (*sperimentare*) to test; (*tentare*) to try, attempt; (*assaggiare*) to try, taste; (*sperimentare in sé*) to experience; (*sentire*) to feel; (*cimentare*) to put to the test; (*dimostrare*) to prove; (*abito*) to try on; **~ a fare** to try *o* attempt to do

proveni'enza [prove'njɛntsa] *sf* origin, source

prove'nire *vi*: **~ da** to come from

pro'venti *smpl* revenue *sg*

prove'nuto, a *pp di* **provenire**

pro'verbio *sm* proverb

pro'vetta *sf* test tube; **bambino in ~** test-tube baby

pro'vetto, a *ag* skilled, experienced

pro'vincia, ce *o* **cie** [pro'vintʃa] *sf* province; **provinci'ale** *ag* provincial; **(strada) provinciale** main road (*BRIT*), highway (*US*)

pro'vino *sm* (*CINEMA*) screen test; (*campione*) specimen

provo'cante *ag* (*attraente*) provocative

provo'care *vt* (*causare*) to cause, bring about; (*eccitare: riso, pietà*) to arouse, (*irritare, sfidare*) to provoke; **provoca'torio, a** *ag* provocative; **provocazi'one** *sf* provocation

provve'dere *vi* (*disporre*): **~ (a)** to provide (for); (*prendere un provvedimento*) to take steps, act; **provvedi'mento** *sm* measure; (*di previdenza*) precaution

provvi'denza [provvi'dɛntsa] *sf*: **la ~** providence; **provvidenzi'ale** *ag* providential

provvigi'one [provvi'dʒone] *sf* (*COMM*) commission

provvi'sorio, a *ag* temporary

prov'vista *sf* provision, supply

'prua *sf* (NAUT) = **prora**

pru'dente *ag* cautious, prudent; (*assennato*) sensible, wise; pru'denza *sf* prudence, caution; wisdom

'prudere *vi* to itch, be itchy

'prugna ['pruɲɲa] *sf* plum; ~ **secca** prune

pruri'gnoso, a [pruridʒi'noso] *ag* itchy

pru'rito *sm* itchiness *no pl*; itch

P.S. *abbr* (= *postscriptum*) P.S.; (*POLIZIA*) = **Pubblica Sicurezza**

pseu'donimo *sm* pseudonym

PSI *sigla m* = **Partito Socialista Italiano**

psicana'lista, i, e *sm/f* psychoanalyst

'psiche ['psike] *sf* (PSIC) psyche

psichi'atra, i, e [psi'kjatra] *sm/f* psychiatrist; psichi'atrico, a, ci, che *ag* psychiatric

'psichico, a, ci, che ['psikiko] *ag* psychological

psicolo'gia [psikolo'dʒia] *sf* psychology; psico'logico, a, ci, che *ag* psychological; psi'cologo, a, gi, ghe *sm/f* psychologist

psico'patico, a, ci, che *ag* psychopathic ♦ *sm/f* psychopath

P.T. *abbr* = **Posta e Telegrafi**

pubbli'care *vt* to publish

pubblicazi'one [pubblikat'tsjone] *sf* publication; ~i (matrimoniali) *sfpl* (marriage) banns

pubbli'cista, i, e [pubbli'tʃista] *sm/f* (STAMPA) occasional contributor

pubblicità [pubblitʃi'ta] *sf* (*diffusione*) publicity; (*attività*) advertising; (*annunci nei giornali*) advertisements *pl*; pubblici'tario, a *ag* advertising *cpd*; (*trovata, film*) publicity *cpd*

'pubblico, a, ci, che *ag* public; (*statale: scuola etc*) state *cpd* ♦ *sm* public; (*spettatori*) audience; in ~ in public; ~ funzionario civil servant; P~ Ministero Public Prosecutor's Office; la P~a Sicurezza the police

'pube *sm* (ANAT) pubis

pubertà *sf* puberty

'pudico, a, ci, che *ag* modest

pu'dore *sm* modesty

puericul'tura *sf* paediatric nursing; infant care

pue'rile *ag* childish

pugi'lato [pudʒi'lato] *sm* boxing

'pugile ['pudʒile] *sm* boxer

pugna'lare [puɲɲa'lare] *vt* to stab

pu'gnale [puɲ'ɲale] *sm* dagger

'pugno ['puɲɲo] *sm* fist; (*colpo*) punch; (*quantità*) fistful

'pulce ['pultʃe] *sf* flea

pul'cino [pul'tʃino] *sm* chick

pu'ledro, a *sm/f* colt/filly

pu'leggia, ge [pu'leddʒa] *sf* pulley

pu'lire *vt* to clean; (*lucidare*) to polish; pu'lita *sf* quick clean; pu'lito, a *ag* (*anche fig*) clean; (*ordinato*) neat, tidy; puli'tura *sf* cleaning; pulitura a secco dry cleaning; puli'zia *sf* cleaning; cleanness; fare le pulizie to do the cleaning o the housework

'pullman *sm inv* coach

pul'lover *sm inv* pullover, jumper

pullu'lare *vi* to swarm, teem

pul'mino *sm* minibus

'pulpito *sm* pulpit

pul'sante *sm* (push-)button

pul'sare *vi* to pulsate, beat; pulsazi'one *sf* beat

pul'viscolo *sm* fine dust

'puma *sm inv* puma

pun'gente [pun'dʒente] *ag* prickly; stinging; (*anche fig*) biting

'pungere ['pundʒere] *vt* to prick; (*sog: insetto, ortica*) to sting; (: *freddo*) to bite

pungigli'one [pundʒiʎ'ʎone] *sm* sting

pu'nire *vt* to punish; punizi'one *sf* punishment; (SPORT) penalty

'punta *sf* point; (*parte terminale*) tip, end; (*di monte*) peak; (*di costa*) promontory; (*minima parte*) touch, trace; in ~ di piedi on tip-toe; ore di ~ peak hours; uomo di ~ front-rank o leading man

pun'tare *vt* (*piedi a terra, gomiti sul tavolo*) to plant; (*dirigere: pistola*) to point; (*scommettere*) to bet ♦ *vi* (*mirare*): ~ a to aim at; ~ su (*dirigersi*) to head o make for; (*fig: contare*) to count o rely on

pun'tata *sf (gita)* short trip; *(scommessa)* bet; *(parte di opera)* instalment; **romanzo a ~e** serial

punteggia'tura [punteddʒa'tura] *sf (LING)* punctuation

pun'teggio [pun'teddʒo] *sm* score

puntel'lare *vt* to support

pun'tello *sm* prop, support

puntigli'oso, a [puntiʎ'ʎoso] *ag* punctilious

pun'tina *sf*: **~ da disegno** drawing pin

pun'tino *sm* dot; **fare qc a ~** to do sth properly

'**punto, a** *pp di* **pungere** ♦ *sm (segno, macchiolina)* dot; *(LING)* full stop; *(MAT, momento, di punteggio, fig: argomento)* point; *(posto)* spot; *(a scuola)* mark; *(nel cucire, nella maglia, MED)* stitch ♦ *av*: **non ... ~** not at all; **due ~i** *sm (LING)* colon; **sul ~ di fare** (just) about to do; **fare il ~** *(NAUT)* to take a bearing; *(fig)*: **fare il ~ della situazione** to take stock of the situation; to sum up the situation; **alle 6 in ~** at 6 o'clock sharp *o* on the dot; **essere a buon ~** to have reached a satisfactory stage; **mettere a ~** to adjust; *(motore)* to tune; *(cannocchiale)* to focus; *(fig)* to settle; **di ~ in bianco** point-blank; **~ cardinale** point of the compass, cardinal point; **~ debole** weak point; **~ esclamativo/ interrogativo** exclamation/question mark; **~ di riferimento** landmark; *(fig)* point of reference; **~ di vendita** retail outlet; **~ e virgola** semicolon; **~ di vista** *(fig)* point of view; **~i di sospensione** suspension points

puntu'ale *ag* punctual; **puntualità** *sf* punctuality

pun'tura *sf (di ago)* prick; *(di insetto)* sting, bite; *(MED)* puncture; *(: iniezione)* injection; *(dolore)* sharp pain

punzecchi'are [puntsek'kjare] *vt* to prick; *(fig)* to tease

'**pupa** *sf* doll

pu'pazzo [pu'pattso] *sm* puppet

pu'pilla *sf (ANAT)* pupil

pu'pillo, a *sm/f (DIR)* ward; *(prediletto)* favourite, pet

purché [pur'ke] *cong* provided that, on condition that

'**pure** *cong (tuttavia)* and yet, nevertheless; *(anche se)* even if ♦ *av (anche)* too, also; **pur di** *(al fine di)* just to; **faccia ~!** go ahead!, please do!

purè *sm (CUC)* purée; *(: di patate)* mashed potatoes

pu'rea *sf* = **purè**

pu'rezza [pu'rettsa] *sf* purity

'**purga, ghe** *sf (MED)* purging *no pl*; purge; *(POL)* purge

pur'gante *sm (MED)* purgative, purge

pur'gare *vt (MED, POL)* to purge; *(pulire)* to clean

purga'torio *sm* purgatory

purifi'care *vt* to purify; *(metallo)* to refine

puri'tano, a *ag, sm/f* puritan

'**puro, a** *ag* pure; *(acqua)* clear, limpid; *(vino)* undiluted; **puro'sangue** *sm/f inv* thoroughbred

pur'troppo *av* unfortunately

'**pustola** *sf* pimple

puti'ferio *sm* rumpus, row

putre'fare *vi* to putrefy, rot; **putre'fatto, a** *pp di* **putrefare**

'**putrido, a** *ag* putrid, rotten

put'tana *(fam!)* *sf* whore *(!)*

'**puzza** ['puttsa] *sf* = **puzzo**

puz'zare [put'tsare] *vi* to stink

'**puzzo** ['puttso] *sm* stink, foul smell

'**puzzola** ['puttsola] *sf* polecat

puzzo'lente [puttso'lente] *ag* stinking

Q, q

qua *av* here; **in ~** *(verso questa parte)* this way; **da un anno in ~** for a year now; **da quando in ~?** since when?; **per di ~** *(passare)* this way; **al di ~ di** *(fiume, strada)* on this side of; **~ dentro/fuori** *etc* in/out here *etc*; *vedi anche* **questo**

qua'derno *sm* notebook; *(per scuola)* exercise book

qua'drante *sm* quadrant; *(di orologio)* face

qua'drare *vi (bilancio)* to balance, tally;

(*descrizione*) to correspond ♦ *vt* (*MAT*) to
square; **non mi quadra** I don't like it;
qua'drato, a *ag* square; (*fig: equilibrato*)
level-headed, sensible; (: *peg*) square ♦ *sm*
(*MAT*) square; (*PUGILATO*) ring; **5 al
quadrato** 5 squared
qua'dretto *sm*: **a ~i** (*tessuto*) checked;
(*foglio*) squared
quadri'foglio [kwadri'fɔʎʎo] *sm* four-leaf
clover
'quadro *sm* (*pittura*) painting, picture;
(*quadrato*) square; (*tabella*) table, chart;
(*TECN*) board, panel; (*TEATRO*) scene; (*fig:
scena, spettacolo*) sight; (: *descrizione*)
outline, description; **~i** *smpl* (*POL*) party
organizers; (*MIL*) cadres; (*COMM*) managerial
staff; (*CARTE*) diamonds
'quadruplo, a *ag, sm* quadruple
quaggiù [kwad'dʒu] *av* down here
'quaglia ['kwaʎʎa] *sf* quail

PAROLA CHIAVE

'qualche ['kwalke] *det* **1** some, a few; (*in
interrogative*) any; **ho comprato ~ libro** I've
bought some *o* a few books; **~ volta**
sometimes; **hai ~ sigaretta?** have you any
cigarettes?
2 (*uno*): **c'è ~ medico?** is there a doctor?;
in ~ modo somehow
3 (*un certo, parecchio*) some; **un
personaggio di ~ rilievo** a figure of some
importance
4: **~ cosa = qualcosa**

qualche'duno [kwalke'duno] *pron* =
qualcuno
qual'cosa *pron* something; (*in espressioni
interrogative*) anything; **qualcos'altro**
something else; anything else; **~ di nuovo**
something new; anything new; **~ da
mangiare** something to eat; anything to
eat; **c'è ~ che non va?** is there something
o anything wrong?
qual'cuno *pron* (*persona*) someone,
somebody; (: *in espressioni interrogative*)
anyone, anybody; (*alcuni*) some; **~ è
favorevole a noi** some are on our side;

qualcun altro someone *o* somebody else;
anyone *o* anybody else

PAROLA CHIAVE

'quale (*spesso troncato in qual*) *det*
1 (*interrogativo*) what; (: *scegliendo tra due
o più cose o persone*) which; **~ uomo/
denaro?** what man/money?; which man/
money?; **~i sono i tuoi programmi?** what
are your plans?; **~ stanza preferisci?**
which room do you prefer?
2 (*relativo: come*): **il risultato fu ~ ci si
aspettava** the result was as expected
3 (*esclamativo*) what; **~ disgrazia!** what
bad luck!
♦ *pron* **1** (*interrogativo*) which; **~ dei due
scegli?** which of the two do you want?
2 (*relativo*): **il(la) ~** (*persona: soggetto*)
who; (: *oggetto, con preposizione*) whom;
(*cosa*) which; (*possessivo*) whose; **suo
padre, il ~ è avvocato, ...** his father, who
is a lawyer, ...; **il signore con il ~ parlavo**
the gentleman to whom I was speaking;
l'albergo al ~ ci siamo fermati the hotel
where we stayed *o* which we stayed at; **la
signora della ~ ammiriamo la bellezza**
the lady whose beauty we admire
3 (*relativo: in elenchi*) such as, like; **piante
~i l'edera** plants like *o* such as ivy; **~
sindaco di questa città** as mayor of this
town

qua'lifica, che *sf* qualification; (*titolo*) title
qualifi'care *vt* to qualify; (*definire*): **~ qn/
qc come** to describe sb/sth as; **~rsi** *vr*
(*anche SPORT*) to qualify; **qualifica'tivo, a**
ag qualifying; **qualificazi'one** *sf*: **gara di
qualificazione** (*SPORT*) qualifying event
qualità *sf inv* quality; **in ~ di** in one's
capacity as
qua'lora *cong* in case, if
qual'siasi *det inv* = **qualunque**
qua'lunque *det inv* any; (*quale che sia*)
whatever; (*discriminativo*) whichever;
(*posposto: mediocre*) poor, indifferent;
ordinary; **mettiti un vestito ~** put on any
old dress; **~ cosa** anything; **~ cosa**

accada whatever happens; **a ~ costo** at any cost, whatever the cost; **l'uomo ~** the man in the street; **~ persona** anyone, anybody

'**quando** *cong, av* when; **~ sarò ricco** when I'm rich; **da ~** (*dacché*) since; (*interrogativo*): **da ~ sei qui?** how long have you been here?; **quand'anche** even if

quantità *sf inv* quantity; (*gran numero*): **una ~ di** a great deal of; a lot of; **in grande ~** in large quantities; **quantita'tivo** *sm* (*COMM*) amount, quantity

---

PAROLA CHIAVE

'**quanto, a** *det* 1 (*interrogativo: quantità*) how much; (*: numero*) how many; **~ pane/denaro?** how much bread/money?; **~i libri/ragazzi?** how many books/boys?; **~ tempo?** how long?; **~i anni hai?** how old are you?

2 (*esclamativo*): **~e storie!** what a lot of nonsense!; **~ tempo sprecato!** what a waste of time!

3 (*relativo: quantità*) as much ... as; (*: numero*) as many ... as; **ho ~ denaro mi occorre** I have as much money as I need; **prendi ~i libri vuoi** take as many books as you like

♦ *pron* 1 (*interrogativo: quantità*) how much; (*: numero*) how many; (*: tempo*) how long; **~ mi dai?** how much will you give me?; **~i me ne hai portati?** how many did you bring me?; **da ~ sei qui?** how long have you been here?; **~i ne abbiamo oggi?** what's the date today?

2 (*relativo: quantità*) as much as; (*: numero*) as many as; **farò ~ posso** I'll do as much as I can; **possono venire ~i sono stati invitati** all those who have been invited can come

♦ *av* 1 (*interrogativo: con ag, av*) how; (*: con vb*) how much; **~ stanco ti sembrava?** how tired did he seem to you?; **~ corre la tua moto?** how fast can your motorbike go?; **~ costa?** how much

does it cost?; **quant'è?** how much is it?

2 (*esclamativo: con ag, av*) how; (*: con vb*) how much; **~ sono felice!** how happy I am!; **sapessi ~ abbiamo camminato!** if you knew how far we've walked!; **studierò ~ posso** I'll study as much as *o* all I can; **~ prima** as soon as possible

3: **in ~** (*in qualità di*) as; (*perché, per il fatto che*) as, since; **(in) ~ a** (*per ciò che riguarda*) as for, as regards

4: **per ~** (*nonostante, anche se*) however; **per ~ si sforzi, non ce la farà** try as he may, he won't manage it; **per ~ sia brava, fa degli errori** however good she may be, she makes mistakes; **per ~ io sappia** as far as I know

---

quan'tunque *cong* although, though
qua'ranta *num* forty
quaran'tena *sf* quarantine
quaran'tesimo, a *num* fortieth
quaran'tina *sf*: **una ~ (di)** about forty
qua'resima *sf*: **la ~** Lent
'**quarta** *sf* (*AUT*) fourth (gear); *vedi anche* **quarto**
quar'tetto *sm* quartet(te)
quarti'ere *sm* district, area; (*MIL*) quarters *pl*; **~ generale** headquarters *pl*
'**quarto, a** *ag* fourth ♦ *sm* fourth; (*quarta parte*) quarter; **le 6 e un ~** a quarter past six; **~ d'ora** quarter of an hour; **~i di finale** quarter final
'**quarzo** ['kwartso] *sm* quartz
'**quasi** *av* almost, nearly ♦ *cong* (*anche: ~ che*) as if; **(non) ... ~ mai** hardly ever; **~ ~ me ne andrei** I've half a mind to leave
quas'sù *av* up here
'**quatto, a** *ag* crouched, squatting; (*silenzioso*) silent; **~ ~** very quietly; stealthily
quat'tordici [kwat'tordit∫i] *num* fourteen
quat'trini *smpl* money *sg*, cash *sg*
'**quattro** *num* four; **in ~ e quattr'otto** in less than no time; **quattro'cento** *num* four hundred ♦ *sm*: **il Quattrocento** the fifteenth century; **quattro'mila** *num* four thousand

---

PAROLA CHIAVE

'**quello, a** (*dav sm* **quel** +*C*, **quell'** +*V*, **quello** +*s impura, gn, pn, ps, x, z; pl* **quei** +*C*, **quegli** +*V o s impura, gn, pn, ps, x, z; dav sf* **quella** +*C*, **quell'** +*V; pl* **quelle**) *det* that; those *pl*; **~a casa** that house; **quegli uomini** those men; **voglio ~a camicia (lì** *o* **là)** I want that shirt
♦ *pron* **1** (*dimostrativo*) that (one); those (ones) *pl*; (*ciò*) that; **conosci ~a?** do you know that woman?; **prendo ~ bianco** I'll take the white one; **chi è ~?** who's that?; **prendi ~ (lì** *o* **là)** take that one (there)
2 (*relativo*): **~(a) che** (*persona*) the one (who); (*cosa*) the one (which), the one (that); **~i(e) che** (*persone*) those who; (*cose*) those which; **è lui ~ che non voleva venire** he's the one who didn't want to come; **ho fatto ~ che potevo** I did what I could

'**quercia, ce** ['kwertʃa] *sf* oak (tree); (*legno*) oak
que'rela *sf* (*DIR*) (legal) action; **quere'lare** *vt* to bring an action against
que'sito *sm* question, query; problem
questio'nario *sm* questionnaire
questi'one *sf* problem, question; (*controversia*) issue; (*litigio*) quarrel; **in ~** in question; **è ~ di tempo** it's a matter *o* question of time

PAROLA CHIAVE

'**questo, a** *det* **1** (*dimostrativo*) this; these *pl*; **~ libro (qui** *o* **qua)** this book; **io prendo ~ cappotto, tu quello** I'll take this coat, you take that one; **quest'oggi** today; **~a sera** this evening
2 (*enfatico*): **non fatemi più prendere di ~e paure** don't frighten me like that again
♦ *pron* (*dimostrativo*) this (one); these (ones) *pl*; (*ciò*) this; **prendo ~ (qui** *o* **qua)** I'll take this one; **preferisci ~i o quelli?** do you prefer these (ones) or those (ones)?; **~ intendevo io** this is what I meant; **vengono Paolo e Luca: ~ da Roma,**

quello da Palermo Paolo and Luca are coming: the former from Palermo, the latter from Rome

---

ques'tore *sm* ≈ chief constable (*BRIT*), ≈ police commissioner (*US*)
'**questua** *sf* collection (of alms)
ques'tura *sf* police headquarters *pl*
qui *av* here; **da** *o* **di ~** from here; **di ~ in avanti** from now on; **di ~ a poco/una settimana** in a little while/a week's time; **~ dentro/sopra/vicino** in/up/near here; *vedi anche* **questo**
quie'tanza [kwje'tantsa] *sf* receipt
quie'tare *vt* to calm, soothe
qui'ete *sf* quiet, quietness; calmness; stillness; peace
qui'eto, a *ag* quiet; (*notte*) calm, still; (*mare*) calm
'**quindi** *av* then ♦ *cong* therefore, so
'**quindici** ['kwinditʃi] *num* fifteen; **~ giorni** a fortnight (*BRIT*), two weeks
quindi'cina [kwindi'tʃina] *sf* (*serie*): **una ~ (di)** about fifteen; **fra una ~ di giorni** in a fortnight
quin'quennio *sm* period of five years
quin'tale *sm* quintal (*100 kg*)
'**quinte** *sfpl* (*TEATRO*) wings
'**quinto, a** *num* fifth

Quirinale

🛈 *The* **Quirinale**, *which takes its name from the hill in Rome on which it stands, is the official residence of the Presidente della Repubblica.*

'**quota** *sf* (*parte*) quota, share; (*AER*) height, altitude; (*IPPICA*) odds *pl*; **prendere/ perdere ~** (*AER*) to gain/lose height *o* altitude; **~ d'iscrizione** enrolment fee; (*a club*) membership fee
quo'tare *vt* (*BORSA*) to quote; **quotazi'one** *sf* quotation
quotidi'ano, a *ag* daily; (*banale*) everyday ♦ *sm* (*giornale*) daily (paper)
quozi'ente [kwot'tsjente] *sm* (*MAT*) quotient; **~ d'intelligenza**

intelligence quotient, IQ

R, r

ra'barbaro *sm* rhubarb

'rabbia *sf* (*ira*) anger, rage; (*accanimento, furia*) fury; (*MED: idrofobia*) rabies *sg*

rab'bino *sm* rabbi

rabbi'oso, a *ag* angry, furious; (*facile all'ira*) quick-tempered; (*forze, acqua etc*) furious, raging; (*MED*) rabid, mad

rabbo'nire *vt* to calm down; ~rsi *vr* to calm down

rabbrivi'dire *vi* to shudder, shiver

rabbui'arsi *vr* to grow dark

raccapez'zarsi [rakkapet'tsarsi] *vr*: **non ~** to be at a loss

raccapricci'ante [rakkaprit'tʃante] *ag* horrifying

raccatta'palle *sm inv* (*SPORT*) ballboy

raccat'tare *vt* to pick up

rac'chetta [rak'ketta] *sf* (*per tennis*) racket; (*per ping-pong*) bat; **~ da neve** snowshoe; **~ da sci** ski stick

racchi'udere [rak'kjudere] *vt* to contain; racchi'uso, a *pp di* racchiudere

rac'cogliere [rak'kɔʎʎere] *vt* to collect; (*raccattare*) to pick up; (*frutti, fiori*) to pick, pluck; (*AGR*) to harvest; (*approvazione, voti*) to win; ~rsi *vr* to gather; (*fig*) to gather one's thoughts; to meditate; raccogli'mento *sm* meditation; raccogli'tore *sm* (*cartella*) folder, binder; **raccoglitore ad anelli** ring binder

rac'colta *sf* collecting *no pl*; collection; (*AGR*) harvesting *no pl*, gathering *no pl*; harvest, crop; (*adunata*) gathering

rac'colto, a *pp di* raccogliere ♦ *ag* (*persona: pensoso*) thoughtful; (*luogo: appartato*) secluded, quiet ♦ *sm* (*AGR*) crop, harvest

raccoman'dare *vt* to recommend; (*affidare*) to entrust; (*esortare*): **~ a qn di non fare** to tell *o* warn sb not to do; ~rsi *vr*: **~rsi a qn** to commend o.s. to sb; **mi raccomando!** don't forget!;

raccoman'data *sf* (*anche*: **lettera raccomandata**) recorded-delivery letter; raccomandazi'one *sf* recommendation

raccon'tare *vt*: **~ (a qn)** (*dire*) to tell (sb); (*narrare*) to relate (to sb), tell (sb) about; rac'conto *sm* telling *no pl*, relating *no pl*; (*fatto raccontato*) story, tale

raccorci'are [rakkor'tʃare] *vt* to shorten

rac'cordo *sm* (*TECN: giunto*) connection, joint; (*AUT: di autostrada*) slip road (*BRIT*), entrance (*o* exit) ramp (*US*); **~ anulare** (*AUT*) ring road (*BRIT*), beltway (*US*)

ra'chitico, a, ci, che [ra'kitiko] *ag* suffering from rickets; (*fig*) scraggy, scrawny

racimo'lare [ratʃimo'lare] *vt* (*fig*) to scrape together, glean

'rada *sf* (natural) harbour

'radar *sm* radar

raddol'cire [raddol'tʃire] *vt* (*persona, carattere*) to soften; ~rsi *vr* (*tempo*) to grow milder; (*persona*) to soften, mellow

raddoppi'are *vt*, *vi* to double

raddriz'zare [raddrit'tsare] *vt* to straighten; (*fig: correggere*) to put straight, correct

'radere *vt* (*barba*) to shave off; (*mento*) to shave; (*fig: rasentare*) to graze; to skim; ~rsi *vr* to shave (o.s.); **~ al suolo** to raze to the ground

radu'are *vi* to strike off

'radia'tore *sm* radiator

radiazi'one [radjat'tsjone] *sf* (*FISICA*) radiation; (*cancellazione*) striking off

radi'cale *ag* radical ♦ *sm* (*LING*) root

ra'dicchio [ra'dikkjo] *sm* chicory

ra'dice [ra'ditʃe] *sf* root

'radio *sf inv* radio ♦ *sm* (*CHIM*) radium; radioat'tivo, a *ag* radioactive; radiodiffusi'one *sf* (*radio*) broadcasting; radiogra'fare *vt* to X-ray; radiogra'fia *sf* radiography; (*foto*) X-ray photograph

radi'oso, a *ag* radiant

'rado, a *ag* (*capelli*) sparse, thin; (*visite*) infrequent; **di ~** rarely

radu'nare *vt*, to gather, assemble; ~rsi *vr* to gather, assemble; ra'duno *sm* meeting

ra'dura *sf* clearing

raffazzo'nato [raffattso'nato] *ag* patched up

raf'fermo, a *ag* stale

'raffica, che *sf* (*METEOR*) gust (of wind); (*di colpi: scarica*) burst of gunfire

raffigu'rare *vt* to represent

raffi'nare *vt* to refine; **raffina'tezza** *sf* refinement; **raffi'nato, a** *ag* refined; **raffine'ria** *sf* refinery

raffor'zare [raffor'tsare] *vt* to reinforce

raffredda'mento *sm* cooling

raffred'dare *vt* to cool; (*fig*) to dampen, have a cooling effect on; **~rsi** *vr* to grow cool *o* cold; (*prendere un raffreddore*) to catch a cold; (*fig*) to cool (off)

raffred'dato, a *ag* (*MED*): **essere ~** to have a cold

raffred'dore *sm* (*MED*) cold

raf'fronto *sm* comparison

'rafia *sf* (*fibra*) raffia

ra'gazzo, a [ra'gattso] *sm/f* boy/girl; (*fam: fidanzato*) boyfriend/girlfriend

raggi'ante [rad'dʒante] *ag* radiant, shining

'raggio ['raddʒo] *sm* (*di sole etc*) ray; (*MAT, distanza*) radius; (*di ruota etc*) spoke; **~ d'azione** range; **~i X** X-rays

raggi'rare [raddʒi'rare] *vt* to take in, trick; **rag'giro** *sm* trick

raggi'ungere [rad'dʒundʒere] *vt* to reach; (*persona: riprendere*) to catch up (with); (*bersaglio*) to hit; (*fig: meta*) to achieve; **raggi'unto, a** *pp di* **raggiungere**

raggomito'larsi *vr* to curl up

raggranel'lare *vt* to scrape together

raggrup'pare *vt* to group (together)

raggu'aglio [rag'gwaʎʎo] *sm* (*informazione*) piece of information

ragguar'devole *ag* (*degno di riguardo*) distinguished, notable; (*notevole: somma*) considerable

ragiona'mento [radʒona'mento] *sm* reasoning *no pl*; arguing *no pl*; argument

ragio'nare [radʒo'nare] *vi* to reason; **~ di** (*discorrere*) to talk about

ragi'one [ra'dʒone] *sf* reason; (*dimostrazione, prova*) argument, reason; (*diritto*) right; **aver ~** to be right; **aver ~ di**

qn to get the better of sb; **dare ~ a qn** to agree with sb; to prove sb right; **perdere la ~** to become insane; (*fig*) to take leave of one's senses; **in ~ di** at the rate of; to the amount of; according to; **a o con ~** rightly, justly; **~ sociale** (*COMM*) corporate name; **a ragion veduta** after due consideration

ragione'ria [radʒone'ria] *sf* accountancy; accounts department

ragio'nevole [radʒo'nevole] *ag* reasonable

ragioni'ere, a [radʒo'njere] *sm/f* accountant

ragli'are [raʎ'ʎare] *vi* to bray

ragna'tela [raɲɲa'tela] *sf* cobweb, spider's web

'ragno ['raɲɲo] *sm* spider

ragù *sm inv* (*CUC*) meat sauce; stew

RAI-TV [raiti'vu] *sigla f* = **Radio televisione italiana**

rallegra'menti *smpl* congratulations

ralle'grare *vt* to cheer up; **~rsi** *vr* to cheer up; (*provare allegrezza*) to rejoice; **~rsi con qn** to congratulate sb

rallen'tare *vt* to slow down; (*fig*) to lessen, slacken ♦ *vi* to slow down

raman'zina [raman'dzina] *sf* lecture, telling-off

'rame *sm* (*CHIM*) copper

rammari'carsi *vr*: **~ (di)** (*rincrescersi*) to be sorry (about), regret; (*lamentarsi*) to complain (about); **ram'marico, chi** *sm* regret

rammen'dare *vt* to mend; (*calza*) to darn; **ram'mendo** *sm* mending *no pl*; darning *no pl*; mend; darn

rammen'tare *vt* to remember, recall; (*richiamare alla memoria*) to remind: **~ qc a qn** to remind sb of sth; **~rsi** *vr*: **~rsi (di qc)** to remember (sth)

rammol'lire *vt* to soften ♦ *vi* (*anche: ~rsi*) to go soft

'ramo *sm* branch

ramo'scello [ramoʃ'ʃello] *sm* twig

'rampa *sf* flight (of stairs); **~ di lancio** launching pad

rampi'cante *ag* (*BOT*) climbing

ram'pone *sm* harpoon; (*ALPINISMO*) crampon

'rana *sf* frog

'rancido, a ['rantʃido] *ag* rancid

ran'core *sm* rancour, resentment

ran'dagio, a, gi, gie *o* ge [ran'dadʒo] *ag* (*gatto, cane*) stray

ran'dello *sm* club, cudgel

'rango, ghi *sm* (*condizione sociale, MIL: riga*) rank

rannicchi'arsi [rannik'kjarsi] *vr* to crouch, huddle

rannuvo'larsi *vr* to cloud over, become overcast

ra'nocchio [ra'nɔkkjo] *sm* (edible) frog

'rantolo *sm* wheeze; (*di agonizzanti*) death rattle

'rapa *sf* (*BOT*) turnip

ra'pace [ra'patʃe] *ag* (*animale*) predatory; (*fig*) rapacious, grasping ♦ *sm* bird of prey

ra'pare *vt* (*capelli*) to crop, cut very short

'rapida *sf* (*di fiume*) rapid; *vedi anche* rapido

rapida'mente *av* quickly, rapidly

rapidità *sf* speed

'rapido, a *ag* fast; (*esame, occhiata*) quick, rapid ♦ *sm* (*FERR*) express (train)

rapi'mento *sm* kidnapping; (*fig*) rapture

ra'pina *sf* robbery; ~ a mano armata armed robbery; rapi'nare *vt* to rob, rapina'tore, 'trice *sm/f* robber

ra'pire *vt* (*cose*) to steal; (*persone*) to kidnap; (*fig*) to enrapture, delight; rapi'tore, 'trice *sm/f* kidnapper

rappor'tare *vt* (*confrontare*) to compare, (*riprodurre*) to reproduce

rap'porto *sm* (*resoconto*) report; (*legame*) relationship; (*MAT, TECN*) ratio; ~i *smpl* (*fra persone, paesi*) relations; ~i sessuali sexual intercourse *sg*

rap'prendersi *vr* to coagulate, clot; (*latte*) to curdle

rappre'saglia [rappre'saʎʎa] *sf* reprisal, retaliation

rappresen'tante *sm/f* representative; rappresen'tanza *sf* delegation, deputation; (*COMM: ufficio, sede*) agency

rappresen'tare *vt* to represent; (*TEATRO*) to perform; rappresentazi'one *sf* representation; performing *no pl*; (*spettacolo*) performance

rap'preso, a *pp di* rapprendere

rapso'dia *sf* rhapsody

rara'mente *av* seldom, rarely

rare'fatto, a *ag* rarefied

'raro, a *ag* rare

ra'sare *vt* (*barba etc*) to shave off; (*siepi, erba*) to trim, cut; ~rsi *vr* to shave (o.s.)

raschi'are [ras'kjare] *vt* to scrape; (*macchia, fango*) to scrape off ♦ *vi* to clear one's throat

rasen'tare *vt* (*andar rasente*) to keep close to; (*sfiorare*) to skim along (*o* over); (*fig*) to border on

ra'sente *prep*: ~ (a) close to, very near

'raso, a *pp di* radere ♦ *ag* (*barba*) shaved; (*capelli*) cropped; (*con misure di capacità*) level; (*pieno: bicchiere*) full to the brim ♦ *sm* (*tessuto*) satin; ~ terra close to the ground; un cucchiaio ~ a level spoonful

ra'soio *sm* razor; ~ elettrico electric shaver *o* razor

ras'segna [ras'seɲɲa] *sf* (*MIL*) inspection, review; (*esame*) inspection; (*resoconto*) review, survey; (*pubblicazione letteraria etc*) review; (*mostra*) exhibition, show; passare in ~ (*MIL, fig*) to review

rasse'gnare [rasseɲ'ɲare] *vt*: ~ le dimissioni to resign, hand in one's resignation; ~rsi *vr* (*accettare*): ~rsi (a qc/ a fare) to resign o.s. (to sth/to doing); rassegnazi'one *sf* resignation

rassere'narsi *vr* (*tempo*) to clear up

rasset'tare *vt* to tidy, put in order; (*aggiustare*) to repair, mend

rassicu'rare *vt* to reassure

rasso'dare *vt* to harden, stiffen

rassomigli'anza [rassomiʎ'ʎantsa] *sf* resemblance

rassomigli'are [rassomiʎ'ʎare] *vi*: ~ a to resemble, look like

rastrel'lare *vt* to rake; (*fig: perlustrare*) to comb

rastrelli'era *sf* rack; (*per piatti*) dish rack

ras'trello *sm* rake

'rata *sf* (*quota*) instalment; **pagare a ~e** to pay by instalments *o* on hire purchase (*BRIT*)

ratifi'care *vt* (*DIR*) to ratify

'ratto *sm* (*DIR*) abduction; (*ZOOL*) rat

rattop'pare *vt* to patch; **rat'toppo** *sm* patching *no pl*; patch

rattrap'pirsi *vr* to get stiff

rattris'tare *vt* to sadden; ~**rsi** *vr* to become sad

'rauco, a, chi, che *ag* hoarse

rava'nello *sm* radish

ravi'oli *smpl* ravioli *sg*

ravve'dersi *vr* to mend one's ways

ravvici'nare [ravvitʃi'nare] *vt* (*avvicinare*): ~ **qc a** to bring sth nearer to; (: *due tubi*) to bring closer together; (*riconciliare*) to reconcile, bring together

ravvi'sare *vt* to recognize

ravvi'vare *vt* to revive; (*fig*) to brighten up, enliven; ~**rsi** *vr* to revive; to brighten up

razio'cinio [ratsjo'tʃinjo] *sm* reasoning *no pl*; reason; (*buon senso*) common sense

razio'nale [rattsjo'nale] *ag* rational

razio'nare [rattsjo'nare] *vt* to ration

razi'one [rat'tsjone] *sf* ration; (*porzione*) portion, share

'razza ['rattsa] *sf* race; (*ZOOL*) breed; (*discendenza, stirpe*) stock, race; (*sorta*) sort, kind

raz'zia [rat'tsia] *sf* raid, foray

razzi'ale [rat'tsjale] *ag* racial

raz'zismo [rat'tsizmo] *sm* racism, racialism

raz'zista, i, e [rat'tsista] *ag, sm/f* racist, racialist

'razzo ['raddzo] *sm* rocket

razzo'lare [rattso'lare] *vi* (*galline*) to scratch about

re *sm inv* king; (*MUS*) D; (: *solfeggiando*) re

rea'gire [rea'dʒire] *vi* to react

re'ale *ag* real; (*di, da re*) royal ♦ *sm*: **il ~** reality; **rea'lismo** *sm* realism; **rea'lista, i, e** *sm/f* realist; (*POL*) royalist

realiz'zare [realid'dzare] *vt* (*progetto etc*) to realize, carry out; (*sogno, desiderio*) to realize, fulfil; (*scopo*) to achieve; (*COMM: titoli etc*) to realize; (*CALCIO etc*) to score; ~**rsi** *vr* to be realized; **realizzazi'one** *sf* realization; fulfilment; achievement

real'mente *av* really, actually

realtà *sf inv* reality

re'ato *sm* offence

reat'tore *sm* (*FISICA*) reactor; (*AER: aereo*) jet; (: *motore*) jet engine

reazio'nario, a [reattsjo'narjo] *ag* (*POL*) reactionary

reazi'one [reat'tsjone] *sf* reaction

recapi'tare *vt* to deliver

re'capito *sm* (*indirizzo*) address; (*consegna*) delivery

re'care *vt* (*portare*) to bring; (*avere su di sé*) to carry, bear; (*cagionare*) to cause, bring; ~**rsi** *vr* to go

re'cedere [re'tʃedere] *vi* to withdraw

recensi'one [retʃen'sjone] *sf* review; **recen'sire** *vt* to review

re'cente [re'tʃente] *ag* recent; **di ~** recently; **recente'mente** *av* recently

recessi'one [retʃes'sjone] *sf* (*ECON*) recession

re'cidere [re'tʃidere] *vt* to cut off, chop off

reci'divo, a [retʃi'divo] *sm/f* (*DIR*) second (*o* habitual) offender, recidivist

re'cinto [re'tʃinto] *sm* enclosure; (*ciò che recinge*) fence; surrounding wall

recipi'ente [retʃi'pjente] *sm* container

re'ciproco, a, ci, che [re'tʃiproko] *ag* reciprocal

re'ciso, a [re'tʃizo] *pp di* **recidere**

'recita ['retʃita] *sf* performance

reci'tare [retʃi'tare] *vt* (*poesia, lezione*) to recite; (*dramma*) to perform; (*ruolo*) to play *o* act (the part of); **recitazi'one** *sf* recitation; (*di attore*) acting

recla'mare *vi* to complain ♦ *vt* (*richiedere*) to demand

ré'clame [re'klam] *sf inv* advertising *no pl*; advertisement, advert (*BRIT*), ad (*fam*)

re'clamo *sm* complaint

reclusi'one *sf* (*DIR*) imprisonment

'recluta *sf* recruit; **reclu'tare** *vt* to recruit

re'condito, a *ag* secluded; (*fig*) secret,

hidden

recriminazi'one [rekriminat'tsjone] *sf* recrimination

recrude'scenza [rekrudeʃʃentsa] *sf* fresh outbreak

recupe'rare *vt* = **ricuperare**

redargu'ire *vt* to rebuke

re'datto, a *pp di* **redigere**; **redat'tore, 'trice** *sm/f* (*STAMPA*) editor; (: *di articolo*) writer; (*di dizionario etc*) compiler; **redattore capo** chief editor; **redazi'one** *sf* editing; writing; (*sede*) editorial office(s); (*personale*) editorial staff; (*versione*) version

reddi'tizio, a [reddi'tittsjo] *ag* profitable

'reddito *sm* income; (*dello Stato*) revenue; (*di un capitale*) yield

re'dento, a *pp di* **redimere**

redenzi'one [reden'tsjone] *sf* redemption

re'digere [re'didʒere] *vt* to write; (*contratto*) to draw up

'redini *sfpl* reins

'reduce ['redutʃe] *ag*: **~ da** returning from, back from ♦ *sm/f* survivor

refe'rendum *sm inv* referendum

refe'renza [refe'rentsa] *sf* reference

re'ferto *sm* medical report

refet'torio *sm* refectory

refrat'tario, a *ag* refractory

refrige'rare [refridʒe'rare] *vt* to refrigerate; (*rinfrescare*) to cool, refresh

rega'lare *vt* to give (as a present), make a present of

re'gale *ag* regal

re'galo *sm* gift, present

re'gata *sf* regatta

reg'gente [red'dʒente] *sm/f* regent

'reggere ['reddʒere] *vt* (*tenere*) to hold; (*sostenere*) to support, bear, hold up; (*portare*) to carry, bear; (*resistere*) to withstand; (*dirigere: impresa*) to manage, run; (*governare*) to rule, govern; (*LING*) to take, be followed by ♦ *vi* (*resistere*): **~ a** to stand up to, hold out against; (*sopportare*): **~ a** to stand; (*durare*) to last; (*fig: teoria etc*) to hold water; **~rsi** *vr* (*stare ritto*) to stand

'reggia, ge ['reddʒa] *sf* royal palace

reggi'calze [reddʒi'kaltse] *sm inv* suspender belt

reggi'mento [reddʒi'mento] *sm* (*MIL*) regiment

reggi'petto [reddʒi'petto] *sm* bra

reggi'seno [reddʒi'seno] *sm* bra

re'gia, 'gie [re'dʒia] *sf* (*TV, CINEMA etc*) direction

re'gime [re'dʒime] *sm* (*POL*) regime; (*DIR: aureo, patrimoniale etc*) system; (*MED*) diet; (*TECN*) (engine) speed

re'gina [re'dʒina] *sf* queen

'regio, a, gi, gie ['redʒo] *ag* royal

regio'nale [redʒo'nale] *ag* regional ♦ *sm* local train (*stopping frequently*)

regi'one [re'dʒone] *sf* region; (*territorio*) region, district, area

re'gista, i, e [re'dʒista] *sm/f* (*TV, CINEMA etc*) director

regis'trare [redʒis'trare] *vt* (*AMM*) to register; (*COMM*) to enter; (*notare*) to note, take note of; (*canzone, conversazione, sog: strumento di misura*) to record; (*mettere a punto*) to adjust, regulate; (*bagagli*) to check in; **registra'tore** *sm* (*strumento*) recorder, register; (*magnetofono*) tape recorder; **registratore di cassa** cash register; **registrazi'one** *sf* recording; (*AMM*) registration; (*COMM*) entry; (*di bagagli*) check-in

re'gistro [re'dʒistro] *sm* (*libro, MUS, TECN*) register; **ledger**; **logbook**; (*DIR*) registry

re'gnare [reɲ'ɲare] *vi* to reign, rule

'regno ['reɲɲo] *sm* kingdom; (*periodo*) reign; (*fig*) realm; **il ~ animale/vegetale** the animal/vegetable kingdom; **il R~ Unito** the United Kingdom

'regola *sf* rule; **a ~ d'arte** duly; perfectly; **in ~** in order

rego'labile *ag* adjustable

regola'mento *sm* (*complesso di norme*) regulations *pl*; (*di debito*) settlement; **~ di conti** (*fig*) settling of scores

rego'lare *ag* regular; (*in regola: domanda*) in order, lawful ♦ *vt* to regulate, control; (*apparecchio*) to adjust, regulate; (*questione, conto, debito*) to settle; **~rsi** *vr* (*moderarsi*): **~rsi nel bere/nello spendere** to control one's drinking/spending; (*comportarsi*) to behave, act; **regolarità** *sf inv* regularity

'regolo *sm* ruler; **~ calcolatore** slide rule

reinte'grare *vt* (*energie*) to recover; (*in una carica*) to reinstate

rela'tivo, a *ag* relative

relazi'one [relat'tsjone] *sf* (*fra cose, persone*) relation(ship); (*resoconto*) report, account; **~i** *sfpl* (*conoscenze*) connections

rele'gare *vt* to banish; (*fig*) to relegate

religi'one [reli'dʒone] *sf* religion; **religi'oso, a** *ag* religious ♦ *sm/f* monk/nun

re'liquia *sf* relic

re'litto *sm* wreck; (*fig*) down-and-out

re'mare *vi* to row

remini'scenze [reminiʃ'ʃentse] *sfpl* reminiscences

remissi'one *sf* remission

remis'sivo, a *ag* submissive, compliant

'remo *sm* oar

re'moto, a *ag* remote

'rendere *vt* (*ridare*) to return, give back; (: *saluto etc*) to return; (*produrre*) to yield, bring in; (*esprimere, tradurre*) to render; **~ qc possibile** to make sth possible; **~rsi utile** to make o.s. useful; **~rsi conto di qc** to realize sth

rendi'conto *sm* (*rapporto*) report, account; (*AMM, COMM*) statement of account

rendi'mento *sm* (*reddito*) yield; (*di manodopera, TECN*) efficiency; (*capacità di produrre*) output; (*di studenti*) performance

'rendita *sf* (*di individuo*) private *o* unearned income; (*COMM*) revenue; **~ annua** annuity

'rene *sm* kidney

'reni *sfpl* back *sg*

reni'tente *ag* reluctant, unwilling; **~ ai consigli di qn** unwilling to follow sb's advice; **essere ~ alla leva** (*MIL*) to fail to report for military service

'renna *sf* reindeer *inv*

'Reno *sm*: **il ~** the Rhine

'reo, a *sm/f* (*DIR*) offender

re'parto *sm* department, section; (*MIL*) detachment

repel'lente *ag* repulsive

repen'taglio [repen'taʎʎo] *sm*: **mettere a ~** to jeopardize, risk

repen'tino, a *ag* sudden, unexpected

repe'rire *vt* to find, trace

re'perto *sm* (*ARCHEOLOGIA*) find; (*MED*) report; (*DIR: anche:* **~ giudiziario**) exhibit

reper'torio *sm* (*TEATRO*) repertory; (*elenco*) index, (alphabetical) list

'replica, che *sf* repetition; reply, answer; (*obiezione*) objection; (*TEATRO, CINEMA*) repeat performance; (*copia*) replica

repli'care *vt* (*ripetere*) to repeat; (*rispondere*) to answer, reply

repressi'one *sf* repression

re'presso, a *pp di* **reprimere**

re'primere *vt* to suppress, repress

re'pubblica, che *sf* republic; **repubbli'cano, a** *ag, sm/f* republican

repu'tare *vt* to consider, judge

reputazi'one [reputat'tsjone] *sf* reputation

'requie *sf*: **senza ~** unceasingly

requi'sire *vt* to requisition

requi'sito *sm* requirement

'resa *sf* (*l'arrendersi*) surrender; (*restituzione, rendimento*) return; **~ dei conti** rendering of accounts; (*fig*) day of reckoning

resi'dente *ag* resident; **resi'denza** *sf* residence; **residenzi'ale** *ag* residential

re'siduo, a *ag* residual, remaining ♦ *sm* remainder; (*CHIM*) residue

'resina *sf* resin

resis'tente *ag* (*che resiste*): **~ a** resistant to; (*forte*) strong; (*duraturo*) long-lasting, durable; **~ al caldo** heat-resistant; **resis'tenza** *sf* resistance; (*di persona: fisica*) stamina, endurance; (: *mentale*) endurance, resistance

---

Resistenza

i The **Resistenza** in Italy fought against the Nazis and the Fascists during the Second World War. Members of the Resistance spanned a wide political spectrum and played a vital role in the Liberation and in the formation of the new democratic government at the end *of the war.*

re'sistere *vi* to resist; ~ **a** (*assalto, tentazioni*) to resist; (*dolore, sog: pianta*) to withstand; (*non patir danno*) to be resistant to; **resis'tito, a** *pp di* **resistere**

'**reso, a** *pp di* **rendere**

reso'conto *sm* report, account

res'pingere [res'pindʒere] *vt* to drive back, repel; (*rifiutare*) to reject; (*INS: bocciare*) to fail; **res'pinto, a** *pp di* **respingere**

respi'rare *vi* to breathe; (*fig*) to get one's breath; to breathe again ♦ *vt* to breathe (in), inhale; **respira'tore** *sm* respirator; **respirazi'one** *sf* breathing; **respirazione artificiale** artificial respiration; **res'piro** *sm* breathing *no pl*; (*singolo atto*) breath; (*fig*) respite, rest; **mandare un respiro di sollievo** to give a sigh of relief

respon'sabile *ag* responsible ♦ *sm/f* person responsible; (*capo*) person in charge; ~ **di** responsible for; (*DIR*) liable for; **responsabilità** *sf inv* responsibility; (*legale*) liability

res'ponso *sm* answer

'**ressa** *sf* crowd, throng

res'tare *vi* (*rimanere*) to remain, stay; (*avanzare*) to be left, remain; ~ **orfano/ cieco** to become an be left an orphan/ become blind; ~ **d'accordo** to agree; **non resta più niente** there's nothing left; **restano pochi giorni** there are only a few days left

restau'rare *vt* to restore; **restaurazi'one** *sf* (*POL*) restoration; **res'tauro** *sm* (*di edifici etc*) restoration

res'tio, a, 'tii, 'tie *ag*: ~ **a** reluctant to

restitu'ire *vt* to return, give back; (*energie, forze*) to restore

'**resto** *sm* remainder, rest; (*denaro*) change; (*MAT*) remainder; ~**i** *smpl* (*di cibo*) leftovers; (*di città*) remains; **del** ~ moreover, besides; ~**i mortali** (*mortal*) remains

res'tringere [res'trindʒere] *vt* to reduce; (*vestito*) to take in; (*stoffa*) to shrink; (*fig*) to restrict, limit; ~**rsi** *vr* (*strada*) to narrow; (*stoffa*) to shrink; **restrizi'one** *sf* restriction

'**rete** *sf* net; (*fig*) trap, snare; (*di recinzione*) wire netting; (*AUT, FERR, di spionaggio etc*) network; **segnare una** ~ (*CALCIO*) to score a goal; ~ **del letto** (*sprung*) bed base

reti'cente [reti'tʃente] *ag* reticent

retico'lato *sm* grid; (*rete*) wire netting; (*di filo spinato*) barbed wire (fence)

'**retina** *sf* (*ANAT*) retina

re'torica *sf* rhetoric

re'torico, a, ci, che *ag* rhetorical

retribu'ire *vt* to pay; **retribuzi'one** *sf* payment

'**retro** *sm inv* back ♦ *av* (*dietro*): **vedi** ~ see over(leaf)

retro'cedere [retro'tʃedere] *vi* to withdraw ♦ *vt* (*CALCIO*) to relegate; (*MIL*) to degrade

re'trogrado, a *ag* (*fig*) reactionary, backward-looking

retro'marcia [retro'martʃa] *sf* (*AUT*) reverse; (: *dispositivo*) reverse gear

retro'scena [retro'ʃena] *sm inv* (*TEATRO*) backstage; **i** ~ (*fig*) the behind-the-scenes activities

retrospet'tivo, a *ag* retrospective

retrovi'sore *sm* (*AUT*) (rear-view) mirror

'**retta** *sf* (*MAT*) straight line; (*di convitto*) charge for bed and board; (*fig: ascolto*): **dar** ~ **a** to listen to, pay attention to

rettango'lare *ag* rectangular

ret'tangolo, a *ag* right-angled ♦ *sm* rectangle

ret'tifica, che *sf* rectification, correction

rettifi'care *vt* (*curva*) to straighten; (*fig*) to rectify, correct

'**rettile** *sm* reptile

retti'lineo, a *ag* rectilinear

retti'tudine *sf* rectitude, uprightness

'**retto, a** *pp di* **reggere** ♦ *ag* straight; (*MAT*): **angolo** ~ right angle; (*onesto*) honest, upright; (*giusto, esatto*) correct, proper, right

ret'tore *sm* (*REL*) rector; (*di università*) ≈ chancellor

reuma'tismo *sm* rheumatism

reve'rendo, a *ag*: **il** ~ **padre Belli** the Reverend Father Belli

rever'sibile *ag* reversible

revisio'nare *vt* (*conti*) to audit; (*TECN*) to overhaul, service; (*DIR: processo*) to review

revisi'one *sf* auditing *no pl*; audit; servicing *no pl*; overhaul; review; revision

revi'sore *sm*: ~ **di conti/bozze** auditor/proofreader

'revoca *sf* revocation

revo'care *vt* to revoke

re'volver *sm inv* revolver

riabili'tare *vt* to rehabilitate

riagganci'are [riaggan'tʃare] *vt* (*TEL*) to hang up

rial'zare [rial'tsare] *vt* to raise, lift; (*alzare di più*) to heighten, raise; (*aumentare: prezzi*) to increase, raise ♦ *vi* (*prezzi*) to rise, increase; **ri'alzo** *sm* (*di prezzi*) increase, rise; (*sporgenza*) rise

rianimazi'one [rianimat'tsjone] *sf* (*MED*) resuscitation; **centro di** ~ intensive care unit

riap'pendere *vt* to rehang; (*TEL*) to hang up

ria'prire *vt* to reopen, open again; **~rsi** *vr* to reopen, open again

ri'armo *sm* (*MIL*) rearmament

rias'setto *sm* (*di stanza etc*) rearrangement; (*ordinamento*) reorganization

rias'sumere *vt* (*riprendere*) to resume; (*impiegare di nuovo*) to re-employ; (*sintetizzare*) to summarize; **rias'sunto, a** *pp di* **riassumere** ♦ *sm* summary

ria'vere *vt* to have again; (*avere indietro*) to get back; (*riacquistare*) to recover; **~rsi** *vr* to recover

riba'dire *vt* (*fig*) to confirm

ri'balta *sf* flap; (*TEATRO: proscenio*) front of the stage; (*fig*) limelight; **luci della** ~ footlights *pl*

ribal'tabile *ag* (*sedile*) tip-up

ribal'tare *vt, vi* (*anche:* **~rsi**) to turn over, tip over

ribas'sare *vt* to lower, bring down ♦ *vi* to come down, fall; **ri'basso** *sm* reduction, fall

ri'battere *vt* to return, hit back; (*confutare*)

to refute; ~ **che** to retort that

ribel'larsi *vr*: ~ **(a)** to rebel (against); **ri'belle** *ag* (*soldati*) rebel; (*ragazzo*) rebellious ♦ *sm/f* rebel; **ribelli'one** *sf* rebellion

'ribes *sm inv* currant; ~ **nero** blackcurrant; ~ **rosso** redcurrant

ribol'lire *vi* (*fermentare*) to ferment; (*fare bolle*) to bubble, boil; (*fig*) to seethe

ri'brezzo [ri'breddzo] *sm* disgust, loathing; **far** ~ **a** to disgust

ribut'tante *ag* disgusting, revolting

rica'dere *vi* to fall again; (*scendere a terra, fig: nel peccato etc*) to fall back; (*vestiti, capelli etc*) to hang (down); (*riversarsi: fatiche, colpe*): ~ **su** to fall on; **rica'duta** *sf* (*MED*) relapse

rical'care *vt* (*disegni*) to trace; (*fig*) to follow faithfully

rica'mare *vt* to embroider

ricambi'are *vt* to change again; (*contraccambiare*) to repay, return; **ri'cambio** *sm* exchange, return; (*FISIOL*) metabolism; **ricambi** *smpl* (*TECN*) spare parts

ri'camo *sm* embroidery

ricapito'lare *vt* to recapitulate, sum up

ricari'care *vt* (*arma, macchina fotografica*) to reload; (*pipa*) to refill; (*orologio*) to rewind; (*batteria*) to recharge

ricat'tare *vt* to blackmail; **ricatta'tore, 'trice** *sm/f* blackmailer; **ri'catto** *sm* blackmail

rica'vare *vt* (*estrarre*) to draw out, extract; (*ottenere*) to obtain, gain; **ri'cavo** *sm* proceeds *pl*

ric'chezza [rik'kettsa] *sf* wealth; (*fig*) richness; ~**e** *sfpl* (*beni*) wealth *sg*, riches

'riccio, a ['rittʃo] *ag* curly ♦ *sm* (*ZOOL*) hedgehog; (: *anche:* ~ **di mare**) sea urchin; **'ricciolo** *sm* curl; **ricci'uto, a** *ag* curly

'ricco, a, chi, che *ag* rich; (*persona, paese*) rich, wealthy ♦ *sm/f* rich man/woman; **i** ~**chi** the rich; ~ **di** full of; rich in

ri'cerca, che [ri'tʃerka] *sf* search; (*indagine*) investigation, inquiry; (*studio*): **la** ~ research; **una** ~ piece of research

ricer'care [ritʃer'kare] *vt* (*motivi, cause*) to look for, try to determine; (*successo, piacere*) to pursue; (*onore, gloria*) to seek; **ricer'cato, a** *ag* (*apprezzato*) much sought-after; (*affettato*) studied, affected ♦ *sm/f* (*POLIZIA*) wanted man/woman

ri'cetta [ri'tʃetta] *sf* (*MED*) prescription; (*CUC*) recipe

ricettazi'one [ritʃettat'tsjone] *sf* (*DIR*) receiving (stolen goods)

ri'cevere [ri'tʃevere] *vt* to receive; (*stipendio, lettera*) to get, receive; (*accogliere: ospite*) to welcome; (*vedere: cliente, rappresentante etc*) to see; **ricevi'mento** *sm* receiving *no pl*; (*festa*) reception; **ricevi'tore** *sm* (*TECN*) receiver; **ricevito'ria** *sf* lottery *o* pools office; **rice'vuta** *sf* receipt; **ricevuta fiscale** receipt for tax purposes; **ricezi'one** [ritʃet'tsjone] *sf* (*RADIO, TV*) reception

richia'mare [rikja'mare] *vt* (*chiamare indietro, ritelefonare*) to call back; (*ambasciatore, truppe*) to recall; (*rimproverare*) to reprimand; (*attirare*) to attract, draw; ~**rsi a** (*riferirsi a*) to refer to; **richi'amo** *sm* call; recall; reprimand; attraction

richi'edere [ri'kjedere] *vt* to ask again for; (*chiedere indietro*): ~ **qc** to ask for sth back; (*chiedere: per sapere*) to ask; (: *per avere*) to ask for; (*AMM: documenti*) to apply for; (*esigere*) to need, require; **richi'esta** *sf* (*domanda*) request; (*AMM*) application, request; (*esigenza*) demand, request; **a richiesta** on request; **richi'esto, a** *pp di* **richiedere**

rici'clare [ritʃi'klare] *vt* to recycle

'ricino [ri'tʃino] *sm*: **olio di** ~ castor oil

ricogni'zi'one [rikoɲɲit'tsjone] *sf* (*MIL*) reconnaissance; (*DIR*) recognition, acknowledgement

ricominci'are [rikomin'tʃare] *vt, vi* to start again, begin again

ricom'pensa *sf* reward

ricompen'sare *vt* to reward

riconcili'are [rikontʃi'ljare] *vt* to reconcile; ~**rsi** *vr* to be reconciled; **riconciliazi'one** *sf* reconciliation

ricono'scente [rikonoʃ'ʃente] *ag* grateful; **ricono'scenza** *sf* gratitude

rico'noscere [riko'noʃʃere] *vt* to recognize; (*DIR: figlio, debito*) to acknowledge; (*ammettere: errore*) to admit, acknowledge; **riconosci'mento** *sm* recognition; acknowledgement; (*identificazione*) identification; **riconosci'uto, a** *pp di* **riconoscere**

ricopi'are *vt* to copy

rico'prire *vt* (*coprire*) to cover; (*occupare: carica*) to hold

ricor'dare *vt* to remember, recall; (*richiamare alla memoria*): ~ **qc a qn** to remind sb of sth; ~**rsi** *vr*: ~**rsi (di)** to remember; ~**rsi di qc/di aver fatto** to remember sth/having done

ri'cordo *sm* memory; (*regalo*) keepsake, souvenir; (*di viaggio*) souvenir; ~**i** *smpl* (*memorie*) memoirs

ricor'rente *ag* recurrent, recurring; **ricor'renza** *sf* recurrence; (*festività*) anniversary

ri'correre *vi* (*ripetersi*) to recur; ~ **a** (*rivolgersi*) to turn to; (: *DIR*) to appeal to; (*servirsi di*) to have recourse to; **ri'corso, a** *pp di* **ricorrere** ♦ *sm* recurrence; (*DIR*) appeal; **far ricorso a** = **ricorrere a**

ricostitu'ente *ag* (*MED*): **cura** ~ tonic

ricostru'ire *vt* (*casa*) to rebuild; (*fatti*) to reconstruct; **ricostruzi'one** *sf* rebuilding *no pl*; reconstruction

ri'cotta *sf* soft white unsalted cheese made from sheep's milk

ricove'rare *vt* to give shelter to; ~ **qn in ospedale** to admit sb to hospital

ri'covero *sm* shelter, refuge; (*MIL*) shelter; (*MED*) admission (to hospital)

ricre'are *vt* to recreate; (*fig: distrarre*) to amuse

ricreazi'one [rikreat'tsjone] *sf* recreation, entertainment; (*INS*) break

ri'credersi *vr* to change one's mind

ricupe'rare *vt* (*rientrare in possesso di*) to recover, get back; (*tempo perduto*) to make up for; (*NAUT*) to salvage; (: *naufraghi*) to rescue; (*delinquente*) to rehabilitate; ~ **lo**

svantaggio (*SPORT*) to close the gap
ridacchi'are [ridak'kjare] *vi* to snigger
ri'dare *vt* to return, give back
'**ridere** *vi* to laugh; (*deridere, beffare*): ~ **di**
to laugh at, make fun of
ri'detto, a *pp di* **ridire**
ri'dicolo, a *ag* ridiculous, absurd
ridimensio'nare *vt* to reorganize; (*fig*) to
see in the right perspective
ri'dire *vt* to repeat; (*criticare*) to find fault
with; to object to; **trova sempre qualcosa**
da ~ he always manages to find fault
ridon'dante *ag* redundant
ri'dotto, a *pp di* **ridurre** ♦ *ag* (*biglietto*)
reduced; (*formato*) small
ri'durre *vt* (*anche CHIM, MAT*) to reduce;
(*prezzo, spese*) to cut, reduce; (*accorciare*:
opera letteraria) to abridge; (: *RADIO, TV*) to
adapt; **ridursi** *vr* (*diminuirsi*) to be reduced,
shrink; **ridursi a** to be reduced to; **ridursi**
pelle e ossa to be reduced to skin and
bone; **ridut'tore** *sm* (*ELEC*) adaptor;
riduzi'one *sf* reduction; abridgement;
adaptation
riem'pire *vt* to fill (up); (*modulo*) to fill in *o*
out; **~rsi** *vr* to fill (up); ~ **qc di** to fill sth
(up) with
rien'tranza [rien'trantsa] *sf* recess;
indentation
rien'trare *vi* (*entrare di nuovo*) to go (*o*
come) back in; (*tornare*) to return; (*fare*
una rientranza) to go in, curve inwards; to
be indented; (*riguardare*): ~ **in** to be
included among, form part of; **ri'entro** *sm*
(*ritorno*) return; (*di astronave*) re-entry
riepilo'gare *vt* to summarize ♦ *vi* to
recapitulate
ri'fare *vt* to do again; (*ricostruire*) to make
again; (*nodo*) to tie again, do up again;
(*imitare*) to imitate, copy; **~rsi** *vr* (*risarcirsi*):
~rsi di to make up for; (*vendicarsi*): **~rsi di**
qc su qn to get one's own back on sb for
sth; (*riferirsi*): **~rsi a** to go back to; to
follow; ~ **il letto** to make the bed; **~rsi una**
vita to make a new life for o.s.; **ri'fatto, a**
pp di **rifare**
riferi'mento *sm* reference; **in** *o* **con** ~ **a**

with reference to
rife'rire *vt* (*riportare*) to report ♦ *vi* to do a
report; **~rsi** *vr*: **~rsi a** to refer to
rifi'nire *vt* to finish off, put the finishing
touches to; **rifini'tura** *sf* finishing touch;
rifiniture *sfpl* (*di mobile, auto*) finish *sg*
rifiu'tare *vt* to refuse; ~ **di fare** to refuse to
do; **rifi'uto** *sm* refusal; **rifiuti** *smpl*
(*spazzatura*) rubbish *sg*, refuse *sg*
riflessi'one *sf* (*FISICA, meditazione*)
reflection; (*il pensare*) thought, reflection;
(*osservazione*) remark
rifles'sivo, a *ag* (*persona*) thoughtful,
reflective; (*LING*) reflexive
ri'flesso, a *pp di* **riflettere** ♦ *sm* (*di luce,*
allo specchio) reflection; (*FISIOL*) reflex; **di** *o*
per ~ indirectly
ri'flettere *vt* to reflect ♦ *vi* to think; **~rsi** *vr*
to be reflected; ~ **su** to think over
riflet'tore *sm* reflector; (*proiettore*)
floodlight; searchlight
ri'flusso *sm* flowing back; (*della marea*)
ebb; **un'epoca di** ~ an era of nostalgia
ri'fondere *vt* to refund, repay
ri'forma *sf* reform; **la R~** (*REL*) the
Reformation
rifor'mare *vt* to re-form; (*REL, POL*) to
reform; (*MIL*: *recluta*) to declare unfit for
service; (: *soldato*) to invalid out, discharge;
riforma'torio *sm* (*DIR*) community home
(*BRIT*), reformatory (*US*)
riforni'mento *sm* supplying, providing;
restocking; **~i** *smpl* (*provviste*) supplies,
provisions
rifor'nire *vt* (*provvedere*): ~ **di** to supply *o*
provide with; (*fornire di nuovo*: *casa etc*) to
restock
rifrazi'one [rifrat'tsjone] *sf* refraction
rifug'gire [rifud'dʒire] *vi* to escape again;
(*fig*): ~ **da** to shun
rifugi'arsi [rifu'dʒarsi] *vr* to take refuge;
rifugi'ato, a *sm/f* refugee
ri'fugio [ri'fudʒo] *sm* refuge, shelter; (*in*
montagna) shelter; ~ **antiaereo** air-raid
shelter
'**riga, ghe** *sf* line; (*striscia*) stripe; (*di*
persone, cose) line, row; (*regolo*) ruler;

(*scriminatura*) parting; **mettersi in ~** to line up; **a ~ghe** (*foglio*) lined; (*vestito*) striped

ri'gagnolo [ri'gaɲɲolo] *sm* rivulet

ri'gare *vt* (*foglio*) to rule ♦ *vi*: **~ diritto** (*fig*) to toe the line

rigatti'ere *sm* junk dealer

riget'tare [ridʒet'tare] *vt* (*gettare indietro*) to throw back; (*fig*: *respingere*) to reject; (*vomitare*) to bring *o* throw up; **ri'getto** *sm* (*anche MED*) rejection

rigidità [ridʒidi'ta] *sf* rigidity; stiffness; severity, rigours *pl*; strictness

'rigido, a [ridʒido] *ag* rigid, stiff; (*membra etc*: *indurite*) stiff; (*METEOR*) harsh, severe; (*fig*) strict

rigi'rare [ridʒi'rare] *vt* to turn; **~rsi** *vr* to turn round; (*nel letto*) to turn over; **~ qc tra le mani** to turn sth over in one's hands; **~ il discorso** to change the subject

'rigo, ghi *sm* line; (*MUS*) staff, stave

rigogli'oso, a [rigoʎ'ʎoso] *ag* (*pianta*) luxuriant; (*fig*: *commercio, sviluppo*) thriving

ri'gonfio, a *ag* swollen

ri'gore *sm* (*METEOR*) harshness, rigours *pl*; (*fig*) severity, strictness; (*anche*: **calcio di ~**) penalty; **di ~** compulsory; **a rigor di termini** strictly speaking; **rigo'roso, a** *ag* (*severo: persona, ordine*) strict; (*preciso*) rigorous

rigover'nare *vt* to wash (up)

riguar'dare *vt* to look at again; (*considerare*) to regard, consider; (*concernere*) to regard, concern; **~rsi** *vr* (*aver cura di sé*) to look after o.s.

rigu'ardo *sm* (*attenzione*) care; (*considerazione*) regard, respect; **~ a** concerning, with regard to; **non aver ~i nell'agire/nel parlare** to act/speak freely

rilasci'are [rilaʃ'ʃare] *vt* (*rimettere in libertà*) to release; (*AMM: documenti*) to issue; **ri'lascio** *sm* release; issue

rilas'sare *vt* to relax; **~rsi** *vr* to relax; (*fig*: *disciplina*) to become slack

rile'gare *vt* (*libro*) to bind; **rilega'tura** *sf* binding

ri'leggere [ri'leddʒere] *vt* to reread, read again; (*rivedere*) to read over

ri'lento: a ~ *av* slowly

rileva'mento *sm* (*topografico, statistico*) survey; (*NAUT*) bearing

rile'vante *ag* considerable; important

rile'vare *vt* (*ricavare*) to find; (*notare*) to notice; (*mettere in evidenza*) to point out; (*venire a conoscere: notizia*) to learn; (*raccogliere: dati*) to gather, collect; (*TOPOGRAFIA*) to survey; (*MIL*) to relieve; (*COMM*) to take over

rili'evo *sm* (*ARTE, GEO*) relief; (*fig*: *rilevanza*) importance; (*TOPOGRAFIA*) survey; **dar ~ a** *o* **mettere in ~ qc** to bring sth out, highlight sth

rilut'tante *ag* reluctant; **rilut'tanza** *sf* reluctance

'rima *sf* rhyme; (*verso*) verse

riman'dare *vt* to send again; (*restituire, rinviare*) to send back, return; (*differire*): **~ qc (a)** to postpone sth *o* put sth off (till); (*fare riferimento*): **~ qn a** to refer sb to; **essere rimandato** (*INS*) to have to repeat one's exams

ri'mando *sm* (*rinvio*) return; (*dilazione*) postponement; (*riferimento*) cross-reference

rima'nente *ag* remaining ♦ *sm* rest, remainder; **i ~i** (*persone*) the rest of them, the others; **rima'nenza** *sf* rest, remainder; **rimanenze** *sfpl* (*COMM*) unsold stock *sg*

rima'nere *vi* (*restare*) to remain, stay; (*avanzare*) to be left, remain; (*restare stupito*) to be amazed; (*restare, mancarc*): **rimangono poche settimane a Pasqua** there are only a few weeks left till Easter; **rimane da vedere se** it remains to be seen whether; (*diventare*): **~ vedovo** to be left a widower; (*trovarsi*): **~ sorpreso** to be surprised

ri'mare *vt, vi* to rhyme

rimargi'nare [rimardʒi'nare] *vt, vi* (*anche*: **~rsi**) to heal

ri'masto, a *pp di* **rimanere**

rima'sugli [rima'suʎʎi] *smpl* leftovers

rimbal'zare [rimbal'tsare] *vi* to bounce back, rebound; (*proiettile*) to ricochet; **rim'balzo** *sm* rebound; ricochet

rimbam'bito, a *ag* senile, in one's dotage

rimboc'care vt (coperta) to tuck in; (maniche, pantaloni) to turn o roll up

rimbom'bare vi to resound

rimbor'sare vt to pay back, repay; **rim'borso** sm repayment

rimedi'are vi: ~ **a** to remedy ♦ vt (fam: procurarsi) to get o scrape together

ri'medio sm (medicina) medicine; (cura, fig) remedy, cure

rimesco'lare vt to mix well, stir well; (carte) to shuffle; **sentirsi ~ il sangue** (per paura) to feel one's blood run cold; (per rabbia) to feel one's blood boil

ri'messa sf (locale: per veicoli) garage; (: per aerei) hangar; (COMM: di merce) consignment; (: di denaro) remittance; (TENNIS) return; (CALCIO: anche: ~ **in gioco**) throw-in

ri'messo, a pp di **rimettere**

ri'mettere vt (mettere di nuovo) to put back; (indossare di nuovo): ~ **qc** to put sth back on, put sth on again; (affidare) to entrust; (: decisione) to refer; (condonare) to remit; (COMM: merci) to deliver; (: denaro) to remit; (vomitare) to bring up; (perdere: anche: **rimetterci**) to lose; **~rsi al bello** (tempo) to clear up; **~rsi in salute** to get better, recover one's health

'rimmel ® sm inv mascara

rimoder'nare vt to modernize

rimon'tare vt (meccanismo) to reassemble; (: tenda) to put up again ♦ vi (salire di nuovo): ~ **in** (macchina, treno) to get back into; (SPORT) to close the gap

rimorchi'are [rimor'kjare] vt to tow; (fig: ragazza) to pick up; **rimorchia'tore** sm (NAUT) tug(boat)

ri'morchio [ri'mɔrkjo] sm tow; (veicolo) trailer

ri'morso sm remorse

rimozi'one [rimot'tsjone] sf removal; (da un impiego) dismissal; (PSIC) repression

rim'pasto sm (POL) reshuffle

rimpatri'are vi to return home ♦ vt to repatriate; **rim'patrio** sm repatriation

rimpi'angere [rim'pjandʒere] vt to regret; (persona) to miss; **rimpi'anto, a** pp di

rimpiangere ♦ sm regret

rimpiat'tino sm hide-and-seek

rimpiaz'zare [rimpjat'tsare] vt to replace

rimpiccio'lire [rimpittʃo'lire] vt to make smaller ♦ vi (anche: **~rsi**) to become smaller

rimpin'zare [rimpin'tsare] vt: ~ **di** to cram o stuff with

rimprove'rare vt to rebuke, reprimand; **rim'provero** sm rebuke, reprimand

rimugi'nare [rimudʒi'nare] vt (fig) to turn over in one's mind

rimunerazi'one [rimunerat'tsjone] sf remuneration; (premio) reward

rimu'overe vt to remove; (destituire) to dismiss

Rinasci'mento [rinaʃʃi'mento] sm: **il ~** the Renaissance

ri'nascita [ri'naʃʃita] sf rebirth, revival

rinca'rare vt to increase the price of ♦ vi to go up, become more expensive

rinca'sare vi to go home

rinchi'udere [rin'kjudere] vt to shut (o lock) up; **~rsi** vr: **~rsi in** to shut o.s. up in; **~rsi in se stesso** to withdraw into o.s.; **rinchi'uso, a** pp di **rinchiudere**

rin'correre vt to chase, run after; **rin'corsa** sf short run; **rin'corso, a** pp di **rincorrere**

rin'crescere [rin'kreʃʃere] vb impers: **mi rincresce che/di non poter fare** I'm sorry that/I can't do, I regret that/being unable to do; **rincresci'mento** sm regret; **rincresci'uto, a** pp di **rincrescere**

rincu'lare vi (arma) to recoil

rinfacci'are [rinfat'tʃare] vt (fig): ~ **qc a qn** to throw sth in sb's face

rinfor'zare [rinfor'tsare] vt to reinforce, strengthen ♦ vi (anche: **~rsi**) to grow stronger; **rin'forzo** sm: **mettere un rinforzo a** to strengthen; **di rinforzo** (asse, sbarra) strengthening; (esercito) supporting; (personale) extra, additional; **rinforzi** smpl (MIL) reinforcements

rinfran'care vt to encourage, reassure

rinfres'care vt (atmosfera, temperatura) to cool (down); (abito, pareti) to freshen up

♦ *vi (tempo)* to grow cooler; **~rsi** *vr (ristorarsi)* to refresh o.s.; *(lavarsi)* to freshen up; **rin'fresco, schi** *sm (festa)* party; **rinfreschi** *smpl* refreshments

rin'fusa *sf:* **alla ~** in confusion, higgledy-piggledy

ringhi'are [rin'gjare] *vi* to growl, snarl

ringhi'era [rin'gjɛra] *sf* railing; *(delle scale)* banister(s *pl*)

ringiova'nire [rindʒova'nire] *vt (sog: vestito, acconciatura etc):* **~ qn** to make sb look younger; *(: vacanze etc)* to rejuvenate ♦ *vi (anche:* **~rsi***)* to become *(o* look*)* younger

ringrazia'mento [ringrattsja'mento] *sm* thanks *pl*

ringrazi'are [ringrat'tsjare] *vt* to thank; **~ qn di qc** to thank sb for sth

rinne'gare *vt (fede)* to renounce; *(figlio)* to disown, repudiate; **rinne'gato, a** *sm/f* renegade

rinnova'mento *sm* renewal; *(economico)* revival

rinno'vare *vt* to renew; *(ripetere)* to repeat, renew; **rin'novo** *sm (di contratto)* renewal; **"chiuso per rinnovo dei locali"** "closed for alterations"

rinoce'ronte [rinotʃe'ronte] *sm* rhinoceros

rino'mato, a *ag* renowned, celebrated

rinsal'dare *vt* to strengthen

rintoc'care *vi (campana)* to toll; *(orologio)* to strike

rintracci'are [rintrat'tʃare] *vt* to track down

rintro'nare *vi* to boom, roar ♦ *vt (assordare)* to deafen; *(stordire)* to stun

ri'nuncia [ri'nuntʃa] *etc* = **rinunzia** *etc*

ri'nunzia [ri'nuntsja] *sf* renunciation

rinunzi'are [rinun'tsjare] *vi:* **~ a** to give up, renounce

rinve'nire *vt* to find, recover; *(scoprire)* to discover, find out ♦ *vi (riprendere i sensi)* to come round; *(fiori)* to revive

rinvi'are *vt (rimandare indietro)* to send back, return; *(differire):* **~ qc (a)** to postpone sth *o* put sth off (till); to adjourn sth (till); *(fare un rimando):* **~ qn a** to refer sb to

rinvigo'rire *vt* to strengthen

rin'vio, 'vii *sm (rimando)* return; *(differimento)* postponement; *(: di seduta)* adjournment; *(in un testo)* cross-reference

ri'one *sm* district, quarter

riordi'nare *vt (rimettere in ordine)* to tidy; *(riorganizzare)* to reorganize

riorganiz'zare [riorganid'dzare] *vt* to reorganize

ripa'gare *vt* to repay

ripa'rare *vt (proteggere)* to protect, defend; *(correggere: male, torto)* to make up for; *(: errore)* to put right; *(aggiustare)* to repair ♦ *vi (mettere rimedio):* **~ a** to make up for; **~rsi** *vr (rifugiarsi)* to take refuge *o* shelter; **riparazi'one** *sf (di un torto)* reparation; *(di guasto, scarpe)* repairing *no pl*; repair; *(risarcimento)* compensation

ri'paro *sm (protezione)* shelter, protection; *(rimedio)* remedy

ripar'tire *vt (dividere)* to divide up; *(distribuire)* to share out ♦ *vi* to set off again; to leave again

ripas'sare *vi* to come *(o* go*)* back ♦ *vt (scritto, lezione)* to go over (again); **ri'passo** *sm* revision (*BRIT*), review (*US*)

ripen'sare *vi* to think; *(cambiare pensiero)* to change one's mind; *(tornare col pensiero):* **~ a** to recall

ripercu'otersi *vr:* **~ su** *(fig)* to have repercussions on

ripercussi'one *sf (fig):* **avere una ~** *o* **delle ~i su** to have repercussions on

ripes'care *vt (pesce)* to catch again; *(persona, cosa)* to fish out; *(fig: ritrovare)* to dig out

ri'petere *vt* to repeat; *(ripassare)* to go over; **ripetizi'one** *sf* repetition; *(di lezione)* revision; **ripetizioni** *sfpl (INS)* private tutoring *o* coaching *sg*

ripi'ano *sm (di mobile)* shelf

ri'picca *sf:* **per ~** out of spite

'ripido, a *ag* steep

ripie'gare *vt* to refold; *(piegare più volte)* to fold (up) ♦ *vi (MIL)* to retreat, fall back; *(fig: accontentarsi):* **~ su** to make do with; **~rsi** *vr* to bend; **ripi'ego, ghi** *sm* expedient

ripi'eno, a *ag* full; (*CUC*) stuffed; (: *panino*) filled ♦ *sm* (*CUC*) stuffing

ri'porre *vt* (*porre al suo posto*) to put back, replace; (*mettere via*) to put away; (*fiducia, speranza*): ~ **qc in qn** to place *o* put sth in sb

ripor'tare *vt* (*portare indietro*) to bring (*o* take) back; (*riferire*) to report; (*citare*) to quote; (*vittoria*) to gain; (*successo*) to have; (*MAT*) to carry; **~rsi a** (*anche fig*) to go back to; (*riferirsi a*) to refer to; ~ **danni** to suffer damage

ripo'sare *vt, vi* to rest; **~rsi** *vr* to rest; **ri'poso** *sm* rest; (*MIL*): **riposo!** at ease!; **a riposo** (*in pensione*) retired; **giorno di riposo** day off

ripos'tiglio [ripos'tiʎʎo] *sm* lumber-room

ri'posto, a *pp di* **riporre**

ri'prendere *vt* (*prigioniero, fortezza*) to recapture; (*prendere indietro*) to take back; (*ricominciare: lavoro*) to resume; (*andare a prendere*) to fetch, come back for; (*riassumere: impiegati*) to take on again, re-employ; (*rimproverare*) to tell off; (*restringere: abito*) to take in; (*CINEMA*) to shoot; **~rsi** *vr* to recover; (*correggersi*) to correct o.s.; **ri'presa** *sf* recapture; resumption; (*economica, da malattia, emozione*) recovery; (*AUT*) acceleration *no pl*; (*TEATRO, CINEMA*) rerun; (*CINEMA: presa*) shooting *no pl*; shot; (*SPORT*) second half; (: *PUGILATO*) round; **a più riprese** on several occasions, several times; **ripreso, a** *pp di* **riprendere**

ripristi'nare *vt* to restore

ripro'durre *vt* to reproduce; **riprodursi** *vr* (*BIOL*) to reproduce; (*riformarsi*) to form again; **riproduzi'one** *sf* reproduction; **riproduzione vietata** all rights reserved

ripudi'are *vt* to repudiate, disown

ripu'gnante [ripuɲ'ɲante] *ag* disgusting, repulsive

ripu'gnare [ripuɲ'ɲare] *vi*: ~ **a qn** to repel *o* disgust sb

ripu'lire *vt* to clean up; (*sog: ladri*) to clean out; (*perfezionare*) to polish, refine

ri'quadro *sm* square; (*ARCHIT*) panel

ri'saia *sf* paddy field

risa'lire *vi* (*ritornare in su*) to go back up; ~ **a** (*ritornare con la mente*) to go back to; (*datare da*) to date back to, go back to

risal'tare *vi* (*fig: distinguersi*) to stand out; (*ARCHIT*) to project, jut out; **ri'salto** *sm* prominence; (*sporgenza*) projection; **mettere** *o* **porre in risalto qc** to make sth stand out

risa'nare *vt* (*guarire*) to heal, cure; (*palude*) to reclaim; (*economia*) to improve; (*bilancio*) to reorganize

risa'puto, a *ag*: **è ~ che ...** everyone knows that ..., it is common knowledge that ...

risarci'mento [risartʃi'mento] *sm*: ~ **(di)** compensation (for)

risar'cire [risar'tʃire] *vt* (*cose*) to pay compensation for; (*persona*): ~ **qn di qc** to compensate sb for sth

ri'sata *sf* laugh

riscalda'mento *sm* heating; ~ **centrale** central heating

riscal'dare *vt* (*scaldare*) to heat; (: *mani, persona*) to warm; (*minestra*) to reheat; **~rsi** *vr* to warm up

riscat'tare *vt* (*prigioniero*) to ransom, pay a ransom for; (*DIR*) to redeem; **~rsi** *vr* (*da disonore*) to redeem o.s.; **ris'catto** *sm* ransom; redemption

rischia'rare [riskja'rare] *vt* (*illuminare*) to light up; (*colore*) to make lighter; **~rsi** *vr* (*tempo*) to clear up; (*cielo*) to clear; (*fig: volto*) to brighten up; **~rsi la voce** to clear one's throat

rischi'are [ris'kjare] *vt* to risk ♦ *vi*: ~ **di fare qc** to risk *o* run the risk of doing sth

'rischio ['riskjo] *sm* risk; **rischi'oso, a** *ag* risky, dangerous

riscia'cquare [riʃʃa'kware] *vt* to rinse

riscon'trare *vt* (*rilevare*) to find; **ris'contro** *sm* confirmation; (*lettera di risposta*) reply

ris'cossa *sf* (*riconquista*) recovery, reconquest; *vedi anche* **riscosso**

riscossi'one *sf* collection

ris'cosso, a *pp di* **riscuotere**

ris'cuotere *vt* (*ritirare: somma*) to collect; (: *stipendio*) to draw, collect; (*assegno*) to cash; (*fig: successo etc*) to win, earn; **~rsi** *vr*: **~rsi (da)** to shake o.s. (out of), rouse o.s. (from)

risenti'mento *sm* resentment

risen'tire *vt* to hear again; (*provare*) to feel ♦ *vi*: **~ di** to feel (*o* show) the effects of; **~rsi** *vr*: **~rsi di** *o* **per** to take offence at, resent

risen'tito, a *ag* resentful

ri'serbo *sm* reserve

ri'serva *sf* reserve; (*di caccia, pesca*) preserve; (*restrizione, di indigeni*) reservation; **di ~** (*provviste etc*) in reserve

riser'vare *vt* (*tenere in serbo*) to keep, put aside; (*prenotare*) to book, reserve; **~rsi** *vr*: **~rsi di fare qc** to intend to do sth

riserva'tezza *sf* reserve

riser'vato, a *ag* (*prenotato, fig: persona*) reserved; (*confidenziale*) confidential

risi'edere *vi*: **~ a** *o* **in** to reside in

'risma *sf* (*di carta*) ream; (*fig*) kind, sort

'riso (*pl(f)* **~a**: *il ridere*) *sm*: **il ~** laughter; (*pianta*) rice ♦ *pp di* **ridere**

riso'lino *sm* snigger

ri'solto, a *pp di* **risolvere**

risolu'tezza [risolu'tettsa] *sf* determinazione

riso'luto, a *ag* determined, resolute

risoluzi'one [risolut'tsjone] *sf* solving *no pl*; (MAT) solution; (*decisione, di immagine*) resolution

ri'solvere *vt* (*difficoltà, controversia*) to resolve; (*problema*) to solve; (*decidere*): **~ di fare** to resolve to do; **~rsi** *vr* (*decidersi*): **~rsi a fare** to make up one's mind to do; (*andare a finire*): **~rsi in** to end up, turn out; **~rsi in nulla** to come to nothing

riso'nanza [riso'nantsa] *sf* resonance; **aver vasta ~** (*fig: fatto etc*) to be known far and wide

riso'nare *vt, vi* = **risuonare**

ri'sorgere [ri'sordʒere] *vi* to rise again; **risorgi'mento** *sm* revival; **il Risorgimento** (STORIA) the Risorgimento

ri'sorsa *sf* expedient, resort; **~e** *sfpl* (*naturali, finanziarie etc*) resources; **persona piena di ~e** resourceful person

ri'sorto, a *pp di* **risorgere**

ri'sotto *sm* (CUC) risotto

risparmi'are *vt* to save; (*non uccidere*) to spare ♦ *vi* to save; **~ qc a qn** to spare sb sth

ris'parmio *sm* saving *no pl*; (*denaro*) savings *pl*

rispec'chiare [rispek'kjare] *vt* to reflect

rispet'tabile *ag* respectable

rispet'tare *vt* to respect; **farsi ~** to command respect

rispet'tivo, a *ag* respective

ris'petto *sm* respect; **~i** *smpl* (*saluti*) respects, regards; **~ a** (*in paragone a*) compared to; (*in relazione a*) as regards, as for; **rispet'toso, a** *ag* respectful

ris'plendere *vi* to shine

ris'pondere *vi* to answer, reply; (*freni*) to respond; **~ a** (*domanda*) to answer, reply to, (*persona*) to answer; (*invito*) to reply to; (*provocazione, sog: veicolo, apparecchio*) to respond to; (*corrispondere a*) to correspond to; (: *speranze, bisogno*) to answer; **~ di** to answer for; **ris'posta** *sf* answer, reply; **in risposta a** in reply to; **risposto, a** *pp di* **rispondere**

'rissa *sf* brawl

ristabi'lire *vt* to re-establish, restore; (*persona: sog: riposo etc*) to restore to health; **~rsi** *vr* to recover

rista'gnare [ristan'ɲare] *vi* (*acqua*) to become stagnant; (*sangue*) to cease flowing; (*fig: industria*) to stagnate; **ris'tagno** *sm* stagnation

ris'tampa *sf* reprinting *no pl*; reprint

risto'rante *sm* restaurant

risto'rarsi *vr* to have something to eat and

drink; (*riposarsi*) to rest, have a rest;
ris'toro *sm* (*bevanda, cibo*) refreshment;
servizio di ristoro (*FERR*) refreshments *pl*
ristret'tezza [ristret'tettsa] *sf* (*strettezza*)
narrowness; (*fig: scarsezza*) scarcity, lack;
(*: meschinità*) meanness; **~e** *sfpl* (*povertà*)
financial straits
ris'tretto, a *pp di* **restringere ♦** *ag*
(*racchiuso*) enclosed, hemmed in; (*angusto*)
narrow; (*limitato*): **~ (a)** restricted *o* limited
(to); (*CUC: brodo*) thick; (*: caffè*) extra
strong
risucchi'are [risuk'kjare] *vt* to suck in
risul'tare *vi* (*dimostrarsi*) to prove (to be),
turn out (to be); (*riuscire*): **~ vincitore** to
emerge as the winner; **~ da** (*provenire*) to
result from, be the result of; **mi risulta che
...** I understand that ...; **non mi risulta** not
as far as I know; **risul'tato** *sm* result
risuo'nare *vi* (*rimbombare*) to resound
risurrezi'one [risurret'tsjone] *sf* (*REL*)
resurrection
risusci'tare [risuʃʃi'tare] *vt* to resuscitate,
restore to life; (*fig*) to revive, bring back
♦ *vi* to rise (from the dead)
ris'veglio [riz'veʎʎo] *sm* waking up; (*fig*)
revival
ris'volto *sm* (*di giacca*) lapel; (*di
pantaloni*) turn-up; (*di manica*) cuff; (*di
tasca*) flap; (*di libro*) inside flap; (*fig*)
implication
ritagli'are [ritaʎ'ʎare] *vt* (*tagliar via*) to cut
out; **ri'taglio** *sm* (*di giornale*) cutting,
clipping; (*di stoffa etc*) scrap; **nei ritagli di
tempo** in one's spare time
ritar'dare *vi* (*persona, treno*) to be late;
(*orologio*) to be slow **♦** *vt* (*rallentare*) to
slow down; (*impedire*) to delay, hold up;
(*differire*) to postpone, delay;
ritarda'tario, a *sm/f* latecomer
ri'tardo *sm* delay; (*di persona aspettata*)
lateness *no pl*; (*fig: mentale*) backwardness;
in ~ late
ri'tegno [ri'teɲɲo] *sm* restraint
rite'nere *vt* (*trattenere*) to hold back;
(*: somma*) to deduct; (*giudicare*) to
consider, believe; **rite'nuta** *sf* (*sul salario*)

deduction
riti'rare *vt* to withdraw; (*POL: richiamare*) to
recall; (*andare a prendere: pacco etc*) to
collect, pick up; **~rsi** *vr* to withdraw; (*da
un'attività*) to retire; (*stoffa*) to shrink;
(*marea*) to recede; **riti'rata** *sf* (*MIL*) retreat;
(*latrina*) lavatory; **ri'tiro** *sm* withdrawal;
recall; collection; (*luogo appartato*) retreat
'ritmo *sm* rhythm; (*fig*) rate; (*: della vita*)
pace, tempo
'rito *sm* rite; **di ~** usual, customary
ritoc'care *vt* (*disegno, fotografia*) to touch
up; (*testo*) to alter; **ri'tocco, chi** *sm*
touching up *no pl*; alteration
ritor'nare *vi* to return, go (*o come*) back;
(*ripresentarsi*) to recur; (*ridiventare*): **~ ricco**
to become rich again **♦** *vt* (*restituire*) to
return, give back
ritor'nello *sm* refrain
ri'torno *sm* return; **essere di ~** to be back;
avere un ~ di fiamma (*AUT*) to backfire;
(*fig: persona*) to be back in love again
ritorsi'one *sf* retaliation
ri'trarre *vt* (*trarre indietro, via*) to withdraw;
(*distogliere: sguardo*) to turn away;
(*rappresentare*) to portray, depict; (*ricavare*)
to get, obtain
ritrat'tare *vt* (*disdire*) to retract, take back;
(*trattare nuovamente*) to deal with again
ri'tratto, a *pp di* **ritrarre ♦** *sm* portrait
ri'troso, a *ag* (*restio*): **~ (a)** reluctant (to);
(*schivo*) shy; **andare a ~** to go backwards
ritro'vare *vt* to find; (*salute*) to regain;
(*persona*) to find; to meet again; **~rsi** *vr*
(*essere, capitare*) to find o.s.; (*raccapezzarsi*)
to find one's way; (*con senso reciproco*) to
meet (again); **ri'trovo** *sm* meeting place;
ritrovo notturno night club
'ritto, a *ag* (*in piedi*) standing, on one's
feet; (*levato in alto*) erect, raised; (*: capelli*)
standing on end; (*posto verticalmente*)
upright
ritu'ale *ag, sm* ritual
riuni'one *sf* (*adunanza*) meeting;
(*riconciliazione*) reunion
riu'nire *vt* (*ricongiungere*) to join (together);
(*riconciliare*) to reunite, bring together

(again); **~rsi** *vr (adunarsi)* to meet; *(tornare insieme)* to be reunited

riu'scire [riuʃˈʃire] *vi (uscire di nuovo)* to go out again, go back out; *(aver esito: fatti, azioni)* to go, turn out; *(aver successo)* to succeed, be successful; *(essere, apparire)* to be, prove; *(raggiungere il fine)* to manage, succeed; **~ a fare qc** to manage to do *o* succeed in doing *o* be able to do sth; **riu'scita** *sf (esito)* result, outcome; *(buon esito)* success

'riva *sf (di fiume)* bank; *(di lago, mare)* shore

ri'vale *sm/f* rival; **rivalità** *sf* rivalry

ri'valsa *sf (rivincita)* revenge

rivalu'tare *vt (ECON)* to revalue

rivan'gare *vt (ricordi etc)* to dig up (again)

rive'dere *vt* to see again; *(ripassare)* to revise; *(verificare)* to check

rive'lare *vt* to reveal; *(divulgare)* to reveal, disclose; *(dare indizio)* to reveal, show; **~rsi** *vr (manifestarsi)* to be revealed; **~rsi onesto** etc to prove to be honest etc; **rivela'tore** *sm (TECN)* detector; *(FOT)* developer; **rivelazi'one** *sf* revelation

rivendi'care *vt* to claim, demand

ri'vendita *sf (bottega)* retailer's (shop)

rivendi'tore, 'trice *sm/f* retailer; **~ autorizzato** *(COMM)* authorized dealer

ri'verbero *sm (di luce, calore)* reflection; *(di suono)* reverberation

rive'renza [rive'rɛntsa] *sf* reverence; *(inchino)* bow; curtsey

rive'rire *vt (rispettare)* to revere; *(salutare)* to pay one's respects to

river'sare *vt (anche fig)* to pour; **~rsi** *vr (fig: persone)* to pour out

rivesti'mento *sm* covering; coating

rives'tire *vt* to dress again; *(ricoprire)* to cover; to coat; *(fig: carica)* to hold; **~rsi** *vr* to get dressed again; to change (one's clothes)

rivi'era *sf* coast; **la ~ ligure** the Italian Riviera

ri'vincita [ri'vintʃita] *sf (SPORT)* return match; *(fig)* revenge

rivis'suto, a *pp di* **rivivere**

ri'vista *sf* review; *(periodico)* magazine, review; *(TEATRO)* revue; variety show

ri'vivere *vi (riacquistare forza)* to come alive again; *(tornare in uso)* to be revived ♦ *vt* to relive

ri'volgere [ri'voldʒere] *vt (attenzione, sguardo)* to turn, direct; *(parole)* to address; **~rsi** *vr* to turn round; *(fig: dirigersi per informazioni)*: **~rsi a** to go and see, go and speak to; *(: ufficio)* to enquire at

ri'volta *sf* revolt, rebellion

rivol'tare *vt* to turn over; *(con l'interno all'esterno)* to turn inside out; *(disgustare: stomaco)* to upset, turn; **~rsi** *vr (ribellarsi)*: **~rsi (a)** to rebel (against)

rivol'tella *sf* revolver

ri'volto, a *pp di* **rivolgere**

rivoluzio'nare [rivoluttsjo'nare] *vt* to revolutionize

rivoluzio'nario, a [rivoluttsjo'narjo] *ag, sm/f* revolutionary

rivoluzi'one [rivolut'tsjone] *sf* revolution

riz'zare [rit'tsare] *vt* to raise, erect; **~rsi** *vr* to stand up; *(capelli)* to stand on end

'roba *sf* stuff, things *pl*; *(possessi, beni)* belongings *pl*, things *pl*, possessions *pl*; **~ da mangiare** things *pl* to eat, food; **~ da matti** sheer madness *o* lunacy

'robot *sm inv* robot

ro'busto, a *ag* robust, sturdy; *(solido: catena)* strong

'rocca, che *sf* fortress

'rocca'forte *sf* stronghold

roc'chetto [rok'ketto] *sm* reel, spool

'roccia, ce ['rɔttʃa] *sf* rock; **fare ~** *(SPORT)* to go rock climbing; **roc'cioso, a** *ag* rocky

ro'daggio [ro'daddʒo] *sm* running *(BRIT) o* breaking *(US)* in; **in ~** running *(BRIT) o* breaking *(US)* in

'Rodano *sm*: **il ~** the Rhone

'rodere *vt* to gnaw (at); *(distruggere poco a poco)* to eat into

rodi'tore *sm (ZOOL)* rodent

rodo'dendro *sm* rhododendron

'rogna ['rɔɲɲa] *sf (MED)* scabies *sg*; *(fig)* bother, nuisance ro'gnone [roɲ'ɲone] *sm* (*CUC*) kidney

'rogo, ghi *sm* (*per cadaveri*) (funeral) pyre; (*supplizio*): il ~ the stake

rol'lio *sm* roll(ing)

'Roma *sf* Rome

Roma'nia *sf*: la ~ Romania

ro'manico, a, ci, che *ag* Romanesque

ro'mano, a *ag, sm/f* Roman

romanti'cismo [romanti'tʃizmo] *sm* romanticism

ro'mantico, a, ci, che *ag* romantic

ro'manza [ro'mandza] *sf* (*MUS, LETTERATURA*) romance

roman'zesco, a, schi, sche [roman'dzesko] *ag* (*stile, personaggi*) fictional; (*fig*) storybook *cpd*

romanzi'ere [roman'dzjere] *sm* novelist

ro'manzo, a [ro'mandzo] *ag* (*LING*) romance *cpd* ♦ *sm* novel; ~ d'appendice serial (story)

rom'bare *vi* to rumble, thunder, roar

'rombo *sm* rumble, thunder, roar; (*MAT*) rhombus; (*ZOOL*) turbot; brill

ro'meno, a *ag, sm/f, sm* = rumeno, a

'rompere *vt* to break; (*fidanzamento*) to break off ♦ *vi* to break; ~rsi *vr* to break; mi rompe le scatole (*fam*) he (*o* she) is a pain in the neck; ~rsi un braccio to break an arm; rompi'capo *sm* worry, headache; (*indovinello*) puzzle; (*in enigmistica*) brainteaser; rompighi'accio *sm* (*NAUT*) icebreaker; rompis'catole (*fam*) *sm/f inv* pest, pain in the neck

'ronda *sf* (*MIL*) rounds *pl*, patrol

ron'della *sf* (*TECN*) washer

'rondine *sf* (*ZOOL*) swallow

ron'done *sm* (*ZOOL*) swift

ron'zare [ron'dzare] *vi* to buzz, hum

ron'zino [ron'dzino] *sm* (*peg: cavallo*) nag

ron'zio [ron'dzio] *sm* buzzing

'rosa *sf* rose ♦ *ag inv, sm* pink; ro'saio *sm* (*pianta*) rosebush, rose tree; (*giardino*) rose garden; ro'sario *sm* (*REL*) rosary; ro'sato, a *ag* pink, rosy ♦ *sm* (*vino*) rosé (wine); ro'seo, a *ag* (*anche fig*) rosy

rosicchi'are [rosik'kjare] *vt* to gnaw (at); (*mangiucchiare*) to nibble (at)

rosma'rino *sm* rosemary

'roso, a *pp di* rodere

roso'lare *vt* (*CUC*) to brown

roso'lia *sf* (*MED*) German measles *sg*, rubella

ro'sone *sm* rosette; (*vetrata*) rose window

'rospo *sm* (*ZOOL*) toad

ros'setto *sm* (*per labbra*) lipstick

'rosso, a *ag, sm, sm/f* red; il mar R~ the Red Sea; ~ d'uovo egg yolk; ros'sore *sm* flush, blush

rosticce'ria [rostittʃe'ria] *sf* shop selling roast meat and other cooked food

ro'tabile *ag* (*percorribile*): strada ~ roadway; (*FERR*): materiale ~ rolling stock

ro'taia *sf* rut, track; (*FERR*) rail

ro'tare *vt, vi* to rotate; rotazi'one *sf* rotation

rote'are *vt, vi* to whirl; ~ gli occhi to roll one's eyes

ro'tella *sf* small wheel; (*di mobile*) castor

roto'lare *vt, vi* to roll; ~rsi *vr* to roll (about)

'rotolo *sm* roll; andare a ~i (*fig*) to go to rack and ruin

ro'tonda *sf* rotunda

ro'tondo, a *ag* round

'rotta *sf* (*AER, NAUT*) course, route; (*MIL*) rout; a ~ di collo at breakneck speed; essere in ~ con qn to be on bad terms with sb

rot'tame *sm* fragment, scrap, broken bit; ~i *smpl* (*di nave, aereo etc*) wreckage *sg*

'rotto, a *pp di* rompere ♦ *ag* broken; (*calzoni*) torn, split; per il ~ della cuffia by the skin of one's teeth

rot'tura *sf* breaking *no pl*; break; breaking off; (*MED*) fracture, break

rou'lotte [ru'lɔt] *sf* caravan

ro'vente *ag* red-hot

'rovere *sm* oak

rovesci'are [rovef'ʃare] *vt* (*versare in giù*) to pour; (: *accidentalmente*) to spill; (*capovolgere*) to turn upside down; (*gettare a terra*) to knock down; (: *fig: governo*) to overthrow; (*piegare all'indietro: testa*) to throw back; ~rsi *vr* (*sedia, macchina*) to overturn; *(barca)* to capsize; *(liquido)* to spill; *(fig: situazione)* to be reversed

ro'vescio, sci [ro'veʃʃo] *sm* other side, wrong side; *(della mano)* back; *(di moneta)* reverse; *(pioggia)* sudden downpour; *(fig)* setback; *(MAGLIA: anche:* **punto ~)** purl (stitch); *(TENNIS)* backhand (stroke); **a ~** upside-down; inside-out; **capire qc a ~** to misunderstand sth

ro'vina *sf* ruin; **andare in ~** *(andare a pezzi)* to collapse; *(fig)* to go to rack and ruin

rovi'nare *vi* to collapse, fall down ♦ *vt* *(danneggiare, fig)* to ruin; **rovi'noso, a** *ag* disastrous; damaging; violent

rovis'tare *vt (casa)* to ransack; *(tasche)* to rummage in *(o* through)

'rovo *sm (BOT)* blackberry bush, bramble bush

'rozzo, a ['roddzo] *ag* rough, coarse

'ruba *sf:* **andare a ~** to sell like hot cakes

ru'bare *vt* to steal; **~ qc a qn** to steal sth from sb

rubi'netto *sm* tap, faucet *(US)*

ru'bino *sm* ruby

ru'brica, che *sf (STAMPA)* column; *(quadernetto)* index book; address book

'rude *ag* tough, rough

'rudere *sm (rovina)* ruins *pl*

rudimen'tale *ag* rudimentary, basic

rudi'menti *smpl* rudiments; basic principles; basic knowledge *sg*

ruffi'ano *sm* pimp

'ruga, ghe *sf* wrinkle

'ruggine ['ruddʒine] *sf* rust

rug'gire [rud'dʒire] *vi* to roar

rugi'ada [ru'dʒada] *sf* dew

ru'goso, a *ag* wrinkled

rul'lare *vi (tamburo, nave)* to roll; *(aereo)* to taxi

rul'lino *sm (FOT)* spool; *(: pellicola)* film

'rullo *sm (di tamburi)* roll; *(arnese cilindrico, TIP)* roller; **~ compressore** steam roller; **~ di pellicola** roll of film

rum *sm* rum

ru'meno, a *ag, sm/f, sm* Romanian

rumi'nare *vt (ZOOL)* to ruminate

ru'more *sm:* **un ~** a noise, a sound; *(fig)* a rumour; **il ~** noise; **rumo'roso, a** *ag* noisy

ru'olo *sm (TEATRO, fig)* role, part; *(elenco)* roll, register, list; **di ~** permanent, on the permanent staff

ru'ota *sf* wheel; **~ anteriore / posteriore** front/back wheel; **~ di scorta** spare wheel

ruo'tare *vt, vi* = **rotare**

'rupe *sf* cliff

ru'rale *ag* rural, country *cpd*

ru'scello [ruʃ'ʃello] *sm* stream

'ruspa *sf* excavator

rus'sare *vi* to snore

'Russia *sf:* **la ~** Russia; **'russo, a** *ag, sm/f, sm* Russian

'rustico, a, ci, che *ag* rustic; *(fig)* rough, unrefined

rut'tare *vi* to belch; **'rutto** *sm* belch

'ruvido, a *ag* rough, coarse

ruzzo'lare [ruttso'lare] *vi* to tumble down; **ruzzo'loni** *av:* **cadere ruzzoloni** to tumble down

S, s

S. *abbr* (= *sud*) S

sa *vb vedi* **sapere**

'sabato *sm* Saturday; **di** *o* **il ~** on Saturdays

'sabbia *sf* sand; **~e mobili** quicksand(s); **sabbi'oso, a** *ag* sandy

sabo'taggio [sabo'taddʒo] *sm* sabotage

sabo'tare *vt* to sabotage

'sacca, che *sf* bag; *(bisaccia)* haversack; **~ da viaggio** travelling bag

sacca'rina *sf* saccharin(e)

sac'cente [sat'tʃente] *sm/f* know-all *(BRIT)*, know-it-all *(US)*

saccheggi'are [sakked'dʒare] *vt* to sack, plunder; **sac'cheggio** *sm* sack(ing)

sac'chetto [sak'ketto] *sm* (small) bag; (small) sack

'sacco, chi *sm* bag; *(per carbone etc)* sack; *(ANAT, BIOL)* sac; *(tela)* sacking; *(saccheggio)* sack(ing); *(fig: grande quantità):* **un ~ di** lots of, heaps of; **~ a pelo** sleeping bag; **~ per i rifiuti** bin bag

sacer'dote [satʃer'dɔte] *sm* priest;
 sacer'dozio *sm* priesthood
sacra'mento *sm* sacrament
sacrifi'care *vt* to sacrifice; **~rsi** *vr* to
 sacrifice o.s.; (*privarsi di qc*) to make
 sacrifices
sacri'ficio [sakri'fitʃo] *sm* sacrifice
sacri'legio [sacri'ledʒo] *sm* sacrilege
'sacro, a *ag* sacred
'sadico, a, ci, che *ag* sadistic ♦ *sm/f*
 sadist
sa'etta *sf* arrow; (*fulmine: anche fig*)
 thunderbolt; flash of lightning
sa'fari *sm inv* safari
sa'gace [sa'gatʃe] *ag* shrewd, sagacious
sag'gezza [sad'dʒettsa] *sf* wisdom
saggi'are [sad'dʒare] *vt* (*metalli*) to assay;
 (*fig*) to test
'saggio, a, gi, ge ['saddʒo] *ag* wise ♦ *sm*
 (*persona*) sage; (*esperimento*) test; (*fig:
 prova*) proof; (*campione*) sample; (*scritto*)
 essay
Sagit'tario [sadʒit'tarjo] *sm* Sagittarius
'sagoma *sf* (*profilo*) outline, profile; (*forma*)
 form, shape; (*TECN*) template; (*bersaglio*)
 target; (*fig: persona*) character
'sagra *sf* festival
sagres'tano *sm* sacristan; sexton
sagres'tia *sf* sacristy
Sa'hara [sa'ara] *sm*: **il (deserto del) ~** the
 Sahara (Desert)
'sai *vb vedi* **sapere**
'sala *sf* hall; (*stanza*) room; **~ d'aspetto**
 waiting room; **~ da ballo** ballroom; **~ per
 concerti** concert hall; **~ da gioco** gaming
 room; **~ operatoria** operating theatre; **~
 da pranzo** dining room
sa'lame *sm* salami *no pl*, salami sausage
sala'moia *sf* (*CUC*) brine
sa'lare *vt* to salt
sa'lario *sm* pay, wages *pl*
sa'lato, a *ag* (*sapore*) salty; (*CUC*) salted,
 salt *cpd*; (*fig: prezzo*) steep, stiff
sal'dare *vt* (*congiungere*) to join, bind;
 (*parti metalliche*) to solder; (: *con saldatura
 autogena*) to weld; (*conto*) to settle, pay;
 salda'tura *sf* soldering; welding; (*punto

 saldato*) soldered joint; weld
sal'dezza [sal'dettsa] *sf* firmness; strength
'saldo, a *ag* (*resistente, forte*) strong, firm;
 (*fermo*) firm, steady, stable; (*fig*) firm,
 steadfast ♦ *sm* (*svendita*) sale; (*di conto*)
 settlement; (*ECON*) balance
'sale *sm* salt; (*fig*): **ha poco ~ in zucca** he
 doesn't have much sense; **~ fino/grosso**
 table/cooking salt
'salice ['salitʃe] *sm* willow; **~ piangente**
 weeping willow
sali'ente *ag* (*fig*) salient, main
sali'era *sf* salt cellar
sa'lina *sf* saltworks *sg*
sa'lino, a *ag* saline
sa'lire *vi* to go (*o come*) up; (*aereo etc*) to
 climb, go up; (*passeggero*) to get on;
 (*sentiero, prezzi, livello*) to go up, rise ♦ *vt*
 (*scale, gradini*) to go (*o come*) up; **~ su** to
 climb (up); **~ sul treno/sull'autobus** to
 board the train/the bus; **~ in macchina** to
 get into the car; **sa'lita** *sf* climb, ascent;
 (*erta*) hill, slope; **in salita** *ag, av* uphill
sa'liva *sf* saliva
'salma *sf* corpse
'salmo *sm* psalm
sal'mone *sm* salmon
sa'lone *sm* (*stanza*) sitting room, lounge;
 (*in albergo*) lounge; (*su nave*) lounge,
 saloon; (*mostra*) show, exhibition; **~ di
 bellezza** beauty salon
sa'lotto *sm* lounge, sitting room; (*mobilio*)
 lounge suite
sal'pare *vi* (*NAUT*) to set sail; (*anche*: **~
 l'ancora**) to weigh anchor
'salsa *sf* (*CUC*) sauce; **~ di pomodoro**
 tomato sauce
sal'siccia, ce [sal'sittʃa] *sf* pork sausage
sal'tare *vi* to jump, leap; (*esplodere*) to
 blow up, explode; (: *valvola*) to blow;
 (*venir via*) to pop off; (*non aver luogo: corso
 etc*) to be cancelled ♦ *vt* to jump (over),
 leap (over); (*fig: pranzo, capitolo*) to skip,
 miss (out); (*CUC*) to sauté; **far ~** to blow
 up; to burst open; **~ fuori** (*fig: apparire
 all'improvviso*) to turn up
saltel'lare *vi* to skip; to hop

saltim'banco *sm* acrobat

'**salto** *sm* jump; (*SPORT*) jumping; **fare un ~** to jump, leap; **fare un ~ da qn** to pop over to sb's (place); **~ in alto/lungo** high/long jump; **~ con l'asta** pole vaulting; **~ mortale** somersault

saltu'ario, a *ag* occasional, irregular

sa'lubre *ag* healthy, salubrious

salume'ria *sf* delicatessen

sa'lumi *smpl* salted pork meats

salu'tare *ag* healthy; (*fig*) salutary, beneficial ♦ *vt* (*incontrandosi*) to greet; (*congedandosi*) to say goodbye to; (*MIL*) to salute

sa'lute *sf* health; **~!** (*a chi starnutisce*) bless you!; (*nei brindisi*) cheers!; **bere alla ~ di qn** to drink (to) sb's health

sa'luto *sm* (*gesto*) wave; (*parola*) greeting; (*MIL*) salute; **~i** *smpl* (*formula di cortesia*) greetings; **cari ~i** best regards; **vogliate gradire i nostri più distinti ~i** Yours faithfully

salvacon'dotto *sm* (*MIL*) safe conduct

salva'gente [salva'dʒɛnte] *sm* (*NAUT*) lifebuoy; (*ciambella*) life belt; (*giubbotto*) lifejacket; (*stradale*) traffic island

salvaguar'dare *vt* to safeguard

sal'vare *vt* to save; (*trarre da un pericolo*) to rescue; (*proteggere*) to protect; **~rsi** *vr* to save o.s.; to escape; **salva'taggio** *sm* rescue; **salva'tore, 'trice** *sm/f* saviour

'**salve** (*fam*) *escl* hi!

sal'vezza [sal'vettsa] *sf* salvation; (*sicurezza*) safety

'**salvia** *sf* (*BOT*) sage

salvi'etta *sf* napkin; **~ umidificata** baby wipe

'**salvo, a** *ag* safe, unhurt, unharmed; (*fuori pericolo*) safe, out of danger ♦ *sm*: **in ~** to save; **mettere qc in ~** to put sth in a safe place; **~ che** (*a meno che*) unless; (*eccetto che*) except (that); **~ imprevisti** barring accidents

sam'buco *sm* elder (tree)

san *ag* *vedi* **santo**

sa'nare *vt* to heal, cure; (*economia*) to put right

san'cire [san'tʃire] *vt* to sanction

'**sandalo** *sm* (*BOT*) sandalwood; (*calzatura*) sandal

'**sangue** *sm* blood; **farsi cattivo ~** to fret, get in a state; **~ freddo** (*fig*) sang-froid, calm; **a ~ freddo** in cold blood; **sangu'igno, a** *ag* blood *cpd*; (*colore*) blood-red; **sangui'nare** *vi* to bleed; **sangui'noso, a** *ag* bloody; **sangui'suga** *sf* leech

sanità *sf* health; (*salubrità*) healthiness; **Ministero della S~** Department of Health; **~ mentale** sanity

sani'tario, a *ag* health *cpd*; (*condizioni*) sanitary ♦ *sm* (*AMM*) doctor; (**impianti**) **~i** *smpl* bathroom *o* sanitary fittings

'**sanno** *vb* *vedi* **sapere**

'**sano, a** *ag* healthy; (*denti, costituzione*) healthy, sound; (*integro*) whole, unbroken; (*fig: politica, consigli*) sound, **~ di mente** sane; **di ~a pianta** completely, entirely; **~ e salvo** safe and sound

sant' *ag* *vedi* **santo**

santifi'care *vt* to sanctify; (*feste*) to observe

santità *sf* sanctity; holiness; **Sua/Vostra ~** (*titolo di Papa*) His/Your Holiness

'**santo, a** *ag* holy; (*fig*) saintly; (*seguito da nome proprio*) saint ♦ *sm/f* saint; **la S~a Sede** the Holy See

santu'ario *sm* sanctuary

sanzio'nare [santsjo'nare] *vt* to sanction

sanzi'one [san'tsjone] *sf* sanction; (*penale, civile*) sanction, penalty

sa'pere *vt* to know; (*essere capace di*): **so nuotare** I know how to swim, I can swim ♦ *vi*: **~ di** (*aver sapore*) to taste of; (*aver odore*) to smell of ♦ *sm* knowledge; **far ~ qc a qn** to inform sb about sth, let sb know sth; **mi sa che non sia vero** I don't think that's true

sapi'enza [sa'pjɛntsa] *sf* wisdom

sa'pone *sm* soap; **~ da bucato** washing soap; **sapo'netta** *sf* cake *o* bar *o* tablet of soap

sa'pore *sm* taste, flavour; **sapo'rito, a** *ag* tasty

sappi'amo *vb vedi* **sapere**

saraci'nesca [saratʃiˈneska] *sf* (*serranda*) rolling shutter

sar'casmo *sm* sarcasm *no pl*; sarcastic remark

Sar'degna [sarˈdeɲɲa] *sf*: **la ~** Sardinia

sar'dina *sf* sardine

'sardo, a *ag, sm/f* Sardinian

'sarto, a *sm/f* tailor/dressmaker; **sarto'ria** *sf* tailor's (shop); dressmaker's (shop); (*casa di moda*) fashion house; (*arte*) couture

'sasso *sm* stone; (*ciottolo*) pebble; (*masso*) rock

sas'sofono *sm* saxophone

sas'soso, a *ag* stony; pebbly

'Satana *sm* Satan; **sa'tanico, a, ci, che** *ag* satanic, fiendish

sa'tellite *sm, ag* satellite

'satira *sf* satire

'saturo, a *ag* saturated; (*fig*): **~ di** full of

'sauna *sf* sauna

Sa'voia *sf* Savoy

savoi'ardo, a *ag* of Savoy, Savoyard ♦ *sm* (*biscotto*) sponge finger

sazi'are [satˈtsjare] *vt* to satisfy, satiate; **~rsi** *vr*: **~rsi (di)** to eat one's fill (of); (*fig*): **~rsi di** to grow tired *o* weary of

'sazio, a [ˈsattsjo] *ag*: **~ (di)** sated (with), full (of); (*fig: stufo*) fed up (with), sick (of)

sba'dato, a *ag* careless, inattentive

sbadigli'are [zbadiʎˈʎare] *vi* to yawn; **sba'diglio** *sm* yawn

sbagli'are [zbaʎˈʎare] *vt* to make a mistake in, get wrong ♦ *vi* to make a mistake, be mistaken, be wrong; (*operare in modo non giusto*) to err; **~rsi** *vr* to make a mistake, be mistaken, be wrong; **~ la mira/strada** to miss one's aim/take the wrong road; **'sbaglio** *sm* mistake, error; (*morale*) error; **fare uno sbaglio** to make a mistake

sbal'lare *vt* (*merce*) to unpack ♦ *vi* (*nel fare un conto*) to overestimate; (*fam: gergo della droga*) to get high

sballot'tare *vt* to toss (about)

sbalor'dire *vt* to stun, amaze ♦ *vi* to be stunned, be amazed; **sbalordi'tivo, a** *ag* amazing; (*prezzo*) incredible, absurd

sbal'zare [zbalˈtsare] *vt* to throw, hurl ♦ *vi* (*balzare*) to bounce; (*saltare*) to leap, bound; **'sbalzo** *sm* (*spostamento improvviso*) jolt, jerk; **a sbalzi** jerkily; (*fig*) in fits and starts; **uno sbalzo di temperatura** a sudden change in temperature

sban'dare *vi* (*NAUT*) to list; (*AER*) to bank; (*AUT*) to skid; **~rsi** *vr* (*folla*) to disperse

sbandie'rare *vt* (*bandiera*) to wave; (*fig*) to parade, show off

sbaragli'are [zbaraʎˈʎare] *vt* (*MIL*) to rout; (*in gare sportive etc*) to beat, defeat

sba'raglio [zbaraˈʎʎo] *sm* rout; defeat; **gettarsi allo ~** to risk everything

sbaraz'zarsi [zbaratˈtsarsi] *vr*: **~ di** to get rid of, rid o.s. of

sbar'care *vt* (*passeggeri*) to disembark; (*merci*) to unload ♦ *vi* to disembark; **'sbarco** *sm* disembarkation; unloading; (*MIL*) landing

'sbarra *sf* bar; (*di passaggio a livello*) barrier; (*DIR*): **presentarsi alla ~** to appear before the court

sbarra'mento *sm* (*stradale*) barrier; (*diga*) dam, barrage; (*MIL*) barrage

sbar'rare *vt* (*strada etc*) to block, bar; (*assegno*) to cross; **~ il passo** to bar the way; **~ gli occhi** to open one's eyes wide

'sbattere *vt* (*porta*) to slam, bang; (*tappeti, ali, CUC*) to beat; (*urtare*) to knock, hit ♦ *vi* (*porta, finestra*) to bang; (*agitarsi: ali, vele etc*) to flap; **me ne sbatto!** (*fam*) I don't give a damn!; **sbat'tuto, a** *ag* (*viso, aria*) dejected, worn out; (*uovo*) beaten

sba'vare *vi* to dribble; (*colore*) to smear, smudge

sbia'dire *vi, vt* to fade; **~rsi** *vr* to fade, **sbia'dito, a** *ag* faded; (*fig*) colourless, dull

sbian'care *vt* to whiten; (*tessuto*) to bleach ♦ *vi* (*impallidire*) to grow pale *o* white

sbi'eco, a, chi, che *ag* (*storto*) squint, askew; **di ~: guardare qn di ~** (*fig*) to look askance at sb; **tagliare una stoffa di ~** to cut a material on the bias

sbigot'tire *vt* to dismay, stun ♦ *vi* (*anche:* **~rsi**) to be dismayed

sbilanci'are [zbilan'tʃare] *vt* to throw off balance; **~rsi** *vr* (*perdere l'equilibrio*) to overbalance, lose one's balance; (*fig: compromettersi*) to compromise o.s.

sbirci'are [zbir'tʃare] *vt* to cast sidelong glances at, eye

'sbirro (*peg*) *sm* cop

sbizzar'rirsi [zbiddzar'rirsi] *vr* to indulge one's whims

sbloc'care *vt* to unblock, free; (*freno*) to release; (*prezzi, affitti*) to decontrol

sboc'care *vi*: **~ in** (*fiume*) to flow into; (*strada*) to lead into; (*persona*) to come (out) into; (*fig: concludersi*) to end (up) in

sboc'cato, a *ag* (*persona*) foul-mouthed; (*linguaggio*) foul

sbocci'are [zbot'tʃare] *vi* (*fiore*) to bloom, open (out)

'sbocco, chi *sm* (*di fiume*) mouth; (*di strada*) end; (*di tubazione, COMM*) outlet; (*uscita: anche fig*) way out; **siamo in una situazione senza ~chi** there's no way out of this for us

sbol'lire *vi* (*fig*) to cool down, calm down

'sbornia (*fam*) *sf*: **prendersi una ~** to get plastered

sbor'sare *vt* (*denaro*) to pay out

sbot'tare *vi*: **~ in una risata/per la collera** to burst out laughing/explode with anger

sbotto'nare *vt* to unbutton, undo

sbrai'are *vi* to yell, bawl

sbra'nare *vt* to tear to pieces

sbricio'lare [zbritʃo'lare] *vt* to crumble; **~rsi** *vr* to crumble

sbri'gare *vt* to deal with; **~rsi** *vr* to hurry (up); **sbriga'tivo, a** *ag* (*persona, modo*) quick, expeditious; (*giudizio*) hasty

sbrindel'lato, a *ag* tattered, in tatters

sbrodo'lare *vt* to stain, dirty

'sbronza ['zbrontsa] (*fam*) *sf* (*ubriaco*): **prendersi una ~** to get plastered

'sbronzo, a ['zbrontso] (*fam*) *ag* plastered

sbruf'fone, a *sm/f* boaster

sbu'care *vi* to come out, emerge; (*improvvisamente*) to pop out (*o* up)

sbucci'are [zbut'tʃare] *vt* (*arancia, patata*) to peel; (*piselli*) to shell; **~rsi un ginocchio** to graze one's knee

sbudel'larsi *vr*: **~ dalle risa** to split one's sides laughing

sbuf'fare *vi* (*persona, cavallo*) to snort; (*: ansimare*) to puff, pant; (*treno*) to puff; **'sbuffo** *sm* (*di aria, fumo, vapore*) puff; **maniche a sbuffo** puff(ed) sleeves

'scabbia *sf* (*MED*) scabies *sg*

sca'broso, a *ag* (*fig: difficile*) difficult, thorny; (*: imbarazzante*) embarrassing; (*: sconcio*) indecent

scacchi'era [skak'kjera] *sf* chessboard

scacci'are [skat'tʃare] *vt* to chase away *o* out, drive away *o* out

'scacco, chi *sm* (*pezzo del gioco*) chessman; (*quadretto di scacchiera*) square; (*fig*) setback, reverse; **~chi** *smpl* (*gioco*) chess *sg*; **a ~chi** (*tessuto*) check(ed); **scacco'matto** *sm* checkmate

sca'dente *ag* shoddy, of poor quality

sca'denza [ska'dentsa] *sf* (*di cambiale, contratto*) maturity; (*di passaporto*) expiry date; **a breve/lunga ~** short-/long-term; **data di ~** expiry date

sca'dere *vi* (*contratto etc*) to expire; (*debito*) to fall due; (*valore, forze, peso*) to decline, go down

sca'fandro *sm* (*di palombaro*) diving suit; (*di astronauta*) space-suit

scaf'fale *sm* shelf; (*mobile*) set of shelves

'scafo *sm* (*NAUT, AER*) hull

scagio'nare [skadʒo'nare] *vt* to exonerate, free from blame

'scaglia ['skaʎʎa] *sf* (*ZOOL*) scale; (*scheggia*) chip, flake

scagli'are [skaʎ'ʎare] *vt* (*lanciare: anche fig*) to hurl, fling; **~rsi** *vr*: **~rsi su *o* contro** to hurl *o* fling o.s. at; (*fig*) to rail at

scaglio'nare [skaʎʎo'nare] *vt* (*pagamenti*) to space out, spread out; (*MIL*) to echelon; **scagli'one** *sm* echelon; (*GEO*) terrace; **a scaglioni** in groups

'scala *sf* (*a gradini etc*) staircase, stairs *pl*; (*a pioli, di corda*) ladder; (*MUS, GEO, di colori, valori, fig*) scale; **~e** *sfpl* (*scalinata*) stairs; **su vasta ~/~ ridotta** on a large/small

scale; ~ **a libretto** stepladder; ~ **mobile**
escalator; (*ECON*) sliding scale; ~ **mobile**
(dei salari) index-linked pay scale

Scala

i Milan's world-famous **la Scala** *theatre*
first opened its doors in 1778 with a
performance of Salieri's opera, "L'Europa
riconosciuta". It suffered serious damage in
the bombing of Milan in 1943 and
reopened in 1946 with a concert conducted
by Toscanini. It also has a famous classical
dance school.

---

sca'lare *vt* (*ALPINISMO, muro*) to climb,
scale; (*debito*) to scale down, reduce;
sca'lata *sf* scaling *no pl*, climbing *no pl*;
(*arrampicata, fig*) climb; scala'tore,
'trice *sm/f* climber
scalda'bagno [skalda'baɲɲo] *sm* water-
heater
scal'dare *vt* to heat; ~rsi *vr* to warm up,
heat up; (*al fuoco, al sole*) to warm o.s.;
(*fig*) to get excited
scal'fire *vt* to scratch
scali'nata *sf* staircase
sca'lino *sm* (*anche fig*) step; (*di scala a
pioli*) rung
'scalo *sm* (*NAUT*) slipway; (*: porto
d'approdo*) port of call; (*AER*) stopover; fare
~ (a) (*NAUT*) to call (at), put in (at); (*AER*) to
land (at), make a stop (at); ~ merci (*FERR*)
goods (*BRIT*) *o* freight yard
scalop'pina *sf* (*CUC*) escalope
scal'pello *sm* chisel
scal'pore *sm* noise, row; far ~ (*notizia*) to
cause a sensation *o* a stir
'scaltro, a *ag* cunning, shrewd
'scalzo, a ['skaltso] *ag* barefoot
scambi'are *vt* to exchange; (*confondere*):
~ qn/qc per to take *o* mistake sb/sth for;
mi hanno scambiato il cappello they've
given me the wrong hat
scambi'evole *ag* mutual, reciprocal
'scambio *sm* exchange; (*FERR*) points *pl*;
fare (uno) ~ to make a swap
scampa'gnata [skampaɲ'ɲata] *sf* trip to

the country
scam'pare *vt* (*salvare*) to rescue, save;
(*evitare: morte, prigione*) to escape ♦ *vi*: ~
(a qc) to survive (sth), escape (sth);
scamparla bella to have a narrow escape
'scampo *sm* (*salvezza*) escape; (*ZOOL*)
prawn; cercare ~ nella fuga to seek safety
in flight
'scampolo *sm* remnant
scanala'tura *sf* (*incavo*) channel, groove
scandagli'are [skandaʎ'ʎare] *vt* (*NAUT*) to
sound; (*fig*) to sound out; to probe
scandaliz'zare [skandalid'dzare] *vt* to
shock, scandalize; ~rsi *vr* to be shocked
'scandalo *sm* scandal
Scandi'navia *sf*: la ~ Scandinavia;
scandi'navo, a *ag, sm/f* Scandinavian
scan'dire *vt* (*versi*) to scan; (*parole*) to
articulate, pronounce distinctly; ~ il tempo
(*MUS*) to beat time
scan'nare *vt* (*animale*) to butcher,
slaughter; (*persona*) to cut *o* slit the throat
of
'scanno *sm* seat, bench
scansafa'tiche [skansafa'tike] *sm/f inv*
idler, loafer
scan'sare *vt* (*rimuovere*) to move (aside),
shift; (*schivare: schiaffo*) to dodge; (*sfuggire*)
to avoid; ~rsi *vr* to move aside
scan'sia *sf* shelves *pl*; (*per libri*) bookcase
'scanso *sm*: a ~ di in order to avoid, as a
precaution against
scanti'nato *sm* basement
scanto'nare *vi* to turn the corner;
(*svignarsela*) to sneak off
scapacci'one [skapat'tʃone] *sm* clout
scapes'trato, a *ag* dissolute
'scapito *sm*: a ~ di to the detriment of
'scapola *sf* shoulder blade
'scapolo *sm* bachelor
scappa'mento *sm* (*AUT*) exhaust
scap'pare *vi* (*fuggire*) to escape; (*andare
via in fretta*) to rush off; lasciarsi ~
un'occasione to let an opportunity go by;
~ di prigione to escape from prison; ~ di
mano (*oggetto*) to slip out of one's hands;
~ di mente a qn to slip sb's mind; mi

scappò detto I let it slip; **scap'pata** *sf* quick visit *o* call; **scappa'tella** *sf* escapade; **scappa'toia** *sf* way out

scara'beo *sm* beetle

scarabocchi'are [skarabok'kjare] *vt* to scribble, scrawl; **scara'bocchio** *sm* scribble, scrawl

scara'faggio [skara'faddʒo] *sm* cockroach

scaraven'tare *vt* to fling, hurl

scarce'rare [skartʃe'rare] *vt* to release (from prison)

scardi'nare *vt*: ~ **una porta** to take a door off its hinges

'scarica, che *sf* (*di più armi*) volley of shots; (*di sassi, pugni*) hail, shower; (*ELETTR*) discharge; ~ **di mitra** burst of machine-gun fire

scari'care *vt* (*merci, camion etc*) to unload; (*passeggeri*) to set down, put off; (*arma*) to unload; (*: sparare, ELETTR*) to discharge; (*sog: corso d'acqua*) to empty, pour; (*fig: liberare da un peso*) to unburden, relieve; ~**rsi** *vr* (*orologio*) to run *o* wind down; (*batteria, accumulatore*) to go flat *o* dead; (*fig: rilassarsi*) to unwind; (*: sfogarsi*) to let off steam; **scarica'tore** *sm* (*di porto*) docker

'scarico, a, chi, che *ag* unloaded; (*orologio*) run down; (*accumulatore*) dead, flat ♦ *sm* (*di merci, materiali*) unloading; (*di immondizie*) dumping, tipping (*BRIT*); (*TECN: deflusso*) draining; (*: dispositivo*) drain; (*AUT*) exhaust

scarlat'tina *sf* scarlet fever

scar'latto, a *ag* scarlet

'scarno, a *ag* thin, bony

'scarpa *sf* shoe; ~**e da ginnastica/tennis** gym/tennis shoes

scar'pata *sf* escarpment

scar'pone *sm* boot; ~**i da sci** ski-boots

scarseggi'are [skarsed'dʒare] *vi* to be scarce; ~ **di** to be short of, lack

scar'sezza [skar'settsa] *sf* scarcity, lack

'scarso, a *ag* (*insufficiente*) insufficient, meagre; (*povero: annata*) poor, lean; (*INS: voto*) poor; ~ **di** lacking in; **3 chili ~i** just under 3 kilos, barely 3 kilos

scarta'mento *sm* (*FERR*) gauge; ~ **normale/ridotto** standard/narrow gauge

scar'tare *vt* (*pacco*) to unwrap; (*idea*) to reject; (*MIL*) to declare unfit for military service; (*carte da gioco*) to discard; (*CALCIO*) to dodge (past) ♦ *vi* to swerve

'scarto *sm* (*cosa scartata, anche COMM*) reject; (*di veicolo*) swerve; (*differenza*) gap, difference

scassi'nare *vt* to break, force

'scasso *sm vedi* **furto**

scate'nare *vt* (*fig*) to incite, stir up; ~**rsi** *vr* (*temporale*) to break; (*rivolta*) to break out; (*persona: infuriarsi*) to rage

'scatola *sf* box; (*di latta*) tin (*BRIT*), can; **cibi in** ~ tinned (*BRIT*) *o* canned foods; ~ **cranica** cranium

scat'tare *vt* (*fotografia*) to take ♦ *vi* (*congegno, molla etc*) to be released; (*balzare*) to spring up; (*SPORT*) to put on a spurt; (*fig: per l'ira*) to fly into a rage; ~ **in piedi** to spring to one's feet

'scatto *sm* (*dispositivo*) release; (*: di arma da fuoco*) trigger mechanism; (*rumore*) click; (*balzo*) jump, start; (*SPORT*) spurt; (*fig: di ira etc*) fit; (*: di stipendio*) increment; **di ~** suddenly

scatu'rire *vi* to gush, spring

scaval'care *vt* (*ostacolo*) to pass (*o* climb) over; (*fig*) to get ahead of, overtake

sca'vare *vt* (*terreno*) to dig; (*legno*) to hollow out; (*pozzo, galleria*) to bore; (*città sepolta etc*) to excavate

'scavo *sm* excavating *no pl*; excavation

'scegliere ['ʃeʎʎere] *vt* to choose, select

sce'icco, chi [ʃe'ikko] *sm* sheik

scelle'rato, a [ʃelle'rato] *ag* wicked, evil

scel'lino [ʃel'lino] *sm* shilling

'scelta ['ʃelta] *sf* choice; selection; **di prima** ~ top grade *o* quality; **frutta o formaggi a** ~ choice of fruit or cheese

'scelto, a ['ʃelto] *pp di* **scegliere** ♦ *ag* (*gruppo*) carefully selected; (*frutta, verdura*) choice, top quality; (*MIL: specializzato*) crack *cpd*, highly skilled

sce'mare [ʃe'mare] *vt, vi* to diminish

'scemo, a ['ʃemo] *ag* stupid, silly

'**scempio** ['ʃɛmpjo] *sm* slaughter, massacre; (*fig*) ruin; **far ~ di** (*fig*) to play havoc with, ruin

'**scena** ['ʃɛna] *sf* (*gen*) scene; (*palcoscenico*) stage; **le ~e** (*fig: teatro*) the stage; **fare una ~** to make a scene; **andare in ~** to be staged *o* put on *o* performed; **mettere in ~** to stage

sce'nario [ʃe'narjo] *sm* scenery; (*di film*) scenario

sce'nata [ʃe'nata] *sf* row, scene

'**scendere** ['ʃɛndere] *vi* to go (*o* come) down; (*strada, sole*) to go down; (*notte*) to fall; (*passeggero: fermarsi*) to get out, alight; (*fig: temperatura, prezzi*) to go *o* come down, fall, drop ♦ *vt* (*scale, pendio*) to go (*o* come) down; **~ dalle scale** to go (*o* come) down the stairs; **~ dal treno** to get off *o* out of the train; **~ dalla macchina** to get out of the car; **~ da cavallo** to dismount, get off one's horse

'**scenico, a, ci, che** ['ʃɛniko] *ag* stage *cpd*, scenic

scervel'lato, a [ʃervel'lato] *ag* feather-brained, scatterbrained

'**sceso, a** ['ʃeso] *pp di* **scendere**

'**scettico, a, ci, che** ['ʃɛttiko] *ag* sceptical

'**scettro** ['ʃɛttro] *sm* sceptre

'**scheda** ['skɛda] *sf* (*index*) card; **~ elettorale** ballot paper; **~ telefonica** phone card; **sche'dare** *vt* (*dati*) to file; (*libri*) to catalogue; (*registrare: anche POLIZIA*) to put on one's files; **sche'dario** *sm* file; (*mobile*) filing cabinet

'**scheggia, ge** ['skɛddʒa] *sf* splinter, sliver

sche'letro ['skɛletro] *sm* skeleton

'**schema, i** ['skɛma] *sm* (*diagramma*) diagram, sketch; (*progetto, abbozzo*) outline, plan

'**scherma** ['skɛrma] *sf* fencing

scher'maglia [sker'maʎʎa] *sf* (*fig*) skirmish

'**schermo** ['skɛrmo] *sm* shield, screen; (*CINEMA, TV*) screen

scher'nire [sker'nire] *vt* to mock, sneer at; '**scherno** *sm* mockery, derision

scher'zare [sker'tsare] *vi* to joke

'**scherzo** ['skɛrtso] *sm* joke; (*tiro*) trick;

(*MUS*) scherzo; **è uno ~!** (*una cosa facile*) it's child's play!, it's easy!; **per ~** in jest; for a joke *o* a laugh; **fare un brutto ~ a qn** to play a nasty trick on sb; **scher'zoso, a** *ag* (*tono, gesto*) playful; (*osservazione*) facetious; **è un tipo scherzoso** he likes a joke

schiaccia'noci [skjattʃa'notʃi] *sm inv* nutcracker

schiacci'are [skjat'tʃare] *vt* (*dito*) to crush; (*noci*) to crack; **~ un pisolino** to have a nap

schiaffeggi'are [skjaffed'dʒare] *vt* to slap

schi'affo ['skjaffo] *sm* slap

schiamaz'zare [skjamat'tsare] *vi* to squawk, cackle

schian'tare [skjan'tare] *vt* to break, tear apart; **~rsi** *vr* to break (up), shatter; **schi'anto** *sm* (*rumore*) crash; tearing sound; **è uno schianto!** (*fam*) it's (*o* he's *o* she's) terrific!; **di schianto** all of a sudden

schia'rire [skja'rire] *vt* to lighten, make lighter ♦ *vi* (*anche*: **~rsi**) to grow lighter; (*tornar sereno*) to clear, brighten up; **~rsi la voce** to clear one's throat

schiavitù [skjavi'tu] *sf* slavery

schi'avo, a ['skjavo] *sm/f* slave

schi'ena ['skjɛna] *sf* (*ANAT*) back; **schie'nale** *sm* (*di sedia*) back

schi'era ['skjɛra] *sf* (*MIL*) rank; (*gruppo*) group, band

schiera'mento [skjera'mento] *sm* (*MIL, SPORT*) formation; (*fig*) alliance

schie'rare [skje'rare] *vt* (*esercito*) to line up, draw up, marshal; **~rsi** *vr* to line up; (*fig*): **~rsi con** *o* **dalla parte di / contro qn** to side with/oppose sb

schi'etto, a ['skjɛtto] *ag* (*puro*) pure; (*fig*) frank, straightforward; sincere

'**schifo** ['skifo] *sm* disgust; **fare ~** (*essere fatto male, dare pessimi risultati*) to be awful; **mi fa ~** it makes me sick, it's disgusting; **quel libro è uno ~** that book's rotten; **schi'foso, a** *ag* disgusting, revolting; (*molto scadente*) rotten, lousy

schioc'care [skjɔk'kare] *vt* (*frusta*) to crack; (*dita*) to snap; (*lingua*) to click; **~ le labbra**

to smack one's lips

schi'udere ['skjudere] *vt* to open; **~rsi** *vr* to open

schi'uma ['skjuma] *sf* foam; (*di sapone*) lather; (*di latte*) froth; (*fig: feccia*) scum; **schiu'mare** *vt* to skim ♦ *vi* to foam

schi'uso, a ['skjuso] *pp di* **schiudere**

schi'vare [ski'vare] *vt* to dodge, avoid

'schivo, a ['skivo] *ag* (*ritroso*) stand-offish, reserved; (*timido*) shy

schiz'zare [skit'tsare] *vt* (*spruzzare*) to spurt, squirt; (*sporcare*) to splash, spatter; (*fig: abbozzare*) to sketch ♦ *vi* to spurt, squirt; (*saltar fuori*) to dart up (*o off etc*)

schizzi'noso, a [skittsi'noso] *ag* fussy, finicky

'schizzo ['skittso] *sm* (*di liquido*) spurt; splash, spatter; (*abbozzo*) sketch

sci [ʃi] *sm* (*attrezzo*) ski; (*attività*) skiing; **~ nautico** water-skiing

'scia ['ʃia] (*pl* **'scie**) *sf* (*di imbarcazione*) wake; (*di profumo*) trail

scià [ʃa] *sm inv* shah

sci'abola ['ʃabola] *sf* sabre

scia'callo [ʃa'kallo] *sm* jackal

sciac'quare [ʃak'kware] *vt* to rinse

scia'gura [ʃa'gura] *sf* disaster, calamity; misfortune; **sciagu'rato, a** *ag* unfortunate; (*malvagio*) wicked

scialac'quare [ʃalak'kware] *vt* to squander

scia'lare [ʃa'lare] *vi* to lead a life of luxury

sci'albo, a ['ʃalbo] *ag* pale, dull; (*fig*) dull, colourless

sci'alle ['ʃalle] *sm* shawl

scia'luppa [ʃa'luppa] *sf* (*anche:* **~ di salvataggio**) lifeboat

sci'ame ['ʃame] *sm* swarm

scian'cato, a [ʃan'kato] *ag* lame

sci'are [ʃi'are] *vi* to ski

sci'arpa ['ʃarpa] *sf* scarf; (*fascia*) sash

scia'tore, 'trice [ʃa'tore] *sm/f* skier

sci'atto, a ['ʃatto] *ag* (*persona*) slovenly, unkempt

scien'tifico, a, ci, che [ʃen'tifiko] *ag* scientific

sci'enza ['ʃentsa] *sf* science; (*sapere*) knowledge; **~e** *sfpl* (*INS*) science *sg*; **~e**

naturali natural sciences; **scienzi'ato, a** *sm/f* scientist

'scimmia ['ʃimmja] *sf* monkey; **scimmiot'tare** *vt* to ape, mimic

scimpanzé [ʃimpan'tse] *sm inv* chimpanzee

scimu'nito, a [ʃimu'nito] *ag* silly, idiotic

'scindere ['ʃindere] *vt* to split (up); **~rsi** *vr* to split (up)

scin'tilla [ʃin'tilla] *sf* spark; **scintil'lare** *vi* to spark; (*acqua, occhi*) to sparkle

scioc'chezza [ʃok'kettsa] *sf* stupidity *no pl*; stupid *o* foolish thing; **dire ~e** to talk nonsense

sci'occo, a, chi, che ['ʃɔkko] *ag* stupid, foolish

sci'ogliere ['ʃɔʎʎere] *vt* (*nodo*) to untie; (*capelli*) to loosen; (*persona, animale*) to untie, release; (*fig: persona*): **~ da** to release from; (*neve*) to melt; (*nell'acqua: zucchero etc*) to dissolve; (*fig: mistero*) to solve; (*porre fine a: contratto*) to cancel; (*: società, matrimonio*) to dissolve; (*: riunione*) to bring to an end; **~rsi** *vr* to loosen, come untied; to melt; to dissolve; (*assemblea etc*) to break up; **~ i muscoli** to limber up

sciol'tezza [ʃol'tettsa] *sf* agility; suppleness; ease

sci'olto, a ['ʃɔlto] *pp di* **sciogliere** ♦ *ag* loose; (*agile*) agile, nimble; supple; (*disinvolto*) free and easy; **versi ~i** (*POESIA*) blank verse

sciope'rante [ʃope'rante] *sm/f* striker

sciope'rare [ʃope'rare] *vi* to strike, go on strike

sci'opero ['ʃopero] *sm* strike; **fare ~** to strike; **~ bianco** work-to-rule (*BRIT*), slowdown (*US*); **~ selvaggio** wildcat strike; **~ a singhiozzo** on-off strike

scip'pare [ʃip'pare] *vt*: **~ qn** to snatch sb's bag; **mi hanno scippato** they snatched my bag

sci'rocco [ʃi'rɔkko] *sm* sirocco

sci'roppo [ʃi'rɔppo] *sm* syrup

'scisma, i ['ʃizma] *sm* (*REL*) schism

scissi'one [ʃis'sjone] *sf* (*anche fig*) split, division; (*FISICA*) fission

'scisso, a ['ʃisso] *pp di* **scindere**

sciu'pare [ʃu'pare] vt (*abito, libro, appetito*) to spoil, ruin; (*tempo, denaro*) to waste; **~rsi** vr to get spoilt o ruined; (*rovinarsi la salute*) to ruin one's health

scivo'lare [ʃivo'lare] vi to slide o glide along; (*involontariamente*) to slip, slide; **'scivolo** sm slide; (*TECN*) chute; **scivo'loso, a** ag slippery

scle'rosi sf sclerosis

scoc'care vt (*freccia*) to shoot ♦ vi (*guizzare*) to shoot up; (*battere: ora*) to strike

scocci'are [skot'tʃare] (*fam*) vt to bother, annoy; **~rsi** vr to be bothered o annoyed

sco'della sf bowl

scodinzo'lare [skodintso'lare] vi to wag its tail

scogli'era [skoʎ'ʎera] sf reef; cliff

'scoglio ['skoʎʎo] sm (*al mare*) rock

scoi'attolo sm squirrel

scolapi'atti sm inv drainer (*for plates*)

sco'lare ag: **età ~** school age ♦ vt to drain ♦ vi to drip

scola'resca sf schoolchildren pl, pupils pl

sco'laro, a sm/f pupil, schoolboy/girl

sco'lastico, a, ci, che ag school cpd; scholastic

scol'lare vt (*staccare*) to unstick; **~rsi** vr to come unstuck

scolla'tura sf neckline

'scolo sm drainage

scolo'rire vt to fade; to discolour ♦ vi (*anche:* **~rsi**) to fade; to become discoloured; (*impallidire*) to turn pale

scol'pire vt to carve, sculpt

scombi'nare vt to mess up, upset

scombusso'lare vt to upset

scom'messa sf bet, wager

scom'messo, a pp di **scommettere**

scom'mettere vt, vi to bet

scomo'dare vt to trouble, bother; to disturb; **~rsi** vr to put o.s. out; **~rsi a fare** to go to the bother o trouble of doing

'scomodo, a ag uncomfortable; (*sistemazione, posto*) awkward, inconvenient

scompa'rire vi (*sparire*) to disappear,

vanish; (*fig*) to be insignificant;

scom'parsa sf disappearance;

scom'parso, a pp di **scomparire**

scomparti'mento sm compartment

scom'parto sm compartment, division

scompigli'are [skompiʎ'ʎare] vt (*cassetto, capelli*) to mess up, disarrange; (*fig: piani*) to upset; **scom'piglio** sm mess, confusion

scom'porre vt (*parola, numero*) to break up; (*CHIM*) to decompose; **scomporsi** vr (*fig*) to get upset, lose one's composure; **scom'posto, a** pp di **scomporre** ♦ ag (*gesto*) unseemly; (*capelli*) ruffled, dishevelled

sco'munica sf excommunication

scomuni'care vt to excommunicate

sconcer'tare [skontʃer'tare] vt to disconcert, bewilder

'sconcio, a, ci, ce ['skontʃo] ag (*osceno*) indecent, obscene ♦ sm disgrace

sconfes'sare vt to renounce, disavow; to repudiate

scon'figgere [skon'fiddʒere] vt to defeat, overcome

sconfi'nare vi to cross the border; (*in proprietà privata*) to trespass; (*fig*): **~ da** to stray o digress from; **sconfi'nato, a** ag boundless, unlimited

scon'fitta sf defeat

scon'fitto, a pp di **sconfiggere**

scon'forto sm despondency

scongiu'rare [skondʒu'rare] vt (*implorare*) to entreat, beseech, implore; (*eludere: pericolo*) to ward off, avert; **scongi'uro** sm entreaty; (*esorcismo*) exorcism; **fare gli scongiuri** to touch wood (*BRIT*), knock on wood (*US*)

scon'nesso, a ag incoherent

sconosci'uto, a [skonoʃ'ʃuto] ag unknown; new, strange ♦ sm/f stranger; unknown person

sconquas'sare vt to shatter, smash

sconside'rato, a ag thoughtless, rash

sconsigli'are [skonsiʎ'ʎare] vt: **~ qc a qn** to advise sb against sth; **~ qn dal fare qc** to advise sb not to do o against doing sth

sconso'lato, a ag inconsolable; desolate

scon'tare *vt* (COMM: *detrarre*) to deduct; (: *debito*) to pay off; (: *cambiale*) to discount; (*pena*) to serve; (*colpa, errori*) to pay for, suffer for

scon'tato, a *ag* (*previsto*) foreseen, taken for granted; **dare per ~ che** to take it for granted that

scon'tento, a *ag*: **~ (di)** dissatisfied (with) ♦ *sm* dissatisfaction

'sconto *sm* discount; **fare uno ~** to give a discount

scon'trarsi *vr* (*treni etc*) to crash, colllde; (*venire ad uno scontro, fig*) to clash; **~ con** to crash into, collide with

scon'trino *sm* ticket

'scontro *sm* clash, encounter; crash, collision

scon'troso, a *ag* sullen, surly; (*permaloso*) touchy

sconveni'ente *ag* unseemly, improper

scon'volgere [skon'vɔldʒere] *vt* to throw into confusion, upset; (*turbare*) to shake, disturb, upset; **scon'volto, a** *pp di* **sconvolgere**

'scopa *sf* broom; (CARTE) Italian card game; **sco'pare** *vt* to sweep

sco'perta *sf* discovery

sco'perto, a *pp di* **scoprire** ♦ *ag* uncovered; (*capo*) uncovered, bare; (*macchina*) open; (MIL) exposed, without cover; (*conto*) overdrawn

'scopo *sm* aim, purpose; **a che ~?** what for?

scoppi'are *vi* (*spaccarsi*) to burst; (*esplodere*) to explode; (*fig*) to break out; **~ in pianto** *o* **a piangere** to burst out crying; **~ dalle risa** *o* **dal ridere** to split one's sides laughing

scoppiet'tare *vi* to crackle

'scoppio *sm* explosion; (*di tuono, arma etc*) crash, bang; (*fig: di risa, ira*) fit, outburst; (: *di guerra*) outbreak; **a ~ ritardato** delayed-action

sco'prire *vt* to discover; (*liberare da ciò che copre*) to uncover; (: *monumento*) to unveil; **~rsi** *vr* to put on lighter clothes; (*fig*) to give o.s. away

scoraggi'are [skorad'dʒare] *vt* to discourage; **~rsi** *vr* to become discouraged, lose heart

scorcia'toia [skortʃa'toja] *sf* short cut

'scorcio ['skortʃo] *sm* (ARTE) foreshortening; (*di secolo, periodo*) end, close

scor'dare *vt* to forget; **~rsi** *vr*: **~rsi di qc/ di fare** to forget sth/to do

'scorgere ['skɔrdʒere] *vt* to make out, distinguish, see

sco'ria *sf* (*di metalli*) slag; (*vulcanica*) scorla; **~e radloattive** (FISICA) radioactlve waste *sg*

'scorno *sm* ignominy, disgrace

scorpacci'ata [skorpat'tʃata] *sf*: **fare una ~ (di)** to stuff o.s. (with), eat one's fill (of)

scorpi'one *sm* scorpion; (*dello zodiaco*): **S~** Scorpio

scorraz'zare [skorrat'tsare] *vi* to run about

'scorrere *vt* (*giornale, lettera*) to run *o* skim through ♦ *vi* (*liquido, fiume*) to run, flow; (*fune*) to run; (*cassetto, porta*) to slide easily; (*tempo*) to pass (by)

scor'retto, a *ag* incorrect; (*sgarbato*) impolite; (*sconveniente*) improper

scor'revole *ag* (*porta*) sliding; (*fig: stile*) fluent, flowing

scorri'banda *sf* (MIL) raid; (*escursione*) trip, excursion

'scorsa *sf* quick look, glance

'scorso, a *pp di* **scorrere** ♦ *ag* last

scor'solo, a *ag*: **nodo ~** noose

'scorta *sf* (*di personalità, convoglio*) escort; (*provvista*) supply, stock; **scor'tare** *vt* to escort

scor'tese *ag* discourteous, rude; **scorte'sia** *sf* discourtesy, rudeness; (*azione*) discourtesy

scorti'care *vt* to skin

'scorto, a *pp di* **scorgere**

'scorza ['skɔrdza] *sf* (*di albero*) bark; (*di agrumi*) peel, skin

sco'sceso, a [skoʃ'ʃeso] *ag* steep

'scossa *sf* jerk, jolt, shake; (ELETTR, *fig*) shock

'scosso, a *pp di* **scuotere** ♦ *ag* (*turbato*) shaken, upset

scos'tante *ag* (*fig*) off-putting (*BRIT*), unpleasant

scos'tare *vt* to move (away), shift; **~rsi** *vr* to move away

scostu'mato, a *ag* immoral, dissolute

scot'tare *vt* (*ustionare*) to burn; (: con liquido bollente) to scald ♦ *vi* to burn; (*caffè*) to be too hot; **scotta'tura** *sf* burn; scald

'scotto, a *ag* overcooked ♦ *sm* (*fig*): **pagare lo ~ (di)** to pay the penalty (for)

sco'vare *vt* to drive out, flush out; (*fig*) to discover

'Scozia ['skɔttsia] *sf*: **la ~** Scotland; **scoz'zese** *ag* Scottish ♦ *sm/f* Scot

scredi'tare *vt* to discredit

screpo'lare *vt* to crack; **~rsi** *vr* to crack; **screpola'tura** *sf* cracking *no pl*; crack

screzi'ato, a [skret'tsjato] *ag* streaked

'screzio ['skrɛttsjo] *sm* disagreement

scricchio'lare [skrikkjo'lare] *vi* to creak, squeak

'scricciolo ['skrittʃolo] *sm* wren

'scrigno ['skriɲɲo] *sm* casket

scrimina'tura *sf* parting

'scritta *sf* inscription

'scritto, a *pp di* **scrivere** ♦ *ag* written ♦ *sm* writing; (*lettera*) letter, note; **~i** *smpl* (*letterari etc*) writing *sg*

scrit'toio *sm* writing desk

scrit'tore, 'trice *sm/f* writer

scrit'tura *sf* writing; (*COMM*) entry; (*contratto*) contract; (*REL*): **la Sacra S~** the Scriptures *pl*; **~e** *sfpl* (*COMM*) accounts, books

scrittu'rare *vt* (*TEATRO, CINEMA*) to sign up, engage; (*COMM*) to enter

scriva'nia *sf* desk

'scrivere *vt* to write; **come si scrive?** how is it spelt?, how do you write it?

scroc'cone, a *sm/f* scrounger

'scrofa *sf* (*ZOOL*) sow

scrol'lare *vt* to shake; **~rsi** *vr* (*anche fig*) to give o.s. a shake; **~ le spalle/il capo** to shrug one's shoulders/shake one's head

scrosci'are [skroʃ'ʃare] *vi* (*pioggia*) to pour down, pelt down; (*torrente, fig: applausi*) to thunder, roar; **'scroscio** *sm* pelting; thunder, roar; (*di applausi*) burst

scros'tare *vt* (*intonaco*) to scrape off, strip; **~rsi** *vr* to peel off, flake off

'scrupolo *sm* scruple; (*meticolosità*) care, conscientiousness

scru'tare *vt* to scrutinize; (*intenzioni, causa*) to examine, scrutinize

scruti'nare *vt* (*voti*) to count; **scru'tinio** *sm* (*votazione*) ballot; (*insieme delle operazioni*) poll; (*INS*) (*meeting for*) assignment of marks at end of a term or year

scu'cire [sku'tʃire] *vt* (*orlo etc*) to unpick, undo

scude'ria *sf* stable

scu'detto *sm* (*SPORT*) (championship) shield; (*distintivo*) badge

'scudo *sm* shield

scul'tore, 'trice *sm/f* sculptor

scul'tura *sf* sculpture

scu'ola *sf* school; **~ elementare/ materna/media** primary (*BRIT*) *o* grade (*US*)/nursery/secondary (*BRIT*) *o* high (*US*) school; **~ guida** driving school; **~ dell'obbligo** compulsory education; **~e serali** evening classes, night school *sg*; **~ tecnica** technical college

scu'otere *vt* to shake; **~rsi** *vr* to jump, be startled; (*fig: muoversi*) to rouse o.s., stir o.s.; (: *turbarsi*) to be shaken

'scure *sf* axe

'scuro, a *ag* dark; (*fig: espressione*) grim ♦ *sm* darkness; dark colour; (*imposta*) (window) shutter; **verde/rosso etc ~** dark green/red *etc*

scur'rile *ag* scurrilous

'scusa *sf* apology; (*pretesto*) excuse; **chiedere ~ a qn (per)** to apologize to sb (for); **chiedo ~** I'm sorry; (*disturbando etc*) excuse me

scu'sare *vt* to excuse; **~rsi** *vr*: **~rsi (di)** to apologize (for); **(mi) scusi** I'm sorry; (*per richiamare l'attenzione*) excuse me

sde'gnato, a [zdeɲ'ɲato] *ag* indignant, angry

'sdegno ['zdeɲɲo] *sm* scorn, disdain;

sde'gnoso, a *ag* scornful, disdainful
sdoga'nare *vt* (*merci*) to clear through customs
sdolci'nato, a [zdoltʃi'nato] *ag* mawkish, oversentimental
sdrai'arsi *vr* to stretch out, lie down
'sdraio *sm*: **sedia a ~** deck chair
sdruccio'levole [zdruttʃo'levole] *ag* slippery

PAROLA CHIAVE
---

se *pron vedi* **si**
  ♦ *cong* **1** (*condizionale, ipotetica*) if; **~ nevica non vengo** I won't come if it snows; **sarei rimasto ~ me l'avessero chiesto** I would have stayed if they'd asked me; **non puoi fare altro ~ non telefonare** all you can do is phone; **~ mai** if, if ever; **siamo noi ~ mai che le siamo grati** it is we who should be grateful to you; **~ no** (*altrimenti*) or (else), otherwise
  2 (*in frasi dubitative, interrogative indirette*) if, whether; **non so ~ scrivere o telefonare** I don't know whether *o* if I should write or phone

---

sé *pron* (*gen*) oneself; (*esso, essa, lui, lei, loro*) itself; himself; herself; themselves; **~ stesso(a)** *pron* oneself; itself; himself; herself; **~ stessi(e)** *pron pl* themselves
seb'bene *cong* although, though
sec. *abbr* (= *secolo*) c
'secca *sf* (*del mare*) shallows *pl*; *vedi anche* **secco**
sec'care *vt* to dry; (*prosciugare*) to dry up; (*fig: importunare*) to annoy, bother ♦ *vi* to dry; to dry up; **~rsi** *vr* to dry; to dry up; (*fig*) to grow annoyed; **secca'tura** *sf* (*fig*) bother *no pl*, trouble *no pl*
secchi'ello *sm* bucket; **~ del ghiaccio** ice bucket
'secchio [*'sekkjo*] *sm* bucket, pail
'secco, a, chi, che *ag* dry; (*fichi, pesce*) dried; (*foglie, ramo*) withered; (*magro: persona*) thin, skinny; (*fig: risposta, modo di fare*) curt, abrupt; (: *colpo*) clean, sharp ♦ *sm* (*siccità*) drought; **restarci ~** (*fig*:

morire sul colpo) to drop dead; **mettere in ~** (*barca*) to beach; **rimanere a ~** (*fig*) to be left in the lurch
seco'lare *ag* age-old, centuries-old; (*laico, mondano*) secular
'secolo *sm* century; (*epoca*) age
se'conda *sf* (*AUT*) second (gear); **viaggiare in ~** to travel second-class; *vedi anche* **secondo**
secon'dario, a *ag* secondary
se'condo, a *ag* second ♦ *sm* second; (*di pranzo*) main course ♦ *prep* according to; (*nel modo prescritto*) in accordance with; **~ me** in my opinion, to my mind; **di ~a classe** second-class; **di ~a mano** second-hand; **a ~a di** according to; in accordance with
'sedano *sm* celery
seda'tivo, a *ag, sm* sedative
'sede *sf* seat; (*di ditta*) head office; (*di organizzazione*) headquarters *pl*; **~ sociale** registered office
seden'tario, a *ag* sedentary
se'dere *vi* to sit, be seated; **~rsi** *vr* to sit down ♦ *sm* (*deretano*) behind, bottom
'sedia *sf* chair
sedi'cente [sedi'tʃente] *ag* self-styled
'sedici ['seditʃi] *num* sixteen
se'dile *sm* seat; (*panchina*) bench
se'dotto, a *pp di* **sedurre**
sedu'cente [sedu'tʃente] *ag* seductive; (*proposta*) very attractive
se'durre *vt* to seduce
se'duta *sf* session, sitting; (*riunione*) meeting; **~ spiritica** séance; **~ stante** (*fig*) immediately
seduzi'one [sedut'tsjone] *sf* seduction; (*fascino*) charm, appeal
'sega, ghe *sf* saw
'segale *sf* rye
se'gare *vt* to saw; (*recidere*) to saw off; **sega'tura** *sf* (*residuo*) sawdust
'seggio ['seddʒo] *sm* seat; **~ elettorale** polling station
'seggiola ['seddʒola] *sf* chair; **seggio'lino** *sm* seat; (*per bambini*) child's chair; **seggio'lone** *sm* (*per bambini*) highchair

seggio'via [seddʒo'via] *sf* chairlift

seghe'ria [sege'ria] *sf* sawmill

segna'lare [seɲɲa'lare] *vt* (*manovra etc*) to signal; to indicate; (*annunciare*) to announce; to report; (*fig: far conoscere*) to point up; (: *persona*) to single out; **~rsi** *vr* (*distinguersi*) to distinguish o.s.

se'gnale [seɲ'ɲale] *sm* signal; (*cartello*): ~ **stradale** road sign; ~ **d'allarme** alarm; (*FERR*) communication cord; ~ **orario** (*RADIO*) time signal; **segna'letica** *sf* signalling, signposting; **segnaletica stradale** road signs *pl*

segna'libro [seɲɲa'libro] *sm* bookmark

se'gnare [seɲ'ɲare] *vt* to mark; (*prendere nota*) to note; (*indicare*) to indicate, mark; (*SPORT: goal*) to score; **~rsi** *vr* (*REL*) to make the sign of the cross, cross o.s.

'**segno** [seɲɲo] *sm* sign; (*impronta, contrassegno*) mark; (*limite*) limit, bounds *pl*; (*bersaglio*) target; **fare ~ di sì/no** to nod (one's head)/shake one's head; **fare ~ a qn di fermarsi** to motion (to) sb to stop; **cogliere** *o* **colpire nel ~** (*fig*) to hit the mark

segre'gare *vt* to segregate, isolate; **segregazi'one** *sf* segregation

segre'tario, a *sm/f* secretary; ~ **comunale** town clerk; **S~ di Stato** Secretary of State

segrete'ria *sf* (*di ditta, scuola*) (secretary's) office; (*d'organizzazione internazionale*) secretariat; (*POL etc: carica*) office of Secretary; ~ **telefonica** answering service

segre'tezza [segre'tettsa] *sf* secrecy

se'greto, a *ag* secret ♦ *sm* secret; secrecy *no pl*; **in ~** in secret, secretly

segu'ace [se'gwatʃe] *sm/f* follower, disciple

segu'ente *ag* following, next

segu'ire *vt* to follow; (*frequentare: corso*) to attend ♦ *vi* to follow; (*continuare: testo*) to continue

segui'tare *vt* to continue, carry on with ♦ *vi* to continue, carry on

'**seguito** *sm* (*scorta*) suite, retinue; (*discepoli*) followers *pl*; (*favore*) following;

(*continuazione*) continuation; (*conseguenza*) result; **di ~** at a stretch, on end; **in ~** later on; **in ~ a, a ~ di** following; (*a causa di*) as a result of, owing to

'**sei** *vb vedi* **essere** ♦ *num* six

sei'cento [sei'tʃento] *num* six hundred ♦ *sm*: **il S~** the seventeenth century

selci'ato [sel'tʃato] *sm* cobbled surface

selezio'nare [selettsjo'nare] *vt* to select

selezi'one [selet'tsjone] *sf* selection

'**sella** *sf* saddle; **sel'lare** *vt* to saddle

selvag'gina [selvad'dʒina] *sf* (*animali*) game

sel'vaggio, a, gi, ge [sel'vaddʒo] *ag* wild; (*tribù*) savage, uncivilized; (*fig*) savage, brutal ♦ *sm/f* savage

sel'vatico, a, ci, che *ag* wild

se'maforo *sm* (*AUT*) traffic lights *pl*

sem'brare *vi* to seem ♦ *vb impers*: **sembra che** it seems that; **mi sembra che** it seems to me that; **I think (that)**; ~ **di essere** to seem to be

'**seme** *sm* seed; (*sperma*) semen; (*CARTE*) suit

se'mestre *sm* half-year, six-month period

'**semi...** *prefisso* semi...; **semi'cerchio** *sm* semicircle; **semifi'nale** *sf* semifinal; **semi'freddo** *sm* ice-cream cake

'**semina** *sf* (*AGR*) sowing

semi'nare *vt* to sow

semi'nario *sm* seminar; (*REL*) seminary

seminter'rato *sm* basement; (*appartamento*) basement flat

sem'mai = **se mai**; *vedi* **se**

'**semola** *sf*: ~ **di grano duro** durum wheat

semo'lino *sm* semolina

'**semplice** ['semplitʃe] *ag* simple; (*di un solo elemento*) single; **semplice'mente** *av* simply; **semplicità** *sf* simplicity

'**sempre** *av* always; (*ancora*) still; **posso ~ tentare** I can always o still try; **da ~** always; **per ~** forever; **una volta per ~** once and for all; ~ **che** provided (that); ~ **più** more and more; ~ **meno** less and less

sempre'verde *ag, sm o f* (*BOT*) evergreen

'**senape** *sf* (*CUC*) mustard

se'nato *sm* senate; **sena'tore, 'trice**

sm/f senator

'**senno** *sm* judgment, (common) sense; **col ~ di poi** with hindsight

sennò *av* = **se no**; *vedi* **se**

'**seno** *sm* (ANAT: *petto, mammella*) breast; (: *grembo, fig*) womb; (: *cavità*) sinus

sen'sato, a *ag* sensible

sensazio'nale [sensattsjo'nale] *ag* sensational

sensazi'one [sensat'tsjone] *sf* feeling, sensation; **avere la ~ che** to have a feeling that; **fare ~** to cause a sensation, create a stir

sen'sibile *ag* sensitive; (*ai sensi*) perceptible; (*rilevante, notevole*) appreciable, noticeable; **~ a** sensitive to; **sensibilità** *sf* sensitivity

'**senso** *sm* (FISIOL, *istinto*) sense; (*impressione, sensazione*) feeling, sensation; (*significato*) meaning, sense; (*direzione*) direction; **~i** *smpl* (*coscienza*) consciousness *sg*; (*sensualità*) senses; **ciò non ha ~** that doesn't make sense, **fare ~** (*ripugnare*) to disgust, repel; **~ comune** common sense; **in ~ orario/antiorario** clockwise/anticlockwise; **a ~ unico** (*strada*) one-way

sensu'ale *ag* sensual; sensuous; **sensualità** *sf* sensuality; sensuousness

sen'tenza [sen'tentsa] *sf* (DIR) sentence; (*massima*) maxim; **sentenzi'are** *vi* (DIR) to pass judgment

senti'ero *sm* path

sentimen'tale *ag* sentimental; (*vita, avventura*) love *cpd*

senti'mento *sm* feeling

senti'nella *sf* sentry

sen'tire *vt* (*percepire al tatto, fig*) to feel; (*udire*) to hear; (*ascoltare*) to listen to; (*odore*) to smell; (*avvertire con il gusto, assaggiare*) to taste ♦ *vi*: **~ di** (*avere sapore*) to taste of; (*avere odore*) to smell of; **~rsi** *vr* (*uso reciproco*) to be in touch; **~rsi bene/male** to feel well/unwell *o* ill; **~rsi di fare qc** (*essere disposto*) to feel like doing sth

sen'tito, a *ag* (*sincero*) sincere, warm; **per ~ dire** by hearsay

'**senza** ['sentsa] *prep, cong* without; **~ dir nulla** without saying a word; **fare ~ qc** to do without sth; **~ di me** without me; **~ che io lo sapessi** without me *o* my knowing; **senz'altro** of course, certainly; **~ dubbio** no doubt; **~ scrupoli** unscrupulous; **~ amici** friendless

sepa'rare *vt* to separate; (*dividere*) to divide; (*tenere distinto*) to distinguish; **~rsi** *vr* (*coniugi*) to separate, part; (*amici*) to part, leave each other; **~rsi da** (*coniuge*) to separate *o* part from; (*amico, socio*) to part company with; (*oggetto*) to part with; **sepa'rato, a** *ag* (*letti, conto etc*) separate; (*coniugi*) separated; **separazi'one** *sf* separation

se'polcro *sm* sepulchre

se'polto, a *pp di* **seppellire**

seppel'lire *vt* to bury

'**seppia** *sf* cuttlefish ♦ *ag inv* sepia

se'quenza [se'kwentsa] *sf* sequence

seques'trare *vt* (DIR) to impound; (*rapire*) to kidnap; **se'questro** *sm* (DIR) impoundment; **sequestro di persona** kidnapping

'**sera** *sf* evening; **di ~** in the evening; **domani ~** tomorrow evening, tomorrow night; **se'rale** *ag* evening *cpd*; **se'rata** *sf* evening; (*ricevimento*) party

ser'bare *vt* to keep; (*mettere da parte*) to put aside; **~ rancore/odio verso qn** to bear sb a grudge/hate sb

serba'toio *sm* tank; (*cisterna*) cistern

'**serbo** *sm*: **mettere/tenere** *o* **avere in ~ qc** to put/keep sth aside

se'reno, a *ag* (*tempo, cielo*) clear; (*fig*) serene, calm

ser'gente [ser'dʒente] *sm* (MIL) sergeant

'**serie** *sf inv* (*successione*) series *inv*; (*gruppo, collezione*) set; (SPORT) division; league; (COMM): **modello di ~/fuori ~** standard/custom-built model; **in ~** in quick succession; (COMM) mass *cpd*

serietà *sf* seriousness; reliability

'**serio, a** *ag* serious; (*impiegato*) responsible, reliable; (*ditta, cliente*) reliable, dependable; **sul ~** (*davvero*) really, truly; (*seriamente*) seriously, in earnest

ser'mone *sm* sermon
serpeggi'are [serped'dʒare] *vi* to wind; (*fig*) to spread
ser'pente *sm* snake; ~ **a sonagli** rattlesnake
'serra *sf* greenhouse; hothouse
ser'randa *sf* roller shutter
ser'rare *vt* to close, shut; (*a chiave*) to lock; (*stringere*) to tighten; ~ **i pugni/i denti** to clench one's fists/teeth; ~ **le file** to close ranks
serra'tura *sf* lock
'serva *sf vedi* **servo**
ser'vire *vt* to serve; (*clienti: al ristorante*) to wait on; (: *al negozio*) to serve, attend to; (*fig: giovare*) to aid, help; (*CARTE*) to deal ♦ *vi* (*TENNIS*) to serve; (*essere utile*): ~ **a qn** to be of use to sb; ~ **a qc/a fare** (*utensile etc*) to be used for sth/for doing; ~ **(a qn) da** to serve as (for sb); ~**rsi** *vr* (*usare*): ~**rsi di** to use; (*prendere: cibo*): ~**rsi (di)** to help o.s. (to); (*essere cliente abituale*): ~**rsi da** to be a regular customer at, to go to
servitù *sf* servitude; slavery; (*personale di servizio*) servants *pl*, domestic staff
servizi'evole [servit'tsjevole] *ag* obliging, willing to help
ser'vizio [ser'vittsjo] *sm* service; (*al ristorante: sul conto*) service (charge); (*STAMPA, TV, RADIO*) report; (*da tè, caffè etc*) set, service; ~**i** *smpl* (*di casa*) kitchen and bathroom; (*ECON*) services; **essere di ~** to be on duty; **fuori ~** (*telefono etc*) out of order; ~ **compreso** service included; ~ **militare** military service; ~**i segreti** secret service *sg*
'servo, a *sm/f* servant
ses'santa *num* sixty; **sessan'tesimo, a** *num* sixtieth
sessan'tina *sf*: **una ~ (di)** about sixty

sessi'one *sf* session
'sesso *sm* sex; **sessu'ale** *ag* sexual, sex *cpd*
ses'tante *sm* sextant
'sesto, a *ag, sm* sixth
'seta *sf* silk
'sete *sf* thirst; **avere ~** to be thirsty
'setola *sf* bristle
'setta *sf* sect
set'tanta *num* seventy; **settan'tesimo, a** *num* seventieth
settan'tina *sf*: **una ~ (di)** about seventy
'sette *num* seven
sette'cento [sette'tʃento] *num* seven hundred ♦ *sm*: **il S~** the eighteenth century
set'tembre *sm* September
settentrio'nale *ag* northern
settentri'one *sm* north
setti'mana *sf* week; **settima'nale** *ag, sm* weekly

'settimo, a *ag, sm* seventh
set'tore *sm* sector
severità *sf* severity
se'vero, a *ag* severe
sevizi'are [sevit'tsjare] *vt* to torture
se'vizie [se'vittsje] *sfpl* torture *sg*
sezio'nare [settsjo'nare] *vt* to divide into sections; (*MED*) to dissect
sezi'one [set'tsjone] *sf* section
sfaccen'dato, a [sfattʃen'dato] *ag* idle
sfacci'ato, a [sfat'tʃato] *ag* (*maleducato*) cheeky, impudent; (*vistoso*) gaudy
sfa'celo [sfa'tʃelo] *sm* (*fig*) ruin, collapse
sfal'darsi *vr* to flake (off)
sfa'mare *vt* to feed; (*sog: cibo*) to fill
'sfarzo ['sfartso] *sm* pomp, splendour
sfasci'are [sfaʃ'ʃare] *vt* (*ferita*) to unbandage; (*distruggere*) to smash, shatter;

~rsi *vr* (*rompersi*) to smash, shatter

sfa'tare *vt* (*leggenda*) to explode

sfavil'lare *vi* to spark, send out sparks; (*risplendere*) to sparkle

sfavo'revole *ag* unfavourable

'sfera *sf* sphere; **'sferico, a, ci, che** *ag* spherical

sfer'rare *vt* (*fig: colpo*) to land, deal; (*: attacco*) to launch

sfer'zare [sfer'tsare] *vt* to whip; (*fig*) to lash out at

sfi'brare *vt* (*indebolire*) to exhaust, enervate

'sfida *sf* challenge

sfi'dare *vt* to challenge; (*fig*) to defy, brave

sfi'ducia [sfi'dutʃa] *sf* distrust, mistrust

sfigu'rare *vt* (*persona*) to disfigure; (*quadro, statua*) to deface ♦ *vi* (*far cattiva figura*) to make a bad impression

sfi'lare *vt* (*ago*) to unthread; (*abito, scarpe*) to slip off ♦ *vi* (*truppe*) to march past; (*atleti*) to parade; **~rsi** *vr* (*perle etc*) to come unstrung; (*orlo, tessuto*) to fray; (*calza*) to run, ladder; **sfi'lata** *sf* march past; parade; **sfilata di moda** fashion show

'sfinge ['sfindʒe] *sf* sphinx

sfi'nito, a *ag* exhausted

sfio'rare *vt* to brush (against); (*argomento*) to touch upon

sfio'rire *vi* to wither, fade

sfo'cato, a *ag* (*FOT*) out of focus

sfoci'are [sfo'tʃare] *vi*: **~ in** to flow into; (*fig: malcontento*) to develop into

sfode'rato, a *ag* (*vestito*) unlined

sfo'gare *vt* to vent, pour out; **~rsi** *vr* (*sfogare la propria rabbia*) to give vent to one's anger; (*confidarsi*): **~rsi (con)** to pour out one's feelings (to); **non sfogarti su di me!** don't take your bad temper out on me!

sfoggi'are [sfod'dʒare] *vt, vi* to show off

'sfoglia ['sfoʎʎa] *sf* sheet of pasta dough; **pasta ~** (*CUC*) puff pastry

sfogli'are [sfoʎ'ʎare] *vt* (*libro*) to leaf through

'sfogo, ghi *sm* (*eruzione cutanea*) rash; (*fig*) outburst; **dare ~ a** (*fig*) to give vent to

sfolgo'rante *ag* (*luce*) blazing; (*fig: vittoria*) brilliant

sfol'lare *vt* to empty, clear ♦ *vi* to disperse; **~ da** (*città*) to evacuate

sfon'dare *vt* (*porta*) to break down; (*scarpe*) to wear a hole in; (*cesto, scatola*) to burst, knock the bottom out of; (*MIL*) to break through ♦ *vi* (*riuscire*) to make a name for o.s.

'sfondo *sm* background

sfor'mato *sm* (*CUC*) type of soufflé

sfor'nare *vt* (*pane etc*) to take out of the oven; (*fig*) to churn out

sfor'nito, a *ag*: **~ di** lacking in, without; (*negozio*) out of

sfor'tuna *sf* misfortune, ill luck *no pl*; **avere ~** to be unlucky; **sfortu'nato, a** *ag* unlucky; (*impresa, film*) unsuccessful

sfor'zare [sfor'tsare] *vt* to force; (*voce, occhi*) to strain; **~rsi** *vr*: **~rsi di** o **a** o **per fare** to try hard to do

'sforzo ['sfortso] *sm* effort; (*tensione eccessiva, TECN*) strain; **fare uno ~** to make an effort

sfrat'tare *vt* to evict; **'sfratto** *sm* eviction

sfrecci'are [sfret'tʃare] *vi* to shoot o flash past

sfregi'are [sfre'dʒare] *vt* to slash, gash; (*persona*) to disfigure; (*quadro*) to deface; **'sfregio** *sm* gash; scar; (*fig*) insult

sfre'nato, a *ag* (*fig*) unrestrained, unbridled

sfron'tato, a *ag* shameless

sfrutta'mento *sm* exploitation

sfrut'tare *vt* (*terreno*) to overwork, exhaust; (*miniera*) to exploit, work; (*fig: operai, occasione, potere*) to exploit

sfug'gire [sfud'dʒire] *vi* to escape; **~ a** (*custode*) to escape (from); (*morte*) to escape; **~ a qn** (*dettaglio, nome*) to escape sb; **~ di mano a qn** to slip out of sb's hand (o hands); **sfug'gita: di sfuggita** *ad* (*rapidamente, in fretta*) in passing

sfu'mare *vt* (*colori, contorni*) to soften, shade off ♦ *vi* to shade (off), fade; (*fig: svanire*) to vanish, disappear; (*: speranze*) to come to nothing

sfuma'tura *sf* shading off *no pl;* (*tonalità*) shade, tone; (*fig*) touch, hint

sfuri'ata *sf* (*scatto di collera*) fit of anger; (*rimprovero*) sharp rebuke

sga'bello *sm* stool

sgabuz'zino [zgabud'dzino] *sm* lumber room

sgambet'tare *vi* to kick one's legs about

sgam'betto *sm:* **far lo ~ a qn** to trip sb up; (*fig*) to oust sb

sganasci'arsi [zganaʃ'ʃarsi] *vr:* **~ dalle risa** to roar with laughter

sganci'are [zgan'tʃare] *vt* to unhook; (*FERR*) to uncouple; (*bombe: da aereo*) to release, drop; (*fig: fam: soldi*) to fork out; **~rsi** *vr* (*fig*): **~rsi (da)** to get away (from)

sganghe'rato, a [zgange'rato] *ag* (*porta*) off its hinges; (*auto*) ramshackle; (*risata*) wild, boisterous

sgar'bato, a *ag* rude, impolite

'sgarbo *sm:* **fare uno ~ a qn** to be rude to sb

sgattaio'lare *vi* to sneak away *o* off

sge'lare [zdʒe'lare] *vi, vt* to thaw

'sghembo, a ['zgembo] *ag* (*obliquo*) slanting; (*storto*) crooked

sghignaz'zare [zgiɲɲat'tsare] *vi* to laugh scornfully

sgob'bare (*fam*) *vi* (*scolaro*) to swot; (*operaio*) to slog

sgoccio'lare [zgottʃo'lare] *vt* (*vuotare*) to drain (to the last drop) ♦ *vi* (*acqua*) to drip; (*recipiente*) to drain; **'sgoccioli** *smpl:* **essere agli ~** (*provviste*) to be nearly finished; (*periodo*) to be nearly over

sgo'larsi *vr* to talk (*o* shout *o* sing) o.s. hoarse

sgomb(e)'rare *vt* to clear; (*andarsene da: stanza*) to vacate; (*evacuare*) to evacuate

'sgombro, a *ag:* **~ (di)** clear (of), free (from) ♦ *sm* (*ZOOL*) mackerel; (*anche:* **sgombero**) clearing; vacating; evacuation; (*: trasloco*) removal

sgomen'tare *vt* to dismay; **sgo'mento, a** *ag* dismayed ♦ *sm* dismay, consternation

sgonfi'are *vt* to let down, deflate; **~rsi** *vr* to go down

'sgorbio *sm* blot; scribble

sgor'gare *vi* to gush (out)

sgoz'zare [zgot'tsare] *vt* to cut the throat of

sgra'devole *ag* unpleasant, disagreeable

sgra'dito, a *ag* unpleasant, unwelcome

sgra'nare *vt* (*piselli*) to shell; **~ gli occhi** to open one's eyes wide

sgran'chirsi [zgran'kirsi] *vr* to stretch; **~ le gambe** to stretch one's legs

sgranocchi'are [zgranok'kjare] *vt* to munch

'sgravio *sm:* **~ fiscale** tax relief

sgrazi'ato, a [zgrat'tsjato] *ag* clumsy, ungainly

sgreto'lare *vt* to cause to crumble; **~rsi** *vr* to crumble

sgri'dare *vt* to scold; **sgri'data** *sf* scolding

sguai'ato, a *ag* coarse, vulgar

sgual'cire [zgwal'tʃire] *vt* to crumple (up), crease

sgual'drina (*peg*) *sf* slut

sgu'ardo *sm* (*occhiata*) look, glance; (*espressione*) look (in one's eye)

'sguattero, a *sm/f* dishwasher (*person*)

squaz'zare [zgwat'tsare] *vi* (*nell'acqua*) to splash about; (*nella melma*) to wallow; **~ nell'oro** to be rolling in money

sguinzagli'are [zgwintsaʎ'ʎare] *vt* to let off the leash; (*fig: persona*): **~ qn dietro a qn** to set sb on sb

sgusci'are [zguʃ'ʃare] *vt* to shell ♦ *vi* (*sfuggire di mano*) to slip; **~ via** to slip *o* slink away

'shampoo ['ʃampo] *sm inv* shampoo

shock [ʃɔk] *sm inv* shock

PAROLA CHIAVE

---

si[1] (*dav lo, la, li, le, ne diventa* **se**) *pron*

1 (*riflessivo: maschile*) himself; (*: femminile*) herself; (*: neutro*) itself; (*: impersonale*) oneself; (*: pl*) themselves; **lavarsi** to wash (oneself); **~ è tagliato** he has cut himself; **~ credono importanti** they think a lot of themselves

2 (*riflessivo: con complemento oggetto*): **lavarsi le mani** to wash one's hands; **~ sta**

lavando i capelli he (*o* she) is washing his (*o* her) hair

3 (*reciproco*) one another, each other; **si amano** they love one another *o* each other

4 (*passivo*): **~ ripara facilmente** it is easily repaired

5 (*impersonale*): **~ dice che ...** they *o* people say that ...; **~ vede che è vecchio** one *o* you can see that it's old

6 (*noi*) we; **tra poco ~ parte** we're leaving soon

si² *sm* (*MUS*) B; (*solfeggiando la scala*) ti

sì *av* yes; **un giorno ~ e uno no** every other day

'sia *cong*: **~ ... ~** (*o ... o*): **~ che lavori, ~ che non lavori** whether he works or not; (*tanto ... quanto*): **verranno ~ Luigi ~ suo fratello** both Luigi and his brother will be coming

si'amo *vb vedi* **essere**

sibi'lare *vi* to hiss; (*fischiare*) to whistle; **si'bilo** hiss, whistle

si'cario *sm* hired killer

sicché [sik'ke] *cong* (*perciò*) so (that), therefore; (*e quindi*) (and) so

siccità [sittʃi'ta] *sf* drought

sic'come *cong* since, as

Si'cilia [si'tʃilja] *sf*: **la ~** Sicily; **sicili'ano, a** *ag, sm/f* Sicilian

si'cura *sf* safety catch; (*AUT*) safety lock

sicu'rezza [siku'rettsa] *sf* safety; security; (*fiducia*) confidence; (*certezza*) certainty; **di ~** safety *cpd*; **~ stradale** road safety

si'curo, a *ag* safe; (*ben difeso*) secure; (*fiducioso*) confident; (*certo*) sure, certain; (*notizia, amico*) reliable; (*esperto*) skilled ♦ *av* (*anche*: **di ~**) certainly; **essere/ mettere al ~** to be safe/put in a safe place; **~ di sé** self-confident, sure of o.s.; **sentirsi ~** to feel safe *o* secure

siderur'gia [siderur'dʒia] *sf* iron and steel industry

'sidro *sm* cider

si'epe *sf* hedge

si'ero *sm* (*MED*) serum; **sieronega'tivo, a** *ag* HIV-negative; **sieroposi'tivo, a** *ag* HIV-positive

si'esta *sf* siesta, (afternoon) nap

si'ete *vb vedi* **essere**

si'filide *sf* syphilis

si'fone *sm* siphon

Sig. *abbr* (= *signore*) Mr

siga'retta *sf* cigarette

'sigaro *sm* cigar

Sigg. *abbr* (= *signori*) Messrs

sigil'lare [sidʒil'lare] *vt* to seal

si'gillo [si'dʒillo] *sm* seal

'sigla *sf* initials *pl*; acronym, abbreviation; **~ automobilistica** *abbreviation of province on vehicle number plate*; **~ musicale** signature tune

si'glare *vt* to initial

Sig.na *abbr* (= *signorina*) Miss

signifi'care [siɲɲifi'kare] *vt* to mean; **significa'tivo, a** *ag* significant; **signifi'cato** *sm* meaning

si'gnora [siɲ'ɲora] *sf* lady; **la ~ X** Mrs X; **buon giorno S~/Signore/Signorina** good morning; (*deferente*) good morning Madam/Sir/Madam; (*quando si conosce il nome*) good morning Mrs/Mr/Miss X; **Gentile S~/Signore/Signorina** (*in una lettera*) Dear Madam/Sir/Madam; **il signor Rossi e ~** Mr Rossi and his wife; **~e e signori** ladies and gentlemen

si'gnore [siɲ'ɲore] *sm* gentleman; (*padrone*) lord, master; (*REL*): **il S~** the Lord; **il signor X** Mr X; **i ~i Bianchi** (*coniugi*) Mr and Mrs Bianchi; *vedi anche* **signora**

signo'rile [siɲɲo'rile] *ag* refined

signo'rina [siɲɲo'rina] *sf* young lady; **la ~ X** Miss X; *vedi anche* **signora**

Sig.ra *abbr* (= *signora*) Mrs

silenzia'tore [silentsja'tore] *sm* silencer

si'lenzio [si'lentsjo] *sm* silence; **fare ~** to be quiet, stop talking; **silenzi'oso, a** *ag* silent, quiet

si'licio [si'litʃo] *sm* silicon

'sillaba *sf* syllable

silu'rare *vt* to torpedo; (*fig: privare del comando*) to oust

si'luro *sm* torpedo

simboleggi'are [simboled'dʒare] *vt* to

symbolize

'simbolo *sm* symbol

'simile *ag* (*analogo*) similar; (*di questo tipo*): **un uomo ~** such a man, a man like this; **libri ~i** such books; **~ a** similar to; **i suoi ~i** one's fellow men; one's peers

simme'tria *sf* symmetry

simpa'tia *sf* (*qualità*) pleasantness; (*inclinazione*) liking; **avere ~ per qn** to like sb, have a liking for sb; **sim'patico, a, ci, che** *ag* (*persona*) nice, pleasant, likeable; (*casa, albergo etc*) nice, pleasant

simpatiz'zare [simpatid'dzare] *vi*: **~ con** to take a liking to

sim'posio *sm* symposium

simu'lare *vt* to sham, simulate; (*TECN*) to simulate; **simulazi'one** *sf* shamming; simulation

simul'taneo, a *ag* simultaneous

sina'goga, ghe *sf* synagogue

sincerità [sintʃeri'ta] *sf* sincerity

sin'cero, a [sin'tʃero] *ag* sincere; genuine; heartfelt

'sincope *sf* syncopation; (*MED*) blackout

sinda'cale *ag* (*trade-*)union *cpd*; **sindaca'lista, i, e** *sm/f* trade unionist

sinda'cato *sm* (*di lavoratori*) (trade) union; (*AMM, ECON, DIR*) syndicate, trust, pool

'sindaco, ci *sm* mayor

sinfo'nia *sf* (*MUS*) symphony

singhioz'zare [singjot'tsare] *vi* to sob; to hiccup

singhi'ozzo [sin'gjottso] *sm* sob; (*MED*) hiccup; **avere il ~** to have the hiccups; **a ~** (*fig*) by fits and starts

singo'lare *ag* (*insolito*) remarkable, singular; (*LING*) singular ♦ *sm* (*LING*) singular; (*TENNIS*): **~ maschile/femminile** men's/women's singles

'singolo, a *ag* single, individual ♦ *sm* (*persona*) individual; (*TENNIS*) = **singolare**

si'nistra *sf* (*POL*) left (wing); **a ~** on the left; (*direzione*) to the left

si'nistro, a *ag* left, left-hand; (*fig*) sinister ♦ *sm* (*incidente*) accident

'sino *prep* = **fino**

si'nonimo *sm* synonym; **~ di** synonymous with

sin'tassi *sf* syntax

'sintesi *sf* synthesis; (*riassunto*) summary, résumé

sin'tetico, a, ci, che *ag* synthetic

sintetiz'zare [sintetid'dzare] *vt* to synthesize; (*riassumere*) to summarize

sinto'matico, a, ci, che *ag* symptomatic

'sintomo *sm* symptom

sinu'oso, a *ag* (*strada*) winding

si'pario *sm* (*TEATRO*) curtain

si'rena *sf* (*apparecchio*) siren; (*nella mitologia, fig*) siren, mermaid

'Siria *sf*: **la ~** Syria

si'ringa, ghe *sf* syringe

'sismico, a, ci, che *ag* seismic

sis'mografo *sm* seismograph

sis'tema, i *sm* system; method, way

siste'mare *vt* (*mettere a posto*) to tidy, put in order; (*risolvere: questione*) to sort out, settle; (*procurare un lavoro a*) to find a job for; (*dare un alloggio a*) to settle, find accommodation for; **~rsi** *vr* (*problema*) to be settled; (*persona: trovare alloggio*) to find accommodation (*BRIT*) *o* accommodations (*US*); (: *trovarsi un lavoro*) to get fixed up with a job; **ti sistemo io!** I'll soon sort you out!

siste'matico, a, ci, che *ag* systematic

sistemazi'one [sistemat'tsjone] *sf* arrangement, order; settlement; employment; accommodation (*BRIT*), accommodations (*US*)

'sito *sm* (*Internet*) Website

situ'are *vt* to site, situate; **situ'ato, a** *ag*: **situato a/su** situated at/on

situazi'one [situat'tsjone] *sf* situation

ski-lift ['ski:lift] *sm inv* ski tow

slacci'are [zlat'tʃare] *vt* to undo, unfasten

slanci'ato, a [zlan'tʃato] *ag* slender

'slancio *sm* dash, leap; (*fig*) surge; **di ~** impetuously

sla'vato, a *ag* faded, washed out; (*fig: viso, occhi*) pale, colourless

'slavo, a *ag* Slav(onic), Slavic

sle'ale *ag* disloyal; (*concorrenza etc*) unfair
sle'gare *vt* to untie
slip [zlip] *sm inv* briefs *pl*
'**slitta** *sf* sledge; (*trainata*) sleigh
slit'tare *vi* to slip, slide; (*AUT*) to skid
slo'gare *vt* (*MED*) to dislocate
sloggi'are [zlod'dʒare] *vt* (*inquilino*) to turn out ♦ *vi* to move out
slo'vacco, a, chi, che *ag, sm/f* Slovak
Slovenia [zlo'vɛnja] *sf* Slovenia
smacchi'are [zmak'kjare] *vt* to remove stains from; **smacchia'tore** *sm* stain remover
'**smacco, chi** *sm* humiliating defeat
smagli'ante [zmaʎ'ʎante] *ag* brilliant, dazzling
smaglia'tura [zmaʎʎa'tura] *sf* (*su maglia, calza*) ladder; (*della pelle*) stretch mark
smalizi'ato, a [zmalit'tsjato] *ag* shrewd, cunning
smal'tare *vt* to enamel; (*ceramica*) to glaze; (*unghie*) to varnish
smal'tire *vt* (*merce*) to sell off; (*rifiuti*) to dispose of; (*cibo*) to digest; (*peso*) to lose; (*rabbia*) to get over; **~ la sbornia** to sober up
'**smalto** *sm* (*anche: di denti*) enamel; (*per ceramica*) glaze; **~ per unghie** nail varnish
'**smania** *sf* agitation, restlessness; (*fig*): **~ di** thirst for, craving for; **avere la ~ addosso** to have the fidgets; **avere la ~ di fare** to be desperate to do
smantel'lare *vt* to dismantle
smarri'mento *sm* loss; (*fig*) bewilderment; dismay
smar'rire *vt* to lose; (*non riuscire a trovare*) to mislay; **~rsi** *vr* (*perdersi*) to lose one's way, get lost; (*: oggetto*) to go astray; **smar'rito, a** *ag* (*sbigottito*) bewildered
smasche'rare [zmaske'rare] *vt* to unmask
smemo'rato, a *ag* forgetful
smen'tire *vt* (*negare*) to deny; (*testimonianza*) to refute; **smen'tita** *sf* denial; retraction
sme'raldo *sm* emerald
smerci'are [zmer'tʃare] *vt* (*COMM*) to sell; (*: svendere*) to sell off

'**smesso, a** *pp di* **smettere**
'**smettere** *vt* to stop; (*vestiti*) to stop wearing ♦ *vi* to stop, cease; **~ di fare** to stop doing
'**smilzo, a** ['zmiltso] *ag* thin, lean
sminu'ire *vt* to diminish, lessen; (*fig*) to belittle
sminuz'zare [zminut'tsare] *vt* to break into small pieces; to crumble
smis'tare *vt* (*pacchi etc*) to sort; (*FERR*) to shunt
smisu'rato, a *ag* boundless, immeasurable; (*grandissimo*) immense, enormous
smobili'tare *vt* to demobilize
smo'dato, a *ag* immoderate
smoking ['smaukıŋ] *sm inv* dinner jacket
smon'tare *vt* (*mobile, macchina etc*) to take to pieces, dismantle; (*fig: scoraggiare*) to dishearten ♦ *vi* (*scendere: da cavallo*) to dismount; (*: da treno*) to get off; (*terminare il lavoro*) to stop (work); **~rsi** *vr* to lose heart; to lose one's enthusiasm
'**smorfia** *sf* grimace; (*atteggiamento lezioso*) simpering; **fare ~e** to make faces; to simper; **smorfi'oso, a** *ag* simpering
'**smorto, a** *ag* (*viso*) pale, wan; (*colore*) dull
smor'zare [zmor'tsare] *vt* (*suoni*) to deaden; (*colori*) to tone down; (*luce*) to dim; (*sete*) to quench; (*entusiasmo*) to dampen; **~rsi** *vr* (*suono, luce*) to fade; (*entusiasmo*) to dampen
'**smosso, a** *pp di* **smuovere**
smotta'mento *sm* landslide
'**smunto, a** *ag* haggard, pinched
smu'overe *vt* to move, shift; (*fig: commuovere*) to move; (*: dall'inerzia*) to rouse, stir; **~rsi** *vr* to move, shift
smus'sare *vt* (*angolo*) to round off, smooth; (*lama etc*) to blunt; **~rsi** *vr* to become blunt
snatu'rato, a *ag* inhuman, heartless
'**snello, a** *ag* (*agile*) agile; (*svelto*) slender, slim
sner'vare *vt* to enervate, wear out
sni'dare *vt* to drive out, flush out
snob'bare *vt* to snub

sno'bismo sm snobbery

snoccio'lare [znottʃo'lare] vt (frutta) to stone; (fig: orazioni) to rattle off

sno'dare vt (rendere agile, mobile) to loosen; ~rsi vr to come loose; (articolarsi) to bend; (strada, fiume) to wind

so vb vedi sapere

so'ave ag sweet, gentle, soft

sobbal'zare [sobbal'tsare] vi to jolt, jerk; (trasalire) to jump, start; sob'balzo sm jerk, jolt; jump, start

sobbar'carsi vr: ~ a to take on, undertake

sob'borgo, ghi sm suburb

sobil'lare vt to stir up, incite

'sobrio, a ag sober

socchi'udere [sok'kjudere] vt (porta) to leave ajar; (occhi) to half-close; socchi'uso, a pp di socchiudere

soc'correre vt to help, assist; soc'corso, a pp di soccorrere ♦ sm help, aid, assistance; soccorsi smpl relief sg, aid sg; soccorso stradale breakdown service

soci'ale [so'tʃale] ag social; (di associazione) club cpd, association cpd

socia'lismo [sotʃa'lizmo] sm socialism; socia'lista, i, e ag, sm/f socialist

società [sotʃe'ta] sf inv society; (sportiva) club; (COMM) company; ~ per azioni limited (BRIT) o incorporated (US) company; ~ a responsabilità limitata type of limited liability company

soci'evole [so'tʃevole] ag sociable

'socio [ˈsɔtʃo] sm (DIR, COMM) partner; (membro di associazione) member

'soda sf (CHIM) soda; (bibita) soda (water)

soda'lizio [soda'littsjo] sm association, society

soddisfa'cente [soddisfa'tʃente] ag satisfactory

soddis'fare vt, vi: ~ a to satisfy; (impegno) to fulfil; (debito) to pay off; (richiesta) to meet, comply with; soddis'fatto, a pp di soddisfare ♦ ag satisfied; soddisfatto di happy o satisfied with; pleased with; soddisfazi'one sf satisfaction

'sodo, a ag firm, hard; (uovo) hard-boiled ♦ av (picchiare, lavorare) hard; (dormire)

soundly

sofà sm inv sofa

soffe'renza [soffe'rentsa] sf suffering

sof'ferto, a pp di soffrire

soffi'are vt to blow; (notizia, segreto) to whisper ♦ vi to blow; (sbuffare) to puff (and blow); ~rsi il naso to blow one's nose; ~ qc/qn a qn (fig) to pinch o steal sth/sb from sb; ~ via qc to blow sth away

'soffice [ˈsɔffitʃe] ag soft

'soffio sm (di vento) breath; ~ al cuore heart murmur

sof'fitta sf attic

sof'fitto sm ceiling

soffo'care vi (anche: ~rsi) to suffocate, choke ♦ vt to suffocate, choke; (fig) to stifle, suppress

sof'friggere [sof'friddʒere] vt to fry lightly

sof'frire vt to suffer, endure; (sopportare) to bear, stand ♦ vi to suffer; to be in pain; ~ (di) qc (MED) to suffer from sth

sof'fritto, a pp di soffriggere ♦ sm (CUC) fried mixture of herbs, bacon and onions

sofisti'cato, a ag sophisticated; (vino) adulterated

sogget'tivo, a [soddʒet'tivo] ag subjective

sog'getto, a [sod'dʒetto] ag: ~ a (sottomesso) subject to; (esposto: a variazioni, danni etc) subject o liable to ♦ sm subject

soggezi'one [soddʒet'tsjone] sf subjection; (timidezza) awe; avere ~ di qn to stand in awe of sb; to be ill at ease in sb's presence

sogghi'gnare [soggin'nare] vi to sneer

soggior'nare [soddʒor'nare] vi to stay; soggi'orno sm (invernale, marino) stay; (stanza) living room

sog'giungere [sod'dʒundʒere] vt to add

'soglia [ˈsɔʎʎa] sf doorstep; (anche fig) threshold

'sogliola [ˈsɔʎʎola] sf (ZOOL) sole

so'gnare [son'nare] vt, vi to dream; ~ a occhi aperti to daydream; sogna'tore, 'trice sm/f dreamer

'sogno [ˈsonno] sm dream

'soia sf (BOT) soya

sol sm (MUS) G; (: solfeggiando) so(h)

so'laio *sm* (*soffitta*) attic
sola'mente *av* only, just
so'lare *ag* solar, sun *cpd*
'solco, chi *sm* (*scavo, fig: ruga*) furrow; (*incavo*) rut, track; (*di disco*) groove
sol'dato *sm* soldier; ~ **semplice** private
'soldo *sm* (*fig*): **non avere un** ~ to be penniless; **non vale un** ~ it's not worth a penny; ~**i** *smpl* (*denaro*) money *sg*
'sole *sm* sun; (*luce*) sun(light); (*tempo assolato*) sun(shine); **prendere il** ~ to sunbathe
soleggi'ato, a [soled'dʒato] *ag* sunny
so'lenne *ag* solemn; **solennità** *sf* solemnity; (*festività*) holiday, feast day
sol'fato *sm* (CHIM) sulphate
soli'dale *ag*: **essere** ~ **(con)** to be in agreement (with)
solidarietà *sf* solidarity
'solido, a *ag* solid; (*forte, robusto*) sturdy, solid; (*fig: ditta*) sound, solid ♦ *sm* (MAT) solid
soli'loquio *sm* soliloquy
so'lista, i, e *ag* solo ♦ *sm/f* soloist
solita'mente *av* usually, as a rule
soli'tario, a *ag* (*senza compagnia*) solitary, lonely; (*solo, isolato*) solitary, lone; (*deserto*) lonely ♦ *sm* (*gioiello, gioco*) solitaire
'solito, a *ag* usual; **essere** ~ **fare** to be in the habit of doing; **di** ~ usually; **più tardi del** ~ later than usual; **come al** ~ as usual
soli'tudine *sf* solitude
solleci'tare [solletʃi'tare] *vt* (*lavoro*) to speed up; (*persona*) to urge on; (*chiedere con insistenza*) to press for, request urgently; (*stimolare*): ~ **qn a fare** to urge sb to do; **sollecitazi'one** *sf* entreaty, request; (*fig*) incentive; (TECN) stress
sol'lecito, a *ag* prompt, quick ♦ *sm* (*lettera*) reminder; **solleci'tudine** *sf* promptness, speed
solleti'care *vt* to tickle
sol'letico *sm* tickling; **soffrire il** ~ to be ticklish
solleva'mento *sm* raising; lifting; revolt; ~ **pesi** (SPORT) weight-lifting
solle'vare *vt* to lift, raise; (*fig: persona:*

alleggerire): ~ **(da)** to relieve (of); (: *dar conforto*) to comfort, relieve; (: *questione*) to raise; (: *far insorgere*) to stir (to revolt); ~**rsi** *vr* to rise; (*fig: riprendersi*) to recover; (: *ribellarsi*) to rise up
solli'evo *sm* relief; (*conforto*) comfort
'solo, a *ag* alone; (*in senso spirituale: isolato*) lonely; (*unico*): **un** ~ **libro** only one book, a single book; (*con ag numerale*): **veniamo noi tre** ~**i** just *o* only the three of us are coming ♦ *av* (*soltanto*) only, just; **non** ~ ... **ma anche** not only ... but also; **fare qc da** ~ to do sth (all) by oneself
sol'tanto *av* only
so'lubile *ag* (*sostanza*) soluble
soluzi'one [solut'tsjone] *sf* solution
sol'vente *ag, sm* solvent
'soma *sf*: **bestia da** ~ beast of burden
so'maro *sm* ass, donkey
somigli'anza [somiʎ'ʎantsa] *sf* resemblance
somigli'are [somiʎ'ʎare] *vi*: ~ **a** to be like, resemble; (*nell'aspetto fisico*): to look like; ~**rsi** *vr* to be (*o* look) alike
'somma *sf* (MAT) sum; (*di denaro*) sum (of money)
som'mare *vt* to add up; (*aggiungere*) to add; **tutto sommato** all things considered
som'mario, a *ag* (*racconto, indagine*) brief; (*giustizia*) summary ♦ *sm* summary
som'mergere [som'mɛrdʒere] *vt* to submerge
sommer'gibile [sommer'dʒibile] *sm* submarine
som'merso, a *pp di* **sommergere**
som'messo, a *ag* (*voce*) soft, subdued
somminis'trare *vt* to give, administer
sommità *sf inv* summit, top; (*fig*) height
'sommo, a *ag* highest; (*rispetto etc*) highest, greatest; (*poeta, artista*) great, outstanding; **per** ~**i capi** briefly, covering the main points
som'mossa *sf* uprising
so'nare *etc* = **suonare** *etc*
son'daggio [son'daddʒo] *sm* sounding; probe; boring, drilling; (*indagine*) survey; ~ **d'opinioni** opinion poll
son'dare *vt* (NAUT) to sound; (*atmosfera,*

piaga) to probe; (*MINERALOGIA*) to bore, drill; (*fig: opinione etc*) to survey, poll

so'netto *sm* sonnet

son'nambulo, a *sm/f* sleepwalker

sonnecchi'are [sonnek'kjare] *vi* to doze, nod

son'nifero *sm* sleeping drug (*o* pill)

'sonno *sm* sleep; **prendere ~** to fall asleep; **aver ~** to be sleepy

'sono *vb vedi* **essere**

so'noro, a *ag* (*ambiente*) resonant; (*voce*) sonorous, ringing; (*onde, film*) sound *cpd*

sontu'oso, a *ag* sumptuous; lavish

sopo'rifero, a *ag* soporific

soppe'sare *vt* to weigh in one's hand(s), feel the weight of; (*fig*) to weigh up

soppi'atto: di ~ *av* secretly; furtively

soppor'tare *vt* (*reggere*) to support; (*subire: perdita, spese*) to bear, sustain; (*soffrire: dolore*) to bear, endure; (*sog: cosa: freddo*) to withstand; (*sog: persona: freddo, vino*) to take; (*tollerare*) to put up with, tolerate

sop'presso, a *pp di* **sopprimere**

sop'primere *vt* (*carica, privilegi, testimone*) to do away with; (*pubblicazione*) to suppress; (*parola, frase*) to delete

'sopra *prep* (*gen*) on; (*al di sopra di, più in alto di*) above; over; (*riguardo a*) on, about ♦ *av* on top; (*attaccato, scritto*) on it; (*al di sopra*) above; (*al piano superiore*) upstairs; **donne ~ i 30 anni** women over 30 (years of age); **abito di ~** I live upstairs; **dormirci ~** (*fig*) to sleep on it

so'prabito *sm* overcoat

soprac'ciglio [soprat'tʃiʎʎo] (*pl(f)* **soprac'ciglia**) *sm* eyebrow

sopracco'perta *sf* (*di letto*) bedspread; (*di libro*) jacket

sopraf'fare *vt* to overcome, overwhelm; **sopraf'fatto, a** *pp di* **sopraffare**

sopraf'fino, a *ag* (*pranzo, vino*) excellent

sopraggi'ungere [soprad'dʒundʒere] *vi* (*giungere all'improvviso*) to arrive (unexpectedly); (*accadere*) to occur (unexpectedly)

sopral'luogo, ghi *sm* (*di esperti*)

inspection; (*di polizia*) on-the-spot investigation

sopram'mobile *sm* ornament

soprannatu'rale *ag* supernatural

sopran'nome *sm* nickname

so'prano, a *sm/f* (*persona*) soprano ♦ *sm* (*voce*) soprano

soprappensi'ero *av* lost in thought

sopras'salto *sm*: **di ~** with a start; suddenly

soprasse'dere *vi*: **~ a** to delay, put off

soprat'tutto *av* (*anzitutto*) above all; (*specialmente*) especially

sopravvalu'tare *vt* to overestimate

soprav'vento *sm*: **avere/prendere il ~ su** to have/get the upper hand over

sopravvis'suto, a *pp di* **sopravvivere**

soprav'vivere *vi* to survive; (*continuare a vivere*): **~ (in)** to live on (in); **~ a** (*incidente etc*) to survive; (*persona*) to outlive

soprele'vata *sf* (*strada*) flyover; (*ferrovia*) elevated railway

soprinten'dente *sm/f* supervisor; (*statale: di belle arti etc*) keeper; **soprinten'denza** *sf* supervision; (*ente*): **soprintendenza alle Belle Arti** government department responsible for monuments and artistic treasures

so'pruso *sm* abuse of power; **subire un ~** to be abused

soq'quadro *sm*: **mettere a ~** to turn upside-down

sor'betto *sm* sorbet, water ice

sor'bire *vt* to sip; (*fig*) to put up with

'sorcio, ci ['sortʃo] *sm* mouse

'sordido, a *ag* sordid; (*fig: gretto*) stingy

sor'dina *sf*: **in ~** softly; (*fig*) on the sly

sordità *sf* deafness

'sordo, a *ag* deaf; (*rumore*) muffled; (*dolore*) dull; (*odio, rancore*) veiled ♦ *sm/f* deaf person; **sordo'muto, a** *ag* deaf-and-dumb ♦ *sm/f* deaf-mute

so'rella *sf* sister; **sorel'lastra** *sf* stepsister

sor'gente [sor'dʒɛnte] *sf* (*d'acqua*) spring; (*di fiume, FISICA, fig*) source

'sorgere ['sordʒere] *vi* to rise; (*scaturire*) to spring, rise; (*fig: difficoltà*) to arise

sormon'tare vt (fig) to overcome, surmount

sorni'one, a ag sly

sorpas'sare vt (AUT) to overtake; (fig) to surpass; (: eccedere) to exceed, go beyond; ~ **in altezza** to be higher than; (persona) to be taller than; **sor'passo** sm (AUT) overtaking

sorpren'dente ag surprising

sor'prendere vt (cogliere: in flagrante etc) to catch; (stupire) to surprise; ~**rsi** vr: ~**rsi (di)** to be surprised (at); **sor'presa** sf surprise; **fare una sorpresa a qn** to give sb a surprise; **sor'preso, a** pp di **sorprendere**

sor'reggere [sor'reddʒere] vt to support, hold up; (fig) to sustain; **sor'retto, a** pp di **sorreggere**

sor'ridere vi to smile; **sor'riso, a** pp di **sorridere ♦** sm smile

'sorso sm sip

'sorta sf sort, kind; **di ~** whatever, of any kind, at all

'sorte sf (fato) fate, destiny; (evento fortuito) chance; **tirare a ~** to draw lots

sor'teggio [sor'teddʒo] sm draw

sorti'legio [sorti'ledʒo] sm witchcraft no pl; (incantesimo) spell; **fare un ~ a qn** to cast a spell on sb

sor'tita sf (MIL) sortie

'sorto, a pp di **sorgere**

sorvegli'anza [sorveʎ'ʎantsa] sf watch; supervision; (POLIZIA, MIL) surveillance

sorvegli'are [sorveʎ'ʎare] vt (bambino, bagagli, prigioniero) to watch, keep an eye on; (malato) to watch over; (territorio, casa) to watch o keep watch over; (lavori) to supervise

sorvo'lare vt (territorio) to fly over ♦ vi: ~ **su** (fig) to skim over

'sosia sm inv double

sos'pendere vt (appendere) to hang (up); (interrompere, privare di una carica) to suspend; (rimandare) to defer; (appendere) to hang; **sospensi'one** sf (anche CHIM, AUT) suspension; deferment; **sos'peso, a** pp di **sospendere ♦** ag (appeso): **sospeso**

a hanging on (o from); (treno, autobus) cancelled; **in sospeso** in abeyance; (conto) outstanding; **tenere in sospeso** (fig) to keep in suspense

sospet'tare vt to suspect ♦ vi: ~ **di** to suspect; (diffidare) to be suspicious of

sos'petto, a ag suspicious ♦ sm suspicion; **sospet'toso, a** ag suspicious

sos'pingere [sos'pindʒere] vt to drive, push; **sos'pinto, a** pp di **sospingere**

sospi'rare vi to sigh ♦ vt to long for, yearn for; **sos'piro** sm sigh

'sosta sf (fermata) stop, halt; (pausa) pause, break; **senza ~** non-stop, without a break

sostan'tivo sm noun, substantive

sos'tanza [sos'tantsa] sf substance; ~**e** sfpl (ricchezze) wealth sg, possessions; **in ~** in short, to sum up; **sostanzi'oso, a** ag (cibo) nourishing, substantial

sos'tare vi (fermarsi) to stop (for a while), stay; (fare una pausa) to take a break

sos'tegno [sos'teɲɲo] sm support

soste'nere vt to support; (prendere su di sé) to take on, bear; (resistere) to withstand, stand up to; (affermare): ~ **che** to maintain that; ~**rsi** vr to hold o.s. up, support o.s.; (fig) to keep up one's strength; ~ **gli esami** to sit exams; **sosteni'tore, 'trice** sm/f supporter

sosten'tamento sm maintenance, support

soste'nuto, a ag (stile) elevated; (velocità, ritmo) sustained; (prezzo) high ♦ sm/f: **fare il(la) ~(a)** to be standoffish, keep one's distance

sostitu'ire vt (mettere al posto di): ~ **qn/qc a** to substitute sb/sth for; (prendere il posto di: persona) to substitute for; (: cosa) to take the place of

sosti'tuto, a sm/f substitute

sostituzi'one [sostitut'tsjone] sf substitution; **in ~ di** as a substitute for, in place of

sotta'ceti [sotta'tʃeti] smpl pickles

sot'tana sf (sottoveste) underskirt; (gonna) skirt; (REL) soutane, cassock

sotter'fugio [sotter'fudʒo] *sm* subterfuge
sotter'raneo, a *ag* underground ♦ *sm* cellar
sotter'rare *vt* to bury
sottigli'ezza [sottiʎ'λettsa] *sf* thinness; slimness; (*fig: acutezza*) subtlety; shrewdness; **~e** *sfpl* (*pedanteria*) quibbles
sot'tile *ag* thin; (*figura, caviglia*) thin, slim, slender; (*fine: polvere, capelli*) fine; (*fig: leggero*) light; (*: vista*) sharp, keen; (*: olfatto*) fine, discriminating; (*: mente*) subtle; shrewd ♦ *sm*: **non andare per il ~** not to mince matters
sottin'tendere *vt* (*intendere qc non espresso*) to understand; (*implicare*) to imply; **sottin'teso, a** *pp di* **sottintendere** ♦ *sm* allusion; **parlare senza sottintesi** to speak plainly
'sotto *prep* (*gen*) under; (*più in basso di*) below ♦ *av* underneath, beneath; below; **(al piano) di ~** downstairs; **~ forma di** in the form of; **~ il monte** at the foot of the mountain; **siamo ~ Natale** it's nearly Christmas; **~ la pioggia / il sole** in the rain/sun(shine); **~ terra** underground; **chiuso ~ vuoto** vacuum-packed
sottoline'are *vt* to underline; (*fig*) to emphasize, stress
sottoma'rino, a *ag* (*flora*) submarine; (*cavo, navigazione*) underwater ♦ *sm* (*NAUT*) submarine
sotto'messo, a *pp di* **sottomettere**
sotto'mettere *vt* to subdue, subjugate; **~rsi** *vr* to submit
sottopas'saggio [sottopas'saddʒo] *sm* (*AUT*) underpass; (*pedonale*) subway, underpass
sotto'porre *vt* (*costringere*) to subject; (*fig: presentare*) to submit; **sottoporsi** *vr* to submit; **sottoporsi a** (*subire*) to undergo; **sotto'posto, a** *pp di* **sottoporre**
sottos'critto, a *pp di* **sottoscrivere**
sottos'crivere *vt* to sign ♦ *vi*: **~ a** to subscribe to; **sottoscrizi'one** *sf* signing; subscription
sottosegre'tario *sm*: **~ di Stato** Under-Secretary of State (*BRIT*), Assistant Secretary of State (*US*)
sotto'sopra *av* upside-down
sotto'terra *av* underground
sotto'titolo *sm* subtitle
sottovalu'tare *vt* to underestimate
sotto'veste *sf* underskirt
sotto'voce [sotto'votʃe] *av* in a low voice
sot'trarre *vt* (*MAT*) to subtract, take away; **~ qn/qc a** (*togliere*) to remove sb/sth from; (*salvare*) to save *o* rescue sb/sth from; **~ qc a qn** (*rubare*) to steal sth from sb; **sottrarsi** *vr*: **sottrarsi a** (*sfuggire*) to escape; (*evitare*) to avoid; **sot'tratto, a** *pp di* **sottrarre**; **sottrazi'one** *sf* subtraction; removal
sovi'etico, a, ci, che *ag* Soviet ♦ *sm/f* Soviet citizen
sovraccari'care *vt* to overload
sovrannatu'rale *ag* = **soprannaturale**
so'vrano, a *ag* sovereign; (*fig: sommo*) supreme ♦ *sm/f* sovereign, monarch
sovrap'porre *vt* to place on top of, put on top of
sovras'tare *vi*: **~ a** (*vallata, fiume*) to overhang; (*fig*) to hang over, threaten ♦ *vt* to overhang; to hang over, threaten
sovrinten'dente *etc* = **soprintendente** *etc*
sovru'mano, a *ag* superhuman
sovvenzi'one [sovven'tsjone] *sf* subsidy, grant
sovver'sivo, a *ag* subversive
'sozzo, a ['sottso] *ag* filthy, dirty
S.p.A. *abbr* = **società per azioni**
spac'care *vt* to split, break; (*legna*) to chop; **~rsi** *vr* to split, break; **spacca'tura** *sf* split
spacci'are [spat'tʃare] *vt* (*vendere*) to sell (off); (*mettere in circolazione*) to circulate; (*droga*) to peddle, push; **~rsi** *vr*: **~rsi per** (*farsi credere*) to pass o.s. off as, pretend to be; **spaccia'tore, 'trice** *sm/f* (*di droga*) pusher; (*di denaro falso*) dealer; **'spaccio** *sm* (*di merce rubata, droga*): **spaccio (di)** trafficking (in); (*in denaro falso*): **spaccio (di)** passing (of); (*vendita*) sale; (*bottega*) shop
'spacco, chi *sm* (*fenditura*) split, crack;

(*strappo*) tear; (*di gonna*) slit

spac'cone *sm/f* boaster, braggart

'spada *sf* sword

spae'sato, a *ag* disorientated, lost

spa'ghetti [spa'getti] *smpl* (*CUC*) spaghetti *sg*

'Spagna ['spanna] *sf*: **la ~** Spain; **spa'gnolo, a** *ag* Spanish ♦ *sm/f* Spaniard ♦ *sm* (*LING*) Spanish; **gli Spagnoli** the Spanish

'spago, ghi *sm* string, twine

spai'ato, a *ag* (*calza, guanto*) odd

spalan'care *vt* to open wide; **~rsi** *vr* to open wide

spa'lare *vt* to shovel

'spalla *sf* shoulder; (*fig: TEATRO*) stooge; **~e** *sfpl* (*dorso*) back; **spalleggi'are** *vt* to back up, support

spalli'era *sf* (*di sedia etc*) back; (*di letto: da capo*) head(board); (: *da piedi*) foot(board); (*GINNASTICA*) wall bars *pl*

spal'lina *sf* (*bretella*) strap; (*imbottita*) shoulder pad

spal'mare *vt* to spread

'spalti *smpl* (*di stadio*) terracing

'spandere *vt* to spread; (*versare*) to pour (out); **~rsi** *vr* to spread; **'spanto, a** *pp di* **spandere**

spa'rare *vt* to fire ♦ *vi* (*far fuoco*) to fire; (*tirare*) to shoot; **spara'toria** *sf* exchange of shots

sparecchi'are [sparek'kjare] *vt*: **~ (la tavola)** to clear the table

spa'reggio [spa'reddʒo] *sm* (*SPORT*) play-off

'spargere ['spardʒere] *vt* (*sparpagliare*) to scatter; (*versare: vino*) to spill; (: *lacrime, sangue*) to shed; (*diffondere*) to spread; (*emanare*) to give off (*o out*); **~rsi** *vr* to spread; **spargi'mento** *sm* scattering, strewing; spilling; shedding; **spargimento di sangue** bloodshed

spa'rire *vi* to disappear, vanish

spar'lare *vi*: **~ di** to run down, speak ill of

'sparo *sm* shot

sparpagli'are [sparpaʎ'ʎare] *vt* to scatter; **~rsi** *vr* to scatter

'sparso, a *pp di* **spargere** ♦ *ag* scattered;

(*sciolto*) loose

spar'tire *vt* (*eredità, bottino*) to share out; (*avversari*) to separate

spar'tito *sm* (*MUS*) score

sparti'traffico *sm inv* (*AUT*) central reservation (*BRIT*), median (strip) (*US*)

spa'ruto, a *ag* (*viso etc*) haggard

sparvi'ero *sm* (*ZOOL*) sparrowhawk

spasi'mante *sm* suitor

'spasimo *sm* pang; **'spasmo** *sm* (*MED*) spasm; **spas'modico, a, ci, che** *ag* (*angoscioso*) agonizing; (*MED*) spasmodic

spassio'nato, a *ag* dispassionate, impartial

'spasso *sm* (*divertimento*) amusement, enjoyment; **andare a ~** to go out for a walk; **essere a ~** (*fig*) to be out of work; **mandare qn a ~** (*fig*) to give sb the sack

'spatola *sf* spatula; (*di muratore*) trowel

spau'racchio [spau'rakkjo] *sm* scarecrow

spau'rire *vt* to frighten, terrify

spa'valdo, a *ag* arrogant, bold

spaven'passeri *sm inv* scarecrow

spaven'tare *vt* to frighten, scare; **~rsi** *vr* to be frightened, be scared; to get a fright; **spa'vento** *sm* fear, fright; **far spavento a qn** to give sb a fright; **spaven'toso, a** *ag* frightening, terrible; (*fig: fam*) tremendous, fantastic

spazien'tire [spattsjen'tire] *vi* (*anche*: **~rsi**) to lose one's patience

'spazio ['spattsjo] *sm* space; **~ aereo** airspace; **spazi'oso, a** *ag* spacious

spazzaca'mino [spattsaka'mino] *sm* chimney sweep

spazza'neve [spattsa'neve] *sm inv* snowplough

spaz'zare [spat'tsare] *vt* to sweep; (*foglie etc*) to sweep up; (*cacciare*) to sweep away; **spazza'tura** *sf* sweepings *pl*; (*immondizia*) rubbish; **spaz'zino** *sm* street sweeper

'spazzola ['spattsola] *sf* brush; **~ per abiti** clothesbrush; **~ da capelli** hairbrush; **spazzo'lare** *vt* to brush; **spazzo'lino** *sm* (small) brush; **spazzolino da denti** toothbrush

specchi'arsi [spek'kjarsi] *vr* to look at o.s. in a mirror; (*riflettersi*) to be mirrored, be reflected

'specchio ['spekkjo] *sm* mirror

speci'ale [spe't∫ale] *ag* special; **specia'lista, i, e** *sm/f* specialist; **specialità** *sf inv* speciality; (*branca di studio*) special field, speciality; **specializ'zarsi** *vr*: **specializzarsi (in)** to specialize (in); **special'mente** *av* especially, particularly

'specie ['spet∫e] *sf inv* (BIOL, BOT, ZOOL) species *inv*; (*tipo*) kind, sort ♦ *av* especially, particularly; **una ~ di** a kind of; **fare ~ a qn** to surprise sb; **la ~ umana** mankind

specifi'care [spet∫ifi'kare] *vt* to specify, state

spe'cifico, a, ci, che [spe't∫ifiko] *ag* specific

specu'lare *vi*: **~ su** (COMM) to speculate in; (*sfruttare*) to exploit; (*meditare*) to speculate on; **speculazi'one** *sf* speculation

spe'dire *vt* to send; **spedizi'one** *sf* sending; (*collo*) consignment; (*scientifica etc*) expedition

'spegnere ['speɲɲere] *vt* (*fuoco, sigaretta*) to put out, extinguish; (*apparecchio elettrico*) to turn *o* switch off; (*gas*) to turn off; (*fig: suoni, passioni*) to stifle; (*debito*) to extinguish; **~rsi** *vr* to go out; to go off; (*morire*) to pass away

spel'lare *vt* (*scuoiare*) to skin; (*scorticare*) to graze; **~rsi** *vr* to peel

'spendere *vt* to spend

spen'nare *vt* to pluck

spensie'rato, a *ag* carefree

'spento, a *pp di* **spegnere** ♦ *ag* (*suono*) muffled; (*colore*) dull; (*sigaretta*) out; (*civiltà, vulcano*) extinct

spe'ranza [spe'rantsa] *sf* hope

spe'rare *vt* to hope for ♦ *vi*: **~ in** to trust in; **~ che/di fare** to hope that/to do; **lo spero, spero di sì** I hope so

sper'duto, a *ag* (*isolato*) out-of-the-way; (*persona: smarrita, a disagio*) lost

spergi'uro, a [sper'dʒuro] *sm/f* perjurer

♦ *sm* perjury

sperimen'tale *ag* experimental

sperimen'tare *vt* to experiment with, test; (*fig*) to test, put to the test

'sperma, i *sm* sperm

spe'rone *sm* spur

sperpe'rare *vt* to squander

'spesa *sf* (*somma di denaro*) expense; (*costo*) cost; (*acquisto*) purchase; (*fam: acquisto del cibo quotidiano*) shopping; **~e** *sfpl* (*soldi spesi*) expenses; (COMM) costs; charges; **fare la ~** to do the shopping; **a ~e di** (*a carico di*) at the expense of; **~e generali** overheads; **~e postali** postage *sg*; **~e di viaggio** travelling expenses

'speso, a *pp di* **spendere**

'spesso, a *ag* (*fitto*) thick; (*frequente*) frequent ♦ *av* often; **~e volte** frequently, often

spes'sore *sm* thickness

spet'tabile (*abbr*: **Spett.**: *in lettere*) *ag*: **~ ditta X** Messrs X and Co.

spet'tacolo *sm* (*rappresentazione*) performance, show; (*vista, scena*) sight; **dare ~ di sé** to make an exhibition *o* a spectacle of o.s.; **spettaco'loso, a** *ag* spectacular

spet'tare *vi*: **~ a** (*decisione*) to be up to; (*stipendio*) to be due to; **spetta a te decidere** it's up to you to decide

spetta'tore, 'trice *sm/f* (CINEMA, TEATRO) member of the audience; (*di avvenimento*) onlooker, witness

spetti'nare *vt*: **~ qn** to ruffle sb's hair; **~rsi** *vr* to get one's hair in a mess

'spettro *sm* (*fantasma*) spectre; (FISICA) spectrum

'spezie ['spettsje] *sfpl* (CUC) spices

spez'zare [spet'tsare] *vt* (*rompere*) to break; (*fig: interrompere*) to break up; **~rsi** *vr* to break

spezza'tino [spettsa'tino] *sm* (CUC) stew

spezzet'tare [spettset'tare] *vt* to break up (*o chop*) into small pieces

'spia *sf* spy; (*confidente della polizia*) informer; (ELETTR) indicating light; warning light; (*fessura*) peep-hole; (*fig: sintomo*) sign, indication

spia'cente [spja'tʃɛnte] *ag* sorry; **essere ~ di qc/di fare qc** to be sorry about sth/for doing sth

spia'cevole [spja'tʃevole] *ag* unpleasant

spi'aggia, ge ['spjaddʒa] *sf* beach; **~ libera** public beach

spia'nare *vt* (*terreno*) to level, make level; (*edificio*) to raze to the ground; (*pasta*) to roll out; (*rendere liscio*) to smooth (out)

spi'ano *sm*: **a tutto ~** (*lavorare*) non-stop, without a break; (*spendere*) lavishly

spian'tato, a *ag* penniless, ruined

spi'are *vt* to spy on

spl'azzo ['spjattso] *sm* open space; (*radura*) clearing

spic'care *vt* (*assegno, mandato di cattura*) to issue ♦ *vi* (*risaltare*) to stand out; **~ il volo** to fly off; (*fig*) to spread one's wings; **~ un balzo** to leap; **spic'cato, a** *ag* (*marcato*) marked, strong; (*notevole*) remarkable

'spicchio ['spikkjo] *sm* (*di agrumi*) segment; (*di aglio*) clove; (*parte*) piece, slice

spicci'are [spit'tʃare] *vt* to finish off quickly; **~rsi** *vr* to hurry up

'spicciolo, a ['spittʃolo] *ag*: **moneta ~a, ~i** *smpl* (small) change

'spicco, chi *sm*: **di ~** outstanding; (*tema*) main, principal; **fare ~** to stand out

spie'dino *sm* (*utensile*) skewer; (*pietanza*) kebab

spi'edo *sm* (*CUC*) spit

spie'gare *vt* (*far capire*) to explain; (*tovaglia*) to unfold; (*vele*) to unfurl; **~rsi** *vr* to explain o.s., make o.s. clear; **~ qc a qn** to explain sth to sb; **spiegazi'one** *sf* explanation

spiegaz'zare [spjegat'tsare] *vt* to crease, crumple

spie'tato, a *ag* ruthless, pitiless

spiffe'rare (*fam*) *vt* to blurt out, blab

'spiga, ghe *sf* (*BOT*) ear

spigli'ato, a [spiʎ'ʎato] *ag* self-possessed, self-confident

'spigolo *sm* corner; (*MAT*) edge

'spilla *sf* brooch; (*da cravatta, cappello*) pin; **~ di sicurezza** *o* **da balia** safety pin

spil'lare *vt* (*vino, fig*) to tap; **~ denaro/ notizie a qn** to tap sb for money/ information

'spillo *sm* pin

spi'lorcio, a, ci, ce [spi'lortʃo] *ag* mean, stingy

'spina *sf* (*BOT*) thorn; (*ZOOL*) spine, prickle; (*di pesce*) bone; (*ELETTR*) plug; (*di botte*) bunghole; **birra alla ~** draught beer; **~ dorsale** (*ANAT*) backbone

spi'nacio [spi'natʃo] *sm* spinach; (*CUC*): **~i** spinach *sg*

'spingere ['spindʒere] *vt* to push; (*condurre: anche fig*) to drive; (*stimolare*): **~ qn a fare** to urge *o* press sb to do; **~rsi** *vr* (*inoltrarsi*) to push on, carry on; **~rsi troppo lontano** (*anche fig*) to go too far

spi'noso, a *ag* thorny, prickly

'spinta *sf* (*urto*) push; (*FISICA*) thrust; (*fig: stimolo*) incentive, spur; (: *appoggio*) string-pulling *no pl*; **dare una ~a a qn** (*fig*) to pull strings for sb

'spinto, a *pp di* **spingere**

spio'naggio [spio'naddʒo] *sm* espionage, spying

spi'overe *vi* to stop raining

'spira *sf* coil

spi'raglio [spi'raʎʎo] *sm* (*fessura*) chink, narrow opening; (*raggio di luce, fig*) glimmer, gleam

spi'rale *sf* spiral; (*contraccettivo*) coil; **a ~** spiral(-shaped)

spi'rare *vi* (*vento*) to blow; (*morire*) to expire, pass away

spiri'tato, a *ag* possessed; (*fig: persona, espressione*) wild

spiri'tismo *sm* spiritualism

'spirito *sm* (*REL, CHIM, disposizione d'animo, di legge etc, fantasma*) spirit; (*pensieri, intelletto*) mind; (*arguzia*) wit; (*umorismo*) humour, wit; **lo S~ Santo** the Holy Spirit *o* Ghost

spirito'saggine [spirito'saddʒine] *sf* witticism; (*peg*) wisecrack

spiri'toso, a *ag* witty

spiritu'ale *ag* spiritual

'splendere *vi* to shine

'splendido, a *ag* splendid; (*splendente*) shining; (*sfarzoso*) magnificent, splendid

splen'dore *sm* splendour; (*luce intensa*) brilliance, brightness

spodes'tare *vt* to deprive of power; (*sovrano*) to depose

spogli'are [spoʎˈʎare] *vt* (*svestire*) to undress; (*privare, fig: depredare*): ~ qn di qc to deprive sb of sth; (*togliere ornamenti: anche fig*): ~ qn/qc di to strip sb/sth of; ~rsi *vr* to undress, strip; ~rsi di (*ricchezze etc*) to deprive o.s. of, give up; (*pregiudizi*) to rid o.s. of; spoglia'toio *sm* dressing room; (*di scuola etc*) cloakroom; (*SPORT*) changing room; 'spoglie ['spɔʎʎe] *sfpl* (*salma*) remains; (*preda*) spoils, booty *sg*; *vedi anche* spoglio; 'spoglio, a *ag* (*pianta, terreno*) bare; (*privo*): spoglio di stripped of; lacking in, without ♦ *sm* (*di voti*) counting

'spola *sf* (*bobina di filo*) cop; fare la ~ (fra) to go to and fro *o* shuttle (between)

spol'pare *vt* to strip the flesh off

spolve'rare *vt* (*anche CUC*) to dust; (*con spazzola*) to brush; (*con battipanni*) to beat; (*fig*) to polish off ♦ *vi* to dust

'sponda *sf* (*di fiume*) bank; (*di mare, lago*) shore; (*bordo*) edge

spon'taneo, a *ag* spontaneous; (*persona*) unaffected, natural

spopo'lare *vt* to depopulate ♦ *vi* (*attirare folla*) to draw the crowds; ~rsi *vr* to become depopulated

spor'care *vt* to dirty, make dirty; (*fig*) to sully, soil; ~rsi *vr* to get dirty

spor'cizia [spor'tʃittsja] *sf* (*stato*) dirtiness; (*sudiciume*) dirt, filth; (*cosa sporca*) dirt *no pl*, something dirty

'sporco, a, chi, che *ag* dirty, filthy

spor'genza [spor'dʒentsa] *sf* projection

'sporgere ['spɔrdʒere] *vt* to put out, stretch out ♦ *vi* (*venire in fuori*) to stick out; ~rsi *vr* to lean out; ~ querela contro qn (DIR) to take legal action against sb

sport *sm inv* sport

'sporta *sf* shopping bag

spor'tello *sm* (*di treno, auto etc*) door; (*di banca, ufficio*) window, counter; ~ automatico (*BANCA*) cash dispenser, automated telling machine

spor'tivo, a *ag* (*gara, giornale, centro*) sports *cpd*; (*persona*) sporty; (*abito*) casual; (*spirito, atteggiamento*) sporting

'sporto, a *pp di* sporgere

'sposa *sf* bride; (*moglie*) wife

sposa'lizio [spoza'littsjo] *sm* wedding

spo'sare *vt* to marry; (*fig: idea, fede*) to espouse; ~rsi *vr* to get married, marry; ~rsi con qn to marry sb, get married to sb; spo'sato, a *ag* married

'sposo *sm* (*bride*)groom; (*marito*) husband; gli ~i *smpl* the newlyweds

spos'sato, a *ag* exhausted, weary

spos'tare *vt* to move, shift; (*cambiare: orario*) to change; ~rsi *vr* to move

'spranga, ghe *sf* (*sbarra*) bar

'sprazzo ['sprattso] *sm* (*di sole etc*) flash; (*fig: di gioia etc*) burst

spre'care *vt* to waste; ~rsi *vr* (*persona*) to waste one's energy; 'spreco *sm* waste

spre'gevole [spre'dʒevole] *ag* contemptible, despicable

spregiudi'cato, a [spredʒudi'kato] *ag* unprejudiced, unbiased; (*peg*) unscrupulous

'spremere *vt* to squeeze

spre'muta *sf* fresh juice; ~ d'arancia fresh orange juice

sprez'zante [spret'tsante] *ag* scornful, contemptuous

sprigio'nare [spridʒo'nare] *vt* to give off, emit; ~rsi *vr* to emanate; (*uscire con impeto*) to burst out

spriz'zare [sprit'tsare] *vt, vi* to spurt; ~ gioia/salute to be bursting with joy/health

sprofon'dare *vi* to sink; (*casa*) to collapse; (*suolo*) to give way, subside; ~rsi *vr*: ~rsi in (*poltrona*) to sink into; (*fig*) to become immersed *o* absorbed in

spro'nare *vt* to spur (on)

'sprone *sm* (*sperone, fig*) spur

sproporzio'nato, a [sproportsjo'nato] *ag* disproportionate, out of all proportion

sproporzi'one [spropor'tsjone] *sf* disproportion

sproposi'tato, a *ag* (*lettera, discorso*) full of mistakes; (*fig: costo*) excessive, enormous

spro'posito *sm* blunder; **a ~** at the wrong time; (*rispondere, parlare*) irrelevantly

sprovve'duto, a *ag* inexperienced, naïve

sprov'visto, a *ag* (*mancante*): **~ di** lacking in, without; **alla ~a** unawares

spruz'zare [sprut'tsare] *vt* (*a nebulizzazione*) to spray; (*aspergere*) to sprinkle; (*inzaccherare*) to splash; **'spruzzo** *sm* spray; splash

'spugna ['spuɲɲa] *sf* (ZOOL) sponge; (*tessuto*) towelling; **spu'gnoso, a** *ag* spongy

'spuma *sf* (*schiuma*) foam; (*bibita*) fizzy drink

spu'mante *sm* sparkling wine

spumeggi'ante [spumed'dʒante] *ag* (*birra*) foaming; (*vino, fig*) sparkling

spu'mone *sm* (CUC) mousse

spun'tare *vt* (*coltello*) to break the point of; (*capelli*) to trim ♦ *vi* (*uscire: germogli*) to sprout; (: *capelli*) to begin to grow; (: *denti*) to come through; (*apparire*) to appear (suddenly); **~rsi** *vr* to become blunt, lose its point; **spuntarla** (*fig*) to make it, win through

spun'tino *sm* snack

'spunto *sm* (TEATRO, MUS) cue; (*fig*) starting point; **dare lo ~ a** (*fig*) to give rise to

spur'gare *vt* (*fogna*) to clean, clear

spu'tare *vt* to spit out; (*fig*) to belch (out) ♦ *vi* to spit; **'sputo** *sm* spittle *no pl*, spit *no pl*

'squadra *sf* (*strumento*) (set) square; (*gruppo*) team, squad; (*di operai*) gang, squad; (MIL) squad; (: AER, NAUT) squadron; (SPORT) team; **lavoro a ~e** teamwork

squa'drare *vt* to square, make square; (*osservare*) to look at closely

squa'driglia [skwa'driʎʎa] *sf* (AER) flight; (NAUT) squadron

squa'drone *sm* squadron

squagli'arsi [skwaʎ'ʎarsi] *vr* to melt; (*fig*) to sneak off

squa'lifica *sf* disqualification

squalifi'care *vt* to disqualify

'squallido, a *ag* wretched, bleak

squal'lore *sm* wretchedness, bleakness

'squalo *sm* shark

'squama *sf* scale; **squa'mare** *vt* to scale; **squamarsi** *vr* to flake *o* peel (off)

squarcia'gola [skwartʃa'gola]: **a ~** *av* at the top of one's voice

squarci'are [skwar'tʃare] *vt* to rip (open); (*fig*) to pierce

squar'tare *vt* to quarter, cut up

squattri'nato, a *ag* penniless

squili'brato, a *ag* (PSIC) unbalanced; **squi'librio** *sm* (*differenza, sbilancio*) imbalance; (PSIC) unbalance

squil'lante *ag* shrill, sharp

squil'lare *vi* (*campanello, telefono*) to ring (out); (*tromba*) to blare; **'squillo** *sm* ring, ringing *no pl*; blare; **ragazza** *f* **squillo** *inv* call girl

squi'sito, a *ag* exquisite; (*cibo*) delicious; (*persona*) delightful

squit'tire *vi* (*uccello*) to squawk; (*topo*) to squeak

sradi'care *vt* to uproot; (*fig*) to eradicate

sragio'nare [zradʒo'nare] *vi* to talk nonsense, rave

srego'lato, a *ag* (*senza ordine: vita*) disorderly; (*smodato*) immoderate; (*dissoluto*) dissolute

S.r.l. *abbr* = **società a responsabilità limitata**

'stabile *ag* stable, steady; (*tempo: non variabile*) settled; (TEATRO: *compagnia*) resident ♦ *sm* (*edificio*) building

stabili'mento *sm* (*edificio*) establishment; (*fabbrica*) plant, factory

stabi'lire *vt* to establish; (*fissare: prezzi, data*) to fix; (*decidere*) to decide; **~rsi** *vr* (*prendere dimora*) to settle

stac'care *vt* (*levare*) to detach, remove; (*separare: anche fig*) to separate, divide; (*strappare*) to tear off (*o* out); (*scandire: parole*) to pronounce clearly; (SPORT) to leave behind; **~rsi** *vr* (*bottone etc*) to come off; (*scostarsi*): **~rsi (da)** to move away (from); (*fig: separarsi*): **~rsi da** to leave; **non ~ gli occhi da qn** not to take one's eyes off sb

'stadio *sm* (*SPORT*) stadium; (*periodo, fase*) phase, stage

'staffa *sf* (*di sella, TECN*) stirrup; **perdere le ~e** (*fig*) to fly off the handle

staf'fetta *sf* (*messo*) dispatch rider; (*SPORT*) relay race

stagio'nale [stadʒo'nale] *ag* seasonal

stagio'nare [stadʒo'nare] *vt* (*legno*) to season; (*formaggi, vino*) to mature

stagi'one [sta'dʒone] *sf* season; **alta/bassa ~** high/low season

stagli'arsi [staʎ'ʎarsi] *vr* to stand out, be silhouetted

'stagno, a ['staɲɲo] *ag* watertight; (*a tenuta d'aria*) airtight ♦ *sm* (*acquitrino*) pond; (*CHIM*) tin

sta'gnola [staɲ'ɲɔla] *sf* tinfoil

'stalla *sf* (*per bovini*) cowshed; (*per cavalli*) stable

stal'lone *sm* stallion

sta'mani *av* = **stamattina**

stamat'tina *av* this morning

stam'becco, chi *sm* ibex

'stampa *sf* (*TIP, FOT: tecnica*) printing; (*impressione, copia fotografica*) print; (*insieme di quotidiani, giornalisti etc*) press; **"~e"** *sfpl* "printed matter"

stam'pante *sf* (*INFORM*) printer

stam'pare *vt* to print; (*pubblicare*) to publish; (*coniare*) to strike, coin; (*imprimere: anche fig*) to impress

stampa'tello *sm* block letters *pl*

stam'pella *sf* crutch

'stampo *sm* mould; (*fig: indole*) type, kind, sort

sta'nare *vt* to drive out

stan'care *vt* to tire, make tired; (*annoiare*) to bore; (*infastidire*) to annoy; **~rsi** *vr* to get tired, tire o.s. out; **~rsi (di)** to grow weary (of), grow tired (of)

stan'chezza [stan'kettsa] *sf* tiredness, fatigue

'stanco, a, chi, che *ag* tired; **~ di** tired of, fed up with

'stanga, ghe *sf* bar; (*di carro*) shaft

stan'gata *sf* (*colpo: anche fig*) blow; (*cattivo risultato*) poor result; (*CALCIO*) shot

sta'notte *av* tonight; (*notte passata*) last night

'stante *prep*: **a sé ~** (*appartamento, casa*) independent, separate

stan'tio, a, 'tii, 'tie *ag* stale; (*burro*) rancid; (*fig*) old

stan'tuffo *sm* piston

'stanza ['stantsa] *sf* room; (*POESIA*) stanza; **~ da letto** bedroom

stanzi'are [stan'tsjare] *vt* to allocate

stap'pare *vt* to uncork; to uncap

'stare *vi* (*restare in un luogo*) to stay, remain; (*abitare*) to stay, live; (*essere situato*) to be, be situated; (*anche: ~ in piedi*) to be, stand; (*essere, trovarsi*) to be; (*dipendere*): **se stesse in me** if it were up to me, if it depended on me; (*seguito da gerundio*): **sta studiando** he's studying; **starci** (*esserci spazio*): **nel baule non ci sta più niente** there's no more room in the boot; (*accettare*) to accept; **ci stai?** is that okay with you?; **~ a** (*attenersi a*) to follow, stick to; (*seguito dall'infinito*): **stiamo a discutere** we're talking; (*toccare a*): **sta a te giocare** it's your turn to play; **~ per fare qc** to be about to do sth; **come sta?** how are you?; **io sto bene/male** I'm very well/not very well; **~ a qn** (*abiti etc*) to fit sb; **queste scarpe mi stanno strette** these shoes are tight for me; **il rosso ti sta bene** red suits you

starnu'tire *vi* to sneeze; **star'nuto** *sm* sneeze

sta'sera *av* this evening, tonight

sta'tale *ag* state *cpd*; government *cpd* ♦ *sm/f* state employee, local authority employee; (*nell'amministrazione*) ≈ civil servant

sta'tista, i *sm* statesman

sta'tistica *sf* statistics *sg*

'stato, a *pp di* **essere; stare** ♦ *sm* (*condizione*) state, condition; (*POL*) state; (*DIR*) status; **essere in ~ d'accusa** (*DIR*) to be committed for trial; **~ d'assedio/**

d'emergenza state of siege/emergency; **~ civile** (*AMM*) marital status; **~ maggiore** (*MIL*) staff; **gli S~i Uniti (d'America)** the United States (of America)

'**statua** *sf* statue

statuni'tense *ag* United States *cpd,* of the United States

sta'tura *sf* (*ANAT*) height, stature; (*fig*) stature

sta'tuto *sm* (*DIR*) statute; constitution

sta'volta *av* this time

stazio'nario, a [stattsjo'narjo] *ag* stationary; (*fig*) unchanged

stazi'one [stat'tsjone] *sf* station; (*balneare, termale*) resort; **~ degli autobus** bus station; **~ balneare** seaside resort; **~ ferroviaria** railway (*BRIT*) o railroad (*US*) station; **~ invernale** winter sports resort; **~ di polizia** police station (*in small town*); **~ di servizio** service o petrol (*BRIT*) o filling station

'**stecca, che** *sf* stick; (*di ombrello*) rib; (*di sigarette*) carton; (*MED*) splint; (*stonatura*): **fare una ~** to sing (o play) a wrong note

stec'cato *sm* fence

stec'chito, a [stek'kito] *ag*: **lasciar ~ qn** (*fig*) to leave sb flabbergasted; **morto ~** stone dead

'**stella** *sf* star; **~ alpina** (*BOT*) edelweiss; **~ di mare** (*ZOOL*) starfish

'**stelo** *sm* stem; (*asta*) rod; **lampada a ~** standard lamp

'**stemma, i** *sm* coat of arms

stempe'rare *vt* to dilute; to dissolve; (*colori*) to mix

sten'dardo *sm* standard

'**stendere** *vt* (*braccia, gambe*) to stretch (out); (*tovaglia*) to spread (out); (*bucato*) to hang out; (*mettere a giacere*) to lay (down); (*spalmare: colore*) to spread; (*mettere per iscritto*) to draw up; **~rsi** *vr* (*coricarsi*) to stretch out, lie down; (*estendersi*) to extend, stretch

stenodatti'lografo, a *sm/f* shorthand typist (*BRIT*), stenographer (*US*)

stenogra'fare *vt* to take down in shorthand; **stenogra'fia** *sf* shorthand

sten'tare *vi*: **~ a fare** to find it hard to do, have difficulty doing

'**stento** *sm* (*fatica*) difficulty; **~i** *smpl* (*privazioni*) hardship *sg*, privation *sg*; **a ~** with difficulty, barely

'**sterco** *sm* dung

stereo('fonico, a, ci, che) *ag* stereo(phonic)

'**sterile** *ag* sterile; (*terra*) barren; (*fig*) futile, fruitless; **sterilità** *sf* sterility

steriliz'zare [sterilid'dzare] *vt* to sterilize; **sterilizzazi'one** *sf* sterilization

ster'lina *sf* pound (sterling)

stermi'nare *vt* to exterminate, wipe out

stermi'nato, a *ag* immense; endless

ster'minio *sm* extermination, destruction

'**sterno** *sm* (*ANAT*) breastbone

'**sterpo** *sm* dry twig; **~i** *smpl* brushwood *sg*

ster'zare [ster'tsare] *vt, vi* (*AUT*) to steer; '**sterzo** *sm* steering; (*volante*) steering wheel

'**steso, a** *pp di* **stendere**

'**stesso, a** *ag* same; (*rafforzativo: in persona, proprio*): **il re ~** the king himself o in person ♦ *pron*: **lo(la) ~(a)** the same (one); **i suoi ~i avversari lo ammirano** even his enemies admire him; **fa lo ~** it doesn't matter; **per me è lo ~** it's all the same to me, it doesn't matter to me; *vedi* **io; tu** *etc*

ste'sura *sf* drafting *no pl*, drawing up *no pl*; draft

'**stigmate** *sfpl* (*REL*) stigmata

sti'lare *vt* to draw up, draft

'**stile** *sm* style; **sti'lista, i** *sm* designer

stil'lare *vi* (*trasudare*) to ooze; (*gocciolare*) to drip; **stilli'cidio** *sm* (*fig*) continual pestering (o moaning *etc*)

stilo'grafica, che *sf* (*anche:* **penna ~**) fountain pen

'**stima** *sf* esteem; valuation; assessment, estimate

sti'mare *vt* (*persona*) to esteem, hold in high regard; (*terreno, casa etc*) to value; (*stabilire in misura approssimativa*) to estimate, assess; (*ritenere*): **~ che** to consider that; **~rsi fortunato** to consider o.s. (to be) lucky

stimo'lare *vt* to stimulate; (*incitare*): ~ **qn (a fare)** to spur sb on (to do)

'stimolo *sm* (*anche fig*) stimulus

'stinco, chi *sm* shin; shinbone

'stingere ['stindʒere] *vt, vi* (*anche*: ~**rsi**) to fade; **'stinto, a** *pp di* **stingere**

sti'pare *vt* to cram, pack; ~**rsi** *vr* (*accalcarsi*) to crowd, throng

sti'pendio *sm* salary

'stipite *sm* (*di porta, finestra*) jamb

stipu'lare *vt* (*redigere*) to draw up

sti'rare *vt* (*abito*) to iron; (*distendere*) to stretch; (*strappare: muscolo*) to strain; ~**rsi** *vr* to stretch (o.s.); **stira'tura** *sf* ironing

'stirpe *sf* birth, stock; descendants *pl*

stiti'chezza [stiti'kettsa] *sf* constipation

'stitico, a, ci, che *ag* constipated

'stiva *sf* (*di nave*) hold

sti'vale *sm* boot

'stizza ['stittsa] *sf* anger, vexation; **stiz'zirsi** *vr* to lose one's temper; **stiz'zoso, a** *ag* (*persona*) quick-tempered, irascible; (*risposta*) angry

stocca'fisso *sm* stockfish, dried cod

stoc'cata *sf* (*colpo*) stab, thrust; (*fig*) gibe, cutting remark

'stoffa *sf* material, fabric; (*fig*): **aver la ~ di** to have the makings of

'stola *sf* stole

'stolto, a *ag* stupid, foolish

'stomaco, chi *sm* stomach; **dare di ~** to vomit; **essere di ~** to be sick

sto'nare *vt* to sing (*o* play) out of tune ♦ *vi* to be out of tune, sing (*o* play) out of tune; (*fig*) to be out of place, jar; (: *colori*) to clash; **stona'tura** *sf* (*suono*) false note

stop *sm inv* (*TEL*) stop; (*AUT: cartello*) stop sign; (: *fanalino d'arresto*) brake-light

'stoppa *sf* tow

stop'pino *sm* wick; (*miccia*) fuse

'storcere ['stɔrtʃere] *vt* to twist; ~**rsi** *vr* to writhe, twist; ~ **il naso** (*fig*) to turn up one's nose; ~**rsi la caviglia** to twist one's ankle

stor'dire *vt* (*intontire*) to stun, daze; ~**rsi** *vr*: ~**rsi col bere** to dull one's senses with

drink; **stor'dito, a** *ag* stunned

'storia *sf* (*scienza, avvenimenti*) history; (*racconto, bugia*) story; (*faccenda, questione*) business *no pl*; (*pretesto*) excuse, pretext; ~**e** *sfpl* (*smancerie*) fuss *sg*; **'storico, a, ci, che** *ag* historic(al) ♦ *sm* historian

stori'one *sm* (*ZOOL*) sturgeon

stor'mire *vi* to rustle

'stormo *sm* (*di uccelli*) flock

stor'nare *vt* (*COMM*) to transfer

'storno *sm* (*ZOOL*) starling

storpi'are *vt* to cripple, maim; (*fig: parole*) to mangle; (: *significato*) to twist

'storpio, a *ag* crippled, maimed

'storta *sf* (*distorsione*) sprain, twist

'storto, a *pp di* **storcere** ♦ *ag* (*chiodo*) twisted, bent; (*gamba, quadro*) crooked

sto'viglie [sto'viʎʎe] *sfpl* dishes *pl*, crockery

'strabico, a, ci, che *ag* squint-eyed; (*occhi*) squint

stra'bismo *sm* squinting

stra'carico, a, chi, che *ag* overloaded

strac'chino [strak'kino] *sm* type of soft cheese

stracci'are [strat'tʃare] *vt* to tear

'straccio, a, ci, ce ['strattʃo] *ag*: **carta ~a** waste paper ♦ *sm* rag; (*per pulire*) cloth, duster

stra'cotto, a *ag* overcooked ♦ *sm* (*CUC*) beef stew

'strada *sf* road; (*di città*) street; (*cammino, via, fig*) way; **farsi ~** (*fig*) to do well for o.s.; **essere fuori ~** (*fig*) to be on the wrong track; ~ **facendo** to be on the way; ~ **senza uscita** dead end; **stra'dale** *ag* road *cpd*

strafalci'one [strafal'tʃone] *sm* blunder, howler

stra'fare *vi* to overdo it; **stra'fatto, a** *pp di* **strafare**

strafot'tente *ag*: **è** ~ he doesn't give a damn, he couldn't care less

'strage ['stradʒe] *sf* massacre, slaughter

stralu'nato, a *ag* (*occhi*) rolling; (*persona*) beside o.s., very upset

stramaz'zare [stramat'tsare] *vi* to fall heavily

'**strambo, a** *ag* strange, queer
strampa'lato, a *ag* odd, eccentric
stra'nezza [stra'nettsa] *sf* strangeness
strango'lare *vt* to strangle; **~rsi** *vr* to choke
strani'ero, a *ag* foreign ♦ *sm/f* foreigner
'**strano, a** *ag* strange, odd
straordi'nario, a *ag* extraordinary; (*treno etc*) special ♦ *sm* (*lavoro*) overtime
strapaz'zare [strapat'tsare] *vt* to ill-treat; **~rsi** *vr* to tire o.s. out, overdo things; **stra'pazzo** *sm* strain, fatigue; **da strapazzo** (*fig*) third-rate
strapi'ombo *sm* overhanging rock; **a ~** overhanging
strapo'tere *sm* excessive power
strap'pare *vt* (*gen*) to tear, rip; (*pagina etc*) to tear off, tear out; (*sradicare*) to pull up; (*togliere*): **~ qc a qn** to snatch sth from sb; (*fig*) to wrest sth from sb; **~rsi** *vr* (*lacerarsi*) to rip, tear; (*rompersi*) to break; **~rsi un muscolo** to tear a muscle; '**strappo** *sm* pull, tug; tear, rip; **fare uno strappo alla regola** to make an exception to the rule; **strappo muscolare** torn muscle
strari'pare *vi* to overflow
strasci'care [straʃʃi'kare] *vt* to trail; (*piedi*) to drag; **~ le parole** to drawl
'**strascico, chi** ['straʃʃiko] *sm* (*di abito*) train; (*conseguenza*) after-effect
strata'gemma, i [strata'dʒɛmma] *sm* stratagem
strate'gia, 'gie [strate'dʒia] *sf* strategy; **stra'tegico, a, ci, che** *ag* strategic
'**strato** *sm* layer; (*rivestimento*) coat, coating; (*GEO, fig*) stratum; (*METEOR*) stratus; **~ di ozono** ozone layer
strava'gante *ag* odd, eccentric; **strava'ganza** *sf* eccentricity
stra'vecchio, a [stra'vekkjo] *ag* very old
stra'vizio [stra'vittsjo] *sm* excess
stra'volgere [stra'vɔldʒere] *vt* (*volto*) to contort; (*fig: animo*) to trouble deeply; (: *verità*) to twist, distort; **stra'volto, a** *pp di* **stravolgere**
strazi'are [strat'tsjare] *vt* to torture,

torment; '**strazio** *sm* torture; (*fig: cosa fatta male*): **essere uno ~** to be appalling
'**strega, ghe** *sf* witch
stre'gare *vt* to bewitch
stre'gone *sm* (*mago*) wizard; (*di tribù*) witch doctor
stregua *sf*: **alla ~ di** by the same standard as
stre'mare *vt* to exhaust
'**stremo** *sm* very end; **essere allo ~** to be at the end of one's tether
'**strenna** *sf* Christmas present
strepi'toso, a *ag* clamorous, deafening; (*fig: successo*) resounding
stres'sante *ag* stressful
'**stretta** *sf* (*di mano*) grasp; (*finanziaria*) squeeze; (*fig: dolore, turbamento*) pang; **una ~a di mano** a handshake; **essere alle ~e** to have one's back to the wall; *vedi anche* **stretto**
stretta'mente *av* tightly; (*rigorosamente*) strictly
stret'tezza [stret'tettsa] *sf* narrowness
'**stretto, a** *pp di* **stringere** ♦ *ag* (*corridoio, limiti*) narrow; (*gonna, scarpe, nodo, curva*) tight; (*intimo: parente, amico*) close; (*rigoroso: osservanza*) strict; (*preciso: significato*) precise, exact ♦ *sm* (*braccio di mare*) strait; **a denti ~i** with clenched teeth; **lo ~ necessario** the bare minimum; **stret'toia** *sf* bottleneck; (*fig*) tricky situation
stri'ato, a *ag* streaked
'**stridere** (*porta*) to squeak; (*animale*) to screech, shriek; (*colori*) to clash; '**stridulo, a** *ag* shrill
stril'lare *vt, vi* to scream, shriek; '**strillo** *sm* scream, shriek
stril'lone *sm* newspaper seller
strimin'zito, a [strimin'tsito] *ag* (*misero*) shabby; (*molto magro*) skinny
strimpel'lare *vt* (*MUS*) to strum
'**stringa, ghe** *sf* lace
strin'gato, a *ag* (*fig*) concise
'**stringere** ['strindʒere] *vt* (*avvicinare due cose*) to press (together), squeeze (together); (*tenere stretto*) to hold tight,

clasp, clutch; (*pugno, mascella, denti*) to clench; (*labbra*) to compress; (*avvitare*) to tighten; (*abito*) to take in; (*sog: scarpe*) to pinch, be tight for; (*fig: concludere: patto*) to make; (*: accelerare: passo, tempo*) to quicken ♦ *vi* (*essere stretto*) to be tight; (*tempo: incalzare*) to be pressing; **~rsi** *vr* (*accostarsi*): **~rsi a** to press o.s. up against; **~ la mano a qn** to shake sb's hand; **~ gli occhi** to screw up one's eyes

'**striscia, sce** ['striʃʃa] *sf* (*di carta, tessuto etc*) strip; (*riga*) stripe; **~sce (pedonali)** zebra crossing *sg*

strisci'are [striʃ'ʃare] *vt* (*piedi*) to drag; (*muro, macchina*) to graze ♦ *vi* to crawl, creep

'**striscio** ['striʃʃo] *sm* graze; (*MED*) smear; **colpire di ~** to graze

strito'lare *vt* to grind

striz'zare [strit'tsare] *vt* (*panni*) to wring (out); **~ l'occhio** to wink

'**strofa** *sf* strophe

strofi'naccio [strofi'nattʃo] *sm* duster, cloth; (*per piatti*) dishcloth; (*per pavimenti*) floorcloth

strofi'nare *vt* to rub

stron'care *vt* to break off; (*fig: ribellione*) to suppress, put down; (*: film, libro*) to tear to pieces

stropicci'are [stropit'tʃare] *vt* to rub

stroz'zare [strot'tsare] *vt* (*soffocare*) to choke, strangle; **~rsi** *vr* to choke; **strozza'tura** *sf* (*restringimento*) narrowing; (*di strada etc*) bottleneck

'**struggersi** ['struddʒersi] *vr* (*fig*): **~ di** to be consumed with

strumen'tale *ag* (*MUS*) instrumental

strumentaliz'zare [strumentalid'dzare] *vt* to exploit, use to one's own ends

stru'mento *sm* (*arnese, fig*) instrument, tool; (*MUS*) instrument; **~ a corda** *o* **ad arco/a fiato** stringed/wind instrument

'**strutto** *sm* lard

strut'tura *sf* structure; **struttu'rare** *vt* to structure

'**struzzo** ['struttso] *sm* ostrich

stuc'care *vt* (*muro*) to plaster; (*vetro*) to

putty; (*decorare con stucchi*) to stucco

stuc'chevole [stuk'kevole] *ag* nauseating; (*fig*) tedious, boring

'**stucco, chi** *sm* plaster; (*da vetri*) putty; (*ornamentale*) stucco; **rimanere di ~** (*fig*) to be dumbfounded

stu'dente, 'essa *sm/f* student; (*scolaro*) pupil, schoolboy/girl; **studen'tesco, a, schi, sche** *ag* student *cpd*; school *cpd*

studi'are *vt* to study

'**studio** *sm* studying; (*ricerca, saggio, stanza*) study; (*di professionista*) office; (*di artista, CINEMA, TV, RADIO*) studio; **~i** *smpl* (*INS*) studies; **~ medico** doctor's surgery (*BRIT*) *o* office (*US*)

studi'oso, a *ag* studious, hard-working ♦ *sm/f* scholar

'**stufa** *sf* stove; **~ elettrica** electric fire *o* heater

stu'fare *vt* (*CUC*) to stew; (*fig: fam*) to bore; **stu'fato** *sm* (*CUC*) stew; '**stufo, a** (*fam*) *ag*: **essere stufo di** to be fed up with, be sick and tired of

stu'oia *sf* mat

stupefa'cente [stupefa'tʃɛnte] *ag* stunning, astounding ♦ *sm* drug, narcotic

stu'pendo, a *ag* marvellous, wonderful

stupi'daggine [stupi'daddʒine] *sf* stupid thing (to do *o* say)

stupidità *sf* stupidity

'**stupido, a** *ag* stupid

stu'pire *vt* to amaze, stun ♦ *vi* (*anche*): **~rsi**: **~ (di)** to be amazed (at), be stunned (by)

stu'pore *sm* amazement, astonishment

'**stupro** *sm* rape

stu'rare *vt* (*lavandino*) to clear

stuzzica'denti [stuttsika'denti] *sm* toothpick

stuzzi'care [stuttsi'kare] *vt* (*ferita etc*) to poke (at), prod (at); (*fig*) to tease; (*: appetito*) to whet; (*: curiosità*) to stimulate; **~ i denti** to pick one's teeth

---

PAROLA CHIAVE

---

su (*su +il* = **sul**, *su +lo* = **sullo**, *su +l'* = **sull'**, *su +la* = **sulla**, *su +i* = **sui**, *su +gli**

= **sugli**, *su* +*le* = **sulle**) *prep* **1** (*gen*) on; (*moto*) on(to); (*in cima a*) on (top of); **mettilo sul tavolo** put it on the table; **un paesino sul mare** a village by the sea **2** (*argomento*) about, on; **un libro ~ Cesare** a book on *o* about Caesar **3** (*circa*) about; **costerà sui 3 milioni** it will cost about 3 million; **una ragazza sui 17 anni** a girl of about 17 (years of age) **4**: **~ misura** made to measure; **~ richiesta** on request; **3 casi ~ dieci** 3 cases out of 10

♦ *av* **1** (*in alto, verso l'alto*) up; **vieni ~** come on up; **guarda ~** look up; **~ le mani!** hands up!; **in ~** (*verso l'alto*) up(wards); (*in poi*) onwards; **dai 20 anni in ~** from the age of 20 onwards **2** (*addosso*) on; **cos'hai ~?** what have you got on?

♦ *escl* come on!; **~ coraggio!** come on, cheer up!

'**sua** *vedi* **suo**

su'bacqueo, a *ag* underwater ♦ *sm* skindiver

sub'buglio [sub'buʎʎo] *sm* confusion, turmoil

subcosci'ente [subkoʃʃɛnte] *ag, sm* subconscious

'**subdolo, a** *ag* underhand, sneaky

suben'trare *vi*: **~ a qn in qc** to take over sth from sb

su'bire *vt* to suffer, endure

subis'sare *vt* (*fig*): **~ di** to overwhelm with, load with

subi'taneo, a *ag* sudden

'**subito** *av* immediately, at once, straight away

subodo'rare *vt* (*insidia etc*) to smell, suspect

subordi'nato, a *ag* subordinate; (*dipendente*): **~ a** dependent on, subject to

subur'bano, a *ag* suburban

suc'cedere [sut'tʃɛdere] *vi* (*prendere il posto di qn*): **~ a** to succeed; (*venire dopo*): **~ a** to follow; (*accadere*) to happen; **~rsi** *vr* to follow each other; **~ al trono** to succeed to

the throne; **successi'one** *sf* succession; **succes'sivo, a** *ag* successive; **suc'cesso, a** *pp di* **succedere** ♦ *sm* (*esito*) outcome; (*buona riuscita*) success; **di successo** (*libro, personaggio*) successful

succhi'are [suk'kjare] *vt* to suck (up); **succhi'otto** *sm* (*per bambino*) dummy

suc'cinto, a [sut'tʃinto] *ag* (*discorso*) succinct; (*abito*) brief

'**succo, chi** *sm* juice; (*fig*) essence, gist; **~ di frutta** fruit juice; **suc'coso, a** *ag* juicy; (*fig*) pithy

succur'sale *sf* branch (office)

sud *sm* south ♦ *ag inv* south; (*lato*) south, southern

Su'dafrica *sm*: **il ~** South Africa; **sudafri'cano, a** *ag, sm/f* South African

Suda'merica *sm*: **il ~** South America; **sudameri'cano, a** *ag, sm/f* South American

su'dare *vi* to perspire, sweat; **~ freddo** to come out in a cold sweat; **su'data** *sf* sweat; **ho fatto una bella sudata per finirlo in tempo** it was a real sweat to get it finished in time

sud'detto, a *ag* above-mentioned

sud'dito, a *sm/f* subject

suddi'videre *vt* to subdivide

su'dest *sm* south-east

'**sudicio, a, ci, ce** ['suditʃo] *ag* dirty, filthy; **sudici'ume** *sm* dirt, filth

su'dore *sm* perspiration, sweat

su'dovest *sm* south-west

'**sue** *vedi* **suo**

suffici'ente [suffi'tʃɛnte] *ag* enough, sufficient; (*borioso*) self-important; (*INS*) satisfactory; **suffici'enza** *sf* self-importance; pass mark; **a sufficienza** enough; **ne ho avuto a sufficienza!** I've had enough of this!

suf'fisso *sm* (*LING*) suffix

suf'fragio [suf'fradʒo] *sm* (*voto*) vote; **~ universale** universal suffrage

suggel'lare [suddʒel'lare] *vt* (*fig*) to seal

suggeri'mento [suddʒeri'mento] *sm* suggestion; (*consiglio*) piece of advice, advice *no pl*

sugge'rire [suddʒe'rire] *vt* (*risposta*) to tell; (*consigliare*) to advise; (*proporre*) to suggest; (*TEATRO*) to prompt; **suggeri'tore, 'trice** *sm/f* (*TEATRO*) prompter

suggestio'nare [suddʒestjo'nare] *vt* to influence

suggesti'one [suddʒes'tjone] *sf* (*PSIC*) suggestion

sugges'tivo, a [suddʒes'tivo] *ag* (*paesaggio*) evocative; (*teoria*) interesting, attractive

'sughero ['sugero] *sm* cork

'sugli ['suʎʎi] *prep* +det vedi **su**

'sugo, ghi *sm* (*succo*) juice; (*di carne*) gravy; (*condimento*) sauce; (*fig*) gist, essence

'sui *prep* +det vedi **su**

sui'cida, i, e [sui'tʃida] *ag* suicidal ♦ *sm/f* suicide

suici'darsi [suitʃi'darsi] *vr* to commit suicide

sui'cidio [sui'tʃidjo] *sm* suicide

su'ino, a *ag*: **carne ~a** pork ♦ *sm* pig; **~i** *smpl* swine *pl*

sul *prep* + det vedi **su**

sull' *prep* + det vedi **su**

'sulla *prep* + det vedi **su**

'sulle *prep* + det vedi **su**

'sullo *prep* + det vedi **su**

sulta'nina *ag f*: (*uva*) ~ sultana

sul'tano, a *sm/f* sultan/sultana

'sunto *sm* summary

'suo (*f* **'sua**, *pl* **'sue, su'oi**) *det*: **il ~, la sua** etc (*di lui*) his; (*di lei*) her; (*di esso*) its; (*con valore indefinito*) one's, his/her; (*forma di cortesia: anche*: **S~**) your ♦ *pron*: **il ~, la sua** etc his; hers; yours; **i suoi** his (*o* her *o* one's *o* your) family

su'ocero, a ['swɔtʃero] *sm/f* father/mother-in-law; **i ~i** *smpl* father-and-mother-in-law

su'oi vedi **suo**

su'ola *sf* (*di scarpa*) sole

su'olo *sm* (*terreno*) ground; (*terra*) soil

suo'nare *vt* (*MUS*) to play; (*campana*) to ring; (*ore*) to strike; (*clacson, allarme*) to sound ♦ *vi* to play; (*telefono, campana*) to ring; (*ore*) to strike; (*clacson, fig: parole*) to sound

suone'ria *sf* alarm

su'ono *sm* sound

su'ora *sf* (*REL*) sister

'super *sf* (*anche*: **benzina ~**) ≈ four-star (petrol) (*BRIT*), premium (*US*)

supe'rare *vt* (*oltrepassare: limite*) to exceed, surpass; (*percorrere*) to cover; (*attraversare: fiume*) to cross; (*sorpassare: veicolo*) to overtake; (*fig: essere più bravo di*) to surpass, outdo; (*: difficoltà*) to overcome; (*: esame*) to get through; **~ qn in altezza/peso** to be taller/heavier than sb; **ha superato la cinquantina** he's over fifty (years of age)

su'perbia *sf* pride; **su'perbo, a** *ag* proud; (*fig*) magnificent, superb

superfici'ale [superfi'tʃale] *ag* superficial

super'ficie, ci [super'fitʃe] *sf* surface

su'perfluo, a *ag* superfluous

superi'ore *ag* (*piano, arto, classi*) upper; (*più elevato: temperatura, livello*): **~ (a)** higher (than); (*migliore*): **~ (a)** superior (to); **~, a** *ag* (*anche REL*) superior; **superiorità** *sf* superiority

superla'tivo, a *ag, sm* superlative

supermer'cato *sm* supermarket

su'perstite *ag* surviving ♦ *sm/f* survivor

superstizi'one [superstit'tsjone] *sf* superstition; **superstizi'oso, a** *ag* superstitious

super'strada *sf* ≈ (toll-free) motorway

su'pino, a *ag* supine

suppel'lettile *sf* furnishings *pl*

suppergiù [supper'dʒu] *av* more or less, roughly

supplemen'tare *ag* extra; (*treno*) relief *cpd*; (*entrate*) additional

supple'mento *sm* supplement

sup'plente *sm/f* temporary member of staff; supply (*o* substitute) teacher

'supplica, che *sf* (*preghiera*) plea; (*domanda scritta*) petition, request

suppli'care *vt* to implore, beseech

sup'plire *vi*: **~ a** to make up for,

compensate for

sup'plizio [sup'plittsjo] *sm* torture

sup'porre *vt* to suppose

sup'porto *sm* (*sostegno*) support

sup'posta *sf* (*MED*) suppository

sup'posto, a *pp di* **supporre**

su'premo, a *ag* supreme

surge'lare [surdʒe'lare] *vt* to (deep-) freeze; **surge'lati** *smpl* frozen food *sg*

sur'plus *sm inv* (*ECON*) surplus

surriscal'dare *vt* to overheat

surro'gato *sm* substitute

suscet'tibile [suʃʃet'tibile] *ag* (*sensibile*) touchy, sensitive

susci'tare [suʃʃi'tare] *vt* to provoke, arouse

su'sina *sf* plum; **su'sino** *sm* plum (tree)

sussegu'ire *vt* to follow; **~rsi** *vr* to follow one another

sus'sidio *sm* subsidy

sus'sistere *vi* to exist; (*essere fondato*) to be valid *o* sound

sussul'tare *vi* to shudder

sussur'rare *vt, vi* to whisper, murmur; **sus'surro** *sm* whisper, murmur

sutu'rare *vt* (*MED*) to stitch up, suture

sva'gare *vt* (*distrarre*) to distract; (*divertire*) to amuse; **~rsi** *vr* to amuse o.s.; to enjoy o.s.

'svago, ghi *sm* (*riposo*) relaxation; (*ricreazione*) amusement; (*passatempo*) pastime

svaligi'are [zvali'dʒare] *vt* to rob, burgle (*BRIT*), burglarize (*US*)

svalu'tare *vt* (*ECON*) to devalue; (*fig*) to belittle; **~rsi** *vr* (*ECON*) to be devalued; **svalutazi'one** *sf* devaluation

sva'nire *vi* to disappear, vanish

svan'taggio [zvan'taddʒo] *sm* disadvantage; (*inconveniente*) drawback, disadvantage

svapo'rare *vi* to evaporate

svari'ato, a *ag* varied; various

'svastica *sf* swastika

sve'dese *ag* Swedish ♦ *sm/f* Swede ♦ *sm* (*LING*) Swedish

'sveglia [zve'ʎʎa] *sf* waking up; (*orologio*) alarm (clock); **~ telefonica** alarm call

svegli'are [zveʎ'ʎare] *vt* to wake up; (*fig*) to awaken, arouse; **~rsi** *vr* to wake up; (*fig*) to be revived, reawaken

'sveglio, a ['zveʎʎo] *ag* awake; (*fig*) quick-witted

sve'lare *vt* to reveal

'svelto, a *ag* (*passo*) quick; (*mente*) quick, alert; **alla ~a** quickly

'svendita *sf* (*COMM*) (clearance) sale

sveni'mento *sm* fainting fit, faint

sve'nire *vi* to faint

sven'tare *vt* to foil, thwart

sven'tato, a *ag* (*distratto*) scatterbrained; (*imprudente*) rash

svento'lare *vt, vi* to wave, flutter

sven'trare *vt* to disembowel

sven'tura *sf* misfortune; **sventu'rato, a** *ag* unlucky, unfortunate

sve'nuto, a *pp di* **svenire**

svergo'gnato, a [zvergoɲ'ɲato] *ag* shameless

sver'nare *vi* to spend the winter

sves'tire *vt* to undress; **~rsi** *vr* to get undressed

'Svezia ['zvettsja] *sf*: **la ~** Sweden

svez'zare [zvet'tsare] *vt* to wean

svi'are *vt* to divert; (*fig*) to lead astray; **~rsi** *vr* to go astray

svi'gnarsela [zviɲ'ɲarsela] *vr* to slip away, sneak off

svilup'pare *vt* to develop; **~rsi** *vr* to develop

svi'luppo *sm* development

'svincolo *sm* (*stradale*) motorway (*BRIT*) *o* expressway (*US*) intersection

svisce'rare [zviʃʃe'rare] *vt* (*fig: argomento*) to examine in depth; **svisce'rato, a** *ag* (*amore*) passionate; (*lodi*) obsequious

'svista *sf* oversight

svi'tare *vt* to unscrew

'Svizzera ['zvittsera] *sf*: **la ~** Switzerland

'svizzero, a ['zvittsero] *ag, sm/f* Swiss

svogli'ato, a [zvoʎ'ʎato] *ag* listless; (*pigro*) lazy

svolaz'zare [zvolat'tsare] *vi* to flutter

'svolgere ['zvɔldʒere] *vt* to unwind; (*srotolare*) to unroll; (*fig: argomento*) to develop; (: *piano, programma*) to carry out; **~rsi** *vr* to unwind; to unroll; (*fig: aver luogo*) to take place; (: *procedere*) to go on; **svolgi'mento** *sm* development; carrying out; (*andamento*) course

'**svolta** *sf* (*atto*) turning *no pl*; (*curva*) turn, bend; (*fig*) turning-point

svol'tare *vi* to turn

'**svolto, a** *pp di* **svolgere**

svuo'tare *vt* to empty (out)

T, t

tabac'caio, a *sm/f* tobacconist
tabacche'ria [tabakke'ria] *sf* tobacconist's (shop)
ta'bacco, chi *sm* tobacco
ta'bella *sf* (*tavola*) table; (*elenco*) list
tabel'lone *sm* (*pubblicitario*) billboard; (*con orario*) timetable board
taber'nacolo *sm* tabernacle
tabu'lato *sm* (*INFORM*) printout
'**tacca, che** *sf* notch, nick
tac'cagno, a [tak'kaɲɲo] *ag* mean, stingy
tac'chino [tak'kino] *sm* turkey
tacci'are [tat'tʃare] *vt*: **~ qn di** to accuse sb of
'**tacco, chi** *sm* heel; **~chi a spillo** stiletto heels
taccu'ino *sm* notebook
ta'cere [ta'tʃere] *vi* to be silent *o* quiet; (*smettere di parlare*) to fall silent ♦ *vt* to keep to oneself, say nothing about; **far ~ qn** to make sb be quiet; (*fig*) to silence sb
ta'chimetro [ta'kimetro] *sm* speedometer
'**tacito, a** ['tatʃito] *ag* silent; (*sottinteso*) tacit, unspoken
ta'fano *sm* horsefly
taffe'ruglio [taffe'ruʎʎo] *sm* brawl, scuffle
taffettà *sm* taffeta
'**taglia** ['taʎʎa] *sf* (*statura*) height; (*misura*) size; (*riscatto*) ransom; (*ricompensa*) reward; **~ forte** (*di abito*) large size
taglia'carte [taʎʎa'karte] *sm inv* paperknife
tagli'ando [taʎ'ʎando] *sm* coupon
tagli'are [taʎ'ʎare] *vt* to cut; (*recidere,

interrompere*) to cut off; (*intersecare*) to cut across, intersect; (*carne*) to carve; (*vini*) to blend ♦ *vi* to cut; (*prendere una scorciatoia*) to take a short-cut; **~ corto** (*fig*) to cut short
taglia'telle [taʎʎa'telle] *sfpl* tagliatelle *pl*
taglia'unghie [taʎʎa'ungje] *sm inv* nail clippers *pl*
tagli'ente [taʎ'ʎente] *ag* sharp
'**taglio** ['taʎʎo] *sm* cutting *no pl*; cut; (*parte tagliente*) cutting edge; (*di abito*) cut, style; (*di stoffa: lunghezza*) length; (*di vini*) blending; **di ~** on edge, edgeways; **banconote di piccolo/grosso ~** notes of small/large denomination
tagli'ola [taʎ'ʎola] *sf* trap, snare
tai'lleur [ta'jœr] *sm inv* suit (*for women*)
'**talco** *sm* talcum powder

PAROLA CHIAVE

'**tale** *det* **1** (*simile, così grande*) such; **un(a) ~ ...** such (a) ...; **non accetto ~i discorsi** I won't allow such talk; **è di una ~ arroganza** he is so arrogant; **fa una ~ confusione!** he makes such a mess!
2 (*persona o cosa indeterminata*) such-and-such; **il giorno ~ all'ora ~** on such-and-such a day at such-and-such a time; **la tal persona** that person; **ha telefonato una ~ Giovanna** somebody called Giovanna phoned
3 (*nelle similitudini*): **~ ... ~** like ... like; **~ padre ~ figlio** like father, like son; **hai il vestito ~ quale il mio** your dress is just *o* exactly like mine
♦ *pron* (*indefinito: persona*): **un(a) ~** someone; **quel** (*o* **quella**) **~** that person, that man (*o* woman); **il tal dei ~i** what's-his-name

---

ta'lento *sm* talent
talis'mano *sm* talisman
tallon'cino [tallon'tʃino] *sm* counterfoil
tal'lone *sm* heel
tal'mente *av* so
ta'lora *av* = **talvolta**
'**talpa** *sf* (*ZOOL*) mole

tal'volta *av* sometimes, at times

tambu'rello *sm* tambourine

tam'buro *sm* drum

Ta'migi [ta'midʒi] *sm*: **il ~** the Thames

tampona'mento *sm* (*AUT*) collision; **~ a catena** pile-up

tampo'nare *vt* (*otturare*) to plug; (*urtare: macchina*) to crash *o* ram into

tam'pone *sm* (*MED*) wad, pad; (*per timbri*) ink-pad; (*respingente*) buffer; **~ assorbente** tampon

'tana *sf* lair, den

'tanfo *sm* stench; musty smell

tan'gente [tan'dʒɛnte] *ag* (*MAT*): **~ a** tangential to ♦ *sf* tangent; (*quota*) share

---
Tangentopoli

i Tangentopoli *describes the corruption scandal involving a large number of politicians, industrialists and businessmen. Investigations exposed a complex system of bribes, some paid from public funds, to gain benefits for private individuals and political parties. The scandal began in Milan which was subsequently called* Tangentopoli *or "Bribesville".*

---

tangenzi'ale [tandʒen'tsjale] *sf* (*AUT*) bypass

'tanica *sf* (*contenitore*) jerry can

tan'tino: un ~ *av* a little, a bit

PAROLA CHIAVE

'tanto, a *det* **1** (*molto: quantità*) a lot of, much; (*: numero*) a lot of, many; (*così ~: quantità*) so much, such a lot of; (*: numero*) so many, such a lot of; **~e volte** so many times, so often; **~i auguri!** all the best!; **~e grazie** many thanks; **~ tempo** so long, such a long time; **ogni ~i chilometri** every so many kilometres

2: **~ ... quanto** (*quantità*) as much ... as; (*numero*) as many ... as; **ho ~a pazienza quanta ne hai tu** I have as much patience as you have *o* as you; **ha ~i amici quanti nemici** he has as many friends as he has enemies

3 (*rafforzativo*) such; **ho aspettato per ~ tempo** I waited so long *o* for such a long time

♦ *pron* **1** (*molto*) much, a lot; (*così ~*) so much, such a lot; **~i, e** many, a lot; so many, such a lot; **credevo ce ne fosse ~** I thought there was (such) a lot, I thought there was plenty

2: **~ quanto** (*denaro*) as much as; (*cioccolatini*) as many as; **ne ho ~ quanto basta** I have as much as I need; **due volte ~** twice as much

3 (*indeterminato*) so much; **~ per l'affitto, ~ per il gas** so much for the rent, so much for the gas; **costa un ~ al metro** it costs so much per metre; **di ~ in ~, ogni ~** every so often; **~ vale che ...** I (*o* we *etc*) may as well ...; **~ meglio!** so much the better!; **~ peggio per lui!** so much the worse for him!

♦ *av* **1** (*molto*) very; **vengo ~ volentieri** I'd be very glad to come; **non ci vuole ~ a capirlo** it doesn't take much to understand it

2 (*così ~: con ag, av*) so; (*: con vb*) so much, such a lot; **è ~ bella!** she's so beautiful!; **non urlare ~** don't shout so much; **sto ~ meglio adesso** I'm so much better now; **~ ... che** so ... (that); **~ ... da** so ... as

3: **~ ... quanto** as ... as; **conosco ~ Carlo quanto suo padre** I know both Carlo and his father; **non è poi ~ complicato quanto sembri** it's not as difficult as it seems; **~ più insisti, ~ più non mollerà** the more you insist, the more stubborn he'll be; **quanto più ... ~ meno** the more ... the less

4 (*solamente*) just; **~ per cambiare/ scherzare** just for a change/a joke; **una volta ~** for once

5 (*a lungo*) (for) long

♦ *cong* after all

'tappa *sf* (*luogo di sosta, fermata*) stop, halt; (*parte di un percorso*) stage, leg; (*SPORT*) lap; **a ~e** in stages

tap'pare _vt_ to plug, stop up; (_bottiglia_) to cork

tap'peto _sm_ carpet; (_anche:_ **tappetino**) rug; (_SPORT_): **andare al ~** to go down for the count; **mettere sul ~** (_fig_) to bring up for discussion

tappez'zare [tappet'tsare] _vt_ (_con carta_) to paper; (_rivestire_): **~ qc (di)** to cover sth (with); **tappezze'ria** _sf_ (_tessuto_) tapestry; (_carta da parati_) wallpaper; (_arte_) upholstery; **far da tappezzeria** (_fig_) to be a wallflower; **tappezzi'ere** _sm_ upholsterer

'tappo _sm_ stopper; (_in sughero_) cork

tarchi'ato, a [tar'kjato] _ag_ stocky, thickset

tar'dare _vi_ to be late ♦ _vt_ to delay; **~ a fare** to delay doing

'tardi _av_ late; **più ~** later (on); **al più ~** at the latest; **sul ~** (_verso sera_) late in the day; **far ~** to be late; (_restare alzato_) to stay up late

tar'divo, a _ag_ (_primavera_) late; (_rimedio_) belated, tardy; (_fig_) retarded

'tardo, a _ag_ (_lento, fig: ottuso_) slow; (_tempo: avanzato_) late

'targa, ghe _sf_ plate; (_AUT_) number (_BRIT_) o license (_US_) plate; **tar'ghetta** _sf_ (_su bagaglio_) name tag; (_su porta_) nameplate

ta'riffa _sf_ (_gen_) rate, tariff; (_di trasporti_) fare; (_elenco_) price list; tariff

'tarlo _sm_ woodworm

'tarma _sf_ moth

ta'rocco, chi _sm_ tarot card; **~chi** _smpl_ (_gioco_) tarot _sg_

tartagli'are [tartaʎ'ʎare] _vi_ to stutter, stammer

'tartaro, a _ag, sm_ (_in tutti i sensi_) tartar

tarta'ruga, ghe _sf_ tortoise; (_di mare_) turtle; (_materiale_) tortoiseshell

tar'tina _sf_ canapé

tar'tufo _sm_ (_BOT_) truffle

'tasca, sche _sf_ pocket; **tas'cabile** _ag_ (_libro_) pocket _cpd_; **tasca'pane** _sm_ haversack; **tas'chino** _sm_ breast pocket

'tassa _sf_ (_imposta_) tax; (_doganale_) duty; (_per iscrizione: a scuola etc_) fee; **~ di circolazione/di soggiorno** road/tourist tax

tas'sametro _sm_ taximeter

tas'sare _vt_ to tax; to levy a duty on

tassa'tivo, a _ag_ peremptory

tassazi'one [tassat'tsjone] _sf_ taxation

tas'sello _sm_ plug; wedge

tassì _sm inv_ = **taxi**; **tas'sista, i, e** _sm/f_ taxi driver

'tasso _sm_ (_di natalità, d'interesse etc_) rate; (_BOT_) yew; (_ZOOL_) badger; **~ di cambio/d'interesse** rate of exchange/interest

tas'tare _vt_ to feel; **~ il terreno** (_fig_) to see how the land lies

tasti'era _sf_ keyboard

'tasto _sm_ key; (_tatto_) touch, feel

tas'toni _av_: **procedere (a) ~** to grope one's way forward

'tattica _sf_ tactics _pl_

'tattico, a, ci, che _ag_ tactical

'tatto _sm_ (_senso_) touch; (_fig_) tact; **duro al ~** hard to the touch; **aver ~** to be tactful, have tact

tatu'aggio [tatu'addʒo] _sm_ tattooing; (_disegno_) tattoo

tatu'are _vt_ to tattoo

'tavola _sf_ table; (_asse_) plank, board; (_lastra_) tablet; (_quadro_) panel (painting); (_illustrazione_) plate; **~ calda** snack bar; **~ a vela** windsurfer

tavo'lato _sm_ boarding; (_pavimento_) wooden floor

tavo'letta _sf_ tablet, bar; **a ~** (_AUT_) flat out

tavo'lino _sm_ small table; (_scrivania_) desk

'tavolo _sm_ table

tavo'lozza [tavo'lɔttsa] _sf_ (_ARTE_) palette

'taxi _sm inv_ taxi

'tazza ['tattsa] _sf_ cup; **~ da caffè/tè** coffee/tea cup; **una ~ di caffè/tè** a cup of coffee/tea

te _pron_ (_soggetto: in forme comparative, oggetto_) you

tè _sm inv_ tea; (_trattenimento_) tea party

tea'trale _ag_ theatrical

te'atro _sm_ theatre

'tecnica, che _sf_ technique; (_tecnologia_) technology

'tecnico, a, ci, che _ag_ technical ♦ _sm/f_ technician

tecnolo'gia [teknolo'dʒia] _sf_ technology

te'desco, a, schi, sche *ag, sm/f, sm* German

'tedio *sm* tedium, boredom

te'game *sm* (*CUC*) pan

'teglia ['teʎʎa] *sf* (*per dolci*) (baking) tin; (*per arrosti*) (roasting) tin

'tegola *sf* tile

tei'era *sf* teapot

'tela *sf* (*tessuto*) cloth; (*per vele, quadri*) canvas; (*dipinto*) canvas, painting; **di ~** (*calzoni*) (heavy) cotton *cpd*; (*scarpe, borsa*) canvas *cpd*; **~ cerata** oilcloth

te'laio *sm* (*apparecchio*) loom; (*struttura*) frame

tele'camera *sf* television camera

teleco'mando *sm* remote control

telecopia'trice *sf* fax (machine)

tele'cronaca *sf* television report

tele'ferica, che *sf* cableway

telefo'nare *vi* to telephone, ring; to make a phone call ♦ *vt* to telephone; **~ a** to phone up, ring up, call up

telefo'nata *sf* (telephone) call; **~ a carico del destinatario** reverse charge (*BRIT*) *o* collect (*US*) call

tele'fonico, a, ci, che *ag* (tele)phone *cpd*

telefon'ino *sm* mobile phone

telefo'nista, i, e *sm/f* telephonist; (*d'impresa*) switchboard operator

te'lefono *sm* telephone; **~ a gettoni** ≈ pay phone

telegior'nale [teledʒor'nale] *sm* television news (programme)

te'legrafo *sm* telegraph

tele'gramma, i *sm* telegram

tele'matica *sf* data transmission; telematics *sg*

teleobiet'tivo *sm* telephoto lens *sg*

telepa'tia *sf* telepathy

teles'copio *sm* telescope

teleselezi'one [teleselet'tsjone] *sf* direct dialling

telespetta'tore, 'trice *sm/f* (television) viewer

televisi'one *sf* television

televi'sore *sm* television set

'telex *sm inv* telex

'telo *sm* cloth; **~ da bagno** bath towel; **~ da spiaggia** beach towel

'tema, i *sm* theme; (*INS*) essay, composition

teme'rario, a *ag* rash, reckless

te'mere *vt* to fear, be afraid of; (*essere sensibile a: freddo, calore*) to be sensitive to ♦ *vi* to be afraid; (*essere preoccupato*): **~ per** to worry about, fear for; **~ di/che** to be afraid of/that

temperama'tite *sm inv* pencil sharpener

tempera'mento *sm* temperament

tempe'rato, a *ag* moderate, temperate; (*clima*) temperate

tempera'tura *sf* temperature

tempe'rino *sm* penknife

tem'pesta *sf* storm; **~ di sabbia/neve** sand/snowstorm

tempes'tare *vt*: **~ qn di domande** to bombard sb with questions; **~ qn di colpi** to rain blows on sb

tempes'tivo, a *ag* timely

tempes'toso, a *ag* stormy

'tempia *sf* (*ANAT*) temple

'tempio *sm* (*edificio*) temple

'tempo *sm* (*METEOR*) weather; (*cronologico*) time; (*epoca*) time, times *pl*; (*di film, gioco: parte*) part; (*MUS*) time; (: *battuta*) beat; (*LING*) tense; **un ~** once; **~ fa** some time ago; **al ~ stesso** *o* **a un ~** at the same time; **per ~** early; **ha fatto il suo ~** it has had its day; **~ libero** free time; **primo/secondo ~** (*TEATRO*) first/second part; (*SPORT*) first/second half; **in ~ utile** in due time *o* course; **a ~ pieno** full-time

tempo'rale *ag* temporal ♦ *sm* (*METEOR*) (thunder)storm

tempo'raneo, a *ag* temporary

temporeggi'are [tempored'dʒare] *vi* to play for time, temporize

tem'prare *vt* to temper

te'nace [te'natʃe] *ag* strong, tough; (*fig*) tenacious; te'nacia *sf* tenacity

te'naglie [te'naʎʎe] *sfpl* pincers *pl*

'tenda *sf* (*riparo*) awning; (*di finestra*) curtain; (*per campeggio etc*) tent

ten'denza [ten'dɛntsa] *sf* tendency; (*orientamento*) trend; **avere ~ a** *o* **per qc** to have a bent for sth

'tendere *vt* (*allungare al massimo*) to stretch, draw tight; (*porgere: mano*) to hold out; (*fig: trappola*) to lay, set ♦ *vi*: **~ a qc/a fare** to tend towards sth/to do; **~ l'orecchio** to prick up one's ears; **il tempo tende al caldo** the weather is getting hot; **un blu che tende al verde** a greenish blue

ten'dina *sf* curtain

'tendine *sm* tendon, sinew

ten'done *sm* (*da circo*) tent

'tenebre *sfpl* darkness *sg*; **tene'broso, a** *ag* dark, gloomy

te'nente *sm* lieutenant

te'nere *vt* to hold; (*conservare, mantenere*) to keep; (*ritenere, considerare*) to consider; (*spazio: occupare*) to take up, occupy; (*seguire: strada*) to keep to ♦ *vi* to hold; (*colori*) to be fast; (*dare importanza*): **~ a** to care about; **~ a fare** to want to do, be keen to do; **~rsi** *vr* (*stare in una determinata posizione*) to stand; (*stimarsi*) to consider o.s.; (*aggrapparsi*): **~rsi a** to hold on to; (*attenersi*): **~rsi a** to stick to; **~ una conferenza** to give a lecture; **~ conto di qc** to take sth into consideration; **~ presente qc** to bear sth in mind

'tenero, a *ag* tender; (*pietra, cera, colore*) soft; (*fig*) tender, loving

'tenia *sf* tapeworm

'tennis *sm* tennis

te'nore *sm* (*tono*) tone; (*MUS*) tenor; **~ di vita** (*livello*) standard of living

tensi'one *sf* tension

ten'tare *vt* (*indurre*) to tempt; (*provare*): **~ qc/di fare** to attempt *o* try sth/to do; **tenta'tivo** *sm* attempt; **tentazi'one** *sf* temptation

tenten'nare *vi* to shake, be unsteady; (*fig*) to hesitate, waver

ten'toni *av*: **andare a ~** (*anche fig*) to grope one's way

'tenue *ag* (*sottile*) fine; (*colore*) soft; (*fig*) slender, slight

te'nuta *sf* (*capacità*) capacity; (*divisa*) uniform; (*abito*) dress; (*AGR*) estate; **a ~ d'aria** airtight; **~ di strada** roadholding power

teolo'gia [teolo'dʒia] *sf* theology; **te'ologo, gi** *sm* theologian

teo'rema, i *sm* theorem

teo'ria *sf* theory; **te'orico, a, ci, che** *ag* theoretic(al)

te'pore *sm* warmth

'teppa *sf* mob, hooligans *pl*; **tep'pismo** *sm* hooliganism; **tep'pista, i** *sm* hooligan

tera'pia *sf* therapy

tergicris'tallo [terdʒikris'tallo] *sm* windscreen (*BRIT*) *o* windshield (*US*) wiper

tergiver'sare [terdʒiver'sare] *vi* to shilly-shally

'tergo *sm*: **a ~** behind; **vedi a ~** please turn over

ter'male *ag* thermal; **stazione** *sf* ~ spa

'terme *sfpl* thermal baths

'termico, a, ci, che *ag* thermic; (*unità*) thermal

termi'nale *ag, sm* terminal

termi'nare *vt* to end; (*lavoro*) to finish ♦ *vi* to end

'termine *sm* term; (*fine, estremità*) end; (*di territorio*) boundary, limit; **contratto a ~** (*COMM*) forward contract; **a breve/lungo ~** short-/long-term; **parlare senza mezzi ~i** to talk frankly, not to mince one's words

ter'mometro *sm* thermometer

termonucle'are *ag* thermonuclear

termosi'fone *sm* radiator

ter'mostato *sm* thermostat

'terra *sf* (*gen, ELETTR*) earth; (*sostanza*) soil, earth; (*opposto al mare*) land *no pl*; (*regione, paese*) land; (*argilla*) clay; **~e** *sfpl* (*possedimento*) lands, land *sg*; **a o per ~** (*stato*) on the ground (*o* floor); (*moto*) to the ground, down; **mettere a ~** (*ELETTR*) to earth

terra'cotta *sf* terracotta; **vasellame** *sm* **di ~** earthenware

terra'ferma *sf* dry land, terra firma; (*continente*) mainland

terrapi'eno *sm* embankment, bank

ter'razza [ter'rattsa] *sf* terrace

ter'razzo [ter'rattso] *sm* = **terrazza**

terre'moto *sm* earthquake

ter'reno, a *ag* (*vita, beni*) earthly ♦ *sm* (*suolo, fig*) ground; (*COMM*) land *no pl*, plot (of land); site; (*SPORT, MIL*) field

ter'restre *ag* (*superficie*) of the earth, earth's; (*di terra: battaglia, animale*) land *cpd*; (*REL*) earthly, worldly

ter'ribile *ag* terrible, dreadful

terrifi'cante *ag* terrifying

ter'rina *sf* tureen

territori'ale *ag* territorial

terri'torio *sm* territory

ter'rore *sm* terror; **terro'rismo** *sm* terrorism; **terro'rista, i, e** *sm/f* terrorist

'terso, a *ag* clear

'terzo, a [ˈtɛrtso] *ag* third ♦ *sm* (*frazione*) third; (*DIR*) third party; **la ~a pagina** (*STAMPA*) the Arts page

'tesa *sf* brim

'teschio [ˈteskjo] *sm* skull

'tesi *sf* thesis

'teso, a *pp di* **tendere** ♦ *ag* (*tirato*) taut, tight; (*fig*) tense

teso'reria *sf* treasury

tesori'ere *sm* treasurer

te'soro *sm* treasure; **il Ministero del T~** the Treasury

'tessera *sf* (*documento*) card

'tessere *vt* to weave; **'tessile** *ag, sm* textile; **'tessitore, 'trice** *sm/f* weaver; **tessi'tura** *sf* weaving

tes'suto *sm* fabric, material; (*BIOL*) tissue

'testa *sf* head; (*di cose: estremità, parte anteriore*) head, front; **di ~** (*vettura etc*) front; **tenere ~ a qn** (*nemico etc*) to stand up to sb; **fare di ~ propria** to go one's own way; **in ~** (*SPORT*) in the lead; **~ o croce?** heads or tails?; **avere la ~ dura** to be stubborn; **~ di serie** (*TENNIS*) seed, seeded player

testa'mento *sm* (*atto*) will; **l'Antico/il Nuovo T~** (*REL*) the Old/New Testament

tes'tardo, a *ag* stubborn, pig-headed

tes'tata *sf* (*parte anteriore*) head; (*intestazione*) heading

'teste *sm/f* witness

tes'ticolo *sm* testicle

testi'mone *sm/f* (*DIR*) witness

testimoni'anza [testimoˈnjantsa] *sf* testimony

testimoni'are *vt* to testify; (*fig*) to bear witness to, testify to ♦ *vi* to give evidence, testify

tes'tina *sf* (*TECN*) head

'testo *sm* text; **fare ~** (*opera, autore*) to be authoritative; **questo libro non fa ~** this book is not essential reading; **testu'ale** *ag* textual; literal, word for word

tes'tuggine [tesˈtuddʒine] *sf* tortoise; (*di mare*) turtle

'tetano *sm* (*MED*) tetanus

'tetro, a *ag* gloomy

'tetto *sm* roof; **tet'toia** *sf* roofing; canopy

'Tevere *sm*: **il ~** the Tiber

Tg *abbr* = **telegiornale**

'thermos ® [ˈtɛrmos] *sm inv* vacuum *o* Thermos ® flask

ti *pron* (*dav lo, la, li, le, ne diventa* **te**) *pron* (*oggetto*) you; (*complemento di termine*) (to) you; (*riflessivo*) yourself

'tibia *sf* tibia, shinbone

tic *sm inv* tic, (nervous) twitch; (*fig*) mannerism

ticchet'tio [tikketˈtio] *sm* (*di macchina da scrivere*) clatter; (*di orologio*) ticking; (*della pioggia*) patter

'ticchio [ˈtikkjo] *sm* (*ghiribizzo*) whim; (*tic*) tic, (nervous) twitch

'tichet *sm inv* (*su farmaci*) prescription charge

ti'epido, a *ag* lukewarm, tepid

ti'fare *vi*: **~ per** to be a fan of; (*parteggiare*) to side with

'tifo *sm* (*MED*) typhus; (*fig*): **fare il ~ per** to be a fan of

tifoi'dea *sf* typhoid

ti'fone *sm* typhoon

ti'foso, a *sm/f* (*SPORT etc*) fan

'tiglio [ˈtiʎʎo] *sm* lime (tree), linden (tree)

'tigre *sf* tiger

tim'ballo *sm* (*strumento*) kettledrum; (*CUC*) timbale

'timbro *sm* stamp; (*MUS*) timbre, tone

'**timido, a** *ag* shy; timid

'**timo** *sm* thyme

ti'**mone** *sm* (*NAUT*) rudder; **timoni'ere** *sm* helmsman

ti'**more** *sm* (*paura*) fear; (*rispetto*) awe; **timo'roso, a** *ag* timid, timorous

'**timpano** *sm* (*ANAT*) eardrum; (*MUS*): **~i** *smpl* kettledrums, timpani

ti'**nello** *sm* small dining room

'**tingere** ['tindʒere] *vt* to dye

'**tino** *sm* vat

ti'**nozza** [ti'nɔttsa] *sf* tub

'**tinta** *sf* (*materia colorante*) dye; (*colore*) colour, shade; **tinta'rella** (*fam*) *sf* (sun)tan

tintin'**nare** *vi* to tinkle

'**tinto, a** *pp di* **tingere**

tinto'**ria** *sf* (*lavasecco*) dry cleaner's (shop)

tin'**tura** *sf* (*operazione*) dyeing; (*colorante*) dye; **~ di iodio** tincture of iodine

'**tipico, a, ci, che** *ag* typical

'**tipo** *sm* type; (*genere*) kind, type; (*fam*) chap, fellow

tipogra'**fia** *sf* typography; (*procedimento*) letterpress (printing); (*officina*) printing house; **tipo'grafico, a, ci, che** *ag* typographic(al); letterpress *cpd*; ti'**pografo** *sm* typographer

ti'**ranno, a** *ag* tyrannical ♦ *sm* tyrant

ti'**rante** *sm* (*per tenda*) guy

ti'**rare** *vt* (*gen*) to pull; (*estrarre*): **~ qc da** to take *o* pull sth out of; to get sth out of; to extract sth from; (*chiudere: tenda etc*) to draw, pull; (*tracciare, disegnare*) to draw, trace; (*lanciare: sasso, palla*) to throw; (*stampare*) to print; (*pistola, freccia*) to fire ♦ *vi* (*pipa, camino*) to draw; (*vento*) to blow; (*abito*) to be tight; (*fare fuoco*) to fire; (*fare del tiro, CALCIO*) to shoot; **~ avanti** *vi* to struggle on ♦ *vt* to keep going; **~ fuori** (*estrarre*) to take out, pull out; **~ giù** (*abbassare*) to bring down; **~ su** to pull up; (*capelli*) to put up; (*fig: bambino*) to bring up; **~rsi indietro** to move back

tira'**tore** *sm* gunman; **un buon ~** a good shot; **~ scelto** marksman

tira'**tura** *sf* (*azione*) printing; (*di libro*) (print) run; (*di giornale*) circulation

'**tirchio, a** ['tirkjo] *ag* mean, stingy

'**tiro** *sm* shooting *no pl*, firing *no pl*; (*colpo, sparo*) shot; (*di palla: lancio*) throwing *no pl*; throw; (*fig*) trick; **cavallo da ~** draught (*BRIT*) *o* draft (*US*) horse; **~ a segno** target shooting; (*luogo*) shooting range

tiro'**cinio** [tiro'tʃinjo] *sm* apprenticeship; (*professionale*) training

ti'**roide** *sf* thyroid (gland)

Tir'**reno** *sm*: **il (mar) ~** the Tyrrhenian Sea

ti'**sana** *sf* herb tea

tito'**lare** *sm/f* incumbent; (*proprietario*) owner; (*CALCIO*) regular player

'**titolo** *sm* title; (*di giornale*) headline; (*diploma*) qualification; (*COMM*) security; (: *azione*) share; **a che ~?** for what reason?; **a ~ di amicizia** out of friendship; **a ~ di premio** as a prize; **~ di credito** share

titu'**bante** *ag* hesitant, irresolute

'**tizio, a** ['tittsjo] *sm/f* fellow, chap

tiz'**zone** [tit'tsone] *sm* brand

toast [toust] *sm inv* toasted sandwich (*generally with ham and cheese*)

toc'**cante** *ag* touching

toc'**care** *vt* to touch; (*tastare*) to feel; (*fig: riguardare*) to concern; (: *commuovere*) to touch, move; (: *pungere*) to hurt, wound; (: *far cenno a: argomento*) to touch on, mention ♦ *vi*: **~ a** (*accadere*) to happen to; (*spettare*) to be up to; **~ (il fondo)** (*in acqua*) to touch the bottom; **tocca a te difenderci** it's up to you to defend us; **a chi tocca?** whose turn is it?; **mi toccò pagare** I had to pay

'**tocco, chi** *sm* touch; (*ARTE*) stroke, touch

'**toga, ghe** *sf* toga; (*di magistrato, professore*) gown

'**togliere** ['tɔʎʎere] *vt* (*rimuovere*) to take away (*o* off), remove; (*riprendere, non concedere più*) to take away, remove; (*MAT*) to take away, subtract; **~ qc a qn** to take sth (away) from sb; **ciò non toglie che** nevertheless, be that as it may; **~rsi il cappello** to take off one's hat

toi'**lette** [twa'lɛt] *sf inv* toilet; (*mobile*) dressing table

to'**letta** *sf* = **toilette**

tolle'ranza [tolle'rantsa] *sf* tolerance

tolle'rare *vt* to tolerate

'**tolto, a** *pp di* **togliere**

to'**maia** *sf (di scarpa)* upper

'**tomba** *sf* tomb

tom'**bino** *sm* manhole cover

'**tombola** *sf (gioco)* tombola; *(ruzzolone)* tumble

'**tomo** *sm* volume

'**tonaca, che** *sf* (REL) habit

'**tondo, a** *ag* round

'**tonfo** *sm* splash; *(rumore sordo)* thud; *(caduta)*: **fare un ~** to take a tumble

'**tonico, a, ci, che** *ag, sm* tonic

tonifi'**care** *vt (muscoli, pelle)* to tone up; *(irrobustire)* to invigorate, brace

tonnel'**laggio** [tonnel'laddʒo] *sm* (NAUT) tonnage

tonnel'**lata** *sf* ton

'**tonno** *sm* tuna (fish)

'**tono** *sm (gen)* tone; *(MUS: di pezzo)* key; *(di colore)* shade, tone

ton'**silla** *sf* tonsil; **tonsil'lite** *sf* tonsillitis

'**tonto, a** *ag* dull, stupid

to'**pazio** [to'pattsjo] *sm* topaz

'**topo** *sm* mouse

topogra'**fia** *sf* topography

'**toppa** *sf (serratura)* keyhole; *(pezza)* patch

to'**race** [to'ratʃe] *sm* chest

'**torba** *sf* peat

'**torbido, a** *ag (liquido)* cloudy; *(: fiume)* muddy; *(fig)* dark; troubled ♦ *sm*: **pescare nel ~** *(fig)* to fish in troubled water

'**torcere** ['tortʃere] *vt* to twist; **~rsi** *vr* to twist, writhe

torchi'**are** [tor'kjare] *vt* to press; '**torchio** *sm* press

'**torcia, ce** ['tortʃa] *sf* torch; **~ elettrica** torch (BRIT), flashlight (US)

torci'**collo** [tortʃi'kɔllo] *sm* stiff neck

'**tordo** *sm* thrush

To'**rino** *sf* Turin

tor'**menta** *sf* snowstorm

tormen'**tare** *vt* to torment; **~rsi** *vr* to fret, worry o.s.; **tor'mento** *sm* torment

torna'**conto** *sm* advantage, benefit

tor'**nado** *sm* tornado

tor'**nante** *sm* hairpin bend

tor'**nare** *vi* to return, go *(o come)* back; *(ridiventare: anche fig)* to become (again); *(riuscire giusto, esatto: conto)* to work out; *(risultare)* to turn out (to be), prove (to be); **~ utile** to prove *o* turn out (to be) useful; **~ a casa** to go *(o come)* home

torna'**sole** *sm inv* litmus

tor'**neo** *sm* tournament

'**tornio** *sm* lathe

'**toro** *sm* bull; *(dello zodiaco)*: **T~** Taurus

tor'**pedine** *sf* torpedo; **torpedini'era** *sf* torpedo boat

'**torre** *sf* tower; *(SCACCHI)* rook, castle; **~ di controllo** (AER) control tower

torrefazi'**one** [torrefat'tsjone] *sf* roasting

tor'**rente** *sm* torrent

tor'**retta** *sf* turret

torri'**one** *sm* keep

tor'**rone** *sm* nougat

torsi'**one** *sf* twisting; torsion

'**torso** *sm* torso, trunk; *(ARTE)* torso

'**torsolo** *sm (di cavolo etc)* stump; *(di frutta)* core

'**torta** *sf* cake

'**torto, a** *pp di* **torcere** ♦ *ag (ritorto)* twisted; *(storto)* twisted, crooked ♦ *sm (ingiustizia)* wrong; *(colpa)* fault; **a ~** wrongly; **aver ~** to be wrong

'**tortora** *sf* turtle dove

tortu'**oso, a** *ag (strada)* twisting, *(fig)* tortuous

tor'**tura** *sf* torture; **tortu'rare** *vt* to torture

'**torvo, a** *ag* menacing, grim

tosa'**erba** *sm o f inv* (lawn)mower

to'**sare** *vt (pecora)* to shear; *(siepe)* to clip

Tos'**cana** *sf*: **la ~** Tuscany; **tos'cano, a** *ag, sm/f* Tuscan ♦ *sm (sigaro)* strong Italian cigar

'**tosse** *sf* cough

'**tossico, a, ci, che** *ag* toxic

tossicodipen'**dente** *sm/f* drug addict

tossi'**comane** *sm/f* drug addict

tos'**sire** *vi* to cough

tosta'**pane** *sm inv* toaster

tos'**tare** *vt* to toast; *(caffè)* to roast

'**tosto, a** *ag*: **faccia ~a** cheek

to'tale *ag, sm* total; **totalità** *sf*: **la totalità di** all of, the total amount (*o number*) of; the whole +*sg*; **totaliz'zare** *vt* to total; (*SPORT: punti*) to score

toto'calcio [toto'kaltʃo] *sm* gambling pool betting on football results, ≈ (football) pools *pl* (*BRIT*)

to'vaglia [to'vaʎʎa] *sf* tablecloth; **tovagli'olo** *sm* napkin

'tozzo, a ['tɔttso] *ag* squat ♦ *sm*: ~ **di pane** crust of bread

tra *prep* (*di due persone, cose*) between; (*di più persone, cose*) among(st); (*tempo: entro*) within, in; ~ **5 giorni** in 5 days' time; **sia detto ~ noi ...** between you and me ...; **litigano ~ (di) loro** they're fighting amongst themselves; ~ **breve** soon; ~ **sé e sé** (*parlare etc*) to oneself

trabal'lare *vi* to stagger, totter

traboc'care *vi* to overflow

traboc'chetto [trabok'ketto] *sm* (*fig*) trap

tracan'nare *vt* to gulp down

'traccia, ce ['trattʃa] *sf* (*segno, striscia*) trail, track; (*orma*) tracks *pl*; (*residuo, testimonianza*) trace, sign; (*abbozzo*) outline

tracci'are [trat'tʃare] *vt* to trace, mark (out); (*disegnare*) to draw; (*fig: abbozzare*) to outline; **tracci'ato** *sm* (*grafico*) layout, plan

tra'chea [tra'kea] *sf* windpipe, trachea

tra'colla *sf* shoulder strap; **borsa a ~** shoulder bag

tra'collo *sm* (*fig*) collapse, crash

tradi'mento *sm* betrayal; (*DIR, MIL*) treason

tra'dire *vt* to betray; (*coniuge*) to be unfaithful to; (*doveri: mancare*) to fail in; (*rivelare*) to give away, reveal; **tradi'tore, 'trice** *sm/f* traitor

tradizio'nale [tradittsjo'nale] *ag* traditional

tradizi'one [tradit'tsjone] *sf* tradition

tra'dotto, a *pp di* **tradurre**

tra'durre *vt* to translate; (*spiegare*) to render, convey; **tradut'tore, 'trice** *sm/f* translator; **traduzi'one** *sf* translation

trafe'lato, a *ag* out of breath

traffi'cante *sm/f* dealer; (*peg*) trafficker

traffi'care *vi* (*commerciare*): ~ **(in)** to trade (in), deal (in); (*affaccendarsi*) to busy o.s. ♦ *vt* (*peg*) to traffic in

'traffico, ci *sm* traffic; (*commercio*) trade, traffic

tra'figgere [tra'fiddʒere] *vt* to run through, stab; (*fig*) to pierce

tra'fitto, a *pp di* **trafiggere**

trafo'rare *vt* to bore, drill; **tra'foro** *sm* (*azione*) boring, drilling; (*galleria*) tunnel

tra'gedia [tra'dʒedja] *sf* tragedy

tra'ghetto [tra'getto] *sm* ferry(boat)

'tragico, a, ci, che ['tradʒiko] *ag* tragic

tra'gitto [tra'dʒitto] *sm* (*passaggio*) crossing; (*viaggio*) journey

tragu'ardo *sm* (*SPORT*) finishing line; (*fig*) goal, aim

traiet'toria *sf* trajectory

trai'nare *vt* to drag, haul; (*rimorchiare*) to tow; **'traino** *sm* (*carro*) wagon; (*slitta*) sledge; (*carico*) load

tralasci'are [tralaʃ'ʃare] *vt* (*studi*) to neglect; (*dettagli*) to leave out, omit

'tralcio ['traltʃo] *sm* (*BOT*) shoot

tra'liccio [tra'littʃo] *sm* (*ELETTR*) pylon

tram *sm inv* tram

'trama *sf* (*filo*) weft, woof; (*fig: argomento, maneggio*) plot

traman'dare *vt* to pass on, hand down

tra'mare *vt* (*fig*) to scheme, plot

tram'busto *sm* turmoil

trames'tio *sm* bustle

tramez'zino [tramed'dzino] *sm* sandwich

tra'mezzo [tra'meddzo] *sm* (*EDIL*) partition

'tramite *prep* through

tramon'tare *vi* to set, go down; **tra'monto** *sm* setting; (*del sole*) sunset

tramor'tire *vi* to faint ♦ *vt* to stun

trampo'lino *sm* (*per tuffi*) springboard, diving board; (*per lo sci*) ski-jump

'trampolo *sm* stilt

tramu'tare *vt*: ~ **in** to change into, turn into

tra'nello *sm* trap

trangugi'are [trangu'dʒare] *vt* to gulp down

'tranne *prep* except (for), but (for); ~ **che**

unless

tranquil'lante *sm* (MED) tranquillizer

tranquillità *sf* calm, stillness; quietness; peace of mind

tranquilliz'zare [trankwillid'dzare] *vt* to reassure

tran'quillo, a *ag* calm, quiet; (*bambino, scolaro*) quiet; (*sereno*) with one's mind at rest; **sta' ~** don't worry

transat'lantico, ci *sm* transatlantic liner

transatlantico

> 🛈 The transatlantico *is a room in the* Palazzo di Montecitorio. *The* deputati *relax in it between parliamentary sessions and give media interviews and press conferences there.*

transazi'one [transat'tsjone] *sf* compromise; (DIR) settlement; (COMM) transaction, deal

tran'senna *sf* barrier

tran'sigere [tran'sidʒere] *vi* (*venire a patti*) to compromise, come to an agreement

tran'sistor *sm inv* transistor

transi'tabile *ag* passable

transi'tare *vi* to pass

transi'tivo, a *ag* transitive

'transito *sm* transit; **di ~** (*merci*) in transit; (*stazione*) transit *cpd*; **"divieto di ~"** "no entry"

transi'torio, a *ag* transitory, transient; (*provvisorio*) provisional

'trapano *sm* (*utensile*) drill; (: MED) trepan

trapas'sare *vt* to pierce

tra'passo *sm* passage

trape'lare *vi* to leak, drip; (*fig*) to leak out

tra'pezio [tra'pettsjo] *sm* (MAT) trapezium; (*attrezzo ginnico*) trapeze

trapian'tare *vt* to transplant; **trapi'anto** *sm* transplanting; (MED) transplant

'trappola *sf* trap

tra'punta *sf* quilt

'trarre *vt* to draw, pull; (*portare*) to take; (*prendere, tirare fuori*) to take (out), draw; (*derivare*) to obtain; **~ origine da qc** to have its origins *o* originate in sth

trasa'lire *vi* to start, jump

trasan'dato, a *ag* shabby

tras'bordo *sm* transfer

trasci'nare [traʃʃi'nare] *vt* to drag; **~rsi** *vr* to drag o.s. along; (*fig*) to drag on

tras'correre *vt* (*tempo*) to spend, pass ♦ *vi* to pass; **tras'corso, a** *pp di* **trascorrere**

tras'critto, a *pp di* **trascrivere**

tras'crivere *vt* to transcribe

trascu'rare *vt* to neglect; (*non considerare*) to disregard; **trascura'tezza** *sf* carelessness, negligence; **trascu'rato, a** *ag* (*casa*) neglected; (*persona*) careless, negligent

trasfe'ribile *ag* transferable; **"non ~"** (*su assegno*) "account payee only"

trasferi'mento *sm* transfer; (*trasloco*) removal, move

trasfe'rire *vt* to transfer; **~rsi** *vr* to move; **tras'ferta** *sf* transfer; (*indennità*) travelling expenses *pl*; (SPORT) away game

trasfigu'rare *vt* to transfigure

trasfor'mare *vt* to transform, change; **trasforma'tore** *sm* (ELEC) transformer

trasfusi'one *sf* (MED) transfusion

trasgre'dire *vt* to disobey, contravene

tras'lato, a *ag* metaphorical, figurative

traslo'care *vt* to move, transfer; **~rsi** *vr* to move; **tras'loco, chi** *sm* removal

tras'messo, a *pp di* **trasmettere**

tras'mettere *vt* (*passare*): **~ qc a qn** to pass sth on to sb, (*mandare*) to send; (TECN, TEL, MED) to transmit; (TV, RADIO) to broadcast; **trasmetti'tore** *sm* transmitter; **trasmissi'one** *sf* (*gen, FISICA, TECN*) transmission; (*passaggio*) transmission, passing on; (TV, RADIO) broadcast; **trasmit'tente** *sf* transmitting *o* broadcasting station

traso'gnato, a [trasoɲ'ɲato] *ag* dreamy

traspa'rente *ag* transparent

traspa'rire *vi* to show (through)

traspi'rare *vi* to perspire; (*fig*) to come to light, leak out; **traspirazi'one** *sf* perspiration

traspor'tare *vt* to carry, move; (*merce*) to

transport, convey; **lasciarsi ~ (da qc)** (*fig*) to let o.s. be carried away (by sth); **tras'porto** *sm* transport

trastul'lare *vt* to amuse; **~rsi** *vr* to amuse o.s.

trasu'dare *vi* (*filtrare*) to ooze; (*sudare*) to sweat ♦ *vt* to ooze with

trasver'sale *ag* transverse, cross(-); running at right angles

trasvo'lare *vt* to fly over

'tratta *sf* (*ECON*) draft; (*di persone*): **la ~ delle bianche** the white slave trade

tratta'mento *sm* treatment; (*servizio*) service

trat'tare *vt* (*gen*) to treat; (*commerciare*) to deal in; (*svolgere: argomento*) to discuss, deal with; (*negoziare*) to negotiate ♦ *vi*: **~ di** to deal with; **~ con** (*persona*) to deal with; **si tratta di ...** it's about ...; **tratta'tive** *sfpl* negotiations; **trat'tato** *sm* (*testo*) treatise; (*accordo*) treaty; **trattazi'one** *sf* treatment

tratteggi'are [tratted'dʒare] *vt* (*disegnare: a tratti*) to sketch, outline; (*: col tratteggio*) to hatch

tratte'nere *vt* (*far rimanere: persona*) to detain; (*intrattenere: ospiti*) to entertain; (*tenere, frenare, reprimere*) to hold back, keep back; (*astenersi dal consegnare*) to hold, keep; (*detrarre: somma*) to deduct; **~rsi** *vr* (*astenersi*) to restrain o.s., stop o.s.; (*soffermarsi*) to stay, remain

tratteni'mento *sm* entertainment; (*festa*) party

tratte'nuta *sf* deduction

trat'tino *sm* dash; (*in parole composte*) hyphen

'tratto, a *pp di* **trarre** ♦ *sm* (*di penna, matita*) stroke; (*parte*) part, piece; (*di strada*) stretch; (*di mare, cielo*) expanse; (*di tempo*) period (of time); **~i** *smpl* (*caratteristiche*) features; (*modo di fare*) ways, manners; **a un ~, d'un ~** suddenly

trat'tore *sm* tractor

tratto'ria *sf* restaurant

'trauma, i *sm* trauma; **trau'matico, a, ci, che** *ag* traumatic

tra'vaglio [tra'vaʎʎo] *sm* (*angoscia*) pain, suffering; (*MED*) pains *pl*

trava'sare *vt* to decant

'trave *sf* beam

tra'versa *sf* (*trave*) crosspiece; (*via*) sidestreet; (*FERR*) sleeper (*BRIT*), (railroad) tie (*US*); (*CALCIO*) crossbar

traver'sare *vt* to cross; **traver'sata** *sf* crossing; (*AER*) flight, trip

traver'sie *sfpl* mishaps, misfortunes

traver'sina *sf* (*FERR*) sleeper (*BRIT*), (railroad) tie (*US*)

tra'verso, a *ag* oblique; **di ~** *ag* askew ♦ *av* sideways; **andare di ~** (*cibo*) to go down the wrong way; **guardare di ~** to look askance at

travesti'mento *sm* disguise

traves'tire *vt* to disguise; **~rsi** *vr* to disguise o.s.

travi'are *vt* (*fig*) to lead astray

travi'sare *vt* (*fig*) to distort, misrepresent

tra'volgere [tra'vɔldʒere] *vt* to sweep away, carry away; (*fig*) to overwhelm; **tra'volto, a** *pp di* **travolgere**

tre *num* three

trebbi'are *vt* to thresh

'treccia, ce ['trettʃa] *sf* plait, braid

tre'cento [tre'tʃento] *num* three hundred ♦ *sm*: **il T~** the fourteenth century

'tredici ['treditʃi] *num* thirteen

'tregua *sf* truce; (*fig*) respite

tre'mare *vi*: **~ di** (*freddo etc*) to shiver *o* tremble with; (*paura, rabbia*) to shake *o* tremble with

tre'mendo, a *ag* terrible, awful

tre'mila *num* three thousand

'tremito *sm* trembling *no pl*; shaking *no pl*; shivering *no pl*

tremo'lare *vi* to tremble; (*luce*) to flicker; (*foglie*) to quiver

tre'more *sm* tremor

'treno *sm* train; **~ di gomme** set of tyres (*BRIT*) *o* tires (*US*); **~ merci** goods (*BRIT*) *o* freight train; **~ viaggiatori** passenger train

'trenta *num* thirty; **tren'tesimo, a** *num* thirtieth; **tren'tina** *sf*: **una trentina (di)** thirty or so, about thirty 'trepi'dante *ag* anxious

treppi'ede *sm* tripod; (CUC) trivet

'tresca, sche *sf* (fig) intrigue; (: *relazione amorosa*) affair

'trespolo *sm* trestle

tri'angolo *sm* triangle

tri'bù *sf inv* tribe

tri'buna *sf* (*podio*) platform; (*in aule etc*) gallery; (*di stadio*) stand

tribu'nale *sm* court

tribu'tare *vt* to bestow

tri'buto *sm* tax; (fig) tribute

tri'checo, chi [tri'keko] *sm* (ZOOL) walrus

tri'ciclo [tri'tʃiklo] *sm* tricycle

trico'lore *ag* three-coloured ♦ *sm* tricolour; (*bandiera italiana*) Italian flag

tri'dente *sm* trident

tri'foglio [tri'fɔʎʎo] *sm* clover

'triglia ['triʎʎa] *sf* red mullet

tril'lare *vi* (MUS) to trill

tri'mestre *sm* period of three months; (INS) term, quarter (US); (COMM) quarter

'trina *sf* lace

trin'cea [trin'tʃea] *sf* trench; trince'rare *vt* to entrench

trinci'are [trin'tʃare] *vt* to cut up

trion'fare *vi* to triumph, win; ~ **su** to triumph over, overcome; tri'onfo *sm* triumph

tripli'care *vt* to triple

'triplice ['triplitʃe] *ag* triple; **in ~ copia** in triplicate

'triplo, a *ag* triple; treble ♦ *sm:* **il ~ (di)** three times as much (as); **la spesa è ~a** it costs three times as much

'trippa *sf* (CUC) tripe

'triste *ag* sad; (*luogo*) dreary, gloomy; tris'tezza *sf* sadness; gloominess

trita'carne *sm inv* mincer, grinder (US)

tri'tare *vt* to mince, grind (US)

'trito, a *ag* (*tritato*) minced, ground (US); ~ **e ritrito** (fig) trite, hackneyed

'trittico, ci *sm* (ARTE) triptych

trivel'lare *vt* to drill

trivi'ale *ag* vulgar, low

tro'feo *sm* trophy

'tromba *sf* (MUS) trumpet; (AUT) horn; ~

d'aria whirlwind; ~ **delle scale** stairwell

trom'bone *sm* trombone

trom'bosi *sf* thrombosis

tron'care *vt* to cut off; (*spezzare*) to break off

'tronco, a, chi, che *ag* cut off; broken off; (LING) truncated; (fig) cut short ♦ *sm* (BOT, ANAT) trunk; (fig: *tratto*) section; **licenziare qn in ~** to fire sb on the spot

troneggi'are [troned'dʒare] *vi:* ~ **(su)** to tower (over)

'tronfio, a *ag* conceited

'trono *sm* throne

tropi'cale *ag* tropical

'tropico, ci *sm* tropic; ~**ci** *smpl* (GEO) tropics

PAROLA CHIAVE

'troppo, a *det* (in *eccesso: quantità*) too much; (: *numero*) too many; **c'era ~a gente** there were too many people; **fa ~ caldo** it's too hot

♦ *pron* (in *eccesso: quantità*) too much; (: *numero*) too many; **ne hai messo ~** you've put in too much; **meglio ~i che pochi** better too many than too few

♦ *av* (*eccessivamente: con ag, av*) too; (: *con vb*) too much; ~ **amaro/tardi** too bitter/late; **lavora ~** he works too much; **di ~** too much; too many; **qualche tazza di ~** a few cups too many; **3000 lire di ~** 3000 lire too much; **essere di ~** to be in the way

---

'trota *sf* trout

trot'tare *vi* to trot; trotterel'lare *vi* to trot along; (*bambino*) to toddle; 'trotto *sm* trot

'trottola *sf* spinning top

tro'vare *vt* to find; (*giudicare*): **trovo che** I find *o* think that; ~**rsi** *vr* (*reciproco: incontrarsi*) to meet; (*essere, stare*) to be; (*arrivare, capitare*) to find o.s.; **andare a ~ qn** to go and see sb; ~ **qn colpevole** to find sb guilty; ~**rsi bene** (*in un luogo, con qn*) to get on well; tro'vata *sf* good idea

truc'care *vt* (*falsare*) to fake; (*attore etc*) to

make up; (*travestire*) to disguise; (*SPORT*) to fix; (*AUT*) to soup up; **~rsi** *vr* to make up (one's face); **trucca'tore, 'trice** *sm/f* (*CINEMA, TEATRO*) make-up artist

'trucco, chi *sm* trick; (*cosmesi*) make-up

'truce ['trutʃe] *ag* fierce

truci'dare [trutʃi'dare] *vt* to slaughter

'truciolo ['trutʃolo] *sm* shaving

'truffa *sf* fraud, swindle; **truf'fare** *vt* to swindle, cheat

'truppa *sf* troop

tu *pron* you; **~ stesso(a)** you yourself; **dare del ~ a qn** to address sb as "tu"

'tua *vedi* **tuo**

'tuba *sf* (*MUS*) tuba; (*cappello*) top hat

tu'bare *vi* to coo

tuba'tura *sf* piping *no pl*, pipes *pl*

tu'betto *sm* tube

'tubo *sm* tube; pipe; **~ digerente** (*ANAT*) alimentary canal, digestive tract; **~ di scappamento** (*AUT*) exhaust pipe

'tue *vedi* **tuo**

tuf'fare *vt* to plunge, dip; **~rsi** *vr* to plunge, dive; **'tuffo** *sm* dive; (*breve bagno*) dip

tu'gurio *sm* hovel

tuli'pano *sm* tulip

tume'farsi *vr* (*MED*) to swell

'tumido, a *ag* swollen

tu'more *sm* (*MED*) tumour

tu'multo *sm* uproar, commotion; (*sommossa*) riot; (*fig*) turmoil; **tumultu'oso, a** *ag* rowdy, unruly; (*fig*) turbulent, stormy

'tunica, che *sf* tunic

Tuni'sia *sf*: **la ~** Tunisia

'tuo (*f* **'tua**, *pl* **tu'oi**, **'tue**) *det*: **il ~, la tua** *etc* your ♦ *pron*: **il ~, la tua** *etc* yours

tuo'nare *vi* to thunder; **tuona** it is thundering, there's some thunder

tu'ono *sm* thunder

tu'orlo *sm* yolk

tu'racciolo [tu'rattʃolo] *sm* cap, top; (*di sughero*) cork

tu'rare *vt* to stop, plug; (*con sughero*) to cork; **~rsi il naso** to hold one's nose

turba'mento *sm* disturbance; (*di animo*) anxiety, agitation

tur'bante *sm* turban

tur'bare *vt* to disturb, trouble

'turbine *sm* whirlwind

turbo'lento, a *ag* turbulent; (*ragazzo*) boisterous, unruly

turbo'lenza *sf* turbulence

tur'chese [tur'kese] *sf* turquoise

Tur'chia [tur'kia] *sf*: **la ~** Turkey

tur'chino, a [tur'kino] *ag* deep blue

'turco, a, chi, che *ag* Turkish ♦ *sm/f* Turk/Turkish woman ♦ *sm* (*LING*) Turkish; **parlare ~** (*fig*) to talk double-dutch

tu'rismo *sm* tourism; tourist industry; **tu'rista, i, e** *sm/f* tourist; **tu'ristico, a, ci, che** *ag* tourist *cpd*

'turno *sm* turn; (*di lavoro*) shift; **di ~** (*soldato, medico, custode*) on duty; **a ~** (*rispondere*) in turn; (*lavorare*) in shifts; **fare a ~ a fare qc** to take turns to do sth; **è il suo ~** it's your (*o his etc*) turn

'turpe *ag* filthy, vile; **turpi'loquio** *sm* obscene language

'tuta *sf* overalls *pl*; (*SPORT*) tracksuit

tu'tela *sf* (*DIR: di minore*) guardianship; (*: protezione*) protection; (*difesa*) defence; **tute'lare** *vt* to protect, defend

tu'tore, 'trice *sm/f* (*DIR*) guardian

tutta'via *cong* nevertheless, yet

PAROLA CHIAVE

'tutto, a *det* **1** (*intero*) all; **~ il latte** all the milk; **~a la notte** all night, the whole night; **~ il libro** the whole book; **~a una bottiglia** a whole bottle

2 (*pl, collettivo*) all; every; **~i i libri** all the books; **~e le notti** every night; **~i i venerdì** every Friday; **~i gli uomini** all the men; (*collettivo*) all men; **~ l'anno** all year long; **~i e due** both *o* each of us (*o* them *o* you); **~i e cinque** all five of us (*o* them *o* you)

3 (*completamente*): **era ~a sporca** she was all dirty; **tremava ~** he was trembling all over; **è ~a sua madre** she's just *o* exactly like her mother

4: **a tutt'oggi** so far, up till now; **a ~a velocità** at full *o* top speed

♦ *pron* **1** (*ogni cosa*) everything, all; (*qualsiasi cosa*) anything; **ha mangiato ~** he's eaten everything; **~ considerato** all things considered; **in ~: 10.000 lire in ~** 10.000 lire in all; **in ~ eravamo 50** there were 50 of us in all

2: ~i, e (*ognuno*) all, everybody; **vengono ~i** they are all coming, everybody's coming; **~i quanti** all and sundry

♦ *av* (*completamente*) entirely, quite; **è ~ il contrario** it's quite *o* exactly the opposite; **tutt'al più: saranno stati tutt'al più una cinquantina** there were about fifty of them at (the very) most; **tutt'al più possiamo prendere un treno** if the worst comes to the worst we can take a train; **tutt'altro** on the contrary; **è tutt'altro che felice** he's anything but happy; **tutt'a un tratto** suddenly

♦ *sm*: **il ~** the whole lot, all of it

tutto'fare *ag inv*: **domestica ~** general maid; **ragazzo ~** office boy ♦ *sm/f inv* handyman/woman
tut'tora *av* still

U, u

ubbidi'ente *ag* obedient; **ubbidi'enza** *sf* obedience
ubbi'dire *vi* to obey; **~ a** to obey; (*sog: veicolo, macchina*) to respond to
ubria'care *vt*: **~ qn** to get sb drunk; (*sog: alcool*) to make sb drunk; (*fig*) to make sb's head spin *o* reel; **~rsi** *vr* to get drunk; **~rsi di** (*fig*) to become intoxicated with
ubri'aco, a, chi, che *ag, sm/f* drunk
uccelli'era [utt∫el'ljɛra] *sf* aviary
uccel'lino [utt∫el'lino] *sm* baby bird, chick
uc'cello [ut't∫ɛllo] *sm* bird
uc'cidere [ut't∫idere] *vt* to kill; **~rsi** *vr* (*suicidarsi*) to kill o.s.; (*perdere la vita*) to be killed; **uccisi'one** *sf* killing; **uc'ciso, a** *pp di* **uccidere**; **ucci'sore** *sm* killer
udi'enza [u'djɛntsa] *sf* audience; (*DIR*) hearing; **dare ~ (a)** to grant an

audience (to)
u'dire *vt* to hear; **udi'tivo, a** *ag* auditory; **u'dito** *sm* (sense of) hearing; **udi'torio** *sm* (*persone*) audience
'uffa *escl* tut!
uffici'ale [uffi't∫ale] *ag* official ♦ *sm* (*AMM*) official, officer; (*MIL*) officer; **~ di stato civile** registrar
uf'ficio [uf'fit∫o] *sm* (*gen*) office; (*dovere*) duty; (*mansione*) task, function, job; (*agenzia*) agency, bureau; (*REL*) service; **d'~** *ag* office *cpd*; official ♦ *av* officially; **~ di collocamento** employment office; **~ informazioni** information bureau; **~ oggetti smarriti** lost property office (*BRIT*), lost and found (*US*); **~ postale** post office
uffici'oso, a [uffi't∫oso] *ag* unofficial
'UFO *sm inv* UFO
'ufo: a ~ *av* free, for nothing
uggi'oso, a [ud'dʒoso] *ag* (*tempo*) dull
uguagli'anza [ugwaʎ'ʎantsa] *sf* equality
uguagli'are [ugwaʎ'ʎare] *vt* to make equal; (*essere uguale*) to equal, be equal to; (*livellare*) to level; **~rsi a** *o* **con qn** (*paragonarsi*) to compare o.s. to sb
ugu'ale *ag* equal; (*identico*) identical, the same; (*uniforme*) level, even ♦ *av*: **costano ~** they cost the same; **sono bravi ~** they're equally good; **ugual'mente** *av* equally; (*lo stesso*) all the same
'ulcera ['ultʃera] *sf* ulcer
u'livo = **olivo**
ulteri'ore *ag* further
ulti'mare *vt* to finish, complete
'ultimo, a *ag* (*finale*) last; (*estremo*) farthest, utmost; (*recente: notizia, moda*) latest; (*fig: sommo, fondamentale*) ultimate ♦ *sm/f* last (one); **fino all'~** to the last, until the end; **da ~, in ~** in the end; **abitare all'~ piano** to live on the top floor; **per ~** (*entrare, arrivare*) last
ulu'lare *vi* to howl; **ulu'lato** *sm* howling *no pl*; howl
umanità *sf* humanity; **umani'tario, a** *ag* humanitarian
u'mano, a *ag* human; (*comprensivo*) humane

umet'tare *vt* to dampen, moisten
umidità *sf* dampness; humidity
'umido, a *ag* damp; (*mano, occhi*) moist; (*clima*) humid ♦ *sm* dampness, damp; **carne in ~** stew
'umile *ag* humble
umili'are *vt* to humiliate; **~rsi** *vr* to humble o.s.; **umiliazi'one** *sf* humiliation
umiltà *sf* humility, humbleness
u'more *sm* (*disposizione d'animo*) mood; (*carattere*) temper; **di buon/cattivo ~** in a good/bad mood
umo'rismo *sm* humour; **avere il senso dell'~** to have a sense of humour; **umo'ristico, a, ci, che** *ag* humorous, funny
un *vedi* **uno**
un' *vedi* **uno**
'una *vedi* **uno**
u'nanime *ag* unanimous; **unanimità** *sf* unanimity; **all'unanimità** unanimously
unci'netto [untʃi'netto] *sm* crochet hook
un'cino [un'tʃino] *sm* hook
'undici ['unditʃi] *num* eleven
'ungere ['undʒere] *vt* to grease, oil; (*REL*) to anoint; (*fig*) to flatter, butter up; **~rsi** *vr* (*sporcarsi*) to get covered in grease; **~rsi con la crema** to put on cream
unghe'rese [unge'rese] *ag, sm/f, sm* Hungarian
Unghe'ria [unge'ria] *sf*: **l'~** Hungary
'unghia ['ungja] *sf* (*ANAT*) nail; (*di animale*) claw; (*di rapace*) talon; (*di cavallo*) hoof; **unghi'ata** *sf* (*graffio*) scratch
ungu'ento *sm* ointment
'unico, a, ci, che *ag* (*solo*) only; (*ineguagliabile*) unique; (*singolo: binario*) single; **figlio(a) ~(a)** only son/daughter, only child
unifamili'are *ag* one-family *cpd*
unifi'care *vt* to unite, unify; (*sistemi*) to standardize; **unificazi'one** *sf* uniting; unification; standardization
uni'forme *ag* uniform; (*superficie*) even ♦ *sf* (*divisa*) uniform
unilate'rale *ag* one-sided; (*DIR*) unilateral
uni'one *sf* union; (*fig: concordia*) unity,

harmony
u'nire *vt* to unite; (*congiungere*) to join, connect; (: *ingredienti, colori*) to combine; (*in matrimonio*) to unite, join together; **~rsi** *vr* to unite; (*in matrimonio*) to be joined together; **~ qc a** to unite sth with; to join *o* connect sth with; to combine sth with; **~rsi a** (*gruppo, società*) to join
unità *sf inv* (*unione, concordia*) unity; (*MAT, MIL, COMM, di misura*) unit; **uni'tario, a** *ag* unitary; **prezzo unitario** price per unit
u'nito, a *ag* (*paese*) united; (*amici, famiglia*) close; **in tinta ~a** plain, self-coloured
univer'sale *ag* universal; general
università *sf inv* university; **universi'tario, a** *ag* university *cpd* ♦ *sm/f* (*studente*) university student; (*insegnante*) academic, university lecturer
uni'verso *sm* universe

PAROLA CHIAVE

'uno, a (*dav sm* **un** *+C, V,* **uno** *+s impura, gn, pn, ps, x, z; dav sf* **un'** *+V,* **una** *+C*) *art indet* **1** a; (*dav vocale*) an; **un bambino** a child; **~a strada** a street; **~ zingaro** a gypsy
2 (*intensivo*): **ho avuto ~a paura!** I got such a fright!
♦ *pron* **1** one; **prendine ~** take one (of them); **l'~ o l'altro** either (of them); **l'~ e l'altro** both (of them); **aiutarsi l'un l'altro** to help one another *o* each other; **sono entrati l'~ dopo l'altro** they came in one after the other
2 (*un tale*) someone, somebody
3 (*con valore impersonale*) one, you; **se ~ vuole** if one wants, if you want
♦ *num* one; **~a mela e due pere** one apple and two pears; **~ più ~ fa due** one plus one equals two, one and one are two
♦ *sf*: **è l'~a** it's one (o'clock)

'unto, a *pp di* **ungere** ♦ *ag* greasy, oily ♦ *sm* grease; **untu'oso, a** *ag* greasy, oily
u'omo (*pl* **u'omini**) *sm* man; **da ~** (*abito, scarpe*) men's, for men; **~ d'affari** businessman; **~ di paglia** stooge; **~ rana** frogman

u'**ovo** (*pl(f)* u'**ova**) *sm* egg; **~ affogato** poached egg; **~ al tegame** fried egg; **~ alla coque** boiled egg; **~ bazzotto/sodo** soft-/hard-boiled egg; **~ di Pasqua** Easter egg; **~ in camicia** poached egg; **~a strapazzate** scrambled eggs

ura'**gano** *sm* hurricane

urba'**nistica** *sf* town planning

ur'**bano, a** *ag* urban, city *cpd*, town *cpd*; (*TEL: chiamata*) local; (*fig*) urbane

ur'**gente** [ur'dʒɛnte] *ag* urgent; **ur'genza** *sf* urgency; **in caso d'urgenza** (in case of) an emergency; **d'urgenza** *ag* emergency ♦ *av* urgently, as a matter of urgency

u'**rina** *sf* = **orina**

ur'**lare** *vi* (*persona*) to scream, yell; (*animale, vento*) to howl ♦ *vt* to scream, yell

'**urlo** (*pl(m)* '**urli**, *pl(f)* '**urla**) *sm* scream, yell; howl

'**urna** *sf* urn; (*elettorale*) ballot-box; **andare alle ~e** to go to the polls

urrà *escl* hurrah!

U.R.S.S. *abbr f*: **l'~** the USSR

ur'**tare** *vt* to bump into, knock against; (*fig: irritare*) to annoy ♦ *vi*: **~ contro o in** to bump into, knock against, crash into; (*fig: imbattersi*) to come up against; **~rsi** *vr* (*reciproco: scontrarsi*) to collide; (*: fig*) to clash; (*irritarsi*) to get annoyed; '**urto** *sm* (*colpo*) knock, bump; (*scontro*) crash, collision; (*fig*) clash

'**U.S.A.** ['uza] *smpl*: **gli ~** the USA

u'**sanza** [u'zantsa] *sf* custom; (*moda*) fashion

u'**sare** *vt* to use, employ ♦ *vi* (*servirsi*): **~ di** to use; (*: diritto*) to exercise; (*essere di moda*) to be fashionable; (*essere solito*): **~ fare** to be in the habit of doing, be accustomed to doing ♦ *vb impers*: **qui usa così** it's the custom round here; u'**sato, a** *ag* used; (*consumato*) worn; (*di seconda mano*) used, second-hand ♦ *sm* second-hand goods *pl*

usci'**ere** [uʃ'fere] *sm* usher

'**uscio** ['uʃo] *sm* door

u'**scire** [uʃ'fire] *vi* (*gen*) to come out; (*partire, andare a passeggio, a uno spettacolo etc*) to go out; (*essere sorteggiato: numero*) to come up; **~ da** (*gen*) to leave; (*posto*) to go (*o come*) out of, leave; (*solco, vasca etc*) to come out of; (*muro*) to stick out of; (*competenza etc*) to be outside; (*infanzia, adolescenza*) to leave behind; (*famiglia nobile etc*) to come from; **~ da o di casa** to go out; (*fig*) to leave home; **~ in automobile** to go out in the car, go for a drive; **~ di strada** (*AUT*) to go off *o* leave the road

u'**scita** [uʃ'fita] *sf* (*passaggio, varco*) exit, way out; (*per divertimento*) outing; (*ECON: somma*) expenditure; (*TEATRO*) entrance; (*fig: battuta*) witty remark; **~ di sicurezza** emergency exit

usi'**gnolo** [uziɲ'ɲɔlo] *sm* nightingale

U.S.L. [uzl] *sigla f* (= *unità sanitaria locale*) local health centre

'**uso** *sm* (*utilizzazione*) use; (*esercizio*) practice; (*abitudine*) custom; **a ~ di** for (the use of); **d'~** (*corrente*) in use; **fuori ~** out of use

usti'**one** *sf* burn

usu'**ale** *ag* common, everyday

u'**sura** *sf* usury; (*logoramento*) wear (and tear)

uten'**sile** *sm* tool, implement; **~i da cucina** kitchen utensils

u'**tente** *sm/f* user

'**utero** *sm* uterus

'**utile** *ag* useful ♦ *sm* (*vantaggio*) advantage, benefit; (*ECON: profitto*) profit; **utilità** *sf* usefulness *no pl*; use; (*vantaggio*) benefit;

utili'**taria** *sf* (*AUT*) economy car

utiliz'**zare** [utilid'dzare] *vt* to use, make use of, utilize

'**uva** *sf* grapes *pl*; **~ passa** raisins *pl*; **~ spina** gooseberry

V, v

v. *abbr* (= *vedi*) v

va *vb vedi* **andare**

va'cante *ag* vacant

va'canza [va'kantsa] *sf* (*l'essere vacante*) vacancy; (*riposo, ferie*) holiday(s *pl*) (*BRIT*), vacation (*US*); (*giorno di permesso*) day off, holiday; **~e** *sfpl* (*periodo di ferie*) holidays (*BRIT*), vacation *sg* (*US*); **essere/andare in ~** to be/go on holiday *o* vacation; **~e estive** summer holiday(s) *o* vacation

'vacca, che *sf* cow

vacci'nare [vattʃi'nare] *vt* to vaccinate

vac'cino [vat'tʃino] *sm* (*MED*) vaccine

vacil'lare [vatʃil'lare] *vi* to sway, wobble; (*luce*) to flicker; (*fig: memoria, coraggio*) to be failing, falter

'vacuo, a *ag* (*fig*) empty, vacuous

'vado *vb vedi* **andare**

vaga'bondo, a *sm/f* tramp, vagrant

va'gare *vi* to wander

va'gina [va'dʒina] *sf* vagina

va'gire [va'dʒire] *vi* to whimper

va'gito [va'dʒito] *sm* cry

'vaglia ['vaʎʎa] *sm inv* money order; **~ postale** postal order

vagli'are [vaʎ'ʎare] *vt* to sift; (*fig*) to weigh up; **'vaglio** *sm* sieve

'vago, a, ghi, ghe *ag* vague

va'gone *sm* (*FERR: per passeggeri*) coach; (*: per merci*) truck, wagon; **~ letto** sleeper, sleeping car; **~ ristorante** dining *o* restaurant car

'vai *vb vedi* **andare**

vai'olo *sm* smallpox

va'langa, ghe *sf* avalanche

va'lente *ag* able, talented

va'lere *vi* (*avere forza, potenza*) to have influence; (*essere valido*) to be valid; (*avere vigore, autorità*) to hold, apply; (*essere capace: poeta, studente*) to be good, be able ♦ *vt* (*prezzo, sforzo*) to be worth; (*corrispondere*) to correspond to; (*procurare*): **~ qc a qn** to earn sb sth; **~rsi**

di to make use of, take advantage of; **far ~** (*autorità etc*) to assert; **vale a dire** that is to say; **~ la pena** to be worth the effort *o* worth it

va'levole *ag* valid

vali'care *vt* to cross

'valico, chi *sm* (*passo*) pass

'valido, a *ag* valid; (*rimedio*) effective; (*aiuto*) real; (*persona*) worthwhile

valige'ria [validʒe'ria] *sf* leather goods *pl*; leather goods factory; leather goods shop

vali'getta [vali'dʒetta] *sf* briefcase

va'ligia, gie *o* **ge** [va'lidʒa] *sf* (suit)case; **fare le ~gie** to pack (up)

val'lata *sf* valley

'valle *sf* valley; **a ~** (*di fiume*) downstream; **scendere a ~** to go downhill

va'lore *sm* (*gen*) value; (*merito*) merit, worth; (*coraggio*) valour, courage; (*COMM: titolo*) security; **~i** *smpl* (*oggetti preziosi*) valuables

valoriz'zare [valorid'dzare] *vt* (*terreno*) to develop; (*fig*) to make the most of

'valso, a *pp di* **valere**

va'luta *sf* currency, money; (*BANCA*): **~ 15 gennaio** interest to run from January 15th

valu'tare *vt* (*casa, gioiello, fig*) to value; (*stabilire: peso, entrate, fig*) to estimate; **valutazi'one** *sf* valuation; estimate

'valvola *sf* (*TECN, ANAT*) valve; (*ELETTR*) fuse

'valzer ['valtser] *sm inv* waltz

vam'pata *sf* (*di fiamma*) blaze; (*di calore*) blast; (*: al viso*) flush

vam'piro *sm* vampire

vanda'lismo *sm* vandalism

'vandalo *sm* vandal

vaneggi'are [vaned'dʒare] *vi* to rave

'vanga, ghe *sf* spade; **van'gare** *vt* to dig

van'gelo [van'dʒelo] *sm* gospel

va'niglia [va'niʎʎa] *sf* vanilla

vanità *sf* vanity; (*di promessa*) emptiness; (*di sforzo*) futility; **vani'toso, a** *ag* vain, conceited

'vanno *vb vedi* **andare**

'vano, a *ag* vain ♦ *sm* (*spazio*) space; (*apertura*) opening; (*stanza*) room

van'taggio [van'taddʒo] *sm* advantage;

essere/portarsi in ~ (*SPORT*) to be in/take the lead; **vantaggi'oso, a** *ag* advantageous; favourable

van'tare *vt* to praise, speak highly of; **~rsi** *vr*: **~rsi (di/di aver fatto)** to boast *o* brag (about/about having done); **vante'ria** *sf* boasting; **'vanto** *sm* boasting; (*merito*) virtue, merit; (*gloria*) pride

'vanvera *sf*: **a ~** haphazardly; **parlare a ~** to talk nonsense

va'pore *sm* vapour; (*anche: ~* **acqueo**) steam; (*nave*) steamer; **a ~** (*turbina etc*) steam *cpd*; **al ~** (*CUC*) steamed; **vapo'retto** *sm* steamer; **vaporiz'zare** *vt* to vaporize; **vapo'roso, a** *ag* (*tessuto*) filmy; (*capelli*) soft and full

va'rare *vt* (*NAUT, fig*) to launch; (*DIR*) to pass

var'care *vt* to cross

'varco, chi *sm* passage; **aprirsi un ~ tra la folla** to push one's way through the crowd

vari'abile *ag* variable; (*tempo, umore*) changeable, variable ♦ *sf* (*MAT*) variable

vari'are *vt, vi* to vary; **~ di opinione** to change one's mind; **variazi'one** *sf* variation; change

va'rice [va'ritʃe] *sf* varicose vein

vari'cella [vari'tʃella] *sf* chickenpox

vari'coso, a *ag* varicose

vario'gato, a *ag* variegated

varie'tà *sf inv* variety ♦ *sm inv* variety show

'vario, a *ag* varied; (*parecchi: col sostantivo al pl*) various; (*mutevole: umore*) changeable; **vario'pinto, a** *ag* multicoloured

'varo *sm* (*NAUT, fig*) launch; (*di leggi*) passing

va'saio *sm* potter

'vasca, sche *sf* basin; (*anche: ~* **da bagno**) bathtub, bath

vase'lina *sf* vaseline

vasel'lame *sm* (*stoviglie*) crockery; (*: di porcellana*) china; **~ d'oro/d'argento** gold/silver plate

'vaso *sm* (*recipiente*) pot; (*: barattolo*) jar; (*: decorativo*) vase; (*ANAT*) vessel; **~ da fiori** vase; (*per piante*) flowerpot

vas'soio *sm* tray

'vasto, a *ag* vast, immense

Vati'cano *sm*: **il ~** the Vatican

ve *pron, av vedi* **vi**

vecchi'aia [vek'kjaja] *sf* old age

'vecchio, a ['vekkjo] *ag* old ♦ *sm/f* old man/woman; **i ~i** the old

'vece ['vetʃe] *sf*: **in ~ di** in the place of, for; **fare le ~i di qn** to take sb's place

ve'dere *vt, vi* to see; **~rsi** *vr* to meet, see one another; **avere a che ~ con** to have something to do with; **far ~ qc a qn** to show sb sth; **farsi ~** to show o.s.; (*farsi vivo*) to show one's face; **vedi di non farlo** make sure *o* see you don't do it; **non (ci) si vede** (*è buio etc*) you can't see a thing; **non lo posso ~** (*fig*) I can't stand him

ve'detta *sf* (*sentinella, posto*) look-out; (*NAUT*) patrol boat

'vedovo, a *sm/f* widower/widow

ve'duta *sf* view

vee'mente *ag* vehement; violent

vege'tale [vedʒe'tale] *ag, sm* vegetable

vegetari'ano, a [vedʒeta'rjano] *ag, sm/f* vegetarian

ve'geto, a ['vedʒeto] *ag* (*pianta*) thriving; (*persona*) strong, vigorous

'veglia ['veʎʎa] *sf* wakefulness; (*sorveglianza*) watch; (*trattenimento*) evening gathering; **fare ~ a un malato** to watch over a sick person

vegli'are [veʎ'ʎare] *vi* to be awake; to stay *o* sit up; (*stare vigile*) to watch; to keep watch ♦ *vt* (*malato, morto*) to watch over, sit up with

ve'icolo *sm* vehicle

'vela *sf* (*NAUT: tela*) sail; (*sport*) sailing

ve'lare *vt* to veil; **~rsi** *vr* (*occhi, luna*) to mist over; (*voce*) to become husky; **~rsi il viso** to cover one's face (with a veil); **ve'lato, a** *ag* veiled

veleggi'are [veled'dʒare] *vi* to sail; (*AER*) to glide

ve'leno *sm* poison; **vele'noso, a** *ag* poisonous

veli'ero *sm* sailing ship

ve'lina sf (anche: **carta** ~: per imballare) tissue paper

ve'livolo sm aircraft

velleità sf inv vain ambition, vain desire

vel'luto sm velvet; ~ **a coste** cord

'velo sm veil; (tessuto) voile

ve'loce [ve'lotʃe] ag fast, quick ♦ av fast, quickly; velo'cista, i, e sm/f (SPORT) sprinter; velocità sf speed; **a forte velocità** at high speed; **velocità di crociera** cruising speed

'vena sf (gen) vein; (filone) vein, seam; (fig: ispirazione) inspiration; (: umore) mood; **essere in ~ di qc** to be in the mood for sth

ve'nale ag (prezzo, valore) market cpd; (fig) venal; mercenary

ven'demmia sf (raccolta) grape harvest; (quantità d'uva) grape crop, grapes pl; (vino ottenuto) vintage; vendemmi'are vt to harvest ♦ vi to harvest the grapes

'vendere vt to sell; **"vendesi"** "for sale"

ven'detta sf revenge

vendi'care vt to avenge; ~**rsi** vr: ~**rsi (di)** to avenge o.s. (for); (per rancore) to take one's revenge (for); ~**rsi su qn** to revenge o.s. on sb; vendica'tivo, a ag vindictive

'vendita sf sale; **la ~** (attività) selling; (smercio) sales pl; **in ~** on sale; ~ **all'asta** sale by auction; vendi'tore sm seller, vendor; (gestore di negozio) trader, dealer

vene'rabile ag venerable

venerando, a ag = venerabile

vene'rare vt to venerate

venerdì sm inv Friday; **di** o **il ~** on Fridays; **V~ Santo** Good Friday

ve'nereo, a ag venereal

've'neto, a ag, sm/f Venetian

Ve'nezia [ve'nettsja] sf Venice; venezi'ana sf Venetian blind; venezi'ano, a ag, sm/f Venetian

veni'ale ag venial

ve'nire vi to come; (riuscire: dolce, fotografia) to turn out; (come ausiliare: essere): **viene ammirato da tutti** he is admired by everyone; ~ **da** to come from; **quanto viene?** how much does it cost?;

far ~ (mandare a chiamare) to send for; ~ **giù** to come down; ~ **meno** (svenire) to faint; ~ **meno a qc** not to fulfil sth; ~ **su** to come up; ~ **a trovare qn** to come and see sb; ~ **via** to come away

ven'taglio [ven'taλλo] sm fan

ven'tata sf gust (of wind)

ven'tenne ag: **una ragazza** ~ a twenty-year-old girl, a girl of twenty

ven'tesimo, a num twentieth

'venti num twenty

venti'lare vt (stanza) to air, ventilate; (fig: idea, proposta) to air; ventila'tore sm ventilator, fan

ven'tina sf: **una** ~ **(di)** around twenty, twenty or so

venti'sette num twenty-seven

'vento sm wind

'ventola sf (AUT, TECN) fan

ven'tosa sf (ZOOL) sucker; (di gomma) suction pad

ven'toso, a ag windy

'ventre sm stomach

ven'tura sf: **soldato di** ~ mercenary

ven'turo, a ag next, coming

ve'nuta sf coming, arrival

ve'nuto, a pp di venire

vera'mente av really

ver'bale ag verbal ♦ sm (di riunione) minutes pl

'verbo sm (LING) verb; (parola) word; (REL): **il V~** the Word

'verde ag, sm green; **essere al** ~ to be broke; ~ **bottiglia/oliva** bottle/olive green

verde'rame sm verdigris

ver'detto sm verdict

ver'dura sf vegetables pl

'verga, ghe sf rod

'vergine ['verdʒine] sf virgin; (dello zodiaco): **V~** Virgo ♦ ag virgin; (ragazza): **essere** ~ to be a virgin

ver'gogna [ver'gonɲa] sf shame; (timidezza) shyness, embarrassment; vergo'gnarsi vr: **vergognarsi (di)** to be o feel ashamed (of); to be shy (about), be embarrassed (about); vergo'gnoso, a ag ashamed; (timido) shy, embarrassed; (causa

di vergogna: azione) shameful
ve'rifica, che *sf* checking *no pl*, check
verifi'care *vt* (*controllare*) to check; (*confermare*) to confirm, bear out
verità *sf inv* truth
veriti'ero, a *ag* (*che dice la verità*) truthful; (*conforme a verità*) true
'verme *sm* worm
vermi'celli [vermi'tʃelli] *smpl* vermicelli *sg*
ver'miglio [ver'miʎʎo] *sm* vermilion, scarlet
'vermut *sm inv* vermouth
ver'nice [ver'nitʃe] *sf* (*colorazione*) paint; (*trasparente*) varnish; (*pelle*) patent leather; **"~ fresca"** ''wet paint''; **vernici'are** *vt* to paint; to varnish
'vero, a *ag* (*veridico: fatti, testimonianza*) true; (*autentico*) real ♦ *sm* (*verità*) truth; (*realtà*) (real) life; **un ~ e proprio delinquente** a real criminal, an out-and-out criminal
vero'simile *ag* likely, probable
ver'ruca, che *sf* wart
versa'mento *sm* (*pagamento*) payment; (*deposito di denaro*) deposit
ver'sante *sm* slopes *pl*, side
ver'sare *vt* (*fare uscire: vino, farina*) to pour (out); (*spargere: lacrime, sangue*) to shed; (*rovesciare*) to spill; (*ECON*) to pay; (: *depositare*) to deposit, pay in; **~rsi** *vr* (*rovesciarsi*) to spill; (*fiume, folla*): **~rsi (in)** to pour (into)
ver'satile *ag* versatile
ver'setto *sm* (*REL*) verse
versi'one *sf* version; (*traduzione*) translation
'verso *sm* (*di poesia*) verse, line; (*di animale, uccello*) cry; (*direzione*) direction; (*modo*) way; (*di foglio di carta*) verso; (*di moneta*) reverse; **~i** *smpl* (*poesia*) verse *sg*; **non c'è ~ di persuaderlo** there's no way of persuading him, he can't be persuaded ♦ *prep* (*in direzione di*) toward(s); (*nei pressi di*) near, around (about); (*in senso temporale*) about, around; (*nei confronti di*) for; **~ di me** towards me; **~ sera** towards evening
'vertebra *sf* vertebra

verti'cale *ag, sf* vertical
'vertice ['vertitʃe] *sm* summit, top; (*MAT*) vertex; **conferenza al ~** (*POL*) summit conference
ver'tigine [ver'tidʒine] *sf* dizziness *no pl*; dizzy spell; (*MED*) vertigo; **avere le ~i** to feel dizzy; **vertigi'noso, a** *ag* (*altezza*) dizzy; (*fig*) breathtakingly high (*o deep etc*)
ve'scica, che [veʃ'ʃika] *sf* (*ANAT*) bladder; (*MED*) blister
'vescovo *sm* bishop
'vespa *sf* wasp
'vespro *sm* (*REL*) vespers *pl*
ves'sillo *sm* standard; (*bandiera*) flag
ves'taglia [ves'taʎʎa] *sf* dressing gown
'veste *sf* garment; (*rivestimento*) covering; (*qualità, facoltà*) capacity; **in ~ ufficiale** (*fig*) in an official capacity; **in ~ di** in the guise of, as; **vesti'ario** *sm* wardrobe, clothes *pl*
ves'tire *vt* (*bambino, malato*) to dress; (*avere indosso*) to have on, wear; **~rsi** *vr* to dress, get dressed; **ves'tito, a** *ag* dressed ♦ *sm* garment; (*da donna*) dress; (*da uomo*) suit; **vestiti** *smpl* (*indumenti*) clothes; **vestito di bianco** dressed in white
Ve'suvio *sm*: **il ~** Vesuvius
vete'rano, a *ag, sm/f* veteran
veteri'naria *sf* veterinary medicine
veteri'nario, a *ag* veterinary ♦ *sm* veterinary surgeon (*BRIT*), veterinarian (*US*), vet
'veto *sm inv* veto
ve'traio *sm* glassmaker; glazier
ve'trata *sf* glass door (*o window*); (*di chiesa*) stained glass window
vetre'ria *sf* (*stabilimento*) glassworks *sg*; (*oggetti di vetro*) glassware
ve'trina *sf* (*di negozio*) (shop) window; (*armadio*) display cabinet; **vetri'nista, i, e** *sm/f* window dresser
vetri'olo *sm* vitriol
'vetro *sm* glass; (*per finestra, porta*) pane (of glass)
'vetta *sf* peak, summit, top
vet'tore *sm* (*MAT, FISICA*) vector; (*chi trasporta*) carrier

vetto'vaglie [vetto'vaʎʎe] *sfpl* supplies

vet'tura *sf* (*carrozza*) carriage; (*FERR*) carriage (*BRIT*), car (*US*); (*auto*) car (*BRIT*), automobile (*US*)

vezzeggia'tivo [vettseddʒa'tivo] *sm* (*LING*) term of endearment

'vezzo ['vettso] *sm* habit; **~i** *smpl* (*smancerie*) affected ways; (*leggiadria*) charms; **vez'zoso, a** *ag* (*grazioso*) charming, pretty; (*lezioso*) affected

vi (*dav lo, la, li, le, ne diventa* **ve**) *pron* (*oggetto*) you; (*complemento di termine*) (to) you; (*riflessivo*) yourselves; (*reciproco*) each other ♦ *av* (*lì*) there; (*qui*) here; (*per questo/quel luogo*) through here/there; **~ è/sono** there is/are

'via *sf* (*gen*) way; (*strada*) street; (*sentiero, pista*) path, track; (*AMM: procedimento*) channels *pl* ♦ *prep* (*passando per*) via, by way of ♦ *av* away ♦ *escl* go away!; (*suvvia*) come on!; (*SPORT*) go! ♦ *sm* (*SPORT*) starting signal; **in ~ di guarigione** on the road to recovery; **per ~ di** (*a causa di*) because of, on account of; **in o per ~** on the way; **per ~ aerea** by air; (*lettere*) by airmail; **andare/essere** to go/be away; **~ ~ che** (*a mano a mano*) as; **dare il ~** (*SPORT*) to give the starting signal; **dare il ~ a** (*fig*) to start; **V~ lattea** (*ASTR*) Milky Way; **~ di mezzo** middle course; **in ~ provvisoria** provisionally

viabilità *sf* (*di strada*) practicability; (*rete stradale*) roads *pl*, road network

via'dotto *sm* viaduct

viaggi'are [viad'dʒare] *vi* to travel; **viaggia'tore, 'trice** *ag* travelling ♦ *sm* traveller; (*passeggero*) passenger

vi'aggio ['vjaddʒo] *sm* travel(ling); (*tragitto*) journey, trip; **buon ~!** have a good trip!; **~ di nozze** honeymoon

vi'ale *sm* avenue

via'vai *sm* coming and going, bustle

vi'brare *vi* to vibrate

vi'cario *sm* (*apostolico etc*) vicar

'vice ['vitʃe] *sm/f* deputy ♦ *prefisso*: **~'console** *sm* vice-consul; **~diret'tore** *sm* assistant manager

vi'cenda [vi'tʃenda] *sf* event; **a ~** in turn; **vicen'devole** *ag* mutual, reciprocal

vice'versa [vitʃe'versa] *av* vice versa; **da Roma a Pisa e ~** from Rome to Pisa and back

vici'nanza [vitʃi'nantsa] *sf* nearness, closeness; **~e** *sfpl* (*paraggi*) neighbourhood, vicinity

vici'nato [vitʃi'nato] *sm* neighbourhood; (*vicini*) neighbours *pl*

vi'cino, a [vi'tʃino] *ag* (*gen*) near; (*nello spazio*) near, nearby; (*accanto*) next; (*nel tempo*) near, close at hand ♦ *sm/f* neighbour ♦ *av* near, close; **da ~** (*guardare*) close up; (*esaminare, seguire*) closely; (*conoscere*) well, intimately; **~ a** near (to), close to; (*accanto a*) beside; **~ di casa** neighbour

'vicolo *sm* alley; **~ cieco** blind alley

'video *sm inv* (*TV: schermo*) screen; **~'camera** *sf* camcorder; **~cas'setta** *sf* videocassette; **~registra'tore** *sm* video (recorder)

vie'tare *vt* to forbid; (*AMM*) to prohibit; **~ a qn di fare** to forbid sb to do; to prohibit sb from doing; **"vietato fumare/ l'ingresso"** "no smoking/admittance"

Viet'nam *sm*: **il ~** Vietnam; **vietna'mita, i, e** *ag, sm/f, sm* Vietnamese *inv*

vi'gente [vi'dʒente] *ag* in force

vigi'lare [vidʒi'lare] *vt* to watch over, keep an eye on; **~ che** to make sure that, see to it that

'vigile ['vidʒile] *ag* watchful ♦ *sm* (*anche:* **~ urbano**) policeman (*in towns*); **~ del fuoco** fireman

vi'gilia [vi'dʒilja] *sf* (*giorno antecedente*) eve; **la ~ di Natale** Christmas Eve

vigli'acco, a, chi, che [viʎ'ʎakko] *ag* cowardly ♦ *sm/f* coward

'vigna ['viɲɲa] *sf* = **vi'gneto**

vi'gneto [viɲ'ɲeto] *sm* vineyard

vi'gnetta [viɲ'ɲetta] *sf* cartoon

vi'gore *sm* vigour; (*DIR*): **essere/entrare in ~** to be in/come into force; **vigo'roso, a** *ag* vigorous

'vile *ag* (*spregevole*) low, mean, base;

(codardo) cowardly

vili'pendio *sm* contempt, scorn; public insult

'villa *sf* villa

vil'laggio [vil'laddʒo] *sm* village

villa'nia *sf* rudeness, lack of manners; **fare** *(o* **dire) una ~ a qn** to be rude to sb

vil'lano, a *ag* rude, ill-mannered

villeggia'tura [villeddʒa'tura] *sf* holiday(s *pl) (BRIT),* vacation *(US)*

vil'lino *sm* small house (with a garden), cottage

vil'loso, a *ag* hairy

viltà *sf* cowardice *no pl;* cowardly act

Viminale

i The **Viminale**, which takes its name from the hill in Rome on which it stands, is the home of the Ministry of the Interior.

'vimine *sm* wicker; **mobili di ~i** wicker furniture *sg*

'vincere ['vintʃere] *vt (in guerra, al gioco, a una gara)* to defeat, beat; *(premio, guerra, partita)* to win; *(fig)* to overcome, conquer ♦ *vi* to win; **~ qn in bellezza** to be better-looking than sb; '**vincita** *sf* win; *(denaro vinto)* winnings *pl;* **vinci'tore** *sm* winner; *(MIL)* victor

vinco'laro *vt* to bind; *(COMM: denaro)* to tie up; '**vincolo** *sm (fig)* bond, tie; *(DIR: servitù)* obligation

vi'nicolo, a *ag* wine *cpd*

'vino *sm* wine; **~ bianco/rosso** white/red wine; **~ da pasto** table wine

'vinto, a *pp di* **vincere**

vi'ola *sf (BOT)* violet; *(MUS)* viola ♦ *ag, sm inv (colore)* purple

vio'lare *vt (chiesa)* to desecrate, violate; *(giuramento, legge)* to violate

violen'tare *vt* to use violence on; *(donna)* to rape

vio'lento, a *ag* violent; **vio'lenza** *sf* violence; **violenza carnale** rape

vio'letta *sf (BOT)* violet

vio'letto, a *ag, sm (colore)* violet

violi'nista, i, e *sm/f* violinist

vio'lino *sm* violin

violon'cello [violon'tʃello] *sm* cello

vi'ottolo *sm* path, track

'vipera *sf* viper, adder

vi'rare *vi (NAUT, AER)* to turn; *(FOT)* to tone; **~ di bordo** *(NAUT)* to tack

'virgola *sf (LING)* comma; *(MAT)* point; **virgo'lette** *sfpl* inverted commas, quotation marks

vi'rile *ag (proprio dell'uomo)* masculine; *(non puerile, da uomo)* manly, virile

virtù *sf inv* virtue; **in** *o* **per ~ di** by virtue of, by

virtu'ale *ag* virtual

virtu'oso, a *ag* virtuous ♦ *sm/f (MUS etc)* virtuoso

'virus *sm inv (anche COMPUT)* virus

'viscere ['viʃʃere] *sfpl (di animale)* entrails *pl;* *(fig)* bowels *pl*

'vischio ['viskjo] *sm (BOT)* mistletoe; *(pania)* birdlime; **vischi'oso, a** *ag* sticky

'viscido, a ['viʃʃido] *ag* slimy

vi'sibile *ag* visible

visi'bilio *sm:* **andare in ~** to go into raptures

visibilità *sf* visibility

visi'era *sf (di elmo)* visor; *(di berretto)* peak

visi'one *sf* vision; **prendere ~ di qc** to examine sth, look sth over; **prima/seconda ~** *(CINEMA)* first/second showing

'visita *sf* visit; *(MED)* visit, call; *(: esame)* examination; **visi'tare** *vt* to visit; *(MED)* to visit, call on; *(: esaminare)* to examine; **visita'tore, 'trice** *sm/f* visitor

vi'sivo, a *ag* visual

'viso *sm* face

vi'sone *sm* mink

'vispo, a *ag* quick, lively

vis'suto, a *pp di* **vivere** ♦ *ag (aria, modo di fare)* experienced

'vista *sf (facoltà)* (eye)sight; *(fatto di vedere):* **la ~ di** the sight of; *(veduta)* view; **sparare a ~** to shoot on sight; **in ~** in sight; **perdere qn di ~** to lose sight of sb; *(fig)* to lose touch with sb; **a ~ d'occhio** as far as the eye can see; *(fig)* before one's very eyes; **far ~ di fare** to pretend to do

'**visto, a** *pp di* **vedere** ♦ *sm* visa; **~ che** seeing (that)

vis'toso, a *ag* gaudy, garish; (*ingente*) considerable

visu'ale *ag* visual; **visualizza'tore** *sm* (*INFORM*) visual display unit, VDU

'**vita** *sf* life; (*ANAT*) waist; **a ~** for life

vi'tale *ag* vital; **vita'lizio, a** *ag* life *cpd* ♦ *sm* life annuity

vita'mina *sf* vitamin

'**vite** *sf* (*BOT*) vine; (*TECN*) screw

vi'tello *sm* (*ZOOL*) calf; (*carne*) veal; (*pelle*) calfskin

vi'ticcio [vi'tittʃo] *sm* (*BOT*) tendril

viticol'tore *sm* wine grower; **viticol'tura** *sf* wine growing

'**vitreo, a** *ag* vitreous; (*occhio, sguardo*) glassy

'**vittima** *sf* victim

'**vitto** *sm* food; (*in un albergo etc*) board; **~ e alloggio** board and lodging

vit'toria *sf* victory

'**viva** *escl*: **~ il re!** long live the king!

vi'vace [vi'vatʃe] *ag* (*vivo, animato*) lively; (: *mente*) lively, sharp; (*colore*) bright; **vivacità** *sf* vivacity; liveliness; brightness

vi'vaio *sm* (*di pesci*) hatchery; (*AGR*) nursery

vi'vanda *sf* food; (*piatto*) dish

vi'vente *ag* living, alive; **i ~i** the living

'**vivere** *vi* to live ♦ *vt* to live; (*passare: brutto momento*) to live through, go through; (*sentire: gioie, pene di qn*) to share ♦ *sm* life; (*anche: modo di ~*) way of life; **~i** *smpl* (*cibo*) food *sg*, provisions; **~ di** to live on

'**vivido, a** *ag* (*colore*) vivid, bright

'**vivo, a** *ag* (*vivente*) alive, living; (: *animale*) live; (*fig*) lively; (: *colore*) bright, brilliant; **i ~i** the living; **~ e vegeto** hale and hearty; **farsi ~** to show one's face; to be heard from; **ritrarre dal ~** to paint from life; **pungere qn nel ~** (*fig*) to cut sb to the quick

vizi'are [vit'tsjare] *vt* (*bambino*) to spoil; (*corrompere moralmente*) to corrupt; **vizi'ato, a** *ag* spoilt; (*aria, acqua*) polluted

'**vizio** ['vittsjo] *sm* (*morale*) vice; (*cattiva abitudine*) bad habit; (*imperfezione*) flaw, defect; (*errore*) fault, mistake; **vizi'oso, a** *ag* depraved; defective; (*inesatto*) incorrect, wrong

vocabo'lario *sm* (*dizionario*) dictionary; (*lessico*) vocabulary

vo'cabolo *sm* word

vo'cale *ag* vocal ♦ *sf* vowel

vocazi'one [vokat'tsjone] *sf* vocation; (*fig*) natural bent

'**voce** ['votʃe] *sf* voice; (*diceria*) rumour; (*di un elenco, in bilancio*) item; **aver ~ in capitolo** (*fig*) to have a say in the matter

voci'are [vo'tʃare] *vi* to shout, yell

'**voga** (*NAUT*) rowing; (*usanza*): **essere in ~** to be in fashion *o* in vogue

vo'gare *vi* to row

'**voglia** ['voλλa] *sf* desire, wish; (*macchia*) birthmark; **aver ~ di qc/di fare** to feel like sth/like doing; (*più forte*) to want sth/to do

'**voi** *pron* you; **voi'altri** *pron* you

vo'lano *sm* (*SPORT*) shuttlecock; (*TECN*) flywheel

vo'lante *ag* flying ♦ *sm* (*steering*) wheel

volan'tino *sm* leaflet

vo'lare *vi* (*uccello, aereo, fig*) to fly; (*cappello*) to blow away *o* off, fly away *o* off; **~ via** to fly away *o* off

vo'latile *ag* (*CHIM*) volatile ♦ *sm* (*ZOOL*) bird

volente'roso, a *ag* willing

volenti'eri *av* willingly; **"~!"** "with pleasure", "I'd be glad to"

PAROLA CHIAVE
---

vo'lere *sm* will, wish(es); **contro il ~ di** against the wishes of; **per ~ di qn** in obedience to sb's will *o* wishes
♦ *vt* 1 (*esigere, desiderare*) to want; **voler fare/che qn faccia** to want to do/sb to do; **volete del caffè?** would you like *o* do you want some coffee?; **vorrei questo/fare** I would *o* I'd like this/to do; **come vuoi** as you like; **senza ~** (*inavvertitamente*) without meaning to, unintentionally
2 (*consentire*): **vogliate attendere, per piacere** please wait; **vogliamo andare?**

shall we go?; **vuole essere così gentile da ...?** would you be so kind as to ...?; **non ha voluto ricevermi** he wouldn't see me **3: volerci** (*essere necessario: materiale, attenzione*) to need; (: *tempo*) to take; **quanta farina ci vuole per questa torta?** how much flour do you need for this cake?; **ci vuole un'ora per arrivare a Venezia** it takes an hour to get to Venice **4: voler bene a qn** (*amore*) to love sb; (*affetto*) to be fond of sb, like sb very much; **voler male a qn** to dislike sb; **volerne a qn** to bear sb a grudge; **voler dire** to mean

vol'gare *ag* vulgar; **volgariz'zare** *vt* to popularize

'volgere ['vɔldʒere] *vt* to turn ♦ *vi* to turn; (*tendere*): ~ **a: il tempo volge al brutto** the weather is breaking; **un rosso che volge al viola** a red verging on purple; **~rsi** *vr* to turn; ~ **al peggio** to take a turn for the worse, ~ **al termine** to draw to an end

'volgo *sm* common people

voli'era *sf* aviary

voli'tivo, a *ag* strong-willed

'volo *sm* flight; **al ~: colpire qc al ~** to hit sth as it flies past; **capire al ~** to understand straight away

volontà *sf* will; **a ~** (*mangiare, bere*) as much as one likes; **buona/cattiva ~** goodwill/lack of goodwill

volon'tario, a *ag* voluntary ♦ *sm* (*MIL*) volunteer

'volpe *sf* fox

'volta *sf* (*momento, circostanza*) time; (*turno, giro*) turn; (*curva*) turn, bend; (*ARCHIT*) vault; (*direzione*): **partire alla ~ di** to set off for; **a mia** (*o tua etc*) ~ in turn; **una ~** once; **una ~ sola** only once; **due ~e** twice; **una cosa per ~** one thing at a time; **una ~ per tutte** once and for all; **a ~e** at times, sometimes; **una ~ che** (*temporale*) once; (*causale*) since; **3 ~e 4** 3 times 4

volta'faccia [volta'fattʃa] *sm inv* (*fig*) volte-face

vol'taggio [vol'taddʒo] *sm* (*ELETTR*) voltage

vol'tare *vt* to turn; (*girare: moneta*) to turn over; (*rigirare*) to turn round ♦ *vi* to turn; **~rsi** *vr* to turn; to turn over; to turn round

volteggi'are [volted'dʒare] *vi* (*volare*) to circle; (*in equitazione*) to do trick riding; (*in ginnastica*) to vault; to perform acrobatics

'volto, a *pp di* **volgere** ♦ *sm* face

vo'lubile *ag* changeable, fickle

vo'lume *sm* volume; **volumi'noso, a** *ag* voluminous, bulky

voluttà *sf* sensual pleasure *o* delight; **voluttu'oso, a** *ag* voluptuous

vomi'tare *vt, vi* to vomit; **'vomito** *sm* vomiting *no pl*; vomit

'vongola *sf* clam

vo'race [vo'ratʃe] *ag* voracious, greedy

vo'ragine [vo'radʒine] *sf* abyss, chasm

'vortice ['vortitʃe] *sm* whirlwind; whirlpool; (*fig*) whirl

'vostro, a *det:* **il(la) ~(a)** *etc* your ♦ *pron:* **il(la) ~(a)** *etc* yours

vo'tante *sm/f* voter

vo'tare *vi* to vote ♦ *vt* (*sottoporre a votazione*) to take a vote on; (*approvare*) to vote for; (*REL*): ~ **qc a** to dedicate sth to; **votazi'one** *sf* vote, voting; **votazioni** *sfpl* (*POL*) votes; (*INS*) marks

'voto *sm* (*POL*) vote; (*INS*) mark; (*REL*) vow; (: *offerta*) votive offering; **aver ~i belli/ brutti** (*INS*) to get good/bad marks

vs. *abbr* (*COMM*) = **vostro**

vul'cano *sm* volcano

vulne'rabile *ag* vulnerable

vuo'tare *vt* to empty; **~rsi** *vr* to empty

vu'oto, a *ag* empty; (*fig: privo*): ~ **di** (*senso etc*) devoid of ♦ *sm* empty space, gap; (*spazio in bianco*) blank; (*FISICA*) vacuum; (*fig: mancanza*) gap, void; **a mani ~e** empty-handed; ~ **d'aria** air pocket; ~ **a rendere** returnable bottle

W, X, Y

'water ['wɔ:tə*] *sm inv* toilet
watt [vat] *sm inv* watt
'weekend ['wi:kend] *sm inv* weekend
'whisky ['wiski] *sm inv* whisky
'windsurf ['windsə:f] *sm inv* (*tavola*) windsurfer; (*sport*) windsurfing
'würstel ['vyrstəl] *sm inv* frankfurter
xi'lofono [ksi'lɔfono] *sm* xylophone
yacht [jɔt] *sm inv* yacht
'yoghurt ['jɔgurt] *sm inv* yoghourt

Z, z

zabai'one [dzaba'jone] *sm dessert made of egg yolks, sugar and marsala*
zaf'fata [tsaf'fata] *sf* (*tanfo*) stench
zaffe'rano [dzaffe'rano] *sm* saffron
zaf'firo [dzaf'firo] *sm* sapphire
'zaino ['dzaino] *sm* rucksack
'zampa ['tsampa] *sf* (*di animale: gamba*) leg; (*: piede*) paw; **a quattro ~e** on all fours
zampil'lare [tsampil'lare] *vi* to gush, spurt; **zam'pillo** *sm* gush, spurt
zam'pogna [tsam'poɲɲa] *sf instrument similar to bagpipes*
'zanna ['tsanna] *sf* (*di elefante*) tusk; (*di carnivori*) fang
zan'zara [dzan'dzara] *sf* mosquito; **zanzari'era** *sf* mosquito net
'zappa ['tsappa] *sf* hoe; **zap'pare** *vt* to hoe
zar, za'rina [tsar, tsa'rina] *sm/f* tsar/tsarina
'zattera ['dzattera] *sf* raft
za'vorra [dza'vɔrra] *sf* ballast
'zazzera ['tsattsera] *sf* shock of hair
'zebra ['dzɛbra] *sf* zebra; **~e** *sfpl* (*AUT*) zebra crossing *sg* (*BRIT*), crosswalk *sg* (*US*)
'zecca, che ['tsekka] *sf* (*ZOOL*) tick; (*officina di monete*) mint
'zelo ['dzɛlo] *sm* zeal
'zenit ['dzɛnit] *sm* zenith
zenzero ['dzɛndzero] *sm* ginger
'zeppa ['tseppa] *sf* wedge

'zeppo, a ['tseppo] *ag*: **~ di** crammed *o* packed with
zer'bino [dzer'bino] *sm* doormat
'zero ['dzɛro] *sm* zero, nought; **vincere per tre a ~** (*SPORT*) to win three-nil
'zeta ['dzɛta] *sm o f* zed, (the letter) z
'zia ['tsia] *sf* aunt
zibel'lino [dzibel'lino] *sm* sable
'zigomo ['dzigomo] *sm* cheekbone
zig'zag [dzig'dzag] *sm inv* zigzag; **andare a ~** to zigzag
zim'bello [dzim'bello] *sm* (*oggetto di burle*) laughing-stock
'zinco ['dzinko] *sm* zinc
'zingaro, a ['dzingaro] *sm/f* gipsy
'zio ['tsio] (*pl* **'zii**) *sm* uncle; **zii** *smpl* (*zio e zia*) uncle and aunt
zi'tella [dzi'tella] *sf* spinster; (*peg*) old maid
'zitto, a ['tsitto] *ag* quiet, silent; **sta' ~!** be quiet!
ziz'zania [dzid'dzanja] *sf* (*fig*): **gettare** *o* **seminare ~** to sow discord
'zoccolo ['tsɔkkolo] *sm* (*calzatura*) clog; (*di cavallo etc*) hoof; (*basamento*) base; plinth
zo'diaco [dzo'diako] *sm* zodiac
'zolfo ['tsolfo] *sm* sulphur
'zolla ['dzɔlla] *sf* clod (of earth)
zol'letta [dzol'letta] *sf* sugar lump
'zona ['dzɔna] *sf* zone, area; **~ di depressione** (*METEOR*) trough of low pressure; **~ disco** (*AUT*) ≈ meter zone; **~ pedonale** pedestrian precinct; **~ verde** (*di abitato*) green area
'zonzo ['dzondzo]: **a ~** *av*: **andare a ~** to wander about, stroll about
zoo ['dzɔo] *sm inv* zoo
zoolo'gia [dzoolo'dʒia] *sf* zoology
zoppi'care [tsoppi'kare] *vi* to limp; to be shaky, rickety
'zoppo, a ['tsɔppo] *ag* lame; (*fig: mobile*) shaky, rickety
zoti'cone [dzoti'kone] *sm* lout
'zucca, che ['tsukka] *sf* (*BOT*) marrow; pumpkin
zucche'rare [tsukke'rare] *vt* to put sugar in; **zucche'rato, a** *ag* sweet, sweetened

zuccheri'era [tsukke'rjera] *sf* sugar bowl

zuccheri'ficio [tsukkeri'fitʃo] *sm* sugar refinery

zucche'rino, a [tsukke'rino] *ag* sugary, sweet

'zucchero ['tsukkero] *sm* sugar

zuc'china [tsuk'kina] *sf* courgette (*BRIT*), zucchini (*US*)

zuc'chino [tsuk'kino] *sm* = **zucchina**

'zuffa ['tsuffa] *sf* brawl

'zuppa ['tsuppa] *sf* soup; (*fig*) mixture, muddle; ~ **inglese** (*CUC*) *dessert made with sponge cake, custard and chocolate*, ≈ trifle (*BRIT*); **zuppi'era** *sf* soup tureen

'zuppo, a ['tsuppo] *ag:* ~ **(di)** drenched (with), soaked (with)

PUZZLES AND WORDGAMES

Introduction

We are delighted that you have decided to invest in this Collins Pocket Dictionary! Whether you intend to use it in school, at home, on holiday or at work, we are sure that you will find it very useful.

The purpose of this supplement is to help you become aware of the wealth of vocabulary and grammatical information your dictionary contains, to explain how this information is presented and also to point out some of the traps one can fall into when using an Italian-English English-Italian dictionary.

In the pages which follow you will find explanations and wordgames (not too difficult!) designed to give you practice in exploring the dictionary's contents and in retrieving information for a variety of purposes. Answers are provided at the end. If you spend a little time on these pages you should be able to use your dictionary more efficiently and effectively. Have fun!

Supplement by
Roy Simon
reproduced by kind permission of
Tayside Region Education Department

PUZZLES AND WORDGAMES

Contents

HOW INFORMATION IS PRESENTED IN YOUR DICTIONARY

A great deal of information is packed into your Collins Pocket Dictionary using colour, various typefaces, sizes of type, symbols, abbreviations and brackets. The purpose of this section is to acquaint you with the conventions used in presenting information.

Headwords

A headword is the word you look up in a dictionary. Headwords are listed in alphabetical order throughout the dictionary. They are printed in colour so that they stand out clearly from all the other words on the dictionary page.

Note that at the top of each page two headwords appear. These tell you which is the first and last word dealt with on the page in question. They are there to help you scan through the dictionary more quickly.

The Italian alphabet consists in practice of the same 26 letters as the English alphabet but j, k, w, x and y are found only in words of foreign origin. Where words are distinguised only by an accent, the unaccented form precedes the accented – e.g. te, tè.

A dictionary entry

An entry is made up of a headword and all the information about that headword. Entries will be short or long depending on how frequently a word is used in either English or Italian and how many meanings it has. Inevitably, the fuller the dictionary entry the more care is needed in sifting through it to find the information you require.

Meanings

The translations of a headword are given in ordinary type. Where there is more than one meaning or usage, a semi-colon separates one from the other.

cannocchi'ale [kannok'kjale] *sm* telescope
can'none *sm* (*MIL*) gun; (: *STORIA*) cannon; (*tubo*) pipe, tube; (*piega*) box pleat; (*fig*) ace
can'nuccia, ce [kan'nuttʃa] *sf* (drinking) straw
ca'noa *sf* canoe

'prua *sf* (*NAUT*) = **prora**
pru'dente *ag* cautious, prudent;

te *pron* (*soggetto: in forme comparative, oggetto*) you
tè *sm inv* tea; (*trattenimento*) tea party

puericul'tura *sf* paediatric nursing; infant care

fu'ori *av* outside; (*all'aperto*) outdoors, outside; (*fuori di casa, SPORT*) out; (*esclamativo*) get out! ♦ *prep*: ~ **(di)** out of, outside ♦ *sm* outside; **lasciar ~ qc/qn** to leave sth/sb out; **far ~ qn** (*fam*) to kill sb, do sb in; **essere ~ di sé** to be beside o.s., ~ **luogo** (*inopportuno*) out of place, uncalled for; ~ **mano** out of the way, remote; ~ **pericolo** out of danger; ~ **uso** old-fashioned; obsolete

'fragola *sf* strawberry

'grande (*qualche volta* **gran** +C, **grand'** +V) *ag* (*grosso, largo, vasto*) big, large; (*alto*) tall; (*lungo*) long; (*in sensi astratti*) great ♦ *sm/f* (*persona adulta*) adult, grown-up; (*chi ha ingegno e potenza*) great man/ woman; **fare le cose in ~** to do things in style; **una gran bella donna** a very beautiful woman; **non è una gran cosa** *o* **un gran che** it's nothing special; **non ne so gran che** I don't know very much about it

In addition, you will often find other words appearing in *italics* in brackets before the translations. These either give some notion of the contexts in which the headword might appear (as with 'alto' opposite – 'una persona alta', 'un suono alto', etc.) or else they provide synonyms (as with 'reggere' opposite – 'tenere', 'sostenere', etc.).

Phonetic spellings

Where an Italian word contains a sound which is difficult for the English speaker, the phonetic spelling of the word – i.e. its pronunciation – is given in square brackets immediately after it. The phonetic transcription of Italian and English vowels and consonants is given on pages xiv to xv at the front of your dictionary.

Additional information about headwords

Information about the form or usage of certain headwords is given in brackets between the headword and the translation or translations. Have a look at the entries for 'A.C.I.', 'camerino', 'materia' and 'leccapiedi' opposite. This information is usually given in abbreviated form. A helpful list of abbreviations is given on pages xi to xiii at the front of your dictionary.

You should be particularly careful with colloquial words or phrases. Words labelled (*fam*) would not normally be used in formal speech, while those labelled (*fam!*) would be considered offensive. Careful consideration of such style labels will help you avoid many an embarrassing situation when using Italian!

Expressions in which the headword appears

An entry will often feature certain common expressions in which the headword appears. These expressions are in **bold** type, but in black as opposed to colour. A swung dash (~) is used instead of repeating a headword in an entry. 'Freno' and 'idea' opposite illustrate this point. Sometimes the swung dash is used with the appropriate ending shown after it; e.g. 'mano', where '~i' is used to indicate the plural form, 'mani'.

Related words

In the Pocket Dictionary words related to certain headwords are sometimes given at the end of an entry, as with 'finestra' and 'accept' opposite. These are easily picked out as they are also in colour. These words are placed in alphabetical order after the headword to which they belong: cf. 'acceptable', 'acceptance' opposite.

'alto, a *ag* high; (*persona*) tall; (*tessuto*) wide, broad; (*sonno, acque*) deep; (*suono*) high(-pitched); (GEO) upper; (*: settentrionale*) northern ♦ *sm* top (part) ♦ *av* high; (*parlare*) aloud, loudly; **il palazzo è ~ 20 metri** the building is 20 metres high;

pron'tezza [pron'tettsa] *sf* readiness; quickness, promptness

A.C.I. ['atʃi] *sigla m* = *Automobile Club d'Italia*

came'rino *sm* (TEATRO) dressing room

scocci'are [skot'tʃare] (*fam*) *vt* to bother, annoy; **~rsi** *vr* to be bothered *o* annoyed

fre'gare *vt* to rub; (*fam: truffare*) to take in, cheat; (*: rubare*) to swipe, pinch; **fregarsene** (*fam!*) **chi se ne frega?** who gives a damn (about it)?

'freno *sm* brake; (*morso*) bit; **~ a disco** disc brake; **~ a mano** handbrake; **tenere a ~** to restrain

i'dea *sf* idea; (*opinione*) opinion, view; (*ideale*) ideal; **dare l'~ di** to seem, look like; **~ fissa** obsession; **neanche** *o* **neppure per** **~** certainly not!

fi'nestra *sf* window; **fines'trino** *sm* (*di treno, auto*) window

accept [ək'sept] *vt* accettare; **~able** *adj* accettabile; **~ance** *n* accettazione *f*

'reggere ['rɛddʒere] *vt* (*tenere*) to hold; (*sostenere*) to support, bear, hold up; (*portare*) to carry, bear; (*resistere*) to withstand; (*dirigere: impresa*) to manage, run; (*governare*) to rule, govern;

reci'tare [retʃi'tare] *vt* (*poesia, lezione*) to recite; (*dramma*) to perform; (*ruolo*) to play *o* act (the part of); **recitazi'one** *sf* recitation; (*di attore*) acting

ma'teria *sf* (FISICA) matter; (TECN, COMM) material, matter *no pl*; (*disciplina*) subject; (*argomento*) subject matter, material;

leccapi'edi (*peg*) *sm/f inv* toady, bootlicker

'rompere *vt* to break; (*fidanzamento*) to break off ♦ *vi* to break; **~rsi** *vr* to break; **mi rompe le scatole** (*fam*) he (*o* she) is a pain in the neck; **~rsi un braccio** to break an arm;

'mano, i *sf* hand; (*strato: di vernice etc*) coat; **di prima ~** (*notizia*) first-hand; **di seconda ~** second-hand; **man ~** little by little, gradually; **man ~ che** as; **darsi** *o* **stringersi la ~** to shake hands; **mettere le ~i avanti** (*fig*) to safeguard o.s.; **restare a ~i vuote** to be left empty-handed; **venire alle ~i** to come to blows; **a ~** by hand; **~i in alto!** hands up!

291

'Key' words

Your Collins Pocket Dictionary gives special status to certain Italian and English words which can be looked on as 'key' words in each language. These are words which have many different usages. 'Molto', 'volere' and 'così' opposite are typical examples in Italian. You are likely to become familiar with them in your day-to-day language studies.

There will be occasions, however, when you want to check on a particular usage. Your dictionary can be very helpful here. Note how with 'volere', for example, different parts of speech and different usages are clearly indicated by a combination of lozenges – ♦ – and numbers. Additionally, further guides to usage are given in the language of the user who needs them. These are bracketed and in italics.

vo'lere *sm* will, wish(es); **contro il ~ di** against the wishes of; **per ~ di qn** in obedience to sb's will *o* wishes

♦ *vt* **1** (*esigere, desiderare*) to want; **voler fare/che qn faccia** to want to do/sb to do; **volete del caffè?** would you like *o* do you want some coffee?; **vorrei questo/ fare** I would *o* I'd like this/to do; **come vuoi** as you like; **senza ~** (*inavvertitamente*) without meaning to, unintentionally
2 (*consentire*): **vogliate attendere, per piacere** please wait; **vogliamo andare?** shall we go?; **vuole essere così gentile da ...?** would you be so kind as to ...?; **non ha voluto ricevermi** he wouldn't see me
3: **volerci** (*essere necessario: materiale, attenzione*) to need; (*: tempo*) to take; **quanta farina ci vuole per questa torta?** how much flour do you need for this cake?; **ci vuole un'ora per arrivare a Venezia** it takes an hour to get to Venice
4: **voler bene a qn** (*amore*) to love sb; (*affetto*) to be fond of sb, like sb very much; **voler male a qn** to dislike sb; **volerne a qn** to bear sb a grudge; **voler dire** to mean

'molto, a *det* (*quantità*) a lot of, much; (*numero*) a lot of, many; **~ pane/carbone** a lot of bread/coal; **~a gente** a lot of people, many people; **~i libri** a lot of books, many books; **non ho ~ tempo** I haven't got much time; **per ~ (tempo)** for a long time

♦ *av* **1** a lot, (very) much; **viaggia ~** he travels a lot; **non viaggia ~** he doesn't travel much *o* a lot
2 (*intensivo: con aggettivi, avverbi*) very; (*: con participio passato*) (very) much; **~ buono** very good; **~ migliore, ~ meglio** much *o* a lot better

♦ *pron* much, a lot; **~i, e** *pron pl* many, a lot; **~i pensano che ...** many (people) think ...

così *av* **1** (*in questo modo*) like this, (in) this way; (*in tal modo*) so; **le cose stanno ~** this is the way things stand; **non ho detto ~!** I didn't say that!; **come stai? – (e) ~** how are you? — so-so; **e ~ via** and so on; **per ~ dire** so to speak
2 (*tanto*) so; **~ lontano** so far away; **un ragazzo ~ intelligente** such an intelligent boy

♦ *ag inv* (*tale*): **non ho mai visto un film ~** I've never seen such a film

♦ *cong* **1** (*perciò*) so, therefore
2: **~ ... come** as ... as; **non è ~ bravo come te** he's not as good as you; **~ ... che** so ... that

HEADWORDS

Study the following sentences. In each sentence a wrong word spelt very similarly to the correct word has deliberately been put in and the sentence doesn't make sense. This word is shaded each time. Write out each sentence again, putting in the <u>correct</u> word which you will find in your dictionary near the wrong word.

Example: Vietato l'ingrosso agli estranei

['ingrosso' ('all'ingrosso' = 'wholesale') is the wrong word and should be replaced by 'ingresso' (= 'entry')]

1. Ha agito contro il volare della maggioranza.

2. Inserire la moneta e pigliare il pulsante.

3. Non dobbiamo molare proprio adesso.

4. Ho dovuto impanare la lezione a memoria.

5. Il prato era circondato da uno stecchito.

6. Vorrei sentire il tuo parare.

7. Vorrei un po' di panno sulle fragole.

8. Qual è l'oratorio d'apertura dell'ufficio?

9. Quel negoziante mi ha imbrigliato!

10. Sedevano fiasco a fiasco.

WORDGAME 2

DICTIONARY ENTRIES

Complete the crossword below by looking up the English words in the list and finding the correct Italian translations. There is a slight catch, however! All the English words can be translated several ways into Italian, but only one translation will fit correctly into each part of the crossword.

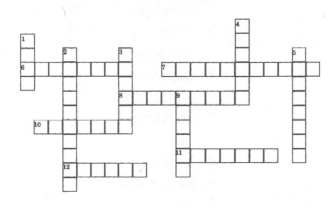

1.	THREAD	7.	COLD
2.	PERMIT	8.	WAIT
3.	PRESENT	9.	NOTICE
4.	WANT	10.	RETURN
5.	JOURNEY	11.	CUT
6.	FREE	12.	REST

FINDING MEANINGS

In this list there are eight pairs of words that have some sort of connection with each other. For example, **'laurea'** (= 'degree') and **'studente'** (= 'student') are linked. Find the other pairs.

1. vestaglia
2. nido
3. pelletteria
4. pantofola
5. campanile
6. studente
7. libro
8. borsetta
9. passerella
10. pinna
11. laurea
12. scaffale
13. gazza
14. nave
15. campana
16. squalo

WORDGAME 4

SYNONYMS

Complete the crossword by supplying SYNONYMS of the words below. You will sometimes find the synonym you are looking for in italics and bracketed at the entries for the words listed below. Sometimes you will have to turn to the English-Italian section for help.

1. RIGUARDO
2. GALA
3. GALLERIA
4. CANCELLARE
5. GALERA
6. BUFFO
7. GIOCARE
8. RAPIDO
9. PAURA
10. MARRONE

SPELLING

You will often use your dictionary to check spellings. The person who has compiled this list of ten Italian words has made <u>three</u> spelling mistakes. Find the three words which have been misspelt and write them out correctly.

1. uccello
2. docia
3. unghia
4. opportuno
5. temporale
6. ortica
7. ovest
8. arabiato
9. folio
10. ossigeno

WORDGAME 6

ANTONYMS

Complete the crossword by supplying ANTONYMS (i.e. opposites) in Italian of the words below. Use your dictionary to help you.

1. ricchezza
2. accettare
3. coraggioso
4. ridere
5. difendere

6. liscio
7. colpevole
8. chiaro
9. bello
10. aperto

WORDGAME 7

PHONETIC SPELLINGS

The phonetic transcriptions of ten Italian words are given below. If you study pages xiv to xv at the front of your dictionary you should be able to work out what the words are.

1. ˈridʒido
2. pitˈtʃone
3. ˈdʒɛlo
4. ˈmattso
5. deˈtʃennjo
6. ˈkjave
7. ˈfɔʎʎa
8. ˈsoɲɲo
9. ˈaʃʃa
10. ˈgjanda

WORDGAME 8

EXPRESSIONS IN WHICH THE HEADWORD APPEARS

If you look up the headword 'colpo' in the Italian-English section of your dictionary you will find that the word can have many meanings. Study the entry carefully and translate the following sentences into English.

1. La sua sconfitta è stata un duro colpo per tutti.

2. Ha preso un brutto colpo in testa.

3. Dammi un colpo di telefono domani mattina.

4. Sparò quattro colpi di pistola.

5. Il rumore cessò di colpo.

6. La sua fuga è stata un colpo di testa.

7. Un colpo di vento fece sbattere le persiane.

8. Gli è preso un colpo ed è morto.

9. Hai fatto colpo col tuo discorso, ieri.

10. Gli ho dato un colpo senza volere ed è caduto.

11. Con questo caldo è facile prendere un colpo di sole.

12. Hanno arrestato gli autori del fallito colpo di Stato.

WORDGAME 9

RELATED WORDS

Fill in the blanks in the pairs of sentences below. The missing words are related to the words on the left. Choose the correct 'relative' each time. You will find it in your dictionary near the headword provided.

HEADWORD	RELATED WORDS
impiegare	1. Fa l' _____ di banca. 2. Ha appena lasciato il suo _____ .
studiare	3. Ha vissuto a Firenze quand'era _____ . 4. Ha uno _____ in centro.
usare	5. Si raccomanda l' _____ delle cinture di sicurezza. 6. La tua macchina è nuova o _____?
unità	7. È una famiglia molto _____ . 8. Vi potete _____ a noi, se volete.
rifiuto	9. È un'offerta che non potrete _____. 10. Dov'è il bidone dei _____?
festeggiare	11. Il negozio è chiuso nei giorni _____ . 12. Ha organizzato una _____ di compleanno.

WORDGAME 10

'KEY' WORDS

Study carefully the entry **'fare'** in your dictionary and find translations for the following:

1. the weather is fine

2. to do psychology

3. go ahead!

4. let me see

5. to get one's hair cut

6. this is the way it's done

7. to do the shopping

8. to be quick

9. to start up the engine

10. he made as if to leave

THE DICTIONARY AND GRAMMAR

While it is true that a dictionary can never be a substitute for a detailed grammar reference book, it nevertheless provides a great deal of grammatical information. If you know how to extract this information you will be able to use Italian more accurately both in speech and in writing.

The Collins Pocket Dictionary presents grammatical information as follows.

Parts of speech

Parts of speech are given in italics immediately after the phonetic spellings of headwords. Abbreviated forms are used. Abbreviations can be checked on pages xi to xiii.

Changes in parts of speech within an entry – for example, from adjective to adverb to noun – are indicated by means of lozenges - ♦ - as with the Italian 'forte' and the English 'act' opposite.

Genders of Italian nouns

The gender of each noun in the Italian-English section of the dictionary is indicated in the following way:

> *sm* = sostantivo maschile
>
> *sf* = sostantivo femminile

You will occasionally see *'sm/f'* beside an entry. This indicates that a noun – 'insegnante', for example – can be either masculine or feminine.

Feminine and *irregular* plural forms of nouns are shown, as with 'bambino', 'autore' and 'bruco' opposite.

So many things depend on your knowing the correct gender of an Italian noun – whether you use 'il' or 'la' etc. to translate 'the'; the way you spell and pronounce certain adjectives; the changes you make to past participles, etc. If you are in any doubt as to the gender of a noun, it is always best to check it in your dictionary.

ono'rare *vt* to honour; *(far onore a)* to do credit to; **~rsi** *vr*: **~rsi di** to feel honoured at, be proud of

quassù *av* up here

perciò [per'tʃɔ] *cong* so, for this (*o* that) reason

'pranzo ['prandzo] *sm* dinner; *(a mezzogiorno)* lunch

'cena ['tʃena] *sf* dinner; *(leggera)* supper

bam'bino, a *sm/f* child

au'tore, 'trice *sm/f* author

'bruco, chi *sm* caterpillar; grub

'forte *ag* strong; *(suono)* loud; *(spesa)* considerable, great; *(passione, dolore)* great, deep ♦ *av* strongly; *(velocemente)* fast; *(a voce alta)* loud(ly); *(violentemente)* hard ♦ *sm* *(edificio)* fort; *(specialità)* forte, strong point; **essere ~ in qc** to be good at sth

act [ækt] *n* atto; *(in music-hall etc)* numero; *(LAW)* decreto ♦ *vi* agire; *(THEATRE)* recitare; *(pretend)* fingere ♦ *vt* *(part)* recitare; **to ~ as** agire da; **~ing** *adj* che fa le funzioni di ♦ *n* *(of actor)* recitazione *f*; *(activity)*: **to do some ~ing** fare del teatro (*ur* del cinema)

inse'gnante [inseɲ'nante] *ag* teaching ♦ *sm/f* teacher

Adjectives

Adjectives are given in both their masculine and feminine forms, where these are different. The usual rule is to drop the 'o' of the masculine form and add an 'a' to make an adjective feminine, as with 'nero' opposite.

Some adjectives have identical masculine and feminine forms, as with 'verde' opposite.

Many Italian adjectives, however, do not follow the regular pattern. Where an adjective has irregular plural forms, this information is clearly provided in your dictionary, usually with the irregular endings, being given. Consider the entries for 'bianco' and 'lungo' opposite.

Adverbs

Advebs are not always listed in your dictionary. The normal rule for forming adverbs in Italian is to add '-mente' to the feminine form of the adjective. Thus:

vero > vera > veramente

The '-mente' ending is often the equivalent of the English '-ly':

veramente – really
certamente – certainly

Adjectives ending in '-e' and '-le' are slightly different:

recente > recentemente
reale > realmente

Where an adverb is very common in Italian, or where its translation(s) cannot be derived from translations for the adjective, it will be listed in alphabetical order, either as a headword or as a subentry. Compare 'solamente' and 'attualmente' opposite.

In many cases, however, Italian adverbs are not given, since the English translation can easily be derived from the relevant translation of the adjective headword: e.g. 'cortese' opposite.

Information about verbs

A major problem facing language learners is that the form of a verb will change according to the subject and/or the tense being used. A typical Italian verb can take on many different forms – too many to list in a dictionary entry.

'nero, a *ag* black; (*scuro*) dark ♦ *sm* black;
il Mar N~ the Black Sea

'verde *ag, sm* green; **essere al ~** to be
broke; **~ bottiglia/oliva** bottle/olive green

bi'anco, a, chi, che *ag* white; (*non
scritto*) blank ♦ *sm* white; (*intonaco*)
whitewash ♦ *sm/f* white, white man/
woman; **in ~** (*foglio, assegno*) blank; (*notte*)
sleepless; **in ~ e nero** (*TV, FOT*) black and
white; **mangiare in ~** to follow a bland
diet; **pesce in ~** boiled fish; **andare in ~**
(*non riuscire*) to fail; **~ dell'uovo** egg-white

'lungo, a, ghi, ghe *ag* long; (*lento:
persona*) slow; (*diluito: caffè, brodo*) weak,
watery, thin ♦ *sm* length ♦ *prep* along; **~ 3
metri** 3 metres long; **a ~** for a long time; **a
~ andare** in the long run; **di gran ~a** (*by far*;
(*molto*) by far; **andare in ~** *o* **per le lunghe**
to drag on; **saperla ~a** to know what's
what; **in ~ e in largo** far and wide, all over;
~ il corso dei secoli throughout the
centuries

vera'mente *av* really

certa'mente [tʃerta'mente] *av* certainly

re'cente [re'tʃente] *ag* recent; **di ~** recently;
recente'mente *av* recently

sola'mente *av* only, just

'solo, a *ag* alone; (*in senso spirituale:
isolato*) lonely; (*unico*): **un ~ libro** only one
book, a single book; (*con ag numerale*):
veniamo noi tre ~i just *o* only the three of
us are coming ♦ *av* (*soltanto*) only, just;
non ~ ... ma anche not only ... but also;
fare qc da ~ to do sth (all) by oneself

cor'tese *ag* courteous; **corte'sia** *sf*
courtesy; **per cortesia ...** excuse me,
please ...

attu'ale *ag* (*presente*) present; (*di attualità*)
topical; (*che è in atto*) actual; **attualità** *sf
inv* topicality; (*avvenimento*) current event;
attual'mente *av* at the moment, at
present

Yet, although verbs are listed in your dictionary in their infinitive forms only, this does not mean that the dictionary is of limited value when it comes to handling the verb system of the Italian language. On the contrary, it contains much valuable information.

First of all, your dictionary will help you with the meanings of unfamiliar verbs. If you came across the word 'riempie' in a text and looked it up in your dictionary you wouldn't find it. You must deduce that it is part of a verb and look for the infinitive form. Thus you will see that 'riempie' is a form of the verb 'riempire'. You now have the basic meaning of the word you are concerned with – something to do with the English verb 'fill' – and this should be enough to help you understand the text you are reading.

It is usually an easy task to make the connection between the form of a verb and the infinitive. For example, 'riempiono', 'riempirò', 'riempissero' and 'reimpii' are all recognisable as parts of the infinitive 'riempire'. However, sometimes it is less obvious – for example, 'vengo', 'vieni' and 'verrò are all parts of 'venire'. The only real solution to this problem is to learn the various forms of the main Italian regular and irregular verbs.

And this is the second source of help offered by your dictionary. The verb tables on page 616 to 617 at the back of the Collins Pocket Dictionary provide a summary of some of the main forms of the main tenses of regular and irregular verbs. Consider the verb 'venire' below where the following information is given:

2	venuto	– Past Participle
3	vengo, vieni, viene, vengono	– Present Tense forms
5	venni, venisti	– Past Tense forms
6	verrò *etc.*	– 1st Person Singular of the Future Tense
8	venga	– 1st, 2nd, 3rd Person of Present Subjunctive

The regular '-are' verb 'parlare' is presented in greater detail, as are the regular '-ire' and '-ere' verbs. The main tenses and the different endings are given in full. This information can be transferred and applied to all verbs in the list. In addition, the main parts of the most common irregular verbs are listed in the body of the dictionary.

PARLARE

1 parlando
2 parlato
3 parlo, parli, parla, parliamo, parlate, parlano
4 parlavo, parlavi, parlava, parlavamo, parlavate, parlavano
5 parlai, parlasti, parlò, parlammo, parlaste, parlarono
6 parlerò, parlerai, parlerà, parleremo, parlerete, parleranno
7 parlerei, parleresti, parlerebbe, parleremmo, parlereste, parlerebbero
8 parli, parli, parli, parliamo, parliate, parlino
9 parlassi, parlassi, parlasse, parlassimo, parlaste, parlassero
10 parla!, parli!, parlate!, parlino!

In order to make maximum use of the information contained in these pages, a good working knowledge of the various rules affecting Italian verbs is required. You will acquire this in the course of your Italian studies and your Collins dictionary will serve as a useful reminder. If you happen to forget how to form the second person singular form of the Future Tense of 'venire' there will be no need to panic – your dictionary contains the information!

WORDGAME 11

PARTS OF SPEECH

In each sentence below a word has been shaded. Put a tick in the appropriate box to indicate the <u>part of speech</u> each time. Remember, different parts of speech are indicated by lozenges within entries.

SENTENCE	Noun	Adj	Adv	Verb
1. Studia diritto a Roma.				
2. Parla più piano! Il bambino dorme.				
3. Ho già versato la minestra nel piatto.				
4. Ho spento il televisore prima della fine del film.				
5. Ha finto di andarsene ed è rimasto ad ascoltare.				
6. Non gli ho permesso di venire.				
7. Vuoi una fetta di dolce?				
8. Abbassi il volume, per favore? Così è troppo forte.				
9. Dopo la notizia sembrava molto scossa.				
10. Hanno assunto un capo del personale per la nostra sezione.				

WORDGAME 12

NOUNS

This list contains the feminine form of some Italian nouns. Use your dictionary to find the **masculine** form.

MASCULINE	FEMININE
	amica
	cantante
	direttrice
	straniera
	regista
	studentessa
	cugina
	lettrice
	professoressa
	collaboratrice

WORDGAME 13

MEANING CHANGES WITH GENDER

There are some pairs of Italian nouns which are distinguished only by
their ending and gender, e.g. 'il partito' and 'la partita'. Fill in the blanks
below with the appropriate member of each pair and the correct article –
'il, la, un' etc – where an article is required.

1. L'ho scritto su _____ da qualche parte   foglio *or*

   Guarda! Sulla pianta è spuntata _____   foglia?

2. Non è questo _____ di fare le cose!   moda *or*

   È un colore che non va più di _____   modo?

3. È arrivato di _____   corso *or*

   Credo che mi iscriverò ad _____   corsa?

   di spagnolo

4. In questa zona ci sono tanti _____   castagne *or*

   Ho comprato un sacchetto di _____   castagni?

5. Fammi vedere _____ della mano!   palma *or*

   Sedevano sulla spiaggia all'ombra di _____   palmo?

6. Ti va di fare _____ a tennis?   partito *or*

   _____ si sta preparando alle elezioni   partita?

7. Devo mettere _____ su questi pantaloni   pezzo *or*

   Vuoi _____ di torta?   pezza?

8. Per oggi basta lavorare! Vado a _____   caso *or*

   Ci siamo conosciuti per _____   casa?

WORDGAME 14

NOUN AND ADJECTIVE FORMS

Use your dictionary to find the following forms of these words.

MASCULINE	FEMININE
1. bianco	
2. fresco	
3. largo	
4. verde	
5. grave	

SINGULAR	PLURAL
6. poca	
7. giovane	
8. grande	
9. veloce	
10. poeta	
11. diadema	
12. triste	
13. tronco	
14. tromba	
15. dialogo	

WORDGAME 15

ADVERBS

Translate the following Italian adverbs into English. Put an asterisk next to those that don't appear in the Italian-English section of the Collins dictionary.

1. recentemente
2. redditiziamente
3. costantemente
4. gentilmente
5. mensilmente
6. naturalmente
7. aggressivamente
8. semplicemente
9. tenacemente
10. esattamente

WORDGAME 16

VERB TENSES

Use your dictionary to help you fill in the blanks in the table below.
(Remember the important pages at the back of your dictionary.)

INFINITIVE	PRESENT TENSE	PAST PARTICIPLE	FUTURE
venire			io
rimanere			
vedere			io
avere	io		
offrire			
muovere			io
finire	io		
uscire	io		
dovere			io
dormire			io
vivere			
potere	io		

WORDGAME 17

PAST PARTICIPLES

Use the verb tables at the back of your dictionary to work out the past participle of these verbs. Check that you have found the correct form by looking in the main text.

INFINITIVE	PAST PARTICIPLE
venire	
contrarre	
coprire	
vivere	
offrire	
sorridere	
prendere	
mettere	
sorprendere	
percorrere	
accogliere	
dipingere	
condurre	
scendere	

WORDGAME 18

IDENTIFYING INFINITIVES

In the sentences below you will see various Italian verbs shaded. Use your dictionary to help you find the **infinitive** form of each verb.

1. Quand'ero a Londra dividevo
   un appartamento con degli amici.

2. I miei amici mi raggiunsero in discoteca.

3. Sua madre lo accompagnava a scuola in macchina.

4. Domani mi alzerò alle nove.

5. Questo fine settimana andremo tutti in campagna.

6. Hanno già venduto la casa.

7. Entrò e si mise a sedere.

8. È nato in Germania.

9. Gli piacerebbe vivere negli Stati Uniti.

10. Faremo una partita a tennis.

11. Ha ricominciato a piovere.

12. Non so cosa gli sia successo.

13. Vorremmo visitare il castello.

14. I bambini avevano freddo.

15. Non so cosa sia meglio fare.

MORE ABOUT MEANING

In this section we will consider some of the problems associated with using a bilingual dictionary.

Overdependence on your dictionary

That the dictionary is an invaluable tool for the language learner is beyond dispute. Nevertheless, it is possible to become overdependent on your dictionary, turning to it in an almost automatic fashion every time you come up against a new Italian word or phrase. Tackling an unfamiliar text in this way will turn reading in Italian into an extremely tedious activity. If you stop to look up every new word you may actually be *hindering* your ability to read in Italian – you are so concerned with the individual words that you pay no attention to the text as a whole and to the context which gives them meaning. It is therefore important to develop appropriate reading skills – using clues such as titles, headlines, illustrations, etc., understanding relations within a sentence, etc. to predict or infer what a text is about.

A detailed study of the development of reading skills is not within the scope of this supplement; we are concerned with knowing how to use a dictionary, which is only one of several important skills involved in reading. Nevertheless, it may be instructive to look at one example. You see the following text in an Italian newspaper and are interested in working out what it is about.

Contextual clues here include the words in large type which you would probably recognise as an Italian name, something that looks like a date in the middle, and the name and address in the bottom right hand corner. The Italian words 'annunciare' and 'clinica' resemble closely the words 'announce' and

> *Siamo lieti di annunciare*
> *la nascito di*
>
> # Mario, Francesco
>
> *il 29 marzo 1999*
>
> *Monica e Fraco ROSSI*
> *Clinca*   *corso Italia n° 18*
> *del Sole*   *34142 Padova*

'clinic' in English, so you would not have to look them up in your dictionary. Other 'form' words such as 'siamo', 'la', 'il', and 'di' will be familiar to you from your general studies in Italian. Given that we are dealing with a newspaper, you will probably have worked out by now that this could be an announcement placed in the 'Personal Column'.

318

So you have used a series of cultural, contextual and word-formation clues to get you to the point where you have understood that Monica and Franco Rossi have placed this notice in the 'Personal Column' of the newspaper and that something happened to Francesco on 29 March 1999, something connected with a hospital. And you have reached this point *without* opening your dictionary once. Common sense and your knowledge of newspaper contents in this country might suggest that this must be an announcement of someone's birth or death. Thus 'lieti' ('happy') and 'nascita' ('birth') become the only words that you need to look up in order to confirm that this is indeed a birth announcement.

When learning Italian we are helped considerably by the fact that many Italian and English words look and sound alike and have exactly the same meaning. Such words are called 'COGNATES'. Many words which look similar in Italian and English come from a common Latin root. Other words are the same or nearly the same in both languages because Italian language has borrowed a word from English or vice versa. The dictionary will often not be necessary where cognates are concerned – provided you know the English word that the Italian word resembles!

Words with more than one meaning

The need to examine with care *all* the information contained in a dictionary entry must be stressed. This is particularly important with the many Italian words which have more than one meaning. For example, the Italian 'giornale' can mean 'diary' as well as 'newspaper'. How you translated the word would depend on the context in which you found it.

Similarly, if you were trying to translate a phrase such as 'era in corso ...', you would have to look through the whole entry for 'corso' to get the right translation. If you restricted your search to the first lines of the entry and saw that the meanings given are 'course' and 'main street', you might be tempted to assume that the phrase meant 'it was in the main street'. But if you examined the entry closely you would see that 'in corso' means 'in progress, under way'. So 'era in corso' means 'it was in progress', as in the phrase 'lavori in corso'.

The same need for care applies when you are using the English-Italian section of your dictionary to translate a word from English into Italian. Watch out in particular for the lozenges indicating changes in parts of speech.

The noun 'sink' is 'lavandino, aquaio', while the verb is 'affondare'. If you don't watch what you are doing, you could end up with ridiculous non-Italian e.g. 'Ha messo i piatti sporchi nell'affondare.'

Phrasal verbs

Another potential source of difficulty is English phrasal verbs. These consist of a common verb ('go', 'make', etc.) plus an adverb and/or a preposition to give English expressions such as 'to make out', 'to take after', etc. Entries for such verbs tend to be fairly full, so close examination of the contents is required. Note how these verbs appear in colour within the entry.

False friends

Many Italian and English words have similar forms *and* meanings. Many Italian words, however, *look* like English words but have a

make [meɪk] (*pt, pp* **made**) *vt* fare; (*manufacture*) fare, fabbricare; (*cause to be*): **to ~ sb sad** *etc* rendere qn triste *etc*; (*force*): **to ~ sb do sth** costringere qn a fare qc, far fare qc a qn; (*equal*): **2 and 2 ~ 4** 2 più 2 fa 4 ♦ *n* fabbricazione *f*; (*brand*) marca; **to ~ a fool of sb** far fare a qn la figura dello scemo; **to ~ a profit** realizzare un profitto; **to ~ a loss** subire una perdita; **to ~ it** (*arrive*) arrivare; (*achieve sth*) farcela; **what time do you ~ it?** che ora fai?; **to ~ do with** arrangiarsi con; **~ for** *vt fus* (*place*) avviarsi verso; **~ out** *vt* (*write out*) scrivere; (: *cheque*) emettere; (*understand*) capire; (*see*) distinguere; (: *numbers*) decifrare; **~ up** *vt* (*constitute*) formare; (*invent*) inventare; (*parcel*) fare ♦ *vi* conciliarsi; (*with cosmetics*) truccarsi; **~ up for** *vt fus* compensare; ricuperare; **~-believe** *n*: **a world of ~-believe** un mondo di favole;

completely *different* meaning. For example, 'attualmente' means 'at the moment, at present'; 'eventuale' means 'possible'. This can easily lead to serious mistranslations.

Sometimes the meaning of the Italian word is *close* to the English. For example, 'la moneta' means 'small change' rather than 'money'; 'il soprannome' means 'nickname' not 'surname'. But some Italian words have two meanings, one the same as the English, the other completely different! 'L'editore' can mean 'publisher' as well as 'editor'; 'la marcia' can mean 'march/running/walking', but also 'the gear (of a car)'.

Such words are often referred to as 'false friends'. You will have to look at the context in which they appear to arrive at the correct meaning. If they seem to fit in with the sense of the passage as a whole, you will probably not need to look them up. If they don't make sense, however, you may well be dealing with 'false friends'.

WORDGAME 19

WORDS IN CONTEXT

Study the sentences below. Translations of the shaded words are given at the bottom. Match the number of the sentence and the letter of the translation correctly each time.

1. In questa zona è proibito cacciare.
2. L'ho visto cacciare i soldi in tasca.
3. È il ritratto di una dama del Settecento.
4. Facciamo una partita a dama?
5. Ha versato il vino nei bicchieri.
6. Hanno versato tutti i soldi sul loro conto.
7. Ti presento il mio fratello maggiore.
8. Aveva il grado di maggiore nell'esercito.
9. Ho finito i dadi per brodo.
10. In un angolo due uomini giocavano a dadi.
11. Sua madre è già partita per il mare.
12. Ti va di fare una partita a carte?
13. Il ladro è stato visto da un passante.
14. Devi infilare la cintura nel passante.
15. È corso verso di me.
16. Leggete ad alta voce il primo verso della poesia.

a. poured	e. loop	i. dice	m. passer-by
b. hunt	f. towards	j. major	n. draughts
c. left	g. paid	k. stock cubes	o. older
d. game	h. line	l. stick	p. lady

321

WORDS WITH MORE THAN ONE MEANING

Look at the advertisements below. The words which are shaded can have more than one meaning. Use your dictionary to help you work out the correct translation in the context.

1

Desidero ricevere maggiori informazioni
per un soggiorno al Lago di Garda

Nome e cognome: _____

Indirizzo:_____

2

Con il patrocinio della

REGIONE TOSCANA e CAMERA DI

COMMERCIO DELLA TOSCANA

3

TRILLO
LA SVEGLIA ELETTRONICA
CHE NON TI TRADISCE
4 funzioni: ore, minuti, secondi,
sveglia
Funzionamento a pile

4

**ECONOMIA E
FINANZA
BORSA E FONDI**

5

Albergo Ristorante
"La Cantina"
cucina casalinga
a 500 metri dalla piazza

6

**SI PREGA DI RITIRARE LO
SCONTRINO ALLA CASSA**

7

Visite guidate al paese
di Alassio

8

CASSA
rurale ed artigiana
Via Basovizza 2
Trieste

9

**Una casa in riva al mare
"CALA DEI TEMPLARI"**
Soggiorno, una camera da letto,
bagno, balcone

10

PRATOLINI
la cucina su misura per te
Pratolini S.p.A. – 57480 Frascati – Roma
Tel (0733) 5581 (10 linee) –
Fax (0733) 5585

WORDGAME 21

FALSE FRIENDS

Look at the advertisements below. The words which are shaded resemble English words but have different meanings here. Find a correct translation for each word in the context.

1

Boutique "La Moda"

Liquidazione di tutti gli articoli

2

Pensione Miramonti

camere con bagno/doccia

parcheggio privato

bar, ristorante

3

ACCENDERE LE LUCI IN GALLERIA

4

LIBRERIA

Il Gabbiano

Libri – Giornali – Articoli
spiaggia – Guide turistiche
– Cartoline

SASSARI
Via Mazzini 46

5

ITALMODA CRAVATTE

LE GRANDI FIRME
Divisione della BST,
Bergamo S.p.A

6

La **direzione** di questo albergo
declina ogni responsabilità per lo
smarrimento di oggetti lasciati
incustoditi

7

Questo **esercizio** resterà
chiuso nei giorni festivi
e il lunedì

8

"Le bollicine"

Locale notturno
– pianobar
– discoteca

9

Lago di Garda
campeggi, sport acquatici,
gite in battello

10

Attenzione: per l'uso leggere
attentamente l'istruzione
interna.
Da vendersi dietro
presentazione di **ricetta** medica.

HAVE FUN WITH YOUR DICTIONARY

Here are some word games for you to try. You will find your dictionary helpful as you attempt the activities.

WORDGAME 22

CODED WORDS

In the boxes below, the letters of eight Italian words have been replaced by numbers. A number represents the same letter each time.

Try to crack the code and find the eight words. If you need help, use your dictionary.

Here is a clue: all the words you are looking for have something to do with TRANSPORT.

1. | T¹ | R² | E³ | ⁴ | ⁵ |

2. | ⁶ | ⁷ | ⁸ | ⁹ | ⁵ | ⁴ |

3. | ⁴ | ⁷ | ¹⁰ | ³ |

4. | ⁷ | ¹¹ | ¹ | ⁵ | ¹² | ¹¹ | ¹⁶ |

5. | ¹ | ² | ⁷ | ¹³ | ¹⁴ | ³ | ¹ | ¹ | ⁵ |

6. | ⁸ | ⁵ | ¹ | ⁵ | ⁶ | ⁹ | ⁶ | ¹⁵ | ³ | ¹ | ¹ | ⁷ |

7. | ¹² | ⁷ | ² | ⁶ | ⁷ |

8. | ⁷ | ¹¹ | ¹ | ⁵ | ⁸ | ⁵ | ¹² | ⁹ | ¹⁵ | ³ |

326

WORDGAME 23

HEADLESS WORDS

If you 'behead' certain Italian words, i.e. take away their first letter, you are left with another Italian word. For example, if you behead **'maglio'** (= 'mallet'), you get **'aglio'** (= 'garlic').

The following words have their heads chopped off, i.e. the first letter has been removed. Use your dictionary to help you form a new Italian word by adding one letter to the start of each word below. Write down the new Italian word and its meaning. There may be more than one new word you can form.

1. arto (= limb)
2. alto (= high)
3. esca (= bait)
4. unto (= greasy)
5. ora (= hour)
6. acca (= letter H)
7. orale (= oral)
8. otto (= eight)
9. orda (= horde)
10. alone (= halo)
11. oca (= goose)
12. anca (= hip)
13. ascia (= axe)
14. anno (= year)
15. rete (= net)

327

WORDGAME 24

CROSSWORD

Complete this crossword by looking up the words listed below in the English-Italian section of your dictionary. Remember to read through the entry carefully to find the word that will fit.

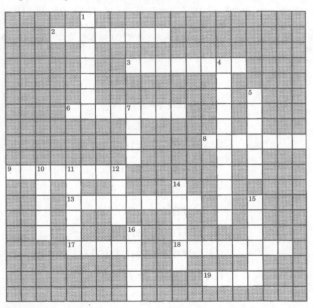

ACROSS

2. to dirty
3. to admire
6. relationship
8. deposit
9. strip
13. employ
17. ebony
18. to take off
19. night

DOWN

1. (a piece of) news
4. to reassure
5. story
7. porthole
10. rough
11. swarm
12. air
14. sad
15. adder
16. harbour

328

WORDGAME 25

SPLIT WORDS

There are twelve Italian words hidden in the grid below. Each word is made up of five letters but has been split into two parts. Find the Italian words. Each group of letters can only be used once. Use your dictionary to help you.

fer	ba	por	sce	za	che
an	mo	to	gam	se	duo
pri	ta	co	ro	fuo	na
fal	sen	men	so	for	mo

KITCHEN WORDS

Here is a list of Italian words for things you will find in the kitchen.
Unfortunately, the letters have all been jumbled up. Try to work out what
each word is and put the word in the boxes on the right. You will see that
there are six shaded boxes below. With the six letters in the shaded boxes
make up <u>another</u> Italian word for an object you can find in the kitchen.

1. zazta   Vuoi una _____
   di caffé?

2. grifo   Metti il burro
   nel _____!

3. vatloa   A _____! È
   pronto!

4. norfo   Cuocere in _____
   per 20 minuti.

5. chiocciau   Assaggia la
   minestra col _____.

6. polacasta   Usa il _____ per gli
   spaghetti.

The word you are looking for is:

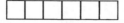

330

WORDGAME 27

GRID WORDS

Take the four letters given each time and put them in the four empty boxes in the centre of each grid. Arrange them in such a way that you form four six-letter words. Use your dictionary to check the words.

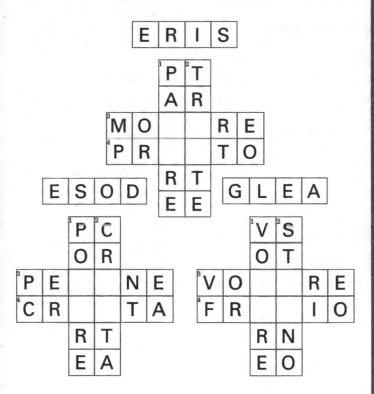

ANSWERS

WORDGAME 1

1	volere	6	parere
2	pigiare	7	panna
3	mollare	8	orario
4	imparare	9	imbrogliato
5	steccato	10	fianco

WORDGAME 2

1	filo	7	raffreddore
2	permettere	8	attendere
3	regalo	9	notare
4	volere	10	ritorno
5	tragitto	11	ridurre
6	liberare	12	riposo

WORDGAME 3

vestaglia + pantofola
nido + gazza
pelletteria + borsetta
campanile + campana
studente + laurea
libro + scaffale
passerella + nave
pinna + squalo

WORDGAME 4

1	attenzione	6	divertente
2	sfarzo	7	ingannare
3	traforo	8	veloce
4	annullare	9	timore
5	prigione	10	bruno

WORDGAME 5

1 doccia 2 arrabbiato 3 foglio

WORDGAME 6

1	povertà	6	ruvido
2	rifiutare	7	innocente
3	vigliacco	8	scuro
4	piangere	9	brutto
5	attaccare	10	chiuso

WORDGAME 7

1	rigido	6	chiave
2	piccione	7	foglia
3	gelo	8	sogno
4	mazzo	9	ascia
5	decennio	10	ghianda

WORDGAME 8

1 shock
2 blow
3 phone call
4 shot
5 suddenly
6 impulse *or* whim
7 gust of wind
8 stroke
9 strong impression
10 knock
11 sunstroke
12 coup d'état

WORDGAME 9

1	impiegato	7	unita
2	impiego	8	unire
3	studente	9	rifiutare
4	studio	10	rifiuti
5	uso	11	festivi
6	usata	12	festa

WORDGAME 10

1 fa bel tempo
2 fare psicologia
3 faccia pure
4 fammi vedere
5 farsi tagliare i capelli
6 si fa così
7 fare la spesa
8 fare presto
9 far partire il motore
10 fece per andarsene

WORDGAME 11

1	n	5	v	8	adj
2	adv	6	v	9	adj
3	n	7	n	10	n
4	n				

WORDGAME 12

1	amico	6	studente
2	cantante	7	cugino
3	direttore	8	lettore
4	straniero	9	professore
5	regista	10	collaboratore

WORDGAME 13

1	un foglio	5	il palmo
	una foglia		una palma
2	il modo	6	una partita
	moda		il partito
3	corsa	7	una pezza
	un corso		un pezzo
4	castagni	8	casa
	castagne		caso

WORDGAME 14

1	bianca	9	veloci
2	fresca	10	poeti
3	larga	11	diademi
4	verde	12	tristi
5	grave	13	tronchi
6	poche	14	trombe
7	giovani	15	dialoghi
8	grandi		

WORDGAME 16

1	io verrò	7	io finisco
2	rimasto	8	io esco
3	io vedrò	9	io dovrò
4	io ho	10	io dormirò
5	offerto	11	vissuto
6	mosso	12	io posso

WORDGAME 17

1	venuto	8	messo
2	contratto	9	sorpreso
3	coperto	10	percorso
4	vissuto	11	accolto
5	offerto	12	dipinto
6	sorriso	13	condotto
7	preso	14	sceso

WORDGAME 18

1	essere	9	piacere
2	raggiungere	10	fare
3	accompagnare	11	ricominciare
4	alzarsi	12	succedere
5	andare	13	volere
6	vendere	14	avere
7	mettersi	15	essere
8	nascere		

WORDGAME 19

1	b	5	a	9	k	13	m
2	l	6	g	10	i	14	e
3	p	7	o	11	c	15	f
4	n	8	j	12	d	16	h

WORDGAME 20

1 stay
2 chamber
3 alarm clock
4 stock exchange; funds
5 cooking
6 checkout (here; till)
7 village (here; town)
8 bank
9 living room
10 kitchen

WORDGAME 21

1 clearance sale
2 boarding house
3 tunnel
4 newspapers
5 ties
6 management
7 business
8 nightclub
9 camp site
10 prescription

WORDGAME 22

1 treno
2 camion
3 nave
4 autobus
5 traghetto
6 motocicletta
7 barca
8 automobile

WORDGAME 23

1 sarto (= tailor)
2 salto (= jump)
3 pesca (= peach)
4 punto (= dot)
5 mora (= blackberry)
6 vacca (= cow)
7 morale (= moral)
8 rotto (= broken)
9 corda (= cord)
10 salone (= sitting room)
11 foca (= seal)
12 panca (= bench)
13 fascia (= band)
14 danno (= damage)
15 prete (= priest)

WORDGAME 24

ACROSS		DOWN	
2	sporcare	1	notizia
3	ammirare	4	rassicurare
6	rapporto	5	favola
8	acconto	7	oblò
9	striscia	10	rozzo
13	impiegare	11	sciame
17	ebano	12	aria
18	togliere	14	triste
19	sera	15	vipera
		16	porto

WORDGAME 25

ferro	senza	duomo
gamba	anche	fuoco
porta	primo	falso
scena	mento	forse

WORDGAME 26

1 tazza
2 frigo
3 tavola
4 forno
5 cucchiaio
6 colapasta

Missing word – FRUSTA

WORDGAME 27

1 parere	1 podere	1 volere
2 triste	2 crosta	2 stagno
3 morire	3 pedone	3 volare
4 presto	4 cresta	4 fregio

ENGLISH – ITALIAN
INGLESE – ITALIANO

A, a

A [eɪ] *n* (*MUS*) la *m*; (*letter*) A, a *f or m inv*; **~-road** *n* strada statale

KEYWORD

a [ə] (*before vowel or silent h*: **an**) *indef art*
1 un (uno +*s impure, gn, pn, ps, x, z*), *f* una (un' +*vowel*); **~ book** un libro; **~ mirror** uno specchio; **an apple** una mela; **she's ~ doctor** è medico
2 (*instead of the number "one"*) un(o), *f* una; **~ year ago** un anno fa; **~ hundred/thousand** *etc* **pounds** cento/mille *etc* sterline
3 (*in expressing ratios, prices etc*) a, per; **3 ~ day/week** 3 al giorno/alla settimana; **10 km an hour** 10 km all'ora; **£5 ~ person** 5 sterline a persona *or* per persona

A.A. *n abbr* (= *Alcoholics Anonymous*) AA; (*BRIT*: = *Automobile Association*) ≈ A.C.I.
A.A.A. (*US*) *n abbr* (= *American Automobile Association*) ≈ A.C.I. *m*
aback [əˈbæk] *adv*: **to be taken ~** essere sbalordito(a)
abandon [əˈbændən] *vt* abbandonare ♦ *n*: **with ~** sfrenatamente, spensieratamente
abate [əˈbeɪt] *vi* calmarsi
abattoir [ˈæbətwɑː*] (*BRIT*) *n* mattatoio
abbey [ˈæbɪ] *n* abbazia, badia
abbot [ˈæbət] *n* abate *m*
abbreviation [əbriːvɪˈeɪʃən] *n* abbreviazione *f*
abdicate [ˈæbdɪkeɪt] *vt* abdicare a ♦ *vi* abdicare
abdomen [ˈæbdəmən] *n* addome *m*
abduct [æbˈdʌkt] *vt* rapire
abide [əˈbaɪd] *vt*: **I can't ~ it/him** non lo posso soffrire *or* sopportare; **~ by** *vt fus* conformarsi a
ability [əˈbɪlɪtɪ] *n* abilità *f inv*

abject [ˈæbdʒekt] *adj* (*poverty*) abietto(a); (*apology*) umiliante
ablaze [əˈbleɪz] *adj* in fiamme
able [ˈeɪbl] *adj* capace; **to be ~ to do sth** essere capace di fare qc, poter fare qc; **~-bodied** *adj* robusto(a); **ably** *adv* abilmente
abnormal [æbˈnɔːməl] *adj* anormale
aboard [əˈbɔːd] *adv* a bordo ♦ *prep* a bordo di
abode [əˈbəʊd] *n*: **of no fixed ~** senza fissa dimora
abolish [əˈbɒlɪʃ] *vt* abolire
abominable [əˈbɒmɪnəbl] *adj* abominevole
aborigine [æbəˈrɪdʒɪnɪ] *n* aborigeno/a
abort [əˈbɔːt] *vt* abortire; **~ion** [əˈbɔːʃən] *n* aborto; **to have an ~ion** abortire; **~ive** *adj* abortivo(a)
abound [əˈbaʊnd] *vi* abbondare; **to ~ in** *or* **with** abbondare di

KEYWORD

about [əˈbaʊt] *adv* **1** (*approximately*) circa, quasi: **~ a hundred/thousand** *etc* un centinaio/migliaio *etc*, circa cento/mille *etc*; **it takes ~ 10 hours** ci vogliono circa 10 ore; **at ~ 2 o'clock** verso le 2; **I've just ~ finished** ho quasi finito
2 (*referring to place*) qua e là, in giro; **to leave things lying ~** lasciare delle cose in giro; **to run ~** correre qua e là; **to walk ~** camminare
3: **to be ~ to do sth** stare per fare qc
♦ *prep* **1** (*relating to*) su, di; **a book ~ London** un libro su Londra; **what is it ~?** di che si tratta?; (*book, film etc*) di cosa tratta?; **we talked ~ it** ne abbiamo parlato; **what** *or* **how ~ doing this?** che ne dici di fare questo?
2 (*referring to place*): **to walk ~ the town**

camminare per la città; **her clothes were scattered ~ the room** i suoi vestiti erano sparsi *or* in giro per tutta la stanza

about-face *n* dietro front *m inv*
about-turn *n* dietro front *m inv*
above [ə'bʌv] *adv, prep* sopra; **mentioned ~** suddetto; **~ all** soprattutto; **~board** *adj* aperto(a); onesto(a)
abrasive [ə'breɪzɪv] *adj* abrasivo(a); (*fig*) caustico(a)
abreast [ə'brɛst] *adv* di fianco; **to keep ~ of** tenersi aggiornato su
abroad [ə'brɔːd] *adv* all'estero
abrupt [ə'brʌpt] *adj* (*sudden*) improvviso(a); (*gruff, blunt*) brusco(a)
abscess ['æbsɪs] *n* ascesso
absence ['æbsəns] *n* assenza
absent ['æbsənt] *adj* assente; **~ee** [-'tiː] *n* assente *m/f*; **~-minded** *adj* distratto(a)
absolute ['æbsəluːt] *adj* assoluto(a); **~ly** [-'luːtlɪ] *adv* assolutamente
absolve [əb'zɔlv] *vt*: **to ~ sb (from)** (*sin*) assolvere qn (da); (*oath*) sciogliere qn (da)
absorb [əb'zɔːb] *vt* assorbire; **to be ~ed in a book** essere immerso in un libro; **~ent cotton** (*US*) *n* cotone *m* idrofilo
absorption [əb'sɔːpʃən] *n* assorbimento
abstain [əb'steɪn] *vi*: **to ~ (from)** astenersi (da)
abstract ['æbstrækt] *adj* astratto(a)
absurd [əb'sɔːd] *adj* assurdo(a)
abuse [*n* ə'bjuːs, *vb* ə'bjuːz] *n* abuso; (*insults*) ingiurie *fpl* ♦ *vt* abusare di; **abusive** *adj* ingiurioso(a)
abysmal [ə'bɪzməl] *adj* spaventoso(a)
abyss [ə'bɪs] *n* abisso
AC *abbr* (= *alternating current*) c.a.
academic [ækə'dɛmɪk] *adj* accademico(a); (*pej: issue*) puramente formale ♦ *n* universitario/a
academy [ə'kædəmɪ] *n* (*learned body*) accademia; (*school*) scuola privata; **~ of music** conservatorio
accelerate [æk'sɛləreɪt] *vt, vi* accelerare; **acceleration** *n* accelerazione *f*; **accelerator** *n* acceleratore *m*

accent ['æksənt] *n* accento
accept [ək'sɛpt] *vt* accettare; **~able** *adj* accettabile; **~ance** *n* accettazione *f*
access ['æksɛs] *n* accesso; **~ible** [æk'sɛsəbl] *adj* accessibile
accessory [æk'sɛsərɪ] *n* accessorio; (*LAW*): **~ to** complice *m/f* di
accident ['æksɪdənt] *n* incidente *m*; (*chance*) caso; **by ~** per caso; **~al** [-'dɛntl] *adj* accidentale; **~ally** [-'dɛntəlɪ] *adv* per caso; **~ insurance** *n* assicurazione *f* contro gli infortuni; **~-prone** *adj*: **he's very ~-prone** è un vero passaguai
acclaim [ə'kleɪm] *n* acclamazione *f*
accommodate [ə'kɔmədeɪt] *vt* alloggiare; (*oblige, help*) favorire
accommodating [ə'kɔmədeɪtɪŋ] *adj* compiacente
accommodation [əkɔmə'deɪʃən] *n* alloggio; **~s** (*US*) *npl* alloggio
accompany [ə'kʌmpənɪ] *vt* accompagnare
accomplice [ə'kʌmplɪs] *n* complice *m/f*
accomplish [ə'kʌmplɪʃ] *vt* compiere; (*goal*) raggiungere; **~ed** *adj* esperto(a); **~ment** *n* compimento; realizzazione *f*
accord [ə'kɔːd] *n* accordo ♦ *vt* accordare; **of his own ~** di propria iniziativa; **~ance** *n*: **in ~ance with** in conformità con; **~ing**: **~ing to** *prep* secondo; **~ingly** *adv* in conformità
accordion [ə'kɔːdɪən] *n* fisarmonica
account [ə'kaʊnt] *n* (*COMM*) conto; (*report*) descrizione *f*; **~s** *npl* (*COMM*) conti *mpl*; **of no ~** di nessuna importanza; **on ~** in acconto; **on no ~** per nessun motivo; **on ~ of** a causa di; **to take into ~, take ~ of** tener conto di; **~ for** *vt fus* spiegare; giustificare; **~able** *adj*: **~able (to)** responsabile (verso)
accountancy [ə'kaʊntənsɪ] *n* ragioneria
accountant [ə'kaʊntənt] *n* ragioniere/a
account number *n* numero di conto
accrued interest [ə'kruːd-] *n* interesse *m* maturato
accumulate [ə'kjuːmjuleɪt] *vt* accumulare ♦ *vi* accumularsi
accuracy ['ækjurəsɪ] *n* precisione *f*

accurate [ˈækjʊrɪt] *adj* preciso(a); **~ly** *adv* precisamente

accusation [ækjuːˈzeɪʃən] *n* accusa

accuse [əˈkjuːz] *vt* accusare; **~d** *n* accusato/a

accustom [əˈkʌstəm] *vt* abituare; **~ed** *adj*: **~ed to** abituato(a) a

ace [eɪs] *n* asso

ache [eɪk] *n* male *m*, dolore *m* ♦ *vi* (*be sore*) far male, dolere; **my head ~s** mi fa male la testa

achieve [əˈtʃiːv] *vt* (*aim*) raggiungere; (*victory, success*) ottenere; **~ment** *n* compimento; successo

acid [ˈæsɪd] *adj* acido(a) ♦ *n* acido; **~ rain** *n* pioggia acida

acknowledge [əkˈnɒlɪdʒ] *vt* (*letter: also:* **~ receipt of**) confermare la ricevuta di; (*fact*) riconoscere; **~ment** *n* conferma; riconoscimento

acne [ˈækni] *n* acne *f*

acorn [ˈeɪkɔːn] *n* ghianda

acoustic [əˈkuːstɪk] *adj* acustico(a); **~s** *n*, *npl* acustica

acquaint [əˈkweɪnt] *vt*: **to ~ sb with sth** far sapere qc a qn; **to be ~ed with** (*person*) conoscere; **~ance** *n* conoscenza; (*person*) conoscente *m/f*

acquire [əˈkwaɪəˈ] *vt* acquistare

acquit [əˈkwɪt] *vt* assolvere; **to ~ o.s. well** comportarsi bene; **~tal** *n* assoluzione *f*

acre [ˈeɪkəˈ] *n* acro (= 4047 *m²*)

acrid [ˈækrɪd] *adj* acre; pungente

acrobat [ˈækrəbæt] *n* acrobata *m/f*

across [əˈkrɒs] *prep* (*on the other side*) dall'altra parte di; (*crosswise*) attraverso ♦ *adv* dall'altra parte; in larghezza; **to run/swim ~** attraversare di corsa/a nuoto; **~ from** di fronte a

acrylic [əˈkrɪlɪk] *adj* acrilico(a)

act [ækt] *n* atto; (*in music-hall etc*) numero; (*LAW*) decreto ♦ *vi* agire; (*THEATRE*) recitare; (*pretend*) fingere ♦ *vt* (*part*) recitare; **to ~ as** agire da; **~ing** *adj* che fa le funzioni di ♦ *n* (*of actor*) recitazione *f*; (*activity*): **to do some ~ing** fare del teatro (*or* del cinema)

action [ˈækʃən] *n* azione *f*; (*MIL*) combattimento; (*LAW*) processo; **out of ~** fuori combattimento; fuori servizio; **to take ~** agire; **~ replay** *n* (*TV*) replay *m inv*

activate [ˈæktɪveɪt] *vt* (*mechanism*) attivare

active [ˈæktɪv] *adj* attivo(a); **~ly** *adv* (*participate*) attivamente; (*discourage, dislike*) vivamente

activity [ækˈtɪvɪtɪ] *n* attività *f inv*; **~ holiday** *n* vacanza organizzata con attività ricreative per ragazzi

actor [ˈæktəˈ] *n* attore *m*

actress [ˈæktrɪs] *n* attrice *f*

actual [ˈæktjʊəl] *adj* reale, vero(a); **~ly** *adv* veramente; (*even*) addirittura

acute [əˈkjuːt] *adj* acuto(a); (*mind, person*) perspicace

ad [æd] *n abbr* = **advertisement**

A.D. *adv abbr* (= *Anno Domini*) d.C.

adamant [ˈædəmənt] *adj* irremovibile

adapt [əˈdæpt] *vt* adattare ♦ *vi*: **to ~ (to)** adattarsi (a); **~able** *adj* (*device*) adattabile; (*person*) che sa adattarsi; **~er** *or* **~or** *n* (*ELEC*) adattatore *m*

add [æd] *vt* aggiungere; (*figures: also:* **~ up**) addizionare ♦ *vi*: **to ~ to** (*increase*) aumentare; **it doesn't ~ up** (*fig*) non quadra, non ha senso

adder [ˈædəˈ] *n* vipera

addict [ˈædɪkt] *n* tossicomane *m/f*; (*fig*) fanatico/a; **~ed** [əˈdɪktɪd] *adj*: **to be ~ed to** (*drink etc*) essere dedito(a) a; (*fig: football etc*) essere tifoso(a) di; **~ion** [əˈdɪkʃən] *n* (*MED*) tossicodipendenza; **~ive** [əˈdɪktɪv] *adj* che dà assuefazione

addition [əˈdɪʃən] *n* addizione *f*; (*thing added*) aggiunta; **in ~** inoltre; **in ~ to** oltre; **~al** *adj* supplementare

additive [ˈædɪtɪv] *n* additivo

address [əˈdrɛs] *n* indirizzo; (*talk*) discorso ♦ *vt* indirizzare; (*speak to*) fare un discorso a; (*issue*) affrontare

adept [ˈædɛpt] *adj*: **~ at** esperto(a) in

adequate [ˈædɪkwɪt] *adj* adeguato(a); sufficiente

adhere [ədˈhɪəˈ] *vi*: **to ~ to** aderire a; (*fig: rule, decision*) seguire

adhesive [ədˈhiːzɪv] *n* adesivo; **~ tape** *n*

(*BRIT: for parcels etc*) nastro adesivo; (*US: MED*) cerotto adesivo

adjective ['ædʒɛktɪv] *n* aggettivo

adjoining [ə'dʒɔɪnɪŋ] *adj* accanto *inv*, adiacente

adjourn [ə'dʒəːn] *vt* rimandare ♦ *vi* essere aggiornato(a)

adjust [ə'dʒʌst] *vt* aggiustare; (*change*) rettificare ♦ *vi*: to ~ (to) adattarsi (a); ~able *adj* regolabile; ~ment *n* (*PSYCH*) adattamento; (*of machine*) regolazione *f*; (*of prices, wages*) modifica

ad-lib [æd'lɪb] *vi* improvvisare ♦ *adv*: ad lib a piacere, a volontà

administer [əd'mɪnɪstə*] *vt* amministrare; (*justice, drug*) somministrare

administration [ədmɪnɪs'treɪʃən] *n* amministrazione *f*

administrative [əd'mɪnɪstrətɪv] *adj* amministrativo(a)

admiral ['ædmərəl] *n* ammiraglio; A~ty (*BRIT*) *n* Ministero della Marina

admiration [ædmə'reɪʃən] *n* ammirazione *f*

admire [əd'maɪə*] *vt* ammirare

admission [əd'mɪʃən] *n* ammissione *f*; (*to exhibition, night club etc*) ingresso; (*confession*) confessione *f*

admit [əd'mɪt] *vt* ammettere; far entrare; (*agree*) riconoscere; to ~ to riconoscere; ~tance *n* ingresso; ~tedly *adv* bisogna pur riconoscere (che)

ad nauseam [æd'nɔːsɪæm] *adv* fino alla nausea, a non finire

ado [ə'duː] *n*: without (any) more ~ senza più indugi

adolescence [ædəu'lɛsns] *n* adolescenza

adolescent [ædəu'lɛsnt] *adj, n* adolescente *m/f*

adopt [ə'dɔpt] *vt* adottare; ~ed *adj* adottivo(a); ~ion [ə'dɔpʃən] *n* adozione *f*

adore [ə'dɔː*] *vt* adorare

Adriatic [eɪdrɪ'ætɪk] *n*: the ~ (Sea) il mare Adriatico, l'Adriatico

adrift [ə'drɪft] *adv* alla deriva

adult ['ædʌlt] *adj* adulto(a); (*work, education*) per adulti ♦ *n* adulto/a

adultery [ə'dʌltərɪ] *n* adulterio

advance [əd'vɑːns] *n* avanzamento; (*money*) anticipo ♦ *adj* (*booking etc*) in anticipo ♦ *vt* (*money*) anticipare ♦ *vi* avanzare; in ~ in anticipo; ~d *adj* avanzato(a); (*SCOL: studies*) superiore

advantage [əd'vɑːntɪdʒ] *n* (*also: TENNIS*) vantaggio; to take ~ of approfittarsi di

advent ['ædvənt] *n* avvento; (*REL*): A~ Avvento

adventure [əd'vɛntʃə*] *n* avventura

adverb ['ædvəːb] *n* avverbio

adverse ['ædvəːs] *adj* avverso(a)

advert ['ædvəːt] (*BRIT*) *n abbr* = advertisement

advertise ['ædvətaɪz] *vi* (*vt*) fare pubblicità *or* réclame (a); fare un'inserzione (per vendere); to ~ for (*staff*) mettere un annuncio sul giornale per trovare

advertisement [əd'vəːtɪsmənt] *n* (*COMM*) réclame *f inv*, pubblicità *f inv*; (*in classified ads*) inserzione *f*

advertising ['ædvətaɪzɪŋ] *n* pubblicità

advice [əd'vaɪs] *n* consigli *mpl*; (*notification*) avviso; piece of ~ consiglio; to take legal ~ consultare un avvocato

advisable [əd'vaɪzəbl] *adj* consigliabile

advise [əd'vaɪz] *vt* consigliare; to ~ sb of sth informare qn di qc; to ~ sb against sth/doing sth sconsigliare qc a qn/a qn di fare qc; ~r *or* advisor *n* consigliere/a; advisory [-ərɪ] *adj* consultivo(a)

advocate [*n* 'ædvəkɪt, *vb* 'ædvəkeɪt] *n* (*upholder*) sostenitore/trice; (*LAW*) avvocato (difensore) ♦ *vt* propugnare

Aegean [ɪ'dʒiːən] *n*: the ~ (Sea) il mar Egeo, l'Egeo

aerial ['ɛərɪəl] *n* antenna ♦ *adj* aereo(a)

aerobics [ɛə'rəubɪks] *n* aerobica

aeroplane ['ɛərəpleɪn] (*BRIT*) *n* aeroplano

aerosol ['ɛərəsɔl] (*BRIT*) *n* aerosol *m inv*

aesthetic [ɪs'θɛtɪk] *adj* estetico(a)

afar [ə'fɑː*] *adv*: from ~ da lontano

affair [ə'fɛə*] *n* affare *m*; (*also:* love ~) relazione *f* amorosa; ~s (*business*) affari

affect [ə'fɛkt] *vt* toccare; (*influence*) influire su, incidere su; (*feign*) fingere; ~ed *adj* affettato(a)

affection [əˈfekʃən] *n* affezione *f*; **~ate** *adj* affettuoso(a)

afflict [əˈflɪkt] *vt* affliggere

affluence [ˈæfluəns] *n* abbondanza; opulenza

affluent [ˈæfluənt] *adj* ricco(a); **the ~ society** la società del benessere

afford [əˈfɔːd] *vt* permettersi; (*provide*) fornire

afloat [əˈfləut] *adv* a galla

afoot [əˈfut] *adv*: **there is something ~** si sta preparando qualcosa

afraid [əˈfreɪd] *adj* impaurito(a); **to be ~ of** *or* **to/that** aver paura di/che; **I am ~ so/ not** ho paura di sì/no

Africa [ˈæfrɪkə] *n* Africa; **~n** *adj, n* africano(a)

after [ˈɑːftə*] *prep, adv* dopo ♦ *conj* dopo che; **what/who are you ~?** che/chi cerca?; **~ he left/having done** dopo che se ne fu andato/dopo aver fatto; **to name sb ~ sb** dare a qn il nome di qn; **it's twenty ~ eight** (*US*) sono le otto e venti; **to ask ~ sb** chiedere di qn; **~ all** dopo tutto; **~ you!** dopo di lei!; **~effects** *npl* conseguenze *fpl*; (*of illness*) postumi *mpl*; **~math** *n* conseguenze *fpl*; (*of illness*) postumi *mpl*; **~math** *n* conseguenze *fpl*; **~math** *n* nel periodo dopo; **~noon** *n* pomeriggio; **~s** *n* (*inf: dessert*) dessert *m inv*; **~-shave (lotion)** *n* dopobarba *m inv*; **~sun (lotion/cream)** *n* doposole *m inv*; **~thought** *n*: **as an ~thought** come aggiunta; **~wards** (*US* **~ward**) *adv* dopo

again [əˈgen] *adv* di nuovo; **to begin/see ~** ricominciare/rivedere; **not ... ~** non ... più; **~ and ~** ripetutamente

against [əˈgenst] *prep* contro

age [eɪdʒ] *n* età *f inv* ♦ *vt, vi* invecchiare; **it's been ~s since** sono secoli che; **he is 20 years of ~** ha 20 anni; **to come of ~** diventare maggiorenne; **~d** [*adj* eɪdʒd, *npl* ˈeɪdʒɪd] *adj*: **~d 10** di 10 anni ♦ *npl* **the ~d** gli anziani; **~ group** *n* generazione *f*; **~ limit** *n* limite *m* d'età

agency [ˈeɪdʒənsɪ] *n* agenzia

agenda [əˈdʒendə] *n* ordine *m* del giorno

agent [ˈeɪdʒənt] *n* agente *m*

aggravate [ˈægrəveɪt] *vt* aggravare; (*person*) irritare

aggregate [ˈægrɪgeɪt] *n* aggregato

aggressive [əˈgresɪv] *adj* aggressivo(a)

agitate [ˈædʒɪteɪt] *vt* turbare; agitare ♦ *vi*: **to ~ for** agitarsi per

AGM *n abbr* = **annual general meeting**

ago [əˈgəu] *adv*: **2 days ~** 2 giorni fa; **not long ~** poco tempo fa; **how long ~?** quanto tempo fa?

agonizing [ˈægənaɪzɪŋ] *adj* straziante

agony [ˈægənɪ] *n* dolore *m* atroce; **to be in ~** avere dolori atroci

agree [əˈgriː] *vt* (*price*) pattuire ♦ *vi*: **to ~ (with)** essere d'accordo (con); (*LING*) concordare (con); **to ~ to sth/to do sth** accettare qc/di fare qc; **to ~ that** (*admit*) ammettere che; **to ~ on sth** accordarsi su qc; **garlic doesn't ~ with me** l'aglio non mi va; **~able** *adj* gradevole; (*willing*) disposto(a); **~d** *adj* (*time, place*) stabilito(a); **~ment** *n* accordo; **in ~ment** d'accordo

agricultural [ægrɪˈkʌltʃərəl] *adj* agricolo(a)

agriculture [ˈægrɪkʌltʃə*] *n* agricoltura

aground [əˈgraund] *adv*: **to run ~** arenarsi

ahead [əˈhed] *adv* avanti; davanti; **~ of** davanti a; (*fig: schedule etc*) in anticipo su; **~ of time** in anticipo; **go right** *or* **straight ~** tiri diritto

aid [eɪd] *n* aiuto ♦ *vt* aiutare; **in ~ of** a favore di

aide [eɪd] *n* (*person*) aiutante *m*

AIDS [eɪdz] *n abbr* (= *acquired immune deficiency syndrome*) AIDS *f*; **~-related** *adj* (*symptoms, illness*) legato(a) all'AIDS; (*research*) sull'AIDS

aim [eɪm] *vt*: **to ~ sth at** (*such as gun*) mirare qc a, puntare qc a; (*camera*) rivolgere qc a; (*missile*) lanciare qc contro ♦ *vi* (*also*: **to take ~**) prendere la mira ♦ *n* mira; **to ~ at** mirare; **to ~ to do** aver l'intenzione di fare; **~less** *adj* senza scopo

ain't [eɪnt] (*inf*) = **am not**; **aren't**; **isn't**

air [eə*] *n* aria ♦ *vt* (*room*) arieggiare; (*clothes*) far prendere aria a; (*grievances, ideas*) esprimere pubblicamente ♦ *cpd* (*currents*) d'aria; (*attack*) aereo(a); **to throw sth into the ~** lanciare qc in aria; **by ~** (*travel*) in aereo; **on the ~** (*RADIO, TV*) in onda; **~bed** (*BRIT*) *n* materasso; **~ conditioning** *n* condizionamento d'aria; **~craft** *n inv* apparecchio; **~craft carrier** *n* portaerei *f inv*; **~field** *n* campo d'aviazione; **A~ Force** *n* aviazione *f* militare; **~ freshener** *n* deodorante *m* per ambienti; **~gun** *n* fucile *m* ad aria compressa; **~ hostess** (*BRIT*) *n* hostess *f inv*; **~ letter** (*BRIT*) *n* aerogramma *m*; **~lift** *n* ponte *m* aereo; **~line** *n* linea aerea; **~liner** *n* aereo di linea; **~mail** *n*: **by ~mail** per via aerea; **~ mattress** *n* materasso gonfiabile; **~plane** (*US*) *n* aeroplano; **~port** *n* aeroporto; **~ raid** *n* incursione *f* aerea; **~sick** *adj*: **to be ~sick** soffrire di mal d'aria; **~tight** *adj* ermetico(a); **~ traffic controller** *n* controllore *m* del traffico aereo; **~y** *adj* arioso(a); (*manners*) noncurante

aisle [aɪl] *n* (*of church*) navata laterale; navata centrale; (*of plane*) corridoio; **~ seat** *n* (*on plane*) posto sul corridoio

ajar [ə'dʒɑː*] *adj* socchiuso(a)

alarm [ə'lɑːm] *n* allarme *m* ♦ *vt* allarmare; **~ call** *n* (*in hotel etc*) sveglia; **~ clock** *n* sveglia

alas [ə'læs] *excl* ohimè!, ahimè!

albeit [ɔːl'biːɪt] *conj* sebbene +*sub*, benché +*sub*

album ['ælbəm] *n* album *m inv*

alcohol ['ælkəhɒl] *n* alcool *m*; **~ic** [-'hɒlɪk] *adj* alcolico(a) ♦ *n* alcolizzato/a

ale [eɪl] *n* birra

alert [ə'ləːt] *adj* vigile ♦ *n* allarme *m* ♦ *vt* avvertire; mettere in guardia; **on the ~** all'erta

algebra ['ældʒɪbrə] *n* algebra

alias ['eɪlɪəs] *adv* alias ♦ *n* pseudonimo, falso nome *m*

alibi ['ælɪbaɪ] *n* alibi *m inv*

alien ['eɪlɪən] *n* straniero/a; (*extraterrestrial*) alieno/a ♦ *adj*: **~ (to)** estraneo(a) (a); **~ate** *vt* alienare

alight [ə'laɪt] *adj* acceso(a) ♦ *vi* scendere;

(*bird*) posarsi

alike [ə'laɪk] *adj* simile ♦ *adv* sia ... sia; **to look ~** assomigliarsi

alimony ['ælɪmənɪ] *n* (*payment*) alimenti *mpl*

alive [ə'laɪv] *adj* vivo(a); (*lively*) vivace

┌─────────────┐
│ KEYWORD │
└─────────────┘

all [ɔːl] *adj* tutto(a); **~ day** tutto il giorno; **~ night** tutta la notte; **~ men** tutti gli uomini; **~ five came** sono venuti tutti e cinque; **~ the books** tutti i libri; **~ the food** tutto il cibo; **~ the time** sempre; tutto il tempo; **~ his life** tutta la vita

♦ *pron* **1** tutto(a); **I ate it ~, I ate ~ of it** l'ho mangiato tutto; **~ of us went** tutti noi siamo andati; **~ of the boys went** tutti i ragazzi sono andati

2 (*in phrases*): **above ~** soprattutto; **after ~** dopotutto; **at ~**: **not at ~** (*in answer to question*) niente affatto; (*in answer to thanks*) prego!, di niente!, s'immagini!; **I'm not at ~ tired** non sono affatto stanco(a); **anything at ~ will do** andrà bene qualsiasi cosa; **~ in ~** tutto sommato

♦ *adv*: **~ alone** tutto(a) solo(a); **it's not as hard as ~ that** non è poi così difficile; **~ the more/the better** tanto più/meglio; **~ but** quasi; **the score is two ~** il punteggio è di due a due

allay [ə'leɪ] *vt* (*fears*) dissipare

all clear *n* (*also fig*) segnale *m* di cessato allarme

allegation [ælɪ'geɪʃən] *n* asserzione *f*

allege [ə'ledʒ] *vt* asserire; **~dly** [ə'ledʒɪdlɪ] *adv* secondo quanto si asserisce

allegiance [ə'liːdʒəns] *n* fedeltà

allergic [ə'ləːdʒɪk] *adj*: **~ to** allergico(a) a

allergy ['ælədʒɪ] *n* allergia

alleviate [ə'liːvɪeɪt] *vt* sollevare

alley ['ælɪ] *n* vicolo

alliance [ə'laɪəns] *n* alleanza

allied ['ælaɪd] *adj* alleato(a)

all-in *adj* (*BRIT*: *also adv*: *charge*) tutto compreso

all-night *adj* aperto(a) (*or che dura*) tutta

la notte

allocate ['æləkeɪt] *vt* assegnare

allot [ə'lɒt] *vt* assegnare; **~ment** *n* assegnazione *f*; (*garden*) lotto di terra

all-out *adj* (*effort etc*) totale ♦ *adv*: **to go all out for** mettercela tutta per

allow [ə'lau] *vt* (*practice, behaviour*) permettere; (*sum to spend etc*) accordare; (*sum, time estimated*) dare; (*concede*): **to ~ that** ammettere che; **to ~ sb to do** permettere a qn di fare; **he is ~ed to** lo può fare; **~ for** *vt fus* tener conto di; **~ance** *n* (*money received*) assegno; indennità *f inv*; (*TAX*) detrazione *f* di imposta; **to make ~ances for** tener conto di

alloy ['ælɔɪ] *n* lega

all right *adv* (*feel, work*) bene; (*as answer*) va bene

all-round *adj* completo(a)

all-time *adj* (*record*) assoluto(a)

alluring [ə'ljuərɪŋ] *adj* seducente

ally ['ælaɪ] *n* alleato

almighty [ɔːl'maɪtɪ] *adj* onnipotente; (*row etc*) colossale

almond ['ɑːmənd] *n* mandorla

almost ['ɔːlməust] *adv* quasi

alone [ə'ləun] *adj, adv* solo(a); **to leave sb ~** lasciare qn in pace; **to leave sth ~** lasciare qc; **let ~ ...** figuriamoci poi ..., tanto meno ....

along [ə'lɒŋ] *prep* lungo ♦ *adv*: **is he coming ~?** viene con noi?; **he was limping ~** veniva zoppicando; **~ with** insieme con; **all ~** (*all the time*) sempre, fin dall'inizio; **~side** *prep* accanto a; lungo ♦ *adv* accanto

aloof [ə'luːf] *adj* distaccato(a) ♦ *adv*: **to stand ~** tenersi a distanza *or* in disparte

aloud [ə'laud] *adv* ad alta voce

alphabet ['ælfəbet] *n* alfabeto

alpine ['ælpaɪn] *adj* alpino(a)

Alps [ælps] *npl*: **the ~** le Alpi

already [ɔːl'redɪ] *adv* già

alright ['ɔːl'raɪt] (*BRIT*) *adv* = **all right**

Alsatian [æl'seɪʃən] (*BRIT*) *n* (*dog*) pastore *m* tedesco, (*cane m*) lupo

also ['ɔːlsəu] *adv* anche

altar ['ɔːltə*] *n* altare *m*

alter ['ɔːltə*] *vt, vi* alterare

alternate [*adj* ɔl'təːnɪt, *vb* 'ɔltəːneɪt] *adj* alterno(a); (*US: plan etc*) alternativo(a) ♦ *vi*: **to ~ (with)** alternarsi (a); **on ~ days** ogni due giorni; **alternating** ['ɔltəːneɪtɪŋ] *adj* (*current*) alternato(a)

alternative [ɔl'təːnətɪv] *adj* alternativo(a) ♦ *n* (*choice*) alternativa; **~ly** *adv*: **~ly one could ...** come alternativa si potrebbe ...; **~ medicine** *n* medicina alternativa

alternator ['ɔltəːneɪtə*] *n* (*AUT*) alternatore *m*

although [ɔːl'ðəu] *conj* benché +*sub*, sebbene +*sub*

altitude ['æltɪtjuːd] *n* altitudine *f*

alto ['æltəu] *n* contralto; (*male*) contraltino

altogether [ɔːltə'geðə*] *adv* del tutto, completamente; (*on the whole*) tutto considerato; (*in all*) in tutto

aluminium [ælju'mɪnɪəm] *n* alluminio

aluminum [ə'luːmɪnəm] (*US*) *n* = **aluminium**

always ['ɔːlweɪz] *adv* sempre

Alzheimer's (disease) ['æltshaɪməz-] *n* (malattia di) Alzheimer

am [æm] *vb see* **be**

a.m. *adv abbr* (= *ante meridiem*) della mattina

amalgamate [ə'mælɡəmeɪt] *vt* amalgamare ♦ *vi* amalgamarsi

amateur ['æmətə*] *n* dilettante *m/f* ♦ *adj* (*SPORT*) dilettante; **~ish** (*pej*) *adj* da dilettante

amaze [ə'meɪz] *vt* stupire; **to be ~d (at)** essere sbalordito (da); **~ment** *n* stupore *m*; **amazing** *adj* sorprendente, sbalorditivo(a)

ambassador [æm'bæsədə*] *n* ambasciatore/trice

amber ['æmbə*] *n* ambra; **at ~** (*BRIT: AUT*) giallo

ambiguous [æm'bɪɡjuəs] *adj* ambiguo(a)

ambition [æm'bɪʃən] *n* ambizione *f*

ambitious [æm'bɪʃəs] *adj* ambizioso(a)

ambulance ['æmbjuləns] *n* ambulanza

ambush ['æmbʊʃ] *n* imboscata ♦ *vt* fare un'imboscata a

amenable [ə'mi:nəbl] *adj*: ~ **to** (*advice etc*) ben disposto(a) a

amend [ə'mɛnd] *vt* (*law*) emendare; (*text*) correggere; **to make ~s** fare ammenda

amenities [ə'mi:nɪtɪz] *npl* attrezzature *fpl* ricreative e culturali

America [ə'mɛrɪkə] *n* America; ~**n** *adj, n* americano(a)

amiable ['eɪmɪəbl] *adj* amabile, gentile

amicable ['æmɪkəbl] *adj* amichevole

amid(st) [ə'mɪd(st)] *prep* fra, tra, in mezzo a

amiss [ə'mɪs] *adj, adv*: **there's something ~** c'è qualcosa che non va bene; **don't take it ~** non prendertela (a male)

ammonia [ə'məʊnɪə] *n* ammoniaca

ammunition [æmju'nɪʃən] *n* munizioni *fpl*

amok [ə'mɔk] *adv*: **to run ~** diventare pazzo(a) furioso(a)

among(st) [ə'mʌŋ(st)] *prep* fra, tra, in mezzo a

amorous ['æmərəs] *adj* amoroso(a)

amount [ə'maʊnt] *n* somma; ammontare *m*; quantità *f inv* ♦ *vi*: **to ~ to** (*total*) ammontare a; (*be same as*) essere come

amp(ère) ['æmp(ɛə*)] *n* ampère *m inv*

ample ['æmpl] *adj* ampio(a); spazioso(a); (*enough*): **this is ~** questo è più che sufficiente

amplifier ['æmplɪfaɪə*] *n* amplificatore *m*

amuse [ə'mju:z] *vt* divertire; ~**ment** *n* divertimento; ~**ment arcade** *n* sala giochi; ~**ment park** *n* luna park *m inv*

an [æn] *indef art see* **a**

anaemic [ə'ni:mɪk] *adj* anemico(a)

anaesthetic [ænɪs'θɛtɪk] *adj* anestetico(a) ♦ *n* anestetico

analog(ue) ['ænəlɔg] *adj* (*watch, computer*) analogico(a)

analyse ['ænəlaɪz] (*BRIT*) *vt* analizzare

analysis [ə'nælɪsɪs] (*pl* **analyses**) *n* analisi *f inv*

analyst ['ænəlɪst] *n* (*POL etc*) analista *m/f*; (*US*) (psic)analista *m/f*

analyze ['ænəlaɪz] (*US*) *vt* = **analyse**

anarchy ['ænəkɪ] *n* anarchia

anatomy [ə'nætəmɪ] *n* anatomia

ancestor ['ænsɪstə*] *n* antenato/a

anchor ['æŋkə*] *n* ancora ♦ *vi* (*also*: **to drop ~**) gettare l'ancora ♦ *vt* ancorare; **to weigh ~** salpare *or* levare l'ancora

anchovy ['æntʃəvɪ] *n* acciuga

ancient ['eɪnʃənt] *adj* antico(a); (*person, car*) vecchissimo(a)

ancillary [æn'sɪlərɪ] *adj* ausiliario(a)

and [ænd] *conj* e (*often* ed *before vowel*); ~ **so on** e così via; **try ~ come** cerca di venire; **he talked ~ talked** non la finiva di parlare; **better ~ better** sempre meglio

anemic [ə'ni:mɪk] (*US*) *adj* = **anaemic**

anesthetic [ænɪs'θɛtɪk] (*US*) *adj, n* = **anaesthetic**

anew [ə'nju:] *adv* di nuovo

angel ['eɪndʒəl] *n* angelo

anger ['æŋgə*] *n* rabbia

angina [æn'dʒaɪnə] *n* angina pectoris

angle ['æŋgl] *n* angolo; **from their ~** dal loro punto di vista

Anglican ['æŋglɪkən] *adj, n* anglicano(a)

angling ['æŋglɪŋ] *n* pesca con la lenza

Anglo- ['æŋgləʊ] *prefix* anglo....

angrily ['æŋgrɪlɪ] *adv* con rabbia

angry ['æŋgrɪ] *adj* arrabbiato(a), furioso(a); (*wound*) infiammato(a); **to be ~ with sb/at sth** essere in collera con qn/per qc; **to get ~** arrabbiarsi; **to make sb ~** fare arrabbiare qn

anguish ['æŋgwɪʃ] *n* angoscia

animal ['ænɪməl] *adj* animale ♦ *n* animale *m*

animate ['ænɪmɪt] *adj* animato(a)

animated ['ænɪmeɪtɪd] *adj* animato(a)

aniseed ['ænɪsiːd] *n* semi *mpl* di anice

ankle ['æŋkl] *n* caviglia; ~ **sock** *n* calzino

annex [*n* 'ænɛks, *vb* ə'nɛks] *n* (*also*: *BRIT*: **annexe**) (edificio) annesso ♦ *vt* annettere

anniversary [ænɪ'vɜːsərɪ] *n* anniversario

announce [ə'naʊns] *vt* annunciare; ~**ment** *n* annuncio; (*letter, card*) partecipazione *f*; ~**r** *n* (*RADIO, TV: between programmes*) annunciatore/ trice; (: *in a programme*) presentatore/trice

annoy [ə'nɔɪ] *vt* dare fastidio a; **don't get**

~ed! non irritarti!; **~ance** n fastidio; (*cause of ~ance*) noia; **~ing** adj noioso(a)

annual ['ænjuəl] adj annuale ♦ n (BOT) pianta annua; (*book*) annuario

annul [ə'nʌl] vt annullare

annum ['ænəm] n see **per**

anonymous [ə'nɔnɪməs] adj anonimo(a)

anorak ['ænəræk] n giacca a vento

anorexia [ænə'rɛksɪə] n (MED: also: ~ **nervosa**) anoressia

another [ə'nʌðə*] adj: ~ **book** (*one more*) un altro libro, ancora un libro; (*a different one*) un altro libro ♦ pron un altro(un'altra), ancora uno(a); see also **one**

answer ['ɑːnsə*] n risposta; soluzione f ♦ vi rispondere ♦ vt (*reply to*) rispondere a; (*problem*) risolvere; (*prayer*) esaudire; **in ~ to your letter** in risposta alla sua lettera; **to ~ the phone** rispondere (al telefono); **to ~ the bell** rispondere al campanello; **to ~ the door** aprire la porta; **~ back** vi ribattere; **~ for** vt fus essere responsabile di; **~ to** vt fus (*description*) corrispondere a; **~able** adj: **~able (to sb/for sth)** responsabile (verso qn/di qc); **~ing machine** n segreteria (telefonica) automatica

ant [ænt] n formica

antagonism [æn'tægənɪzəm] n antagonismo

antagonize [æn'tægənaɪz] vt provocare l'ostilità di

Antarctic [ænt'ɑːktɪk] n: **the ~** l'Antartide f

antenatal ['æntɪ'neɪtl] adj prenatale; **~ clinic** n assistenza medica preparto

anthem ['ænθəm] n: **national ~** inno nazionale

antibiotic ['æntɪbaɪ'ɔtɪk] n antibiotico

antibody ['æntɪbɔdɪ] n anticorpo

anticipate [æn'tɪsɪpeɪt] vt prevedere; pregustare; (*wishes, request*) prevenire

anticipation [æntɪsɪ'peɪʃən] n anticipazione f; (*expectation*) aspettativa fpl

anticlimax ['æntɪ'klaɪmæks] n: **it was an ~** fu una completa delusione

anticlockwise ['æntɪ'klɔkwaɪz] adj, adv in senso antiorario

antics ['æntɪks] npl buffonerie fpl

antifreeze ['æntɪ'friːz] n anticongelante m

antihistamine [æntɪ'hɪstəmɪn] n antistaminico

antiquated ['æntɪkweɪtɪd] adj antiquato(a)

antique [æn'tiːk] n antichità f inv ♦ adj antico(a); **~ dealer** n antiquario/a; **~ shop** n negozio d'antichità

anti-Semitism ['æntɪ'semɪtɪzəm] n antisemitismo

antiseptic [æntɪ'septɪk] n antisettico

antisocial ['æntɪ'səuʃəl] adj asociale

antlers ['æntləz] npl palchi mpl

anvil ['ænvɪl] n incudine f

anxiety [æŋ'zaɪətɪ] n ansia; (*keenness*): **~ to do** smania di fare

anxious ['æŋkʃəs] adj ansioso(a), inquieto(a); (*worrying*) angosciante; (*keen*): **~ to do/that** impaziente di fare/che +sub

KEYWORD

any ['enɪ] adj **1** (*in questions etc*): **have you ~ butter?** hai del burro?, hai un po' di burro?; **have you ~ children?** hai bambini?; **if there are ~ tickets left** se ci sono ancora (dei) biglietti, se c'è ancora qualche biglietto

2 (*with negative*): **I haven't ~ money/books** non ho soldi/libri

3 (*no matter which*) qualsiasi, qualunque; **choose ~ book you like** scegli un libro qualsiasi

4 (*in phrases*): **in ~ case** in ogni caso; **~ day now** da un giorno all'altro; **at ~ moment** in qualsiasi momento, da un momento all'altro; **at ~ rate** ad ogni modo

♦ pron **1** (*in questions, with negative*): **have you got ~?** ne hai?; **can ~ of you sing?** qualcuno di voi sa cantare?; **I haven't ~ (of them)** non ne ho

2 (*no matter which one(s)*): **take ~ of those books (you like)** prendi uno qualsiasi di quei libri

♦ adv **1** (*in questions etc*): **do you want ~ more soup/sandwiches?** vuoi ancora un po' di minestra/degli altri panini?; **are you feeling ~ better?** ti senti meglio?

2 (*with negative*): **I can't hear him ~ more**

non lo sento più; **don't wait ~ longer** non aspettate più

anybody ['ɛnɪbɔdɪ] *pron* (*in questions etc*) qualcuno, nessuno; (*with negative*) nessuno; (*no matter who*) chiunque; **can you see ~?** vedi qualcuno *or* nessuno?; **if ~ should phone ...** se telefona qualcuno ...; **I can't see ~** non vedo nessuno; **~ could do it** chiunque potrebbe farlo

anyhow ['ɛnɪhau] *adv* (*at any rate*) ad ogni modo, comunque; (*haphazard*): **do it ~ you like** fallo come ti pare; **I shall go ~** ci andrò lo stesso *or* comunque; **she leaves things just ~** lascia tutto come una capita

anyone ['ɛnɪwʌn] *pron* = **anybody**

anything ['ɛnɪθɪŋ] *pron* (*in question etc*) qualcosa, niente; (*with negative*) niente; (*no matter what*): **you can say ~ you like** puoi dire quello che ti pare; **can you see ~?** vedi niente *or* qualcosa?; **if ~ happens to me ...** se mi dovesse succedere qualcosa ...; **I can't see ~** non vedo niente; **~ will do** va bene qualsiasi cosa *or* tutto

anyway ['ɛnɪweɪ] *adv* (*at any rate*) ad ogni modo, comunque; (*besides*) ad ogni modo

anywhere ['ɛnɪwɛə*] *adv* (*in questions etc*) da qualche parte; (*with negative*) da nessuna parte; (*no matter where*) da qualsiasi *or* qualunque parte, dovunque; **can you see him ~?** lo vedi da qualche parte?; **I can't see him ~** non lo vedo da nessuna parte; **~ in the world** dovunque nel mondo

apart [ə'pɑːt] *adv* (*to one side*) a parte; (*separately*) separatamente; **with one's legs ~** con le gambe divaricate; **10 miles ~** a 10 miglia di distanza (l'uno dall'altro); **to take ~** smontare; **~ from** a parte, eccetto

apartheid [ə'pɑːteɪt] *n* apartheid *f*

apartment [ə'pɑːtmənt] *n* (*US*) appartamento; (*room*) locale *m*; **~ building** (*US*) *n* stabile *m*, caseggiato

ape [eɪp] *n* scimmia ♦ *vt* scimmiottare

apéritif [ə'pɛrɪtv] *n* aperitivo

aperture ['æpətʃjuə*] *n* apertura

APEX *n abbr* (= *advance purchase*

excursion) APEX *m inv*

apologetic [əpɔlə'dʒɛtɪk] *adj* (*tone, letter*) di scusa

apologize [ə'pɔlədʒaɪz] *vi*: **to ~ (for sth to sb)** scusarsi (di qc a qn), chiedere scusa (a qn per qc)

apology [ə'pɔlədʒɪ] *n* scuse *fpl*

apostle [ə'pɔsl] *n* apostolo

apostrophe [ə'pɔstrəfɪ] *n* (*sign*) apostrofo

appal [ə'pɔːl] *vt* scioccare; **~ling** *adj* spaventoso(a)

apparatus [æpə'reɪtəs] *n* apparato; (*in gymnasium*) attrezzatura

apparel [ə'pærl] (*US*) *n* abbigliamento, confezioni *fpl*

apparent [ə'pærənt] *adj* evidente; **~ly** *adv* evidentemente

appeal [ə'piːl] *vi* (*LAW*) appellarsi alla legge ♦ *n* (*LAW*) appello; (*request*) richiesta; (*charm*) attrattiva; **to ~ for** chiedere (con insistenza); **to ~ to** (*subj: person*) appellarsi a; (*subj: thing*) piacere a; **it doesn't ~ to me** mi dice poco; **~ing** *adj* (*nice*) attraente

appear [ə'pɪə*] *vi* apparire; (*LAW*) comparire; (*publication*) essere pubblicato(a); (*seem*) sembrare; **it would ~ that** sembra che; **~ance** *n* apparizione *f*; apparenza *f*; (*look, aspect*) aspetto

appease [ə'piːz] *vt* calmare, appagare

appendicitis [əpendɪ'saɪtɪs] *n* appendicite *f*

appendix [ə'pendɪks] (*pl* **appendices**) *n* appendice *f*

appetite ['æpɪtaɪt] *n* appetito

appetizer ['æpɪtaɪzə*] *n* stuzzichino

applaud [ə'plɔːd] *vt, vi* applaudire

applause [ə'plɔːz] *n* applauso

apple ['æpl] *n* mela; **~ tree** *n* melo

appliance [ə'plaɪəns] *n* apparecchio

applicant ['æplɪkənt] *n* candidato/a

application [æplɪ'keɪʃən] *n* applicazione *f*; (*for a job, a grant etc*) domanda; **~ form** *n* modulo per la domanda

applied [ə'plaɪd] *adj* applicato(a)

apply [ə'plaɪ] *vt*: **to ~ (to)** (*paint, ointment*) dare (a); (*theory, technique*) applicare (a) ♦ *vi*: **to ~ to** (*ask*) rivolgersi a; (*be suitable for, relevant to*) riguardare, riferirsi a; **to ~**

(for) (*permit, grant, job*) fare domanda (per); **to ~ o.s. to** dedicarsi a

appoint [ə'pɔɪnt] *vt* nominare; **~ed** *adj*: **at the ~ed time** all'ora stabilita; **~ment** *n* nomina; (*arrangement to meet*) appuntamento; **to make an ~ment (with)** prendere un appuntamento (con)

appraisal [ə'preɪzl] *n* valutazione *f*

appreciate [ə'priːʃɪeɪt] *vt* (*like*) apprezzare; (*be grateful for*) essere riconoscente di; (*be aware of*) rendersi conto di ♦ *vi* (FINANCE) aumentare; **I'd ~ your help** ti sono grato per l'aiuto

appreciation [əpriːʃɪ'eɪʃən] *n* apprezzamento; (FINANCE) aumento del valore

appreciative [ə'priːʃɪətɪv] *adj* (*person*) sensibile; (*comment*) elogiativo(a)

apprehend [æprɪ'hɛnd] *vt* (*arrest*) arrestare

apprehension [æprɪ'hɛnʃən] *n* (*fear*) inquietudine *f*

apprehensive [æprɪ'hɛnsɪv] *adj* apprensivo(a)

apprentice [ə'prɛntɪs] *n* apprendista *m/f*; **~ship** *n* apprendistato

approach [ə'prəutʃ] *vi* avvicinarsi ♦ *vt* (*come near*) avvicinarsi a; (*ask, apply to*) rivolgersi a; (*subject, passer-by*) avvicinare ♦ *n* approccio; accesso; (*to problem*) modo di affrontare; **~able** *adj* accessibile

appropriate [*adj* ə'prəuprɪɪt, *vb* ə'prəuprɪeɪt] *adj* appropriato(a); adatto(a) ♦ *vt* (*take*) appropriarsi

approval [ə'pruːvəl] *n* approvazione *f*; **on ~** (COMM) in prova, in esame

approve [ə'pruːv] *vt, vi* approvare; **~ of** *vt fus* approvare

approximate [ə'prɔksɪmɪt] *adj* approssimativo(a); **~ly** *adv* circa

apricot ['eɪprɪkɔt] *n* albicocca

April ['eɪprəl] *n* aprile *m*; **~ fool!** pesce d'aprile!

i **April Fool's Day** è il primo aprile, il giorno degli scherzi e delle burle. Il nome deriva dal fatto che, se una persona cade nella trappola che gli è stata tesa, fa la figura del **fool**, cioè dello sciocco.

apron ['eɪprən] *n* grembiule *m*

apt [æpt] *adj* (*suitable*) adatto(a); (*able*) capace; (*likely*): **to be ~ to do** avere tendenza a fare

aquarium [ə'kwɛərɪəm] *n* acquario

Aquarius [ə'kwɛərɪəs] *n* Acquario

Arab ['ærəb] *adj, n* arabo(a)

Arabian [ə'reɪbɪən] *adj* arabo(a)

Arabic ['ærəbɪk] *adj* arabico(a), arabo(a) ♦ *n* arabo; **~ numerals** numeri *mpl* arabi

arbitrary ['ɑːbɪtrərɪ] *adj* arbitrario(a)

arbitration [ɑːbɪ'treɪʃən] *n* (LAW) arbitrato; (INDUSTRY) arbitraggio

arcade [ɑː'keɪd] *n* portico, (*passage with shops*) galleria

arch [ɑːtʃ] *n* arco; (*of foot*) arco plantare ♦ *vt* inarcare

archaeologist [ɑːkɪ'ɔlədʒɪst] *n* archeologo/a

archaeology [ɑːkɪ'ɔlədʒɪ] *n* archeologia

archbishop [ɑːtʃ'bɪʃəp] *n* arcivescovo

archeology [ɑːkɪ'ɔlədʒɪ] *etc* (US) = **archaeology** *etc*

archery ['ɑːtʃərɪ] *n* tiro all'arco

architect ['ɑːkɪtɛkt] *n* architetto; **~ure** ['ɑːkɪtɛktʃə*] *n* architettura

archives ['ɑːkaɪvz] *npl* archivi *mpl*

Arctic ['ɑːktɪk] *adj* artico(a) ♦ *n* **the ~** l'Artico

ardent ['ɑːdənt] *adj* ardente

are [ɑː*] *vb see* **be**; **~n't** [ɑːnt] = **~ not**

area ['ɛərɪə] *n* (GEOM) area; (*zone*) zona; (: *smaller*) settore *m*

Argentina [ɑːdʒən'tiːnə] *n* Argentina; **Argentinian** [-'tɪnɪən] *adj, n* argentino(a)

arguably ['ɑːgjuəblɪ] *adv*: **it is ~ ...** si può sostenere che sia ....

argue ['ɑːgjuː] *vi* (*quarrel*) litigare; (*reason*) ragionare; **to ~ that** sostenere che

argument ['ɑːgjumənt] *n* (*reasons*) argomento; (*quarrel*) lite *f*; **~ative** [ɑːgju'mɛntətɪv] *adj* litigioso(a)

Aries ['ɛərɪz] *n* Ariete *m*

arise [ə'raɪz] (*pt* **arose**, *pp* **arisen**) *vi* (*opportunity, problem*) presentarsi

aristocrat ['ærɪstəkræt] n aristocratico/a
arithmetic [ə'rɪθmətɪk] n aritmetica
ark [ɑːk] n: **Noah's A~** l'arca di Noè
arm [ɑːm] n braccio ♦ vt armare; **~s** npl
(weapons) armi fpl; **~ in ~** a braccetto
armaments ['ɑːməmənts] npl armamenti
mpl
arm: **~chair** n poltrona; **~ed** adj
armato(a); **~ed robbery** n rapina a mano
armata
armour ['ɑːmə*] (US **armor**) n armatura;
(MIL: tanks) mezzi mpl blindati; **~ed car** n
autoblinda f inv
armpit ['ɑːmpɪt] n ascella
armrest ['ɑːmrest] n bracciolo
army ['ɑːmɪ] n esercito
aroma [ə'rəumə] n aroma; **~therapy** n
aromaterapia
arose [ə'rəuz] pt of **arise**
around [ə'raund] adv attorno, intorno
♦ prep intorno a; (fig: about): **~ £5/**
3 o'clock circa 5 sterline/le 3; **is he ~?** è in
giro?
arouse [ə'rauz] vt (sleeper) svegliare;
(curiosity, passions) suscitare
arrange [ə'reɪndʒ] vt sistemare;
(programme) preparare; **to ~ to do sth**
mettersi d'accordo per fare qc; **~ment** n
sistemazione f; (agreement) accordo;
~ments npl (plans) progetti mpl, piani mpl
array [ə'reɪ] n: **~ of** fila di
arrears [ə'rɪəz] npl arretrati mpl; **to be in ~**
with one's rent essere in arretrato con
l'affitto
arrest [ə'rest] vt arrestare; (sb's attention)
attirare ♦ n arresto; **under ~** in arresto
arrival [ə'raɪvəl] n arrivo; (person) arrivato/a;
a new ~ un nuovo venuto; (baby) un
neonato
arrive [ə'raɪv] vi arrivare
arrogant ['ærəgənt] adj arrogante
arrow ['ærəu] n freccia
arse [ɑːs] (infl) n culo (!)
arson ['ɑːsn] n incendio doloso
art [ɑːt] n arte f; (craft) mestiere m; **A~s** npl
(SCOL) Lettere fpl
artery ['ɑːtərɪ] n arteria

art gallery n galleria d'arte
arthritis [ɑː'θraɪtɪs] n artrite f
artichoke ['ɑːtɪtʃəuk] n carciofo; **Jerusalem**
~ topinambur m inv
article ['ɑːtɪkl] n articolo; **~s** npl (BRIT: LAW:
training) contratto di tirocinio; **~ of**
clothing capo di vestiario
articulate [adj ɑː'tɪkjulɪt, vb ɑː'tɪkjuleɪt] adj
(person) che si esprime forbitamente;
(speech) articolato(a) ♦ vi articolare; **~d**
lorry (BRIT) n autotreno
artificial [ɑːtɪ'fɪʃəl] adj artificiale; **~**
respiration n respirazione f artificiale
artist ['ɑːtɪst] n artista m/f; **~ic** [ɑː'tɪstɪk] adj
artistico(a); **~ry** n arte f
art school n scuola d'arte

KEYWORD

as [æz] conj 1 (referring to time) mentre; **~**
the years went by col passare degli anni;
he came in ~ I was leaving arrivò mentre
stavo uscendo; **~ from tomorrow** da
domani
2 (in comparisons): **~ big ~** grande come;
twice ~ big ~ due volte più grande di; **~**
much/many ~ tanto quanto/tanti quanti;
~ soon ~ possible prima possibile
3 (since, because) dal momento che,
siccome
4 (referring to manner, way) come; **do ~**
you wish fa' come vuoi; **~ she said** come
ha detto lei
5 (concerning): **~ for or to that** per quanto
riguarda or quanto a quello
6: **~ if or though** come se; **he looked ~ if**
he was ill sembrava stare male; see also
long; such; well
♦ prep: **he works ~ a driver** fa l'autista; **~**
chairman of the company, he ... come
presidente della compagnia, lui ...; **he**
gave me it ~ a present me lo ha regalato

a.s.a.p. abbr = **as soon as possible**
ascend [ə'send] vt salire
ascertain [æsə'teɪn] vt accertare
ash [æʃ] n (dust) cenere f; (wood, tree)
frassino

ashamed [ə'feɪmd] *adj* vergognoso(a); **to be ~ of** vergognarsi di

ashore [ə'ʃɔ:*] *adv* a terra

ashtray ['æʃtreɪ] *n* portacenere *m*

Ash Wednesday *n* mercoledì *m inv* delle Ceneri

Asia ['eɪʃə] *n* Asia; **~n** *adj*, *n* asiatico(a)

aside [ə'saɪd] *adv* da parte ♦ *n* a parte *m*

ask [ɑ:sk] *vt* (*question*) domandare; (*invite*) invitare; **to ~ sb sth/sb to do sth** chiedere qc a qn/a qn di fare qc; **to ~ sb about sth** chiedere a qn di qc; **to ~ (sb) a question** fare una domanda (a qn); **to ~ sb out to dinner** invitare qn a mangiare fuori; **~ after** *vt fus* chiedere di; **~ for** *vt fus* chiedere; (*trouble etc*) cercare

asleep [ə'sli:p] *adj* addormentato(a); **to be ~** dormire; **to fall ~** addormentarsi

asparagus [əs'pærəgəs] *n* asparagi *mpl*

aspect ['æspekt] *n* aspetto

aspersions [əs'pə:ʃənz] *npl*: **to cast ~ on** diffamare

asphyxiation [æsfɪksɪ'eɪʃən] *n* asfissia

aspire [əs'paɪə*] *vi*: **to ~ to** aspirare a

aspirin ['æsprɪn] *n* aspirina

ass [æs] *n* asino; (*inf*) scemo/a; (*US: inf!*) culo (*!*)

assailant [ə'seɪlənt] *n* assalitore *m*

assassinate [ə'sæsɪneɪt] *vt* assassinare; **assassination** [əsæsɪ'neɪʃən] *n* assassinio

assault [ə'sɔ:lt] *n* (*MIL*) assalto; (*gen: attack*) aggressione / ♦ *vt* assaltare; aggredire; (*sexually*) violentare

assemble [ə'sembl] *vt* riunire; (*TECH*) montare ♦ *vi* riunirsi

assembly [ə'semblɪ] *n* (*meeting*) assemblea; (*construction*) montaggio; **~ line** *n* catena di montaggio

assent [ə'sent] *n* assenso, consenso

assert [ə'sə:t] *vt* asserire; (*insist on*) far valere

assess [ə'ses] *vt* valutare; **~ment** *n* valutazione *f*

asset ['æset] *n* vantaggio; **~s** *npl* (*FINANCE: of individual*) beni *mpl*; (: *of company*) attivo

assign [ə'saɪn] *vt*: **to ~ (to)** (*task*) assegnare

(a); (*resources*) riservare (a); (*cause, meaning*) attribuire (a); **to ~ a date to sth** fissare la data di qc; **~ment** *n* compito

assist [ə'sɪst] *vt* assistere, aiutare; **~ance** *n* assistenza, aiuto; **~ant** *n* assistente *m/f*; (*BRIT: also: shop ~ant*) commesso/a

associate [*adj, n* ə'səʊʃɪɪt, *vb* ə'səʊʃɪeɪt] *adj* associato(a); (*member*) aggiunto(a) ♦ *n* collega *m/f* ♦ *vt* associare ♦ *vi*: **to ~ with sb** frequentare qn

association [əsəʊsɪ'eɪʃən] *n* associazione *f*

assorted [ə'sɔ:tɪd] *adj* assortito(a)

assortment [ə'sɔ:tmənt] *n* assortimento

assume [ə'sju:m] *vt* supporre; (*responsibilities etc*) assumere; (*attitude, name*) prendere

assumption [ə'sʌmpʃən] *n* supposizione *f*, ipotesi *f inv*; (*of power*) assunzione *f*

assurance [ə'ʃʊərəns] *n* assicurazione *f*; (*self-confidence*) fiducia in se stesso

assure [ə'ʃʊə*] *vt* assicurare

asthma ['æsmə] *n* asma

astonish [ə'stɒnɪʃ] *vt* stupire; **~ment** *n* stupore *m*

astound [ə'staʊnd] *vt* sbalordire

astray [ə'streɪ] *adv*: **to go ~** smarrirsi; **to lead ~** portare sulla cattiva strada

astride [ə'straɪd] *prep* a cavalcioni di

astrology [əs'trɒlədʒɪ] *n* astrologia

astronaut ['æstrənɔ:t] *n* astronauta *m/f*

astronomy [əs'trɒnəmɪ] *n* astronomia

asylum [ə'saɪləm] *n* asilo; (*building*) manicomio

KEYWORD

---

at [æt] *prep* **1** (*referring to position, direction*) a; **~ the top** in cima; **~ the desk** al banco, alla scrivania; **~ home/school** a casa/ scuola; **~ the baker's** dal panettiere; **to look ~ sth** guardare qc; **to throw sth ~ sb** lanciare qc a qn

2 (*referring to time*) a; **~ 4 o'clock** alle 4; **~ night** di notte; **~ Christmas** a Natale; **~ times** a volte

3 (*referring to rates, speed etc*) a; **~ £1 a kilo** a 1 sterlina al chilo; **two ~ a time** due alla volta, due per volta; **~ 50 km/h** a

50 km/h

4 (*referring to manner*): ~ **a stroke** d'un solo colpo; ~ **peace** in pace

5 (*referring to activity*): **to be ~ work** essere al lavoro; **to play ~ cowboys** giocare ai cowboy; **to be good ~ sth/doing sth** essere bravo in qc/a fare qc

6 (*referring to cause*): **shocked/ surprised/annoyed ~ sth** colpito da/ sorpreso da/arrabbiato per qc; **I went ~ his suggestion** ci sono andato dietro suo consiglio

ate [eɪt] *pt of* **eat**

atheist ['eɪθɪɪst] *n* ateo/a

Athens ['æθɪnz] *n* Atene *f*

athlete ['æθliːt] *n* atleta *m/f*

athletic [æθ'lɛtɪk] *adj* atletico(a); **~s** *n* atletica

Atlantic [ət'læntɪk] *adj* atlantico(a) ♦ *n*: **the ~ (Ocean)** l'Atlantico, l'Oceano Atlantico

atlas ['ætləs] *n* atlante *m*

ATM *n abbr* (= *automated telling machine*) cassa automatica prelievi, sportello automatico

atmosphere ['ætməsfɪə*] *n* atmosfera

atom ['ætəm] *n* atomo; **~ic** [ə'tɒmɪk] *adj* atomico(a); **~(ic) bomb** *n* bomba atomica; **~izer** ['ætəmaɪzə*] *n* atomizzatore *m*

atone [ə'təʊn] *vi*: **to ~ for** espiare

atrocious [ə'trəʊʃəs] *adj* pessimo(a), atroce

attach [ə'tætʃ] *vt* attaccare; (*document, letter*) allegare; (*importance etc*) attribuire; **to be ~ed to sb/sth** (*to like*) essere affezionato(a) a qn/qc

attaché case [ə'tæʃeɪ-] *n* valigetta per documenti

attachment [ə'tætʃmənt] *n* (*tool*) accessorio; (*love*): ~ **(to)** affetto (per)

attack [ə'tæk] *vt* attaccare; (*person*) aggredire; (*task etc*) iniziare; (*problem*) affrontare ♦ *n* attacco; **heart ~** infarto; **~er** *n* aggressore *m*

attain [ə'teɪn] *vt* (*also*: **to ~ to**) arrivare a, raggiungere

attempt [ə'tɛmpt] *n* tentativo ♦ *vt* tentare;

to make an ~ on sb's life attentare alla vita di qn

attend [ə'tɛnd] *vt* frequentare; (*meeting, talk*) andare a; (*patient*) assistere; ~ **to** *vt fus* (*needs, affairs etc*) prendersi cura di; (*customer*) occuparsi di; **~ance** *n* (*being present*) presenza; (*people present*) gente *f* presente; **~ant** *n* custode *m/f*; persona di servizio ♦ *adj* concomitante

attention [ə'tɛnʃən] *n* attenzione *f* ♦ *excl* (*MIL*) attenti!; **for the ~ of** (*ADMIN*) per l'attenzione di

attentive [ə'tɛntɪv] *adj* attento(a); (*kind*) premuroso(a)

attic ['ætɪk] *n* soffitta

attitude ['ætɪtjuːd] *n* atteggiamento; posa

attorney [ə'tɜːnɪ] *n* (*lawyer*) avvocato; (*having proxy*) mandatario; **A~ General** *n* (*BRIT*) Procuratore *m* Generale; (*US*) Ministro della Giustizia

attract [ə'trækt] *vt* attirare; **~ion** [ə'trækʃən] *n* (*gen pl: pleasant things*) attrattiva; (*PHYSICS, fig: towards sth*) attrazione *f*; **~ive** *adj* attraente

attribute [*n* 'ætrɪbjuːt, *vb* ə'trɪbjuːt] *n* attributo ♦ *vt*: **to ~ sth to** attribuire qc a

attrition [ə'trɪʃən] *n*: **war of ~** guerra di logoramento

aubergine ['əʊbəʒiːn] *n* melanzana

auburn ['ɔːbən] *adj* tizianesco(a)

auction ['ɔːkʃən] *n* (*also*: **sale by ~**) asta ♦ *vt* (*also*: **to sell by ~**) vendere all'asta; (*also*: **to put up for ~**) mettere all'asta; **~eer** [-'nɪə*] *n* banditore *m*

audible ['ɔːdɪbl] *adj* udibile

audience ['ɔːdɪəns] *n* (*people*) pubblico; spettatori *mpl*; ascoltatori *mpl*; (*interview*) udienza

audio-typist ['ɔːdɪəʊ'taɪpɪst] *n* dattilografo/a che trascrive da nastro

audio-visual [ɔːdɪəʊ'vɪzjuəl] *adj* audiovisivo(a); ~ **aid** *n* sussidio audiovisivo

audit ['ɔːdɪt] *vt* rivedere, verificare

audition [ɔː'dɪʃən] *n* audizione *f*

auditor ['ɔːdɪtə*] *n* revisore *m*

augment [ɔːg'mɛnt] *vt, vi* aumentare

augur ['ɔːgə*] *vi*: **it ~s well** promette bene

August ['ɔːgəst] n agosto
aunt [ɑːnt] n zia; **~ie** or **~y** n zietta
au pair ['əu'peə*] n (also: **~ girl**) (ragazza f)
   alla pari inv
auspicious [ɔːs'pɪʃəs] adj propizio(a)
Australia [ɔs'treɪlɪə] n Australia; **~n** adj, n
   australiano(a)
Austria ['ɔstrɪə] n Austria; **~n** adj, n
   austriaco(a)
authentic [ɔː'θentɪk] adj autentico(a)
author ['ɔːθə*] n autore/trice
authoritarian [ɔːθɔrɪ'teərɪən] adj
   autoritario(a)
authoritative [ɔː'θɔrɪtətɪv] adj (account etc)
   autorevole; (manner) autoritario(a)
authority [ɔː'θɔrɪtɪ] n autorità f inv;
   (permission) autorizzazione f; **the**
   authorities npl (government etc) le autorità
authorize ['ɔːθəraɪz] vt autorizzare
auto ['ɔːtəu] (US) n auto f inv
autobiography [ɔːtəbaɪ'ɔgrəfɪ] n
   autobiografia
autograph ['ɔːtəgrɑːf] n autografo ♦ vt
   firmare
automatic [ɔːtə'mætɪk] adj automatico(a)
   ♦ n (gun) arma automatica; (washing
   machine) lavatrice f automatica; (car)
   automobile f con cambio automatico;
   ~ally adv automaticamente
automation [ɔːtə'meɪʃən] n automazione f
automobile ['ɔːtəməbiːl] (US) n automobile
   f
autonomy [ɔː'tɔnəmɪ] n autonomia
autumn ['ɔːtəm] n autunno
auxiliary [ɔːg'zɪlɪərɪ] adj ausiliario(a) ♦ n
   ausiliare m/f
Av. abbr = **avenue**
avail [ə'veɪl] vt: **to ~ o.s. of** servirsi di;
   approfittarsi di ♦ n: **to no ~** inutilmente
available [ə'veɪləbl] adj disponibile
avalanche ['ævəlɑːnʃ] n valanga
avant-garde ['ævɑ̃'gɑːd] adj
   d'avanguardia
Ave. abbr = **avenue**
avenge [ə'vendʒ] vt vendicare
avenue ['ævənjuː] n viale m; (fig) strada, via
average ['ævərɪdʒ] n media ♦ adj medio(a)

♦ vt (a certain figure) fare di or in media;
on ~ in media; **~ out** vi: **to ~ out at**
   aggirarsi in media su, essere in media di
averse [ə'vɜːs] adj: **to be ~ to sth/doing**
   essere contrario a qc/a fare
avert [ə'vɜːt] vt evitare, prevenire; (one's
   eyes) distogliere
aviary ['eɪvɪərɪ] n voliera, uccelliera
avid ['ævɪd] adj (supporter etc) accanito(a)
avocado [ævə'kɑːdəu] n (also: BRIT: **~ pear**)
   avocado m inv
avoid [ə'vɔɪd] vt evitare
await [ə'weɪt] vt aspettare
awake [ə'weɪk] (pt **awoke**, pp **awoken**,
   awaked) adj sveglio(a) ♦ vt svegliare ♦ vi
   svegliarsi; **~ning** [ə'weɪknɪŋ] n risveglio
award [ə'wɔːd] n premio; (LAW) risarcimento
   ♦ vt assegnare; (LAW: damages) accordare
aware [ə'weə*] adj: **~ of** (conscious)
   conscio(a) di; (informed) informato(a) di; **to**
   become ~ of accorgersi di; **~ness** n
   consapevolezza
away [ə'weɪ] adj, adv vla; lontano(a); **two**
   kilometres ~ a due chilometri di distanza;
   two hours ~ by car a due ore di distanza
   in macchina; **the holiday was two weeks**
   ~ mancavano due settimane alle vacanze;
   he's ~ for a week è andato via per una
   settimana; **to take ~** togliere; **he was**
   working/pedalling etc la particella
   indica la continuità e l'energia dell'azione.
   lavorava/pedalava etc più che poteva; **to**
   fade/wither etc **~** la particella rinforza
   l'idea della diminuzione; **~ game** n
   (SPORT) partita fuori casa
awe [ɔː] n timore m; **~-inspiring**
   imponente; **~some** adj imponente
awful ['ɔːfəl] adj terribile; **an ~ lot of** un
   mucchio di; **~ly** adv (very) terribilmente
awkward ['ɔːkwəd] adj (clumsy) goffo(a);
   (inconvenient) scomodo(a); (embarrassing)
   imbarazzante
awning ['ɔːnɪŋ] n (of shop, hotel etc) tenda
awoke [ə'wəuk] pt of **awake**
awoken [ə'wəukn] pp of **awake**
awry [ə'raɪ] adv di traverso
axe [æks] (US **ax**) n scure f ♦ vt (project etc)

abolire; (*jobs*) sopprimere

axes ['æksiːz] *npl of* **axis**

axis ['æksɪs] (*pl* **axes**) *n* asse *m*

axle ['æksl] *n* (*also*: ~**-tree**) asse *m*

ay(e) [aɪ] *excl* (*yes*) sì

B, b

B [biː] *n* (*MUS*) si *m*; (*letter*) B, b *f or m inv*; ~**-road** *n* (*BRIT*: *AUT*) strada secondaria

B.A. *n abbr* = **Bachelor of Arts**

baby ['beɪbɪ] *n* bambino/a; ~ **carriage** (*US*) *n* carrozzina; ~ **food** *n* omogeneizzati *mpl*; ~**-sit** *vi* fare il (*or* la) baby-sitter; ~**-sitter** *n* baby-sitter *m/f inv*; ~**-sitting** *n*: **to go** ~**-sitting** fare il (*or* la) baby-sitter; ~ **wipe** *n* salvietta umidificata

bachelor ['bætʃələ*] *n* scapolo; **B~ of Arts/ Science** ≈ laureato/a in lettere/scienze

back [bæk] *n* (*of person, horse*) dorso, schiena; (*as opposed to front*) dietro; (*of hand*) dorso; (*of train*) coda; (*of chair*) schienale *m*; (*of page*) rovescio; (*of book*) retro; (*FOOTBALL*) difensore *m* ♦ *vt* (*candidate: also*: ~ **up**) appoggiare; (*horse: at races*) puntare su; (*car*) guidare a marcia indietro ♦ *vi* indietreggiare; (*car etc*) fare marcia indietro ♦ *cpd* posteriore, di dietro; (*AUT*: *seat, wheels*) posteriore ♦ *adv* (*not forward*) indietro; (*returned*): **he's** ~ è tornato; **he ran** ~ tornò indietro di corsa; (*restitution*): **throw the ball** ~ ritira la palla; **can I have it** ~? posso riaverlo?; (*again*): **he called** ~ ha richiamato; ~ **down** *vi* fare marcia indietro; ~ **out** *vi* (*of promise*) tirarsi indietro; ~ **up** *vt* (*support*) appoggiare, sostenere; (*COMPUT*) fare una copia di riserva di; ~**bencher** (*BRIT*) *n membro del Parlamento senza potere amministrativo*; ~**bone** *n* spina dorsale; ~**date** *vt* (*letter*) retrodatare; ~**dated pay rise** aumento retroattivo; ~**fire** *vi* (*AUT*) dar ritorni di fiamma; (*plans*) fallire; ~**ground** *n* sfondo; (*of events*) background *m inv*; (*basic knowledge*) base *f*; (*experience*) esperienza; **family** ~**ground** ambiente *m* familiare;

~**hand** *n* (*TENNIS*: *also*: ~**hand stroke**) rovescio; ~**handed** *adj* (*fig*) ambiguo(a); ~**hander** (*BRIT*) *n* (*bribe*) bustarella; ~**ing** *n* (*fig*) appoggio; ~**lash** *n* contraccolpo, ripercussione *f*; ~**log** *n*: ~**log of work** lavoro arretrato; ~ **number** *n* (*of magazine etc*) numero arretrato; ~**pack** *n* zaino; ~**packer** *n* chi viaggia con zaino e sacco a pelo; ~ **pay** *n* arretrato di paga; ~ **payments** *npl* arretrati *mpl*; ~**side** (*inf*) *n* sedere *m*; ~**stage** *adv* nel retroscena; ~**stroke** *n* nuoto sul dorso; ~**up** *adj* (*train, plane*) supplementare; (*COMPUT*) di riserva ♦ *n* (*support*) appoggio, sostegno; (*also*: ~**up file**) file *m inv* di riserva; ~**ward** *adj* (*movement*) indietro *inv*; (*person*) tardivo(a); (*country*) arretrato(a); ~**wards** *adv* indietro; (*fall, walk*) all'indietro; ~**yard** *n* cortile *m* dietro la casa

bacon ['beɪkən] *n* pancetta

bad [bæd] *adj* cattivo(a); (*accident, injury*) brutto(a); (*meat, food*) andato(a) a male; **his** ~ **leg** la sua gamba malata; **to go** ~ andare a male

badge [bædʒ] *n* insegna; (*of policeman*) stemma *m*

badger ['bædʒə*] *n* tasso

badly ['bædlɪ] *adv* (*work, dress etc*) male; ~ **wounded** gravemente ferito; **he needs it** ~ ne ha un gran bisogno; ~ **off** *adj* povero(a)

badminton ['bædmɪntən] *n* badminton *m*

bad-tempered ['bæd'tɛmpəd] *adj* irritabile; di malumore

baffle ['bæfl] *vt* (*puzzle*) confondere

bag [bæg] *n* sacco; (*handbag etc*) borsa; ~**s of** (*inf*: *lots of*) un sacco di; ~**gage** *n* bagagli *mpl*; ~**gage allowance** *n* franchigia *f* bagaglio *inv*; ~**gage reclaim** *n* ritiro *m* bagaglio *inv*; ~**gy** *adj* largo(a), sformato(a); ~**pipes** *npl* cornamusa

bail [beɪl] *n* cauzione *f* ♦ *vt* (*prisoner: also*: **grant ~ to**) concedere la libertà provvisoria su cauzione a; (*boat: also*: ~ **out**) aggottare; **on** ~ in libertà provvisoria su cauzione; ~ **out** *vt* (*prisoner*) ottenere la libertà provvisoria su cauzione di; *see also* **bale**

bailiff ['beɪlɪf] n (LAW: BRIT) ufficiale m giudiziario; (: US) usciere m

bait [beɪt] n esca ♦ vt (hook) innescare; (trap) munire di esca; (fig) tormentare

bake [beɪk] vt cuocere al forno ♦ vi cuocersi al forno; ~d beans npl fagioli mpl in salsa di pomodoro; ~d potato npl patata cotta al forno con la buccia; ~r n fornaio/a, panettiere/a; ~ry n panetteria; **baking** n cottura (al forno); **baking powder** n lievito in polvere

balance ['bæləns] n equilibrio; (COMM: sum) bilancio; (remainder) resto; (scales) bilancia ♦ vt tenere in equilibrio; (budget) far quadrare; (account) pareggiare; (compensate) contrappesare; ~ **of trade/payments** bilancia commerciale/dei pagamenti; ~d adj (personality, diet) equilibrato(a); ~ **sheet** n bilancio

balcony ['bælkənɪ] n balcone m; (in theatre) balconata

bald [bɔːld] adj calvo(a); (tyre) liscio(a)

bale [beɪl] n balla, ~ **out** vi (of a plane) gettarsi col paracadute

ball [bɔːl] n palla; (football) pallone m; (for golf) pallina; (of wool, string) gomitolo; (dance) ballo; **to play** ~ (fig) stare al gioco

ballast ['bæləst] n zavorra

ball bearings npl cuscinetti a sfere

ballerina [bælə'riːnə] n ballerina

ballet ['bæleɪ] n balletto; ~ **dancer** n ballerino(a) classico(a)

balloon [bə'luːn] n pallone m

ballot paper ['bælət-] n scheda

ball-point pen n penna a sfera

ballroom ['bɔːlrum] n sala da ballo

balm [bɑːm] n balsamo

ban [bæn] n interdizione f ♦ vt interdire

banana [bə'nɑːnə] n banana

band [bænd] n banda; (at a dance) orchestra; (MIL) fanfara; ~ **together** vi collegarsi

bandage ['bændɪdʒ] n benda, fascia

Bandaid ® ['bændeɪd] (US) n cerotto

bandy-legged [-'legɪd] adj dalle gambe storte

bang [bæŋ] n (of door) lo sbattere; (of gun,

blow) colpo ♦ vt battere (violentemente); (door) sbattere ♦ vi scoppiare; sbattere

Bangladesh [bɑːŋglə'deʃ] n Bangladesh m

bangle ['bæŋgl] n braccialetto

bangs [bæŋz] (US) npl (fringe) frangia, frangetta

banish ['bænɪʃ] vt bandire

banister(s) ['bænɪstə(z)] n(pl) ringhiera

bank [bæŋk] n banca, banco; (of river, lake) riva, sponda; (of earth) banco ♦ vi (AVIAT) inclinarsi in virata; ~ **on** vt fus contare su; ~ **account** n conto in banca; ~ **card** n carta f assegni inv; ~**er** n banchiere m; ~**er's card** (BRIT) n = **bank card**; B~ **holiday** (BRIT) n giorno di festa; ~**ing** n attività bancaria; professione f di banchiere; ~**note** n banconota; ~ **rate** n tasso bancario

---
bank holiday
---

i Una **bank holiday**, in Gran Bretagna, è una giornata in cui banche e negozi sono chiusi. Generalmente le **bank holiday** cadono di lunedì e molti ne approfittano per fare una breve vacanza fuori città.

---

bankrupt ['bæŋkrʌpt] adj fallito(a); **to go** ~ fallire; ~**cy** n fallimento

bank statement n estratto conto

banner ['bænə*] n striscione m

baptism ['bæptɪzəm] n battesimo

bar [bɑː*] n (place) bar m inv; (counter) banco; (rod) barra; (of window etc) sbarra; (of chocolate) tavoletta; (fig) ostacolo; restrizione f; (MUS) battuta ♦ vt (road, window) sbarrare; (person) escludere; (activity) interdire; ~ **of soap** saponetta; **the B~** (LAW) l'Ordine m degli avvocati; **behind** ~**s** (prisoner) dietro le sbarre; ~ **none** senza eccezione

barbaric [bɑː'bærɪk] adj barbarico(a)

barbecue ['bɑːbɪkjuː] n barbecue m inv

barbed wire ['bɑːbd-] n filo spinato

barber ['bɑːbə*] n barbiere m

bar code n (on goods) codice m a barre

bare [beə*] adj nudo(a) ♦ vt scoprire,

denudare; (*teeth*) mostrare; **the ~ necessities** lo stretto necessario; **~back** *adv* senza sella; **~faced** *adj* sfacciato(a); **~foot** *adj, adv* scalzo(a); **~ly** *adv* appena

bargain ['bɑːgɪn] *n* (*transaction*) contratto; (*good buy*) affare *m* ♦ *vi* trattare; **into the ~** per giunta; **~ for** *vt fus*: **he got more than he ~ed for** gli è andata peggio di quel che si aspettasse

barge [bɑːdʒ] *n* chiatta; **~ in** *vi* (*walk in*) piombare dentro; (*interrupt talk*) intromettersi a sproposito

bark [bɑːk] *n* (*of tree*) corteccia; (*of dog*) abbaio ♦ *vi* abbaiare

barley ['bɑːlɪ] *n* orzo

barmaid ['bɑːmeɪd] *n* cameriera al banco

barman ['bɑːmən] *n* barista *m*

bar meal *n* spuntino servito al bar

barn [bɑːn] *n* granaio

barometer [bə'rɒmɪtə*] *n* barometro

baron ['bærən] *n* barone *m*; **~ess** *n* baronessa

barracks ['bærəks] *npl* caserma

barrage ['bærɑːʒ] *n* (*MIL, dam*) sbarramento; (*fig*) fiume *m*

barrel ['bærəl] *n* barile *m*; (*of gun*) canna

barren ['bærən] *adj* sterile; (*soil*) arido(a)

barricade [bærɪ'keɪd] *n* barricata

barrier ['bærɪə*] *n* barriera

barring ['bɑːrɪŋ] *prep* salvo

barrister ['bærɪstə*] (*BRIT*) *n* avvocato/essa (*con diritto di parlare davanti a tutte le corti*)

barrow ['bærəʊ] *n* (*cart*) carriola

bartender ['bɑːtendə*] (*US*) *n* barista *m*

barter ['bɑːtə*] *vt*: **to ~ sth for** barattare qc con

base [beɪs] *n* base *f* ♦ *vt*: **to ~ sth on** basare qc su ♦ *adj* vile

baseball ['beɪsbɔːl] *n* baseball *m*

basement ['beɪsmənt] *n* seminterrato; (*of shop*) interrato

bases[1] ['beɪsiːz] *npl of* **basis**

bases[2] ['beɪsɪz] *npl of* **base**

bash [bæʃ] (*inf*) *vt* picchiare

bashful ['bæʃfʊl] *adj* timido(a)

basic ['beɪsɪk] *adj* rudimentale; essenziale; **~ally** [-lɪ] *adv* fondamentalmente;

sostanzialmente; **~s** *npl*: **the ~s** l'essenziale *m*

basil ['bæzl] *n* basilico

basin ['beɪsn] *n* (*vessel, also GEO*) bacino; (*also:* **wash~**) lavabo

basis ['beɪsɪs] (*pl* **bases**) *n* base *f*; **on a part-time ~** part-time; **on a trial ~** in prova

bask [bɑːsk] *vi*: **to ~ in the sun** crogiolarsi al sole

basket ['bɑːskɪt] *n* cesta; (*smaller*) cestino; (*with handle*) paniere *m*; **~ball** *n* pallacanestro *f*

bass [beɪs] *n* (*MUS*) basso

bassoon [bə'suːn] *n* fagotto

bastard ['bɑːstəd] *n* bastardo/a; (*inf!*) stronzo (!)

bat [bæt] *n* pipistrello; (*for baseball etc*) mazza; (*BRIT: for table tennis*) racchetta ♦ *vt*: **he didn't ~ an eyelid** non battè ciglio

batch [bætʃ] *n* (*of bread*) infornata; (*of papers*) cumulo

bated ['beɪtɪd] *adj*: **with ~ breath** col fiato sospeso

bath [bɑːθ] *n* bagno; (*bathtub*) vasca da bagno ♦ *vt* far fare il bagno a; **to have a ~** fare un bagno; *see also* **baths**

bathe [beɪð] *vi* fare il bagno ♦ *vt* (*wound*) lavare; **~r** *n* bagnante *m/f*

bathing ['beɪðɪŋ] *n* bagni *mpl*; **~ costume** (*US* **~ suit**) *n* costume *m* da bagno

bathrobe ['bɑːθrəʊb] *n* accappatoio

bathroom ['bɑːθrʊm] *n* stanza da bagno

baths [bɑːðz] *npl* bagni *mpl* pubblici

bath towel *n* asciugamano da bagno

baton ['bætən] *n* (*MUS*) bacchetta; (*ATHLETICS*) testimone *m*; (*club*) manganello

batter ['bætə*] *vt* battere ♦ *n* pastetta; **~ed** *adj* (*hat*) sformato(a); (*pan*) ammaccato(a)

battery ['bætərɪ] *n* batteria; (*of torch*) pila; **~ farming** *n* allevamento in batteria

battle ['bætl] *n* battaglia ♦ *vi* battagliare, lottare; **~field** *n* campo di battaglia; **~ship** *n* nave *f* da guerra

bawl [bɔːl] *vi* urlare

bay [beɪ] *n* (*of sea*) baia; **to hold sb at ~** tenere qn a bada; **~ leaf** *n* foglia d'alloro;

~ **window** n bovindo
bazaar [bə'zɑ:*] n bazar m inv; vendita di
beneficenza
B. & B. abbr = **bed and breakfast**
BBC n abbr (= British Broadcasting
Corporation) rete nazionale di
radiotelevisione in Gran Bretagna
B.C. adv abbr (= before Christ) a.C.

KEYWORD

be [bi:] (pt was, were, pp been) aux vb
1 (with present participle: forming continuous tenses): **what are you doing?** che fa?,
che sta facendo?; **they're coming tomorrow** vengono domani; **I've been waiting
for her for hours** sono ore che l'aspetto
2 (with pp: forming passives) essere; **to ~
killed** essere or venire ucciso(a); **the box
had been opened** la scatola era stata
aperta; **the thief was nowhere to ~ seen**
il ladro non si trovava da nessuna parte
3 (in tag questions): **it was fun, wasn't it?**
è stato divertente, no?; **he's good-looking,
isn't he?** è un bell'uomo, vero?; **she's
back, is she?** così è tornata, eh?
4 (+to +infinitive): **the house is to ~ sold**
abbiamo (or hanno etc) intenzione di
vendere casa; **you're to ~ congratulated
for all your work** dovremo farvi i
complimenti per tutto il vostro lavoro; **he's
not to open it** non deve aprirlo
♦ vb +complement 1 (gen) essere; **I'm
English** sono inglese; **I'm tired** sono
stanco(a); **I'm hot/cold** ho caldo/freddo;
he's a doctor è medico; **2 and 2 are 4** 2
più 2 fa 4; **~ careful!** sta attento(a)!; **~
good** sii buono(a)
2 (of health) stare; **how are you?** come
sta?; **he's very ill** sta molto male
3 (of age): **how old are you?** quanti anni
hai?; **I'm sixteen (years old)** ho sedici
anni
4 (cost) costare; **how much was the
meal?** quant'era or quanto costava il
pranzo?; **that'll ~ £5, please** (fa) 5 sterline,
per favore
♦ vi 1 (exist, occur etc) essere, esistere; **the

best singer that ever was** il migliore
cantante mai esistito or di tutti tempi; **~
that as it may** comunque sia, sia come sia;
so ~ it sia pure, e sia
2 (referring to place) essere, trovarsi; **I
won't ~ here tomorrow** non ci sarò
domani; **Edinburgh is in Scotland**
Edimburgo si trova in Scozia
3 (referring to movement): **where have you
been?** dov'è stato?; **I've been to China**
sono stato in Cina
♦ impers vb 1 (referring to time, distance)
essere; **it's 5 o'clock** sono le 5; **it's the
28th of April** è il 28 aprile; **it's 10 km to
the village** di qui al paese sono 10 km
2 (referring to the weather) fare; **it's too
hot/cold** fa troppo caldo/freddo; **it's
windy** c'è vento
3 (emphatic): **it's me** sono io; **it was
Maria who paid the bill** è stata Maria che
ha pagato il conto

beach [bi:tʃ] n spiaggia ♦ vt tirare in secco
beacon ['bi:kən] n (lighthouse) faro;
(marker) segnale m
bead [bi:d] n perlina
beak [bi:k] n becco
beaker ['bi:kə*] n coppa
beam [bi:m] n trave f; (of light) raggio ♦ vi
brillare
bean [bi:n] n fagiolo; (of coffee) chicco;
runner ~ fagiolino; **broad ~** fava;
~sprouts npl germogli mpl di soia
bear [bεə*] (pt bore, pp borne) n orso ♦ vt
portare; (endure) sopportare; (produce)
generare ♦ vi: **to ~ right/left** piegare a
destra/sinistra; **~ out** vt (suspicions)
confermare, convalidare; (person) dare il
proprio appoggio a; **~ up** vi (person) fare
buon viso a cattiva sorte
beard [bɪəd] n barba
bearer ['bεərə*] n portatore m
bearing ['bεərɪŋ] n portamento;
(connection) rapporto; **~s** npl (also: **ball ~s**)
cuscinetti mpl a sfere; **to take a ~** fare un
rilevamento; **to find one's ~s** orientarsi
beast [bi:st] n bestia; **~ly** adj meschino(a);

(*weather*) da cani

beat [bi:t] (*pt* **beat**, *pp* **beaten**) *n* colpo; (*of heart*) battito; (*MUS*) tempo; battuta; (*of policeman*) giro ♦ *vt* battere; (*eggs, cream*) sbattere ♦ *vi* battere; **off the ~en track** fuori mano; **~ it!** (*inf*) fila!, fuori dai piedi!; **~ off** *vt* respingere; **~ up** *vt* (*person*) picchiare; (*eggs*) sbattere; **beaten** *pp* of **beat**; **~ing** *n* bastonata

beautiful ['bju:tiful] *adj* bello(a); **~ly** *adv* splendidamente

beauty ['bju:tɪ] *n* bellezza; **~ salon** *n* istituto di bellezza; **~ spot** (*BRIT*) *n* (*TOURISM*) luogo pittoresco

beaver ['bi:vɔ*] *n* castoro

became [bɪ'keɪm] *pt* of **become**

because [bɪ'kɔz] *conj* perché; **~ of** a causa di

beckon ['bekən] *vt* (*also*: **~ to**) chiamare con un cenno

become [bɪ'kʌm] (*irreg: like* **come**) *vt* diventare; **to ~ fat/thin** ingrassarsi/dimagrire

becoming [bɪ'kʌmɪŋ] *adj* (*behaviour*) che si conviene; (*clothes*) grazioso(a)

bed [bed] *n* letto; (*of flowers*) aiuola; (*of coal, clay*) strato; **single/double ~** letto a una piazza/a due piazze *or* matrimoniale; **~ and breakfast** *n* (*place*) ≈ pensione *f* familiare; (*terms*) camera con colazione; **~clothes** ['bedkləuðz] *npl* biancheria e coperte *fpl* da letto; **~ding** *n* coperte e lenzuola *fpl*

---
bed and breakfast

ⓘ *I* **bed and breakfast**, *anche* B & B, *sono piccole pensioni a conduzione familiare, più economiche rispetto agli alberghi, dove al mattino viene servita la tradizionale colazione all'inglese.*

---

bed linen *n* biancheria da letto
bedraggled [bɪ'dræɡld] *adj* fradicio(a)
bed: ~ridden *adj* costretto(a) a letto; **~room** *n* camera da letto; **~side** *n*: **at sb's ~side** al capezzale di qn; **~sit(ter)** (*BRIT*) *n* monolocale *m*; **~spread** *n*

copriletto; **~time** *n*: **it's ~time** è ora di andare a letto

bee [bi:] *n* ape *f*

beech [bi:tʃ] *n* faggio

beef [bi:f] *n* manzo; **roast ~** arrosto di manzo; **~burger** *n* hamburger *m inv*; **B~eater** *n* guardia della Torre di Londra

beehive ['bi:haɪv] *n* alveare *m*

beeline ['bi:laɪn] *n*: **to make a ~ for** buttarsi a capo fitto verso

been [bi:n] *pp* of **be**

beer [bɪə*] *n* birra

beetle ['bi:tl] *n* scarafaggio; coleottero

beetroot ['bi:tru:t] (*BRIT*) *n* barbabietola

before [bɪ'fɔ:*] *prep* (*in time*) prima di; (*in space*) davanti a ♦ *conj* prima che +*sub*; prima di ♦ *adv* prima; **~ going** prima di andare; **~ she goes** prima che vada; **the week ~** la settimana prima; **I've seen it ~** l'ho già visto; **I've never seen it ~** è la prima volta che lo vedo; **~hand** *adv* in anticipo

beg [beg] *vi* chiedere l'elemosina ♦ *vt* (*also*: **~ for**) chiedere in elemosina; (: *favour*) chiedere; **to ~ sb to do qc** pregare qn di fare

began [bɪ'ɡæn] *pt* of **begin**

beggar ['beɡə*] *n* mendicante *m/f*

begin [bɪ'ɡɪn] (*pt* **began**, *pp* **begun**) *vt, vi* cominciare; **to ~ doing** *or* **to do sth** incominciare a fare qc; **~ner** *n* principiante *m/f*; **~ning** *n* inizio, principio

begun [bɪ'ɡʌn] *pp* of **begin**

behalf [bɪ'hɑ:f] *n*: **on ~ of** per conto di; a nome di

behave [bɪ'heɪv] *vi* comportarsi; (*well: also*: **~ o.s.**) comportarsi bene

behaviour [bɪ'heɪvjə*] (*US* **behavior**) *n* comportamento, condotta

behind [bɪ'haɪnd] *prep* dietro; (*followed by pronoun*) dietro di; (*time*) in ritardo con ♦ *adv* dietro; (*leave, stay*) indietro ♦ *n* didietro; **to be ~ (schedule)** essere in ritardo rispetto al programma; **~ the scenes** (*fig*) dietro le quinte

behold [bɪ'həuld] (*irreg: like* **hold**) *vt* vedere, scorgere

beige [beɪʒ] *adj* beige *inv*

Beijing ['beɪ'dʒɪŋ] n Pechino f

being ['biːŋ] n essere m

Beirut [beɪ'ruːt] n Beirut f

Belarus [belə'rus] n Bielorussia

belated [bɪ'leɪtɪd] adj tardo(a)

belch [beltʃ] vi ruttare ♦ vt (gen: ~ out: smoke etc) eruttare

Belgian ['beldʒən] adj, n belga m/f

Belgium ['beldʒəm] n Belgio

belie [bɪ'laɪ] vt smentire

belief [bɪ'liːf] n (opinion) opinione f, convinzione f; (trust, faith) fede f

believe [bɪ'liːv] vt, vi credere; **to ~ in** (God) credere in; (ghosts) credere a; (method) avere fiducia in; **~r** n (REL) credente m/f; (in idea, activity): **to be a ~r in** credere in

belittle [bɪ'lɪtl] vt sminuire

bell [bel] n campana; (small, on door, electric) campanello

belligerent [bɪ'lɪdʒərənt] adj bellicoso(a)

bellow ['beləu] vi muggire

bellows ['beləuz] npl soffietto

belly ['belɪ] n pancia

belong [bɪ'lɒŋ] vi: **to ~ to** appartenere a; (club etc) essere socio di; **this book ~s here** questo libro va qui; **~ings** npl cose fpl, roba

beloved [bɪ'lʌvɪd] adj adorato(a)

below [bɪ'ləu] prep sotto, al di sotto di ♦ adv sotto, di sotto; giù; **see ~** vedi sotto or oltre

belt [belt] n cintura; (TECH) cinghia ♦ vt (thrash) picchiare ♦ vi (inf) filarsela; **~way** (US) n (AUT: ring road) circonvallazione f; (: motorway) autostrada

bemused [bɪ'mjuːzd] adj perplesso(a), stupito(a)

bench [bentʃ] n panca; (in workshop, POL) banco; **the B~** (LAW) la Corte

bend [bend] (pt, pp bent) vt curvare; (leg, arm) piegare ♦ vi curvarsi; piegarsi ♦ n (BRIT: in road) curva; (in pipe, river) gomito; **~ down** vi chinarsi; **~ over** vi piegarsi

beneath [bɪ'niːθ] prep sotto, al di sotto di; (unworthy of) indegno(a) di ♦ adv sotto, di sotto

benefactor ['benɪfæktə*] n benefattore m

beneficial [benɪ'fɪʃəl] adj che fa bene; vantaggioso(a)

benefit ['benɪfɪt] n beneficio, vantaggio; (allowance of money) indennità f inv ♦ vt far bene a ♦ vi: **he'll ~ from it** ne trarrà beneficio or profitto

benevolent [bɪ'nevələnt] adj benevolo(a)

benign [bɪ'naɪn] adj (person, smile) benevolo(a); (MED) benigno(a)

bent [bent] pt, pp of **bend** ♦ n inclinazione f ♦ adj (inf: dishonest) losco(a); **to be ~ on** essere deciso(a) a

bequest [bɪ'kwest] n lascito

bereaved [bɪ'riːvd] n: **the ~** i familiari in lutto

beret ['bereɪ] n berretto

Berlin [bəː'lɪn] n Berlino f

berm [bəːm] (US) n (AUT) corsia d'emergenza

berry ['berɪ] n bacca

berserk [bə'səːk] adj: **to go ~** montare su tutte le furie

berth [bəːθ] n (bed) cuccetta; (for ship) ormeggio ♦ vi (in harbour) entrare in porto; (at anchor) gettare l'ancora

beseech [bɪ'siːtʃ] (pt, pp besought) vt implorare

beset [bɪ'set] (pt, pp beset) vt assalire

beside [bɪ'saɪd] prep accanto a; **to be ~ o.s. (with anger)** essere fuori di sé (dalla rabbia); **that's ~ the point** non c'entra

besides [bɪ'saɪdz] adv inoltre, per di più ♦ prep oltre a; a parte

besiege [bɪ'siːdʒ] vt (town) assediare; (fig) tempestare

best [best] adj migliore ♦ adv meglio; **the ~ part of** (quantity) la maggior parte di; **at ~** tutt'al più; **to make the ~ of sth** cavare il meglio possibile da qc; **to do one's ~** fare del proprio meglio; **to the ~ of my knowledge** per quel che ne so; **to the ~ of my ability** al massimo delle mie capacità; **~-before date** n scadenza; **~ man** n testimone m dello sposo

bestow [bɪ'stəu] vt accordare; (title) conferire

bet [bet] (pt, pp bet or betted) n scommessa ♦ vt, vi scommettere; **to ~ sb sth**

scommettere qc con qn

betray [bɪ'treɪ] *vt* tradire; **~al** *n* tradimento

better ['betə*] *adj* migliore ♦ *adv* meglio ♦ *vt* migliorare ♦ *n*: **to get the ~ of** avere la meglio su; **you had ~ do it** è meglio che lo faccia; **he thought ~ of it** cambiò idea; **to get ~** migliorare; **~ off** *adj* più ricco(a); *(fig)*: **you'd be ~ off this way** starebbe meglio così

betting ['betɪŋ] *n* scommesse *fpl*; **~ shop** *(BRIT)* *n* ufficio dell'allibratore

between [bɪ'twi:n] *prep* tra ♦ *adv* in mezzo, nel mezzo

beverage ['bevərɪdʒ] *n* bevanda

beware [bɪ'weə*] *vt*, *vi*: **to ~ (of)** stare attento(a) (a); **"~ of the dog"** "attenti al cane"

bewildered [bɪ'wɪldəd] *adj* sconcertato(a), confuso(a)

beyond [bɪ'jɒnd] *prep* *(in space)* oltre; *(exceeding)* al di sopra di ♦ *adv* di là; **~ doubt** senza dubbio; **~ repair** irreparabile

bias ['baɪəs] *n* *(prejudice)* pregiudizio; *(preference)* preferenza; **~(s)ed** *adj* parziale

bib [bɪb] *n* bavaglino

Bible ['baɪbl] *n* Bibbia

bicarbonate of soda [baɪ'kɑ:bənɪt-] *n* bicarbonato (di sodio)

bicker ['bɪkə*] *vi* bisticciare

bicycle ['baɪsɪkl] *n* bicicletta

bid [bɪd] *(pt* **bade** *or* **bid**, *pp* **bidden** *or* **bid**) *n* offerta; *(attempt)* tentativo ♦ *vi* fare un'offerta ♦ *vt* fare un'offerta di; **to ~ sb good day** dire buon giorno a qn; **~der** *n*: **the highest ~der** il maggior offerente; **~ding** *n* offerte *fpl*

bide [baɪd] *vt*: **to ~ one's time** aspettare il momento giusto

bifocals [baɪ'fəuklz] *npl* occhiali *mpl* bifocali

big [bɪg] *adj* grande; grosso(a)

big dipper [-'dɪpə*] *n* montagne *fpl* russe, otto *m inv* volante

bigheaded ['bɪg'hedɪd] *adj* presuntuoso(a)

bigot ['bɪgət] *n* persona gretta; **~ed** *adj* gretto(a); **~ry** *n* grettezza

big top *n* tendone *m* del circo

bike [baɪk] *n* bici *f inv*

bikini [bɪ'ki:nɪ] *n* bikini *m inv*

bilingual [baɪ'lɪŋgwəl] *adj* bilingue

bill [bɪl] *n* conto; *(POL)* atto; *(US: banknote)* banconota; *(of bird)* becco; *(of show)* locandina; **"post no ~s"** "divieto di affissione"; **to fit** *or* **fill the ~** *(fig)* fare al caso; **~board** *n* tabellone *m*

billet ['bɪlɪt] *n* alloggio

billfold ['bɪlfəuld] *(US)* *n* portafoglio

billiards ['bɪljədz] *n* biliardo

billion ['bɪljən] *n* *(BRIT)* bilione *m*; *(US)* miliardo

bimbo ['bɪmbəu] *n* *(pej, col)* pollastrella, svampitella

bin [bɪn] *n* *(for coal, rubbish)* bidone *m*; *(for bread)* cassetta; *(dust~)* pattumiera; *(litter ~)* cestino

bind [baɪnd] *(pt, pp* **bound**) *vt* legare; *(oblige)* obbligare ♦ *n* *(inf)* scocciatura; **~ing** *adj* *(contract)* vincolante

binge [bɪndʒ] *(inf)* *n*: **to go on a ~** fare baldoria

bingo ['bɪŋgəu] *n* gioco simile alla tombola

binoculars [bɪ'nɔkjuləz] *npl* binocolo

bio... [baɪə'...] *prefix*: **~chemistry** *n* biochimica; **~degradable** *adj* biodegradabile; **~graphy** *n* biografia; **~logical** *adj* biologico(a); **~logy** [baɪ'ɔlədʒɪ] *n* biologia

birch [bə:tʃ] *n* betulla

bird [bə:d] *n* uccello; *(BRIT: inf: girl)* bambola; **~'s eye view** *n* vista panoramica; **~ watcher** *n* ornitologo/a dilettante

Biro ® ['baɪrəu] *n* biro ® *f inv*

birth [bə:θ] *n* nascita; **to give ~ to** partorire; **~ certificate** *n* certificato di nascita; **~ control** *n* controllo delle nascite; contraccezione *f*; **~day** *n* compleanno ♦ *cpd* di compleanno; **~ rate** *n* indice *m* di natalità

biscuit ['bɪskɪt] *(BRIT)* *n* biscotto

bisect [baɪ'sekt] *vt* tagliare in due (parti)

bishop ['bɪʃəp] *n* vescovo

bit [bɪt] *pt of* **bite** ♦ *n* pezzo; *(COMPUT)* bit *m inv*; *(of horse)* morso; **a ~ of** un po' di; **a ~ mad** un po' matto; **~ by ~** a poco a poco

bitch [bɪtʃ] *n* *(dog)* cagna; *(inf!)* vacca

bite [baɪt] (*pt* **bit**, *pp* **bitten**) *vt*, *vi* mordere; (*subj: insect*) pungere ♦ *n* morso; (*insect ~*) puntura; (*mouthful*) boccone *m*; **let's have a ~ (to eat)** mangiamo un boccone; **to ~ one's nails** mangiarsi le unghie; **bitten** ['bɪtn] *pp of* **bite**

bitter ['bɪtə*] *adj* amaro(a); (*wind, criticism*) pungente ♦ *n* (*BRIT: beer*) birra amara; **~ness** *n* amarezza; gusto amaro

black [blæk] *adj* nero(a) ♦ *n* nero; (*person*): **B~** negro/a ♦ *vt* (*BRIT: INDUSTRY*) boicottare; **to give sb a ~ eye** fare un occhio nero a qn; **in the ~** (*bank account*) in attivo; **~ and blue** *adj* tutto(a) pesto(a); **~berry** *n* mora; **~bird** *n* merlo; **~board** *n* lavagna; **~ coffee** *n* caffè *m inv* nero; **~currant** *n* ribes *m inv*; **~en** *vt* annerire; **~ ice** *n* strato trasparente di ghiaccio; **~leg** *n* (*BRIT*) crumiro; **~list** *n* lista nera; **~mail** *n* ricatto ♦ *vt* ricattare; **~market** *n* mercato nero; **~out** *n* oscuramento; (*TV, RADIO*) interruzione *f* delle trasmissioni; (*fainting*) svenimento; **B~ Sea** *n*: **the B~ Sea** il Mar Nero; **~ sheep** *n* pecora nera; **~smith** *n* fabbro ferraio; **~ spot** *n* (*AUT*) luogo famigerato per gli incidenti; (*for unemployment etc*) zona critica

bladder ['blædə*] *n* vescica

blade [bleɪd] *n* lama; (*of oar*) pala; **~ of grass** filo d'erba

blame [bleɪm] *n* colpa ♦ *vt*: **to ~ sb/sth for sth** dare la colpa di qc a qn/qc; **who's to ~?** chi è colpevole?

bland [blænd] *adj* mite; (*taste*) blando(a)

blank [blæŋk] *adj* bianco(a); (*look*) distratto(a) ♦ *n* spazio vuoto; (*cartridge*) cartuccia a salve; **~ cheque** *n* assegno in bianco

blanket ['blæŋkɪt] *n* coperta

blare [blɛə*] *vi* strombettare

blasphemy ['blæsfɪmɪ] *n* bestemmia

blast [blɑːst] *n* (*of wind*) raffica; (*of bomb etc*) esplosione *f* ♦ *vt* far saltare; **~-off** *n* (*SPACE*) lancio

blatant ['bleɪtənt] *adj* flagrante

blaze [bleɪz] *n* (*fire*) incendio; (*fig*) vampata;

splendore *m* ♦ *vi* (*fire*) ardere, fiammeggiare; (*guns*) sparare senza sosta; (*fig: eyes*) ardere ♦ *vt*: **to ~ a trail** (*fig*) tracciare una via nuova; **in a ~ of publicity** circondato da grande pubblicità

blazer ['bleɪzə*] *n* blazer *m inv*

bleach [bliːtʃ] *n* (*also: household ~*) varechina ♦ *vt* (*material*) candeggiare; **~ed** *adj* (*hair*) decolorato(a); **~ers** (*US*) *npl* (*SPORT*) posti *mpl* di gradinata

bleak [bliːk] *adj* tetro(a)

bleat [bliːt] *vi* belare

bled [bled] *pt*, *pp of* **bleed**

bleed [bliːd] (*pt*, *pp* **bled**) *vi* sanguinare; **my nose is ~ing** mi viene fuori sangue dal naso

bleeper ['bliːpə*] *n* (*device*) cicalino

blemish ['blemɪʃ] *n* macchia

blend [blend] *n* miscela ♦ *vt* mescolare ♦ *vi* (*colours etc: also: ~ in*) armonizzare

bless [bles] (*pt*, *pp* **blessed** *or* **blest**) *vt* benedire; **~ you!** (*after sneeze*) salute!; **~ing** *n* benedizione *f*; fortuna; **blest** [blest] *pt*, *pp of* **bless**

blew [bluː] *pt of* **blow**

blight [blaɪt] *vt* (*hopes etc*) deludere; (*life*) rovinare

blimey ['blaɪmɪ] (*BRIT: inf*) *excl* accidenti!

blind [blaɪnd] *adj* cieco(a) ♦ *n* (*for window*) avvolgibile *m*; (*Venetian ~*) veneziana ♦ *vt* accecare; **the ~** *npl* i ciechi; **~ alley** *n* vicolo cieco; **~ corner** (*BRIT*) *n* svolta cieca; **~fold** *n* benda ♦ *adj*, *adv* bendato(a) ♦ *vt* bendare gli occhi a; **~ly** *adv* ciecamente; **~ness** *n* cecità; **~ spot** *n* (*AUT etc*) punto cieco; (*fig*) punto debole

blink [blɪŋk] *vi* battere gli occhi; (*light*) lampeggiare; **~ers** *npl* paraocchi *mpl*

bliss [blɪs] *n* estasi *f*

blister ['blɪstə*] *n* (*on skin*) vescica; (*on paintwork*) bolla ♦ *vi* (*paint*) coprirsi di bolle

blizzard ['blɪzəd] *n* bufera di neve

bloated ['bləʊtɪd] *adj* gonfio(a)

blob [blɔb] *n* (*drop*) goccia; (*stain, spot*) macchia

bloc [blɔk] *n* (*POL*) blocco

block [blɔk] *n* blocco; (*in pipes*) ingombro; (*toy*) cubo; (*of buildings*) isolato ♦ *vt* bloccare; ~**ade** [-'keɪd] *n* blocco; ~**age** *n* ostacolo; ~**buster** *n* (*film, book*) grande successo; ~ **letters** *npl* stampatello; ~ **of flats** (*BRIT*) *n* caseggiato.

bloke [bləuk] (*BRIT: inf*) *n* tizio

blond(e) [blɔnd] *adj, n* biondo(a)

blood [blʌd] *n* sangue *m*; ~ **donor** *n* donatore/trice di sangue; ~ **group** *n* gruppo sanguigno; ~**hound** *n* segugio; ~ **poisoning** *n* setticemia; ~ **pressure** *n* pressione *f* sanguigna; ~**shed** *n* spargimento di sangue; ~**shot** *adj*: ~**shot eyes** occhi iniettati di sangue; ~**stream** *n* flusso del sangue; ~ **test** *n* analisi *f inv* del sangue; ~**thirsty** *adj* assetato(a) di sangue; ~**y** *adj* (*fight*) sanguinoso(a); (*nose*) sanguinante; (*BRIT: inf!*): **this** ~**y ...** questo maledetto ...; ~**y awful/good** (*inf!*) veramente terribile/forte; ~**y-minded** (*BRIT: inf*) *adj* indisponente

bloom [bluːm] *n* fiore *m* ♦ *vi* (*tree*) essere in fiore; (*flower*) aprirsi

blossom ['blɔsəm] *n* fiore *m*; (*with pl sense*) fiori *mpl* ♦ *vi* essere in fiore

blot [blɔt] *n* macchia ♦ *vt* macchiare; ~ **out** *vt* (*memories*) cancellare; (*view*) nascondere

blotchy ['blɔtʃi] *adj* (*complexion*) coperto(a) di macchie

blotting paper ['blɔtɪŋ-] *n* carta assorbente

blouse [blauz] *n* (*feminine garment*) camicetta

blow [bləu] (*pt* **blew**, *pp* **blown**) *n* colpo ♦ *vi* soffiare ♦ *vt* (*fuse*) far saltare; (*subj: wind*) spingere; (*instrument*) suonare; **to ~ one's nose** soffiarsi il naso; **to ~ a whistle** fischiare; ~ **away** *vt* portare via; ~ **down** *vt* abbattere; ~ **off** *vt* far volare via; ~ **out** *vi* scoppiare; ~ **over** *vi* calmarsi; ~ **up** *vi* saltare in aria ♦ *vt* far saltare in aria; (*tyre*) gonfiare; (*PHOT*) ingrandire; ~**-dry** *n* messa in piega a föhn; ~**lamp** (*BRIT*) *n* lampada a benzina per saldare; **blown** *pp of* **blow**; ~**-out** *n* (*of tyre*) scoppio; ~**torch** *n* = ~**lamp**

blue [bluː] *adj* azzurro(a); (*depressed*) giù *inv*; ~ **film/joke** film/ barzelletta pornografico(a); **out of the** ~ (*fig*) all'improvviso; ~**bell** *n* giacinto dei boschi; ~**bottle** *n* moscone *m*; ~**print** *n* (*fig*): ~**print (for)** formula (di)

bluff [blʌf] *vi* bluffare ♦ *n* bluff *m inv* ♦ *adj* (*person*) brusco(a); **to call sb's** ~ mettere alla prova il bluff di qn

blunder ['blʌndə*] *n* abbaglio ♦ *vi* prendere un abbaglio

blunt [blʌnt] *adj* smussato(a); spuntato(a); (*person*) brusco(a)

blur [bləː*] *n* forma indistinta ♦ *vt* offuscare

blush [blʌʃ] *vi* arrossire ♦ *n* rossore *m*

blustering ['blʌstərɪŋ] *adj* infuriato(a)

blustery ['blʌstəri] *adj* (*weather*) burrascoso(a)

boar [bɔː*] *n* cinghiale *m*

board [bɔːd] *n* tavola; (*on wall*) tabellone *m*; (*committee*) consiglio; (*in firm*) consiglio d'amministrazione; (*NAUT, AVIAT*): **on ~** a bordo ♦ *vt* (*ship*) salire a bordo di; (*train*) salire su; **full ~** (*BRIT*) pensione completa; **half ~** (*BRIT*) mezza pensione; ~ **and lodging** *n* vitto e alloggio; **which goes by the ~** (*fig*) che viene abbandonato; ~ **up** *vt* (*door*) chiudere con assi; ~**er** *n* (*SCOL*) convittore/trice; ~**ing card** *n* = ~**ing pass**; ~**ing house** *n* pensione *f*; ~**ing pass** *n* (*AVIAT, NAUT*) carta d'imbarco; ~**ing school** *n* collegio; ~ **room** *n* sala del consiglio

boast [bəust] *vi*: **to ~ (about** *or* **of)** vantarsi (di)

boat [bəut] *n* nave *f*; (*small*) barca; ~**swain** ['bəusn] *n* nostromo

bob [bɔb] *vi* (*boat, cork on water: also:* ~ **up and down**) andare su e giù; ~ **up** *vi* saltare fuori

bobby ['bɔbi] (*BRIT: inf*) *n* poliziotto

bobsleigh ['bɔbsleɪ] *n* bob *m inv*

bode [bəud] *vi*: **to ~ well/ill (for)** essere di buon/cattivo auspicio (per)

bodily ['bɔdɪli] *adj* fisico(a), corporale ♦ *adv* corporalmente; interamente; in persona

body ['bɔdi] *n* corpo; (*of car*) carrozzeria; (*of*

plane) fusoliera; (*fig: group*) gruppo; (: *organization*) organizzazione *f*; (: *quantity*) quantità *f inv*; **~-building** *n* culturismo; **~guard** *n* guardia del corpo; **~work** *n* carrozzeria

bog [bɔg] *n* palude *f* ♦ *vt*: **to get ~ged down** (*fig*) impantanarsi

bogus ['bəugəs] *adj* falso(a); finto(a)

boil [bɔɪl] *vt, vi* bollire ♦ *n* (*MED*) foruncolo; **to come to the** (*BRIT*) **or a** (*US*) **~** raggiungere l'ebollizione; **~ down to** *vt fus* (*fig*) ridursi a; **~ over** *vi* traboccare (bollendo); **~ed egg** *n* uovo alla coque; **~ed potatoes** *npl* patate *fpl* bollite *or* lesse; **~er** *n* caldaia; **~er suit** (*BRIT*) *n* tuta; **~ing point** *n* punto di ebollizione

boisterous ['bɔɪstərəs] *adj* chiassoso(a)

bold [bəuld] *adj* audace; (*child*) impudente; (*colour*) deciso(a)

bollard ['bɔləd] (*BRIT*) *n* (*AUT*) colonnina luminosa

bolt [bəult] *n* chiavistello; (*with nut*) bullone *m* ♦ *adv*: **~ upright** diritto(a) come un fuso ♦ *vt* serrare; (*also*: **~ together**) imbullonare; (*food*) mangiare in fretta ♦ *vi* scappare via

bomb [bɔm] *n* bomba ♦ *vt* bombardare

bombastic [bɔm'bæstɪk] *adj* magniloquente

bomb: **~ disposal unit** *n* corpo degli artificieri; **~er** *n* (*AVIAT*) bombardiere *m*; **~shell** *n* (*fig*) notizia bomba

bond [bɔnd] *n* legame *m*; (*binding promise, FINANCE*) obbligazione *f*; (*COMM*): **in ~** in attesa di sdoganamento

bondage ['bɔndɪdʒ] *n* schiavitù *f*

bone [bəun] *n* osso; (*of fish*) spina, lisca ♦ *vt* disossare; togliere le spine a; **~ idle** *adj* pigrissimo(a); **~ marrow** *n* midollo osseo

bonfire ['bɔnfaɪə*] *n* falò *m inv*

bonnet ['bɔnɪt] *n* cuffia; (*BRIT: of car*) cofano

bonus ['bəunəs] *n* premio; (*fig*) sovrappiù *m inv*

bony ['bəunɪ] *adj* (*MED: tissue*) osseo(a); (*arm, face*) ossuto(a); (*meat*) pieno(a) di ossi; (*fish*) pieno(a) di spine

boo [bu:] *excl* ba! ♦ *vt* fischiare

booby trap ['bu:bɪ-] *n* trappola

book [buk] *n* libro; (*of stamps etc*)

blocchetto ♦ *vt* (*ticket, seat, room*) prenotare; (*driver*) multare; (*football player*) ammonire; **~s** *npl* (*COMM*) conti *mpl*; **~case** *n* scaffale *m*; **~ing office** (*BRIT*) *n* (*RAIL*) biglietteria; (*THEATRE*) botteghino; **~-keeping** *n* contabilità; **~let** *n* libricino; **~maker** *n* allibratore *m*; **~seller** *n* libraio; **~shop**, **~store** *n* libreria

boom [bu:m] *n* (*noise*) rimbombo; (*in prices etc*) boom *m inv* ♦ *vi* rimbombare; andare a gonfie vele

boon [bu:n] *n* vantaggio

boost [bu:st] *n* spinta ♦ *vt* spingere; **~er** *n* (*MED*) richiamo

boot [bu:t] *n* stivale *m*; (*for hiking*) scarpone *m* da montagna; (*for football etc*) scarpa; (*BRIT: of car*) portabagagli *m inv* ♦ *vt* (*COMPUT*) inizializzare; **to ~** (*in addition*) per giunta, in più

booth [bu:ð] *n* cabina; (*at fair*) baraccone *m*

booty ['bu:tɪ] *n* bottino

booze [bu:z] (*inf*) *n* alcool *m*

border ['bɔ:də*] *n* orlo; margine *m*; (*of a country*) frontiera; (*for flowers*) aiuola (laterale) ♦ *vt* (*road*) costeggiare; (*another country: also*: **~ on**) confinare con; **the B~s** la zona di confine tra l'Inghilterra e la Scozia; **~ on** *vt fus* (*fig: insanity etc*) sfiorare; **~line** *n* (*fig*): **on the ~line** incerto(a); **~line case** *n* caso incerto

bore [bɔ:*] *pt of* **bear** ♦ *vt* (*hole etc*) scavare; (*person*) annoiare ♦ *n* (*person*) seccatore/trice; (*of gun*) calibro; **to be ~d** annoiarsi; **~dom** *n* noia; **boring** *adj* noioso(a)

born [bɔ:n] *adj*: **to be ~** nascere; **I was ~ in 1960** sono nato nel 1960

borne [bɔ:n] *pp of* **bear**

borough ['bʌrə] *n* comune *m*

borrow ['bɔrəu] *vt*: **to ~ sth (from sb)** prendere in prestito qc (da qn)

Bosnia(-Herzegovina) ['bɔznɪə-(herzə'gəuvi:nə)] *n* Bosnia-Erzegovina

Bosnian ['bɔznɪən] *n, adj* bosniaco(a) *m/f*

boss [bɔs] *n* capo ♦ *vt* comandare; **~y** *adj* prepotente

bosun ['bəusn] *n* nostromo

botany ['bɔtənɪ] *n* botanica

botch [bɔtʃ] *vt* (*also:* ~ **up**) fare un pasticcio di

both [bəuθ] *adj* entrambi(e), tutt'e due ♦ *pron:* ~ (**of them**) entrambi(e); ~ **of us went, we** ~ **went** ci siamo andati tutt'e due ♦ *adv:* **they sell** ~ **meat and poultry** vendono insieme la carne ed il pollame

bother ['bɔðə*] *vt* (*worry*) preoccupare; (*annoy*) infastidire ♦ *vi* (*also:* ~ **o.s.**) preoccuparsi ♦ *n:* **it is a** ~ **to have to do** è una seccatura dover fare; **it was no** ~ non c'era problema; **to** ~ **doing sth** darsi la pena di fare qc

bottle ['bɔtl] *n* bottiglia; (*baby's*) biberon *m inv* ♦ *vt* imbottigliare; ~ **up** *vt* contenere; ~ **bank** *n* contenitore *m* per la raccolta del vetro; ~**neck** *n* imbottigliamento; ~ **opener** *n* apribottiglie *m inv*

bottom ['bɔtəm] *n* fondo; (*buttocks*) sedere *m* ♦ *adj* più basso(a); ultimo(a); **at the** ~ **of** in fondo a

bough [bau] *n* ramo

bought [bɔːt] *pt, pp of* **buy**

boulder ['bəuldə*] *n* masso (tondeggiante)

bounce [bauns] *vi* (*ball*) rimbalzare; (*cheque*) essere restituito(a) ♦ *vt* far rimbalzare ♦ *n* (*rebound*) rimbalzo; ~**r** (*inf*) *n* buttafuori *m inv*

bound [baund] *pt, pp of* **bind** ♦ *n* (*gen pl*) limite *m*; (*leap*) salto ♦ *vi* saltare ♦ *vt* (*limit*) delimitare ♦ *adj:* ~ **by law** obbligato(a) per legge; **to be** ~ **to do sth** (*obliged*) essere costretto(a) a fare qc; **he's** ~ **to fail** (*likely*) fallirà di certo; ~ **for** diretto(a) a; **out of** ~**s** il cui accesso è vietato

boundary ['baundrɪ] *n* confine *m*

boundless ['baundlɪs] *adj* senza limiti

bourgeois ['buəʒwɑː] *adj* borghese

bout [baut] *n* periodo; (*of malaria etc*) attacco; (*BOXING etc*) incontro

bow[1] [bəu] *n* nodo; (*weapon*) arco; (*MUS*) archetto

bow[2] [bau] *n* (*with body*) inchino; (*NAUT: also:* ~**s**) prua ♦ *vi* inchinarsi; (*yield*): **to** ~ **to** *or* **before** sottomettersi a

bowels ['bauəlz] *npl* intestini *mpl*; (*fig*) viscere *fpl*

bowl [bəul] *n* (*for eating*) scodella; (*for washing*) bacino; (*ball*) boccia ♦ *vi* (*CRICKET*) servire (la palla)

bow-legged ['bəu'legɪd] *adj* dalle gambe storte

bowler ['bəulə*] *n* (*CRICKET, BASEBALL*) lanciatore *m*; (*BRIT: also:* ~ **hat**) bombetta

bowling ['bəulɪŋ] *n* (*game*) gioco delle bocce; ~ **alley** *n* pista da bowling; ~ **green** *n* campo di bocce

bowls [bəulz] *n* gioco delle bocce

bow tie *n* cravatta a farfalla

box [bɔks] *n* scatola; (*also:* **cardboard** ~) cartone *m*; (*THEATRE*) palco ♦ *vt* inscatolare ♦ *vi* fare del pugilato; ~**er** *n* (*person*) pugile *m*; ~**ing** *n* (*SPORT*) pugilato; **B**~**ing Day** (*BRIT*) *n* ≈ Santo Stefano; ~**ing gloves** *npl* guantoni *mpl* da pugile; ~**ing ring** *n* ring *m inv*; ~ **office** *n* biglietteria; ~ **room** *n* ripostiglio

---

Boxing Day

---

i   *Il* **Boxing Day** *è il primo giorno infrasettimanale dopo Natale. Prende il nome dalla tradizionale usanza di donare pacchi regalo natalizi, un tempo chiamati "Christmas boxes", a fornitori e dipendenti.*

---

boy [bɔɪ] *n* ragazzo

boycott ['bɔɪkɔt] *n* boicottaggio ♦ *vt* boicottare

boyfriend ['bɔɪfrend] *n* ragazzo

boyish ['bɔɪʃ] *adj* da ragazzo

B.R. *abbr* (*formerly*) = **British Rail**

bra [brɑː] *n* reggipetto, reggiseno

brace [breɪs] *n* (*on teeth*) apparecchio correttore; (*tool*) trapano ♦ *vt* rinforzare, sostenere; ~**s** (*BRIT*) *npl* (*DRESS*) bretelle *fpl*; **to** ~ **o.s.** (*also fig*) tenersi forte

bracelet ['breɪslɪt] *n* braccialetto

bracing ['breɪsɪŋ] *adj* invigorante

bracken ['brækən] *n* felce *f*

bracket ['brækɪt] *n* (*TECH*) mensola; (*group*) gruppo; (*TYP*) parentesi *f inv* ♦ *vt* mettere fra parentesi

brag [bræg] *vi* vantarsi

braid [breɪd] *n* (*trimming*) passamano; (*of*

hair) treccia

brain [breɪn] *n* cervello; **~s** *npl* (*intelligence*) cervella *fpl*; **he's got ~s** è intelligente; **~wash** *vt* fare un lavaggio di cervello a; **~wave** *n* lampo di genio; **~y** *adj* intelligente

braise [breɪz] *vt* brasare

brake [breɪk] *n* (*on vehicle*) freno ♦ *vi* frenare; **~ fluid** *n* liquido dei freni; **~ light** *n* (fanalino dello) stop *m inv*

bramble ['bræmbl] *n* rovo

bran [bræn] *n* crusca

branch [brɑːntʃ] *n* ramo; (*COMM*) succursale *f*; **~ out** *vi* (*fig*) intraprendere una nuova attività

brand [brænd] *n* (*also:* **~ name**) marca; (*fig*) tipo ♦ *vt* (*cattle*) marcare (a ferro rovente)

brand-new *adj* nuovo(a) di zecca

brandy ['brændɪ] *n* brandy *m inv*

brash [bræʃ] *adj* sfacciato(a)

brass [brɑːs] *n* ottone *m*; **the ~** (*MUS*) gli ottoni; **~ band** *n* fanfara

brat [bræt] (*pej*) *n* marmocchio, monello/a

bravado [brəˈvɑːdəu] *n* spavalderia

brave [breɪv] *adj* coraggioso(a) ♦ *vt* affrontare; **~ry** *n* coraggio

brawl [brɔːl] *n* rissa

brawny ['brɔːnɪ] *adj* muscoloso(a)

bray [breɪ] *vi* ragliare

brazen ['breɪzn] *adj* sfacciato(a) ♦ *vt*: **to ~ it out** fare lo sfacciato

brazier ['breɪzɪə*] *n* braciere *m*

Brazil [brəˈzɪl] *n* Brasile *m*

breach [briːtʃ] *vt* aprire una breccia in ♦ *n* (*gap*) breccia, varco; (*breaking*): **~ of contract** rottura di contratto; **~ of the peace** violazione *f* dell'ordine pubblico

bread [bred] *n* pane *m*; **~ and butter** *n* pane e burro; (*fig*) mezzi *mpl* di sussistenza; **~bin** *n* cassetta *f* portapane *inv*; **~crumbs** *npl* briciole *fpl*; (*CULIN*) pangrattato; **~line** *n*: **to be on the ~line** avere appena il denaro per vivere

breadth [bretθ] *n* larghezza; (*fig: of knowledge etc*) ampiezza

breadwinner ['bredwɪnə*] *n* chi guadagna il pane per tutta la famiglia

break [breɪk] (*pt* **broke**, *pp* **broken**) *vt* rompere; (*law*) violare; (*record*) battere ♦ *vi* rompersi; (*storm*) scoppiare; (*weather*) cambiare; (*dawn*) spuntare; (*news*) saltare fuori ♦ *n* (*gap*) breccia; (*fracture*) rottura; (*rest, also SCOL*) intervallo; (: *short*) pausa; (*chance*) possibilità *f inv*; **to ~ one's leg** *etc* rompersi la gamba *etc*; **to ~ the news to sb** comunicare per primo la notizia a qn; **to ~ even** coprire le spese; **to ~ free** *or* **loose** spezzare i legami; **to ~ open** (*door etc*) sfondare; **~ down** *vt* (*figures, data*) analizzare ♦ *vi* (*person*) avere un esaurimento (nervoso); (*AUT*) guastarsi; **~ in** *vt* (*horse etc*) domare ♦ *vi* (*burglar*) fare irruzione; (*interrupt*) interrompere; **~ into** *vt fus* (*house*) fare irruzione in; **~ off** *vi* (*speaker*) interrompersi; (*branch*) troncarsi; **~ out** *vi* evadere; (*war, fight*) scoppiare; **to ~ out in spots** coprirsi di macchie; **~ up** *vi* (*ship*) sfondarsi; (*meeting*) sciogliersi; (*crowd*) disperdersi; (*marriage*) andare a pezzi; (*SCOL*) chiudere ♦ *vt* fare a pezzi, spaccare; (*fight etc*) interrompere, far cessare; **~age** *n* rottura; (*object broken*) cosa rotta; **~down** *n* (*AUT*) guasto; (*in communications*) interruzione *f*; (*of marriage*) rottura; (*MED: also:* **nervous ~down**) esaurimento nervoso; (*of statistics*) resoconto; **~down van** (*BRIT*) *n* carro *m* attrezzi *inv*; **~er** *n* frangente *m*

breakfast ['brekfəst] *n* colazione *f*

break: **~-in** *n* irruzione *f*; **~ing and entering** *n* (*LAW*) violazione *f* di domicilio con scasso; **~through** *n* (*fig*) passo avanti; **~water** *n* frangiflutti *m inv*

breast [brest] *n* (*of woman*) seno; (*chest, CULIN*) petto; **~-feed** (*irreg: like* **feed**) *vt, vi* allattare (al seno); **~-stroke** *n* nuoto a rana

breath [breθ] *n* respiro; **out of ~** senza fiato

Breathalyser ® ['breθəlaɪzə*] (*BRIT*) *n* alcoltest *m inv*

breathe [briːð] *vt, vi* respirare; **~ in** *vt* respirare ♦ *vi* inspirare; **~ out** *vt, vi* espirare; **~r** *n* attimo di respiro; **breathing** *n* respiro, respirazione *f*

breathless ['breθlɪs] *adj* senza fiato
breathtaking ['breθteɪkɪŋ] *adj* mozzafiato *inv*
bred [bred] *pt, pp of* **breed**
breed [briːd] (*pt, pp* **bred**) *vt* allevare ♦ *vi* riprodursi ♦ *n* razza; (*type, class*) varietà *f inv*; **~ing** *n* riproduzione *f*; allevamento; (*upbringing*) educazione *f*
breeze [briːz] *n* brezza
breezy ['briːzɪ] *adj* allegro(a); ventilato(a)
brew [bruː] *vt* (*tea*) fare un infuso di; (*beer*) fare ♦ *vi* (*storm, fig: trouble etc*) prepararsi; **~ery** *n* fabbrica di birra
bribe [braɪb] *n* bustarella ♦ *vt* comprare; **~ry** *n* corruzione *f*
brick [brɪk] *n* mattone *m*; **~layer** *n* muratore *m*
bridal ['braɪdl] *adj* nuziale
bride [braɪd] *n* sposa; **~groom** *n* sposo; **~smaid** *n* damigella d'onore
bridge [brɪdʒ] *n* ponte *m*; (*NAUT*) ponte di comando; (*of nose*) dorso; (*CARDS*) bridge *m inv* ♦ *vt* (*fig: gap*) colmare
bridle ['braɪdl] *n* briglia; **~ path** *n* sentiero (per cavalli)
brief [briːf] *adj* breve ♦ *n* (*LAW*) comparsa; (*gen*) istruzioni *fpl* ♦ *vt* mettere al corrente; **~s** *npl* (*underwear*) mutande *fpl*; **~case** *n* cartella; **~ing** *n* briefing *m inv*; **~ly** *adv* (*glance*) di sfuggita; (*explain, say*) brevemente
bright [braɪt] *adj* luminoso(a); (*clever*) sveglio(a); (*lively*) vivace; **~en** (*also:* **~en up**) *vt* (*room*) rendere luminoso(a) ♦ *vi* schiarirsi; (*person*) rallegrarsi
brilliance ['brɪljəns] *n* splendore *m*
brilliant ['brɪljənt] *adj* brillante; (*light, smile*) radioso(a); (*inf*) splendido(a)
brim [brɪm] *n* orlo
brine [braɪn] *n* (*CULIN*) salamoia
bring [brɪŋ] (*pt, pp* **brought**) *vt* portare; **~ about** *vt* causare; **~ back** *vt* riportare; **~ down** *vt* portare giù; abbattere; **~ forward** *vt* (*proposal*) avanzare; (*meeting*) anticipare; **~ off** *vt* (*task, plan*) portare a compimento; **~ out** *vt* tirar fuori; (*meaning*) mettere in evidenza; (*book,*

album) far uscire; **~ round** *vt* (*unconscious person*) far rinvenire; **~ up** *vt* (*carry up*) portare su; (*child*) allevare; (*question*) introdurre; (*food: vomit*) rimettere, rigurgitare
brink [brɪŋk] *n* orlo
brisk [brɪsk] *adj* (*manner*) spiccio(a); (*trade*) vivace; (*pace*) svelto(a)
bristle ['brɪsl] *n* setola ♦ *vi* rizzarsi; **bristling with** irto(a) di
Britain ['brɪtən] *n* (*also:* **Great ~**) Gran Bretagna
British ['brɪtɪʃ] *adj* britannico(a); **the ~** *npl* i Britannici; **the ~ Isles** *npl* le Isole Britanniche; **~ Rail** *n* compagnia ferroviaria britannica, ≈ Ferrovie *fpl* dello Stato
Briton ['brɪtən] *n* britannico/a
brittle ['brɪtl] *adj* fragile
broach [brəʊtʃ] *vt* (*subject*) affrontare
broad [brɔːd] *adj* largo(a); (*distinction*) generale; (*accent*) spiccato(a); **in ~ daylight** in pieno giorno; **~cast** (*pt, pp* **~cast**) *n* trasmissione *f* ♦ *vt* trasmettere per radio (*or* per televisione) ♦ *vi* fare una trasmissione; **~en** *vt* allargare ♦ *vi* allargarsi; **~ly** *adv* (*fig*) in generale; **~-minded** *adj* di mente aperta
broccoli ['brɔkəlɪ] *n* broccoli *mpl*
brochure ['brəʊʃjʊə*] *n* dépliant *m inv*
broil [brɔɪl] *vt* cuocere a fuoco vivo
broke [brəʊk] *pt of* **break** ♦ *adj* (*inf*) squattrinato(a)
broken ['brəʊkn] *pp of* **break** ♦ *adj* rotto(a); **a ~ leg** una gamba rotta; **in ~ English** in un inglese stentato; **~-hearted** *adj*: **to be ~-hearted** avere il cuore spezzato
broker ['brəʊkə*] *n* agente *m*
brolly ['brɔlɪ] (*BRIT: inf*) *n* ombrello
bronchitis [brɔŋ'kaɪtɪs] *n* bronchite *f*
bronze [brɔnz] *n* bronzo
brooch [brəʊtʃ] *n* spilla
brood [bruːd] *n* covata ♦ *vi* (*person*) rimuginare
brook [bruk] *n* ruscello
broom [brum] *n* scopa; (*BOT*) ginestra
Bros. *abbr* (= *Brothers*) F.lli

broth [brɔθ] *n* brodo

brothel ['brɔθl] *n* bordello

brother ['brʌðə*] *n* fratello; **~-in-law** *n* cognato

brought [brɔːt] *pt, pp of* **bring**

brow [brau] *n* fronte *f*; (*rare, gen: eye~*) sopracciglio; (*of hill*) cima

brown [braun] *adj* bruno(a), marrone; (*tanned*) abbronzato(a) ♦ *n* (*colour*) color *m* bruno *or* marrone ♦ *vt* (CULIN) rosolare; **~ bread** *n* pane *m* integrale, pane nero

Brownie ['brauni] *n* giovane esploratrice *f*; **b~** (US: *cake*) dolce al cioccolato e nocciole

brown paper *n* carta da pacchi *or* da imballaggio

brown sugar *n* zucchero greggio

browse [brauz] *vi* (*among books*) curiosare fra i libri; **to ~ through a book** sfogliare un libro

bruise [bruːz] *n* (*on person*) livido ♦ *vt* farsi un livido a

brunette [bruːˈnet] *n* bruna

brunt [brʌnt] *n*: **the ~ of** (*attack, criticism etc*) il peso maggiore di

brush [brʌʃ] *n* spazzola; (*for painting, shaving*) pennello; (*quarrel*) schermaglia ♦ *vt* spazzolare; (*also:* **~ against**) sfiorare; **~ aside** *vt* scostare; **~ up** *vt* (*knowledge*) rinfrescare; **~wood** *n* macchia

Brussels ['brʌslz] *n* Bruxelles *f*; **~ sprout** *n* cavolo di Bruxelles

brutal ['bruːtl] *adj* brutale

brute [bruːt] *n* bestia ♦ *adj*: **by ~ force** con la forza, a viva forza

B.Sc. *n abbr* (UNIV) = **Bachelor of Science**

BSE *n abbr* (= *bovine spongiform encephalopathy*) encefalite *f* bovina spongiforme

bubble ['bʌbl] *n* bolla ♦ *vi* ribollire; (*sparkle, fig*) essere effervescente; **~ bath** *n* bagnoschiuma *m inv*; **~ gum** *n* gomma americana

buck [bʌk] *n* maschio (*di camoscio, caprone, coniglio etc*); (US: *inf*) dollaro ♦ *vi* sgroppare; **to pass the ~ (to sb)** scaricare (su di qn) la propria responsabilità; **~ up** *vi* (*cheer up*) rianimarsi

bucket ['bʌkɪt] *n* secchio

Buckingham Palace

ⓘ **Buckingham Palace** è la residenza ufficiale a Londra del sovrano britannico. Fu costruita nel 1703 per il duca di Buckingham.
---

buckle ['bʌkl] *n* fibbia ♦ *vt* allacciare ♦ *vi* (*wheel etc*) piegarsi

bud [bʌd] *n* gemma; (*of flower*) bocciolo ♦ *vi* germogliare; (*flower*) sbocciare

Buddhism ['budɪzəm] *n* buddismo

budding ['bʌdɪŋ] *adj* (*poet etc*) in erba

buddy ['bʌdɪ] (US) *n* compagno

budge [bʌdʒ] *vt* scostare; (*fig*) smuovere ♦ *vi* spostarsi; smuoversi

budgerigar ['bʌdʒərɪgɑː*] *n* pappagallino

budget ['bʌdʒɪt] *n* bilancio preventivo ♦ *vi*: **to ~ for sth** fare il bilancio per qc

budgie ['bʌdʒɪ] *n* = **budgerigar**

buff [bʌf] *adj* color camoscio ♦ *n* (*inf*: *enthusiast*) appassionato/a

buffalo ['bʌfələu] (*pl* **~** *or* **~es**) *n* bufalo; (US) bisonte *m*

buffer ['bʌfə*] *n* respingente *m*; (COMPUT) memoria tampone, buffer *m inv*

buffet¹ ['bufeɪ] *n* (*food, BRIT: bar*) buffet *m inv*; **~ car** (BRIT) *n* (RAIL) ≈ servizio ristoro

buffet² ['bʌfɪt] *vt* sferzare

bug [bʌg] *n* (*esp US: insect*) insetto; (COMPUT, *fig: germ*) virus *m inv*; (*spy device*) microfono spia ♦ *vt* mettere sotto controllo; (*inf: annoy*) scocciare

buggy ['bʌgɪ] *n* (*baby ~*) passeggino

bugle ['bjuːgl] *n* tromba

build [bɪld] (*pt, pp* **built**) *n* (*of person*) corporatura ♦ *vt* costruire; **~ up** *vt* accumulare; aumentare; **~er** *n* costruttore *m*; **~ing** *n* costruzione *f*; edificio; (*industry*) edilizia; **~ing society** (BRIT) *n* società *f inv* immobiliare

built [bɪlt] *pt, pp of* **build** ♦ *adj*: **~-in** (*cupboard*) a muro; (*device*) incorporato(a); **~-up area** *n* abitato

bulb [bʌlb] *n* (BOT) bulbo; (ELEC) lampadina

bulge [bʌldʒ] *n* rigonfiamento ♦ *vi* essere

protuberante *or* rigonfio(a); **to be bulging with** essere pieno(a) *or* zeppo(a) di

bulk [bʌlk] *n* massa, volume *m*; **in ~ a** pacchi (*or* cassette *etc*); (*COMM*) all'ingrosso; **the ~ of** il grosso di; **~y** *adj* grosso(a); voluminoso(a)

bull [bul] *n* toro; (*male elephant, whale*) maschio; **~dog** *n* bulldog *m inv*

bulldozer ['buldəuzə*] *n* bulldozer *m inv*

bullet ['bulɪt] *n* pallottola

bulletin ['bulɪtɪn] *n* bollettino

bulletproof ['bulɪtpruːf] *adj* (*car*) blindato(a); (*vest etc*) antiproiettile *inv*

bullfight ['bulfaɪt] *n* corrida; **~er** *n* torero; **~ing** *n* tauromachia

bullion ['buljən] *n* oro *or* argento in lingotti

bullock ['bulək] *n* manzo

bullring ['bulrɪŋ] *n* arena (per corride)

bull's-eye ['bulzaɪ] *n* centro del bersaglio

bully ['bulɪ] *n* prepotente *m* ♦ *vt* angariare; (*frighten*) intimidire

bum [bʌm] (*inf*) *n* (*backside*) culo; (*tramp*) vagabondo/a

bumblebee ['bʌmblbiː] *n* bombo

bump [bʌmp] *n* (*in car*) piccolo tamponamento; (*jolt*) scossa; (*on road etc*) protuberanza; (*on head*) bernoccolo ♦ *vt* battere; **~ into** *vt fus* scontrarsi con; (*person*) imbattersi in; **~er** *n* paraurti *m inv* ♦ *adj*: **~er harvest** raccolto eccezionale; **~er cars** *npl* autoscontri *mpl*

bumpy ['bʌmpɪ] *adj* (*road*) dissestato(a)

bun [bʌn] *n* focaccia; (*of hair*) crocchia

bunch [bʌntʃ] *n* (*of flowers, keys*) mazzo; (*of bananas*) casco; (*of people*) gruppo; **~ of grapes** grappolo d'uva; **~es** *npl* (*in hair*) codine *fpl*

bundle ['bʌndl] *n* fascio ♦ *vt* (*also: ~ up*) legare in un fascio; (*put*): **to ~ sth/sb into** spingere qc/qn in

bungalow ['bʌŋgələu] *n* bungalow *m inv*

bungle ['bʌŋgl] *vt* fare un pasticcio di

bunion ['bʌnjən] *n* callo (al piede)

bunk [bʌŋk] *n* cuccetta; **~ beds** *npl* letti *mpl* a castello

bunker ['bʌŋkə*] *n* (*coal store*) ripostiglio per il carbone; (*MIL, GOLF*) bunker *m inv*

bunny ['bʌnɪ] *n* (*also: ~ rabbit*) coniglietto

bunting ['bʌntɪŋ] *n* pavesi *mpl*, bandierine *fpl*

buoy [bɔɪ] *n* boa; **~ant** *adj* galleggiante; (*fig*) vivace

burden ['bəːdn] *n* carico, fardello ♦ *vt*: **to ~ sb with** caricare qn di

bureau [bjuə'rəu] (*pl* **bureaux**) *n* (*BRIT: writing desk*) scrivania; (*US: chest of drawers*) cassettone *m*; (*office*) ufficio, agenzia

bureaucracy [bjuə'rɔkrəsɪ] *n* burocrazia

bureaux [bjuə'rəuz] *npl of* **bureau**

burglar ['bəːglə*] *n* scassinatore *m*; **~ alarm** *n* campanello antifurto; **~y** *n* furto con scasso

burial ['berɪəl] *n* sepoltura

burly ['bəːlɪ] *adj* robusto(a)

Burma ['bəːmə] *n* Birmania

burn [bəːn] (*pt, pp* **burned** *or* **burnt**) *vt, vi* bruciare ♦ *n* bruciatura, scottatura; **~ down** *vt* distruggere col fuoco; **~er** *n* (*on cooker*) fornello; (*TECH*) bruciatore *m*, becco (a gas); **~ing** *adj* in fiamme; (*sand*) che scotta; (*ambition*) bruciante; **burnt** *pt, pp of* **burn**

burrow ['bʌrəu] *n* tana ♦ *vt* scavare

bursary ['bəːsərɪ] (*BRIT*) *n* (*SCOL*) borsa di studio

burst [bəːst] (*pt, pp* **burst**) *vt* far scoppiare ♦ *vi* esplodere; (*tyre*) scoppiare ♦ *n* scoppio; (*also: ~ pipe*) rottura nel tubo, perdita; **a ~ of speed** uno scatto di velocità; **to ~ into flames/tears** scoppiare in fiamme/lacrime; **to ~ out laughing** scoppiare a ridere; **to be ~ing with** scoppiare di; **~ into** *vt fus* (*room etc*) irrompere in

bury ['berɪ] *vt* seppellire

bus [bʌs] (*pl* **~es**) *n* autobus *m inv*

bush [buʃ] *n* cespuglio; (*scrub land*) macchia; **to beat about the ~** menare il cane per l'aia

bushy ['buʃɪ] *adj* cespuglioso(a)

busily ['bɪzɪlɪ] *adv* con impegno, alacremente

business ['bɪznɪs] *n* (*matter*) affare *m*; (*trading*) affari *mpl*; (*firm*) azienda; (*job,* duty) lavoro; **to be away on ~** essere andato via per affari; **it's none of my ~** questo non mi riguarda; **he means ~** non scherza; **~like** adj serio(a); efficiente; **~man/woman** (irreg) n uomo/donna d'affari; **~ trip** n viaggio d'affari

busker ['bʌskə*] (BRIT) n suonatore/trice ambulante

bus: ~ shelter n pensilina (alla fermata dell'autobus); **~ station** n stazione f delle corriere, autostazione f; **~-stop** n fermata d'autobus

bust [bʌst] n busto; (ANAT) seno ♦ adj (inf: broken) rotto(a); **to go ~** fallire

bustle ['bʌsl] n movimento, attività ♦ vi darsi da fare; **bustling** adj movimentato(a)

busy ['bɪzɪ] adj occupato(a); (shop, street) molto frequentato(a) ♦ vt: **to ~ o.s.** darsi da fare; **~body** n ficcanaso m/f inv; **~ signal** (US) n (TEL) segnale m di occupato

but [bʌt] conj ma; **I'd love to come, ~ I'm busy** vorrei tanto venire, ma ho da fare ♦ prep (apart from, except) eccetto, tranne, meno; **he was nothing ~ trouble** non dava altro che guai; **no-one ~ him can do it** nessuno può farlo tranne lui; **~ for you/your help** se non fosse per te/per il tuo aiuto; **anything ~ that** tutto ma non questo ♦ adv (just, only) solo, soltanto; **she's a child ~** è solo una bambina; **had I ~ known** se solo avessi saputo; **I can ~ try** tentar non nuoce; **all ~ finished** quasi finito

butcher ['butʃə*] n macellaio ♦ vt macellare; **~'s (shop)** n macelleria

butler ['bʌtlə*] n maggiordomo

butt [bʌt] n (cask) grossa botte f; (of gun) calcio; (of cigarette) mozzicone m; (BRIT: fig: target) oggetto ♦ vt cozzare; **~ in** vi (interrupt) interrompere

butter ['bʌtə*] n burro ♦ vt imburrare; **~cup** n ranuncolo

butterfly ['bʌtəflaɪ] n farfalla; (SWIMMING:

also: **~ stroke**) (nuoto a) farfalla

buttocks ['bʌtəks] npl natiche fpl

button ['bʌtn] n bottone m; (US: badge) distintivo ♦ vt (also: **~ up**) abbottonare ♦ vi abbottonarsi

buttress ['bʌtrɪs] n contrafforte f

buy [baɪ] (pt, pp bought) vt comprare ♦ n acquisto; **to ~ sb sth/sth from sb** comprare qc per qn/qc da qn; **to ~ sb a drink** offrire da bere a qn; **~er** n compratore/trice

buzz [bʌz] n ronzio; (inf: phone call) colpo di telefono ♦ vi ronzare

buzzer ['bʌzə*] n cicalino

buzz word (inf) n termine m di gran moda

by [baɪ] prep **1** (referring to cause, agent) da; **killed ~ lightning** ucciso da un fulmine; **surrounded ~ a fence** circondato da uno steccato; **a painting ~ Picasso** un quadro di Picasso

2 (referring to method, manner, means): **~ bus/car/train** in autobus/macchina/treno, con l'autobus/la macchina/il treno; **to pay ~ cheque** pagare con (un) assegno; **~ moonlight** al chiaro di luna; **~ saving hard, he ...** risparmiando molto, lui ...

3 (via, through) per; **we came ~ Dover** siamo venuti via Dover

4 (close to, past) accanto a; **the house ~ the river** la casa sul fiume; **a holiday ~ the sea** una vacanza al mare; **she sat ~ his bed** si sedette accanto al suo letto; **she rushed ~ me** mi è passata accanto correndo; **I go ~ the post office every day** passo davanti all'ufficio postale ogni giorno

5 (not later than) per, entro; **~ 4 o'clock** per or entro le 4; **~ this time tomorrow** domani a quest'ora; **~ the time I got here it was too late** quando sono arrivato era ormai troppo tardi

6 (during): **~ day/night** di giorno/notte

7 (amount) a; **~ the kilo/metre** a chili/metri; **paid ~ the hour** pagato all'ora; **one ~ one** uno per uno; **little ~ little** a poco a poco

8 (*MATH, measure*): **to divide/multiply ~ 3** dividere/moltiplicare per 3; **it's broader ~ a metre** è un metro più largo, è più largo di un metro

9 (*according to*) per; **to play ~ the rules** attenersi alle regole; **it's all right ~ me** per me va bene

10: (**all**) **~ oneself** *etc* (tutto(a)) solo(a); **he did it** (**all**) **~ himself** lo ha fatto (tutto) da solo

11: **~ the way** a proposito; **this wasn't my idea ~ the way** tra l'altro l'idea non è stata mia

♦ *adv* **1** *see* **go; pass** *etc*

2: **~ and ~** (*in past*) poco dopo; (*in future*) fra breve; **~ and large** nel complesso

---

bye(-bye) ['baɪ('baɪ)] *excl* ciao!, arrivederci!

by(e)-law *n* legge *f* locale

by-election (*BRIT*) *n* elezione *f* straordinaria

bygone ['baɪgɔn] *adj* passato(a) ♦ *n*: **let ~s be ~s** mettiamoci una pietra sopra

bypass ['baɪpɑːs] *n* circonvallazione *f*; (*MED*) by-pass *m inv* ♦ *vt* fare una deviazione intorno a

by-product *n* sottoprodotto *m*; (*fig*) conseguenza secondaria

bystander ['baɪstændə*] *n* spettatore/trice

byte [baɪt] *n* (*COMPUT*) byte *m inv*, bicarattere *m*

byword ['baɪwəːd] *n*: **to be a ~ for** essere sinonimo di

C, c

C [siː] *n* (*MUS*) do

C. *abbr* (= *centigrade*) C.

C.A. *n abbr* = **chartered accountant**

cab [kæb] *n* taxi *m inv*; (*of train, truck*) cabina

cabaret ['kæbəreɪ] *n* cabaret *m inv*

cabbage ['kæbɪdʒ] *n* cavolo

cabin ['kæbɪn] *n* capanna; (*on ship*) cabina; **~ crew** *n* equipaggio; **~ cruiser** *n* cabinato

cabinet ['kæbɪnɪt] *n* (*POL*) consiglio dei ministri; (*furniture*) armadietto; (*also:* **display ~**) vetrinetta

cable ['keɪbl] *n* cavo; fune *f*; (*TEL*) cablogramma *m* ♦ *vt* telegrafare; **~-car** *n* funivia; **~ television** *n* televisione *f* via cavo

cache [kæʃ] *n* deposito segreto

cackle ['kækl] *vi* schiamazzare

cactus ['kæktəs] (*pl* **cacti**) *n* cactus *m inv*

cadet [kə'dɛt] *n* (*MIL*) cadetto

cadge [kædʒ] (*inf*) *vt* scroccare

café ['kæfeɪ] *n* caffè *m inv*

cafeteria [kæfɪ'tɪərɪə] *n* self-service *m inv*

cage [keɪdʒ] *n* gabbia

cagey ['keɪdʒɪ] (*inf*) *adj* chiuso(a); guardingo(a)

cagoule [kə'guːl] *n* K-way ® *m inv*

cajole [kə'dʒəʊl] *vt* allettare

cake [keɪk] *n* (*large*) torta; (*small*) pasticcino; **~ of soap** saponetta; **~d** *adj*: **~d with** incrostato(a) di

calculate ['kælkjuleɪt] *vt* calcolare; **calculation** [-'leɪʃən] *n* calcolo; **calculator** *n* calcolatrice *f*

calendar ['kæləndə*] *n* calendario; **~ year** *n* anno civile

calf [kɑːf] (*pl* **calves**) *n* (*of cow*) vitello; (*of other animals*) piccolo; (*also:* **~skin**) (pelle *f* di) vitello; (*ANAT*) polpaccio

calibre ['kælɪbə*] (*US* **caliber**) *n* calibro

call [kɔːl] *vt* (*gen, also TEL*) chiamare; (*meeting*) indire ♦ *vi* chiamare; (*visit: also:* **~ in, ~ round**) passare ♦ *n* (*shout*) grido, urlo; (*TEL*) telefonata; **to be ~ed** (*person, object*) chiamarsi; **to be on ~** essere a disposizione; **~ back** *vi* (*return*) ritornare; (*TEL*) ritelefonare, richiamare; **~ for** *vt fus* richiedere; (*fetch*) passare a prendere; **~ off** *vt* disdire; **~ on** *vt fus* (*visit*) passare da; (*appeal to*) chiedere a; **~ out** *vi* (*in pain*) urlare; (*to person*) chiamare; **~ up** *vt* (*MIL*) richiamare; (*TEL*) telefonare a; **~box** (*BRIT*) *n* cabina telefonica; **~er** *n* persona che chiama; visitatore/trice; **~ girl** *n* ragazza *f* squillo *inv*; **~-in** (*US*) *n* (*phone-in*) trasmissione *f* a filo diretto con gli ascoltatori; **~ing** *n* vocazione *f*; **~ing card**

(*US*) *n* biglietto da visita

callous ['kæləs] *adj* indurito(a), insensibile

calm [kɑːm] *adj* calmo(a) ♦ *n* calma ♦ *vt* calmare; ~ **down** *vi* calmarsi ♦ *vt* calmare

Calor gas ® ['kælə*-*] *n* butano

calorie ['kælərɪ] *n* caloria

calves [kɑːvz] *npl of* **calf**

Cambodia [kæm'bəʊdʒə] *n* Cambogia

camcorder ['kæmkɔːdə*] *n* camcorder *f inv*

came [keɪm] *pt of* **come**

camel ['kæməl] *n* cammello

camera ['kæmərə] *n* macchina fotografica; (*CINEMA, TV*) cinepresa; **in** ~ a porte chiuse; **~man** (*irreg*) *n* cameraman *m inv*

camouflage ['kæməflɑːʒ] *n* (*MIL, ZOOL*) mimetizzazione *f* ♦ *vt* mimetizzare

camp [kæmp] *n* campeggio; (*MIL*) campo ♦ *vi* accamparsi ♦ *adj* effeminato(a)

campaign [kæm'peɪn] *n* (*MIL, POL etc*) campagna ♦ *vi* (*also fig*) fare una campagna

camp bed (*BRIT*) *n* brandina

camper ['kæmpə*] *n* campeggiatore/trice; (*vehicle*) camper *m inv*

camping ['kæmpɪŋ] *n* campeggio; **to go** ~ andare in campeggio

campsite ['kæmpsaɪt] *n* campeggio

campus ['kæmpəs] *n* campus *m inv*

can[1] [kæn] *n* (*of milk*) scatola; (*of oil*) bidone *m*; (*of water*) tanica; (*tin*) scatola ♦ *vt* mettere in scatola

can[2] [kæn] (*negative* **cannot, can't**; *conditional and pt* **could**) *aux vb* 1 (*be able to*) potere; **I ~'t go any further** non posso andare oltre; **you ~ do it if you try** sei in grado di farlo — basta provarci; **I'll help you all I ~** ti aiuterò come potrò; **I ~'t see you** non ti vedo

2 (*know how to*) sapere, essere capace di; **I ~ swim** so nuotare; ~ **you speak French?** parla francese?

3 (*may*) potere; **could I have a word with you?** posso parlarle un momento?

4 (*expressing disbelief, puzzlement etc*): **it ~'t be true!** non può essere vero!; **what**

CAN he want? cosa può mai volere?

5 (*expressing possibility, suggestion etc*): **he could be in the library** può darsi che sia in biblioteca; **she could have been delayed** può aver avuto un contrattempo

Canada ['kænədə] *n* Canada *m*

Canadian [kə'neɪdɪən] *adj, n* canadese *m/f*

canal [kə'næl] *n* canale *m*

canary [kə'nɛərɪ] *n* canarino

cancel ['kænsəl] *vt* annullare; (*train*) sopprimere; (*cross out*) cancellare; **~lation** [-'leɪʃən] *n* annullamento; soppressione *f*; cancellazione *f*; (*TOURISM*) prenotazione *f* annullata

cancer ['kænsə*] *n* cancro; **C~** (*sign*) Cancro

candid ['kændɪd] *adj* onesto(a)

candidate ['kændɪdeɪt] *n* candidato/a

candle ['kændl] *n* candela; (*in church*) cero; **~light** *n*: **by ~light** a lume di candela; **~stick** *n* bugia; (*bigger, ornate*) candeliere *m*

candour ['kændə*] (*US* **candor**) *n* sincerità

candy ['kændɪ] *n* zucchero candito; (*US*) caramella; caramelle *fpl*; **~-floss** (*BRIT*) *n* zucchero filato

cane [keɪn] *n* canna; (*for furniture*) bambù *m*; (*stick*) verga ♦ *vt* (*BRIT: SCOL*) punire a colpi di verga

canister ['kænɪstə*] *n* scatola metallica

cannabis ['kænəbɪs] *n* canapa indiana

canned ['kænd] *adj* (*food*) in scatola

cannon ['kænən] (*pl* ~ *or* ~**s**) *n* (*gun*) cannone *m*

cannot ['kænɒt] = **can not**

canny ['kænɪ] *adj* furbo(a)

canoe [kə'nuː] *n* canoa; **~ing** *n* canottaggio

canon ['kænən] *n* (*clergyman*) canonico; (*standard*) canone *m*

can opener [-'əʊpnə*] *n* apriscatole *m inv*

canopy ['kænəpɪ] *n* baldacchino

cant [kænt] *n* gergo ♦ *vt* inclinare ♦ *vi* inclinarsi

can't [kænt] = **can not**

canteen [kæn'tiːn] *n* mensa; (*BRIT: of cutlery*) portaposate *m inv*

canter ['kæntə*] *vi* andare al piccolo

galoppo

canvas ['kænvəs] *n* tela

canvass ['kænvəs] *vi* (*POL*): **to ~ for** raccogliere voti per ♦ *vt* fare un sondaggio di

cap [kæp] *n* (*hat*) berretto; (*of pen*) coperchio; (*of bottle, toy gun*) tappo; (*contraceptive*) diaframma *m* ♦ *vt* (*outdo*) superare; (*limit*) fissare un tetto (a)

capability [keɪpə'bɪlɪtɪ] *n* capacità *f inv*, abilità *f inv*

capable ['keɪpəbl] *adj* capace

capacity [kə'pæsɪtɪ] *n* capacità *f inv*; (*of lift etc*) capienza

cape [keɪp] *n* (*garment*) cappa; (*GEO*) capo

caper ['keɪpə*] *n* (*CULIN*) cappero; (*prank*) scherzetto

capital ['kæpɪtl] *n* (*also*: ~ **city**) capitale *f*; (*money*) capitale *m*; (*also*: ~ **letter**) maiuscola; ~ **gains tax** *n* imposta sulla plusvalenza; **~ism** *n* capitalismo; **~ist** *adj*, *n* capitalista (*m/f*); **~ize**: **to ~ize on** *vt fus* trarre vantaggio da; ~ **punishment** *n* pena capitale

Capitol ['kæpɪtl] *n*: **the ~** il Campidoglio

⎡ **Capitol** ⎤

ⓘ *Il* **Capitol** *è l'edificio dove si svolgono le riunioni del Congresso degli Stati Uniti. È situato sull'omonimo colle, Capitol Hill, a Washington D.C.*

Capricorn ['kæprɪkɔːn] *n* Capricorno

capsize [kæp'saɪz] *vt* capovolgere ♦ *vi* capovolgersi

capsule ['kæpsjuːl] *n* capsula

captain ['kæptɪn] *n* capitano

caption ['kæpʃən] *n* leggenda

captivate ['kæptɪveɪt] *vt* avvincere

captive ['kæptɪv] *adj, n* prigioniero(a)

captivity [kæp'tɪvɪtɪ] *n* cattività

capture ['kæptʃə*] *vt* catturare; (*COMPUT*) registrare ♦ *n* cattura; (*data ~*) registrazione *f* or rilevazione *f* di dati

car [kɑː*] *n* (*AUT*) macchina, automobile *f*; (*RAIL*) vagone *m*

carafe [kə'ræf] *n* caraffa

caramel ['kærəməl] *n* caramello

caravan ['kærəvæn] *n* (*BRIT*) roulotte *f inv*; (*of camels*) carovana; **~ning** *n* vacanze *fpl* in roulotte; ~ **site** (*BRIT*) *n* campeggio per roulotte

carbohydrates [kɑːbəu'haɪdreɪts] *npl* (*foods*) carboidrati *mpl*

carbon ['kɑːbən] *n* carbonio; ~ **paper** *n* carta carbone

car boot sale *n* mercatino dell'usato dove la merce viene esposta nei bagagliai delle macchine

carburettor [kɑːbju'retə*] (*US* **carburetor**) *n* carburatore *m*

card [kɑːd] *n* carta; (*visiting ~ etc*) biglietto; (*Christmas ~ etc*) cartolina; **~board** *n* cartone *m*; ~ **game** *n* gioco di carte

cardiac ['kɑːdɪæk] *adj* cardiaco(a)

cardigan ['kɑːdɪgən] *n* cardigan *m inv*

cardinal ['kɑːdɪnl] *adj* cardinale ♦ *n* cardinale *m*

card index *n* schedario

cardphone ['kɑːdfəun] *n* telefono a scheda

care [keə*] *n* cura, attenzione *f*; (*worry*) preoccupazione *f* ♦ *vi*: **to ~ about** curarsi di; (*thing, idea*) interessarsi di; ~ **of** presso; **in sb's ~** alle cure di qn; **to take ~** (**to do**) fare attenzione (a fare); **to take ~ of** curarsi di; (*bill, problem*) occuparsi di; **I don't ~** non me ne importa; **I couldn't ~ less** non m'interessa affatto; ~ **for** *vt fus* aver cura di; (*like*) volere bene a

career [kə'rɪə*] *n* carriera ♦ *vi* (*also*: ~ **along**) andare di (gran) carriera

carefree ['keəfriː] *adj* sgombro(a) di preoccupazioni

careful ['keəful] *adj* attento(a); (*cautious*) cauto(a); (**be**) **~!** attenzione!; **~ly** *adv* con cura; cautamente

careless ['keəlɪs] *adj* negligente; (*heedless*) spensierato(a)

carer ['keərə*] *n* assistente *m/f* (*di persone malata o handicappata*)

caress [kə'res] *n* carezza ♦ *vt* accarezzare

caretaker ['keəteɪkə*] *n* custode *m*

car-ferry *n* traghetto

cargo ['kɑːgəu] (*pl* **~es**) *n* carico

car hire *n* autonoleggio
Caribbean [kærɪ'bi:ən] *adj*: **the ~ (Sea)** il
Mar dei Caraibi
caring ['kɛərɪŋ] *adj* (*person*) premuroso(a);
(*society, organization*) umanitario(a)
carnage ['kɑ:nɪdʒ] *n* carneficina
carnation [kɑ:'neɪʃən] *n* garofano
carnival ['kɑ:nɪvəl] *n* (*public celebration*)
carnevale *m*; (*US: funfair*) luna park *m inv*
carol ['kærəl] *n*: (**Christmas**) ~ canto di
Natale
carp [kɑ:p] *n* (*fish*) carpa
car park (*BRIT*) *n* parcheggio
carpenter ['kɑ:pɪntə*] *n* carpentiere *m*
carpentry ['kɑ:pɪntrɪ] *n* carpenteria
carpet ['kɑ:pɪt] *n* tappeto ♦ *vt* coprire con
tappeto
car phone *n* telefonino per auto, cellulare
m per auto
car rental (*US*) *n* autonoleggio
carriage ['kærɪdʒ] *n* vettura; (*of goods*)
trasporto; **~way** (*BRIT*) *n* (*part of road*)
carreggiata
carrier ['kærɪə*] *n* (*of disease*) portatore/
trice; (*COMM*) impresa di trasporti; **~ bag**
(*BRIT*) *n* sacchetto
carrot ['kærət] *n* carota
carry ['kærɪ] *vt* (*subj: person*) portare;
(*: vehicle*) trasportare; (*involve:
responsibilities etc*) comportare; (*MED*) essere
portatore/trice di ♦ *vi* (*sound*) farsi sentire:
to be *or* **get carried away** (*fig*)
entusiasmarsi; **~ on** *vi*: **to ~ on with sth**/
doing continuare qc/a fare ♦ *vt* mandare
avanti; **~ out** *vt* (*orders*) eseguire;
(*investigation*) svolgere; **~cot** (*BRIT*) *n* culla
portabile; **~-on** (*inf*) *n* (*fuss*) casino,
confusione *f*
cart [kɑ:t] *n* carro ♦ *vt* (*inf*) trascinare
carton ['kɑ:tən] *n* (*box*) scatola di cartone;
(*of yogurt*) cartone *m*; (*of cigarettes*) stecca
cartoon [kɑ:'tu:n] *n* (*PRESS*) disegno
umoristico; (*comic strip*) fumetto; (*CINEMA*)
disegno animato
cartridge ['kɑ:trɪdʒ] *n* (*for gun, pen*)
cartuccia; (*music tape*) cassetta
carve [kɑ:v] *vt* (*meat*) trinciare; (*wood,
stone*) intagliare; **~ up** *vt* (*fig: country*)
suddividere; **carving** *n* (*in wood etc*)
scultura; **carving knife** *n* trinciante *m*
car wash *n* lavaggio auto
cascade [kæs'keɪd] *n* cascata
case [keɪs] *n* caso; (*LAW*) causa, processo;
(*box*) scatola; (*BRIT: also: suit~*) valigia; **in ~
of** in caso di; **in ~ he** caso mai lui; **in any ~**
in ogni caso; **just in ~** in caso di bisogno
cash [kæʃ] *n* denaro; (*coins, notes*) denaro
liquido ♦ *vt* incassare; **to pay (in) ~** pagare
in contanti; **~ on delivery** pagamento alla
consegna; **~-book** *n* giornale *m* di cassa;
~ card (*BRIT*) *n* tesserino di prelievo; **~
desk** (*BRIT*) *n* cassa; **~ dispenser** (*BRIT*)
n sportello automatico
cashew [kæ'ʃu:] *n* (*also:* **~ nut**) anacardio
cashier [kæ'ʃɪə*] *n* cassiere/a
cashmere ['kæʃmɪə*] *n* cachemire *m*
cash register *n* registratore *m* di cassa
casing ['keɪsɪŋ] *n* rivestimento
casino [kə'si:nəu] *n* casinò *m inv*
cask [kɑ:sk] *n* botte *f*
casket ['kɑ:skɪt] *n* cofanetto; (*US: coffin*)
bara
casserole ['kæsərəul] *n* casseruola; (*food*):
chicken ~ pollo in casseruola
cassette [kæ'set] *n* cassetta; **~ player** *n*
riproduttore *m* a cassette; **~ recorder** *n*
registratore *m* a cassette
cast [kɑ:st] (*pt, pp* **cast**) *vt* (*throw*) gettare;
(*metal*) gettare, fondere; (*THEATRE*): **to ~ sb
as Hamlet** scegliere qn per la parte di
Amleto ♦ *n* (*THEATRE*) cast *m inv*; (*also:
plaster ~*) ingessatura; **to ~ one's vote**
votare, dare il voto; **~ off** *vi* (*NAUT*) salpare;
(*KNITTING*) calare; **~ on** *vi* (*KNITTING*) avviare
le maglie
castaway ['kɑ:stəwei] *n* naufrago/a
caster sugar ['kɑ:stə*-] (*BRIT*) *n* zucchero
semolato
casting vote ['kɑ:stɪŋ-] (*BRIT*) *n* voto
decisivo
cast iron *n* ghisa
castle ['kɑ:sl] *n* castello
castor oil ['kɑ:stə*-] *n* olio di ricino
casual ['kæʒjul] *adj* (*by chance*) casuale,

fortuito(a); (*irregular: work etc*)
avventizio(a); (*unconcerned*) noncurante,
indifferente; ~ **wear** casual *m*; ~**ly** *adv* (*in
a relaxed way*) con noncuranza; (*dress*)
casual

casualty ['kæʒjultɪ] *n* ferito/a; (*dead*)
morto/a, vittima; (*MED: department*) pronto
soccorso

cat [kæt] *n* gatto

catalogue ['kætələg] (*US* **catalog**) *n*
catalogo ♦ *vt* catalogare

catalyst ['kætəlɪst] *n* catalizzatore *m*

catalytic convertor [kætəlɪtɪk-] *n*
marmitta catalitica, catalizzatore *m*

catapult ['kætəpʌlt] *n* catapulta; fionda

cataract ['kætərækt] *n* (*also MED*) cateratta

catarrh [kə'tɑːʳ] *n* catarro

catastrophe [kə'tæstrəfɪ] *n* catastrofe *f*

catch [kætʃ] (*pt, pp* **caught**) *vt* prendere;
(*ball*) afferrare; (*surprise: person*)
sorprendere; (*attention*) attirare; (*comment,
whisper*) cogliere; (*person: also:* ~ **up**)
raggiungere ♦ *vi* (*fire*) prendere ♦ *n* (*fish
etc caught*) retata; (*of ball*) presa; (*trick*)
inganno; (*TECH*) gancio; (*game*) catch *m
inv*; **to** ~ **fire** prendere fuoco; **to** ~ **sight of**
scorgere; ~ **on** *vi* capire; (*become popular*)
affermarsi, far presa; ~ **up** *vi* mettersi in
pari ♦ *vt* (*also:* ~ **up with**) raggiungere

catching ['kætʃɪŋ] *adj* (*MED*) contagioso(a)

catchment area ['kætʃmənt-] *n* (*BRIT*)
(*SCOL*) circoscrizione *f* scolare

catch phrase *n* slogan *m inv*; frase *f* fatta

catchy ['kætʃɪ] *adj* orecchiabile

category ['kætɪgərɪ] *n* categoria

cater ['keɪtəʳ] *vi*: ~ **for** (*BRIT: needs*)
provvedere a; (: *readers, consumers*)
incontrare i gusti di; (*COMM: provide food*)
provvedere alla ristorazione di; ~**er** *n*
fornitore *m*; ~**ing** *n* approvvigionamento

caterpillar ['kætəpɪləʳ] *n* bruco

cathedral [kə'θiːdrəl] *n* cattedrale *f*, duomo

catholic ['kæθəlɪk] *adj* universale; aperto(a);
eclettico(a); **C~** *adj, n* (*REL*) cattolico(a)

CAT scan *n* (= *computerized axial
tomography*) TAC *f inv*

Catseye ® [kæts'aɪ] (*BRIT*) *n* (*AUT*) cata-

rifrangente *m*

cattle ['kætl] *npl* bestiame *m*, bestie *fpl*

catty ['kætɪ] *adj* maligno(a), dispettoso(a)

caucus ['kɔːkəs] *n* (*POL: group*) comitato di
dirigenti; (: *US*) (riunione *f* del) comitato
elettorale

caught [kɔːt] *pt, pp of* **catch**

cauliflower ['kɔlɪflauəʳ] *n* cavolfiore *m*

cause [kɔːz] *n* causa ♦ *vt* causare

caution ['kɔːʃən] *n* prudenza; (*warning*)
avvertimento ♦ *vt* avvertire; ammonire

cautious ['kɔːʃəs] *adj* cauto(a), prudente

cavalry ['kævəlrɪ] *n* cavalleria

cave [keɪv] *n* caverna, grotta; ~ **in** *vi* (*roof
etc*) crollare; ~**man** (*irreg*) *n* uomo delle
caverne

caviar(e) ['kævɪɑːʳ] *n* caviale *m*

CB *n abbr* (= *Citizens' Band (Radio)*): ~
radio (set) baracchino

CBI *n abbr* (= *Confederation of British
Industries*) ≈ Confindustria

cc *abbr* = **cubic centimetres; carbon copy**

CD *abbr* (*disc*) CD *m inv*; (*player*) lettore *m*
CD *inv*

CDI *n abbr* (= *compact disk interactive*) CD-I
m inv, compact disc *m inv* interattivo

CD player *n* lettore *m* CD

CD-ROM [-rɔm] *n abbr* CD-ROM *m inv*

cease [siːs] *vt, vi* cessare; ~**fire** *n* cessate il
fuoco *m inv*; ~**less** *adj* incessante,
continuo(a)

cedar ['siːdəʳ] *n* cedro

ceiling ['siːlɪŋ] *n* soffitto; (*on wages etc*)
tetto

celebrate ['sɛlɪbreɪt] *vt, vi* celebrare; ~**d** *adj*
celebre; **celebration** [-'breɪʃən] *n*
celebrazione *f*

celery ['sɛlərɪ] *n* sedano

cell [sɛl] *n* cella; (*of revolutionaries, BIOL*)
cellula; (*ELEC*) elemento (di batteria)

cellar ['sɛləʳ] *n* sottosuolo; cantina

'cello ['tʃɛləu] *n* violoncello

cellphone [sɛl,fəun] *n* cellulare *m*

Celt [kɛlt, sɛlt] *n* celta *m/f*

Celtic ['kɛltɪk, 'sɛltɪk] *adj* celtico(a)

cement [sə'mɛnt] *n* cemento; ~ **mixer** *n*
betoniera

cemetery ['semitri] n cimitero

censor ['sensə*] n censore m ♦ vt censurare; **~ship** n censura

censure ['senʃə*] vt riprovare, censurare

census ['sensəs] n censimento

cent [sent] n (US: coin) centesimo (= 1:100 di un dollaro); see also **per**

centenary [sen'ti:nəri] n centenario

center ['sentə*] (US) n, vt = **centre**

centigrade ['sentigreid] adj centigrado(a)

centimetre ['sentimi:tə*] (US **centimeter**) n centimetro

centipede ['sentipi:d] n centopiedi m inv

central ['sentrəl] adj centrale; **C~ America** n America centrale; **~ heating** n riscaldamento centrale; **~ize** vt accentrare

centre ['sentə*] (US **center**) n centro ♦ vt centrare; **~-forward** n (SPORT) centroavanti m inv; **~-half** n (SPORT) centromediano

century ['sentjuri] n secolo; **20th ~** ventesimo secolo

ceramic [si'ræmik] adj ceramico(a); **~s** npl ceramica

cereal ['si:riəl] n cereale m

ceremony ['seriməni] n cerimonia; **to stand on ~** fare complimenti

certain ['sə:tən] adj certo(a); **to make ~ of** assicurarsi di; **for ~** per certo, di sicuro; **~ly** adv certamente, certo; **~ty** n certezza

certificate [sə'tifikit] n certificato; diploma m

certified ['sə:tifaid]: **~ mail** (US) n posta raccomandata con ricevuta di ritorno; **~ public accountant** (US) n ≈ commercialista m/f

certify ['sə:tifai] vt certificare; (award diploma to) conferire un diploma a; (declare insane) dichiarare pazzo(a)

cervical ['sə:vikl] adj: **~ cancer** cancro della cervice; **~ smear** Pap-test m inv

cervix ['sə:viks] n cervice f

cf. abbr (= compare) cfr

CFC n (= chlorofluorocarbon) CFC m inv

ch. abbr (= chapter) cap

chafe [tʃeif] vt fregare, irritare

chain [tʃein] n catena ♦ vt (also: **~ up**) incatenare; **~ reaction** n reazione f a catena; **~-smoke** vi fumare una sigaretta dopo l'altra; **~ store** n negozio a catena

chair [tʃeə*] n sedia; (armchair) poltrona; (of university) cattedra; (of meeting) presidenza ♦ vt (meeting) presiedere; **~lift** n seggiovia; **~man** (irreg) n presidente m

chalet ['ʃælei] n chalet m inv

chalk [tʃɔ:k] n gesso

challenge ['tʃælindʒ] n sfida ♦ vt sfidare; (statement, right) mettere in dubbio; **to ~ sb to do** sfidare qn a fare; **challenging** adj (task) impegnativo(a); (look) di sfida

chamber ['tʃeimbə*] n camera; **~ of commerce** n camera del commercio; **~maid** n cameriera; **~ music** n musica da camera

chamois ['ʃæmwa:] n camoscio; (also: **~ leather**) panno in pelle di camoscio

champagne [ʃæm'pein] n champagne m inv

champion ['tʃæmpiən] n campione/essa; **~ship** n campionato

chance [tʃa:ns] n caso; (opportunity) occasione f; (likelihood) possibilità f inv ♦ vt: **to ~ it** rischiare, provarci ♦ adj fortuito(a); **to take a ~** rischiare; **by ~** per caso

chancellor ['tʃa:nsələ*] n cancelliere m; **C~ of the Exchequer** (BRIT) n Cancelliere dello Scacchiere

chandelier [ʃændə'liə*] n lampadario

change [tʃeindʒ] vt cambiare; (transform): **to ~ sb into** trasformare qn in ♦ vi cambiare; (~ one's clothes) cambiarsi; (be transformed): **to ~ into** trasformarsi in ♦ n cambiamento; (of clothes) cambio; (money) resto; **to ~ one's mind** cambiare idea; **for a ~** tanto per cambiare; **~able** adj (weather) variabile; **~ machine** n distributore automatico di monete; **~over** n cambiamento, passaggio

changing ['tʃeindʒiŋ] adj che cambia; (colours) cangiante; **~ room** n (BRIT: in shop) camerino; (: SPORT) spogliatoio

channel ['tʃænl] n canale m; (of river, sea) alveo ♦ vt canalizzare; **the (English) C~**

n la Manica; **~-hopping** *n* (*TV*) zapping *m inv*; **the C~ Islands** *npl* le Isole Normanne; **the C~ Tunnel** *n* il tunnel sotto la Manica

chant [tʃɑːnt] *n* canto; salmodia ♦ *vt* cantare; salmodiare

chaos [ˈkeɪɔs] *n* caos *m*

chap [tʃæp] (*BRIT: inf*) *n* (*man*) tipo

chapel [ˈtʃæpəl] *n* cappella

chaperone [ˈʃæpərəun] *n* accompagnatrice *f* ♦ *vt* accompagnare

chaplain [ˈtʃæplɪn] *n* cappellano

chapped [tʃæpt] *adj* (*skin, lips*) screpolato(a)

chapter [ˈtʃæptə*] *n* capitolo

char [tʃɑː*] *vt* (*burn*) carbonizzare

character [ˈkærɪktə*] *n* carattere *m*; (*in novel, film*) personaggio; **~istic** [-ˈrɪstɪk] *adj* caratteristico(a) ♦ *n* caratteristica

charcoal [ˈtʃɑːkəul] *n* carbone *m* di legna

charge [tʃɑːdʒ] *n* accusa; (*cost*) prezzo; (*responsibility*) responsabilità ♦ *vt* (*gun, battery, MIL: enemy*) caricare; (*customer*) fare pagare a; (*sum*) fare pagare; (*LAW*): **to ~ sb (with)** accusare qn (di) ♦ *vi* (*gen with: up, along etc*) lanciarsi; **~s** *npl* (*bank ~s etc*) tariffe *fpl*; **to reverse the ~s** (*TEL*) fare una telefonata a carico del destinatario; **to take ~ of** incaricarsi di; **to be in ~ of** essere responsabile per; **how much do you ~?** quanto chiedete?; **to ~ an expense (up) to sb** addebitare una spesa a qn; **~ card** *n* carta *f* clienti *inv*

charitable [ˈtʃærɪtəbl] *adj* caritatevole

charity [ˈtʃærɪtɪ] *n* carità; (*organization*) opera pia

charm [tʃɑːm] *n* fascino; (*on bracelet*) ciondolo ♦ *vt* affascinare, incantare; **~ing** *adj* affascinante

chart [tʃɑːt] *n* tabella; grafico; (*map*) carta nautica ♦ *vt* fare una carta nautica di; **~s** *npl* (*MUS*) hit parade *f*

charter [ˈtʃɑːtə*] *vt* (*plane*) noleggiare ♦ *n* (*document*) carta; **~ed accountant** (*BRIT*) *n* ragioniere/a professionista; **~ flight** *n* volo *m* charter *inv*

charwoman [ˈtʃɑːwumən] *n* = **charlady**

chase [tʃeɪs] *vt* inseguire; (*also:* **~ away**) cacciare ♦ *n* caccia

chasm [ˈkæzəm] *n* abisso

chassis [ˈʃæsɪ] *n* telaio

chat [tʃæt] *vi* (*also:* **have a ~**) chiacchierare ♦ *n* chiacchierata; **~ show** (*BRIT*) *n* talk show *m inv*

chatter [ˈtʃætə*] *vi* (*person*) ciarlare; (*bird*) cinguettare; (*teeth*) battere ♦ *n* ciarle *fpl*; cinguettio; **~box** (*inf*) *n* chiacchierone/a

chatty [ˈtʃætɪ] *adj* (*style*) familiare; (*person*) chiacchierino/a

chauffeur [ˈʃəufə*] *n* autista *m*

chauvinist [ˈʃəuvɪnɪst] *n* (*male ~*) maschilista *m*; (*nationalist*) sciovinista *m/f*

cheap [tʃiːp] *adj* a buon mercato; (*joke*) grossolano(a); (*poor quality*) di cattiva qualità ♦ *adv* a buon mercato; **~ day return** *n* biglietto ridotto di andata e ritorno valido in giornata; **~er** *adj* meno caro(a); **~ly** *adv* a buon prezzo, a buon mercato

cheat [tʃiːt] *vi* imbrogliare; (*at school*) copiare ♦ *vt* ingannare ♦ *n* imbroglione *m*; **to ~ sb out of sth** defraudare qn di qc

check [tʃɛk] *vt* verificare; (*passport, ticket*) controllare; (*halt*) fermare; (*restrain*) contenere ♦ *n* verifica; controllo; (*curb*) freno; (*US: bill*) conto; (*pattern: gen pl*) quadretti *mpl*; (*US*) = **cheque** ♦ *adj* (*pattern, cloth*) a quadretti; **~ in** *vi* (*in hotel*) registrare; (*at airport*) presentarsi all'accettazione ♦ *vt* (*luggage*) depositare; **~ out** *vi* (*in hotel*) saldare il conto; **~ up** *vi*: **to ~ up (on sth)** investigare (qc); **to ~ up on sb** informarsi sul conto di qn; **~ered** (*US*) *adj* = **chequered**; **~ers** (*US*) *n* dama; **~-in (desk)** *n* check-in *m inv*, accettazione *f* (bagagli *inv*); **~ing account** (*US*) *n* conto corrente; **~mate** *n* scaccomatto; **~out** *n* (*in supermarket*) cassa; **~point** *n* posto di blocco; **~room** (*US*) *n* deposito *m* bagagli *inv*; **~up** *n* (*MED*) controllo medico

cheek [tʃiːk] *n* guancia; (*impudence*) faccia tosta; **~bone** *n* zigomo; **~y** *adj* sfacciato(a)

cheep [tʃiːp] *vi* pigolare

cheer [tʃɪə*] *vt* applaudire; (*gladden*) rallegrare ♦ *vi* applaudire ♦ *n* grido (di incoraggiamento); **~s** *npl* (*of approval, encouragement*) applausi *mpl*; evviva *mpl*; **~s!** salute!; **~ up** *vi* rallegrarsi, farsi animo ♦ *vt* rallegrare; **~ful** *adj* allegro(a)

cheerio [tʃɪərɪˈaʊ] (*BRIT*) *excl* ciao!

cheese [tʃiːz] *n* formaggio; **~board** *n* piatto del (*or* per il) formaggio

cheetah [tʃiːtə] *n* ghepardo

chef [ʃef] *n* capocuoco

chemical [ˈkemɪkəl] *adj* chimico(a) ♦ *n* prodotto chimico

chemist [ˈkemɪst] *n* (*BRIT: pharmacist*) farmacista *m/f*; (*scientist*) chimico/a; **~ry** *n* chimica; **~'s (shop)** (*BRIT*) *n* farmacia

cheque [tʃek] (*BRIT*) *n* assegno; **~book** *n* libretto degli assegni; **~ card** *n* carta *f* assegni *inv*

chequered [ˈtʃekəd] (*US* **checkered**) *adj* (*fig*) movimentato(a)

cherish [ˈtʃerɪʃ] *vt* aver caro

cherry [ˈtʃerɪ] *n* ciliegia; (*also:* **~ tree**) ciliegio

chess [tʃes] *n* scacchi *mpl*; **~board** *n* scacchiera

chest [tʃest] *n* petto; (*box*) cassa; **~ of drawers** *n* cassettone *m*

chestnut [ˈtʃesnʌt] *n* castagna; (*also:* **~ tree**) castagno

chew [tʃuː] *vt* masticare; **~ing gum** *n* chewing gum *m*

chic [ʃiːk] *adj* elegante

chick [tʃɪk] *n* pulcino; (*inf*) pollastrella

chicken [ˈtʃɪkɪn] *n* pollo; (*inf: coward*) coniglio; **~ out** (*inf*) *vi* avere fifa; **~pox** *n* varicella

chicory [ˈtʃɪkərɪ] *n* cicoria

chief [tʃiːf] *n* capo ♦ *adj* principale; **~ executive** *n* direttore *m* generale; **~ly** *adv* per lo più, soprattutto

chilblain [ˈtʃɪlbleɪn] *n* gelone *m*

child [tʃaɪld] (*pl* **~ren**) *n* bambino/a; **~birth** *n* parto; **~hood** *n* infanzia; **~ish** *adj* puerile; **~like** *adj* fanciullesco(a); **~minder** (*BRIT*) *n* bambinaia

children [ˈtʃɪldrən] *npl of* **child**

child seat *n* seggiolino per bambini (*in auto*)

Chile [ˈtʃɪlɪ] *n* Cile *m*

chill [tʃɪl] *n* freddo; (*MED*) infreddatura ♦ *vt* raffreddare

chilli [ˈtʃɪlɪ] *n* peperoncino

chilly [ˈtʃɪlɪ] *adj* freddo(a), fresco(a); **to feel ~** sentirsi infreddolito(a)

chime [tʃaɪm] *n* carillon *m inv* ♦ *vi* suonare, scampanare

chimney [ˈtʃɪmnɪ] *n* camino; **~ sweep** *n* spazzacamino

chimpanzee [tʃɪmpænˈziː] *n* scimpanzé *m inv*

chin [tʃɪn] *n* mento

China [ˈtʃaɪnə] *n* Cina

china [ˈtʃaɪnə] *n* porcellana

Chinese [tʃaɪˈniːz] *adj* cinese ♦ *n inv* cinese *m/f*; (*LING*) cinese *m*

chink [tʃɪŋk] *n* (*opening*) fessura; (*noise*) tintinnio

chip [tʃɪp] *n* (*gen pl: CULIN*) patatina fritta; (: *US: also:* **potato ~**) patatina; (*of wood, glass, stone*) scheggia; (*also:* **micro~**) chip *m inv* ♦ *vt* (*cup, plate*) scheggiare

chip shop

> ***i*** I **chip shops**, anche chiamati "fish and chip shops", sono friggitorie che vendono principalmente filetti di pesce impanati e patatine fritte.

chiropodist [kɪˈrɔpədɪst] (*BRIT*) *n* pedicure *m/f inv*

chirp [tʃəːp] *vi* cinguettare; fare cri cri

chisel [ˈtʃɪzl] *n* cesello

chit [tʃɪt] *n* biglietto

chitchat [ˈtʃɪttʃæt] *n* chiacchiere *fpl*

chivalry [ˈʃɪvəlrɪ] *n* cavalleria; cortesia

chives [tʃaɪvz] *npl* erba cipollina

chock-a-block [ˈtʃɔk-] *adj* pieno(a) zeppo(a)

chock-full [ˈtʃɔk-] *adj* = **chock-a-block**

chocolate [ˈtʃɔklɪt] *n* (*substance*) cioccolato, cioccolata; (*drink*) cioccolata; (*a sweet*) cioccolatino

choice [tʃɔɪs] *n* scelta ♦ *adj* scelto(a)

choir ['kwaɪə*] n coro; **~boy** n corista m fanciullo

choke [tʃəuk] vi soffocare ♦ vt soffocare; (*block*): **to be ~d with** essere intasato(a) di ♦ n (AUT) valvola dell'aria

cholera ['kɔlərə] n colera m

cholesterol [kə'lestərɔl] n colesterolo

choose [tʃuːz] (pt **chose,** pp **chosen**) vt scegliere; **to ~ to do** decidere di fare; preferire fare

choosy ['tʃuːzɪ] adj schizzinoso(a)

chop [tʃɔp] vt (*wood*) spaccare; (*CULIN: also*: **~ up**) tritare ♦ n (*CULIN*) costoletta; **~s** npl (*jaws*) mascelle fpl

chopper ['tʃɔpə*] n (*helicopter*) elicottero

choppy ['tʃɔpɪ] adj (*sea*) mosso(a)

chopsticks ['tʃɔpstɪks] npl bastoncini mpl cinesi

choral ['kɔːrəl] adj corale

chord [kɔːd] n (*MUS*) accordo

chore [tʃɔː*] n faccenda; **household ~s** faccende fpl domestiche

chortle ['tʃɔːtl] vi ridacchiare

chorus ['kɔːrəs] n coro; (*repeated part of song, also fig*) ritornello

chose [tʃəuz] pt of **choose**

chosen ['tʃəuzn] pp of **choose**

chowder ['tʃaudə*] n (*esp US*) zuppa di pesce

Christ [kraɪst] n Cristo

christen ['krɪsn] vt battezzare

Christian ['krɪstɪən] adj, n cristiano(a); **~ity** [-'ænɪtɪ] n cristianesimo; **~ name** n nome m (di battesimo)

Christmas ['krɪsməs] n Natale m; **Merry ~!** Buon Natale!; **~ card** n cartolina di Natale; **~ Day** n il giorno di Natale; **~ Eve** n la vigilia di Natale; **~ tree** n albero di Natale

chrome [krəum] n cromo

chromium ['krəumɪəm] n cromo

chronic ['krɔnɪk] adj cronico(a)

chronological [krɔnə'lɔdʒɪkəl] adj cronologico(a)

chrysanthemum [krɪ'sænθəməm] n crisantemo

chubby ['tʃʌbɪ] adj paffuto(a)

chuck [tʃʌk] (*inf*) vt buttare, gettare; (*BRIT: also*: **~ up**) piantare; **~ out** vt buttar fuori

chuckle ['tʃʌkl] vi ridere sommessamente

chug [tʃʌg] vi fare ciuf ciuf

chum [tʃʌm] n compagno/a

chunk [tʃʌŋk] n pezzo

church [tʃəːtʃ] n chiesa; **~yard** n sagrato

churn [tʃəːn] n (*for butter*) zangola; (*for milk*) bidone m; **~ out** vt sfornare

chute [ʃuːt] n (*also*: **rubbish ~**) canale m di scarico; (*BRIT: children's slide*) scivolo

chutney ['tʃʌtnɪ] n salsa piccante (*di frutta, zucchero e spezie*)

CIA (*US*) n abbr (= *Central Intelligence Agency*) CIA f

CID (*BRIT*) n abbr (= *Criminal Investigation Department*) ≈ polizia giudiziaria

cider ['saɪdə*] n sidro

cigar [sɪ'gɑː*] n sigaro

cigarette [sɪgə'ret] n sigaretta; **~ case** n portasigarette m inv; **~ end** n mozzicone m

Cinderella [sɪndə'relə] n Cenerentola

cinders ['sɪndəz] npl ceneri fpl

cine camera ['sɪnɪ-] (*BRIT*) n cinepresa

cine film ['sɪnɪ-] (*BRIT*) n pellicola

cinema ['sɪnəmə] n cinema m inv

cinnamon ['sɪnəmən] n cannella

cipher ['saɪfə*] n cifra

circle ['səːkl] n cerchio; (*of friends etc*) circolo; (*in cinema*) galleria ♦ vi girare in circolo ♦ vt (*surround*) circondare; (*move round*) girare intorno a

circuit ['səːkɪt] n circuito; **~ous** [səː'kjuɪtəs] adj indiretto(a)

circular ['səːkjulə*] adj circolare ♦ n circolare f

circulate ['səːkjuleɪt] vi circolare ♦ vt far circolare; **circulation** [-'leɪʃən] n circolazione f; (*of newspaper*) tiratura

circumstances ['səːkəmstənsɪz] npl circostanze fpl; (*financial condition*) condizioni fpl finanziarie

circus ['səːkəs] n circo

CIS n abbr (= *Commonwealth of Independent States*) CSI f

cistern ['sɪstən] n cisterna; (*in toilet*)

serbatoio d'acqua

citizen ['sitizn] *n* (*of country*) cittadino/a; (*of town*) abitante *m/f*; **~ship** *n* cittadinanza

citrus fruit ['sitrəs-] *n* agrume *m*

city ['siti] *n* città *f inv*; **the C~** la Città di Londra (*centro commerciale*)

civic ['sivik] *adj* civico(a); **~ centre** (*BRIT*) *n* centro civico

civil ['sivil] *adj* civile; **~ engineer** *n* ingegnere *m* civile; **~ian** [si'viliən] *adj*, *n* borghese *m/f*

civilization [sivilar'zeiʃən] *n* civiltà *f inv*

civilized ['sivilaizd] *adj* civilizzato(a); (*fig*) cortese

civil: ~ law *n* codice *m* civile; (*study*) diritto civile; **~ servant** *n* impiegato/a statale; **C~ Service** *n* amministrazione *f* statale; **~ war** *n* guerra civile

clad [klæd] *adj*: **~ (in)** vestito(a) (di)

claim [kleim] *vt* (*assert*): **to ~ (that)/to be** sostenere (che)/di essere; (*credit, rights etc*) rivendicare; (*damages*) richiedere ♦ *vi* (*for insurance*) fare una domanda d'indennizzo ♦ *n* pretesa; rivendicazione *f*; richiesta; **~ant** *n* (*ADMIN, LAW*) richiedente *m/f*

clairvoyant [kleə'vɔiənt] *n* chiaroveggente *m/f*

clam [klæm] *n* vongola

clamber ['klæmbə*] *vi* arrampicarsi

clammy ['klæmi] *adj* (*weather*) caldo(a) umido(a); (*hands*) viscido(a)

clamour ['klæmə*] (*US* **clamor**) *vi*: **to ~ for** chiedere a gran voce

clamp [klæmp] *n* pinza; morsa ♦ *vt* stringere con una morsa; (*AUT: wheel*) applicare i ceppi bloccaruote a; **~ down on** *vt fus* dare un giro di vite a

clan [klæn] *n* clan *m inv*

clang [klæŋ] *vi* emettere un suono metallico

clap [klæp] *vi* applaudire; **~ping** *n* applausi *mpl*

claret ['klærət] *n* vino di Bordeaux

clarify ['klærifai] *vt* chiarificare, chiarire

clarinet [klæri'net] *n* clarinetto

clarity ['klæriti] *n* clarità

clash [klæʃ] *n* frastuono; (*fig*) scontro ♦ *vi* scontrarsi; cozzare

clasp [klɑːsp] *n* (*hold*) stretta; (*of necklace, bag*) fermaglio, fibbia ♦ *vt* stringere

class [klɑːs] *n* classe *f* ♦ *vt* classificare

classic ['klæsik] *adj* classico(a) ♦ *n* classico; **~al** *adj* classico(a)

classified ['klæsifaid] *adj* (*information*) segreto(a), riservato(a); **~ advertisement** *n* annuncio economico

classmate ['klɑːsmeit] *n* compagno/a di classe

classroom ['klɑːsrum] *n* aula

clatter ['klætə*] *n* tintinnio; scalpitio ♦ *vi* tintinnare; scalpitare

clause [klɔːz] *n* clausola; (*LING*) proposizione *f*

claw [klɔː] *n* (*of bird of prey*) artiglio; (*of lobster*) pinza

clay [klei] *n* argilla

clean [kliːn] *adj* pulito(a); (*clear, smooth*) liscio(a) ♦ *vt* pulire; **~ out** *vt* ripulire; **~ up** *vt* (*also fig*) ripulire; **~-cut** *adj* (*man*) curato(a); **~er** *n* (*person*) donna delle pulizie; **~er's** *n* (*also:* **dry ~er's**) tintoria; **~ing** *n* pulizia; **~liness** ['klenlimis] *n* pulizia

cleanse [klenz] *vt* pulire; purificare; **~r** *n* detergente *m*

clean-shaven [-'ʃeivn] *adj* sbarbato(a)

cleansing department ['klenziŋ-] (*BRIT*) *n* nettezza urbana

clear [kliə*] *adj* chiaro(a); (*glass etc*) trasparente; (*road, way*) libero(a); (*conscience*) pulito(a) ♦ *vt* sgombrare; liberare; (*table*) sparecchiare; (*cheque*) fare la compensazione di; (*LAW: suspect*) discolpare; (*obstacle*) superare ♦ *vi* (*weather*) rasserenarsi; (*fog*) andarsene ♦ *adv*: **~ of** distante da; **~ up** *vt* mettere in ordine; (*mystery*) risolvere; **~ance** *n* (*removal*) sgombro; (*permission*) autorizzazione *f*, permesso; **~-cut** *adj* ben delineato(a), distinto(a); **~ing** *n* radura; **~ing bank** (*BRIT*) *n* banca (che fa uso della camera di compensazione); **~ly** *adv* chiaramente; **~way** (*BRIT*) *n* strada con divieto di sosta

cleaver ['kliːvə*] *n* mannaia

clef [klɛf] n (MUS) chiave f

cleft [klɛft] n (in rock) crepa, fenditura

clench [klɛntʃ] vt stringere

clergy ['klɜːdʒɪ] n clero; ~man (irreg) n ecclesiastico

clerical ['klɛrɪkəl] adj d'impiegato; (REL) clericale

clerk [klɑːk, (US) klɜːrk] n (BRIT) impiegato/a; (US) commesso/a

clever ['klɛvə*] adj (mentally) intelligente; (deft, skilful) abile; (device, arrangement) ingegnoso(a)

click [klɪk] vi scattare ♦ vt (heels etc) battere; (tongue) far schioccare

client ['klaɪənt] n cliente m/f

cliff [klɪf] n scogliera scoscesa, rupe f

climate ['klaɪmɪt] n clima m

climax ['klaɪmæks] n culmine m; (sexual) orgasmo

climb [klaɪm] vi salire; (clamber) arrampicarsi ♦ vt salire; (CLIMBING) scalare ♦ n salita; arrampicata; scalata; ~-down n marcia indietro; ~er n rocciatore/trice; alpinista m/f; ~ing n alpinismo

clinch [klɪntʃ] vt (deal) concludere

cling [klɪŋ] (pt, pp clung) vi: to ~ (to) aggrapparsi (a); (of clothes) aderire strettamente (a)

clinic ['klɪnɪk] n clinica; ~al adj clinico(a); (fig) distaccato(a); (: room) freddo(a)

clink [klɪŋk] vi tintinnare

clip [klɪp] n (for hair) forcina; (also: paper ~) graffetta; (TV, CINEMA) sequenza ♦ vt attaccare insieme; (hair, nails) tagliare; (hedge) tosare; ~pers npl (for gardening) cesoie fpl; (also: nail ~pers) forbicine fpl per le unghie; ~ping n (from newspaper) ritaglio

clique [kliːk] n cricca

cloak [kləuk] n mantello ♦ vt avvolgere; ~room n (for coats etc) guardaroba m inv; (BRIT: W.C.) gabinetti mpl

clock [klɔk] n orologio; ~ in or on vi timbrare il cartellino (all'entrata); ~ off or out vi timbrare il cartellino (all'uscita); ~wise adv in senso orario; ~work n movimento or meccanismo a orologeria

♦ adj a molla

clog [klɔg] n zoccolo ♦ vt intasare ♦ vi (also: ~ up) intasarsi, bloccarsi

cloister ['klɔɪstə*] n chiostro

clone [kləun] n clone m

close¹ [kləus] adj: ~ (to) vicino(a) (a); (watch, link, relative) stretto(a); (examination) attento(a); (contest) combattuto(a); (weather) afoso(a) ♦ adv vicino, dappresso; ~ to vicino a; ~ by, ~ at hand a portata di mano; a ~ friend un amico intimo; to have a ~ shave (fig) scamparla bella

close² [kləuz] vt chiudere ♦ vi (shop etc) chiudere; (lid, door etc) chiudersi; (end) finire ♦ n (end) fine f; ~ down vi cessare (definitivamente); ~d adj chiuso(a); ~d shop n azienda o fabbrica che impiega solo aderenti ai sindacati

close-knit [kləus'nɪt] adj (family, community) molto unito(a)

closely ['kləuslɪ] adv (examine, watch) da vicino; (related) strettamente

closet ['klɔzɪt] n (cupboard) armadio

close-up ['kləusʌp] n primo piano

closure ['kləuʒə*] n chiusura

clot [klɔt] n (also: blood ~) coagulo; (inf: idiot) scemo/a ♦ vi coagularsi

cloth [klɔθ] n (material) tessuto, stoffa; (rag) strofinaccio

clothe [kləuð] vt vestire; ~s npl abiti mpl, vestiti mpl; ~s brush n spazzola per abiti; ~s line n corda (per stendere il bucato); ~s peg (US ~s pin) n molletta

clothing ['kləuðɪŋ] n = clothes

cloud [klaud] n nuvola; ~burst n acquazzone m; ~y adj nuvoloso(a); (liquid) torbido(a)

clout [klaut] vt dare un colpo a

clove [kləuv] n chiodo di garofano; ~ of garlic spicchio d'aglio

clover ['kləuvə*] n trifoglio

clown [klaun] n pagliaccio ♦ vi (also: ~ about, ~ around) fare il pagliaccio

cloying ['klɔɪɪŋ] adj (taste, smell) nauseabondo(a)

club [klʌb] n (society) club m inv, circolo;

(*weapon*, GOLF) mazza ♦ *vt* bastonare ♦ *vi*: **to ~ together** associarsi; **~s** *npl* (CARDS) fiori *mpl*; **~ class** *n* (AVIAT) classe *f* club *inv*; **~house** *n* sede *f* del circolo

cluck [klʌk] *vi* chiocciare

clue [kluː] *n* indizio; (*in crosswords*) definizione *f*; **I haven't a ~** non ho la minima idea

clump [klʌmp] *n* (*of flowers, trees*) gruppo; (*of grass*) ciuffo

clumsy ['klʌmzi] *adj* goffo(a)

clung [klʌŋ] *pt, pp of* **cling**

cluster ['klʌstə*] *n* gruppo ♦ *vi* raggrupparsi

clutch [klʌtʃ] *n* (*grip, grasp*) presa, stretta; (AUT) frizione *f* ♦ *vt* afferrare, stringere forte

clutter ['klʌtə*] *vt* ingombrare

CND *n abbr* = **Campaign for Nuclear Disarmament**

Co. *abbr* = **county; company**

c/o *abbr* (= *care of*) presso

coach [kəutʃ] *n* (*bus*) pullman *m inv*; (*horse-drawn, of train*) carrozza; (SPORT) allenatore/trice; (*tutor*) chi dà ripetizioni ♦ *vt* allenare; dare ripetizioni a; **~ trip** *n* viaggio in pullman

coal [kəul] *n* carbone *m*; **~ face** *n* fronte *f*; **~field** *n* bacino carbonifero

coalition [kəuə'lɪʃən] *n* coalizione *f*

coalman ['kəulmən] (*irreg*) *n* negoziante *m* di carbone

coalmine ['kəulmaɪn] *n* miniera di carbone

coarse [kɔːs] *adj* (*salt, sand etc*) grosso(a), (*cloth, person*) rozzo(a)

coast [kəust] *n* costa ♦ *vi* (*with cycle etc*) scendere a ruota libera; **~al** *adj* costiero(a); **~guard** *n* guardia costiera; **~line** *n* linea costiera

coat [kəut] *n* cappotto; (*of animal*) pelo; (*of paint*) mano *f* ♦ *vt* coprire; **~ hanger** *n* attaccapanni *m inv*; **~ing** *n* rivestimento; **~ of arms** *n* stemma *m*

coax [kəuks] *vt* indurre (con moine)

cobbler ['kɔblə*] *n* calzolaio

cobbles ['kɔblz] *npl* ciottoli *mpl*

cobblestones ['kɔblstəunz] *npl* ciottoli *mpl*

cobweb ['kɔbweb] *n* ragnatela

cocaine [kə'keɪn] *n* cocaina

cock [kɔk] *n* (*rooster*) gallo; (*male bird*) maschio ♦ *vt* (*gun*) armare; **~erel** *n* galletto

cockle ['kɔkl] *n* cardio

cockney ['kɔknɪ] *n* cockney *m/f inv* (*abitante dei quartieri popolari dell'East End di Londra*)

cockpit ['kɔkpɪt] *n* abitacolo

cockroach ['kɔkrəutʃ] *n* blatta

cocktail ['kɔkteɪl] *n* cocktail *m inv*; **~ cabinet** *n* mobile *m* bar *inv*; **~ party** *n* cocktail *m inv*

cocoa ['kəukəu] *n* cacao

coconut ['kəukənʌt] *n* noce *f* di cocco

cocoon [kə'kuːn] *n* bozzolo

cod [kɔd] *n* merluzzo

C.O.D. *abbr* = **cash on delivery**

code [kəud] *n* codice *m*

cod-liver oil *n* olio di fegato di merluzzo

coercion [kəu'əːʃən] *n* coercizione *f*

coffee ['kɔfɪ] *n* caffè *m inv*; **~ bar** *n* (BRIT) caffè *m inv*; **~ break** *n* pausa per il caffè; **~pot** *n* caffettiera; **~ table** *n* tavolino

coffin ['kɔfɪn] *n* bara

cog [kɔg] *n* dente *m*

cogent ['kəudʒənt] *adj* convincente

coherent [kəu'hɪərənt] *adj* coerente

coil [kɔɪl] *n* rotolo; (ELEC) bobina; (*contraceptive*) spirale *f* ♦ *vt* avvolgere

coin [kɔɪn] *n* moneta ♦ *vt* (*word*) coniare; **~age** *n* sistema *m* monetario; **~-box** *n* (BRIT) telefono a gettoni

coincide [kəuɪn'saɪd] *vi* coincidere; **coincidence** [kəu'ɪnsɪdəns] *n* combinazione *f*

Coke ® [kəuk] *n* coca

coke [kəuk] *n* coke *m*

colander ['kɔləndə*] *n* colino

cold [kəuld] *adj* freddo(a) ♦ *n* freddo; (MED) raffreddore *m*; **it's ~** fa freddo; **to be ~** (*person*) aver freddo; (*object*) essere freddo(a); **to catch ~** prendere freddo; **to catch a ~** prendere un raffreddore; **in ~ blood** a sangue freddo; **~-shoulder** *vt* trattare con freddezza; **~ sore** *n* erpete *m*

coleslaw ['kəulslɔ:] n insalata di cavolo bianco

colic ['kɒlik] n colica

collapse [kə'læps] vi crollare ♦ n crollo; (MED) collasso

collapsible [kə'læpsəbl] adj pieghevole

collar ['kɒlə*] n (of coat, shirt) colletto; (of dog, cat) collare m; **~bone** n clavicola

collateral [kə'lætərl] n garanzia

colleague ['kɒli:g] n collega m/f

collect [kə'lekt] vt (gen) raccogliere; (as a hobby) fare collezione di; (BRIT: call and pick up) prendere; (money owed, pension) riscuotere; (donations, subscriptions) fare una colletta di ♦ vi adunarsi, riunirsi; ammucchiarsi; **to call ~** (US: TEL) fare una chiamata a carico del destinatario; **~ion** [kə'lekʃən] n raccolta; collezione f; (for money) colletta

collector [kə'lektə*] n collezionista m/f

college ['kɒlidʒ] n college m inv; (of technology etc) istituto superiore

collide [kə'laid] vi: **to ~ (with)** scontrarsi (con)

colliery ['kɒliəri] (BRIT) n miniera di carbone

collision [kə'liʒən] n collisione f, scontro

colloquial [kə'ləukwiəl] adj familiare

colon ['kəulən] n (sign) due punti mpl; (MED) colon m inv

colonel ['kə:nl] n colonnello

colonial [kə'ləuniəl] adj coloniale

colony ['kɒləni] n colonia

colour ['kʌlə*] (US **color**) n colore m ♦ vt colorare; (tint, dye) tingere; (fig: affect) influenzare ♦ vi (blush) arrossire; **~s** npl (of party, club) colori mpl; **in ~** a colori; **~ in** vt colorare; **~ bar** n discriminazione f razziale (in locali etc); **~-blind** adj daltonico(a); **~ed** adj (photo) a colori; (person) di colore; **~ film** n (for camera) pellicola a colori; **~ful** adj pieno(a) di colore, a vivaci colori; (personality) colorato(a); **~ing** n (substance) colorante m; (complexion) colorito; **~ scheme** n combinazione f di colori; **~ television** n televisione f a colori

colt [kəult] n puledro

column ['kɒləm] n colonna; **~ist** ['kɒləmnist] n articolista m/f

coma ['kəumə] n coma m inv

comb [kəum] n pettine m ♦ vt (hair) pettinare; (area) battere a tappeto

combat ['kɒmbæt] n combattimento ♦ vt combattere, lottare contro

combination [kɒmbi'neiʃən] n combinazione f

combine [vb kəm'bain, n 'kɒmbain] vt: **to ~ (with)** combinare (con); (one quality with another) unire (a) ♦ vi unirsi; (CHEM) combinarsi ♦ n (ECON) associazione f; **~ (harvester)** n mietitrebbia

come [kʌm] (pt **came**, pp **come**) vi venire; arrivare; **to ~ to** (decision etc) raggiungere; **I've ~ to like him** ha cominciato a piacermi; **to ~ undone** slacciarsi; **to ~ loose** allentarsi; **~ about** vi succedere; **~ across** vt fus trovare per caso; **~ away** vi venire via; staccarsi; **~ back** vi ritornare; **~ by** vt fus (acquire) ottenere; procurarsi; **~ down** vi scendere; (prices) calare; (buildings) essere demolito(a); **~ forward** vi farsi avanti; presentarsi; **~ from** vt fus venire da; provenire da; **~ in** vi entrare; **~ in for** vt fus (criticism etc) ricevere; **~ into** vt fus (money) ereditare; **~ off** vi (button) staccarsi; (stain) andar via; (attempt) riuscire; **~ on** vi (pupil, work, project) fare progressi; (lights) accendersi; (electricity) entrare in funzione; **~ on!** avanti!, andiamo!, forza!; **~ out** vi uscire; (stain) andare via; **~ round** vi (after faint, operation) riprendere conoscenza, rinvenire; **~ to** vi rinvenire; **~ up** vi (sun) salire; (problem) sorgere; (event) essere in arrivo; (in conversation) saltar fuori; **~ up against** vt fus (resistance, difficulties) urtare contro; **~ up with** vt fus: **he came up with an idea** venne fuori con un'idea; **~ upon** vt fus trovare per caso; **~back** n (THEATRE etc) ritorno

comedian [kə'mi:diən] n comico

comedienne [kəmi:di'en] n attrice f comica

comedy ['kɒmidi] n commedia

comeuppance [kʌm'ʌpəns] n: **to get**

one's ~ ricevere ciò che si merita

comfort ['kʌmfət] n comodità f inv,
benessere m; (relief) consolazione f,
conforto ♦ vt consolare, confortare; ~s npl
comodità fpl; ~able adj comodo(a);
(financially) agiato(a); ~ably adv (sit etc)
comodamente; (live) bene; ~ station (US)
n gabinetti mpl

comic ['kɔmɪk] adj (also: ~al) comico(a) ♦ n
comico; (BRIT: magazine) giornaletto; ~
strip n fumetto

coming ['kʌmɪŋ] n arrivo ♦ adj (next)
prossimo(a); (future) futuro(a); ~(s) and
going(s) n(pl) andirivieni m inv

comma ['kɔmə] n virgola

command [kə'mɑːnd] n ordine m,
comando; (MIL: authority) comando;
(mastery) padronanza ♦ vt comandare; to ~
sb to do ordinare a qn di fare; ~eer
[kɔmən'dɪə*] vt requisire; ~er n capo; (MIL)
comandante m

commando [kə'mɑːndəu] n commando m
inv; membro di un commando

commence [kə'mens] vt, vi cominciare

commend [kə'mend] vt lodare;
raccomandare

commensurate [kə'menʃərɪt] adj: ~ with
proporzionato(a) a

comment ['kɔment] n commento ♦ vi: to ~
(on) fare commenti (su); ~ary ['kɔməntəri]
n commentario; (SPORT) radiocronaca;
telecronaca; ~ator ['kɔməntertə*] n
commentatore/trice; radiocronista m/f;
telecronista m/f

commerce ['kɔmə:s] n commercio

commercial [kə'mə:ʃəl] adj commerciale
♦ n (TV, RADIO: advertisement) pubblicità f
inv; ~ radio/television n radio f inv/
televisione f privata

commiserate [kə'mɪzəreɪt] vi: to ~ with
partecipare al dolore di

commission [kə'mɪʃən] n commissione f
♦ vt (work of art) commissionare; out of ~
(NAUT) in disarmo; ~aire [kəmɪʃə'neə*] (BRIT)
n (at shop, cinema etc) portiere m in livrea;
~er n (POLICE) questore m

commit [kə'mɪt] vt (act) commettere; (to

sb's care) affidare; to ~ o.s. (to do)
impegnarsi (a fare); to ~ suicide suicidarsi;
~ment n impegno; promessa

committee [kə'mɪtɪ] n comitato

commodity [kə'mɔdɪtɪ] n prodotto, articolo

common ['kɔmən] adj comune; (pej)
volgare; (usual) normale ♦ n terreno
comune; the C~s (BRIT) npl la Camera dei
Comuni; in ~ in comune; ~er n cittadino/a
(non nobile); ~ law n diritto
consuetudinario; ~ly adv comunemente,
usualmente; C~ Market n Mercato
Comune; ~place adj banale, ordinario(a);
~room n sala di riunione; (SCOL) sala dei
professori; ~ sense n buon senso; the
C~wealth n il Commonwealth

commotion [kə'məuʃən] n confusione f,
tumulto

communal ['kɔmju:nl] adj (for common
use) pubblico(a)

commune [n 'kɔmju:n, vb kə'mju:n] n
(group) comune f ♦ vi: to ~ with mettersi
in comunione con

communicate [kə'mju:nɪkeɪt] vt
comunicare, trasmettere ♦ vi: to ~ (with)
comunicare (con)

communication [kəmju:nɪ'keɪʃən] n
comunicazione f; ~ cord (BRIT) n segnale
m d'allarme

communion [kə'mju:nɪən] n (also: Holy
C~) comunione f

communiqué [kə'mju:nɪkeɪ] n comunicato

communism ['kɔmjunɪzəm] n comunismo;
communist adj, n comunista m/f

community [kə'mju:nɪtɪ] n comunità f inv;
~ centre n circolo ricreativo; ~ chest
(US) n fondo di beneficenza

commutation ticket [kɔmju'teɪʃən-] (US) n
biglietto di abbonamento

commute [kə'mju:t] vi fare il pendolare
♦ vt (LAW) commutare; ~r n pendolare m/f

compact [adj kəm'pækt, n 'kɔmpækt] adj
compatto(a) ♦ n (also: powder ~)
portacipria m inv; ~ disc n compact disc
m inv; ~ disc player n lettore m CD inv

companion [kəm'pænɪən] n compagno/a;
~ship n compagnia

company [ˈkʌmpənɪ] n (also COMM, MIL, THEATRE) compagnia; **to keep sb ~** tenere compagnia a qn; **~ secretary** (BRIT) n segretario/a generale

comparable [ˈkɔmpərəbl] adj simile

comparative [kəmˈpærətɪv] adj relativo(a); (adjective etc) comparativo(a); **~ly** adv relativamente

compare [kəmˈpɛə*] vt: **to ~ sth/sb with/ to** confrontare qc/qn con/a ♦ vi: **to ~ (with)** reggere il confronto (con); **comparison** [-ˈpærɪsn] n confronto; **in comparison (with)** in confronto (a)

compartment [kəmˈpɑːtmənt] n compartimento; (RAIL) scompartimento

compass [ˈkʌmpəs] n bussola; **~es** npl (MATH) compasso

compassion [kəmˈpæʃən] n compassione f

compatible [kəmˈpætɪbl] adj compatibile

compel [kəmˈpɛl] vt costringere, obbligare

compensate [ˈkɔmpənseɪt] vt risarcire ♦ vi: **to ~ for** compensare; **compensation** [-ˈseɪʃən] n compensazione f; (money) risarcimento

compère [ˈkɔmpɛə*] n presentatore/trice

compete [kəmˈpiːt] vi (take part) concorrere; (vie): **to ~ (with)** fare concorrenza (a)

competent [ˈkɔmpɪtənt] adj competente

competition [kɔmpɪˈtɪʃən] n gara; concorso; (ECON) concorrenza

competitive [kəmˈpetɪtɪv] adj (ECON) concorrenziale; (sport) agonistico(a); (person) che ha spirito di competizione; che ha spirito agonistico

competitor [kəmˈpetɪtə*] n concorrente m/f

complacency [kəmˈpleɪsnsɪ] n compiacenza di sé

complain [kəmˈpleɪn] vi lagnarsi, lamentarsi; **~t** n lamento; (in shop etc) reclamo; (MED) malattia

complement [n ˈkɔmplɪmənt, vb ˈkɔmplɪment] n complemento; (especially of ship's crew etc) effettivo ♦ vt (enhance) accompagnarsi bene a; **~ary** [kɔmplɪˈmentərɪ] adj complementare

complete [kəmˈpliːt] adj completo(a) ♦ vt completare; (a form) riempire; **~ly** adv completamente; **completion** [-ˈpliːʃən] n completamento

complex [ˈkɔmpleks] adj complesso(a) ♦ n (PSYCH, buildings etc) complesso

complexion [kəmˈplekʃən] n (of face) carnagione f

compliance [kəmˈplaɪəns] n acquiescenza; **in ~ with** (orders, wishes etc) in conformità con

complicate [ˈkɔmplɪkeɪt] vt complicare; **~d** adj complicato(a); **complication** [-ˈkeɪʃən] n complicazione f

compliment [n ˈkɔmplɪmənt, vb ˈkɔmplɪment] n complimento ♦ vt fare un complimento a; **~s** npl (greetings) complimenti mpl; rispetti mpl; **to pay sb a ~** fare un complimento a qn; **~ary** [-ˈmentərɪ] adj complimentoso(a), elogiativo(a); (free) in omaggio; **~ary ticket** n biglietto omaggio

comply [kəmˈplaɪ] vi: **to ~ with** assentire a; conformarsi a

component [kəmˈpəunənt] adj componente ♦ n componente m

compose [kəmˈpəuz] vt (form): **to be ~d of** essere composto di; (music, poem etc) comporre; **to ~ o.s.** ricomporsi; **~d** adj calmo(a); **~r** n (MUS) compositore/trice

composition [kɔmpəˈzɪʃən] n composizione f

composure [kəmˈpəuʒə*] n calma

compound [ˈkɔmpaund] n (CHEM, LING) composto; (enclosure) recinto ♦ adj composto(a); **~ fracture** n frattura esposta

comprehend [kɔmprɪˈhend] vt comprendere, capire; **comprehension** [-ˈhenʃən] n comprensione f

comprehensive [kɔmprɪˈhensɪv] adj comprensivo(a); **~ policy** n (INSURANCE) polizza che copre tutti i rischi; **~ (school)** (BRIT) n scuola secondaria aperta a tutti

compress [vb kəmˈpres, n ˈkɔmpres] vt comprimere ♦ n (MED) compressa

comprise [kəmˈpraɪz] vt (also: **be ~d of**) comprendere

compromise [ˈkɒmprəmaɪz] *n* compromesso ♦ *vt* compromettere ♦ *vi* venire a un compromesso

compulsion [kəmˈpʌlʃən] *n* costrizione *f*

compulsive [kəmˈpʌlsɪv] *adj* (*liar, gambler*) che non riesce a controllarsi; (*viewing, reading*) cui non si può fare a meno

compulsory [kəmˈpʌlsərɪ] *adj* obbligatorio(a)

computer [kəmˈpjuːtə*] *n* computer *m inv*, elaboratore *m* elettronico; ~ **game** *n* gioco per computer; ~**-generated** *adj* realizzato(a) al computer; ~**ize** *vt* computerizzare; ~ **programmer** *n* programmatore/trice; ~ **programming** *n* programmazione *f* di computer; ~ **science** *n* informatica; **computing** *n* informatica

comrade [ˈkɒmrɪd] *n* compagno/a; ~**ship** *n* cameratismo

con [kɒn] (*inf*) *vt* truffare ♦ *n* truffa

conceal [kənˈsiːl] *vt* nascondere

concede [kənˈsiːd] *vt* ammettere

conceit [kənˈsiːt] *n* presunzione *f*, vanità; ~**ed** *adj* presuntuoso(a), vanitoso(a)

conceive [kənˈsiːv] *vt* concepire ♦ *vi* concepire un bambino

concentrate [ˈkɒnsəntreɪt] *vi* concentrarsi ♦ *vt* concentrare

concentration [kɒnsənˈtreɪʃən] *n* concentrazione *f*; ~ **camp** *n* campo di concentramento

concept [ˈkɒnsept] *n* concetto

concern [kənˈsɜːn] *n* affare *m*; (*COMM*) azienda, ditta; (*anxiety*) preoccupazione *f* ♦ *vt* riguardare; **to be ~ed (about)** preoccuparsi (di); ~**ing** *prep* riguardo a, circa

concert [ˈkɒnsət] *n* concerto; ~**ed** [kənˈsɜːtɪd] *adj* concertato(a); ~ **hall** *n* sala da concerti

concertina [kɒnsəˈtiːnə] *n* piccola fisarmonica

conclude [kənˈkluːd] *vt* concludere; **conclusion** [-ˈkluːʒən] *n* conclusione *f*; **conclusive** [-ˈkluːsɪv] *adj* conclusivo(a)

concoct [kənˈkɒkt] *vt* inventare; ~**ion** [-ˈkɒkʃən] *n* miscuglio

concourse [ˈkɒnkɔːs] *n* (*hall*) atrio

concrete [ˈkɒnkriːt] *n* calcestruzzo ♦ *adj* concreto(a); di calcestruzzo

concur [kənˈkɜː*] *vi* concordare

concurrently [kənˈkʌrntlɪ] *adv* simultaneamente

concussion [kənˈkʌʃən] *n* commozione *f* cerebrale

condemn [kənˈdem] *vt* condannare; (*building*) dichiarare pericoloso(a)

condensation [kɒndenˈseɪʃən] *n* condensazione *f*

condense [kənˈdens] *vi* condensarsi ♦ *vt* condensare; ~**d milk** *n* latte *m* condensato

condescending [kɒndɪˈsendɪŋ] *adj* (*person*) che ha un'aria di superiorità

condition [kənˈdɪʃən] *n* condizione *f*; (*MED*) malattia ♦ *vt* condizionare; **on ~ that** a condizione che +*sub*, a condizione di; ~**er** *n* (*for hair*) balsamo; (*for fabrics*) ammorbidente *m*

condolences [kənˈdəʊlənsɪz] *npl* condoglianze *fpl*

condom [ˈkɒndəm] *n* preservativo

condominium [kɒndəˈmɪnɪəm] (*US*) *n* condominio

conducive [kənˈdjuːsɪv] *adj*: ~ **to** favorevole a

conduct [*n* ˈkɒndʌkt, *vb* kənˈdʌkt] *n* condotta ♦ *vt* condurre; (*manage*) dirigere; amministrare; (*MUS*) dirigere; **to ~ o.s.** comportarsi; ~**ed tour** *n* gita accompagnata; ~**or** *n* (*of orchestra*) direttore *m* d'orchestra; (*on bus*) bigliettaio; (*US: on train*) controllore *m*; (*ELEC*) conduttore *m*; ~**ress** *n* (*on bus*) bigliettaia

cone [kəʊn] *n* cono; (*BOT*) pigna; (*traffic ~*) birillo

confectioner [kənˈfekʃənə*] *n* pasticciere *m*; ~**'s (shop)** *n* ≈ pasticceria; ~**y** *n* dolciumi *mpl*

confer [kənˈfɜː*] *vt*: **to ~ sth on** conferire qc a ♦ *vi* conferire

conference [ˈkɒnfərns] *n* congresso

confess [kənˈfes] *vt* confessare, ammettere

♦ *vi* confessare; **~ion** [-'feʃən] *n* confessione *f*

confetti [kən'feti] *n* coriandoli *mpl*

confide [kən'faɪd] *vi*: **to ~ in** confidarsi con

confidence ['kɒnfɪdns] *n* confidenza; (*trust*) fiducia; (*self-assurance*) sicurezza di sé; **in ~** (*speak, write*) in confidenza, confidenzialmente; **~ trick** *n* truffa; **confident** *adj* sicuro(a); sicuro(a) di sé; **confidential** [kɒnfɪ'denʃəl] *adj* riservato(a), confidenziale

confine [kən'faɪn] *vt* limitare; (*shut up*) rinchiudere; **~d** *adj* (*space*) ristretto(a); **~ment** *n* prigionia; **~s** ['kɒnfaɪnz] *npl* confini *mpl*

confirm [kən'fəːm] *vt* confermare; **~ation** [kɒnfə'meɪʃən] *n* conferma; (*REL*) cresima; **~ed** *adj* inveterato(a)

confiscate ['kɒnfɪskeɪt] *vt* confiscare

conflict [*n* 'kɒnflɪkt, *vb* kən'flɪkt] *n* conflitto ♦ *vi* essere in conflitto; **~ing** *adj* contrastante

conform [kən'fɔːm] *vi*: **to ~ (to)** conformarsi (a)

confound [kən'faʊnd] *vt* confondere

confront [kən'frʌnt] *vt* (*enemy, danger*) affrontare; **~ation** [kɒnfrən'teɪʃən] *n* scontro

confuse [kən'fjuːz] *vt* (*one thing with another*) confondere; **~d** *adj* confuso(a); **confusing** *adj* che fa confondere; **confusion** [-'fjuːʒən] *n* confusione *f*

congeal [kən'dʒiːl] *vi* (*blood*) congelarsi

congenial [kən'dʒiːnɪəl] *adj* (*person*) simpatico(a); (*thing*) congeniale

congested [kən'dʒestɪd] *adj* congestionato(a)

congestion [kən'dʒestʃən] *n* congestione *f*

congratulate [kən'grætjuleɪt] *vt*: **to ~ sb (on)** congratularsi con qn (per *or* di); **congratulations** [-'leɪʃənz] *npl* auguri *mpl*; (*on success*) complimenti *mpl*, congratulazioni *fpl*

congregate ['kɒŋgrɪgeɪt] *vi* congregarsi, riunirsi

congress ['kɒŋgres] *n* congresso; **C~man** (*US*) *n* membro del Congresso

conjunction [kən'dʒʌŋkʃən] *n* congiunzione *f*

conjunctivitis [kəndʒʌŋktɪ'vaɪtɪs] *n* congiuntivite *f*

conjure ['kʌndʒə*] *vi* fare giochi di prestigio; **~ up** *vt* (*ghost, spirit*) evocare; (*memories*) rievocare; **~r** *n* prestidigitatore/ trice, prestigiatore/trice

conk out [kɒŋk-] (*inf*) *vi* andare in panne

con man *n* truffatore *m*

connect [kə'nekt] *vt* connettere, collegare; (*ELEC, TEL*) collegare; (*fig*) associare ♦ *vi* (*train*): **to ~ with** essere in coincidenza con; **to be ~ed with** (*associated*) aver rapporti con; **~ion** [-ʃən] *n* relazione *f*, rapporto; (*ELEC*) connessione *f*; (*train, plane*) coincidenza; (*TEL*) collegamento

connive [kə'naɪv] *vi*: **to ~ at** essere connivente in

connoisseur [kɒnɪ'sə*] *n* conoscitore/trice

conquer ['kɒŋkə*] *vt* conquistare; (*feelings*) vincere

conquest ['kɒŋkwest] *n* conquista

cons [kɒnz] *npl see* **convenience; pro**

conscience ['kɒnʃəns] *n* coscienza

conscientious [kɒnʃi'enʃəs] *adj* coscienzioso(a)

conscious ['kɒnʃəs] *adj* consapevole; (*MED*) cosciente; **~ness** *n* consapevolezza; coscienza

conscript ['kɒnskrɪpt] *n* coscritto; **~ion** [-'skrɪpʃən] *n* arruolamento (obbligatorio)

consent [kən'sent] *n* consenso ♦ *vi*: **to ~ (to)** acconsentire (a)

consequence ['kɒnsɪkwəns] *n* conseguenza, risultato; importanza

consequently ['kɒnsɪkwəntlɪ] *adv* di conseguenza, dunque

conservation [kɒnsə'veɪʃən] *n* conservazione *f*

conservative [kən'sə:vətɪv] *adj* conservatore(trice); (*cautious*) cauto(a); **C~** (*BRIT*) *adj*, *n* (*POL*) conservatore(trice)

conservatory [kən'sə:vətrɪ] *n* (*greenhouse*) serra; (*MUS*) conservatorio

conserve [kən'sə:v] *vt* conservare ♦ *n* conserva

consider [kən'sɪdə*] *vt* considerare; (*take*

into account) tener conto di; **to ~ doing sth** considerare la possibilità di fare qc

considerable [kən'sɪdərəbl] *adj* considerevole, notevole; **considerably** *adv* notevolmente, decisamente

considerate [kən'sɪdərɪt] *adj* premuroso(a)

consideration [kənsɪdə'reɪʃən] *n* considerazione *f*

considering [kən'sɪdərɪŋ] *prep* in considerazione di

consign [kən'saɪn] *vt*: **to ~ to** (*sth unwanted*) relegare in; (*person: to sb's care*) consegnare a; (*: to poverty*) condannare a; **~ment** *n* (*of goods*) consegna; spedizione *f*

consist [kən'sɪst] *vi*: **to ~ of** constare di, essere composto(a) di

consistency [kən'sɪstənsɪ] *n* consistenza; (*fig*) coerenza

consistent [kən'sɪstənt] *adj* coerente

consolation [kɒnsə'leɪʃən] *n* consolazione *f*

console[1] [kən'səʊl] *vt* consolare

console[2] ['kɒnsəʊl] *n* quadro di comando

consonant ['kɒnsənənt] *n* consonante *f*

consortium [kən'sɔːtɪəm] *n* consorzio

conspicuous [kən'spɪkjʊəs] *adj* cospicuo(a)

conspiracy [kən'spɪrəsɪ] *n* congiura, cospirazione *f*

constable ['kʌnstəbl] (*BRIT*) *n* ≈ poliziotto, agente *m* di polizia; **chief ~** ≈ questore *m*

constabulary [kən'stæbjʊlərɪ] *n* forze *fpl* dell'ordine

constant ['kɒnstənt] *adj* costante; continuo(a); **~ly** *adv* costantemente; continuamente

constipated ['kɒnstɪpeɪtɪd] *adj* stitico(a)

constipation [kɒnstɪ'peɪʃən] *n* stitichezza

constituency [kən'stɪtjʊənsɪ] *n* collegio elettorale

constituent [kən'stɪtjʊənt] *n* elettore/trice; (*part*) elemento componente

constitution [kɒnstɪ'tjuːʃən] *n* costituzione *f*; **~al** *adj* costituzionale

constraint [kən'streɪnt] *n* costrizione *f*

construct [kən'strʌkt] *vt* costruire; **~ion** [-ʃən] *n* costruzione *f*; **~ive** *adj* costruttivo(a)

consul ['kɒnsl] *n* console *m*; **~ate**

['kɒnsjʊlɪt] *n* consolato

consult [kən'sʌlt] *vt* consultare; **~ant** *n* (*MED*) consulente *m* medico; (*other specialist*) consulente; **~ation** [-'teɪʃən] *n* (*MED*) consulto; (*discussion*) consultazione *f*; **~ing room** (*BRIT*) *n* ambulatorio

consume [kən'sjuːm] *vt* consumare; **~r** *n* consumatore/trice; **~r goods** *npl* di consumo; **~r society** *n* società dei consumi

consumption [kən'sʌmpʃən] *n* consumo

cont. *abbr* = **continued**

contact ['kɒntækt] *n* contatto; (*person*) conoscenza ♦ *vt* mettersi in contatto con; **~ lenses** *npl* lenti *fpl* a contatto

contagious [kən'teɪdʒəs] *adj* (*also fig*) contagioso(a)

contain [kən'teɪn] *vt* contenere; **to ~ o.s.** contenersi; **~er** *n* recipiente *m*; (*for shipping etc*) container *m inv*

contaminate [kən'tæmɪneɪt] *vt* contaminare

cont'd *abbr* = **continued**

contemplate ['kɒntəmpleɪt] *vt* contemplare; (*consider*) pensare a (*or* di)

contemporary [kən'tempərərɪ] *adj, n* contemporaneo(a)

contempt [kən'tempt] *n* disprezzo; **~ of court** (*LAW*) oltraggio alla Corte; **~ible** *adj* deprecabile

contend [kən'tend] *vt*: **to ~ that** sostenere che ♦ *vi*: **to ~ with** lottare contro; **~er** *n* contendente *m/f*; concorrente *m/f*

content[1] ['kɒntent] *n* contenuto; **~s** *npl* (*of box, case etc*) contenuto; **(table of) ~s** indice *m*

content[2] [kən'tent] *adj* contento(a), soddisfatto(a) ♦ *vt* contentare, soddisfare; **~ed** *adj* contento(a), soddisfatto(a)

contention [kən'tenʃən] *n* contesa; (*assertion*) tesi *f inv*

contentment [kən'tentmənt] *n* contentezza

contest [*n* 'kɒntest, *vb* kən'test] *n* lotta; (*competition*) gara, concorso ♦ *vt* contestare; impugnare; (*compete for*) essere in lizza per; **~ant** [kən'testənt] *n* concorrente *m/f*; (*in fight*) avversario/a

context ['kɔntɛkst] *n* contesto
continent ['kɔntɪnənt] *n* continente *m*; **the C~** (*BRIT*) l'Europa continentale; **~al** [-'nɛntl] *adj* continentale; **~al breakfast** *n* colazione *f* all'europea (*senza piatti caldi*); **~al quilt** (*BRIT*) *n* piumino
contingency [kən'tɪndʒənsɪ] *n* eventualità *f inv*
continual [kən'tɪnjuəl] *adj* continuo(a)
continuation [kəntɪnju'eɪʃən] *n* continuazione *f*; (*after interruption*) ripresa; (*of story*) seguito
continue [kən'tɪnju:] *vi* continuare ♦ *vt* continuare; (*start again*) riprendere
continuity [kɔntɪ'nju:ɪtɪ] *n* continuità; (*TV, CINEMA*) (ordine *m* della) sceneggiatura
continuous [kən'tɪnjuəs] *adj* continuo(a); ininterrotto(a)
contort [kən'tɔːt] *vt* contorcere
contour ['kɔntuə*] *n* contorno, profilo; (*also*: ~ *line*) curva di livello
contraband ['kɔntrəbænd] *n* contrabbando
contraceptive [kɔntrə'sɛptɪv] *adj* contraccettivo(a) ♦ *n* contraccettivo
contract [*n* 'kɔntrækt, *vb* kən'trækt] *n* contratto ♦ *vi* (*become smaller*) contrarsi; (*COMM*): **to ~ to do sth** fare un contratto per fare qc ♦ *vt* (*illness*) contrarre; **~ion** [-ʃən] *n* contrazione *f*; **~or** *n* imprenditore *m*
contradict [kɔntrə'dɪkt] *vt* contraddire
contraflow ['kɔntrəfləu] *n* (*AUT*) senso unico alternato
contraption [kən'træpʃən] (*pej*) *n* aggeggio
contrary¹ ['kɔntrərɪ] *adj* contrario(a); (*unfavourable*) avverso(a), contrario(a) ♦ *n* contrario; **on the ~** al contrario; **unless you hear to the ~** salvo contrordine
contrary² [kən'trɛərɪ] *adj* (*perverse*) bisbetico(a)
contrast [*n* 'kɔntrɑːst, *vb* kən'trɑːst] *n* contrasto ♦ *vt* mettere in contrasto; **in ~ to** contrariamente a
contribute [kən'trɪbjuːt] *vi* contribuire ♦ *vt*: **to ~ £10/an article to** dare 10 sterline/un articolo a; **to ~ to** contribuire a; (*newspaper*) scrivere per; **contribution** [kɔntrɪ'bjuːʃən] *n* contributo; **contributor**

n (*to newspaper*) collaboratore/trice
contrivance [kən'traɪvəns] *n* congegno; espediente *m*
contrive [kən'traɪv] *vi*: **to ~ to do** fare in modo di fare
control [kən'trəul] *vt* controllare; (*firm, operation etc*) dirigere ♦ *n* controllo; **~s** *npl* (*of vehicle etc*) comandi *mpl*; (*governmental*) controlli *mpl*; **under ~** sotto controllo; **to be in ~ of** avere il controllo di; **to go out of ~** (*car*) non rispondere ai comandi; (*situation*) sfuggire di mano; **~led substance** *n* sostanza stupefacente; **~ panel** *n* quadro dei comandi; **~ room** *n* (*NAUT, MIL*) sala di comando; (*RADIO, TV*) sala di regia; **~ tower** *n* (*AVIAT*) torre *f* di controllo
controversial [kɔntrə'vəːʃl] *adj* controverso(a), polemico(a)
controversy ['kɔntrəvəːsɪ] *n* controversia, polemica
convalesce [kɔnvə'lɛs] *vi* rimettersi in salute
convene [kən'viːn] *vt* convocare ♦ *vi* convenire, adunarsi
convenience [kən'viːnɪəns] *n* comodità *f inv*; **at your ~** a suo comodo; **all modern ~s**, (*BRIT*) **all mod cons** tutte le comodità moderne
convenient [kən'viːnɪənt] *adj* conveniente, comodo(a)
convent ['kɔnvənt] *n* convento
convention [kən'vɛnʃən] *n* convenzione *f*; (*meeting*) convegno; **~al** *adj* convenzionale
conversant [kən'vəːsnt] *adj*: **to be ~ with** essere al corrente di; essere pratico(a) di
conversation [kɔnvə'seɪʃən] *n* conversazione *f*; **~al** *adj* non formale
converse¹ [kən'vəːs] *vi* conversare
converse² ['kɔnvəːs] *n* contrario, opposto; **~ly** [-'vəːslɪ] *adv* al contrario, per contro
convert [*vb* kən'vəːt, *n* 'kɔnvəːt] *vt* (*COMM, REL*) convertire; (*alter*) trasformare ♦ *n* convertito/a; **~ible** *n* macchina decappottabile
convex ['kɔnvɛks] *adj* convesso(a)
convey [kən'veɪ] *vt* trasportare; (*thanks*)

comunicare; (*idea*) dare; **~or belt** *n* nastro trasportatore

convict [*vb* kən'vɪkt, *n* 'kɒnvɪkt] *vt* dichiarare colpevole ♦ *n* carcerato/a; **~ion** [-ʃən] *n* condanna; (*belief*) convinzione *f*

convince [kən'vɪns] *vt* convincere, persuadere; **convincing** *adj* convincente

convoluted [kɒnvə'luːtɪd] *adj* (*argument etc*) involuto(a)

convoy ['kɒnvɔɪ] *n* convoglio

convulse [kən'vʌls] *vt*: **to be ~d with laughter** contorcersi dalle risa

cook [kuk] *vt* cucinare, cuocere ♦ *vi* cuocere; (*person*) cucinare ♦ *n* cuoco/a; **~book** *n* libro di cucina; **~er** *n* fornello, cucina; **~ery** *n* cucina; **~ery book** (*BRIT*) *n* = **~book**; **~ie** (*US*) *n* biscotto; **~ing** *n* cucina

cool [kuːl] *adj* fresco(a); (*not afraid, calm*) calmo(a); (*unfriendly*) freddo(a) ♦ *vt* raffreddare; (*room*) rinfrescare ♦ *vi* (*water*) raffreddarsi; (*air*) rinfrescarsi

coop [kuːp] *n* stia ♦ *vt*: **to ~ up** (*fig*) rinchiudere

cooperate [kəu'ɔpəreɪt] *vi* cooperare, collaborare; **cooperation** [-'reɪʃən] *n* cooperazione *f*, collaborazione *f*

cooperative [kəu'ɔpərətɪv] *adj* cooperativo(a) ♦ *n* cooperativa

coordinate [*vb* kəu'ɔːdɪneɪt, *n* kəu'ɔːdɪnət] *vt* coordinare ♦ *n* (*MATH*) coordinata; **~s** *npl* (*clothes*) coordinati *mpl*

co-ownership [kəu'əunəʃɪp] *n* comproprietà

cop [kɒp] (*inf*) *n* sbirro

cope [kəup] *vi*: **to ~ with** (*problems*) far fronte a

copper ['kɒpə*] *n* rame *m*; (*inf: policeman*) sbirro; **~s** *npl* (*coins*) spiccioli *mpl*

copse [kɒps] *n* bosco ceduo

copy ['kɒpɪ] *n* copia ♦ *vt* copiare; **~right** *n* diritto d'autore

coral ['kɒrəl] *n* corallo

cord [kɔːd] *n* corda; (*ELEC*) filo

cordial ['kɔːdɪəl] *adj* cordiale ♦ *n* (*BRIT*) cordiale *m*

cordon ['kɔːdn] *n* cordone *m*; **~ off** *vt* fare

cordone a

corduroy ['kɔːdərɔɪ] *n* fustagno

core [kɔː*] *n* (*of fruit*) torsolo; (*of organization etc*) cuore *m* ♦ *vt* estrarre il torsolo da

cork [kɔːk] *n* sughero; (*of bottle*) tappo; **~screw** *n* cavatappi *m inv*

corn [kɔːn] *n* (*BRIT: wheat*) grano; (*US: maize*) granturco; (*on foot*) callo; **~ on the cob** (*CULIN*) pannocchia cotta

corned beef ['kɔːnd-] *n* carne *f* di manzo in scatola

corner ['kɔːnə*] *n* angolo; (*AUT*) curva ♦ *vt* intrappolare; mettere con le spalle al muro; (*COMM: market*) accaparrare ♦ *vi* prendere una curva; **~stone** *n* pietra angolare

cornet ['kɔːnɪt] *n* (*MUS*) cornetta; (*BRIT: of ice-cream*) cono

cornflakes ['kɔːnfleɪks] *npl* fiocchi *mpl* di granturco

cornflour ['kɔːnflauə*] (*BRIT*) *n* farina finissima di granturco

cornstarch ['kɔːnstɑːt] (*US*) *n* = **cornflour**

Cornwall ['kɔːnwəl] *n* Cornovaglia

corny ['kɔːnɪ] (*inf*) *adj* trito(a)

coronary ['kɔrənərɪ] *n*: **~ (thrombosis)** trombosi *f* coronaria

coronation [kɔrə'neɪʃən] *n* incoronazione *f*

coroner ['kɔrənə*] *n* magistrato incaricato di indagare le cause di morte in circostanze sospette

coronet ['kɔrənɪt] *n* diadema *m*

corporal ['kɔːpərl] *n* caporalmaggiore *m* ♦ *adj*: **~ punishment** pena corporale

corporate ['kɔːpərɪt] *adj* costituito(a) (in corporazione); comune

corporation [kɔːpə'reɪʃən] *n* (*of town*) consiglio comunale; (*COMM*) ente *m*

corps [kɔː*, *pl* kɔːz] *n inv* corpo

corpse [kɔːps] *n* cadavere *m*

correct [kə'rɛkt] *adj* (*accurate*) corretto(a), esatto(a); (*proper*) corretto(a) ♦ *vt* correggere; **~ion** [-ʃən] *n* correzione *f*

correspond [kɒrɪs'pɒnd] *vi* corrispondere; **~ence** *n* corrispondenza; **~ence course** *n* corso per corrispondenza; **~ent** *n* corrispondente *m/f*

corridor ['kɔrɪdɔ:*] n corridoio

corrode [kə'rəud] vt corrodere ♦ vi corrodersi

corrugated ['kɔrəgeɪtɪd] adj increspato(a); ondulato(a); ~ **iron** n lamiera di ferro ondulata

corrupt [kə'rʌpt] adj corrotto(a); (COMPUT) alterato(a) ♦ vt corrompere

corset ['kɔ:sɪt] n busto

Corsica ['kɔ:sɪkə] n Corsica

cosh [kɔʃ] (BRIT) n randello (corto)

cosmetic [kɔz'metɪk] n cosmetico ♦ adj (fig: measure etc) superficiale

cost [kɔst] (pt, pp cost) n costo ♦ vt costare; (find out the ~ of) stabilire il prezzo di; ~**s** npl (COMM, LAW) spese fpl; **how much does it ~?** quanto costa?; **at all ~s** a ogni costo

co-star ['kəu-] n attore/trice della stessa importanza del protagonista

cost-effective adj conveniente

costly ['kɔstlɪ] adj costoso(a), caro(a)

cost-of-living adj: ~ **allowance** indennità f inv di contingenza

cost price (BRIT) n prezzo all'ingrosso

costume ['kɔstju:m] n costume m; (lady's suit) tailleur m inv; (BRIT: also: **swimming** ~) costume da bagno; ~ **jewellery** n bigiotteria

cosy ['kəuzɪ] (US **cozy**) adj intimo(a); **I'm very ~ here** sto proprio bene qui

cot [kɔt] n (BRIT: child's) lettino; (US: campbed) brandina

cottage ['kɔtɪdʒ] n cottage m inv; ~ **cheese** n fiocchi mpl di latte magro

cotton ['kɔtn] n cotone m; ~ **on to** (inf) vt fus afferrare; ~ **candy** (US) n zucchero filato; ~ **wool** (BRIT) n cotone idrofilo

couch [kautʃ] n sofà m inv

couchette [ku:'ʃet] n (on train, boat) cuccetta

cough [kɔf] vi tossire ♦ n tosse f; ~ **drop** n pasticca per la tosse

could [kud] pt of **can²**; ~**n't** = **could not**

council ['kaunsl] n consiglio; **city** or **town** ~ consiglio comunale; ~ **estate** (BRIT) n quartiere m di case popolari; ~ **house**

(BRIT) n casa popolare; ~**lor** n consigliere/a

counsel ['kaunsl] n avvocato; consultazione f ♦ vt consigliare; ~**lor** n (US: ~**or**) consigliere/a; (US) avvocato

count [kaunt] vt, vi contare ♦ n (of votes etc) conteggio; (of pollen etc) livello; (nobleman) conte m; ~ **on** vt fus contare su; ~**down** n conto alla rovescia

countenance ['kauntɪnəns] n volto, aspetto ♦ vt approvare

counter ['kauntə*] n banco ♦ vt opporsi a ♦ adv: ~ **to** contro; in opposizione a; ~**act** vt agire in opposizione a; (poison etc) annullare gli effetti di; ~-**espionage** n controspionaggio

counterfeit ['kauntəfɪt] n contraffazione f, falso ♦ vt contraffare, falsificare ♦ adj falso(a)

counterfoil ['kauntəfɔɪl] n matrice f

counterpart ['kauntəpɑ:t] n (of document etc) copia; (of person) corrispondente m/f

counter-productive [-prə'dʌktɪv] adj controproducente

countersign ['kauntəsaɪn] vt controfirmare

countess ['kauntɪs] n contessa

countless ['kauntlɪs] adj innumerevole

country ['kʌntrɪ] n paese m; (native land) patria; (as opposed to town) campagna; (region) regione f; ~ **dancing** (BRIT) n danza popolare; ~ **house** n villa in campagna; ~**man** (irreg) n (national) compatriota m; (rural) contadino; ~**side** n campagna

county ['kauntɪ] n contea

coup [ku:] (pl **coups**) n colpo; (also: ~ **d'état**) colpo di Stato

couple ['kʌpl] n coppia; **a ~ of** un paio di

coupon ['ku:pɔn] n buono; (detachable form) coupon m inv

courage ['kʌrɪdʒ] n coraggio

courgette [kuə'ʒet] (BRIT) n zucchina

courier ['kurɪə*] n corriere m; (for tourists) guida

course [kɔ:s] n corso; (of ship) rotta; (for golf) campo; (part of meal) piatto; **of ~** senz'altro, naturalmente; ~ **of action** modo d'agire; **a ~ of treatment** (MED) una cura

court [kɔːt] n corte f; (TENNIS) campo ♦ vt (woman) fare la corte a; **to take to ~** citare in tribunale

courteous ['kɜːtɪəs] adj cortese

courtesy ['kɜːtəsɪ] n cortesia; **(by) ~ of** per gentile concessione di; **~ bus, ~ coach** n autobus m inv gratuito (di hotel, aeroporto)

court-house (US) n palazzo di giustizia

courtier ['kɔːtɪə*] n cortigiano/a

court-martial [-'mɑːʃəl] (pl courts-martial) n corte f marziale

courtroom ['kɔːtrum] n tribunale m

courtyard ['kɔːtjɑːd] n cortile m

cousin ['kʌzn] n cugino/a; **first ~** cugino di primo grado

cove [kəuv] n piccola baia

covenant ['kʌvənənt] n accordo

cover ['kʌvə*] vt coprire; (book, table) rivestire; (include) comprendere; (PRESS) fare un servizio su ♦ n (of pan) coperchio; (over furniture) fodera; (of bed) copriletto; (of book) copertina; (shelter) riparo; (COMM, INSURANCE, and spy) copertura; **to take ~** (shelter) ripararsi; **under ~** al riparo; **under ~ of darkness** protetto dall'oscurità; **under separate ~** (COMM) a parte, in plico separato; **~ up** vi: **to ~ up for sb** coprire qn; **~age** n (PRESS, RADIO, TV): **to give full ~age to sth** fare un ampio servizio su qc; **~ charge** n coperto; **~ing** n copertura; **~ing letter** (US ~ **letter**) n lettera d'accompagnamento; **~ note** n (INSURANCE) polizza (di assicurazione) provvisoria

covert ['kʌvət] adj (hidden) nascosto(a); (glance) furtivo(a)

cover-up n occultamento (di informazioni)

cow [kau] n vacca ♦ vt (person) intimidire

coward ['kauəd] n vigliacco/a; **~ice** [-ɪs] n vigliaccheria; **~ly** adj vigliacco(a)

cowboy ['kaubɔɪ] n cow-boy m inv

cower ['kauə*] vi acquattarsi

coxswain ['kɔksn] (abbr: **cox**) n timoniere m

coy [kɔɪ] adj falsamente timido(a)

cozy ['kəuzɪ] (US) adj = **cosy**

CPA (US) n abbr = **certified public accountant**

crab [kræb] n granchio; **~ apple** n mela selvatica

crack [kræk] n fessura, crepa; incrinatura; (noise) schiocco; (: of gun) scoppio; (drug) crack m inv ♦ vt spaccare; incrinare; (whip) schioccare; (nut) schiacciare; (problem) risolvere; (code) decifrare ♦ adj (troops) fuori classe; **to ~ a joke** fare una battuta; **~ down on** vt fus porre freno a; **~ up** vi crollare; **~er** n cracker m inv; petardo

crackle ['krækl] vi crepitare

cradle ['kreɪdl] n culla

craft [krɑːft] n mestiere m; (cunning) astuzia; (boat) naviglio; **~sman** (irreg) n artigiano; **~smanship** n abilità; **~y** adj furbo(a), astuto(a)

crag [kræg] n roccia

cram [kræm] vt (fill): **to ~ sth with** riempire qc di; (put): **to ~ sth into** stipare qc in ♦ vi (for exams) prepararsi (in gran fretta)

cramp [kræmp] n crampo; **~ed** adj ristretto(a)

crampon ['kræmpən] n (CLIMBING) rampone m

cranberry ['krænbəri] n mirtillo

crane [kreɪn] n gru f inv

crank [kræŋk] n manovella; (person) persona stramba

cranny ['krænɪ] n see **nook**

crash [kræʃ] n fragore m; (of car) incidente m; (of plane) caduta; (of business etc) crollo ♦ vt fracassare ♦ vi (plane) fracassarsi; (car) avere un incidente, (two cars) scontrarsi; (business etc) fallire, andare in rovina; **~ course** n corso intensivo; **~ helmet** n casco; **~ landing** n atterraggio di fortuna

crate [kreɪt] n cassa

cravat(e) [krə'væt] n fazzoletto da collo

crave [kreɪv] vt, vi: **to ~ (for)** desiderare ardentemente

crawl [krɔːl] vi strisciare carponi; (vehicle) avanzare lentamente ♦ n (SWIMMING) crawl m

crayfish ['kreɪfɪʃ] n inv (freshwater) gambero (d'acqua dolce); (saltwater) gambero

crayon ['kreɪən] n matita colorata

craze [kreɪz] n mania

crazy ['kreɪzɪ] adj matto(a); (inf: keen): ~ **about sb** pazzo(a) di qn; ~ **about sth** matto(a) per qc

creak [kri:k] vi cigolare, scricchiolare

cream [kri:m] n crema; (fresh) panna ♦ adj (colour) color crema inv; ~ **cake** n torta alla panna; ~ **cheese** n formaggio fresco; **~y** adj cremoso(a)

crease [kri:s] n grinza; (deliberate) piega ♦ vt sgualcire ♦ vi sgualcirsi

create [kri:'eɪt] vt creare; **creation** [-ʃən] n creazione f; **creative** adj creativo(a)

creature ['kri:tʃə*] n creatura

crèche [kreʃ] n asilo infantile

credence ['kri:dns] n: **to lend** or **give** ~ **to** prestar fede a

credentials [krɪ'denʃlz] npl credenziali fpl

credit ['kredɪt] n credito; onore m ♦ vt (COMM) accreditare; (believe: also: **give** ~ **to**) credere, prestar fede a; **~s** npl (CINEMA) titoli mpl; **to** ~ **sb with** (fig) attribuire a qn; **to be in** ~ (person) essere creditore(trice); (bank account) essere coperto(a); ~ **card** n carta di credito; **~or** n creditore/trice

creed [kri:d] n credo; dottrina

creek [kri:k] n insenatura; (US) piccolo fiume m

creep [kri:p] (pt, pp **crept**) vi avanzare furtivamente (or pian piano); **~er** n pianta rampicante; **~y** adj (frightening) che fa accapponare la pelle

crematorium [kremə'tɔ:rɪəm] (pl **crematoria**) n forno crematorio

crêpe [kreɪp] n crespo; ~ **bandage** (BRIT) n fascia elastica

crept [krept] pt, pp of **creep**

crescent ['kresnt] n (shape) mezzaluna; (street) strada semicircolare

cress [kres] n crescione m

crest [krest] n cresta; (of coat of arms) cimiero; **~fallen** adj mortificato(a)

Crete [kri:t] n Creta

crevasse [krɪ'væs] n crepaccio

crevice ['krevɪs] n fessura, crepa

crew [kru:] n equipaggio; **~-cut** n: **to have a ~-cut** avere i capelli a spazzola; **~-neck** n girocollo

crib [krɪb] n culla ♦ vt (inf) copiare

crick [krɪk] n crampo

cricket ['krɪkɪt] n (insect) grillo; (game) cricket m

crime [kraɪm] n crimine m; **criminal** ['krɪmɪnl] adj, n criminale m/f

crimson ['krɪmzn] adj color cremisi inv

cringe [krɪndʒ] vi acquattarsi; (in embarrassment) sentirsi sprofondare

crinkle ['krɪŋkl] vt arricciare, increspare

cripple ['krɪpl] n zoppo/a ♦ vt azzoppare

crises ['kraɪsi:z] npl of **crisis**

crisis ['kraɪsɪs] (pl **crises**) n crisi f inv

crisp [krɪsp] adj croccante; (fig) frizzante; vivace; deciso(a); **~s** (BRIT) npl patatine fpl

criss-cross ['krɪs-] adj incrociato(a)

criteria [kraɪ'tɪərɪə] npl of **criterion**

criterion [kraɪ'tɪərɪən] (pl **criteria**) n criterio

critic ['krɪtɪk] n critico; **~al** adj critico(a); **~ally** adv (speak etc) criticamente; **~ally ill** gravemente malato; **~ism** ['krɪtɪsɪzm] n critica; **~ize** ['krɪtɪsaɪz] vt criticare

croak [krəuk] vi gracchiare; (frog) gracidare

Croatia [krəu'eɪʃə] n Croazia

crochet ['krəuʃeɪ] n lavoro all'uncinetto

crockery ['krɔkərɪ] n vasellame m

crocodile ['krɔkədaɪl] n coccodrillo

crocus ['krəukəs] n croco

croft [krɔft] (BRIT) n piccolo podere m

crony ['krəunɪ] (inf: pej) n compare m

crook [kruk] n truffatore m; (of shepherd) bastone m; **~ed** ['krukɪd] adj curvo(a), storto(a); (action) disonesto(a)

crop [krɔp] n (produce) coltivazione f; (amount produced) raccolto; (riding ~) frustino ♦ vt (hair) rapare; ~ **up** vi presentarsi

croquette [krə'ket] n crocchetta

cross [krɔs] n croce f; (BIOL) incrocio ♦ vt (street etc) attraversare; (arms, legs, BIOL) incrociare; (cheque) sbarrare ♦ adj di cattivo umore; ~ **out** vt cancellare; ~ **over** vi attraversare; **~bar** n traversa; **~country (race)** n cross-country m inv; **~-examine**

vt (LAW) interrogare in contraddittorio; ~-**eyed** adj strabico(a); ~**fire** n fuoco incrociato; ~**ing** n incrocio; (sea passage) traversata; (also: **pedestrian ~ing**) passaggio pedonale; ~**ing guard** (US) n dipendente comunale che aiuta i bambini ad attraversare la strada; ~ **purposes** npl: **to be at ~ purposes** non parlare della stessa cosa; ~**reference** n rinvio, rimando; ~**roads** n incrocio; ~ **section** n sezione f trasversale; (in population) settore m rappresentativo; ~**walk** (US) n strisce fpl pedonali, passaggio pedonale; ~**wind** n vento di traverso; ~**word** n cruciverba m inv

crotch [krɔtʃ] n (ANAT) inforcatura; (of garment) pattina

crotchet ['krɔtʃɪt] n (MUS) semiminima

crouch [krautʃ] vi acquattarsi; rannicchiarsi

crow [krəu] n (bird) cornacchia; (of cock) canto del gallo ♦ vi (cock) cantare

crowbar ['krəubɑ:ʳ] n piede m di porco

crowd [kraud] n folla ♦ vt affollare, stipare ♦ vi: **to ~ round/in** affollarsi intorno a/in; ~**ed** adj affollato(a); ~**ed with** stipato(a) di

crown [kraun] n corona; (of head) calotta cranica; (of hat) cocuzzolo; (of hill) cima ♦ vt incoronare; (fig: career) coronare; ~ **jewels** npl gioielli mpl della Corona; ~ **prince** n principe m ereditario

crow's feet npl zampe fpl di gallina

crucial ['kru:ʃl] adj cruciale, decisivo(a)

crucifix ['kru:sɪfɪks] n crocifisso; ~**ion** [-'fɪkʃən] n crocifissione f

crude [kru:d] adj (materials) greggio(a); non raffinato(a); (fig: basic) crudo(a), primitivo(a); (: vulgar) rozzo(a), grossolano(a); ~ **(oil)** n (petrolio) greggio

cruel ['kruəl] adj crudele; ~**ty** n crudeltà f inv

cruise [kru:z] n crociera ♦ vi andare a velocità di crociera; (taxi) circolare; ~**r** n incrociatore m

crumb [krʌm] n briciola

crumble ['krʌmbl] vt sbriciolare ♦ vi sbriciolarsi; (plaster etc) sgretolarsi; (land, earth) franare; (building, fig) crollare;

crumbly adj friabile

crumpet ['krʌmpɪt] n specie di frittella

crumple ['krʌmpl] vt raggrinzare, spiegazzare

crunch [krʌntʃ] vt sgranocchiare; (underfoot) scricchiolare ♦ n (fig) punto or momento cruciale; ~**y** adj croccante

crusade [kru:'seɪd] n crociata

crush [krʌʃ] n folla; (love): **to have a ~ on sb** avere una cotta per qn; (drink): **lemon ~** spremuta di limone ♦ vt schiacciare; (crumple) sgualcire

crust [krʌst] n crosta

crutch [krʌtʃ] n gruccia

crux [krʌks] n nodo

cry [kraɪ] vi piangere; (shout: also: ~ **out**) urlare ♦ n urlo, grido; ~ **off** vi ritirarsi

cryptic ['krɪptɪk] adj ermetico(a)

crystal ['krɪstl] n cristallo; ~-**clear** adj cristallino(a)

cub [kʌb] n cucciolo; (also: ~ **scout**) lupetto

Cuba ['kju:bə] n Cuba

cube [kju:b] n cubo ♦ vt (MATH) elevare al cubo; **cubic** adj cubico(a); (metre, foot) cubo(a); **cubic capacity** n cilindrata

cubicle ['kju:bɪkl] n scompartimento separato; cabina

cuckoo ['kuku:] n cucù m inv; ~ **clock** n orologio a cucù

cucumber ['kju:kʌmbəʳ] n cetriolo

cuddle ['kʌdl] vt abbracciare, coccolare ♦ vi abbracciarsi

cue [kju:] n (snooker ~) stecca; (THEATRE etc) segnale m

cuff [kʌf] n (BRIT: of shirt, coat etc) polsino; (US: of trousers) risvolto; **off the ~** improvvisando; ~**link** n gemello

cuisine [kwɪ'zi:n] n cucina

cul-de-sac ['kʌldəsæk] n vicolo cieco

cull [kʌl] vt (ideas etc) scegliere ♦ n (of animals) abbattimento selettivo

culminate ['kʌlmɪneɪt] vi: **to ~ in** culminare con; **culmination** [-'neɪʃən] n culmine m

culottes [kju:'lɔts] npl gonna f pantalone inv

culpable ['kʌlpəbl] adj colpevole

culprit ['kʌlprɪt] *n* colpevole *m/f*

cult [kʌlt] *n* culto

cultivate ['kʌltɪveɪt] *vt* (*also fig*) coltivare; **cultivation** [-'veɪʃən] *n* coltivazione *f*

cultural ['kʌltʃərəl] *adj* culturale

culture ['kʌltʃə*] *n* (*also fig*) cultura; ~**d** *adj* colto(a)

cumbersome ['kʌmbəsəm] *adj* ingombrante

cunning ['kʌnɪŋ] *n* astuzia, furberia ♦ *adj* astuto(a), furbo(a)

cup [kʌp] *n* tazza; (*prize, of bra*) coppa

cupboard ['kʌbəd] *n* armadio

cup-tie (*BRIT*) *n* partita di coppa

curate ['kjuərɪt] *n* cappellano

curator [kjuə'reɪtə*] *n* direttore *m* (*di museo etc*)

curb [kə:b] *vt* tenere a freno ♦ *n* freno; (*US*) bordo del marciapiede

curdle ['kə:dl] *vi* cagliare

cure [kjuə*] *vt* guarire; (*CULIN*) trattare; affumicare; essiccare ♦ *n* rimedio

curfew ['kə:fju:] *n* coprifuoco

curiosity [kjuərɪ'ɔsɪtɪ] *n* curiosità

curious ['kjuərɪəs] *adj* curioso(a)

curl [kə:l] *n* riccio ♦ *vt* ondulare; (*tightly*) arricciare ♦ *vi* arricciarsi; (*tightly*) rannicchiarsi; ~ **up** *vi* rannicchiarsi; ~**er** *n* bigodino

curly ['kə:lɪ] *adj* ricciuto(a)

currant ['kʌrnt] *n* (*dried*) sultanina; (*bush, fruit*) ribes *m inv*

currency ['kʌrnsɪ] *n* moneta; **to gain** ~ (*fig*) acquistare larga diffusione

current ['kʌrnt] *adj* corrente ♦ *n* corrente *f*; ~ **account** (*BRIT*) *n* conto corrente; ~ **affairs** *npl* attualità *fpl*; ~**ly** *adv* attualmente

curricula [kə'rɪkjulə] *npl of* **curriculum**

curriculum [kə'rɪkjuləm] (*pl* ~**s** *or* **curricula**) *n* curriculum *m inv*; ~ **vitae** *n* curriculum vitae *m inv*

curry ['kʌrɪ] *n* curry *m inv* ♦ *vt*: **to** ~ **favour with** cercare di attirarsi i favori di; ~ **powder** *n* curry *m*

curse [kə:s] *vt* maledire ♦ *vi* bestemmiare ♦ *n* maledizione *f*; bestemmia

cursor ['kə:sə*] *n* (*COMPUT*) cursore *m*

cursory ['kə:sərɪ] *adj* superficiale

curt [kə:t] *adj* secco(a)

curtail [kə:'teɪl] *vt* (*freedom etc*) limitare; (*visit etc*) accorciare; (*expenses etc*) ridurre, decurtare

curtain ['kə:tn] *n* tenda; (*THEATRE*) sipario

curts(e)y ['kə:tsɪ] *vi* fare un inchino *or* una riverenza

curve [kə:v] *n* curva ♦ *vi* curvarsi

cushion ['kuʃən] *n* cuscino ♦ *vt* (*shock*) fare da cuscinetto a

custard ['kʌstəd] *n* (*for pouring*) crema

custodian [kʌs'təudɪən] *n* custode *m/f*

custody ['kʌstədɪ] *n* (*of child*) tutela; **to take into** ~ (*suspect*) mettere in detenzione preventiva

custom ['kʌstəm] *n* costume *m*, consuetudine *f*; (*COMM*) clientela; ~**ary** *adj* consueto(a)

customer ['kʌstəmə*] *n* cliente *m/f*

customized ['kʌstəmaɪzd] *adj* (*car etc*) fuoriserie *inv*

custom-made *adj* (*clothes*) fatto(a) su misura; (*other goods*) fatto(a) su ordinazione

customs ['kʌstəmz] *npl* dogana; ~ **duty** *n* tassa doganale; ~ **officer** *n* doganiere *m*

cut [kʌt] (*pt, pp* **cut**) *vt* tagliare; (*shape, make*) intagliare; (*reduce*) ridurre ♦ *vi* tagliare ♦ *n* taglio; (*in salary etc*) riduzione *f*; **to** ~ **a tooth** mettere un dente; ~ **down** *vt* (*tree etc*) abbattere ♦ *vt fus* (*also*: ~ **down on**) ridurre; ~ **off** *vt* tagliare; (*fig*) isolare; ~ **out** *vt* tagliare fuori; eliminare; ritagliare; ~ **up** *vt* (*paper, meat*) tagliare a pezzi; ~**back** *n* riduzione *f*

cute [kju:t] *adj* (*sweet*) carino(a)

cuticle ['kju:tɪkl] *n* (*on nail*) pellicina, cuticola

cutlery ['kʌtlərɪ] *n* posate *fpl*

cutlet ['kʌtlɪt] *n* costoletta; (*nut etc* ~) cotoletta vegetariana

cut: ~**out** *n* interruttore *m*; (*cardboard* ~*out*) ritaglio; ~**-price** (*US* ~**-rate**) *adj* a prezzo ridotto; ~**throat** *n* assassino ♦ *adj* (*competition*) spietato(a)

cutting ['kʌtɪŋ] *adj* tagliente ♦ *n* (*from*

newspaper) ritaglio (di giornale); (*from plant*) talea

CV *n abbr* = **curriculum vitae**

cwt *abbr* = **hundredweight(s)**

cyanide ['saɪənaɪd] *n* cianuro

cycle ['saɪkl] *n* ciclo; (*bicycle*) bicicletta ♦ *vi* andare in bicicletta; **~ hire** *n* noleggio *m* biciclette *inv*; **~ lane**, **~ path** *n* pista ciclabile

cycling ['saɪklɪŋ] *n* ciclismo

cyclist ['saɪklɪst] *n* ciclista *m/f*

cygnet ['sɪgnɪt] *n* cigno giovane

cylinder ['sɪlɪndə*] *n* cilindro; **~-head gasket** *n* guarnizione *f* della testata del cilindro

cymbals ['sɪmblz] *npl* cembali *mpl*

cynic ['sɪnɪk] *n* cinico/a; **~al** *adj* cinico(a); **~ism** ['sɪnɪsɪzəm] *n* cinismo

Cyprus ['saɪprəs] *n* Cipro

cyst [sɪst] *n* cisti *f inv*

cystitis [sɪs'taɪtɪs] *n* cistite *f*

czar [zɑ:*] *n* zar *m inv*

Czech [tʃek] *adj* ceco(a) ♦ *n* ceco/a; (*LING*) ceco

Czech Republic *n*: **the ~** la Repubblica Ceca

D, d

D [di:] *n* (*MUS*) re *m*

dab [dæb] *vt* (*eyes, wound*) tamponare; (*paint, cream*) applicare (con leggeri colpetti)

dabble ['dæbl] *vi*: **to ~ in** occuparsi (da dilettante) di

dad(dy) [dæd(ɪ)] (*inf*) *n* babbo, papà *m inv*

daffodil ['dæfədɪl] *n* trombone *m*, giunchiglia

daft [dɑ:ft] *adj* sciocco(a)

dagger ['dægə*] *n* pugnale *m*

daily ['deɪlɪ] *adj* quotidiano(a), giornaliero(a) ♦ *n* quotidiano ♦ *adv* tutti i giorni

dainty ['deɪntɪ] *adj* delicato(a), grazioso(a)

dairy ['dɛərɪ] *n* (*BRIT: shop*) latteria; (*on farm*) caseificio ♦ *adj* caseario(a); **~ farm** *n* caseificio; **~ products** *npl* latticini *mpl*; **~**

store (*US*) *n* latteria

daisy ['deɪzɪ] *n* margherita

dale [deɪl] (*BRIT*) *n* valle *f*

dam [dæm] *n* diga ♦ *vt* sbarrare; costruire dighe su

damage ['dæmɪdʒ] *n* danno, danni *mpl*; (*fig*) danno ♦ *vt* danneggiare; **~s** *npl* (*LAW*) danni

damn [dæm] *vt* condannare; (*curse*) maledire ♦ *n* (*inf*): **I don't give a ~** non me ne frega niente ♦ *adj* (*inf: also:* **~ed**): **this ~ ...** questo maledetto ...; **~ (it)!** accidenti!; **~ing** *adj* (*evidence*) schiacciante

damp [dæmp] *adj* umido(a) ♦ *n* umidità, umido ♦ *vt* (*also:* **~en: cloth, rag**) inumidire, bagnare; (*enthusiasm etc*) spegnere

damson ['dæmzən] *n* susina damaschina

dance [dɑ:ns] *n* danza, ballo; (*ball*) ballo ♦ *vi* ballare; **~ hall** *n* dancing *m inv*, sala da ballo; **~r** *n* danzatore/trice; (*professional*) ballerino/a

dancing ['dɑ:nsɪŋ] *n* danza, ballo

dandelion ['dændɪlaɪən] *n* dente *m* di leone

dandruff ['dændrəf] *n* forfora

Dane [deɪn] *n* danese *m/f*

danger ['deɪndʒə*] *n* pericolo; **there is a ~ of fire** c'è pericolo di incendio; **in ~** in pericolo; **he was in ~ of falling** rischiava di cadere; **~ous** *adj* pericoloso(a)

dangle ['dæŋgl] *vt* dondolare; (*fig*) far balenare ♦ *vi* pendolare

Danish ['deɪnɪʃ] *adj* danese ♦ *n* (*LING*) danese *m*

dare [dɛə*] *vt*: **to ~ sb to do** sfidare qn a fare ♦ *vi*: **to ~ (to) do sth** osare fare qc; **I ~ say** (*I suppose*) immagino (che); **daring** *adj* audace, ardito(a) ♦ *n* audacia

dark [dɑ:k] *adj* (*night, room*) buio(a), scuro(a); (*colour, complexion*) scuro(a); (*fig*) cupo(a), tetro(a), nero(a) ♦ *n*: **in the ~** al buio; **in the ~ about** (*fig*) all'oscuro di; **after ~** a notte fatta; **~en** *vt* (*colour*) scurire ♦ *vi* (*sky, room*) oscurarsi; **~ glasses** *npl* occhiali *mpl* scuri; **~ness** *n* oscurità, buio; **~room** *n* camera oscura

darling ['dɑ:lɪŋ] *adj* caro(a) ♦ *n* tesoro

darn [dɑ:n] *vt* rammendare

dart [dɑːt] *n* freccetta; (SEWING) pince *f inv*
♦ *vi*: **to ~ towards** precipitarsi verso; **to ~ away/along** sfrecciare via/lungo; **~board** *n* bersaglio (per freccette); **~s** *n* tiro al bersaglio (con freccette)

dash [dæʃ] *n* (*sign*) lineetta; (*small quantity*) punta ♦ *vt* (*missile*) gettare; (*hopes*) infrangere ♦ *vi*: **to ~ towards** precipitarsi verso; **~ away** *or* **off** *vi* scappare via

dashboard ['dæʃbɔːd] *n* (AUT) cruscotto

dashing ['dæʃɪŋ] *adj* ardito(a)

data ['deɪtə] *npl* dati *mpl*; **~base** *n* base *f* di dati, data base *m inv*; **~ processing** *n* elaborazione *f* (elettronica) dei dati

date [deɪt] *n* data; appuntamento; (*fruit*) dattero ♦ *vt* datare; (*person*) uscire con; **~ of birth** data di nascita; **to ~** (*until now*) fino a oggi; **~d** *adj* passato(a) di moda; **~ rape** *n* stupro perpetrato da persona conosciuta

daub [dɔːb] *vt* imbrattare

daughter ['dɔːtə*] *n* figlia; **~-in-law** *n* nuora

daunting ['dɔːntɪŋ] *adj* non invidiabile

dawdle ['dɔːdl] *vi* bighellonare

dawn [dɔːn] *n* alba ♦ *vi* (*day*) spuntare; (*fig*): **it ~ed on him that ...** gli è venuto in mente che ....

day [deɪ] *n* giorno; (*as duration*) giornata; (*period of time, age*) tempo, epoca; **the ~ before** il giorno avanti *or* prima; **the ~ after, the following ~** il giorno dopo *or* seguente; **the ~ after tomorrow** dopodomani; **the ~ before yesterday** l'altroieri; **by ~** di giorno; **~break** *n* spuntar *m* del giorno; **~dream** *vi* sognare a occhi aperti; **~light** *n* luce *f* del giorno; **~ return** (BRIT) *n* biglietto giornaliero di andata e ritorno; **~time** *n* giorno; **~-to-~** *adj* (*life, organization*) quotidiano(a)

daze [deɪz] *vt* (*subj: drug*) inebetire; (: *blow*) stordire ♦ *n*: **in a ~** inebetito(a); stordito(a)

dazzle ['dæzl] *vt* abbagliare

DC *abbr* (= *direct current*) c.c.

D-day *n* giorno dello sbarco alleato in Normandia

dead [ded] *adj* morto(a); (*numb*) intirizzito(a); (*telephone*) muto(a); (*battery*) scarico(a) ♦ *adv* assolutamente, perfettamente ♦ *npl*: **the ~** i morti; **he was shot ~** fu colpito a morte; **~ tired** stanco(a) morto(a); **to stop ~** fermarsi di colpo; **~en** *vt* (*blow, sound*) ammortire; **~ end** *n* vicolo cieco; **~ heat** *n* (SPORT): **to finish in a ~ heat** finire alla pari; **~line** *n* scadenza; **~lock** *n* punto morto; **~ loss** *n*: **to be a ~ loss** (*inf: person, thing*) non valere niente; **~ly** *adj* mortale; (*weapon, poison*) micidiale; **~pan** *adj* a faccia impassibile

deaf [def] *adj* sordo(a); **~en** *vt* assordare; **~ness** *n* sordità

deal [diːl] (*pt, pp* **dealt**) *n* accordo; (*business ~*) affare *m* ♦ *vt* (*blow, cards*) dare; **a great ~ (of)** molto(a); **~ in** *vt fus* occuparsi di; **~ with** *vt fus* fare affari con, trattare con; (COMM) fare affari con, trattare con; (*handle*) occuparsi di; (*be about: book etc*) trattare di; **~er** *n* commerciante *m/f*; **~ings** *npl* (COMM) relazioni *fpl*; (*relations*) rapporti *mpl*; **dealt** [delt] *pt, pp of* **deal**

dean [diːn] *n* (REL) decano; (SCOL) preside *m* di facoltà (*or* di collegio)

dear [dɪə*] *adj* caro(a) ♦ *n*: **my ~** caro mio/cara mia ♦ *excl*: **~ me!** Dio mio!; **D~ Sir/Madam** (*in letter*) Egregio Signore/Egregia Signora; **D~ Mr/Mrs X** Gentile Signor/Signora X; **~ly** *adv* (*love*) moltissimo; (*pay*) a caro prezzo

death [deθ] *n* morte *f*; (ADMIN) decesso; **~ certificate** *n* atto di decesso; **~ly** *adj* di morte; **~ penalty** *n* pena di morte; **~ rate** *n* indice *m* di mortalità; **~ toll** *n* vittime *fpl*

debacle [dɪ'bækl] *n* fiasco

debase [dɪ'beɪs] *vt* (*currency*) adulterare; (*person*) degradare

debatable [dɪ'beɪtəbl] *adj* discutibile

debate [dɪ'beɪt] *n* dibattito ♦ *vt* dibattere; discutere

debit ['debɪt] *n* debito ♦ *vt*: **to ~ a sum to sb** *or* **to sb's account** addebitare una somma a qn

debris ['debriː] *n* detriti *mpl*

debt [det] *n* debito; **to be in ~** essere

indebitato(a); **~or** n debitore/trice

début ['deɪbjuː] n debutto

decade ['dekeɪd] n decennio

decadence ['dekədəns] n decadenza

decaff ['diːkæf] (inf) n decaffeinato

decaffeinated [dɪ'kæfɪneɪtɪd] adj
decaffeinato(a)

decanter [dɪ'kæntə*] n caraffa

decay [dɪ'keɪ] n decadimento; (also: **tooth
~**) carie f ♦ vi (rot) imputridire

deceased [dɪ'siːst] n defunto/a

deceit [dɪ'siːt] n inganno; **~ful** adj
ingannevole, perfido(a)

deceive [dɪ'siːv] vt ingannare

December [dɪ'sembə*] n dicembre m

decent ['diːsənt] adj decente; (respectable)
per bene; (kind) gentile

deception [dɪ'sepʃən] n inganno

deceptive [dɪ'septɪv] adj ingannevole

decide [dɪ'saɪd] vt (person) far prendere una
decisione a; (question, argument) risolvere,
decidere ♦ vi decidere, decidersi; **to ~ to
do/that** decidere di fare/che; **to ~ on**
decidere per; **~d** adj (resolute) deciso(a);
(clear, definite) netto(a), chiaro(a); **~dly**
[-dɪdlɪ] adv indubbiamente; decisamente

decimal ['desɪməl] adj decimale ♦ n
decimale m; **~ point** n ≈ virgola

decipher [dɪ'saɪfə*] vt decifrare

decision [dɪ'sɪʒən] n decisione f

decisive [dɪ'saɪsɪv] adj decisivo(a), (person)
deciso(a)

deck [dek] n (NAUT) ponte m; (of bus): **top ~**
imperiale m; (record ~) piatto; (of cards)
mazzo; **~chair** n sedia a sdraio

declaration [deklə'reɪʃən] n dichiarazione f

declare [dɪ'kleə*] vt dichiarare

decline [dɪ'klaɪn] n (decay) declino;
(lessening) ribasso ♦ vt declinare; rifiutare
♦ vi declinare; diminuire

decode [diː'kəud] vt decifrare

decoder [diː'kəudə*] n (TV) decodificatore
m

decompose [diːkəm'pəuz] vi decomporre

décor ['deɪkɔː*] n decorazione f

decorate ['dekəreɪt] vt (adorn, give a medal
to) decorare; (paint and paper) tinteggiare

e tappezzare; **decoration** [-'reɪʃən] n
(medal etc, adornment) decorazione f;
decorator n decoratore m

decorum [dɪ'kɔːrəm] n decoro

decoy ['diːkɔɪ] n zimbello

decrease [n 'diːkriːs, vb diː'kriːs] n
diminuzione f ♦ vt, vi diminuire

decree [dɪ'kriː] n decreto; **~ nisi** [-'naɪsaɪ] n
sentenza provvisoria di divorzio

dedicate ['dedɪkeɪt] vt consacrare; (book
etc) dedicare

dedication [dedɪ'keɪʃən] n (devotion)
dedizione f; (in book etc) dedica

deduce [dɪ'djuːs] vt dedurre

deduct [dɪ'dʌkt] vt: **to ~ sth (from)** dedurre
qc (da); **~ion** [dɪ'dʌkʃən] n deduzione f

deed [diːd] n azione f, atto; (LAW) atto

deep [diːp] adj profondo(a); **4 metres ~**
profondo(a) 4 metri ♦ adv: **spectators
stood 20 ~** c'erano 20 file di spettatori;
~en vt (hole) approfondire ♦ vi
approfondirsi; (darkness) farsi più buio; **~
end** n: **the ~ end** (of swimming pool) la
parte più profonda; **~-freeze** n
congelatore m; **~-fry** vt friggere in olio
abbondante; **~ly** adv profondamente; **~-
sea diving** n immersione f in alto mare;
~-seated adj radicato(a)

deer [dɪə*] n inv: **the ~** i cervidi; **(red) ~**
cervo; **(fallow) ~** daino; **(roe) ~** capriolo;
~skin n pelle f di daino

deface [dɪ'feɪs] vt imbrattare

default [dɪ'fɔːlt] n (COMPUT: also: **~ value**)
default m inv; **by ~** (SPORT) per abbandono

defeat [dɪ'fiːt] n sconfitta ♦ vt (team,
opponents) sconfiggere; **~ist** adj, n
disfattista m/f

defect [n 'diːfekt, vb dɪ'fekt] n difetto ♦ vi: **to
~ to the enemy** passare al nemico; **~ive**
[dɪ'fektɪv] adj difettoso(a)

defence [dɪ'fens] (US **defense**) n difesa;
~less adj senza difesa

defend [dɪ'fend] vt difendere; **~ant** n
imputato/a; **~er** n difensore/a

defense [dɪ'fens] (US) n = **defence**

defensive [dɪ'fensɪv] adj difensivo(a) ♦ n:
on the ~ sulla difensiva

defer [dɪ'fəː*] vt (*postpone*) differire, rinviare

defiance [dɪ'faɪəns] n sfida; **in ~ of** a dispetto di

defiant [dɪ'faɪənt] adj (*attitude*) di sfida; (*person*) ribelle

deficiency [dɪ'fɪʃənsɪ] n deficienza; carenza

deficit ['dɛfɪsɪt] n deficit m inv

define [dɪ'faɪn] vt definire

definite ['dɛfɪnɪt] adj (*fixed*) definito(a), preciso(a); (*clear, obvious*) ben definito(a), esatto(a); (*LING*) determinativo(a); **he was ~ about it** ne era sicuro; **~ly** adv indubbiamente

definition [dɛfɪ'nɪʃən] n definizione f

deflate [diː'fleɪt] vt sgonfiare

deflect [dɪ'flɛkt] vt deflettere, deviare

deformed [dɪ'fɔːmd] adj deforme

defraud [dɪ'frɔːd] vt defraudare

defrost [diː'frɔst] vt (*fridge*) disgelare; **~er** (*US*) n (*demister*) sbrinatore m

deft [dɛft] adj svelto(a), destro(a)

defunct [dɪ'fʌŋkt] adj che non esiste più

defuse [diː'fjuːz] vt disinnescare; (*fig*) distendere

defy [dɪ'faɪ] vt sfidare; (*efforts etc*) resistere a; **it defies description** supera ogni descrizione

degenerate [vb dɪ'dʒɛnəreɪt, adj dɪ'dʒɛnərɪt] vi degenerare ♦ adj degenere

degree [dɪ'griː] n grado; (*SCOL*) laurea (universitaria); **a (first) ~ in maths** una laurea in matematica; **by ~s** (*gradually*) gradualmente, a poco a poco; **to some ~** fino a un certo punto, in certa misura

dehydrated [diːhaɪ'dreɪtɪd] adj disidratato(a); (*milk, eggs*) in polvere

de-ice [diː'aɪs] vt (*windscreen*) disgelare

deign [deɪn] vi: **to ~ to do** degnarsi di fare

deity ['diːɪtɪ] n divinità f inv

dejected [dɪ'dʒɛktɪd] adj abbattuto(a), avvilito(a)

delay [dɪ'leɪ] vt ritardare ♦ vi: **to ~ (in doing sth)** ritardare (a fare qc) ♦ n ritardo; **to be ~ed** subire un ritardo; (*person*) essere trattenuto(a)

delectable [dɪ'lɛktəbl] adj (*person, food*) delizioso(a)

delegate [n 'dɛlɪgɪt, vb 'dɛlɪgeɪt] n delegato/a ♦ vt delegare; **delegation** [-'geɪʃən] n (*group*) delegazione f; (*by manager*) delega

delete [dɪ'liːt] vt cancellare

deliberate [adj dɪ'lɪbərɪt, vb dɪ'lɪbəreɪt] adj (*intentional*) intenzionale; (*slow*) misurato(a) ♦ vi deliberare, riflettere; **~ly** adv (*on purpose*) deliberatamente

delicacy ['dɛlɪkəsɪ] n delicatezza

delicate ['dɛlɪkɪt] adj delicato(a)

delicatessen [dɛlɪkə'tɛsn] n ≈ salumeria

delicious [dɪ'lɪʃəs] adj delizioso(a), squisito(a)

delight [dɪ'laɪt] n delizia, gran piacere m ♦ vt dilettare; **to take (a) ~ in** dilettarsi in; **~ed** adj: **~ed (at or with)** contentissimo(a) (di), felice (di); **~ed to do** felice di fare; **~ful** adj delizioso(a); incantevole

delinquent [dɪ'lɪŋkwənt] adj, n delinquente m/f

delirious [dɪ'lɪrɪəs] adj: **to be ~** delirare

deliver [dɪ'lɪvə*] vt (*mail*) distribuire; (*goods*) consegnare; (*speech*) pronunciare; (*MED*) far partorire; **~y** n distribuzione f; consegna; (*of speaker*) dizione f; (*MED*) parto

delude [dɪ'luːd] vt illudere

deluge ['dɛljuːdʒ] n diluvio

delusion [dɪ'luːʒən] n illusione f

demand [dɪ'mɑːnd] vt richiedere; (*rights*) rivendicare ♦ n domanda; (*claim*) rivendicazione f; **in ~** ricercato(a), richiesto(a); **on ~** a richiesta; **~ing** adj (*boss*) esigente; (*work*) impegnativo(a)

demean [dɪ'miːn] vt: **to ~ o.s.** umiliarsi

demeanour [dɪ'miːnə*] (*US* **demeanor**) n comportamento; contegno

demented [dɪ'mɛntɪd] adj demente, impazzito(a)

demise [dɪ'maɪz] n decesso

demister [diː'mɪstə*] (*BRIT*) n (*AUT*) sbrinatore m

demo ['dɛməu] (*inf*) n abbr (= *demonstration*) manifestazione f

democracy [dɪ'mɔkrəsɪ] n democrazia

democrat ['dɛməkræt] n democratico/a; **~ic** [dɛmə'krætɪk] adj democratico(a)

demolish [dɪ'mɔlɪʃ] *vt* demolire
demonstrate ['dɛmənstreɪt] *vt* dimostrare, provare ♦ *vi* dimostrare, manifestare; **demonstration** [-'streɪʃən] *n* dimostrazione *f*; (*POL*) dimostrazione, manifestazione *f*; **demonstrator** *n* (*POL*) dimostrante *m/f*; (*COMM*) dimostratore/trice
demote [dɪ'məut] *vt* far retrocedere
demure [dɪ'mjuə*] *adj* contegnoso(a)
den [dɛn] *n* tana, covo; (*room*) buco
denial [dɪ'naɪəl] *n* diniego; rifiuto
denim ['dɛnɪm] *n* tessuto di cotone ritorto; **~s** *npl* (*jeans*) blue jeans *mpl*
Denmark ['dɛnmɑːk] *n* Danimarca
denomination [dɪnɔmɪ'neɪʃən] *n* (*money*) valore *m*; (*REL*) confessione *f*
denounce [dɪ'nauns] *vt* denunciare
dense [dɛns] *adj* fitto(a); (*smoke*) denso(a); (*inf: person*) ottuso(a), duro(a)
density ['dɛnsɪtɪ] *n* densità *f inv*
dent [dɛnt] *n* ammaccatura ♦ *vt* (*also*: **make a ~ in**) ammaccare
dental ['dɛntl] *adj* dentale; **~ surgeon** *n* medico/a dentista
dentist ['dɛntɪst] *n* dentista *m/f*
dentures ['dɛntʃəz] *npl* dentiera
deny [dɪ'naɪ] *vt* negare; (*refuse*) rifiutare
deodorant [diː'əudərənt] *n* deodorante *m*
depart [dɪ'pɑːt] *vi* partire; **to ~ from** (*fig*) deviare da
department [dɪ'pɑːtmənt] *n* (*COMM*) reparto; (*SCOL*) sezione *f*, dipartimento; (*POL*) ministero; **~ store** *n* grande magazzino
departure [dɪ'pɑːtʃə*] *n* partenza; (*fig*): **~ from** deviazione *f* da; **a new ~** una svolta (decisiva); **~ lounge** *n* (*at airport*) sala d'attesa
depend [dɪ'pɛnd] *vi*: **to ~ on** dipendere da; (*rely on*) contare su; **it ~s** dipende; **~ing on the result ...** a seconda del risultato ...; **~able** *adj* fidato(a); (*car etc*) affidabile; **~ant** *n* persona a carico; **~ent** *adj*: **to be ~ent on** dipendere da; (*child, relative*) essere a carico di ♦ *n* = **~ant**
depict [dɪ'pɪkt] *vt* (*in picture*) dipingere; (*in words*) descrivere

depleted [dɪ'pliːtɪd] *adj* diminuito(a)
deploy [dɪ'plɔɪ] *vt* dispiegare
depopulation ['diːpɔpju'leɪʃən] *n* spopolamento
deport [dɪ'pɔːt] *vt* deportare; espellere
deportment [dɪ'pɔːtmənt] *n* portamento
deposit [dɪ'pɔzɪt] *n* (*COMM, GEO*) deposito; (*of ore, oil*) giacimento; (*CHEM*) sedimento; (*part payment*) acconto; (*for hired goods etc*) cauzione *f* ♦ *vt* depositare; dare in acconto; mettere *or* lasciare in deposito; **~ account** *n* conto vincolato
depot ['dɛpəu] *n* deposito; (*US*) stazione *f* ferroviaria
depreciate [dɪ'priːʃɪeɪt] *vi* svalutarsi
depress [dɪ'prɛs] *vt* deprimere; (*price, wages*) abbassare; (*press down*) premere; **~ed** *adj* (*person*) depresso(a), abbattuto(a); (*price*) in ribasso; (*industry*) in crisi; **~ing** *adj* deprimente; **~ion** [dɪ'prɛʃən] *n* depressione *f*
deprivation [dɛprɪ'veɪʃən] *n* privazione *f*
deprive [dɪ'praɪv] *vt*: **to ~ sb of** privare qn di; **~d** *adj* disgraziato(a)
depth [dɛpθ] *n* profondità *f inv*; **in the ~s of** nel profondo di; nel cuore di; **out of one's ~** (*in water*) dove non si tocca; (*fig*) a disagio
deputize ['dɛpjutaɪz] *vi*: **to ~ for** svolgere le funzioni di
deputy ['dɛpjutɪ] *adj*: **~ head** (*BRIT, SCOL*) vicepreside *m/f* ♦ *n* (*assistant*) vice *m/f inv*; (*US: also*: **~ sheriff**) vice-sceriffo
derail [dɪ'reɪl] *vt*: **to be ~ed** deragliare
deranged [dɪ'reɪndʒd] *adj*: **to be (mentally) ~** essere pazzo(a)
derby ['dəːbɪ] (*US*) *n* (*bowler hat*) bombetta
derelict ['dɛrɪlɪkt] *adj* abbandonato(a)
derisory [dɪ'raɪsərɪ] *adj* (*sum*) irrisorio(a); (*laughter, person*) beffardo(a)
derive [dɪ'raɪv] *vt*: **to ~ sth from** derivare qc da; trarre qc da ♦ *vi*: **to ~ from** derivare da
derogatory [dɪ'rɔgətərɪ] *adj* denigratorio(a)
derv [dəːv] (*BRIT*) *n* gasolio
descend [dɪ'sɛnd] *vt, vi* discendere, scendere; **to ~ from** discendere da; **to ~ to** (*lying, begging*) abbassarsi a; **~ant** *n*

discendente *m/f*

descent [dɪ'sɛnt] *n* discesa; *(origin)* discendenza, famiglia

describe [dɪs'kraɪb] *vt* descrivere; **description** [-'krɪpʃən] *n* descrizione *f*; *(sort)* genere *m*, specie *f*

desecrate ['dɛsɪkreɪt] *vt* profanare

desert [*n* 'dɛzət, *vb* dɪ'zə:t] *n* deserto ♦ *vt* lasciare, abbandonare ♦ *vi* (MIL) disertare; **~er** *n* disertore *m*; **~ion** [dɪ'zə:ʃən] *n* (MIL) diserzione *f*; (LAW) abbandono del tetto coniugale; **~ island** *n* isola deserta; **~s** [dɪ'zə:ts] *npl*: **to get one's just ~s** avere ciò che si merita

deserve [dɪ'zə:v] *vt* meritare; **deserving** *adj (person)* meritevole, degno(a); *(cause)* meritorio(a)

design [dɪ'zaɪn] *n (art, sketch)* disegno; *(layout, shape)* linea; *(pattern)* fantasia; *(intention)* intenzione *f* ♦ *vt* disegnare; progettare

designer [dɪ'zaɪnə*] *n* (ART, TECH) disegnatore/trice; *(of fashion)* modellista *m/f*

desire [dɪ'zaɪə*] *n* desiderio, voglia ♦ *vt* desiderare, volere

desk [dɛsk] *n (in office)* scrivania; *(for pupil)* banco; *(BRIT: in shop, restaurant)* cassa; *(in hotel)* ricevimento; *(at airport)* accettazione *f*

desolate ['dɛsəlɪt] *adj* desolato(a)

despair [dɪs'pɛə*] *n* disperazione *f* ♦ *vi*: **to ~ of** disperare di

despatch [dɪs'pætʃ] *n, vt* = **dispatch**

desperate ['dɛspərɪt] *adj* disperato(a); *(fugitive)* capace di tutto; **to be ~ for sth/ to do** volere disperatamente qc/fare; **~ly** *adv* disperatamente; *(very)* terribilmente, estremamente

desperation [dɛspə'reɪʃən] *n* disperazione *f*

despicable [dɪs'pɪkəbl] *adj* disprezzabile

despise [dɪs'paɪz] *vt* disprezzare, sdegnare

despite [dɪs'paɪt] *prep* malgrado, a dispetto di, nonostante

despondent [dɪs'pɔndənt] *adj* abbattuto(a), scoraggiato(a)

dessert [dɪ'zə:t] *n* dolce *m*; frutta; **~spoon** *n* cucchiaio da dolci

destination [dɛstɪ'neɪʃən] *n* destinazione *f*

destined ['dɛstɪnd] *adj*: **to be ~ to do/for** essere destinato(a) a fare/per

destiny ['dɛstɪnɪ] *n* destino

destitute ['dɛstɪtjuːt] *adj* indigente, bisognoso(a)

destroy [dɪs'trɔɪ] *vt* distruggere; **~er** *n* (NAUT) cacciatorpediniere *m*

destruction [dɪs'trʌkʃən] *n* distruzione *f*

detach [dɪ'tætʃ] *vt* staccare, distaccare; **~ed** *adj (attitude)* distante; **~ed house** *n* villa; **~ment** *n* (MIL) distaccamento; *(fig)* distacco

detail ['di:teɪl] *n* particolare *m*, dettaglio ♦ *vt* dettagliare, particolareggiare; **in ~** nei particolari; **~ed** *adj* particolareggiato(a)

detain [dɪ'teɪn] *vt* trattenere; *(in captivity)* detenere

detect [dɪ'tɛkt] *vt* scoprire, scorgere; *(MED, POLICE, RADAR etc)* individuare; **~ion** [dɪ'tɛkʃən] *n* scoperta; individuazione *f*; **~ive** *n* investigatore/trice; **~ive story** *n* giallo

détente [deɪ'tɑ:nt] *n* (POL) distensione *f*

detention [dɪ'tɛnʃən] *n* detenzione *f*; (SCOL) permanenza forzata per punizione

deter [dɪ'tə:*] *vt* dissuadere

detergent [dɪ'tə:dʒənt] *n* detersivo

deteriorate [dɪ'tɪərɪəreɪt] *vi* deteriorarsi

determine [dɪ'tə:mɪn] *vt* determinare; **~d** *adj (person)* risoluto(a), deciso(a); **~d to do** deciso(a) a fare

detour ['di:tuə*] *n* deviazione *f*

detract [dɪ'trækt] *vi*: **to ~ from** detrarre da

detriment ['dɛtrɪmənt] *n*: **to the ~ of a** detrimento di; **~al** [dɛtrɪ'mɛntl] *adj*: **~al to** dannoso(a), nocivo(a) a

devaluation [dɪvæljʊ'eɪʃən] *n* svalutazione *f*

devastate ['dɛvəsteɪt] *vt* devastare; *(fig)*: **~d by** sconvolto(a) da; **devastating** *adj* devastatore(trice); sconvolgente

develop [dɪ'vɛləp] *vt* sviluppare; *(habit)* prendere (gradualmente) ♦ *vi* svilupparsi; *(facts, symptoms: appear)* manifestarsi, rivelarsi; **~er** *n* (also: **property ~er**) costruttore *m* edile; **~ing country** *n* paese *m* in via di sviluppo; **~ment** *n* sviluppo

device [dɪ'vaɪs] *n (apparatus)* congegno

devil ['dɛvl] *n* diavolo; demonio

devious ['diːvɪəs] *adj (person)* subdolo(a)

devise [dɪ'vaɪz] *vt* escogitare, concepire

devoid [dɪ'vɔɪd] *adj*: ~ **of** privo(a) di

devolution [diːvə'luːʃən] *n (POL)* decentramento

devote [dɪ'vəʊt] *vt*: **to ~ sth to** dedicare qc a; **~d** *adj* devoto(a); **to be ~d to sb** essere molto affezionato(a) a qn; **~e** [dɛvəʊ'tiː] *n (MUS, SPORT)* appassionato/a

devotion [dɪ'vəʊʃən] *n* devozione *f*, attaccamento; *(REL)* atto di devozione, preghiera

devour [dɪ'vaʊə*] *vt* divorare

devout [dɪ'vaʊt] *adj* pio(a), devoto(a)

dew [djuː] *n* rugiada

dexterity [dɛks'tɛrɪtɪ] *n* destrezza

diabetes [daɪə'biːtiːz] *n* diabete *m*; **diabetic** [-'bɛtɪk] *adj, n* diabetico(a)

diabolical [daɪə'bɒlɪkl] *(inf) adj (weather, behaviour)* orribile

diagnosis [daɪəg'nəʊsɪs] *(pl diagnoses) n* diagnosi *f inv*

diagonal [daɪ'ægənl] *adj* diagonale ♦ *n* diagonale *f*

diagram ['daɪəgræm] *n* diagramma *m*

dial ['daɪəl] *n* quadrante *m*; *(on radio)* lancetta; *(on telephone)* disco combinatore ♦ *vt (number)* fare

dialect ['daɪəlɛkt] *n* dialetto

dialling code ['daɪəlɪŋ-] *(US* **area code***) n* prefisso

dialling tone ['daɪəlɪŋ-] *(US* **dial tone***) n* segnale *m* di linea libera

dialogue ['daɪəlɒg] *(US* **dialog***) n* dialogo

diameter [daɪ'æmɪtə*] *n* diametro

diamond ['daɪəmənd] *n* diamante *m*; *(shape)* rombo; **~s** *npl (CARDS)* quadri *mpl*

diaper ['daɪəpə*] *(US) n* pannolino

diaphragm ['daɪəfræm] *n* diaframma *m*

diarrhoea [daɪə'riːə] *(US* **diarrhea***) n* diarrea

diary ['daɪərɪ] *n (daily account)* diario; *(book)* agenda

dice [daɪs] *n inv* dado ♦ *vt (CULIN)* tagliare a dadini

Dictaphone ® ['dɪktəfəʊn] *n* dittafono ®

dictate [dɪk'teɪt] *vt* dettare

dictation [dɪk'teɪʃən] *n* dettatura; *(SCOL)* dettato

dictator [dɪk'teɪtə*] *n* dittatore *m*; **~ship** *n* dittatura

dictionary ['dɪkʃənrɪ] *n* dizionario

did [dɪd] *pt of* do

didn't = **did not**

die [daɪ] *vi* morire; **to be dying for sth/to do sth** morire dalla voglia di qc/di fare qc; **~ away** *vi* spegnersi a poco a poco; **~ down** *vi* abbassarsi; **~ out** *vi* estinguersi

diesel ['diːzəl] *n (vehicle)* diesel *m inv*; **~ engine** *n* motore *m* diesel *inv*; **~ (oil)** *n* gasolio (per motori diesel), diesel *m inv*

diet ['daɪət] *n* alimentazione *f*; *(restricted food)* dieta ♦ *vi (also:* **be on a ~***)* stare a dieta

differ ['dɪfə*] *vi*: **to ~ from sth** differire da qc; essere diverso(a) da qc; **to ~ from sb over sth** essere in disaccordo con qn su qc; **~ence** *n* differenza; *(disagreement)* screzio; **~ent** *adj* diverso(a); **~entiate** [-'rɛnʃɪeɪt] *vi*: **to ~entiate between** discriminare *or* fare differenza fra

difficult ['dɪfɪkəlt] *adj* difficile; **~y** *n* difficoltà *f inv*

diffident ['dɪfɪdənt] *adj* sfiduciato(a)

diffuse [*adj* dɪ'fjuːs, *vb* dɪ'fjuːz] *adj* diffuso(a) ♦ *vt* diffondere

dig [dɪg] *(pt, pp* **dug***) vt (hole)* scavare; *(garden)* vangare ♦ *n (prod)* gomitata; *(archaeological)* scavo; *(fig)* frecciata; **~ into** *vt fus (savings)* scavare in; **to ~ one's nails into** conficcare le unghie in; **~ up** *vt (tree etc)* sradicare; *(information)* scavare fuori

digest [*vb* daɪ'dʒɛst, *n* 'daɪdʒɛst] *vt* digerire ♦ *n* compendio; **~ion** [dɪ'dʒɛstʃən] *n* digestione *f*; **~ive** *adj (juices, system)* digerente

digit ['dɪdʒɪt] *n* cifra; *(finger)* dito; **~al** *adj* digitale

dignified ['dɪgnɪfaɪd] *adj* dignitoso(a)

dignity ['dɪgnɪtɪ] *n* dignità

digress [daɪˈgrɛs] vi: **to ~ from** divagare da

digs [dɪgz] (BRIT: inf) npl camera ammobiliata

dike [daɪk] n = **dyke**

dilapidated [dɪˈlæpɪdeɪtɪd] adj cadente

dilemma [daɪˈlɛmə] n dilemma m

diligent [ˈdɪlɪdʒənt] adj diligente

dilute [daɪˈluːt] vt diluire; (with water) annacquare

dim [dɪm] adj (light) debole; (outline, figure) vago(a); (room) in penombra; (inf: person) tonto(a) ♦ vt (light) abbassare

dime [daɪm] (US) n = 10 cents

dimension [daɪˈmɛnʃən] n dimensione f

diminish [dɪˈmɪnɪʃ] vt, vi diminuire

diminutive [dɪˈmɪnjutɪv] adj minuscolo(a) ♦ n (LING) diminutivo

dimmers [ˈdɪməz] (US) npl (AUT) anabbaglianti mpl; luci fpl di posizione

dimple [ˈdɪmpl] n fossetta

din [dɪn] n chiasso, fracasso

dine [daɪn] vi pranzare; **~r** n (person) cliente m/f; (US: place) tavola calda

dinghy [ˈdɪŋgɪ] n battello pneumatico; (also: **rubber ~**) gommone m

dingy [ˈdɪndʒɪ] adj grigio(a)

dining car [ˈdaɪnɪŋ-] (BRIT) n vagone m ristorante

dining room [ˈdaɪnɪŋ-] n sala da pranzo

dinner [ˈdɪnə*] n (lunch) pranzo; (evening meal) cena; (public) banchetto; **~ jacket** n smoking m inv; **~ party** n cena; **~ time** n ora di pranzo (or cena)

dip [dɪp] n discesa; (in sea) bagno; (CULIN) salsetta ♦ vt immergere; bagnare; (BRIT: AUT: lights) abbassare ♦ vi abbassarsi

diploma [dɪˈpləumə] n diploma m

diplomacy [dɪˈpləuməsɪ] n diplomazia

diplomat [ˈdɪpləmæt] n diplomatico; **~ic** [dɪpləˈmætɪk] adj diplomatico(a)

diprod [ˈdɪprɒd] (US) n = **dipstick**

dipstick [ˈdɪpstɪk] n (AUT) indicatore m di livello dell'olio

dipswitch [ˈdɪpswɪtʃ] (BRIT) n (AUT) levetta dei fari

dire [daɪə*] adj terribile; estremo(a)

direct [daɪˈrɛkt] adj diretto(a) ♦ vt dirigere; (order): **to ~ sb to do sth** dare direttive a qn di fare qc ♦ adv direttamente; **can you ~ me to ...?** mi può indicare la strada per ...?

direction [dɪˈrɛkʃən] n direzione f; **~s** npl (advice) chiarimenti mpl; **sense of ~** senso dell'orientamento; **~s for use** istruzioni fpl

directly [dɪˈrɛktlɪ] adv (in straight line) direttamente; (at once) subito

director [dɪˈrɛktə*] n direttore/trice; amministratore/trice; (THEATRE, CINEMA) regista m/f

directory [dɪˈrɛktərɪ] n elenco; **~ enquiries**, **~ assistance** (US) n informazioni fpl elenco abbonati inv

dirt [dəːt] n sporcizia; immondizia; (earth) terra; **~-cheap** adj da due soldi; **~y** adj sporco(a) ♦ vt sporcare; **~y trick** n brutto scherzo

disability [dɪsəˈbɪlɪtɪ] n invalidità f inv; (LAW) incapacità f inv

disabled [dɪsˈeɪbld] adj invalido(a); (mentally) ritardato(a) ♦ npl: **the ~** gli invalidi

disadvantage [dɪsədˈvɑːntɪdʒ] n svantaggio

disagree [dɪsəˈgriː] vi (differ) discordare; (be against, think otherwise): **to ~ (with)** essere in disaccordo (con), dissentire (da); **~able** adj sgradevole; (person) antipatico(a); **~ment** n disaccordo; (argument) dissapore m

disallow [dɪsəˈlau] vt (appeal) respingere

disappear [dɪsəˈpɪə*] vi scomparire; **~ance** n scomparsa

disappoint [dɪsəˈpɔɪnt] vt deludere; **~ed** adj deluso(a); **~ing** adj deludente; **~ment** n delusione f

disapproval [dɪsəˈpruːvəl] n disapprovazione f

disapprove [dɪsəˈpruːv] vi: **to ~ of** disapprovare

disarm [dɪsˈɑːm] vt disarmare; **~ament** n disarmo

disarray [dɪsəˈreɪ] n: **in ~** (army) in rotta; (organization) in uno stato di confusione; (clothes, hair) in disordine

disaster [dɪˈzɑːstə*] n disastro
disband [dɪsˈbænd] vt sbandare; (MIL) congedare ♦ vi sciogliersi
disbelief [ˈdɪsbəˈliːf] n incredulità
disc [dɪsk] n disco; (COMPUT) = **disk**
discard [dɪsˈkɑːd] vt (old things) scartare; (fig) abbandonare
discern [dɪˈsəːn] vt discernere, distinguere; **~ing** adj perspicace
discharge [vb dɪsˈtʃɑːdʒ, n ˈdɪstʃɑːdʒ] vt (duties) compiere; (ELEC, waste etc) scaricare; (MED) emettere; (patient) dimettere; (employee) licenziare; (soldier) congedare; (defendant) liberare ♦ n (ELEC) scarica; (MED) emissione f; (dismissal) licenziamento; congedo; liberazione f
disciple [dɪˈsaɪpl] n discepolo
discipline [ˈdɪsɪplɪn] n disciplina ♦ vt disciplinare; (punish) punire
disc jockey n disc jockey m inv
disclaim [dɪsˈkleɪm] vt negare, smentire
disclose [dɪsˈkləʊz] vt rivelare, svelare; **disclosure** [-ˈkləʊʒə*] n rivelazione f
disco [ˈdɪskəʊ] n abbr = **discotheque**
discoloured [dɪsˈkʌləd] (US **discolored**) adj scolorito(a); ingiallito(a)
discomfort [dɪsˈkʌmfət] n disagio; (lack of comfort) scomodità f inv
disconcert [dɪskənˈsəːt] vt sconcertare
disconnect [dɪskəˈnekt] vt sconnettere, staccare; (ELEC, RADIO) staccare; (gas, water) chiudere
discontent [dɪskənˈtent] n scontentezza; **~ed** adj scontento(a)
discontinue [dɪskənˈtɪnjuː] vt smettere, cessare; **"~d"** (COMM) "fuori produzione"
discord [ˈdɪskɔːd] n disaccordo; (MUS) dissonanza
discotheque [ˈdɪskəʊtek] n discoteca
discount [n ˈdɪskaʊnt, vb dɪsˈkaʊnt] n sconto ♦ vt scontare; (idea) non badare a
discourage [dɪsˈkʌrɪdʒ] vt scoraggiare
discourteous [dɪsˈkəːtɪəs] adj scortese
discover [dɪsˈkʌvə*] vt scoprire; **~y** n scoperta
discredit [dɪsˈkredɪt] vt screditare; mettere in dubbio

discreet [dɪsˈkriːt] adj discreto(a)
discrepancy [dɪsˈkrepənsɪ] n discrepanza
discriminate [dɪsˈkrɪmɪneɪt] vi: **to ~ between** distinguere tra; **to ~ against** discriminare contro; **discriminating** adj fine, giudizioso(a); **discrimination** [-ˈneɪʃən] n discriminazione f; (judgment) discernimento
discuss [dɪsˈkʌs] vt discutere; (debate) dibattere; **~ion** [dɪsˈkʌʃən] n discussione f
disdain [dɪsˈdeɪn] n disdegno
disease [dɪˈziːz] n malattia
disembark [dɪsɪmˈbɑːk] vt, vi sbarcare
disentangle [dɪsɪnˈtæŋgl] vt liberare; (wool etc) sbrogliare
disfigure [dɪsˈfɪgə*] vt sfigurare
disgrace [dɪsˈgreɪs] n vergogna; (disfavour) disgrazia ♦ vt disonorare, far cadere in disgrazia; **~ful** adj scandaloso(a), vergognoso(a)
disgruntled [dɪsˈgrʌntld] adj scontento(a), di cattivo umore
disguise [dɪsˈgaɪz] n travestimento ♦ vt: **to ~ (as)** travestire (da); **in ~** travestito(a)
disgust [dɪsˈgʌst] n disgusto, nausea ♦ vt disgustare, far schifo a; **~ing** adj disgustoso(a); ripugnante
dish [dɪʃ] n piatto; **to do** or **wash the ~es** fare i piatti; **~ out** vt distribuire; **~ up** vt servire; **~cloth** n strofinaccio
dishearton [dɪsˈhɑːtn] vt scoraggiare
dishevelled [dɪˈʃevəld] (US **disheveled**) adj arruffato(a); scapigliato(a)
dishonest [dɪsˈɔnɪst] adj disonesto(a)
dishonour [dɪsˈɔnə*] (US **dishonor**) n disonore m; **~able** adj disonorevole
dishtowel [ˈdɪʃtaʊəl] (US) n strofinaccio dei piatti
dishwasher [ˈdɪʃwɔʃə*] n lavastoviglie f inv
disillusion [dɪsɪˈluːʒən] vt disilludere, disingannare
disinfect [dɪsɪnˈfekt] vt disinfettare; **~ant** n disinfettante m
disintegrate [dɪsˈɪntɪgreɪt] vi disintegrarsi
disinterested [dɪsˈɪntrəstɪd] adj disinteressato(a)
disjointed [dɪsˈdʒɔɪntɪd] adj sconnesso(a)

disk [dɪsk] n (COMPUT) disco; **single-/
double-sided ~** disco a facciata singola/
doppia; **~ drive** n lettore m; **~ette** (US) n
= **disk**

dislike [dɪs'laɪk] n antipatia, avversione f;
(gen pl) cosa che non piace ♦ vt: **he ~s it**
non gli piace

dislocate ['dɪsləkeɪt] vt slogare

dislodge [dɪs'lɔdʒ] vt rimuovere

disloyal [dɪs'lɔɪəl] adj sleale

dismal ['dɪzml] adj triste, cupo(a)

dismantle [dɪs'mæntl] vt (machine)
smontare

dismay [dɪs'meɪ] n costernazione f ♦ vt
sgomentare

dismiss [dɪs'mɪs] vt congedare; (employee)
licenziare; (idea) scacciare; (LAW)
respingere; **~al** n congedo; licenziamento

dismount [dɪs'maunt] vi scendere

disobedience [dɪsə'biːdɪəns] n
disubbidienza

disobedient [dɪsə'biːdɪənt] adj
disubbidiente

disobey [dɪsə'beɪ] vt disubbidire a

disorder [dɪs'ɔːdə*] n disordine m; (rioting)
tumulto; (MED) disturbo; **~ly** adj
disordinato(a); tumultuoso(a)

disorientated [dɪs'ɔːrɪɛnteɪtɪd] adj
disorientato(a)

disown [dɪs'əun] vt rinnegare

disparaging [dɪs'pærɪdʒɪŋ] adj
spregiativo(a), sprezzante

dispassionate [dɪs'pæʃənət] adj calmo(a),
freddo(a); imparziale

dispatch [dɪs'pætʃ] vt spedire, inviare ♦ n
spedizione f, invio; (MIL, PRESS) dispaccio

dispel [dɪs'pel] vt dissipare, scacciare

dispense [dɪs'pens] vt distribuire,
amministrare; **~ with** vt fus fare a meno
di; **~r** n (container) distributore m;
dispensing chemist (BRIT) n farmacista
m/f

disperse [dɪs'pəːs] vt disperdere;
(knowledge) disseminare ♦ vi disperdersi

dispirited [dɪs'pɪrɪtɪd] adj scoraggiato(a),
abbattuto(a)

displace [dɪs'pleɪs] vt spostare; **~d person**

n (POL) profugo/a

display [dɪs'pleɪ] n esposizione f; (of feeling
etc) manifestazione f; (screen) schermo ♦ vt
mostrare; (goods) esporre; (pej) ostentare

displease [dɪs'pliːz] vt dispiacere a,
scontentare; **~d with** scontento di;
displeasure [-'pleʒə*] n dispiacere m

disposable [dɪs'pəuzəbl] adj (pack etc) a
perdere; (income) disponibile; **~ nappy** n
pannolino di carta

disposal [dɪs'pəuzl] n eliminazione f; (of
property) cessione f; **at one's ~** alla sua
disposizione

dispose [dɪs'pəuz] vi: **~ of** sbarazzarsi di;
~d to do disposto(a) a fare;
disposition [-'zɪʃən] n disposizione f;
(temperament) carattere m

disproportionate [dɪsprə'pɔːʃənət] adj
sproporzionato(a)

disprove [dɪs'pruːv] vt confutare

dispute [dɪs'pjuːt] n disputa; (also: industrial ~) controversia (sindacale) ♦ vt contestare; (matter) discutere; (victory) disputare

disqualify [dɪs'kwɔlɪfaɪ] vt (SPORT)
squalificare; **to ~ sb from sth/from doing**
rendere qn incapace a qc/a fare;
squalificare qn da qc/da fare; **to ~ sb from
driving** ritirare la patente a qn

disquiet [dɪs'kwaɪət] n inquietudine f

disregard [dɪsrɪ'gɑːd] vt non far caso a, non
badare a

disrepair [dɪsrɪ'pɛə*] n: **to fall into ~**
(building) andare in rovina; (machine)
deteriorarsi

disreputable [dɪs'repjutəbl] adj poco
raccomandabile; indecente

disrupt [dɪs'rʌpt] vt disturbare; creare
scompiglio in

dissatisfaction [dɪssætɪs'fækʃən] n
scontentezza, insoddisfazione f

dissect [dɪ'sekt] vt sezionare

dissent [dɪ'sent] n dissenso

dissertation [dɪsə'teɪʃən] n tesi f inv,
dissertazione f

disservice [dɪs'səːvɪs] n: **to do sb a ~** fare
un cattivo servizio a qn

dissimilar [dɪ'sɪmɪlə*] adj: **~ (to)** dissimile

or diverso(a) (da)

dissipate ['dɪsɪpeɪt] *vt* dissipare

dissolve [dɪ'zɔlv] *vt* dissolvere, sciogliere; (*POL, marriage etc*) sciogliere ♦ *vi* dissolversi, sciogliersi

distance ['dɪstns] *n* distanza; **in the ~** in lontananza

distant ['dɪstnt] *adj* lontano(a), distante; (*manner*) riservato(a), freddo(a)

distaste [dɪs'teɪst] *n* ripugnanza; **~ful** *adj* ripugnante, sgradevole

distended [dɪs'tendɪd] *adj* (*stomach*) dilatato(a)

distil [dɪs'tɪl] (*US* **distill**) *vt* distillare; **~lery** *n* distilleria

distinct [dɪs'tɪŋkt] *adj* distinto(a); **as ~ from** a differenza di; **~ion** [dɪs'tɪŋkʃən] *n* distinzione *f*; (*in exam*) lode *f*; **~ive** *adj* distintivo(a)

distinguish [dɪs'tɪŋgwɪʃ] *vt* distinguere; discernere; **~ed** *adj* (*eminent*) eminente; **~ing** *adj* (*feature*) distinto(a), caratteristico(a)

distort [dɪs'tɔːt] *vt* distorcere; (*TECH*) deformare

distract [dɪs'trækt] *vt* distrarre; **~ed** *adj* distratto(a); **~ion** [dɪs'trækʃən] *n* distrazione *f*

distraught [dɪs'trɔːt] *adj* stravolto(a)

distress [dɪs'tres] (*US*) *n* angoscia ♦ *vt* affliggere; **~ing** *adj* doloroso(a); **~ signal** *n* segnale *m* di soccorso

distribute [dɪs'trɪbjuːt] *vt* distribuire; **distribution** [-'bjuːʃən] *n* distribuzione *f*; **distributor** *n* distributore *m*

district ['dɪstrɪkt] *n* (*of country*) regione *f*; (*of town*) quartiere *m*; (*ADMIN*) distretto; **~ attorney** (*US*) *n* ≈ sostituto procuratore *m* della Repubblica; **~ nurse** (*BRIT*) *n* infermiera di quartiere

distrust [dɪs'trʌst] *n* diffidenza, sfiducia ♦ *vt* non aver fiducia in

disturb [dɪs'təːb] *vt* disturbare; **~ance** *n* disturbo; (*political etc*) disordini *mpl*; **~ed** *adj* (*worried, upset*) turbato(a); **emotionally ~ed** con turbe emotive; **~ing** *adj* sconvolgente

disuse [dɪs'juːs] *n*: **to fall into ~** cadere in disuso

disused [dɪs'juːzd] *adj* abbandonato(a)

ditch [dɪtʃ] *n* fossa ♦ *vt* (*inf*) piantare in asso

dither ['dɪðə*] (*pej*) *vi* vacillare

ditto ['dɪtəu] *adv* idem

dive [daɪv] *n* tuffo; (*of submarine*) immersione *f* ♦ *vi* tuffarsi; immergersi; **~r** *n* tuffatore/trice; palombaro

diverse [daɪ'vəːs] *adj* vario(a)

diversion [daɪ'vəːʃən] *n* (*BRIT: AUT*) deviazione *f*; (*distraction*) divertimento

divert [daɪ'vəːt] *vt* deviare

divide [dɪ'vaɪd] *vt* dividere; (*separate*) separare ♦ *vi* dividersi; **~d highway** (*US*) *n* strada a doppia carreggiata

dividend ['dɪvɪdend] *n* dividendo; (*fig*): **to pay ~s** dare dei frutti

divine [dɪ'vaɪn] *adj* divino(a)

diving ['daɪvɪŋ] *n* tuffo; **~ board** *n* trampolino

divinity [dɪ'vɪnɪtɪ] *n* divinità *f inv*; teologia

division [dɪ'vɪʒən] *n* divisione *f*; separazione *f*; (*esp FOOTBALL*) serie *f*

divorce [dɪ'vɔːs] *n* divorzio ♦ *vt* divorziare da; (*dissociate*) separare; **~d** *adj* divorziato(a); **~e** [-'siː] *n* divorziato/a

D.I.Y. (*BRIT*) *n abbr* = **do-it-yourself**

dizzy ['dɪzɪ] *adj*: **to feel ~** avere il capogiro

DJ *n abbr* = **disc jockey**

━━━ KEYWORD ━━━

do [duː] (*pt* **did**, *pp* **done**) *n* (*inf: party etc*) festa; **it was rather a grand ~** è stato un ricevimento piuttosto importante
♦ *vb* **1** (*in negative constructions*) *non tradotto*; **I don't understand** non capisco
2 (*to form questions*) *non tradotto*; **didn't you know?** non lo sapevi?; **why didn't you come?** perché non sei venuto?
3 (*for emphasis, in polite expressions*): **she does seem rather late** sembra essere piuttosto in ritardo; **~ sit down** si accomodi la prego, prego si sieda; **~ take care!** mi raccomando, sta attento!
4 (*used to avoid repeating vb*): **she swims better than I ~** lei nuota meglio di me; **~**

you agree? — yes, I ~/no, I don't sei d'accordo? — sì/no; **she lives in Glasgow — so ~ I** lei vive a Glasgow — anch'io; **he asked me to help him and I did** mi ha chiesto di aiutarlo ed io l'ho fatto
5 (*in question tags*): **you like him, don't you?** ti piace, vero?; **I don't know him, ~ I?** non lo conosco, vero?
♦ *vt* (*gen, carry out, perform etc*) fare; **what are you ~ing tonight?** che fa stasera?; **to ~ the cooking** cucinare; **to ~ the washing-up** fare i piatti; **to ~ one's teeth** lavarsi i denti; **to ~ one's hair/nails** farsi i capelli/le unghie; **the car was ~ing 100** la macchina faceva i 100 all'ora
♦ *vi* **1** (*act, behave*) fare; **~ as I ~** faccia come me, faccia come faccio io
2 (*get on, fare*) andare; **he's ~ing well/badly at school** va bene/male a scuola; **how ~ you ~?** piacere!
3 (*suit*) andare bene; **this room will ~** questa stanza va bene
4 (*be sufficient*) bastare; **will £10 ~?** basteranno 10 sterline?; **that'll ~** basta così; **that'll ~!** (*in annoyance*) ora basta!; **to make ~ (with)** arrangiarsi (con)
do away with *vt fus* (*kill*) far fuori; (*abolish*) abolire
do up *vt* (*laces*) allacciare; (*dress, buttons*) abbottonare; (*renovate: room, house*) rimettere a nuovo, rifare
do with *vt fus* (*need*) aver bisogno di; (*be connected*): **what has it got to ~ with you?** e tu che c'entri?; **I won't have anything to ~ with it** non voglio avere niente a che farci; **it has to ~ with money** si tratta di soldi
do without *vi* fare senza ♦ *vt fus* fare a meno di

dock [dɔk] *n* (*NAUT*) bacino; (*LAW*) banco degli imputati ♦ *vi* entrare in bacino; (*SPACE*) agganciarsi; **~s** *npl* (*NAUT*) dock *m inv*; **~er** *n* scaricatore *m*; **~yard** *n* cantiere *m* (navale)
doctor ['dɔktə*] *n* medico/a; (*Ph.D. etc*) dottore/essa ♦ *vt* (*drink etc*) adulterare; **D~**

of Philosophy *n* dottorato di ricerca; (*person*) titolare *m/f* di un dottorato di ricerca
doctrine ['dɔktrɪn] *n* dottrina
document ['dɔkjumənt] *n* documento; **~ary** [-'mentərɪ] *adj* (*evidence*) documentato(a) ♦ *n* documentario
dodge [dɔdʒ] *n* trucco; schivata ♦ *vt* schivare, eludere
dodgems ['dɔdʒəmz] (*BRIT*) *npl* autoscontri *mpl*
doe [dəu] *n* (*deer*) femmina di daino; (*rabbit*) coniglia
does [dʌz] *vb see* **do; doesn't = does not**
dog [dɔg] *n* cane *m* ♦ *vt* (*follow closely*) pedinare; (*fig: memory etc*) perseguitare; **~ collar** *n* collare *m* di cane; (*fig*) collarino; **~-eared** *adj* (*book*) con orecchie
dogged ['dɔgɪd] *adj* ostinato(a), tenace
dogsbody ['dɔgzbɔdɪ] (*BRIT: inf*) *n* factotum *m inv*
doing ['du:ɪŋ] *n*: **this is your ~** è opera tua, sei stato tu
do-it-yourself *n* il far da sé
doldrums ['dɔldrəmz] *npl* (*fig*): **to be in the ~** avere un brutto periodo
dole [dəul] (*BRIT*) *n* sussidio di disoccupazione; **to be on the ~** vivere del sussidio; **~ out** *vt* distribuire
doll [dɔl] *n* bambola; **~ed up** (*inf*) *adj* in ghingheri
dollar ['dɔlə*] *n* dollaro
dolly ['dɔlɪ] *n* bambola
dolphin ['dɔlfɪn] *n* delfino
domain [də'meɪn] *n* dominio
dome [dəum] *n* cupola
domestic [də'mestɪk] *adj* (*duty, happiness, animal*) domestico(a); (*policy, affairs, flights*) nazionale; **~ated** *adj* addomesticato(a)
dominant ['dɔmɪnənt] *adj* dominante
dominate ['dɔmɪneɪt] *vt* dominare
domineering [dɔmɪ'nɪərɪŋ] *adj* dispotico(a), autoritario(a)
dominion [də'mɪnɪən] *n* dominio; sovranità; dominion *m inv*
domino ['dɔmɪnəu] (*pl* **~es**) *n* domino; **~es** *n* (*game*) gioco del domino

don [dɔn] (BRIT) n docente m/f universitario(a)

donate [də'neɪt] vt donare

done [dʌn] pp of **do**

donkey ['dɒŋkɪ] n asino

donor ['dəʊnə*] n donatore/trice; **~ card** n tessera di donatore di organi

don't [dəʊnt] = **do not**

doodle ['du:dl] vi scarabocchiare

doom [du:m] n destino; rovina ♦ vt: **to be ~ed (to failure)** essere predestinato(a) (a fallire)

door [dɔ:*] n porta; **~bell** n campanello; **~ handle** n maniglia; **~man** (irreg) n (in hotel) portiere m in livrea; **~mat** n stuoia della porta; **~step** n gradino della porta; **~way** n porta

dope [dəʊp] n (inf: drugs) roba ♦ vt (horse etc) drogare

dormant ['dɔ:mənt] adj inattivo(a)

dormitory ['dɔ:mɪtrɪ] n dormitorio; (US) casa dello studente

dormouse ['dɔ:maʊs] (pl **dormice**) n ghiro

dosage ['dəʊsɪdʒ] n posologia

dose [dəʊs] n dose f; (bout) attacco

doss house ['dɔs-] (BRIT) n asilo notturno

dot [dɒt] n punto; **~ted with** punteggiato(a) di; **on the ~** in punto; **~ted line** ['dɒtɪd-] n linea punteggiata

double ['dʌbl] adj doppio(a) ♦ adv (twice): **to cost ~ (sth)** costare il doppio (di qc) ♦ n sosia m inv ♦ vt raddoppiare; (fold) piegare doppio or in due ♦ vi raddoppiarsi; **at the ~** (BRIT), **on the ~** a passo di corsa; **~ bass** n contrabbasso; **~ bed** n letto matrimoniale; **~-breasted** adj a doppio petto; **~cross** vt fare il doppio gioco con; **~decker** n autobus m inv a due piani; **~ glazing** (BRIT) n doppi vetri mpl; **~ room** n camera per due; **~s** n (TENNIS) doppio; **doubly** adv doppiamente

doubt [daʊt] n dubbio ♦ vt dubitare di; **to ~ that** dubitare che +sub; **~ful** adj dubbioso(a), incerto(a); (person) equivoco(a); **~less** adv indubbiamente

dough [dəʊ] n pasta, impasto; **~nut** n bombolone m

dove [dʌv] n colombo/a

Dover ['dəʊvə*] n Dover f

dovetail ['dʌvteɪl] vi (fig) combaciare

dowdy ['daʊdɪ] adj trasandato(a); malvestito(a)

down [daʊn] n piume fpl ♦ adv giù, di sotto ♦ prep giù per ♦ vt (inf: drink) scolarsi; **~ with X!** abbasso X!; **~-and-out** n barbone m; **~-at-heel** adj scalcagnato(a); **~cast** adj abbattuto(a); **~fall** n caduta; rovina; **~hearted** adj scoraggiato(a); **~hill** adv: **to go ~hill** andare in discesa; (fig) lasciarsi andare; andare a rotoli; **~ payment** n acconto; **~pour** n scroscio di pioggia; **~right** adj franco(a); (refusal) assoluto(a); **~size** vi (ECON: company) ridurre il personale; **~stairs** adv di sotto; al piano inferiore; **~stream** adv a valle; **~-to-earth** adj pratico(a); **~town** adv in città; **~ under** adv (Australia etc) agli antipodi; **~ward** ['daʊnwəd] adj, adv in giù, in discesa; **~wards** ['daʊnwədz] adv = **~ward**

ⓘ Al numero 10 di **Downing Street**, nel quartiere di Westminster a Londra, si trova la residenza del primo ministro inglese, al numero 11 quella del **Chancellor of the Exchequer**.

dowry ['daʊrɪ] n dote f

doz. abbr = **dozen**

doze [dəʊz] vi sonnecchiare; **~ off** vi appisolarsi

dozen ['dʌzn] n dozzina; **a ~ books** una dozzina di libri; **~s of** decine fpl di

Dr. abbr (= doctor) dott.; (in street names) = **drive**

drab [dræb] adj tetro(a), grigio(a)

draft [drɑ:ft] n abbozzo; (POL) bozza; (COMM) tratta; (US: call-up) leva ♦ vt abbozzare; see also **draught**

draftsman ['drɑ:ftsmən] (US) n = **draughtsman**

drag [dræg] vt trascinare; (river) dragare ♦ vi trascinarsi ♦ n (inf) noioso/a; noia, fatica; (women's clothing): **in ~** travestito (da donna); ~ **on** vi tirar avanti lentamente

dragon ['drægən] n drago

dragonfly ['drægənflaɪ] n libellula

drain [dreɪn] n (for sewage) fogna; (on resources) salasso ♦ vt (land, marshes) prosciugare; (vegetables) scolare ♦ vi (water) defluire (via); ~**age** n prosciugamento; fognatura; ~**ing board** (US ~**board**) n piano del lavello; ~**pipe** n tubo di scarico

drama ['drɑːmə] n (art) dramma m, teatro; (play) commedia; (event) dramma; ~**tic** [drə'mætɪk] adj drammatico(a); ~**tist** ['dræmətɪst] n drammaturgo/a; ~**tize** ['dræmətaɪz] vt (events) drammatizzare

drank [dræŋk] pt of **drink**

drape [dreɪp] vt drappeggiare; ~**r** (BRIT) n negoziante m/f di stoffe; ~**s** (US) npl (curtains) tende fpl

drastic ['dræstɪk] adj drastico(a)

draught [drɑːft] (US **draft**) n corrente f d'aria; (NAUT) pescaggio; **on** ~ (beer) alla spina; ~ **beer** n birra alla spina; ~**board** (BRIT) n scacchiera; ~**s** (BRIT) n (gioco della) dama

draughtsman ['drɑːftsmən] (US **draftsman**) (irreg) n disegnatore m

draw [drɔː] (pt **drew**, pp **drawn**) vt tirare; (take out) estrarre; (attract) attirare; (picture) disegnare; (line, circle) tracciare; (money) ritirare ♦ vi (SPORT) pareggiare ♦ n pareggio; (in lottery) estrazione f; **to ~ near** avvicinarsi; ~ **out** vi (lengthen) allungarsi ♦ vt (money) ritirare; ~ **up** vi (stop) arrestarsi, fermarsi ♦ vt (chair) avvicinare; (document) compilare; ~**back** n svantaggio, inconveniente m; ~**bridge** n ponte m levatoio

drawer [drɔː*] n cassetto

drawing ['drɔːɪŋ] n disegno; ~ **board** n tavola da disegno; ~ **pin** (BRIT) n puntina da disegno; ~ **room** n salotto

drawl [drɔːl] n pronuncia strascicata

drawn [drɔːn] pp of **draw**

dread [dred] n terrore m ♦ vt tremare all'idea di; ~**ful** adj terribile

dream [driːm] (pt, pp **dreamed** or **dreamt**)

n sogno ♦ vt, vi sognare; ~**y** adj sognante

dreary ['drɪərɪ] adj tetro(a); monotono(a)

dredge [dredʒ] vt dragare

dregs [dregz] npl feccia

drench [drentʃ] vt inzuppare

dress [dres] n vestito; (no pl: clothing) abbigliamento ♦ vt vestire; (wound) fasciare ♦ vi vestirsi; **to get ~ed** vestirsi; ~ **up** vi vestirsi a festa; (in fancy dress) vestirsi in costume; ~ **circle** (BRIT) n prima galleria; ~**er** n (BRIT: cupboard) credenza; (US) cassettone m; ~**ing** n (MED) benda; (CULIN) condimento; ~**ing gown** (BRIT) n vestaglia; ~**ing room** n (THEATRE) camerino; (SPORT) spogliatoio; ~**ing table** n toilette f inv; ~**maker** n sarta; ~ **rehearsal** n prova generale; ~**y** (inf) adj elegante

drew [druː] pt of **draw**

dribble ['drɪbl] vi (baby) sbavare ♦ vt (ball) dribblare

dried [draɪd] adj (fruit, beans) secco(a); (eggs, milk) in polvere

drier ['draɪə*] n = **dryer**

drift [drɪft] n (of current etc) direzione f; forza; (of snow) cumulo; turbine m; (general meaning) senso ♦ vi (boat) essere trasportato(a) dalla corrente; (sand, snow) ammucchiarsi; ~**wood** n resti mpl della mareggiata

drill [drɪl] n trapano; (MIL) esercitazione f ♦ vt trapanare; (troops) addestrare ♦ vi (for oil) fare trivellazioni

drink [drɪŋk] (pt **drank**, pp **drunk**) n bevanda, bibita; (alcoholic ~) bicchierino; (sip) sorso ♦ vt, vi bere; **to have a ~** bere qualcosa; **a ~ of water** un po' d'acqua; ~**er** n bevitore/trice; ~**ing water** n acqua potabile

drip [drɪp] n goccia; gocciolamento; (MED) fleboclisi f inv ♦ vi gocciolare; (tap) sgocciolare; ~**-dry** adj (shirt) che non si stira; ~**ping** n grasso d'arrosto

drive [draɪv] (pt **drove**, pp **driven**) n passeggiata or giro in macchina; (also: ~**way**) viale m d'accesso; (energy) energia; (campaign) campagna; (also: disk ~) lettore m ♦ vt guidare; (nail) piantare; (push) cacciare, spingere; (TECH: motor) azionare; far funzionare ♦ vi (AUT: at controls) guidare; (: travel) andare in macchina; **left-/right-hand ~** guida a sinistra/destra; **to ~ sb mad** far impazzire qn

drivel ['drɪvl] (inf) n idiozie fpl

driven ['drɪvn] pp of **drive**

driver ['draɪvə*] n conducente m/f; (of taxi) tassista m; (chauffeur, of bus) autista m/f; **~'s license** (US) n patente f di guida

driveway ['draɪvweɪ] n viale m d'accesso

driving ['draɪvɪŋ] n ~ **instructor** n istruttore/trice di scuola guida; **~ lesson** n lezione f di guida; **~ licence** (BRIT) n patente f di guida; **~ mirror** n specchietto retrovisore; **~ school** n scuola f guida inv; **~ test** n esame m di guida

drizzle ['drɪzl] n pioggerella

drool [druːl] vi sbavare

droop [druːp] vi (flower) appassire; (head, shoulders) chinarsi

drop [drɒp] n (of water) goccia; (lessening) diminuzione f; (fall) caduta ♦ vt lasciare cadere; (voice, eyes, price) abbassare; (set down from car) far scendere; (name from list) lasciare fuori ♦ vi cascare; (wind) abbassarsi; **~s** npl (MED) gocce fpl; **~ off** vi (sleep) addormentarsi ♦ vt (passenger) far scendere; **~ out** vi (withdraw) ritirarsi; (student etc) smettere di studiare; **~-out** n (from society/from university) chi ha abbandonato (la società/gli studi); **~per** n contagocce m inv; **~pings** npl sterco

drought [draut] n siccità f inv

drove [drəʊv] pt of **drive**

drown [draun] vt affogare; (fig: noise) soffocare ♦ vi affogare

drowsy ['drauzɪ] adj sonnolento(a), assonnato(a)

drug [drʌg] n farmaco; (narcotic) droga ♦ vt drogare; **to be on ~s** drogarsi; (MED) prendere medicinali; **hard/soft ~s** droghe pesanti/leggere; **~ addict** n tossicomane m/f; **~gist** (US) n persona che gestisce un drugstore; **~store** (US) n drugstore m inv

drum [drʌm] n tamburo; (for oil, petrol)

fusto ♦ vi tamburellare; **~s** npl (set of ~s) batteria; **~mer** n batterista m/f

drunk [drʌŋk] pp of **drink** ♦ adj ubriaco(a); ebbro(a) ♦ n (also: **~ard**) ubriacone/a; **~en** adj ubriaco(a); da ubriaco

dry [draɪ] adj secco(a); (day, clothes) asciutto(a) ♦ vt seccare; (clothes, hair, hands) asciugare ♦ vi asciugarsi; **~ up** vi seccarsi; **~-cleaner's** n lavasecco m inv; **~-cleaning** n pulitura a secco; **~er** n (for hair) föhn m inv, asciugacapelli m inv; (for clothes) asciugabiancheria; (US: spin-dryer) centrifuga; **~ goods store** (US) n negozio di stoffe; **~ rot** n fungo del legno

DSS n abbr (= Department of Social Security) ministero della Previdenza sociale

DTP n abbr (= desk-top publishing) desktop publishing m inv

dual ['djuəl] adj doppio(a); **~ carriageway** (BRIT) n strada a doppia carreggiata; **~-purpose** adj a doppio uso

dubbed [dʌbd] adj (CINEMA) doppiato(a)

dubious ['djuːbɪəs] adj dubbio(a)

Dublin ['dʌblɪn] n Dublino f

duchess ['dʌtʃɪs] n duchessa

duck [dʌk] n anatra ♦ vi abbassare la testa; **~ling** n anatroccolo

duct [dʌkt] n condotto; (ANAT) canale m

dud [dʌd] n (object, tool): **it's a ~** è inutile, non funziona ♦ adj: **~ cheque** (BRIT) assegno a vuoto

due [djuː] adj dovuto(a); (expected) atteso(a); (fitting) giusto(a) ♦ n dovuto ♦ adv: **~ north** diritto verso nord; **~s** npl (for club, union) quota; (in harbour) diritti mpl di porto; **in ~ course** a tempo debito; finalmente; **~ to** dovuto a; a causa di; **to be ~ to do** dover fare

duet [djuː'ɛt] n duetto

duffel bag ['dʌfl-] n sacca da viaggio di tela

duffel coat ['dʌfl-] n montgomery m inv

dug [dʌg] pt, pp of **dig**

duke [djuːk] n duca m

dull [dʌl] adj (light) debole; (boring) noioso(a); (slow-witted) ottuso(a); (sound, pain) sordo(a); (weather, day) fosco(a), scuro(a) ♦ vt (pain, grief) attutire; (mind, senses) intorpidire

duly ['dju:lɪ] adv (on time) a tempo debito; (as expected) debitamente

dumb [dʌm] adj muto(a); (pej) stupido(a); **~founded** [dʌm'faundɪd] adj stupito(a), stordito(a)

dummy ['dʌmɪ] n (tailor's model) manichino; (TECH, COMM) riproduzione f; (BRIT: for baby) tettarella ♦ adj falso(a), finto(a)

dump [dʌmp] n (also: **rubbish ~**) discarica di rifiuti; (inf: place) buco ♦ vt (put down) scaricare; mettere giù; (get rid of) buttar via

dumpling ['dʌmplɪŋ] n specie di gnocco

dumpy ['dʌmpɪ] adj tracagnotto(a)

dunce [dʌns] n (SCOL) somaro/a

dung [dʌŋ] n concime m

dungarees [dʌŋgə'ri:z] npl tuta

dungeon ['dʌndʒən] n prigione f sotterranea

dupe [dju:p] n zimbello ♦ vt gabbare, ingannare

duplex ['dju:pleks] (US) n (house) casa con muro divisorio in comune con un'altra; (apartment) appartamento su due piani

duplicate [n 'dju:plɪkət, vb 'dju:plɪkeɪt] n doppio ♦ vt duplicare; **in ~** in doppia copia

durable ['djuərəbl] adj durevole; (clothes, metal) resistente

duration [djuə'reɪʃən] n durata

during ['djuərɪŋ] prep durante, nel corso di

dusk [dʌsk] n crepuscolo

dust [dʌst] n polvere f ♦ vt (furniture) spolverare; (cake etc) to ~ **with** cospargere con; **~bin** (BRIT) n pattumiera; **~er** n straccio per la polvere; **~man** (BRIT: irreg) n netturbino; **~y** adj polveroso(a)

Dutch [dʌtʃ] adj olandese ♦ n (LING) olandese m; **the ~** npl gli Olandesi; **to go ~** (inf) fare alla romana; **~man/woman** (irreg) n olandese m/f

duty ['dju:tɪ] n dovere m; (tax) dazio, tassa; **on ~** di servizio; **off ~** libero(a), fuori servizio; **~ chemist's** n farmacia di turno; **~-free** adj esente da dazio

duvet ['du:veɪ] (BRIT) n piumino, piumone m

dwarf [dwɔ:f] n nano/a ♦ vt far apparire piccolo

dwell [dwel] (pt, pp **dwelt**) vi dimorare; **~ on** vt fus indugiare su

dwindle ['dwɪndl] vi diminuire, decrescere

dye [daɪ] n tinta ♦ vt tingere

dying ['daɪɪŋ] adj morente, moribondo(a)

dyke [daɪk] (BRIT) n diga

dynamic [daɪ'næmɪk] adj dinamico(a)

dynamite ['daɪnəmaɪt] n dinamite f

dynamo ['daɪnəməu] n dinamo f inv

dyslexia [dɪs'leksɪə] n dislessia

E, e

E [i:] n (MUS) mi m

each [i:tʃ] adj ogni, ciascuno(a) ♦ pron ciascuno(a), ognuno(a); **~ one** ognuno(a); **~ other** si (or ci etc); **they hate ~ other** si odiano (l'un l'altro); **you are jealous of ~ other** siete gelosi l'uno dell'altro; **they have 2 books ~** hanno 2 libri ciascuno

eager ['i:gə*] adj impaziente; desideroso(a); ardente; **to be ~ for** essere desideroso di, aver gran voglia di

eagle ['i:gl] n aquila

ear [ɪə*] n orecchio; (of corn) pannocchia; **~ache** n mal m d'orecchi; **~drum** n timpano

earl [ə:l] (BRIT) n conte m

earlier ['ə:lɪə*] adj precedente ♦ adv prima

early ['ə:lɪ] adv presto, di buon'ora; (ahead of time) in anticipo ♦ adj (near the beginning) primo(a); (sooner than expected) prematuro(a); (quick: reply) veloce; **at an ~ hour** di buon'ora; **to have an ~ night** andare a letto presto; **in the ~** or **~ in the spring/19th century** all'inizio della primavera/dell'Ottocento; **~ retirement** n ritiro anticipato

earmark ['ɪəmɑ:k] vt: **to ~ sth for** destinare qc a

earn [ə:n] vt guadagnare; (rest, reward) meritare

earnest ['ə:nɪst] adj serio(a); **in ~** sul serio

earnings ['ə:nɪŋz] npl guadagni mpl;

(*salary*) stipendio

earphones ['ɪəfəʊnz] *npl* cuffia

earring ['ɪərɪŋ] *n* orecchino

earshot ['ɪəʃɔt] *n*: **within ~** a portata d'orecchio

earth [əːθ] *n* terra ♦ *vt* (*BRIT: ELEC*) mettere a terra; **~enware** *n* terracotta; stoviglie *fpl* di terracotta; **~quake** *n* terremoto; **~y** *adj* (*fig*) grossolano(a)

ease [iːz] *n* agio, comodo ♦ *vt* (*soothe*) calmare; (*loosen*) allentare; **to ~ sth out/in** tirare fuori/infilare qc con delicatezza; facilitare l'uscita/l'entrata di qc; **at ~** a proprio agio; (*MIL*) a riposo; **~ off** *or* **up** *vi* diminuire; (*slow down*) rallentare

easel ['iːzl] *n* cavalletto

easily ['iːzɪlɪ] *adv* facilmente

east [iːst] *n* est *m* ♦ *adj* dell'est ♦ *adv* a oriente; **the E~** l'Oriente *m*; (*POL*) l'Est

Easter ['iːstə*] *n* Pasqua; **~ egg** *n* uovo di Pasqua

easterly ['iːstəlɪ] *adj* dall'est, d'oriente

eastern ['iːstən] *adj* orientale, d'oriente; dell'est

East Germany *n* Germania dell'Est

eastward(s) ['iːstwəd(z)] *adv* verso est, verso levante

easy ['iːzɪ] *adj* facile; (*manner*) disinvolto(a) ♦ *adv*: **to take it** *or* **things ~** prendersela con calma; **~ chair** *n* poltrona; **~-going** *adj* accomodante

eat [iːt] (*pt* **ate**, *pp* **eaten**) *vt*, *vi* mangiare; **~ away at** *vt fus* rodere; **~ into** *vt fus* rodere

eaves [iːvz] *npl* gronda

eavesdrop ['iːvzdrɔp] *vi*: **to ~ (on a conversation)** origliare (una conversazione)

ebb [ɛb] *n* riflusso ♦ *vi* rifluire; (*fig: also: ~ away*) declinare

ebony ['ɛbənɪ] *n* ebano

EC *n abbr* (= *European Community*) CEE *f*

eccentric [ɪk'sɛntrɪk] *adj*, *n* eccentrico(a)

echo ['ɛkəʊ] (*pl* **~es**) *n* eco *m or f* ♦ *vt* ripetere; fare eco a ♦ *vi* echeggiare; dare un eco

éclair [eɪ'klɛə*] *n* ≈ bignè *m inv*

eclipse [ɪ'klɪps] *n* eclissi *f inv*

ecology [ɪ'kɔlədʒɪ] *n* ecologia

economic [iːkə'nɔmɪk] *adj* economico(a); **~al** *adj* economico(a); (*person*) economo(a); **~s** *n* economia ♦ *npl* lato finanziario

economize [ɪ'kɔnəmaɪz] *vi* risparmiare, fare economia

economy [ɪ'kɔnəmɪ] *n* economia; **~ class** *n* (*AVIAT*) classe *f* turistica; **~ size** *n* (*COMM*) confezione *f* economica

ecstasy ['ɛkstəsɪ] *n* estasi *f inv*

ECU ['eɪkjuː] *n abbr* (= *European Currency Unit*) ECU *m inv*

eczema ['ɛksɪmə] *n* eczema *m*

edge [ɛdʒ] *n* margine *m*; (*of table, plate, cup*) orlo; (*of knife etc*) taglio ♦ *vt* bordare; **on ~** (*fig*) = **edgy; to ~ away from** sgattaiolare da; **~ways** *adv*: **he couldn't get a word in ~ways** non riuscì a dire una parola; **edgy** *adj* nervoso(a)

edible ['ɛdɪbl] *adj* commestibile; (*meal*) mangiabile

edict ['iːdɪkt] *n* editto

Edinburgh ['ɛdɪnbərə] *n* Edimburgo *f*

edit ['ɛdɪt] *vt* curare; **~ion** [ɪ'dɪʃən] *n* edizione *f*; **~or** *n* (*in newspaper*) redattore/trice; redattore/trice capo; (*of sb's work*) curatore/trice; **~orial** [-'tɔːrɪəl] *adj* redazionale, editoriale ♦ *n* editoriale *m*

educate ['ɛdjukeɪt] *vt* istruire; educare

education [ɛdju'keɪʃən] *n* educazione *f*; (*schooling*) istruzione *f*; **~al** *adj* pedagogico(a); scolastico(a); istruttivo(a)

EEC *n abbr* = **EC**

eel [iːl] *n* anguilla

eerie ['ɪərɪ] *adj* che fa accapponare la pelle

effect [ɪ'fɛkt] *n* effetto ♦ *vt* effettuare; **to take ~** (*law*) entrare in vigore; (*drug*) fare effetto; **in ~** effettivamente; **~ive** *adj* efficace; (*actual*) effettivo(a); **~ively** *adv* efficacemente; effettivamente; **~iveness** *n* efficacia

effeminate [ɪ'fɛmɪnɪt] *adj* effeminato(a)

efficiency [ɪ'fɪʃənsɪ] *n* efficienza; rendimento effettivo

efficient [ɪ'fɪʃənt] *adj* efficiente

effort ['ɛfət] *n* sforzo

effusive [ɪ'fjuːsɪv] *adj* (*handshake, welcome*) caloroso(a)

e.g. *adv abbr* (= *exempli gratia*) per esempio, p.es.

egg [ɛg] *n* uovo; **hard-boiled / soft-boiled ~** uovo sodo/alla coque; **~ on** *vt* incitare; **~cup** *n* portauovo *m inv*; **~plant** *n* (*esp US*) melanzana; **~shell** *n* guscio d'uovo

ego ['iːgəu] *n* ego *m inv*

egotism ['ɛgəutɪzəm] *n* egotismo

Egypt ['iːdʒɪpt] *n* Egitto; **~ian** [ɪ'dʒɪpʃən] *adj, n* egiziano(a)

eiderdown ['aɪdədaun] *n* piumino

eight [eɪt] *num* otto; **~een** *num* diciotto; **~eenth** [eɪtθ] *num* ottavo(a); **~y** *num* ottanta

Eire ['ɛərə] *n* Repubblica d'Irlanda

either ['aɪðə*] *adj* l'uno(a) o l'altro(a); (*both, each*) ciascuno(a) ♦ *pron:* **~ (of them)** (o) l'uno(a) o l'altro(a) ♦ *adv* neanche ♦ *conj:* **~ good or bad** o buono o cattivo; **on ~ side** su ciascun lato; **I don't like ~** non mi piace né l'uno né l'altro; **no, I don't ~** no, neanch'io

eject [ɪ'dʒɛkt] *vt* espellere; lanciare

elaborate [*adj* ɪ'læbərɪt, *vb* ɪ'læbəreɪt] *adj* elaborato(a), minuzioso(a) ♦ *vt* elaborare ♦ *vi* fornire i particolari

elastic [ɪ'læstɪk] *adj* elastico(a) ♦ *n* elastico; **~ band** (*BRIT*) *n* elastico

elated [ɪ'leɪtɪd] *adj* pieno(a) di gioia

elbow ['ɛlbəu] *n* gomito

elder ['ɛldə*] *adj* maggiore, più vecchio(a) ♦ *n* (*tree*) sambuco; **one's ~s** i più anziani; **~ly** *adj* anziano(a) ♦ *npl:* **the ~ly** gli anziani

eldest ['ɛldɪst] *adj, n:* **the ~ (child)** il(la) maggiore (dei bambini)

elect [ɪ'lɛkt] *vt* eleggere ♦ *adj:* **the president ~** il presidente designato; **to ~ to do** decidere di fare; **~ion** [ɪ'lɛkʃən] *n* elezione *f;* **~ioneering** [ɪlɛkʃə'nɪərɪŋ] *n* propaganda elettorale; **~or** *n* elettore/trice; **~orate** *n* elettorato

electric [ɪ'lɛktrɪk] *adj* elettrico(a); **~al** *adj*

elettrico(a); **~ blanket** *n* coperta elettrica; **~ fire** *n* stufa elettrica

electrician [ɪlɛk'trɪʃən] *n* elettricista *m*

electricity [ɪlɛk'trɪsɪtɪ] *n* elettricità

electrify [ɪ'lɛktrɪfaɪ] *vt* (*RAIL*) elettrificare; (*audience*) elettrizzare

electrocute [ɪ'lɛktrəukjuːt] *vt* fulminare

electronic [ɪlɛk'trɔnɪk] *adj* elettronico(a); **~ mail** *n* posta elettronica; **~s** *n* elettronica

elegant ['ɛlɪgənt] *adj* elegante

element ['ɛlɪmənt] *n* elemento; (*of heater, kettle etc*) resistenza; **~ary** [-'mɛntərɪ] *adj* elementare

elephant ['ɛlɪfənt] *n* elefante/essa

elevation [ɛlɪ'veɪʃən] *n* elevazione *f*

elevator ['ɛlɪveɪtə*] *n* elevatore *m;* (*US: lift*) ascensore *m*

eleven [ɪ'lɛvn] *num* undici; **~ses** (*BRIT*) *n* caffè *m* a metà mattina; **~th** *adj* undicesimo(a)

elicit [ɪ'lɪsɪt] *vt:* **to ~ (from)** trarre (da), cavare fuori (da)

eligible ['ɛlɪdʒəbl] *adj* eleggibile; (*for membership*) che ha i requisiti

elm [ɛlm] *n* olmo

elocution [ɛlə'kjuːʃən] *n* dizione *f*

elongated ['iːlɔŋgeɪtɪd] *adj* allungato(a)

elope [ɪ'ləup] *vi* (*lovers*) scappare; **~ment** *n* fuga

eloquent ['ɛləkwənt] *adj* eloquente

else [ɛls] *adv* altro; **something ~** qualcos'altro; **somewhere ~** altrove; **everywhere ~** in qualsiasi altro luogo; **nobody ~** nessun altro; **where ~?** in quale altro luogo?; **little ~** poco altro; **~where** *adv* altrove

elude [ɪ'luːd] *vt* eludere

elusive [ɪ'luːsɪv] *adj* elusivo(a)

emaciated [ɪ'meɪsɪeɪtɪd] *adj* emaciato(a)

E-mail, e-mail *n abbr* (= *electronic mail*) posta elettronica

emanate ['ɛməneɪt] *vi:* **to ~ from** provenire da

emancipate [ɪ'mænsɪpeɪt] *vt* emancipare

embankment [ɪm'bæŋkmənt] *n* (*of road, railway*) terrapieno

embark [ɪm'bɑːk] *vi:* **to ~ (on)** imbarcarsi

(su) ♦ vt imbarcare; **to ~ on** (fig) imbarcarsi in; **~ation** [embɑ:'keɪʃən] n imbarco

embarrass [ɪm'bærəs] vt imbarazzare; **~ed** adj imbarazzato(a); **~ing** adj imbarazzante; **~ment** n imbarazzo

embassy ['embəsɪ] n ambasciata

embrace [ɪm'bedɪd] adj incastrato(a)

embellish [ɪm'belɪʃ] vt abbellire

embers ['embəz] npl braci fpl

embezzle [ɪm'bezl] vt appropriarsi indebitamente di

embitter [ɪm'bɪtə*] vt amareggiare; inasprire

embody [ɪm'bɔdɪ] vt (features) racchiudere, comprendere; (ideas) dar forma concreta a, esprimere

embossed [ɪm'bɔst] adj in rilievo; goffrato(a)

embrace [ɪm'breɪs] vt abbracciare ♦ vi abbracciarsi ♦ n abbraccio

embroider [ɪm'brɔɪdə*] vt ricamare; **~y** n ricamo

embryo ['embrɪəu] n embrione m

emerald ['emərəld] n smeraldo

emerge [ɪ'mɜːdʒ] vi emergere

emergency [ɪ'mɜːdʒənsɪ] n emergenza; **in an ~** in caso di emergenza; **~ cord** (US) n segnale m d'allarme; **~ exit** n uscita di sicurezza; **~ landing** n atterraggio forzato; **~ services** npl (fire, police, ambulance) servizi mpl di pronto intervento

emery board ['emərɪ-] n limetta di carta smerigliata

emigrate ['emɪɡreɪt] vi emigrare

eminent ['emɪnənt] adj eminente

emissions [ɪ'mɪʃənz] npl emissioni fpl

emit [ɪ'mɪt] vt emettere

emotion [ɪ'məuʃən] n emozione f; **~al** adj (person) emotivo(a); (scene) commovente; (tone, speech) carico(a) d'emozione

emperor ['empərə*] n imperatore m

emphasis ['emfəsɪs] (pl **-ases**) n enfasi f inv; importanza

emphasize ['emfəsaɪz] vt (word, point) sottolineare; (feature) mettere in evidenza

emphatic [em'fætɪk] adj (strong) vigoroso(a); (unambiguous, clear) netto(a)

empire ['empaɪə*] n impero

employ [ɪm'plɔɪ] vt impiegare; **~ee** [-'iː] n impiegato/a; **~er** n principale m/f, datore m di lavoro; **~ment** n impiego; **~ment agency** n agenzia di collocamento

empower [ɪm'pauə*] vt: **to ~ sb to do** concedere autorità a qn di fare

empress ['emprɪs] n imperatrice f

emptiness ['emptɪnɪs] n vuoto

empty ['emptɪ] adj vuoto(a); (threat, promise) vano(a) ♦ vt vuotare ♦ vi vuotarsi; (liquid) scaricarsi; **~-handed** adj a mani vuote

EMU n abbr (= economic and monetary union) unione f economica e monetaria

emulate ['emjuleɪt] vt emulare

emulsion [ɪ'mʌlʃən] n emulsione f; **~ (paint)** n colore m a tempera

enable [ɪ'neɪbl] vt: **to ~ sb to do** permettere a qn di fare

enamel [ɪ'næməl] n smalto; (also: **~ paint**) vernice f a smalto

enchant [ɪn'tʃɑːnt] vt incantare; (subj: magic spell) catturare; **~ing** adj incantevole, affascinante

encircle [ɪn'sɜːkl] vt accerchiare

encl. abbr (= enclosed) all

enclave ['enkleɪv] n enclave f

enclose [ɪn'kləuz] vt (land) circondare, recingere; (letter etc): **to ~ (with)** allegare (con); **please find ~d** trovi qui accluso

enclosure [ɪn'kləuʒə*] n recinto

encompass [ɪn'kʌmpəs] vt comprendere

encore [ɒŋ'kɔː*] excl bis ♦ n bis m inv

encounter [ɪn'kauntə*] n incontro ♦ vt incontrare

encourage [ɪn'kʌrɪdʒ] vt incoraggiare; **~ment** n incoraggiamento

encroach [ɪn'krəutʃ] vi: **to ~ (up)on** (rights) usurpare; (time) abusare di; (land) oltrepassare i limiti di

encyclop(a)edia [ensaɪkləu'piːdɪə] n enciclopedia

end [end] n fine f; (aim) fine m; (of table) bordo estremo; (of pointed object) punta ♦ vt finire; (also: **bring to an ~, put an ~ to**) mettere fine a ♦ vi finire; **in the ~** alla

fine; **on ~** (*object*) ritto(a); **to stand on ~**
(*hair*) rizzarsi; **for hours on ~** per ore ed
ore; **~ up** *vi*: **to ~ up in** finire in
endanger [ɪn'deɪndʒə*] *vt* mettere in
pericolo
endearing [ɪn'dɪərɪŋ] *adj* accattivante
endeavour [ɪn'devə*] (*US* **endeavor**) *n*
sforzo, tentativo ♦ *vi*: **to ~ to do** cercare *or*
sforzarsi di fare
ending ['endɪŋ] *n* fine *f*, conclusione *f*;
(*LING*) desinenza
endive ['endaɪv] *n* (*curly*) indivia (riccia);
(*smooth, flat*) indivia belga
endless ['endlɪs] *adj* senza fine
endorse [ɪn'dɔːs] *vt* (*cheque*) girare;
(*approve*) approvare, appoggiare; **~ment** *n*
approvazione *f*; (*on driving licence*)
contravvenzione registrata sulla patente
endurance [ɪn'djuərəns] *n* resistenza;
pazienza
endure [ɪn'djuə*] *vt* sopportare, resistere a
♦ *vi* durare
enemy ['enəmɪ] *adj, n* nemico(a)
energetic [enə'dʒetɪk] *adj* energico(a);
attivo(a)
energy ['enədʒɪ] *n* energia
enforce [ɪn'fɔːs] *vt* (*LAW*) applicare, far
osservare
engage [ɪn'geɪdʒ] *vt* (*hire*) assumere;
(*lawyer*) incaricare; (*attention, interest*)
assorbire; (*TECH*): **to ~ gear/the clutch**
innestare la marcia/la frizione ♦ *vi* (*TECH*)
ingranare; **to ~ in** impegnarsi in; **~d** *adj*
(*BRIT*: *busy, in use*) occupato(a); (*betrothed*)
fidanzato(a); **to get ~d** fidanzarsi; **~d tone**
(*BRIT*) *n* (*TEL*) segnale *m* di occupato;
~ment *n* impegno, obbligo;
appuntamento; (*to marry*) fidanzamento;
~ment ring *n* anello di fidanzamento
engaging [ɪn'geɪdʒɪŋ] *adj* attraente
engine ['endʒɪn] *n* (*AUT*) motore *m*; (*RAIL*)
locomotiva; **~ driver** *n* (*of train*)
macchinista *m*
engineer [endʒɪ'nɪə*] *n* ingegnere *m*; (*BRIT*:
for repairs) tecnico; (*on ship, US*: *RAIL*)
macchinista *m*; **~ing** *n* ingegneria
England ['ɪŋglənd] *n* Inghilterra

English ['ɪŋglɪʃ] *adj* inglese ♦ *n* (*LING*)
inglese *m*; **the ~** *npl* gli Inglesi; **the ~
Channel** *n* la Manica; **~man/woman**
(*irreg*) *n* inglese *m/f*
engraving [ɪn'greɪvɪŋ] *n* incisione *f*
engrossed [ɪn'grəust] *adj*: **~ in** assorbito(a)
da, preso(a) da
engulf [ɪn'gʌlf] *vt* inghiottire
enhance [ɪn'hɑːns] *vt* accrescere
enjoy [ɪn'dʒɔɪ] *vt* godere; (*have*: *success,
fortune*) avere; **to ~ o.s.** godersela,
divertirsi; **~able** *adj* piacevole; **~ment** *n*
piacere *m*, godimento
enlarge [ɪn'lɑːdʒ] *vt* ingrandire ♦ *vi*: **to ~
on** (*subject*) dilungarsi su
enlighten [ɪn'laɪtn] *vt* illuminare; dare
schiarimenti a; **~ed** *adj* illuminato(a);
~ment *n*: **the E~ment** (*HISTORY*)
l'Illuminismo
enlist [ɪn'lɪst] *vt* arruolare; (*support*)
procurare ♦ *vi* arruolarsi
enmity ['enmɪtɪ] *n* inimicizia
enormous [ɪ'nɔːməs] *adj* enorme
enough [ɪ'nʌf] *adj, n*: **~ time/books** assai
tempo/libri; **have you got ~?** ne ha
abbastanza *or* a sufficienza? ♦ *adv*: **big ~**
abbastanza grande; **he has not worked ~**
non ha lavorato abbastanza; **~!** basta!;
that's ~, thanks basta così, grazie; **I've
had ~ of him** ne ho abbastanza di lui; **...
which, funnily *or* oddly ~** ... che, strano a
dirsi
enquire [ɪn'kwaɪə*] *vt, vi* = **inquire**
enrage [ɪn'reɪdʒ] *vt* fare arrabbiare
enrich [ɪn'rɪtʃ] *vt* arricchire
enrol [ɪn'rəul] (*US* **enroll**) *vt* iscrivere ♦ *vi*
iscriversi; **~ment** (*US* **enrollment**) *n*
iscrizione *f*
en suite [ɒn'swiːt] *adj*: **room with ~
bathroom** camera con bagno
ensure [ɪn'ʃuə*] *vt* assicurare; garantire
entail [ɪn'teɪl] *vt* comportare
entangled [ɪn'tæŋgld] *adj*: **to become ~
(in)** impigliarsi (in)
enter ['entə*] *vt* entrare in; (*army*) arruolarsi
in; (*competition*) partecipare a; (*sb for a
competition*) iscrivere; (*write down*)

registrare; (*COMPUT*) inserire ♦ *vi* entrare; ~
for *vt fus* iscriversi a; ~ **into** *vt fus*
(*explanation*) cominciare a dare; (*debate*)
partecipare a; (*agreement*) concludere
enterprise ['ɛntəpraɪz] *n* (*undertaking,
company*) impresa; (*spirit*) iniziativa; **free ~**
liberalismo economico; **private ~** iniziativa
privata
enterprising ['ɛntəpraɪzɪŋ] *adj*
intraprendente
entertain [ɛntə'teɪn] *vt* divertire; (*invite*)
ricevere; (*idea, plan*) nutrire; **~er** *n*
comico/a; **~ing** *adj* divertente; **~ment** *n*
(*amusement*) divertimento; (*show*)
spettacolo
enthralled [ɪn'θrɔːld] *adj* affascinato(a)
enthusiasm [ɪn'θuːzɪæzəm] *n* entusiasmo
enthusiast [ɪn'θuːzɪæst] *n* entusiasta *m/f*;
~ic [-'æstɪk] *adj* entusiastico(a);
to be ~ic about sth/sb essere
appassionato(a) di qc/entusiasta di qn
entire [ɪn'taɪə*] *adj* intero(a); **~ly** *adv*
completamente, interamente; **~ty**
[ɪn'taɪərətɪ] *n*: **in its ~ty** nel suo complesso
entitle [ɪn'taɪtl] *vt* (*give right*): **to ~ sb to
sth/to do** dare diritto a qn a qc/a fare; **~d**
adj (*book*) che si intitola; **to be ~d to do**
avere il diritto di fare
entrails ['ɛntreɪlz] *npl* interiora *fpl*
entrance [*n* 'ɛntrns, *vb* ɪn'trɑːns] *n* entrata,
ingresso; (*of person*) entrata ♦ *vt* incantare,
rapire; **to gain ~ to** (*university etc*) essere
ammesso a; ~ **examination** *n* esame *m*
di ammissione; ~ **fee** *n* tassa d'iscrizione;
(*to museum etc*) prezzo d'ingresso; ~ **ramp**
(*US*) *n* (*AUT*) rampa di accesso
entrant ['ɛntrnt] *n* partecipante *m/f*;
concorrente *m/f*
entreat [ɛn'triːt] *vt* supplicare
entrenched [ɛn'trɛntʃt] *adj* radicato(a)
entrepreneur [ɔntrəprə'nəː*] *n*
imprenditore *m*
entrust [ɪn'trʌst] *vt*: **to ~ sth to** affidare qc a
entry ['ɛntrɪ] *n* entrata; (*way in*) entrata,
ingresso; (*item: on list*) iscrizione *f*; (*in
dictionary*) voce *f*; **no ~** vietato l'ingresso;
(*AUT*) divieto di accesso; ~ **form** *n* modulo

d'iscrizione; ~ **phone** *n* citofono
envelop [ɪn'vɛləp] *vt* avvolgere, avviluppare
envelope ['ɛnvələup] *n* busta
envious ['ɛnvɪəs] *adj* invidioso(a)
environment [ɪn'vaɪərnmənt] *n* ambiente
m; **~al** [-'mɛntl] *adj* ecologico(a);
ambientale; **~-friendly** *adj* che rispetta
l'ambiente
envisage [ɪn'vɪzɪdʒ] *vt* immaginare;
prevedere
envoy ['ɛnvɔɪ] *n* inviato/a
envy ['ɛnvɪ] *n* invidia ♦ *vt* invidiare; **to ~ sb
sth** invidiare qn per qc
epic ['ɛpɪk] *n* poema *m* epico ♦ *adj* epico(a)
epidemic [ɛpɪ'dɛmɪk] *n* epidemia
epilepsy ['ɛpɪlɛpsɪ] *n* epilessia
episode ['ɛpɪsəud] *n* episodio
epistle [ɪ'pɪsl] *n* epistola
epitome [ɪ'pɪtəmɪ] *n* epitome *f*;
quintessenza; **epitomize** *vt* (*fig*) incarnare
equal ['iːkwl] *adj* uguale ♦ *n* pari *m/f inv*
♦ *vt* uguagliare; ~ **to** (*task*) all'altezza di;
~ity [iː'kwɔlɪtɪ] *n* uguaglianza; **~ize** *vi*
pareggiare; **~ly** *adv* ugualmente
equanimity [ɛkwə'nɪmɪtɪ] *n* serenità
equate [ɪ'kweɪt] *vt*: **to ~ sth with**
considerare qc uguale a; (*compare*)
paragonare qc con; **equation** [ɪ'kweɪʃən] *n*
(*MATH*) equazione *f*
equator [ɪ'kweɪtə*] *n* equatore *m*
equilibrium [iːkwɪ'lɪbrɪəm] *n* equilibrio
equip [ɪ'kwɪp] *vt* equipaggiare, attrezzare; **to
~ sb/sth with** fornire qn/qc di; **to be well
~ped** (*office etc*) essere ben attrezzato(a);
he is well ~ped for the job ha i requisiti
necessari per quel lavoro; **~ment** *n*
attrezzatura; (*electrical etc*) apparecchiatura
equitable ['ɛkwɪtəbl] *adj* equo(a), giusto(a)
equities ['ɛkwɪtɪz] *npl* (*BRIT*) (*COMM*) azioni
fpl ordinarie
equivalent [ɪ'kwɪvəlnt] *adj* equivalente ♦ *n*
equivalente *m*; **to be ~ to** equivalere a
era ['ɪərə] *n* era, età *f inv*
eradicate [ɪ'rædɪkeɪt] *vt* sradicare
erase [ɪ'reɪz] *vt* cancellare; **~r** *n* gomma
erect [ɪ'rɛkt] *adj* eretto(a) ♦ *vt* costruire;
(*assemble*) montare; **~ion** [ɪ'rɛkʃən] *n*

costruzione f; montaggio; (PHYSIOL)
erezione f

ERM n (= Exchange Rate Mechanism) ERM
m

ermine ['əːmɪn] n ermellino

erode [ɪ'rəud] vt erodere; (metal) corrodere

erotic [ɪ'rɔtɪk] adj erotico(a)

errand ['ɛrnd] n commissione f

erratic [ɪ'rætɪk] adj imprevedibile; (person,
mood) incostante

error ['ɛrə*] n errore m

erupt [ɪ'rʌpt] vi (volcano) mettersi (or essere)
in eruzione; (war, crisis) scoppiare; ~**ion**
[ɪ'rʌpʃən] n eruzione f; scoppio

escalate ['ɛskəleɪt] vi intensificarsi

escalator ['ɛskəleɪtə*] n scala mobile

escapade [ɛskə'peɪd] n scappatella;
avventura

escape [ɪ'skeɪp] n evasione f; fuga; (of gas
etc) fuga, fuoriuscita ♦ vi fuggire; (from jail)
evadere, scappare; (leak) uscire ♦ vt
sfuggire a; **to ~ from** (place) fuggire da;
(person) sfuggire a; **escapism** n evasione
f (dalla realtà)

escort [n 'ɛskɔːt, vb ɪ'skɔːt] n scorta; (male
companion) cavaliere m ♦ vt scortare;
accompagnare

Eskimo ['ɛskɪməu] n eschimese m/f

especially [ɪ'spɛʃlɪ] adv specialmente;
soprattutto; espressamente

espionage ['ɛspɪənɑːʒ] n spionaggio

esplanade [ɛsplə'neɪd] n lungomare m inv

Esq. abbr = Esquire

Esquire [ɪ'skwaɪə*] n: **J. Brown, ~** Signor J.
Brown

essay ['ɛseɪ] n (SCOL) composizione f;
(LITERATURE) saggio

essence ['ɛsns] n essenza

essential [ɪ'sɛnʃl] adj essenziale ♦ n
elemento essenziale; ~**ly** adv
essenzialmente

establish [ɪ'stæblɪʃ] vt stabilire; (business)
mettere su; (one's power etc) affermare;
~**ed** adj (business etc) affermato(a);
~**ment** n stabilimento; **the E~ment** la
classe dirigente, l'establishment m

estate [ɪ'steɪt] n proprietà f inv; beni mpl,

patrimonio; (BRIT: also: **housing ~**)
complesso edilizio; ~ **agent** (BRIT) n
agente m immobiliare; ~ **car** (BRIT) n
giardiniera

esteem [ɪ'stiːm] n stima ♦ vt (think highly
of) stimare; (consider) considerare

esthetic [ɪs'θetɪk] (US) adj = **aesthetic**

estimate [n 'ɛstɪmət, vb 'ɛstɪmeɪt] n stima;
(COMM) preventivo ♦ vt stimare, valutare;
estimation [-'meɪʃən] n stima; opinione f

estranged [ɪ'streɪndʒd] adj separato(a)

etc abbr (= et cetera) etc, ecc

eternal [ɪ'təːnl] adj eterno(a)

eternity [ɪ'təːnɪtɪ] n eternità

ether ['iːθə*] n etere m

ethical ['ɛθɪkl] adj etico(a), morale

ethics ['ɛθɪks] n etica ♦ npl morale f

Ethiopia [iːθɪ'əupɪə] n Etiopia

ethnic ['ɛθnɪk] adj etnico(a); ~ **minority** n
minoranza etnica

ethos ['iːθɔs] n norma di vita

etiquette ['ɛtɪkɛt] n etichetta

EU n abbr (= European Union) UE

Eurocheque ['juərəutʃɛk] n eurochèque m
inv

Europe ['juərəp] n Europa; **European**
[-'piːən] adj, n europeo(a); **European
Community** n Comunità Europea

evacuate [ɪ'vækjueɪt] vt evacuare

evade [ɪ'veɪd] vt (tax) evadere; (duties etc)
sottrarsi a; (person) schivare

evaluate [ɪ'væljueɪt] vt valutare

evaporate [ɪ'væpəreɪt] vi evaporare; ~**d
milk** n latte m concentrato

evasion [ɪ'veɪʒən] n evasione f

evasive [ɪ'veɪsɪv] adj evasivo(a)

eve [iːv] n: **on the ~ of** alla vigilia di

even ['iːvn] adj regolare; (number) pari inv
♦ adv anche, perfino; ~ **if**, ~ **though** anche
se; ~ **more** ancora di più; ~ **so** ciò
nonostante; **not** ~ nemmeno; **to get ~ with
sb** dare la pari a qn

evening ['iːvnɪŋ] n sera; (as duration, event)
serata; **in the ~** la sera; ~ **class** n corso
serale; ~ **dress** n (woman's) abito da sera;
in ~ dress (man) in abito scuro; (woman)
in abito lungo

event [ɪ'vɛnt] *n* avvenimento; (*SPORT*) gara; **in the ~ of** in caso di; **~ful** *adj* denso(a) di eventi

eventual [ɪ'vɛntʃuəl] *adj* finale; **~ity** [-'ælɪtɪ] *n* possibilità *f inv*, eventualità *f inv*; **~ly** *adv* alla fine

ever ['ɛvə*] *adv* mai; (*at all times*) sempre; **the best ~** il migliore che ci sia mai stato; **have you ~ seen it?** l'ha mai visto?; **~ since** *adv* da allora ♦ *conj* sin da quando; **~ so pretty** così bello(a); **~green** *n* sempreverde *m*; **~lasting** *adj* eterno(a)

every ['ɛvrɪ] *adj* ogni; **~ day** tutti i giorni, ogni giorno; **~ other/third day** ogni due/ tre giorni; **~ other car** una macchina su due; **~ now and then** ogni tanto, di quando in quando; **~body** *pron* = **~one**; **~day** *adj* quotidiano(a); di ogni giorno; **~one** *pron* ognuno, tutti *pl*; **~thing** *pron* tutto, ogni cosa; **~where** *adv* (*gen*) dappertutto; (*wherever*) ovunque

evict [ɪ'vɪkt] *vt* sfrattare

evidence ['ɛvɪdns] *n* (*proof*) prova; (*of witness*) testimonianza; (*sign*): **to show ~ of** dare segni di; **to give ~** deporre

evident ['ɛvɪdnt] *adj* evidente; **~ly** *adv* evidentemente

evil ['iːvl] *adj* cattivo(a), maligno(a) ♦ *n* male *m*

evoke [ɪ'vəuk] *vt* evocare

evolution [iːvə'luːʃən] *n* evoluzione *f*

evolve [ɪ'vɔlv] *vt* elaborare ♦ *vi* svilupparsi, evolversi

ewe [juː] *n* pecora

ex- [ɛks] *prefix* ex

exacerbate [ɛks'æsəbeɪt] *vt* aggravare

exact [ɪg'zækt] *adj* esatto(a) ♦ *vt*: **to ~ sth (from)** estorcere qc (da); esigere qc (da); **~ing** *adj* esigente; (*work*) faticoso(a); **~ly** *adv* esattamente

exaggerate [ɪg'zædʒəreɪt] *vt, vi* esagerare; **exaggeration** [-'reɪʃən] *n* esagerazione *f*

exalted [ɪg'zɔːltɪd] *adj* esaltato(a); elevato(a)

exam [ɪg'zæm] *n abbr* (*SCOL*) = **examination**

examination [ɪgzæmɪ'neɪʃən] *n* (*SCOL*) esame *m*; (*MED*) controllo

examine [ɪg'zæmɪn] *vt* esaminare; **~r** *n* esaminatore/trice

example [ɪg'zɑːmpl] *n* esempio; **for ~** ad *or* per esempio

exasperate [ɪg'zɑːspəreɪt] *vt* esasperare; **exasperating** *adj* esasperante; **exasperation** [-'reɪʃən] *n* esasperazione *f*

excavate ['ɛkskəveɪt] *vt* scavare

exceed [ɪk'siːd] *vt* superare; (*one's powers, time limit*) oltrepassare; **~ingly** *adv* eccessivamente

excellent ['ɛksələnt] *adj* eccellente

except [ɪk'sɛpt] *prep* (*also*: **~ for**, **~ing**) salvo, all'infuori di, eccetto ♦ *vt* escludere; **~ if/when** salvo se/quando; **~ that** salvo che; **~ion** [ɪk'sɛpʃən] *n* eccezione *f*; **to take ~ion to** trovare a ridire su; **~ional** [ɪk'sɛpʃənl] *adj* eccezionale

excerpt ['ɛksɜːpt] *n* estratto

excess [ɪk'sɛs] *n* eccesso; **~ baggage** *n* bagaglio in eccedenza; **~ fare** *n* supplemento; **~ive** *adj* eccessivo(a)

exchange [ɪks'tʃeɪndʒ] *n* scambio; (*also*: **telephone ~**) centralino ♦ *vt*: **to ~ (for)** scambiare (con); **~ rate** *n* tasso di cambio

Exchequer [ɪks'tʃɛkə*] *n*: **the ~** (*BRIT*) lo Scacchiere, ≈ il ministero delle Finanze

excise ['ɛksaɪz] *n* imposta, dazio

excite [ɪk'saɪt] *vt* eccitare; **to get ~d** eccitarsi; **~ment** *n* eccitazione *f*; agitazione *f*; **exciting** *adj* avventuroso(a); (*film, book*) appassionante

exclaim [ɪk'skleɪm] *vi* esclamare; **exclamation** [ɛksklə'meɪʃən] *n* esclamazione *f*; **exclamation mark** *n* punto esclamativo

exclude [ɪk'skluːd] *vt* escludere

exclusive [ɪk'skluːsɪv] *adj* esclusivo(a); **~ of VAT** I.V.A. esclusa

excommunicate [ɛkskə'mjuːnɪkeɪt] *vt* scomunicare

excruciating [ɪk'skruːʃɪeɪtɪŋ] *adj* straziante, atroce

excursion [ɪk'skɜːʃən] *n* escursione *f*, gita

excuse [*n* ɪk'skjuːs, *vb* ɪk'skjuːz] *n* scusa ♦ *vt* scusare; **to ~ sb from** (*activity*) dispensare qn da; **~ me!** mi scusi!; **now, if you will ~**

me ... ora, mi scusi ma ....

ex-directory (*BRIT*) *adj* (*TEL*): **to be ~** non essere sull'elenco

execute ['ɛksɪkjuːt] *vt* (*prisoner*) giustiziare; (*plan etc*) eseguire

execution [ɛksɪ'kjuːʃən] *n* esecuzione *f*; **~er** *n* boia *m inv*

executive [ɪg'zɛkjutɪv] *n* (*COMM*) dirigente *m*; (*POL*) esecutivo ♦ *adj* esecutivo(a)

exemplify [ɪg'zɛmplɪfaɪ] *vt* esemplificare

exempt [ɪg'zɛmpt] *adj* esentato(a) ♦ *vt*: **to ~ sb from** esentare qn da; **~ion** [ɪg'zɛmpʃən] *n* esenzione *f*

exercise ['ɛksəsaɪz] *n* (*keep fit*) moto; (*SCOL*, *MIL etc*) esercizio ♦ *vt* esercitare; (*patience*) usare; (*dog*) portar fuori ♦ *vi* (*also*: **take ~**) fare del moto; **~bike** *n* cyclette *f inv*; **~ book** *n* quaderno

exert [ɪg'zəːt] *vt* esercitare; **to ~ o.s.** sforzarsi; **~ion** [-ʃən] *n* sforzo

exhale [ɛks'heɪl] *vt*, *vi* espirare

exhaust [ɪg'zɔːst] *n* (*also*: **~ fumes**) scappamento; (*also*: **~ pipe**) tubo di scappamento ♦ *vt* esaurire; **~ed** *adj* esaurito(a); **~ion** [ɪg'zɔːstʃən] *n* esaurimento; **nervous ~ion** sovraffaticamento mentale; **~ive** *adj* esauriente

exhibit [ɪg'zɪbɪt] *n* (*ART*) oggetto esposto; (*LAW*) documento *or* oggetto esibito ♦ *vt* esporre; (*courage*, *skill*) dimostrare; **~ion** [ɛksɪ'bɪʃən] *n* mostra, esposizione *f*

exhilarating [ɪg'zɪləreɪtɪŋ] *adj* esilarante; stimolante

exhort [ɪg'zɔːt] *vt* esortare

exile ['ɛksaɪl] *n* esilio; (*person*) esiliato/a ♦ *vt* esiliare

exist [ɪg'zɪst] *vi* esistere; **~ence** *n* esistenza; **~ing** *adj* esistente

exit ['ɛksɪt] *n* uscita ♦ *vi* (*THEATRE*, *COMPUT*) uscire; **~ poll** *n* exit poll *m inv*; **~ ramp** *n* (*US*) (*AUT*) rampa di uscita

exodus ['ɛksədəs] *n* esodo

exonerate [ɪg'zɔnəreɪt] *vt*: **to ~ from** discolpare da

exotic [ɪg'zɔtɪk] *adj* esotico(a)

expand [ɪk'spænd] *vt* espandere; estendere;

allargare ♦ *vi* (*business*, *gas*) espandersi; (*metal*) dilatarsi

expanse [ɪk'spæns] *n* distesa, estensione *f*

expansion [ɪk'spænʃən] *n* (*gen*) espansione *f*; (*of town*, *economy*) sviluppo; (*of metal*) dilatazione *f*

expect [ɪk'spɛkt] *vt* (*anticipate*) prevedere, aspettarsi, prevedere *or* aspettarsi che +*sub*; (*require*) richiedere, esigere; (*suppose*) supporre; (*await*, *also baby*) aspettare ♦ *vi*: **to be ~ing** essere in stato interessante; **to ~ sb to do** aspettarsi che qn faccia; **~ancy** *n* (*anticipation*) attesa; **life ~ancy** probabilità *fpl* di vita; **~ant mother** *n* gestante *f*; **~ation** [ɛkspɛk'teɪʃən] *n* aspettativa; speranza

expediency [ɪk'spiːdɪənsɪ] *n* convenienza

expedient [ɪk'spiːdɪənt] *adj* conveniente; vantaggioso(a) ♦ *n* espediente *m*

expedition [ɛkspə'dɪʃən] *n* spedizione *f*

expel [ɪk'spɛl] *vt* espellere

expend [ɪk'spɛnd] *vt* spendere; (*use up*) consumare; **~iture** [ɪk'spɛndɪtʃə*] *n* spesa

expense [ɪk'spɛns] *n* spesa; (*high cost*) costo; **~s** *npl* (*COMM*) spese *fpl*, indennità *fpl*; **at the ~ of** a spese di; **~ account** *n* conto *m* spese *inv*

expensive [ɪk'spɛnsɪv] *adj* caro(a), costoso(a)

experience [ɪk'spɪərɪəns] *n* esperienza ♦ *vt* (*pleasure*) provare; (*hardship*) soffrire; **~d** *adj* esperto(a)

experiment [*n* ɪk'spɛrɪmənt, *vb* ɪk'spɛrɪment] *n* esperimento, esperienza ♦ *vi*: **to ~ (with/on)** fare esperimenti (con/su)

expert ['ɛkspəːt] *adj*, *n* esperto(a); **~ise** [-'tiːz] *n* competenza

expire [ɪk'spaɪə*] *vi* (*period of time*, *licence*) scadere; **expiry** *n* scadenza

explain [ɪk'spleɪn] *vt* spiegare; **explanation** [ɛksplə'neɪʃən] *n* spiegazione *f*; **explanatory** [ɪk'splænətrɪ] *adj* esplicativo(a)

explicit [ɪk'splɪsɪt] *adj* esplicito(a)

explode [ɪk'spləud] *vi* esplodere

exploit [*n* 'ɛksplɔɪt, *vb* ɪk'splɔɪt] *n* impresa ♦ *vt* sfruttare; **~ation** [-'teɪʃən] *n* sfruttamento

exploratory [ɪk'splɔːrətrɪ] *adj* esplorativo(a)

explore [ɪk'splɔː*] *vt* esplorare; (*possibilities*) esaminare; **~r** *n* esploratore/trice

explosion [ɪk'spləʊʒən] *n* esplosione *f*

explosive [ɪk'spləʊsɪv] *adj* esplosivo(a) ♦ *n* esplosivo

exponent [ɪk'spəʊnənt] *n* esponente *m/f*

export [*vb* ɛk'spɔːt, *n* 'ɛkspɔːt] *vt* esportare ♦ *n* esportazione *f*; articolo di esportazione ♦ *cpd* d'esportazione; **~er** *n* esportatore *m*

expose [ɪk'spəʊz] *vt* esporre; (*unmask*) smascherare; **~d** *adj* (*position*) esposto(a)

exposure [ɪk'spəʊʒə*] *n* esposizione *f*; (*PHOT*) posa; (*MED*) assideramento; **~ meter** *n* esposimetro

express [ɪk'sprɛs] *adj* (*definite*) chiaro(a), espresso(a); (*BRIT: letter etc*) espresso *inv* ♦ *n* (*train*) espresso ♦ *vt* esprimere; **~ion** [ɪk'sprɛʃən] *n* espressione *f*; **~ive** *adj* espressivo(a); **~ly** *adv* espressamente; **~way** (*US*) *n* (*urban motorway*) autostrada che attraversa la città

exquisite [ɛk'skwɪzɪt] *adj* squisito(a)

extend [ɪk'stɛnd] *vt* (*visit*) protrarre; (*road, deadline*) prolungare; (*building*) ampliare; (*offer*) offrire, porgere ♦ *vi* (*land, period*) estendersi

extension [ɪk'stɛnʃən] *n* (*of road, term*) prolungamento; (*of contract, deadline*) proroga; (*building*) annesso; (*to wire, table*) prolunga; (*telephone*) interno; (*: in private house*) apparecchio supplementare

extensive [ɪk'stɛnsɪv] *adj* esteso(a), ampio(a); (*damage*) su larga scala; (*coverage, discussion*) esauriente; (*use*) grande; **~ly** *adv*: **he's travelled ~ly** ha viaggiato molto

extent [ɪk'stɛnt] *n* estensione *f*; **to some ~** fino a un certo punto; **to such an ~ that ...** a un tal punto che ...; **to what ~?** fino a che punto?; **to the ~ of ...** fino al punto di ...

extenuating [ɪks'tɛnjʊeɪtɪŋ] *adj*: **~ circumstances** attenuanti *fpl*

exterior [ɛk'stɪərɪə*] *adj* esteriore, esterno(a) ♦ *n* esteriore *m*, esterno; aspetto (esteriore)

exterminate [ɪk'stə:mɪneɪt] *vt* sterminare

external [ɛk'stə:nl] *adj* esterno(a), esteriore

extinct [ɪk'stɪŋkt] *adj* estinto(a)

extinguish [ɪk'stɪŋgwɪʃ] *vt* estinguere; **~er** *n* estintore *m*

extort [ɪk'stɔːt] *vt*: **to ~ sth (from)** estorcere qc (da); **~ionate** [ɪk'stɔːʃənɪt] *adj* esorbitante

extra ['ɛkstrə] *adj* extra *inv*, supplementare ♦ *adv* (*in addition*) di più ♦ *n* extra *m inv*; (*surcharge*) supplemento; (*CINEMA, THEATRE*) comparsa

extra... ['ɛkstrə] *prefix* extra...

extract [*vb* ɪk'strækt, *n* 'ɛkstrækt] *vt* estrarre; (*money, promise*) strappare ♦ *n* estratto; (*passage*) brano

extracurricular ['ɛkstrəkə'rɪkjʊlə*] *adj* extrascolastico(a)

extradite ['ɛkstrədaɪt] *vt* estradare

extramarital [ɛkstrə'mærɪtl] *adj* extraconiugale

extramural [ɛkstrə'mjʊərl] *adj* fuori dell'università

extraordinary [ɪk'strɔːdnrɪ] *adj* straordinario(a)

extravagance [ɪk'strævəgəns] *n* sperpero; stravaganza

extravagant [ɪk'strævəgənt] *adj* (*lavish*) prodigo(a); (*wasteful*) dispendioso(a)

extreme [ɪk'striːm] *adj* estremo(a) ♦ *n* estremo; **~ly** *adv* estremamente

extricate ['ɛkstrɪkeɪt] *vt*: **to ~ sth (from)** districare qc (da)

extrovert ['ɛkstrəvə:t] *n* estroverso/a

exude [ɪg'zjuːd] *vt* trasudare; (*fig*) emanare

eye [aɪ] *n* occhio; (*of needle*) cruna ♦ *vt* osservare; **to keep an ~ on** tenere d'occhio; **~brow** *n* sopracciglio; **~drops** *npl* gocce *fpl* oculari, collirio; **~lash** *n* ciglio; **~lid** *n* palpebra; **~liner** *n* eye-liner *m inv*; **~-opener** *n* rivelazione *f*; **~shadow** *n* ombretto; **~sight** *n* vista; **~sore** *n* pugno nell'occhio; **~ witness** *n* testimone *m/f* oculare

F, f

F [ɛf] *n* (MUS) fa *m*
fable ['feɪbl] *n* favola
fabric ['fæbrɪk] *n* stoffa, tessuto
fabulous ['fæbjuləs] *adj* favoloso(a); (*super*) favoloso(a), fantastico(a)
façade [fə'sɑːd] *n* (*also fig*) facciata
face [feɪs] *n* faccia, viso, volto; (*expression*) faccia; (*of clock*) quadrante *m*; (*of building*) facciata ♦ *vt* essere di fronte a; (*facts, situation*) affrontare; **~ down** a faccia in giù; **to make** *or* **pull a ~** fare una smorfia; **in the ~ of** (*difficulties etc*) di fronte a; **on the ~ of it** a prima vista; **~ to ~** faccia a faccia; **~ up to** *vt fus* affrontare, far fronte a; **~ cloth** (BRIT) *n* guanto di spugna; **~ cream** *n* crema per il viso; **~ lift** *n* lifting *m inv*; (*of façade etc*) ripulita; **~ powder** *n* cipria; **~-saving** *adj* per salvare la faccia
facet ['fæsɪt] *n* sfaccettatura
facetious [fə'siːʃəs] *adj* faceto(a)
face value *n* (*of coin*) valore *m* facciale *or* nominale; **to take sth at ~** (*fig*) giudicare qc dalle apparenze
facial ['feɪʃəl] *adj* del viso
facile ['fæsaɪl] *adj* superficiale
facilities [fə'sɪlɪtɪz] *npl* attrezzature *fpl*; **credit ~** facilitazioni *fpl* di credito
facing ['feɪsɪŋ] *prep* di fronte a
facsimile [fæk'sɪmɪlɪ] *n* facsimile *m inv*; **~ machine** *n* telecopiatrice *f*
fact [fækt] *n* fatto; **in ~** infatti
factor ['fæktə*] *n* fattore *m*
factory ['fæktərɪ] *n* fabbrica, stabilimento
factual ['fæktjuəl] *adj* che si attiene ai fatti
faculty ['fækəltɪ] *n* facoltà *f inv*; (US) corpo insegnante
fad [fæd] *n* mania; capriccio
fade [feɪd] *vi* sbiadire, sbiadirsi; (*light, sound, hope*) attenuarsi, affievolirsi; (*flower*) appassire
fag [fæg] (BRIT: *inf*) *n* (*cigarette*) cicca
fail [feɪl] *vt* (*exam*) non superare; (*candidate*) bocciare; (*subj: courage, memory*) mancare

a ♦ *vi* fallire; (*student*) essere respinto(a); (*eyesight, health, light*) venire a mancare; **to ~ to do sth** (*neglect*) mancare di fare qc; (*be unable*) non riuscire a fare qc; **without ~** senza fallo; certamente; **~ing** *n* difetto ♦ *prep* in mancanza di; **~ure** ['feɪljə*] *n* fallimento; (*person*) fallito/a; (*mechanical etc*) guasto
faint [feɪnt] *adj* debole; (*recollection*) vago(a); (*mark*) indistinto(a) ♦ *n* (MED) svenimento ♦ *vi* svenire; **to feel ~** sentirsi svenire
fair [fɛə*] *adj* (*person, decision*) giusto(a), equo(a); (*quite large, quite good*) discreto(a); (*hair etc*) biondo(a); (*skin, complexion*) chiaro(a); (*weather*) bello(a), clemente ♦ *adv* (*play*) lealmente ♦ *n* fiera; (BRIT: *funfair*) luna park *m inv*; **~ly** *adv* equamente; (*quite*) abbastanza; **~ness** *n* equità, giustizia; **~ play** *n* correttezza
fairy ['fɛərɪ] *n* fata; **~ tale** *n* fiaba
faith [feɪθ] *n* fede *f*; (*trust*) fiducia; (*sect*) religione *f*, fede *f*; **~ful** *adj* fedele; **~fully** *adv* fedelmente; **yours ~fully** (BRIT: *in letters*) distinti saluti
fake [feɪk] *n* imitazione *f*; (*picture*) falso; (*person*) impostore/a ♦ *adj* falso(a) ♦ *vt* (*accounts*) falsificare; (*illness*) fingere; (*painting*) contraffare
fall [fɔːl] (*pt* fell, *pp* fallen) *n* caduta; (*in temperature*) abbassamento; (*in price*) ribasso; (US: *autumn*) autunno ♦ *vi* cadere; (*temperature, price, night*) scendere; **~s** *npl* (*waterfall*) cascate *fpl*; **to ~ flat** (*on one's face*) cadere bocconi; (*joke*) fare cilecca; (*plan*) fallire; **~ back** *vi* (*retreat*) indietreggiare; (MIL) ritirarsi; **~ back on** *vt fus* (*remedy etc*) ripiegare su; **~ behind** *vi* rimanere indietro; **~ down** *vi* (*person*) cadere; (*building*) crollare; **~ for** *vt fus* (*person*) prendere una cotta per; **to ~ for a trick** (*or a story etc*) cascarci; **~ in** *vi* crollare; (MIL) mettersi in riga; **~ off** *vi* cadere; (*diminish*) diminuire, abbassarsi; **~ out** *vi* (*hair, teeth*) cadere; (*friends etc*) litigare; **~ through** *vi* (*plan, project*) fallire
fallacy ['fæləsɪ] *n* errore *m*

fallen ['fɔːlən] pp of **fall**

fallout ['fɔːlaut] n fall-out m

fallow ['fæləu] adj incolto(a), a maggese

false [fɔːls] adj falso(a); **under ~ pretences** con l'inganno; **~ teeth** (BRIT) npl denti mpl finti

falter ['fɔːltə*] vi esitare, vacillare

fame [feim] n fama, celebrità

familiar [fə'mɪlɪə*] adj familiare; (close) intimo(a); **to be ~ with** (subject) conoscere; **~ize** [fə'mɪlɪəraɪz] vt: **to ~ize o.s. with** familiarizzare con

family ['fæmɪlɪ] n famiglia; **~ business** n ditta a conduzione familiare

famine ['fæmɪn] n carestia

famished ['fæmɪʃt] adj affamato(a)

famous ['feiməs] adj famoso(a); **~ly** adv (get on) a meraviglia

fan [fæn] n (folding) ventaglio; (ELEC) ventilatore m; (person) ammiratore/trice; tifoso/a ♦ vt far vento a; (fire, quarrel) alimentare

fanatic [fə'nætɪk] n fanatico/a

fan belt n cinghia del ventilatore

fanciful ['fænsɪful] adj fantasioso(a)

fancy ['fænsɪ] n immaginazione f, fantasia; (whim) capriccio ♦ adj (hat) stravagante; (hotel, food) speciale ♦ vt (feel like, want) aver voglia di; (imagine, think) immaginare; **to take a ~ to** incapricciarsi di; **he fancies her** (inf) gli piace; **~ dress** n costume m (per maschera); **~-dress ball** n ballo in maschera

fang [fæŋ] n zanna; (of snake) dente m

fantastic [fæn'tæstɪk] adj fantastico(a)

fantasy ['fæntəsɪ] n fantasia, immaginazione f; fantasticheria; chimera

far [fɑː*] adj lontano(a) ♦ adv lontano; (much, greatly) molto; **~ away, ~ off** lontano, distante; **~ better** assai migliore; **~ from** lontano da; **by ~** di gran lunga; **go as ~ as the farm** vada fino alla fattoria; **as ~ as I know** per quel che so; **how ~?** quanto lontano?; (referring to activity etc) fino a dove?; **~away** adj lontano(a)

farce [fɑːs] n farsa

fare [fɛə*] n (on trains, buses) tariffa; (in taxi)

prezzo della corsa; (food) vitto, cibo; **half ~** metà tariffa; **full ~** tariffa intera

Far East n: **the ~** l'Estremo Oriente m

farewell [fɛə'wɛl] excl, n addio

farm [fɑːm] n fattoria, podere m ♦ vt coltivare; **~er** n coltivatore/trice; agricoltore/trice; **~hand** n bracciante m agricolo; **~house** n fattoria; **~ing** n (gen) agricoltura; (of crops) coltivazione f; (of animals) allevamento; **~land** n terreno coltivabile; **~ worker** n = **~hand**; **~yard** n aia

far-reaching [-'riːtʃɪŋ] adj di vasta portata

fart [fɑːt] (inf!) vi scoreggiare (!)

farther ['fɑːðə*] adv più lontano ♦ adj più lontano(a)

farthest ['fɑːðɪst] superl of **far**

fascinate ['fæsɪneɪt] vt affascinare; **fascinating** adj affascinante; **fascination** [-'neɪʃən] n fascino

fascism ['fæʃɪzəm] n fascismo

fashion ['fæʃən] n moda; (manner) maniera, modo ♦ vt foggiare, formare; **in ~** alla moda; **out of ~** passato(a) di moda; **~able** adj alla moda, di moda; **~ show** n sfilata di moda

fast [fɑːst] adj rapido(a), svelto(a), veloce; (clock): **to be ~** andare avanti; (dye, colour) solido(a) ♦ adv rapidamente; (stuck, held) saldamente ♦ n digiuno ♦ vi digiunare; **~ asleep** profondamente addormentato

fasten ['fɑːsn] vt chiudere, fissare; (coat) abbottonare, allacciare ♦ vi chiudersi, fissarsi; abbottonarsi, allacciarsi; **~er** n fermaglio, chiusura; **~ing** n = **~er**

fast food n fast food m

fastidious [fæs'tɪdɪəs] adj esigente, difficile

fat [fæt] adj grasso(a); (book, profit etc) grosso(a) ♦ n grasso

fatal ['feɪtl] adj fatale; mortale; disastroso(a); **~ity** [fə'tælɪtɪ] n (road death etc) morto/a, vittima; **~ly** adv a morte

fate [feɪt] n destino; (of person) sorte f; **~ful** adj fatidico(a)

father ['fɑːðə*] n padre m; **~-in-law** n suocero; **~ly** adj paterno(a)

fathom ['fæðəm] n braccio (= 1828 mm)

♦ *vt* (*mystery*) penetrare, sondare

fatigue [fə'ti:g] *n* stanchezza

fatten ['fætn] *vt*, *vi* ingrassare

fatty ['fæti] *adj* (*food*) grasso(a) ♦ *n* (*inf*) ciccione/a

fatuous ['fætjuəs] *adj* fatuo(a)

faucet ['fɔ:sɪt] (*US*) *n* rubinetto

fault [fɔ:lt] *n* colpa; (*TENNIS*) fallo; (*defect*) difetto; (*GEO*) faglia ♦ *vt* criticare; **it's my ~** è colpa mia; **to find ~ with** trovare da ridire su; **at ~** in fallo; **~y** *adj* difettoso(a)

fauna ['fɔ:nə] *n* fauna

favour ['feɪvə*] (*US* **favor**) *n* favore *m* ♦ *vt* (*proposition*) favorire, essere favorevole a; (*pupil etc*) favorire; (*team, horse*) dare per vincente; **to do sb a ~** fare un favore *or* una cortesia a qn; **to find ~ with** (*subj: person*) entrare nelle buone grazie di; (: *suggestion*) avere l'approvazione di; **in ~ of** in favore di; **~able** *adj* favorevole; **~ite** [-rɪt] *adj, n* favorito(a)

fawn [fɔ:n] *n* daino ♦ *adj* (*also*: **~-coloured**) marrone chiaro *inv* ♦ *vi*: **to ~ (up)on** adulare servilmente

fax [fæks] *n* (*document*) facsimile *m inv*, telecopia; (*machine*) telecopiatrice *f* ♦ *vt* telecopiare, trasmettere in facsimile

FBI (*US*) *n abbr* (= *Federal Bureau of Investigation*) F.B.I. *f*

fear [fɪə*] *n* paura, timore *m* ♦ *vt* aver paura di, temere; **for ~ of** per paura di; **~ful** *adj* pauroso(a); (*sight, noise*) terribile, spaventoso(a)

feasible ['fi:zəbl] *adj* possibile, realizzabile

feast [fi:st] *n* festa, banchetto; (*REL: also*: **~ day**) festa ♦ *vi* banchettare

feat [fi:t] *n* impresa, fatto insigne

feather ['feðə*] *n* penna

feature ['fi:tʃə*] *n* caratteristica; (*PRESS, TV*) articolo ♦ *vt* (*subj: film*) avere come protagonista ♦ *vi* figurare; **~s** *npl* (*of face*) fisionomia; **~ film** *n* film *m inv* principale

February ['februəri] *n* febbraio

fed [fed] *pt, pp of* **feed**

federal ['fedərəl] *adj* federale

fed-up *adj*: **to be ~** essere stufo(a)

fee [fi:] *n* pagamento; (*of doctor, lawyer*)

onorario; (*for examination*) tassa d'esame; **school ~s** tasse *fpl* scolastiche

feeble ['fi:bl] *adj* debole

feed [fi:d] (*pt, pp* **fed**) *n* (*of baby*) pappa; (*of animal*) mangime *m*; (*on printer*) meccanismo di alimentazione ♦ *vt* nutrire; (*baby*) allattare; (*horse etc*) dare da mangiare a; (*fire, machine*) alimentare; (*data, information*): **to ~ into** inserire in; **~ on** *vt fus* nutrirsi di; **~back** *n* feed-back *m*

feel [fi:l] (*pt, pp* **felt**) *n* consistenza; (*sense of touch*) tatto ♦ *vt* toccare; palpare; tastare; (*cold, pain, anger*) sentire; (*think, believe*): **to ~ (that)** pensare che; **to ~ hungry/cold** aver fame/freddo; **to ~ lonely/better** sentirsi solo/meglio; **I don't ~ well** non mi sento bene; **it ~s soft** è morbido al tatto; **to ~ like** (*want*) aver voglia di; **to ~ about** *or* **around for** cercare a tastoni; **~er** *n* (*of insect*) antenna; **~ing** *n* sensazione *f*; (*emotion*) sentimento

feet [fi:t] *npl of* **foot**

feign [feɪn] *vt* fingere, simulare

fell [fel] *pt of* **fall** ♦ *vt* (*tree*) abbattere

fellow ['feləu] *n* individuo, tipo; compagno; (*of learned society*) membro ♦ *cpd*: **~ citizen** *n* concittadino/a; **~ countryman** (*irreg*) *n* compatriota *m*; **~ men** *npl* simili *mpl*; **~ship** *n* associazione *f*; compagnia; specie di borsa di studio universitaria

felony ['feləni] *n* reato, crimine *m*

felt [felt] *pt, pp of* **feel** ♦ *n* feltro; **~-tip pen** *n* pennarello

female ['fi:meɪl] *n* (*ZOOL*) femmina; (*pej: woman*) donna, femmina ♦ *adj* (*BIOL, ELEC*) femmina *inv*; (*sex, character*) femminile; (*vote etc*) di donne

feminine ['femɪnɪn] *adj* femminile

feminist ['femɪnɪst] *n* femminista *m/f*

fence [fens] *n* recinto ♦ *vt* (*also*: **~ in**) recingere ♦ *vi* (*SPORT*) tirare di scherma; **fencing** *n* (*SPORT*) scherma

fend [fend] *vi*: **to ~ for o.s.** arrangiarsi; **~ off** *vt* (*attack, questions*) respingere, difendersi da

fender ['fendə*] *n* parafuoco; (*on boat*) parabordo; (*US*) parafango; paraurti *m inv*

ferment [vb fə'mɛnt, n 'fɛːmɛnt] vi fermentare ♦ n (fig) agitazione f, eccitazione f

fern [fɜːn] n felce f

ferocious [fə'rəʊʃəs] adj feroce

ferret ['fɛrɪt] n furetto; ~ **out** vt (information) scovare

ferry ['fɛrɪ] n (small) traghetto; (large: also: ~**boat**) nave f traghetto inv ♦ vt traghettare

fertile ['fɜːtaɪl] adj fertile; (BIOL) fecondo(a); **fertilizer** ['fɜːtɪlaɪzə*] n fertilizzante m

fester ['fɛstə*] vi suppurare

festival ['fɛstɪvəl] n (REL) festa; (ART, MUS) festival m inv

festive ['fɛstɪv] adj di festa; **the ~ season** (BRIT: Christmas) il periodo delle feste

festivities [fɛs'tɪvɪtɪz] npl festeggiamenti mpl

festoon [fɛs'tuːn] vt: **to ~ with** ornare di

fetch [fɛtʃ] vt andare a prendere; (sell for) essere venduto(a) per

fête [feɪt] n festa

fetus ['fiːtəs] (US) n = **foetus**

feud [fjuːd] n contesa, lotta

feudal ['fjuːdl] adj feudale

fever ['fiːvə*] n febbre f; ~**ish** adj febbrile

few [fjuː] adj pochi(e); **a ~** adj qualche inv ♦ pron alcuni(e); ~**er** adj meno inv; meno numerosi(e); ~**est** adj il minor numero di

fiancé [fɪ'ɑːŋseɪ] n fidanzato; ~**e** n fidanzata

fib [fɪb] n piccola bugia

fibre ['faɪbə*] (US **fiber**) n fibra; F~**glass** ® n fibra di vetro

fickle ['fɪkl] adj incostante, capriccioso(a)

fiction ['fɪkʃən] n narrativa, romanzi mpl; (sth made up) finzione f; ~**al** adj immaginario(a)

fictitious [fɪk'tɪʃəs] adj fittizio(a)

fiddle ['fɪdl] n (MUS) violino; (cheating) imbroglio; truffa ♦ vt (BRIT: accounts) falsificare, falsare; ~ **with** vt fus gingillarsi con

fidelity [fɪ'dɛlɪtɪ] n fedeltà; (accuracy) esattezza

fidget ['fɪdʒɪt] vi agitarsi

field [fiːld] n campo; ~ **marshal** n feldmaresciallo; ~**work** n ricerche fpl esterne

fiend [fiːnd] n demonio

fierce [fɪəs] adj (animal, person, fighting) feroce; (loyalty) assoluto(a); (wind) furioso(a); (heat) intenso(a)

fiery ['faɪərɪ] adj ardente; infocato(a)

fifteen [fɪf'tiːn] num quindici

fifth [fɪfθ] num quinto(a)

fifty ['fɪftɪ] num cinquanta; ~-~ adj: **a ~-~ chance** una possibilità su due ♦ adv fifty-fifty, metà per ciascuno

fig [fɪg] n fico

fight [faɪt] (pt, pp **fought**) n zuffa, rissa; (MIL) battaglia, combattimento; (against cancer etc) lotta ♦ vt (person) azzuffarsi con; (enemy: also: MIL) combattere; (cancer, alcoholism, emotion) lottare contro, combattere; (election) partecipare a ♦ vi combattere; ~**er** n combattente m; (plane) aeroplano da caccia; ~**ing** n combattimento

figment ['fɪgmənt] n: **a ~ of the imagination** un parto della fantasia

figurative ['fɪgjʊrətɪv] adj figurato(a)

figure ['fɪgə*] n figura; (number, cipher) cifra ♦ vt (think: esp US) pensare ♦ vi (appear) figurare; ~ **out** vt riuscire a capire; calcolare; ~**head** n (NAUT) polena; (pej) prestanome m/f inv; ~ **of speech** n figura retorica

file [faɪl] n (tool) lima; (dossier) incartamento; (folder) cartellina; (COMPUT) archivio; (row) fila ♦ vt (nails, wood) limare; (papers) archiviare; (LAW: claim) presentare; passare agli atti; ~ **in/out** vi entrare/uscire in fila

filing cabinet ['faɪlɪŋ-] n casellario

fill [fɪl] vt riempire; (job) coprire ♦ n: **to eat one's ~** mangiare a sazietà; ~ **in** vt (hole) riempire; (form) compilare; ~ **up** vt riempire ♦ vi (AUT) fare il pieno

fillet ['fɪlɪt] n filetto; ~ **steak** n bistecca di filetto

filling ['fɪlɪŋ] n (CULIN) impasto, ripieno; (for tooth) otturazione f; ~ **station** n stazione f di rifornimento

film [fɪlm] n (CINEMA) film m inv; (PHOT) pellicola; (of powder, liquid) sottile strato ♦ vt, vi girare; ~ **star** n divo/a dello schermo

filter ['fɪltə*] n filtro ♦ vt filtrare; ~ **lane** (BRIT) n (AUT) corsia di svincolo; ~**-tipped** adj con filtro

filth [fɪlθ] n sporcizia; ~**y** adj lordo(a), sozzo(a); (language) osceno(a)

fin [fɪn] n (of fish) pinna

final ['faɪnl] adj finale, ultimo(a); definitivo(a) ♦ n (SPORT) finale f; ~**s** npl (SCOL) esami mpl finali

finale [fɪ'nɑːlɪ] n finale m

finalize ['faɪnəlaɪz] vt mettere a punto

finally ['faɪnəlɪ] adv (lastly) alla fine; (eventually) finalmente

finance [faɪ'næns] n finanza; (capital) capitale m ♦ vt finanziare; ~**s** npl (funds) finanze fpl

financial [faɪ'nænʃəl] adj finanziario(a)

financier [faɪ'nænsɪə*] n finanziatore m

find [faɪnd] (pt, pp found) vt trovare; (lost object) ritrovare ♦ n trovata, scoperta; **to ~ sb guilty** (LAW) giudicare qn colpevole; ~ **out** vt (truth, secret) scoprire; (person) cogliere in fallo; **to ~ out about** informarsi su; (by chance) scoprire; ~**ings** npl (LAW) sentenza, conclusioni fpl; (of report) conclusioni

fine [faɪn] adj bello(a); ottimo(a); (thin, subtle) fine ♦ adv (well) molto bene ♦ n (LAW) multa ♦ vt (LAW) multare; **to be ~** (person) stare bene; (weather) far bello; ~ **arts** npl belle arti fpl

finery ['faɪnərɪ] n abiti mpl eleganti

finger ['fɪŋgə*] n dito ♦ vt toccare, tastare; **little/index ~** mignolo/(dito) indice m; ~**nail** n unghia; ~**print** n impronta digitale; ~**tip** n punta del dito

finish ['fɪnɪʃ] n fine f; (polish etc) finitura ♦ vt, vi finire; **to ~ doing sth** finire di fare qc; **to ~ third** arrivare terzo(a); ~ **off** vt compiere; (kill) uccidere; ~ **up** vi, vt finire; ~**ing line** n linea d'arrivo

finite ['faɪnaɪt] adj limitato(a); (verb) finito(a)

Finland ['fɪnlənd] n Finlandia

Finn [fɪn] n finlandese m/f; ~**ish** adj finlandese ♦ n (LING) finlandese m

fir [fəː*] n abete m

fire [faɪə*] n fuoco; (destructive) incendio; (gas ~, electric ~) stufa ♦ vt (gun) far fuoco con; (arrow) sparare; (fig) infiammare; (inf: dismiss) licenziare ♦ vi sparare, far fuoco; **on ~** in fiamme; ~ **alarm** n allarme m d'incendio; ~**arm** n arma da fuoco; ~ **brigade** (US ~ **department**) n (corpo dei) pompieri mpl; ~ **engine** n autopompa; ~ **escape** n scala di sicurezza; ~ **extinguisher** n estintore m; ~**guard** n parafuoco; ~**man** (irreg) n pompiere m; ~**place** n focolare m; ~**side** n angolo del focolare; ~ **station** n caserma dei pompieri; ~**wood** n legna; ~**works** npl fuochi mpl d'artificio

firing squad ['faɪərɪŋ-] n plotone m d'esecuzione

firm [fəːm] adj fermo(a) ♦ n ditta, azienda; ~**ly** adv fermamente

first [fəːst] adj primo(a) ♦ adv (before others) il primo, la prima; (before other things) per primo; (when listing reasons etc) per prima cosa ♦ n (person: in race) primo/a; (BRIT: SCOL) laurea con lode; (AUT) prima; **at ~** dapprima, all'inizio; ~ **of all** prima di tutto; ~ **aid** n pronto soccorso; ~**-aid kit** n cassetta pronto soccorso; ~**-class** adj di prima classe; ~ **floor** n il primo piano (BRIT); il pianterreno (US); ~**-hand** adj di prima mano; ~ **lady** (US) n moglie f del presidente; ~**ly** adv in primo luogo; ~ **name** n prenome m; ~**-rate** adj di prima qualità, ottimo(a)

fish [fɪʃ] n inv pesce m ♦ vt (river, area) pescare in ♦ vi pescare; **to go ~ing** andare a pesca; ~**erman** n pescatore m; ~ **farm** n vivaio; ~ **fingers** (BRIT) npl bastoncini mpl di pesce (surgelati); ~**ing boat** n barca da pesca; ~**ing line** n lenza; ~**ing rod** n canna da pesca; ~**monger** n pescivendolo; ~**monger's (shop)** n pescheria; ~ **sticks** (US) npl = ~ **fingers**; ~**y** (inf) adj (tale, story) sospetto(a)

fist [fɪst] n pugno

fit [fɪt] *adj* (MED, SPORT) in forma; (*proper*) adatto(a), appropriato(a); conveniente ♦ *vt* (*subj: clothes*) stare bene a; (*put in, attach*) mettere; installare; (*equip*) fornire, equipaggiare ♦ *vi* (*clothes*) stare bene; (*parts*) andare bene, adattarsi; (*in space, gap*) entrare ♦ *n* (MED) accesso, attacco; ~ **to** in grado di; ~ **for** adatto(a) a; degno(a) di; **a ~ of anger** un accesso d'ira; **this dress is a good ~** questo vestito sta bene; **by ~s and starts** a sbalzi; ~ **in** *vi* accordarsi; adattarsi; ~**ful** *adj* saltuario(a); ~**ness** *n* forma fisica; ~**ted carpet** *n* moquette *f*; ~**ted kitchen** *n* cucina componibile; ~**ter** *n* aggiustatore *m or* montatore *m* meccanico; ~**ting** *adj* appropriato(a) ♦ *n* (*of dress*) prova; (*of piece of equipment*) montaggio, aggiustaggio; ~**tings** *npl* (*in building*) impianti *mpl*; ~**ting room** *n* camerino

five [faɪv] *num* cinque; ~**r** (*inf*) *n* (BRIT) biglietto da cinque sterline; (US) biglietto da cinque dollari

fix [fɪks] *vt* fissare; (*mend*) riparare; (*meal, drink*) preparare ♦ *n*: **to be in a ~** essere nei guai; ~ **up** *vt* (*meeting*) fissare; **to ~ sb up with sth** procurare qc a qn; ~**ation** *n* fissazione *f*; ~**ed** [fɪkst] *adj* fisso(a); ~**ture** ['fɪkstʃə*] *n* impianto (fisso); (SPORT) incontro (del calendario sportivo)

fizzy ['fɪzɪ] *adj* frizzante; gassato(a)

flabbergasted ['flæbəɡɑːstɪd] *adj* sbalordito(a)

flabby ['flæbɪ] *adj* flaccido(a)

flag [flæɡ] *n* bandiera; (*also*: ~**stone**) pietra da lastricare ♦ *vi* stancarsi; affievolirsi; ~ **down** *vt* fare segno (di fermarsi) a

flagpole ['flæɡpəʊl] *n* albero

flagship ['flæɡʃɪp] *n* nave *f* ammiraglia

flair [flɛə*] *n* (*for business etc*) fiuto; (*for languages etc*) facilità; (*style*) stile *m*

flak [flæk] *n* (MIL) fuoco d'artiglieria; (*inf: criticism*) critiche *fpl*

flake [fleɪk] *n* (*of rust, paint*) scaglia; (*of snow, soap powder*) fiocco ♦ *vi* (*also*: ~ **off**) sfaldarsi

flamboyant [flæm'bɔɪənt] *adj* sgargiante

flame [fleɪm] *n* fiamma

flamingo [flə'mɪŋɡəʊ] *n* fenicottero, fiammingo

flammable ['flæməbl] *adj* infiammabile

flan [flæn] (BRIT) *n* flan *m inv*

flank [flæŋk] *n* fianco ♦ *vt* fiancheggiare

flannel ['flænl] *n* (BRIT: *also*: **face ~**) guanto di spugna; (*fabric*) flanella

flap [flæp] *n* (*of pocket*) patta; (*of envelope*) lembo ♦ *vt* (*wings*) battere ♦ *vi* (*sail, flag*) sbattere; (*inf: also*: **be in a ~**) essere in agitazione

flare [flɛə*] *n* razzo; (*in skirt etc*) svasatura; ~ **up** *vi* andare in fiamme; (*fig: person*) infiammarsi di rabbia; (*: revolt*) scoppiare

flash [flæʃ] *n* vampata; (*also*: **news ~**) notizia *f* lampo *inv*; (PHOT) flash *m inv* ♦ *vt* accendere e spegnere; (*send: message*) trasmettere; (*: look, smile*) lanciare ♦ *vi* brillare; (*light on ambulance, eyes etc*) lampeggiare; **in a ~** in un lampo; **to ~ one's headlights** lampeggiare; **he ~ed by** *or* **past** ci passò davanti come un lampo; ~**bulb** *n* cubo *m* flash *inv*; ~**cube** *n* flash *m inv*; ~**light** *n* lampadina tascabile

flashy ['flæʃɪ] (*pej*) *adj* vistoso(a)

flask [flɑːsk] *n* fiasco; (*also*: **vacuum ~**) thermos ® *m inv*

flat [flæt] *adj* piatto(a); (*tyre*) sgonfio(a), a terra; (*battery*) scarico(a); (*beer*) svampito(a); (*denial*) netto(a); (MUS) bemolle *inv*; (*: voice*) stonato(a); (*rate, fee*) unico(a) ♦ *n* (BRIT: *rooms*) appartamento; (AUT) pneumatico sgonfio; (MUS) bemolle *m*; **to work ~ out** lavorare a più non posso; ~**ly** *adv* categoricamente; ~**ten** *vt* (*also*: ~**ten out**) appiattire; (*building, city*) spianare

flatter ['flætə*] *vt* lusingare; ~**ing** *adj* lusinghiero(a); (*dress*) che dona; ~**y** *n* adulazione *f*

flaunt [flɔːnt] *vt* fare mostra di

flavour ['fleɪvə*] (US **flavor**) *n* gusto ♦ *vt* insaporire, aggiungere sapore a; **strawberry-~ed** al gusto di fragola; ~**ing** *n* essenza (artificiale)

flaw [flɔː] *n* difetto

flax [flæks] *n* lino

flea [fliː] n pulce f

fleck [flɛk] n (mark) macchiolina; (pattern) screziatura

fled [flɛd] pt, pp of **flee**

flee [fliː] (pt, pp **fled**) vt fuggire da ♦ vi fuggire, scappare

fleece [fliːs] n vello ♦ vt (inf) pelare

fleet [fliːt] n flotta; (of lorries etc) convoglio, parco

fleeting ['fliːtɪŋ] adj fugace, fuggitivo(a); (visit) volante

Flemish ['flɛmɪʃ] adj fiammingo(a)

flesh [flɛʃ] n carne f; (of fruit) polpa; ~ **wound** n ferita superficiale

flew [fluː] pt of **fly**

flex [flɛks] n filo (flessibile) ♦ vt flettere; (muscles) contrarre; ~**ible** adj flessibile

flick [flɪk] n colpetto; scarto ♦ vt dare un colpetto a; ~ **through** vt fus sfogliare

flicker ['flɪkə*] vi tremolare

flier ['flaɪə*] n aviatore m

flight [flaɪt] n volo; (escape) fuga; (also: ~ **of steps**) scalinata; ~ **attendant** (US) n steward m inv, hostess f inv; ~ **deck** n (AVIAT) cabina di controllo; (NAUT) ponte m di comando

flimsy ['flɪmzɪ] adj (shoes, clothes) leggero(a); (building) poco solido(a); (excuse) che non regge

flinch [flɪntʃ] vi ritirarsi; to ~ **from** tirarsi indietro di fronte a

fling [flɪŋ] (pt, pp **flung**) vt lanciare, gettare

flint [flɪnt] n selce f; (in lighter) pietrina

flip [flɪp] vt (switch) far scattare; (coin) lanciare in aria

flippant ['flɪpənt] adj senza rispetto, irriverente

flipper ['flɪpə*] n pinna

flirt [fləːt] vi flirtare ♦ n civetta

float [fləut] n galleggiante m; (in procession) carro; (money) somma ♦ vi galleggiare

flock [flɔk] n (of sheep, REL) gregge m; (of birds) stormo ♦ vi: to ~ **to** accorrere in massa

flog [flɔg] vt flagellare

flood [flʌd] n alluvione m; (of letters etc) marea ♦ vt allagare; (subj: people) invadere ♦ vi (place) allagarsi; (people): to ~ **into** riversarsi in; ~**ing** n inondazione f; ~**light** n riflettore m ♦ vt illuminare a giorno

floor [flɔː*] n pavimento; (storey) piano; (of sea, valley) fondo ♦ vt (subj: blow) atterrare; (: question) ridurre al silenzio; **ground** ~, (US) **first** ~ pianterreno; **first** ~, (US) **second** ~ primo piano; ~**board** n tavellone m di legno; ~ **show** n spettacolo di varietà

flop [flɔp] n fiasco ♦ vi far fiasco; (fall) lasciarsi cadere

floppy ['flɔpɪ] adj floscio(a), molle; ~ **(disk)** n (COMPUT) floppy disk m inv

Florence ['flɔrəns] n Firenze f; **Florentine** ['flɔrəntaɪn] adj fiorentino(a)

florid ['flɔrɪd] adj (complexion) florido(a); (style) fiorito(a)

florist ['flɔrɪst] n fioraio/a

flounder ['flaundə*] vi annaspare ♦ n (ZOOL) passera di mare

flour ['flauə*] n farina

flourish ['flʌrɪʃ] vi fiorire ♦ n (bold gesture): **with a** ~ con ostentazione; ~**ing** adj florido(a)

flout [flaut] vt (order) contravvenire a

flow [fləu] n flusso; circolazione f ♦ vi fluire; (traffic, blood in veins) circolare; (hair) scendere; ~ **chart** n schema m di flusso

flower ['flauə*] n fiore m ♦ vi fiorire; ~ **bed** n aiuola; ~**pot** n vaso da fiori; ~**y** adj (perfume) di fiori; (pattern) a fiori; (speech) fiorito(a)

flown [fləun] pp of **fly**

flu [fluː] n influenza

fluctuate ['flʌktjueɪt] vi fluttuare, oscillare

fluent ['fluːənt] adj (speech) facile, sciolto(a); corrente; **he speaks ~ Italian, he's ~ in Italian** parla l'italiano correntemente

fluff [flʌf] n lanugine f; ~**y** adj lanuginoso(a); (toy) di peluche

fluid ['fluːɪd] adj fluido(a) ♦ n fluido

fluke [fluːk] n (inf) colpo di fortuna

flung [flʌŋ] pt, pp of **fling**

fluoride ['fluəraɪd] n fluoruro; ~ **toothpaste** dentifricio al fluoro

flurry ['flʌrɪ] n (of snow) tempesta; **a ~ of**

activity uno scoppio di attività

flush [flʌʃ] n rossore m; (fig: of youth, beauty etc) rigoglio, pieno vigore ♦ vt ripulire con un getto d'acqua ♦ vi arrossire ♦ adj: ~ **with** a livello di, pari a; **to ~ the toilet** tirare l'acqua; ~**ed** adj tutto(a) rosso(a)

flustered ['flʌstəd] adj sconvolto(a)

flute [fluːt] n flauto

flutter ['flʌtə*] n agitazione f; (of wings) battito ♦ vi (bird) battere le ali

flux [flʌks] n: **in a state of ~** in continuo mutamento

fly [flaɪ] (pt **flew**, pp **flown**) n (insect) mosca; (on trousers: also: **flies**) chiusura ♦ vt pilotare; (passengers, cargo) trasportare (in aereo); (distances) percorrere ♦ vi volare; (escape) fuggire; (flag) sventolare; ~ **away** or **off** vi volare via; ~**ing** n (activity) aviazione f; (action) volo ♦ adj: ~ **visit** visita volante; **with ~ing colours** con risultati brillanti; ~**ing saucer** n disco volante; ~**ing start** n: **to get off to a ~ing start** partire come un razzo; ~**over** (BRIT) n (bridge) cavalcavia m inv; ~**sheet** n (for tent) sopratetto

foal [fəul] n puledro

foam [fəum] n schiuma; (also: ~ **rubber**) gommapiuma ® ♦ vi schiumare; (soapy water) fare la schiuma

fob [fɒb] vt: **to ~ sb off with** rifilare a qn

focus ['fəukəs] (pl ~**es**) n fuoco; (of interest) centro ♦ vt (field glasses etc) mettere a fuoco ♦ vi: **to ~ on** (with camera) mettere a fuoco; (person) fissare lo sguardo su; **in ~** a fuoco; **out of ~** sfocato(a)

fodder ['fɒdə*] n foraggio

foe [fəu] n nemico

foetus ['fiːtəs] (US **fetus**) n feto

fog [fɒg] n nebbia; ~**gy** adj: **it's ~gy** c'è nebbia; ~ **lamp** (US ~ **light**) n (AUT) faro m antinebbia inv

foil [fɔɪl] vt confondere, frustrare ♦ n lamina di metallo; (kitchen ~) foglio di alluminio; (FENCING) fioretto; **to act as a ~ to** (fig) far risaltare

fold [fəuld] n (bend, crease) piega; (AGR) ovile m; (fig) gregge m ♦ vt piegare; (arms)

incrociare; ~ **up** vi (map, bed, table) piegarsi; (business) crollare ♦ vt (map etc) piegare, ripiegare; ~**er** n (for papers) cartella; cartellina; ~**ing** adj (chair, bed) pieghevole

foliage ['fəulɪdʒ] n fogliame m

folk [fəuk] npl gente f ♦ adj popolare; ~**s** npl (family) famiglia; ~**lore** ['fəuklɔ:*] n folclore m; ~ **song** n canto popolare

follow ['fɒləu] vt seguire ♦ vi seguire; (result) conseguire, risultare; **to ~ suit** fare lo stesso; ~ **up** vt (letter, offer) fare seguito a; (case) seguire; ~**er** n seguace m/f, discepolo/a; ~**ing** adj seguente ♦ n seguito, discepoli mpl; ~**-on call** n chiamata successiva

folly ['fɒlɪ] n pazzia, follia

fond [fɒnd] adj (memory, look) tenero(a), affettuoso(a); **to be ~ of sb** volere bene a qn; **he's ~ of walking** gli piace fare camminate

fondle ['fɒndl] vt accarezzare

font [fɒnt] n (in church) fonte m battesimale; (TYP) caratteri mpl

food [fuːd] n cibo; ~ **mixer** n frullatore m; ~ **poisoning** n intossicazione f; ~ **processor** n tritatutto m inv elettrico; ~**stuffs** npl generi fpl alimentari

fool [fuːl] n sciocco/a; (CULIN) frullato ♦ vt ingannare ♦ vi (gen: ~ **around**) fare lo sciocco; ~**hardy** adj avventato(a); ~**ish** adj scemo(a), stupido(a); imprudente; ~**proof** adj (plan etc) sicurissimo(a)

foot [fut] (pl **feet**) n piede m; (measure) piede (= 304 mm; 12 inches); (of animal) zampa ♦ vt (bill) pagare; **on ~** a piedi; ~**age** n (CINEMA: length) ≈ metraggio; (: material) sequenza; ~**ball** n pallone m; (sport: BRIT) calcio; (: US) football m americano; ~**ball player** n (BRIT: also: ~**baller**) calciatore m; (US) giocatore m di football americano; ~**brake** n freno a pedale; ~**bridge** n passerella; ~**hills** npl contrafforti fpl; ~**hold** n punto d'appoggio; ~**ing** n (fig) posizione f; **to lose one's ~ing** mettere un piede in fallo; ~**note** n nota (a piè di pagina); ~**path** n sentiero; (*in street*) marciapiede *m*; **~print** *n* orma, impronta; **~step** *n* passo; (*~print*) orma, impronta; **~wear** *n* calzatura

KEYWORD

for [fɔː*] *prep* **1** (*indicating destination, intention, purpose*) per; **the train ~ London** il treno per Londra; **he went ~ the paper** è andato a prendere il giornale; **it's time ~ lunch** è ora di pranzo; **what's it ~?** a che serve?; **what ~?** (*why*) perché?

2 (*on behalf of, representing*) per; **to work ~ sb/sth** lavorare per qn/qc; **I'll ask him ~ you** glielo chiederò a nome tuo; **G ~ George** G come George

3 (*because of*) per, a causa di; **~ this reason** per questo motivo

4 (*with regard to*) per; **it's cold ~ July** è freddo per luglio; **~ everyone who voted yes, 50 voted no** per ogni voto a favore ce n'erano 50 contro

5 (*in exchange for*) per; **I sold it ~ £5** l'ho venduto per 5 sterline

6 (*in favour of*) per, a favore di; **are you ~ or against us?** è con noi o contro di noi?; **I'm all ~ it** sono completamente a favore

7 (*referring to distance, time*) per; **there are roadworks ~ 5 km** ci sono lavori in corso per 5 km; **he was away ~ 2 years** è stato via per 2 anni; **she will be away ~ a month** starà via un mese; **it hasn't rained ~ 3 weeks** non piove da 3 settimane; **can you do it ~ tomorrow?** può farlo per domani?

8 (*with infinitive clauses*): **it is not ~ me to decide** non sta a me decidere; **it would be best ~ you to leave** sarebbe meglio che lei se ne andasse; **there is still time ~ you to do it** ha ancora tempo per farlo; **~ this to be possible ...** perché ciò sia possibile ...

9 (*in spite of*) nonostante; **~ all his complaints, he's very fond of her** nonostante tutte le sue lamentele, le vuole molto bene

♦ *conj* (*since, as: rather formal*) dal momento che, poiché

forage ['fɔrɪdʒ] *vi*: **to ~ (for)** andare in cerca (di)

foray ['fɔreɪ] *n* incursione *f*

forbid [fə'bɪd] (*pt* **forbad(e)**, *pp* **forbidden**) *vt* vietare, interdire; **to ~ sb to do sth** proibire a qn di fare qc; **~ding** *adj* minaccioso(a)

force [fɔːs] *n* forza ♦ *vt* forzare; **the F~s** (*BRIT*) *npl* le forze armate; **to ~ o.s. to do** costringersi a fare; **in ~** (*in large numbers*) in gran numero; (*law*) in vigore; **~d** *adj* forzato(a); **~-feed** *vt* (*animal, prisoner*) sottoporre ad alimentazione forzata; **~ful** *adj* forte, vigoroso(a)

forceps ['fɔːsɛps] *npl* forcipe *m*

forcibly ['fɔːsəblɪ] *adv* con la forza; (*vigorously*) vigorosamente

ford [fɔːd] *n* guado

fore [fɔː*] *n*: **to come to the ~** mettersi in evidenza

forearm ['fɔːrɑːm] *n* avambraccio

foreboding [fɔː'bəudɪŋ] *n* cattivo presagio

forecast ['fɔːkɑːst] (*irreg: like* **cast**) *n* previsione *f* ♦ *vt* prevedere

forecourt ['fɔːkɔːt] *n* (*of garage*) corte *f* esterna

forefinger ['fɔːfɪŋɡə*] *n* (*dito*) indice *m*

forefront ['fɔːfrʌnt] *n*: **in the ~ of** all'avanguardia in

forego [fɔː'ɡəu] (*irreg: like* **go**) *vt* rinunciare a

foregone [fɔː'ɡɔn] *pp of* **forego** ♦ *adj*: **it's a ~ conclusion** è una conclusione scontata

foreground ['fɔːɡraund] *n* primo piano

forehead ['fɔrɪd] *n* fronte *f*

foreign ['fɔrɪn] *adj* straniero(a); (*trade*) estero(a); (*object, matter*) estraneo(a); **~er** *n* straniero/a; **~ exchange** *n* cambio con l'estero; (*currency*) valuta estera; **F~ Office** (*BRIT*) *n* Ministero degli Esteri; **F~ Secretary** (*BRIT*) *n* ministro degli Affari esteri

foreleg ['fɔːlɛɡ] *n* zampa anteriore

foreman ['fɔːmən] (*irreg*) *n* caposquadra *m*

foremost ['fɔːməust] *adj* principale; più in vista ♦ *adv*: **first and ~** innanzitutto

forensic [fə'rɛnsɪk] *adj*: ~ **medicine** medicina legale

forerunner ['fɔ:rʌnə*] *n* precursore *m*

foresaw [fɔ:'sɔ:] *pt of* **foresee**

foresee [fɔ:'si:] (*irreg: like* **see**) *vt* prevedere; **~able** *adj* prevedibile; **foreseen** *pp of* **foresee**

foreshadow [fɔ:'ʃædəu] *vt* presagire, far prevedere

foresight ['fɔ:saɪt] *n* previdenza

forest ['fɔrɪst] *n* foresta

forestry ['fɔrɪstrɪ] *n* silvicoltura

foretaste ['fɔ:teɪst] *n* pregustazione *f*

foretell [fɔ:'tɛl] (*irreg: like* **tell**) *vt* predire; **foretold** [fɔ:'təuld] *pt, pp of* **foretell**

forever [fə'rɛvə*] *adv* per sempre; (*endlessly*) sempre, di continuo

foreword ['fɔ:wə:d] *n* prefazione *f*

forfeit ['fɔ:fɪt] *vt* perdere; (*one's happiness, health*) giocarsi

forgave [fə'geɪv] *pt of* **forgive**

forge [fɔdʒ] *n* fucina ♦ *vt* (*signature, money*) contraffare, falsificare; (*wrought iron*) fucinare, foggiare; ~ **ahead** *vi* tirare avanti; **~ry** *n* falso; (*activity*) contraffazione *f*

forget [fə'gɛt] (*pt* **forgot**, *pp* **forgotten**) *vt, vi* dimenticare; **~ful** *adj* di corta memoria; **~ful of** dimentico(a) di; **~-me-not** *n* nontiscordardimé *m inv*

forgive [fə'gɪv] (*pt* **forgave**, *pp* **forgiven**) *vt* perdonare; **to ~ sb for sth** perdonare qc a qn; **~ness** *n* perdono

forgo [fɔ:'gəu] = **forego**

forgot [fə'gɔt] *pt of* **forget**

forgotten [fə'gɔtn] *pp of* **forget**

fork [fɔ:k] *n* (*for eating*) forchetta; (*for gardening*) forca; (*of roads, rivers, railways*) biforcazione *f* ♦ *vi* (*road etc*) biforcarsi; ~ **out** (*inf*) *vt* (*pay*) sborsare; **~-lift truck** *n* carrello elevatore

forlorn [fə'lɔ:n] *adj* (*person*) sconsolato(a); (*place*) abbandonato(a); (*attempt*) disperato(a); (*hope*) vano(a)

form [fɔ:m] *n* forma; (*SCOL*) classe *f*; (*questionnaire*) scheda ♦ *vt* formare; **in top ~** in gran forma

formal ['fɔ:məl] *adj* formale; (*gardens*) simmetrico(a), regolare; **~ly** *adv* formalmente

format ['fɔ:mæt] *n* formato ♦ *vt* (*COMPUT*) formattare

formation [fɔ:'meɪʃən] *n* formazione *f*

formative ['fɔ:mətɪv] *adj*: ~ **years** anni *mpl* formativi

former ['fɔ:mə*] *adj* vecchio(a) (*before n*), ex *inv* (*before n*); **the ~ ... the latter** quello ... questo; **~ly** *adv* in passato

formula ['fɔ:mjulə] *n* formula

forsake [fə'seɪk] (*pt* **forsook**, *pp* **forsaken**) *vt* abbandonare

fort [fɔ:t] *n* forte *m*

forth [fɔ:θ] *adv* in avanti; **back and ~** avanti e indietro; **and so ~** e così via; **~coming** *adj* (*event*) prossimo(a); (*help*) disponibile; (*character*) aperto(a), comunicativo(a); **~right** *adj* franco(a), schietto(a); **~with** *adv* immediatamente, subito

fortify ['fɔ:tɪfaɪ] *vt* (*city*) fortificare; (*person*) armare

fortitude ['fɔ:tɪtju:d] *n* forza d'animo

fortnight ['fɔ:tnaɪt] (*BRIT*) *n* quindici giorni *mpl*, due settimane *fpl*; **~ly** *adj* bimensile ♦ *adv* ogni quindici giorni

fortress ['fɔ:trɪs] *n* fortezza, rocca

fortunate ['fɔ:tʃənɪt] *adj* fortunato(a); **it is ~ that** è una fortuna che; **~ly** *adv* fortunatamente

fortune ['fɔ:tʃən] *n* fortuna; **~-teller** *n* indovino/a

forty ['fɔ:tɪ] *num* quaranta

forum ['fɔ:rəm] *n* foro

forward ['fɔ:wəd] *adj* (*ahead of schedule*) in anticipo; (*movement, position*) in avanti; (*not shy*) aperto(a); diretto(a) ♦ *n* (*SPORT*) avanti *m inv* ♦ *vt* (*letter*) inoltrare; (*parcel, goods*) spedire; (*career, plans*) promuovere, appoggiare; **to move ~** avanzare; **~(s)** *adv* avanti

fossil ['fɔsl] *adj* fossile ♦ *n* fossile *m*

foster ['fɔstə*] *vt* incoraggiare, nutrire; (*child*) avere in affidamento; ~ **child** *n* bambino(a) preso(a) in affidamento

fought [fɔ:t] *pt, pp of* **fight**

foul [faul] *adj* (*smell, food, temper etc*) cattivo(a); (*weather*) brutto(a); (*language*) osceno(a) ♦ *n* (*SPORT*) fallo ♦ *vt* sporcare; ~ **play** *n* (*LAW*): **the police suspect ~ play** la polizia sospetta un atto criminale

found [faund] *pt, pp of* **find** ♦ *vt* (*establish*) fondare; **~ation** [-'deɪʃən] *n* (*act*) fondazione *f*; (*base*) base *f*; (*also:* **~ation cream**) fondo tinta; **~ations** *npl* (*of building*) fondamenta *fpl*

founder ['faundə*] *n* fondatore/trice ♦ *vi* affondare

foundry ['faundrɪ] *n* fonderia

fountain ['fauntɪn] *n* fontana; ~ **pen** *n* penna stilografica

four [fɔː*] *num* quattro; **on all ~s** a carponi; **~-poster** *n* (*also:* **~-poster bed**) letto a quattro colonne; **~teen** *num* quattordici; **~th** *num* quarto(a)

fowl [faul] *n* pollame *m*; volatile *m*

fox [fɔks] *n* volpe *f* ♦ *vt* confondere

foyer ['fɔɪeɪ] *n* atrio; (*THEATRE*) ridotto

fraction ['frækʃən] *n* frazione *f*

fracture ['fræktʃə*] *n* frattura

fragile ['frædʒaɪl] *adj* fragile

fragment ['frægmənt] *n* frammento

fragrant ['freɪgrənt] *adj* fragrante, profumato(a)

frail [freɪl] *adj* debole, delicato(a)

frame [freɪm] *n* (*of building*) armatura; (*of human, animal*) ossatura, corpo; (*of picture*) cornice *f*; (*of door, window*) telaio; (*of spectacles: also:* **~s**) montatura ♦ *vt* (*picture*) incorniciare; ~ **of mind** *n* stato d'animo; **~work** *n* struttura

France [frɑːns] *n* Francia

franchise ['fræntʃaɪz] *n* (*POL*) diritto di voto; (*COMM*) concessione *f*

frank [fræŋk] *adj* franco(a), aperto(a) ♦ *vt* (*letter*) affrancare; **~ly** *adv* francamente, sinceramente

frantic ['fræntɪk] *adj* frenetico(a)

fraternity [frə'tɜːnɪtɪ] *n* (*club*) associazione *f*; (*spirit*) fratellanza

fraud [frɔːd] *n* truffa; (*LAW*) frode *f*; (*person*) impostore/a

fraught [frɔːt] *adj*: ~ **with** pieno(a) di, intriso(a) da

fray [freɪ] *vt* logorare ♦ *vi* logorarsi

freak [friːk] *n* fenomeno, mostro

freckle ['frekl] *n* lentiggine *f*

free [friː] *adj* libero(a); (*gratis*) gratuito(a) ♦ *vt* (*prisoner, jammed person*) liberare; (*jammed object*) districare; ~ (**of charge**), **for ~** gratuitamente; **~dom** ['friːdəm] *n* libertà; **F~fone** ® *n* numero verde; **~-for-all** *n* parapiglia *m* generale; ~ **gift** *n* regalo, omaggio; **~hold** *n* proprietà assoluta; ~ **kick** *n* calcio libero; **~lance** *adj* indipendente; **~ly** *adv* liberamente; (*liberally*) liberalmente; **F~mason** *n* massone *m*; **F~post** ® *n* affrancatura a carico del destinatario; **~-range** *adj* (*hen*) ruspante; (*eggs*) di gallina ruspante; **~style** *n* (*SPORT*) stile *m* libero; ~ **trade** *n* libero scambio; **~way** (*US*) *n* superstrada; ~ **will** *n* libero arbitrio; **of one's own ~ will** di spontanea volontà

freeze [friːz] (*pt* **froze**, *pp* **frozen**) *vi* gelare ♦ *vt* gelare; (*food*) congelare; (*prices, salaries*) bloccare ♦ *n* gelo; blocco; **~-dried** *adj* liofilizzato(a); **~r** *n* congelatore *m*

freezing ['friːzɪŋ] *adj* (*wind, weather*) gelido(a); ~ **point** *n* punto di congelamento; **3 degrees below ~ point** 3 gradi sotto zero

freight [freɪt] *n* (*goods*) merce *f*, merci *fpl*; (*money charged*) spese *fpl* di trasporto; ~ **train** (*US*) *n* treno *m* merci *inv*

French [frentʃ] *adj* francese ♦ *n* (*LING*) francese *m*; **the ~** *npl* i Francesi; ~ **bean** *n* fagiolino; ~ **fried potatoes** (*US* **~ fries**) *npl* patate *fpl* fritte; **~man** (*irreg*) *n* francese *m*; ~ **window** *n* portafinestra; **~woman** (*irreg*) *n* francese *f*

frenzy ['frenzɪ] *n* frenesia

frequency ['friːkwənsɪ] *n* frequenza

frequent [*adj* 'friːkwənt, *vb* frɪ'kwent] *adj* frequente ♦ *vt* frequentare; **~ly** *adv* frequentemente, spesso

fresco ['freskəu] *n* affresco

fresh [freʃ] *adj* fresco(a); (*new*) nuovo(a); (*cheeky*) sfacciato(a); **~en** *vi* (*wind, air*)

rinfrescare; ~**en up** *vi* rinfrescarsi; ~**er**
(*BRIT: inf*) *n* (*SCOL*) matricola; ~**ly** *adv* di
recente, di fresco; ~**man** (*irreg*) (*US*) *n*
= ~**er**; ~**ness** *n* freschezza; ~**water** *adj*
(*fish*) d'acqua dolce
fret [frɛt] *vi* agitarsi, affliggersi
friar ['fraɪə*] *n* frate *m*
friction ['frɪkʃən] *n* frizione *f*, attrito
Friday ['fraɪdɪ] *n* venerdì *m inv*
fridge [frɪdʒ] (*BRIT*) *n* frigo, frigorifero
fried [fraɪd] *pt, pp of* **fry** ♦ *adj* fritto(a)
friend [frɛnd] *n* amico/a; ~**ly** *adj*
amichevole; ~**ly fire** *n* (*MIL*) fuoco amico;
~**ship** *n* amicizia
frieze [friːz] *n* fregio
fright [fraɪt] *n* paura, spavento; **to take** ~
spaventarsi; ~**en** *vt* spaventare, far paura
a; ~**ened** *adj* spaventato(a); ~**ening** *adj*
spaventoso(a), pauroso(a); ~**ful** *adj* orribile
frill [frɪl] *n* balza
fringe [frɪndʒ] *n* (*decoration, BRIT: of hair*)
frangia; (*edge: of forest etc*) margine *m*; ~
benefits *npl* vantaggi *mpl*
frisk [frɪsk] *vt* perquisire
frisky ['frɪskɪ] *adj* vivace, vispo(a)
fritter ['frɪtə*] *n* frittella; ~ **away** *vt* sprecare
frivolous ['frɪvələs] *adj* frivolo(a)
frizzy ['frɪzɪ] *adj* crespo(a)
fro [frəu] *see* **to**
frock [frɔk] *n* vestito
frog [frɔg] *n* rana; ~**man** (*irreg*) *n* uomo *m*
rana *inv*
frolic ['frɔlɪk] *vi* sgambettare

| KEYWORD |

from [frɔm] *prep* **1** (*indicating starting place,
origin etc*) da; **where do you come ~?,
where are you ~?** da dove viene?, di
dov'è?; ~ **London to Glasgow** da Londra a
Glasgow; **a letter ~ my sister** una lettera
da mia sorella; **tell him ~ me that ...** gli
dica da parte mia che ...
2 (*indicating time*) da; ~ **one o'clock to** *or*
until *or* **till two** dall'una alle due; ~
January (on) da gennaio, a partire da
gennaio
3 (*indicating distance*) da; **the hotel is**

1 km ~ the beach l'albergo è a 1 km dalla
spiaggia
4 (*indicating price, number etc*) da; **prices
range ~ £10 to £50** i prezzi vanno dalle 10
alle 50 sterline
5 (*indicating difference*) da; **he can't tell
red ~ green** non sa distinguere il rosso dal
verde
6 (*because of, on the basis of*): ~ **what he
says** da quanto dice lui; **weak ~ hunger**
debole per la fame

---

front [frʌnt] *n* (*of house, dress*) davanti *m
inv*; (*of train*) testa; (*of book*) copertina; (*promenade: also:* **sea ~**) lungomare *m*;
(*MIL, POL, METEOR*) fronte *m*; (*fig:
appearances*) fronte *f* ♦ *adj* primo(a);
anteriore, davanti *inv*; **in ~ of** davanti a; ~
door *n* porta d'entrata; (*of car*) sportello
anteriore; ~**ier** ['frʌntɪə*] *n* frontiera; ~
page *n* prima pagina; ~ **room** (*BRIT*) *n*
salotto; ~-**wheel drive** *n* trasmissione *f*
anteriore
frost [frɔst] *n* gelo; (*also:* **hoar~**) brina;
~**bite** *n* congelamento; ~**ed** *adj* (*glass*)
smerigliato(a); ~**y** *adj* (*weather, look*)
gelido(a)
froth ['frɔθ] *n* spuma; schiuma
frown [fraun] *vi* acciigliarsi
froze [frəuz] *pt of* **freeze**; **frozen** *pp of*
freeze
fruit [fruːt] *n inv* (*also fig*) frutto; (*collectively*)
frutta; ~**erer** *n* fruttivendolo; ~**erer's
(shop)** *n*: **at the ~erer's (shop)** dal
fruttivendolo; ~**ful** *adj* fruttuoso(a); ~**ion**
[fruː'ɪʃən] *n*: **to come to ~ion** realizzarsi; ~
juice *n* succo di frutta; ~ **machine** (*BRIT*)
n macchina *f* mangiasoldi *inv*; ~ **salad** *n*
macedonia
frustrate [frʌs'treɪt] *vt* frustrare
fry [fraɪ] (*pt, pp* **fried**) *vt* friggere; *see also*
small; ~**ing pan** *n* padella
ft. *abbr* = **foot; feet**
fudge [fʌdʒ] *n* (*CULIN*) specie di caramella a
base di latte, burro e zucchero
fuel [fjuəl] *n* (*for heating*) combustibile *m*;
(*for propelling*) carburante *m*; ~ **tank** *n*

deposito *m* nafta *inv*; (*on vehicle*) serbatoio (della benzina)

fugitive ['fju:dʒɪtɪv] *n* fuggitivo/a, profugo/a

fulfil [ful'fɪl] *vt* (*function*) compiere; (*order*) eseguire; (*wish, desire*) soddisfare, appagare; **~ment** (*US* **fulfillment**) *n* (*of wishes*) soddisfazione *f*, appagamento; **sense of ~ment** soddisfazione

full [ful] *adj* pieno(a); (*details, skirt*) ampio(a) ♦ *adv*: **to know ~ well that** sapere benissimo che; **I'm ~ (up)** sono pieno; **a ~ two hours** due ore intere; **at ~ speed** a tutta velocità; **in ~** per intero; **~ board** (*BRIT*) *n* pensione *f* completa; **~ employment** *n* piena occupazione; **~-length** *adj* (*film*) a lungometraggio; (*coat, novel*) lungo(a); (*portrait*) in piedi; **~ moon** *n* luna piena; **~-scale** *adj* (*attack, war*) su larga scala; (*model*) in grandezza naturale; **~ stop** *n* punto; **~-time** *adj, adv* (*work*) a tempo pieno; **~y** *adv* interamente, pienamente, completamente; (*at least*) almeno; **~y-fledged** *adj* (*teacher, member etc*) a tutti gli effetti; **~y licensed** *adj* (*hotel, restaurant*) autorizzato(a) alla vendita di alcolici

fumble ['fʌmbl] *vi*: **to ~ with sth** armeggiare con qc

fume [fju:m] *vi* essere furioso(a); **~s** *npl* esalazioni *fpl*, vapori *mpl*

fun [fʌn] *n* divertimento, spasso; **to have ~** divertirsi; **for ~** per scherzo; **to make ~ of** prendersi gioco di

function ['fʌŋkʃən] *n* funzione *f*, cerimonia, ricevimento ♦ *vi* funzionare; **~al** *adj* funzionale

fund [fʌnd] *n* fondo, cassa; (*source*) fondo; (*store*) riserva; **~s** *npl* (*money*) fondi *mpl*

fundamental [fʌndə'mentl] *adj* fondamentale

funeral ['fju:nərəl] *n* funerale *m*; **~ parlour** *n* impresa di pompe funebri; **~ service** *n* ufficio funebre

fun fair (*BRIT*) *n* luna park *m inv*

fungus ['fʌŋgəs] (*pl* **fungi**) *n* fungo; (*mould*) muffa

funnel ['fʌnl] *n* imbuto; (*of ship*) ciminiera

funny ['fʌnɪ] *adj* divertente, buffo(a); (*strange*) strano(a), bizzarro(a)

fur [fə:*] *n* pelo; pelliccia; (*BRIT*: *in kettle etc*) deposito calcare; **~ coat** *n* pelliccia

furious ['fjuərɪəs] *adj* furioso(a); (*effort*) accanito(a)

furlong ['fə:lɒŋ] *n* = 201.17 m (*termine ippico*)

furnace ['fə:nɪs] *n* fornace *f*

furnish ['fə:nɪʃ] *vt* ammobiliare; (*supply*) fornire; **~ings** *npl* mobili *mpl*, mobilia

furniture ['fə:nɪtʃə*] *n* mobili *mpl*; **piece of ~** mobile *m*

furrow ['fʌrəu] *n* solco

furry ['fə:rɪ] *adj* (*animal*) peloso(a)

further ['fə:ðə*] *adj* supplementare, altro(a); nuovo(a); più lontano(a) ♦ *adv* più lontano; (*more*) di più; (*moreover*) inoltre ♦ *vt* favorire, promuovere; **college of ~ education** *n* istituto statale con corsi specializzati (*di formazione professionale, aggiornamento professionale etc*); **~more** [fə:ðə'mɔ:*] *adv* inoltre, per di più

furthest ['fə:ðɪst] *superl of* **far**

fury ['fjuərɪ] *n* furore *m*

fuse [fju:z] *n* fusibile *m*; (*for bomb etc*) miccia, spoletta ♦ *vt* fondere ♦ *vi* fondersi; **to ~ the lights** (*BRIT*: *ELEC*) far saltare i fusibili; **~ box** *n* cassetta dei fusibili

fuselage ['fju:zəlɑ:ʒ] *n* fusoliera

fuss [fʌs] *n* agitazione *f*; (*complaining*) storie *fpl*; **to make a ~** fare delle storie; **~y** *adj* (*person*) puntiglioso(a), esigente; che fa le storie; (*dress*) carico(a) di fronzoli; (*style*) elaborato(a)

future ['fju:tʃə*] *adj* futuro(a) ♦ *n* futuro, avvenire *m*; (*LING*) futuro; **in ~** in futuro

fuze [fju:z] (*US*) = **fuse**

fuzzy ['fʌzɪ] *adj* (*PHOT*) indistinto(a), sfocato(a); (*hair*) crespo(a)

G, g

G [dʒi:] n (MUS) sol m

G7 abbr (= Group of Seven) G7

gabble ['gæbl] vi borbottare; farfugliare

gable ['geɪbl] n frontone m

gadget ['gædʒɪt] n aggeggio

Gaelic ['geɪlɪk] adj gaelico(a) ♦ n (LING) gaelico

gag [gæg] n bavaglio; (joke) facezia, scherzo ♦ vt imbavagliare

gaiety ['geɪtɪ] n gaiezza

gaily ['geɪlɪ] adv allegramente

gain [geɪn] n guadagno, profitto ♦ vt guadagnare ♦ vi (clock, watch) andare avanti; (benefit): **to ~ (from)** trarre beneficio (da); **to ~ 3lbs (in weight)** aumentare di 3 libbre; **to ~ on sb** (in race etc) guadagnare su qn

gal. abbr = **gallon**

galaxy ['gæləksɪ] n galassia

gale [geɪl] n vento forte; burrasca

gallant ['gælənt] adj valoroso(a); (towards ladies) galante, cortese

gall bladder ['gɔ:l-] n cistifellea

gallery ['gælərɪ] n galleria

gallon ['gælən] n gallone m (= 8 pints; BRIT = 4.543l; US = 3.785l)

gallop ['gæləp] n galoppo ♦ vi galoppare

gallows ['gæləuz] n forca

gallstone ['gɔ:lstəun] n calcolo biliare

galore [gə'lɔ:*] adv a iosa, a profusione

galvanize ['gælvənaɪz] vt galvanizzare

gambit ['gæmbɪt] n (fig): **(opening) ~** prima mossa

gamble ['gæmbl] n azzardo, rischio calcolato ♦ vt, vi giocare; **to ~ on** (fig) giocare su; **~r** n giocatore/trice d'azzardo; **gambling** n gioco d'azzardo

game [geɪm] n gioco; (event) partita; (TENNIS) game m inv; (CULIN, HUNTING) selvaggina ♦ adj (ready): **to be ~ (for sth/ to do)** essere pronto(a) (a qc/a fare); **big ~** selvaggina grossa; **~keeper** n guardacaccia m inv

gammon ['gæmən] n (bacon) quarto di maiale; (ham) prosciutto affumicato

gamut ['gæmət] n gamma

gang [gæŋ] n banda, squadra ♦ vi: **to ~ up on sb** far combutta contro qn

gangrene ['gæŋgri:n] n cancrena

gangster ['gæŋstə*] n gangster m inv

gangway ['gæŋweɪ] n passerella; (BRIT: of bus) corridoio

gaol [dʒeɪl] (BRIT) n, vt = **jail**

gap [gæp] n (space) buco; (in time) intervallo; (difference): **~ (between)** divario (tra)

gape [geɪp] vi (person) restare a bocca aperta; (shirt, hole) essere spalancato(a); **gaping** adj spalancato(a)

garage ['gærɑ:ʒ] n garage m inv

garbage ['gɑ:bɪdʒ] n (US) immondizie fpl, rifiuti mpl; (inf) sciocchezze fpl; **~ can** (US) n bidone m della spazzatura

garbled ['gɑ:bld] adj deformato(a); ingarbugliato(a)

garden ['gɑ:dn] n giardino; **~s** npl (public park) giardini pubblici; **~er** n giardiniere/a; **~ing** n giardinaggio

gargle ['gɑ:gl] vi fare gargarismi

garish ['gɛərɪʃ] adj vistoso(a)

garland ['gɑ:lənd] n ghirlanda; corona

garlic ['gɑ:lɪk] n aglio

garment ['gɑ:mənt] n indumento

garnish ['gɑ:nɪʃ] vt (food) guarnire

garrison ['gærɪsn] n guarnigione f

garter ['gɑ:tə*] n giarrettiera

gas [gæs] n gas m inv; (US: gasoline) benzina ♦ vt asfissiare con il gas; **~ cooker** (BRIT) n cucina a gas; **~ cylinder** n bombola del gas; **~ fire** (BRIT) n radiatore m a gas

gash [gæʃ] n sfregio ♦ vt sfregiare

gasket ['gæskɪt] n (AUT) guarnizione f

gas mask n maschera f antigas inv

gas meter n contatore m del gas

gasoline ['gæsəli:n] (US) n benzina

gasp [gɑ:sp] n respiro affannoso, ansito ♦ vi ansare, ansimare; (in surprise) restare senza fiato

gas station (US) n distributore m di benzina

gassy ['gæsɪ] *adj* gassoso(a)

gate [geɪt] *n* cancello; (*at airport*) uscita; **~crash** (*BRIT*) *vt* partecipare senza invito a; **~way** *n* porta

gather ['gæðə*] *vt* (*flowers, fruit*) cogliere; (*pick up*) raccogliere; (*assemble*) radunare; raccogliere; (*understand*) capire; (*SEWING*) increspare ♦ *vi* (*assemble*) radunarsi; **to ~ speed** acquistare velocità; **~ing** *n* adunanza

gauche [gəʊʃ] *adj* goffo(a), maldestro(a)

gaudy ['gɔːdɪ] *adj* vistoso(a)

gauge [geɪdʒ] *n* (*instrument*) indicatore *m* ♦ *vt* misurare; (*fig*) valutare

gaunt [gɔːnt] *adj* scarno(a); (*grim, desolate*) desolato(a)

gauntlet ['gɔːntlɪt] *n* guanto; (*fig*): **to run the ~ through an angry crowd** passare sotto il fuoco di una folla ostile; **to throw down the ~** gettare il guanto

gauze [gɔːz] *n* garza

gave [geɪv] *pt of* **give**

gay [geɪ] *adj* (*homosexual*) omosessuale; (*cheerful*) gaio(a), allegro(a); (*colour*) vivace, vivo(a)

gaze [geɪz] *n* sguardo fisso ♦ *vi*: **to ~ at** guardare fisso

GB *abbr* = **Great Britain**

GCE (*BRIT*) *n abbr* (= *General Certificate of Education*) ≈ maturità

GCSE (*BRIT*) *n abbr* = *General Certificate of Secondary Education*

gear [gɪə*] *n* attrezzi *mpl*, equipaggiamento; (*TECH*) ingranaggio; (*AUT*) marcia ♦ *vt* (*fig: adapt*): **to ~ sth to** adattare qc a; **in top** *or* (*US*) **high/low ~** in quarta (*or* quinta)/seconda; **in ~** in marcia; **~ box** *n* scatola del cambio; **~ lever** (*US* **~ shift**) *n* leva del cambio

geese [giːs] *npl of* **goose**

gel [dʒel] *n* gel *m inv*

gem [dʒem] *n* gemma

Gemini ['dʒemɪnaɪ] *n* Gemelli *mpl*

gender ['dʒendə*] *n* genere *m*

general ['dʒenərl] *n* generale *m* ♦ *adj* generale; **in ~** in genere; **~ delivery** (*US*) *n* fermo posta *m*; **~ election** *n* elezioni *fpl* generali; **~ly** *adv* generalmente; **~ practitioner** *n* medico generico

generate ['dʒenəreɪt] *vt* generare

generation [dʒenə'reɪʃən] *n* generazione *f*

generator ['dʒenəreɪtə*] *n* generatore *m*

generosity [dʒenə'rɒsɪtɪ] *n* generosità

generous ['dʒenərəs] *adj* generoso(a); (*copious*) abbondante

genetic engineering [dʒɪ'netɪk-] *n* ingegneria genetica

genetic fingerprinting [dʒɪ'netɪk-] *n* rilevamento delle impronte genetiche

Geneva [dʒɪ'niːvə] *n* Ginevra

genial ['dʒiːnɪəl] *adj* geniale, cordiale

genitals ['dʒenɪtlz] *npl* genitali *mpl*

genius ['dʒiːnɪəs] *n* genio

Genoa ['dʒenəʊə] *n* Genova

gent [dʒent] *n abbr* = **gentleman**

genteel [dʒen'tiːl] *adj* raffinato(a), distinto(a)

gentle ['dʒentl] *adj* delicato(a); (*person*) dolce

gentleman ['dʒentlmən] *n* signore *m*; (*well-bred man*) gentiluomo

gently ['dʒentlɪ] *adv* delicatamente

gentry ['dʒentrɪ] *n* nobiltà minore

gents [dʒents] *n* W.C. *m* (per signori)

genuine ['dʒenjuɪn] *adj* autentico(a); sincero(a)

geography [dʒɪ'ɒgrəfɪ] *n* geografia

geology [dʒɪ'ɒlədʒɪ] *n* geologia

geometric(al) [dʒɪə'metrɪk(l)] *adj* geometrico(a)

geometry [dʒɪ'ɒmətrɪ] *n* geometria

geranium [dʒɪ'reɪnjəm] *n* geranio

geriatric [dʒerɪ'ætrɪk] *adj* geriatrico(a)

germ [dʒɜːm] *n* (*MED*) microbo; (*BIOL, fig*) germe *m*

German ['dʒɜːmən] *adj* tedesco(a) ♦ *n* tedesco/a; (*LING*) tedesco; **~ measles** (*BRIT*) *n* rosolia

Germany ['dʒɜːmənɪ] *n* Germania

gesture ['dʒestjə*] *n* gesto

KEYWORD

---

get [get] (*pt, pp* **got**, (*US*) *pp* **gotten**) *vi*
1 (*become, be*) diventare, farsi; **to ~ old**

invecchiare; **to ~ tired** stancarsi; **to ~ drunk** ubriacarsi; **to ~ killed** venire or rimanere ucciso(a); **when do I ~ paid?** quando mi pagate? **it's ~ting late** si sta facendo tardi
2 (go): **to ~ to/from** andare a/da; **to ~ home** arrivare or tornare a casa; **how did you ~ here?** come sei venuto?
3 (begin) mettersi a, cominciare a; **to ~ to know sb** incominciare a conoscere qn; **let's ~ going** or **started** muoviamoci
4 (modal aux vb): **you've got to do it** devi farlo
♦ vt 1: **to ~ sth done** (do) fare qc; (have done) far fare qc; **to ~ one's hair cut** farsi tagliare i capelli; **to ~ sb to do sth** far fare qc a qn
2 (obtain: money, permission, results) ottenere; (find: job, flat) trovare; (fetch: person, doctor) chiamare; (: object) prendere; **to ~ sth for sb** prendere or procurare qc a qn; **~ me Mr Jones, please** (TEL) mi passi il signor Jones, per favore; **can I ~ you a drink?** le posso offrire da bere?
3 (receive: present, letter, prize) ricevere; (acquire: reputation) farsi; **how much did you ~ for the painting?** quanto le hanno dato per il quadro?
4 (catch) prendere; (hit: target etc) colpire; **to ~ sb by the arm/throat** afferrare qn per un braccio/alla gola; **~ him!** prendetelo!
5 (take, move) portare; **to ~ sth to sb** far avere qc a qn; **do you think we'll ~ it through the door?** pensi che riusciremo a farlo passare per la porta?
6 (catch, take: plane, bus etc) prendere
7 (understand) afferrare; (hear) sentire; **I've got it!** ci sono arrivato!, ci sono!; **I'm sorry, I didn't ~ your name** scusi, non ho capito (or sentito) il suo nome
8 (have, possess): **to have got** avere; **how many have you got?** quanti ne ha?
get about vi muoversi; (news) diffondersi
get along vi (agree) andare d'accordo; (depart) andarsene; (manage) = **get by**
get at vt fus (attack) prendersela con; (reach) raggiungere, arrivare a

get away vi partire, andarsene; (escape) scappare
get away with vt fus cavarsela; farla franca
get back vi (return) ritornare, tornare ♦ vt riottenere, riavere
get by vi (pass) passare; (manage) farcela
get down vi, vt fus scendere ♦ vt far scendere; (depress) buttare giù
get down to vt fus (work) mettersi a (fare)
get in vi entrare; (train) arrivare; (arrive home) ritornare, tornare
get into vt fus entrare in; **to ~ into a rage** incavolarsi
get off vi (from train etc) scendere; (depart: person, car) andare via; (escape) cavarsela ♦ vt (remove: clothes, stain) levare ♦ vt fus (train, bus) scendere da
get on vi (at exam etc) andare; (agree): **to ~ on (with)** andare d'accordo (con) ♦ vt fus montare in; (horse) montare su
get out vi uscire; (of vehicle) scendere ♦ vt tirar fuori, far uscire
get out of vt fus uscire da; (duty etc) evitare
get over vt fus (illness) riaversi da
get round vt fus aggirare; (fig: person) rigirare
get through vi (TEL) avere la linea
get through to vt fus (TEL) parlare a
get together vi riunirsi ♦ vt raccogliere; (people) adunare
get up vi (rise) alzarsi ♦ vt fus salire su per
get up to vt fus (reach) raggiungere; (prank etc) fare

getaway ['getəweɪ] n fuga
geyser ['giːzə*] n (BRIT) scaldabagno; (GEO) geyser m inv
Ghana ['gɑːnə] n Ghana m
ghastly ['gɑːstlɪ] adj orribile, orrendo(a); (pale) spettrale
gherkin ['gɜːkɪn] n cetriolino
ghetto blaster ['getəublɑːstə*] n maxistereo m inv portatile
ghost [gəust] n fantasma m, spettro

giant ['dʒaɪənt] *n* gigante *m* ♦ *adj* gigantesco(a), enorme

gibberish ['dʒɪbərɪʃ] *n* parole *fpl* senza senso

gibe [dʒaɪb] *n* = **jibe**

giblets ['dʒɪblɪts] *npl* frattaglie *fpl*

Gibraltar [dʒɪ'brɔːltə*] *n* Gibilterra

giddy ['gɪdɪ] *adj* (*dizzy*): **to be ~** aver le vertigini

gift [gɪft] *n* regalo; (*donation, ability*) dono; **~ed** *adj* dotato(a); **~ token** *n* buono *m* omaggio *inv*; **~ voucher** *n* = **~ token**

gigantic [dʒaɪ'gæntɪk] *adj* gigantesco(a)

giggle ['gɪgl] *vi* ridere scioccamente

gill [dʒɪl] *n* (*measure*) = 0.25 pints (*BRIT* = 0.148l, *US* = 0.118l)

gills [gɪlz] *npl* (*of fish*) branchie *fpl*

gilt [gɪlt] *n* doratura ♦ *adj* dorato(a); **~-edged** *adj* (*COMM*) della massima sicurezza

gimmick ['gɪmɪk] *n* trucco

gin [dʒɪn] *n* (*liquor*) gin *m inv*

ginger ['dʒɪndʒə*] *n* zenzero; **~ ale**, **~ beer** *n* bibita gassosa allo zenzero; **~bread** *n* pan *m* di zenzero

gingerly ['dʒɪndʒəlɪ] *adv* cautamente

gipsy ['dʒɪpsɪ] *n* zingaro/a

giraffe [dʒɪ'rɑːf] *n* giraffa

girder ['gəːdə*] *n* trave *f*

girl [gəːl] *n* ragazza; (*young unmarried woman*) signorina; (*daughter*) figlia, figliola; **~friend** *n* (*of girl*) amica; (*of boy*) ragazza; **~ish** *adj* da ragazza

giro ['dʒaɪrəu] *n* (*bank ~*) versamento bancario; (*post office ~*) postagiro; (*BRIT: welfare cheque*) assegno del sussidio di assistenza sociale

gist [dʒɪst] *n* succo

give [gɪv] (*pt* **gave**, *pp* **given**) *vt* dare ♦ *vi* cedere; **to ~ sb sth**, **~ sth to sb** dare qc a qn; **I'll ~ you £5 for it** te lo pago 5 sterline; **to ~ a cry/sigh** emettere un grido/sospiro; **to ~ a speech** fare un discorso; **~ away** *vt* dare via; (*disclose*) rivelare; (*bride*) condurre all'altare; **~ back** *vt* rendere; **~ in** *vi* cedere ♦ *vt* consegnare; **~ off** *vt* emettere; **~ out** *vt* distribuire;

~ up *vi* rinunciare ♦ *vt* rinunciare a; **to ~ up smoking** smettere di fumare; **to ~ o.s. up** arrendersi; **~ way** *vi* cedere; (*BRIT: AUT*) dare la precedenza

glacier ['glæsɪə*] *n* ghiacciaio

glad [glæd] *adj* lieto(a), contento(a)

gladly ['glædlɪ] *adv* volentieri

glamorous ['glæmərəs] *adj* affascinante, seducente

glamour ['glæmə*] *n* fascino

glance [glɑːns] *n* occhiata, sguardo ♦ *vi*: **to ~ at** dare un'occhiata a; **to ~ off** (*bullet*) rimbalzare su; **glancing** *adj* (*blow*) che colpisce di striscio

gland [glænd] *n* ghiandola

glare [glɛə*] *n* (*of anger*) sguardo furioso; (*of light*) riverbero, luce *f* abbagliante; (*of publicity*) chiasso ♦ *vi* abbagliare; **to ~ at** guardare male; **glaring** *adj* (*mistake*) madornale

glass [glɑːs] *n* (*substance*) vetro; (*tumbler*) bicchiere *m*; **~es** *npl* (*spectacles*) occhiali *mpl*; **~ware** *n* vetrame *m*; **~y** *adj* (*eyes*) vitreo(a)

glaze [gleɪz] *vt* (*door*) fornire di vetri; (*pottery*) smaltare ♦ *n* smalto; **~d** *adj* (*eyes*) vitreo(a); (*pottery*) smaltato(a)

glazier ['gleɪzɪə*] *n* vetraio

gleam [gliːm] *vi* luccicare

glean [gliːn] *vt* (*information*) racimolare

glee [gliː] *n* allegrezza, gioia

glen [glɛn] *n* valletta

glib [glɪb] *adj* dalla parola facile; facile

glide [glaɪd] *vi* scivolare; (*AVIAT, birds*) planare; **~r** *n* (*AVIAT*) aliante *m*; **gliding** *n* (*AVIAT*) volo a vela

glimmer ['glɪmə*] *n* barlume *m*

glimpse [glɪmps] *n* impressione *f* fugace ♦ *vt* vedere al volo

glint [glɪnt] *vi* luccicare

glisten ['glɪsn] *vi* luccicare

glitter ['glɪtə*] *vi* scintillare

gloat [gləut] *vi*: **to ~ (over)** gongolare di piacere (per)

global ['gləubl] *adj* globale; **~ warming** *n* effetto *m* serra *inv*

globe [gləub] *n* globo, sfera

gloom [gluːm] n oscurità, buio; (sadness) tristezza, malinconia; **~y** adj scuro(a); fosco(a), triste

glorious ['glɔːrɪəs] adj glorioso(a); magnifico(a)

glory ['glɔːrɪ] n gloria; splendore m

gloss [glɔs] n (shine) lucentezza; (also: ~ **paint**) vernice f a olio; **~ over** vt fus scivolare su

glossary ['glɔsərɪ] n glossario

glossy ['glɔsɪ] adj lucente

glove [glʌv] n guanto; **~ compartment** n (AUT) vano portaoggetti

glow [gləu] vi ardere; (face) essere luminoso(a)

glower ['glauə*] vi: **to ~ (at sb)** guardare (qn) in cagnesco

glucose ['gluːkəus] n glucosio

glue [gluː] n colla ♦ vt incollare

glum [glʌm] adj abbattuto(a)

glut [glʌt] n eccesso

glutton ['glʌtn] n ghiottone/a; **a ~ for work** un(a) patito(a) del lavoro

gnat [næt] n moscerino

gnaw [nɔː] vt rodere

go [gəu] (pt **went**, pp **gone**; pl **~es**) vi andare; (depart) partire, andarsene; (work) funzionare; (time) passare; (break etc) rompersi; (be sold): **to ~ for £10** essere venduto per 10 sterline; (fit, suit): **to ~ with** andare bene con; (become): **to ~ pale** diventare pallido(a); **to ~ mouldy** ammuffire ♦ n: **to have a ~ (at)** provare; **to be on the ~** essere in moto; **whose ~ is it?** a chi tocca?; **he's going to do** sta per fare; **to ~ for a walk** andare a fare una passeggiata; **to ~ dancing/shopping** andare a ballare/fare la spesa; **just then the bell went** proprio allora suonò il campanello; **how did it ~?** com'è andato?; **to ~ round the back/by the shop** passare da dietro/davanti al negozio; **~ about** vi (also: **~ round**: rumour) correre, circolare ♦ vt fus: **how do I ~ about this?** qual è la prassi per questo?; **~ ahead** vi andare avanti; **~ along** vi andare, avanzare ♦ vt fus percorrere; **to ~ along with** (plan, idea)

appoggiare; **~ away** vi partire, andarsene; **~ back** vi tornare, ritornare; **~ back on** vt fus (promise) non mantenere; **~ by** vi (years, time) scorrere ♦ vt fus attenersi a, seguire (alla lettera); prestar fede a; **~ down** vi scendere; (ship) affondare; (sun) tramontare ♦ vt fus scendere; **~ for** vt fus (fetch) andare a prendere; (like) andar matto(a) per; (attack) attaccare; saltare addosso a; **~ in** vi entrare; **~ in for** vt fus (competition) iscriversi a; (be interested in) interessarsi di; **~ into** vt fus entrare in, (investigate) indagare, esaminare; (embark on) lanciarsi in; **~ off** vi partire, andar via; (food) guastarsi; (explode) esplodere, scoppiare; (event) passare ♦ vt fus: **I've gone off chocolate** la cioccolata non mi piace più; **the gun went off** il fucile si scaricò; **~ on** vi continuare; (happen) succedere; **to ~ on doing** continuare a fare; **~ out** vi uscire; (couple): **they went out for 3 years** sono stati insieme per 3 anni; (fire, light) spegnersi; **~ over** vi (ship) ribaltarsi ♦ vt fus (check) esaminare; **~ through** vt fus (town etc) attraversare; (files, papers) passare in rassegna; (examine: list etc) leggere da cima a fondo; **~ up** vi salire; **~ without** vt fus fare a meno di

goad [gəud] vt spronare

go-ahead adj intraprendente ♦ n via m

goal [gəul] n (SPORT) gol m, rete f; (: place) porta; (fig: aim) fine m, scopo; **~keeper** n portiere m; **~-post** n palo (della porta)

goat [gəut] n capra

gobble ['gɔbl] vt (also: **~ down**, **~ up**) ingoiare

go-between n intermediario/a

god [gɔd] n dio; **G~** n Dio; **~child** n figlioccio/a; **~daughter** n figlioccia; **~dess** n dea; **~father** n padrino; **~-forsaken** adj desolato(a), sperduto(a); **~mother** n madrina; **~send** n dono del cielo; **~son** n figlioccio

goggles ['gɔglz] npl occhiali mpl (di protezione)

going ['gəuɪŋ] n (conditions) andare m, stato del terreno ♦ adj: **the ~ rate** la tariffa in vigore

gold [gəuld] n oro ♦ adj d'oro; **~en** adj (*made of ~*) d'oro; (*~ in colour*) dorato(a); **~fish** n pesce m dorato or rosso; **~mine** n (*also fig*) miniera d'oro; **~-plated** adj placcato(a) oro *inv*; **~smith** n orefice m, orafo

golf [gɔlf] n golf m; **~ ball** n (*for game*) pallina da golf; (*on typewriter*) pallina; **~ club** n circolo di golf; (*stick*) bastone m or mazza da golf; **~ course** n campo di golf; **~er** n giocatore/trice di golf

gondola ['gɔndələ] n gondola

gone [gɔn] pp of **go** ♦ adj partito(a)

gong [gɔŋ] n gong m *inv*

good [gud] adj buono(a); (*kind*) buono(a), gentile; (*child*) bravo(a) ♦ n bene m; **~s** npl (*COMM etc*) beni mpl; merci fpl; **~!** bene!, ottimo!; **to be ~ at** essere bravo(a) in; **to be ~ for** andare bene per; **it's ~ for you** fa bene; **would you be ~ enough to ...?** avrebbe la gentilezza di ...?; **a ~ deal (of)** molto(a), una buona quantità (di); **a ~ many** molti(e); **to make ~** (*loss, damage*) compensare; **it's no ~ complaining** brontolare non serve a niente; **for ~** per sempre, definitivamente; **~ morning!** buon giorno!; **~ afternoon/evening!** buona sera!; **~ night!** buona notte!; **~bye** excl arrivederci!; **G~ Friday** n Venerdì Santo; **~-looking** adj bello(a); **~-natured** adj affabile; **~ness** n (*of person*) bontà; **for ~ness sake!** per amor di Dio!; **~ness gracious!** santo cielo!, mamma mia!; **~s train** (*BRIT*) n treno m merci *inv*; **~will** n amicizia, benevolenza

goose [gu:s] (pl **geese**) n oca

gooseberry ['guzbərɪ] n uva spina; **to play ~** (*BRIT*) tenere la candela

gooseflesh ['gu:sfleʃ] n pelle f d'oca

goose pimples npl pelle f d'oca

gore [gɔ:*] vt incornare ♦ n sangue m (coagulato)

gorge [gɔ:dʒ] n gola ♦ vt: **to ~ o.s. (on)** ingozzarsi (di)

gorgeous ['gɔ:dʒəs] adj magnifico(a)

gorilla [gə'rɪlə] n gorilla m *inv*

gorse [gɔ:s] n ginestrone m

gory ['gɔ:rɪ] adj sanguinoso(a)

go-slow (*BRIT*) n rallentamento dei lavori (*per agitazione sindacale*)

gospel ['gɔspl] n vangelo

gossip ['gɔsɪp] n chiacchiere fpl; pettegolezzi mpl; (*person*) pettegolo/a ♦ vi chiacchierare

got [gɔt] pt, pp of **get**; **~ten** (*US*) pp of **get**

gout [gaut] n gotta

govern ['gʌvn] vt governare

governess ['gʌvənɪs] n governante f

government ['gʌvnmənt] n governo

governor ['gʌvənə*] n (*of state, bank*) governatore m; (*of school, hospital*) amministratore m; (*BRIT: of prison*) direttore/trice

gown [gaun] n vestito lungo; (*of teacher, BRIT: of judge*) toga

G.P. n abbr = **general practitioner**

grab [græb] vt afferrare, arraffare; (*property, power*) impadronirsi di ♦ vi: **to ~ at** cercare di afferrare

grace [greɪs] n grazia ♦ vt onorare; **5 days' ~** dilazione f di 5 giorni; **~ful** adj elegante, aggraziato(a); **gracious** ['greɪʃəs] adj grazioso(a); misericordioso(a)

grade [greɪd] n (*COMM*) qualità f *inv*; classe f; categoria; (*in hierarchy*) grado; (*SCOL: mark*) voto; (*US: school class*) classe ♦ vt classificare; ordinare; graduare; **~ crossing** (*US*) n passaggio a livello; **~ school** (*US*) n scuola elementare

gradient ['greɪdɪənt] n pendenza, inclinazione f

gradual ['grædjuəl] adj graduale; **~ly** adv man mano, a poco a poco

graduate [n 'grædjuət, vb 'grædjueɪt] n (*of university*) laureato/a; (*US: of high school*) diplomato/a ♦ vi laurearsi; diplomarsi; **graduation** [-'eɪʃən] n (*ceremony*) consegna delle lauree (*or dei diplomi*)

graffiti [grə'fi:tɪ] npl graffiti mpl

graft [grɑ:ft] n (*AGR, MED*) innesto; (*bribery*) corruzione f; (*BRIT: hard work*): **it's hard ~** è un lavoraccio ♦ vt innestare

grain [greɪn] n grano; (*of sand*) granello; (*of*

wood) venatura

gram [græm] *n* grammo

grammar ['græmə*] *n* grammatica; ~ **school** (*BRIT*) *n* ≈ liceo

grammatical [grə'mætɪkl] *adj* grammaticale

gramme [græm] *n* = **gram**

grand [grænd] *adj* grande, magnifico(a); grandioso(a); ~**children** *npl* nipoti *mpl*; ~**dad** (*inf*) *n* nonno; ~**daughter** *n* nipote *f*; ~**eur** ['grændjə*] *n* grandiosità; ~**father** *n* nonno; ~**ma** (*inf*) *n* nonna; ~**mother** *n* nonna; ~**pa** (*inf*) *n* = ~**dad**; ~**parents** *npl* nonni *mpl*; ~ **piano** *n* pianoforte *m* a coda; ~**son** *n* nipote *m*; ~**stand** *n* (*SPORT*) tribuna

granite ['grænɪt] *n* granito

granny ['grænɪ] (*inf*) *n* nonna

grant [grɑ:nt] *vt* accordare; (*a request*) accogliere; (*admit*) ammettere, concedere ♦ *n* (*SCOL*) borsa; (*ADMIN*) sussidio, sovvenzione *f*; **to take sth for ~ed** dare qc per scontato; **to take sb for ~ed** dare per scontata la presenza di qn

granulated ['grænjuleɪtɪd] *adj*: ~ **sugar** zucchero cristallizzato

granule ['grænju:l] *n* granello

grape [greɪp] *n* chicco d'uva, acino

grapefruit ['greɪpfru:t] *n* pompelmo

graph [grɑ:f] *n* grafico; ~**ic** *adj* grafico(a); (*vivid*) vivido(a); ~**ics** *n* grafica ♦ *npl* illustrazioni *fpl*

grapple ['græpl] *vi*: **to ~ with** essere alle prese con

grasp [grɑ:sp] *vt* afferrare ♦ *n* (*grip*) presa; (*fig*) potere *m*; comprensione *f*; ~**ing** *adj* avido(a)

grass [grɑ:s] *n* erba; ~**hopper** *n* cavalletta; ~**-roots** *adj* di base

grate [greɪt] *n* graticola (del focolare) ♦ *vi* cigolare, stridere ♦ *vt* (*CULIN*) grattugiare

grateful ['greɪtful] *adj* grato(a), riconoscente

grater ['greɪtə*] *n* grattugia

grating ['greɪtɪŋ] *n* (*iron bars*) grata ♦ *adj* (*noise*) stridente, stridulo(a)

gratitude ['grætɪtju:d] *n* gratitudine *f*

gratuity [grə'tju:ɪtɪ] *n* mancia

grave [greɪv] *n* tomba ♦ *adj* grave, serio(a)

gravel ['grævl] *n* ghiaia

gravestone ['greɪvstəun] *n* pietra tombale

graveyard ['greɪvjɑ:d] *n* cimitero

gravity ['grævɪtɪ] *n* (*PHYSICS*) gravità; pesantezza; (*seriousness*) gravità, serietà

gravy ['greɪvɪ] *n* intingolo della carne; salsa

gray [greɪ] *adj* = **grey**

graze [greɪz] *vi* pascolare, pascere ♦ *vt* (*touch lightly*) sfiorare; (*scrape*) escoriare ♦ *n* (*MED*) escoriazione *f*

grease [gri:s] *n* (*fat*) grasso; (*lubricant*) lubrificante *m* ♦ *vt* ingrassare; lubrificare; ~**proof paper** (*BRIT*) *n* carta oleata; **greasy** *adj* grasso(a), untuoso(a)

great [greɪt] *adj* grande; (*inf*) magnifico(a), meraviglioso(a); **G~ Britain** *n* Gran Bretagna; ~**-grandfather** *n* bisnonno; ~**-grandmother** *n* bisnonna; ~**ly** *adv* molto; ~**ness** *n* grandezza

Greece [gri:s] *n* Grecia

greed [gri:d] *n* (*also*: ~**iness**) avarizia; (*for food*) golosità, ghiottoneria; ~**y** *adj* avido(a); goloso(a), ghiotto(a)

Greek [gri:k] *adj* greco(a) ♦ *n* greco/a; (*LING*) greco

green [gri:n] *adj* verde; (*inexperienced*) inesperto(a), ingenuo(a) ♦ *n* verde *m*; (*stretch of grass*) prato; (*on golf course*) green *m inv*; ~**s** *npl* (*vegetables*) verdura; ~ **belt** *n* (*round town*) cintura di verde; ~ **card** *n* (*BRIT: AUT*) carta verde; (*US: ADMIN*) *permesso di soggiorno e di lavoro*; ~**ery** *n* verde *m*; ~**grocer** (*BRIT*) *n* fruttivendolo/a, erbivendolo/a; ~**house** *n* serra; ~**house effect** *n* effetto serra; ~**house gas** *n* gas responsabile dell'effetto serra; ~**ish** *adj* verdastro(a)

Greenland ['gri:nlənd] *n* Groenlandia

greet [gri:t] *vt* salutare; ~**ing** *n* saluto; ~**ing(s) card** *n* cartolina d'auguri

gregarious [grə'gɛərɪəs] *adj* (*person*) socievole

grenade [grə'neɪd] *n* (*also*: **hand ~**) granata

grew [gru:] *pt of* **grow**

grey [greɪ] *adj* grigio(a); ~**haired** *adj* dai

capelli grigi; **~hound** n levriere m
grid [grɪd] n grata; (ELEC) rete f
gridlock ['grɪdlɒk] n (traffic jam) paralisi f
inv del traffico; **~ed** adj paralizzato(a) dal
traffico; (talks etc) in fase di stallo
grief [griːf] n dolore m
grievance ['griːvəns] n lagnanza
grieve [griːv] vi addolorarsi; rattristarsi ♦ vt
addolorare; **to ~ for sb** (dead person)
piangere qn
grievous ['griːvəs] adj: **~ bodily harm** (LAW)
aggressione f
grill [grɪl] n (on cooker) griglia; (also: **mixed
~**) grigliata mista ♦ vt (BRIT) cuocere ai ferri;
(inf: question) interrogare senza sosta
grille [grɪl] n grata; (AUT) griglia
grim [grɪm] adj sinistro(a), brutto(a)
grimace [grɪ'meɪs] n smorfia ♦ vi fare
smorfie; fare boccacce
grime [graɪm] n sudiciume m
grin [grɪn] n sorriso smagliante ♦ vi fare un
gran sorriso
grind [graɪnd] (pt, pp **ground**) vt macinare;
(make sharp) arrotare ♦ n (work) sgobbata
grip [grɪp] n impugnatura; presa; (holdall)
borsa da viaggio ♦ vt (object) afferrare;
(attention) catturare; **to come to ~s with**
affrontare; cercare di risolvere
gripping ['grɪpɪŋ] adj avvincente
grisly ['grɪzlɪ] adj macabro(a), orrido(a)
gristle ['grɪsl] n cartilagine f
grit [grɪt] n ghiaia; (courage) fegato ♦ vt
(road) coprire di sabbia; **to ~ one's teeth**
stringere i denti
groan [grəʊn] n gemito ♦ vi gemere
grocer ['grəʊsə*] n negoziante m di generi
alimentari; **~ies** npl provviste fpl; **~'s
(shop)** n negozio di (generi) alimentari
groggy ['grɒgɪ] adj barcollante
groin [grɔɪn] n inguine m
groom [gruːm] n palafreniere m; (also:
bride~) sposo ♦ vt (horse) strigliare; (fig):
to ~ sb for avviare qn a; **well-~ed** (person)
curato(a)
groove [gruːv] n scanalatura, solco
grope [grəʊp] vi: **to ~ for** cercare a tastoni
gross [grəʊs] adj grossolano(a); (COMM)

lordo(a); **~ly** adv (greatly) molto
grotesque [grəʊ'tɛsk] adj grottesco(a)
grotto ['grɒtəʊ] n grotta
grotty ['grɒtɪ] (inf) adj terribile
ground [graʊnd] pt, pp of **grind** ♦ n suolo,
terra; (land) terreno; (SPORT) campo;
(reason: gen pl) ragione f; (US: also: **~ wire**)
terra f (plane) tenere a terra; (US: ELEC)
mettere la presa a terra a; **~s** npl (of coffee
etc) fondi mpl; (gardens etc) terreno,
giardini mpl; **on/to the ~** per/a terra; **to
gain/lose ~** guadagnare/perdere terreno;
~ cloth (US) n = **~sheet**; **~ing** n (in
education) basi fpl; **~less** adj infondato(a);
~sheet (BRIT) n telone m impermeabile; **~
staff** n personale m di terra; **~work** n
preparazione f
group [gruːp] n gruppo ♦ vt (also: **~
together**) raggruppare ♦ vi (also: **~
together**) raggrupparsi
grouse [graʊs] n inv (bird) tetraone m ♦ vi
(complain) brontolare
grove [grəʊv] n boschetto
grovel ['grɒvl] vi (fig): **to ~ (before)**
strisciare (di fronte a)
grow [grəʊ] (pt **grew**, pp **grown**) vi
crescere; (increase) aumentare; (develop)
svilupparsi; (become): **to ~ rich/weak**
arricchirsi/indebolirsi ♦ vt coltivare, far
crescere; **~ up** vi farsi grande, crescere;
~er n coltivatore/trice; **~ing** adj (fear,
amount) crescente
growl [graʊl] vi ringhiare
grown [grəʊn] pp of **grow**; **~-up** n adulto/
a, grande m/f
growth [grəʊθ] n crescita, sviluppo; (what
has grown) crescita; (MED) escrescenza,
tumore m
grub [grʌb] n larva; (inf: food) roba (da
mangiare)
grubby ['grʌbɪ] adj sporco(a)
grudge [grʌdʒ] n rancore m ♦ vt: **to ~ sb
sth** dare qc a qn di malavoglia; invidiare qc
a qn; **to bear sb a ~ (for)** serbar rancore a
qn (per)
gruelling ['grʊəlɪŋ] (US **grueling**) adj
estenuante

gruesome ['gru:səm] *adj* orribile

gruff [grʌf] *adj* rozzo(a)

grumble ['grʌmbl] *vi* brontolare, lagnarsi

grumpy ['grʌmpɪ] *adj* scorbutico(a)

grunt [grʌnt] *vi* grugnire

G-string *n* tanga *m inv*

guarantee [gærən'ti:] *n* garanzia ♦ *vt* garantire

guard [gɑ:d] *n* guardia; (*one man*) guardia, sentinella; (*BRIT: RAIL*) capotreno; (*on machine*) schermo protettivo; (*also:* **fire~**) parafuoco ♦ *vt* fare la guardia a; (*protect*): **to ~ (against)** proteggere (da); **to be on one's ~** stare in guardia; **~ against** *vt fus* guardarsi da; **~ed** *adj* (*fig*) cauto(a), guardingo(a); **~ian** *n* custode *m*; (*of minor*) tutore/trice; **~'s van** (*BRIT*) *n* (*RAIL*) vagone *m* di servizio

guerrilla [gə'rɪlə] *n* guerrigliero

guess [gɛs] *vi* indovinare ♦ *vt* indovinare; (*US*) credere, pensare ♦ *n*: **to take** *or* **have a ~** provare a indovinare; **~work** *n*: **I got the answer by ~work** ho azzeccato la risposta

guest [gɛst] *n* ospite *m/f*; (*in hotel*) cliente *m/f*; **~-house** *n* pensione *f*; **~ room** *n* camera degli ospiti

guffaw [gʌ'fɔ:] *vi* scoppiare in una risata sonora

guidance ['gaɪdəns] *n* guida, direzione *f*

guide [gaɪd] *n* (*person, book etc*) guida; (*BRIT: also:* **girl ~**) giovane esploratrice *f* ♦ *vt* guidare; **~book** *n* guida; **~ dog** *n* cane *m* guida *inv*; **~lines** *npl* (*fig*) indicazioni *fpl*, linee *fpl* direttive

guild [gɪld] *n* arte *f*, corporazione *f*; associazione *f*

guillotine ['gɪləti:n] *n* ghigliottina; (*for paper*) taglierina

guilt [gɪlt] *n* colpevolezza; **~y** *adj* colpevole

guinea pig ['gɪnɪ-] *n* cavia

guise [gaɪz] *n* maschera

guitar [gɪ'tɑ:*] *n* chitarra

gulf [gʌlf] *n* golfo; (*abyss*) abisso

gull [gʌl] *n* gabbiano

gullible ['gʌlɪbl] *adj* credulo(a)

gully ['gʌlɪ] *n* burrone *m*; gola; canale *m*

gulp [gʌlp] *vi* deglutire; (*from emotion*) avere il nodo in gola ♦ *vt* (*also:* **~ down**) tracannare, inghiottire

gum [gʌm] *n* (*ANAT*) gengiva; (*glue*) colla; (*also:* **~drop**) caramella gommosa; (*also:* **chewing ~**) chewing-gum *m* ♦ *vt*: **to ~ (together)** incollare; **~boots** (*BRIT*) *npl* stivali *mpl* di gomma

gumption ['gʌmpʃən] *n* spirito d'iniziativa, buonsenso

gun [gʌn] *n* fucile *m*; (*small*) pistola, rivoltella; (*rifle*) carabina; (*shotgun*) fucile da caccia; (*cannon*) cannone *m*; **~boat** *n* cannoniera; **~fire** *n* spari *mpl*; **~man** *n* bandito armato; **~point** *n*: **at ~point** sotto minaccia di fucile; **~powder** *n* polvere *f* da sparo; **~shot** *n* sparo

gurgle ['gə:gl] *vi* gorgogliare

gush [gʌʃ] *vi* sgorgare; (*fig*) abbandonarsi ad effusioni

gusset ['gʌsɪt] *n* gherone *m*

gust [gʌst] *n* (*of wind*) raffica; (*of smoke*) buffata

gusto ['gʌstəu] *n* entusiasmo

gut [gʌt] *n* intestino, budello; **~s** *npl* (*ANAT*) interiora *fpl*; (*courage*) fegato

gutter ['gʌtə*] *n* (*of roof*) grondaia; (*in street*) cunetta

guy [gaɪ] *n* (*inf: man*) tipo, elemento; (*also:* **~rope**) cavo *or* corda di fissaggio; (*figure*) effigie di Guy Fawkes

---
Guy Fawkes' Night

ⓘ Il 5 novembre si festeggia con falò e fuochi d'artificio la **Guy Fawkes' Night**, la notte in cui, nel 1605, fallì la Congiura delle Polveri contro Giacomo I; **Guy Fawkes** era il nome di uno dei cospiratori.

---

guzzle ['gʌzl] *vt* tranguglare

gym [dʒɪm] *n* (*also:* **gymnasium**) palestra; (*also:* **gymnastics**) ginnastica

gymnast ['dʒɪmnæst] *n* ginnasta *m/f*; **~ics** [-'næstɪks] *n*, *npl* ginnastica

gym shoes *npl* scarpe *fpl* da ginnastica

gym slip (*BRIT*) *n* grembiule *m* da scuola

(*per ragazze*)

gynaecologist [gaɪnɪ'kɔlədʒɪst] (*US* **gynecologist**) *n* ginecologo/a

gypsy ['dʒɪpsɪ] *n* = **gipsy**

gyrate [dʒaɪ'reɪt] *vi* girare

H, h

haberdashery ['hæbə'dæʃərɪ] (*BRIT*) *n* merceria

habit ['hæbɪt] *n* abitudine *f*; (*costume*) abito; (*REL*) tonaca

habitual [hə'bɪtjuəl] *adj* abituale; (*drinker, liar*) inveterato(a)

hack [hæk] *vt* tagliare, fare a pezzi ♦ *n* (*pej: writer*) scribacchino/a

hacker ['hækə*] *n* (*COMPUT*) pirata *m* informatico

hackney cab ['hæknɪ-] *n* carrozza a nolo

hackneyed ['hæknɪd] *adj* comune, trito(a)

had [hæd] *pt, pp of* **have**

haddock ['hædək] (*pl* ~ *or* ~**s**) *n* eglefino

hadn't ['hædnt] = **had not**

haemorrhage ['hemərɪdʒ] (*US* **hemorrhage**) *n* emorragia

haemorrhoids ['hemərɔɪdz] (*US* **hemorrhoids**) *npl* emorroidi *fpl*

haggard ['hægəd] *adj* smunto(a)

haggle ['hægl] *vi* mercanteggiare

Hague [heɪg] *n*: **The ~** L'Aia

hail [heɪl] *n* grandine *f*; (*of criticism etc*) pioggia ♦ *vt* (*call*) chiamare; (*flag down: taxi*) fermare; (*greet*) salutare ♦ *vi* grandinare; ~**stone** *n* chicco di grandine

hair [hɛə*] *n* capelli *mpl*; (*single hair: on head*) capello; (: *on body*) pelo; **to do one's ~** pettinarsi; ~**brush** *n* spazzola per capelli; ~**cut** *n* taglio di capelli; ~**do** ['hɛədu:] *n* acconciatura, pettinatura; ~**dresser** *n* parrucchiere/a; ~**dryer** *n* asciugacapelli *m inv*; ~ **grip** *n* forcina; ~**net** *n* retina per capelli; ~**pin** *n* forcina; ~**pin bend** (*US* ~**pin curve**) *n* tornante *m*; ~**raising** *adj* orripilante; ~ **removing cream** *n* crema depilatoria; ~ **spray** *n* lacca per capelli; ~**style** *n* pettinatura,

acconciatura; ~**y** *adj* irsuto(a); peloso(a); (*inf: frightening*) spaventoso(a)

hake [heɪk] (*pl* ~ *or* ~**s**) *n* nasello

half [hɑːf] (*pl* **halves**) *n* mezzo, metà *f inv* ♦ *adj* mezzo(a) ♦ *adv* a mezzo, a metà; ~ **an hour** mezz'ora; ~ **a dozen** mezza dozzina; ~ **a pound** mezza libbra; **two and a ~** due e mezzo; **a week and a ~** una settimana e mezza; ~ **(of it)** la metà; ~ **(of)** la metà di; **to cut sth in ~** tagliare qc in due; ~ **asleep** mezzo(a) addormentato(a); ~-**baked** *adj* (*scheme*) che non sta in piedi; ~ **board** (*BRIT*) *n* mezza pensione; ~-**caste** ['hɑːfkɑːst] *n* meticcio/a; ~ **fare** *n* tariffa a metà prezzo; ~-**hearted** *adj* tiepido(a); ~-**hour** *n* mezz'ora; ~-**mast**: **at** ~-**mast** *adv* (*flag*) a mezz'asta; ~**penny** ['heɪpnɪ] (*BRIT*) *n* mezzo penny *m inv*; ~-**price** *adj, adv* a metà prezzo; ~ **term** (*BRIT*) *n* (*SCOL*) vacanza a *or* di metà trimestre; ~-**time** *n* (*SPORT*) intervallo; ~**way** *adv* a metà strada

halibut ['hælɪbət] *n inv* ippoglosso

hall [hɔːl] *n* sala, salone *m*; (*entrance way*) entrata; ~ **of residence** (*BRIT*) *n* casa dello studente

hallmark ['hɔːlmɑːk] *n* marchio di garanzia; (*fig*) caratteristica

hallo [hə'ləu] *excl* = **hello**

Hallowe'en [hæləu'iːn] *n* vigilia d'Ognissanti

┌─────────────────────────────┐
│ **Hallowe'en** │
└─────────────────────────────┘

i *Negli Stati Uniti e in Scozia il 31 ottobre si festeggia* **Hallowe'en**, *la notte delle streghe e dei fantasmi; i bambini, travestiti da fantasmi e con lanterne ricavate da zucche, bussano alle porte e raccolgono dolci e piccoli doni.*

hallucination [həluːsɪ'neɪʃən] *n* allucinazione *f*

hallway ['hɔːlweɪ] *n* corridoio; (*entrance*) ingresso

halo ['heɪləu] *n* (*of saint etc*) aureola

halt [hɔːlt] *n* fermata ♦ *vt* fermare ♦ *vi* fermarsi

halve [hɑːv] *vt* (*apple etc*) dividere a metà; (*expense*) ridurre di metà

halves [hɑːvz] *npl of* **half**

ham [hæm] *n* prosciutto

Hamburg ['hæmbəːg] *n* Amburgo *f*

hamburger ['hæmbəːgə*] *n* hamburger *m inv*

hamlet ['hæmlɪt] *n* paesetto

hammer ['hæmə*] *n* martello ♦ *vt* martellare ♦ *vi*: **to ~ on** *or* **at the door** picchiare alla porta

hammock ['hæmək] *n* amaca

hamper ['hæmpə*] *vt* impedire ♦ *n* cesta

hamster ['hæmstə*] *n* criceto

hand [hænd] *n* mano *f*; (*of clock*) lancetta; (*handwriting*) scrittura; (*at cards*) mano; (: *game*) partita; (*worker*) operaio/a ♦ *vt* dare, passare; **to give sb a ~** dare una mano a qn; **at ~** a portata di mano; **in ~** a disposizione; (*work*) in corso; **on ~** (*person*) disponibile; (*services*) pronto(a) a intervenire; **to ~** (*information etc*) a portata di mano; **on the one ~ ..., on the other ~** da un lato ..., dall'altro; **~ in** *vt* consegnare; **~ out** *vt* distribuire; **~ over** *vt* passare; cedere; **~bag** *n* borsetta; **~book** *n* manuale *m*; **~brake** *n* freno a mano; **~cuffs** *npl* manette *fpl*; **~ful** *n* manciata, pugno

handicap ['hændɪkæp] *n* handicap *m inv* ♦ *vt* handicappare; **to be physically ~ped** essere handicappato(a); **to be mentally ~ped** essere un(a) handicappato(a) mentale

handicraft ['hændɪkrɑːft] *n* lavoro d'artigiano

handiwork ['hændɪwəːk] *n* opera

handkerchief ['hæŋkətʃɪf] *n* fazzoletto

handle ['hændl] *n* (*of door etc*) maniglia; (*of cup etc*) ansa; (*of knife etc*) impugnatura; (*of saucepan*) manico; (*for winding*) manovella ♦ *vt* toccare, maneggiare; (*deal with*) occuparsi di; (*treat: people*) trattare; "**~ with care**" "fragile"; **to fly off the ~** (*fig*) perdere le staffe, uscire dai gangheri; **~bar(s)** *n(pl)* manubrio

hand: **~ luggage** *n* bagagli *mpl* a mano;

~made *adj* fatto(a) a mano; **~out** *n* (*money, food*) elemosina; (*leaflet*) volantino; (*at lecture*) prospetto; **~rail** *n* corrimano; **~set** *n* (*TEL*) ricevitore *m*; **please replace the ~set** riagganciare il ricevitore; **~shake** *n* stretta di mano

handsome ['hænsəm] *adj* bello(a); (*profit, fortune*) considerevole

handwriting ['hændraɪtɪŋ] *n* scrittura

handy ['hændɪ] *adj* (*person*) bravo(a); (*close at hand*) a portata di mano; (*convenient*) comodo(a)

hang [hæŋ] (*pt, pp* **hung**) *vt* appendere; (*criminal: pt, pp* **hanged**) impiccare ♦ *vi* (*painting*) essere appeso(a); (*hair*) scendere; (*drapery*) cadere; **to get the ~ of sth** (*inf*) capire come qc funziona; **~ about** *or* **around** *vi* bighellonare, ciondolare; **~ on** *vi* (*wait*) aspettare; **~ up** *vi* (*TEL*) riattaccare ♦ *vt* appendere

hangar ['hæŋə*] *n* hangar *m inv*

hanger ['hæŋə*] *n* gruccia

hanger-on *n* parassita *m*

hang-gliding ['-glaɪdɪŋ] *n* volo col deltaplano

hangover ['hæŋəuvə*] *n* (*after drinking*) postumi *mpl* di sbornia

hang-up *n* complesso

hanker ['hæŋkə*] *vi*: **to ~ after** bramare

hankie ['hæŋkɪ] *n abbr* = **handkerchief**

hanky ['hæŋkɪ] *n abbr* = **handkerchief**

haphazard [hæp'hæzəd] *adj* a casaccio, alla carlona

happen ['hæpən] *vi* accadere, succedere; (*chance*): **to ~ to do sth** fare qc per caso; **as it ~s** guarda caso; **~ing** *n* avvenimento

happily ['hæpɪlɪ] *adv* felicemente; fortunatamente

happiness ['hæpɪnɪs] *n* felicità, contentezza

happy ['hæpɪ] *adj* felice, contento(a); **~ with** (*arrangements etc*) soddisfatto(a) di; **to be ~ to do** (*willing*) fare volentieri; **~ birthday!** buon compleanno!; **~-go-lucky** *adj* spensierato(a); **~ hour** *n orario in cui i bar hanno prezzi ridotti*

harangue [hə'ræŋ] *vt* arringare

harass ['hærəs] *vt* molestare; **~ment** *n*

molestia

harbour ['hɑːbə*] (*US* **harbor**) *n* porto ♦ *vt* (*hope, fear*) nutrire; (*criminal*) dare rifugio a

hard [hɑːd] *adj* duro(a) ♦ *adv* (*work*) sodo; (*think, try*) bene; **to look ~ at** guardare fissamente; esaminare attentamente; **no ~ feelings!** senza rancore!; **to be ~ of hearing** essere duro(a) d'orecchio; **to be ~ done by** essere trattato(a) ingiustamente; **~back** *n* libro rilegato; **~ cash** *n* denaro in contanti; **~ disk** *n* (*COMPUT*) disco rigido; **~en** *vt, vi* indurire; **~-headed** *adj* pratico(a); **~ labour** *n* lavori forzati *mpl*

hardly ['hɑːdlɪ] *adv* (*scarcely*) appena; **it's ~ the case** non è proprio il caso; **~ anyone/anywhere** quasi nessuno/da nessuna parte; **~ ever** quasi mai

hardship ['hɑːdʃɪp] *n* avversità *f inv*; privazioni *fpl*

hard shoulder (*BRIT*) *n* (*AUT*) corsia d'emergenza

hard-up (*inf*) *adj* al verde

hardware ['hɑːdwɛə*] *n* ferramenta *fpl*; (*COMPUT*) hardware *m*; (*MIL*) armamenti *mpl*; **~ shop** *n* (negozio di) ferramenta *fpl*

hard-wearing [-'wɛərɪŋ] *adj* resistente; (*shoes*) robusto(a)

hard-working [-'wəːkɪŋ] *adj* lavoratore(trice)

hardy ['hɑːdɪ] *adj* robusto(a); (*plant*) resistente al gelo

hare [hɛə*] *n* lepre *f*; **~-brained** *adj* folle; scervellato(a)

harm [hɑːm] *n* male *m*; (*wrong*) danno ♦ *vt* (*person*) fare male a; (*thing*) danneggiare; **out of ~'s way** al sicuro; **~ful** *adj* dannoso(a); **~less** *adj* innocuo(a); inoffensivo(a)

harmonica [hɑːˈmɔnɪkə] *n* armonica

harmonious [hɑːˈməunɪəs] *adj* armonioso(a)

harmony ['hɑːmənɪ] *n* armonia

harness ['hɑːnɪs] *n* (*for horse*) bardatura, finimenti *mpl*; (*for child*) briglie *fpl*; (*safety ~*) imbracatura ♦ *vt* (*horse*) bardare; (*resources*) sfruttare

harp [hɑːp] *n* arpa ♦ *vi*: **to ~ on about**

insistere tediosamente su

harpoon [hɑːˈpuːn] *n* arpione *m*

harrowing ['hærəuŋ] *adj* straziante

harsh [hɑːʃ] *adj* (*life, winter*) duro(a); (*judge, criticism*) severo(a); (*sound*) rauco(a); (*light*) violento(a)

harvest ['hɑːvɪst] *n* raccolto; (*of grapes*) vendemmia ♦ *vt* fare il raccolto di, raccogliere; vendemmiare

has [hæz] *vb see* **have**

hash [hæʃ] *n* (*CULIN*) specie di spezzatino fatto con carne già cotta; (*fig: mess*) pasticcio

hasn't ['hæznt] = **has not**

hassle ['hæsl] (*inf*) *n* sacco di problemi

haste [heɪst] *n* fretta; precipitazione *f*; **~n** ['heɪsn] *vt* affrettare ♦ *vi*: **to ~n (to)** affrettarsi (a); **hastily** *adv* in fretta; precipitosamente; **hasty** *adj* affrettato(a); precipitoso(a)

hat [hæt] *n* cappello

hatch [hætʃ] *n* (*NAUT: also:* **~way**) boccaporto; (*also:* **service ~**) portello di servizio ♦ *vi* (*bird*) uscire dal guscio; (*egg*) schiudersi

hatchback ['hætʃbæk] *n* (*AUT*) tre (*or* cinque) porte *f inv*

hatchet ['hætʃɪt] *n* accetta

hate [heɪt] *vt* odiare, detestare ♦ *n* odio; **~ful** *adj* odioso(a), detestabile

hatred ['heɪtrɪd] *n* odio

haughty ['hɔːtɪ] *adj* altero(a), arrogante

haul [hɔːl] *vt* trascinare, tirare ♦ *n* (*of fish*) pescata; (*of stolen goods etc*) bottino; **~age** *n* trasporto; autotrasporto; **~ier** (*US* **~er**) *n* trasportatore *m*

haunch [hɔːntʃ] *n* anca; (*of meat*) coscia

haunt [hɔːnt] *vt* (*subj: fear*) pervadere; (*: person*) frequentare ♦ *n* rifugio; **this house is ~ed** questa casa è abitata da un fantasma

---

KEYWORD

---

have [hæv] (*pt, pp* **had**) *aux vb* **1** (*gen*) avere; essere; **to ~ arrived/gone** essere arrivato(a)/andato(a); **to ~ eaten/slept** avere mangiato/dormito; **he has been**

kind/promoted è stato gentile/promosso; **having finished** or **when he had finished, he left** dopo aver finito, se n'è andato
2 (in tag questions): **you've done it, ~n't you?** l'ha fatto, (non è) vero?; **he hasn't done it, has he?** non l'ha fatto, vero?
3 (in short answers and questions): **you've made a mistake – no I ~n't/so I ~** ha fatto un errore — ma no, niente affatto/sì, è vero; **we ~n't paid – yes we ~!** non abbiamo pagato — ma sì che abbiamo pagato!; **I've been there before, ~ you?** ci sono già stato, e lei?

♦ modal aux vb (be obliged): **to ~ (got) to do sth** dover fare qc; **I ~n't got** or **I don't ~ to wear glasses** non ho bisogno di portare gli occhiali

♦ vt 1 (possess, obtain) avere; **he has (got) blue eyes/dark hair** ha gli occhi azzurri/i capelli scuri; **do you ~** or **you got a car/phone?** ha la macchina/il telefono?; **may I ~ your address?** potrebbe darmi il suo indirizzo?; **you can ~ it for £5** te lo lascio per 5 sterline
2 (+noun: take, hold etc): **to ~ breakfast/a swim/a bath** fare colazione/una nuotata/un bagno; **to ~ lunch** pranzare; **to ~ dinner** cenare; **to ~ a drink** bere qualcosa; **to ~ a cigarette** fumare una sigaretta
3: **to ~ sth done** far fare qc; **to ~ one's hair cut** farsi tagliare i capelli; **to ~ sb do sth** far fare qc a qn
4 (experience, suffer) avere; **to ~ a cold/flu** avere il raffreddore/l'influenza; **she had her bag stolen** le hanno rubato la borsa
5 (inf: dupe): **you've been had!** ci sei cascato!
have out vt: **to ~ it out with sb** (settle a problem etc) mettere le cose in chiaro con qn

haven ['heɪvn] n porto; (fig) rifugio
haven't ['hævnt] = **have not**
havoc ['hævək] n caos m
hawk [hɔːk] n falco
hay [heɪ] n fieno; **~ fever** n febbre f da fieno; **~stack** n pagliaio

haywire ['heɪwaɪə*] (inf) adj: **to go ~** impazzire
hazard ['hæzəd] n azzardo, ventura; pericolo, rischio ♦ vt (guess etc) azzardare; **~ous** adj pericoloso(a); **~ (warning) lights** npl (AUT) luci fpl di emergenza
haze [heɪz] n foschia
hazelnut ['heɪzlnʌt] n nocciola
hazy ['heɪzɪ] adj fosco(a); (idea) vago(a)
he [hiː] pronoun lui, egli; **it is ~ who ...** è lui che ....
head [hɛd] n testa; (leader) capo; (of school) preside m/f ♦ vt (list) essere in testa a; (group) essere a capo di; **~s (or tails)** testa (o croce), pari (o dispari); **~ first** a capofitto, di testa; **~ over heels in love** pazzamente innamorato(a); **to ~ the ball** colpire una palla di testa; **~ for** vt fus dirigersi verso; **~ache** n mal m di testa; **~dress** (BRIT) n (of bride) acconciatura; **~ing** n titolo; intestazione f; **~lamp** (BRIT) n = **~light**; **~land** n promontorio; **~light** n fanale m; **~line** n titolo; **~long** adv (fall) a capofitto; (rush) precipitosamente; **~master/mistress** n preside m/f; **~ office** n sede f (centrale); **~-on** adj (collision) frontale; **~phones** npl cuffia; **~quarters** npl ufficio centrale; (MIL) quartiere m generale; **~-rest** n poggiacapo; **~room** n (in car) altezza dell'abitacolo; (under bridge) altezza limite; **~scarf** n foulard m inv; **~strong** adj testardo(a); **~ waiter** n capocameriere m; **~way** n: **to make ~way** fare progressi; **~wind** n controvento; **~y** adj (experience, period) inebriante
heal [hiːl] vt, vi guarire
health [hɛlθ] n salute f; **~ centre** (BRIT) n poliambulatorio; **~ food(s)** n(pl) cibo macrobiotico; **~ food store** n negozio di alimenti dietetici e macrobiotici; **the H~ Service** (BRIT) n ≈ il Servizio Sanitario Statale; **~y** adj (person) sano(a), in buona salute; (climate) salubre; (appetite, economy etc) sano(a)
heap [hiːp] n mucchio ♦ vt (stones, sand): **to ~ (up)** ammucchiare; (plate, sink): **to ~**

sth with riempire qc di; **~s of** (*inf*) un mucchio di

hear [hɪə*] (*pt, pp* **heard**) *vt* sentire; (*news*) ascoltare ♦ *vi* sentire; **to ~ about** avere notizie di; sentire parlare di; **to ~ from sb** ricevere notizie da qn; **~ing** *n* (*sense*) udito; (*of witnesses*) audizione *f*; (*of a case*) udienza; **~ing aid** *n* apparecchio acustico; **~say** *n* dicerie *fpl*, chiacchiere *fpl*

hearse [həːs] *n* carro funebre

heart [hɑːt] *n* cuore *m*; **~s** *npl* (*CARDS*) cuori *mpl*; **to lose ~** scoraggiarsi; **to take ~** farsi coraggio; **at ~** in fondo; **by ~** (*learn, know*) a memoria; **~ attack** *n* attacco di cuore; **~beat** *n* battito del cuore; **~breaking** *adj* straziante; **~broken** *adj*: **to be ~broken** avere il cuore spezzato; **~burn** *n* bruciore *m* di stomaco; **~ failure** *n* arresto cardiaco; **~felt** *adj* sincero(a)

hearth [hɑːθ] *n* focolare *m*

heartland ['hɑːtlænd] *n* regione *f* centrale

heartless ['hɑːtlɪs] *adj* senza cuore

hearty ['hɑːtɪ] *adj* caloroso(a); robusto(a), sano(a); vigoroso(a)

heat [hiːt] *n* calore *m*; (*fig*) ardore *m*; fuoco; (*SPORT: also*: **qualifying ~**) prova eliminatoria ♦ *vt* scaldare; **~ up** *vi* (*liquids*) scaldarsi; (*room*) riscaldarsi ♦ *vt* scaldare; **~ed** *adj* riscaldato(a); (*argument*) acceso(a); **~er** *n* radiatore *m*; (*stove*) stufa

heath [hiːθ] *n* (*BRIT*) landa

heathen ['hiːðən] *n* pagano/a

heather ['hɛðə*] *n* erica

heating ['hiːtɪŋ] *n* riscaldamento

heatstroke ['hiːtstrəuk] *n* colpo di sole

heatwave ['hiːtweɪv] *n* ondata di caldo

heave [hiːv] *vt* (*pull*) tirare (con forza); (*push*) spingere (con forza); (*lift*) sollevare (con forza) ♦ *vi* sollevarsi; (*retch*) aver conati di vomito ♦ *n* (*push*) grande spinta; **to ~ a sigh** emettere un sospiro

heaven ['hɛvn] *n* paradiso, cielo; **~ly** *adj* divino(a), celeste

heavily ['hɛvɪlɪ] *adv* pesantemente; (*drink, smoke*) molto

heavy ['hɛvɪ] *adj* pesante; (*sea*) grosso(a); (*rain, blow*) forte; (*weather*) afoso(a);

(*drinker, smoker*) gran (*before noun*); **~ goods vehicle** *n* veicolo per trasporti pesanti; **~weight** *n* (*SPORT*) peso massimo

Hebrew ['hiːbruː] *adj* ebreo(a) ♦ *n* (*LING*) ebraico

Hebrides ['hɛbrɪdiːz] *npl*: **the ~** le Ebridi

heckle ['hɛkl] *vt* interpellare e dare noia a (*un oratore*)

hectic ['hɛktɪk] *adj* movimentato(a)

he'd [hiːd] = **he would; he had**

hedge [hɛdʒ] *n* siepe *f* ♦ *vi* essere elusivo(a); **to ~ one's bets** (*fig*) coprirsi dai rischi

hedgehog ['hɛdʒhɒg] *n* riccio

heed [hiːd] *vt* (*also*: **take ~ of**) badare a, far conto di; **~less** *adj*: **~less (of)** sordo(a) (a)

heel [hiːl] *n* (*ANAT*) calcagno; (*of shoe*) tacco ♦ *vt* (*shoe*) rifare i tacchi a

hefty ['hɛftɪ] *adj* (*person*) robusto(a); (*parcel*) pesante; (*profit*) grosso(a)

heifer ['hɛfə*] *n* giovenca

height [haɪt] *n* altezza; (*high ground*) altura; (*fig: of glory*) apice *m*; (: *of stupidity*) colmo; **~en** *vt* (*fig*) accrescere

heir [ɛə*] *n* erede *m*; **~ess** *n* erede *f*; **~loom** *n* mobile *m* (*or* gioiello *or* quadro) di famiglia

held [hɛld] *pt, pp of* **hold**

helicopter ['hɛlɪkɒptə*] *n* elicottero

heliport ['hɛlɪpɔːt] *n* eliporto

helium ['hiːlɪəm] *n* elio

hell [hɛl] *n* inferno; **~!** (*inf*) porca miseria!, accidenti!

he'll [hiːl] = **he will; he shall**

hellish ['hɛlɪʃ] (*inf*) *adj* infernale

hello [hə'ləu] *excl* buon giorno!; ciao! (*to sb one addresses as "tu"*); (*surprise*) ma guarda!

helm [hɛlm] *n* (*NAUT*) timone *m*

helmet ['hɛlmɪt] *n* casco

help [hɛlp] *n* aiuto; (*charwoman*) donna di servizio ♦ *vt* aiutare; **~!** aiuto!; **~ yourself (to bread)** si serva (del pane); **he can't ~ it** non ci può far niente; **~er** *n* aiutante *m/f*, assistente *m/f*; **~ful** *adj* di grande aiuto; (*useful*) utile; **~ing** *n* porzione *f*; **~less** *adj* impotente; debole

hem [hem] *n* orlo ♦ *vt* fare l'orlo a; **~ in** *vt* cingere

hemisphere ['hemɪsfɪə*] *n* emisfero

hemorrhage ['hemərɪdʒ] *(US) n* = **haemorrhage**

hemorrhoids ['hemərɔɪdz] *(US) npl* = **haemorrhoids**

hen [hen] *n* gallina; *(female bird)* femmina

hence [hens] *adv (therefore)* dunque; **2 years ~** di qui a 2 anni; **~forth** *adv* d'ora in poi

henpecked ['henpekt] *adj* dominato dalla moglie

hepatitis [hepə'taɪtɪs] *n* epatite *f*

her [hə:*] *pron (direct)* la, l' +*vowel; (indirect)* le; *(stressed, after prep)* lei ♦ *adj* il(la) suo(a), i(le) suoi(sue); *see also* **me; my**

herald ['herəld] *n* araldo ♦ *vt* annunciare

heraldry ['herəldrɪ] *n* araldica

herb [hə:b] *n* erba

herd [hə:d] *n* mandria

here [hɪə*] *adv* qui, qua ♦ *excl* ehi!; **~!** *(at roll call)* presente!; **~ is/are** ecco; **~ he/ she is** eccolo/eccola; **~after** *adv* in futuro; dopo questo; **~by** *adv (in letter)* con la presente

hereditary [hɪ'redɪtrɪ] *adj* ereditario(a)

heresy ['herəsɪ] *n* eresia

heretic ['herətɪk] *n* eretico/a

heritage ['herɪtɪdʒ] *n* eredità; *(fig)* retaggio

hermetically [hə:'metɪklɪ] *adv*: **~ sealed** ermeticamente chiuso(a)

hermit ['hə:mɪt] *n* eremita *m*

hernia ['hə:nɪə] *n* ernia

hero ['hɪərəu] *(pl ~es) n* eroe *m*

heroin ['herəuɪn] *n* eroina

heroine ['herəuɪn] *n* eroina

heron ['herən] *n* airone *m*

herring ['herɪŋ] *n* aringa

hers [hə:z] *pron* il(la) suo(a), i(le) suoi(sue); *see also* **mine**¹

herself [hə:'self] *pron (reflexive)* si; *(emphatic)* lei stessa; *(after prep)* se stessa, sé; *see also* **oneself**

he's [hi:z] = **he is; he has**

hesitant ['hezɪtənt] *adj* esitante, indeciso(a)

hesitate ['hezɪteɪt] *vi*: **to ~ (about/to do)**

esitare (su/a fare); **hesitation** [-'teɪʃən] *n* esitazione *f*

heterosexual ['hetərəu'seksjuəl] *adj, n* eterosessuale *m/f*

hexagonal [hek'sægənəl] *adj* esagonale

heyday ['heɪdeɪ] *n*: **the ~ of** i bei giorni di, l'età d'oro di

HGV *n abbr* = **heavy goods vehicle**

hi [haɪ] *excl* ciao!

hiatus [haɪ'eɪtəs] *n* vuoto; *(LING)* iato

hibernate ['haɪbəneɪt] *vi* ibernare

hiccough ['hɪkʌp] *vi* singhiozzare; **~s** *npl*: **to have ~s** avere il singhiozzo

hiccup ['hɪkʌp] = **hiccough**

hid [hɪd] *pt of* **hide**; **~den** ['hɪdn] *pp of* **hide**

hide [haɪd] *(pt* **hid**, *pp* **hidden**) *n (skin)* pelle *f* ♦ *vt*: **to ~ sth (from sb)** nascondere qc (a qn) ♦ *vi*: **to ~ (from sb)** nascondersi (da qn); **~-and-seek** *n* rimpiattino

hideous ['hɪdɪəs] *adj* laido(a); orribile

hiding ['haɪdɪŋ] *n (beating)* bastonata; **to be in ~** *(concealed)* tenersi nascosto(a)

hierarchy ['haɪərɑːkɪ] *n* gerarchia

hi-fi ['haɪfaɪ] *n* stereo ♦ *adj* ad alta fedeltà, hi-fi *inv*

high [haɪ] *adj* alto(a); *(speed, respect, number)* grande; *(wind)* forte; *(voice)* acuto(a) ♦ *adv* alto, in alto; **20m ~** alto(a) 20m; **~brow** *adj, n* intellettuale *m/f*; **~chair** *n* seggiolone *m*; **~er education** *n* studi *mpl* superiori; **~-handed** *adj* prepotente; **~-heeled** *adj* con i tacchi alti; **~ jump** *n (SPORT)* salto in alto; **the H~lands** *npl* le Highlands scozzesi; **~light** *n (fig: of event)* momento culminante; *(in hair)* colpo di sole ♦ *vt* mettere in evidenza; **~ly** *adv* molto; **to speak ~ly of** parlare molto bene di; **~ly strung** *adj* teso(a) di nervi, eccitabile; **~ness** *n*: **Her H~ness** Sua Altezza; **~-pitched** *adj* acuto(a); **~-rise block** *n* palazzone *m*; **~ school** *n* scuola secondaria; *(US)* istituto superiore d'istruzione; **~ season** *(BRIT) n* alta stagione; **~ street** *(BRIT) n* strada principale

highway ['haɪweɪ] *n* strada maestra; **H~ Code** *(BRIT) n* codice *m* della strada

hijack [ˈhaɪdʒæk] *vt* dirottare; **~er** *n* dirottatore/trice

hike [haɪk] *vi* fare un'escursione a piedi ♦ *n* escursione *f* a piedi; **~r** *n* escursionista *m/f*; **hiking** *n* escursioni *fpl* a piedi

hilarious [hɪˈlɛərɪəs] *adj* (*behaviour, event*) spassosissimo(a)

hill [hɪl] *n* collina, colle *m*; (*fairly high*) montagna; (*on road*) salita; **~side** *n* fianco della collina; **~ walking** *n* escursioni *fpl* in collina; **~y** *adj* collinoso(a); montagnoso(a)

hilt [hɪlt] *n* (*of sword*) elsa; **to the ~** (*fig: support*) fino in fondo

him [hɪm] *pron* (*direct*) lo, l' +*vowel*; (*indirect*) gli; (*stressed, after prep*) lui; *see also* **me**; **~self** *pron* (*reflexive*) si; (*emphatic*) lui stesso; (*after prep*) se stesso, sé; *see also* **oneself**

hinder [ˈhɪndə*] *vt* ostacolare; **hindrance** [ˈhɪndrəns] *n* ostacolo, impedimento

hindsight [ˈhaɪndsaɪt] *n*: **with ~** con il senno di poi

Hindu [ˈhɪnduː] *n* indù *m/f inv*

hinge [hɪndʒ] *n* cardine *m* ♦ *vi* (*fig*): **to ~ on** dipendere da

hint [hɪnt] *n* (*suggestion*) allusione *f*; (*advice*) consiglio; (*sign*) accenno ♦ *vt*: **to ~ that** lasciar capire che ♦ *vi*: **to ~ at** alludere a

hip [hɪp] *n* anca, fianco

hippopotamus [hɪpəˈpɒtəməs] (*pl* **~es** *or* **hippopotami**) *n* ippopotamo

hire [ˈhaɪə*] *vt* (*BRIT: car, equipment*) noleggiare; (*worker*) assumere, dare lavoro a ♦ *n* nolo, noleggio; **for ~** da nolo; (*taxi*) libero(a); **~(d) car** (*BRIT*) *n* macchina a nolo; **~ purchase** (*BRIT*) *n* acquisto (*or* vendita) rateale

his [hɪz] *adj, pron* il(la) suo(sua), i(le) suoi(sue); *see also* **my**; **mine¹**

hiss [hɪs] *vi* fischiare; (*cat, snake*) sibilare

historic(al) [hɪˈstɔrɪk(l)] *adj* storico(a)

history [ˈhɪstərɪ] *n* storia

hit [hɪt] (*pt, pp* **hit**) *vt* colpire, picchiare; (*knock against*) battere; (*reach: target*) raggiungere; (*collide with: car*) urtare contro; (*fig: affect*) colpire; (*find: problem etc*) incontrare ♦ *n* colpo; (*success, song*)

successo; **to ~ it off with sb** andare molto d'accordo con qn; **~-and-run driver** *n* pirata *m* della strada

hitch [hɪtʃ] *vt* (*fasten*) attaccare; (*also:* **~ up**) tirare su ♦ *n* (*difficulty*) intoppo, difficoltà *f inv*; **to ~ a lift** fare l'autostop

hitch-hike *vi* fare l'autostop; **~r** *n* autostoppista *m/f*; **hitch-hiking** *n* autostop *m*

hi-tech [ˈhaɪtek] *adj* di alta tecnologia ♦ *n* alta tecnologia

hitherto [hɪðəˈtuː] *adv* in precedenza

HIV *abbr*: **HIV-negative/-positive** *adj* sieronegativo(a)/sieropositivo(a)

hive [haɪv] *n* alveare *m*

H.M.S. *abbr* = **His(Her) Majesty's Ship**

hoard [hɔːd] *n* (*of food*) provviste *fpl*; (*of money*) gruzzolo ♦ *vt* ammassare

hoarding [ˈhɔːdɪŋ] (*BRIT*) *n* (*for posters*) tabellone *m* per affissioni

hoarse [hɔːs] *adj* rauco(a)

hoax [həuks] *n* scherzo; falso allarme

hob [hɒb] *n* piastra (con fornelli)

hobble [ˈhɒbl] *vi* zoppicare

hobby [ˈhɒbɪ] *n* hobby *m inv*, passatempo

hobo [ˈhəubəu] (*US*) *n* vagabondo

hockey [ˈhɒkɪ] *n* hockey *m*

hoe [həu] *n* zappa

hog [hɒg] *n* maiale *m* ♦ *vt* (*fig*) arraffare; **to go the whole ~** farlo fino in fondo

hoist [hɔɪst] *n* paranco ♦ *vt* issare

hold [həuld] (*pt, pp* **held**) *vt* tenere; (*contain*) contenere; (*keep back*) trattenere; (*believe*) mantenere; considerare; (*possess*) avere, possedere; detenere ♦ *vi* (*withstand pressure*) tenere; (*be valid*) essere valido(a) ♦ *n* presa; (*control*): **to have a ~ over** avere controllo su; (*NAUT*) stiva; **~ the line!** (*TEL*) resti in linea!; **to ~ one's own** (*fig*) difendersi bene; **to catch** *or* **get (a) ~ of** afferrare; **~ back** *vt* trattenere; (*secret*) tenere celato(a); **~ down** *vt* (*person*) tenere a terra; (*job*) tenere; **~ off** *vt* tener lontano; **~ on** *vi* tener fermo; (*wait*) aspettare; **~ on!** (*TEL*) resti in linea!; **~ on to** *vt fus* tenersi stretto a; (*keep*) conservare; **~ out** *vt* offrire ♦ *vi* (*resist*) resistere; ~ **up** vt (raise) alzare; (support) sostenere; (delay) ritardare; (rob) assaltire; ~**all** (BRIT) n borsone m; ~**er** n (container) contenitore m; (of ticket, title) possessore/posseditrice; (of office etc) incaricato/a; (of record) detentore/trice; ~**ing** n (share) azioni fpl, titoli mpl; (farm) podere m, tenuta; ~**up** n (robbery) rapina a mano armata; (delay) ritardo; (BRIT: in traffic) blocco

hole [həul] n buco, buca

holiday ['hɔlədɪ] n vacanza; (day off) giorno di vacanza; (public) giorno festivo; **on ~** in vacanza; ~ **camp** (BRIT) n (also: ~ **centre**) ≈ villaggio (di vacanze); ~**maker** (BRIT) n villeggiante m/f; ~ **resort** n luogo di villeggiatura

holiness ['həulɪnɪs] n santità

Holland ['hɔlənd] n Olanda

hollow ['hɔləu] adj cavo(a); (container, claim) vuoto(a); (laugh, sound) cupo(a) ♦ n cavità f inv; (in land) valletta, depressione f ♦ vt: **to ~ out** scavare

holly ['hɔlɪ] n agrifoglio

holocaust ['hɔləkɔːst] n olocausto

holster ['həulstə*] n fondina (di pistola)

holy ['həulɪ] adj santo(a); (bread) benedetto(a), consacrato(a); (ground) consacrato(a)

homage ['hɔmɪdʒ] n omaggio; **to pay ~ to** rendere omaggio a

home [həum] n casa; (country) patria, (institution) casa, ricovero ♦ cpd familiare; (cooking etc) casalingo(a); (ECON, POL) nazionale, interno(a); (SPORT) di casa ♦ adv a casa; in patria; (right in: nail etc) fino in fondo; **at ~** a casa; (in situation) a proprio agio; **to go (or come) ~** tornare a casa (or in patria); **make yourself at ~** si metta a suo agio; ~ **address** n indirizzo di casa; ~**land** n patria; ~**less** adj senza tetto; spatriato(a); ~**ly** adj semplice, alla buona; accogliente; ~-**made** adj casalingo(a); **H~ Office** (BRIT) n ministero degli Interni; ~ **rule** n autogoverno; **H~ Secretary** (BRIT) n ministro degli Interni; ~**sick** adj: **to be ~sick** avere la nostalgia; ~ **town** n città f

inv natale; ~**ward** ['həumwəd] adj (journey) di ritorno; ~**work** n compiti mpl (per casa)

homicide ['hɔmɪsaɪd] (US) n omicidio

homoeopathic [həumɪə'pæθɪk] (US **homeopathic**) adj omeopatico(a)

homosexual [hɔməu'sɛksjuəl] adj, n omosessuale m/f

honest ['ɔnɪst] adj onesto(a); sincero(a); ~**ly** adv onestamente; sinceramente; ~**y** n onestà

honey ['hʌnɪ] n miele m; ~**comb** n favo; ~**moon** n luna di miele, viaggio di nozze; ~**suckle** n (BOT) caprifoglio

honk [hɔŋk] vi suonare il clacson

honorary ['ɔnərərɪ] adj onorario(a); (duty, title) onorifico(a)

honour ['ɔnə*] (US **honor**) vt onorare ♦ n onore m; ~**able** adj onorevole; ~**s degree** n (SCOL) laurea specializzata

hood [hud] n cappuccio; (on cooker) cappa; (BRIT: AUT) capote f; (US: AUT) cofano

hoodlum ['huːdləm] n teppista m/f

hoof [huːf] (pl **hooves**) n zoccolo

hook [huk] n gancio; (for fishing) amo ♦ vt uncinare; (dress) agganciare

hooligan ['huːlɪgən] n giovinastro, teppista m

hoop [huːp] n cerchio

hooray [huː'reɪ] excl = **hurray**

hoot [huːt] vi (AUT) suonare il clacson; (siren) ululare; (owl) gufare; ~**er** n (BRIT: AUT) clacson m inv; (NAUT) sirena

Hoover ® ['huːvə*] (BRIT) n aspirapolvere m inv ♦ vt: **h~** pulire con l'aspirapolvere

hooves [huːvz] npl of **hoof**

hop [hɔp] vi saltellare, saltare; (on one foot) saltare su una gamba

hope [həup] vt: **to ~ that/to do** sperare che/di fare ♦ vi sperare ♦ n speranza; **I ~ so/not** spero di sì/no; ~**ful** adj (person) pieno(a) di speranza; (situation) promettente; ~**fully** adv con speranza; ~**fully he will recover** speriamo che si riprenda; ~**less** adj senza speranza, disperato(a); (useless) inutile

hops [hɔps] npl luppoli mpl

horde [hɔːd] n orda

horizon [həˈraɪzn] n orizzonte m; ~**tal** [hɒrɪˈzɒntl] adj orizzontale

hormone [ˈhɔːməun] n ormone m

horn [hɔːn] n (ZOOL, MUS) corno; (AUT) clacson m inv

hornet [ˈhɔːnɪt] n calabrone m

horoscope [ˈhɒrəskəup] n oroscopo

horrendous [həˈrendəs] adj orrendo(a)

horrible [ˈhɒrɪbl] adj orribile, tremendo(a)

horrid [ˈhɒrɪd] adj orrido(a); (person) odioso(a)

horrify [ˈhɒrɪfaɪ] vt scandalizzare

horror [ˈhɒrə*] n orrore m; ~ **film** n film m inv dell'orrore

hors d'œuvre [ɔːˈdəːvrə] n antipasto

horse [hɔːs] n cavallo; ~**back: on** ~**back** adj, adv a cavallo; ~ **chestnut** n ippocastano; ~**man** (irreg) n cavaliere m; ~**power** n cavallo (vapore); ~-**racing** n ippica; ~**radish** n rafano; ~**shoe** n ferro di cavallo; ~**woman** (irreg) n amazzone f

horticulture [ˈhɔːtɪkʌltʃə*] n orticoltura

hose [həuz] n (also: ~**pipe**) tubo; (also: **garden** ~) tubo per annaffiare

hosiery [ˈhəuʒərɪ] n maglieria

hospice [ˈhɒspɪs] n ricovero, ospizio

hospitable [hɒsˈpɪtəbl] adj ospitale

hospital [ˈhɒspɪtl] n ospedale m

hospitality [hɒspɪˈtælɪtɪ] n ospitalità

host [həust] n ospite m; (REL) ostia; (large number): **a ~ of** una schiera di

hostage [ˈhɒstɪdʒ] n ostaggio/a

hostel [ˈhɒstl] n ostello; (also: **youth ~**) ostello della gioventù

hostess [ˈhəustɪs] n ospite f; (BRIT: **air ~**) hostess f inv

hostile [ˈhɒstaɪl] adj ostile

hostility [hɒˈstɪlɪtɪ] n ostilità f inv

hot [hɒt] adj caldo(a); (as opposed to only warm) molto caldo(a); (spicy) piccante; (fig) accanito(a); ardente; violento(a), focoso(a); **to be ~** (person) aver caldo; (object) essere caldo(a); (weather) far caldo; ~**bed** n (fig) focolaio; ~ **dog** n hot dog m inv

hotel [həuˈtel] n albergo; ~**ier** n albergatore/trice

hot: ~**house** n serra; ~ **line** n (POL)

telefono rosso; ~**ly** adv violentemente; ~**plate** n (on cooker) piastra riscaldante; ~**pot** n (BRIT) stufato coperto da uno strato di patate; ~-**water bottle** n borsa dell'acqua calda

hound [haund] vt perseguitare ♦ n segugio

hour [ˈauə*] n ora; ~**ly** adj all'ora

house [n haus, pl ˈhauzɪz, vb hauz] n (also firm) casa; (POL) camera; (THEATRE) sala; pubblico; spettacolo; (dynasty) casata ♦ vt (person) ospitare, alloggiare; **on the ~** (fig) offerto(a) dalla casa; ~ **arrest** n arresti mpl domiciliari; ~**boat** n house boat f inv; ~**bound** adj confinato(a) in casa; ~**breaking** n furto con scasso; ~**hold** n famiglia; casa; ~**keeper** n governante f; ~**keeping** n (work) governo della casa; (money) soldi mpl per le spese di casa; ~-**warming party** n festa per inaugurare la casa nuova; ~**wife** (irreg) n massaia, casalinga; ~**work** n faccende fpl domestiche

housing [ˈhauzɪŋ] n alloggio; ~ **development** (BRIT ~ **estate**) n zona residenziale con case popolari e/o private

hovel [ˈhɒvl] n casupola

hover [ˈhɒvə*] vi (bird) librarsi; ~**craft** n hovercraft m inv

how [hau] adv come; ~ **are you?** come sta?; ~ **do you do?** piacere!; ~ **far is it to the river?** quanto è lontano il fiume?; ~ **long have you been here?** da quando è qui?; ~ **lovely!/awful!** che bello!/orrore!; ~ **many?** quanti(e)?; ~ **much?** quanto(a)?; ~ **much milk?** quanto latte?; ~ **many people?** quante persone?; ~ **old are you?** quanti anni ha?; ~**ever** adv in qualsiasi modo or maniera che; (+adjective) per quanto +sub; (in questions) come ♦ conj comunque, però

howl [haul] vi ululare; (baby, person) urlare

H.P. abbr = **hire purchase**; **horsepower**

h.p. n abbr = **H.P**

HQ n abbr = **headquarters**

hub [hʌb] n (of wheel) mozzo; (fig) fulcro

hubcap [ˈhʌbkæp] n coprimozzo

huddle [ˈhʌdl] vi: **to ~ together** rannicchiarsi l'uno contro l'altro

hue [hju:] n tinta

huff [hʌf] n: **in a ~** stizzito(a)

hug [hʌg] vt abbracciare; (shore, kerb) stringere

huge [hju:dʒ] adj enorme, immenso(a)

hulk [hʌlk] n (ship) nave f in disarmo; (building, car) carcassa; (person) mastodonte m

hull [hʌl] n (of ship) scafo

hullo [hə'ləu] excl = **hello**

hum [hʌm] vt (tune) canticchiare ♦ vi canticchiare; (insect, plane, tool) ronzare

human ['hju:mən] adj umano(a) ♦ n essere m umano

humane [hju:'mein] adj umanitario(a)

humanitarian [hju:mæni'teəriən] adj umanitario(a)

humanity [hju:'mæniti] n umanità

humble ['hʌmbl] adj umile, modesto(a) ♦ vt umiliare

humdrum ['hʌmdrʌm] adj monotono(a), tedioso(a)

humid ['hju:mid] adj umido(a)

humiliate [hju:'milieit] vt umiliare; **humiliation** [-'eiʃən] n umiliazione f

humility [hju:'militi] n umiltà

humorous ['hju:mərəs] adj umoristico(a); (person) buffo(a)

humour ['hju:mə*] (US **humor**) n umore m ♦ vt accontentare

hump [hʌmp] n gobba

hunch [hʌntʃ] n (premonition) intuizione f; **~ed** adj incurvato(a)

hundred ['hʌndrəd] num cento; **~s of** centinaia fpl di; **~weight** n (BRIT) = 50.8 kg; 112 lb; (US) = 45.3 kg; 100 lb

hung [hʌŋ] pt, pp of **hang**

Hungary ['hʌŋgəri] n Ungheria

hunger ['hʌŋgə*] n fame f ♦ vi: **to ~ for** desiderare ardentemente; **~ strike** n sciopero della fame

hungry ['hʌŋgri] adj affamato(a); (avid): **~ for** avido(a) di; **to be ~** aver fame

hunk [hʌŋk] n (of bread etc) bel pezzo

hunt [hʌnt] vt (seek) cercare; (SPORT) cacciare ♦ vi: **to ~ (for)** andare a caccia (di) ♦ n caccia; **~er** n cacciatore m; **~ing** n

caccia

hurdle ['hə:dl] n (SPORT, fig) ostacolo

hurl [hə:l] vt lanciare con violenza

hurrah [hu'rɑ:] excl = **hurray**

hurray [hu'rei] excl urra!, evviva!

hurricane ['hʌrikən] n uragano

hurried ['hʌrid] adj affrettato(a); (work) fatto(a) in fretta; **~ly** adv in fretta

hurry ['hʌri] n fretta ♦ vi (also: ~ up) affrettarsi ♦ vt (also: ~ up: person) affrettare; (: work) far in fretta; **to be in a ~** aver fretta

hurt [hə:t] (pt, pp **hurt**) vt (cause pain to) far male a; (injure, fig) ferire ♦ vi far male; **~ful** adj (remark) che ferisce

hurtle ['hə:tl] vi: **to ~ past/down** passare/ scendere a razzo

husband ['hʌzbənd] n marito

hush [hʌʃ] n silenzio, calma ♦ vt zittire; **~!** zitto(a)!; **~ up** vt (scandal) mettere a tacere

husk [hʌsk] n (of wheat) cartoccio; (of rice, maize) buccia

husky ['hʌski] adj roco(a) ♦ n cane m eschimese

hustle ['hʌsl] vt spingere, incalzare ♦ n: **~ and bustle** trambusto

hut [hʌt] n rifugio; (shed) ripostiglio

hutch [hʌtʃ] n gabbia

hyacinth ['haiəsinθ] n giacinto

hybrid ['haibrid] n ibrido

hydrant ['haidrənt] n (also: **fire ~**) idrante m

hydraulic [hai'drɔ:lik] adj idraulico(a)

hydroelectric [haidrəu'lektrik] adj idroelettrico(a)

hydrofoil ['haidrəufɔil] n aliscafo

hydrogen ['haidrədʒən] n idrogeno

hyena [hai'i:nə] n iena

hygiene ['haidʒi:n] n igiene f

hymn [him] n inno; cantica

hype [haip] (inf) n campagna pubblicitaria

hypermarket ['haipəmɑ:kit] (BRIT) n ipermercato

hyphen ['haifn] n trattino

hypnotize ['hipnətaiz] vt ipnotizzare

hypocrisy [hi'pɔkrisi] n ipocrisia

hypocrite ['hipəkrit] n ipocrita m/f; **hypocritical** [-'kritikl] adj ipocrita

hypothermia [haɪpəʊ'θə:mɪə] _n_ ipotermia
hypothesis [haɪ'pɒθɪsɪs] (_pl_ **hypotheses**) _n_ ipotesi _f inv_
hypothetical [haɪpəʊ'θetɪkl] _adj_ ipotetico(a)
hysterical [hɪ'sterɪkl] _adj_ isterico(a)
hysterics [hɪ'sterɪks] _npl_ accesso di isteria; (_laughter_) attacco di riso

I, i

I [aɪ] _pron_ io
ice [aɪs] _n_ ghiaccio; (_on road_) gelo; (~ _cream_) gelato ♦ _vt_ (_cake_) glassare ♦ _vi_ (_also:_ ~ **over**) ghiacciare; (_also:_ ~ **up**) gelare; **~berg** _n_ iceberg _m inv_; **~box** _n_ (_US_) frigorifero; (_BRIT_) reparto ghiaccio; (_insulated box_) frigo portatile; ~ **cream** _n_ gelato; ~ **hockey** _n_ hockey _m_ su ghiaccio
Iceland ['aɪslənd] _n_ Islanda
ice: ~ **lolly** (_BRIT_) _n_ ghiacciolo; ~ **rink** _n_ pista di pattinaggio; ~ **skating** _n_ pattinaggio sul ghiaccio
icicle ['aɪsɪkl] _n_ ghiacciolo
icing ['aɪsɪŋ] _n_ (_CULIN_) glassa; ~ **sugar** (_BRIT_) _n_ zucchero a velo
icy ['aɪsɪ] _adj_ ghiacciato(a); (_weather, temperature_) gelido(a)
I'd [aɪd] = **I would; I had**
idea [aɪ'dɪə] _n_ idea
ideal [aɪ'dɪəl] _adj_ ideale ♦ _n_ ideale _m_
identical [aɪ'dentɪkl] _adj_ identico(a)
identification [aɪdentɪfɪ'keɪʃən] _n_ identificazione _f_; **(means of)** ~ carta d'identità
identify [aɪ'dentɪfaɪ] _vt_ identificare
Identikit picture ® [aɪ'dentɪkɪt-] _n_ identikit _m inv_
identity [aɪ'dentɪtɪ] _n_ identità _f inv_; ~ **card** _n_ carta d'identità
ideology [aɪdɪ'ɔlədʒɪ] _n_ ideologia
idiom ['ɪdɪəm] _n_ idioma _m_; (_phrase_) espressione _f_ idiomatica
idiot ['ɪdɪət] _n_ idiota _m/f_; ~**ic** [-'ɔtɪk] _adj_ idiota
idle ['aɪdl] _adj_ inattivo(a); (_lazy_) pigro(a),

ozioso(a); (_unemployed_) disoccupato(a); (_question, pleasures_) ozioso(a) ♦ _vi_ (_engine_) girare al minimo
idol ['aɪdl] _n_ idolo; ~**ize** _vt_ idoleggiare
i.e. _adv abbr_ (= _that is_) cioè
if [ɪf] _conj_ se; ~ **I were you ...** se fossi in te ..., io al tuo posto ...; ~ **so** se è così; ~ **not** se no; ~ **only** se solo _or_ soltanto
ignite [ɪg'naɪt] _vt_ accendere ♦ _vi_ accendersi
ignition [ɪg'nɪʃən] _n_ (_AUT_) accensione _f_; **to switch on/off the** ~ accendere/spegnere il motore; ~ **key** _n_ (_AUT_) chiave _f_ dell'accensione
ignorant ['ɪgnərənt] _adj_ ignorante; **to be** ~ **of** (_subject_) essere ignorante in; (_events_) essere ignaro(a) di
ignore [ɪg'nɔ:*] _vt_ non tener conto di; (_person, fact_) ignorare
I'll [aɪl] = **I will; I shall**
ill [ɪl] _adj_ (_sick_) malato(a); (_bad_) cattivo(a) ♦ _n_ male _m_ ♦ _adv_: **to speak** _etc_ ~ **of sb** parlare _etc_ male di qn; **to take** _or_ **be taken** ~ ammalarsi; ~**-advised** _adj_ (_decision_) poco giudizioso(a); (_person_) mal consigliato(a); ~**-at-ease** _adj_ a disagio
illegal [ɪ'li:gl] _adj_ illegale
illegible [ɪ'ledʒɪbl] _adj_ illeggibile
illegitimate [ɪlɪ'dʒɪtɪmət] _adj_ illegittimo(a)
ill-fated [ɪl'feɪtɪd] _adj_ nefasto(a)
ill feeling _n_ rancore _m_
illiterate [ɪ'lɪtərət] _adj_ analfabeta, illetterato(a); (_letter_) scorretto(a)
ill-mannered [ɪl'mænəd] _adj_ maleducato(a)
illness ['ɪlnɪs] _n_ malattia
ill-treat _vt_ maltrattare
illuminate [ɪ'lu:mɪneɪt] _vt_ illuminare; **illumination** [-'neɪʃən] _n_ illuminazione _f_; **illuminations** _npl_ (_decorative_) luminarie _fpl_
illusion [ɪ'lu:ʒən] _n_ illusione _f_
illustrate ['ɪləstreɪt] _vt_ illustrare
illustration [ɪlə'streɪʃən] _n_ illustrazione _f_
I'm [aɪm] = **I am**
image ['ɪmɪdʒ] _n_ immagine _f_; (_public face_) immagine (pubblica); ~**ry** _n_ immagini _fpl_
imaginary [ɪ'mædʒɪnərɪ] _adj_ immaginario(a)
imagination [ɪmædʒɪ'neɪʃən] _n_ immaginazione _f_, fantasia

imaginative [ɪˈmædʒɪnətɪv] *adj* immaginoso(a)

imagine [ɪˈmædʒɪn] *vt* immaginare

imbalance [ɪmˈbæləns] *n* squilibrio

imbue [ɪmˈbjuː] *vt*: **to ~ sb/sth with** permeare qn/qc di

imitate [ˈɪmɪteɪt] *vt* imitare; **imitation** [-ˈteɪʃən] *n* imitazione *f*

immaculate [ɪˈmækjulət] *adj* immacolato(a); (*dress, appearance*) impeccabile

immaterial [ɪməˈtɪərɪəl] *adj* immateriale, indifferente

immature [ɪməˈtjuə*] *adj* immaturo(a)

immediate [ɪˈmiːdɪət] *adj* immediato(a); **~ly** *adv* (*at once*) subito, immediatamente; **~ly next to** proprio accanto a

immense [ɪˈmɛns] *adj* immenso(a); enorme

immerse [ɪˈmɜːs] *vt* immergere

immersion heater [ɪˈmɜːʃən] (*BRIT*) *n* scaldaacqua *m inv* a immersione

immigrant [ˈɪmɪɡrənt] *n* immigrante *m/f*; immigrato/a

immigration [ɪmɪˈɡreɪʃən] *n* immigrazione *f*

imminent [ˈɪmɪnənt] *adj* imminente

immoral [ɪˈmɔrl] *adj* immorale

immortal [ɪˈmɔːtl] *adj*, *n* immortale *m/f*

immune [ɪˈmjuːn] *adj*: **~ (to)** immune (da); **immunity** *n* immunità

impact [ˈɪmpækt] *n* impatto

impair [ɪmˈpɛə*] *vt* danneggiare

impart [ɪmˈpɑːt] *vt* (*make known*) comunicare; (*bestow*) impartire

impartial [ɪmˈpɑːʃl] *adj* imparziale

impassable [ɪmˈpɑːsəbl] *adj* insuperabile; (*road*) impraticabile

impassive [ɪmˈpæsɪv] *adj* impassibile

impatience [ɪmˈpeɪʃəns] *n* impazienza

impatient [ɪmˈpeɪʃənt] *adj* impaziente; **to get** *or* **grow ~** perdere la pazienza

impeccable [ɪmˈpekəbl] *adj* impeccabile

impede [ɪmˈpiːd] *vt* impedire

impediment [ɪmˈpedɪmənt] *n* impedimento; (*also*: **speech ~**) difetto di pronuncia

impending [ɪmˈpendɪŋ] *adj* imminente

imperative [ɪmˈperətɪv] *adj* imperativo(a);

necessario(a), urgente; (*voice*) imperioso(a)

imperfect [ɪmˈpɜːfɪkt] *adj* imperfetto(a); (*goods etc*) difettoso(a) ♦ *n* (*LING*: *also*: **~ tense**) imperfetto

imperial [ɪmˈpɪərɪəl] *adj* imperiale; (*measure*) legale

impersonal [ɪmˈpɜːsənl] *adj* impersonale

impersonate [ɪmˈpɜːsəneɪt] *vt* impersonare; (*THEATRE*) fare la mimica di

impertinent [ɪmˈpɜːtɪnənt] *adj* insolente, impertinente

impervious [ɪmˈpɜːvɪəs] *adj* (*fig*): **~ to** insensibile a; impassibile di fronte a

impetuous [ɪmˈpetjuəs] *adj* impetuoso(a), precipitoso(a)

impetus [ˈɪmpətəs] *n* impeto

impinge on [ɪmˈpɪndʒ-] *vt fus* (*person*) colpire; (*rights*) ledere

implement [*n* ˈɪmplɪmənt, *vb* ˈɪmplɪment] *n* attrezzo; (*for cooking*) utensile *m* ♦ *vt* effettuare

implicit [ɪmˈplɪsɪt] *adj* implicito(a); (*complete*) completo(a)

imply [ɪmˈplaɪ] *vt* insinuare; suggerire

impolite [ɪmpəˈlaɪt] *adj* scortese

import [*vb* ɪmˈpɔːt, *n* ˈɪmpɔːt] *vt* importare ♦ *n* (*COMM*) importazione *f*

importance [ɪmˈpɔːtns] *n* importanza

important [ɪmˈpɔːtnt] *adj* importante; **it's not ~** non ha importanza

importer [ɪmˈpɔːtə*] *n* importatore/trice

impose [ɪmˈpəuz] *vt* imporre ♦ *vi*: **to ~ on sb** sfruttare la bontà di qn

imposing [ɪmˈpəuzɪŋ] *adj* imponente

imposition [ɪmpəˈzɪʃən] *n* (*of tax etc*) imposizione *f*; **to be an ~ on** (*person*) abusare della gentilezza di

impossibility [ɪmpɔsəˈbɪlɪtɪ] *n* impossibilità

impossible [ɪmˈpɔsɪbl] *adj* impossibile

impotent [ˈɪmpətnt] *adj* impotente

impound [ɪmˈpaund] *vt* confiscare

impoverished [ɪmˈpɔvərɪʃt] *adj* impoverito(a)

impracticable [ɪmˈpræktɪkəbl] *adj* inattuabile

impractical [ɪmˈpræktɪkl] *adj* non pratico(a)

impress [ɪmˈpres] *vt* impressionare; (*mark*)

imprimere, stampare; **to ~ sth on sb** far capire qc a qn

impression [ɪmˈprɛʃən] *n* impressione *f*; **to be under the ~ that** avere l'impressione che

impressive [ɪmˈprɛsɪv] *adj* notevole

imprint [ˈɪmprɪnt] *n* (*of hand etc*) impronta; (*PUBLISHING*) sigla editoriale

imprison [ɪmˈprɪzn] *vt* imprigionare; **~ment** *n* imprigionamento

improbable [ɪmˈprɒbəbl] *adj* improbabile; (*excuse*) inverosimile

impromptu [ɪmˈprɒmptjuː] *adj* improvvisato(a)

improper [ɪmˈprɒpə*] *adj* scorretto(a); (*unsuitable*) inadatto(a), improprio(a); sconveniente, indecente

improve [ɪmˈpruːv] *vt* migliorare ♦ *vi* migliorare; (*pupil etc*) fare progressi; **~ment** *n* miglioramento; progresso

improvise [ˈɪmprəvaɪz] *vt, vi* improvvisare

impudent [ˈɪmpjudnt] *adj* impudente, sfacciato(a)

impulse [ˈɪmpʌls] *n* impulso; **on ~** d'impulso, impulsivamente

impulsive [ɪmˈpʌlsɪv] *adj* impulsivo(a)

KEYWORD

in [ɪn] *prep* **1** (*indicating place, position*) in; **~ the house/garden** in casa/giardino; **~ the box** nella scatola; **~ the fridge** nel frigorifero; **I have it ~ my hand** ce l'ho in mano; **~ town/the country** in città/campagna; **~ school** a scuola; **~ here/there** qui/lì dentro

2 (*with place names: of town, region, country*): **~ London** a Londra; **~ England** in Inghilterra; **~ the United States** negli Stati Uniti; **~ Yorkshire** nello Yorkshire

3 (*indicating time: during, in the space of*) in; **~ spring/summer** in primavera/estate; **~ 1999** nel 1999; **~ May** in *or* a maggio; **I'll see you ~ July** ci vediamo a luglio; **~ the afternoon** nel pomeriggio; **at 4 o'clock ~ the afternoon** alle 4 del pomeriggio; **I did it ~ 3 hours/days** l'ho fatto in 3 ore/giorni; **I'll see you ~ 2**

weeks *or* **~ 2 weeks' time** ci vediamo tra 2 settimane

4 (*indicating manner etc*) a; **~ a loud/soft voice** a voce alta/bassa; **~ pencil** a matita; **~ English/French** in inglese/francese; **the boy ~ the blue shirt** il ragazzo con la camicia blu

5 (*indicating circumstances*): **~ the sun** al sole; **~ the shade** all'ombra; **~ the rain** sotto la pioggia; **a rise ~ prices** un aumento dei prezzi

6 (*indicating mood, state*): **~ tears** in lacrime; **~ anger** per la rabbia; **~ despair** disperato(a); **~ good condition** in buono stato, in buone condizioni; **to live ~ luxury** vivere nel lusso

7 (*with ratios, numbers*): **1 ~ 10** 1 su 10; **20 pence ~ the pound** 20 pence per sterlina; **they lined up ~ twos** si misero in fila a due a due

8 (*referring to people, works*) in; **the disease is common ~ children** la malattia è comune nei bambini; **~ (the works of) Dickens** in Dickens

9 (*indicating profession etc*) in; **to be ~ teaching** fare l'insegnante, insegnare; **to be ~ publishing** essere nell'editoria

10 (*after superlative*) di; **the best ~ the class** il migliore della classe

11 (*with present participle*): **~ saying this** dicendo questo, nel dire questo

♦ *adv*: **to be ~** (*person: at home, work*) esserci; (*train, ship, plane*) essere arrivato(a); (*in fashion*) essere di moda; **to ask sb ~** invitare qn ad entrare; **to run/limp** *etc* **~** entrare di corsa/zoppicando *etc*

♦ *n*: **the ~s and outs of the problem** tutti i particolari del problema

---

in. *abbr* = **inch**

inability [ɪnəˈbɪlɪtɪ] *n*: **~ (to do)** incapacità (di fare)

inaccurate [ɪnˈækjʊrət] *adj* inesatto(a), impreciso(a)

inadequate [ɪnˈædɪkwət] *adj* insufficiente

inadvertently [ɪnədˈvəːtntlɪ] *adv* senza volerlo

inadvisable [ɪnəd'vaɪzəbl] *adj* consigliabile

inane [ɪ'neɪn] *adj* vacuo(a), stupido(a)

inanimate [ɪn'ænɪmət] *adj* inanimato(a)

inappropriate [ɪnə'prəʊprɪət] *adj* non adatto(a); (*word, expression*) improprio(a)

inarticulate [ɪnɑː'tɪkjʊlət] *adj* (*person*) che si esprime male; (*speech*) inarticolato(a)

inasmuch as [ɪnəz'mʌtʃæz] *adv* in quanto che; (*insofar as*) poiché

inaudible [ɪn'ɔːdɪbl] *adj* che non si riesce a sentire

inauguration [ɪnɔːgjʊ'reɪʃən] *n* inaugurazione *f*; insediamento in carica

in-between *adj* fra i (*or* le) due

inborn [ɪn'bɔːn] *adj* innato(a)

inbred [ɪn'bred] *adj* innato(a); (*family*) connaturato(a)

Inc. (*US*) *abbr* (= *incorporated*) S.A

incapable [ɪn'keɪpəbl] *adj* incapace

incapacitate [ɪnkə'pæsɪteɪt] *vt*: **to ~ sb from doing** rendere qn incapace di fare

incense [*n* 'ɪnsens, *vb* ɪn'sens] *n* incenso ♦ *vt* (*anger*) infuriare

incentive [ɪn'sentɪv] *n* incentivo

incessant [ɪn'sesnt] *adj* incessante; **~ly** *adv* di continuo, senza sosta

inch [ɪntʃ] *n* pollice *m* (= *25 mm; 12 in a foot*); **within an ~ of** a un pelo da; **he didn't give an ~** non ha ceduto di un millimetro

incidence ['ɪnsɪdns] *n* (*of crime, disease*) incidenza

incident ['ɪnsɪdnt] *n* incidente *m*; (*in book*) episodio

incidental [ɪnsɪ'dentl] *adj* accessorio(a), d'accompagnamento; (*unplanned*) incidentale; **~ to** marginale a; **~ly** [-'dentəlɪ] *adv* (*by the way*) a proposito

inclination [ɪnklɪ'neɪʃən] *n* inclinazione *f*

incline [*n* 'ɪnklaɪn, *vb* ɪn'klaɪn] *n* pendenza, pendio ♦ *vt* inclinare ♦ *vi* (*surface*) essere inclinato(a); **to be ~d to do** tendere a fare; essere propenso(a) a fare

include [ɪn'kluːd] *vt* includere, comprendere; **including** *prep* compreso(a), incluso(a)

inclusive [ɪn'kluːsɪv] *adj* incluso(a),

compreso(a); **~ of tax** *etc* tasse *etc* comprese

incoherent [ɪnkəʊ'hɪərənt] *adj* incoerente

income ['ɪnkʌm] *n* reddito; **~ tax** *n* imposta sul reddito

incoming ['ɪnkʌmɪŋ] *adj* (*flight, mail*) in arrivo; (*government*) subentrante; (*tide*) montante

incompetent [ɪn'kɒmpɪtnt] *adj* incompetente, incapace

incomplete [ɪnkəm'pliːt] *adj* incompleto(a)

incongruous [ɪn'kɒŋgruəs] *adj* poco appropriato(a); (*remark, act*) incongruo(a)

inconsiderate [ɪnkən'sɪdərət] *adj* sconsiderato(a)

inconsistency [ɪnkən'sɪstənsɪ] *n* incoerenza

inconsistent [ɪnkən'sɪstənt] *adj* incoerente; **~ with** non coerente con

inconspicuous [ɪnkən'spɪkjuəs] *adj* incospicuo(a); (*colour*) poco appariscente; (*dress*) dimesso(a)

inconvenience [ɪnkən'viːnjəns] *n* inconveniente *m*; (*trouble*) disturbo ♦ *vt* disturbare

inconvenient [ɪnkən'viːnjənt] *adj* scomodo(a)

incorporate [ɪn'kɔːpəreɪt] *vt* incorporare; (*contain*) contenere; **~d** *adj*: **~d company** (*US*) società *f inv* anonima

incorrect [ɪnkə'rekt] *adj* scorretto(a); (*statement*) Inesatto(a)

increase [*n* 'ɪnkriːs, *vb* ɪn'kriːs] *n* aumento ♦ *vi*, *vt* aumentare

increasing [ɪn'kriːsɪŋ] *adj* (*number*) crescente; **~ly** *adv* sempre più

incredible [ɪn'kredɪbl] *adj* incredibile

increment ['ɪnkrɪmənt] *n* aumento, incremento

incriminate [ɪn'krɪmɪneɪt] *vt* comprometter

incubator ['ɪnkjubeɪtə*] *n* incubatrice *f*

incumbent [ɪn'kʌmbənt] *adj*: **to be ~ on sb** spettare a qn

incur [ɪn'kəː*] *vt* (*expenses*) incorrere; (*anger, risk*) esporsi a; (*debt*) contrarre; (*loss*) subire

indebted [ɪn'detɪd] *adj*: **to be ~ to sb (for)** essere obbligato(a) verso qn (per)

indecent [ɪn'diːsnt] *adj* indecente; ~
assault (*BRIT*) *n* aggressione *f* a scopo di
violenza sessuale; ~ **exposure** *n* atti *mpl*
osceni in luogo pubblico
indecisive [ɪndɪ'saɪsɪv] *adj* indeciso(a)
indeed [ɪn'diːd] *adv* infatti; veramente; **yes**
~**!** certamente!
indefinite [ɪn'dɛfɪnɪt] *adj* indefinito(a);
(*answer*) vago(a); (*period, number*)
indeterminato(a); ~**ly** *adv* (*wait*)
indefinitamente
indemnity [ɪn'dɛmnɪtɪ] *n* (*insurance*)
assicurazione *f*; (*compensation*) indennità,
indennizzo
independence [ɪndɪ'pɛndns] *n*
indipendenza

Independence Day
---

i *Negli Stati Uniti il 4 luglio si festeggia*
l'Independence Day, giorno in cui,
nel 1776, 13 colonie britanniche
proclamarono la propria indipendenza dalla
Gran Bretagna ed entrarono ufficialmente a
far parte degli Stati Uniti d'America.

---

independent [ɪndɪ'pɛndnt] *adj*
indipendente
index ['ɪndɛks] (*pl* ~**es**) *n* (*in book*) indice *m*;
(: *in library etc*) catalogo; (*pl* **indices**: *ratio,
sign*) indice *m*; ~ **card** *n* scheda; ~ **finger**
n (*dito*) indice *m*; ~**-linked** (*US* ~**ed**) *adj*
legato(a) al costo della vita
India ['ɪndɪə] *n* India; ~**n** *adj*, *n* indiano(a)
indicate ['ɪndɪkeɪt] *vt* indicare; **indication**
[-'keɪʃən] *n* indicazione *f*, segno
indicative [ɪn'dɪkətɪv] *adj*: ~ **of** indicativo(a)
di
indicator ['ɪndɪkeɪtə*] *n* indicatore *m*; (*AUT*)
freccia
indices ['ɪndɪsiːz] *npl of* **index**
indictment [ɪn'daɪtmənt] *n* accusa
indifference [ɪn'dɪfrəns] *n* indifferenza
indifferent [ɪn'dɪfrənt] *adj* indifferente;
(*poor*) mediocre
indigenous [ɪn'dɪdʒɪnəs] *adj* indigeno(a)
indigestion [ɪndɪ'dʒɛstʃən] *n* indigestione *f*
indignant [ɪn'dɪgnənt] *adj*: ~ (**at sth/with**

sb) indignato(a) (per qc/contro qn)
indignity [ɪn'dɪgnɪtɪ] *n* umiliazione *f*
indigo ['ɪndɪgəʊ] *n* indaco
indirect [ɪndɪ'rɛkt] *adj* indiretto(a)
indiscreet [ɪndɪ'skriːt] *adj* indiscreto(a);
(*rash*) imprudente
indiscriminate [ɪndɪ'skrɪmɪnət] *adj*
indiscriminato(a)
indisputable [ɪndɪ'spjuːtəbl] *adj*
incontestabile, indiscutibile
individual [ɪndɪ'vɪdjʊəl] *n* individuo ♦ *adj*
individuale; (*characteristic*) particolare,
originale
indoctrination [ɪndɔktrɪ'neɪʃən] *n*
indottrinamento
Indonesia [ɪndə'niːzɪə] *n* Indonesia
indoor ['ɪndɔː*] *adj* da interno; (*plant*)
d'appartamento; (*swimming pool*)
coperto(a); (*sport, games*) fatto(a) al
coperto; ~**s** [ɪn'dɔːz] *adv* all'interno
induce [ɪn'djuːs] *vt* persuadere; (*bring
about, MED*) provocare
indulge [ɪn'dʌldʒ] *vt* (*whim*) compiacere,
soddisfare; (*child*) viziare ♦ *vi*: **to** ~ **in sth**
concedersi qc; abbandonarsi a qc; ~**nce** *n*
lusso (*leniency*) indulgenza; ~**nt** *adj* indulgente
industrial [ɪn'dʌstrɪəl] *adj* industriale;
(*injury*) sul lavoro; ~ **action** *n* azione *f*
rivendicativa; ~ **estate** (*BRIT*) *n* zona
industriale; ~ **park** (*US*) *n* = ~ **estate**
industrious [ɪn'dʌstrɪəs] *adj* industrioso(a),
assiduo(a)
industry ['ɪndəstrɪ] *n* industria; (*diligence*)
operosità
inedible [ɪn'ɛdɪbl] *adj* immangiabile;
(*poisonous*) non commestibile
ineffective [ɪnɪ'fɛktɪv] *adj* inefficace;
incompetente
ineffectual [ɪnɪ'fɛktʃʊəl] *adj* inefficace;
incompetente
inefficient [ɪnɪ'fɪʃənt] *adj* inefficiente
inept [ɪ'nɛpt] *adj* inetto(a)
inequality [ɪnɪ'kwɒlɪtɪ] *n* ineguaglianza
inescapable [ɪnɪ'skeɪpəbl] *adj* inevitabile
inevitable [ɪn'ɛvɪtəbl] *adj* inevitabile;
inevitably *adv* inevitabilmente

inexact [ɪnɪg'zækt] *adj* inesatto(a)

inexcusable [ɪnɪks'kju:zəbl] *adj* ingiustificabile

inexpensive [ɪnɪk'spensɪv] *adj* poco costoso(a)

inexperienced [ɪnɪks'pɪərɪənst] *adj* inesperto(a), senza esperienza

infallible [ɪn'fælɪbl] *adj* infallibile

infamous ['ɪnfəməs] *adj* infame

infancy ['ɪnfənsɪ] *n* infanzia

infant ['ɪnfənt] *n* bambino/a; **~ school** (*BRIT*) scuola elementare (*per bambini dall'età di 5 a 7 anni*)

infantry ['ɪnfəntrɪ] *n* fanteria

infatuated [ɪn'fætjueɪtɪd] *adj*: **~ with** infatuato(a) di

infatuation [ɪnfætju'eɪʃən] *n* infatuazione *f*

infect [ɪn'fekt] *vt* infettare; **~ion** [ɪn'fekʃən] *n* infezione *f*; **~ious** [ɪn'fekʃəs] *adj* (*disease*) infettivo(a), contagioso(a); (*person, fig*: *enthusiasm*) contagioso(a)

infer [ɪn'fə:*] *vt* inferire, dedurre

inferior [ɪn'fɪərɪə*] *adj* inferiore; (*goods*) di qualità scadente ♦ *n* inferiore *m/f*; (*in rank*) subalterno/a; **~ity** [ɪnfɪərɪ'ɔrətɪ] *n* inferiorità; **~ity complex** *n* complesso di inferiorità

infertile [ɪn'fə:taɪl] *adj* sterile

in-fighting ['ɪnfaɪtɪŋ] *n* lotte *fpl* intestine

infiltrate ['ɪnfɪltreɪt] *vt* infiltrarsi in

infinite ['ɪnfɪnɪt] *adj* infinito(a)

infinitive [ɪn'fɪnɪtɪv] *n* infinito

infinity [ɪn'fɪnɪtɪ] *n* infinità, (*also MATH*) infinito

infirmary [ɪn'fə:mərɪ] *n* ospedale *m*; (*in school, factory*) infermeria

inflamed [ɪn'fleɪmd] *adj* infiammato(a)

inflammable [ɪn'flæməbl] *adj* infiammabile

inflammation [ɪnflə'meɪʃən] *n* infiammazione *f*

inflatable [ɪn'fleɪtəbl] *adj* gonfiabile

inflate [ɪn'fleɪt] *vt* (*tyre, balloon*) gonfiare; (*fig*) esagerare; gonfiare; **inflation** [ɪn'fleɪʃən] *n* (*ECON*) inflazione *f*; **inflationary** [ɪn'fleɪʃnərɪ] *adj* inflazionistico(a)

inflict [ɪn'flɪkt] *vt*: **to ~ on** infliggere a

influence ['ɪnfluəns] *n* influenza ♦ *vt* influenzare; **under the ~ of alcohol** sotto l'effetto dell'alcool

influential [ɪnflu'enʃl] *adj* influente

influenza [ɪnflu'enzə] *n* (*MED*) influenza

influx ['ɪnflʌks] *n* afflusso

inform [ɪn'fɔ:m] *vt*: **to ~ sb (of)** informare qn (di) ♦ *vi*: **to ~ on sb** denunciare qn

informal [ɪn'fɔ:ml] *adj* informale; (*announcement, invitation*) non ufficiale; **~ity** [-'mælɪtɪ] *n* informalità; carattere *m* non ufficiale

informant [ɪn'fɔ:mənt] *n* informatore/trice

information [ɪnfə'meɪʃən] *n* informazioni *fpl*; particolari *mpl*; **a piece of ~** un'informazione; **~ desk** *n* banco *m* informazioni *inv*; **~ office** *n* ufficio *m* informazioni *inv*

informative [ɪn'fɔ:mətɪv] *adj* istruttivo(a)

informer [ɪn'fɔ:mə*] *n* (*also*: **police ~**) informatore/trice

infringe [ɪn'frɪndʒ] *vt* infrangere ♦ *vi*: **to ~ on** calpestare; **~ment** *n* infrazione *f*

infuriating [ɪn'fjuərɪeɪtɪŋ] *adj* molto irritante

ingenious [ɪn'dʒi:njəs] *adj* ingegnoso(a)

ingenuity [ɪndʒɪ'nju:ɪtɪ] *n* ingegnosità

ingenuous [ɪn'dʒenjuəs] *adj* ingenuo(a)

ingot ['ɪŋgət] *n* lingotto

ingrained [ɪn'greɪnd] *adj* radicato(a)

ingratiate [ɪn'greɪʃɪeɪt] *vt*: **to ~ o.s. with sb** ingraziarsi qn

ingredient [ɪn'gri:dɪənt] *n* ingrediente *m*; elemento

inhabit [ɪn'hæbɪt] *vt* abitare

inhabitant [ɪn'hæbɪtnt] *n* abitante *m/f*

inhale [ɪn'heɪl] *vt* inalare ♦ *vi* (*in smoking*) aspirare

inherent [ɪn'hɪərənt] *adj*: **~ (in or to)** inerente (a)

inherit [ɪn'herɪt] *vt* ereditare; **~ance** *n* eredità

inhibit [ɪn'hɪbɪt] *vt* (*PSYCH*) inibire; **~ion** [-'bɪʃən] *n* inibizione *f*

inhospitable [ɪnhɔs'pɪtəbl] *adj* inospitale

inhuman [ɪn'hju:mən] *adj* inumano(a)

initial [ɪ'nɪʃl] *adj* iniziale ♦ *n* iniziale *f* ♦ *vt* siglare; **~s** *npl* (*of name*) iniziali *fpl*; (*as signature*) sigla; **~ly** *adv* inizialmente, all'inizio

initiate [ɪ'nɪʃɪeɪt] *vt* (*start*) avviare; intraprendere; iniziare; (*person*) iniziare; **to ~ sb into a secret** mettere qn a parte di un segreto; **to ~ proceedings against sb** (*LAW*) intentare causa contro qn

initiative [ɪ'nɪʃətɪv] *n* iniziativa

inject [ɪn'dʒɛkt] *vt* (*liquid*) iniettare; (*patient*): **to ~ sb with sth** fare a qn un'iniezione di qc; (*funds*) immettere; **~ion** [ɪn'dʒɛkʃən] *n* iniezione *f*, puntura

injure ['ɪndʒə*] *vt* ferire; (*damage: reputation etc*) nuocere a; **~d** *adj* ferito(a)

injury ['ɪndʒərɪ] *n* ferita; **~ time** *n* (*SPORT*) tempo di recupero

injustice [ɪn'dʒʌstɪs] *n* ingiustizia

ink [ɪŋk] *n* inchiostro

inkling ['ɪŋklɪŋ] *n* sentore *m*, vaga idea

inlaid ['ɪnleɪd] *adj* incrostato(a); (*table etc*) intarsiato(a)

inland [*adj* 'ɪnlənd, *adv* ɪn'lænd] *adj* interno(a) ♦ *adv* all'interno; **I~ Revenue** (*BRIT*) *n* Fisco

in-laws ['ɪnlɔːz] *npl* suoceri *mpl*; famiglia del marito (*or* della moglie)

inlet ['ɪnlɛt] *n* (*GEO*) insenatura, baia

inmate ['ɪnmeɪt] *n* (*in prison*) carcerato/a; (*in asylum*) ricoverato/a

inn [ɪn] *n* locanda

innate [ɪ'neɪt] *adj* innato(a)

inner ['ɪnə*] *adj* interno(a), interiore; **~ city** *n* centro di una zona urbana; **~ tube** *n* camera d'aria

innings ['ɪnɪŋz] *n* (*CRICKET*) turno di battuta

innocence ['ɪnəsns] *n* innocenza

innocent ['ɪnəsnt] *adj* innocente

innocuous [ɪ'nɔkjuəs] *adj* innocuo(a)

innuendo [ɪnju'ɛndəu] (*pl* **~es**) *n* insinuazione *f*

innumerable [ɪ'njuːmrəbl] *adj* innumerevole

in-patient *n* ricoverato/a

input ['ɪnput] *n* input *m*

inquest ['ɪnkwɛst] *n* inchiesta

inquire [ɪn'kwaɪə*] *vi* informarsi ♦ *vt* domandare, informarsi su; **~ about** *vt fus* informarsi di *or* su; **~ into** *vt fus* fare indagini su; **inquiry** *n* domanda; (*LAW*) indagine *f*, investigazione *f*; **"inquiries"** "informazioni"; **inquiry office** (*BRIT*) *n* ufficio *m* informazioni *inv*

inquisitive [ɪn'kwɪzɪtɪv] *adj* curioso(a)

ins. *abbr* = **inches**

insane [ɪn'seɪn] *adj* matto(a), pazzo(a); (*MED*) alienato(a)

insanity [ɪn'sænɪtɪ] *n* follia; (*MED*) alienazione *f* mentale

inscription [ɪn'skrɪpʃən] *n* iscrizione *f*; dedica

insect ['ɪnsɛkt] *n* insetto; **~icide** [ɪn'sɛktɪsaɪd] *n* insetticida *m*; **~ repellent** *n* insettifugo

insecure [ɪnsɪ'kjuə*] *adj* malsicuro(a); (*person*) insicuro(a)

insemination [ɪnsɛmɪ'neɪʃən] *n*: **artificial ~** fecondazione *f* artificiale

insensible [ɪn'sɛnsɪbl] *adj* (*unconscious*) privo(a) di sensi

insensitive [ɪn'sɛnsɪtɪv] *adj* insensibile

insert [ɪn'səːt] *vt* inserire, introdurre; **~ion** [ɪn'səːʃən] *n* inserzione *f*

in-service *adj* (*training, course*) durante l'orario di lavoro

inshore [ɪn'ʃɔː*] *adj* costiero(a) ♦ *adv* presso la riva; verso la riva

inside ['ɪn'saɪd] *n* interno, parte *f* interiore ♦ *adj* interno(a), interiore ♦ *adv* dentro, all'interno ♦ *prep* dentro, all'interno di; (*of time*): **~ 10 minutes** entro 10 minuti; **~s** *npl* (*inf: stomach*) ventre *m*; **~ forward** *n* (*SPORT*) mezzala, interno; **~ lane** *n* (*AUT*) corsia di marcia; **~ out** *adv* (*turn*) a rovescio; (*know*) a fondo; **~r dealing** *n* insider dealing *m inv*; **~r trading** *n* insider trading *m inv*

insight ['ɪnsaɪt] *n* acume *m*, perspicacia; (*glimpse, idea*) percezione *f*

insignia [ɪn'sɪgnɪə] *npl* insegne *fpl*

insignificant [ɪnsɪg'nɪfɪknt] *adj* insignificante

insincere [ɪnsɪn'sɪə*] *adj* insincero(a)

insinuate [ɪn'sɪnjueɪt] *vt* insinuare

insist [ɪnˈsɪst] *vi* insistere; **to ~ on doing** insistere per fare; **to ~ that** insistere perché +*sub*; (*claim*) sostenere che; **~ent** *adj* insistente

insole [ˈɪnsəʊl] *n* soletta

insolent [ˈɪnsələnt] *adj* insolente

insomnia [ɪnˈsɒmnɪə] *n* insonnia

inspect [ɪnˈspekt] *vt* ispezionare; (*BRIT: ticket*) controllare; **~ion** [ɪnˈspekʃən] *n* ispezione *f*; controllo; **~or** *n* ispettore/trice; (*BRIT: on buses, trains*) controllore *m*

inspire [ɪnˈspaɪə*] *vt* ispirare

install [ɪnˈstɔːl] *vt* installare; **~ation** [ɪnstəˈleɪʃən] *n* installazione *f*

installment [ɪnˈstɔːlmənt] (*US* **installment**) *n* rata; (*of TV serial etc*) puntata; **in ~s** (*pay*) a rate; (*receive*) una parte per volta; (: *publication*) a fascicoli

instance [ˈɪnstəns] *n* esempio, caso; **for ~** per *or* ad esempio; **in the first ~** in primo luogo

instant [ˈɪnstənt] *n* istante *m*, attimo ♦ *adj* immediato(a); urgente; (*coffee, food*) in polvere; **~ly** *adv* immediatamente, subito

instead [ɪnˈsted] *adv* invece; **~ of** invece di

instep [ˈɪnstep] *n* collo del piede; (*of shoe*) collo della scarpa

instil [ɪnˈstɪl] *vt*: **to ~ (into)** inculcare (in)

instinct [ˈɪnstɪŋkt] *n* istinto

institute [ˈɪnstɪtjuːt] *n* istituto ♦ *vt* istituire, stabilire; (*inquiry*) avviare; (*proceedings*) iniziare

institution [ɪnstɪˈtjuːʃən] *n* istituzione *f*; (*educational ~, mental ~*) istituto

instruct [ɪnˈstrʌkt] *vt*: **to ~ sb in sth** insegnare qc a qn; **to ~ sb to do** dare ordini a qn di fare; **~ion** [ɪnˈstrʌkʃən] *n* istruzione *f*; **~ions (for use)** istruzioni per l'uso; **~or** *n* istruttore/trice; (*for skiing*) maestro/a

instrument [ˈɪnstrəmənt] *n* strumento; **~al** [-ˈmentl] *adj* (*MUS*) strumentale; **to be ~al in** essere d'aiuto in; **~ panel** *n* quadro *m* portastrumenti *inv*

insufferable [ɪnˈsʌfərəbl] *adj* insopportabile

insufficient [ɪnsəˈfɪʃənt] *adj* insufficiente

insular [ˈɪnsjʊlə*] *adj* insulare; (*person*) di mente ristretta

insulate [ˈɪnsjʊleɪt] *vt* isolare; **insulation** [-ˈleɪʃən] *n* isolamento

insulin [ˈɪnsjʊlɪn] *n* insulina

insult [*n* ˈɪnsʌlt, *vb* ɪnˈsʌlt] *n* insulto, affronto ♦ *vt* insultare; **~ing** *adj* offensivo(a), ingiurioso(a)

insuperable [ɪnˈsjuːprəbl] *adj* insormontabile, insuperabile

insurance [ɪnˈʃʊərəns] *n* assicurazione *f*; **fire/life ~** assicurazione contro gli incendi/ sulla vita; **~ policy** *n* polizza d'assicurazione

insure [ɪnˈʃʊə*] *vt* assicurare

intact [ɪnˈtækt] *adj* intatto(a)

intake [ˈɪnteɪk] *n* (*TECH*) immissione *f*; (*of food*) consumo; (*BRIT: of pupils etc*) afflusso

integral [ˈɪntɪɡrəl] *adj* integrale; (*part*) integrante

integrate [ˈɪntɪɡreɪt] *vt* integrare ♦ *vi* integrarsi

integrity [ɪnˈtɛɡrɪtɪ] *n* integrità

intellect [ˈɪntəlekt] *n* intelletto; **~ual** [-ˈlektjʊəl] *adj*, *n* intellettuale *m/f*

intelligence [ɪnˈtelɪdʒəns] *n* intelligenza; (*MIL etc*) informazioni *fpl*; **~ service** *n* servizio segreto

intelligent [ɪnˈtelɪdʒənt] *adj* intelligente

intend [ɪnˈtend] *vt* (*gift etc*): **to ~ sth for** destinare qc a; **to ~ to do** aver l'intenzione di fare, **~ed** *adj* (*effect*) voluto(a)

intense [ɪnˈtens] *adj* intenso(a); (*person*) di forti sentimenti; **~ly** *adv* intensamente; profondamente

intensive [ɪnˈtensɪv] *adj* intensivo(a); **~ care unit** *n* reparto terapia intensiva

intent [ɪnˈtent] *n* intenzione *f* ♦ *adj*: **~ (on)** intento(a) (a), immerso(a) (in); **to all ~s and purposes** a tutti gli effetti; **to be ~ on doing sth** essere deciso a fare qc

intention [ɪnˈtenʃən] *n* intenzione *f*; **~al** *adj* intenzionale, deliberato(a); **~ally** *adv* apposta

intently [ɪnˈtentlɪ] *adv* attentamente

interact [ɪntərˈækt] *vi* interagire

interactive *adj* (*COMPUT*) interattivo(a)

interchange [ˈɪntətʃeɪndʒ] *n* (*exchange*)

scambio; (*on motorway*) incrocio pluridirezionale; **~able** [-'tʃeɪndʒəbl] *adj* intercambiabile

intercom ['ɪntəkɒm] *n* interfono

intercourse ['ɪntəkɔːs] *n* rapporti *mpl*

interest ['ɪntrɪst] *n* interesse *m*; (COMM: *stake, share*) interessi *mpl* ♦ *vt* interessare; **~ed** *adj* interessato(a); **to be ~ed in** interessarsi di; **~ing** *adj* interessante; **~ rate** *n* tasso di interesse

interface [ɪn'təfeɪs] *n* (COMPUT) interfaccia

interfere [ɪntə'fɪə*] *vi*: **to ~ in** (*quarrel, other people's business*) immischiarsi in; **to ~ with** (*object*) toccare; (*plans, duty*) interferire con

interference [ɪntə'fɪərəns] *n* interferenza

interim ['ɪntərɪm] *adj* provvisorio(a) ♦ *n*: **in the ~** nel frattempo

interior [ɪn'tɪərɪə*] *n* interno; (*of country*) entroterra ♦ *adj* interno(a); (*minister*) degli Interni; **~ designer** *n* arredatore/trice

interlock [ɪntə'lɒk] *vi* ingranarsi

interlude ['ɪntəluːd] *n* intervallo; (THEATRE) intermezzo

intermediate [ɪntə'miːdɪət] *adj* intermedio(a)

intermission [ɪntə'mɪʃən] *n* pausa; (THEATRE, CINEMA) intermissione *f*, intervallo

intern [*vb* ɪn'tɜːn, *n* 'ɪntɜːn] *vt* internare ♦ *n* (US) medico interno

internal [ɪn'tɜːnl] *adj* interno(a); **~ly** *adv*: "**not to be taken ~ly**" "per uso esterno"; **I~ Revenue Service** (US) *n* Fisco

international [ɪntə'næʃənl] *adj* internazionale ♦ *n* (BRIT: SPORT) incontro internazionale

interplay ['ɪntəpleɪ] *n* azione e reazione *f*

interpret [ɪn'tɜːprɪt] *vt* interpretare ♦ *vi* fare da interprete; **~er** *n* interprete *m/f*

interrelated [ɪntərɪ'leɪtɪd] *adj* correlato(a)

interrogate [ɪn'terəugeɪt] *vt* interrogare; **interrogation** [-'geɪʃən] *n* interrogazione *f*; (*of suspect etc*) interrogatorio

interrupt [ɪntə'rʌpt] *vt, vi* interrompere; **~ion** [-'rʌpʃən] *n* interruzione *f*

intersect [ɪntə'sekt] *vi* (*roads*) incrociarsi; **~ion** [-'sekʃən] *n* intersezione *f*; (*of roads*) incrocio

intersperse [ɪntə'spɜːs] *vt*: **to ~ with** costellare di

intertwine [ɪntə'twaɪn] *vi* intrecciarsi

interval ['ɪntəvl] *n* intervallo; **at ~s** a intervalli

intervene [ɪntə'viːn] *vi* (*time*) intercorrere; (*event, person*) intervenire; **intervention** [-'venʃən] *n* intervento

interview ['ɪntəvjuː] *n* (RADIO, TV *etc*) intervista; (*for job*) colloquio ♦ *vt* intervistare; avere un colloquio con; **~er** *n* intervistatore/trice

intestine [ɪn'testɪn] *n* intestino

intimacy ['ɪntɪməsɪ] *n* intimità

intimate [*adj* 'ɪntɪmət, *vb* 'ɪntɪmeɪt] *adj* intimo(a); (*knowledge*) profondo(a) ♦ *vt* lasciar capire

into ['ɪntuː] *prep* dentro, in; **come ~ the house** entra in casa; **he worked late ~ the night** lavorò fino a tarda notte; **~ Italian** in italiano

intolerable [ɪn'tɒlərəbl] *adj* intollerabile

intolerance [ɪn'tɒlərns] *n* intolleranza

intolerant [ɪn'tɒlərnt] *adj*: **~ of** intollerante di

intoxicated [ɪn'tɒksɪkeɪtɪd] *adj* inebriato(a)

intractable [ɪn'træktəbl] *adj* intrattabile

intransitive [ɪn'trænsɪtɪv] *adj* intransitivo(a)

intravenous [ɪntrə'viːnəs] *adj* endovenoso(a)

in-tray *n* contenitore *m* per la corrispondenza in arrivo

intricate ['ɪntrɪkət] *adj* intricato(a), complicato(a)

intrigue [ɪn'triːg] *n* intrigo ♦ *vt* affascinare; **intriguing** *adj* affascinante

intrinsic [ɪn'trɪnsɪk] *adj* intrinseco(a)

introduce [ɪntrə'djuːs] *vt* introdurre; **to ~ sb (to sb)** presentare qn (a qn); **to ~ sb to** (*pastime, technique*) iniziare qn a; **introduction** [-'dʌkʃən] *n* introduzione *f*; (*of person*) presentazione *f*; (*to new experience*) iniziazione *f*; **introductory** *adj* introduttivo(a)

intrude [ɪn'truːd] *vi* (*person*): **to ~ (on)** intromettersi (in); **~r** *n* intruso/a

intuition [ɪntjuː'ɪʃən] *n* intuizione *f*

inundate ['mʌndeɪt] *vt*: **to ~ with** inondare di

invade [ɪn'veɪd] *vt* invadere

invalid [*n* 'ɪnvəlɪd, *adj* ɪn'vælɪd] *n* malato/a; (*with disability*) invalido/a ♦ *adj* (*not valid*) invalido(a), non valido(a)

invaluable [ɪn'væljuəbl] *adj* prezioso(a); inestimabile

invariably [ɪn'veərɪəblɪ] *adv* invariabilmente; sempre

invasion [ɪn'veɪʒən] *n* invasione *f*

invent [ɪn'vent] *vt* inventare; **~ion** [ɪn'venʃən] *n* invenzione *f*; **~ive** *adj* inventivo(a); **~or** *n* inventore *m*

inventory ['ɪnvəntrɪ] *n* inventario

invert [ɪn'vəːt] *vt* invertire; (*cup, object*) rovesciare; **~ed commas** (*BRIT*) *npl* virgolette *fpl*

invest [ɪn'vest] *vt* investire ♦ *vi*: **to ~ (in)** investire (in)

investigate [ɪn'vestɪgeɪt] *vt* investigare, indagare; (*crime*) fare indagini su; **investigation** [-'geɪʃən] *n* investigazione *f*; (*of crime*) indagine *f*

investment [ɪn'vestmənt] *n* investimento

investor [ɪn'vestə*] *n* investitore/trice; azionista *m/f*

invidious [ɪn'vɪdɪəs] *adj* odioso(a); (*task*) spiacevole

invigilator [ɪn'vɪdʒɪleɪtə*] *n* (*in exam*) sorvegliante *m/f*

invigorating [ɪn'vɪgəreɪtɪŋ] *adj* stimolante; vivificante

invisible [ɪn'vɪzɪbl] *adj* invisibile

invitation [ɪnvɪ'teɪʃən] *n* invito

invite [ɪn'vaɪt] *vt* invitare; (*opinions etc*) sollecitare; **inviting** *adj* invitante, attraente

invoice ['ɪnvɔɪs] *n* fattura ♦ *vt* fatturare

involuntary [ɪn'vɔləntrɪ] *adj* involontario(a)

involve [ɪn'vɔlv] *vt* (*entail*) richiedere, comportare; (*associate*): **to ~ sb (in)** implicare qn (in); coinvolgere qn (in); **~d** *adj* involuto(a), complesso(a); **to be ~d in** essere coinvolto(a) in; **~ment** *n* implicazione *f*; coinvolgimento

inward ['ɪnwəd] *adj* (*movement*) verso l'interno; (*thought, feeling*) interiore,

intimo(a); **~(s)** *adv* verso l'interno

I/O *abbr* (*COMPUT*: = *input/output*) I/O

iodine ['aɪəudiːn] *n* iodio

ioniser ['aɪənaɪzə*] *n* ionizzatore *m*

iota [aɪ'əutə] *n* (*fig*) briciolo

IOU *n abbr* (= *I owe you*) pagherò *m inv*

IQ *n abbr* (= *intelligence quotient*) quoziente *m* d'intelligenza

IRA *n abbr* (= *Irish Republican Army*) IRA *f*

Iran [ɪ'rɑːn] *n* Iran *m*; **~ian** *adj, n* iraniano(a)

Iraq [ɪ'rɑːk] *n* Iraq *m*; **~i** *adj, n* iracheno(a)

irate [aɪ'reɪt] *adj* adirato(a)

Ireland ['aɪələnd] *n* Irlanda

iris ['aɪrɪs] (*pl* **~es**) *n* iride *f*; (*BOT*) giaggiolo, iride

Irish ['aɪrɪʃ] *adj* irlandese ♦ *npl*: **the ~** gli Irlandesi; **~man** (*irreg*) *n* irlandese *m*; **~ Sea** *n* Mar *m* d'Irlanda; **~woman** (*irreg*) *n* irlandese *f*

irksome ['əːksəm] *adj* seccante

iron ['aɪən] *n* ferro; (*for clothes*) ferro da stiro ♦ *adj* di or in ferro ♦ *vt* (*clothes*) stirare; **~ out** *vt* (*crease*) appianare; (*fig*) spianare; far sparire

ironic(al) [aɪ'rɔnɪk(l)] *adj* ironico(a)

ironing ['aɪənɪŋ] *n* (*act*) stirare *m*; (*clothes*) roba da stirare; **~ board** *n* asse *f* da stiro

ironmonger's (shop) ['aɪənmʌŋgəz] (*BRIT*) *n* negozio di ferramenta

irony ['aɪrənɪ] *n* ironia

irrational [ɪ'ræʃənl] *adj* irrazionale

irregular [ɪ'regjulə*] *adj* irregolare

irrelevant [ɪ'reləvənt] *adj* non pertinente

irreplaceable [ɪrɪ'pleɪsəbl] *adj* insostituibile

irrepressible [ɪrɪ'presəbl] *adj* irrefrenabile

irresistible [ɪrɪ'zɪstɪbl] *adj* irresistibile

irrespective [ɪrɪ'spektɪv]: **~ of** *prep* senza riguardo a

irresponsible [ɪrɪ'spɔnsɪbl] *adj* irresponsabile

irrigate ['ɪrɪgeɪt] *vt* irrigare; **irrigation** [-'geɪʃən] *n* irrigazione *f*

irritable ['ɪrɪtəbl] *adj* irritabile

irritate ['ɪrɪteɪt] *vt* irritare; **irritating** *adj* (*person, sound etc*) irritante; **irritation** [-'teɪʃən] *n* irritazione *f*

IRS (US) n abbr = **Internal Revenue Service**

is [ɪz] vb see **be**

Islam ['ɪzlɑːm] n Islam m

island ['aɪlənd] n isola; **~er** n isolano/a

isle [aɪl] n isola

isn't ['ɪznt] = **is not**

isolate ['aɪsəleɪt] vt isolare; **~d** adj isolato(a); **isolation** [-'leɪʃən] n isolamento

Israel ['ɪzreɪl] n Israele m; **~i** [ɪz'reɪlɪ] adj, n israeliano(a)

issue ['ɪʃuː] n questione f, problema m; (of banknotes etc) emissione f; (of newspaper etc) numero ♦ vt (statement) rilasciare; (rations, equipment) distribuire; (book) pubblicare; (banknotes, cheques, stamps) emettere; **at ~** in gioco, in discussione; **to take ~ with sb (over sth)** prendere posizione contro qn (riguardo a qc); **to make an ~ of sth** fare un problema di qc

isthmus ['ɪsməs] n istmo

KEYWORD

---

it [ɪt] pron **1** (specific: subject) esso(a); (: direct object) lo(la), l'; (: indirect object) gli(le); **where's my book? — ~'s on the table** dov'è il mio libro? — è sulla tavola; **I can't find ~** non lo (or la) trovo; **give ~ to me** dammelo (or dammela); **about/from/ of ~** ne; **I spoke to him about ~** gliene ho parlato; **what did you learn from ~?** quale insegnamento ne hai tratto?; **I'm proud of ~** ne sono fiero; **did you go to ~?** ci sei andato?; **put the book in ~** mettici il libro **2** (impers): **~'s raining** piove; **~'s Friday tomorrow** domani è venerdì; **~'s 6 o'clock** sono le 6; **who is ~? — ~'s me** chi è? — sono io

Italian [ɪ'tæljən] adj italiano(a) ♦ n italiano/a; (LING) italiano; **the ~s** gli Italiani

italics [ɪ'tælɪks] npl corsivo

Italy ['ɪtəlɪ] n Italia

itch [ɪtʃ] n prurito ♦ vi (person) avere il prurito; (part of body) prudere; **to ~ to do sth** aver una gran voglia di fare qc; **~y** adj che prude; **to be ~y** = **to ~**

it'd ['ɪtd] = **it would**; **it had**

item ['aɪtəm] n articolo; (on agenda) punto; (also: **news ~**) notizia; **~ize** vt specificare, dettagliare

itinerant [ɪ'tɪnərənt] adj ambulante

itinerary [aɪ'tɪnərərɪ] n itinerario

it'll ['ɪtl] = **it will**; **it shall**

its [ɪts] adj il(la) suo(a), i(le) suoi(sue)

it's [ɪts] = **it is**; **it has**

itself [ɪt'self] pron (emphatic) esso(a) stesso(a); (reflexive) si

ITV (BRIT) n abbr (= Independent Television) rete televisiva in concorrenza con la BBC

I.U.D. n abbr (= intra-uterine device) spirale f

I've [aɪv] = **I have**

ivory ['aɪvərɪ] n avorio

ivy ['aɪvɪ] n edera

J, j

jab [dʒæb] vt dare colpetti a ♦ n (MED: inf) puntura; **to ~ sth into** affondare or piantare qc dentro

jack [dʒæk] n (AUT) cricco; (CARDS) fante m; **~ up** vt sollevare col cricco

jackal ['dʒækl] n sciacallo

jackdaw ['dʒækdɔː] n taccola

jacket ['dʒækɪt] n giacca; (of book) copertina

jack-knife vi: **the lorry ~d** l'autotreno si è piegato su se stesso

jack plug n (ELEC) jack m inv

jackpot ['dʒækpɔt] n primo premio (in denaro)

jade [dʒeɪd] n (stone) giada

jaded ['dʒeɪdɪd] adj sfinito(a), spossato(a)

jagged ['dʒægɪd] adj seghettato(a); (cliffs etc) frastagliato(a)

jail [dʒeɪl] n prigione f ♦ vt mandare in prigione

jam [dʒæm] n marmellata; (also: **traffic ~**) ingorgo; (inf) pasticcio ♦ vt (passage etc) ingombrare, ostacolare; (mechanism, drawer etc) bloccare; (RADIO) disturbare con interferenze ♦ vi incepparsi; **to ~ sth into** forzare qc dentro; infilare qc a forza dentro

Jamaica [dʒə'meɪkə] *n* Giamaica
jangle ['dʒæŋgl] *vi* risuonare; (*bracelet*) tintinnare
janitor ['dʒænɪtə*] *n* (*caretaker*) portiere *m*; (: *SCOL*) bidello
January ['dʒænjuərɪ] *n* gennaio
Japan [dʒə'pæn] *n* Giappone *m*; **~ese** [dʒæpə'niːz] *adj* giapponese ♦ *n inv* giapponese *m/f*; (*LING*) giapponese *m*
jar [dʒɑː*] *n* (*glass*) barattolo, vasetto ♦ *vi* (*sound*) stonare; (*colours etc*) stonare
jargon ['dʒɑːgən] *n* gergo
jasmin(e) ['dʒæzmɪn] *n* gelsomino
jaundice ['dʒɔːndɪs] *n* itterizia
jaunt [dʒɔːnt] *n* gita
javelin ['dʒævlɪn] *n* giavellotto
jaw [dʒɔː] *n* mascella
jay [dʒeɪ] *n* ghiandaia
jaywalker ['dʒeɪwɔːkə*] *n* pedone(a) indisciplinato(a)
jazz [dʒæz] *n* jazz *m*; **~ up** *vt* rendere vivace
jealous ['dʒeləs] *adj* geloso(a); **~y** *n* gelosia
jeans [dʒiːnz] *npl* jeans *mpl* (blue-)jeans *mpl*
jeer [dʒɪə*] *vi*: **to ~ (at)** fischiare; beffeggiare
jelly ['dʒelɪ] *n* gelatina; **~fish** *n* medusa
jeopardy ['dʒepədɪ] *n*: **in ~** in pericolo
jerk [dʒəːk] *n* sobbalzo, scossa; sussulto; (*inf: idiot*) tonto/a ♦ *vt* dare una scossa a ♦ *vi* (*vehicles*) sobbalzare
jersey ['dʒəːzɪ] *n* maglia; (*fabric*) jersey *m*
jest [dʒest] *n* scherzo
Jesus ['dʒiːzəs] *n* Gesù *m*
jet [dʒet] *n* (*of gas, liquid*) getto; (*AVIAT*) aviogetto; **~-black** *adj* nero(a) come l'ebano, corvino(a); **~ engine** *n* motore *m* a reazione; **~ lag** *n* (problemi *mpl* dovuti allo) sbalzo dei fusi orari
jettison ['dʒetɪsn] *vt* gettare in mare
jetty ['dʒetɪ] *n* molo
Jew [dʒuː] *n* ebreo
jewel ['dʒuːəl] *n* gioiello; **~ler** (*US* **~er**) *n* orefice *m*, gioielliere/a; **~(l)er's (shop)** *n* oreficeria, gioielleria; **~lery** (*US* **~ery**) *n* gioielli *mpl*
Jewess ['dʒuːɪs] *n* ebrea
Jewish ['dʒuːɪʃ] *adj* ebreo(a), ebraico(a)
jibe [dʒaɪb] *n* beffa

jiffy ['dʒɪfɪ] (*inf*) *n*: **in a ~** in un batter d'occhio
jig [dʒɪg] *n* giga
jigsaw ['dʒɪgsɔː] *n* (*also*: **~ puzzle**) puzzle *m inv*
jilt [dʒɪlt] *vt* piantare in asso
jingle ['dʒɪŋgl] *n* (*for advert*) sigla pubblicitaria ♦ *vi* tintinnare, scampanellare
jinx [dʒɪŋks] *n* iettatura; (*person*) iettatore/trice
jitters ['dʒɪtəz] (*inf*) *npl*: **to get the ~** aver fifa
job [dʒɔb] *n* lavoro; (*employment*) impiego, posto; **it's not my ~** (*duty*) non è compito mio; **it's a good ~ that ...** meno male che ...; **just the ~!** proprio quello che ci vuole; **~ centre** (*BRIT*) *n* ufficio di collocamento; **~less** *adj* senza lavoro, disoccupato(a)
jockey ['dʒɔkɪ] *n* fantino, jockey *m inv* ♦ *vi*: **to ~ for position** manovrare per una posizione di vantaggio
jog [dʒɔg] *vt* urtare ♦ *vi* (*SPORT*) fare footing, fare jogging; **to ~ sb's memory** rinfrescare la memoria a qn; **to ~ along** trottare; (*fig*) andare avanti piano piano; **~ging** *n* footing *m*, jogging *m*
join [dʒɔɪn] *vt* unire, congiungere; (*become member of*) iscriversi a; (*meet*) raggiungere; riunirsi a ♦ *vi* (*roads, rivers*) confluire ♦ *n* giuntura; **~ in** *vi* partecipare ♦ *vt fus* unirsi a; **~ up** *vi* incontrarsi; (*MIL*) arruolarsi
joiner ['dʒɔɪnə*] (*BRIT*) *n* falegname *m*
joint [dʒɔɪnt] *n* (*TECH*) giuntura; giunto; (*ANAT*) articolazione *f*, giuntura; (*BRIT: CULIN*) arrosto; (*inf: place*) locale *m*; (: *of cannabis*) spinello ♦ *adj* comune; **~ account** *n* (*at bank etc*) conto in partecipazione, conto comune
joist [dʒɔɪst] *n* trave *f*
joke [dʒəuk] *n* scherzo; (*funny story*) barzelletta; (*also*: **practical ~**) beffa ♦ *vi* scherzare; **to play a ~ on sb** fare uno scherzo a qn; **~r** *n* (*CARDS*) matta, jolly *m inv*
jolly ['dʒɔlɪ] *adj* allegro(a), gioioso(a) ♦ *adv* (*BRIT: inf*) veramente, proprio
jolt [dʒəult] *n* scossa, sobbalzo ♦ *vt* urtare

Jordan ['dʒɔːdən] n (country) Giordania; (river) Giordano

jostle ['dʒɔsl] vt spingere coi gomiti

jot [dʒɔt] n: **not one ~** nemmeno un po'; **~ down** vt annotare in fretta, buttare giù; **~ter** (BRIT) n blocco

journal ['dʒəːnl] n giornale m; rivista; diario; **~ism** n giornalismo; **~ist** n giornalista m/f

journey ['dʒəːnɪ] n viaggio; (distance covered) tragitto

joy [dʒɔɪ] n gioia; **~ful** adj gioioso(a), allegro(a); **~rider** n chi ruba un'auto per farvi un giro; **~stick** n (AVIAT) barra di comando; (COMPUT) joystick m inv

JP n abbr = **Justice of the Peace**

Jr abbr = **junior**

jubilant ['dʒuːbɪlnt] adj giubilante; trionfante

jubilee ['dʒuːbɪliː] n giubileo; **silver ~** venticinquesimo anniversario

judge [dʒʌdʒ] n giudice m/f ♦ vt giudicare; **judg(e)ment** n giudizio

judiciary [dʒuːˈdɪʃərɪ] n magistratura

judo ['dʒuːdəu] n judo

jug [dʒʌg] n brocca, bricco

juggernaut ['dʒʌgənɔːt] (BRIT) n (huge truck) bestione m

juggle ['dʒʌgl] vi fare giochi di destrezza; **~r** n giocoliere/a

juice [dʒuːs] n succo

juicy ['dʒuːsɪ] adj succoso(a)

jukebox ['dʒuːkbɔks] n juke-box m inv

July [dʒuːˈlaɪ] n luglio

jumble ['dʒʌmbl] n miscuglio ♦ vt (also: **~ up**) mischiare; **~ sale** (BRIT) n vendita di beneficenza

---
jumble sale

ℹ️ *Una* **jumble sale** *è un mercatino di oggetti di seconda mano organizzato in chiese, scuole o in circoli ricreativi, i cui proventi vengono devoluti in beneficenza.*

jumbo (jet) ['dʒʌmbəu-] n jumbo-jet m inv

jump [dʒʌmp] vi saltare, balzare; (start) sobbalzare; (increase) rincarare ♦ vt saltare ♦ n salto, balzo; sobbalzo

jumper ['dʒʌmpə*] n (BRIT: pullover) maglione m, pullover m inv; (US: dress) scamiciato; **~ cables** (US) npl = **jump leads**

jump leads (BRIT) npl cavi mpl per batteria

jumpy ['dʒʌmpɪ] adj nervoso(a), agitato(a)

Jun. abbr = **junior**

junction ['dʒʌŋkʃən] n (BRIT: of roads) incrocio; (of rails) nodo ferroviario

juncture ['dʒʌŋktʃə*] n: **at this ~** in questa congiuntura

June [dʒuːn] n giugno

jungle ['dʒʌŋgl] n giungla

junior ['dʒuːnɪə*] adj, n: **he's ~ to me (by 2 years), he's my ~ (by 2 years)** è più giovane di me (di 2 anni); **he's ~ to me** (seniority) è al di sotto di me, ho più anzianità di lui; **~ school** (BRIT) n scuola elementare (da 8 a 11 anni)

junk [dʒʌŋk] n cianfrusaglie fpl; (cheap goods) robaccia; **~ food** n porcherie fpl

junkie ['dʒʌŋkɪ] (inf) n drogato/a

junk mail n stampe fpl pubblicitarie

junk shop n chincaglieria

Junr abbr = **junior**

juror ['dʒuərə*] n giurato/a

jury ['dʒuərɪ] n giuria

just [dʒʌst] adj giusto(a) ♦ adv: **he's ~ done it/left** lo ha appena fatto/è appena partito; **~ right** proprio giusto; **~ 2 o'clock** le 2 precise; **she's ~ as clever as you** è in gamba proprio quanto te; **it's ~ as well that ...** meno male che ...; **~ as I arrived** proprio mentre arrivavo; **it was ~ before/ enough/here** era poco prima/appena assai/proprio qui; **it's ~ me** sono solo io; **~ missed/caught** appena perso/preso; **~ listen to this!** senta un po' questo!

justice ['dʒʌstɪs] n giustizia; **J~ of the Peace** n giudice m conciliatore

justify ['dʒʌstɪfaɪ] vt giustificare

jut [dʒʌt] vi (also: **~ out**) sporgersi

juvenile ['dʒuːvənaɪl] adj giovane, giovanile; (court) dei minorenni; (books) per ragazzi ♦ n giovane m/f, minorenne m/f

juxtapose ['dʒʌkstəpəuz] vt giustapporre

K, k

K *abbr* (= *one thousand*) mille; (= *kilobyte*) K
Kampuchea [kæmpu'tʃɪə] *n* Cambogia
kangaroo [kæŋgə'ruː] *n* canguro
karate [kə'rɑːtɪ] *n* karatè *m*
kebab [kə'bæb] *n* spiedino
keel [kiːl] *n* chiglia; **on an even ~** (*fig*) in uno stato normale
keen [kiːn] *adj* (*interest, desire*) vivo(a); (*eye, intelligence*) acuto(a); (*competition*) serrato(a); (*edge*) affilato(a); (*eager*) entusiasta; **to be ~ to do** *or* **on doing sth** avere una gran voglia di fare qc; **to be ~ on sth** essere appassionato(a) di qc; **to be ~ on sb** avere un debole per qn
keep [kiːp] (*pt, pp* **kept**) *vt* tenere; (*hold back*) trattenere; (*feed: one's family etc*) mantenere, sostenere; (*a promise*) mantenere; (*chickens, bees, pigs etc*) allevare ♦ *vi* (*food*) mantenersi; (*remain: in a certain state or place*) restare ♦ *n* (*of castle*) maschio; (*food etc*): **enough for his ~** abbastanza per vitto e alloggio; (*inf*): **for ~s** per sempre; **to ~ doing sth** continuare a fare qc; fare qc di continuo; **to ~ sb from doing** impedire a qn di fare; **to ~ sb busy/a place tidy** tenere qn occupato(a)/un luogo in ordine; **to ~ sth to o.s.** tenere qc per sé; **to ~ sth (back) from sb** celare qc a qn; **to ~ time** (*clock*) andar bene; **~ on** *vi*: **to ~ on doing** continuare a fare; **to ~ on (about sth)** continuare a insistere (su qc); **~ out** *vt* tener fuori; **"~ out"** "vietato l'accesso"; **~ up** *vt* continuare, mantenere ♦ *vi*: **to ~ up with** tener dietro a, andare di pari passo con; (*work etc*) farcela a seguire; **~er** *n* custode *m/f*, guardiano/a; **~-fit** *n* ginnastica; **~ing** *n* (*care*) custodia; **in ~ing with** in armonia con; in accordo con; **~sake** *n* ricordo
kennel ['kɛnl] *n* canile *m*; **to put a dog in ~s** mettere un cane al canile
kept [kɛpt] *pt, pp of* **keep**
kerb [kəːb] (*BRIT*) *n* orlo del marciapiede

kernel ['kəːnl] *n* nocciolo
kettle ['kɛtl] *n* bollitore *m*
kettle drum *n* timpano
key [kiː] *n* (*gen, MUS*) chiave *f*; (*of piano, typewriter*) tasto ♦ *adj* chiave *inv* ♦ *vt* (*also: ~ in*) digitare; **~board** *n* tastiera; **~ed up** *adj* (*person*) agitato(a); **~hole** *n* buco della serratura; **~hole surgery** *n* chirurgia non invasiva; **~note** *n* (*MUS*) tonica; (*fig*) nota dominante; **~ring** *n* portachiavi *m inv*
khaki ['kɑːkɪ] *adj* cachi ♦ *n* cachi *m*
kick [kɪk] *vt* calciare, dare calci a; (*inf: habit etc*) liberarsi di ♦ *vi* (*horse*) tirar calci ♦ *n* calcio; (*thrill*): **he does it for ~s** lo fa giusto per il piacere di farlo; **~ off** *vi* (*SPORT*) dare il primo calcio
kid [kɪd] *n* (*inf: child*) ragazzino/a; (*animal, leather*) capretto ♦ *vi* (*inf*) scherzare
kidnap ['kɪdnæp] *vt* rapire, sequestrare; **~per** *n* rapitore/trice; **~ping** *n* sequestro (di persona)
kidney ['kɪdnɪ] *n* (*ANAT*) rene *m*; (*CULIN*) rognone *m*
kill [kɪl] *vt* uccidere, ammazzare ♦ *n* uccisione *f*; **~er** *n* uccisore *m*, killer *m inv*; assassino/a; **~ing** *n* assassinio; **to make a ~ing** (*inf*) fare un bel colpo; **~joy** *n* guastafeste *m/f inv*
kiln [kɪln] *n* forno
kilo ['kiːləu] *n* chilo; **~byte** *n* (*COMPUT*) kilobyte *m inv*; **~gram(me)** ['kɪləugræm] *n* chilogrammo; **~metre** ['kɪləmiːtə*] (*US* **~meter**) *n* chilometro; **~watt** ['kɪləuwɔt] *n* chilowatt *m inv*
kilt [kɪlt] *n* gonnellino scozzese
kin [kɪn] *n see* **next**; **kith**
kind [kaɪnd] *adj* gentile, buono(a) ♦ *n* sorta, specie *f*; (*species*) genere *m*; **to be two of a ~** essere molto simili; **in ~** (*COMM*) in natura
kindergarten ['kɪndəgɑːtn] *n* giardino d'infanzia
kind-hearted [-'hɑːtɪd] *adj* di buon cuore
kindle ['kɪndl] *vt* accendere, infiammare
kindly ['kaɪndlɪ] *adj* pieno(a) di bontà, benevolo(a) ♦ *adv* con bontà, gentilmente; **will you ~ ...** vuole ... per favore
kindness ['kaɪndnɪs] *n* bontà, gentilezza

king [kɪŋ] *n* re *m inv*; ~**dom** *n* regno, reame *m*; ~**fisher** *n* martin *m inv* pescatore; ~**size** *adj* super *inv*; gigante

kiosk ['kiːɔsk] *n* edicola, chiosco; (*BRIT: TEL*) cabina (telefonica)

kipper ['kɪpə*] *n* aringa affumicata

kiss [kɪs] *n* bacio ♦ *vt* baciare; **to ~ (each other)** baciarsi; ~ **of life** *n* respirazione *f* bocca a bocca

kit [kɪt] *n* equipaggiamento, corredo; (*set of tools etc*) attrezzi *mpl*; (*for assembly*) scatola di montaggio

kitchen ['kɪtʃɪn] *n* cucina; ~ **sink** *n* acquaio

kite [kaɪt] *n* (*toy*) aquilone *m*

kitten ['kɪtn] *n* gattino, micino/a

kitty ['kɪtɪ] *n* (*money*) fondo comune

knack [næk] *n*: **to have the ~ of** avere l'abilità di

knapsack ['næpsæk] *n* zaino, sacco da montagna

knead [niːd] *vt* impastare

knee [niː] *n* ginocchio; ~**cap** *n* rotula

kneel [niːl] (*pt, pp* **knelt**) *vi* (*also*: ~ **down**) inginocchiarsi

knew [njuː] *pt of* **know**

knickers ['nɪkəz] (*BRIT*) *npl* mutandine *fpl*

knife [naɪf] (*pl* **knives**) *n* coltello ♦ *vt* accoltellare, dare una coltellata a

knight [naɪt] *n* cavaliere *m*; (*CHESS*) cavallo; ~**hood** (*BRIT*) *n* (*title*): **to get a ~hood** essere fatto cavaliere

knit [nɪt] *vt* fare a maglia ♦ *vi* lavorare a maglia; (*broken bones*) saldarsi; **to ~ one's brows** aggrottare le sopracciglia; ~**ting** *n* lavoro a maglia; ~**ting machine** *n* macchina per maglieria; ~**ting needle** *n* ferro (da calza); ~**wear** *n* maglieria

knives [naɪvz] *npl of* **knife**

knob [nɔb] *n* bottone *m*; manopola

knock [nɔk] *vt* colpire; urtare; (*fig: inf*) criticare ♦ *vi* (*at door etc*): **to ~ at/on** bussare a ♦ *n* bussata; colpo, botta; ~ **down** *vt* abbattere; ~ **off** *vi* (*inf: finish*) smettere (di lavorare) ♦ *vt* (*from price*) far abbassare; (*inf: steal*) sgraffignare; ~ **out** *vt* stendere; (*BOXING*) mettere K.O.; (*defeat*) battere; ~ **over** *vt* (*person*) investire;

(*object*) far cadere; ~**er** *n* (*on door*) battente *m*; ~**out** *n* (*BOXING*) knock out *m inv* ♦ *cpd* a eliminazione

knot [nɔt] *n* nodo ♦ *vt* annodare

know [nəu] (*pt* **knew**, *pp* **known**) *vt* sapere; (*person, author, place*) conoscere; **to ~ how to do** sapere fare; **to ~ about** *or* **of sth/sb** conoscere qc/qn; ~**all** *n* sapientone/a; ~-**how** *n* tecnica; pratica; ~**ing** *adj* (*look etc*) d'intesa; ~**ingly** *adv* (*purposely*) consapevolmente; (*smile, look*) con aria d'intesa

knowledge ['nɔlɪdʒ] *n* consapevolezza; (*learning*) conoscenza, sapere *m*; ~**able** *adj* ben informato(a)

known [nəun] *pp of* **know**

knuckle ['nʌkl] *n* nocca

Koran [kɔ'rɑːn] *n* Corano

Korea [kə'rɪə] *n* Corea

kosher ['kəuʃə*] *adj* kasher *inv*

L, l

L (*BRIT*) *abbr* = **learner driver**

lab [læb] *n abbr* (= *laboratory*) laboratorio

label ['leɪbl] *n* etichetta, cartellino; (*brand: of record*) casa ♦ *vt* etichettare

labor *etc* ['leɪbə*] (*US*) = **labour** *etc*

laboratory [lə'bɔrətərɪ] *n* laboratorio

labour ['leɪbə*] (*US* **labor**) *n* (*task*) lavoro; (*workmen*) manodopera; (*MED*): **to be in ~** avere le doglie ♦ *vi*: **to ~ (at)** lavorare duro (a); **L~, the L~ party** (*BRIT*) il partito laburista, i laburisti; **hard ~** lavori *mpl* forzati; ~**ed** *adj* (*breathing*) affannoso(a); ~**er** *n* manovale *m*; **farm ~er** lavoratore *m* agricolo

lace [leɪs] *n* merletto, pizzo; (*of shoe etc*) laccio ♦ *vt* (*shoe: also*: ~ **up**) allacciare

lack [læk] *n* mancanza ♦ *vt* mancare di; **through** *or* **for ~ of** per mancanza di; **to be ~ing** mancare; **to be ~ing in** mancare di

lackadaisical [lækə'deɪzɪkl] *adj* disinteressato(a), noncurante

lacquer ['lækə*] *n* lacca

lad [læd] *n* ragazzo, giovanotto

ladder ['lædə*] n scala; (BRIT: in tights) smagliatura

laden ['leɪdn] adj: ~ (with) carico(a) or caricato(a) (di)

ladle ['leɪdl] n mestolo

lady ['leɪdɪ] n signora; dama; L~ Smith lady Smith; **the ladies' (room)** i gabinetti per signore; ~**bird** (US ~**bug**) n coccinella; ~**like** adj da signora, distinto(a); ~**ship** n: **your ~ship** signora contessa (or baronessa etc)

lag [læg] n (of time) lasso, intervallo ♦ vi (also: ~ **behind**) trascinarsi ♦ vt (pipes) rivestire di materiale isolante

lager ['lɑːgə*] n lager m inv

lagoon [ləˈguːn] n laguna

laid [leɪd] pt, pp of **lay**; ~ **back** (inf) adj rilassato(a), tranquillo(a); ~ **up** adj: ~ **up (with)** costretto(a) a letto (da)

lain [leɪn] pp of **lie**

lair [lɛə*] n covo, tana

lake [leɪk] n lago

lamb [læm] n agnello

lame [leɪm] adj zoppo(a); (excuse etc) zoppicante

lament [ləˈment] n lamento ♦ vt lamentare, piangere

laminated ['læmɪneɪtɪd] adj laminato(a)

lamp [læmp] n lampada

lamppost ['læmppəust] (BRIT) n lampione m

lampshade ['læmpʃeɪd] n paralume m

lance [lɑːns] vt (MED) incidere

land [lænd] n (as opposed to sea) terra (ferma); (country) paese m; (soil) terreno; suolo; (estate) terreni mpl, terre fpl ♦ vi (from ship) sbarcare; (AVIAT) atterrare; (fig: fall) cadere ♦ vt (passengers) sbarcare; (goods) scaricare; **to ~ sb with sth** affibbiare qc a qn; ~ **up** vi andare a finire; ~**fill site** n discarica; ~**ing** n atterraggio; (of staircase) pianerottolo; ~**ing gear** n carrello di atterraggio; ~**lady** n padrona or proprietaria di casa; ~**locked** adj senza sbocco sul mare; ~**lord** n padrone m or proprietario di casa; (of pub etc) padrone m; ~**mark** n punto di riferimento; (fig) pietra miliare; ~**owner** n proprietario(a)

terriero(a); ~**scape** n paesaggio; ~**slide** n (GEO) frana; (fig: POL) valanga

lane [leɪn] n stradina; (AUT, in race) corsia; **"get in lane"** "immettersi in corsia"

language ['læŋgwɪdʒ] n lingua; (way one speaks) linguaggio; **bad ~** linguaggio volgare; ~ **laboratory** n laboratorio linguistico

languid ['læŋgwɪd] adj languido(a)

lank [læŋk] adj (hair) liscio(a) e opaco(a)

lanky ['læŋkɪ] adj allampanato(a)

lantern ['læntn] n lanterna

lap [læp] n (of track) giro; (of body): **in** or **on one's ~** in grembo ♦ vt (also: ~ **up**) papparsi, leccare ♦ vi (waves) sciabordare; ~ **up** vt (fig) bearsi di

lapel [ləˈpɛl] n risvolto

Lapland ['læplænd] n Lapponia

lapse [læps] n lapsus m inv; (longer) caduta ♦ vi (law) cadere; (membership, contract) scadere; **to ~ into bad habits** pigliare cattive abitudini; ~ **of time** spazio di tempo

laptop (computer) ['læp,tɒp-] n laptop m inv

larch [lɑːtʃ] n larice m

lard [lɑːd] n lardo

larder ['lɑːdə*] n dispensa

large [lɑːdʒ] adj grande; (person, animal) grosso(a); **at ~** (free) in libertà; (generally) in generale; nell'insieme; ~**ly** adv in gran parte

largesse [lɑːˈʒɛs] n generosità

lark [lɑːk] n (bird) allodola; (joke) scherzo, gioco

laryngitis [lærɪnˈdʒaɪtɪs] n laringite f

laser ['leɪzə*] n laser m; ~ **printer** n stampante f laser inv

lash [læʃ] n frustata; (also: **eye~**) ciglio ♦ vt frustare; (tie): **to ~ to/together** legare a/insieme; ~ **out** vi: **to ~ out (at** or **against sb)** attaccare violentemente (qn)

lass [læs] n ragazza

lasso [læˈsuː] n laccio

last [lɑːst] adj ultimo(a); (week, month, year) scorso(a), passato(a) ♦ adv per ultimo ♦ vi durare; ~ **week** la settimana scorsa; ~ **night** ieri sera, la notte scorsa; **at ~** finalmente, alla fine; **~ but one** penultimo(a); **~-ditch** *adj* (*attempt*) estremo(a); **~ing** *adj* durevole; **~ly** *adv* infine, per finire; **~-minute** *adj* fatto(a) (*or* preso(a) *etc*) all'ultimo momento

latch [lætʃ] *n* chiavistello

late [leɪt] *adj* (*not on time*) in ritardo; (*far on in day etc*) tardi *inv*; tardo(a); (*former*) ex; (*dead*) defunto(a) ♦ *adv* tardi; (*behind time, schedule*) in ritardo; **of ~** di recente; **in the ~ afternoon** nel tardo pomeriggio; **in ~ May** verso la fine di maggio; **~comer** *n* ritardatario/a; **~ly** *adv* recentemente

later ['leɪtə*] *adj* (*date etc*) posteriore; (*version etc*) successivo(a) ♦ *adv* più tardi; **~ on** più avanti

lateral ['lætərl] *adj* laterale

latest ['leɪtɪst] *adj* ultimo(a), più recente; **at the ~** al più tardi

lathe [leɪð] *n* tornio

lather ['lɑːðə*] *n* schiuma di sapone ♦ *vt* insaponare

Latin ['lætɪn] *n* latino ♦ *adj* latino(a); **~ America** *n* America Latina; **~-American** *adj*, *n* sudamericano(a)

latitude ['lætɪtjuːd] *n* latitudine *f*; (*fig*) libertà d'azione

latter ['lætə*] *adj* secondo(a); più recente ♦ *n*: **the ~** quest'ultimo, il secondo; **~ly** *adv* recentemente, negli ultimi tempi

lattice ['lætɪs] *n* traliccio; graticolato

laudable ['lɔːdəbl] *adj* lodevole

laugh [lɑːf] *n* risata ♦ *vi* ridere; **~ at** *vt fus* (*misfortune etc*) ridere di; **~ off** *vt* prendere alla leggera; **~able** *adj* ridicolo(a); **~ing stock** *n*: **the ~ing stock of** lo zimbello di; **~ter** *n* riso; risate *fpl*

launch [lɔːntʃ] *n* (*of rocket*, COMM) lancio; (*of new ship*) varo; (*also*: **motor ~**) lancia ♦ *vt* (*rocket*, COMM) lanciare; (*ship*, *plan*) varare; **~ into** *vt fus* lanciarsi in; **~(ing) pad** *n* rampa di lancio

launder ['lɔːndə*] *vt* lavare e stirare

launderette [lɔːn'drɛt] (BRIT) *n* lavanderia (automatica)

Laundromat ® ['lɔːndrəmæt] (US) *n* lavanderia automatica

laundry ['lɔːndrɪ] *n* lavanderia; (*clothes*) biancheria; (: *dirty*) panni *mpl* da lavare

laurel ['lɔrl] *n* lauro

lava ['lɑːvə] *n* lava

lavatory ['lævətərɪ] *n* gabinetto

lavender ['lævəndə*] *n* lavanda

lavish ['lævɪʃ] *adj* copioso(a); abbondante; (*giving freely*): **~ with** prodigo(a) di, largo(a) in ♦ *vt*: **to ~ sth on sb** colmare qn di qc

law [lɔː] *n* legge *f*; **civil/criminal ~** diritto civile/penale; **~-abiding** *adj* ubbidiente alla legge; **~ and order** *n* l'ordine *m* pubblico; **~ court** *n* tribunale *m*, corte *f* di giustizia; **~ful** *adj* legale; lecito(a); **~less** *adj* che non conosce nessuna legge

lawn [lɔːn] *n* tappeto erboso; **~ mower** *n* tosaerba *m or f inv*; **~ tennis** *n* tennis *m* su prato

law school *n* facoltà *f inv* di legge

lawsuit ['lɔːsuːt] *n* processo, causa

lawyer ['lɔːjə*] *n* (*for sales, wills etc*) ≈ notaio; (*partner, in court*) ≈ avvocato/essa

lax [læks] *adj* rilassato(a); negligente

laxative ['læksətɪv] *n* lassativo

lay [leɪ] (*pt, pp* **laid**) *pt of* **lie** ♦ *adj* laico(a); (*not expert*) profano(a) ♦ *vt* posare, mettere; (*eggs*) fare; (*trap*) tendere; (*plans*) fare, elaborare; **to ~ the table** apparecchiare la tavola; **~ aside** *or* **by** *vt* mettere da parte; **~ down** *vt* mettere giù; (*rules etc*) formulare, fissare; **to ~ down the law** dettar legge; **to ~ down one's life** dare la propria vita; **~ off** *vt* (*workers*) licenziare; **~ on** *vt* (*provide*) fornire; **~ out** *vt* (*display*) presentare, disporre; **~about** *n* sfaccendato/a, fannullone/a; **~-by** (BRIT) *n* piazzola (di sosta)

layer ['leɪə*] *n* strato

layman ['leɪmən] *n* laico; profano

layout ['leɪaut] *n* lay-out *m inv*, disposizione *f*; (PRESS) impaginazione *f*

laze [leɪz] *vi* oziare

lazy ['leɪzɪ] *adj* pigro(a)

lb. *abbr* = **pound** (*weight*)

lead¹ [liːd] (*pt, pp* **led**) *n* (*front position*)

posizione f di testa; (distance, time ahead) vantaggio; (clue) indizio; (ELEC) filo (elettrico); (for dog) guinzaglio; (THEATRE) parte f principale ♦ vt guidare, condurre; (induce) indurre; (be leader of) essere a capo di ♦ vi condurre; (SPORT) essere in testa; **in the ~** in testa; **to ~ the way** fare strada; **~ away** vt condurre via; **~ back** vt: **to ~ back to** ricondurre a; **~ on** vt (tease) tenere sulla corda; **~ to** vt fus condurre a; portare a; **~ up to** vt fus portare a

lead² [lɛd] n (metal) piombo; (in pencil) mina; **~ed petrol** n benzina con piombo

leaden ['lɛdn] adj (sky, sea) plumbeo(a)

leader ['li:də*] n capo; leader m inv; (in newspaper) articolo di fondo; (SPORT) chi è in testa; **~ship** n direzione f; capacità di comando

leading ['li:dɪŋ] adj primo(a); principale ♦ **light** n (person) personaggio di primo piano; **~ man/lady** n (THEATRE) primo attore/prima attrice

lead singer n cantante alla testa di un gruppo

leaf [li:f] n (pl **leaves**) foglia ♦ vi: **to ~ through** sfogliare qc; **to turn over a new ~** cambiar vita

leaflet ['li:flɪt] n dépliant m inv; (POL, REL) volantino

league [li:g] n lega; (FOOTBALL) campionato; **to be in ~ with** essere in lega con

leak [li:k] n (out) fuga; (in) infiltrazione f; (security ~) fuga d'informazioni ♦ vi (roof, bucket) perdere; (liquid) uscire; (shoes) lasciar passare l'acqua ♦ vt (information) divulgare; **~ out** vi uscire; (information) trapelare

lean [li:n] (pt, pp **leaned** or **leant**) adj magro(a) ♦ vt: **to ~ sth on sth** appoggiare qc su qc ♦ vi (slope) pendere; (rest): **to ~ against** appoggiarsi contro; essere appoggiato(a) a; **to ~ on** appoggiarsi a; **~ back/forward** vi sporgersi indietro/in avanti; **~ out** vi sporgersi; **~ over** vi inclinarsi; **~ing** n: **~ing (towards)** propensione f (per)

leap [li:p] (pt, pp **leaped** or **leapt**) n salto, balzo ♦ vi saltare, balzare; **~frog** n gioco della cavallina; **~ year** n anno bisestile

learn [lə:n] (pt, pp **learned** or **learnt**) vt, vi imparare; **to ~ about sth** (hear, read) apprendere qc; **to ~ to do sth** imparare a fare qc; **~ed** ['lə:nɪd] adj erudito(a), dotto(a); **~er** n principiante m/f; apprendista m/f; (BRIT: also: **~er driver**) guidatore/trice principiante; **~ing** n erudizione f, sapienza

lease [li:s] n contratto d'affitto ♦ vt affittare

leash [li:ʃ] n guinzaglio

least [li:st] adj: **the ~** (+noun) il(la) più piccolo(a), il(la) minimo(a); (smallest amount of) il(la) meno ♦ adv (+verb) meno; **the ~** (+adjective): **the ~ beautiful girl** la ragazza meno bella; **the ~ possible effort** il minimo sforzo possibile; **I have the ~ money** ho meno denaro di tutti; **at ~** almeno; **not in the ~** affatto, per nulla

leather ['lɛðə*] n cuoio

leave [li:v] (pt, pp **left**) vt lasciare; (go away from) partire da ♦ vi partire, andarsene; (bus, train) partire ♦ n (time off) congedo; (MIL, also: consent) licenza; **to be left** rimanere; **there's some milk left over** c'è rimasto del latte; **on ~** in congedo; **~ behind** vt (person, object) lasciare; (: forget) dimenticare; **~ out** vt omettere, tralasciare; **~ of absence** n congedo

leaves [li:vz] npl of **leaf**

Lebanon ['lɛbənən] n Libano

lecherous ['lɛtʃərəs] adj lascivo(a), lubrico(a)

lecture ['lɛktʃə*] n conferenza; (SCOL) lezione f ♦ vi fare conferenze; fare lezioni ♦ vt (scold): **to ~ sb on** or **about sth** rimproverare qn or fare una ramanzina a qn per qc; **to give a ~ on** tenere una conferenza su

lecturer ['lɛktʃərə*] (BRIT) n (at university) professore/essa, docente m/f

led [lɛd] pt, pp of **lead**

ledge [lɛdʒ] n (of window) davanzale m; (on wall etc) sporgenza; (of mountain) cornice f, cengia

ledger ['lɛdʒə*] n libro maestro, registro

lee [li:] n lato sottovento

leech [li:tʃ] n sanguisuga

leek [li:k] n porro

leer [lɪə*] vi: **to ~ at sb** gettare uno sguardo voglioso (or maligno) su qn

leeway ['li:weɪ] n (fig): **to have some ~** avere una certa libertà di azione

left [lɛft] pt, pp of **leave** ♦ adj sinistro(a) ♦ adv a sinistra ♦ n sinistra; **on the ~, to the ~** a sinistra; **the L~** (POL) la sinistra; **~-hand drive** n guida a sinistra; **~-handed** adj mancino(a); **~-hand side** n lato or fianco sinistro; **~-luggage locker** n armadietto per deposito bagagli; **~-luggage (office)** (BRIT) n deposito m bagagli inv; **~overs** npl avanzi mpl, resti mpl; **~-wing** adj (POL) di sinistra

leg [lɛg] n gamba; (of animal) zampa; (of furniture) piede m; (CULIN: of chicken) coscia; (of journey) tappa; **lst/2nd ~** (SPORT) partita di andata/ritorno

legacy ['lɛgəsɪ] n eredità f inv

legal ['li:gl] adj legale; **~ holiday** (US) n giorno festivo, festa nazionale; **~ tender** n moneta legale

legend ['lɛdʒənd] n leggenda

legislation [lɛdʒɪs'leɪʃən] n legislazione f; **legislature** ['lɛdʒɪslətʃə*] n corpo legislativo

legitimate [lɪ'dʒɪtɪmət] adj legittimo(a)

leg-room n spazio per le gambe

leisure ['lɛʒə*] n agio, tempo libero; ricreazioni fpl; **at ~** con comodo; **~ centre** n centro di ricreazione; **~ly** adj tranquillo(a); fatto(a) con comodo or senza fretta

lemon ['lɛmən] n limone m; **~ade** [-'neɪd] n limonata; **~ tea** n tè m inv al limone

lend [lɛnd] (pt, pp lent) vt: **to ~ sth (to sb)** prestare qc a qn); **~ing library** n biblioteca che consente prestiti di libri

length [lɛŋθ] n lunghezza; (distance) distanza; (section: of road, pipe etc) pezzo, tratto; (of time) periodo; **at ~** (at last) finalmente, alla fine; (lengthily) a lungo; **~en** vt allungare, prolungare ♦ vi

allungarsi; **~ways** adv per il lungo; **~y** adj molto lungo(a)

lenient ['li:nɪənt] adj indulgente, clemente

lens [lɛnz] n lente f; (of camera) obiettivo

Lent [lɛnt] n Quaresima

lent [lɛnt] pt, pp of **lend**

lentil ['lɛntl] n lenticchia

Leo ['li:əu] n Leone m

leotard ['li:ətɑ:d] n calzamaglia

leprosy ['lɛprəsɪ] n lebbra

lesbian ['lɛzbɪən] n lesbica

less [lɛs] adj, pron, adv meno ♦ prep: **~ tax/10% discount** meno tasse/il 10% di sconto; **~ than ever** meno che mai; **~ than half** meno della metà; **~ and ~** sempre meno; **the ~ he works ...** meno lavora ....

lessen ['lɛsn] vi diminuire, attenuarsi ♦ vt diminuire, ridurre

lesser ['lɛsə*] adj minore, più piccolo(a); **to a ~ extent** in grado or misura minore

lesson ['lɛsn] n lezione f; **to teach sb a ~** dare una lezione a qn

let [lɛt] (pt, pp let) vt lasciare; (BRIT: lease) dare in affitto; **to ~ sb do sth** lasciar fare qc a qn, lasciare che qn faccia qc; **to ~ sb know sth** far sapere qc a qn; **~'s go** andiamo; **~ him come** lo lasci venire; **"to ~"** "affittasi"; **~ down** vt (lower) abbassare; (dress) allungare; (hair) sciogliere; (tyre) sgonfiare; (disappoint) deludere; **~ go** vt, vi mollare; **~ in** vt lasciare entrare; (visitor etc) far entrare; **~ off** vt (allow to go) lasciare andare; (firework etc) far partire; **~ on** (inf) vi dire; **~ out** vt lasciare uscire; (scream) emettere; **~ up** vi diminuire

lethal ['li:θl] adj letale, mortale

lethargic [lɛ'θɑ:dʒɪk] adj letargico(a)

letter ['lɛtə*] n lettera; **~ bomb** n lettera esplosiva; **~box** (BRIT) n buca delle lettere; **~ing** n iscrizione f; caratteri mpl

lettuce ['lɛtɪs] n lattuga, insalata

let-up n pausa

leukaemia [lu:'ki:mɪə] (US **leukemia**) n leucemia

level ['lɛvl] adj piatto(a), piano(a); orizzontale ♦ adv: **to draw ~ with** mettersi alla pari di ♦ *n* livello ♦ *vt* livellare, spianare; **to be ~ with** essere alla pari di; **A ~s** (*BRIT*) *npl* ≈ esami *mpl* di maturità; **O ~s** (*BRIT*) *npl esami fatti in Inghilterra all'età di 16 anni*; **on the ~** piatto(a); (*fig*) onesto(a); **~ off** *or* **out** *vi* (*prices etc*) stabilizzarsi; **~ crossing** (*BRIT*) *n* passaggio a livello; **~-headed** *adj* equilibrato(a)

lever ['li:və*] *n* leva; **~age** *n*: **~age (on** *or* **with)** forza (su); (*fig*) ascendente *m* (su)

levy ['levi] *n* tassa, imposta ♦ *vt* imporre

lewd [lu:d] *adj* osceno(a), lascivo(a)

liability [laiə'biləti] *n* responsabilità *f inv*; (*handicap*) peso; **liabilities** *npl* debiti *mpl*; (*on balance sheet*) passivo

liable ['laiəbl] *adj* (*subject*): **~ to** soggetto(a) a; passibile di; (*responsible*): **~ (for)** responsabile (di); (*likely*): **~ to do** propenso(a) a fare

liaise [li:'eiz] *vi*: **to ~ (with)** mantenere i contatti (con)

liaison [li:'eizɔn] *n* relazione *f*; (*MIL*) collegamento

liar ['laiə*] *n* bugiardo/a

libel ['laibl] *n* libello, diffamazione *f* ♦ *vt* diffamare

liberal ['libərl] *adj* liberale; (*generous*): **to be ~ with** distribuire liberalmente

liberation [libə'reiʃən] *n* liberazione *f*

liberty ['libəti] *n* libertà *f inv*; **at ~** (*criminal*) in libertà; **at ~ to do** libero(a) di fare

Libra ['li:brə] *n* Bilancia

librarian [lai'breəriən] *n* bibliotecario/a

library ['laibrəri] *n* biblioteca

Libya ['libiə] *n* Libia; **~n** *adj*, *n* libico(a)

lice [lais] *npl of* **louse**

licence ['laisns] (*US* **license**) *n* autorizzazione *f*, permesso; (*COMM*) licenza; (*RADIO, TV*) canone *m*, abbonamento; (*also*: **driving ~**, (*US*) **driver's ~**) patente *f* di guida; (*excessive freedom*) licenza; **~ number** *n* numero di targa; **~ plate** *n* targa

license ['laisns] *n* (*US*) = **licence** ♦ *vt* dare una licenza a; **~d** *adj* (*for alcohol*) che ha la licenza di vendere bibite alcoliche

lick [lik] *vt* leccare; (*inf*: *defeat*) stracciare; **to**

~ one's lips (*fig*) leccarsi i baffi

licorice ['likəris] (*US*) *n* = **liquorice**

lid [lid] *n* coperchio; (*eye~*) palpebra

lie [lai] (*pt* **lay**, *pp* **lain**) *vi* (*rest*) giacere; star disteso(a); (*of object*: *be situated*) trovarsi, essere; (*tell lies*: *pt, pp* **lied**) mentire, dire bugie ♦ *n* bugia, menzogna; **to ~ low** (*fig*) latitare; **~ about** *or* **around** (*things*) essere in giro; (*person*) bighellonare; **~-down** (*BRIT*) *n*: **to have a ~-down** sdraiarsi, riposarsi; **~-in** (*BRIT*) *n*: **to have a ~-in** rimanere a letto

lieu [lu:]: **in ~ of** *prep* invece di, al posto di

lieutenant [lef'tenant, (*US*) lu:'tenənt] *n* tenente *m*

life [laif] (*pl* **lives**) *n* vita ♦ *cpd* di vita; della vita; a vita; **to come to ~** rianimarsi; **~ assurance** (*BRIT*) *n* = **~ insurance**; **~-belt** (*BRIT*) *n* salvagente *m*; **~-boat** *n* scialuppa di salvataggio; **~guard** *n* bagnino; **~ imprisonment** *n* carcere *m* a vita; **~ insurance** *n* assicurazione *f* sulla vita; **~ jacket** *n* giubbotto di salvataggio; **~less** *adj* senza vita; **~like** *adj* verosimile; rassomigliante; **~long** *adj* per tutta la vita; **~ preserver** (*US*) *n* salvagente *m*; giubbotto di salvataggio; **~ sentence** *n* ergastolo; **~-size(d)** *adj* a grandezza naturale; **~ span** *n* (durata della) vita; **~style** *n* stile *m* di vita; **~ support system** *n* respiratore *m* automatico; **~time** *n*: **in his ~time** durante la sua vita; **once in a ~time** una volta nella vita

lift [lift] *vt* sollevare; (*ban, rule*) levare ♦ *vi* (*fog*) alzarsi ♦ *n* (*BRIT*: *elevator*) ascensore *m*; **to give sb a ~** (*BRIT*) dare un passaggio a qn; **~-off** *n* decollo

light [lait] (*pt, pp* **lighted** *or* **lit**) *n* luce *f*, lume *m*; (*daylight*) luce *f*, giorno; (*lamp*) lampada; (*AUT*: *rear ~*) luce *f* di posizione; (: *headlamp*) fanale *m*; (*for cigarette etc*): **have you got a ~?** ha da accendere?; **~s** *npl* (*AUT*: *traffic ~s*) semaforo ♦ *vt* (*candle, cigarette, fire*) accendere; (*room*): **to be lit by** essere illuminato(a) da ♦ *adj* (*room, colour*) chiaro(a); (*not heavy, also fig*) leggero(a); **to come to ~** venire alla luce,

emergere; ~ **up** _vi_ illuminarsi ♦ _vt_
illuminare; ~ **bulb** _n_ lampadina; **~en** _vt_
(_make less heavy_) alleggerire; **~er** _n_ (_also:_
cigarette ~er) accendino; **~-headed** _adj_
stordito(a); **~-hearted** _adj_ gioioso(a),
gaio(a); **~house** _n_ faro; **~ing** _n_
illuminazione _f_; **~ly** _adv_ leggermente; **to
get off ~ly** cavarsela a buon mercato; ~
meter _n_ (_PHOT_) esposimetro; **~ness** _n_
chiarezza; (_in weight_) leggerezza
lightning ['laɪtnɪŋ] _n_ lampo, fulmine _m_; ~
conductor (_US_ ~ **rod**) _n_ parafulmine _m_
light pen _n_ penna ottica
lightweight ['laɪtweɪt] _adj_ (_suit_) leggero(a)
♦ _n_ (_BOXING_) peso leggero
light year _n_ anno _m_ luce _inv_
like [laɪk] _vt_ (_person_) volere bene a; (_activity,
object, food_): **I ~ swimming/that book/
chocolate** mi piace nuotare/quel libro/il
cioccolato ♦ _prep_ come ♦ _adj_ simile,
uguale ♦ _n_: **the ~** uno(a) uguale; **his ~s
and dislikes** i suoi gusti; **I would ~, I'd ~**
mi piacerebbe, vorrei; **would you ~ a
coffee?** gradirebbe un caffè?; **to be/look ~
sb/sth** somigliare a qn/qc; **what does it
look/taste ~?** come ha aspetto/gusto ha?;
what does it sound ~? come fa?; **that's
just ~ him** è proprio da lui; **do it ~ this**
fallo così; **it is nothing ~ ...** non è affatto
come ...; **~able** _adj_ simpatico(a)
likelihood ['laɪklɪhud] _n_ probabilità
likely ['laɪklɪ] _adj_ probabile; plausibile; **he's
~ to leave** probabilmente partirà, è
probabile che parta; **not ~!** neanche per
sogno!
likeness ['laɪknɪs] _n_ somiglianza
likewise ['laɪkwaɪz] _adv_ similmente, nello
stesso modo
liking ['laɪkɪŋ] _n_: ~ (**for**) debole _m_ (per); **to
be to sb's ~** piacere a qn
lilac ['laɪlək] _n_ lilla _m inv_
lily ['lɪlɪ] _n_ giglio; ~ **of the valley** _n_
mughetto
limb [lɪm] _n_ arto
limber up ['lɪmbə*-] _vi_ riscaldarsi i muscoli
limbo ['lɪmbəu] _n_: **to be in ~** (_fig_) essere
lasciato(a) nel dimenticatoio

lime [laɪm] _n_ (_tree_) tiglio; (_fruit_) limetta;
(_GEO_) calce _f_
limelight ['laɪmlaɪt] _n_: **in the ~** (_fig_) alla
ribalta, in vista
limerick ['lɪmərɪk] _n_ poesiola umoristica di
5 versi
limestone ['laɪmstəun] _n_ pietra calcarea;
(_GEO_) calcare _m_
limit ['lɪmɪt] _n_ limite _m_ ♦ _vt_ limitare; **~ed**
adj limitato(a), ristretto(a); **to be ~ed to**
limitarsi a; **~ed (liability) company**
(_BRIT_) ≈ società _f inv_ a responsabilità
limitata
limp [lɪmp] _n_: **to have a ~** zoppicare ♦ _vi_
zoppicare ♦ _adj_ floscio(a), flaccido(a)
limpet ['lɪmpɪt] _n_ patella
line [laɪn] _n_ linea; (_rope_) corda; (_for fishing_)
lenza; (_wire_) filo; (_of poem_) verso; (_row,
series_) fila, riga; coda; (_on face_) ruga ♦ _vt_
(_clothes_): **to ~ (with)** foderare (di); (_box_): **to
~ (with)** rivestire _or_ foderare (di); (_subj:
trees, crowd_) fiancheggiare; ~ **of business**
settore _m or_ ramo d'attività; **in ~ with** in
linea con; ~ **up** _vi_ allinearsi, mettersi in fila
♦ _vt_ mettere in fila; (_event, celebration_)
preparare
lined [laɪnd] _adj_ (_face_) rugoso(a); (_paper_) a
righe, rigato(a)
linen ['lɪnɪn] _n_ biancheria, panni _mpl_; (_cloth_)
tela di lino
liner ['laɪnə*] _n_ nave _f_ di linea; (_for bin_)
sacchetto
linesman ['laɪnzmən] _n_ guardalinee _m inv_
line-up _n_ allineamento, fila; (_SPORT_)
formazione _f_ di gioco
linger ['lɪŋgə*] _vi_ attardarsi; indugiare;
(_smell, tradition_) persistere
lingerie ['lænʒəri:] _n_ biancheria intima
femminile
linguistics [lɪŋ'gwɪstɪks] _n_ linguistica
lining ['laɪnɪŋ] _n_ fodera
link [lɪŋk] _n_ (_of a chain_) anello; (_relationship_)
legame _m_; (_connection_) collegamento ♦ _vt_
collegare, unire, congiungere; (_associate_):
to ~ with _or_ **to** collegare a; **~s** _npl_ (_GOLF_)
pista _or_ terreno da golf; ~ **up** _vt_ collegare,
unire ♦ _vi_ riunirsi; associarsi

lino ['laɪnəu] n = **linoleum**

linoleum [lɪ'nəulɪəm] n linoleum m inv

lion ['laɪən] n leone m; **~ess** n leonessa

lip [lɪp] n labbro; (of cup etc) orlo

liposuction ['lɪpəusʌkʃən] n liposuzione f

lip: ~read vi leggere sulle labbra; **~ salve** n burro di cacao; **~ service** n: **to pay ~ service to sth** essere favorevole a qc solo a parole; **~stick** n rossetto

liqueur [lɪ'kjuə*] n liquore m

liquid ['lɪkwɪd] n liquido ♦ adj liquido(a)

liquidize ['lɪkwɪdaɪz] vt (CULIN) passare al frullatore; **~r** n frullatore m (a brocca)

liquor ['lɪkə*] n alcool m

liquorice ['lɪkərɪs] (BRIT) n liquirizia

liquor store (US) n negozio di liquori

lisp [lɪsp] n pronuncia blesa della ''s''

list [lɪst] n lista, elenco ♦ vt (write down) mettere in lista; fare una lista di; (enumerate) elencare; **~ed building** (BRIT) n edificio sotto la protezione delle Belle Arti

listen ['lɪsn] vi ascoltare; **to ~ to** ascoltare; **~er** n ascoltatore/trice

listless ['lɪstlɪs] adj apatico(a)

lit [lɪt] pt, pp of **light**

liter ['li:tə*] (US) n = **litre**

literacy ['lɪtərəsɪ] n il sapere leggere e scrivere

literal ['lɪtərl] adj letterale; **~ly** adv alla lettera, letteralmente

literary ['lɪtərərɪ] adj letterario(a)

literate ['lɪtərət] adj che sa leggere e scrivere

literature ['lɪtərɪtʃə*] n letteratura; (brochures etc) materiale m

lithe [laɪð] adj agile, snello(a)

litigation [lɪtɪ'geɪʃən] n causa

litre ['li:tə*] (US **liter**) n litro

litter ['lɪtə*] n (rubbish) rifiuti mpl; (young animals) figliata; **~ bin** (BRIT) n cestino per rifiuti; **~ed** adj: **~ed with** coperto(a) di

little ['lɪtl] adj (small) piccolo(a); (not much) poco(a) ♦ adv poco; **a ~** un po' (di); **a ~ bit** un pochino; **~ by ~** a poco a poco; **~ finger** n mignolo

live¹ [lɪv] vi vivere; (reside) vivere, abitare;

~ down vt far dimenticare (alla gente); **~ on** vt fus (food) vivere di; **~ together** vi vivere insieme, convivere; **~ up to** vt fus tener fede a, non venir meno a

live² [laɪv] adj (animal) vivo(a); (wire) sotto tensione; (bullet, missile) inesploso(a); (broadcast) diretto(a); (performance) dal vivo

livelihood ['laɪvlɪhud] n mezzi mpl di sostentamento

lively ['laɪvlɪ] adj vivace, vivo(a)

liven up ['laɪvn'ʌp] vt (discussion, evening) animare ♦ vi ravvivarsi

liver ['lɪvə*] n fegato

lives [laɪvz] npl of **life**

livestock ['laɪvstɔk] n bestiame m

livid ['lɪvɪd] adj livido(a); (furious) livido(a) di rabbia, furibondo(a)

living ['lɪvɪŋ] adj vivo(a), vivente ♦ n: **to earn** or **make a ~** guadagnarsi la vita; **~ conditions** npl condizioni fpl di vita; **~ room** n soggiorno; **~ standards** npl tenore m di vita; **~ wage** n salario sufficiente per vivere

lizard ['lɪzəd] n lucertola

load [ləud] n (weight) peso; (thing carried) carico ♦ vt (also: **~ up**): **to ~ (with)** (lorry, ship) caricare (di); (gun, camera, COMPUT) caricare (con); **a ~ of, ~s of** (fig) un sacco di, **un** sacco di, (vehicle): **~ed (with)** carico(a) (di), (question) capzioso(a); (inf: rich) carico(a) di soldi

loaf [ləuf] (pl **loaves**) n pane m, pagnotta

loan [ləun] n prestito ♦ vt dare in prestito; **on ~** in prestito

loath [ləuθ] adj: **to be ~ to do** essere restio(a) a fare

loathe [ləuð] vt detestare, aborrire

loaves [ləuvz] npl of **loaf**

lobby ['lɔbɪ] n atrio, vestibolo; (POL: pressure group) gruppo di pressione ♦ vt fare pressione su

lobster ['lɔbstə*] n aragosta

local ['ləukl] adj locale ♦ n (BRIT: pub) ≈ bar m inv all'angolo; **the ~s** npl (local inhabitants) la gente della zona; **~ anaesthetic** n anestesia locale; **~**

authority *n* ente *m* locale; ~ **call** *n* (TEL) telefonata urbana; ~ **government** *n* amministrazione *f* locale

locality [ləu'kælɪtɪ] *n* località *f inv*; (*position*) posto, luogo

locally ['ləukəlɪ] *adv* da queste parti; nel vicinato

locate [ləu'keɪt] *vt* (*find*) trovare; (*situate*) collocare; situare

location [ləu'keɪʃən] *n* posizione *f*; **on** ~ (CINEMA) all'esterno

loch [lɔx] *n* lago

lock [lɔk] *n* (*of door, box*) serratura; (*of canal*) chiusa; (*of hair*) ciocca, riccio ♦ *vt* (*with key*) chiudere a chiave ♦ *vi* (*door etc*) chiudersi; (*wheels*) bloccarsi, incepparsi; ~ **in** *vt* chiudere dentro (a chiave); ~ **out** *vt* chiudere fuori; ~ **up** *vt* (*criminal, mental patient*) rinchiudere; (*house*) chiudere (a chiave) ♦ *vi* chiudere tutto (a chiave)

locker ['lɔkə*] *n* armadietto

locket ['lɔkɪt] *n* medaglione *m*

locksmith ['lɔksmɪθ] *n* magnano

lockup ['lɔkʌp] *n* (US) prigione *f*; guardina

locum ['ləukəm] *n* (MED) medico sostituto

locust ['ləukəst] *n* locusta

lodge [lɔdʒ] *n* casetta, portineria; (*hunting* ~) casino di caccia ♦ *vi* (*person*): **to** ~ (**with**) essere a pensione (presso *or* da); (*bullet etc*) conficcarsi ♦ *vt* (*appeal etc*) presentare, fare; **to** ~ **a complaint** presentare un reclamo; ~**r** *n* affittuario/a; (*with room and meals*) pensionante *m/f*

lodgings ['lɔdʒɪŋz] *npl* camera d'affitto; camera ammobiliata

loft [lɔft] *n* solaio, soffitta

lofty ['lɔftɪ] *adj* alto(a); (*haughty*) altezzoso(a)

log [lɔg] *n* (*of wood*) ceppo; (*book*) = **logbook** ♦ *vt* registrare

logbook ['lɔgbuk] *n* (NAUT, AVIAT) diario di bordo; (AUT) libretto di circolazione

loggerheads ['lɔgəhɛdz] *npl*: **at** ~ (**with**) ai ferri corti (con)

logic ['lɔdʒɪk] *n* logica; ~**al** *adj* logico(a)

loin [lɔɪn] *n* (CULIN) lombata

loiter ['lɔɪtə*] *vi* attardarsi

loll [lɔl] *vi* (*also*: ~ **about**) essere stravaccato(a)

lollipop ['lɔlɪpɔp] *n* lecca lecca *m inv*; ~ **man/lady** (BRIT: *irreg*) *n* impiegato/a che aiuta i bambini ad attraversare la strada

---

lollipop man/lady

In Gran Bretagna il **lollipop man** *e la* **lollipop lady** *sono persone incaricate di aiutare i bambini ad attraversare la strada in prossimità delle scuole; usano una paletta la cui forma ricorda quella di un lecca lecca, in inglese* **lollipop**.

London ['lʌndən] *n* Londra; ~**er** *n* londinese *m/f*

lone [ləun] *adj* solitario(a)

loneliness ['ləunlɪnɪs] *n* solitudine *f*, isolamento

lonely ['ləunlɪ] *adj* solo(a); solitario(a), isolato(a)

long [lɔŋ] *adj* lungo(a) ♦ *adv* a lungo, per molto tempo ♦ *vi*: **to** ~ **for sth/to do** desiderare qc/di fare; non veder l'ora di aver qc/di fare; **so** *or* **as** ~ **as** (*while*) finché; (*provided that*) sempre che +*sub*; **don't be** ~! fai presto!; **how** ~ **is this river/course?** quanto è lungo questo fiume/corso?; **6 metres** ~ lungo 6 metri; **6 months** ~ che dura 6 mesi, di 6 mesi; **all night** ~ tutta la notte; **he no** ~**er comes** non viene più; ~ **before** molto tempo prima; **before** ~ (+*future*) presto, fra poco; (+*past*) poco tempo dopo; **at** ~ **last** finalmente; ~**-distance** *adj* (*race*) di fondo; (*call*) interurbano(a); ~**-haired** *adj* dai capelli lunghi; ~**ing** *n* desiderio, voglia, brama

longitude ['lɔŋgɪtjuːd] *n* longitudine *f*

long: ~ **jump** *n* salto in lungo; ~**-life** *adj* (*milk*) a lunga conservazione; (*batteries*) di lunga durata; ~**-lost** *adj* perduto(a) da tempo; ~**-range** *adj* a lunga portata; ~**-sighted** *adj* presbite; ~**-standing** *adj* di vecchia data; ~**-suffering** *adj* estremamente paziente; infinitamente tollerante; ~**-term** *adj* a lungo termine; ~

wave n onde fpl lunghe; **~-winded** adj prolisso(a), interminabile

loo [luː] (BRIT: inf) n W.C. m inv, cesso

look [luk] vi guardare; (seem) sembrare, parere; (building etc): **to ~ south/on to the sea** dare a sud/sul mare ♦ n sguardo; (appearance) aspetto, aria; **~s** npl (good ~s) bellezza; **~ after** vt fus occuparsi di, prendere cura di; (keep an eye on) guardare, badare a; **~ at** vt fus guardare; **~ back** vi: **to ~ back on** (event etc) ripensare a; **~ down on** vt fus (fig) guardare dall'alto, disprezzare; **~ for** vt fus cercare; **~ forward to** vt fus non veder l'ora di; (in letters): **we ~ forward to hearing from you** in attesa di una vostra gentile risposta; **~ into** vt fus esaminare; **~ on** vi fare da spettatore; **~ out** vi (beware): **to ~ out (for)** stare in guardia (per); **~ out for** vt fus cercare; **~ round** vi (turn) girarsi, voltarsi; (in shop) dare un'occhiata; **~ to** vt fus (rely on) contare su; **~ up** vi alzare gli occhi, (improve) migliorare ♦ vt (word) cercare; (friend) andare a trovare; **~ up to** vt fus avere rispetto per; **~-out** n posto d'osservazione; guardia; **to be on the ~-out (for)** stare in guardia (per)

loom [luːm] n telaio ♦ vi (also: **~ up**) apparire minaccioso(a); (event) essere imminente

loony ['luːnɪ] (inf) n pazzo/a

loop [luːp] n cappio ♦ vt: **to ~ sth round sth** passare qc intorno a qc; **~hole** n via d'uscita; scappatoia

loose [luːs] adj (knot) sciolto(a); (screw) allentato(a); (stone) cadente; (clothes) ampio(a), largo(a); (animal) in libertà, scappato(a); (life, morals) dissoluto(a) ♦ n: **to be on the ~** essere in libertà; **~ change** n spiccioli mpl, moneta; **~ chippings** npl (on road) ghiaino; **~ end** n: **to be at a ~ end** (BRIT) or **at ~ ends** (US) non saper che fare; **~ly** adv senza stringere; approssimativamente; **~n** vt sciogliere; (belt etc) allentare

loot [luːt] n bottino ♦ vt saccheggiare

lop [lɔp] vt (also: **~ off**) tagliare via, recidere

lop-sided ['lɔp'saɪdɪd] adj non equilibrato(a), asimmetrico(a)

lord [lɔːd] n signore m; **L~ Smith** lord Smith; **the L~** il Signore; **good L~!** buon Dio!; **the (House of) L~s** (BRIT) la Camera dei Lord; **~ship** n: **your L~ship** Sua Eccellenza

lore [lɔː*] n tradizioni fpl

lorry ['lɔrɪ] (BRIT) n camion m inv; **~ driver** (BRIT) n camionista m

lose [luːz] (pt, pp lost) vt perdere ♦ vi perdere; **to ~ (time)** (clock) ritardare; **~r** n perdente m/f

loss [lɔs] n perdita; **to be at a ~** essere perplesso(a)

lost [lɔst] pt, pp of **lose** ♦ adj perduto(a); **~ property** (US **~ and found**) n oggetti mpl smarriti

lot [lɔt] n (at auctions) lotto; (destiny) destino, sorte f; **the ~** tutto(a) quanto(a); tutti(e) quanti(e); **a ~** molto; **a ~ of** una gran quantità di, un sacco di; **~s of** molto(a); **to draw ~s (for sth)** tirare a sorte (per qc)

lotion ['ləʊʃən] n lozione f

lottery ['lɔtərɪ] n lotteria

loud [laud] adj forte, alto(a); (gaudy) vistoso(a), sgargiante ♦ adv (speak etc) forte, out ~ (read etc) ad alta voce; **~hailer** (BRIT) n portavoce m inv; **~ly** adv fortemente, ad alta voce; **~speaker** n altoparlante m

lounge [laundʒ] n salotto, soggiorno; (at airport, station) sala d'attesa; (BRIT: also: **~ bar**) bar m inv con servizio a tavolino ♦ vi oziare; **~ about** or **around** vi starsene colle mani in mano

louse [laus] (pl lice) n pidocchio

lousy ['lauzɪ] (inf) adj orrendo(a), schifoso(a); **to feel ~** stare da cani

lout [laut] n zoticone m

lovable ['lʌvəbl] adj simpatico(a), carino(a); amabile

love [lʌv] n amore m ♦ vt amare; voler bene a; **to ~ to do: I ~ to do** mi piace fare; **to be/fall in ~ with** essere innamorato(a)/

innamorarsi di; **to make ~** fare l'amore; **"15 ~"** (TENNIS) "15 a zero"; **~ affair** n relazione f; **~ life** n vita sentimentale

lovely ['lʌvlɪ] adj bello(a); (delicious: smell, meal) buono(a)

lover ['lʌvə*] n amante m/f; (person in love) innamorato/a; (amateur): **a ~ of** un(un')amante di; un(un')appassionato(a) di

loving ['lʌvɪŋ] adj affettuoso(a)

low [ləu] adj basso(a) ♦ adv in basso ♦ n (METEOR) depressione f; **to be ~ on** (supplies etc) avere scarsità di; **to feel ~** sentirsi giù; **~-alcohol** adj a basso contenuto alcolico; **~-calorie** adj a basso contenuto calorico; **~-cut** adj (dress) scollato(a); **~er** adj (bottom: of 2 things) più basso; (less important) meno importante ♦ vt calare; (prices, eyes, voice) abbassare; **~-fat** adj magro(a); **~lands** npl (GEO) pianura; **~ly** adj umile, modesto(a)

loyal ['lɔɪəl] adj fedele, leale; **~ty** n fedeltà, lealtà

lozenge ['lɔzɪndʒ] n (MED) pastiglia

L.P. n abbr = **long-playing record**

L-plates (BRIT) npl contrassegno P principiante

---L-plates---

> *Le **L-plates** sono delle tabelle bianche con una L rossa che in Gran Bretagna i guidatori principianti, **learner drivers**, devono applicare alla propria autovettura finché non ottengono la patente.*

Ltd abbr (= **limited**) ≈ S.r.l.

lubricate ['lu:brɪkeɪt] vt lubrificare

luck [lʌk] n fortuna, sorte f; **bad ~** sfortuna, mala sorte; **good ~!** buona fortuna!; **~ily** adv fortunatamente, per fortuna; **~y** adj fortunato(a); (number etc) che porta fortuna

ludicrous ['lu:dɪkrəs] adj ridicolo(a)

lug [lʌg] (inf) vt trascinare

luggage ['lʌgɪdʒ] n bagagli mpl; **~ rack** n portabagagli m inv

lukewarm ['lu:kwɔ:m] adj tiepido(a)

lull [lʌl] n intervallo di calma ♦ vt: **to ~ sb to sleep** cullare qn finché si addormenta; **to be ~ed into a false sense of security** illudersi che tutto vada bene

lullaby ['lʌləbaɪ] n ninnananna

lumbago [lʌm'beɪɡəu] n lombaggine f

lumber ['lʌmbə*] n (wood) legname m; (junk) roba vecchia; **~ with** vt: **to be ~ed with sth** doversi sorbire qc; **~jack** n boscaiolo

luminous ['lu:mɪnəs] adj luminoso(a)

lump [lʌmp] n pezzo; (in sauce) grumo; (swelling) gonfiore m; (also: **sugar ~**) zolletta ♦ vt (also: **~ together**) riunire, mettere insieme; **a ~ sum** una somma globale; **~y** adj (sauce) pieno(a) di grumi; (bed) bitorzoluto(a)

lunatic ['lu:nətɪk] adj pazzo(a), matto(a)

lunch [lʌntʃ] n pranzo, colazione f

luncheon ['lʌntʃən] n pranzo; **~ voucher** (BRIT) n buono m pasto inv

lunch time n ora di pranzo

lung [lʌŋ] n polmone m

lunge [lʌndʒ] vi (also: **~ forward**) fare un balzo in avanti; **to ~ at** balzare su

lurch [lə:tʃ] vi vacillare, barcollare ♦ n scatto improvviso; **to leave sb in the ~** piantare in asso qn

lure [luə*] n richiamo; lusinga ♦ vt attirare (con l'inganno)

lurid ['luərɪd] adj sgargiante; (details etc) impressionante

lurk [lə:k] vi stare in agguato

luscious ['lʌʃəs] adj succulento(a); delizioso(a)

lush [lʌʃ] adj lussureggiante

lust [lʌst] n lussuria; cupidigia; desiderio; (fig): **~ for** sete f di

lusty ['lʌstɪ] adj vigoroso(a), robusto(a)

Luxembourg ['lʌksəmbə:g] n (state) Lussemburgo m; (city) Lussemburgo f

luxuriant [lʌg'zjuərɪənt] adj lussureggiante; (hair) folto(a)

luxurious [lʌg'zjuərɪəs] adj sontuoso(a), di lusso

luxury ['lʌkʃərɪ] n lusso ♦ cpd di lusso

lying ['laɪɪŋ] n bugie fpl, menzogne fpl

♦ *adj* bugiardo(a)
lynch [lɪntʃ] *vt* linciare
lyrical ['lɪrɪkl] *adj* lirico(a); (*fig*) entusiasta
lyrics ['lɪrɪks] *npl* (*of song*) parole *fpl*

M, m

m. *abbr* = **metre; mile; million**
M.A. *abbr* = **Master of Arts**
mac [mæk] (*BRIT*) *n* impermeabile *m*
macaroni [mækə'rəʊnɪ] *n* maccheroni *mpl*
machine [mə'ʃiːn] *n* macchina ♦ *vt* (*TECH*)
lavorare a macchina; (*dress etc*) cucire a
macchina; **~ gun** *n* mitragliatrice *f*; **~ry** *n*
macchinario, macchine *fpl*; (*fig*) macchina
mackerel ['mækrl] *n inv* sgombro
mackintosh ['mækɪntɔʃ] (*BRIT*) *n*
impermeabile *m*
mad [mæd] *adj* matto(a), pazzo(a); (*foolish*)
sciocco(a); (*angry*) furioso(a); **to be ~**
about (*keen*) andare pazzo(a) per
madam ['mædəm] *n* signora
madden ['mædn] *vt* fare infuriare
made [meɪd] *pt, pp of* **make**
Madeira [mə'dɪərə] *n* (*GEO*) Madera; (*wine*)
madera
made-to-measure (*BRIT*) *adj* fatto(a) su
misura
madly ['mædlɪ] *adv* follemente
madman ['mædmən] (*irreg*) *n* pazzo,
alienato
madness ['mædnɪs] *n* pazzia
magazine [mægə'ziːn] *n* (*PRESS*) rivista;
(*RADIO, TV*) rubrica
maggot ['mægət] *n* baco, verme *m*
magic ['mædʒɪk] *n* magia ♦ *adj* magico(a);
~al *adj* magico(a); **~ian** [mə'dʒɪʃən] *n*
mago/a
magistrate ['mædʒɪstreɪt] *n* magistrato;
giudice *m/f*
magnet ['mægnɪt] *n* magnete *m*, calamita;
~ic [-'netɪk] *adj* magnetico(a)
magnificent [mæg'nɪfɪsnt] *adj* magnifico(a)
magnify ['mægnɪfaɪ] *vt* ingrandire; **~ing**
glass *n* lente *f* d'ingrandimento
magnitude ['mægnɪtjuːd] *n* grandezza;

importanza
magpie ['mægpaɪ] *n* gazza
mahogany [mə'hɔgənɪ] *n* mogano
maid [meɪd] *n* domestica; (*in hotel*)
cameriera
maiden ['meɪdn] *n* fanciulla ♦ *adj* (*aunt etc*)
nubile; (*speech, voyage*) inaugurale; **~**
name *n* nome *m* da nubile *or* da ragazza
mail [meɪl] *n* posta ♦ *vt* spedire (per posta);
~box (*US*) *n* cassetta delle lettere; **~ing**
list *n* elenco d'indirizzi; **~-order** *n* vendita
(*or* acquisto) per corrispondenza
maim [meɪm] *vt* mutilare
main [meɪn] *adj* principale ♦ *n* (*pipe*)
conduttura principale; **the ~s** *npl* (*ELEC*) la
linea principale; **in the ~** nel complesso,
nell'insieme; **~frame** *n* (*COMPUT*)
mainframe *m inv*; **~land** *n* continente *m*;
~ly *adv* principalmente, soprattutto; **~**
road *n* strada principale; **~stay** *n* (*fig*)
sostegno principale; **~stream** *n* (*fig*)
corrente *f* principale
maintain [meɪn'teɪn] *vt* mantenere; (*affirm*)
sostenere; **maintenance** ['meɪntənəns] *n*
manutenzione *f*; (*alimony*) alimenti *mpl*
maize [meɪz] *n* granturco, mais *m*
majestic [mə'dʒestɪk] *adj* maestoso(a)
majesty ['mædʒɪstɪ] *n* maestà *f inv*
major ['meɪdʒə*] *n* (*MIL*) maggiore *m* ♦ *adj*
(*greater, MUS*) maggiore; (*in importance*)
principale, importante
Majorca [mə'jɔːkə] *n* Maiorca
majority [mə'dʒɔrɪtɪ] *n* maggioranza
make [meɪk] (*pt, pp* **made**) *vt* fare;
(*manufacture*) fare, fabbricare; (*cause to*
be): **to ~ sb sad** *etc* rendere qn triste *etc*;
(*force*): **to ~ sb do sth** costringere qn a fare
qc, far fare qc a qn; (*equal*): **2 and 2 ~ 4** 2
più 2 fa 4 ♦ *n* fabbricazione *f*; (*brand*)
marca; **to ~ a fool of sb** far fare a qn la
figura dello scemo; **to ~ a profit** realizzare
un profitto; **to ~ a loss** subire una perdita;
to ~ it (*arrive*) arrivare; (*achieve sth*) farcela;
what time do you ~ it? che ora fai?; **to ~**
do with arrangiarsi con; **~ for** *vt fus*
(*place*) avviarsi verso; **~ out** *vt* (*write out*)
scrivere; (: *cheque*) emettere; (*understand*)

capire; (*see*) distinguere; (: *numbers*) decifrare; ~ **up** *vt* (*constitute*) formare; (*invent*) inventare; (*parcel*) fare ♦ *vi* conciliarsi; (*with cosmetics*) truccarsi; ~ **up for** *vt fus* compensare; ricuperare; ~**believe** *n*: **a world of** ~**-believe** un mondo di favole; **it's just** ~**-believe** è tutta un'invenzione; ~**r** *n* (*of programme etc*) creatore/trice; (*manufacturer*) fabbricante *m*; ~**shift** *adj* improvvisato(a); ~**-up** *n* trucco; ~**-up remover** *n* struccatore *m*

making ['meɪkɪŋ] *n* (*fig*): **in the** ~ in formazione; **to have the** ~**s of** (*actor, athlete etc*) avere la stoffa di

maladjusted [mælə'dʒʌstɪd] *adj* disadattato(a)

malaria [mə'lɛərɪə] *n* malaria

Malaysia [mə'leɪzɪə] *n* Malaysia

male [meɪl] *n* (*BIOL*) maschio ♦ *adj* maschile; maschio(a)

malfunction [mæl'fʌŋkʃən] *n* funzione *f* difettosa

malice ['mælɪs] *n* malevolenza; **malicious** [mə'lɪʃəs] *adj* malevolo(a); (*LAW*) doloso(a)

malignant [mə'lɪgnənt] *adj* (*MED*) maligno(a)

mall [mɔːl] *n* (*also*: **shopping** ~) centro commerciale

mallet ['mælɪt] *n* maglio

malnutrition [mælnjuː'trɪʃən] *n* denutrizione *f*

malpractice [mæl'præktɪs] *n* prevaricazione *f*; negligenza

malt [mɔːlt] *n* malto

Malta ['mɔːltə] *n* Malta

mammal ['mæml] *n* mammifero

mammoth ['mæməθ] *adj* enorme, gigantesco(a)

man [mæn] (*pl* **men**) *n* uomo ♦ *vt* fornire d'uomini; stare a; **an old** ~ un vecchio; ~ **and wife** marito e moglie

manage ['mænɪdʒ] *vi* farcela ♦ *vt* (*be in charge of*) occuparsi di; gestire; **to** ~ **to do sth** riuscire a far qc; ~**able** *adj* maneggevole; fattibile; ~**ment** *n* amministrazione *f*, direzione *f*; ~**r** *n* direttore *m*; (*of shop, restaurant*) gerente

m; (*of artist, SPORT*) manager *m inv*; ~**ress** [-ə'rɛs] *n* direttrice *f*; gerente *f*; ~**rial** [-ə'dʒɪərɪəl] *adj* dirigenziale; **managing director** *n* amministratore *m* delegato

mandarin ['mændərɪn] *n* (*person, fruit*) mandarino

mandatory ['mændətərɪ] *adj* obbligatorio(a); ingiuntivo(a)

mane [meɪn] *n* criniera

maneuver *etc* [mə'nuːvə*] (*US*) = **manoeuvre** *etc*

manfully ['mænfəlɪ] *adv* valorosamente

mangle ['mæŋgl] *vt* straziare; mutilare

mango ['mæŋgəu] (*pl* ~**es**) *n* mango

mangy ['meɪndʒɪ] *adj* rognoso(a)

manhandle ['mænhændl] *vt* malmenare

manhole ['mænhəul] *n* botola stradale

manhood ['mænhud] *n* età virile; virilità

man-hour *n* ora di lavoro

manhunt ['mænhʌnt] *n* caccia all'uomo

mania ['meɪnɪə] *n* mania; ~**c** ['meɪnɪæk] *n* maniaco/a

manic ['mænɪk] *adj* (*behaviour, activity*) maniacale

manicure ['mænɪkjuə*] *n* manicure *f inv*; ~ **set** *n* trousse *f inv* della manicure

manifest ['mænɪfɛst] *vt* manifestare ♦ *adj* manifesto(a), palese

manifesto [mænɪ'fɛstəu] *n* manifesto

manipulate [mə'nɪpjuleɪt] *vt* manipolare

mankind [mæn'kaɪnd] *n* umanità, genere *m* umano

manly ['mænlɪ] *adj* virile; coraggioso(a)

man-made *adj* sintetico(a); artificiale

manner ['mænə*] *n* maniera, modo; (*behaviour*) modo di fare; (*type, sort*): **all** ~ **of things** ogni genere di cosa; ~**s** *npl* (*conduct*) maniere *fpl*; **bad** ~**s** maleducazione *f*; ~**ism** *n* vezzo, tic *m inv*

manoeuvre [mə'nuːvə*] (*US* **maneuver**) *vt* manovrare ♦ *vi* far manovre ♦ *n* manovra

manor ['mænə*] *n* (*also*: ~ **house**) maniero

manpower ['mænpauə*] *n* manodopera

mansion ['mænʃən] *n* casa signorile

manslaughter ['mænslɔːtə*] *n* omicidio preterintenzionale

mantelpiece ['mæntlpiːs] *n* mensola del

caminetto

manual ['mænjuəl] *adj* manuale ♦ *n* manuale *m*

manufacture [mænju'fæktʃə*] *vt* fabbricare ♦ *n* fabbricazione *f*, manifattura; **~r** *n* fabbricante *m*

manure [mə'njuə*] *n* concime *m*

manuscript ['mænjuskrɪpt] *n* manoscritto

many ['menɪ] *adj* molti(e) ♦ *pron* molti(e); **a great ~** moltissimi(e), un gran numero (di); **~ a time** molte volte

map [mæp] *n* carta (geografica); **~ out** *vt* tracciare un piano di

maple ['meɪpl] *n* acero

mar [mɑ:*] *vt* sciupare

marathon ['mærəθən] *n* maratona

marauder [mə'rɔ:də*] *n* saccheggiatore *m*

marble ['mɑ:bl] *n* marmo; (*toy*) pallina, bilia

March [mɑ:tʃ] *n* marzo

march [mɑ:tʃ] *vi* marciare; sfilare ♦ *n* marcia

mare [mɛə*] *n* giumenta

margarine [mɑ:dʒə'ri:n] *n* margarina

margin ['mɑ:dʒɪn] *n* margine *m*; **~al (seat)** *n* (*POL*) seggio elettorale ottenuto con una stretta maggioranza

marigold ['mærɪgəʊld] *n* calendola

marina [mə'ri:nə] *n* marina

marine [mə'ri:n] *adj* (*animal, plant*) marino(a); (*forces, engineering*) marittimo(a) ♦ *n* (*BRIT*) fante *m* di marina; (*US*) marine *m* *inv*

marital ['mærɪtl] *adj* maritale, coniugale; **~ status** stato coniugale

mark [mɑ:k] *n* segno; (*stain*) macchia; (*of skid etc*) traccia; (*BRIT: SCOL*) voto; (*SPORT*) bersaglio; (*currency*) marco ♦ *vt* segnare; (*stain*) macchiare; (*indicate*) indicare; (*BRIT: SCOL*) dare un voto a; correggere; **to ~ time** segnare il passo; **~ed** *adj* spiccato(a), chiaro(a); **~er** *n* (*sign*) segno; (*bookmark*) segnalibro

market ['mɑ:kɪt] *n* mercato ♦ *vt* (*COMM*) mettere in vendita; **~ garden** (*BRIT*) *n* orto industriale; **~ing** *n* marketing *m*; **~ place** *n* piazza del mercato; (*COMM*) piazza, mercato; **~ research** *n* indagine *f* *or* ricerca di mercato

marksman ['mɑ:ksmən] *n* tiratore *m* scelto

marmalade ['mɑ:məleɪd] *n* marmellata d'arance

maroon [mə'ru:n] *vt* (*also fig*): **to be ~ed (in** *or* **at)** essere abbandonato(a) (in) ♦ *adj* bordeaux *inv*

marquee [mɑ:'ki:] *n* padiglione *m*

marquess ['mɑ:kwɪs] *n* = **marquis**

marquis ['mɑ:kwɪs] *n* marchese *m*

marriage ['mærɪdʒ] *n* matrimonio; **~ certificate** *n* certificato di matrimonio

married ['mærɪd] *adj* sposato(a); (*life, love*) coniugale, matrimoniale

marrow ['mærəʊ] *n* midollo; (*vegetable*) zucca

marry ['mærɪ] *vt* sposare, sposarsi con; (*subj: vicar, priest etc*) dare in matrimonio ♦ *vi* (*also*: **get married**) sposarsi

Mars [mɑ:z] *n* (*planet*) Marte *m*

marsh [mɑ:ʃ] *n* palude *f*

marshal ['mɑ:ʃl] *n* maresciallo; (*US: fire*) capo; (: *police*) capitano ♦ *vt* (*thoughts, support*) ordinare; (*soldiers*) adunare

martyr ['mɑ:tə*] *n* martire *m/f*; **~dom** *n* martirio

marvel ['mɑ:vl] *n* meraviglia ♦ *vi*: **to ~ (at)** meravigliarsi (di); **~lous** (*US* **~ous**) *adj* meraviglioso(a)

Marxist ['mɑ:ksɪst] *adj*, *n* marxista *m/f*

marzipan ['mɑ:zɪpæn] *n* marzapane *m*

mascara [mæs'kɑ:rə] *n* mascara *m*

masculine ['mæskjʊlɪn] *adj* maschile; (*woman*) mascolino(a)

mash [mæʃ] *vt* passare, schiacciare; **~ed potatoes** *npl* purè *m* di patate

mask [mɑ:sk] *n* maschera ♦ *vt* mascherare

mason ['meɪsn] *n* (*also*: **stone~**) scalpellino; (*also*: **free~**) massone *m*; **~ry** *n* muratura

masquerade [mæskə'reɪd] *vi*: **to ~ as** farsi passare per

mass [mæs] *n* moltitudine *f*, massa; (*PHYSICS*) massa; (*REL*) messa ♦ *cpd* di massa ♦ *vi* ammassarsi; **the ~es** *npl* (*ordinary people*) le masse; **~es of** (*inf*) una montagna di

massacre ['mæsəkə*] *n* massacro

massage ['mæsɑ:ʒ] *n* massaggio

masseur [mæ'sə:*] n massaggiatore m;
  masseuse [-'sə:z] n massaggiatrice f
massive ['mæsɪv] adj enorme, massiccio(a)
mass media npl mass media mpl
mass-production n produzione f in serie
mast [mɑːst] n albero
master ['mɑːstə*] n padrone m; (ART etc,
  teacher: in primary school) maestro; (: in
  secondary school) professore m; (title for
  boys): **M~ X** Signorino X ♦ vt domare;
  (learn) imparare a fondo; (understand)
  conoscere a fondo; ~ **key** n chiave f
  maestra; ~**ly** adj magistrale; ~**mind** n
  mente f superiore ♦ vt essere il cervello di;
  M~ of Arts/Science n Master m inv in
  lettere/scienze; ~**piece** n capolavoro; ~**y**
  n dominio; padronanza
mat [mæt] n stuoia; (also: **door~**) stoino,
  zerbino; (also: **table ~**) sottopiatto ♦ adj
  = **matt**
match [mætʃ] n fiammifero; (game) partita,
  incontro; (fig) uguale m/f; matrimonio;
  partito ♦ vt intonare; (go well with) andare
  benissimo con; (equal) uguagliare;
  (correspond to) corrispondere a; (pair: also:
  ~ **up**) accoppiare ♦ vi combaciare; **to be a
  good ~** andare bene; ~**box** n scatola per
  fiammiferi; ~**ing** adj ben assortito(a)
mate [meɪt] n compagno/a di lavoro; (inf:
  friend) amico/a; (animal) compagno/a; (in
  merchant navy) secondo ♦ vi accoppiarsi
material [mə'tɪərɪəl] n (substance) materiale
  m, materia; (cloth) stoffa ♦ adj materiale;
  ~**s** npl (equipment) materiali mpl
maternal [mə'tə:nl] adj materno(a)
maternity [mə'tə:nɪtɪ] n maternità; ~
  dress n vestito m pre-maman inv; ~
  hospital n ≈ clinica ostetrica
math [mæθ] (US) n = **maths**
mathematical [mæθə'mætɪkl] adj
  matematico(a)
mathematics [mæθə'mætɪks] n matematica
maths [mæθs] (US **math**) n matematica
matinée ['mætɪneɪ] n matinée f inv
mating call ['meɪtɪŋ-] n richiamo sessuale
matriculation [mətrɪkjuˈleɪʃən] n
  immatricolazione f

matrimonial [mætrɪˈməʊnɪəl] adj
  matrimoniale, coniugale
matrimony ['mætrɪmənɪ] n matrimonio
matron ['meɪtrən] n (in hospital)
  capoinfermiera; (in school) infermiera
mat(t) [mæt] adj opaco(a)
matted ['mætɪd] adj ingarbugliato(a)
matter ['mætə*] n questione f; (PHYSICS)
  materia, sostanza; (content) contenuto;
  (MED: pus) pus m ♦ vi importare; **it doesn't
  ~** non importa; (I don't mind) non fa
  niente; **what's the ~?** che cosa c'è?; **no ~
  what** qualsiasi cosa accada; **as a ~ of
  course** come cosa naturale; **as a ~ of fact**
  in verità; ~**-of-fact** adj prosaico(a)
mattress ['mætrɪs] n materasso
mature [mə'tjuə*] adj maturo(a); (cheese)
  stagionato(a) ♦ vi maturare; stagionare
maul [mɔːl] vt lacerare
mauve [məʊv] adj malva inv
maxim ['mæksɪm] n massima
maximum ['mæksɪməm] (pl **maxima**) adj
  massimo(a) ♦ n massimo
May [meɪ] n maggio
may [meɪ] (conditional: **might**) vi (indicating
  possibility): **he ~ come** può darsi che
  venga; (be allowed to): ~ **I smoke?** posso
  fumare?; (wishes): ~ **God bless you!** Dio ti
  benedica!; **you ~ as well go** tanto vale che
  tu te ne vada
maybe ['meɪbiː] adv forse, può darsi; ~
  he'll ... può darsi che lui ... +sub, forse lui
  ....
May Day n il primo maggio
mayhem ['meɪhem] n cagnara
mayonnaise [meɪə'neɪz] n maionese f
mayor [mɛə*] n sindaco; ~**ess** n sindaco
  (donna); moglie f del sindaco
maze [meɪz] n labirinto, dedalo
M.D. abbr = **Doctor of Medicine**
me [miː] pron mi, m' +vowel or silent "h";
  (stressed, after prep) me; **he heard ~** mi ha
  or m'ha sentito; **give ~ a book** dammi (or
  mi dia) un libro; **it's ~** sono io; **with ~** con
  me; **without ~** senza di me
meadow ['mɛdəʊ] n prato
meagre ['miːgə*] (US **meager**) adj magro(a)

meal [miːl] *n* pasto; (*flour*) farina; **~time** *n* l'ora di mangiare

mean [miːn] (*pt, pp* **meant**) *adj* (*with money*) avaro(a), gretto(a); (*unkind*) meschino(a), maligno(a); (*shabby*) misero(a); (*average*) medio(a) ♦ *vt* (*signify*) significare, voler dire; (*intend*): **to ~ to do** aver l'intenzione di fare ♦ *n* mezzo; (*MATH*) media; **~s** *npl* (*way, money*) mezzi *mpl*; **by ~s of** per mezzo di; **by all ~s** ma certo, prego; **to be meant for** essere destinato(a) a; **do you ~ it?** dice sul serio?; **what do you ~?** che cosa vuol dire?

meander [mɪˈændə*] *vi* far meandri

meaning [ˈmiːnɪŋ] *n* significato, senso; **~ful** *adj* significativo(a); **~less** *adj* senza senso

means [miːnz] *npl* mezzi *mpl*; **by ~ of** per mezzo di; (*person*) a mezzo di; **by all ~** ma certo, prego

meant [mɛnt] *pt, pp of* **mean**

meantime [ˈmiːntaɪm] *adv* (*also:* **in the ~**) nel frattempo

meanwhile [ˈmiːnwaɪl] *adv* nel frattempo

measles [ˈmiːzlz] *n* morbillo

measure [ˈmɛʒə*] *vt, vi* misurare ♦ *n* misura; (*also:* **tape ~**) metro; **~ments** *npl* (*size*) misure *fpl*

meat [miːt] *n* carne *f*; **cold ~** affettato; **~ball** *n* polpetta di carne; **~ pie** *n* pasticcio di carne in crosta

Mecca [ˈmɛkə] *n* (*also fig*) la Mecca

mechanic [mɪˈkænɪk] *n* meccanico; **~al** *adj* meccanico(a); **~s** *n* meccanica ♦ *npl* meccanismo

mechanism [ˈmɛkənɪzəm] *n* meccanismo

medal [ˈmɛdl] *n* medaglia; **~lion** [mɪˈdælɪən] *n* medaglione *m*; **~list** (*US* **~ist**) *n* (*SPORT*): **to be a gold ~list** essere medaglia d'oro

meddle [ˈmɛdl] *vi*: **to ~ in** immischiarsi in, mettere le mani in; **to ~ with** toccare

media [ˈmiːdɪə] *npl* media *mpl*

mediaeval [mɛdɪˈiːvl] *adj* = **medieval**

median [ˈmiːdɪən] (*US*) *n* (*also:* **~ strip**) banchina *f* spartitraffico

mediate [ˈmiːdɪeɪt] *vi* fare da mediatore/trice

Medicaid ® [ˈmɛdɪkeɪd] (*US*) *n* assistenza medica ai poveri

medical [ˈmɛdɪkl] *adj* medico(a) ♦ *n* visita medica

Medicare ® [ˈmɛdɪkeə*] (*US*) *n* assistenza medica agli anziani

medication [mɛdɪˈkeɪʃən] *n* medicinali *mpl*, farmaci *mpl*

medicine [ˈmɛdsɪn] *n* medicina

medieval [mɛdɪˈiːvl] *adj* medievale

mediocre [miːdɪˈəʊkə*] *adj* mediocre

meditate [ˈmɛdɪteɪt] *vi*: **to ~ (on)** meditare (su)

Mediterranean [mɛdɪtəˈreɪnɪən] *adj* mediterraneo(a); **the ~ (Sea)** il (mare) Mediterraneo

medium [ˈmiːdɪəm] (*pl* **media**) *adj* medio(a) ♦ *n* (*means*) mezzo; (*pl* **mediums**: *person*) medium *m inv*; **~ wave** *n* onde *fpl* medie

meek [miːk] *adj* dolce, umile

meet [miːt] (*pt, pp* **met**) *vt* incontrare; (*for the first time*) fare la conoscenza di; (*go and fetch*) andare a prendere; (*fig*) affrontare; soddisfare; raggiungere ♦ *vi* incontrarsi; (*in session*) riunirsi; (*join: objects*) unirsi; **~ with** *vt fus* incontrare; **~ing** *n* incontro; (*session: of club etc*) riunione *f*; (*interview*) intervista; **she's at a ~ing** (*COMM*) è in riunione

megabyte [ˈmɛgəbaɪt] *n* (*COMPUT*) megabyte *m inv*

megaphone [ˈmɛgəfəʊn] *n* megafono

melancholy [ˈmɛlənkəlɪ] *n* malinconia ♦ *adj* malinconico(a)

mellow [ˈmɛləʊ] *adj* (*wine, sound*) ricco(a); (*light*) dolce; (*colour*) caldo(a) ♦ *vi* (*person*) addolcirsi

melody [ˈmɛlədɪ] *n* melodia

melon [ˈmɛlən] *n* melone *m*

melt [mɛlt] *vi* (*gen*) sciogliersi, struggersi; (*metals*) fondersi ♦ *vt* sciogliere, struggere; fondere; **~ down** *vt* fondere; **~down** *n* (*in nuclear reactor*) fusione *f* (dovuta a surriscaldamento); **~ing pot** *n* (*fig*) crogiolo

member [ˈmɛmbə*] *n* membro; **M~ of the European Parliament** (*BRIT*) *n* eurodeputato; **M~ of Parliament** (*BRIT*) *n* deputato; **~ship** *n* iscrizione *f*; (numero d')iscritti *mpl*, membri *mpl*; **~ship card** *n* tessera (di iscrizione)

memento [mə'mɛntəʊ] *n* ricordo, souvenir *m inv*

memo ['mɛməʊ] *n* appunto; (*COMM etc*) comunicazione *f* di servizio

memoirs ['mɛmwɑːz] *npl* memorie *fpl*, ricordi *mpl*

memoranda [mɛmə'rændə] *npl of* **memorandum**

memorandum [mɛmə'rændəm] (*pl* **memoranda**) *n* appunto; (*COMM etc*) comunicazione *f* di servizio

memorial [mɪ'mɔːrɪəl] *n* monumento commemorativo ♦ *adj* commemorativo(a)

memorize ['mɛmərɑɪz] *vt* memorizzare

memory ['mɛmərɪ] *n* (*also COMPUT*) memoria; (*recollection*) ricordo

men [mɛn] *npl of* **man**

menace ['mɛnəs] *n* minaccia ♦ *vt* minacciare

mend [mɛnd] *vt* aggiustare, riparare; (*darn*) rammendare ♦ *n*: **on the ~** in via di guarigione; **to ~ one's ways** correggersi

menial ['miːnɪəl] *adj* da servo, domestico(a); umile

meningitis [mɛnɪn'dʒɑɪtɪs] *n* meningite *f*

menopause ['mɛnəʊpɔːz] *n* menopausa

menstruation [mɛnstru'eɪʃən] *n* mestruazione *f*

mental ['mɛntl] *adj* mentale

mentality [mɛn'tælɪtɪ] *n* mentalità *f inv*

menthol ['mɛnθɒl] *n* mentolo

mention ['mɛnʃən] *n* menzione *f* ♦ *vt* menzionare, far menzione di; **don't ~ it!** non c'è di che!, prego!

menu ['mɛnjuː] *n* (*set ~*, *COMPUT*) menù *m inv*; (*printed*) carta

MEP *n abbr* = **Member of the European Parliament**

merchandise ['mɜːtʃəndɑɪz] *n* merci *fpl*

merchant ['mɜːtʃənt] *n* mercante *m*, commerciante *m*; **~ bank** (*BRIT*) *n* banca d'affari; **~ navy** (*US* **~ marine**) *n* marina mercantile

merciful ['mɜːsɪful] *adj* pietoso(a), clemente

merciless ['mɜːsɪlɪs] *adj* spietato(a)

mercury ['mɜːkjʊrɪ] *n* mercurio

mercy ['mɜːsɪ] *n* pietà *f*; (*REL*) misericordia; **at the ~ of** alla mercè di

mere [mɪə*] *adj* semplice; **by a ~ chance** per mero caso; **~ly** *adv* semplicemente, non ... che

merge [mɜːdʒ] *vt* unire ♦ *vi* fondersi, unirsi; (*COMM*) fondersi; **~r** *n* (*COMM*) fusione *f*

meringue [mə'ræŋ] *n* meringa

merit ['mɛrɪt] *n* merito, valore *m* ♦ *vt* meritare

mermaid ['mɜːmeɪd] *n* sirena

merry ['mɛrɪ] *adj* gaio(a), allegro(a); **M~ Christmas!** Buon Natale!; **~-go-round** *n* carosello

mesh [mɛʃ] *n* maglia; rete *f*

mesmerize ['mɛzmərɑɪz] *vt* ipnotizzare; affascinare

mess [mɛs] *n* confusione *f*, disordine *m*; (*fig*) pasticcio; (*dirt*) sporcizia; (*MIL*) mensa; **~ about** (*inf*) *vi* (*also*: **~ around**) trastullarsi; **~ about with** (*inf*) *vt fus* (*also*: **~ around with**) gingillarsi con; (*plans*) fare un pasticcio di; **~ up** *vt* sporcare; fare un pasticcio di; rovinare

message ['mɛsɪdʒ] *n* messaggio

messenger ['mɛsɪndʒə*] *n* messaggero/a

Messrs ['mɛsəz] *abbr* (*on letters*) Spett

messy ['mɛsɪ] *adj* sporco(a); disordinato(a)

met [mɛt] *pt, pp of* **meet**

metal ['mɛtl] *n* metallo; **~lic** [-'tælɪk] *adj* metallico(a)

metaphor ['mɛtəfə*] *n* metafora

meteorology [miːtɪə'rɒlədʒɪ] *n* meteorologia

meter ['miːtə*] *n* (*instrument*) contatore *m*; (*parking ~*) parchimetro; (*US: unit*) = **metre**

method ['mɛθəd] *n* metodo; **~ical** [mɪ'θɒdɪkl] *adj* metodico(a)

Methodist ['mɛθədɪst] *n* metodista *m/f*

meths [mɛθs] (*BRIT*) *n* = **methylated spirit**

methylated spirit ['mɛθɪleɪtɪd-] (*BRIT*) *n* alcool *m* denaturato

metre ['miːtə*] (*US* **meter**) *n* metro

metric ['mɛtrɪk] *adj* metrico(a)

metropolitan [mɛtrə'pɒlɪtən] *adj*

metropolitano(a); **the M~ Police** (*BRIT*) *n* la polizia di Londra

mettle ['metl] *n*: **to be on one's ~** essere pronto(a) a dare il meglio di se stesso(a)

mew [mju:] *vi* (*cat*) miagolare

mews [mju:z] (*BRIT*) *n*: **~ flat** appartamento ricavato da un'antica scuderia

Mexico ['meksɪkəʊ] *n* Messico

miaow [mi:'aʊ] *vi* miagolare

mice [maɪs] *npl of* **mouse**

micro... ['maɪkrəʊ] *prefix* micro...; **~chip** *n* microcircuito integrato; **~(computer)** *n* microcomputer *m inv*; **~phone** *n* microfono; **~scope** *n* microscopio; **~wave** *n* (*also*: **~wave oven**) forno a microonde

mid [mɪd] *adj*: **~ May** metà maggio; **~ afternoon** metà pomeriggio; **in ~ air** a mezz'aria; **~day** *n* mezzogiorno

middle ['mɪdl] *n* mezzo; centro; (*waist*) vita ♦ *adj* di mezzo; **in the ~ of the night** nel bel mezzo della notte; **~-aged** *adj* di mezza età; **the M~ Ages** *npl* il Medioevo; **~-class** *adj* ≈ borghese; **the ~ class(es)** *n(pl)* ≈ la borghesia; **M~ East** *n* Medio Oriente *m*; **~man** (*irreg*) *n* intermediario; agente *m* rivenditore; **~ name** *n* secondo nome *m*; **~-of-the-road** *adj* moderato(a); **~weight** *n* (*BOXING*) peso medio

middling ['mɪdlɪŋ] *adj* medio(a)

midge [mɪdʒ] *n* moscerino

midget ['mɪdʒɪt] *n* nano/a

Midlands ['mɪdləndz] *npl* contee del centro dell'Inghilterra

midnight ['mɪdnaɪt] *n* mezzanotte *f*

midriff ['mɪdrɪf] *n* diaframma *m*

midst [mɪdst] *n*: **in the ~ of** in mezzo a

midsummer [mɪd'sʌmə*] *n* mezza *or* piena estate *f*

midway [mɪd'weɪ] *adj, adv*: **~ (between)** a mezza strada (fra); **~ (through)** a metà (di)

midweek [mɪd'wi:k] *adv* a metà settimana

midwife ['mɪdwaɪf] (*pl* **midwives**) *n* levatrice *f*

might [maɪt] *vb see* **may** ♦ *n* potere *m*, forza; **~y** *adj* forte, potente

migraine ['mi:greɪn] *n* emicrania

migrant ['maɪgrənt] *adj* (*bird*) migratore(trice); (*worker*) emigrato(a)

migrate [maɪ'greɪt] *vi* (*bird*) migrare; (*person*) emigrare

mike [maɪk] *n abbr* (= *microphone*) microfono

Milan [mɪ'læn] *n* Milano *f*

mild [maɪld] *adj* mite; (*person, voice*) dolce; (*flavour*) delicato(a); (*illness*) leggero(a); (*interest*) blando(a) ♦ *n* (*beer*) birra leggera

mildew ['mɪldju:] *n* muffa

mildly ['maɪldlɪ] *adv* mitemente; dolcemente; delicatamente; leggermente; blandamente; **to put it ~** a dire poco

mile [maɪl] *n* miglio; **~age** *n* distanza in miglia, ≈ chilometraggio

mileometer [maɪ'lɒmɪtə*] *n* ≈ conta-chilometri *m inv*

milestone ['maɪlstəʊn] *n* pietra miliare

milieu ['mi:ljə:] *n* ambiente *m*

militant ['mɪlɪtnt] *adj* militante

military ['mɪlɪtərɪ] *adj* militare

milk [mɪlk] *n* latte *m* ♦ *vt* (*cow*) mungere; (*fig*) sfruttare; **~ chocolate** *n* cioccolato al latte; **~man** (*irreg*) *n* lattaio; **~ shake** *n* frappé *m inv*; **~y** *adj* lattiginoso(a); (*colour*) latteo(a); **M~y Way** *n* Via Lattea

mill [mɪl] *n* mulino; (*small: for coffee, pepper etc*) macinino; (*factory*) fabbrica; (*spinning ~*) filatura ♦ *vt* macinare ♦ *vi* (*also*: **~ about**) brulicare

miller ['mɪlə*] *n* mugnaio

milli... ['mɪlɪ] *prefix*: **~gram(me)** *n* milligrammo; **~metre** (*US* **~meter**) *n* millimetro

million ['mɪljən] *n* milione *m*; **~aire** *n* milionario, ≈ miliardario

milometer [maɪ'lɒmɪtə*] *n* = **mileometer**

mime [maɪm] *n* mimo ♦ *vt, vi* mimare

mimic ['mɪmɪk] *n* imitatore/trice ♦ *vt* fare la mimica di

min. *abbr* = **minute(s)**; **minimum**

mince [mɪns] *vt* tritare, macinare ♦ *n* (*BRIT: CULIN*) carne *f* tritata *or* macinata; **~meat** *n* frutta secca tritata per uso in pasticceria; (*US*) carne *f* tritata *or* macinata; **~ pie** *n*

specie di torta con frutta secca; **~r** n
tritacarne m inv

mind [maɪnd] n mente f ♦ vt (attend to, look
after) badare a, occuparsi di; (be careful)
fare attenzione a, stare attento(a) a; (object
to): **I don't ~ the noise** il rumore non mi
dà alcun fastidio; **I don't ~** non m'importa;
it is on my ~ mi preoccupa; **to my ~**
secondo me, a mio parere; **to be out of
one's ~** essere uscito(a) di mente; **to keep
or bear sth in ~** non dimenticare qc; **to
make up one's ~** decidersi; **~ you, ...** sì,
però va detto che ...; **never ~** non importa,
non fa niente; (don't worry) non
preoccuparti; **"~ the step"** "attenzione
allo scalino"; **~er** n (child ~er) bambinaia;
(bodyguard) guardia del corpo; **~ful** adj:
~ful of attento(a) a; memore di; **~less** adj
idiota

mine¹ [maɪn] pron il(la) mio(a), pl i(le)
miei(mie); **that book is ~** quel libro è mio;
yours is red, ~ is green il tuo è rosso, il
mio è verde; **a friend of ~** un mio amico

mine² [maɪn] n miniera; (explosive) mina
♦ vt (coal) estrarre; (ship, beach) minare;
~field n (also fig) campo minato

miner ['maɪnə*] n minatore m

mineral ['mɪnərəl] adj minerale ♦ n
minerale m; **~s** npl (BRIT: soft drinks)
bevande fpl gasate; **~ water** n acqua
minerale

mingle ['mɪŋgl] vi: **to ~ with** mescolarsi a,
mischiarsi con

miniature ['mɪnətʃə*] adj in miniatura ♦ n
miniatura

minibus ['mɪnɪbʌs] n minibus m inv

minim ['mɪnɪm] n (MUS) minima

minimum ['mɪnɪməm] (pl minima) n
minimo ♦ adj minimo(a)

mining ['maɪnɪŋ] n industria mineraria

miniskirt ['mɪnɪskə:t] n minigonna

minister ['mɪnɪstə*] n (BRIT: POL) ministro;
(REL) pastore m ♦ vi: **to ~ to sb** assistere
qn; **to ~ to sb's needs** provvedere ai
bisogni di qn

ministry ['mɪnɪstrɪ] n (BRIT: POL) ministero;
(REL): **to go into the ~** diventare pastore

mink [mɪŋk] n visone m

minnow ['mɪnəu] n pesciolino d'acqua
dolce

minor ['maɪnə*] adj minore, di poca
importanza; (MUS) minore ♦ n (LAW)
minorenne m/f

minority [maɪ'nɔrɪtɪ] n minoranza

mint [mɪnt] n (plant) menta; (sweet) pasticca
di menta ♦ vt (coins) battere; **the (Royal)
M~** (BRIT), **the (US) M~** (US) la Zecca; **in ~
condition** come nuovo(a) di zecca

minus ['maɪnəs] n (also: **~ sign**) segno
meno ♦ prep meno

minute [adj maɪ'nju:t, n 'mɪnɪt] adj
minuscolo(a); (detail) minuzioso(a) ♦ n
minuto; **~s** npl (of meeting) verbale m

miracle ['mɪrəkl] n miracolo

mirage ['mɪrɑ:ʒ] n miraggio

mirror ['mɪrə*] n specchio; (in car)
specchietto

mirth [mə:θ] n ilarità

misadventure [mɪsəd'ventʃə*] n
disavventura; **death by ~** morte f
accidentale

misapprehension ['mɪsæprɪ'henʃən] n
malinteso

misappropriate [mɪsə'prəuprɪeɪt] vt
appropriarsi indebitamente di

misbehave [mɪsbɪ'heɪv] vi comportarsi
male

miscarriage ['mɪskærɪdʒ] n (MED) aborto
spontaneo; **~ of justice** errore m
giudiziario

miscellaneous [mɪsɪ'leɪnɪəs] adj (items)
vario(a); (selection) misto(a)

mischance [mɪs'tʃɑ:ns] n sfortuna

mischief ['mɪstʃɪf] n (naughtiness)
birichineria; (maliciousness) malizia;
mischievous adj birichino(a)

misconception ['mɪskən'sepʃən] n idea
sbagliata

misconduct [mɪs'kɔndʌkt] n cattiva
condotta; **professional ~** reato
professionale

misdemeanour [mɪsdɪ'mi:nə*] (US
misdemeanor) n misfatto; infrazione f

miser ['maɪzə*] n avaro

miserable ['mɪzərəbl] *adj* infelice; (*wretched*) miserabile; (*weather*) deprimente; (*offer, failure*) misero(a)

miserly ['maɪzəlɪ] *adj* avaro(a)

misery ['mɪzərɪ] *n* (*unhappiness*) tristezza; (*wretchedness*) miseria

misfire [mɪs'faɪə*] *vi* far cilecca; (*car engine*) perdere colpi

misfit ['mɪsfɪt] *n* (*person*) spostato/a

misfortune [mɪs'fɔːtʃən] *n* sfortuna

misgiving [mɪs'gɪvɪŋ] *n* apprensione *f*; **to have ~s about** avere dei dubbi per quanto riguarda

misguided [mɪs'gaɪdɪd] *adj* sbagliato(a); poco giudizioso(a)

mishandle [mɪs'hændl] *vt* (*mismanage*) trattare male

mishap ['mɪshæp] *n* disgrazia

misinterpret [mɪsɪn'tɜːprɪt] *vt* interpretare male

misjudge [mɪs'dʒʌdʒ] *vt* giudicare male

mislay [mɪs'leɪ] (*irreg*) *vt* smarrire

mislead [mɪs'liːd] (*irreg*) *vt* sviare; **~ing** *adj* ingannevole

mismanage [mɪs'mænɪdʒ] *vt* gestire male

misplace [mɪs'pleɪs] *vt* smarrire

misprint ['mɪsprɪnt] *n* errore *m* di stampa

Miss [mɪs] *n* Signorina

miss [mɪs] *vt* (*fail to get*) perdere; (*fail to hit*) mancare; (*fail to see*): **you can't ~ it** non puoi non vederlo; (*regret the absence of*): **I ~ him** sento la sua mancanza ♦ *vi* mancare ♦ *n* (*shot*) colpo mancato; **~ out** (*BRIT*) *vt* omettere

misshapen [mɪs'ʃeɪpən] *adj* deforme

missile ['mɪsaɪl] *n* (*MIL*) missile *m*; (*object thrown*) proiettile *m*

missing ['mɪsɪŋ] *adj* perso(a), smarrito(a); (*person*) scomparso(a); (*: after disaster, MIL*) disperso(a); (*removed*) mancante; **to be ~** mancare

mission ['mɪʃən] *n* missione *f*; **~ary** *n* missionario/a

mist [mɪst] *n* nebbia, foschia ♦ *vi* (*also: ~ over, ~ up*) annebbiarsi; (*: BRIT: windows*) appannarsi

mistake [mɪs'teɪk] (*irreg: like* **take**) *n* sbaglio, errore *m* ♦ *vt* sbagliarsi di; fraintendere; **to make a ~** fare uno sbaglio, sbagliare; **by ~** per sbaglio; **to ~ for** prendere per; **mistaken** *pp of* **mistake** ♦ *adj* (*idea etc*) sbagliato(a); **to be mistaken** sbagliarsi

mister ['mɪstə*] (*inf*) *n* signore *m*; *see* **Mr**

mistletoe ['mɪsltəʊ] *n* vischio

mistook [mɪs'tʊk] *pt of* **mistake**

mistress ['mɪstrɪs] *n* padrona; (*lover*) amante *f*; (*BRIT: SCOL*) insegnante *f*

mistrust [mɪs'trʌst] *vt* diffidare di

misty ['mɪstɪ] *adj* nebbioso(a), brumoso(a)

misunderstand [mɪsʌndə'stænd] (*irreg*) *vt*, *vi* capire male, fraintendere; **~ing** *n* malinteso, equivoco

misuse [*n* mɪs'juːs, *vb* mɪs'juːz] *n* cattivo uso; (*of power*) abuso ♦ *vt* far cattivo uso di; abusare di

mitigate ['mɪtɪgeɪt] *vt* mitigare

mitt(en) ['mɪt(n)] *n* mezzo guanto; manopola

mix [mɪks] *vt* mescolare ♦ *vi* (*people*): **to ~ with** avere a che fare con ♦ *n* mescolanza; preparato; **~ up** *vt* mescolare; (*confuse*) confondere; **~ed** *adj* misto(a); **~ed-up** *adj* (*confused*) confuso(a); **~er** *n* (*for food: electric*) frullatore *m*; (*: hand*) frullino; (*person*): **he is a good ~er** è molto socievole; **~ture** *n* mescolanza; (*blend: of tobacco etc*) miscela; (*MED*) sciroppo; **~-up** *n* confusione *f*

moan [məʊn] *n* gemito ♦ *vi* (*inf: complain*): **to ~ (about)** lamentarsi (di)

moat [məʊt] *n* fossato

mob [mɒb] *n* calca ♦ *vt* accalcarsi intorno a

mobile ['məʊbaɪl] *adj* mobile ♦ *n* (*decoration*) mobile *m*; **~ home** *n* grande roulotte *f inv* (*utilizzata come domicilio*); **~ phone** telefono portatile, telefonino

mock [mɒk] *vt* deridere, burlarsi di ♦ *adj* falso(a); **~ery** *n* derisione *f*; **to make a ~ery of** burlarsi di; (*exam*) rendere una farsa; **~-up** *n* modello

mod [mɒd] *adj see* **convenience**

mode [məʊd] *n* modo

model ['mɒdl] *n* modello; (*person: for*

fashion) indossatore/trice; (: *for artist*) modello/a ♦ *adj* (*small-scale: railway etc*) in miniatura; (*child, factory*) modello *inv* ♦ *vt* modellare ♦ *vi* fare l'indossatore (*or* l'indossatrice); **to ~ clothes** presentare degli abiti

modem ['məudem] *n* modem *m inv*

moderate [*adj* 'mɒdərət, *vb* 'mɒdəreɪt] *adj* moderato(a) ♦ *vi* moderarsi, placarsi ♦ *vt* moderare

modern ['mɒdən] *adj* moderno(a); **~ize** *vt* modernizzare

modest ['mɒdɪst] *adj* modesto(a); **~y** *n* modestia

modify ['mɒdɪfaɪ] *vt* modificare

mogul ['məugl] *n* (*fig*) magnate *m*, pezzo grosso

mohair ['məuhɛə*] *n* mohair *m*

moist [mɒɪst] *adj* umido(a); **~en** ['mɒɪsn] *vt* inumidire; **~ure** ['mɒɪstʃə*] *n* umidità; (*on glass*) goccioline *fpl* di vapore; **~urizer** ['mɒɪstʃəraɪzə*] *n* idratante *f*

molar ['məulə*] *n* molare *m*

mold [məuld] (*US*) *n, vt* = **mould**

mole [məul] *n* (*animal, fig*) talpa; (*spot*) neo

molest [məu'lest] *vt* molestare

mollycoddle ['mɒlɪkɒdl] *vt* coccolare, vezzeggiare

molt [məult] (*US*) *vi* = **moult**

molten ['məultən] *adj* fuso(a)

mom [mɒm] (*US*) *n* = **mum**

moment ['məumənt] *n* momento, istante *m*; **at that ~** in quel momento; **at the ~** al momento, in questo momento; **~ary** *adj* momentaneo(a), passeggero(a); **~ous** [-'mentəs] *adj* di grande importanza

momentum [məu'mentəm] *n* (*PHYSICS*) momento; (*fig*) impeto; **to gather ~** aumentare di velocità

mommy ['mɒmɪ] (*US*) *n* = **mummy**

Monaco ['mɒnəkəu] *n* Principato di Monaco

monarch ['mɒnək] *n* monarca *m*; **~y** *n* monarchia

monastery ['mɒnəstərɪ] *n* monastero

Monday ['mʌndɪ] *n* lunedì *m inv*

monetary ['mʌnɪtərɪ] *adj* monetario(a)

money ['mʌnɪ] *n* denaro, soldi *mpl*; **~ belt**

n marsupio (*per soldi*); **~ order** *n* vaglia *m inv*; **~-spinner** (*inf*) *n* miniera d'oro (*fig*)

mongol ['mɒŋgəl] *adj, n* (*MED*) mongoloide *m/f*

mongrel ['mʌŋgrəl] *n* (*dog*) cane *m* bastardo

monitor ['mɒnɪtə*] *n* (*TV, COMPUT*) monitor *m inv* ♦ *vt* controllare

monk [mʌŋk] *n* monaco

monkey ['mʌŋkɪ] *n* scimmia; **~ nut** (*BRIT*) *n* nocciolina americana; **~ wrench** *n* chiave *f* a rullino

mono ['mɒnəu] *adj* (*recording*) (in) mono *inv*

monopoly [mə'nɒpəlɪ] *n* monopolio

monotone ['mɒnətəun] *n* pronunzia (*or* voce *f*) monotona

monotonous [mə'nɒtənəs] *adj* monotono(a)

monsoon [mɒn'su:n] *n* monsone *m*

monster ['mɒnstə*] *n* mostro

monstrous ['mɒnstrəs] *adj* mostruoso(a); (*huge*) gigantesco(a)

month [mʌnθ] *n* mese *m*; **~ly** *adj* mensile ♦ *adv* al mese; ogni mese

monument ['mɒnjumənt] *n* monumento

moo [mu:] *vi* muggire, mugghiare

mood [mu:d] *n* umore *m*; **to be in a good/bad ~** essere di buon/cattivo umore; **~y** *adj* (*variable*) capriccioso(a), lunatico(a); (*sullen*) imbronciato(a)

moon [mu:n] *n* luna; **~light** *n* chiaro di luna; **~lighting** *n* lavoro nero; **~lit** *adj*: **a ~lit night** una notte rischiarata dalla luna

Moor [muə*] *n* moro/a

moor [muə*] *n* brughiera ♦ *vt* (*ship*) ormeggiare ♦ *vi* ormeggiarsi

moorland ['muələnd] *n* brughiera

moose [mu:s] *n inv* alce *m*

mop [mɒp] *n* lavapavimenti *m inv*; (*also*: **~ of hair**) zazzera ♦ *vt* lavare con lo straccio; (*face*) asciugare; **~ up** *vt* asciugare con uno straccio

mope [məup] *vi* fare il broncio

moped ['məuped] *n* (*BRIT*) ciclomotore *m*

moral ['mɒrl] *adj* morale ♦ *n* morale *f*; **~s** *npl* (*principles*) moralità

morality [mə'ræliti] *n* moralità

morass [mə'ræs] *n* palude *f*, pantano

morbid ['mɔːbɪd] *adj* morboso(a)

KEYWORD

more [mɔː*] *adj* **1** (*greater in number etc*) più; **~ people/letters than we expected** più persone/lettere di quante ne aspettavamo; **I have ~ wine/money than you** ho più vino/soldi di te; **I have ~ wine than beer** ho più vino che birra **2** (*additional*) altro(a), ancora; **do you want (some) ~ tea?** vuole dell'altro tè?, vuole ancora del tè?; **I have no** *or* **I don't have any ~ money** non ho più soldi
♦ *pron* **1** (*greater amount*) più; **~ than 10** più di 10; **it cost ~ than we expected** ha costato più di quanto ci aspettavamo **2** (*further or additional amount*) ancora; **is there any ~?** ce n'è ancora?; **there's no ~** non ce n'è più; **a little ~** ancora un po'; **many/much ~** molti(e)/molto(a) di più
♦ *adv*: **~ dangerous/easily (than)** più pericoloso/facilmente (di); **~ and ~** sempre di più; **~ and ~ difficult** sempre più difficile; **~ or less** più o meno; **~ than ever** più che mai

---

moreover [mɔː'rəuvə*] *adv* inoltre, di più

morgue [mɔːg] *n* obitorio

morning ['mɔːnɪŋ] *n* mattina, mattino; (*duration*) mattinata ♦ *cpd* del mattino; **in the ~** la mattina; **7 o'clock in the ~** le 7 di *or* della mattina; **~ sickness** *n* nausee *fpl* mattutine

Morocco [mə'rɔkəu] *n* Marocco

moron ['mɔːrɔn] (*inf*) *n* deficiente *m/f*

morose [mə'rəus] *adj* cupo(a), tetro(a)

Morse [mɔːs] *n* (*also*: **~ code**) alfabeto Morse

morsel ['mɔːsl] *n* boccone *m*

mortal ['mɔːtl] *adj* mortale ♦ *n* mortale *m*

mortgage ['mɔːgɪdʒ] *n* ipoteca; (*loan*) prestito ipotecario ♦ *vt* ipotecare; **~ company** (*US*) *n* società *f inv* di credito immobiliare

mortuary ['mɔːtjuəri] *n* camera mortuaria;

obitorio

mosaic [məu'zeɪɪk] *n* mosaico

Moscow ['mɔskəu] *n* Mosca

Moslem ['mɔzləm] *adj, n* = **Muslim**

mosque [mɔsk] *n* moschea

mosquito [mɔs'kiːtəu] (*pl* **~es**) *n* zanzara

moss [mɔs] *n* muschio

most [məust] *adj* (*almost all*) la maggior parte di; (*largest, greatest*): **who has (the) ~ money?** chi ha più soldi di tutti? ♦ *pron* la maggior parte ♦ *adv* più; (*work, sleep etc*) di più; (*very*) molto, estremamente; **the ~** (*also*: +*adjective*) il(la) più; **~ of** la maggior parte di; **~ of them** quasi tutti; **I saw (the) ~** ho visto più io; **at the (very) ~** al massimo; **to make the ~ of** trarre il massimo vantaggio da; **a ~ interesting book** un libro estremamente interessante; **~ly** *adv* per lo più

MOT (*BRIT*) *n abbr* (= *Ministry of Transport*): **the ~ (test)** *revisione annuale obbligatoria degli autoveicoli*

motel [məu'tɛl] *n* motel *m inv*

moth [mɔθ] *n* farfalla notturna; tarma

mother ['mʌðə*] *n* madre *f* ♦ *vt* (*care for*) fare da madre a; **~hood** *n* maternità; **~-in-law** *n* suocera; **~ly** *adj* materno(a); **~-of-pearl** [mʌðərəv'pəːl] *n* madreperla; **~-to-be** [mʌðətə'biː] *n* futura mamma; **~ tongue** *n* madrelingua

motion ['məuʃən] *n* movimento, moto; (*gesture*) gesto; (*at meeting*) mozione *f* ♦ *vt, vi*: **to ~ (to) sb to do** fare cenno a qn di fare; **~less** *adj* immobile; **~ picture** *n* film *m inv*

motivated ['məutɪveɪtɪd] *adj* motivato(a)

motive ['məutɪv] *n* motivo

motley ['mɔtlɪ] *adj* eterogeneo(a), molto vario(a)

motor ['məutə*] *n* motore *m*; (*BRIT: inf: vehicle*) macchina ♦ *cpd* automobilistico(a); **~bike** *n* moto *f inv*; **~boat** *n* motoscafo; **~car** (*BRIT*) *n* automobile *f*; **~cycle** *n* motocicletta; **~cyclist** *n* motociclista *m/f*; **~ing** (*BRIT*) *n* turismo automobilistico; **~ist** *n* automobilista *m/f*; **~ racing** (*BRIT*) *n* corse *fpl* automobilistiche; **~way** (*BRIT*) *n* autostrada

mottled ['mɔtld] *adj* chiazzato(a), marezzato(a)

motto ['mɔtəu] (*pl* **~es**) *n* motto

mould [məuld] (*US* **mold**) *n* forma, stampo; (*mildew*) muffa ♦ *vt* formare; (*fig*) foggiare; **~y** *adj* ammuffito(a); (*smell*) di muffa

moult [məult] (*US* **molt**) *vi* far la muta

mound [maund] *n* rialzo, collinetta; (*heap*) mucchio

mount [maunt] *n* (*GEO*) monte *m* ♦ *vt* montare; (*horse*) montare a ♦ *vi* (*increase*) aumentare; **~ up** *vi* (*build up*) accumularsi

mountain ['mauntɪn] *n* montagna ♦ *cpd* di montagna; **~ bike** *n* mountain bike *f inv*; **~eer** [-'nɪə*] *n* alpinista *m/f*; **~eering** [-'nɪərɪŋ] *n* alpinismo; **~ous** *adj* montagnoso(a); **~ rescue team** *n* squadra di soccorso alpino; **~side** *n* fianco della montagna

mourn [mɔːn] *vt* piangere, lamentare ♦ *vi*: **to ~ (for sb)** piangere (la morte di qn); **~er** *n* parente *m/f or* amico/a del defunto; **~ing** *n* lutto; **in ~ing** in lutto

mouse [maus] (*pl* **mice**) *n* topo; (*COMPUT*) mouse *m inv*; **~trap** *n* trappola per i topi

mousse [muːs] *n* mousse *f inv*

moustache [məs'tɑːʃ] (*US* **mustache**) *n* baffi *mpl*

mousy ['mausɪ] *adj* (*hair*) né chiaro(a) né scuro(a)

mouth [mauθ, *pl* mauðz] *n* bocca; (*of river*) bocca, foce *f*; (*opening*) orifizio; **~ful** *n* boccata; **~ organ** *n* armonica; **~piece** *n* (*of musical instrument*) imboccatura, bocchino; (*spokesman*) portavoce *m/f inv*; **~wash** *n* collutorio; **~-watering** *adj* che fa venire l'acquolina in bocca

movable ['muːvəbl] *adj* mobile

move [muːv] *n* (*movement*) movimento; (*in game*) mossa; (*: turn to play*) turno; (*change: of house*) trasloco; (*: of job*) cambiamento ♦ *vt* muovere, spostare; (*emotionally*) commuovere; (*POL: resolution etc*) proporre ♦ *vi* (*gen*) muoversi, spostarsi; (*also: ~ house*) cambiar casa, traslocare; **to get a ~ on** affrettarsi, sbrigarsi; **to ~ sb to**

do sth indurre *or* spingere qn a fare qc; **to ~ towards** andare verso; **~ about** *or* **around** *vi* spostarsi; **~ along** *vi* muoversi avanti; **~ away** *vi* allontanarsi, andarsene; **~ back** *vi* (*return*) ritornare; **~ forward** *vi* avanzare; **~ in** *vi* (*to a house*) entrare (in una nuova casa); (*police etc*) intervenire; **~ on** *vi* riprendere la strada; **~ out** *vi* (*of house*) sgombrare; **~ over** *vi* spostarsi; **~ up** *vi* avanzare

moveable ['muːvəbl] *adj* = **movable**

movement ['muːvmənt] *n* (*gen*) movimento; (*gesture*) gesto; (*of stars, water, physical*) moto

movie ['muːvɪ] *n* film *m inv*; **the ~s** il cinema

moviecamera *n* cinepresa

moving ['muːvɪŋ] *adj* mobile; (*causing emotion*) commovente

mow [məu] (*pt* **mowed**, *pp* **mowed** *or* **mown**) *vt* (*grass*) tagliare; (*corn*) mietere; **~ down** *vt* falciare; **~er** *n* (*also:* **lawn-mower**) tagliaerba *m inv*

MP *n abbr* = **Member of Parliament**

m.p.h. *n abbr* = **miles per hour** (*60 m.p.h. = 96 km/h*)

Mr ['mɪstə*] (*US* **Mr.**) *n*: **~ X** Signor X, Sig. X

Mrs ['mɪsɪz] (*US* **Mrs.**) *n*: **~ X** Signora X, Sig.ra X

Ms [mɪz] (*US* **Ms.**) *n* (= *Miss or Mrs*): **~ X** ≈ Signora X, Sig.ra X

M.Sc. *abbr* = **Master of Science**

KEYWORD
---

much [mʌtʃ] *adj, pron* molto(a); **he's done so ~ work** ha lavorato così tanto; **I have as ~ money as you** ho tanti soldi quanti ne hai tu; **how ~ is it?** quant'è?; **it costs too ~** costa troppo; **as ~ as you want** quanto vuoi

♦ *adv* **1** (*greatly*) molto, tanto; **thank you very ~** molte grazie; **he's very ~ the gentleman** è il vero gentiluomo; **I read as ~ as I can** leggo quanto posso; **as ~ as you** tanto quanto te

2 (*by far*) molto; **it's ~ the biggest company in Europe** è di gran lunga la più

grossa società in Europa
3 (*almost*) grossomodo, praticamente;
they're ~ the same sono praticamente
uguali

muck [mʌk] *n* (*dirt*) sporcizia; **~ about** *or*
around (*inf*) *vi* fare lo stupido; (*waste
time*) gingillarsi; **~ up** (*inf*) *vt* (*ruin*)
rovinare
mud [mʌd] *n* fango
muddle [ˈmʌdl] *n* confusione *f*, disordine
m; pasticcio ♦ *vt* (*also:* **~ up**) confondere;
~ through *vi* cavarsela alla meno peggio
muddy [ˈmʌdɪ] *adj* fangoso(a)
mudguard [ˈmʌdɡɑːd] *n* parafango
muesli [ˈmjuːzlɪ] *n* muesli *m*
muffin [ˈmʌfɪn] *n* specie di pasticcino soffice
da tè
muffle [ˈmʌfl] *vt* (*sound*) smorzare, attutire;
(*against cold*) imbacuccare
muffler [ˈmʌflə*] (*US*) *n* (*AUT*) marmitta;
(: *on motorbike*) silenziatore *m*
mug [mʌɡ] *n* (*cup*) tazzone *m*; (*for beer*)
boccale *m*; (*inf: face*) muso; (: *fool*) scemo/
a ♦ *vt* (*assault*) assalire; **~ging** *n* assalto
muggy [ˈmʌɡɪ] *adj* afoso(a)
mule [mjuːl] *n* mulo
multi-level [ˈmʌltɪ-] (*US*) *adj* = **multistorey**
multiple [ˈmʌltɪpl] *adj* multiplo(a);
molteplice ♦ *n* multiplo; **~ sclerosis** *n*
sclerosi *f* a placche
multiplex cinema [ˈmʌltɪpleks-] *n* cinema
m inv multisala *inv*
multiplication [mʌltɪplɪˈkeɪʃən] *n*
moltiplicazione *f*
multiply [ˈmʌltɪplaɪ] *vt* moltiplicare ♦ *vi*
moltiplicarsi
multistorey [ˈmʌltɪˈstɔːrɪ] (*BRIT*) *adj*
(*building, car park*) a più piani
mum [mʌm] (*BRIT: inf*) *n* mamma ♦ *adj:* **to
keep ~** non aprire bocca
mumble [ˈmʌmbl] *vt, vi* borbottare
mummy [ˈmʌmɪ] *n* (*BRIT: mother*) mamma;
(*embalmed*) mummia
mumps [mʌmps] *n* orecchioni *mpl*
munch [mʌntʃ] *vt, vi* sgranocchiare
mundane [mʌnˈdeɪn] *adj* terra a terra *inv*

municipal [mjuːˈnɪsɪpl] *adj* municipale
mural [ˈmjuərl] *n* dipinto murale
murder [ˈmɜːdə*] *n* assassinio, omicidio ♦ *vt*
assassinare; **~er** *n* omicida *m*, assassino;
~ous *adj* omicida
murky [ˈmɜːkɪ] *adj* tenebroso(a)
murmur [ˈmɜːmə*] *n* mormorio ♦ *vt, vi*
mormorare
muscle [ˈmʌsl] *n* muscolo; (*fig*) forza; **~ in**
vi immischiarsi
muscular [ˈmʌskjulə*] *adj* muscolare;
(*person, arm*) muscoloso(a)
muse [mjuːz] *vi* meditare, sognare ♦ *n*
musa
museum [mjuːˈzɪəm] *n* museo
mushroom [ˈmʌʃrum] *n* fungo ♦ *vi*
crescere in fretta
music [ˈmjuːzɪk] *n* musica; **~al** *adj* musicale;
(*person*) portato(a) per la musica ♦ *n*
(*show*) commedia musicale; **~al
instrument** *n* strumento musicale; **~ hall**
n teatro di varietà; **~ian** [-ˈzɪʃən] *n*
musicista *m/f*
Muslim [ˈmazlɪm] *adj, n* musulmano(a)
muslin [ˈmazlɪn] *n* mussola
mussel [ˈmasl] *n* cozza
must [mast] *aux vb* (*obligation*): **I ~ do it**
devo farlo; (*probability*): **he ~ be there by
now** dovrebbe essere arrivato ormai; **I ~
have made a mistake** devo essermi
sbagliato ♦ *n*: **it's a ~** è d'obbligo
mustache [ˈmastæʃ] (*US*) *n* = **moustache**
mustard [ˈmastəd] *n* senape *f*, mostarda
muster [ˈmastə*] *vt* radunare
mustn't [ˈmasnt] = **must not**
musty [ˈmastɪ] *adj* che sa di muffa *or* di
rinchiuso
mute [mjuːt] *adj, n* muto(a)
muted [ˈmjuːtɪd] *adj* smorzato(a)
mutiny [ˈmjuːtɪnɪ] *n* ammutinamento
mutter [ˈmatə*] *vt, vi* borbottare, brontolare
mutton [ˈmatn] *n* carne *f* di montone
mutual [ˈmjuːtʃuəl] *adj* mutuo(a),
reciproco(a); **~ly** *adv* reciprocamente
muzzle [ˈmazl] *n* muso; (*protective device*)
museruola; (*of gun*) bocca ♦ *vt* mettere la
museruola a

my [maɪ] adj il(la) mio(a), pl i(le) miei(mie); ~ **house** la mia casa; ~ **books** i miei libri; ~ **brother** mio fratello; **I've washed ~ hair/cut ~ finger** mi sono lavato i capelli/tagliato il dito

myself [maɪ'sɛlf] pron (reflexive) mi; (emphatic) io stesso(a); (after prep) me; see also **oneself**

mysterious [mɪs'tɪərɪəs] adj misterioso(a)

mystery ['mɪstərɪ] n mistero

mystify ['mɪstɪfaɪ] vt mistificare; (puzzle) confondere

mystique [mɪs'tiːk] n fascino

myth [mɪθ] n mito

mythology [mɪ'θɔlədʒɪ] n mitologia

N, n

n/a abbr = **not applicable**

nag [næg] vt tormentare ♦ vi brontolare in continuazione; ~**ging** adj (doubt, pain) persistente

nail [neɪl] n (human) unghia; (metal) chiodo ♦ vt inchiodare; **to ~ sb down to (doing) sth** costringere qn a (fare) qc; ~ **brush** n spazzolino da or per unghie; ~**file** n lima da or per unghie; ~ **polish** n smalto da or per unghie; ~ **polish remover** n acetone m, solvente m; ~ **scissors** npl forbici fpl da or per unghie; ~ **varnish** (BRIT) n = ~ **polish**

naïve [naɪ'iːv] adj ingenuo(a)

naked ['neɪkɪd] adj nudo(a)

name [neɪm] n nome m; (reputation) nome, reputazione f ♦ vt (baby etc) chiamare; (plant, illness) nominare; (person, object) identificare; (price, date) fissare; **what's your ~?** come si chiama?; **by ~** di nome; **she knows them all by ~** li conosce tutti per nome; ~**ly** adv cioè; ~**sake** n omonimo

nanny ['nænɪ] n bambinaia

nap [næp] n (sleep) pisolino; (of cloth) peluria; **to be caught ~ping** essere preso alla sprovvista

nape [neɪp] n: ~ **of the neck** nuca

napkin ['næpkɪn] n (also: **table ~**) tovagliolo

nappy ['næpɪ] (BRIT) n pannolino; ~ **rash** n arrossamento (causato dal pannolino)

narcissus [naː'sɪsəs] (pl **narcissi**) n narciso

narcotic [naː'kɔtɪk] n narcotico ♦ adj narcotico(a)

narrative ['nærətɪv] n narrativa

narrow ['nærəʊ] adj stretto(a); (fig) limitato(a), ristretto(a) ♦ vi restringersi; **to have a ~ escape** farcela per un pelo; **to ~ sth down** to ridurre qc a; ~**ly** adv per un pelo; (time) per poco; ~**-minded** adj meschino(a)

nasty ['naːstɪ] adj (person, remark: unpleasant) cattivo(a); (: rude) villano(a); (smell, wound, situation) brutto(a)

nation ['neɪʃən] n nazione f

national ['næʃənl] adj nazionale ♦ n cittadino/a; ~ **dress** n costume m nazionale; **N~ Health Service** (BRIT) n servizio nazionale di assistenza sanitaria, ≈ S.S.N. m; **N~ Insurance** (BRIT) n ≈ Previdenza Sociale; ~**ism** n nazionalismo; ~**ity** [-'nælɪtɪ] n nazionalità f inv; ~**ize** vt nazionalizzare; ~**ly** adv a livello nazionale; ~ **park** n parco nazionale

---

National Trust

Fondato nel 1895, il National Trust è un'organizzazione che si occupa della tutela e della salvaguardia di luoghi di interesse storico o ambientale

---

nationwide ['neɪʃənwaɪd] adj diffuso(a) in tutto il paese ♦ adv in tutto il paese

native ['neɪtɪv] n abitante m/f del paese ♦ adj indigeno(a); (country) natio(a); (ability) innato(a); **a ~ of Russia** un nativo della Russia; **a ~ speaker of French** una persona di madrelingua francese; **N~ American** n discendente di tribù dell'America settentrionale; ~ **language** n madrelingua

Nativity [nə'tɪvɪtɪ] n: **the ~** la Natività

NATO ['neɪtəʊ] n abbr (= North Atlantic Treaty Organization) N.A.T.O. f

natural ['nætʃrəl] adj naturale; (ability)

innato(a); (*manner*) semplice; ~ **gas** *n* gas *m* metano; **~ly** *adv* naturalmente; (*by nature: gifted*) di natura

nature ['neɪtʃə*] *n* natura; (*character*) natura, indole *f*; **by ~** di natura

naught [nɔːt] *n* = **nought**

naughty ['nɔːtɪ] *adj* (*child*) birichino(a), cattivello(a); (*story, film*) spinto(a)

nausea ['nɔːsɪə] *n* (MED) nausea; (*fig: disgust*) schifo

nautical ['nɔːtɪkl] *adj* nautico(a)

naval ['neɪvl] *adj* navale; **~ officer** *n* ufficiale *m* di marina

nave [neɪv] *n* navata centrale

navel ['neɪvl] *n* ombelico

navigate ['nævɪɡeɪt] *vt* percorrere navigando ♦ *vi* navigare; (AUT) fare da navigatore; **navigation** [-'ɡeɪʃən] *n* navigazione *f*; (NAUT, AVIAT) ufficiale *m* di rotta; (*explorer*) navigatore *m*; (AUT) copilota *m/f*

navvy ['nævɪ] (BRIT) *n* manovale *m*

navy ['neɪvɪ] *n* marina; **~(-blue)** *adj* blu scuro *inv*

Nazi ['nɑːtsɪ] *n* nazista *m/f*

NB *abbr* (= *nota bene*) N.B.

near [nɪə*] *adj* vicino(a); (*relation*) prossimo(a) ♦ *adv* vicino ♦ *prep* (*also*: ~ **to**) vicino a, presso; (: *time*) verso ♦ *vt* avvicinarsi a; **~by** [nɪə'baɪ] *adj* vicino(a) ♦ *adv* vicino; **~ly** *adv* quasi; **I ~ly fell** per poco non sono caduto; **~ miss** *n*: **that was a ~ miss** c'è mancato poco; **~side** *n* (AUT: *in Britain*) lato sinistro; (: *in US, Europe etc*) lato destro; **~-sighted** [nɪə'saɪtɪd] *adj* miope

neat [niːt] *adj* (*person, room*) ordinato(a); (*work*) pulito(a); (*solution, plan*) ben indovinato(a), azzeccato(a); (*spirits*) liscio(a); **~ly** *adv* con ordine; (*skilfully*) abilmente

necessarily ['nesɪsrɪlɪ] *adv* necessariamente

necessary ['nesɪsrɪ] *adj* necessario(a)

necessity [nɪ'sesɪtɪ] *n* necessità *f inv*

neck [nek] *n* collo; (*of garment*) colletto ♦ *vi* (*inf*) pomiciare, sbaciucchiarsi; **~ and ~** testa a testa

necklace ['neklɪs] *n* collana

neckline ['neklaɪn] *n* scollatura

necktie ['nektaɪ] *n* cravatta

née [neɪ] *adj*: **~ Scott** nata Scott

need [niːd] *n* bisogno ♦ *vt* aver bisogno di; **to ~ to do** dover fare; aver bisogno di fare; **you don't ~ to go** non devi andare, non c'è bisogno che tu vada

needle ['niːdl] *n* ago; (*on record player*) puntina ♦ *vt* punzecchiare

needless ['niːdlɪs] *adj* inutile

needlework ['niːdlwɜːk] *n* cucito

needn't ['niːdnt] = **need not**

needy ['niːdɪ] *adj* bisognoso(a)

negative ['negətɪv] *n* (LING) negazione *f*; (PHOT) negativo ♦ *adj* negativo(a); **~ equity** *n* situazione in cui l'ammontare del mutuo su un immobile supera il suo valore sul mercato

neglect [nɪ'ɡlekt] *vt* trascurare ♦ *n* (*of person, duty*) negligenza; (*of child, house etc*) scarsa cura; **state of ~** stato di abbandono

negligence ['negendʒəns] *n* negligenza

negligible ['neglɪdʒɪbl] *adj* insignificante, trascurabile

negotiable [nɪ'ɡəuʃɪəbl] *adj* (*cheque*) trasferibile

negotiate [nɪ'ɡəuʃɪeɪt] *vi*: **to ~ (with)** negoziare (con) ♦ *vt* (COMM) negoziare; (*obstacle*) superare; **negotiation** [-'eɪʃən] *n* negoziato, trattativa

Negro ['niːɡrəu] (*pl* **~es**) *n* negro(a)

neigh [neɪ] *vi* nitrire

neighbour ['neɪbə*] (US **neighbor**) *n* vicino/a; **~hood** *n* vicinato; **~ing** *adj* vicino(a); **~ly** *adj*: **he is a ~ly person** è un buon vicino

neither ['naɪðə*] *adj, pron* né l'uno(a) né l'altro(a), nessuno(a) dei(delle) due ♦ *conj* neanche, nemmeno, neppure ♦ *adv*: **~ good nor bad** né buono né cattivo; **I didn't move and ~ did Claude** io non mi mossi e nemmeno Claude; **..., ~ did I refuse** ..., ma non ho nemmeno rifiutato

neon light ['niːɔn-] *n* luce *f* al neon

nephew ['nevjuː] *n* nipote *m*

nerve [nə:v] n nervo; (fig) coraggio; (impudence) faccia tosta; **a fit of ~s** una crisi di nervi; **~-racking** adj che spezza i nervi

nervous ['nə:vəs] adj nervoso(a); (anxious) agitato(a), in apprensione; **~ breakdown** n esaurimento nervoso

nest [nɛst] n nido ♦ vi fare il nido, nidificare; **~ egg** n (fig) gruzzolo

nestle ['nɛsl] vi accoccolarsi

net [nɛt] n rete f ♦ adj netto(a) ♦ vt (fish etc) prendere con la rete; (profit) ricavare un utile netto di; **~ball** n specie di pallacanestro

Netherlands ['nɛðələndz] npl: **the ~** i Paesi Bassi

nett [nɛt] adj = **net**

netting ['nɛtɪŋ] n (for fence etc) reticolato

nettle ['nɛtl] n ortica

network ['nɛtwə:k] n rete f

neurotic [njuə'rɔtɪk] adj, n nevrotico(a)

neuter ['nju:tə*] adj neutro(a) ♦ vt (cat etc) castrare

neutral ['nju:trəl] adj neutro(a); (person, nation) neutrale ♦ n (AUT): **in ~** in folle; **~ize** vt neutralizzare

never ['nɛvə*] adv (non...) mai; **~ again** mai più; **I'll ~ go there again** non ci vado più; **~ in my life** mai in vita mia; see also **mind**; **~-ending** adj interminabile; **~theless** [nɛvəðə'lɛs] adv tuttavia, ciò nondimeno, ciò nonostante, ciò nondimeno

new [nju:] adj nuovo(a); (brand new) nuovo(a) di zecca; **N~ Age** n New Age f inv; **~born** adj neonato(a); **~comer** ['nju:kʌmə*] n nuovo(a) venuto(a); **~-fangled** ['nju:fæŋgld] (pej) adj stramoderno(a); **~-found** adj nuovo(a); **~ly** adv di recente; **~ly-weds** npl sposini mpl, sposi mpl novelli

news [nju:z] n notizie fpl; (RADIO) giornale m radio; (TV) telegiornale m; **a piece of ~** una notizia; **~ agency** n agenzia di stampa; **~agent** (BRIT) n giornalaio; **~caster** n (RADIO, TV) annunciatore/trice; **~ flash** n notizia f lampo inv; **~letter** n bollettino; **~paper** n giornale m; **~print** n

carta da giornale; **~reader** n = **~caster**; **~reel** n cinegiornale m; **~ stand** n edicola

newt [nju:t] n tritone m

New Year n Anno Nuovo; **~'s Day** n il Capodanno; **~'s Eve** n la vigilia di Capodanno

New York [-'jɔ:k] n New York f

New Zealand [-'zi:lənd] n Nuova Zelanda; **~er** n neozelandese m/f

next [nɛkst] adj prossimo(a) ♦ adv accanto; (in time) dopo; **the ~ day** il giorno dopo, l'indomani; **~ time** la prossima volta; **~ year** l'anno prossimo; **when do we meet ~?** quando ci rincontriamo?; **~ to** accanto a; **~ to nothing** quasi niente; **~ please!** (avanti il prossimo!; **~ door** adv, adj accanto inv; **~-of-kin** n parente m/f prossimo(a)

NHS n abbr = **National Health Service**

nib [nɪb] n (of pen) pennino

nibble ['nɪbl] vt mordicchiare

Nicaragua [nɪkə'ræɡjuə] n Nicaragua m

nice [naɪs] adj (holiday, trip) piacevole; (flat, picture) bello(a); (person) simpatico(a), gentile; **~ly** adv bene

niceties ['naɪsɪtɪz] npl finezze fpl

nick [nɪk] n taglietto; tacca ♦ vt (inf) rubare; **in the ~ of time** appena in tempo

nickel ['nɪkl] n nichel m; (US) moneta da cinque centesimi di dollaro

nickname ['nɪkneɪm] n soprannome m

niece [ni:s] n nipote f

Nigeria [naɪ'dʒɪərɪə] n Nigeria

niggling ['nɪglɪŋ] adj insignificante; (annoying) irritante

night [naɪt] n notte f; (evening) sera; **at ~** la sera; **by ~** di notte; **the ~ before last** l'altro ieri notte (or sera); **~cap** n bicchierino prima di andare a letto; **~ club** n locale m notturno; **~dress** n camicia da notte; **~fall** n crepuscolo; **~gown** n = **~dress**; **~ie** ['naɪtɪ] n = **~dress**

nightingale ['naɪtɪŋɡeɪl] n usignolo

nightlife ['naɪtlaɪf] n vita notturna

nightly ['naɪtlɪ] adj di ogni notte or sera; (by night) notturno(a) ♦ adv ogni notte or sera

nightmare ['naɪtmeə*] n incubo
night: ~ **porter** n portiere m di notte; ~ **school** n scuola serale; ~ **shift** n turno di notte; **~-time** n notte f
nil [nɪl] n nulla m; (BRIT: SPORT) zero
Nile [naɪl] n: **the** ~ il Nilo
nimble ['nɪmbl] adj agile
nine [naɪn] num nove; **~teen** num diciannove; **~ty** num novanta
ninth [naɪnθ] adj nono(a)
nip [nɪp] vt pizzicare; (bite) mordere
nipple ['nɪpl] n (ANAT) capezzolo
nitrogen ['naɪtrədʒən] n azoto

KEYWORD

no [nəu] (pl **~es**) adv (opposite of "yes") no; **are you coming? – ~ (I'm not)** viene? — no (non vengo); **would you like some more? – ~ thank you** ne vuole ancora un po'? — no, grazie
♦ adj (not any) nessuno(a); **I have ~ money/time/books** non ho soldi/tempo/libri; ~ **student would have done it** nessuno studente lo avrebbe fatto; **"~ parking"** "divieto di sosta"; **"~ smoking"** "vietato fumare"
♦ n no m inv

nobility [nəu'bɪlɪtɪ] n nobiltà
noble ['nəubl] adj nobile
nobody ['nəubədɪ] pron nessuno
nod [nɔd] vi accennare col capo, fare un cenno; (in agreement) annuire con un cenno del capo; (sleep) sonnecchiare ♦ vt: **to ~ one's head** fare di sì col capo ♦ n cenno; ~ **off** vi assopirsi
noise [nɔɪz] n rumore m; (din, racket) chiasso; **noisy** adj (street, car) rumoroso(a); (person) chiassoso(a)
nominal ['nɔmɪnl] adj nominale; (rent) simbolico(a)
nominate ['nɔmɪneɪt] vt (propose) proporre come candidato; (elect) nominare
nominee [nɔmɪ'ni:] n persona nominata; candidato/a
non... [nɔn] prefix non...; **~-alcoholic** adj analcolico(a)

nonchalant ['nɔnʃələnt] adj disinvolto(a), noncurante
non-committal ['nɔnkə'mɪtl] adj evasivo(a)
nondescript ['nɔndɪskrɪpt] adj qualunque inv
none [nʌn] pron (not one thing) niente; (not one person) nessuno(a); ~ **of you** nessuno(a) di voi; **I've ~ left** non ne ho più; **he's ~ the worse for it** non ne ha risentito
nonentity [nɔ'nentɪtɪ] n persona insignificante
nonetheless [nʌnðə'les] adv nondimeno
non-existent [-ɪg'zɪstənt] adj inesistente
non-fiction n saggistica
nonplussed [nɔn'plʌst] adj sconcertato(a)
nonsense ['nɔnsəns] n sciocchezze fpl
non: **~-smoker** n non fumatore/trice; **~-smoking** adj (person) che non fuma; (area, section) per non fumatori; **~-stick** adj antiaderente, antiadesivo(a); **~-stop** adj continuo(a); (train, bus) direttissimo(a) ♦ adv senza sosta
noodles ['nu:dlz] npl taglierini mpl
nook [nuk] n: **~s and crannies** angoli mpl
noon [nu:n] n mezzogiorno
no one ['nəuwʌn] pron = **nobody**
noose [nu:s] n nodo scorsoio; (hangman's) cappio
nor [nɔ:*] conj = **neither** ♦ adv see **neither**
norm [nɔ:m] n norma
normal ['nɔ:ml] adj normale; **~ly** adv normalmente
north [nɔ:θ] n nord m, settentrione m ♦ adj nord inv, del nord, settentrionale ♦ adv verso nord; **N~ America** n America del Nord; **~-east** n nord-est m; **~erly** ['nɔ:ðəlɪ] adj (point, direction) verso nord; **~ern** ['nɔ:ðən] adj del nord, settentrionale; **N~ern Ireland** n Irlanda del Nord; **N~ Pole** n Polo Nord; **N~ Sea** n Mare m del Nord; **~ward(s)** ['nɔ:θwəd(z)] adv verso nord; **~-west** n nord-ovest m
Norway ['nɔ:weɪ] n Norvegia
Norwegian [nɔ:'wi:dʒən] adj norvegese ♦ n norvegese m/f; (LING) norvegese m
nose [nəuz] n naso; (of animal) muso ♦ vi:

to ~ **about** aggirarsi; **~bleed** *n* emorragia nasale; **~-dive** *n* picchiata; **~y** (*inf*) *adj* = **nosy**

nostalgia [nɔsˈtældʒɪə] *n* nostalgia

nostril [ˈnɔstrɪl] *n* narice *f*; (*of horse*) frogia

nosy [ˈnəʊzɪ] (*inf*) *adj* curioso(a)

not [nɔt] *adv* non; **he is ~** *or* **isn't here** non è qui, non c'è; **you must ~** *or* **you mustn't do that** non devi fare quello; **it's too late, isn't it** *or* **is it ~?** è troppo tardi, vero?; **~ that I don't like him** non che (lui) non mi piaccia; **~ yet/now** non ancora/ora; *see also* **all; only**

notably [ˈnəʊtəblɪ] *adv* (*markedly*) notevolmente; (*particularly*) in particolare

notary [ˈnəʊtərɪ] *n* notaio

notch [nɔtʃ] *n* tacca; (*in saw*) dente *m*

note [nəʊt] *n* nota; (*letter, banknote*) biglietto ♦ *vt* (*also:* **~ down**) prendere nota di; **to take ~s** prendere appunti; **~book** *n* taccuino; **~d** [ˈnəʊtɪd] *adj* celebre; **~pad** *n* bloc-notes *m inv*; **~paper** *n* carta da lettere

nothing [ˈnʌθɪŋ] *n* nulla *m*, niente *m*; (*zero*) zero; **he does ~** non fa niente; **~ new/ much** *etc* niente di nuovo/speciale *etc*; **for ~** per niente

notice [ˈnəʊtɪs] *n* avviso; (*of leaving*) preavviso ♦ *vt* notare, accorgersi di; **to take ~ of** fare attenzione a; **to bring sth to sb's ~** far notare qc a qn; **at short ~** con un breve preavviso; **until further ~** fino a nuovo avviso; **to hand in one's ~** licenziarsi; **~able** *adj* evidente; **~ board** (*BRIT*) *n* tabellone *m* per affissi

notify [ˈnəʊtɪfaɪ] *vt*: **to ~ sth to sb** far sapere qc a qn; **to ~ sb of sth** avvisare qn di qc

notion [ˈnəʊʃən] *n* idea; (*concept*) nozione *f*

notorious [nəʊˈtɔːrɪəs] *adj* famigerato(a)

nougat [ˈnuːgaː] *n* torrone *m*

nought [nɔːt] *n* zero

noun [naʊn] *n* nome *m*, sostantivo

nourish [ˈnʌrɪʃ] *vt* nutrire

novel [ˈnɔvl] *n* romanzo ♦ *adj* nuovo(a); **~ist** *n* romanziere/a; **~ty** *n* novità *f inv*

November [nəʊˈvɛmbə*] *n* novembre *m*

novice [ˈnɔvɪs] *n* principiante *m/f*; (*REL*) novizio/a

now [naʊ] *adv* ora, adesso ♦ *conj*: **~ (that)** adesso che, ora che; **by ~** ormai; **just ~** proprio ora; **right ~** subito, immediatamente; **~ and then**, **~ and again** ogni tanto; **from ~ on** da ora in poi; **~adays** [ˈnaʊədeɪz] *adv* oggidì

nowhere [ˈnəʊwɛə*] *adv* in nessun luogo, da nessuna parte

nozzle [ˈnɔzl] *n* (*of hose etc*) boccaglio; (*of fire extinguisher*) lancia

nuance [ˈnjuːɑːns] *n* sfumatura

nuclear [ˈnjuːklɪə*] *adj* nucleare

nucleus [ˈnjuːklɪəs] (*pl* **nuclei**) *n* nucleo

nude [njuːd] *adj* nudo(a) ♦ *n* (*ART*) nudo; **in the ~** tutto(a) nudo(a)

nudge [nʌdʒ] *vt* dare una gomitata a

nudist [ˈnjuːdɪst] *n* nudista *m/f*

nuisance [ˈnjuːsns] *n*: **it's a ~** è una seccatura; **he's a ~** è uno scocciatore

null [nʌl] *adj*: **~ and void** nullo(a)

numb [nʌm] *adj*: **~ (with)** intorpidito(a) (da); (*with fear*) impietrito(a) (da); **~ with cold** intirizzito(a) (dal freddo)

number [ˈnʌmbə*] *n* numero ♦ *vt* numerare; (*include*) contare; **a ~ of** un certo numero di; **to be ~ed among** venire annoverato(a) tra; **they were 10 in ~** erano in tutto 10; **~ plate** (*BRIT*) *n* (*AUT*) targa

numeral [ˈnjuːmərəl] *n* numero, cifra

numerate [ˈnjuːmərɪt] *adj*: **to be ~** avere nozioni di aritmetica

numerical [njuːˈmerɪkl] *adj* numerico(a)

numerous [ˈnjuːmərəs] *adj* numeroso(a)

nun [nʌn] *n* suora, monaca

nurse [nəːs] *n* infermiere/a; (*also:* **~maid**) bambinaia ♦ *vt* (*patient, cold*) curare; (*baby: BRIT*) cullare; (: *US*) allattare, dare il latte a

nursery [ˈnəːsərɪ] *n* (*room*) camera dei bambini; (*institution*) asilo; (*for plants*) vivaio; **~ rhyme** *n* filastrocca; **~ school** *n* scuola materna; **~ slope** (*BRIT*) *n* (*SKI*) pista per principianti

nursing [ˈnəːsɪŋ] *n* (*profession*) professione *f* di infermiere (*or* di infermiera); (*care*) cura; **~ home** *n* casa di cura

nurture ['nə:tʃə*] vt allevare; nutrire

nut [nʌt] n (of metal) dado; (fruit) noce f; **~crackers** npl schiaccianoci m inv

nutmeg ['nʌtmeg] n noce f moscata

nutritious [nju:'trɪʃəs] adj nutriente

nuts [nʌts] (inf) adj matto(a)

nutshell ['nʌtʃel] n: **in a ~** in poche parole

nylon ['naɪlɔn] n nailon m ♦ adj di nailon

O, o

oak [əuk] n quercia ♦ adj di quercia

O.A.P. (BRIT) n abbr = **old age pensioner**

oar [ɔ:*] n remo

oasis [əu'eɪsɪs] (pl **oases**) n oasi f inv

oath [əuθ] n giuramento; (swear word) bestemmia

oatmeal ['əutmi:l] n farina d'avena

oats [əuts] npl avena

obedience [ə'bi:dɪəns] n ubbidienza

obedient [ə'bi:dɪənt] adj ubbidiente

obey [ə'beɪ] vt ubbidire a; (instructions, regulations) osservare

obituary [ə'bɪtjuərɪ] n necrologia

object [n 'ɔbdʒɪkt, vb əb'dʒɛkt] n oggetto; (purpose) scopo, intento; (LING) complemento oggetto ♦ vi: **to ~ to** (attitude) disapprovare; (proposal) protestare contro, sollevare delle obiezioni contro; **expense is no ~** non si bada a spese; **to ~ that** obiettare che; **I ~!** mi oppongo!; **~ion** [əb'dʒɛkʃən] n obiezione f; **~ionable** [əb'dʒɛkʃənəbl] adj antipatico(a); (language) scostumato(a); **~ive** n obiettivo

obligation [ɔblɪ'geɪʃən] n obbligo, dovere m; **without ~** senza impegno

oblige [ə'blaɪdʒ] vt (force): **to ~ sb to do** costringere qn a fare; (do a favour) fare una cortesia a; **to be ~d to sb for sth** essere grato a qn per qc; **obliging** adj servizievole, compiacente

oblique [ə'bli:k] adj obliquo(a); (allusion) indiretto(a)

obliterate [ə'blɪtəreɪt] vt cancellare

oblivion [ə'blɪvɪən] n oblio

oblivious [ə'blɪvɪəs] adj: **~ of** incurante di;

inconscio(a) di

oblong ['ɔblɔŋ] adj oblungo(a) ♦ n rettangolo

obnoxious [əb'nɔkʃəs] adj odioso(a); (smell) disgustoso(a), ripugnante

oboe ['əubəu] n oboe m

obscene [əb'si:n] adj osceno(a)

obscure [əb'skjuə*] adj oscuro(a) ♦ vt oscurare; (hide: sun) nascondere

observant [əb'zə:vnt] adj attento(a)

observation [ɔbzə'veɪʃən] n osservazione f; (by police etc) sorveglianza

observatory [əb'zə:vətrɪ] n osservatorio

observe [əb'zə:v] vt osservare; (remark) fare osservare; **~r** n osservatore/trice

obsess [əb'sɛs] vt ossessionare; **~ive** adj ossessivo(a)

obsolescence [ɔbsə'lɛsns] n obsolescenza

obsolete ['ɔbsəli:t] adj obsoleto(a)

obstacle ['ɔbstəkl] n ostacolo

obstinate ['ɔbstɪnɪt] adj ostinato(a)

obstruct [əb'strʌkt] vt (block) ostruire, ostacolare; (halt) fermare; (hinder) impedire

obtain [əb'teɪn] vt ottenere; **~able** adj ottenibile

obvious ['ɔbvɪəs] adj ovvio(a), evidente; **~ly** adv ovviamente; certo

occasion [ə'keɪʒən] n occasione f; (event) avvenimento; **~al** adj occasionale; **~ally** adv ogni tanto

occupation [ɔkju'peɪʃən] n occupazione f; (job) mestiere m, professione f; **~al hazard** n rischio del mestiere

occupier ['ɔkjupaɪə*] n occupante m/f

occupy ['ɔkjupaɪ] vt occupare; **to ~ o.s. in doing** occuparsi a fare

occur [ə'kə:*] vi accadere, capitare; **to ~ to sb** venire in mente a qn; **~rence** n caso, fatto; presenza

ocean ['əuʃən] n oceano

o'clock [ə'klɔk] adv: **it is 5 ~** sono le 5

OCR n abbr (= optical character recognition) lettura ottica; (= optical character reader) lettore m ottico

octave ['ɔktɪv] n ottavo

October [ɔk'təubə*] n ottobre m

octopus ['ɔktəpəs] n polpo, piovra

odd [ɔd] _adj_ (_strange_) strano(a), bizzarro(a); (_number_) dispari _inv_; (_not of a set_) spaiato(a); **60-~** 60 e oltre; **at ~ times** di tanto in tanto; **the ~ one out** l'eccezione _f_; **~ity** _n_ bizzarria; (_person_) originale _m_; **~-job man** _n_ tuttofare _m inv_; **~ jobs** _npl_ lavori _mpl_ occasionali; **~ly** _adv_ stranamente; **~ments** _npl_ (_COMM_) rimanenze _fpl_; **~s** _npl_ (_in betting_) quota; **~s and ends** _npl_ avanzi _mpl_; **it makes no ~s** non importa; **at ~s** in contesa

odometer [ɔ'dɔmɪtə*] _n_ odometro

odour ['əudə*] (_US_ **odor**) _n_ odore _m_; (_unpleasant_) cattivo odore

KEYWORD

of [ɔv, əv] _prep_ **1** (_gen_) di; **a boy ~ 10** un ragazzo di 10 anni; **a friend ~ ours** un nostro amico; **that was kind ~ you** è stato molto gentile da parte sua

2 (_expressing quantity, amount, dates etc_) di; **a kilo ~ flour** un chilo di farina; **how much ~ this do you need?** quanto gliene serve?; **there were 3 ~ them** (_people_) erano in 3; (_objects_) ce n'erano 3; **3 ~ us went** 3 di noi sono andati; **the 5th ~ July** il 5 luglio

3 (_from, out of_) di, in; **made ~ wood** (fatto) di _or_ in legno

KEYWORD

off [ɔf] _adv_ **1** (_distance, time_): **it's a long way ~** è lontano; **the game is 3 days ~** la partita è tra 3 giorni

2 (_departure, removal_) via; **to go ~ to Paris** andarsene a Parigi; **I must be ~** devo andare via; **to take ~ one's coat** togliersi il cappotto; **the button came ~** il bottone è venuto via _or_ si è staccato; **10% ~** con lo sconto del 10%

3 (_not at work_): **to have a day ~** avere un giorno libero; **to be ~ sick** essere assente per malattia

♦ _adj_ (_engine_) spento(a); (_tap_) chiuso(a); (_cancelled_) sospeso(a); (_BRIT: food_) andato(a) a male; **on the ~ chance** nel caso; **to have**

an ~ day non essere in forma

♦ _prep_ **1** (_motion, removal etc_) da; (_distant from_) a poca distanza da; **a street ~ the square** una strada che parte dalla piazza

2: **to be ~ meat** non mangiare più la carne

offal ['ɔfl] _n_ (_CULIN_) frattaglie _fpl_

off-colour (_BRIT_) _adj_ (_ill_) malato(a), indisposto(a)

offence [ə'fɛns] (_US_ **offense**) _n_ (_LAW_) contravvenzione _f_; (: _more serious_) reato; **to take ~ at** offendersi per

offend [ə'fɛnd] _vt_ (_person_) offendere; **~er** _n_ delinquente _m/f_; (_against regulations_) contravventore/trice

offense [ə'fɛns] (_US_) _n_ = **offence**

offensive [ə'fɛnsɪv] _adj_ offensivo(a); (_smell etc_) sgradevole, ripugnante ♦ _n_ (_MIL_) offensiva

offer ['ɔfə*] _n_ offerta, proposta ♦ _vt_ offrire; **"on ~"** (_COMM_) "in offerta speciale"; **~ing** _n_ offerta

offhand [ɔf'hænd] _adj_ disinvolto(a), noncurante ♦ _adv_ su due piedi

office ['ɔfɪs] _n_ (_place_) ufficio; (_position_) carica; **doctor's ~** (_US_) studio; **to take ~** entrare in carica; **~ automation** _n_ automazione _f_ d'ufficio; burotica; **~ block** (_US_ **~ building**) _n_ complesso di uffici; **~ hours** _npl_ orario d'ufficio; (_US: MED_) orario di visite

officer ['ɔfɪsə*] _n_ (_MIL etc_) ufficiale _m_; (_also:_ **police ~**) agente _m_ di polizia; (_of organization_) funzionario

office worker _n_ impiegato/a d'ufficio

official [ə'fɪʃl] _adj_ (_authorized_) ufficiale ♦ _n_ ufficiale _m_; (_civil servant_) impiegato/a statale; funzionario

officiate [ə'fɪʃɪeɪt] _vi_ presenziare

officious [ə'fɪʃəs] _adj_ invadente

offing ['ɔfɪŋ] _n_: **in the ~** (_fig_) in vista

off: **~-licence** (_BRIT_) _n_ (_shop_) spaccio di bevande alcoliche; **~-line** _adj, adv_ (_COMPUT_) off-line _inv_, fuori linea; (: _switched off_) spento(a); **~-peak** _adj_ (_ticket, heating etc_) a tariffa ridotta; (_time_) non di punta; **~-putting** (_BRIT_) _adj_ sgradevole, antipatico(a); **~-road vehicle** *n* fuoristrada *m inv*; **~-season** *adj, adv* fuori stagione

off-licence

In Gran Bretagna e in Irlanda, gli off-licence sono rivendite di vini, liquori e superalcolici, spesso aperti fino a tarda ora.

offset ['ɔfset] (*irreg*) *vt* (*counteract*) controbilanciare, compensare

offshoot ['ɔfʃuːt] *n* (*fig*) diramazione *f*

offshore [ɔf'ʃɔː*] *adj* (*breeze*) di terra; (*island*) vicino alla costa; (*fishing*) costiero(a)

offside [ɔf'saɪd] *adj* (*SPORT*) fuori gioco; (*AUT: in Britain*) destro(a); (: *in Italy etc*) sinistro(a)

offspring ['ɔfsprɪŋ] *n inv* prole *f*, discendenza

off: **~stage** *adv* dietro le quinte; **~-the-peg** (*US* **~-the-rack**) *adv* prêt à porter; **~-white** *adj* bianco sporco *inv*

often ['ɔfn] *adv* spesso; **how ~ do you go?** quanto spesso ci vai?

oh [əu] *excl* oh!

oil [ɔɪl] *n* olio; (*petroleum*) petrolio; (*for central heating*) nafta ♦ *vt* (*machine*) lubrificare; **~can** *n* oliatore *m* a mano; (*for storing*) latta da olio; **~field** *n* giacimento petrolifero; **~ filter** *n* (*AUT*) filtro dell'olio; **~ painting** *n* quadro a olio; **~ refinery** [-rɪ'faɪnərɪ] *n* raffineria di petrolio; **~ rig** *n* derrick *m inv*; (*at sea*) piattaforma per trivellazioni subacquee; **~ tanker** *n* (*ship*) petroliera; (*truck*) autocisterna per petrolio; **~ well** *n* pozzo petrolifero; **~y** *adj* unto(a), oleoso(a); (*food*) grasso(a)

ointment ['ɔɪntmənt] *n* unguento

O.K. ['əu'keɪ] *excl* d'accordo! ♦ *adj* non male *inv* ♦ *vt* approvare; **is it ~?, are you ~?** tutto bene?

okay ['əu'keɪ] *excl, adj, vt* = **O.K.**

old [əuld] *adj* vecchio(a); (*ancient*) antico(a), vecchio(a); (*person*) vecchio(a), anziano(a); **how ~ are you?** quanti anni ha?; **he's 10 years ~** ha 10 anni; **~er brother** fratello

maggiore; **~ age** *n* vecchiaia; **~ age pensioner** (*BRIT*) *n* pensionato/a; **~-fashioned** *adj* antiquato(a), fuori moda; (*person*) all'antica

olive ['ɔlɪv] *n* (*fruit*) oliva; (*tree*) olivo ♦ *adj* (*also:* **~-green**) verde oliva *inv*; **~ oil** *n* olio d'oliva

Olympic [əu'lɪmpɪk] *adj* olimpico(a); **the ~ Games, the ~s** i giochi olimpici, le Olimpiadi

omelet(te) ['ɔmlɪt] *n* omelette *f inv*

omen ['əumən] *n* presagio, augurio

ominous ['ɔmɪnəs] *adj* minaccioso(a); (*event*) di malaugurio

omit [əu'mɪt] *vt* omettere

KEYWORD

on [ɔn] *prep* 1 (*indicating position*) su; **~ the wall** sulla parete; **~ the left** a *or* sulla sinistra

2 (*indicating means, method, condition etc*): **~ foot** a piedi; **~ the train/plane** in treno/aereo; **~ the telephone** al telefono; **~ the radio/television** alla radio/televisione; **to be ~ drugs** drogarsi; **~ holiday** in vacanza

3 (*of time*): **~ Friday** venerdì; **~ Fridays** il *or* di venerdì; **~ June 20th** il 20 giugno; **~ Friday, June 20th** venerdì, 20 giugno; **a week ~ Friday** venerdì a otto; **~ his arrival** al suo arrivo; **~ seeing this** vedendo ciò

4 (*about, concerning*) su, di; **information ~ train services** informazioni sui collegamenti ferroviari; **a book ~ Goldoni/physics** un libro su Goldoni/di *or* sulla fisica

♦ *adv* 1 (*referring to dress, covering*): **to have one's coat ~** avere indosso il cappotto; **to put one's coat ~** mettersi il cappotto; **what's she got ~?** cosa indossa?; **she put her boots/gloves/hat ~** si mise gli stivali/i guanti/il cappello; **screw the lid ~ tightly** avvita bene il coperchio

2 (*further, continuously*): **to walk ~, go ~** *etc* continuare, proseguire *etc*; **to read ~** continuare a leggere; **~ and off** ogni tanto

♦ *adj* 1 (*in operation: machine, TV, light*)

acceso(a); (: *tap*) aperto(a); (: *brake*)
inserito(a); **is the meeting still ~?** (*in
progress*) la riunione è ancora in corso?;
(*not cancelled*) è confermato l'incontro?;
there's a good film ~ at the cinema
danno un buon film al cinema

2 (*inf*): **that's not ~!** (*not acceptable*) non si
fa così!; (*not possible*) non se ne parla
neanche!

once [wʌns] *adv* una volta ♦ *conj* non
appena, quando; **~ he had left/it was
done** dopo che se n'era andato/fu fatto; **at
~** subito; (*simultaneously*) a un tempo; **~ a
week** una volta per settimana; **~ more**
ancora una volta; **~ and for all** una volta
per sempre; **~ upon a time** c'era una volta

oncoming [ˈɒnkʌmɪŋ] *adj* (*traffic*) che viene
in senso opposto

────────────
KEYWORD
────────────

one [wʌn] *num* uno(a); **~ hundred and fifty**
centocinquanta; **~ day** un giorno
♦ *adj* **1** (*sole*) unico(a); **the ~ book which**
l'unico libro che; **the ~ man who** l'unico
che **2** (*same*) stesso(a); **they came in the ~
car** sono venuti nella stessa macchina
♦ *pron* **1**: **this ~** questo/a; **that ~** quello/a;
I've already got ~/a red ~ ne ho già
uno/uno rosso; **~ by ~** uno per uno
2: **~ another** l'un l'altro; **to look at ~
another** guardarsi; **to help ~ another**
aiutarsi l'un l'altro *or* a vicenda
3 (*impersonal*) si; **~ never knows** non si sa
mai; **to cut ~'s finger** tagliarsi un dito; **~
needs to eat** bisogna mangiare

one: ~-day excursion (*US*) *n* biglietto
giornaliero di andata e ritorno; **~-man** *adj*
(*business*) diretto(a) *etc* da un solo uomo;
~-man band *n* suonatore ambulante con
vari strumenti; **~-off** (*BRIT*: *inf*) *n* fatto
eccezionale

oneself [wʌnˈsɛlf] *pron* (*reflexive*) si; (*after
prep*) se stesso(a), sé; **to do sth (by) ~** fare
qc da sé; **to hurt ~** farsi male; **to keep sth
for ~** tenere qc per sé; **to talk to ~** parlare

da solo

one: ~-sided *adj* (*argument*) unilaterale;
~-to-~ *adj* (*relationship*) univoco(a); **~-
way** *adj* (*street, traffic*) a senso unico

ongoing [ˈɒngəʊɪŋ] *adj* in corso; in
attuazione

onion [ˈʌnjən] *n* cipolla

on-line *adj, adv* (*COMPUT*) on-line *inv*

onlooker [ˈɒnlʊkə*] *n* spettatore/trice

only [ˈəʊnlɪ] *adv* solo, soltanto ♦ *adj* solo(a),
unico(a) ♦ *conj* solo che, ma; **an ~ child**
un figlio unico; **not ~ ... but also** non solo
... ma anche

onset [ˈɒnsɛt] *n* inizio

onshore [ˈɒnʃɔː*] *adj* (*wind*) di mare

onslaught [ˈɒnslɔːt] *n* attacco, assalto

onto [ˈɒntu] *prep* = **on to**

onus [ˈəʊnəs] *n* onere *m*, peso

onward(s) [ˈɒnwəd(z)] *adv* (*move*) in avanti;
from that time ~ da quella volta in poi

ooze [uːz] *vi* stillare

open [ˈəʊpn] *adj* aperto(a); (*road*) libero(a);
(*meeting*) pubblico(a) ♦ *vt* aprire ♦ *vi* (*eyes,
door, debate*) aprirsi; (*flower*) sbocciare;
(*shop, bank, museum*) aprire; (*book etc*:
commence) cominciare; **in the ~ (air)**
all'aperto; **~ on to** *vt fus* (*subj: room, door*)
dare su; **~ up** *vt* aprire; (*blocked road*)
sgombrare ♦ *vi* (*shop, business*) aprire;
~ing *adj* (*speech*) di apertura ♦ *n* apertura;
(*opportunity*) occasione *f*, opportunità *f inv*;
sbocco; **~ing hours** *npl* orario d'apertura;
~ learning centre *n* sistema educativo
nel quale lo studente ha maggiore controllo
e gestione delle modalità di apprendimento;
~ly *adv* apertamente; **~-minded** *adj* che
ha la mente aperta; **~-necked** *adj* col
collo slacciato; **~-plan** *adj* senza pareti
divisorie

────────────
Open University
────────────

i *La* **Open University**, *fondata in Gran
Bretagna nel 1969, organizza corsi
universitari per corrispondenza, basati
anche su lezioni trasmesse per radio e per
televisione e su corsi estivi.*

opera ['ɔpərə] n opera

operate ['ɔpəreɪt] vt (machine) azionare, far funzionare; (system) usare ♦ vi funzionare; (drug) essere efficace; **to ~ on sb (for)** (MED) operare qn (di)

operatic [ɔpə'rætɪk] adj dell'opera, lirico(a)

operating ['ɔpəreɪtɪŋ] adj: **~ table** tavolo operatorio; **~ theatre** sala operatoria

operation [ɔpə'reɪʃən] n operazione f; **to be in ~** (machine) essere in azione or funzionamento; (system) essere in vigore; **to have an ~** (MED) subire un'operazione; **~al** adj in funzione; d'esercizio

operative ['ɔpərətɪv] adj (measure) operativo(a)

operator ['ɔpəreɪtə*] n (of machine) operatore/trice; (TEL) centralinista m/f

opinion [ə'pɪnɪən] n opinione f, parere m; **in my ~** secondo me, a mio avviso; **~ated** adj dogmatico(a); **~ poll** n sondaggio di opinioni

opium ['əupɪəm] n oppio

opponent [ə'pəunənt] n avversario/a

opportunist [ɔpə'tjuːnɪst] n opportunista m/f

opportunity [ɔpə'tjuːnɪtɪ] n opportunità f inv, occasione f; **to take the ~ of doing** cogliere l'occasione per fare

oppose [ə'pəuz] vt opporsi a; **~d to** contrario(a) a; **as ~d to** in contrasto con; **opposing** adj opposto(a); (team) avversario(a)

opposite ['ɔpəzɪt] adj opposto(a); (house etc) di fronte ♦ adv di fronte, dirimpetto ♦ prep di fronte a ♦ n: **the ~** il contrario, l'opposto; **the ~ sex** l'altro sesso

opposition [ɔpə'zɪʃən] n opposizione f

opt [ɔpt] vi: **to ~ for** optare per; **to ~ to do** scegliere di fare; **~ out** vi: **to ~ out of** ritirarsi da

optical ['ɔptɪkl] adj ottico(a)

optician [ɔp'tɪʃən] n ottico

optimist ['ɔptɪmɪst] n ottimista m/f; **~ic** [-'mɪstɪk] adj ottimistico(a)

optimum ['ɔptɪməm] adj ottimale

option ['ɔpʃən] n scelta; (SCOL) materia facoltativa; (COMM) opzione f; **~al** adj facoltativo(a); (COMM) a scelta

or [ɔː*] conj o, oppure; (with negative): **he hasn't seen ~ heard anything** non ha visto né sentito niente; **~ else** se no, altrimenti; oppure

oral ['ɔːrəl] adj orale ♦ n esame m orale

orange ['ɔrɪndʒ] n (fruit) arancia ♦ adj arancione

orbit ['ɔːbɪt] n orbita ♦ vt orbitare intorno a

orbital (motorway) ['ɔːbɪtl-] n raccordo anulare

orchard ['ɔːtʃəd] n frutteto

orchestra ['ɔːkɪstrə] n orchestra; (US: seating) platea

orchid ['ɔːkɪd] n orchidea

ordain [ɔː'deɪn] vt (REL) ordinare; (decide) decretare

ordeal [ɔː'diːl] n prova, travaglio

order ['ɔːdə*] n ordine m; (COMM) ordinazione f ♦ vt ordinare; **in ~** in ordine; (of document) in regola; **in (working) ~** funzionante; **in ~ to do** per fare; **in ~ that** affinché +sub; **on ~** (COMM) in ordinazione; **out of ~** non in ordine; (not working) guasto; **to ~ sb to do** ordinare a qn di fare; **~ form** n modulo d'ordinazione; **~ly** n (MIL) attendente m; (MED) inserviente m ♦ adj (room) in ordine; (mind) metodico(a); (person) ordinato(a), metodico(a)

ordinary ['ɔːdnrɪ] adj normale, comune; (pej) mediocre; **out of the ~** diverso dal solito, fuori dell'ordinario

Ordnance Survey ['ɔːdnəns-] (BRIT) n istituto cartografico britannico

ore [ɔː*] n minerale m grezzo

organ ['ɔːgən] n organo; **~ic** [ɔː'gænɪk] adj organico(a); (of food) biologico(a)

organization [ɔːgənaɪ'zeɪʃən] n organizzazione f

organize ['ɔːgənaɪz] vt organizzare; **to get ~d** organizzarsi; **~r** n organizzatore/trice

orgasm ['ɔːgæzəm] n orgasmo

orgy ['ɔːdʒɪ] n orgia

Orient ['ɔːrɪənt] n: **the ~** l'Oriente m; **oriental** [-'entl] adj, n orientale m/f

origin ['ɔrɪdʒɪn] n origine f

original [ə'rɪdʒɪnl] adj originale; (earliest)

originario(a) ♦ n originale m; ~**ly** adv (at first) all'inizio

originate [ə'rɪdʒɪneɪt] vi: **to ~ from** essere originario(a) di; (suggestion) provenire da; **to ~ in** avere origine in

Orkneys ['ɔːknɪz] npl: **the ~** (also: **the Orkney Islands**) le Orcadi

ornament ['ɔːnəmənt] n ornamento; (trinket) ninnolo; ~**al** [-'mɛntl] adj ornamentale

ornate [ɔː'neɪt] adj molto ornato(a)

orphan ['ɔːfn] n orfano/a

orthodox ['ɔːθədɒks] adj ortodosso(a)

orthopaedic [ɔːθə'piːdɪk] (US **orthopedic**) adj ortopedico(a)

ostensibly [ɒs'tɛnsɪblɪ] adv all'apparenza

ostentatious [ɒstɛn'teɪʃəs] adj pretenzioso(a); ostentato(a)

ostrich ['ɒstrɪtʃ] n struzzo

other ['ʌðə*] adj altro(a) ♦ pron: **the ~ (one)** l'altro(a); ~**s** (~ people) altri mpl; **~ than** altro che; a parte; ~**wise** adv, conj altrimenti

otter ['ɒtə*] n lontra

ouch [autʃ] excl ohi!, ahi!

ought [ɔːt] (pt **ought**) aux vb: **I ~ to do it** dovrei farlo; **this ~ to have been corrected** questo avrebbe dovuto essere corretto; **he ~ to win** dovrebbe vincere

ounce [auns] n oncia (= 28.35 g; 16 in a pound)

our ['auə*] adj il(la) nostro(a), pl i(le) nostri(e); see also **my**; ~**s** pron il(la) nostro(a), pl i(le) nostri(e); see also **mine**; ~**selves** pron pl (reflexive) ci; (after preposition) noi; (emphatic) noi stessi(e); see also **oneself**

oust [aust] vt cacciare, espellere

<hr>

KEYWORD

out [aut] adv (gen) fuori; **~ here/there** qui/là fuori; **to speak ~ loud** parlare forte; **to have a night ~** uscire una sera; **the boat was 10 km ~** la barca era a 10 km dalla costa; **3 days ~ from Plymouth** a 3 giorni da Plymouth

♦ adj: **to be ~** (gen) essere fuori;

(unconscious) aver perso i sensi; (style, singer) essere fuori moda; **before the week was ~** prima che la settimana fosse finita; **to be ~ to do sth** avere intenzione di fare qc; **to be ~ in one's calculations** aver sbagliato i calcoli

♦ **out of** prep **1** (outside, beyond) fuori di; **to go ~ of the house** uscire di casa; **to look ~ of the window** guardare fuori dalla finestra

2 (because of) per

3 (origin) da; **to drink ~ of a cup** bere da una tazza

4 (from among): **~ of 10** su 10

5 (without) senza; **~ of petrol** senza benzina

<hr>

out-and-out adj (liar, thief etc) vero(a) e proprio(a)

outback ['autbæk] n (in Australia) interno, entroterra

outboard ['autbɔːd] n: **~ (motor)** (motore m) fuoribordo

outbreak ['autbreɪk] n scoppio; epidemia

outburst ['autbəːst] n scoppio

outcast ['autkɑːst] n esule m/f; (socially) paria m inv

outcome ['autkʌm] n esito, risultato

outcrop ['autkrɒp] n (of rock) affioramento

outcry ['autkraɪ] n protesta, clamore m

outdated [aut'deɪtɪd] adj (custom, clothes) fuori moda; (idea) sorpassato(a)

outdo [aut'duː] (irreg) vt sorpassare

outdoor [aut'dɔː*] adj all'aperto; ~**s** adv fuori; all'aria aperta

outer ['autə*] adj esteriore; **~ space** n spazio cosmico

outfit ['autfɪt] n (clothes) completo; (: for sport) tenuta

outgoing ['autgəuɪŋ] adj (character) socievole; ~**s** (BRIT) npl (expenses) spese fpl, uscite fpl

outgrow [aut'grəu] (irreg) vt: **he has ~n his clothes** tutti i vestiti gli sono diventati piccoli

outhouse ['authaus] n costruzione f annessa

outing ['autɪŋ] *n* gita; escursione *f*

outlaw ['autlɔː] *n* fuorilegge *m/f* ♦ *vt* bandire

outlay ['autleɪ] *n* spese *fpl*; (*investment*) sborsa, spesa

outlet ['autlet] *n* (*for liquid etc*) sbocco, scarico; (*US: ELEC*) presa di corrente; (*also:* **retail ~**) punto di vendita

outline ['autlaɪn] *n* contorno, profilo; (*summary*) abbozzo, grandi linee *fpl* ♦ *vt* (*fig*) descrivere a grandi linee

outlive [aut'lɪv] *vt* sopravvivere a

outlook ['autluk] *n* prospettiva, vista

outlying ['autlaɪɪŋ] *adj* periferico(a)

outmoded [aut'məudɪd] *adj* passato(a) di moda; antiquato(a)

outnumber [aut'nʌmbə*] *vt* superare in numero

out-of-date *adj* (*passport*) scaduto(a); (*clothes*) fuori moda *inv*

out-of-the-way *adj* (*place*) fuori mano *inv*

outpatient ['autpeɪʃənt] *n* paziente *m/f* esterno(a)

outpost ['autpəust] *n* avamposto

output ['autput] *n* produzione *f*; (*COMPUT*) output *m inv*

outrage ['autreɪdʒ] *n* oltraggio; scandalo ♦ *vt* oltraggiare; **~ous** [-'reɪdʒəs] *adj* oltraggioso(a); scandaloso(a)

outreach worker ['autriːtʃ-] *n* assistente *sociale che opera direttamente nei luoghi di aggregazione di emarginati, tossicodipendenti ecc*

outright [*adv* aut'raɪt, *adj* 'autraɪt] *adv* completamente; schiettamente; apertamente; sul colpo ♦ *adj* completo(a); schietto(a) e netto(a)

outset ['autset] *n* inizio

outside [aut'saɪd] *n* esterno, esteriore *m* ♦ *adj* esterno(a), esteriore ♦ *adv* fuori, all'esterno ♦ *prep* fuori di, all'esterno di; **at the ~** (*fig*) al massimo; **~ lane** *n* (*AUT*) corsia di sorpasso; **~ line** *n* (*TEL*) linea esterna; **~r** *n* (*in race etc*) outsider *m inv*; (*stranger*) estraneo/a

outsize ['autsaɪz] *adj* (*clothes*) per taglie forti

outskirts ['autskəːts] *npl* sobborghi *mpl*

outspoken [aut'spəukən] *adj* molto franco(a)

outstanding [aut'stændɪŋ] *adj* eccezionale, di rilievo; (*unfinished*) non completo(a); non evaso(a); non regolato(a)

outstay [aut'steɪ] *vt*: **to ~ one's welcome** diventare un ospite sgradito

outstretched [aut'stretʃt] *adj* (*hand*) teso(a); (*body*) disteso(a)

outstrip [aut'strɪp] *vt* (*competitors, demand*) superare

out-tray *n* contenitore *m* per la corrispondenza in partenza

outward ['autwəd] *adj* (*sign, appearances*) esteriore; (*journey*) d'andata

outweigh [aut'weɪ] *vt* avere maggior peso di

outwit [aut'wɪt] *vt* superare in astuzia

oval ['əuvl] *adj* ovale ♦ *n* ovale *m*

Oval Office
---

i L'Oval Office *è una grande sala di forma ovale nella* White House, *la Casa Bianca, dove ha sede l'ufficio del Presidente degli Stati Uniti*

---

ovary ['əuvərɪ] *n* ovaia

oven ['ʌvn] *n* forno; **~proof** *adj* da forno

over ['əuvə*] *adv* al di sopra ♦ *adj* (*or adv*) (*finished*) finito(a), terminato(a); (*too*) troppo; (*remaining*) che avanza ♦ *prep* su; sopra; (*above*) al di sopra di; (*on the other side of*) di là di; (*more than*) più di; (*during*) durante; **~ here** qui; **~ there** là; **all ~** (*everywhere*) dappertutto; (*finished*) tutto(a) finito(a); **~ and ~ (again)** più e più volte; **~ and above** oltre (a); **to ask sb ~** invitare qn (a passare)

overall [*adj, n* 'əuvərɔːl, *adv* əuvə'rɔːl] *adj* totale ♦ *n* (*BRIT*) grembiule *m* ♦ *adv* nell'insieme, complessivamente; **~s** *npl* (*worker's ~s*) tuta (da lavoro)

overawe [əuvər'ɔː] *vt* intimidire

overbalance [əuvə'bæləns] *vi* perdere l'equilibrio

overboard ['əuvəbɔːd] *adv* (*NAUT*) fuori bordo, in mare

overbook [əʊvə'buk] *vt*: **the hotel was ~ed** le prenotazioni all'albergo superavano i posti disponibili

overcast ['əʊvəkɑːst] *adj* (*sky*) coperto(a)

overcharge [əʊvə'tʃɑːdʒ] *vt*: **to ~ sb for sth** far pagare troppo caro a qn per qc

overcoat ['əʊvəkəʊt] *n* soprabito, cappotto

overcome [əʊvə'kʌm] (*irreg*) *vt* superare; sopraffare

overcrowded [əʊvə'kraʊdɪd] *adj* sovraffollato(a)

overdo [əʊvə'duː] (*irreg*) *vt* esagerare; (*overcook*) cuocere troppo

overdose ['əʊvədəʊs] *n* dose *f* eccessiva

overdraft ['əʊvədrɑːft] *n* scoperto (di conto)

overdrawn [əʊvə'drɔːn] *adj* (*account*) scoperto(a)

overdue [əʊvə'djuː] *adj* in ritardo

overestimate [əʊvər'ɛstɪmeɪt] *vt* sopravvalutare

overflow [*vb* əʊvə'fləʊ, *n* 'əʊvəfləʊ] *vi* traboccare ♦ *n* (*also*: **~ pipe**) troppopieno

overgrown [əʊvə'grəʊn] *adj* (*garden*) ricoperto(a) di vegetazione

overhaul [*vb* əʊvə'hɔːl, *n* 'əʊvəhɔːl] *vt* revisionare ♦ *n* revisione *f*

overhead [*adv* əʊvə'hɛd, *adj, n* 'əʊvəhɛd] *adv* di sopra ♦ *adj* aereo(a); (*lighting*) verticale ♦ *n* (*US*): **~s**; **~s** *npl* spese *fpl* generali

overhear [əʊvə'hɪə*] (*irreg*) *vt* sentire (per caso)

overheat [əʊvə'hiːt] *vi* (*engine*) surriscaldare

overjoyed [əʊvə'dʒɔɪd] *adj* pazzo(a) di gioia

overlap [əʊvə'læp] *vi* sovrapporsi

overleaf [əʊvə'liːf] *adv* a tergo

overload [əʊvə'ləʊd] *vt* sovraccaricare

overlook [əʊvə'lʊk] *vt* (*have view of*) dare su; (*miss*) trascurare; (*forgive*) passare sopra a

overnight [əʊvə'naɪt] *adv* (*happen*) durante la notte; (*fig*) tutto ad un tratto ♦ *adj* di notte; **he stayed there ~** ci ha passato la notte

overpass ['əʊvəpɑːs] *n* cavalcavia *m inv*

overpower [əʊvə'paʊə*] *vt* sopraffare; **~ing** *adj* irresistibile; (*heat, stench*) soffocante

overrate [əʊvə'reɪt] *vt* sopravvalutare

override [əʊvə'raɪd] (*irreg*: *like* ride) *vt* (*order, objection*) passar sopra a; (*decision*) annullare; **overriding** *adj* preponderante

overrule [əʊvə'ruːl] *vt* (*decision*) annullare; (*claim*) respingere

overrun [əʊvə'rʌn] (*irreg*: *like* run) *vt* (*country*) invadere; (*time limit*) superare

overseas [əʊvə'siːz] *adv* oltremare; (*abroad*) all'estero ♦ *adj* (*trade*) estero(a); (*visitor*) straniero(a)

overshadow [əʊvə'ʃædəʊ] *vt* far ombra su; (*fig*) eclissare

overshoot [əʊvə'ʃuːt] (*irreg*) *vt* superare

oversight ['əʊvəsaɪt] *n* omissione *f*, svista

oversleep [əʊvə'sliːp] (*irreg*) *vt* dormire troppo a lungo

overstep [əʊvə'stɛp] *vt*: **to ~ the mark** superare ogni limite

overt [əʊ'vəːt] *adj* palese

overtake [əʊvə'teɪk] (*irreg*) *vt* sorpassare

overthrow [əʊvə'θrəʊ] (*irreg*) *vt* (*government*) rovesciare

overtime ['əʊvətaɪm] *n* (*lavoro*) straordinario

overtone ['əʊvətəʊn] *n* sfumatura

overture ['əʊvətʃʊə*] *n* (*MUS*) ouverture *f inv*; (*fig*) approccio

overturn [əʊvə'təːn] *vt* rovesciare ♦ *vi* rovesciarsi

overweight [əʊvə'weɪt] *adj* (*person*) troppo grasso(a)

overwhelm [əʊvə'wɛlm] *vt* sopraffare; sommergere; schiacciare; **~ing** *adj* (*victory, defeat*) schiacciante; (*heat, desire*) intenso(a)

overwrought [əʊvə'rɔːt] *adj* molto agitato(a)

owe [əʊ] *vt*: **to ~ sb sth**, **to ~ sth to sb** dovere qc a qn; **owing to** *prep* a causa di

owl [aʊl] *n* gufo

own [əʊn] *vt* possedere ♦ *adj* proprio(a); **a room of my ~** la mia propria camera; **to get one's ~ back** vendicarsi; **on one's ~** tutto(a) solo(a); **~ up** *vi* confessare; **~er** *n* proprietario/a; **~ership** *n* possesso

ox [ɔks] (*pl* **oxen**) *n* bue *m*

oxen ['ɔksn] *npl* of **ox**
oxtail ['ɔksteɪl] *n*: ~ **soup** minestra di coda di bue
oxygen ['ɔksɪdʒən] *n* ossigeno; ~ **mask/tent** *n* maschera/tenda ad ossigeno
oyster ['ɔɪstə*] *n* ostrica
oz. *abbr* = **ounce(s)**
ozone ['əʊzəun] *n* ozono; ~**-friendly** *adj* che non danneggia l'ozono; ~ **hole** *n* buco nell'ozono

P, p

p [piː] *abbr* = **penny; pence**
P.A. *n abbr* = **personal assistant; public address system**
p.a. *abbr* = **per annum**
pa [pɑː] (*inf*) *n* papà *m inv*, babbo
pace [peɪs] *n* passo; (*speed*) passo; velocità ♦ *vi*: **to ~ up and down** camminare su e giù; **to keep ~ with** camminare di pari passo a; (*events*) tenersi al corrente di; ~**maker** *n* (*MED*) segnapasso; (*SPORT: also*: ~ **setter**) battistrada *m inv*
pacific [pə'sɪfɪk] *n*: **the P~ (Ocean)** il Pacifico, l'Oceano Pacifico
pacify ['pæsɪfaɪ] *vt* calmare, placare
pack [pæk] *n* pacco; (*US: of cigarettes*) pacchetto; (*back~*) zaino; (*of hounds*) muta; (*of thieves etc*) banda; (*of cards*) mazzo ♦ *vt* (*in suitcase etc*) mettere; (*fill*) riempire, (*cram*) supare, pigiare; **to ~ (one's bags)** fare la valigia; **to ~ sb off** spedire via qn; ~ **it in!** (*inf*) dacci un taglio!
package ['pækɪdʒ] *n* pacco; balla; (*also*: ~ **deal**) pacchetto; forfait *m inv*; ~ **holiday** *n* vacanza organizzata; ~ **tour** *n* viaggio organizzato
packed lunch *n* pranzo al sacco
packet ['pækɪt] *n* pacchetto
packing ['pækɪŋ] *n* imballaggio; ~ **case** *n* cassa da imballaggio
pact [pækt] *n* patto, accordo; trattato
pad [pæd] *n* blocco; (*to prevent friction*) cuscinetto; (*inf: flat*) appartamentino ♦ *vt* imbottire; ~**ding** *n* imbottitura

paddle ['pædl] *n* (*oar*) pagaia; (*US: for table tennis*) racchetta da ping-pong ♦ *vi* sguazzare ♦ *vt*: **to ~ a canoe** *etc* vogare con la pagaia; **paddling pool** (*BRIT*) *n* piscina per bambini
paddock ['pædək] *n* prato recintato; (*at racecourse*) paddock *m inv*
padlock ['pædlɔk] *n* lucchetto
paediatrics [piːdɪ'ætrɪks] (*US* **pediatrics**) *n* pediatria
pagan ['peɪgən] *adj*, *n* pagano(a)
page [peɪdʒ] *n* pagina; (*also*: ~ **boy**) paggio ♦ *vt* (*in hotel etc*) (far) chiamare
pageant ['pædʒənt] *n* spettacolo storico; grande cerimonia; ~**ry** *n* pompa
pager ['peɪdʒə*] *n* (*TEL*) cercapersone *m inv*
paging device ['peɪdʒɪŋ-] *n* (*TEL*) cercapersone *m inv*
paid [peɪd] *pt, pp* of **pay** ♦ *adj* (*work, official*) rimunerato(a); **to put ~ to** (*BRIT*) mettere fine a
pail [peɪl] *n* secchio
pain [peɪn] *n* dolore *m*; **to be in ~** soffrire, aver male; **to take ~s to do** mettercela tutta per fare; ~**ed** *adj* addolorato(a), afflitto(a); ~**ful** *adj* doloroso(a), che fa male; difficile, penoso(a); ~**fully** *adv* (*fig: very*) fin troppo; ~**killer** *n* antalgico, antidolorifico; ~**less** *adj* indolore
painstaking ['peɪnzteɪkɪŋ] *adj* (*person*) sollecito(a); (*work*) accurato(a)
paint [peɪnt] *n* vernice *f*, colore *m* ♦ *vt* dipingere; (*walls, door etc*) verniciare; **to ~ the door blue** verniciare la porta di azzurro; ~**brush** *n* pennello; ~**er** *n* (*artist*) pittore *m*; (*decorator*) imbianchino; ~**ing** *n* pittura, verniciatura; (*picture*) dipinto, quadro; ~**work** *n* tinta; (*of car*) vernice *f*
pair [pɛə*] *n* (*of shoes, gloves etc*) paio; (*of people*) coppia; duo *m inv*; **a ~ of scissors/trousers** un paio di forbici/pantaloni
pajamas [pɪ'dʒɑːməz] (*US*) *npl* pigiama *m*
Pakistan [pɑːkɪ'stɑːn] *n* Pakistan *m*; ~**i** *adj*, *n* pakistano(a)
pal [pæl] (*inf*) *n* amico/a, compagno/a
palace ['pæləs] *n* palazzo

palatable ['pælɪtəbl] adj gustoso(a)
palate ['pælɪt] n palato
palatial [pə'leɪʃəl] adj sontuoso(a), sfarzoso(a)
pale [peɪl] adj pallido(a) ♦ n: **to be beyond the ~** aver oltrepassato ogni limite
Palestine ['pælɪstaɪn] n Palestina; **Palestinian** [-'tɪnɪən] adj, n palestinese m/f
palette ['pælɪt] n tavolozza
palings ['peɪlɪŋz] npl (fence) palizzata
pallet ['pælɪt] n (for goods) paletta
pallid ['pælɪd] adj pallido(a), smorto(a)
pallor ['pælə*] n pallore m
palm [pɑːm] n (ANAT) palma, palmo; (also: ~ **tree**) palma ♦ vt: **to ~ sth off on sb** (inf) rifilare qc a qn; **P~ Sunday** n Domenica delle Palme
paltry ['pɔːltrɪ] adj irrisorio(a); insignificante
pamper ['pæmpə*] vt viziare, coccolare
pamphlet ['pæmflət] n dépliant m inv
pan [pæn] n (also: **sauce~**) casseruola; (also: **frying ~**) padella
panache [pə'næʃ] n stile m
pancake ['pænkeɪk] n frittella
pancreas ['pæŋkrɪəs] n pancreas m inv
panda ['pændə] n panda m inv; **~ car** (BRIT) n auto f della polizia
pandemonium [pændɪ'məunɪəm] n pandemonio
pander ['pændə*] vi: **to ~ to** lusingare; concedere tutto a
pane [peɪn] n vetro
panel ['pænl] n (of wood, cloth etc) pannello; (RADIO, TV) giuria; **~ling** (US **~ing**) n rivestimento a pannelli
pang [pæŋ] n: **a ~ of regret** un senso di rammarico; **hunger ~s** morsi mpl della fame
panic ['pænɪk] n panico ♦ vi perdere il sangue freddo; **~ky** adj (person) pauroso(a); **~-stricken** adj (person) preso(a) dal panico, in preda al panico; (look) terrorizzato(a)
pansy ['pænzɪ] n (BOT) viola del pensiero, pensée f inv; (inf: pej) femminuccia
pant [pænt] vi ansare

panther ['pænθə*] n pantera
panties ['pæntɪz] npl slip m, mutandine fpl
pantihose ['pæntɪhəuz] (US) n collant m inv
pantomime ['pæntəmaɪm] (BRIT) n pantomima

---
pantomime

ⓘ In Gran Bretagna la **pantomime** è una sorta di libera interpretazione delle favole più conosciute, che vengono messe in scena a teatro durante il periodo natalizio. È uno spettacolo per tutta la famiglia che prevede la partecipazione del pubblico.

---

pantry ['pæntrɪ] n dispensa
pants [pænts] npl mutande fpl, slip m; (US: trousers) pantaloni mpl
papal ['peɪpəl] adj papale, pontificio(a)
paper ['peɪpə*] n carta; (also: **wall~**) carta da parati, tappezzeria; (also: **news~**) giornale m; (study, article) saggio; (exam) prova scritta ♦ adj di carta ♦ vt tappezzare; **~s** npl (also: **identity ~s**) carte fpl, documenti mpl; **~back** n tascabile m; edizione f economica; **~ bag** n sacchetto di carta; **~ clip** n graffetta, clip f inv; **~ hankie** n fazzolettino di carta; **~weight** n fermacarte m inv; **~work** n lavoro amministrativo
papier-mâché ['pæpɪeɪ'mæʃeɪ] n cartapesta
par [pɑː*] n parità, pari f; (GOLF) norma; **on a ~ with** alla pari con
parachute ['pærəʃuːt] n paracadute m inv
parade [pə'reɪd] n parata ♦ vt (fig) fare sfoggio di ♦ vi sfilare in parata
paradise ['pærədaɪs] n paradiso
paradox ['pærədɔks] n paradosso; **~ically** [-'dɔksɪklɪ] adv paradossalmente
paraffin ['pærəfɪn] (BRIT) n: **~ (oil)** paraffina
paragon ['pærəgən] n modello di perfezione or di virtù
paragraph ['pærəgrɑːf] n paragrafo
parallel ['pærəlel] adj parallelo(a); (fig) analogo(a) ♦ n (line) parallela; (fig, GEO) parallelo
paralyse ['pærəlaɪz] (US **paralyze**) vt paralizzare

paralysis [pə'rælisis] *n* paralisi *f inv*

paralyze ['pærəlaiz] (*US*) *vt* = **paralyse**

paramount ['pærəmaunt] *adj*: **of ~ importance** di capitale importanza

paranoid ['pærənɔid] *adj* paranoico(a)

paraphernalia [pærəfə'neiliə] *n* attrezzi *mpl*, roba

parasol ['pærəsɔl] *n* parasole *m*

paratrooper ['pærətru:pə*] *n* paracadutista *m* (*soldato*)

parcel ['pɑ:sl] *n* pacco, pacchetto ♦ *vt* (*also:* **~ up**) impaccare

parched [pɑ:tʃt] *adj* (*person*) assetato(a)

parchment ['pɑ:tʃmənt] *n* pergamena

pardon ['pɑ:dn] *n* perdono; grazia ♦ *vt* perdonare; (*LAW*) graziare; **~ me!** mi scusi!; **I beg your ~!** scusi!; **I beg your ~?** (*BRIT*), **~ me?** (*US*) prego?

parent ['pɛərənt] *n* genitore *m*; **~s** *npl* (*mother and father*) genitori *mpl*; **~al** [pə'rɛntl] *adj* dei genitori

parentheses [pə'rɛnθisi:z] *npl of* **parenthesis**

parenthesis [pə'rɛnθisis] (*pl* **parentheses**) *n* parentesi *f inv*

Paris ['pæris] *n* Parigi *f*

parish ['pæriʃ] *n* parrocchia; (*BRIT: civil*) ≈ municipio

park [pɑ:k] *n* parco ♦ *vt, vi* parcheggiare

parka ['pɑ:kə] *n* eskimo

parking ['pɑ:kiŋ] *n* parcheggio; **"no ~"** "sosta vietata"; **~ lot** (*US*) *n* posteggio, parcheggio; **~ meter** *n* parchimetro; **~ ticket** *n* multa per sosta vietata

parliament ['pɑ:ləmənt] *n* parlamento

parliamentary [pɑ:lə'mɛntəri] *adj* parlamentare

parlour ['pɑ:lə*] (*US* **parlor**) *n* salotto

parochial [pə'rəukiəl] (*pej*) *adj* provinciale

parole [pə'rəul] *n*: **on ~** in libertà per buona condotta

parrot ['pærət] *n* pappagallo

parry ['pæri] *vt* parare

parsley ['pɑ:sli] *n* prezzemolo

parsnip ['pɑ:snip] *n* pastinaca

parson ['pɑ:sn] *n* prete *m*; (*Church of England*) parroco

part [pɑ:t] *n* parte *f*; (*of machine*) pezzo; (*US: in hair*) scriminatura ♦ *adj* in parte ♦ *adv* = **partly** ♦ *vt* separare ♦ *vi* (*people*) separarsi; **to take ~ in** prendere parte a; **for my ~** per parte mia; **to take sth in good ~** prendere bene qc; **to take sb's ~** parteggiare per *or* prendere le parti di qn; **for the most ~** in generale; nella maggior parte dei casi; **~ with** *vt fus* separarsi da; rinunciare a; **~ exchange** (*BRIT*) *n*: **in ~ exchange** in pagamento parziale

partial ['pɑ:ʃl] *adj* parziale; **to be ~ to** avere un debole per

participate [pɑ:'tisipeit] *vi*: **to ~ (in)** prendere parte (a), partecipare (a); **participation** [-'peiʃən] *n* partecipazione *f*

participle ['pɑ:tisipl] *n* participio

particle ['pɑ:tikl] *n* particella

particular [pə'tikjulə*] *adj* particolare; speciale; (*fussy*) difficile; meticoloso(a); **in ~** in particolare, particolarmente; **~ly** *adv* particolarmente; in particolare; **~s** *npl* particolari *mpl*, dettagli *mpl*; (*information*) informazioni *fpl*

parting ['pɑ:tiŋ] *n* separazione *f*; (*BRIT: in hair*) scriminatura ♦ *adj* d'addio

partisan [pɑ:ti'zæn] *n* partigiano/a ♦ *adj* partigiano(a); di parte

partition [pɑ:'tiʃən] *n* (*POL*) partizione *f*; (*wall*) tramezzo

partly ['pɑ:tli] *adv* parzialmente; in parte

partner ['pɑ:tnə*] *n* (*COMM*) socio/a; (*wife, husband etc, SPORT*) compagno/a; (*at dance*) cavaliere/dama; **~ship** *n* associazione *f*; (*COMM*) società *f inv*

partridge ['pɑ:tridʒ] *n* pernice *f*

part-time *adj, adv* a orario ridotto

party ['pɑ:ti] *n* (*POL*) partito; (*group*) gruppo; (*LAW*) parte *f*; (*celebration*) ricevimento; serata; festa ♦ *cpd* (*POL*) del partito, di partito; **~ dress** *n* vestito della festa

pass [pɑ:s] *vt* (*gen*) passare; (*place*) passare davanti a; (*exam*) passare, superare; (*candidate*) promuovere; (*overtake, surpass*) sorpassare, superare; (*approve*) approvare ♦ *vi* passare ♦ *n* (*permit*) lasciapassare *m inv*; permesso; (*in mountains*) passo, gola;

(*SPORT*) passaggio; (*SCOL*): **to get a ~** prendere la sufficienza; **to ~ sth through a hole** *etc* far passare qc attraverso un buco *etc*; **to make a ~ at sb** (*inf*) fare delle proposte *or* delle avances a qn; **~ away** *vi* morire; **~ by** *vi* passare ♦ *vt* trascurare; **~ on** *vt* passare; **~ out** *vi* svenire; **~ up** *vt* (*opportunity*) lasciarsi sfuggire, perdere; **~able** *adj* (*road*) praticabile; (*work*) accettabile

passage ['pæsɪdʒ] *n* (*gen*) passaggio; (*also:* **~way**) corridoio; (*in book*) brano, passo; (*by boat*) traversata

passbook ['pɑːsbuk] *n* libretto di risparmio

passenger ['pæsɪndʒə*] *n* passeggero/a

passer-by [pɑːsə'baɪ] *n* passante *m/f*

passing ['pɑːsɪŋ] *adj* (*fig*) fuggevole; **to mention sth in ~** accennare a qc di sfuggita; **~ place** *n* (*AUT*) piazzola di sosta

passion ['pæʃən] *n* passione *f*; amore *m*; **~ate** *adj* appassionato(a)

passive ['pæsɪv] *adj* (*also* LING) passivo(a); **~ smoking** *n* fumo passivo

Passover ['pɑːsəuvə*] *n* Pasqua ebraica

passport ['pɑːspɔːt] *n* passaporto; **~ control** *n* controllo *m* passaporti *inv*; **~ office** *n* ufficio *m* passaporti *inv*

password ['pɑːswɔːd] *n* parola d'ordine

past [pɑːst] *prep* (*further than*) oltre, di là di; dopo; (*later than*) dopo ♦ *adj* passato(a); (*president etc*) ex *inv* ♦ *n* passato; **he's ~ forty** ha più di quarant'anni; **ten ~ eight** le otto e dieci; **for the ~ few days** da qualche giorno; in questi ultimi giorni; **to run ~** passare di corsa

pasta ['pæstə] *n* pasta

paste [peɪst] *n* (*glue*) colla; (*CULIN*) pâté *m inv*; pasta ♦ *vt* incollare

pastel ['pæstl] *adj* pastello *inv*

pasteurized ['pæstəraɪzd] *adj* pastorizzato(a)

pastille ['pæstl] *n* pastiglia

pastime ['pɑːstaɪm] *n* passatempo

pastry ['peɪstrɪ] *n* pasta

pasture ['pɑːstʃə*] *n* pascolo

pasty¹ ['pæstɪ] *n* pasticcio di carne

pasty² ['peɪstɪ] *adj* (*face etc*) smorto(a)

pat [pæt] *vt* accarezzare, dare un colpetto (affettuoso) a

patch [pætʃ] *n* (*of material, on tyre*) toppa; (*eye ~*) benda; (*spot*) macchia ♦ *vt* (*clothes*) rattoppare; **(to go through) a bad ~** (attraversare) un brutto periodo; **~ up** *vt* rappezzare; (*quarrel*) appianare; **~y** *adj* irregolare

pâté ['pæteɪ] *n* pâté *m inv*

patent ['peɪtnt] *n* brevetto ♦ *vt* brevettare ♦ *adj* patente, manifesto(a); **~ leather** *n* cuoio verniciato

paternal [pə'tɜːnl] *adj* paterno(a)

path [pɑːθ] *n* sentiero, viottolo; viale *m*; (*fig*) via, strada; (*of planet, missile*) traiettoria

pathetic [pə'θetɪk] *adj* (*pitiful*) patetico(a); (*very bad*) penoso(a)

pathological [pæθə'lɒdʒɪkl] *adj* patologico(a)

pathway ['pɑːθweɪ] *n* sentiero

patience ['peɪʃns] *n* pazienza; (*BRIT*: CARDS) solitario

patient ['peɪʃnt] *n* paziente *m/f*; malato/a ♦ *adj* paziente

patio ['pætɪəu] *n* terrazza

patriot ['peɪtrɪət] *n* patriota *m/f*; **~ic** [pætrɪ'ɔtɪk] *adj* patriottico(a); **~ism** *n* patriottismo

patrol [pə'trəul] *n* pattuglia ♦ *vt* pattugliare; **~ car** *n* autoradio *f inv* (della polizia); **~man** (*US: irreg*) *n* poliziotto

patron ['peɪtrən] *n* (*in shop*) cliente *m/f*; (*of charity*) benefattore/trice; **~ of the arts** mecenate *m/f*; **~ize** ['pætrənaɪz] *vt* essere cliente abituale di; (*fig*) trattare dall'alto in basso

patter ['pætə*] *n* picchiettio; (*sales talk*) propaganda di vendita ♦ *vi* picchiettare; **a ~ of footsteps** un rumore di passi

pattern ['pætən] *n* modello; (*design*) disegno, motivo

pauper ['pɔːpə*] *n* indigente *m/f*

pause [pɔːz] *n* pausa ♦ *vi* fare una pausa, arrestarsi

pave [peɪv] *vt* pavimentare; **to ~ the way for** aprire la via a

pavement ['peɪvmənt] (*BRIT*) *n* marciapiede

m

pavilion [pə'vɪlɪən] *n* (SPORT) *edificio annesso a campo sportivo*

paving ['peɪvɪŋ] *n* pavimentazione *f*; ~ **stone** *n* lastra di pietra

paw [pɔː] *n* zampa

pawn [pɔːn] *n* (CHESS) pedone *m*; (fig) pedina ♦ *vt* dare in pegno; ~**broker** *n* prestatore *m* su pegno; ~**shop** *n* monte *m* di pietà

pay [peɪ] (*pt, pp* paid) *n* stipendio; paga ♦ *vt* pagare ♦ *vi* (*be profitable*) rendere; to ~ **attention** (**to**) fare attenzione (a); to ~ **sb a visit** far visita a qn; to ~ **one's respects to sb** porgere i propri rispetti a qn; ~ **back** *vt* rimborsare; ~ **for** *vt fus* pagare; ~ **in** *vt* versare; ~ **off** *vt* (*debt*) saldare; (*person*) pagare; (*employee*) pagare e licenziare ♦ *vi* (*scheme, decision*) dare dei frutti; ~ **up** *vt* saldare; ~**able** *adj* pagabile; ~**ee** *n* beneficiario/a; ~ **envelope** (US) *n* = ~ **packet**; ~**ing** *adj*: ~**ing guest** ospite *m/f* pagante, pensionante *m/f*; ~**ment** *n* pagamento; versamento; saldo; ~ **packet** (BRIT) *n* busta *f* paga *inv*; ~ **phone** *n* cabina telefonica; ~**roll** *n* ruolo (organico); ~ **slip** *n* foglio *m* paga *inv*; ~ **television** *n* televisione *f* a pagamento, pay-tv *f inv*

PC *n abbr* = **personal computer**; *adv abbr* = **politically correct**

p.c. *abbr* = **per cent**

pea [piː] *n* pisello

peace [piːs] *n* pace *f*; ~**ful** *adj* pacifico(a), calmo(a)

peach [piːtʃ] *n* pesca

peacock ['piːkɔk] *n* pavone *m*

peak [piːk] *n* (*of mountain*) cima, vetta; (*mountain itself*) picco; (*of cap*) visiera; (fig) apice *m*, culmine *m*; ~ **hours** *npl* ore *fpl* di punta; ~ **period** *n* = ~ **hours**

peal [piːl] *n* (*of bells*) scampanio, carillon *m inv*; ~**s of laughter** scoppi *mpl* di risa

peanut ['piːnʌt] *n* arachide *f*, nocciolina americana; ~ **butter** *n* burro di arachidi

pear [pɛə*] *n* pera

pearl [pɜːl] *n* perla

peasant ['pɛznt] *n* contadino/a

peat [piːt] *n* torba

pebble ['pɛbl] *n* ciottolo

peck [pɛk] *vt* (*also*: ~ **at**) beccare ♦ *n* colpo di becco; (*kiss*) bacetto; ~**ing order** *n* ordine *m* gerarchico; ~**ish** (BRIT: *inf*) *adj*: **I feel ~ish** ho un languorino

peculiar [pɪ'kjuːlɪə*] *adj* strano(a), bizzarro(a); peculiare; ~ **to** peculiare di

pedal ['pɛdl] *n* pedale *m* ♦ *vi* pedalare

pedantic [pɪ'dæntɪk] *adj* pedantesco(a)

peddler ['pɛdlə*] *n* (*also*: **drug** ~) spacciatore/trice

pedestal ['pɛdəstl] *n* piedestallo

pedestrian [pɪ'dɛstrɪən] *n* pedone/a ♦ *adj* pedonale; (fig) prosaico(a), pedestre; ~ **crossing** (BRIT) *n* passaggio pedonale; ~ **precinct** (BRIT), ~ **zone** (US) *n* zona pedonale

pediatrics [piːdɪ'ætrɪks] (US) *n* = **paediatrics**

pedigree ['pɛdɪɡriː] *n* (*of animal*) pedigree *m inv*; (fig) background *m inv* ♦ *cpd* (*animal*) di razza

pee [piː] (*inf*) *vi* pisciare

peek [piːk] *vi* guardare furtivamente

peel [piːl] *n* buccia; (*of orange, lemon*) scorza ♦ *vt* sbucciare ♦ *vi* (*paint etc*) staccarsi

peep [piːp] *n* (BRIT: *look*) sguardo furtivo, sbirciata; (*sound*) pigolio ♦ *vi* (BRIT) guardare furtivamente; ~ **out** *vi* mostrarsi furtivamente; ~**hole** *n* spioncino

peer [pɪə*] *vi*: to ~ **at** scrutare ♦ *n* (*noble*) pari *m inv*; (*equal*) pari *m/f inv*, uguale *m/f*; (*contemporary*) contemporaneo/a; ~**age** *n* dignità di pari; pari *mpl*

peeved [piːvd] *adj* stizzito(a)

peevish ['piːvɪʃ] *adj* stizzoso(a)

peg [pɛɡ] *n* caviglia; (*for coat etc*) attaccapanni *m inv*; (BRIT: *also*: **clothes** ~) molletta

Peking [piː'kɪŋ] *n* Pechino *f*

pelican ['pɛlɪkən] *n* pellicano; ~ **crossing** (BRIT) *n* (AUT) *attraversamento pedonale con semaforo a controllo manuale*

pellet ['pɛlɪt] *n* pallottola, pallina

pelt [pɛlt] *vt*: to ~ **sb (with)** bombardare qn

(con); ♦ *vi* (*rain*) piovere a dirotto; (*inf: run*) filare ♦ *n* pelle *f*

pelvis ['pelvɪs] *n* pelvi *f inv,* bacino

pen [pen] *n* penna; (*for sheep*) recinto

penal ['piːnl] *adj* penale; **~ize** *vt* punire; (*SPORT, fig*) penalizzare

penalty ['penltɪ] *n* penalità *f inv*; sanzione *f* penale; (*fine*) ammenda; (*SPORT*) penalizzazione *f*; **~ (kick)** *n* (*SPORT*) calcio di rigore

penance ['penəns] *n* penitenza

pence [pens] (*BRIT*) *npl of* **penny**

pencil ['pensl] *n* matita; **~ case** *n* astuccio per matite; **~ sharpener** *n* temperamatite *m inv*

pendant ['pendnt] *n* pendaglio

pending ['pendɪŋ] *prep* in attesa di ♦ *adj* in sospeso

pendulum ['pendjuləm] *n* pendolo

penetrate ['penɪtreɪt] *vt* penetrare

penfriend ['penfrend] (*BRIT*) *n* corrispondente *m/f*

penguin ['peŋgwɪn] *n* pinguino

penicillin [penɪ'sɪlɪn] *n* penicillina

peninsula [pə'nɪnsjulə] *n* penisola

penis ['piːnɪs] *n* pene *m*

penitentiary [penɪ'tenʃərɪ] (*US*) *n* carcere *m*

penknife ['pennaɪf] *n* temperino

pen name *n* pseudonimo

penniless ['penɪlɪs] *adj* senza un soldo

penny ['penɪ] (*pl* **pennies** *or* **pence** (*BRIT*)) *n* penny *m*; (*US*) centesimo

penpal ['penpæl] *n* corrispondente *m/f*

pension ['penʃən] *n* pensione *f*; **~er** (*BRIT*) *n* pensionato/a

pensive ['pensɪv] *adj* pensoso(a)

penthouse ['penthaus] *n* appartamento (di lusso) nell'attico

pent-up ['pentʌp] *adj* (*feelings*) represso(a)

people ['piːpl] *npl* gente *f*; persone *fpl*; (*citizens*) popolo ♦ *n* (*nation, race*) popolo; **4/several ~ came** 4/parecchie persone sono venute; **~ say that ...** si dice che ....

pep [pep] (*inf*): **~ up** *vt* vivacizzare; (*food*) rendere più gustoso(a)

pepper ['pepə*] *n* pepe *m*; (*vegetable*) peperone *m* ♦ *vt* (*fig*): **to ~ with** spruzzare

di; **~mint** *n* (*sweet*) pasticca di menta

peptalk ['peptɔːk] (*inf*) *n* discorso di incoraggiamento

per [pɜː*] *prep* per; a; **~ hour** all'ora; **~ kilo** *etc* il chilo *etc*; **~ day** al giorno; **~ annum** *adv* all'anno; **~ capita** *adj, adv* pro capite *inv*

perceive [pə'siːv] *vt* percepire; (*notice*) accorgersi di

per cent [pə'sent] *adv* per cento

percentage [pə'sentɪdʒ] *n* percentuale *f*

perception [pə'sepʃən] *n* percezione *f*; sensibilità; perspicacia

perceptive [pə'septɪv] *adj* percettivo(a); perspicace

perch [pɜːtʃ] *n* (*fish*) pesce *m* persico; (*for bird*) sostegno, ramo ♦ *vi* appollaiarsi

percolator ['pɜːkəleɪtə*] *n* (*also:* **coffee ~**) caffettiera a pressione; caffettiera elettrica

percussion [pə'kʌʃən] *n* percussione *f*; (*MUS*) strumenti *mpl* a percussione

perennial [pə'renɪəl] *adj* perenne

perfect [*adj, n* 'pɜːfɪkt, *vb* pə'fekt] *adj* perfetto(a) ♦ *n* (*also:* **~ tense**) perfetto, passato prossimo ♦ *vt* perfezionare; mettere a punto; **~ly** *adv* perfettamente, alla perfezione

perforate ['pɜːfəreɪt] *vt* perforare; **perforation** [-'reɪʃən] *n* perforazione *f*

perform [pə'fɔːm] *vt* (*carry out*) eseguire, fare; (*symphony etc*) suonare; (*play, ballet*) dare; (*opera*) fare ♦ *vi* suonare; recitare; **~ance** *n* esecuzione *f*; (*at theatre etc*) rappresentazione *f*, spettacolo; (*of an artist*) interpretazione *f*; (*of player etc*) performance *f*; (*of car, engine*) prestazione *f*; **~er** *n* artista *m/f*

perfume ['pɜːfjuːm] *n* profumo

perhaps [pə'hæps] *adv* forse

peril ['perɪl] *n* pericolo

perimeter [pə'rɪmɪtə*] *n* perimetro

period ['pɪərɪəd] *n* periodo; (*HISTORY*) epoca; (*SCOL*) lezione *f*; (*full stop*) punto; (*MED*) mestruazioni *fpl* ♦ *adj* (*costume, furniture*) d'epoca; **~ic(al)** [-'ɔdɪk(l)] *adj* periodico(a); **~ical** [-'ɔdɪkl] *n* periodico

peripheral [pə'rɪfərəl] *adj* periferico(a) ♦ *n*

(COMPUT) unità f inv periferica
perish ['perɪʃ] vi perire, morire; (decay) deteriorarsi; **~able** adj deperibile
perjury ['pɜːdʒərɪ] n spergiuro
perk [pɜːk] (inf) n vantaggio; **~ up** vi (cheer up) rianimarsi
perm [pɜːm] n (for hair) permanente f
permanent ['pɜːmənənt] adj permanente
permeate ['pɜːmɪeɪt] vi penetrare ♦ vt permeare
permissible [pə'mɪsɪbl] adj permissibile, ammissibile
permission [pə'mɪʃən] n permesso
permissive [pə'mɪsɪv] adj permissivo(a)
permit [n 'pɜːmɪt, vb pə'mɪt] n permesso ♦ vt permettere; **to ~ sb to do** permettere a qn di fare
perpendicular [pɜːpən'dɪkjulə*] adj perpendicolare ♦ n perpendicolare f
perplex [pə'pleks] vt lasciare perplesso(a)
persecute ['pɜːsɪkjuːt] vt perseguitare
persevere [pɜːsɪ'vɪə*] vi perseverare
Persian ['pɜːʃən] adj persiano(a) ♦ n (LING) persiano; **the (~) Gulf** n il Golfo Persico
persist [pə'sɪst] vi: **to ~ (in doing)** persistere (nel fare); ostinarsi (a fare); **~ent** adj persistente; ostinato(a)
person ['pɜːsn] n persona; **in ~** di or in persona, personalmente; **~al** adj personale; individuale; **~al assistant** n segretaria personale; **~al column** n = messaggi mpl personali; **~al computer** n personal computer m inv; **~ality** [-'nælɪtɪ] n personalità f inv; **~ally** adv personalmente; **to take sth ~ally** prendere qc come una critica personale; **~al organizer** n (Filofax ®) Fulltime ®; (electronic) agenda elettronica; **~al stereo** n Walkman ® m inv
personnel [pɜːsə'nel] n personale m
perspective [pə'spektɪv] n prospettiva
Perspex ® ['pɜːspeks] (BRIT) n tipo di resina termoplastica
perspiration [pɜːspɪ'reɪʃən] n traspirazione f, sudore m
persuade [pə'sweɪd] vt: **to ~ sb to do sth** persuadere qn a fare qc

perturb [pə'tɜːb] vt turbare
pervert [n 'pɜːvəːt, vb pə'vəːt] n pervertito/a ♦ vt pervertire
pessimism ['pesɪmɪzəm] n pessimismo
pessimist ['pesɪmɪst] n pessimista m/f; **~ic** [-'mɪstɪk] adj pessimistico(a)
pest [pest] n animale m (or insetto) pestifero; (fig) peste f
pester ['pestə*] vt tormentare, molestare
pet [pet] n animale m domestico ♦ cpd favorito(a) ♦ vt accarezzare; **teacher's ~** favorito/a del maestro
petal ['petl] n petalo
peter ['piːtə*]: **to ~ out** vi esaurirsi; estinguersi
petite [pə'tiːt] adj piccolo(a) e aggraziato(a)
petition [pə'tɪʃən] n petizione f
petrified ['petrɪfaɪd] adj (fig) morto(a) di paura
petrol ['petrəl] (BRIT) n benzina; **two/four-star ~** ≈ benzina normale/super; **~ can** n tanica per benzina
petroleum [pə'trəuləm] n petrolio
petrol: ~ pump (BRIT) n (in car, at garage) pompa di benzina; **~ station** (BRIT) n stazione f di rifornimento; **~ tank** (BRIT) n serbatoio della benzina
petticoat ['petɪkəut] n sottana
petty ['petɪ] adj (mean) meschino(a); (unimportant) insignificante; **~ cash** n piccola cassa; **~ officer** n sottufficiale m di marina
petulant ['petjulənt] adj irritabile
pew [pjuː] n (in chiesa)
pewter ['pjuːtə*] n peltro
phallic ['fælɪk] adj fallico(a)
phantom ['fæntəm] n fantasma m
pharmaceutical [fɑːmə'sjuːtɪkl] adj farmaceutico(a)
pharmacy ['fɑːməsɪ] n farmacia
phase [feɪz] n fase f, periodo ♦ vt: **to ~ sth in/out** introdurre/eliminare qc progressivamente
Ph.D. n abbr = **Doctor of Philosophy**
pheasant ['feznt] n fagiano
phenomena [fə'nɔmɪnə] npl of **phenomenon**

phenomenon [fə'nɔmɪnən] (*pl* **phenomena**) *n* fenomeno
Philippines ['fɪlɪpiːnz] *npl*: **the ~** le Filippine
philosophical [fɪlə'sɔfɪkl] *adj* filosofico(a)
philosophy [fɪ'lɔsəfɪ] *n* filosofia
phobia ['fəubjə] *n* fobia
phone [fəun] *n* telefono ♦ *vt* telefonare; **to be on the ~** avere il telefono; (*be calling*) essere al telefono; **~ back** *vt, vi* richiamare; **~ up** *vt* telefonare a ♦ *vi* telefonare; **~ book** *n* guida del telefono, elenco telefonico; **~ booth** *n* = **~ box**; **~ box** *n* cabina telefonica; **~ call** *n* telefonata; **~card** *n* scheda telefonica; **~-in** *n* (BRIT: RADIO, TV) trasmissione *f* a filo diretto con gli ascoltatori
phonetics [fə'netɪks] *n* fonetica
phoney ['fəunɪ] *adj* falso(a), fasullo(a)
phosphorus ['fɔsfərəs] *n* fosforo
photo ['fəutəu] *n* foto *f inv*
photo... ['fəutəu] *prefix*: **~copier** *n* fotocopiatrice *f*; **~copy** *n* fotocopia ♦ *vt* fotocopiare; **~graph** *n* fotografia ♦ *vt* fotografare; **~grapher** [fə'tɔɡrəfə*] *n* fotografo; **~graphy** [fə'tɔɡrəfɪ] *n* fotografia
phrase [freɪz] *n* espressione *f*; (LING) locuzione *f*; (MUS) frase *f* ♦ *vt* esprimere; **~ book** *n* vocabolarietto
physical ['fɪzɪkl] *adj* fisico(a); **~ education** *n* educazione *f* fisica; **~ly** *adv* fisicamente
physician [fɪ'zɪʃən] *n* medico
physicist ['fɪzɪsɪst] *n* fisico
physics ['fɪzɪks] *n* fisica
physiology [fɪzɪ'ɔlədʒɪ] *n* fisiologia
physique [fɪ'ziːk] *n* fisico; costituzione *f*
pianist ['pɪ:ənɪst] *n* pianista *m/f*
piano [pɪ'ænəu] *n* pianoforte *m*
piccolo ['pɪkələu] *n* ottavino
pick [pɪk] *n* (*tool: also*: **~-axe**) piccone *m* ♦ *vt* scegliere; (*gather*) cogliere; (*remove*) togliere; (*lock*) far scattare; **take your ~** scelga; **the ~ of** il fior fiore di; **to ~ one's nose** mettersi le dita nel naso; **to ~ one's teeth** pulirsi i denti con lo stuzzicadenti; **to ~ a quarrel** attaccar briga; **~ at** *vt fus*: **to ~ at one's food** piluccare; **~ on** *vt fus*

(*person*) avercela con; **~ out** *vt* scegliere; (*distinguish*) distinguere; **~ up** *vi* (*improve*) migliorarsi ♦ *vt* raccogliere; (POLICE, RADIO) prendere; (*collect*) passare a prendere; (AUT: *give lift to*) far salire; (*person: for sexual encounter*) rimorchiare; (*learn*) imparare; **to ~ up speed** acquistare velocità; **to ~ o.s. up** rialzarsi
picket ['pɪkɪt] *n* (*in strike*) scioperante *m/f* che fa parte di un picchetto; picchetto ♦ *vt* picchettare
pickle ['pɪkl] *n* (*also*: **~s**: *as condiment*) sottaceti *mpl*; (*fig: mess*) pasticcio ♦ *vt* mettere sottaceto; mettere in salamoia
pickpocket ['pɪkpɔkɪt] *n* borsaiolo
pickup ['pɪkʌp] *n* (*small truck*) camioncino
picnic ['pɪknɪk] *n* picnic *m inv*
picture ['pɪktʃə*] *n* quadro; (*painting*) pittura; (*photograph*) foto(grafia); (*drawing*) disegno; (*film*) film *m inv* ♦ *vt* raffigurarsi; **~s** (BRIT) *npl* (*cinema*): **the ~s** il cinema; **~ book** *n* libro illustrato
picturesque [pɪktʃə'resk] *adj* pittoresco(a)
pie [paɪ] *n* torta; (*of meat*) pasticcio
piece [piːs] *n* pezzo; (*of land*) appezzamento; (*item*): **a ~ of furniture/ advice** un mobile/consiglio ♦ *vt*: **to ~ together** mettere insieme; **to take to ~s** smontare; **~meal** *adv* pezzo a pezzo, a spizzico; **~work** *n* (lavoro a) cottimo
pie chart *n* grafico a torta
pier [pɪə*] *n* molo; (*of bridge etc*) pila
pierce [pɪəs] *vt* forare; (*with arrow etc*) trafiggere
piercing ['pɪəsɪŋ] *adj* (*cry*) acuto(a); (*eyes*) penetrante; (*wind*) pungente
pig [pɪɡ] *n* maiale *m*, porco
pigeon ['pɪdʒən] *n* piccione *m*; **~hole** *n* casella
piggy bank ['pɪɡɪ-] *n* salvadanaro
pigheaded ['pɪɡ'hedɪd] *adj* caparbio(a), cocciuto(a)
piglet ['pɪɡlɪt] *n* porcellino
pigskin ['pɪɡskɪn] *n* cinghiale *m*
pigsty ['pɪɡstaɪ] *n* porcile *m*
pigtail ['pɪɡteɪl] *n* treccina
pike [paɪk] *n* (*fish*) luccio

pilchard ['pɪltʃəd] n *specie di sardina*

pile [paɪl] n (*pillar, of books*) pila; (*heap*) mucchio; (*of carpet*) pelo ♦ vt (*also:* ~ **up**) ammucchiare ♦ vi (*also:* ~ **up**) ammucchiarsi; **to** ~ **into** (*car*) stiparsi *or* ammucchiarsi in

piles [paɪlz] npl emorroidi fpl

pile-up ['paɪlʌp] n (AUT) tamponamento a catena

pilfering ['pɪlfərɪŋ] n rubacchiare m

pilgrim ['pɪlgrɪm] n pellegrino/a; **~age** n pellegrinaggio

pill [pɪl] n pillola; **the** ~ la pillola

pillage ['pɪlɪdʒ] vt saccheggiare

pillar ['pɪlə*] n colonna; ~ **box** (BRIT) n cassetta postale

pillion ['pɪljən] n: **to ride** ~ (*on motor cycle*) viaggiare dietro

pillow ['pɪləʊ] n guanciale m; **~case** n federa

pilot ['paɪlət] n pilota m/f ♦ cpd (*scheme etc*) pilota inv ♦ vt pilotare; ~ **light** n fiamma pilota

pimp [pɪmp] n mezzano

pimple ['pɪmpl] n foruncolo

pin [pɪn] n spillo; (TECH) perno ♦ vt attaccare con uno spillo; **~s and needles** formicolio; **to** ~ **sb down** (*fig*) obbligare qn a pronunziarsi; **to** ~ **sth on sb** (*fig*) addossare la colpa di qc a qn

pinafore ['pɪnəfɔ:*] n (*also:* ~ **dress**) grembiule m (senza maniche)

pinball ['pɪnbɔ:l] n flipper m inv

pincers ['pɪnsəz] npl pinzette fpl

pinch [pɪntʃ] n pizzicotto, pizzico ♦ vt pizzicare; (*inf: steal*) grattare; **at a** ~ in caso di bisogno

pincushion ['pɪnkʊʃən] n puntaspilli m inv

pine [paɪn] n (*also:* ~ **tree**) pino ♦ vi: **to** ~ **for** struggersi dal desiderio di; ~ **away** vi languire

pineapple ['paɪnæpl] n ananas m inv

ping [pɪŋ] n (*noise*) tintinnio; **~-pong** ® n ping-pong ® m

pink [pɪŋk] adj rosa inv ♦ n (*colour*) rosa m inv; (BOT) garofano

PIN (number) [pɪn-] n abbr codice m

segreto

pinpoint ['pɪnpɔɪnt] vt indicare con precisione

pint [paɪnt] n pinta (BRIT = 0.57l; US = 0.47l); (BRIT: inf) ≈ birra da mezzo

pioneer [paɪə'nɪə*] n pioniere/a

pious ['paɪəs] adj pio(a)

pip [pɪp] n (*seed*) seme m; (BRIT: *time signal on radio*) segnale m orario

pipe [paɪp] n tubo; (*for smoking*) pipa ♦ vt portare per mezzo di tubazione; ~**s** npl (*also:* **bag~s**) cornamusa (scozzese); ~ **cleaner** n scovolino; ~ **dream** n vana speranza; **~line** n conduttura; (*for oil*) oleodotto; **~r** n piffero; suonatore/trice di cornamusa

piping ['paɪpɪŋ] adv: ~ **hot** caldo bollente

pique [pi:k] n picca

pirate ['paɪərət] n pirata m ♦ vt riprodurre abusivamente

Pisces ['paɪsi:z] n Pesci mpl

piss [pɪs] (*inf*) vi pisciare; **~ed** (*inf*) adj (*drunk*) ubriaco(a) fradicio(a)

pistol ['pɪstl] n pistola

piston ['pɪstən] n pistone m

pit [pɪt] n buca, fossa; (*also:* **coal** ~) miniera; (*quarry*) cava ♦ vt: **to** ~ **sb against sb** opporre qn a qn; ~**s** npl (AUT) box m

pitch [pɪtʃ] n (BRIT: SPORT) campo; (MUS) tono; (*tar*) pece f; (*fig*) grado, punto ♦ vt (*throw*) lanciare ♦ vi (*fall*) cascare; **to** ~ **a tent** piantare una tenda; **~ed battle** n battaglia campale

pitfall ['pɪtfɔ:l] n trappola

pith [pɪθ] n (*of plant*) midollo; (*of orange*) parte f interna della scorza; (*fig*) essenza, succo; vigore m

pithy ['pɪθɪ] adj conciso(a); vigoroso(a)

pitiful ['pɪtɪful] adj (*touching*) pietoso(a)

pitiless ['pɪtɪlɪs] adj spietato(a)

pittance ['pɪtns] n miseria, magro salario

pity ['pɪtɪ] n pietà ♦ vt aver pietà di; **what a** ~! che peccato!

pivot ['pɪvət] n perno

pizza ['pi:tsə] n pizza

placard ['plækɑ:d] n affisso

placate [plə'keɪt] vt placare, calmare

place [pleɪs] *n* posto, luogo; (*proper position, rank, seat*) posto; (*house*) casa, alloggio; (*home*): **at/to his ~** a casa sua ♦ *vt* (*object*) posare, mettere; (*identify*) riconoscere; individuare; **to take ~** aver luogo; succedere; **to change ~s with sb** scambiare il posto con qn; **out of ~** (*not suitable*) inopportuno(a); **in the first ~** in primo luogo; **to ~ an order** dare un'ordinazione; **to be ~d** (*in race, exam*) classificarsi

placid [ˈplæsɪd] *adj* placido(a), calmo(a)

plagiarism [ˈpleɪdʒərɪzəm] *n* plagio

plague [pleɪg] *n* peste *f* ♦ *vt* tormentare

plaice [pleɪs] *n inv* pianuzza

plaid [plæd] *n* plaid *m inv*

plain [pleɪn] *adj* (*clear*) chiaro(a), palese; (*simple*) semplice; (*frank*) franco(a), aperto(a); (*not handsome*) bruttino(a); (*without seasoning etc*) scondito(a); naturale; (*in one colour*) tinta unita *inv* ♦ *adv* francamente, chiaramente ♦ *n* pianura; **~ chocolate** *n* cioccolato fondente; **~ clothes** *npl*: **in ~ clothes** (*police*) in borghese; **~ly** *adv* chiaramente; (*frankly*) francamente

plaintiff [ˈpleɪntɪf] *n* attore/trice

plaintive [ˈpleɪntɪv] *adj* (*cry, voice*) dolente, lamentoso(a)

plait [plæt] *n* treccia

plan [plæn] *n* pianta; (*scheme*) progetto, piano ♦ *vt* (*think in advance*) progettare; (*prepare*) organizzare ♦ *vi* far piani *or* progetti; **to ~ to do** progettare di fare

plane [pleɪn] *n* (*AVIAT*) aereo; (*tree*) platano; (*tool*) pialla; (*ART, MATH etc*) piano ♦ *adj* piano(a), piatto(a) ♦ *vt* (*with tool*) piallare

planet [ˈplænɪt] *n* pianeta *m*

plank [plæŋk] *n* tavola, asse *f*

planner [ˈplænə*] *n* pianificatore/trice

planning [ˈplænɪŋ] *n* progettazione *f*; **family ~** pianificazione *f* delle nascite; **~ permission** *n* permesso di costruzione

plant [plɑːnt] *n* pianta; (*machinery*) impianto; (*factory*) fabbrica ♦ *vt* piantare; (*bomb*) mettere

plantation [plænˈteɪʃən] *n* piantagione *f*

plaque [plæk] *n* placca

plaster [ˈplɑːstə*] *n* intonaco; (*also*: **~ of Paris**) gesso; (*BRIT: also*: **sticking ~**) cerotto ♦ *vt* intonacare; ingessare; (*cover*): **to ~ with** coprire di; **~ed** (*inf*) *adj* ubriaco(a) fradicio(a)

plastic [ˈplæstɪk] *n* plastica ♦ *adj* (*made of ~*) di *or* in plastica; **~ bag** *n* sacchetto di plastica

Plasticine ® [ˈplæstɪsiːn] *n* plastilina ®

plastic surgery *n* chirurgia plastica

plate [pleɪt] *n* (*dish*) piatto; (*in book*) tavola; (*dental ~*) dentiera; **gold/silver ~** vasellame *m* d'oro/d'argento

plateau [ˈplætəʊ] (*pl* **~s** *or* **~x**) *n* altipiano

plateaux [ˈplætəʊz] *npl of* **plateau**

plate glass *n* vetro piano

platform [ˈplætfɔːm] *n* (*stage, at meeting*) palco; (*RAIL*) marciapiede *m*; (*BRIT: of bus*) piattaforma

platinum [ˈplætɪnəm] *n* platino

platitude [ˈplætɪtjuːd] *n* luogo comune

platoon [pləˈtuːn] *n* plotone *m*

platter [ˈplætə*] *n* piatto

plausible [ˈplɔːzɪbl] *adj* plausibile, credibile; (*person*) convincente

play [pleɪ] *n* gioco; (*THEATRE*) commedia ♦ *vt* (*game*) giocare a; (*team, opponent*) giocare contro; (*instrument, piece of music*) suonare; (*record, tape*) ascoltare; (*role, part*) interpretare ♦ *vi* giocare; suonare; recitare; **to ~ safe** giocare sul sicuro; **~ down** *vt* minimizzare; **~ up** *vi* (*cause trouble*) fare i capricci; **~boy** *n* playboy *m inv*; **~er** *n* giocatore/trice; (*THEATRE*) attore/trice; (*MUS*) musicista *m/f*; **~ful** *adj* giocoso(a); **~ground** *n* (*in school*) cortile *m* per la ricreazione; (*in park*) parco *m* giochi *inv*; **~group** *n* giardino d'infanzia; **~ing card** *n* carta da gioco; **~ing field** *n* campo sportivo; **~mate** *n* compagno/a di gioco; **~-off** *n* (*SPORT*) bella; **~pen** *n* box *m inv*; **~thing** *n* giocattolo; **~time** *n* (*SCOL*) ricreazione *f*; **~wright** *n* drammaturgo/a

plc *abbr* (= *public limited company*) *società per azioni a responsabilità limitata quotata in borsa*

plea [pli:] *n* (*request*) preghiera, domanda; (*LAW*) (argomento di) difesa; **~ bargaining** *n* (*LAW*) patteggiamento (della pena)

plead [pli:d] *vt* patrocinare; (*give as excuse*) adducere a pretesto ♦ *vi* (*LAW*) perorare la causa; (*beg*): **to ~ with sb** implorare qn

pleasant ['plɛznt] *adj* piacevole, gradevole; **~ries** *npl* (*polite remarks*): **to exchange ~ries** scambiarsi i convenevoli

please [pli:z] *excl* per piacere!, per favore!; (*acceptance*): **yes, ~** sì, grazie ♦ *vt* piacere a ♦ *vi* piacere; (*think fit*): **do as you ~** faccia come le pare; **~ yourself!** come ti (*or* le) pare!; **~d** *adj*: **~d (with)** contento(a) (di); **~d to meet you!** piacere!; **pleasing** *adj* piacevole, che fa piacere

pleasure ['plɛʒə*] *n* piacere *m*; "**it's a ~**" "prego"

pleat [pli:t] *n* piega

pledge [plɛdʒ] *n* pegno; (*promise*) promessa ♦ *vt* impegnare; promettere

plentiful ['plɛntɪful] *adj* abbondante, copioso(a)

plenty ['plɛntɪ] *n*: **~ of** tanto(a), molto(a); un'abbondanza di

pleurisy ['pluərɪsɪ] *n* pleurite *f*

pliable ['plaɪəbl] *adj* flessibile; (*fig: person*) malleabile

pliant ['plaɪənt] *adj* = **pliable**

pliers ['plaɪəz] *npl* pinza

plight [plaɪt] *n* situazione *f* critica

plimsolls ['plɪmsəlz] (*BRIT*) *npl* scarpe *fpl* da tennis

plinth [plɪnθ] *n* plinto; piedistallo

plod [plɒd] *vi* camminare a stento; (*fig*) sgobbare

plonk [plɒŋk] (*inf*) *n* (*BRIT: wine*) vino da poco ♦ *vt*: **to ~ sth down** buttare giù qc bruscamente

plot [plɒt] *n* congiura, cospirazione *f*; (*of story, play*) trama; (*of land*) lotto ♦ *vt* (*mark out*) fare la pianta di; rilevare; (: *diagram etc*) tracciare; (*conspire*) congiurare, cospirare ♦ *vi* congiurare

plough [plau] (*US* **plow**) *n* aratro ♦ *vt* (*earth*) arare; **to ~ money into** (*company*

etc) investire danaro in; **~ through** *vt fus* (*snow etc*) procedere a fatica in; **~man's lunch** (*BRIT*) *n* pasto a base di pane, formaggio e birra

ploy [plɔɪ] *n* stratagemma *m*

pluck [plʌk] *vt* (*fruit*) cogliere; (*musical instrument*) pizzicare; (*bird*) spennare; (*hairs*) togliere ♦ *n* coraggio, fegato; **to ~ up courage** farsi coraggio

plug [plʌg] *n* tappo; (*ELEC*) spina; (*AUT: also*: **spark(ing) ~**) candela ♦ *vt* (*hole*) tappare; (*inf: advertise*) spingere; **~ in** *vt* (*ELEC*) attaccare a una presa

plum [plʌm] *n* (*fruit*) susina

plumb [plʌm] *vt*: **to ~ the depths** (*fig*) toccare il fondo

plumber ['plʌmə*] *n* idraulico

plumbing ['plʌmɪŋ] *n* (*trade*) lavoro di idraulico; (*piping*) tubature *fpl*

plummet ['plʌmɪt] *vi*: **to ~ (down)** cadere a piombo

plump [plʌmp] *adj* grassoccio(a) ♦ *vi*: **to ~ for** (*inf: choose*) decidersi per; **~ up** *vt* (*cushion etc*) sprimacciare

plunder ['plʌndə*] *n* saccheggio ♦ *vt* saccheggiare

plunge [plʌndʒ] *n* tuffo; (*fig*) caduta ♦ *vt* immergere ♦ *vi* (*fall*) cadere, precipitare; (*dive*) tuffarsi; **to take the ~** saltare il fosso; **plunging** *adj* (*neckline*) profondo(a)

pluperfect [plu:'pə:fɪkt] *n* piuccheperfetto

plural ['pluərl] *adj* plurale ♦ *n* plurale *m*

plus [plʌs] *n* (*also*: **~ sign**) segno più ♦ *prep* più; **ten/twenty ~** più di dieci/venti

plush [plʌʃ] *adj* lussuoso(a)

ply [plaɪ] *vt* (*a trade*) esercitare ♦ *vi* (*ship*) fare il servizio ♦ *n* (*of wool, rope*) capo; **to ~ sb with drink** dare di bere continuamente a qn; **~wood** *n* legno compensato

P.M. *n abbr* = **prime minister**

p.m. *adv abbr* (= *post meridiem*) del pomeriggio

pneumatic drill [nju:'mætɪk-] *n* martello pneumatico

pneumonia [nju:'məunɪə] *n* polmonite *f*

poach [pəutʃ] *vt* (*cook: egg*) affogare; (: *fish*) cuocere in bianco; (*steal*) cacciare (*or*

pescare) di frodo ♦ *vi* fare il bracconiere;
~er *n* bracconiere *m*

P.O. Box *n abbr* = Post Office Box

pocket ['pɔkɪt] *n* tasca ♦ *vt* intascare; **to be out of ~** (*BRIT*) rimetterci; **~book** (*US*) *n* (*wallet*) portafoglio; **~ knife** *n* temperino; **~ money** *n* paghetta, settimana

pod [pɔd] *n* guscio

podgy ['pɔdʒɪ] *adj* grassoccio(a)

podiatrist [pɔ'diːətrɪst] (*US*) *n* callista *m/f*, pedicure *m/f*

poem ['pəʊɪm] *n* poesia

poet ['pəʊɪt] *n* poeta/essa; **~ic** [-'ɛtɪk] *adj* poetico(a); **~ry** *n* poesia

poignant ['pɔɪnjənt] *adj* struggente

point [pɔɪnt] *n* (*gen*) punto; (*tip: of needle etc*) punta; (*in time*) punto, momento; (*SCOL*) voto; (*main idea, important part*) nocciolo; (*ELEC*) presa (di corrente); (*also*: **decimal ~**): **2 ~ 3 (2.3)** 2 virgola 3 (2,3) ♦ *vt* (*show*) indicare; (*gun etc*): **to ~ sth at** puntare qc contro ♦ *vi*: **to ~ at** mostrare a dito; **~s** *npl* (*AUT*) puntine *fpl*; (*RAIL*) scambio; **to be on the ~ of doing sth** essere sul punto di *or* stare per fare qc; **to make a ~** fare un'osservazione; **to get/miss the ~** capire/non capire; **to come to the ~** venire al fatto; **there's no ~ (in doing)** è inutile (fare); **~ out** *vt* far notare; **~ to** *vt fus* indicare; (*fig*) dimostrare; **~-blank** *adv* (*also*: **at ~-blank range**) a bruciapelo; (*fig*) categoricamente; **~ed** *adj* (*shape*) aguzzo(a), appuntito(a); (*remark*) specifico(a); **~edly** *adv* in maniera inequivocabile; **~er** *n* (*needle*) lancetta; (*fig*) indicazione *f*, consiglio; **~less** *adj* inutile, vano(a); **~ of view** *n* punto di vista

poise [pɔɪz] *n* (*composure*) portamento; **~d** *adj*: **to be ~d to do** tenersi pronto(a) a fare

poison ['pɔɪzn] *n* veleno ♦ *vt* avvelenare; **~ing** *n* avvelenamento; **~ous** *adj* velenoso(a)

poke [pəʊk] *vt* (*fire*) attizzare; (*jab with finger, stick etc*) punzecchiare; (*put*): **to ~ sth in(to)** spingere qc dentro; **~ about** *vi* frugare

poker ['pəʊkə*] *n* attizzatoio; (*CARDS*) poker *m*

poky ['pəʊkɪ] *adj* piccolo(a) e stretto(a)

Poland ['pəʊlənd] *n* Polonia

polar ['pəʊlə*] *adj* polare; **~ bear** *n* orso bianco

Pole [pəʊl] *n* polacco/a

pole [pəʊl] *n* (*of wood*) palo; (*ELEC, GEO*) polo; **~ bean** (*US*) *n* (*runner bean*) fagiolino; **~ vault** *n* salto con l'asta

police [pə'liːs] *n* polizia ♦ *vt* mantenere l'ordine in; **~ car** *n* macchina della polizia; **~man** (*irreg*) *n* poliziotto, agente *m* di polizia; **~ station** *n* posto di polizia; **~woman** (*irreg*) *n* donna *f* poliziotto *inv*

policy ['pɔlɪsɪ] *n* politica; (*also*: **insurance ~**) polizza (d'assicurazione)

polio ['pəʊlɪəʊ] *n* polio *f*

Polish ['pəʊlɪʃ] *adj* polacco(a) ♦ *n* (*LING*) polacco

polish ['pɔlɪʃ] *n* (*for shoes*) lucido; (*for floor*) cera; (*for nails*) smalto; (*shine*) lucentezza, lustro; (*fig: refinement*) raffinatezza ♦ *vt* lucidare; (*fig: improve*) raffinare; **~ off** *vt* (*food*) mangiarsi; **~ed** *adj* (*fig*) raffinato(a)

polite [pə'laɪt] *adj* cortese; **~ness** *n* cortesia

political [pə'lɪtɪkl] *adj* politico(a); **~ly** *adv* politicamente; **~ly correct** politicamente corretto(a)

politician [pɔlɪ'tɪʃən] *n* politico

politics ['pɔlɪtɪks] *n* politica ♦ *npl* (*views, policies*) idee *fpl* politiche

poll [pəʊl] *n* scrutinio; (*votes cast*) voti *mpl*; (*also*: **opinion ~**) sondaggio (d'opinioni) ♦ *vt* ottenere

pollen ['pɔlən] *n* polline *m*

polling day ['pəʊlɪŋ-] (*BRIT*) *n* giorno delle elezioni

polling station ['pəʊlɪŋ-] (*BRIT*) *n* sezione *f* elettorale

pollute [pə'luːt] *vt* inquinare

pollution [pə'luːʃən] *n* inquinamento

polo ['pəʊləʊ] *n* polo; **~-necked** *adj* a collo alto risvoltato; **~ shirt** *n* polo *f inv*

polyester [pɔlɪ'ɛstə*] *n* poliestere *m*

polystyrene [pɔlɪ'staɪriːn] *n* polistirolo

polytechnic [pɔlɪ'tɛknɪk] *n* (*college*) istituto

superiore ad indirizzo tecnologico

polythene ['pɒliθiːn] *n* politene *m*; ~ **bag** *n* sacco di plastica

pomegranate ['pɒmɪgrænɪt] *n* melagrana

pomp [pɒmp] *n* pompa, fasto

pompom ['pɒmpɒm] *n* pompon *m inv*

pompon ['pɒmpɒn] *n* = **pompom**

pompous ['pɒmpəs] *adj* pomposo(a)

pond [pɒnd] *n* pozza; stagno

ponder ['pɒndə*] *vt* ponderare, riflettere su; **~ous** *adj* ponderoso(a), pesante

pong [pɒŋ] (*BRIT: inf*) *n* puzzo

pony ['pəʊnɪ] *n* pony *m inv*; **~tail** *n* coda di cavallo; ~ **trekking** (*BRIT*) *n* escursione *f* a cavallo

poodle ['puːdl] *n* barboncino, barbone *m*

pool [puːl] *n* (*puddle*) pozza; (*pond*) stagno; (*also*: **swimming** ~) piscina; (*fig: of light*) cerchio; (*billiards*) specie di biliardo a buca ♦ *vt* mettere in comune; **~s** *npl* (*football* ~s) ≈ totocalcio; **typing** ~ servizio comune di dattilografia

poor [pʊə*] *adj* povero(a); (*mediocre*) mediocre, cattivo(a) ♦ *npl*: **the** ~ i poveri; ~ **in** povero(a) di; **~ly** *adv* poveramente; male ♦ *adj* indisposto(a), malato(a)

pop [pɒp] *n* (*noise*) schiocco; (*MUS*) musica pop; (*drink*) bibita gasata; (*US: inf: father*) babbo ♦ *vt* (*put*) mettere (in fretta) ♦ *vi* scoppiare; (*cork*) schioccare; ~ **in** *vi* passare; ~ **out** *vi* fare un salto fuori; ~ **up** *vi* apparire, sorgere; **~corn** *n* pop-corn *m*

pope [pəʊp] *n* papa *m*

poplar ['pɒplə*] *n* pioppo

popper ['pɒpə*] *n* bottone *m* a pressione

poppy ['pɒpɪ] *n* papavero

Popsicle ® ['pɒpsɪkl] (*US*) *n* (*ice lolly*) ghiacciolo

populace ['pɒpjʊləs] *n* popolino

popular ['pɒpjʊlə*] *adj* popolare; (*fashionable*) in voga; **~ity** [-'lærɪtɪ] *n* popolarità

population [pɒpjʊ'leɪʃən] *n* popolazione *f*

porcelain ['pɔːslɪn] *n* porcellana

porch [pɔːtʃ] *n* veranda

porcupine ['pɔːkjʊpaɪn] *n* porcospino

pore [pɔː*] *n* poro ♦ *vi*: **to** ~ **over** essere immerso(a) in

pork [pɔːk] *n* carne *f* di maiale

pornographic [pɔːnə'græfɪk] *adj* pornografico(a)

pornography [pɔː'nɒgrəfɪ] *n* pornografia

porpoise ['pɔːpəs] *n* focena

porridge ['pɒrɪdʒ] *n* porridge *m*

port [pɔːt] *n* (*gen, wine*) porto; (*NAUT: left side*) babordo; ~ **of call** (porto di) scalo

portable ['pɔːtəbl] *adj* portatile

porter ['pɔːtə*] *n* (*for luggage*) facchino, portabagagli *m inv*; (*doorkeeper*) portiere *m*, portinaio

portfolio [pɔːt'fəʊlɪəʊ] *n* (*case*) cartella; (*POL, FINANCE*) portafoglio; (*of artist*) raccolta dei propri lavori

porthole ['pɔːthəʊl] *n* oblò *m inv*

portion ['pɔːʃən] *n* porzione *f*

portrait ['pɔːtreɪt] *n* ritratto

portray [pɔː'treɪ] *vt* fare il ritratto di; (*character on stage*) rappresentare; (*in writing*) ritrarre

Portugal ['pɔːtjʊgl] *n* Portogallo

Portuguese [pɔːtjʊ'giːz] *adj* portoghese ♦ *n inv* portoghese *m/f*; (*LING*) portoghese *m*

pose [pəʊz] *n* posa ♦ *vi* posare; (*pretend*): **to** ~ **as** atteggiarsi a, posare a ♦ *vt* porre

posh [pɒʃ] (*inf*) *adj* elegante; (*family*) per bene

position [pə'zɪʃən] *n* posizione *f*; (*job*) posto ♦ *vt* sistemare

positive ['pɒzɪtɪv] *adj* positivo(a); (*certain*) sicuro(a), certo(a); (*definite*) preciso(a); definitivo(a)

posse ['pɒsɪ] (*US*) *n* drappello

possess [pə'zes] *vt* possedere; **~ion** [pə'zeʃən] *n* possesso; **~ions** *npl* (*belongings*) beni *mpl*; **~ive** *adj* possessivo(a)

possibility [pɒsɪ'bɪlɪtɪ] *n* possibilità *f inv*

possible ['pɒsɪbl] *adj* possibile; **as big as** ~ il più grande possibile

possibly ['pɒsɪblɪ] *adv* (*perhaps*) forse; **if you** ~ **can** se le è possibile; **I cannot** ~ **come** proprio non posso venire

post [pəʊst] *n* (*BRIT*) posta; (*: collection*) levata; (*job, situation*) posto; (*MIL*) postazione f; (pole) palo ♦ vt (BRIT: send by post) impostare; (: appoint): **to ~ to** assegnare a; **~age** n affrancatura; **~age stamp** n francobollo; **~al order** n vaglia m inv postale; **~box** (BRIT) n cassetta postale; **~card** n cartolina; **~ code** (BRIT) n codice m (di avviamento) postale

poster ['pəustə*] n manifesto, affisso

poste restante [pəust'restã:nt] (BRIT) n fermo posta m

postgraduate ['pəust'grædjuət] n laureato/a che continua gli studi

posthumous ['pɔstjuməs] adj postumo(a)

postman ['pəustmən] (irreg) n postino

postmark ['pəustmɑ:k] n bollo or timbro postale

post-mortem [-'mɔ:təm] n autopsia

post office n (building) ufficio postale; (organization): **the Post Office** ≈ le Poste e Telecomunicazioni; **Post Office Box** n casella postale

postpone [pəs'pəun] vt rinviare

postscript ['pəustskrɪpt] n poscritto

posture ['pɔstʃə*] n portamento; (pose) posa, atteggiamento

postwar ['pəust'wɔ:*] adj del dopoguerra

posy ['pəuzɪ] n mazzetto di fiori

pot [pɔt] n (for cooking) pentola; casseruola; (tea~) teiera; (coffee~) caffettiera; (for plants, jam) vaso; (inf: marijuana) erba ♦ vt (plant) piantare in vaso; **a ~ of tea for two** tè per due; **to go to ~** (inf: work, performance) andare in malora

potato [pə'teɪtəu] (pl **~es**) n patata; **~ peeler** n sbucciapatate m inv

potent ['pəutnt] adj potente, forte

potential [pə'tɛnʃl] adj potenziale ♦ n possibilità fpl

pothole ['pɔthəul] n (in road) buca; (BRIT: underground) caverna; **potholing** (BRIT) n: **to go potholing** fare speleologia

potluck [pɔt'lʌk] n: **to take ~** tentare la sorte

potted ['pɔtɪd] adj (food) in conserva; (plant) in vaso; (account etc) condensato(a)

potter ['pɔtə*] n vasaio ♦ vi: **to ~ around, ~ about** (BRIT) lavoracchiare; **~y** n ceramiche

fpl; (factory) fabbrica di ceramiche

potty ['pɔtɪ] adj (inf: mad) tocco(a) ♦ n (child's) vasino

pouch [pautʃ] n borsa; (ZOOL) marsupio

poultry ['pəultrɪ] n pollame m

pounce [pauns] vi: **to ~ (on)** piombare (su)

pound [paund] n (weight) libbra; (money) (lira) sterlina ♦ vt (beat) battere; (crush) pestare, polverizzare ♦ vi (beat) battere, martellare; **~ sterling** n sterlina (inglese)

pour [pɔ:*] vt versare ♦ vi riversarsi; (rain) piovere a dirotto; **~ away** vt vuotare; **~ in** vi affluire in gran quantità; **~ off** vt vuotare; **~ out** vi (people) uscire a fiumi ♦ vt vuotare; versare; (fig) sfogare; **~ing** adj: **~ing rain** pioggia torrenziale

pout [paut] vi sporgere le labbra; fare il broncio

poverty ['pɔvətɪ] n povertà, miseria; **~-stricken** adj molto povero(a), misero(a)

powder ['paudə*] n polvere f ♦ vt: **to ~ one's face** incipriarsi il viso; **~ compact** n portacipria m inv; **~ed milk** n latte m in polvere; **~ room** n toilette f inv (per signore)

power ['pauə*] n (strength) potenza, forza; (ability, POL: of party, leader) potere m; (ELEC) corrente f; **to be in ~** (POL etc) essere al potere; **~ cut** (BRIT) n interruzione f or mancanza di corrente; **~ed** adj: **~ed by** azionato(a) da; **~ failure** n interruzione f della corrente elettrica; **~ful** adj potente, forte; **~less** adj impotente; **~less to do** impossibilitato(a) a fare; **~ point** (BRIT) n presa di corrente; **~ station** n centrale f elettrica

p.p. abbr (= per procurationem): **~ J. Smith** per J. Smith; (= pages) p.p.

PR abbr = **public relations**

practicable ['præktɪkəbl] adj (scheme) praticabile

practical ['præktɪkl] adj pratico(a); **~ity** [-'kælɪtɪ] (no pl) n (of situation etc) lato pratico; **~ joke** n beffa; **~ly** adv praticamente

practice ['præktɪs] n pratica; (of profession) esercizio; (at football etc) allenamento;

(*business*) gabinetto; clientela ♦ *vt, vi* (*US*) = **practise; in ~** (*in reality*) in pratica; **out of ~** fuori esercizio

practise ['præktɪs] (*US* **practice**) *vt* (*work at: piano, one's backhand etc*) esercitarsi a; (*train for: skiing, running etc*) allenarsi a; (*a sport, religion*) praticare; (*method*) usare; (*profession*) esercitare ♦ *vi* esercitarsi; (*train*) allenarsi; (*lawyer, doctor*) esercitare; **practising** *adj* (*Christian etc*) praticante; (*lawyer*) che esercita la professione

practitioner [præk'tɪʃənə*] *n* professionista *m/f*

pragmatic [præg'mætɪk] *adj* pragmatico(a)

prairie ['prɛərɪ] *n* prateria

praise [preɪz] *n* elogio, lode *f* ♦ *vt* elogiare, lodare; **~worthy** *adj* lodevole

pram [præm] (*BRIT*) *n* carrozzina

prank [præŋk] *n* burla

prawn [prɔːn] *n* gamberetto

pray [preɪ] *vi* pregare

prayer [prɛə*] *n* preghiera

preach [priːtʃ] *vt, vi* predicare

precarious [prɪ'kɛərɪəs] *adj* precario(a)

precaution [prɪ'kɔːʃən] *n* precauzione *f*

precede [prɪ'siːd] *vt* precedere

precedent ['prɛsɪdənt] *n* precedente *m*

precept ['priːsɛpt] *n* precetto

precinct ['priːsɪŋkt] *n* (*US*) circoscrizione *f*; **~s** *npl* (*of building*) zona recintata; **pedestrian ~** (*BRIT*) zona pedonale; **shopping ~** (*BRIT*) centro commerciale (chiuso al traffico)

precious ['prɛʃəs] *adj* prezioso(a)

precipitate [prɪ'sɪpɪteɪt] *vt* precipitare

precise [prɪ'saɪs] *adj* preciso(a); **~ly** *adv* precisamente

precocious [prɪ'kəʊʃəs] *adj* precoce

precondition [priːkən'dɪʃən] *n* condizione *f* necessaria

predecessor ['priːdɪsɛsə*] *n* predecessore/a

predicament [prɪ'dɪkəmənt] *n* situazione *f* difficile

predict [prɪ'dɪkt] *vt* predire; **~able** *adj* prevedibile

predominantly [prɪ'dɒmɪnəntlɪ] *adv* in maggior parte; soprattutto

predominate [prɪ'dɒmɪneɪt] *vi* predominare

pre-empt [priː'ɛmpt] *vt* pregiudicare

preen [priːn] *vt*: **to ~ itself** (*bird*) lisciarsi le penne; **to ~ o.s.** agghindarsi

prefab ['priːfæb] *n* casa prefabbricata

preface ['prɛfəs] *n* prefazione *f*

prefect ['priːfɛkt] *n* (*BRIT: in school*) studente/essa con funzioni disciplinari; (*French etc, Admin*) prefetto

prefer [prɪ'fɜː*] *vt* preferire; **to ~ doing** *or* **to do** preferire fare; **~ably** ['prɛfrəblɪ] *adv* preferibilmente; **~ence** ['prɛfrəns] *n* preferenza; **~ential** [prɛfə'rɛnʃəl] *adj* preferenziale

prefix ['priːfɪks] *n* prefisso

pregnancy ['prɛgnənsɪ] *n* gravidanza

pregnant ['prɛgnənt] *adj* incinta *af*

prehistoric ['priːhɪs'tɒrɪk] *adj* preistorico(a)

prejudice ['prɛdʒʊdɪs] *n* pregiudizio; (*harm*) torto, danno; **~d** *adj*: **~d (against)** prevenuto(a) (contro); **~d (in favour of)** ben disposto(a) (verso)

preliminary [prɪ'lɪmɪnərɪ] *adj* preliminare

premarital ['priː'mærɪtl] *adj* prematrimoniale

premature ['prɛmətʃʊə*] *adj* prematuro(a)

premenstrual syndrome [priː'mɛnstruəl-] *n* (*MED*) sindrome *f* premestruale

premier ['prɛmɪə*] *adj* primo(a) ♦ *n* (*POL*) primo ministro

première ['prɛmɪɛə*] *n* prima

premise ['prɛmɪs] *n* premessa; **~s** *npl* (*of business, institution*) locale *m*; **on the ~s** sul posto

premium ['priːmɪəm] *n* premio; **to be at a ~** essere ricercatissimo; **~ bond** (*BRIT*) *n* obbligazione *f* a premio

premonition [prɛmə'nɪʃən] *n* premonizione *f*

preoccupied [priː'ɒkjʊpaɪd] *adj* preoccupato(a)

prep [prɛp] *n* (*SCOL: study*) studio

prepaid [priː'peɪd] *adj* pagato(a) in anticipo

preparation [prɛpə'reɪʃən] *n* preparazione *f*; **~s** *npl* (*for trip, war*) preparativi *mpl*

preparatory [prɪˈpærətərɪ] *adj*
preparatorio(a); **~ school** *n* scuola
elementare privata
prepare [prɪˈpɛə*] *vt* preparare ♦ *vi*: **to ~
for** prepararsi a; **~d to** pronto(a) a
preposition [prɛpəˈzɪʃən] *n* preposizione *f*
preposterous [prɪˈpɒstərəs] *adj* assurdo(a)
prep school *n* = **preparatory school**
prerequisite [priːˈrɛkwɪzɪt] *n* requisito
indispensabile
prescribe [prɪˈskraɪb] *vt* (*MED*) prescrivere
prescription [prɪˈskrɪpʃən] *n* prescrizione *f*;
(*MED*) ricetta
presence [ˈprɛzns] *n* presenza; **~ of mind**
presenza di spirito
present [*adj, n* ˈprɛznt, *vb* prɪˈzɛnt] *adj*
presente; (*wife, residence, job*) attuale ♦ *n*
(*actuality*): **the ~** il presente; (*gift*) regalo
♦ *vt* presentare; (*give*): **to ~ sb with sth**
offrire qc a qn; **to give sb a ~** fare un
regalo a qn; **at ~** al momento; **~ation**
[-ˈteɪʃən] *n* presentazione *f*; (*ceremony*)
consegna ufficiale; **~-day** *adj* attuale,
d'oggigiorno; **~er** *n* (*RADIO, TV*)
presentatore/trice; **~ly** *adv* (*soon*) fra poco,
presto; (*at present*) al momento
preservative [prɪˈzɜːvətɪv] *n* conservante *m*
preserve [prɪˈzɜːv] *vt* (*keep safe*) preservare,
proteggere; (*maintain*) conservare; (*food*)
mettere in conserva ♦ *n* (*often pl: jam*)
marmellata; (: *fruit*) frutta sciroppata
preside [prɪˈzaɪd] *vi*: **to ~ (over)** presiedere
(a)
president [ˈprɛzɪdənt] *n* presidente *m*; **~ial**
[-ˈdɛnʃl] *adj* presidenziale
press [prɛs] *n* (*newspapers etc*): **the P~** la
stampa; (*tool, machine*) pressa; (*for wine*)
torchio ♦ *vt* (*push*) premere, pigiare;
(*squeeze*) spremere; (: *hand*) stringere;
(*clothes: iron*) stirare; (*pursue*) incalzare;
(*insist*): **to ~ sth on sb** far accettare qc da
qn ♦ *vi* premere; accalcare; **we are ~ed
for time** ci manca il tempo; **to ~ for sth**
insistere per avere qc; **~ on** *vi* continuare;
~ conference *n* conferenza *f* stampa *inv*;
~ing *adj* urgente; **~ stud** (*BRIT*) *n* bottone
m a pressione; **~-up** (*BRIT*) *n* flessione *f*

sulle braccia
pressure [ˈprɛʃə*] *n* pressione *f*; **to put ~
on sb (to do)** mettere qn sotto pressione
(affinché faccia); **~ cooker** *n* pentola a
pressione; **~ gauge** *n* manometro; **~
group** *n* gruppo di pressione
prestige [prɛsˈtiːʒ] *n* prestigio
presumably [prɪˈzjuːməblɪ] *adv*
presumibilmente
presume [prɪˈzjuːm] *vt* supporre
presumption [prɪˈzʌmpʃən] *n* presunzione
f
presumptuous [prɪˈzʌmpfəs] *adj*
presuntuoso(a)
pretence [prɪˈtɛns] (*US* **pretense**) *n* (*claim*)
pretesa; **to make a ~ of doing** far finta di
fare; **under false ~s** con l'inganno
pretend [prɪˈtɛnd] *vt* (*feign*) fingere ♦ *vi* far
finta; **to ~ to do** far finta di fare
pretense [prɪˈtɛns] (*US*) *n* = **pretence**
pretentious [prɪˈtɛnfəs] *adj* pretenzioso(a)
pretext [ˈpriːtɛkst] *n* pretesto
pretty [ˈprɪtɪ] *adj* grazioso(a), carino(a)
♦ *adv* abbastanza, assai
prevail [prɪˈveɪl] *vi* (*win, be usual*) prevalere;
(*persuade*): **to ~ (up)on sb to do**
persuadere qn a fare; **~ing** *adj* dominante
prevalent [ˈprɛvələnt] *adj* (*belief*)
predominante; (*customs*) diffuso(a);
(*fashion*) corrente; (*disease*) comune
prevent [prɪˈvɛnt] *vt*: **to ~ sb from doing**
impedire a qn di fare; **to ~ sth from
happening** impedire che qc succeda;
~ative *adj* = **~ive**; **~ion** [-ˈvɛnʃən] *n*
prevenzione *f*; **~ive** *adj* preventivo(a)
preview [ˈpriːvjuː] *n* (*of film*) anteprima
previous [ˈpriːvɪəs] *adj* precedente;
anteriore; **~ly** *adv* prima
prewar [ˈpriːˈwɔː*] *adj* anteguerra *inv*
prey [preɪ] *n* preda ♦ *vi*: **to ~ on** far preda
di; **it was ~ing on his mind** lo stava
ossessionando
price [praɪs] *n* prezzo ♦ *vt* (*goods*) fissare il
prezzo di; valutare; **~less** *adj*
inapprezzabile; **~ list** *n* listino (dei) prezzi
prick [prɪk] *n* puntura ♦ *vt* pungere; **to ~ up
one's ears** drizzare gli orecchi

prickle ['prɪkl] n (of plant) spina; (sensation) pizzicore m

prickly ['prɪklɪ] adj spinoso(a); ~ **heat** n sudamina

pride [praɪd] n orgoglio; superbia ♦ vt: **to ~ o.s. on** essere orgoglioso(a) di; vantarsi di

priest [priːst] n prete m, sacerdote m; ~**hood** n sacerdozio

prim [prɪm] adj pudico(a); contegnoso(a)

primarily ['praɪmərɪlɪ] adv principalmente, essenzialmente

primary ['praɪmərɪ] adj primario(a); (first in importance) primo(a) ♦ n (US: election) primarie fpl; ~ **school** (BRIT) n scuola elementare

prime [praɪm] adj primario(a), fondamentale; (excellent) di prima qualità ♦ vt (wood) preparare; (fig) mettere al corrente ♦ n: **in the ~ of life** nel fiore della vita; **P~ Minister** n primo ministro

primeval [praɪ'miːvl] adj primitivo(a)

primitive ['prɪmɪtɪv] adj primitivo(a)

primrose ['prɪmrəuz] n primavera

primus (stove) ® ['praɪməs(-)] (BRIT) n fornello a petrolio

prince [prɪns] n principe m

princess [prɪn'ses] n principessa

principal ['prɪnsɪpl] adj principale ♦ n (headmaster) preside m

principle ['prɪnsɪpl] n principio; **in ~** in linea di principio; **on ~** per principio

print [prɪnt] n (mark) impronta; (letters) caratteri mpl; (fabric) tessuto stampato; (ART, PHOT) stampa ♦ vt imprimere; (publish) stampare, pubblicare; (write in capitals) scrivere in stampatello; **out of ~** esaurito(a); ~**ed matter** n stampe fpl; ~**er** n tipografo; (machine) stampante f; ~**ing** n stampa; ~**-out** n (COMPUT) tabulato

prior ['praɪə*] adj precedente; (claim etc) più importante; ~ **to doing** prima di fare

priority [praɪ'ɔrɪtɪ] n priorità f inv; precedenza

prise [praɪz] vt: **to ~ open** forzare

prison ['prɪzn] n prigione f ♦ cpd (system) carcerario(a); (conditions, food) nelle or delle prigioni; ~**er** n prigioniero/a

pristine ['prɪstiːn] adj immacolato(a)

privacy ['prɪvəsɪ] n solitudine f, intimità

private ['praɪvɪt] adj privato(a); personale ♦ n soldato semplice; **"~"** (on envelope) "riservata"; (on door) "privato"; **in ~** in privato; ~ **enterprise** n iniziativa privata; ~ **eye** n investigatore m privato; ~**ly** adv in privato; (within oneself) dentro di sé; ~ **property** n proprietà privata; **privatize** vt privatizzare

privet ['prɪvɪt] n ligustro

privilege ['prɪvɪlɪdʒ] n privilegio

privy ['prɪvɪ] adj: **to be ~ to** essere al corrente di

prize [praɪz] n premio ♦ adj (example, idiot) perfetto(a); (bull, novel) premiato(a) ♦ vt apprezzare, pregiare; ~**-giving** n premiazione f; ~**winner** n premiato/a

probability [prɔbə'bɪlɪtɪ] n probabilità f inv; **in all ~** con tutta probabilità

probable ['prɔbəbl] adj probabile; **probably** adv probabilmente

probation [prə'beɪʃən] n: **on ~** (employee) in prova; (LAW) in libertà vigilata

probe [prəub] n (MED, SPACE) sonda; (enquiry) indagine f, investigazione f ♦ vt sondare, esplorare; indagare

problem ['prɔbləm] n problema m

procedure [prə'siːdʒə*] n (ADMIN, LAW) procedura; (method) metodo, procedimento

proceed [prə'siːd] vi (go forward) avanzare, andare avanti; (go about it) procedere; (continue): **to ~ (with)** continuare; **to ~ to** andare a; passare a; **to ~ to do** mettersi a fare; ~**ings** npl misure fpl; (LAW) procedimento; (meeting) riunione f; (records) rendiconti mpl; atti mpl; ~**s** ['prəusiːdz] npl profitto, incasso

process ['prəuses] n processo; (method) metodo, sistema m ♦ vt trattare; (information) elaborare; ~**ing** n trattamento; elaborazione f

procession [prə'seʃən] n processione f,

corteo; **funeral** ~ corteo funebre

pro-choice [prəʊ'tʃɔɪs] *adj* per la libertà di scelta di gravidanza

proclaim [prə'kleɪm] *vt* proclamare, dichiarare

procrastinate [prəʊ'kræstɪneɪt] *vi* procrastinare

prod [prɒd] *vt* dare un colpetto a; pungolare ♦ *n* colpetto

prodigal ['prɒdɪgl] *adj* prodigo(a)

prodigy ['prɒdɪdʒɪ] *n* prodigio

produce [*n* 'prɒdjuːs, *vb* prə'djuːs] *n* (*AGR*) prodotto, prodotti *mpl* ♦ *vt* produrre; (*to show*) esibire, mostrare; (*cause*) cagionare, causare; **~r** *n* (*THEATRE*) regista *m/f*; (*AGR*, *CINEMA*) produttore *m*

product ['prɒdʌkt] *n* prodotto

production [prə'dʌkʃən] *n* produzione *f*; **~ line** *n* catena di lavorazione

productivity [prɒdʌk'tɪvɪtɪ] *n* produttività

profane [prə'feɪn] *adj* profano(a); (*language*) empio(a)

profess [prə'fes] *vt* (*claim*) dichiarare; (*opinion etc*) professare

profession [prə'feʃən] *n* professione *f*; **~al** *n* professionista *m/f* ♦ *adj* professionale; (*work*) da professionista

professor [prə'fesə*] *n* professore *m* (*titolare di una cattedra*); (*US*) professore/essa

proficiency [prə'fɪʃənsɪ] *n* competenza, abilità

profile ['prəʊfaɪl] *n* profilo

profit ['prɒfɪt] *n* profitto; beneficio ♦ *vi*: **to ~ (by** *or* **from)** approfittare (di); **~ability** [-'bɪlɪtɪ] *n* redditività; **~able** *adj* redditizio(a)

profound [prə'faʊnd] *adj* profondo(a)

profusely [prə'fjuːslɪ] *adv* con grande effusione

programme ['prəʊgræm] (*US* **program**) *n* programma *m* ♦ *vt* programmare; **~r** (*US* **programer**) *n* programmatore/trice

progress [*n* 'prəʊgrɛs, *vb* prə'grɛs] *n* progresso ♦ *vi* avanzare, procedere; **in** ~ in corso; **to make** ~ far progressi; **~ive** [-'grɛsɪv] *adj* progressivo(a); (*person*) progressista

prohibit [prə'hɪbɪt] *vt* proibire, vietare; **~ion** [prəʊɪ'bɪʃən] *n* proibizione *f*, divieto; (*US*): **P~ion** proibizionismo; **~ive** *adj* (*price etc*) proibitivo(a)

project [*n* 'prɒdʒɛkt, *vb* prə'dʒɛkt] *n* (*plan*) piano; (*venture*) progetto; (*SCOL*) studio ♦ *vt* proiettare *vi* (*stick out*) sporgere

projectile [prə'dʒɛktaɪl] *n* proiettile *m*

projector [prə'dʒɛktə*] *n* proiettore *m*

pro-life [prəʊ'laɪf] *adj* per il diritto alla vita

prolific [prə'lɪfɪk] *adj* (*artist etc*) fecondo(a)

prolong [prə'lɒŋ] *vt* prolungare

Prom

ⓘ *In Gran Bretagna i* **Prom** *(promenade concert) sono concerti di musica classica, i più noti dei quali sono quelli eseguiti nella Royal Albert Hall a Londra. Un tempo il pubblico seguiva i concerti in piedi, passeggiando. Negli Stati Uniti, invece, con* **prom** *si intende il ballo studentesco di un'università o di un college.*

prom [prɒm] *n abbr* = **promenade**; (*US*: *ball*) ballo studentesco

promenade [prɒmə'nɑːd] *n* (*by sea*) lungomare *m*; **~ concert** *n* concerto (*con posti in piedi*)

prominent ['prɒmɪnənt] *adj* (*standing out*) prominente; (*important*) importante

promiscuous [prə'mɪskjʊəs] *adj* (*sexually*) di facili costumi

promise ['prɒmɪs] *n* promessa ♦ *vt*, *vi* promettere; **to ~ sb sth**, **~ sth to sb** promettere qc a qn; **to ~ (sb) that/to do sth** promettere (a qn) che/di fare qc; **promising** *adj* promettente

promote [prə'məʊt] *vt* promuovere; (*venture, event*) organizzare; **~r** *n* promotore/trice; (*of sporting event*) organizzatore/trice; **promotion** [-'məʊʃən] *n* promozione *f*

prompt [prɒmpt] *adj* rapido(a), svelto(a); puntuale; (*reply*) sollecito(a) ♦ *adv* (*punctually*) in punto ♦ *n* (*COMPUT*) prompt *m* ♦ *vt* incitare; provocare; (*THEATRE*) suggerire a; **to ~ sb to do** incitare qn a fare; **~ly** adv prontamente; puntualmente

prone [prəun] adj (lying) prono(a); **~ to** propenso(a) a, incline a

prong [prɒŋ] n rebbio, punta

pronoun ['prəunaun] n pronome m

pronounce [prə'nauns] vt pronunciare

pronunciation [prənʌnsɪ'eɪʃən] n pronuncia

proof [pru:f] n prova; (of book) bozza; (PHOT) provino ♦ adj: **~ against** a prova di

prop [prɒp] n sostegno, appoggio ♦ vt (also: **~ up**) sostenere, appoggiare; (lean): **to ~ sth against** appoggiare qc contro or a

propaganda [prɒpə'gændə] n propaganda

propel [prə'pel] vt spingere (in avanti), muovere; **~ler** n elica

propensity [prə'pensɪtɪ] n tendenza

proper ['prɒpə*] adj (suited, right) adatto(a), appropriato(a); (seemly) decente; (authentic) vero(a); (inf: real) noun +vero(a) e proprio(a); **~ly** ['prɒpəlɪ] adv (eat, study) bene; (behave) come si deve; **~ noun** n nome m proprio

property ['prɒpətɪ] n (things owned) beni mpl; (land, building) proprietà f inv; (CHEM etc: quality) proprietà; **~ owner** n proprietario/a

prophecy ['prɒfɪsɪ] n profezia

prophesy ['prɒfɪsaɪ] vt predire

prophet ['prɒfɪt] n profeta m

proportion [prə'pɔ:ʃən] n proporzione f; (share) parte f; **~al** adj proporzionale; **~ate** adj proporzionato(a)

proposal [prə'pəuzl] n proposta; (plan) progetto; (of marriage) proposta di matrimonio

propose [prə'pəuz] vt proporre, suggerire ♦ vi fare una proposta di matrimonio; **to ~ to do** proporsi di fare, aver l'intenzione di fare

proposition [prɒpə'zɪʃən] n (offer) proposta

proprietor [prə'praɪətə*] n proprietario/a

propriety [prə'praɪətɪ] n (seemliness) decoro, rispetto delle convenienze sociali

pro rata ['prəu'rɑ:tə] adv in proporzione

prose [prəuz] n prosa

prosecute ['prɒsɪkju:t] vt processare;

prosecution [-'kju:ʃən] n processo; (accusing side) accusa; **prosecutor** n (also: public prosecutor) ≈ procuratore m della Repubblica

prospect [n 'prɒspekt, vb prə'spekt] n prospettiva; (hope) speranza ♦ vi: **to ~ for** cercare; **~s** npl (for work etc) prospettive fpl; **~ive** [-'spektɪv] adj possibile; futuro(a)

prospectus [prə'spektəs] n prospetto, programma m

prosperity [prɒ'sperɪtɪ] n prosperità

prostitute ['prɒstɪtju:t] n prostituta; **male ~** uomo che si prostituisce

protect [prə'tekt] vt proteggere, salvaguardare; **~ed species** n specie f protetta; **~ion** n protezione f; **~ive** adj protettivo(a)

protégé ['prəutəʒeɪ] n protetto

protein ['prəuti:n] n proteina

protest [n 'prəutest, vb prə'test] n protesta ♦ vt, vi protestare

Protestant ['prɒtɪstənt] adj, n protestante m/f

protester [prə'testə*] n dimostrante m/f

prototype ['prəutətaɪp] n prototipo

protracted [prə'træktɪd] adj tirato(a) per le lunghe

protrude [prə'tru:d] vi sporgere

proud [praud] adj fiero(a), orgoglioso(a); (pej) superbo(a)

prove [pru:v] vt provare, dimostrare ♦ vi: **to ~ (to be) correct** etc risultare vero(a) etc; **to ~ o.s.** mostrare le proprie capacità

proverb ['prɒvə:b] n proverbio

provide [prə'vaɪd] vt fornire, provvedere; **to ~ sb with sth** fornire or provvedere qn di qc; **~ for** vt fus provvedere a; (future event) prevedere; **~d (that)** conj purché +sub, a condizione che +sub

providing [prə'vaɪdɪŋ] conj purché +sub, a condizione che +sub

province ['prɒvɪns] n provincia; **provincial** [prə'vɪnʃəl] adj provinciale

provision [prə'vɪʒən] n (supply) riserva; (supplying) provvista; rifornimento; (stipulation) condizione f; **~s** npl (food) provviste fpl; **~al** adj provvisorio(a)

proviso [prə'vaɪzəu] n condizione f
provocative [prə'vɔkətɪv] adj (aggressive) provocatorio(a); (thought-provoking) stimolante; (seductive) provocante
provoke [prə'vəuk] vt provocare; incitare
prowess ['prauɪs] n prodezza
prowl [praul] vi (also: ~ about, ~ around) aggirarsi ♦ n: **to be on the ~** aggirarsi; **~er** n tipo sospetto (che s'aggira con l'intenzione di rubare, aggredire etc)
proximity [prɔk'sɪmɪtɪ] n prossimità
proxy ['prɔksɪ] n: **by ~** per procura
prude [pru:d] n puritano/a
prudent ['pru:dnt] adj prudente
prudish ['pru:dɪʃ] adj puritano(a)
prune [pru:n] n prugna secca ♦ vt potare
pry [praɪ] vi: **to ~ into** ficcare il naso in
PS abbr (= postscript) P.S.
psalm [sɑ:m] n salmo
pseudonym ['sju:dənɪm] n pseudonimo
psyche ['saɪkɪ] n psiche f
psychiatric [saɪkɪ'ætrɪk] adj psichiatrico(a)
psychiatrist [saɪ'kaɪətrɪst] n psichiatra m/f
psychic ['saɪkɪk] adj (also: ~al) psichico(a); (person) dotato(a) di qualità telepatiche
psychoanalyst [saɪkəu'ænəlɪst] n psicanalista m/f
psychological [saɪkə'lɔdʒɪkl] adj psicologico(a)
psychologist [saɪ'kɔlədʒɪst] n psicologo/a
psychology [saɪ'kɔlədʒɪ] n psicologia
psychopath ['saɪkəupæθ] n psicopatico/a
P.T.O. abbr (= please turn over) v.r.
pub [pʌb] n abbr (= public house) pub m inv

> *In Gran Bretagna e in Irlanda i pub sono locali dove vengono servite bevande alcoliche ed analcoliche e dove spesso è possibile anche mangiare, giocare a biliardo o a freccette e guardare la televisione.*

---

pubic ['pju:bɪk] adj pubico(a), del pube
public ['pʌblɪk] adj pubblico(a) ♦ n pubblico; **in ~** in pubblico; **~ address system** n impianto di amplificazione

publican ['pʌblɪkən] n proprietario di un pub
publication [pʌblɪ'keɪʃən] n pubblicazione f
public: **~ company** n società f inv per azioni (costituita tramite pubblica sottoscrizione); **~ convenience** (BRIT) n gabinetti mpl; **~ holiday** n giorno festivo, festa nazionale; **~ house** (BRIT) n pub m inv
publicity [pʌb'lɪsɪtɪ] n pubblicità
publicize ['pʌblɪsaɪz] vt rendere pubblico(a)
publicly ['pʌblɪklɪ] adv pubblicamente
public: **~ opinion** n opinione f pubblica; **~ relations** n pubbliche relazioni fpl; **~ school** n (BRIT) scuola privata; (US) scuola statale; **~-spirited** adj che ha senso civico; **~ transport** n mezzi mpl pubblici
publish ['pʌblɪʃ] vt pubblicare; **~er** n editore m; **~ing** n (industry) editoria; (of a book) pubblicazione f
pub lunch n pranzo semplice ed economico servito nei pub
puce [pju:s] adj marroncino rosato inv
pucker ['pʌkə*] vt corrugare
pudding ['pudɪŋ] n budino; (BRIT: dessert) dolce m; **black ~**, (US) **blood ~** sanguinaccio
puddle ['pʌdl] n pozza, pozzanghera
puff [pʌf] n sbuffo ♦ vt: **to ~ one's pipe** tirare sboccate di fumo ♦ vi (pant) ansare; **~ out** vt (cheeks etc) gonfiare; **~ pastry** n pasta sfoglia; **~y** adj gonfio(a)
pull [pul] n (tug): **to give sth a ~** tirare su qc ♦ vt tirare; (muscle) strappare; (trigger) premere ♦ vi tirare; **to ~ to pieces** fare a pezzi; **to ~ one's punches** (BOXING) risparmiare l'avversario; **to ~ one's weight** dare il proprio contributo; **to ~ o.s. together** ricomporsi, riprendersi; **to ~ sb's leg** prendere in giro qn; **~ apart** vt (break) fare a pezzi; **~ down** vt (house) demolire; (tree) abbattere; **~ in** vi (AUT: at the kerb) accostarsi; (RAIL) entrare in stazione; **~ off** vt (clothes) togliere; (deal etc) portare a compimento; **~ out** vi partire; (AUT: come out of line) spostarsi sulla mezzeria ♦ vt staccare; far uscire; (withdraw) ritirare; **~**

over vi (AUT) accostare; ~ **through** vi
farcela; ~ **up** vi (stop) fermarsi ♦ vt (raise)
sollevare; (uproot) sradicare
pulley ['pulɪ] n puleggia, carrucola
pullover ['pulauva*] n pullover m inv
pulp [pʌlp] n (of fruit) polpa
pulpit ['pulpɪt] n pulpito
pulsate [pʌl'seɪt] vi battere, palpitare
pulse [pʌls] n polso; (BOT) legume m
pummel ['pʌml] vt dare pugni a
pump [pʌmp] n pompa; (shoe) scarpetta
♦ vt pompare; ~ **up** vt gonfiare
pumpkin ['pʌmpkɪn] n zucca
pun [pʌn] n gioco di parole
punch [pʌntʃ] n (blow) pugno; (tool)
punzone m; (drink) ponce m ♦ vt (hit): to
~ **sb/sth** dare un pugno a qn/qc; ~ **line**
(of joke) battuta finale; ~**-up** (BRIT: inf) n
rissa
punctual ['pʌŋktjuəl] adj puntuale
punctuation [pʌŋktju'eɪʃən] n
interpunzione f, punteggiatura
puncture ['pʌŋktʃə*] n foratura ♦ vt forare
pundit ['pʌndɪt] n sapientone/a
pungent ['pʌndʒənt] adj pungente
punish ['pʌnɪʃ] vt punire; ~**ment** n
punizione f
punk [pʌŋk] n (also: ~ **rocker**) punk m/f
inv; (also: ~ **rock**) musica punk, punk rock
m; (US: inf: hoodlum) teppista m
punt [pʌnt] n (boat) barchino
punter ['pʌntə*] n (BRIT) (gambler)
scommettitore/trice; (: inf) cliente m/f
puny ['pju:nɪ] adj gracile
pup [pʌp] n cucciolo/a
pupil ['pju:pl] n allievo/a; (ANAT) pupilla
puppet ['pʌpɪt] n burattino
puppy ['pʌpɪ] n cucciolo/a, cagnolino/a
purchase ['pə:tʃɪs] n acquisto, compera
♦ vt comprare; ~**r** n compratore/trice
pure [pjuə*] adj puro(a)
purée ['pjuəreɪ] n (of potatoes) purè m; (of
tomatoes) passato; (of apples) crema
purely ['pjuəlɪ] adv puramente
purge [pə:dʒ] n (MED) purga; (POL)
epurazione f ♦ vt purgare
puritan ['pjuərɪtən] adj, n puritano(a)

purity ['pjuərɪtɪ] n purezza
purple ['pə:pl] adj di porpora; viola inv
purpose ['pə:pəs] n intenzione f, scopo; **on**
~ apposta; ~**ful** adj deciso(a), risoluto(a)
purr [pə:*] vi fare le fusa
purse [pə:s] n (BRIT) borsellino; (US) borsetta
♦ vt contrarre
purser ['pə:sə*] n (NAUT) commissario di
bordo
pursue [pə'sju:] vt inseguire; (fig: activity
etc) continuare con; (: aim etc) perseguire
pursuit [pə'sju:t] n inseguimento; (fig)
ricerca; (pastime) passatempo
push [puʃ] n spinta; (effort) grande sforzo;
(drive) energia ♦ vt spingere; (button)
premere; (thrust): to ~ **sth (into)** ficcare qc
(in); (fig) fare pubblicità a ♦ vi spingere;
premere; to ~ **for** (fig) insistere per; ~
aside vt scostare; ~ **off** (inf) vi filare; ~
on vi (continue) continuare; ~ **through** vi
farsi largo spingendo ♦ vt (measure) far
approvare; ~ **up** vt (total, prices) far salire;
~**chair** (BRIT) n passeggino; ~**er** n (drug
~er) spacciatore/trice; ~**over** (inf) n: **it's a**
~**over** è un lavoro da bambini; ~**-up** (US) n
(press-up) flessione f sulle braccia; ~**y** (pej)
adj opportunista
puss [pus] (inf) n = **pussy(-cat)**
pussy(-cat) ['pusɪ(-)] (inf) n micio
put [put] (pt, pp **put**) vt mettere, porre; (say)
dire, esprimere; (a question) fare; (estimate)
stimare; ~ **about** or **around** vt (rumour)
diffondere; ~ **across** vt (ideas etc)
comunicare; far capire; ~ **away** vt (return)
mettere a posto; ~ **back** vt (replace)
rimettere (a posto); (postpone) rinviare;
(delay) ritardare; ~ **by** vt (money) mettere
da parte; ~ **down** vt (parcel etc) posare,
mettere giù; (pay) versare; (in writing)
mettere per iscritto; (revolt, animal)
sopprimere; (attribute) attribuire; ~
forward vt (ideas) avanzare, proporre; ~
in vt (application, complaint) presentare;
(time, effort) mettere; ~ **off** vt (postpone)
rimandare, rinviare; (discourage) dissuadere;
~ **on** vt (clothes, lipstick etc) mettere; (light
etc) accendere; (play etc) mettere in scena;

(food, meal) mettere su; *(brake)* mettere; **to ~ on weight** ingrassare; **to ~ on airs** darsi delle arie; **~ out** *vt* mettere fuori; *(one's hand)* porgere; *(light etc)* spegnere; *(person: inconvenience)* scomodare; **~ through** *vt* *(TEL: call)* passare; *(: person)* mettere in comunicazione; *(plan)* far approvare; **~ up** *vt* *(raise)* sollevare, alzare; *(: umbrella)* aprire; *(: tent)* montare; *(pin up)* affiggere; *(hang)* appendere; *(build)* costruire, erigere; *(increase)* aumentare; *(accommodate)* alloggiare; **~ up with** *vt fus* sopportare

putt [pʌt] *n* colpo leggero; **~ing green** *n* green *m inv*; campo da putting

putty ['pʌtɪ] *n* stucco

puzzle ['pʌzl] *n* enigma *m*, mistero; *(jigsaw)* puzzle *m*; *(also:* **crossword ~***)* parole *fpl* incrociate, cruciverba *m inv* ♦ *vt* confondere, rendere perplesso(a) ♦ *vi* scervellarsi

pyjamas [pɪ'dʒɑːməz] *(BRIT) npl* pigiama *m*

pylon ['paɪlən] *n* pilone *m*

pyramid ['pɪrəmɪd] *n* piramide *f*

Pyrenees [pɪrɪ'niːz] *npl:* **the ~** i Pirenei

Q, q

quack [kwæk] *n* *(of duck)* qua qua *m inv*; *(pej: doctor)* dottoruccio/a

quad [kwɔd] *n abbr* = **quadrangle**; **quadruplet**

quadrangle ['kwɔdræŋgl] *n* *(courtyard)* cortile *m*

quadruple [kwɔ'druːpl] *vt* quadruplicare ♦ *vi* quadruplicarsi

quadruplets [kwɔ'druːplɪts] *npl* quattro gemelli *mpl*

quail [kweɪl] *n* *(ZOOL)* quaglia ♦ *vi* *(person):* **to ~ at** *or* **before** perdersi d'animo davanti a

quaint [kweɪnt] *adj* bizzarro(a); *(old-fashioned)* antiquato(a); grazioso(a), pittoresco(a)

quake [kweɪk] *vi* tremare ♦ *n abbr* = **earthquake**

Quaker ['kweɪkə*] *n* quacchero/a

qualification [kwɔlɪfɪ'keɪʃən] *n* *(degree etc)* qualifica, titolo; *(ability)* competenza, qualificazione *f*; *(limitation)* riserva, restrizione *f*

qualified ['kwɔlɪfaɪd] *adj* qualificato(a); *(able):* **~ to** competente in, qualificato(a) a; *(limited)* condizionato(a)

qualify ['kwɔlɪfaɪ] *vt* abilitare; *(limit: statement)* modificare, precisare ♦ *vi:* **to ~ (as)** qualificarsi (come); **to ~ (for)** acquistare i requisiti necessari (per); *(SPORT)* qualificarsi (per *or* a)

quality ['kwɔlɪtɪ] *n* qualità *f inv*

| quality press |

i *Il termine* **quality press** *si riferisce ai quotidiani e ai settimanali che offrono un'informazione più seria ed approfondita rispetto ai* **tabloid***, i giornali popolari; vedi anche* **tabloid press***.*

qualm [kwɑːm] *n* dubbio; scrupolo

quandary ['kwɔndrɪ] *n:* **in a ~** in un dilemma

quantity ['kwɔntɪtɪ] *n* quantità *f inv*

quantity surveyor [-sə'veɪə*] *n* geometra *m (specializzato nel calcolare la quantità e il costo del materiale da costruzione)*

quarantine ['kwɔrəntiːn] *n* quarantena

quarrel ['kwɔrl] *n* lite *f*, disputa ♦ *vi* litigare

quarry ['kwɔrɪ] *n* *(for stone)* cava; *(animal)* preda

quart [kwɔːt] *n* ≈ litro

quarter ['kwɔːtə*] *n* quarto; *(US: coin)* quarto di dollaro; *(of year)* trimestre *m*; *(district)* quartiere *m* ♦ *vt* dividere in quattro; *(MIL)* alloggiare; **~s** *npl* *(living ~s)* alloggio; *(MIL)* alloggi *mpl*, quadrato; **a ~ of an hour** un quarto d'ora; **~ final** *n* quarto di finale; **~ly** *adj* trimestrale ♦ *adv* trimestralmente

quartet(te) [kwɔː'tet] *n* quartetto

quartz [kwɔːts] *n* quarzo

quash [kwɔʃ] *vt* *(verdict)* annullare

quaver ['kweɪvə*] *n* *(BRIT: MUS)* croma ♦ *vi* tremolare

quay [kiː] *n* *(also:* **~side***)* banchina

queasy ['kwi:zɪ] adj (stomach) delicato(a); **to feel ~** aver la nausea

queen [kwi:n] n (gen) regina; (CARDS etc) regina, donna; **~ mother** n regina madre

queer [kwɪə*] adj strano(a), curioso(a) ♦ n (inf) finocchio

quell [kwel] vt domare

quench [kwentʃ] vt: **to ~ one's thirst** dissetarsi

query ['kwɪərɪ] n domanda, questione f ♦ vt mettere in questione

quest [kwest] n cerca, ricerca

question ['kwestʃən] n domanda, questione f ♦ vt (person) interrogare; (plan, idea) mettere in questione or in dubbio; **it's a ~ of doing** si tratta di fare; **beyond ~** fuori di dubbio; **out of the ~** fuori discussione, impossibile; **~able** adj discutibile; **~ mark** n punto interrogativo

questionnaire [kwestʃə'neə*] n questionario

queue [kju:] (BRIT) n coda, fila ♦ vi fare la coda

quibble ['kwɪbl] vi cavillare

quiche [ki:ʃ] n torta salata a base di uova, formaggio, prosciutto o altro

quick [kwɪk] adj rapido(a), veloce; (reply) pronto(a); (mind) pronto(a), acuto(a) ♦ n: **cut to the ~** (fig) toccato(a) sul vivo; **be ~!** fa presto!; **~en** vt accelerare, affrettare ♦ vi accelerare, affrettarsi; **~ly** adv rapidamente, velocemente; **~sand** n sabbie fpl mobili; **~ witted** adj pronto(a) d'ingegno

quid [kwɪd] (BRIT: inf) n inv sterlina

quiet ['kwaɪət] adj tranquillo(a), quieto(a); (ceremony) semplice ♦ n tranquillità, calma ♦ vt, vi (US) = **~en; keep ~!** sta zitto!; **~en** (also: **~en down**) vi calmarsi, chetarsi ♦ vt calmare, chetare; **~ly** adv tranquillamente, calmamente; sommessamente

quilt [kwɪlt] n trapunta; (continental ~) piumino

quin [kwɪn] n abbr = **quintuplet**

quintuplets [kwɪn'tju:plɪts] npl cinque gemelli mpl

quip [kwɪp] n frizzo

quirk [kwə:k] n ghiribizzo

quit [kwɪt] (pt, pp **quit** or **quitted**) vt mollare; (premises) lasciare, partire da ♦ vi (give up) mollare; (resign) dimettersi

quite [kwaɪt] adv (rather) assai; (entirely) completamente, del tutto; **I ~ understand** capisco perfettamente; **that's not ~ big enough** non è proprio sufficiente; **~ a few of them** non pochi di loro; **~ (so)!** esatto!

quits [kwɪts] adj: **~ (with)** pari (con); **let's call it ~** adesso siamo pari

quiver ['kwɪvə*] vi tremare, fremere

quiz [kwɪz] n (game) quiz m inv; indovinello ♦ vt interrogare; **~zical** adj enigmatico(a)

quota ['kwəutə] n quota

quotation [kwəu'teɪʃən] n citazione f; (of shares etc) quotazione f; (estimate) preventivo; **~ marks** npl virgolette fpl

quote [kwəut] n citazione f ♦ vt (sentence) citare; (price) dare, fissare; (shares) quotare ♦ vi: **to ~ from** citare; **~s** npl = **quotation marks**

R, r

rabbi ['ræbaɪ] n rabbino

rabbit ['ræbɪt] n coniglio; **~ hutch** n conigliera

rabble ['ræbl] (pej) n canaglia, plebaglia

rabies ['reɪbi:z] n rabbia

RAC (BRIT) n abbr = **Royal Automobile Club**

rac(c)oon [rə'ku:n] n procione m

race [reɪs] n razza; (competition, rush) corsa ♦ vt (horse) far correre ♦ vi correre; (engine) imballarsi; **~ car** (US) n = **racing car**; **~ car driver** (US) n = **racing driver**; **~course** n campo di corse, ippodromo; **~horse** n cavallo da corsa; **~track** n pista

racial ['reɪʃl] adj razziale

racing ['reɪsɪŋ] n corsa; **~ car** (BRIT) n macchina da corsa; **~ driver** (BRIT) n corridore m automobilista

racism ['reɪsɪzəm] n razzismo; **racist** adj, n razzista m/f

rack [ræk] n rastrelliera; (also: **luggage ~**) rete f, portabagagli m inv; (also: **roof ~**)

portabagagli; (*dish ~*) scolapiatti *m inv*
♦ *vt*: **~ed by** torturato(a) da; **to ~ one's
brains** scervellarsi

racket ['rækɪt] *n* (*for tennis*) racchetta;
(*noise*) fracasso; baccano; (*swindle*)
imbroglio, truffa; (*organized crime*) racket
m inv

racoon [rə'kuːn] *n* = **raccoon**

racquet ['rækɪt] *n* racchetta

racy ['reɪsɪ] *adj* brioso(a); piccante

radar ['reɪdɑːʳ] *n* radar *m*

radial ['reɪdɪəl] *adj* (*also*: **~-ply**) radiale

radiant ['reɪdɪənt] *adj* raggiante; (*PHYSICS*)
radiante

radiate ['reɪdɪeɪt] *vt* (*heat*) irraggiare,
irradiare ♦ *vi* (*lines*) irradiarsi

radiation [reɪdɪ'eɪʃən] *n* irradiamento;
(*radioactive*) radiazione *f*

radiator ['reɪdɪeɪtəʳ] *n* radiatore *m*

radical ['rædɪkl] *adj* radicale

radii ['reɪdɪaɪ] *npl of* **radius**

radio ['reɪdɪəu] *n* radio *f inv*; **on the ~** alla
radio

radioactive [reɪdɪəu'æktɪv] *adj*
radioattivo(a)

radio station *n* stazione *f* radio *inv*

radish ['rædɪʃ] *n* ravanello

radius ['reɪdɪəs] *n* (*pl* **radii**) *n* raggio

RAF *n abbr* = **Royal Air Force**

raffle ['ræfl] *n* lotteria

raft [rɑːft] *n* zattera; (*also*: **life ~**) zattera di
salvataggio

rafter ['rɑːftəʳ] *n* trave *f*

rag [ræg] *n* straccio, cencio; (*pej*: *newspaper*)
giornalaccio, bandiera; (*for charity*)
iniziativa studentesca a scopo benefico; **~s**
npl (*torn clothes*) stracci *mpl*, brandelli *mpl*;
~ doll *n* bambola di pezza

rage [reɪdʒ] *n* (*fury*) collera, furia ♦ *vi*
(*person*) andare su tutte le furie; (*storm*)
infuriare; **it's all the ~** fa furore

ragged ['rægɪd] *adj* (*edge*) irregolare;
(*clothes*) logoro(a); (*appearance*) pezzente

raid [reɪd] *n* (*MIL*) incursione *f*; (*criminal*)
rapina; (*by police*) irruzione *f* ♦ *vt* fare
un'incursione in; rapinare; fare irruzione in

rail [reɪl] *n* (*on stair*) ringhiera; (*on bridge,*
balcony) parapetto; (*of ship*) battagliola; **~s**
npl (*for train*) binario, rotaie *fpl*; **by ~** per
ferrovia; **~ing(s)** *n(pl)* ringhiere *fpl*; **~road**
(*US*) *n* = **~way**; **~way** (*BRIT*) *n* ferrovia;
~way line (*BRIT*) *n* linea ferroviaria;
~wayman (*BRIT*: *irreg*) *n* ferroviere *m*;
~way station (*BRIT*) *n* stazione *f*
ferroviaria

rain [reɪn] *n* pioggia ♦ *vi* piovere; **in the ~**
sotto la pioggia; **it's ~ing** piove; **~bow** *n*
arcobaleno; **~coat** *n* impermeabile *m*;
~drop *n* goccia di pioggia; **~fall** *n*
pioggia; (*measurement*) piovosità; **~forest**
n foresta pluviale; **~y** *adj* piovoso(a)

raise [reɪz] *n* aumento ♦ *vt* (*lift*) alzare;
sollevare; (*increase*) aumentare; (*a protest,*
doubt, question) sollevare; (*cattle, family*)
allevare; (*crop*) coltivare; (*army, funds*)
raccogliere; (*loan*) ottenere; **to ~ one's
voice** alzare la voce

raisin ['reɪzn] *n* uva secca

rake [reɪk] *n* (*tool*) rastrello ♦ *vt* (*garden*)
rastrellare

rally ['rælɪ] *n* (*POL etc*) riunione *f*; (*AUT*) rally
m inv; (*TENNIS*) scambio ♦ *vt* riunire,
radunare ♦ *vi* (*sick person, Stock Exchange*)
riprendersi; **~ round** *vt fus* raggrupparsi
intorno a; venire in aiuto di

RAM [ræm] *n abbr* (= *random access*
memory) memoria ad accesso casuale

ram [ræm] *n* montone *m*, ariete *m* ♦ *vt*
conficcare; (*crash into*) cozzare, sbattere
contro; percuotere; speronare

ramble ['ræmbl] *n* escursione *f* ♦ *vi* (*pej*:
also: **~ on**) divagare; **~r** *n* escursionista
m/f; (*BOT*) rosa rampicante; **rambling** *adj*
(*speech*) sconnesso(a); (*house*) tutto(a) a
nicchie e corridoi; (*BOT*) rampicante

ramp [ræmp] *n* rampa; **on/off ~** (*US*: *AUT*)
raccordo di entrata/uscita

rampage [ræm'peɪdʒ] *n*: **to go on the ~**
scatenarsi in modo violento

rampant ['ræmpənt] *adj* (*disease etc*) che
infierisce

rampart ['ræmpɑːt] *n* bastione *m*

ram raiding *n* il rapinare un negozio o
una banca sfondandone la vetrina con

un'auto-ariete

ramshackle ['ræmʃækl] *adj* (*house*) cadente; (*car etc*) sgangherato(a)

ran [ræn] *pt of* **run**

ranch [rɑːntʃ] *n* ranch *m inv*; **~er** *n* proprietario di un ranch; cowboy *m inv*

rancid ['rænsɪd] *adj* rancido(a)

rancour ['ræŋkə*] (*US* **rancor**) *n* rancore *m*

random ['rændəm] *adj* fatto(a) *or* detto(a) per caso; (*COMPUT, MATH*) casuale ♦ *n*: **at ~** a casaccio; **~ access** *n* (*COMPUT*) accesso casuale

randy ['rændɪ] (*BRIT: inf*) *adj* arrapato(a); lascivo(a)

rang [ræŋ] *pt of* **ring**

range [reɪndʒ] *n* (*of mountains*) catena; (*of missile, voice*) portata; (*of proposals, products*) gamma; (*MIL: also*: **shooting ~**) campo di tiro; (*also*: **kitchen ~**) fornello, cucina economica ♦ *vt* disporre ♦ *vi*: **to ~ over** coprire; **to ~ from ... to** andare da ... a

ranger ['reɪndʒə*] *n* guardia forestale

rank [ræŋk] *n* filla; (*status, MIL*) grado; (*BRIT: also*: **taxi ~**) posteggio di taxi ♦ *vi*: **to ~ among** essere tra ♦ *adj* puzzolente; vero(a) e proprio(a); **the ~ and file** (*fig*) la gran massa

ransack ['rænsæk] *vt* rovistare; (*plunder*) saccheggiare

ransom ['rænsəm] *n* riscatto; **to hold sb to ~** (*fig*) esercitare pressione su qn

rant [rænt] *vi* vociare

rap [ræp] *vt* bussare a; picchiare su ♦ *n* (*music*) rap *m inv*

rape [reɪp] *n* violenza carnale, stupro; (*BOT*) ravizzone *m* ♦ *vt* violentare; **~(seed) oil** *n* olio di ravizzone

rapid ['ræpɪd] *adj* rapido(a); **~s** *npl* (*GEO*) rapida; **~ly** *adv* rapidamente

rapist ['reɪpɪst] *n* violentatore *m*

rapport [ræ'pɔː*] *n* rapporto

rare [reə*] *adj* raro(a); (*CULIN: steak*) al sangue

rarely ['reəlɪ] *adv* raramente

raring ['reərɪŋ] *adj*: **to be ~ to go** (*inf*) non veder l'ora di cominciare

rascal ['rɑːskl] *n* mascalzone *m*

rash [ræʃ] *adj* imprudente, sconsiderato(a) ♦ *n* (*MED*) eruzione *f*; (*of events etc*) scoppio

rasher ['ræʃə*] *n* fetta sottile (di lardo *or* prosciutto)

raspberry ['rɑːzbərɪ] *n* lampone *m*

rasping ['rɑːspɪŋ] *adj* stridulo(a)

rat [ræt] *n* ratto

rate [reɪt] *n* (*proportion*) tasso, percentuale *f*; (*speed*) velocità *f inv*; (*price*) tariffa ♦ *vt* giudicare; stimare; **~s** *npl* (*BRIT: property tax*) imposte *fpl* comunali; (*fees*) tariffe *fpl*; **to ~ sb/sth as** valutare qn/qc come; **~able value** (*BRIT*) *n* valore *m* imponibile *or* locativo (di una proprietà); **~payer** (*BRIT*) *n* contribuente *m/f* (che paga le imposte comunali)

rather ['rɑːðə*] *adv* piuttosto; **it's ~ expensive** è piuttosto caro; (*too*) è un po' caro; **there's ~ a lot** ce n'è parecchio; **I would** *or* **I'd ~ go** preferirei andare

rating ['reɪtɪŋ] *n* (*assessment*) valutazione *f*, (*score*) punteggio di merito

ratio ['reɪʃɪəʊ] *n* proporzione *f*, rapporto

ration ['ræʃən] *n* (*gen pl*) razioni *fpl* ♦ *vt* razionare

rational ['ræʃənl] *adj* razionale, ragionevole; (*solution, reasoning*) logico(a); **~e** [-'nɑːl] *n* fondamento logico; giustificazione *f*; **~ize** *vt* razionalizzare

rat race *n* carrierismo, corsa al successo

rattle ['rætl] *n* tintinnio; (*louder*) strepito; (*for baby*) sonaglino ♦ *vi* risuonare, tintinnare; fare un rumore di ferraglia ♦ *vt* scuotere (con strepito); **~snake** *n* serpente *m* a sonagli

raucous ['rɔːkəs] *adj* rumoroso(a), fragoroso(a)

ravage ['rævɪdʒ] *vt* devastare; **~s** *npl* danni *mpl*

rave [reɪv] *vi* (*in anger*) infuriarsi; (*with enthusiasm*) andare in estasi; (*MED*) delirare ♦ (*BRIT: inf*) *n* (*party*) rave *m inv*

raven ['reɪvən] *n* corvo

ravenous ['rævənəs] *adj* affamato(a)

ravine [rə'viːn] *n* burrone *m*

raving ['reɪvɪŋ] *adj*: **~ lunatic** pazzo(a)

furioso(a)

ravishing [ˈrævɪʃɪŋ] *adj* incantevole

raw [rɔː] *adj* (*uncooked*) crudo(a); (*not processed*) greggio(a); (*sore*) vivo(a); (*inexperienced*) inesperto(a); (*weather, day*) gelido(a); ~ **deal** (*inf*) *n* bidonata; ~ **material** *n* materia prima

ray [reɪ] *n* raggio; **a ~ of hope** un barlume di speranza

rayon [ˈreɪɒn] *n* raion *m*

raze [reɪz] *vt* radere, distruggere

razor [ˈreɪzə*] *n* rasoio; ~ **blade** *n* lama di rasoio

Rd *abbr* = **road**

re [riː] *prep* con riferimento a

reach [riːtʃ] *n* portata; (*of river etc*) tratto ♦ *vt* raggiungere; arrivare a ♦ *vi* stendersi; **out of/within** ~ fuori/a portata di mano; **within ~ of the shops/station** vicino ai negozi/alla stazione; ~ **out** *vt* (*hand*) allungare ♦ *vi*: **to ~ out for** stendere la mano per prendere

react [riːˈækt] *vi* reagire; **~ion** [-ˈækʃən] *n* reazione *f*

reactor [riːˈæktə*] *n* reattore *m*

read [riːd, *pt, pp* red] *vi* leggere ♦ *vt* leggere; (*understand*) intendere, interpretare; (*study*) studiare; ~ **out** *vt* leggere ad alta voce; **~able** *adj* (*writing*) leggibile; (*book etc*) che si legge volentieri; **~er** *n* lettore/trice; (*BRIT: at university*) *professore con funzioni preminenti di ricerca*; **~ership** *n* (*of paper etc*) numero di lettori

readily [ˈredɪlɪ] *adv* volentieri; (*easily*) facilmente; (*quickly*) prontamente

readiness [ˈredɪnɪs] *n* prontezza; **in ~** (*prepared*) pronto(a)

reading [ˈriːdɪŋ] *n* lettura; (*understanding*) interpretazione *f*; (*on instrument*) indicazione *f*

readjust [riːəˈdʒʌst] *vt* riaggiustare ♦ *vi* (*person*): **to ~ (to)** riadattarsi (a)

ready [ˈredɪ] *adj* pronto(a); (*willing*) pronto(a), disposto(a); (*available*) disponibile ♦ *n*: **at the ~** (*MIL*) pronto a sparare; **to get ~** *vi* prepararsi ♦ *vt*

preparare; **~-made** *adj* prefabbricato(a); (*clothes*) confezionato(a); ~ **reckoner** *n* prontuario di calcolo; **~-to-wear** *adj* prêt-à-porter *inv*

reaffirm [riːəˈfɜːm] *vt* riaffermare

real [rɪəl] *adj* reale; vero(a); **in ~ terms** in realtà; ~ **estate** *n* beni *mpl* immobili; **~ism** *n* (*also ART*) realismo; **~ist** *n* realista *m/f*; **~istic** [-ˈlɪstɪk] *adj* realistico(a)

reality [riːˈælɪtɪ] *n* realtà *f inv*

realization [rɪəlaɪˈzeɪʃən] *n* presa di coscienza; realizzazione *f*

realize [ˈrɪəlaɪz] *vt* (*understand*) rendersi conto di

really [ˈrɪəlɪ] *adv* veramente, davvero; **~!** (*indicating annoyance*) oh, insomma!

realm [relm] *n* reame *m*, regno

Realtor ® [ˈrɪəltɔː*] (*US*) *n* agente *m* immobiliare

reap [riːp] *vt* mietere; (*fig*) raccogliere

reappear [riːəˈpɪə*] *vi* ricomparire, riapparire

rear [rɪə*] *adj* di dietro; (*AUT: wheel etc*) posteriore ♦ *n* didietro, parte *f* posteriore ♦ *vt* (*cattle, family*) allevare ♦ *vi* (*also*: ~ **up**: *animal*) impennarsi

rearmament [riːˈɑːməmənt] *n* riarmo

rearrange [riːəˈreɪndʒ] *vt* riordinare

rear-view: ~ **mirror** *n* (*AUT*) specchio retrovisore

reason [ˈriːzn] *n* ragione *f*; (*cause, motive*) ragione, motivo ♦ *vi*: **to ~ with sb** far ragionare qn; **it stands to ~ that** è ovvio che; **~able** *adj* ragionevole; (*not bad*) accettabile; **~ably** *adv* ragionevolmente; **~ed** *adj*: **a well-~ed argument** una forte argomentazione; **~ing** *n* ragionamento

reassurance [riːəˈʃuərəns] *n* rassicurazione *f*

reassure [riːəˈʃuə*] *vt* rassicurare; **to ~ sb of** rassicurare qn di *or* su

rebate [ˈriːbeɪt] *n* (*on tax etc*) sgravio

rebel [*n* ˈrebl, *vb* rɪˈbel] *n* ribelle *m/f* ♦ *vi* ribellarsi; **~lion** *n* ribellione *f*; **~lious** *adj* ribelle

rebound [*vb* rɪˈbaund, *n* ˈriːbaund] *vi* (*ball*) rimbalzare ♦ *n*: **on the ~** di rimbalzo

rebuff [rɪ'bʌf] n secco rifiuto
rebuke [rɪ'bjuːk] vt rimproverare
rebut [rɪ'bʌt] vt rifiutare
recall [rɪ'kɔːl] vt richiamare; (remember) ricordare, richiamare alla mente ♦ n richiamo
recap ['riːkæp], **recapitulate** [riːkə'pɪtjuleɪt] vt ricapitolare ♦ vi riassumere
rec'd abbr = **received**
recede [rɪ'siːd] vi allontanarsi; ritirarsi; calare; **receding** adj (forehead, chin) sfuggente; **he's got a receding hairline** sta stempiando
receipt [rɪ'siːt] n (document) ricevuta; (act of receiving) ricevimento; **~s** npl (COMM) introiti mpl
receive [rɪ'siːv] vt ricevere; (guest) ricevere, accogliere
receiver [rɪ'siːvə*] n (TEL) ricevitore m; (RADIO, TV) apparecchio ricevente; (of stolen goods) ricettatore/trice; (COMM) curatore m fallimentare
recent ['riːsnt] adj recente; **~ly** adv recentemente
receptacle [rɪ'septɪkl] n recipiente m
reception [rɪ'sepʃən] n ricevimento; (welcome) accoglienza; (TV etc) ricezione f; **~ desk** n (in hotel) reception f inv; (in hospital, at doctor's) accettazione f; (in offices etc) portineria; **~ist** n receptionist m/f inv
receptive [rɪ'septɪv] adj ricettivo(a)
recess [rɪ'ses] n (in room, secret place) alcova; (POL etc: holiday) vacanze fpl; **~ion** [-'seʃən] n recessione f
recharge [riː'tʃɑːdʒ] vt (battery) ricaricare
recipe ['resɪpɪ] n ricetta
recipient [rɪ'sɪpɪənt] n beneficiario/a; (of letter) destinatario/a
recital [rɪ'saɪtl] n recital m inv
recite [rɪ'saɪt] vt (poem) recitare
reckless ['rekləs] adj (driver etc) spericolato(a); (spending) folle
reckon ['rekən] vt (count) calcolare; (think): **I ~ that ...** penso che ...; **~ on** vt fus contare su; **~ing** n conto; stima
reclaim [rɪ'kleɪm] vt (demand back)

richiedere, reclamare; (land) bonificare; (materials) recuperare; **reclamation** [reklə'meɪʃən] n bonifica
recline [rɪ'klaɪn] vi stare sdraiato(a); **reclining** adj (seat) ribaltabile
recognition [rekəg'nɪʃən] n riconoscimento; **transformed beyond ~** irriconoscibile
recognize ['rekəgnaɪz] vt: **to ~ (by/as)** riconoscere (a or da/come)
recoil [rɪ'kɔɪl] vi (person): **to ~ from doing sth** rifuggire dal fare qc ♦ n (of gun) rinculo
recollect [rekə'lekt] vt ricordare; **~ion** [-'lekʃən] n ricordo
recommend [rekə'mend] vt raccomandare; (advise) consigliare
reconcile ['rekənsaɪl] vt (two people) riconciliare; (two facts) conciliare, quadrare; **to ~ o.s. to** rassegnarsi a
recondition [riːkən'dɪʃən] vt rimettere a nuovo
reconnoitre [rekə'nɔɪtə*] (US **reconnoiter**) vt (MIL) fare una ricognizione di
reconstruct [riːkən'strʌkt] vt ricostruire
record [n 'rekɔːd, vb rɪ'kɔːd] n ricordo, documento; (of meeting etc) nota, verbale m; (register) registro; (file) pratica, dossier m inv; (COMPUT) record m inv; (also: **criminal ~**) fedina penale sporca; (MUS: disc) disco; (SPORT) record m inv, primato ♦ vt (set down) prendere nota di, registrare; (MUS: song etc) registrare; **in ~ time** a tempo di record; **off the ~** adj ufficioso(a) ♦ adv ufficiosamente; **~ card** n (in file) scheda; **~ed delivery** (BRIT) n (POST): **~ed delivery letter** etc lettera etc raccomandata; **~er** n (MUS) flauto diritto; **~ holder** n (SPORT) primatista m/f; **~ing** n (MUS) registrazione f; **~ player** n giradischi m inv
recount [rɪ'kaunt] vt raccontare, narrare
re-count ['riːkaunt] n (POL: of votes) nuovo computo
recoup [rɪ'kuːp] vt ricuperare
recourse [rɪ'kɔːs] n: **to have ~ to** ricorrere a, far ricorso a
recover [rɪ'kʌvə*] vt ricuperare ♦ vi: **to ~**

(from) riprendersi (da)

recovery [rɪˈkʌvərɪ] *n* ricupero; ristabilimento; ripresa

recreation [rɛkrɪˈeɪʃən] *n* ricreazione *f*; svago; **~al** *adj* ricreativo(a); **~al drug** *n* *sostanza stupefacente usata a scopo ricreativo*

recrimination [rɪkrɪmɪˈneɪʃən] *n* recriminazione *f*

recruit [rɪˈkruːt] *n* recluta; *(in company)* nuovo(a) assunto(a) ♦ *vt* reclutare

rectangle [ˈrɛktæŋgl] *n* rettangolo; **rectangular** [-ˈtæŋgjulə*] *adj* rettangolare

rectify [ˈrɛktɪfaɪ] *vt (error)* rettificare; *(omission)* riparare

rector [ˈrɛktə*] *n (REL)* parroco *(anglicano)*; **~y** *n* presbiterio

recuperate [rɪˈkjuːpəreɪt] *vi* ristabilirsi

recur [rɪˈkəː*] *vi* riaccadere; *(symptoms)* ripresentarsi; **~rent** *adj* ricorrente, periodico(a)

recycle [riːˈsaɪkl] *vt* riciclare

red [rɛd] *n* rosso; *(POL: pej)* rosso/a ♦ *adj* rosso(a); **in the ~** *(account)* scoperto; *(business)* in deficit; **~ carpet treatment** *n* cerimonia di gran pavese; **R~ Cross** *n* Croce *f* Rossa; **~currant** *n* ribes *m inv*; **~den** *vt* arrossare ♦ *vi* arrossire

redeem [rɪˈdiːm] *vt (debt)* riscattare; *(sth in pawn)* ritirare; *(fig, also REL)* redimere; **~ing** *adj*: **~ing feature** unico aspetto positivo

redeploy [riːdɪˈplɔɪ] *vt (resources)* riorganizzare

red-haired [-ˈhɛəd] *adj* dai capelli rossi

red-handed [-ˈhændɪd] *adj*: **to be caught ~** essere preso(a) in flagrante *or* con le mani nel sacco

redhead [ˈrɛdhɛd] *n* rosso/a

red herring *n (fig)* falsa pista

red-hot *adj* arroventato(a)

redirect [riːdaɪˈrɛkt] *vt (mail)* far seguire

red light *n*: **to go through a ~** *(AUT)* passare col rosso; **red-light district** *n* quartiere *m* a luci rosse

redo [riːˈduː] *vt (irreg)* rifare

redouble [riːˈdʌbl] *vt*: **to ~ one's efforts** raddoppiare gli sforzi

redress [rɪˈdrɛs] *vt* riparare

Red Sea *n*: **the ~** il Mar Rosso

redskin [ˈrɛdskɪn] *n* pellerossa *m/f*

red tape *n (fig)* burocrazia

reduce [rɪˈdjuːs] *vt* ridurre; *(lower)* ridurre, abbassare; **"~ speed now"** *(AUT)* "rallentare"; **at a ~d price** scontato(a); **reduction** [rɪˈdʌkʃən] *n* riduzione *f*; *(of price)* ribasso; *(discount)* sconto

redundancy [rɪˈdʌndənsɪ] *n* licenziamento

redundant [rɪˈdʌndnt] *adj (worker)* licenziato(a); *(detail, object)* superfluo(a); **to be made ~** essere licenziato (per eccesso di personale)

reed [riːd] *n (BOT)* canna; *(MUS: of clarinet etc)* ancia

reef [riːf] *n (at sea)* scogliera

reek [riːk] *vi*: **to ~ (of)** puzzare (di)

reel [riːl] *n* bobina, rocchetto; *(FISHING)* mulinello; *(CINEMA)* rotolo; *(dance) danza veloce scozzese* ♦ *vi (sway)* barcollare; **~ in** *vt* tirare su

ref [rɛf] *(inf) n abbr (= referee)* arbitro

refectory [rɪˈfɛktərɪ] *n* refettorio

refer [rɪˈfəː*] *vt*: **to ~ sth to** *(dispute, decision)* deferire qc a; **to ~ sb to** *(inquirer, MED: patient)* indirizzare qn a; *(reader: to text)* rimandare qn a ♦ *vi*: **~ to** *(allude to)* accennare a; *(consult)* rivolgersi a

referee [rɛfəˈriː] *n* arbitro; *(BRIT: for job application)* referenza ♦ *vt* arbitrare

reference [ˈrɛfrəns] *n* riferimento; *(mention)* menzione *f*, allusione *f*; *(for job application)* referenza; **with ~ to** *(COMM: in letter)* in *or* con riferimento a; **~ book** *n* libro di consultazione; **~ number** *n* numero di riferimento

referenda [rɛfəˈrɛndə] *npl of* **referendum**

referendum [rɛfəˈrɛndəm] *(pl* **referenda***) n* referendum *m inv*

refill [*vb* riːˈfɪl, *n* ˈriːfɪl] *vt* riempire di nuovo; *(pen, lighter etc)* ricaricare ♦ *n (for pen etc)* ricambio

refine [rɪˈfaɪn] *vt* raffinare; **~d** *adj (person, taste)* raffinato(a)

reflect [rɪˈflɛkt] *vt (light, image)* riflettere; *(fig)* rispecchiare ♦ *vi (think)* riflettere, considerare; **it ~s badly/well on him** si ripercuote su di lui in senso negativo/positivo; **~ion** [-'flekʃən] n riflessione f; (image) riflesso; (criticism): **~ion on** giudizio su; attacco a; **on ~ion** pensandoci sopra

reflex ['ri:fleks] adj riflesso(a) ♦ n riflesso; **~ive** [rɪ'fleksɪv] adj (LING) riflessivo(a)

reform [rɪ'fɔːm] n (of sinner etc) correzione f; (of law etc) riforma ♦ vt correggere; riformare; **~atory** (US) n riformatorio

refrain [rɪ'freɪn] vi: **to ~ from doing** trattenersi dal fare ♦ n ritornello

refresh [rɪ'freʃ] vt rinfrescare; (subj: food, sleep) ristorare; **~er course** (BRIT) n corso di aggiornamento; **~ing** adj (drink) rinfrescante; (sleep) riposante, ristoratore(trice); **~ments** npl rinfreschi mpl

refrigerator [rɪ'frɪdʒəreɪtə*] n frigorifero

refuel [ri:'fjuəl] vi far rifornimento (di carburante)

refuge ['refjuːdʒ] n rifugio; **to take ~ in** rifugiarsi in

refugee [refjuˈdʒiː] n rifugiato/a, profugo/a

refund [n 'ri:fʌnd, vb rɪ'fʌnd] n rimborso ♦ vt rimborsare

refurbish [ri:'fɜːbɪʃ] vt rimettere a nuovo

refusal [rɪ'fjuːzəl] n rifiuto; **to have first ~ on** avere il diritto d'opzione su

refuse [n 'refjuːs, vb rɪ'fjuːz] n rifiuti mpl ♦ vt, vi rifiutare; **to ~ to do** rifiutare di fare; **~ collection** n raccolta di rifiuti

refute [rɪ'fjuːt] vt confutare

regain [rɪ'geɪn] vt riguadagnare; riacquistare, ricuperare

regal ['ri:gl] adj regale; **~ia** [rɪ'geɪlɪə] n insegne fpl regie

regard [rɪ'gɑːd] n riguardo, stima ♦ vt considerare, stimare; **to give one's ~s to** porgere i suoi saluti a; **"with kindest ~s"** "cordiali saluti"; **~ing, as ~s, with ~ to** riguardo a; **~less** adv lo stesso; **~less of** a dispetto di, nonostante

regenerate [rɪ'dʒenəreɪt] vt rigenerare

régime [reɪ'ʒiːm] n regime m

regiment ['redʒɪmənt] n reggimento; **~al** [-'mentl] adj reggimentale

region ['ri:dʒən] n regione f; **in the ~ of** (fig) all'incirca di; **~al** adj regionale

register ['redʒɪstə*] n registro; (also: **electoral ~**) lista elettorale ♦ vt registrare; (vehicle) immatricolare; (letter) assicurare; (subj: instrument) segnare ♦ vi iscriversi; (at hotel) firmare il registro; (make impression) entrare in testa; **~ed** (BRIT) adj (letter) assicurato(a); **~ed trademark** n marchio depositato

registrar ['redʒɪstrɑː*] n ufficiale m di stato civile; segretario

registration [redʒɪs'treɪʃən] n (act) registrazione f; iscrizione f; (AUT: also: **~ number**) numero di targa

registry ['redʒɪstrɪ] n ufficio del registro; **~ office** (BRIT) n anagrafe f; **to get married in a ~ office** ≈ sposarsi in municipio

regret [rɪ'gret] n rimpianto, rincrescimento ♦ vt rimpiangere; **~fully** adv con rincrescimento; **~table** adj deplorevole

regular ['regjulə*] adj regolare; (usual) abituale, normale; (soldier) dell'esercito regolare ♦ n (client etc) cliente m/f abituale; **~ly** adv regolarmente

regulate ['regjuleɪt] vt regolare; **regulation** [-'leɪʃən] n regolazione f; (rule) regola, regolamento

rehabilitation ['ri:həbɪlɪ'teɪʃən] n (of offender) riabilitazione f; (of disabled) riadattamento

rehearsal [rɪ'hɜːsəl] n prova

rehearse [rɪ'hɜːs] vt provare

reign [reɪn] n regno ♦ vi regnare

reimburse [ri:ɪm'bɜːs] vt rimborsare

rein [reɪn] n (for horse) briglia

reindeer ['reɪndɪə*] n inv renna

reinforce [ri:ɪn'fɔːs] vt rinforzare; **~d concrete** n cemento armato; **~ment** n rinforzo; **~ments** npl (MIL) rinforzi mpl

reinstate [ri:ɪn'steɪt] vt reintegrare

reiterate [ri:'ɪtəreɪt] vt reiterare, ripetere

reject [n 'ri:dʒekt, vb rɪ'dʒekt] n (COMM) scarto ♦ vt rifiutare, respingere; (COMM: goods) scartare; **~ion** [rɪ'dʒekʃən] n rifiuto

rejoice [rɪ'dʒɔɪs] vi: **to ~ (at or over)** provare diletto in

rejuvenate [rɪˈdʒuːvəneɪt] *vt* ringiovanire

relapse [rɪˈlæps] *n* (*MED*) ricaduta

relate [rɪˈleɪt] *vt* (*tell*) raccontare; (*connect*) collegare ♦ *vi*: **to ~ to** (*connect*) riferirsi a; (*get on with*) stabilire un rapporto con; **relating to** che riguarda, rispetto a; **~d** *adj*: **~d (to)** imparentato(a) (con); collegato(a) *or* connesso(a) (a)

relation [rɪˈleɪʃən] *n* (*person*) parente *m/f*; (*link*) rapporto, relazione *f*; **~ship** *n* rapporto; (*personal ties*) rapporti *mpl*, relazioni *fpl*; (*also*: **family ~ship**) legami *mpl* di parentela

relative [ˈrelətɪv] *n* parente *m/f* ♦ *adj* relativo(a); (*respective*) rispettivo(a); **~ly** *adv* relativamente; (*fairly, rather*) abbastanza

relax [rɪˈlæks] *vi* rilasciarsi; (*person: unwind*) rilassarsi ♦ *vt* rilasciare; (*mind, person*) rilassare; **~ation** [riːlækˈseɪʃən] *n* rilasciamento; rilassamento; (*entertainment*) ricreazione *f*, svago; **~ed** *adj* rilassato(a); **~ing** *adj* rilassante

relay [ˈriːleɪ] *n* (*SPORT*) corsa a staffetta ♦ *vt* (*message*) trasmettere

release [rɪˈliːs] *n* (*from prison*) rilascio; (*from obligation*) liberazione *f*; (*of gas etc*) emissione *f*; (*of film etc*) distribuzione *f*; (*record*) disco; (*device*) disinnesto ♦ *vt* (*prisoner*) rilasciare; (*from obligation, wreckage etc*) liberare; (*book, film*) fare uscire; (*news*) rendere pubblico(a); (*gas etc*) emettere; (*TECH: catch, spring etc*) disinnestare

relegate [ˈrelɪgeɪt] *vt* relegare; (*BRIT: SPORT*): **to be ~d** essere retrocesso(a)

relent [rɪˈlent] *vi* cedere; **~less** *adj* implacabile

relevant [ˈreləvənt] *adj* pertinente, in questione; **~ to** pertinente a

reliability [rɪlaɪəˈbɪlɪtɪ] *n* (*of person*) serietà; (*of machine*) affidabilità

reliable [rɪˈlaɪəbl] *adj* (*person, firm*) fidato(a), che dà affidamento; (*method*) sicuro(a); (*machine*) affidabile; **reliably** *adv*: **to be reliably informed** sapere da fonti sicure

reliance [rɪˈlaɪəns] *n*: **~ (on)** fiducia (in); bisogno (di)

relic [ˈrelɪk] *n* (*REL*) reliquia; (*of the past*) resto

relief [rɪˈliːf] *n* (*from pain, anxiety*) sollievo; (*help, supplies*) soccorsi *mpl*; (*ART, GEO*) rilievo

relieve [rɪˈliːv] *vt* (*pain, patient*) sollevare; (*bring help*) soccorrere; (*take over from: gen*) sostituire; (: *guard*) rilevare; **to ~ sb of sth** (*load*) alleggerire qn di qc; **to ~ o.s.** fare i propri bisogni

religion [rɪˈlɪdʒən] *n* religione *f*; **religious** *adj* religioso(a)

relinquish [rɪˈlɪŋkwɪʃ] *vt* abbandonare; (*plan, habit*) rinunziare a

relish [ˈrelɪʃ] *n* (*CULIN*) condimento; (*enjoyment*) gran piacere *m* ♦ *vt* (*food etc*) godere; **to ~ doing** adorare fare

relocate [ˈriːləʊkeɪt] *vt* trasferire ♦ *vi* trasferirsi

reluctance [rɪˈlʌktəns] *n* riluttanza

reluctant [rɪˈlʌktənt] *adj* riluttante, mal disposto(a); **~ly** *adv* di mala voglia, a malincuore

rely [rɪˈlaɪ]: **to ~ on** *vt fus* contare su; (*be dependent*) dipendere da

remain [rɪˈmeɪn] *vi* restare, rimanere; **~der** *n* resto; (*COMM*) rimanenza; **~ing** *adj* che rimane; **~s** *npl* resti *mpl*

remand [rɪˈmɑːnd] *n*: **on ~** in detenzione preventiva ♦ *vt*: **to ~ in custody** rinviare in carcere; trattenere a disposizione della legge; **~ home** (*BRIT*) *n* riformatorio, casa di correzione

remark [rɪˈmɑːk] *n* osservazione *f* ♦ *vt* osservare, dire; **~able** *adj* notevole; eccezionale

remedial [rɪˈmiːdɪəl] *adj* (*tuition, classes*) di riparazione; (*exercise*) correttivo(a)

remedy [ˈremədɪ] *n*: **~ (for)** rimedio (per) ♦ *vt* rimediare a

remember [rɪˈmembə*] *vt* ricordare, ricordarsi di; **~ me to him** salutalo da parte mia; **remembrance** *n* memoria; ricordo; **Remembrance Day** *n* 11 novembre, *giorno della commemorazione dei caduti in* *guerra*

Remembrance Day

🛈 *In Gran Bretagna, il* **Remembrance Day** *è un giorno di commemorazione dei caduti in guerra. Si celebra ogni anno la domenica più vicina all'11 novembre, anniversario della firma dell'armistizio con la Germania nel 1918.*

---

remind [rɪ'maɪnd] *vt*: **to ~ sb of sth** ricordare qc a qn; **to ~ sb to do** ricordare a qn di fare; **~er** *n* richiamo; (*note etc*) promemoria *m inv*

reminisce [remɪ'nɪs] *vi*: **to ~ (about)** abbandonarsi ai ricordi (di)

reminiscent [remɪ'nɪsnt] *adj*: **~ of** che fa pensare a, che richiama

remiss [rɪ'mɪs] *adj* negligente

remission [rɪ'mɪʃən] *n* remissione *f*

remit [rɪ'mɪt] *vt* (*send: money*) rimettere; **~tance** *n* rimessa

remnant ['remnənt] *n* resto, avanzo; **~s** *npl* (*COMM*) scampoli *mpl*; fine *f* serie

remorse [rɪ'mɔːs] *n* rimorso; **~ful** *adj* pieno(a) di rimorsi; **~less** *adj* (*fig*) spietato(a)

remote [rɪ'məʊt] *adj* remoto(a), lontano(a); (*person*) distaccato(a); **~ control** *n* telecomando; **~ly** *adv* remotamente; (*slightly*) vagamente

remould ['riːməʊld] (*BRIT*) *n* (*tyre*) gomma ricostruita

removable [rɪ'muːvəbl] *adj* (*detachable*) staccabile

removal [rɪ'muːvəl] *n* (*taking away*) rimozione *f*; soppressione *f*; (*BRIT: from house*) trasloco; (*from office: dismissal*) destituzione *f*; (*MED*) ablazione *f*; **~ van** (*BRIT*) *n* furgone *m* per traslochi

remove [rɪ'muːv] *vt* togliere, rimuovere; (*employee*) destituire; (*stain*) far sparire; (*doubt, abuse*) sopprimere, eliminare; **~rs** (*BRIT*) *npl* (*company*) ditta *or* impresa di traslochi

Renaissance [rɪ'neɪsɑːns] *n*: **the ~** il Rinascimento

render ['rendə*] *vt* rendere; **~ing** *n* (*MUS etc*) interpretazione *f*

rendez-vous ['rɒndɪvuː] *n* appuntamento; (*place*) luogo d'incontro; (*meeting*) incontro

renegade ['renɪgeɪd] *n* rinnegato/a

renew [rɪ'njuː] *vt* rinnovare; (*negotiations*) riprendere; **~able** *adj* rinnovabile; **~al** *n* rinnovo; ripresa

renounce [rɪ'naʊns] *vt* rinunziare a

renovate ['renəveɪt] *vt* rinnovare; (*art work*) restaurare; **renovation** [-'veɪʃən] *n* rinnovamento; restauro

renown [rɪ'naʊn] *n* rinomanza; **~ed** *adj* rinomato(a)

rent [rent] *n* affitto ♦ *vt* (*take for ~*) prendere in affitto; (*also: ~ out*) dare in affitto; **~al** *n* (*for television, car*) fitto

renunciation [rɪnʌnsɪ'eɪʃən] *n* rinunzia

rep [rep] *n abbr* (*COMM*: = *representative*) rappresentante *m/f*; (*THEATRE*: = *repertory*) teatro di repertorio

repair [rɪ'peə*] *n* riparazione *f* ♦ *vt* riparare; **in good/bad ~** in buone/cattive condizioni; **~ kit** *n* corredo per riparazioni

repatriate [riː'pætrɪeɪt] *vt* rimpatriare

repay [riː'peɪ] (*irreg*) *vt* (*money, creditor*) rimborsare, ripagare; (*sb's efforts*) ricompensare; (*favour*) ricambiare; **~ment** *n* pagamento; rimborso

repeal [rɪ'piːl] *n* (*of law*) abrogazione *f* ♦ *vt* abrogare

repeat [rɪ'piːt] *n* (*RADIO, TV*) replica ♦ *vt* ripetere; (*pattern*) riprodurre; (*promise, attack, also COMM: order*) rinnovare ♦ *vi* ripetere; **~edly** *adv* ripetutamente, spesso

repel [rɪ'pel] *vt* respingere; (*disgust*) ripugnare a; **~lent** *adj* repellente ♦ *n*: **insect ~lent** prodotto *m* anti-insetti *inv*

repent [rɪ'pent] *vi*: **to ~ (of)** pentirsi (di); **~ance** *n* pentimento

repertoire ['repətwɑː*] *n* repertorio

repertory ['repətərɪ] *n* (*also: ~ theatre*) teatro di repertorio

repetition [repɪ'tɪʃən] *n* ripetizione *f*

repetitive [rɪ'petɪtɪv] *adj* (*movement*) che si ripete; (*work*) monotono(a); (*speech*) pieno(a) di ripetizioni

replace [rɪ'pleɪs] vt (put back) rimettere a posto; (take the place of) sostituire; **~ment** n rimessa; sostituzione f; (person) sostituto/a

replay ['riːpleɪ] n (of match) partita ripetuta; (of tape, film) replay m inv

replenish [rɪ'plenɪʃ] vt (glass) riempire; (stock etc) rifornire

replete [rɪ'pliːt] adj (well-fed) sazio(a)

replica ['replɪkə] n replica, copia

reply [rɪ'plaɪ] n risposta ♦ vi rispondere; **~ coupon** n buono di risposta

report [rɪ'pɔːt] n rapporto; (PRESS etc) cronaca; (BRIT: also: **school ~**) pagella; (of gun) sparo ♦ vt riportare; (PRESS etc) fare una cronaca su; (bring to notice: occurrence) segnalare; (: person) denunciare ♦ vi (make a report) fare un rapporto (or una cronaca); (present o.s.): **to ~ (to sb)** presentarsi (a qn); **~ card** (US, SCOTTISH) n pagella; **~edly** adv stando a quanto si dice; **he ~edly told them to ...** avrebbe detto loro di ...; **~er** n reporter m inv

repose [rɪ'pəuz] n: **in ~** (face, mouth) in riposo

reprehensible [reprɪ'hensɪbl] adj riprovevole

represent [reprɪ'zent] vt rappresentare; **~ation** [-'teɪʃən] n rappresentazione f; (petition) rappresentanza; **~ations** npl (protest) protesta; **~ative** n rappresentante m/f; (US: POL) deputato/a ♦ adj rappresentativo(a)

repress [rɪ'pres] vt reprimere; **~ion** [-'preʃən] n repressione f

reprieve [rɪ'priːv] n (LAW) sospensione f dell'esecuzione della condanna; (fig) dilazione f

reprimand ['reprɪmɑːnd] n rimprovero ♦ vt rimproverare

reprint ['riːprɪnt] n ristampa

reprisal [rɪ'praɪzl] n rappresaglia

reproach [rɪ'prəutʃ] n rimprovero ♦ vt: **to ~ sb for sth** rimproverare qn di qc; **~ful** adj di rimprovero

reproduce [riːprə'djuːs] vt riprodurre ♦ vi riprodursi; **reproduction** [-'dʌkʃən] n riproduzione f

reproof [rɪ'pruːf] n riprovazione f

reprove [rɪ'pruːv] vt: **to ~ (for)** biasimare (per)

reptile ['reptaɪl] n rettile m

republic [rɪ'pʌblɪk] n repubblica, **~an** adj, n repubblicano(a)

repudiate [rɪ'pjuːdɪeɪt] vt (accusation) respingere

repulse [rɪ'pʌls] vt respingere

repulsive [rɪ'pʌlsɪv] adj ripugnante, ripulsivo(a)

reputable ['repjutəbl] adj di buona reputazione; (occupation) rispettabile

reputation [repju'teɪʃən] n reputazione f

reputed [rɪ'pjuːtɪd] adj reputato(a); **~ly** adv secondo quanto si dice

request [rɪ'kwest] n domanda; (formal) richiesta ♦ vt: **to ~ (of or from sb)** chiedere (a qn); **~ stop** (BRIT) n (for bus) fermata facoltativa or a richiesta

require [rɪ'kwaɪə*] vt (need: subj: person) aver bisogno di; (: thing, situation) richiedere; (want) volere; esigere; (order): **to ~ sb to do sth** ordinare a qn di fare qc; **~ment** n esigenza; bisogno; requisito

requisition [rekwɪ'zɪʃən] n: **~ (for)** richiesta (di) ♦ vt (MIL) requisire

rescue ['reskjuː] n salvataggio; (help) soccorso ♦ vt salvare; **~ party** n squadra di salvataggio; **~r** n salvatore/trice

research [rɪ'səːtʃ] n ricerca, ricerche fpl ♦ vt fare ricerche su; **~er** n ricercatore/trice

resemblance [rɪ'zembləns] n somiglianza

resemble [rɪ'zembl] vt assomigliare a

resent [rɪ'zent] vt risentirsi di; **~ful** adj pieno(a) di risentimento; **~ment** n risentimento

reservation [rezə'veɪʃən] n (booking) prenotazione f; (doubt) dubbio; (protected area) riserva; (BRIT: on road: also: **central ~**) spartitraffico m inv

reserve [rɪ'zəːv] n riserva ♦ vt (seats etc) prenotare; **~s** npl (MIL) riserve fpl; **in ~** in serbo; **~d** adj (shy) riservato(a)

reservoir ['rezəvwɑː*] n serbatoio

reshuffle [riː'ʃʌfl] n: **Cabinet ~** (POL) rimpasto governativo

reside [rɪ'zaɪd] vi risiedere

residence ['rezidəns] n residenza; **~ permit** (BRIT) n permesso di soggiorno

resident ['rezidənt] n residente m/f; (in hotel) cliente m/f fisso(a); (doctor) fisso(a); (course, college) a tempo pieno con pernottamento; **~ial** [-'denʃəl] adj di residenza; (area) residenziale

residue ['rezidjuː] n resto; (CHEM, PHYSICS) residuo

resign [rɪ'zaɪn] vt (one's post) dimettersi da ♦ vi dimettersi; **to ~ o.s. to** rassegnarsi a; **~ation** [rezɪg'neɪʃən] n dimissioni fpl; rassegnazione f; **~ed** adj rassegnato(a)

resilience [rɪ'zɪlɪəns] n (of material) elasticità, resilienza; (of person) capacità di recupero

resilient [rɪ'zɪlɪənt] adj elastico(a); (person) che si riprende facilmente

resin ['rezɪn] n resina

resist [rɪ'zɪst] vt resistere a; **~ance** n resistenza

resolution [rezə'luːʃən] n risoluzione f

resolve [rɪ'zɔlv] n risoluzione f ♦ vi (decide): **to ~ to do** decidere di fare ♦ vt (problem) risolvere

resort [rɪ'zɔːt] n (town) stazione f; (recourse) ricorso m; **to ~ to** aver ricorso a; **in the last ~** come ultima risorsa

resounding [rɪ'zaʊndɪŋ] adj risonante; (fig) clamoroso(a)

resource [rɪ'sɔːs] n risorsa; **~s** npl (coal, iron etc) risorse fpl; **~ful** adj pieno(a) di risorse, intraprendente

respect [rɪs'pekt] n rispetto ♦ vt rispettare; **~s** npl (greetings) ossequi mpl; **with ~ to** rispetto a, riguardo a; **in this ~** per questo riguardo; **~able** adj rispettabile; **~ful** adj rispettoso(a)

respective [rɪs'pektɪv] adj rispettivo(a)

respite ['respaɪt] n respiro, tregua

respond [rɪs'pɔnd] vi rispondere

response [rɪs'pɔns] n risposta

responsibility [rɪspɔnsɪ'bɪlɪtɪ] n responsabilità f inv

responsible [rɪs'pɔnsɪbl] adj (trustworthy) fidato(a); (job) di (grande) responsabilità; **~ (for)** responsabile (di)

responsive [rɪs'pɔnsɪv] adj che reagisce

rest [rest] n riposo; (stop) sosta, pausa; (MUS) pausa; (object: to support sth) appoggio, sostegno; (remainder) resto, avanzi mpl ♦ vi riposarsi; (remain) rimanere, restare; (be supported): **to ~ on** appoggiarsi su ♦ vt (far) riposare; (lean): **to ~ sth on/against** appoggiare qc su/contro; **the ~ of them** gli altri; **it ~s with him to decide** sta a lui decidere

restaurant ['restərɔŋ] n ristorante m; **~ car** (BRIT) n vagone m ristorante

restful ['restful] adj riposante

rest home n casa di riposo

restitution [restɪ'tjuːʃən] n: **to make ~ to sb for sth** compensare qn di qc

restive ['restɪv] adj agitato(a), impaziente

restless ['restlɪs] adj agitato(a), irrequieto(a)

restoration [restə'reɪʃən] n restauro; restituzione f

restore [rɪ'stɔː*] vt (building, to power) restaurare; (sth stolen) restituire; (peace, health) ristorare

restrain [rɪs'treɪn] vt (feeling, growth) contenere, frenare; (person): **to ~ (from doing)** trattenere (dal fare); **~ed** adj (style) contenuto(a), sobrio(a), (person) riservato(a); **~t** n (restriction) limitazione f; (moderation) ritegno; (of style) contenutezza

restrict [rɪs'trɪkt] vt restringere, limitare; **~ion** [-kʃən] n: **~ion (on)** restrizione f (di), limitazione f

rest room (US) n toletta

restructure [riː'strʌktʃə*] vt ristrutturare

result [rɪ'zʌlt] n risultato ♦ vi: **to ~ in** avere per risultato; **as a ~ of** in or di conseguenza a, in seguito a

resume [rɪ'zjuːm] vt, vi (work, journey) riprendere

résumé ['reɪzjumeɪ] n riassunto; (US) curriculum m inv vitae

resumption [rɪ'zʌmpʃən] n ripresa

resurgence [rɪ'sə:dʒəns] *n* rinascita
resurrection [rezə'rekʃən] *n* risurrezione *f*
resuscitate [rɪ'sʌsɪteɪt] *vt* (MED) risuscitare;
resuscitation [-'teɪʃən] *n* rianimazione *f*
retail ['ri:teɪl] *adj, adv* al minuto ♦ *vt*
vendere al minuto; **~er** *n* commerciante
m/f al minuto, dettagliante *m/f*; **~ price** *n*
prezzo al minuto
retain [rɪ'teɪn] *vt* (*keep*) tenere, serbare; **~er**
n (*fee*) onorario
retaliate [rɪ'tælɪeɪt] *vi*: **to ~ (against)**
vendicarsi (di); **retaliation** [-'eɪʃən] *n*
rappresaglie *fpl*
retarded [rɪ'tɑ:dɪd] *adj* ritardato(a)
retch [retʃ] *vi* aver conati di vomito
retire [rɪ'taɪə*] *vi* (*give up work*) andare in
pensione; (*withdraw*) ritirarsi, andarsene;
(*go to bed*) andare a letto, ritirarsi; **~d** *adj*
(*person*) pensionato(a); **~ment** *n* pensione
f; (*act*) pensionamento; **retiring** *adj*
(*leaving*) uscente; (*shy*) riservato(a)
retort [rɪ'tɔ:t] *vi* rimbeccare
retrace [ri:'treɪs] *vt*: **to ~ one's steps**
tornare sui passi
retract [rɪ'trækt] *vt* (*statement*) ritrattare;
(*claws, undercarriage, aerial*) ritrarre, ritirare
retrain [ri:'treɪn] *vt* (*worker*) riaddestrare
retread ['ri:tred] *n* (*tyre*) gomma rigenerata
retreat [rɪ'tri:t] *n* ritirata; (*place*) rifugio ♦ *vi*
battere in ritirata
retribution [retrɪ'bju:ʃən] *n* castigo
retrieval [rɪ'tri:vəl] *n* (*see vb*) ricupero;
riparazione *f*
retrieve [rɪ'tri:v] *vt* (*sth lost*) ricuperare,
ritrovare; (*situation, honour*) salvare; (*error,
loss*) rimediare a; **~r** *n* cane *m* da riporto
retrospect ['retrəspekt] *n*: **in ~** guardando
indietro; **~ive** [-'spektɪv] *adj*
retrospettivo(a); (*law*) retroattivo(a)
return [rɪ'tə:n] *n* (*going or coming back*)
ritorno; (*of sth stolen etc*) restituzione *f*;
(*FINANCE: from land, shares*) profitto, reddito
♦ *cpd* (*journey, match*) di ritorno; (*BRIT:
ticket*) di andata e ritorno ♦ *vi* tornare,
ritornare ♦ *vt* rendere, restituire; (*bring
back*) riportare; (*send back*) mandare
indietro; (*put back*) rimettere; (*POL:*

candidate) eleggere; **~s** *npl* (COMM) incassi
mpl; profitti *mpl*; **in ~ (for)** in cambio (di);
by ~ of post a stretto giro di posta; **many
happy ~s (of the day)!** cento di questi
giorni!
reunion [ri:'ju:nɪən] *n* riunione *f*
reunite [ri:ju:'naɪt] *vt* riunire
rev [rev] *n abbr* (AUT: = *revolution*) giro ♦ *vt*
(*also: ~ up*) imballare
revamp ['ri:'væmp] *vt* (*firm*) riorganizzare
reveal [rɪ'vi:l] *vt* (*make known*) rivelare,
svelare; (*display*) rivelare, mostrare; **~ing**
adj rivelatore(trice); (*dress*) scollato(a)
revel ['revl] *vi*: **to ~ in sth/in doing**
dilettarsi di qc/a fare
revelation [revə'leɪʃən] *n* rivelazione *f*
revenge [rɪ'vendʒ] *n* vendetta ♦ *vt*
vendicare; **to take ~ on** vendicarsi di
revenue ['revənju:] *n* reddito
reverberate [rɪ'və:bəreɪt] *vi* (*sound*)
rimbombare; (*light*) riverberarsi; (*fig*)
ripercuotersi
revere [rɪ'vɪə*] *vt* venerare
reverence ['revərəns] *n* venerazione *f*,
riverenza
Reverend ['revərənd] *adj* (*in titles*)
reverendo(a)
reverie ['revəri] *n* fantasticheria
reversal [rɪ'və:sl] *n* capovolgimento
reverse [rɪ'və:s] *n* contrario, opposto; (*back,
defeat*) rovescio; (AUT: *also:* **~ gear**) marcia
indietro ♦ *adj* (*order, direction*) contrario(a),
opposto(a) ♦ *vt* (*turn*) invertire, rivoltare;
(*change*) capovolgere, rovesciare; (LAW:
judgment) cassare; (*car*) fare marcia indietro
con ♦ *vi* (BRIT: AUT, *person etc*) fare marcia
indietro; **~d charge call** (BRIT) *n* (TEL)
telefonata con addebito al ricevente;
reversing lights (BRIT) *npl* (AUT) luci *fpl*
per la retromarcia
revert [rɪ'və:t] *vi*: **to ~ to** tornare a
review [rɪ'vju:] *n* rivista; (*of book, film*)
recensione *f*; (*of situation*) esame *m* ♦ *vt*
passare in rivista; fare la recensione di; fare
il punto di; **~er** *n* recensore/a
revise [rɪ'vaɪz] *vt* (*manuscript*) rivedere,
correggere; (*opinion*) emendare,

modificare; (study: subject, notes) ripassare;
revision [rɪ'vɪʒən] n revisione f; ripasso
revitalize [riː'vaɪtəlaɪz] vt ravvivare
revival [rɪ'vaɪvl] n ripresa; ristabilimento;
(of faith) risveglio
revive [rɪ'vaɪv] vt (person) rianimare;
(custom) far rivivere; (hope, courage,
economy) ravvivare; (play, fashion)
riesumare ♦ vi (person) rianimarsi; (hope)
ravvivarsi; (activity) riprendersi
revolt [rɪ'vəʊlt] n rivolta, ribellione f ♦ vi
rivoltarsi, ribellarsi ♦ vt (far) rivoltare; ~**ing**
adj ripugnante
revolution [revə'luːʃən] n rivoluzione f; (of
wheel etc) rivoluzione, giro; ~**ary** adj, n
rivoluzionario(a)
revolve [rɪ'vɒlv] vi girare
revolver [rɪ'vɒlvə*] n rivoltella
revolving [rɪ'vɒlvɪŋ] adj girevole
revue [rɪ'vjuː] n (THEATRE) rivista
revulsion [rɪ'vʌlʃən] n ripugnanza
reward [rɪ'wɔːd] n ricompensa, premio ♦ vt:
to ~ (for) ricompensare (per); ~**ing** adj
(fig) gratificante
rewind [riː'waɪnd] (irreg) vt (watch)
ricaricare; (ribbon etc) riavvolgere
rewire [riː'waɪə*] vt (house) rifare l'impianto
elettrico
reword [riː'wɜːd] vt formulare or esprimere
con altre parole
rheumatism ['ruːmətɪzəm] n reumatismo
Rhine [raɪn] n: **the ~** il Reno
rhinoceros [raɪ'nɒsərəs] n rinoceronte m
rhododendron [rəʊdə'dendrən] n
rododendro
Rhone [rəʊn] n: **the ~** il Rodano
rhubarb ['ruːbɑːb] n rabarbaro
rhyme [raɪm] n rima; (verse) poesia
rhythm ['rɪðm] n ritmo
rib [rɪb] n (ANAT) costola ♦ vt (tease)
punzecchiare
ribbon ['rɪbən] n nastro; **in ~s** (torn) a
brandelli
rice [raɪs] n riso; ~ **pudding** n budino di
riso
rich [rɪtʃ] adj ricco(a); (clothes) sontuoso(a);
(abundant): ~ **in** ricco(a) di; **the ~** npl

(wealthy people) i ricchi; ~**es** npl ricchezze
fpl; ~**ly** adv riccamente; (dressed)
sontuosamente; (deserved) pienamente
rickets ['rɪkɪts] n rachitismo
ricochet ['rɪkəʃeɪ] vi rimbalzare
rid [rɪd] (pt, pp rid) vt: **to ~ sb of** sbarazzare
or liberare qn di; **to get ~ of** sbarazzarsi di
ridden ['rɪdn] pp of ride
riddle ['rɪdl] n (puzzle) indovinello ♦ vt: **to
be ~d with** (holes) essere crivellato(a) di;
(doubts) essere pieno(a) di
ride [raɪd] (pt rode, pp ridden) n (on horse)
cavalcata; (outing) passeggiata; (distance
covered) cavalcata, corsa ♦ vi (as sport)
cavalcare; (go somewhere: on horse, bicycle)
andare (a cavallo or in bicicletta etc);
(journey: on bicycle, motorcycle, bus) andare,
viaggiare ♦ vt (a horse) montare, cavalcare;
to take sb for a ~ (fig) prendere in giro
qn; fregare qn; **to ~ a horse/bicycle/
camel** montare a cavallo/in bicicletta/in
groppa a un cammello; ~**r** n cavalcatore/
trice; (in race) fantino; (on bicycle) ciclista
m/f; (on motorcycle) motociclista m/f
ridge [rɪdʒ] n (of hill) cresta; (of roof) colmo;
(on object) riga (in rilievo)
ridicule ['rɪdɪkjuːl] n ridicolo; scherno ♦ vt
mettere in ridicolo
ridiculous [rɪ'dɪkjuləs] adj ridicolo(a)
riding ['raɪdɪŋ] n equitazione f; ~ **school** n
scuola d'equitazione
rife [raɪf] adj diffuso(a); **to be ~ with**
abbondare di
riffraff ['rɪfræf] n canaglia
rifle ['raɪfl] n carabina ♦ vt vuotare; ~
through vt fus frugare tra; ~ **range** n
campo di tiro; (at fair) tiro a segno
rift [rɪft] n fessura, crepatura; (fig:
disagreement) incrinatura, disaccordo
rig [rɪg] n (also: **oil ~**: on land) derrick m inv;
(: at sea) piattaforma di trivellazione ♦ vt
(election etc) truccare; ~ **out** (BRIT) vt: **to ~
out as/in** vestire da/in; ~ **up** vt allestire;
~**ging** n (NAUT) attrezzatura
right [raɪt] adj giusto(a); (suitable)
appropriato(a); (not left) destro(a) ♦ n
giusto; (title, claim) diritto; (not left) destra

♦ *adv* (*answer*) correttamente; (*not on the left*) a destra ♦ *vt* raddrizzare; (*fig*) riparare ♦ *excl* bene!; **to be ~** (*person*) aver ragione; (*answer*) essere giusto(a) *or* corretto(a); **by ~s** di diritto; **on the ~** a destra; **to be in the ~** aver ragione, essere nel giusto; **~ now** proprio adesso; subito; **~ away** subito; **~ angle** *n* angolo retto; **~eous** ['raɪtʃəs] *adj* retto(a), virtuoso(a); (*anger*) giusto(a), giustificato(a); **~ful** *adj* (*heir*) legittimo(a); **~-handed** *adj* (*person*) che adopera la mano destra; **~-hand man** *n* braccio destro; **~-hand side** *n* il lato destro; **~ly** *adv* bene, correttamente; (*with reason*) a ragione; **~ of way** *n* diritto di passaggio; (*AUT*) precedenza; **~-wing** *adj* (*POL*) di destra

rigid ['rɪdʒɪd] *adj* rigido(a); (*principle*) rigoroso(a)

rigmarole ['rɪgmərəʊl] *n* tiritera; commedia

rile [raɪl] *vt* irritare, seccare

rim [rɪm] *n* orlo; (*of spectacles*) montatura; (*of wheel*) cerchione *m*

rind [raɪnd] *n* (*of bacon*) cotenna; (*of lemon etc*) scorza

ring [rɪŋ] (*pt* **rang**, *pp* **rung**) *n* anello; (*of people, objects*) cerchio; (*of spies*) giro; (*of smoke etc*) spirale *m*; (*arena*) pista, arena; (*for boxing*) ring *m inv*; (*sound of bell*) scampanio ♦ *vi* (*person, bell, telephone*) suonare; (*also: ~ out: voice, words*) risuonare; (*TEL*) telefonare; (*ears*) fischiare ♦ *vt* (*BRIT: TEL*) telefonare a; (*bell, doorbell*) suonare; **to give sb a ~** (*BRIT: TEL*) dare un colpo di telefono a qn; **~ back** *vt, vi* (*TEL*) richiamare; **~ off** (*BRIT*) *vi* (*TEL*) mettere giù, riattaccare; **~ up** (*BRIT*) *vt* (*TEL*) telefonare a; **~ing** *n* (*of bell*) scampanio; (*of telephone*) squillo; (*in ears*) ronzio; **~ing tone** (*BRIT*) *n* (*TEL*) segnale *m* di libero; **~leader** *n* (*of gang*) capobanda *m*

ringlets ['rɪŋlɪts] *npl* boccoli *mpl*

ring road (*BRIT*) *n* raccordo anulare

rink [rɪŋk] *n* (*also: **ice ~***) pista di pattinaggio

rinse [rɪns] *n* risciacquatura; (*hair tint*) cachet *m inv* ♦ *vt* sciacquare

riot ['raɪət] *n* sommossa, tumulto; (*of colours*)

orgia ♦ *vi* tumultuare; **to run ~** creare disordine; **~ous** *adj* tumultuoso(a); (*living*) sfrenato(a); (*party*) scatenato(a)

rip [rɪp] *n* strappo ♦ *vt* strappare ♦ *vi* strapparsi; **~cord** *n* cavo di sfilamento

ripe [raɪp] *adj* (*fruit, grain*) maturo(a); (*cheese*) stagionato(a); **~n** *vt* maturare ♦ *vi* maturarsi

ripple ['rɪpl] *n* increspamento, ondulazione *f*; mormorio ♦ *vi* incresparsi

rise [raɪz] (*pt* **rose**, *pp* **risen**) *n* (*slope*) salita, pendio; (*hill*) altura; (*increase: in wages: BRIT*) aumento; (: *in prices, temperature*) rialzo, aumento; (*fig: to power etc*) ascesa ♦ *vi* alzarsi, levarsi; (*prices*) aumentare; (*waters, river*) crescere; (*sun, wind, person: from chair, bed*) levarsi; (*also: ~ up: building*) ergersi; (: *rebel*) insorgere; ribellarsi; (*in rank*) salire; **to give ~ to** provocare, dare origine a; **to ~ to the occasion** essere all'altezza; **risen** ['rɪzn] *pp* of **rise**; **rising** *adj* (*increasing: number*) sempre crescente; (: *prices*) in aumento; (*tide*) montante; (*sun, moon*) nascente, che sorge

risk [rɪsk] *n* rischio; pericolo ♦ *vt* rischiare; **to take** *or* **run the ~ of doing** correre il rischio di fare; **at ~** in pericolo; **at one's own ~** a proprio rischio e pericolo; **~y** *adj* rischioso(a)

risqué ['riːskeɪ] *adj* (*joke*) spinto(a)

rissole ['rɪsəʊl] *n* crocchetta

rite [raɪt] *n* rito; **last ~s** l'estrema unzione

ritual ['rɪtjʊəl] *adj* rituale ♦ *n* rituale *m*

rival ['raɪvl] *n* rivale *m/f*; (*in business*) concorrente *m/f* ♦ *adj* rivale; che fa concorrenza ♦ *vt* essere in concorrenza con; **to ~ sb/sth in** competere con qn/qc in; **~ry** *n* rivalità; concorrenza

river ['rɪvə*] *n* fiume *m* ♦ *cpd* (*port, traffic*) fluviale; **up/down ~** a monte/valle; **~bank** *n* argine *m*; **~bed** *n* letto di fiume

rivet ['rɪvɪt] *n* ribattino, rivetto ♦ *vt* (*fig*) concentrare, fissare

Riviera [rɪvɪ'eərə] *n*: **the (French) ~** la Costa Azzurra; **the Italian ~** la Riviera

road [rəʊd] *n* strada; (*small*) cammino; (*in town*) via ♦ *cpd* stradale; **major/minor ~**

strada con/senza diritto di precedenza; ~ **accident** n incidente m stradale; ~**block** n blocco stradale; ~**hog** n guidatore m egoista e spericolato; ~ **map** n carta stradale; ~ **rage** n comportamento aggressivo al volante; ~ **safety** n sicurezza sulle strade; ~**side** n margine m della strada; ~**sign** n cartello stradale; ~**user** n chi usa la strada; ~**way** n carreggiata; ~**works** npl lavori mpl stradali; ~**worthy** adj in buono stato di marcia

roam [rəum] vi errare, vagabondare

roar [rɔː*] n ruggito; (of crowd) tumulto; (of thunder, storm) muggito; (of laughter) scoppio ♦ vi ruggire; tumultuare; muggire; **to ~ with laughter** scoppiare dalle risa; **to do a ~ing trade** fare affari d'oro

roast [rəust] n arrosto ♦ vt arrostire; (coffee) tostare, torrefare; ~ **beef** n arrosto di manzo

rob [rɔb] vt (person) rubare; (bank) svaligiare; **to ~ sb of sth** derubare qn di qc; (fig: deprive) privare qn di qc; ~**ber** n ladro; (armed) rapinatore m; ~**bery** n furto; rapina

robe [rəub] n (for ceremony etc) abito; (also: **bath** ~) accappatoio; (US: also: **lap** ~) coperta

robin ['rɔbɪn] n pettirosso

robot ['rəubɔt] n robot m inv

robust [rəu'bʌst] adj robusto(a); (economy) solido(a)

rock [rɔk] n (substance) roccia; (boulder) masso; roccia; (in sea) scoglio; (US: pebble) ciottolo; (BRIT: sweet) zucchero candito ♦ vt (swing gently: cradle) dondolare; (: child) cullare; (shake) scrollare, far tremare ♦ vi dondolarsi; scrollarsi, tremare; **on the ~s** (drink) col ghiaccio; (marriage etc) in crisi; ~ **and roll** n rock and roll m; ~**-bottom** adj bassissimo(a); ~**ery** n giardino roccioso

rocket ['rɔkɪt] n razzo

rock fall n parete f della roccia

rocking ['rɔkɪŋ]: ~ **chair** n sedia a dondolo; ~ **horse** n cavallo a dondolo

rocky ['rɔkɪ] adj (hill) roccioso(a); (path) sassoso(a); (marriage etc) instabile

rod [rɔd] n (metallic, TECH) asta; (wooden) bacchetta; (also: **fishing** ~) canna da pesca

rode [rəud] pt of **ride**

rodent ['rəudnt] n roditore m

rodeo ['rəudɪəu] n rodeo

roe [rəu] n (species: also: ~ **deer**) capriolo; (of fish, also: **hard** ~) uova fpl di pesce; **soft** ~ latte m di pesce

rogue [rəug] n mascalzone m

role [rəul] n ruolo

roll [rəul] n rotolo; (of banknotes) mazzo; (also: **bread** ~) panino; (register) lista; (sound: of drums etc) rullo ♦ vt rotolare; (also: ~ **up**: string) aggomitolare; (also: ~ **up**: sleeves) rimboccare; (cigarettes) arrotolare; (eyes) roteare; (also: ~ **out**: pastry) stendere; (lawn, road etc) spianare ♦ vi rotolare; (wheel) girare; (drum) rullare; (vehicle; also: ~ **along**) avanzare; (ship) rollare; ~ **about** or **around** vi rotolare qua e là; (person) rotolarsi; ~ **by** vi (time) passare; ~ **over** vi rivoltarsi; ~ **up** vi (inf: arrive) arrivare ♦ vt (carpet) arrotolare; ~ **call** n appello; ~**er** n rullo; (wheel) rotella; (for hair) bigodino; ~**er blades** npl pattini mpl in linea; ~**er coaster** n montagne fpl russe; ~**er skates** npl pattini mpl a rotelle

rolling ['rəulɪŋ] adj (landscape) ondulato(a); ~ **pin** n matterello; ~ **stock** n (RAIL) materiale m rotabile

ROM [rɔm] n abbr (= read only memory) memoria di sola lettura

Roman ['rəumən] adj, n romano(a); ~ **Catholic** adj, n cattolico(a)

romance [rə'mæns] n storia (or avventura or film m inv) romantico(a); (charm) poesia; (love affair) idillio

Romania [rəu'meɪnɪə] n = **Rumania**

Roman numeral n numero romano

romantic [rə'mæntɪk] adj romantico(a); sentimentale

Rome [rəum] n Roma

romp [rɔmp] n gioco rumoroso ♦ vi (also: ~ **about**) far chiasso, giocare in un modo rumoroso

rompers ['rɔmpəz] npl pagliaccetto

roof [ruːf] n tetto; (of tunnel, cave) volta ♦ vt

coprire (con un tetto); **~ of the mouth** palato; **~ing** n materiale m per copertura; **~ rack** n (AUT) portabagagli m inv

rook [ruk] n (bird) corvo nero; (CHESS) torre f

room [ru:m] n (in house) stanza; (bed~, in hotel) camera; (in school etc) sala; (space) posto, spazio; **~s** npl (lodging) alloggio; **"~s to let"** (BRIT), **"~s for rent"** (US) "si affittano camere"; **there is ~ for improvement** si potrebbe migliorare; **~ing house** (US) n casa in cui si affittano camere o appartamentini ammobiliati; **~mate** n compagno/a di stanza; **~ service** n servizio da camera; **~y** adj spazioso(a); (garment) ampio(a)

roost [ru:st] vi appollaiarsi

rooster ['ru:stə*] n gallo

root [ru:t] n radice f ♦ vi (plant, belief) attecchire; **~ about** vi (fig) frugare; **~ for** vt fus fare il tifo per; **~ out** vt estirpare

rope [rəup] n corda, fune f; (NAUT) cavo ♦ vt (box) legare; (climbers) legare in cordata; (area: also: **~ off**) isolare cingendo con cordoni; **to know the ~s** (fig) conoscere i trucchi del mestiere; **~ in** vt (fig) coinvolgere; **~ ladder** n scala a corda

rosary ['rəuzəri] n rosario; roseto

rose [rəuz] pt of **rise** ♦ n rosa; (also: **~ bush**) rosaio; (on watering can) rosetta

rosé ['rəuzei] n vino rosato

rosebud ['rəuzbʌd] n bocciolo di rosa

rosebush ['rəuzbuʃ] n rosaio

rosemary ['rəuzməri] n rosmarino

rosette [rəu'zet] n coccarda

roster ['rɒstə*] n: **duty ~** ruolino di servizio

rostrum ['rɒstrəm] n tribuna

rosy ['rəuzi] adj roseo(a)

rot [rɒt] n (decay) putrefazione f; (inf: nonsense) stupidaggini fpl ♦ vt, vi imputridire, marcire

rota ['rəutə] n tabella dei turni

rotary ['rəutəri] adj rotante

rotate [rəu'teit] vt (revolve) far girare; (change round: jobs) fare a turno ♦ vi (revolve) girare; **rotating** adj (movement) rotante

rotten ['rɒtn] adj (decayed) putrido(a),

marcio(a); (dishonest) corrotto(a); (inf: bad) brutto(a); (: action) vigliacco(a); **to feel ~** (ill) sentirsi da cani

rouble ['ru:bl] (US **ruble**) n rublo

rouge [ru:ʒ] n belletto

rough [rʌf] adj (skin, surface) ruvido(a); (terrain, road) accidentato(a); (voice) rauco(a); (person, manner: coarse) rozzo(a), aspro(a); (: violent) brutale; (district) malfamato(a); (weather) cattivo(a); (sea) mosso(a); (plan) abbozzato(a); (guess) approssimativo(a) ♦ n (GOLF) macchia; **to ~ it** far vita dura; **to sleep ~** (BRIT) dormire all'addiaccio; **~age** n alimenti mpl ricchi in cellulosa; **~-and-ready** adj rudimentale; **~cast** n intonaco grezzo; **~ copy** n brutta copia; **~ly** adv (handle) rudemente, brutalmente; (make) grossolanamente; (speak) bruscamente; (approximately) approssimativamente; **~ness** n ruvidità; (of manner) rozzezza

roulette [ru:'let] n roulette f

Roumania [ru:'meiniə] n = **Rumania**

round [raund] adj rotondo(a); (figures) tondo(a) ♦ n (BRIT: of toast) fetta; (duty: of policeman, milkman etc) giro; (: of doctor) visite fpl; (game: of cards, golf, in competition) partita; (of ammunition) cartuccia; (BOXING) round m inv; (of talks) serie f inv ♦ vt (corner) girare; (bend) prendere ♦ prep intorno a ♦ adv: **all ~** tutt'attorno; **to go the long way ~** fare il giro più lungo; **all the year ~** tutto l'anno; **it's just ~ the corner** (also fig) è dietro l'angolo; **~ the clock** ininterrottamente; **to go ~ to sb's house** andare da qn; **go ~ the back** passi dietro; **enough to go ~** abbastanza per tutti; **~ of applause** applausi mpl; **~ of drinks** giro di bibite; **~ of sandwiches** sandwich m inv; **~ off** vt (speech etc) finire; **~ up** vt radunare; (criminals) fare una retata di; (prices) arrotondare; **~about** n (BRIT: AUT) rotatoria; (: at fair) giostra ♦ adj (route, means) indiretto(a); **~ers** npl (game) gioco simile al baseball; **~ly** adv (fig) chiaro e tondo; **~ trip** n (viaggio di) andata e

ritorno; ~**up** n raduno; (of criminals) retata
rouse [rauz] vt (wake up) svegliare; (stir up)
destare; provocare; risvegliare; **rousing**
adj (speech, applause) entusiastico(a)
route [ru:t] n itinerario; (of bus) percorso
routine [ru:'ti:n] adj (work) corrente,
abituale; (procedure) solito(a) ♦ n (pej)
routine f, tran tran m; (THEATRE) numero
rove [rəuv] vt vagabondare per
row[1] [rəu] n (line) riga, fila; (KNITTING) ferro;
(behind one another: of cars, people) fila; (in
boat) remata ♦ vi (in boat) remare; (as
sport) vogare ♦ vt (boat) manovrare a remi;
in a ~ (fig) di fila
row[2] [rau] n (racket) baccano, chiasso;
(dispute) lite f; (scolding) sgridata ♦ vi
(argue) litigare
rowboat ['rəubəut] (US) n barca a remi
rowdy ['raudi] adj chiassoso(a);
turbolento(a) ♦ n teppista m/f
rowing ['rəuɪŋ] n canottaggio; ~ **boat**
(BRIT) n barca a remi
royal ['rɔɪəl] adj reale; **R~ Air Force** n
aeronautica militare britannica
royalty ['rɔɪəltɪ] n (royal persons) (membri
mpl della) famiglia reale; (payment: to
author) diritti mpl d'autore
r.p.m. abbr (= revolutions per minute) giri/
min
R.S.V.P. abbr (= répondez s'il vous plaît)
R.S.V.P.
Rt Hon. (BRIT) abbr (= Right Honourable)
≈ Onorevole
rub [rʌb] n: **to give sth a ~** strofinare qc;
(sore place) massaggiare qc ♦ vt strofinare;
massaggiare; (hands: also: ~ **together**)
sfregarsi; **to ~ sb up** (BRIT) or ~ **sb the
wrong way** (US) lisciare qn contro pelo; ~
off vi andare via; ~ **off on** vt fus lasciare
una traccia su; ~ **out** vt cancellare
rubber ['rʌbə*] n gomma; ~ **band** n
elastico; ~ **plant** n ficus m inv
rubbish ['rʌbɪʃ] n (from household)
immondizie fpl, rifiuti mpl; (fig: pej) cose
fpl senza valore; robaccia; sciocchezze fpl;
~ **bin** (BRIT) n pattumiera; ~ **dump** n (in
town) immondezzaio

rubble ['rʌbl] n macerie fpl; (smaller)
pietrisco
ruble ['ru:bl] (US) n = **rouble**
ruby ['ru:bɪ] n rubino
rucksack ['rʌksæk] n zaino
rudder ['rʌdə*] n timone m
ruddy ['rʌdɪ] adj (face) rubicondo(a); (inf:
damned) maledetto(a)
rude [ru:d] adj (impolite: person) scortese,
rozzo(a); (: word, manners) grossolano(a),
rozzo(a); (shocking) indecente; ~**ness** n
scortesia; grossolanità
ruffle ['rʌfl] vt (hair) scompigliare; (clothes,
water) increspare; (fig: person) turbare
rug [rʌg] n tappeto; (BRIT: for knees) coperta
rugby ['rʌgbɪ] n (also: ~ **football**) rugby m
rugged ['rʌgɪd] adj (landscape) aspro(a);
(features, determination) duro(a); (character)
brusco(a)
ruin ['ru:ɪn] n rovina ♦ vt rovinare; ~**s** npl (of
building, castle etc) rovine fpl, ruderi mpl;
~**ous** adj rovinoso(a); (expenditure)
inverosimile
rule [ru:l] n regola; (regulation)
regolamento, regola; (government)
governo; (~r) riga ♦ vt (country) governare;
(person) dominare ♦ vi regnare; decidere;
(LAW) dichiarare; **as a ~** normalmente; ~
out vt escludere; ~**d** adj (paper)
vergato(a); ~**r** n (sovereign) sovrano/a; (for
measuring) regolo, riga; **ruling** adj (party)
al potere; (class) dirigente ♦ n (LAW)
decisione f
rum [rʌm] n rum m
Rumania [ru:'meɪnɪə] n Romania
rumble ['rʌmbl] n rimbombo; brontolio ♦ vi
rimbombare; (stomach, pipe) brontolare
rummage ['rʌmɪdʒ] vi frugare
rumour ['ru:mə*] (US **rumor**) n voce f ♦ vt:
it is ~ed that corre voce che
rump [rʌmp] n groppa; ~ **steak** n bistecca
di girello
rumpus ['rʌmpəs] (inf) n baccano; (quarrel)
rissa
run [rʌn] (pt **ran**, pp **run**) n corsa; (outing)
gita (in macchina); (distance travelled)
percorso, tragitto; (SKI) pista; (CRICKET,

BASEBALL) meta; (*series*) serie *f*; (*THEATRE*) periodo di rappresentazione; (*in tights, stockings*) smagliatura ♦ *vt* (*distance*) correre; (*operate: business*) gestire, dirigere; (*: competition, course*) organizzare; (*: hotel*) gestire; (*: house*) governare; (*COMPUT*) eseguire; (*water, bath*) far scorrere; (*force through: rope, pipe*): **to ~ sth through** far passare qc attraverso; (*pass: hand, finger*): **to ~ sth over** passare qc su; (*PRESS: feature*) presentare ♦ *vi* correre; (*flee*) scappare; (*pass: road etc*) passare; (*work: machine, factory*) funzionare, andare; (*bus, train: operate*) far scorrere; (*: travel*) circolare; (*: house*) governare; (*COMPUT*) (*slide: drawer; flow: river, bath*) scorrere; (*colours, washing*) stemperarsi; (*in election*) presentarsi candidato; (*nose*) colare; **there was a ~ on ...** c'era una corsa a ...; **in the long ~** a lungo andare; **on the ~** in fuga; **to ~ a race** partecipare ad una gara; **I'll ~ you to the station** ti porto alla stazione; **to ~ a risk** correre un rischio; **~ about** *or* **around** *vi* (*children*) correre qua e là; **~ across** *vt fus* (*find*) trovare per caso; **~ away** *vi* fuggire; **~ down** *vt* (*production*) ridurre gradualmente; (*factory*) rallentare l'attività di; (*AUT*) investire; (*criticize*) criticare; **to be ~ down** (*person: tired*) essere esausto(a); **~ in** (*BRIT*) *vt* (*car*) rodare, fare il rodaggio di; **~ into** *vt fus* (*meet: person*) incontrare per caso; (*: trouble*) incontrare, trovare; (*collide with*) andare a sbattere contro; **~ off** *vi* fuggire ♦ *vt* (*water*) far scolare; (*copies*) fare; **~ out** *vi* (*person*) uscire di corsa; (*liquid*) colare; (*lease*) scadere; (*money*) esaurirsi; **~ out of** *vt fus* rimanere a corto di; **~ over** *vt* (*AUT*) investire, mettere sotto ♦ *vt fus* (*revise*) rivedere; **~ through** *vt fus* (*instructions*) dare una scorsa a; (*rehearse: play*) riprovare, ripetere; **~ up** *vt* (*debt*) lasciar accumulare; **to ~ up against** (*difficulties*) incontrare; **~away** *adj* (*person*) fuggiasco(a); (*horse*) in libertà; (*truck*) fuori controllo

rung [rʌŋ] *pp of* **ring** ♦ *n* (*of ladder*) piolo

runner ['rʌnə*] *n* (*in race*) corridore *m*; (*: horse*) partente *m/f*; (*on sledge*) pattino; (*for drawer etc*) guida; **~ bean** (*BRIT*) *n* fagiolo rampicante; **~-up** *n* secondo(a) arrivato(a)

running ['rʌnɪŋ] *n* corsa; direzione *f*; organizzazione *f*; funzionamento ♦ *adj* (*water*) corrente; (*commentary*) simultaneo(a); **to be in/out of the ~ for sth** essere/non essere più in lizza per qc; **6 days** ~ 6 giorni di seguito; **~ costs** *npl* costi *mpl* d'esercizio; (*of car*) spese *fpl* di mantenimento

runny ['rʌni] *adj* che cola

run-of-the-mill *adj* solito(a), banale

runt [rʌnt] *n* (*also pej*) omuncolo; (*ZOOL*) animale *m* più piccolo del normale

run-through *n* prova

run-up *n*: **~ to** (*election etc*) periodo che precede

runway ['rʌnwei] *n* (*AVIAT*) pista (di decollo)

rupture ['rʌptʃə*] *n* (*MED*) ernia

rural ['rʊərəl] *adj* rurale

ruse [ruːz] *n* trucco

rush [rʌʃ] *n* corsa precipitosa; (*hurry*) furia, fretta; (*sudden demand*): **~ for** corsa a; (*current*) flusso; (*of emotion*) impeto; (*BOT*) giunco ♦ *vt* mandare *or* spedire velocemente; (*attack: town etc*) prendere d'assalto ♦ *vi* precipitarsi; **~ hour** *n* ora di punta

rusk [rʌsk] *n* biscotto

Russia ['rʌʃə] *n* Russia; **~n** *adj* russo(a) ♦ *n* russo/a; (*LING*) russo

rust [rʌst] *n* ruggine *f* ♦ *vi* arrugginirsi

rustic ['rʌstik] *adj* rustico(a)

rustle ['rʌsl] *vi* frusciare ♦ *vt* (*paper*) far frusciare

rustproof ['rʌstpruːf] *adj* inossidabile

rusty ['rʌsti] *adj* arrugginito(a)

rut [rʌt] *n* solco; (*ZOOL*) fregola; **to get into a ~** (*fig*) adagiarsi troppo

ruthless ['ruːθlis] *adj* spietato(a)

rye [rai] *n* segale *f*; **~ bread** *n* pane *m* di segale

S, s

Sabbath ['sæbəθ] n (*Jewish*) sabato; (*Christian*) domenica

sabotage ['sæbɑtɑːʒ] n sabotaggio ♦ vt sabotare

saccharin(e) ['sækərɪn] n saccarina

sachet ['sæʃeɪ] n bustina

sack [sæk] n (*bag*) sacco ♦ vt (*dismiss*) licenziare, mandare a spasso; (*plunder*) saccheggiare; **to get the ~** essere mandato a spasso; **~ing** n tela di sacco; (*dismissal*) licenziamento

sacrament ['sækrəmənt] n sacramento

sacred ['seɪkrɪd] adj sacro(a)

sacrifice ['sækrɪfaɪs] n sacrificio ♦ vt sacrificare

sad [sæd] adj triste

saddle ['sædl] n sella ♦ vt (*horse*) sellare; **to be ~d with sth** (*inf*) avere qc sulle spalle; **~bag** n (*on bicycle*) borsa

sadistic [sə'dɪstɪk] adj sadico(a)

sadness ['sædnɪs] n tristezza

s.a.e. n abbr = **stamped addressed envelope**

safe [seɪf] adj sicuro(a); (*out of danger*) salvo(a), al sicuro; (*cautious*) prudente ♦ n cassaforte f; **~ from** al sicuro da; **~ and sound** sano(a) e salvo(a); **(just) to be on the ~ side** per non correre rischi; **~-conduct** n salvacondotto; **~-deposit** n (*vault*) caveau m inv; (*box*) cassetta di sicurezza; **~guard** n salvaguardia ♦ vt salvaguardare; **~keeping** n custodia; **~ly** adv sicuramente; sano(a) e salvo(a); prudentemente; **~ sex** n sesso sicuro

safety ['seɪftɪ] n sicurezza; **~ belt** n cintura di sicurezza; **~ pin** n spilla di sicurezza; **~ valve** n valvola di sicurezza

saffron ['sæfrən] n zafferano

sag [sæg] vi incurvarsi; afflosciarsi

sage [seɪdʒ] n (*herb*) salvia; (*man*) saggio

Sagittarius [sædʒɪ'tɛərɪəs] n Sagittario

Sahara [sə'hɑːrə] n: **the ~ (Desert)** il (deserto del) Sahara

said [sɛd] pt, pp of **say**

sail [seɪl] n (*on boat*) vela; (*trip*): **to go for a ~** fare un giro in barca a vela ♦ vt (*boat*) condurre, governare ♦ vi (*travel: ship*) navigare; (: *passenger*) viaggiare per mare; (*set off*) salpare; (*sport*) fare della vela; **they ~ed into Genoa** entrarono nel porto di Genova; **~ through** vt fus (*fig*) superare senza difficoltà; **~boat** n (*US*) barca a vela; **~ing** n (*sport*) vela; **to go ~ing** fare della vela; **~ing boat** n barca a vela; **~ing ship** n veliero; **~or** n marinaio

saint [seɪnt] n santo/a; **~ly** adj santo(a)

sake [seɪk] n: **for the ~ of** per, per amore di

salad ['sæləd] n insalata; **~ bowl** n insalatiera; **~ cream** (*BRIT*) n (tipo di) maionese f; **~ dressing** n condimento per insalata

salami [sə'lɑːmɪ] n salame m

salary ['sælərɪ] n stipendio

sale [seɪl] n vendita; (*at reduced prices*) svendita, liquidazione f; (*auction*) vendita all'asta; **"for ~"** "in vendita"; **on ~** in vendita; **on ~ or return** da vendere o rimandare; **~room** n sala delle aste; **~s assistant** (*US* **~s clerk**) n commesso/a; **~sman/ ~swoman** (*irreg*) n commesso/a; (*representative*) rappresentante m/f

salmon ['sæmən] n inv salmone m

saloon [sə'luːn] n (*US*) saloon m inv, bar m inv; (*BRIT: AUT*) berlina; (*ship's lounge*) salone m

salt [sɔlt] n sale m ♦ vt salare; **~ cellar** n saliera; **~water** adj di mare; **~y** adj salato(a)

salute [sə'luːt] n saluto ♦ vt salutare

salvage ['sælvɪdʒ] n (*saving*) salvataggio; (*things saved*) beni mpl salvati or recuperati ♦ vt salvare, mettere in salvo

salvation [sæl'veɪʃən] n salvezza; **S~ Army** n Esercito della Salvezza

same [seɪm] adj stesso(a), medesimo(a) ♦ pron: **the ~** lo(la) stesso(a), gli(le) stessi(e); **the ~ book as** lo stesso libro di (o che); **at the ~ time** allo stesso tempo; **all or just the ~** tuttavia; **to do the ~ as sb** fare come qn; **the ~ to you!** altrettanto a te!

sample ['sɑːmpl] n campione m ♦ vt (food)
assaggiare; (wine) degustare
sanction ['sæŋkʃən] n sanzione f ♦ vt
sancire, sanzionare
sanctity ['sæŋktɪtɪ] n santità
sanctuary ['sæŋktjuərɪ] n (holy place)
santuario; (refuge) rifugio; (for wildlife)
riserva
sand [sænd] n sabbia ♦ vt (also: ~ **down**)
cartavetrare
sandal ['sændl] n sandalo
sandbox ['sændbɒks] (US) n = **sandpit**
sandcastle ['sændkɑːsl] n castello di sabbia
sandpaper ['sændpeɪpə*] n carta vetrata
sandpit ['sændpɪt] n (for children) buca di
sabbia
sandstone ['sændstəun] n arenaria
sandwich ['sændwɪtʃ] n tramezzino, panino,
sandwich m inv ♦ vt: ~**ed between**
incastrato(a) fra; **cheese/ham** ~ sandwich
al formaggio/prosciutto; ~ **course** (BRIT)
n corso di formazione professionale
sandy ['sændɪ] adj sabbioso(a); (colour)
color sabbia inv, biondo(a) o rossiccio(a)
sane [seɪn] adj (person) sano di mente;
(outlook) sensato(a)
sang [sæŋ] pt of **sing**
sanitary ['sænɪtərɪ] adj (system,
arrangements) sanitario(a); (clean)
igienico(a); ~ **towel** (US ~ **napkin**) n
assorbente m (igienico)
sanitation [sænɪ'teɪʃən] n (in house)
impianti mpl sanitari; (in town) fognature
fpl; ~ **department** (US) n nettezza urbana
sanity ['sænɪtɪ] n sanità mentale; (common
sense) buon senso
sank [sæŋk] pt of **sink**
Santa Claus [sæntə'klɔːz] n Babbo Natale
sap [sæp] n (of plants) linfa ♦ vt (strength)
fiaccare
sapling ['sæplɪŋ] n alberello
sapphire ['sæfaɪə*] n zaffiro
sarcasm ['sɑːkæzm] n sarcasmo
sardine [sɑː'diːn] n sardina
Sardinia [sɑː'dɪnɪə] n Sardegna
sash [sæʃ] n fascia

sat [sæt] pt, pp of **sit**
Satan ['seɪtən] n Satana m
satchel ['sætʃl] n cartella
satellite ['sætəlaɪt] adj satellite ♦ n satellite
m; ~ **dish** n antenna parabolica; ~
television n televisione f via satellite
satin ['sætɪn] n raso ♦ adj di raso
satire ['sætaɪə*] n satira
satisfaction [sætɪs'fækʃən] n soddisfazione f
satisfactory [sætɪs'fæktərɪ] adj
soddisfacente
satisfy ['sætɪsfaɪ] vt soddisfare; (convince)
convincere; ~**ing** adj soddisfacente
Saturday ['sætədɪ] n sabato
sauce [sɔːs] n salsa; (containing meat, fish)
sugo; ~**pan** n casseruola
saucer ['sɔːsə*] n sottocoppa m, piattino
Saudi ['saudɪ]: ~ **Arabia** n Arabia Saudita;
~ **(Arabian)** adj, n arabo(a) saudita
sauna ['sɔːnə] n sauna
saunter ['sɔːntə*] vi andare a zonzo,
bighellonare
sausage ['sɒsɪdʒ] n salsiccia; ~ **roll** n rotolo
di pasta sfoglia ripieno di salsiccia
sauté ['səuteɪ] adj: ~ **potatoes** patate fpl
saltate in padella
savage ['sævɪdʒ] adj (cruel, fierce)
selvaggio(a), feroce; (primitive) primitivo(a)
♦ n selvaggio/a ♦ vt attaccare
selvaggiamente
save [seɪv] vt (person, belongings, COMPUT)
salvare; (money) risparmiare, mettere da
parte; (time) risparmiare; (food) conservare;
(avoid: trouble) evitare; (SPORT) parare ♦ vi
(also: ~ **up**) economizzare ♦ n (SPORT)
parata ♦ prep salvo, a eccezione di
saving ['seɪvɪŋ] n risparmio ♦ adj: **the** ~
grace of l'unica cosa buona di; ~**s** npl
(money) risparmi mpl; ~**s account** n
libretto di risparmio; ~**s bank** n cassa di
risparmio
saviour ['seɪvjə*] (US **savior**) n salvatore m
savour ['seɪvə*] (US **savor**) vt gustare; ~**y**
adj (dish: not sweet) salato(a)
saw [sɔː] (pt **sawed**, pp **sawed** or **sawn**) pt
of **see** ♦ n (tool) sega ♦ vt segare; ~**dust**
n segatura; ~**mill** n segheria; **sawn** pp of

saw; **~n-off shotgun** *n* fucile *m* a canne mozze

saxophone ['sæksəfəʊn] *n* sassofono

say [seɪ] (*pt*, *pp* **said**) *n*: **to have one's ~** fare sentire il proprio parere; **to have a** *or* **some ~** avere voce in capitolo ♦ *vt* dire; **could you ~ that again?** potrebbe ripeterlo?; **that goes without ~ing** va da sé; **~ing** *n* proverbio, detto

scab [skæb] *n* crosta; (*pej*) crumiro/a

scaffold ['skæfəʊld] *n* (*gallows*) patibolo; **~ing** *n* impalcatura

scald [skɔːld] *n* scottatura ♦ *vt* scottare

scale [skeɪl] *n* scala; (*of fish*) squama ♦ *vt* (*mountain*) scalare; **~s** *npl* (*for weighing*) bilancia; **on a large ~** su vasta scala; **~ of charges** tariffa; **~ down** *vt* ridurre (proporzionalmente)

scallop ['skɒləp] *n* (*ZOOL*) pettine *m*; (*SEWING*) smerlo

scalp [skælp] *n* cuoio capelluto ♦ *vt* scotennare

scalpel ['skælpl] *n* bisturi *m inv*

scampi ['skæmpɪ] *npl* scampi *mpl*

scan [skæn] *vt* scrutare; (*glance at quickly*) scorrere, dare un'occhiata a; (*TV*) analizzare; (*RADAR*) esplorare ♦ *n* (*MED*) ecografia

scandal ['skændl] *n* scandalo; (*gossip*) pettegolezzi *mpl*

Scandinavia [skændɪ'neɪvɪə] *n* Scandinavia; **~n** *adj*, *n* scandinavo/a

scant [skænt] *adj* scarso(a); **~y** *adj* insufficiente; (*swimsuit*) ridotto(a)

scapegoat ['skeɪpgəʊt] *n* capro espiatorio

scar [skɑː] *n* cicatrice *f* ♦ *vt* sfregiare

scarce [skɛəs] *adj* scarso(a); (*copy, edition*) raro(a); **to make o.s. ~** (*inf*) squagliarsela; **~ly** *adv* appena; **scarcity** *n* scarsità, mancanza

scare [skɛə*] *n* spavento; panico ♦ *vt* spaventare, atterrire; **there was a bomb ~ at the bank** hanno evacuato la banca per paura di un attentato dinamitardo; **to ~ sb stiff** spaventare a morte qn; **~ off** *or* **away** *vt* mettere in fuga; **~crow** *n* spaventapasseri *m inv*; **~d** *adj*: **to be ~d**

aver paura

scarf [skɑːf] (*pl* **scarves** *or* **~s**) *n* (*long*) sciarpa; (*square*) fazzoletto da testa, foulard *m inv*

scarlet ['skɑːlɪt] *adj* scarlatto(a); **~ fever** *n* scarlattina

scarves [skɑːvz] *npl* of **scarf**

scary ['skɛərɪ] *adj* che spaventa

scathing ['skeɪðɪŋ] *adj* aspro(a)

scatter ['skætə*] *vt* spargere; (*crowd*) disperdere ♦ *vi* disperdersi; **~brained** *adj* sbadato(a)

scavenger ['skævɪndʒə*] *n* (*person*) accattone/a

scenario [sɪ'nɑːrɪəʊ] *n* (*THEATRE, CINEMA*) copione *m*; (*fig*) situazione *f*

scene [siːn] *n* (*THEATRE, fig etc*) scena; (*of crime, accident*) scena, luogo; (*sight, view*) vista, veduta; **~ry** *n* (*THEATRE*) scenario; (*landscape*) panorama *m*; **scenic** *adj* scenico(a); panoramico(a)

scent [sɛnt] *n* profumo; (*sense of smell*) olfatto, odorato; (*fig: track*) pista

sceptical ['skɛptɪkəl] (*US* **skeptical**) *adj* scettico(a)

sceptre ['sɛptə*] (*US* **scepter**) *n* scettro

schedule ['ʃedjuːl, (*US*) 'skedjuːl] *n* programma *m*, piano; (*of trains*) orario; (*of prices etc*) lista, tabella ♦ *vt* fissare; **on ~** in orario; **to be ahead of/behind ~** essere in anticipo/ritardo sul previsto; **~d flight** *n* volo di linea

scheme [skiːm] *n* piano, progetto; (*method*) sistema *m*; (*dishonest plan, plot*) intrigo, trama; (*arrangement*) disposizione *f*, sistemazione *f*; (*pension ~ etc*) programma *m* ♦ *vi* fare progetti; (*intrigue*) complottare; **scheming** *adj* intrigante ♦ *n* intrighi *mpl*, macchinazioni *fpl*

schism ['skɪzəm] *n* scisma *m*

scholar ['skɒlə*] *n* erudito/a; (*pupil*) scolaro/a; **~ship** *n* erudizione *f*; (*grant*) borsa di studio

school [skuːl] *n* (*primary, secondary*) scuola; (*university: US*) università *f inv* ♦ *cpd* scolare, scolastico(a) ♦ *vt* (*animal*) addestrare; **~ age** *n* età scolare; **~bag** *n* cartella; **~book** n libro scolastico; **~boy** n scolaro; **~children** npl scolari mpl; **~girl** n scolara; **~ing** n istruzione f; **~master** n (*primary*) maestro; (*secondary*) insegnante m; **~mistress** n maestra; insegnante f; **~teacher** n insegnante m/f, docente m/f; (*primary*) maestro/a

sciatica [saɪˈætɪkə] n sciatica

science [ˈsaɪəns] n scienza; **~ fiction** n fantascienza; **scientific** [-ˈtɪfɪk] adj scientifico(a); **scientist** n scienziato/a

scissors [ˈsɪzəz] npl forbici fpl

scoff [skɒf] vt (*BRIT: inf: eat*) tranguiare, ingozzare ♦ vi: **to ~ (at)** (*mock*) farsi beffe (di)

scold [skəʊld] vt rimproverare

scone [skɒn] n focaccina da tè

scoop [sku:p] n mestolo; (*for ice cream*) cucchiaio dosatore; (*PRESS*) colpo giornalistico, notizia (in) esclusiva; **~ out** vt scavare; **~ up** vt tirare su, sollevare

scooter [ˈsku:tə*] n (*motor cycle*) motoretta, scooter m inv; (*toy*) monopattino

scope [skəʊp] n (*capacity: of plan, undertaking*) portata; (*: of person*) capacità fpl; (*opportunity*) possibilità fpl

scorch [skɔ:tʃ] vt (*clothes*) strinare, bruciacchiare; (*earth, grass*) seccare, bruciare

score [skɔ:*] n punti mpl, punteggio; (*MUS*) partitura, spartito; (*twenty*) venti ♦ vt (*goal, point*) segnare, fare; (*success*) ottenere ♦ vi segnare; (*FOOTBALL*) fare un goal; (*keep score*) segnare i punti; **~s of** (*very many*) un sacco di; **on that ~** a questo riguardo; **to ~ 6 out of 10** prendere 6 su 10; **~ out** vt cancellare con un segno; **~board** n tabellone m segnapunti

scorn [skɔ:n] n disprezzo ♦ vt disprezzare

scornful [ˈskɔ:nful] adj sprezzante

Scorpio [ˈskɔ:pɪəʊ] n Scorpione m

scorpion [ˈskɔ:pɪən] n scorpione m

Scot [skɒt] n scozzese m/f

Scotch [skɒtʃ] n whisky m scozzese, scotch m

scot-free adv: **to get off ~** farla franca

Scotland [ˈskɒtlənd] n Scozia

Scots [skɒts] adj scozzese; **~man/woman** (*irreg*) n scozzese m/f

Scottish [ˈskɒtɪʃ] adj scozzese

scoundrel [ˈskaundrl] n farabutto/a; (*child*) furfantello/a

scour [ˈskauə*] vt (*search*) battere, perlustrare

scout [skaut] n (*MIL*) esploratore m; (*also*: **boy ~**) giovane esploratore, scout m inv; **~ around** vi cercare in giro; **girl ~** (*US*) n giovane esploratrice f

scowl [skaul] vi accigliarsi, aggrottare le sopracciglia; **to ~ at** guardare torvo

scrabble [ˈskræbl] vi (*claw*): **to ~ (at)** graffiare, grattare; (*also*: **~ around**: *search*) cercare a tentoni ♦ n: **S~** ® Scarabeo ®

scraggy [ˈskrægɪ] adj scarno(a), molto magro(a)

scram [skræm] (*inf*) vi filare via

scramble [ˈskræmbl] n arrampicata ♦ vi inerpicarsi; **to ~ out** etc uscire etc in fretta; **to ~ for** azzuffarsi per; **~d eggs** npl uova fpl strapazzate

scrap [skræp] n pezzo, pezzetto; (*fight*) zuffa; (*also*: **~ iron**) rottami mpl di ferro, ferraglia ♦ vt demolire; (*fig*) scartare ♦ vi: **to ~ (with sb)** fare a botte (con qn); **~s** npl (*waste*) scarti mpl; **~book** n album m inv di ritagli; **~ dealer** n commerciante m di ferraglia

scrape [skreɪp] vt, vi raschiare, grattare ♦ n: **to get into a ~** cacciarsi in un guaio; **~ through** vi farcela per un pelo; **~ together** vt (*money*) raggranellare; **~r** n raschietto

scrap: ~ heap n: **on the ~ heap** (*fig*) nel dimenticatoio; **~ merchant** (*BRIT*) n commerciante m di ferraglia; **~ paper** n cartaccia

scratch [skrætʃ] n graffio ♦ cpd: **~ team** squadra raccogliticcia ♦ vt graffiare, rigare ♦ vi grattare; (*paint, car*) graffiare; **to start from ~** cominciare or partire da zero; **to be up to ~** essere all'altezza

scrawl [skrɔ:l] n scarabocchio ♦ vi scarabocchiare

scrawny [ˈskrɔ:nɪ] adj scarno(a), pelle e

ossa *inv*

scream [skri:m] *n* grido, urlo ♦ *vi* urlare, gridare

scree [skri:] *n* ghiaione *m*

screech [skri:tʃ] *vi* stridere

screen [skri:n] *n* schermo; (*fig*) muro, cortina, velo ♦ *vt* schermare, fare schermo a; (*from the wind etc*) riparare; (*film*) proiettare; (*book*) adattare per lo schermo; (*candidates etc*) selezionare; **~ing** *n* (*MED*) dépistage *m inv*; **~play** *n* sceneggiatura

screw [skru:] *n* vite *f* ♦ *vt* avvitare; **~ up** *vt* (*paper etc*) spiegazzare; (*inf: ruin*) rovinare; **to ~ up one's eyes** strizzare gli occhi; **~driver** *n* cacciavite *m*

scribble ['skrɪbl] *n* scarabocchio ♦ *vt* scribacchiare in fretta ♦ *vi* scarabocchiare

script [skrɪpt] *n* (*CINEMA etc*) copione *m*; (*in exam*) elaborato *or* compito d'esame

scripture(s) ['skrɪptʃə(z)] *n(pl)* sacre Scritture *fpl*

scroll [skrəul] *n* rotolo di carta

scrounge [skraundʒ] (*inf*) *vt*: **to ~ sth (off *or* from sb)** scroccare qc (a qn) ♦ *n*: **on the ~** a sbafo

scrub [skrʌb] *n* (*land*) boscaglia ♦ *vt* pulire strofinando; (*reject*) annullare

scruff [skrʌf] *n*: **by the ~ of the neck** per la collottola

scruffy ['skrʌfɪ] *adj* sciatto(a)

scrum(mage) ['skrʌm(ɪdʒ)] *n* mischia

scruple ['skru:pl] *n* scrupolo

scrutiny ['skru:tɪnɪ] *n* esame *m* accurato

scuff [skʌf] *vt* (*shoes*) consumare strascicando

scuffle ['skʌfl] *n* baruffa, tafferuglio

sculptor ['skʌlptə*] *n* scultore *m*

sculpture ['skʌlptʃə*] *n* scultura

scum [skʌm] *n* schiuma; (*pej: people*) feccia

scupper ['skʌpə*] (*BRIT: inf*) *vt* far naufragare

scurry ['skʌrɪ] *vi* sgambare, affrettarsi; **~ off** *vi* andarsene a tutta velocità

scuttle ['skʌtl] *n* (*also: coal ~*) secchio del carbone ♦ *vt* (*ship*) autoaffondare ♦ *vi* (*scamper*): **to ~ away, ~ off** darsela a gambe, scappare

scythe [saɪð] *n* falce *f*

SDP (*BRIT*) *n abbr* = **Social Democratic Party**

sea [si:] *n* mare *m* ♦ *cpd* marino(a), del mare; (*bird, fish*) di mare; (*route, transport*) marittimo(a); **by ~** (*travel*) per mare; **on the ~** (*boat*) in mare; (*town*) di mare; **to be all at ~** (*fig*) non sapere che pesci pigliare; **out to ~** al largo; (**out**) **at ~** in mare; **~board** *n* costa; **~food** *n* frutti *mpl* di mare; **~ front** *n* lungomare *m*; **~gull** *n* gabbiano

seal [si:l] *n* (*animal*) foca; (*stamp*) sigillo; (*impression*) impronta del sigillo ♦ *vt* sigillare; **~ off** *vt* (*close*) sigillare; (*forbid entry to*) bloccare l'accesso a

sea level *n* livello del mare

seam [si:m] *n* cucitura; (*of coal*) filone *m*

seaman ['si:mən] (*irreg*) *n* marinaio

seance ['seɪɒns] *n* seduta spiritica

seaplane ['si:pleɪn] *n* idrovolante *m*

seaport ['si:pɔ:t] *n* porto di mare

search [sə:tʃ] *n* ricerca; (*LAW: at sb's home*) perquisizione *f* ♦ *vt* frugare ♦ *vi*: **to ~ for** ricercare; **in ~ of** alla ricerca di; **~ through** *vt fus* frugare; **~ing** *adj* minuzioso(a); penetrante; **~light** *n* proiettore *m*; **~ party** *n* squadra di soccorso; **~ warrant** *n* mandato di perquisizione

seashore ['si:ʃɔ:*] *n* spiaggia

seasick ['si:sɪk] *adj* che soffre il mal di mare

seaside ['si:saɪd] *n* spiaggia; **~ resort** *n* stazione *f* balneare

season ['si:zn] *n* stagione *f* ♦ *vt* condire, insaporire; **~al** *adj* stagionale; **~ed** *adj* (*fig*) con esperienza; **~ing** *n* condimento; **~ ticket** *n* abbonamento

seat [si:t] *n* sedile *m*; (*in bus, train: place*) posto; (*PARLIAMENT*) seggio; (*buttocks*) didietro; (*of trousers*) fondo ♦ *vt* far sedere; (*have room for*) avere *or* essere fornito(a) di posti a sedere per; **to be ~ed** essere seduto(a); **~ belt** *n* cintura di sicurezza

sea water *n* acqua di mare

seaweed ['si:wi:d] *n* alghe *fpl*

seaworthy ['si:wə:ðɪ] *adj* atto(a) alla navigazione

sec. *abbr* = **second(s)**

secluded [sɪˈkluːdɪd] *adj* isolato(a), appartato(a)

seclusion [sɪˈkluːʒən] *n* isolamento

second[1] [sɪˈkɒnd] (*BRIT*) *vt* (*worker*) distaccare

second[2] [ˈsɛkənd] *num* secondo(a) ♦ *adv* (*in race etc*) al secondo posto ♦ *n* (*unit of time*) secondo; (*AUT*: *also*: **~ gear**) seconda; (*COMM*: *imperfect*) scarto; (*BRIT*: *SCOL*: *degree*) laurea con punteggio discreto ♦ *vt* (*motion*) appoggiare; **~ary** *adj* secondario(a); **~ary school** *n* scuola secondaria; **~-class** *adj* di seconda classe ♦ *adv* in seconda classe; **~er** *n* sostenitore/trice; **~hand** *adj* di seconda mano, usato(a); **~ hand** *n* (*on clock*) lancetta dei secondi; **~ly** *adv* in secondo luogo; **~-rate** *adj* scadente; **~ thoughts** *npl* ripensamenti *mpl*; **on ~ thoughts** (*BRIT*) *or* **thought** (*US*) ripensandoci bene

secrecy [ˈsiːkrəsɪ] *n* segretezza

secret [ˈsiːkrɪt] *adj* segreto(a) ♦ *n* segreto; **in ~** in segreto

secretarial [sɛkrɪˈtɛərɪəl] *adj* di segretario(a)

secretariat [sɛkrɪˈtɛərɪət] *n* segretariato

secretary [ˈsɛkrətrɪ] *n* segretario/a; **S~ of State (for)** (*BRIT*: *POL*) ministro (di)

secretive [ˈsiːkrətɪv] *adj* riservato(a)

sect [sɛkt] *n* setta; **~arian** [-ˈtɛərɪən] *adj* settario(a)

section [ˈsɛkʃən] *n* sezione *f*

sector [ˈsɛktə*] *n* settore *m*

secure [sɪˈkjuə*] *adj* sicuro(a); (*firmly fixed*) assicurato(a), ben fermato(a); (*in safe place*) al sicuro ♦ *vt* (*fix*) fissare, assicurare; (*get*) ottenere, assicurarsi

security [sɪˈkjuərɪtɪ] *n* sicurezza; (*for loan*) garanzia

sedate [sɪˈdeɪt] *adj* posato(a); calmo(a) ♦ *vt* calmare

sedation [sɪˈdeɪʃən] *n* (*MED*) effetto dei sedativi

sedative [ˈsɛdɪtɪv] *n* sedativo, calmante *m*

seduce [sɪˈdjuːs] *vt* sedurre; **seduction** [-ˈdʌkʃən] *n* seduzione *f*; **seductive** [-ˈdʌktɪv] *adj* seducente

see [siː] (*pt* **saw**, *pp* **seen**) *vt* vedere; (*accompany*): **to ~ sb to the door** accompagnare qn alla porta ♦ *vi* vedere; (*understand*) capire ♦ *n* sede *f* vescovile; **to ~ that** (*ensure*) badare che +*sub*, fare in modo che +*sub*; **~ you soon!** a presto!; **~ about** *vt fus* occuparsi di; **~ off** *vt* salutare alla partenza; **~ through** *vt* portare a termine ♦ *vt fus* non lasciarsi ingannare da; **~ to** *vt fus* occuparsi di

seed [siːd] *n* seme *m*; (*fig*) germe *m*; (*TENNIS etc*) testa di serie; **to go to ~** fare seme; (*fig*) scadere; **~ling** *n* piantina di semenzaio; **~y** *adj* (*shabby*: *person*) sciatto(a); (: *place*) cadente

seeing [ˈsiːɪŋ] *conj*: **~ (that)** visto che

seek [siːk] (*pt*, *pp* **sought**) *vt* cercare

seem [siːm] *vi* sembrare, parere; **there ~s to be ...** sembra che ci sia ...; **~ingly** *adv* apparentemente

seen [siːn] *pp of* **see**

seep [siːp] *vi* filtrare, trapelare

seesaw [ˈsiːsɔː] *n* altalena a bilico

seethe [siːð] *vi* ribollire; **to ~ with anger** fremere di rabbia

see-through [ˈsiːθruː] *adj* trasparente

segregate [ˈsɛgrɪgeɪt] *vt* segregare, isolare

seize [siːz] *vt* (*grasp*) afferrare; (*take possession of*) impadronirsi di; (*LAW*) sequestrare; **~ (up)on** *vt fus* ricorrere a; **~ up** *vi* (*TECH*) grippare

seizure [ˈsiːʒə*] *n* (*MED*) attacco; (*LAW*) confisca, sequestro

seldom [ˈsɛldəm] *adv* raramente

select [sɪˈlɛkt] *adj* scelto(a) ♦ *vt* scegliere, selezionare; **~ion** [-ˈlɛkʃən] *n* selezione *f*, scelta

self [sɛlf] *n*: **the ~** l'io *m* ♦ *prefix* auto...; **~-assured** *adj* sicuro(a) di sé; **~-catering** (*BRIT*) *adj* in cui ci si cucina da sé; **~-centred** (*US* **~-centered**) *adj* egocentrico(a); **~-confidence** *n* sicurezza di sé; **~-conscious** *adj* timido(a); **~-contained** (*BRIT*) *adj* (*flat*) indipendente; **~-control** *n* autocontrollo; **~-defence** (*US* **~-defense**) *n* autodifesa; (*LAW*) legittima difesa; **~-discipline** *n* autodisciplina; **~-employed** *adj* che lavora in proprio; **~-evident** *adj* evidente; **~-governing** *adj* autonomo(a); **~-indulgent** *adj* indulgente verso se stesso(a); **~-interest** *n* interesse *m* personale; **~ish** *adj* egoista; **~ishness** *n* egoismo; **~less** *adj* dimentico(a) di sé, altruista; **~-pity** *n* autocommiserazione *f*; **~-portrait** *n* autoritratto; **~-possessed** *adj* controllato(a); **~-preservation** *n* istinto di conservazione; **~-respect** *n* rispetto di sé, amor proprio; **~-righteous** *adj* soddisfatto(a) di sé; **~-sacrifice** *n* abnegazione *f*; **~-satisfied** *adj* compiaciuto(a) di sé; **~-service** *n* autoservizio, self-service *m*; **~-sufficient** *adj* autosufficiente; **~-taught** *adj* autodidatta

sell [sɛl] (*pt, pp* **sold**) *vt* vendere ♦ *vi* vendersi; **to ~ at** *or* **for 1000 lire** essere in vendita a 1000 lire; **~ off** *vt* svendere, liquidare; **~ out** *vi*: **to ~ out (of sth)** esaurire (qc); **the tickets are all sold out** i biglietti sono esauriti; **~-by date** *n* data di scadenza; **~er** *n* venditore/trice; **~ing price** *n* prezzo di vendita

Sellotape ® ['sɛləʊteɪp] (*BRIT*) *n* nastro adesivo, scotch ® *m*

selves [sɛlvz] *npl of* **self**

semaphore ['sɛməfɔː*] *n* segnalazioni *fpl* con bandierine, (*RAIL*) semaforo (ferroviario)

semblance ['sɛmbləns] *n* parvenza, apparenza

semen ['siːmən] *n* sperma *m*

semester [sɪ'mɛstə*] (*US*) *n* semestre *m*

semi... ['sɛmɪ] *prefix* semi...; **~circle** *n* semicerchio; **~colon** *n* punto e virgola; **~detached (house)** (*BRIT*) *n* casa gemella; **~final** *n* semifinale *f*

seminar ['sɛmɪnɑː*] *n* seminario

seminary ['sɛmɪnərɪ] *n* (*REL*) seminario

semiskilled ['sɛmɪ'skɪld] *adj* (*worker*) parzialmente qualificato(a); (*work*) che richiede una qualificazione parziale

semi-skimmed ['sɛmɪ'skɪmd] *adj* (*milk*) parzialmente scremato(a)

senate ['sɛnɪt] *n* senato; **senator** *n* senatore/trice

send [sɛnd] (*pt, pp* **sent**) *vt* mandare; **~ away** *vt* (*letter, goods*) spedire; (*person*) mandare via; **~ away for** *vt fus* richiedere per posta, farsi spedire; **~ back** *vt* rimandare; **~ for** *vt fus* mandare a chiamare, far venire; **~ off** *vt* (*goods*) spedire; (*BRIT: SPORT: player*) espellere; **~ out** *vt* (*invitation*) diramare; **~ up** *vt* (*person, price*) far salire; (*BRIT: parody*) mettere in ridicolo; **~er** *n* mittente *m/f*; **~-off** *n*: **to give sb a good ~-off** festeggiare la partenza di qn

senior ['siːnɪə*] *adj* (*older*) più vecchio(a); (*of higher rank*) di grado più elevato; **~ citizen** *n* persona anziana; **~ity** [-'ɒrɪtɪ] *n* anzianità

sensation [sɛn'seɪʃən] *n* sensazione *f*; **~al** *adj* sensazionale; (*marvellous*) eccezionale

sense [sɛns] *n* senso; (*feeling*) sensazione *f*, senso; (*meaning*) senso, significato; (*wisdom*) buonsenso ♦ *vt* sentire, percepire; **it makes ~** ha senso; **~less** *adj* sciocco(a); (*unconscious*) privo(a) di sensi

sensible ['sɛnsɪbl] *adj* sensato(a), ragionevole

sensitive ['sɛnsɪtɪv] *adj* sensibile; (*skin, question*) delicato(a)

sensual ['sɛnsjʊəl] *adj* sensuale

sensuous ['sɛnsjʊəs] *adj* sensuale

sent [sɛnt] *pt, pp of* **send**

sentence ['sɛntns] *n* (*LING*) frase *f*; (*LAW: judgment*) sentenza; (: *punishment*) condanna ♦ *vt*: **to ~ sb to death/to 5 years** condannare qn a morte/a 5 anni

sentiment ['sɛntɪmənt] *n* sentimento; (*opinion*) opinione *f*; **~al** [-'mɛntl] *adj* sentimentale

sentry ['sɛntrɪ] *n* sentinella

separate [*adj* 'sɛprɪt, *vb* 'sɛpəreɪt] *adj* separato(a) ♦ *vt* separare ♦ *vi* separarsi; **~ly** *adv* separatamente; **~s** *npl* (*clothes*) coordinati *mpl*; **separation** [-'reɪʃən] *n* separazione *f*

September [sɛp'tɛmbə*] *n* settembre *m*

septic ['sɛptɪk] *adj* settico(a); (*wound*) infettato(a); **~ tank** *n* fossa settica

sequel ['si:kwl] *n* conseguenza; (*of story*) seguito; (*of film*) sequenza

sequence ['si:kwəns] *n* (*series*) serie *f*; (*order*) ordine *m*

sequin ['si:kwɪn] *n* lustrino, paillette *f inv*

serene [sə'ri:n] *adj* sereno(a), calmo(a)

sergeant ['sɑ:dʒənt] *n* sergente *m*; (*POLICE*) brigadiere *m*

serial ['sɪərɪəl] *n* (*PRESS*) romanzo a puntate; (*RADIO, TV*) trasmissione *f* a puntate, serial *m inv*; **~ize** *vt* pubblicare (*or* trasmettere) a puntate; ~ **killer** *n* serial-killer *m/f inv*; ~ **number** *n* numero di serie

series ['sɪəri:z] *n inv* serie *f inv*; (*PUBLISHING*) collana

serious ['sɪərɪəs] *adj* serio(a), grave; **~ly** *adv* seriamente

sermon ['sə:mən] *n* sermone *m*

serrated [sɪ'reɪtɪd] *adj* seghettato(a)

serum ['sɪərəm] *n* siero

servant ['sə:vənt] *n* domestico/a

serve [sə:v] *vt* (*employer etc*) servire, essere a servizio di; (*purpose*) servire a; (*customer, food, meal*) servire; (*apprenticeship*) fare; (*prison term*) scontare ♦ *vi* (*also TENNIS*) servire; (*be useful*): **to ~ as/for/to do** servire da/per/per fare ♦ *n* (*TENNIS*) servizio; **it ~s him right** ben gli sta, se l'è meritata; ~ **out**, ~ **up** *vt* (*food*) servire

service ['sə:vɪs] *n* servizio; (*AUT: maintenance*) assistenza, revisione *f* ♦ *vt* (*car, washing machine*) revisionare; **the S~s** le forze armate; **to be of ~ to sb** essere d'aiuto a qn; ~ **included/not included** servizio compreso/escluso; **~able** *adj* pratico(a), utile; ~ **area** *n* (*on motorway*) area di servizio; ~ **charge** (*BRIT*) *n* servizio; **~man** (*irreg*) *n* militare *m*; ~ **station** *n* stazione *f* di servizio

serviette [sə:vɪ'et] (*BRIT*) *n* tovagliolo

session ['seʃən] *n* (*sitting*) seduta, sessione *f*; (*SCOL*) anno scolastico (*or* accademico)

set [set] (*pt, pp* **set**) *n* serie *f inv*; (*of cutlery etc*) servizio; (*RADIO, TV*) apparecchio; (*TENNIS*) set *m inv*; (*group of people*) mondo, ambiente *m*; (*CINEMA*) scenario; (*THEATRE: stage*) scene *fpl*; (: *scenery*)

scenario; (*MATH*) insieme *m*; (*HAIRDRESSING*) messa in piega ♦ *adj* (*fixed*) stabilito(a), determinato(a); (*ready*) pronto(a) ♦ *vt* (*place*) posare, mettere; (*arrange*) sistemare; (*fix*) fissare; (*adjust*) regolare; (*decide: rules etc*) stabilire, fissare ♦ *vi* (*sun*) tramontare; (*jam, jelly*) rapprendersi; (*concrete*) fare presa; **to be ~ on doing** essere deciso a fare; **to ~ to music** mettere in musica; **to ~ on fire** dare fuoco a; **to ~ free** liberare; **to ~ sth going** mettere in moto qc; **to ~ sail** prendere il mare; ~ **about** *vt fus* (*task*) intraprendere, mettersi a; ~ **aside** *vt* mettere da parte; ~ **back** *vt* (*in time*): **to ~ back (by)** mettere indietro (di); (*inf: cost*): **it ~ me back £5** mi è costato la bellezza di 5 sterline; ~ **off** *vi* partire ♦ *vt* (*bomb*) far scoppiare; (*cause to start*) mettere in moto; (*show up well*) dare risalto a; ~ **out** *vi* partire ♦ *vt* (*arrange*) disporre; (*state*) esporre, presentare; **to ~ out to do** proporsi di fare; ~ **up** *vt* (*organization*) fondare, costituire; **~back** *n* (*hitch*) contrattempo, inconveniente *m*; ~ **menu** *n* menù *m inv* fisso

settee [se'ti:] *n* divano, sofà *m inv*

setting ['setɪŋ] *n* (*background*) ambiente *m*; (*of controls*) posizione *f*; (*of sun*) tramonto; (*of jewel*) montatura

settle ['setl] *vt* (*argument, matter*) appianare; (*accounts*) regolare; (*MED: calm*) calmare ♦ *vi* (*bird, dust etc*) posarsi; (*sediment*) depositarsi; (*also:* ~ **down**) sistemarsi, stabilirsi; calmarsi; **to ~ for sth** accontentarsi di qc; **to ~ on sth** decidersi per qc; ~ **in** *vi* sistemarsi; ~ **up** *vi*: **to ~ up with sb** regolare i conti con qn; **~ment** *n* (*payment*) pagamento, saldo; (*agreement*) accordo; (*colony*) colonia; (*village etc*) villaggio, comunità *f inv*; **~r** *n* colonizzatore/trice

setup ['setʌp] *n* (*arrangement*) sistemazione *f*; (*situation*) situazione *f*

seven ['sevn] *num* sette; **~teen** *num* diciassette; **~th** *num* settimo(a); **~ty** *num* settanta

sever ['sevə*] *vt* recidere, tagliare; (*relations*)

troncare

several ['sevərl] *adj*, *pron* alcuni(e), diversi(e); **~ of us** alcuni di noi

severance ['sevərəns] *n* (*of relations*) rottura; **~ pay** *n* indennità di licenziamento

severe [sɪ'vɪə*] *adj* severo(a); (*serious*) serio(a), grave; (*hard*) duro(a); (*plain*) semplice, sobrio(a); **severity** [sɪ'vɛrɪtɪ] *n* severità; gravità; (*of weather*) rigore *m*

sew [səʊ] (*pt* **sewed**, *pp* **sewn**) *vt*, *vi* cucire; **~ up** *vt* ricucire

sewage ['suːɪdʒ] *n* acque *fpl* di scolo

sewer ['suːə*] *n* fogna

sewing ['səʊɪŋ] *n* cucitura; cucito; **~ machine** *n* macchina da cucire

sewn [səʊn] *pp of* **sew**

sex [sɛks] *n* sesso; **to have ~ with** avere rapporti sessuali con; **~ist** *adj*, *n* sessista *m/f*

sexual ['sɛksjʊəl] *adj* sessuale

sexy ['sɛksɪ] *adj* provocante, sexy *inv*

shabby ['ʃæbɪ] *adj* malandato(a); (*behaviour*) vergognoso(a)

shack [ʃæk] *n* baracca, capanna

shackles ['ʃæklz] *npl* ferri *mpl*, catene *fpl*

shade [ʃeɪd] *n* ombra; (*for lamp*) paralume *m*; (*of colour*) tonalità *f inv*; (*small quantity*): **a ~ (more/too large)** un po' (di più/troppo grande) ♦ *vt* ombreggiare, fare ombra a; **in the ~** all'ombra

shadow ['ʃædəʊ] *n* ombra ♦ *vt* (*follow*) pedinare; **~ cabinet** (*BRIT*) *n* (*POL*) governo *m* ombra *inv*; **~y** *adj* ombreggiato(a), ombroso(a); (*dim*) vago(a), indistinto(a)

shady ['ʃeɪdɪ] *adj* ombroso(a); (*fig: dishonest*) losco(a), equivoco(a)

shaft [ʃɑːft] *n* (*of arrow, spear*) asta; (*AUT, TECH*) albero; (*of mine*) pozzo; (*of lift*) tromba; (*of light*) raggio

shaggy ['ʃægɪ] *adj* ispido(a)

shake [ʃeɪk] (*pt* **shook**, *pp* **shaken**) *vt* scuotere; (*bottle, cocktail*) agitare ♦ *vi* tremare; **to ~ one's head** (*in refusal, dismay*) scuotere la testa; **to ~ hands with sb** stringere *or* dare la mano a qn; **~ off** *vt* scrollare (via); (*fig*) sbarazzarsi di; **~ up** *vt*

scuotere; **~n** *pp of* **shake**; **shaky** *adj* (*hand, voice*) tremante; (*building*) traballante

shall [ʃæl] *aux vb*: **I ~ go** andrò; **~ I open the door?** apro io la porta?; **I'll get some, ~ I?** ne prendo un po', va bene?

shallow ['ʃæləʊ] *adj* poco profondo(a); (*fig*) superficiale

sham [ʃæm] *n* finzione *f*, messinscena; (*jewellery, furniture*) imitazione *f*

shambles ['ʃæmblz] *n* confusione *f*, baraonda, scompiglio

shame [ʃeɪm] *n* vergogna ♦ *vt* far vergognare; **it is a ~ (that/to do)** è un peccato (che +*sub*/fare); **what a ~!** che peccato!; **~ful** *adj* vergognoso(a); **~less** *adj* sfrontato(a); (*immodest*) spudorato(a)

shampoo [ʃæm'puː] *n* shampoo *m inv* ♦ *vt* fare lo shampoo a; **~ and set** *n* shampoo e messa in piega

shamrock ['ʃæmrɔk] *n* trifoglio (*simbolo nazionale dell'Irlanda*)

shandy ['ʃændɪ] *n* birra con gassosa

shan't [ʃɑːnt] = **shall not**

shanty town ['ʃæntɪ-] *n* bidonville *f inv*

shape [ʃeɪp] *n* forma ♦ *vt* formare; (*statement*) formulare; (*sb's ideas*) condizionare; **to take ~** prendere forma; **~ up** *vi* (*events*) andare, mettersi; (*person*) cavarsela; **-shaped** *suffix*: **heart-shaped** a forma di cuore; **~less** *adj* senza forma, informe; **~ly** *adj* ben proporzionato(a)

share [ʃɛə*] *n* (*thing received, contribution*) parte *f*; (*COMM*) azione *f* ♦ *vt* dividere; (*have in common*) condividere, avere in comune; **~ out** *vi* dividere; **~holder** *n* azionista *m/f*

shark [ʃɑːk] *n* squalo, pescecane *m*

sharp [ʃɑːp] *adj* (*razor, knife*) affilato(a); (*point*) acuto(a), acuminato(a); (*nose, chin*) aguzzo(a); (*outline, contrast*) netto(a); (*cold, pain*) pungente; (*voice*) stridulo(a); (*person: quick-witted*) sveglio(a); (: *unscrupulous*) disonesto(a); (*MUS*): **C ~ do** diesis ♦ *n* (*MUS*) diesis *m inv* ♦ *adv*: **at 2 o'clock ~** alle due in punto; **~en** *vt* affilare; (*pencil*) fare la punta a; (*fig*) acuire; **~ener** *n* (*also*: **pencil**

~ener) temperamatite m inv; ~-eyed adj dalla vista acuta; ~ly adv (turn, stop) bruscamente; (stand out, contrast) nettamente; (criticize, retort) duramente, aspramente

shatter ['ʃætə*] vt mandare in frantumi, frantumare; (fig: upset) distruggere; (: ruin) rovinare ♦ vi frantumarsi, andare in pezzi

shave [ʃeɪv] vt radere, rasare ♦ vi radersi, farsi la barba ♦ n: **to have a ~** farsi la barba; ~r n (also: **electric ~r**) rasoio elettrico

shaving ['ʃeɪvɪŋ] n (action) rasatura; ~s npl (of wood etc) trucioli mpl; ~ **brush** n pennello da barba; ~ **cream** n crema da barba; ~ **foam** n = ~ **cream**

shawl [ʃɔːl] n scialle m

she [ʃiː] pron ella, lei; ~-**cat** gatta; ~-**elephant** elefantessa

sheaf [ʃiːf] (pl **sheaves**) n covone m; (of papers) fascio

shear [ʃɪə*] (pt ~ed, pp ~ed or **shorn**) vt (sheep) tosare; ~s npl (for hedge) cesoie fpl

sheath [ʃiːθ] n fodero, guaina; (contraceptive) preservativo

sheaves [ʃiːvz] npl of **sheaf**

shed [ʃed] (pt, pp **shed**) n capannone m ♦ vt (leaves, fur etc) perdere; (tears, blood) versare; (workers) liberarsi di

she'd [ʃiːd] = **she had**; **she would**

sheen [ʃiːn] n lucentezza

sheep [ʃiːp] n inv pecora; ~**dog** n cane m da pastore; ~**skin** n pelle f di pecora

sheer [ʃɪə*] adj (utter) vero(a) (e proprio(a)); (steep) a picco, perpendicolare; (almost transparent) sottile ♦ adv a picco

sheet [ʃiːt] n (on bed) lenzuolo; (of paper) foglio; (of glass, ice) lastra; (of metal) foglio, lamina; ~ **lightning** n lampo diffuso

sheik(h) [ʃeɪk] n sceicco

shelf [ʃelf] (pl **shelves**) n scaffale m, mensola

shell [ʃel] n (on beach) conchiglia; (of egg, nut etc) guscio; (explosive) granata; (of building) scheletro ♦ vt (peas) sgranare; (MIL) bombardare; ~ **suit** n (lightweight) tuta di acetato; (heavier) tuta di trilobato

she'll [ʃiːl] = **she will**; **she shall**

shellfish ['ʃelfɪʃ] n inv (crab etc) crostaceo; (scallop etc) mollusco; (pl: as food) crostacei; molluschi

shelter ['ʃeltə*] n riparo, rifugio ♦ vt riparare, proteggere; (give lodging to) dare rifugio or asilo a ♦ vi ripararsi, mettersi al riparo; ~**ed** adj riparato(a); ~**ed housing** (BRIT) n alloggi dotati di strutture per anziani or handicappati

shelve [ʃelv] vt (fig) accantonare, rimandare; ~s npl of **shelf**

shepherd ['ʃepəd] n pastore m ♦ vt (guide) guidare; ~'s **pie** (BRIT) n timballo di carne macinata e purè di patate

sheriff ['ʃerɪf] (US) n sceriffo

sherry ['ʃerɪ] n sherry m inv

she's [ʃiːz] = **she is**; **she has**

Shetland ['ʃetlənd] n (also: **the ~s, the ~ Isles**) le isole Shetland, le Shetland

shield [ʃiːld] n scudo; (trophy) scudetto; (protection) schermo ♦ vt: **to ~ (from)** riparare (da), proteggere (da or contro)

shift [ʃɪft] n (change) cambiamento; (of workers) turno ♦ vt spostare, muovere; (remove) rimuovere ♦ vi spostarsi, muoversi; ~ **work** n lavoro a squadre; ~**y** adj ambiguo(a); (eyes) sfuggente

shilling ['ʃɪlɪŋ] (BRIT) n scellino (= 12 old pence; 20 in a pound)

shimmer ['ʃɪmə*] vi brillare, luccicare

shin [ʃɪn] n tibia

shine [ʃaɪn] (pt, pp **shone**) n splendore m, lucentezza ♦ vi (ri)splendere, brillare ♦ vt far brillare, far risplendere; (torch): **to ~ sth on** puntare qc verso

shingle ['ʃɪŋgl] n (on beach) ciottoli mpl; ~s n (MED) herpes zoster m

shiny ['ʃaɪnɪ] adj lucente, lucido(a)

ship [ʃɪp] n nave f ♦ vt trasportare (via mare); (send) spedire (via mare); ~**building** n costruzione f navale; ~**ment** n carico; ~**ping** n (ships) naviglio; (traffic) navigazione f; ~**shape** adj in perfetto ordine; ~**wreck** n relitto; (event) naufragio ♦ vt: **to be ~wrecked** naufragare, fare naufragio; ~**yard** n cantiere m navale

shire [ˈʃaɪə*] (BRIT) n contea

shirt [ʃəːt] n camicia; **in ~ sleeves** in maniche di camicia

shit [ʃɪt] (infl) excl merda (!)

shiver [ˈʃɪvə*] n brivido ♦ vi rabbrividire, tremare

shoal [ʃəul] n (of fish) banco; (fig) massa

shock [ʃɔk] n (impact) urto, colpo; (ELEC) scossa; (emotional) colpo, shock m inv; (MED) shock ♦ vt colpire, scioccare; scandalizzare; **~ absorber** n ammortizzatore m; **~ing** adj scioccante, traumatizzante; scandaloso(a)

shoddy [ˈʃɔdɪ] adj scadente

shoe [ʃuː] n scarpa; (also: **horse~**) ferro di cavallo ♦ vt (horse) ferrare; **~brush** n spazzola per scarpe; **~lace** n stringa; **~ polish** n lucido per scarpe; **~shop** n calzoleria; **~string** n (fig): **on a ~string** con quattro soldi

shone [ʃɔn] pt, pp of **shine**

shook [ʃuk] pt of **shake**

shoot [ʃuːt] (pt, pp **shot**) n (on branch, seedling) germoglio ♦ vt (game) cacciare, andare a caccia di; (person) sparare a; (execute) fucilare; (film) girare ♦ vi (with gun): **to ~ (at)** sparare (a), fare fuoco (su); (with bow): **to ~ (at)** tirare (su); (FOOTBALL) sparare, tirare (forte); **~ down** vt (plane) abbattere; **~ in/out** vi entrare/uscire come una freccia; **~ up** vi (fig) salire alle stelle; **~ing** n (shots) sparatoria; (HUNTING) caccia; **~ing star** n stella cadente

shop [ʃɔp] n negozio; (workshop) officina ♦ vi (also: **go ~ping**) fare spese; **~ assistant** (BRIT) n commesso/a; **~ floor** n officina; (BRIT: fig) operai mpl, maestranze fpl; **~keeper** n negoziante m/f, bottegaio/a; **~lifting** n taccheggio; **~per** n compratore/trice; **~ping** n (goods) spesa, acquisti mpl; **~ping bag** n borsa per la spesa; **~ping centre** (US **~ping center**) n centro commerciale; **~-soiled** adj sciupato(a) a forza di stare in vetrina; **~ steward** (BRIT) n (INDUSTRY) rappresentante m sindacale; **~ window** n vetrina

shore [ʃɔː*] n (of sea) riva, spiaggia; (of lake) riva ♦ vt: **to ~ (up)** puntellare; **on ~** a riva

shorn [ʃɔːn] pp of **shear**

short [ʃɔːt] adj (not long) corto(a); (soon finished) breve; (person) basso(a); (curt) brusco(a), secco(a); (insufficient) insufficiente ♦ n (also: **~ film**) cortometraggio; **(a pair of) ~s** (i) calzoncini; **to be ~ of sth** essere a corto di or mancare di qc; **in ~** in breve; **~ of doing** a meno che non si faccia; **everything ~ of** tutto fuorché; **it is ~ for** l'abbreviazione or il diminutivo di; **to cut ~** (speech, visit) accorciare, abbreviare; **to fall ~ of** venir meno a; non soddisfare; **to run ~ of** rimanere senza; **to stop ~** fermarsi di colpo; **to stop ~ of** non arrivare fino a; **~age** n scarsezza, carenza; **~bread** n biscotto di pasta frolla; **~change** vt: **to ~-change sb** imbrogliare qn sul resto; **~circuit** n cortocircuito; **~coming** n difetto; **~(crust) pastry** (BRIT) n pasta frolla; **~cut** n scorciatoia; **~en** vt accorciare, ridurre; **~fall** n deficit m; **~hand** (BRIT) n stenografia; **~hand typist** (BRIT) n stenodattilografo/a; **~ list** (BRIT) n (for job) rosa dei candidati; **~-lived** adj di breve durata; **~ly** adv fra poco; **~-sighted** (BRIT) adj miope; **~-staffed** adj a corto di personale; **~-stay** adj (car park) a tempo limitato; **~ story** n racconto, novella; **~-tempered** adj irascibile; **~-term** adj (effect) di or a breve durata; (borrowing) a breve scadenza; **~ wave** n (RADIO) onde fpl corte

shot [ʃɔt] pt, pp of **shoot** ♦ n sparo, colpo; (try) prova; (FOOTBALL) tiro; (injection) iniezione f; (PHOT) foto f inv; **like a ~** come un razzo; (very readily) immediatamente; **~gun** n fucile m da caccia

should [ʃud] aux vb: **I ~ go now** dovrei andare ora; **he ~ be there now** dovrebbe essere arrivato ora; **I ~ go if I were you** se fossi in te andrei; **I ~ like to** mi piacerebbe

shoulder [ˈʃəuldə*] n spalla; (BRIT: of road): **hard ~** banchina ♦ vt (fig) addossarsi, prendere sulle proprie spalle; **~ bag** n borsa a tracolla; ~ **blade** n scapola

shouldn't ['ʃudnt] = **should not**

shout [ʃaut] n urlo, grido ♦ vt gridare ♦ vi (*also*: ~ **out**) urlare, gridare; ~ **down** vt zittire gridando; ~**ing** n urli mpl

shove [ʃʌv] vt spingere; (*inf*: put): **to ~ sth in** ficcare qc in; ~ **off** (*inf*) vi sloggiare, smammare

shovel ['ʃʌvl] n pala ♦ vt spalare

show [ʃəu] (pt ~**ed**, pp **shown**) n (*of emotion*) dimostrazione f, manifestazione f; (*semblance*) apparenza; (*exhibition*) mostra, esposizione f; (*THEATRE, CINEMA*) spettacolo ♦ vt far vedere, mostrare; (*courage etc*) dimostrare, dar prova di; (*exhibit*) esporre ♦ vi vedersi, essere visibile; **for ~** per fare scena; **on ~** (*exhibits etc*) esposto(a); ~ **in** vt (*person*) far entrare; ~ **off** vi (*pej*) esibirsi, mettersi in mostra ♦ vt (*display*) mettere in risalto; (*pej*) mettere in mostra; ~ **out** vt (*person*) accompagnare alla porta; ~ **up** vi (*stand out*) essere ben visibile; (*inf*: turn up) farsi vedere ♦ vt mettere in risalto; ~ **business** n industria dello spettacolo; ~**down** n prova di forza

shower ['ʃauə*] n (*rain*) acquazzone m; (*of stones etc*) pioggia; (*also*: ~**bath**) doccia ♦ vi fare la doccia ♦ vt: **to ~ sb with** (*gifts, abuse etc*) coprire qn di; (*missiles*) lanciare contro qn una pioggia di; **to have a ~** fare la doccia; ~**proof** adj impermeabile

showing ['ʃəuɪŋ] n (*of film*) proiezione f

show jumping n concorso ippico (di salto ad ostacoli)

shown [ʃəun] pp of **show**

show-off (*inf*) n (*person*) esibizionista m/f

showpiece ['ʃəupi:s] n pezzo forte

showroom ['ʃəurum] n sala d'esposizione

shrank [ʃræŋk] pt of **shrink**

shrapnel ['ʃræpnl] n shrapnel m

shred [ʃred] n (*gen pl*) brandello ♦ vt fare a brandelli; (*CULIN*) sminuzzare, tagliuzzare; ~**der** n (*vegetable* ~der) grattugia; (*document* ~der) distruttore m di documenti

shrewd [ʃru:d] adj astuto(a), scaltro(a)

shriek [ʃri:k] n strillo ♦ vi strillare

shrill [ʃrɪl] adj acuto(a), stridulo(a), stridente

shrimp [ʃrɪmp] n gamberetto

shrine [ʃraɪn] n reliquario; (*place*) santuario

shrink [ʃrɪŋk] (pt **shrank**, pp **shrunk**) vi restringersi; (*fig*) ridursi; (*also*: ~ **away**) ritrarsi ♦ vt (*wool*) far restringere ♦ n (*inf*: pej) psicanalista m/f; **to ~ from doing sth** rifuggire dal fare qc; ~**wrap** vt confezionare con pellicola di plastica

shrivel ['ʃrɪvl] (*also*: ~ **up**) vt raggrinzare, avvizzire ♦ vi raggrinzirsi, avvizzire

shroud [ʃraud] n lenzuolo funebre ♦ vt: ~**ed in mystery** avvolto(a) nel mistero

Shrove Tuesday ['ʃrəuv-] n martedì m grasso

shrub [ʃrʌb] n arbusto; ~**bery** n arbusti mpl

shrug [ʃrʌg] n scrollata di spalle ♦ vt, vi: **to ~ (one's shoulders)** alzare le spalle, fare spallucce; ~ **off** vt passare sopra a

shrunk [ʃrʌŋk] pp of **shrink**

shudder ['ʃʌdə*] n brivido ♦ vi rabbrividire

shuffle ['ʃʌfl] vt (*cards*) mescolare; **to ~ (one's feet)** strascicare i piedi

shun [ʃʌn] vt sfuggire, evitare

shunt [ʃʌnt] vt (*RAIL*: direct) smistare; (: divert) deviare; (*object*) spostare

shut [ʃʌt] (pt, pp **shut**) vt chiudere ♦ vi chiudersi, chiudere; ~ **down** vt, vi chiudere definitivamente; ~ **off** vt fermare, bloccare; ~ **up** vi (*inf*: keep quiet) stare zitto(a), fare silenzio ♦ vt (*close*) chiudere; (*silence*) far tacere; ~**ter** n imposta; (*PHOT*) otturatore m

shuttle ['ʃʌtl] n spola, navetta; (*space ~*) navetta (spaziale); (*also*: ~ **service**) servizio m navetta inv

shuttlecock ['ʃʌtlkɔk] n volano

shuttle diplomacy n la gestione dei rapporti diplomatici caratterizzata da frequenti viaggi e incontri dei rappresentanti del governo

shy [ʃaɪ] adj timido(a)

Sicily ['sɪsɪlɪ] n Sicilia

sick [sɪk] adj (*ill*) malato(a); (*vomiting*): **to be ~** vomitare; (*humour*) macabro(a); **to feel ~** avere la nausea; **to be ~ of** (*fig*) averne abbastanza di; ~ **bay** n infermeria; ~**en** vt nauseare ♦ vi: **to be ~ening for sth** (cold etc) covare qc

sickle ['sɪkl] n falcetto

sick: ~ **leave** n congedo per malattia; ~**ly** adj malaticcio(a); (causing nausea) nauseante; ~**ness** n malattia; (vomiting) vomito; ~ **pay** n sussidio per malattia

side [saɪd] n lato; (of lake) riva; (team) squadra ♦ cpd (door, entrance) laterale ♦ vi: **to ~ with sb** parteggiare per qn, prendere le parti di qn; **by the ~ of** a fianco di; (road) sul ciglio di; ~ **by ~** fianco a fianco; **from ~ to ~** da una parte all'altra; **to take ~s (with)** schierarsi (con); ~**board** n credenza; ~**burns** (BRIT ~**boards**) npl (whiskers) basette fpl; ~ **effect** n (MED) effetto collaterale; ~**light** n (AUT) luce f di posizione; ~**line** n (SPORT) linea laterale; (fig) attività secondaria; ~**long** adj obliquo(a); ~ **order** n contorno (pietanza); ~ **show** n attrazione f; ~**step** vt (question) eludere; (problem) scavalcare; ~ **street** n traversa; ~**track** vt (fig) distrarre; ~**walk** (US) n marciapiede m; ~**ways** adv (move) di lato, di fianco

siding ['saɪdɪŋ] n (RAIL) binario di raccordo

siege [siːdʒ] n assedio

sieve [sɪv] n setaccio ♦ vt setacciare

sift [sɪft] vt passare al crivello; (fig) vagliare

sigh [saɪ] n sospiro ♦ vi sospirare

sight [saɪt] n (faculty) vista, (spectacle) spettacolo; (on gun) mira ♦ vt avvistare; **in ~** in vista; **on ~** a vista; **out of ~** non visibile; ~**seeing** n giro turistico; **to go ~seeing** visitare una località

sign [saɪn] n segno; (with hand etc) segno, gesto; (notice) insegna, cartello ♦ vt firmare; (player) ingaggiare; ~ **on** vi (MIL) arruolarsi; (as unemployed) iscriversi sulla lista (dell'ufficio di collocamento) ♦ vt (MIL) arruolare; (employee) assumere; ~ **over** vt: **to ~ sth over to sb** cedere qc con scrittura legale a qn; ~ **up** vi (MIL) arruolarsi; (for course) iscriversi ♦ vt (player) ingaggiare; (recruits) reclutare

signal ['sɪgnl] n segnale m ♦ vi (AUT) segnalare, mettere la freccia ♦ vt (person)

fare segno a; (message) comunicare per mezzo di segnali; ~**man** (irreg) n (RAIL) deviatore m

signature ['sɪgnətʃə*] n firma; ~ **tune** n sigla musicale

signet ring ['sɪgnət-] n anello con sigillo

significance [sɪg'nɪfɪkəns] n significato; importanza

significant [sɪg'nɪfɪkənt] adj significativo(a)

sign language n linguaggio dei muti

signpost ['saɪnpəust] n cartello indicatore

silence ['saɪləns] n silenzio ♦ vt far tacere, ridurre al silenzio; ~**r** n (on gun, BRIT: AUT) silenziatore m

silent ['saɪlnt] adj silenzioso(a); (film) muto(a); **to remain** ~ tacere, stare zitto; ~ **partner** n (COMM) socio inattivo

silhouette [sɪluː'et] n silhouette f inv

silicon chip ['sɪlɪkən] n piastrina di silicio

silk [sɪlk] n seta ♦ adj di seta; ~**y** adj di seta

silly ['sɪlɪ] adj stupido(a), sciocco(a)

silt [sɪlt] n limo

silver ['sɪlvə*] n argento; (money) monete da 5, 10 or 50 pence; (also: ~**ware**) argenteria ♦ adj d'argento; ~ **paper** n (BRIT) carta argentata, (carta) stagnola; ~-**plated** adj argentato(a); ~**smith** n argentiere m; ~**y** adj (colour) argenteo(a); (sound) argentino(a)

similar [sɪmɪlə*] adj: ~ **(to)** simile (a); ~**ly** adv allo stesso modo; così pure

simmer ['sɪmə*] vi cuocere a fuoco lento

simple ['sɪmpl] adj semplice; **simplicity** [-'plɪsɪtɪ] n semplicità; **simply** adv semplicemente

simultaneous [sɪməl'teɪnɪəs] adj simultaneo(a)

sin [sɪn] n peccato ♦ vi peccare

since [sɪns] adv da allora ♦ prep da ♦ conj (time) da quando; (because) poiché, dato che; ~ **then, ever** ~ da allora

sincere [sɪn'sɪə*] adj sincero(a); ~**ly** adv: **yours** ~**ly** (in letters) distinti saluti; **sincerity** [-'sɛrɪtɪ] n sincerità

sinew ['sɪnjuː] n tendine m

sing [sɪŋ] (pt **sang**, pp **sung**) vt, vi cantare

singe [sɪndʒ] vt bruciacchiare

singer ['sɪŋə*] *n* cantante *m/f*

singing ['sɪŋɪŋ] *n* canto

single ['sɪŋgl] *adj* solo(a), unico(a); (*unmarried: man*) celibe; (: *woman*) nubile; (*not double*) semplice ♦ *n* (*BRIT: also:* ~ **ticket**) biglietto di (sola) andata; (*record*) 45 giri *m*; ~**s** *n* (*TENNIS*) singolo; ~ **out** *vt* scegliere; (*distinguish*) distinguere; ~ **bed** *n* letto singolo; ~-**breasted** *adj* a un petto; ~ **file** *n*: **in** ~ **file** in fila indiana; ~-**handed** *adv* senza aiuto, da solo(a); ~-**minded** *adj* tenace, risoluto(a); ~ **parent** *n* (*mother*) ragazza *f* madre *inv*; (*father*) ragazzo *m* padre *inv*; ~ **room** *n* camera singola; ~-**track road** *n* strada a una carreggiata

singly ['sɪŋglɪ] *adv* separatamente

singular ['sɪŋgjulə*] *adj* (*exceptional, LING*) singolare ♦ *n* (*LING*) singolare *m*

sinister ['sɪnɪstə*] *adj* sinistro(a)

sink [sɪŋk] (*pt* **sank**, *pp* **sunk**) *n* lavandino, acquaio ♦ *vt* (*ship*) (fare) affondare, colare a picco; (*foundations*) scavare; (*piles etc*): **to** ~ **sth into** conficcare qc in ♦ *vi* affondare, andare a fondo; (*ground etc*) cedere, avvallarsi; **my heart sank** mi sentii venir meno; ~ **in** *vi* penetrare

sinner ['sɪnə*] *n* peccatore/trice

sinus ['saɪnəs] *n* (*ANAT*) seno

sip [sɪp] *n* sorso ♦ *vt* sorseggiare

siphon ['saɪfən] *n* sifone *m*; ~ **off** *vt* travasare (con un sifone)

sir [sə*] *n* signore *m*; **S~ John Smith** Sir John Smith; **yes** ~ sì, signore

sirloin ['sə:lɔɪn] *n* controfiletto

sissy ['sɪsɪ] (*inf*) *n* femminuccia

sister ['sɪstə*] *n* sorella; (*nun*) suora; (*BRIT: nurse*) infermiera *f* caposala *inv*; ~-**in-law** *n* cognata

sit [sɪt] (*pt, pp* **sat**) *vi* sedere, sedersi; (*assembly*) essere in seduta; (*for painter*) posare ♦ *vt* (*exam*) sostenere, dare; ~ **down** *vi* sedersi; ~ **in on** *vt fus* assistere a; ~ **up** *vi* tirarsi su a sedere; (*not go to bed*) stare alzato(a) fino a tardi

sitcom ['sɪtkɔm] *n abbr* (= *situation comedy*) commedia di situazione; (*TV*)

telefilm *m inv* comico d'interni

site [saɪt] *n* posto; (*also*: **building** ~) cantiere *m* ♦ *vt* situare

sit-in *n* (*demonstration*) sit-in *m inv*

sitting ['sɪtɪŋ] *n* (*of assembly etc*) seduta; (*in canteen*) turno; ~ **room** *n* soggiorno

situated ['sɪtjueɪtɪd] *adj* situato(a)

situation [sɪtju'eɪʃən] *n* situazione *f*; (*job*) lavoro; (*location*) posizione *f*; **"~s vacant"** (*BRIT*) "offerte *fpl* di impiego"

six [sɪks] *num* sei; ~**teen** *num* sedici; ~**th** *num* sesto(a); ~**ty** *num* sessanta

size [saɪz] *n* dimensioni *fpl*; (*of clothing*) taglia, misura; (*of shoes*) numero; (*glue*) colla; ~ **up** *vt* giudicare, farsi un'idea di; ~**able** *adj* considerevole

sizzle ['sɪzl] *vi* sfrigolare

skate [skeɪt] *n* pattino; (*fish: pl inv*) razza ♦ *vi* pattinare; ~**board** *n* skateboard *m inv*; ~**r** *n* pattinatore/trice; **skating** *n* pattinaggio; **skating rink** *n* pista di pattinaggio

skeleton ['skelɪtn] *n* scheletro; ~ **staff** *n* personale *m* ridotto

skeptical ['skeptɪkl] (*US*) *adj* = **sceptical**

sketch [sketʃ] *n* (*drawing*) schizzo, abbozzo; (*THEATRE*) scenetta comica, sketch *m inv* ♦ *vt* abbozzare, schizzare; ~ **book** *n* album *m inv* per schizzi; ~**y** *adj* incompleto(a), lacunoso(a)

skewer ['skju:ə*] *n* spiedo

ski [ski:] *n* sci *m inv* ♦ *vi* sciare; ~ **boot** *n* scarpone *m* da sci

skid [skɪd] *n* slittamento ♦ *vi* slittare

skier ['ski:ə*] *n* sciatore/trice

skiing ['ski:ɪŋ] *n* sci *m*

ski jump *n* (*ramp*) trampolino; (*event*) salto con gli sci

skilful ['skɪlful] (*US* **skillful**) *adj* abile

ski lift ['ski:lɪft] *n* sciovia

skill [skɪl] *n* abilità *f inv*, capacità *f inv*; ~**ed** *adj* esperto(a); (*worker*) qualificato(a), specializzato(a); ~**ful** (*US*) *adj* = **skilful**

skim [skɪm] *vt* (*milk*) scremare; (*glide over*) sfiorare ♦ *vi*: **to** ~ **through** (*fig*) scorrere, dare una scorsa a; ~**med milk** *n* latte *m* scremato

skimp [skɪmp] vt (work: also: ~ **on**) fare alla carlona; (cloth etc) lesinare; ~**y** adj misero(a); striminzito(a); frugale

skin [skɪn] n pelle f ♦ vt (fruit etc) sbucciare; (animal) scuoiare, spellare; ~ **cancer** n cancro alla pelle; ~-**deep** adj superficiale; ~ **diving** n nuoto subacqueo; ~**ny** adj molto magro(a), pelle e ossa inv; ~**tight** adj (dress etc) aderente

skip [skɪp] n saltello, balzo; (BRIT: container) benna ♦ vi saltare; (with rope) saltare la corda ♦ vt saltare

ski pole n racchetta (da sci)

skipper ['skɪpə*] n (NAUT, SPORT) capitano

skipping rope ['skɪpɪŋ-] (BRIT) n corda per saltare

skirmish ['skəːmɪʃ] n scaramuccia

skirt [skəːt] n gonna, sottana ♦ vt fiancheggiare, costeggiare; ~**ing board** (BRIT) n zoccolo

ski slope n pista da sci

ski suit n tuta da sci

skit [skɪt] n parodia; scenetta satirica

ski tow n sciovia, ski-lift m inv

skittle ['skɪtl] n birillo; ~**s** n (game) (gioco dei) birilli mpl

skive [skaɪv] (BRIT: inf) vi fare il lavativo

skull [skʌl] n cranio, teschio

skunk [skʌŋk] n moffetta

sky [skaɪ] n cielo; ~**light** n lucernario; ~**scraper** n grattacielo

slab [slæb] n lastra; (of cake, cheese) fetta

slack [slæk] adj (loose) allentato(a); (slow) lento(a); (careless) negligente; (also: ~**en off**) vi rallentare, diminuire ♦ vt allentare; (speed) diminuire; ~**s** npl (trousers) pantaloni mpl

slag heap [slæg-] n ammasso di scorie

slag off [slæg-] (BRIT: inf) vt sparlare di

slam [slæm] vt (door) sbattere; (throw) scaraventare; (criticize) stroncare ♦ vi sbattere

slander ['slɑːndə*] n calunnia; diffamazione f

slang [slæŋ] n gergo, slang m

slant [slɑːnt] n pendenza, inclinazione f; (fig) angolazione f, punto di vista; ~**ed** adj in pendenza, inclinato(a); (eyes) obliquo(a); ~**ing** adj = ~**ed**

slap [slæp] n manata, pacca; (on face) schiaffo ♦ vt dare una manata a; schiaffeggiare ♦ adv (directly) in pieno; ~ **a coat of paint on it** dagli una mano di vernice; ~**dash** adj negligente; (work) raffazzonato(a); ~**stick** n (comedy) farsa grossolana; ~-**up** (BRIT) adj: **a ~-up meal** un pranzo (or una cena) coi fiocchi

slash [slæʃ] vt tagliare; (face) sfregiare; (fig: prices) ridurre drasticamente, tagliare

slat [slæt] n (of wood) stecca; (of plastic) lamina

slate [sleɪt] n ardesia; (piece) lastra di ardesia ♦ vt (fig: criticize) stroncare, distruggere

slaughter ['slɔːtə*] n strage f, massacro ♦ vt (animal) macellare; (people) trucidare, massacrare

slave [sleɪv] n schiavo/a ♦ vi (also: ~ **away**) lavorare come uno schiavo; ~**ry** n schiavitù f; **slavish** adj servile; (copy) pedissequo(a)

slay [sleɪ] (pt **slew**, pp **slain**) vt (formal) uccidere

sleazy ['sliːzɪ] adj trasandato(a)

sledge [sledʒ] n slitta; ~**hammer** n mazza, martello da fabbro

sleek [sliːk] adj (hair, fur) lucido(a), lucente; (car, boat) slanciato(a), affusolato(a)

sleep [sliːp] (pt, pp **slept**) n sonno ♦ vi dormire; **to go to** ~ addormentarsi; ~ **around** vi andare a letto con tutti; ~ **in** vi (oversleep) dormire fino a tardi; ~**er** (BRIT) n (RAIL: on track) traversina; (: train) treno di vagoni letto; ~**ing bag** n sacco a pelo; ~**ing car** n vagone m letto inv, carrozza f letto inv; ~**ing partner** (BRIT) n (COMM) socio inattivo; ~**ing pill** n sonnifero; ~**less** adj: **a ~less night** una notte in bianco; ~**walker** n sonnambulo/a; ~**y** adj assonnato(a), sonnolento(a); (fig) addormentato(a)

sleet [sliːt] n nevischio

sleeve [sliːv] n manica; (of record) copertina

sleigh [sleɪ] n slitta

sleight [slaɪt] n: ~ **of hand** gioco di destrezza

slender ['slɛndə*] adj snello(a), sottile; (not enough) scarso(a), esiguo(a)

slept [slɛpt] pt, pp of **sleep**

slew [slu:] pt of **slay** ♦ vi (BRIT) girare

slice [slaɪs] n fetta ♦ vt affettare, tagliare a fette

slick [slɪk] adj (skilful) brillante; (clever) furbo(a) ♦ n (also: **oil ~**) chiazza di petrolio

slide [slaɪd] (pt, pp **slid**) n scivolone m; (in playground) scivolo; (PHOT) diapositiva; (BRIT: also: **hair ~**) fermaglio (per capelli) ♦ vt far scivolare ♦ vi scivolare; **~ rule** n regolo calcolatore; **sliding** adj (door) scorrevole; **sliding scale** n scala mobile

slight [slaɪt] adj (slim) snello(a), sottile; (frail) delicato(a), fragile; (trivial) insignificante; (small) piccolo(a) ♦ n offesa, affronto; **not in the ~est** affatto, neppure per sogno; **~ly** adv lievemente, un po'

slim [slɪm] adj magro(a), snello(a) ♦ vi dimagrire; fare (or seguire) una dieta dimagrante

slime [slaɪm] n limo, melma; viscidume m

slimming ['slɪmɪŋ] adj (diet) dimagrante; (food) ipocalorico(a)

sling [slɪŋ] (pt, pp **slung**) n (MED) fascia al collo; (for baby) marsupio ♦ vt lanciare, tirare

slip [slɪp] n scivolata, scivolone m; (mistake) errore m, sbaglio; (underskirt) sottoveste f; (of paper) striscia di carta; tagliando, scontrino ♦ vt (slide) far scivolare ♦ vi (slide) scivolare; (move smoothly): **to ~ into/out of** scivolare in/fuori da; (decline) declinare; **to ~ sth on/off** infilarsi/togliersi qc; **to give sb the ~** sfuggire a qn; **a ~ of the tongue** un lapsus linguae; **~ away** vi svignarsela; **~ in** vt infilare ♦ vi (error) scivolare; **~ out** vi scivolare fuori; **~ up** vi sbagliarsi; **~ped disc** n spostamento delle vertebre

slipper ['slɪpə*] n pantofola

slippery ['slɪpərɪ] adj scivoloso(a)

slip road (BRIT) n (to motorway) rampa di accesso

slip-up n granchio (fig)

slipway ['slɪpweɪ] n scalo di costruzione

slit [slɪt] (pt, pp **slit**) n fessura, fenditura; (cut) taglio ♦ vt fendere; tagliare

slither ['slɪðə*] vi scivolare, sdrucciolare

sliver ['slɪvə*] n (of glass, wood) scheggia; (of cheese etc) fettina

slob [slɒb] (inf) n sciattone/a

slog [slɒg] (BRIT) n faticata ♦ vi lavorare con accanimento, sgobbare

slogan ['sləʊgən] n motto, slogan m inv

slope [sləʊp] n pendio; (side of mountain) versante m; (ski ~) pista; (of roof) pendenza; (of floor) inclinazione f ♦ vi: **to ~ down** declinare; **to ~ up** essere in salita; **sloping** adj inclinato(a)

sloppy ['slɒpɪ] adj (work) tirato(a) via; (appearance) sciatto(a)

slot [slɒt] n fessura ♦ vt: **to ~ sth into** infilare qc in

sloth [sləʊθ] n (laziness) pigrizia, accidia

slot machine n (BRIT: vending machine) distributore m automatico; (for gambling) slot-machine f inv

slouch [slaʊtʃ] vi (when walking) camminare dinoccolato(a); **she was ~ing in a chair** era sprofondata in una poltrona

Slovenia [sləʊ'vi:nɪə] n Slovenia

slovenly ['slʌvənlɪ] adj sciatto(a), trasandato(a)

slow [sləʊ] adj lento(a); (watch): **to be ~** essere indietro ♦ adv lentamente ♦ vt, vi (also: **~ down**, **~ up**) rallentare; **"~"** (road sign) "rallentare"; **~ly** adv lentamente; **~ motion** n: **in ~ motion** al rallentatore

sludge [slʌdʒ] n fanghiglia

slug [slʌg] n lumaca; (bullet) pallottola; **~gish** adj lento(a); (trading) stagnante

sluice [slu:s] n chiusa

slum [slʌm] n catapecchia

slumber ['slʌmbə*] n sonno

slump [slʌmp] n crollo, caduta; (economic) depressione f, crisi f inv ♦ vi crollare

slung [slʌŋ] pt, pp of **sling**

slur [slə:*] n (fig): **~ (on)** calunnia (su) ♦ vt pronunciare in modo indistinto

slush [slʌʃ] n neve f mista a fango; **~ fund** n fondi mpl neri

slut [slʌt] n donna trasandata, sciattona

sly [slaɪ] *adj* (*smile, remark*) sornione(a); (*person*) furbo(a)

smack [smæk] *n* (*slap*) pacca; (*on face*) schiaffo ♦ *vt* schiaffeggiare; (*child*) picchiare ♦ *vi*: **to ~ of** puzzare di

small [smɔ:l] *adj* piccolo(a); **~ ads** (*BRIT*) *npl* piccola pubblicità; **~ change** *n* moneta, spiccioli *mpl*; **~-holder** *n* piccolo proprietario; **~ hours** *npl*: **in the ~ hours** alle ore piccole; **~pox** *n* vaiolo; **~ talk** *n* chiacchiere *fpl*

smart [smɑ:t] *adj* elegante; (*fashionable*) alla moda; (*clever*) intelligente; (*quick*) sveglio(a) ♦ *vi* bruciare; **~ card** *n* carta intelligente; **~en up** *vi* farsi bello(a) ♦ *vt* (*people*) fare bello(a); (*things*) abbellire

smash [smæʃ] *n* (*also*: **~-up**) scontro, collisione *f*; (**~ hit**) successore *m* ♦ *vt* frantumare, fracassare; (*SPORT: record*) battere ♦ *vi* frantumarsi, andare in pezzi; **~ing** (*inf*) *adj* favoloso(a), formidabile

smattering ['smætərɪŋ] *n*: **a ~ of** un'infarinatura di

smear [smɪə*] *n* macchia; (*MED*) striscio ♦ *vt* spalmare; (*make dirty*) sporcare; **~ campaign** *n* campagna diffamatoria

smell [smɛl] (*pt, pp* **smelt** *or* **smelled**) *n* odore *m*; (*sense*) olfatto, odorato ♦ *vt* sentire (l')odore di ♦ *vi* (*food etc*): **to ~ (of)** avere odore (di); (*pej*) puzzare, avere un cattivo odore; **~y** *adj* puzzolente

smile [smaɪl] *n* sorriso ♦ *vi* sorridere

smirk [smə:k] *n* sorriso furbo; sorriso compiaciuto

smog [smɔg] *n* smog *m*

smoke [sməuk] *n* fumo ♦ *vt, vi* fumare; **~d** *adj* (*bacon, glass*) affumicato(a); **~r** *n* (*person*) fumatore/trice; (*RAIL*) carrozza per fumatori; **~ screen** *n* (*MIL*) cortina fumogena *or* di fumo; (*fig*) copertura; **smoking** *n* fumo; **"no smoking"** (*sign*) "vietato fumare"; **smoking compartment** (*BRIT*), **smoking car** (*US*) *n* scompartimento (per) fumatori; **smoky** *adj* fumoso(a); (*taste*) affumicato(a)

smolder ['sməuldə*] (*US*) *vi* = **smoulder**

smooth [smu:ð] *adj* liscio(a); (*sauce*) omogeneo(a); (*flavour, whisky*) amabile; (*movement*) regolare; (*person*) mellifluo(a) ♦ *vt* (*also*: **~ out**) lisciare, spianare; (: *difficulties*) appianare

smother ['smʌðə*] *vt* soffocare

smoulder ['sməuldə*] (*US* **smolder**) *vi* covare sotto la cenere

smudge [smʌdʒ] *n* macchia; sbavatura ♦ *vt* imbrattare, sporcare

smug [smʌg] *adj* soddisfatto(a), compiaciuto(a)

smuggle ['smʌgl] *vt* contrabbandare; **~r** *n* contrabbandiere/a; **smuggling** *n* contrabbando

smutty ['smʌtɪ] *adj* (*fig*) osceno(a), indecente

snack [snæk] *n* spuntino; **~ bar** *n* tavola calda, snack bar *m inv*

snag [snæg] *n* intoppo, ostacolo imprevisto

snail [sneɪl] *n* chiocciola

snake [sneɪk] *n* serpente *m*

snap [snæp] *n* (*sound*) schianto, colpo secco; (*photograph*) istantanea ♦ *adj* improvviso(a) ♦ *vt* (*far*) schioccare; (*break*) spezzare di netto ♦ *vi* spezzarsi con un rumore secco; (*fig: person*) parlare con tono secco; **to ~ shut** chiudersi di scatto; **~ at** *vt fus* (*subj: dog*) cercare di mordere; **~ off** *vt* (*break*) schiantare; **~ up** *vt* afferrare; **~py** (*inf*) *adj* (*answer, slogan*) d'effetto; **make it ~py!** (*hurry up*) sbrigati!, svelto!; **~shot** *n* istantanea

snare [snɛə*] *n* trappola

snarl [snɑ:l] *vi* ringhiare

snatch [snætʃ] *n* (*small amount*) frammento ♦ *vt* strappare (con violenza); (*fig*) rubare

sneak [sni:k] (*pt* (*US*) **snuck**) *vi*: **to ~ in/out** entrare/uscire di nascosto ♦ *n* spione/a; **to ~ up on sb** avvicinarsi quatto quatto a qn; **~ers** *npl* scarpe *fpl* da ginnastica

sneer [snɪə*] *vi* sogghignare; **to ~ at** farsi beffe di

sneeze [sni:z] *n* starnuto ♦ *vi* starnutire

sniff [snɪf] *n* fiutata, annusata ♦ *vi* tirare su col naso ♦ *vt* fiutare, annusare

snigger ['snɪgə*] *vi* ridacchiare, ridere sotto i baffi

snip [snɪp] *n* pezzetto; (*bargain*) (buon) affare *m*, occasione *f* ♦ *vt* tagliare

sniper ['snaɪpə*] *n* (*marksman*) franco tiratore *m*, cecchino

snippet ['snɪpɪt] *n* frammento

snob [snɔb] *n* snob *m/f inv*; **~bery** *n* snobismo; **~bish** *adj* snob *inv*

snooker ['snu:kə*] *n* tipo di gioco del biliardo

snoop [snu:p] *vi*: **to ~ about** curiosare

snooze [snu:z] *n* sonnellino, pisolino ♦ *vi* fare un sonnellino

snore [snɔ:*] *vi* russare

snorkel ['snɔ:kl] *n* (*of swimmer*) respiratore *m* a tubo

snort [snɔ:t] *n* sbuffo ♦ *vi* sbuffare

snout [snaʊt] *n* muso

snow [snəʊ] *n* neve *f* ♦ *vi* nevicare; **~ball** *n* palla di neve ♦ *vi* (*fig*) crescere a vista d'occhio; **~bound** *adj* bloccato(a) dalla neve; **~drift** *n* cumulo di neve (ammucchiato dal vento); **~drop** *n* bucaneve *m inv*; **~fall** *n* nevicata; **~flake** *n* fiocco di neve; **~man** (*irreg*) *n* pupazzo di neve; **~plough** (*US* **~plow**) *n* spazzaneve *m inv*; **~shoe** *n* racchetta da neve; **~storm** *n* tormenta

snub [snʌb] *vt* snobbare ♦ *n* offesa, affronto; **~-nosed** *adj* dal naso camuso

snuff [snʌf] *n* tabacco da fiuto

snug [snʌg] *adj* comodo(a); (*room, house*) accogliente, comodo(a)

snuggle ['snʌgl] *vi*: **to ~ up to sb** stringersi a qn

KEYWORD

so [səʊ] *adv* **1** (*thus, likewise*) così; **if ~** se è così, quand'è così; **I didn't do it — you did ~!** non l'ho fatto io — sì che l'hai fatto!; **~ do I, ~ am I** *etc* anch'io; **it's 5 o'clock – ~ it is!** sono le 5 — davvero!; **I hope ~** lo spero; **I think ~** penso di sì; **~ far** finora, fin qui; (*in past*) fino ad allora

2 (*in comparisons etc: to such a degree*) così; **~ big** così grande (che); **she's not ~ clever as her brother** lei non è (così) intelligente come suo fratello

3: **~ much** *adj* tanto(a) ♦ *adv* tanto; **I've got ~ much work/money** ho tanto lavoro/tanti soldi; **I love you ~ much** ti amo tanto; **~ many** tanti(e)

4 (*phrases*): **10 or ~** circa 10; **~ long!** (*inf: goodbye*) ciao!, ci vediamo!

♦ *conj* **1** (*expressing purpose*): **~ as to do** in modo *or* così da fare; **we hurried ~ as not to be late** ci affrettammo per non fare tardi; **~ (that)** affinché +*sub*, perché +*sub*

2 (*expressing result*): **he didn't arrive ~ I left** non è venuto così me ne sono andata; **~ you see, I could have gone** vedi, sarei potuto andare

---

soak [səʊk] *vt* inzuppare; (*clothes*) mettere a mollo ♦ *vi* (*clothes etc*) essere a mollo; **~ in** *vi* penetrare; **~ up** *vt* assorbire

soap [səʊp] *n* sapone *m*; **~flakes** *npl* sapone *m* in scaglie; **~ opera** *n* soap opera *f inv*; **~ powder** *n* detersivo; **~y** *adj* insaponato(a)

soar [sɔ:*] *vi* volare in alto; (*price etc*) salire alle stelle; (*building*) ergersi

sob [sɔb] *n* singhiozzo ♦ *vi* singhiozzare

sober ['səʊbə*] *adj* sobrio(a); (*not drunk*) non ubriaco(a); (*moderate*) moderato(a); **~ up** *vt* far passare la sbornia a ♦ *vi* farsi passare la sbornia

so-called ['səʊ'kɔ:ld] *adj* cosiddetto(a)

soccer ['sɔkə*] *n* calcio

sociable ['səʊʃəbl] *adj* socievole

social ['səʊʃl] *adj* sociale ♦ *n* festa, serata; **~ club** *n* club *m inv* sociale; **~ism** *n* socialismo; **~ist** *adj, n* socialista *m/f*; **~ize** *vi*: **to ~ize (with)** socializzare (con); **~ security** (*BRIT*) *n* previdenza sociale; **~ work** *n* servizio sociale; **~ worker** *n* assistente *m/f* sociale

society [sə'saɪətɪ] *n* società *f inv*; (*club*) società, associazione *f*; (*also*: **high ~**) alta società

sociology [səʊsɪ'ɒlədʒɪ] *n* sociologia

sock [sɔk] *n* calzino

socket ['sɔkɪt] *n* cavità *f inv*; (*of eye*) orbita; (*BRIT: ELEC: also*: **wall ~**) presa di corrente

sod [sɔd] *n* (*of earth*) zolla erbosa; (*BRIT: inf!*)

bastardo/a (!)

soda ['səudə] n (CHEM) soda; (also: ~ **water**) acqua di seltz; (US: also: ~ **pop**) gassosa

sodium ['səudɪəm] n sodio

sofa ['səufə] n sofà m inv

soft [sɒft] adj (not rough) morbido(a); (not hard) soffice; (not loud) sommesso(a); (not bright) tenue; (kind) gentile; ~ **drink** n analcolico; **~en** ['sɒfn] vt ammorbidire; addolcire; attenuare ♦ vi ammorbidirsi; addolcirsi; attenuarsi; **~ly** adv dolcemente; morbidamente; **~ness** n dolcezza; morbidezza

software ['sɒftweə*] n (COMPUT) software m

soggy ['sɒgɪ] adj inzuppato(a)

soil [sɔɪl] n terreno ♦ vt sporcare

solar ['səulə*] adj solare; ~ **panel** n pannello solare; ~ **power** n energie solare

sold [səuld] pt, pp of **sell**; ~ **out** adj (COMM) esaurito(a)

solder ['səuldə*] vt saldare ♦ n saldatura

soldier ['səuldʒə*] n soldato, militare m

sole [səul] n (of foot) pianta (del piede); (of shoe) suola; (fish: pl inv) sogliola ♦ adj solo(a), unico(a)

solemn ['sɒləm] adj solenne

sole trader n (COMM) commerciante m in proprio

solicit [sə'lɪsɪt] vt (request) richiedere, sollecitare ♦ vi (prostitute) adescare i passanti

solicitor [sə'lɪsɪtə*] n (BRIT) (for wills etc) ≈ notaio; (in court) ≈ avvocato

solid ['sɒlɪd] adj solido(a); (not hollow) pieno(a); (meal) sostanzioso(a) ♦ n solido

solidarity [sɒlɪ'dærɪtɪ] n solidarietà

solitaire [sɒlɪ'teə*] n (games, gem) solitario

solitary ['sɒlɪtərɪ] adj solitario(a); ~ **confinement** n (LAW) isolamento

solo ['səuləu] n assolo; **~ist** n solista m/f

soluble ['sɒljubl] adj solubile

solution [sə'lu:ʃən] n soluzione f

solve [sɒlv] vt risolvere

solvent ['sɒlvənt] adj (COMM) solvibile ♦ n (CHEM) solvente m

sombre ['sɒmbə*] (US **somber**) adj scuro(a); (mood, person) triste

┌─────────────────┐
│ KEYWORD │
└─────────────────┘

some [sʌm] adj 1 (a certain amount or number of): ~ **tea/water/cream** del tè/dell'acqua/della panna; ~ **children/apples** dei bambini/delle mele

2 (certain: in contrasts) certo(a); ~ **people say that ...** alcuni dicono che ..., certa gente dice che ...

3 (unspecified) un(a) certo(a), qualche; ~ **woman was asking for you** una tale chiedeva di lei; ~ **day** un giorno; ~ **day next week** un giorno della prossima settimana

♦ pron 1 (a certain number) alcuni(e), certi(e); **I've got ~** (books etc) ne ho alcuni; ~ **(of them) have been sold** alcuni sono stati venduti

2 (a certain amount) un po'; **I've got ~** (money, milk) ne ho un po'; **I've read ~ of the book** ho letto parte del libro

♦ adv: ~ **10 people** circa 10 persone

somebody ['sʌmbədɪ] pron = **someone**

somehow ['sʌmhau] adv in un modo o nell'altro, in qualche modo; (for some reason) per qualche ragione

someone ['sʌmwʌn] pron qualcuno

someplace ['sʌmpleɪs] (US) adv = **somewhere**

somersault ['sʌməsɔːlt] n capriola; salto mortale ♦ vi fare una capriola (or un salto mortale); (car) cappottare

something ['sʌmθɪŋ] pron qualcosa, qualche cosa; ~ **nice** qualcosa di bello; ~ **to do** qualcosa da fare

sometime ['sʌmtaɪm] adv (in future) una volta o l'altra; (in past): ~ **last month** durante il mese scorso

sometimes ['sʌmtaɪmz] adv qualche volta

somewhat ['sʌmwɒt] adv piuttosto

somewhere ['sʌmweə*] adv in or da qualche parte

son [sʌn] n figlio

song [sɒŋ] n canzone f

sonic ['sɒnɪk] adj (boom) sonico(a)

son-in-law n genero

sonnet ['sɒnɪt] *n* sonetto

sonny ['sʌnɪ] (*inf*) *n* ragazzo mio

soon [suːn] *adv* presto, fra poco; (*early, a short time after*) presto; ~ **afterwards** poco dopo; *see also* **as**; ~**er** *adv* (*time*) prima; (*preference*): **I would** ~**er do** preferirei fare; ~**er or later** prima o poi

soot [sut] *n* fuliggine *f*

soothe [suːð] *vt* calmare

sophisticated [sə'fɪstɪkeɪtɪd] *adj* sofisticato(a); raffinato(a); complesso(a)

sophomore ['sɒfəmɔː*] (*US*) *n* studente/ essa del secondo anno

sopping ['sɒpɪŋ] *adj* (*also:* ~ **wet**) bagnato(a) fradicio(a)

soppy ['sɒpɪ] (*pej*) *adj* sentimentale

soprano [sə'prɑːnəʊ] *n* (*voice*) soprano *m*; (*singer*) soprano *m/f*

sorcerer ['sɔːsərə*] *n* stregone *m*, mago

sore [sɔː*] *adj* (*painful*) dolorante ♦ *n* piaga; ~**ly** *adv* (*tempted*) fortemente

sorrow ['sɒrəʊ] *n* dolore *m*; ~**ful** *adj* doloroso(a)

sorry ['sɒrɪ] *adj* spiacente; (*condition, excuse*) misero(a); ~! scusa! (*or* scusi! *or* scusate!); **to feel** ~ **for sb** rincrescersi per qn

sort [sɔːt] *n* specie *f*, genere *m* ♦ *vt* (*also:* ~ **out**: *papers*) classificare; ordinare; (: *letters etc*) smistare; (: *problems*) risolvere; ~**ing office** *n* ufficio *m* smistamento *inv*

SOS *n abbr* (= *save our souls*) S.O.S. *m inv*

so-so *adv* così così

sought [sɔːt] *pt, pp of* **seek**

soul [səʊl] *n* anima; ~**ful** *adj* pieno(a) di sentimento

sound [saʊnd] *adj* (*healthy*) sano(a); (*safe, not damaged*) solido(a), in buono stato; (*reliable, not superficial*) solido(a); (*sensible*) giudizioso(a), di buon senso ♦ *adv*: ~ **asleep** profondamente addormentato ♦ *n* suono; (*noise*) rumore *m*; (*GEO*) stretto ♦ *vt* (*alarm*) suonare ♦ *vi* suonare; (*fig: seem*) sembrare; **to** ~ **like** rassomigliare a; ~ **out** *vt* sondare; ~ **barrier** *n* muro del suono; ~**bite** *n* dichiarazione breve ed incisiva (*trasmessa per radio o per TV*); ~ **effects** *npl* effetti sonori; ~**ly** *adv* (*sleep*)

profondamente; (*beat*) duramente; ~**proof** *adj* insonorizzato(a), isolato(a) acusticamente; ~**track** *n* (*of film*) colonna sonora

soup [suːp] *n* minestra; brodo; zuppa; ~ **plate** *n* piatto fondo; ~**spoon** *n* cucchiaio da minestra

sour ['saʊə*] *adj* aspro(a); (*fruit*) acerbo(a); (*milk*) acido(a); (*fig*) arcigno(a); acido(a); **it's** ~ **grapes** è soltanto invidia

source [sɔːs] *n* fonte *f*, sorgente *f*; (*fig*) fonte

south [saʊθ] *n* sud *m*, meridione *m*, mezzogiorno ♦ *adj* del sud, sud *inv*, meridionale ♦ *adv* verso sud; S~ **Africa** *n* Sudafrica *m*; S~ **African** *adj*, *n* sudafricano(a); S~ **America** *n* Sudamerica *m*, America del sud; S~ **American** *adj*, *n* sudamericano(a); ~**east** *n* sud-est *m*; ~**erly** ['sʌðəlɪ] *adj* del sud; ~**ern** ['sʌðən] *adj* del sud, meridionale; esposto(a) a sud; S~ **Pole** *n* Polo Sud; ~**ward(s)** *adv* verso sud; ~**west** *n* sud-ovest *m*

souvenir [suːvə'nɪə*] *n* ricordo, souvenir *m inv*

sovereign ['sɒvrɪn] *adj, n* sovrano(a)

soviet ['səʊvɪət] *adj* sovietico(a); **the S~ Union** l'Unione *f* Sovietica

sow[1] [səʊ] (*pt* ~**ed**, *pp* **sown**) *vt* seminare

sow[2] [saʊ] *n* scrofa

sown [səʊn] *pp of* **sow**

soy [sɔɪ] (*US*) *n* = **soya**

soya ['sɔɪə] (*US* **soy**) *n*: ~ **bean** *n* seme *m* di soia; ~ **sauce** *n* salsa di soia

spa [spɑː] *n* (*resort*) stazione *f* termale; (*US: also:* **health** ~) centro di cure estetiche

space [speɪs] *n* spazio; (*room*) posto; spazio; (*length of time*) intervallo ♦ *cpd* spaziale ♦ *vt* (*also:* ~ **out**) distanziare; ~**craft** *n inv* veicolo spaziale; ~**man/woman** (*irreg*) *n* astronauta *m/f*, cosmonauta *m/f*; ~**ship** *n* = ~**craft**; **spacing** *n* spaziatura

spacious ['speɪʃəs] *adj* spazioso(a), ampio(a)

spade [speɪd] *n* (*tool*) vanga; pala; (*child's*) paletta; ~**s** *npl* (*CARDS*) picche *fpl*

Spain [speɪn] *n* Spagna

span [spæn] *n* (*of bird, plane*) apertura alare; (*of arch*) campata; (*in time*) periodo; durata ♦ *vt* attraversare; (*fig*) abbracciare

Spaniard ['spænjəd] *n* spagnolo/a

spaniel ['spænjəl] *n* spaniel *m inv*

Spanish ['spænɪʃ] *adj* spagnolo(a) ♦ *n* (*LING*) spagnolo; **the ~** *npl* gli Spagnoli

spank [spæŋk] *vt* sculacciare

spanner ['spænə*] (*BRIT*) *n* chiave *f* inglese

spare [speə*] *adj* di riserva, di scorta; (*surplus*) in più, d'avanzo ♦ *n* (*part*) pezzo di ricambio ♦ *vt* (*do without*) fare a meno di; (*afford to give*) concedere; (*refrain from hurting, using*) risparmiare; **to ~** (*surplus*) d'avanzo; **~ part** *n* pezzo di ricambio; **~ time** *n* tempo libero; **~ wheel** *n* (*AUT*) ruota di scorta

sparingly ['speərɪŋlɪ] *adv* moderatamente

spark [spɑːk] *n* scintilla; **~(ing) plug** *n* candela

sparkle ['spɑːkl] *n* scintillio, sfavillio ♦ *vi* scintillare, sfavillare; **sparkling** *adj* scintillante, sfavillante; (*conversation, wine, water*) frizzante

sparrow ['spærəu] *n* passero

sparse [spɑːs] *adj* sparso(a), rado(a)

spartan ['spɑːtən] *adj* (*fig*) spartano(a)

spasm ['spæzəm] *n* (*MED*) spasmo; (*fig*) accesso, attacco; **~odic** [spæz'mɔdɪk] *adj* spasmodico(a); (*fig*) intermittente

spastic ['spæstɪk] *n* spastico/a

spat [spæt] *pt, pp of* **spit**

spate [speɪt] *n* (*fig*): **~ of** diluvio *or* fiume *m* di

spawn [spɔːn] *vi* deporre le uova ♦ *n* uova *fpl*

speak [spiːk] (*pt* **spoke**, *pp* **spoken**) *vt* (*language*) parlare; (*truth*) dire ♦ *vi* parlare; **to ~ to sb/of** *or* **about sth** parlare a qn/di qc; **~ up!** parla più forte!; **~er** *n* (*in public*) oratore/trice; (*also:* **loud~er**) altoparlante *m*; (*POL*): **the S~er** il presidente della Camera dei Comuni (*BRIT*) *or* dei Rappresentanti (*US*)

spear [spɪə*] *n* lancia ♦ *vt* infilzare; **~head** *vt* (*attack etc*) condurre

spec [spɛk] (*inf*) *n*: **on ~** sperando bene

special ['spɛʃl] *adj* speciale; **~ist** *n* specialista *m/f*; **~ity** [spɛʃɪ'ælɪtɪ] *n* specialità *f inv*; **~ize** *vi*: **to ~ize (in)** specializzarsi (in); **~ly** *adv* specialmente, particolarmente; **~ needs** *adj*: **~ needs children** bambini *mpl* con difficoltà di apprendimento; **~ty** *n* = **speciality**

species ['spiːʃiːz] *n inv* specie *f inv*

specific [spə'sɪfɪk] *adj* specifico(a); preciso(a); **~ally** *adv* esplicitamente; (*especially*) appositamente

specimen ['spɛsɪmən] *n* esemplare *m*, modello; (*MED*) campione *m*

speck [spɛk] *n* puntino, macchiolina; (*particle*) granello

speckled ['spɛkld] *adj* macchiettato(a)

specs [spɛks] (*inf*) *npl* occhiali *mpl*

spectacle ['spɛktəkl] *n* spettacolo; **~s** *npl* (*glasses*) occhiali *mpl*; **spectacular** [-'tækjulə*] *adj* spettacolare

spectator [spɛk'teɪtə*] *n* spettatore *m*

spectra ['spɛktrə] *npl of* **spectrum**

spectre ['spɛktə*] (*US* **specter**) *n* spettro

spectrum ['spɛktrəm] (*pl* **spectra**) *n* spettro

speculation [spɛkju'leɪʃən] *n* speculazione *f*; congetture *fpl*

speech [spiːtʃ] *n* (*faculty*) parola; (*talk, THEATRE*) discorso; (*manner of speaking*) parlata; **~less** *adj* ammutolito(a), muto(a)

speed [spiːd] *n* velocità *f inv*; (*promptness*) prontezza; **at full** *or* **top ~** a tutta velocità; **~ up** *vi, vt* accelerare; **~boat** *n* motoscafo; **~ily** *adv* velocemente; prontamente; **~ing** *n* (*AUT*) eccesso di velocità; **~ limit** *n* limite *m* di velocità; **~ometer** [spɪ'dɔmɪtə*] *n* tachimetro; **~way** *n* (*sport*) corsa motociclistica (su pista); **~y** *adj* veloce, rapido(a); pronto(a)

spell [spɛl] (*pt, pp* **spelt** (*BRIT*) *or* **~ed**) *n* (*also:* **magic ~**) incantesimo; (*period of time*) (breve) periodo ♦ *vt* (*in writing*) scrivere (lettera per lettera); (*aloud*) dire lettera per lettera; (*fig*) significare; **to cast a ~ on sb** fare un incantesimo a qn; **he can't ~** fa errori di ortografia; **~bound** *adj*

incantato(a); affascinato(a); **~ing** n
ortografia; **spelt** (BRIT) pt, pp of **spell**
spend [spɛnd] (pt, pp **spent**) vt (money)
spendere; (time, life) passare; **~thrift** n
spendaccione/a; **spent** pt, pp of **spend**
sperm [spə:m] n sperma m
sphere [sfɪə*] n sfera
spice [spaɪs] n spezia ♦ vt aromatizzare
spicy ['spaɪsɪ] adj piccante
spider ['spaɪdə*] n ragno
spike [spaɪk] n punta
spill [spɪl] (pt, pp **spilt** or **~ed**) vt versare,
rovesciare ♦ vi versarsi, rovesciarsi; **~ over**
vi (liquid) versarsi; (crowd) riversarsi; **spilt**
pt, pp of **spill**
spin [spɪn] (pt, pp **spun**) n (revolution of
wheel) rotazione f; (AVIAT) avvitamento;
(trip in car) giretto ♦ vt (wool etc) filare;
(wheel) far girare ♦ vi girare
spinach ['spɪnɪtʃ] n spinacio; (as food)
spinaci mpl
spinal ['spaɪnl] adj spinale; **~ cord** n
midollo spinale
spin doctor n pierre addetto alla difesa di
provvedimenti impopolari con interviste,
interventi in TV ecc.
spin-dryer (BRIT) n centrifuga
spine [spaɪn] n spina dorsale; (thorn) spina
spinning ['spɪnɪŋ] n filatura; **~ top** n
trottola
spin-off n (product) prodotto secondario
spinster ['spɪnstə*] n nubile f; zitella
spiral ['spaɪərl] n spirale f ♦ vi (fig) salire a
spirale; **~ staircase** n scala a chiocciola
spire [spaɪə*] n guglia
spirit ['spɪrɪt] n spirito; (ghost) spirito,
fantasma m; (mood) stato d'animo, umore
m; (courage) coraggio; **~s** npl (drink)
alcolici mpl; **in good ~s** di buon umore;
~ed adj vivace, vigoroso(a); (horse)
focoso(a); **~ level** n livella a bolla (d'aria)
spiritual ['spɪrɪtjuəl] adj spirituale
spit [spɪt] (pt, pp **spat**) n (for roasting)
spiedo; (saliva) sputo; saliva ♦ vi sputare;
(fire, fat) scoppiettare
spite [spaɪt] n dispetto ♦ vt contrariare, far
dispetto a; **in ~ of** nonostante, malgrado;

~ful adj dispettoso(a)
spittle ['spɪtl] n saliva; sputo
splash [splæʃ] n spruzzo; (sound) splash m
inv; (of colour) schizzo ♦ vt spruzzare ♦ vi
(also: **~ about**) sguazzare
spleen [spli:n] n (ANAT) milza
splendid ['splendɪd] adj splendido(a),
magnifico(a)
splint [splɪnt] n (MED) stecca
splinter ['splɪntə*] n scheggia ♦ vi
scheggiarsi
split [splɪt] (pt, pp **split**) n spaccatura; (fig:
division, quarrel) scissione f ♦ vt spaccare;
(party) dividere; (work, profits) spartire,
ripartire ♦ vi (divide) dividersi; **~ up** vi
(couple) separarsi, rompere; (meeting)
sciogliersi
spoil [spɔɪl] (pt, pp **spoilt** or **~ed**) vt
(damage) rovinare, guastare; (mar)
sciupare; (child) viziare; **~s** npl bottino;
~sport n guastafeste m/f inv; **spoilt** pt,
pp of **spoil**
spoke [spəuk] pt of **speak** ♦ n raggio
spoken ['spəukn] pp of **speak**
spokesman ['spəuksmən] (irreg) n
portavoce m inv
spokeswoman ['spəukswumən] (irreg) n
portavoce f inv
sponge [spʌndʒ] n spugna; (also: **~ cake**)
pan m di spagna ♦ vt spugnare, pulire con
una spugna ♦ vi: **to ~ off** or **on** scroccare
a; **~ bag** (BRIT) n nécessaire m inv
sponsor ['spɒnsə*] n (RADIO, TV, SPORT etc)
sponsor m inv; (POL: of bill) promotore/trice
♦ vt sponsorizzare; (bill) presentare; **~ship**
n sponsorizzazione f
spontaneous [spɒn'teɪnɪəs] adj
spontaneo(a)
spooky ['spu:kɪ] (inf) adj che fa
accapponare la pelle
spool [spu:l] n bobina
spoon [spu:n] n cucchiaio; **~-feed** vt
nutrire con il cucchiaio; (fig) imboccare;
~ful n cucchiaiata
sport [spɔ:t] n sport m inv; (person) persona
di spirito ♦ vt sfoggiare; **~ing** adj
sportivo(a); **to give sb a ~ing chance** dare

a qn una possibilità (di vincere); ~ **jacket** (*US*) *n* = ~**s jacket**; ~**s jacket** (*BRIT*) *n* giacca sportiva; ~**s jacket** (*BRIT*) *n* giacca sportiva; ~**sman** (*irreg*) *n* sportivo; ~**smanship** *n* spirito sportivo; ~**swear** *n* abiti *mpl* sportivi; ~**swoman** (*irreg*) *n* sportiva; ~**y** *adj* sportivo/a

spot [spɔt] *n* punto; (*mark*) macchia; (*dot: on pattern*) pallino; (*pimple*) foruncolo; (*place*) posto; (*RADIO, TV*) spot *m inv*; (*small amount*): **a** ~ **of** un po' di ♦ *vt* (*notice*) individuare, distinguere; **on the** ~ sul posto; (*immediately*) su due piedi; (*in difficulty*) nei guai; ~ **check** *n* controllo senza preavviso; ~**less** *adj* immacolato(a); ~**light** *n* proiettore *m*; (*AUT*) faro ausiliario; ~**ted** *adj* macchiato(a); a puntini, a pallini; ~**ty** *adj* (*face*) foruncoloso(a)

spouse [spauz] *n* sposo/a

spout [spaut] *n* (*of jug*) beccuccio; (*of pipe*) scarico ♦ *vi* zampillare

sprain [sprein] *n* storta, distorsione *f* ♦ *vt*: **to** ~ **one's ankle** storcersi una caviglia

sprang [spræŋ] *pt of* **spring**

sprawl [sprɔːl] *vi* sdraiarsi (in modo scomposto); (*place*) estendersi (disordinatamente)

spray [sprei] *n* spruzzo; (*container*) nebulizzatore *m*, spray *m inv*; (*of flowers*) mazzetto ♦ *vt* spruzzare; (*crops*) irrorare

spread [spred] (*pt, pp* **spread**) *n* diffusione *f*; (*distribution*) distribuzione *f*; (*CULIN*) pasta (da spalmare); (*inf: food*) banchetto ♦ *vt* (*cloth*) stendere, distendere; (*butter etc*) spalmare; (*disease, knowledge*) propagare, diffondere ♦ *vi* stendersi, distendersi; spalmarsi; propagarsi, diffondersi; ~ **out** *vi* (*move apart*) separarsi; ~**-eagled** ['spredi:gld] *adj* a gambe e braccia aperte; ~**sheet** *n* foglio elettronico ad espansione

spree [spriː] *n*: **to go on a** ~ fare baldoria

sprightly ['spraitli] *adj* vivace

spring [spriŋ] (*pt* **sprang**, *pp* **sprung**) *n* (*leap*) salto, balzo; (*coiled metal*) molla; (*season*) primavera; (*of water*) sorgente *f* ♦ *vi* saltare, balzare; ~ **up** *vi* (*problem*) presentarsi; ~**board** *n* trampolino; ~-

clean(ing) *n* grandi pulizie *fpl* di primavera; ~**time** *n* primavera

sprinkle ['spriŋkl] *vt* spruzzare; spargere; **to** ~ **water etc on**, ~ **with water etc** spruzzare dell'acqua *etc* su; ~**r** *n* (*for lawn*) irrigatore *m*; (*to put out fire*) sprinkler *m inv*

sprint [sprint] *n* scatto ♦ *vi* scattare; ~**er** *n* (*SPORT*) velocista *m/f*

sprout [spraut] *vi* germogliare; ~**s** *npl* (*also*: **Brussels** ~**s**) cavolini *mpl* di Bruxelles

spruce [spruːs] *n inv* abete *m* rosso ♦ *adj* lindo(a); azzimato(a)

sprung [sprʌŋ] *pp of* **spring**

spun [spʌn] *pt, pp of* **spin**

spur [spəː*] *n* sperone *m*; (*fig*) sprone *m*, incentivo ♦ *vt* (*also*: ~ **on**) spronare; **on the** ~ **of the moment** lì per lì

spurious ['spjuəriəs] *adj* falso(a)

spurn [spəːn] *vt* rifiutare con disprezzo, sdegnare

spurt [spəːt] *n* (*of water*) getto; (*of energy*) scatto ♦ *vi* sgorgare

spy [spai] *n* spia ♦ *vi*: **to** ~ **on** spiare ♦ *vt* (*see*) scorgere; ~**ing** *n* spionaggio

sq. *abbr* = **square**

squabble ['skwɔbl] *vi* bisticciarsi

squad [skwɔd] *n* (*MIL*) plotone *m*; (*POLICE*) squadra

squadron ['skwɔdrn] *n* (*MIL*) squadrone *m*; (*AVIAT, NAUT*) squadriglia

squalid ['skwɔlid] *adj* squallido(a)

squall [skwɔːl] *n* raffica; burrasca

squalor ['skwɔlə*] *n* squallore *m*

squander ['skwɔndə*] *vt* dissipare

square [skwɛə*] *n* quadrato; (*in town*) piazza ♦ *adj* quadrato(a); (*inf: ideas, person*) di vecchio stampo ♦ *vt* (*arrange*) regolare; (*MATH*) elevare al quadrato; (*reconcile*) conciliare; **all** ~ pari; **a** ~ **meal** un pasto abbondante; **2 metres** ~ di 2 metri per 2; **1** ~ **metre** 1 metro quadrato; ~**ly** *adv* diritto; fermamente

squash [skwɔʃ] *n* (*SPORT*) squash *m*; (*BRIT: drink*): **lemon/orange** ~ sciroppo di limone/arancia; (*US*) zucca; (*SPORT*) squash *m* ♦ *vt* schiacciare

squat [skwɔt] *adj* tarchiato(a), tozzo(a) ♦ *vi*

(*also:* ~ **down**) accovacciarsi; ~**ter** *n*
occupante *m/f* abusivo(a)

squeak [skwi:k] *vi* squittire

squeal [skwi:l] *vi* strillare

squeamish ['skwi:mɪʃ] *adj* schizzinoso(a);
disgustato(a)

squeeze [skwi:z] *n* pressione *f*; (*also ECON*)
stretta ♦ *vt* premere; (*hand, arm*) stringere;
~ **out** *vt* spremere

squelch [skwɛltʃ] *vi* fare ciac; sguazzare

squid [skwɪd] *n* calamaro

squiggle ['skwɪgl] *n* ghirigoro

squint [skwɪnt] *vi* essere strabico(a) ♦ *n:* **he
has a** ~ è strabico

squirm [skwə:m] *vi* contorcersi

squirrel ['skwɪrəl] *n* scoiattolo

squirt [skwə:t] *vi* schizzare; zampillare ♦ *vt*
spruzzare

Sr *abbr* = **senior**

St *abbr* = **saint; street**

stab [stæb] *n* (*with knife etc*) pugnalata; (*of
pain*) fitta; (*inf: try*): **to have a** ~ **at (doing)
sth** provare a (fare) qc ♦ *vt* pugnalare

stable ['steɪbl] *n* (*for horses*) scuderia; (*for
cattle*) stalla ♦ *adj* stabile

stack [stæk] *n* catasta, pila ♦ *vt* accatastare,
ammucchiare

stadium ['steɪdɪəm] *n* stadio

staff [stɑ:f] *n* (*work force: gen*) personale *m*;
(: *BRIT: SCOL*) personale insegnante ♦ *vt*
fornire di personale

stag [stæg] *n* cervo

stage [steɪdʒ] *n* palcoscenico; (*profession*):
the ~ il teatro, la scena; (*point*) punto;
(*platform*) palco ♦ *vt* (*play*) allestire,
mettere in scena; (*demonstration*)
organizzare; **in** ~**s** per gradi; a tappe;
~**coach** *n* diligenza; ~ **manager** *n*
direttore *m* di scena

stagger ['stægə*] *vi* barcollare ♦ *vt* (*person*)
sbalordire; (*hours, holidays*) scaglionare;
~**ing** *adj* (*amazing*) sbalorditivo(a)

stagnate [stæg'neɪt] *vi* stagnare

stag party *n* festa di addio al celibato

staid [steɪd] *adj* posato(a), serio(a)

stain [steɪn] *n* macchia; (*colouring*) colorante
m ♦ *vt* macchiare; (*wood*) tingere; ~**ed**

glass window *n* vetrata; ~**less** *adj*
(*steel*) inossidabile; ~ **remover** *n*
smacchiatore *m*

stair [steə*] *n* (*step*) gradino; ~**s** *npl* (*flight of
~s*) scale *fpl*, scala; ~**case** *n* scale *fpl*,
scala; ~**way** *n* = ~**case**

stake [steɪk] *n* palo, piolo; (*COMM*) interesse
m; (*BETTING*) puntata, scommessa ♦ *vt* (*bet*)
scommettere; (*risk*) rischiare; **to be at** ~
essere in gioco

stale [steɪl] *adj* (*bread*) raffermo(a); (*food*)
stantio(a); (*air*) viziato(a); (*beer*)
svaporato(a); (*smell*) di chiuso

stalemate ['steɪlmeɪt] *n* stallo; (*fig*) punto
morto

stalk [stɔ:k] *n* gambo, stelo ♦ *vt* inseguire; ~
off *vi* andarsene impettito(a)

stall [stɔ:l] *n* bancarella; (*in stable*) box *m
inv* di stalla ♦ *vt* (*AUT*) far spegnere; (*fig*)
bloccare ♦ *vi* (*AUT*) spegnersi, fermarsi; (*fig*)
temporeggiare; ~**s** *npl* (*BRIT: in cinema,
theatre*) platea

stallion ['stælɪən] *n* stallone *m*

stalwart ['stɔ:lwət] *adj* fidato(a); risoluto(a)

stamina ['stæmɪnə] *n* vigore *m*, resistenza

stammer ['stæmə*] *n* balbuzie *f* ♦ *vi*
balbettare

stamp [stæmp] *n* (*postage* ~) francobollo;
(*implement*) timbro; (*mark, also fig*)
marchio, impronta; (*on document*) bollo;
timbro ♦ *vi* (*also:* ~ **one's foot**) battere il
piede ♦ *vt* battere; (*letter*) affrancare; (*mark
with a* ~) timbrare; ~ **album** *n* album *m
inv* per francobolli; ~ **collecting** *n*
filatelia

stampede [stæm'pi:d] *n* fuggi fuggi *m inv*

stance [stæns] *n* posizione *f*

stand [stænd] (*pt, pp* **stood**) *n* (*position*)
posizione *f*; (*for taxis*) posteggio; (*structure*)
supporto, sostegno; (*at exhibition*) stand *m
inv*; (*in shop*) banco; (*at market*) bancarella;
(*booth*) chiosco; (*SPORT*) tribuna ♦ *vi* stare
in piedi; (*rise*) alzarsi in piedi; (*be placed*)
trovarsi ♦ *vt* (*place*) mettere, porre;
(*tolerate, withstand*) resistere, sopportare;
(*treat*) offrire; **to make a** ~ prendere
posizione; **to** ~ **for parliament** (*BRIT*)

presentarsi come candidato (per il parlamento); ~ **by** *vi* (*be ready*) tenersi pronto(a) ♦ *vt fus* (*opinion*) sostenere; ~ **down** *vi* (*withdraw*) ritirarsi; ~ **for** *vt fus* (*signify*) rappresentare, significare; (*tolerate*) sopportare, tollerare; ~ **in for** *vt fus* sostituire; ~ **out** *vi* (*be prominent*) spiccare; ~ **up** *vi* (*rise*) alzarsi in piedi; ~ **up for** *vt fus* difendere; ~ **up to** *vt fus* tener testa a, resistere a

standard ['stændəd] *n* modello, standard *m inv*; (*level*) livello; (*flag*) stendardo ♦ *adj* (*size etc*) normale, standard *inv*; ~**s** *npl* (*morals*) principi *mpl*, valori *mpl*; ~ **lamp** (*BRIT*) *n* lampada a stelo; ~ **of living** *n* livello di vita

stand-by *n* riserva, sostituto; **to be on** ~ (*gen*) tenersi pronto(a); (*doctor*) essere di guardia; ~ **ticket** *n* (*AVIAT*) biglietto senza garanzia

stand-in *n* sostituto/a

standing ['stændɪŋ] *adj* diritto(a), in piedi; (*permanent*) permanente ♦ *n* rango, condizione *f*, posizione *f*; **of many years'** ~ che esiste da molti anni; ~ **joke** *n* barzelletta; ~ **order** (*BRIT*) *n* (*at bank*) ordine *m* di pagamento (permanente); ~ **room** *n* posto all'impiedi

standpoint ['stændpɔɪnt] *n* punto di vista

standstill ['stændstɪl] *n*: **at a** ~ fermo(a), (*fig*) a un punto morto; **to come to a** ~ fermarsi; giungere a un punto morto

stank [stæŋk] *pt of* **stink**

staple ['steɪpl] *n* (*for papers*) graffetta ♦ *adj* (*food etc*) di base ♦ *vt* cucire; ~**r** *n* cucitrice *f*

star [stɑː*] *n* stella; (*celebrity*) divo/a ♦ *vi*: **to** ~ **(in)** essere il (*or* la) protagonista (di) ♦ *vt* (*CINEMA*) essere interpretato(a) da

starboard ['stɑːbəd] *n* dritta

starch [stɑːtʃ] *n* amido

stardom ['stɑːdəm] *n* celebrità

stare [stɛə*] *n* sguardo fisso ♦ *vi*: **to** ~ **at** fissare

starfish ['stɑːfɪʃ] *n* stella di mare

stark [stɑːk] *adj* (*bleak*) desolato(a) ♦ *adv*: ~ **naked** completamente nudo(a)

starling ['stɑːlɪŋ] *n* storno

starry ['stɑːrɪ] *adj* stellato(a); ~**-eyed** *adj* (*innocent*) ingenuo(a)

start [stɑːt] *n* inizio; (*of race*) partenza; (*sudden movement*) sobbalzo; (*advantage*) vantaggio ♦ *vt* cominciare, iniziare; (*car*) mettere in moto ♦ *vi* cominciare; (*on journey*) partire, mettersi in viaggio; (*jump*) sobbalzare; **to** ~ **doing** *or* **to do sth** (in)cominciare a fare qc; ~ **off** *vi* cominciare; (*leave*) partire; ~ **up** *vi* cominciare; (*car*) avviarsi ♦ *vt* iniziare; (*car*) avviare; ~**er** *n* (*AUT*) motorino d'avviamento; (*SPORT: official*) starter *m inv*; (*BRIT: CULIN*) primo piatto; ~**ing point** *n* punto di partenza

startle ['stɑːtl] *vt* far trasalire; **startling** *adj* sorprendente

starvation [stɑː'veɪʃən] *n* fame *f*, inedia

starve [stɑːv] *vi* morire di fame; soffrire la fame ♦ *vt* far morire di fame, affamare

state [steɪt] *n* stato ♦ *vt* dichiarare, affermare; annunciare; **the S~s** (*USA*) gli Stati Uniti; **to be in a** ~ essere agitato(a); ~**ly** *adj* maestoso(a), imponente; ~**ly home** *n* residenza nobiliare (*d'interesse storico e artistico*); ~**ment** *n* dichiarazione *f*; ~**sman** (*irreg*) *n* statista *m*

static ['stætɪk] *n* (*RADIO*) scariche *fpl* ♦ *adj* statico(a)

station ['steɪʃən] *n* stazione *f* ♦ *vt* collocare, disporre

stationary ['steɪʃənərɪ] *adj* fermo(a), immobile

stationer ['steɪʃənə*] *n* cartolaio/a; ~**'s (shop)** *n* cartoleria; ~**y** *n* articoli *mpl* di cancelleria

station master *n* (*RAIL*) capostazione *m*

station wagon (*US*) *n* giardinetta

statistic [stə'tɪstɪk] *n* statistica; ~**s** *n* (*science*) statistica

statue ['stætjuː] *n* statua

status ['steɪtəs] *n* posizione *f*, condizione *f* sociale; prestigio; stato; ~ **symbol** *n* simbolo di prestigio

statute ['stætjuːt] *n* legge *f*; **statutory** *adj* stabilito(a) dalla legge, statutario(a)

staunch [stɔːntʃ] *adj* fidato(a), leale
stay [steɪ] *n* (*period of time*) soggiorno, permanenza ♦ *vi* rimanere; (*reside*) alloggiare, stare; (*spend some time*) trattenersi, soggiornare; **to ~ put** non muoversi; **to ~ the night** fermarsi per la notte; **~ behind** *vi* restare indietro; **~ in** *vi* (*at home*) stare in casa; **~ on** *vi* restare, rimanere; **~ out** *vi* (*of house*) rimanere fuori (di casa); **~ up** *vi* (*at night*) rimanere alzato(a); **~ing power** *n* capacità di resistenza
stead [stɛd] *n*: **in sb's ~** al posto di qn; **to stand sb in good ~** essere utile a qn
steadfast ['stɛdfɑːst] *adj* fermo(a), risoluto(a)
steadily ['stɛdɪlɪ] *adv* (*firmly*) saldamente; (*constantly*) continuamente; (*fixedly*) fisso; (*walk*) con passo sicuro
steady ['stɛdɪ] *adj* (*not wobbling*) fermo(a); (*regular*) costante; (*person, character*) serio(a); (: *calm*) calmo(a), tranquillo(a) ♦ *vt* stabilizzare; calmare
steak [steɪk] *n* (*meat*) bistecca; (*fish*) trancia
steal [stiːl] (*pt* **stole**, *pp* **stolen**) *vt* rubare ♦ *vi* rubare; (*move*) muoversi furtivamente
stealth [stɛlθ] *n*: **by ~** furtivamente; **~y** *adj* furtivo(a)
steam [stiːm] *n* vapore *m* ♦ *vt* (*CULIN*) cuocere a vapore ♦ *vi* fumare; **~ engine** *n* macchina a vapore; (*RAIL*) locomotiva a vapore; **~er** *n* piroscafo, vapore *m*; **~roller** *n* rullo compressore; **~ship** *n* = **~er**; **~y** *adj* (*room*) pieno(a) di vapore; (*window*) appannato(a)
steel [stiːl] *n* acciaio ♦ *adj* di acciaio; **~works** *n* acciaieria
steep [stiːp] *adj* ripido(a), scosceso(a); (*price*) eccessivo(a) ♦ *vt* inzuppare; (*washing*) mettere a mollo
steeple ['stiːpl] *n* campanile *m*
steer [stɪə*] *vt* guidare ♦ *vi* (*NAUT*: *person*) governare; (*car*) guidarsi; **~ing** *n* (*AUT*) sterzo; **~ing wheel** *n* volante *m*
stem [stɛm] *n* (*of flower, plant*) stelo; (*of tree*) fusto; (*of glass*) gambo; (*of fruit, leaf*) picciolo ♦ *vt* contenere, arginare; **~ from**

vt fus provenire da, derivare da
stench [stɛntʃ] *n* puzzo, fetore *m*
stencil ['stɛnsl] *n* (*of metal, cardboard*) stampino, mascherina; (*in typing*) matrice *f* ♦ *vt* disegnare con stampino
stenographer [stɛ'nɔgrəfə*] (*US*) *n* stenografo/a
step [stɛp] *n* passo; (*stair*) gradino, scalino; (*action*) mossa, azione *f* ♦ *vi*: **to ~ forward/back** fare un passo avanti/indietro; **~s** *npl* = **stepladder**; **to be in/out of ~ (with)** stare/non stare al passo (con); **~ down** *vi* (*fig*) ritirarsi; **~ on** *vt fus* calpestare; **~ up** *vt* aumentare; intensificare; **~brother** *n* fratellastro; **~daughter** *n* figliastra; **~father** *n* patrigno; **~ladder** *n* scala a libretto; **~mother** *n* matrigna; **~ping stone** *n* pietra di un guado; **~sister** *n* sorellastra; **~son** *n* figliastro
stereo ['stɛrɪəʊ] *n* (*system*) sistema *m* stereofonico; (*record player*) stereo *m inv* ♦ *adj* (*also*: **~phonic**) stereofonico(a)
sterile ['stɛraɪl] *adj* sterile; **sterilize** ['stɛrɪlaɪz] *vt* sterilizzare
sterling ['stɜːlɪŋ] *adj* (*gold, silver*) di buona lega ♦ *n* (*ECON*) (lira) sterlina; **a pound ~** una lira sterlina
stern [stɜːn] *adj* severo(a) ♦ *n* (*NAUT*) poppa
stew [stjuː] *n* stufato ♦ *vt* cuocere in umido
steward ['stjuːəd] *n* (*AVIAT, NAUT, RAIL*) steward *m inv*; (*in club etc*) dispensiere *m*; **~ess** *n* assistente *f* di volo, hostess *f inv*
stick [stɪk] (*pt*, *pp* **stuck**) *n* bastone *m*; (*of rhubarb, celery*) gambo; (*of dynamite*) candelotto ♦ *vt* (*glue*) attaccare; (*thrust*): **to ~ sth into** conficcare *or* piantare *or* infiggere qc in; (*inf*: *put*) ficcare; (*inf*: *tolerate*) sopportare ♦ *vi* attaccarsi; (*remain*) restare, rimanere; **~ out** *vi* sporgere, spuntare; **~ up** *vi* sporgere, spuntare; **~ up for** *vt fus* difendere; **~er** *n* cartellino adesivo; **~ing plaster** *n* cerotto adesivo
stick-up (*inf*) *n* rapina a mano armata
sticky ['stɪkɪ] *adj* attaccaticcio(a), vischioso(a); (*label*) adesivo(a); (*fig*: *situation*) difficile

stiff [stɪf] *adj* rigido(a), duro(a); (*muscle*) legato(a), indolenzito(a); (*difficult*) difficile, arduo(a); (*cold*) freddo(a), formale; (*strong*) forte; (*high: price*) molto alto(a) ♦ *adv*: **bored ~** annoiato(a) a morte; **~en** *vt* irrigidire; rinforzare ♦ *vi* irrigidirsi; indurirsi; **~ neck** *n* torcicollo

stifle ['staɪfl] *vt* soffocare

stigma ['stɪgmə] *n* (*fig*) stigma *m*

stile [staɪl] *n* cavalcasiepe *m*; cavalcasteccato

stiletto [stɪ'letəʊ] (*BRIT*) *n* (*also*: **~ heel**) tacco a spillo

still [stɪl] *adj* fermo(a); silenzioso(a) ♦ *adv* (*up to this time, even*) ancora; (*nonetheless*) tuttavia, ciò nonostante; **~born** *adj* nato(a) morto(a); **~ life** *n* natura morta

stilt [stɪlt] *n* trampolo; (*pile*) palo

stilted ['stɪltɪd] *adj* freddo(a), formale; artificiale

stimulate ['stɪmjʊleɪt] *vt* stimolare

stimuli ['stɪmjʊlaɪ] *npl of* **stimulus**

stimulus ['stɪmjʊləs] (*pl* **stimuli**) *n* stimolo

sting [stɪŋ] (*pt, pp* **stung**) *n* puntura; (*organ*) pungiglione *m* ♦ *vt* pungere

stingy ['stɪndʒɪ] *adj* spilorcio(a), tirchio(a)

stink [stɪŋk] (*pt* **stank**, *pp* **stunk**) *n* fetore *m*, puzzo ♦ *vi* puzzare; **~ing** (*inf*) *adj* (*fig*): **a ~ing ...** uno schifo di ..., un(a) maledetto(a) ....

stint [stɪnt] *n* lavoro, compito ♦ *vi*: **to ~ on** lesinare su

stir [stə:*] *n* agitazione *f*, clamore *m* ♦ *vt* mescolare; (*fig*) risvegliare ♦ *vi* muoversi; **~ up** *vt* provocare, suscitare

stirrup ['stɪrəp] *n* staffa

stitch [stɪtʃ] *n* (*SEWING*) punto; (*KNITTING*) maglia; (*MED*) punto (di sutura); (*pain*) fitta ♦ *vt* cucire, attaccare; suturare

stoat [stəʊt] *n* ermellino

stock [stɒk] *n* riserva, provvista; (*COMM*) giacenza, stock *m inv*; (*AGR*) bestiame *m*; (*CULIN*) brodo; (*descent*) stirpe *f*; (*FINANCE*) titoli *mpl*, azioni *fpl* ♦ *adj* (*fig: reply etc*) consueto(a); classico(a) ♦ *vt* (*have in stock*) avere, vendere; **~s and shares** valori *mpl* di borsa; **in ~** in magazzino; **out of ~** esaurito(a); **~ up** *vi*: **to ~ up (with)** fare

provvista (di)

stockbroker ['stɒkbrəʊkə*] *n* agente *m* di cambio

stock cube (*BRIT*) *n* dado

stock exchange *n* Borsa (valori)

stocking ['stɒkɪŋ] *n* calza

stock: **~ market** *n* Borsa, mercato finanziario; **~pile** *n* riserva ♦ *vt* accumulare riserve di; **~taking** (*BRIT*) *n* (*COMM*) inventario

stocky ['stɒkɪ] *adj* tarchiato(a), tozzo(a)

stodgy ['stɒdʒɪ] *adj* pesante, indigesto(a)

stoke [stəʊk] *vt* alimentare

stole [stəʊl] *pt of* **steal** ♦ *n* stola

stolen ['stəʊln] *pp of* **steal**

stomach ['stʌmək] *n* stomaco; (*belly*) pancia ♦ *vt* sopportare, digerire; **~ ache** *n* mal *m* di stomaco

stone [stəʊn] *n* pietra; (*pebble*) sasso, ciottolo; (*in fruit*) nocciolo; (*MED*) calcolo; (*BRIT: weight*) = 6.348 kg.; 14 libbre ♦ *adj* di pietra ♦ *vt* lapidare; (*fruit*) togliere il nocciolo a; **~-cold** *adj* gelido(a); **~-deaf** *adj* sordo(a) come una campana; **~work** *n* muratura; **stony** *adj* sassoso(a); (*fig*) di pietra

stood [stʊd] *pt, pp of* **stand**

stool [stu:l] *n* sgabello

stoop [stu:p] *vi* (*also*: **have a ~**) avere una curvatura; (*bend*) chinarsi, curvarsi

stop [stɒp] *n* arresto; (*stopping place*) fermata; (*in punctuation*) punto ♦ *vt* arrestare, fermare; (*break off*) interrompere; (*also*: **put a ~ to**) porre fine a ♦ *vi* fermarsi; (*rain, noise etc*) cessare, finire; **to ~ doing sth** cessare *or* finire di fare qc; **to ~ dead** fermarsi di colpo; **~ off** *vi* sostare brevemente; **~ up** *vt* (*hole*) chiudere, turare; **~gap** *n* tappabuchi *m inv*; **~lights** *npl* (*AUT*) stop *mpl*; **~over** *n* breve sosta; (*AVIAT*) scalo

stoppage ['stɒpɪdʒ] *n* arresto, fermata; (*of pay*) trattenuta; (*strike*) interruzione *f* del lavoro

stopper ['stɒpə*] *n* tappo

stop press *n* ultimissime *fpl*

stopwatch ['stɒpwɒtʃ] *n* cronometro

storage ['stɔ:rɪdʒ] n immagazzinamento; ~ **heater** n radiatore m elettrico che accumula calore

store [stɔ:ʳ] n provvista, riserva; (depot) deposito; (BRIT: department ~) grande magazzino; (US: shop) negozio ♦ vt immagazzinare; ~**s** npl (provisions) rifornimenti mpl, scorte fpl; **in** ~ di riserva; in serbo; ~ **up** vt conservare; mettere in serbo; ~**room** n dispensa

storey ['stɔ:rɪ] (US **story**) n piano

stork [stɔ:k] n cicogna

storm [stɔ:m] n tempesta, temporale m, burrasca; uragano ♦ vi (fig) infuriarsi ♦ vt prendere d'assalto; ~**y** adj tempestoso(a), burrascoso(a)

story ['stɔ:rɪ] n storia; favola; racconto; (US) = **storey**; ~**book** n libro di racconti

stout [staut] adj solido(a), robusto(a); (friend, supporter) tenace; (fat) corpulento(a), grasso(a) ♦ n birra scura

stove [stəuv] n (for cooking) fornello; (: small) fornelletto; (for heating) stufa

stow [stəu] vt (also: ~ **away**) mettere via; ~**away** n passeggero(a) clandestino(a)

straddle ['strædl] vt stare a cavalcioni di; (fig) essere a cavallo di

straggle ['strægl] vi crescere (or estendersi) disordinatamente; trascinarsi; rimanere indietro; ~**ly** (hair) in disordine

straight [streɪt] adj dritto(a); (frank) onesto(a), franco(a); (simple) semplice ♦ adv diritto; (drink) liscio; **to put** or **get** ~ mettere in ordine, mettere ordine in; ~ **away**, ~ **off** (at once) immediatamente; ~**en** vt (also: ~**en out**) raddrizzare; ~-**faced** adj impassibile, imperturbabile; ~**forward** adj semplice; onesto(a), franco(a)

strain [streɪn] n (TECH) sollecitazione f; (physical) sforzo; (mental) tensione f; (MED) strappo; distorsione f; (streak, trace) tendenza; elemento ♦ vt tendere; (muscle) sforzare; (ankle) storcere; (resources) pesare su; (food) colare; passare; ~**s** npl (MUS) note fpl; ~**ed** adj (muscle) stirato(a); (laugh etc) forzato(a); (relations) teso(a); ~**er** n

passino, colino

strait [streɪt] n (GEO) stretto; ~**s** npl: **to be in dire** ~**s** (fig) essere nei guai; ~**jacket** n camicia di forza; ~-**laced** adj bacchettone(a)

strand [strænd] n (of thread) filo; ~**ed** adj nei guai; senza mezzi di trasporto

strange [streɪndʒ] adj (not known) sconosciuto(a); (odd) strano(a), bizzarro(a); ~**ly** adv stranamente; ~**r** n sconosciuto/a; estraneo/a

strangle ['stræŋgl] vt strangolare; ~**hold** n (fig) stretta (mortale)

strap [stræp] n cinghia; (of slip, dress) spallina, bretella

strategic [strə'ti:dʒɪk] adj strategico(a)

strategy ['strætɪdʒɪ] n strategia

straw [strɔ:] n paglia; (drinking ~) cannuccia; **that's the last** ~**!** è la goccia che fa traboccare il vaso!

strawberry ['strɔ:bərɪ] n fragola

stray [streɪ] adj (animal) randagio(a); (bullet) vagante; (scattered) sparso(a) ♦ vi perdersi

streak [stri:k] n striscia; (of hair) mèche f inv ♦ vt striare, screziare ♦ vi: **to** ~ **past** passare come un fulmine

stream [stri:m] n ruscello; corrente f; (of people, smoke etc) fiume m ♦ vt (SCOL) dividere in livelli di rendimento ♦ vi scorrere; **to** ~ **in/out** entrare/uscire a fiotti

streamer ['stri:mə*] n (of paper) stella filante

streamlined ['stri:mlaɪnd] adj aerodinamico(a), affusolato(a)

street [stri:t] n strada, via; ~**car** (US) n tram m inv; ~ **lamp** n lampione m; ~ **plan** n pianta (di una città); ~**wise** (inf) adj esperto(a) dei bassifondi

strength [streŋθ] n forza; ~**en** vt rinforzare; fortificare; consolidare

strenuous ['strenjuəs] adj vigoroso(a), energico(a); (tiring) duro(a), pesante

stress [stres] n (force, pressure) pressione f; (mental strain) tensione f; (accent) accento ♦ vt insistere su, sottolineare; accentare

stretch [stretʃ] n (of sand etc) distesa ♦ vi stirarsi; (extend): **to** ~ **to** or **as far as**

estendersi fino a ♦ *vt* tendere, allungare; (*spread*) distendere; (*fig*) spingere (al massimo); ~ **out** *vi* allungarsi, estendersi ♦ *vt* (*arm etc*) allungare, tendere; (*to spread*) distendere

stretcher ['stretʃə*] *n* barella, lettiga

strewn [stru:n] *adj*: ~ **with** cosparso(a) di

stricken ['strɪkən] *adj* (*person*) provato(a); (*city, industry etc*) colpito(a); ~ **with** (*disease etc*) colpito(a) da

strict [strɪkt] *adj* (*severe*) rigido(a), severo(a); (*precise*) preciso(a), stretto(a); ~**ly** *adv* severamente; rigorosamente; strettamente

stridden ['strɪdn] *pp of* **stride**

stride [straɪd] (*pt* **strode**, *pp* **stridden**) *n* passo lungo ♦ *vi* camminare a grandi passi

strife [straɪf] *n* conflitto; litigi *mpl*

strike [straɪk] (*pt, pp* **struck**) *n* sciopero; (*of oil etc*) scoperta; (*attack*) attacco ♦ *vt* colpire; (*oil etc*) scoprire, trovare (*bargain*) fare; (*fig*): **the thought** *or* **it ~s me that ...** mi viene in mente che ... ♦ *vi* scioperare; (*attack*) attaccare; (*clock*) suonare; **on** ~ (*workers*) in sciopero; **to** ~ **a match** accendere un fiammifero; ~ **down** *vt* (*fig*) atterrare; ~ **up** *vt* (*MUS, conversation*) attaccare; **to** ~ **up a friendship with** fare amicizia con; ~**r** *n* scioperante *m/f*; (*SPORT*) attaccante *m*; **striking** *adj* che colpisce

string [strɪŋ] (*pt, pp* **strung**) *n* spago; (*row*) fila; sequenza; (*MUS*) corda ♦ *vt*: **to** ~ **out** disporre di fianco; **to** ~ **together** (*words, ideas*) mettere insieme; **the** ~**s** *npl* (*MUS*) gli archi; **to pull ~s for sb** raccomandare qn; ~ **bean** *n* fagiolino; ~**(ed) instrument** *n* (*MUS*) strumento a corda

stringent ['strɪndʒənt] *adj* rigoroso(a)

strip [strɪp] *n* striscia ♦ *vt* spogliare; (*paint*) togliere; (*also*: ~ **down**: *machine*) smontare ♦ *vi* spogliarsi; ~ **cartoon** *n* fumetto

stripe [straɪp] *n* striscia, riga; (*MIL, POLICE*) gallone *m*; ~**d** *adj* a strisce *or* righe

strip lighting *n* illuminazione *f* al neon

stripper ['strɪpə*] *n* spogliarellista *m/f*

strip-search ['strɪpsə:tʃ] *vt*: **to** ~ **sb** perquisire qn facendolo(a) spogliare ♦ *n*

perquisizione (*facendo spogliare il perquisto*)

striptease ['strɪpti:z] *n* spogliarello

strive [straɪv] (*pt* **strove**, *pp* **striven**) *vi*: **to** ~ **to do** sforzarsi di fare; **striven** ['strɪvn] *pp of* **strive**

strode [strəud] *pt of* **stride**

stroke [strəuk] *n* colpo; (*SWIMMING*) bracciata; (: *style*) stile *m*; (*MED*) colpo apoplettico ♦ *vt* accarezzare; **at a** ~ in un attimo

stroll [strəul] *n* giretto, passeggiatina ♦ *vi* andare a spasso; ~**er** (*US*) *n* passeggino

strong [strɔŋ] *adj* (*gen*) forte; (*sturdy*: *table, fabric etc*) robusto(a); **they are 50** ~ sono in 50; ~**box** *n* cassaforte *f*; ~**hold** *n* (*also fig*) roccaforte *f*; ~**ly** *adv* fortemente, con forza; energicamente; vivamente; ~**room** *n* camera di sicurezza

strove [strəuv] *pt of* **strive**

struck [strʌk] *pt, pp of* **strike**

structural ['strʌktʃərəl] *adj* strutturale

structure ['strʌktʃə*] *n* struttura; (*building*) costruzione *f*, fabbricato

struggle ['strʌgl] *n* lotta ♦ *vi* lottare

strum [strʌm] *vt* (*guitar*) strimpellare

strung [strʌŋ] *pt, pp of* **string**

strut [strʌt] *n* sostegno, supporto ♦ *vi* pavoneggiarsi

stub [stʌb] *n* mozzicone *m*; (*of ticket etc*) matrice *f*, talloncino ♦ *vt*: **to** ~ **one's toe** urtare *or* sbattere il dito del piede; ~ **out** *vt* schiacciare

stubble ['stʌbl] *n* stoppia; (*on chin*) barba ispida

stubborn ['stʌbən] *adj* testardo(a), ostinato(a)

stuck [stʌk] *pt, pp of* **stick** ♦ *adj* (*jammed*) bloccato(a); ~**-up** *adj* presuntuoso(a)

stud [stʌd] *n* bottoncino, borchia; (*also*: ~ **earring**) orecchino a pressione; (*also*: ~ **farm**) scuderia, allevamento di cavalli; (*also*: ~ **horse**) stallone *m* ♦ *vt* (*fig*): ~**ded with** tempestato(a) di

student ['stju:dənt] *n* studente/essa ♦ *cpd* studentesco(a); universitario(a); degli studenti; ~ **driver** (*US*) *n* conducente *m/f* principiante

studio ['stju:dɪəu] *n* studio; ~ **flat** (*US* ~ **apartment**) *n* monolocale *m*

studious ['stju:dɪəs] *adj* studioso(a); (*studied*) studiato(a), voluto(a); ~**ly** *adv* (*carefully*) deliberatamente, di proposito

study ['stʌdɪ] *n* studio ♦ *vt* studiare; esaminare ♦ *vi* studiare

stuff [stʌf] *n* roba; (*substance*) sostanza, materiale *m* ♦ *vt* imbottire; (*CULIN*) farcire; (*dead animal*) impagliare; (*inf: push*) ficcare; ~**ing** *n* imbottitura; (*CULIN*) ripieno; ~**y** *adj* (*room*) mal ventilato(a), senz'aria; (*ideas*) antiquato(a)

stumble ['stʌmbl] *vi* inciampare; **to** ~ **across** (*fig*) imbattersi in; **stumbling block** *n* ostacolo, scoglio

stump [stʌmp] *n* ceppo; (*of limb*) moncone *m* ♦ *vt*: **to be** ~**ed** essere sconcertato(a)

stun [stʌn] *vt* stordire; (*amaze*) sbalordire

stung [stʌŋ] *pt, pp of* **sting**

stunk [stʌŋk] *pp of* **stink**

stunning ['stʌnɪŋ] *adj* sbalorditivo(a); (*girl etc*) fantastico(a)

stunt [stʌnt] *n* bravata; trucco pubblicitario; ~**man** (*irreg*) *n* cascatore *m*

stupefy ['stju:pɪfaɪ] *vt* stordire; intontire; (*fig*) stupire

stupendous [stju:'pɛndəs] *adj* stupendo(a), meraviglioso(a)

stupid ['stju:pɪd] *adj* stupido(a); ~**ity** [-'pɪdɪtɪ] *n* stupidità *f inv*, stupidaggine *f*

stupor ['stju:pə*] *n* torpore *m*

sturdy ['stɜ:dɪ] *adj* robusto(a), vigoroso(a); solido(a)

stutter ['stʌtə*] *n* balbuzie *f* ♦ *vi* balbettare

sty [staɪ] *n* (*of pigs*) porcile *m*

stye [staɪ] *n* (*MED*) orzaiolo

style [staɪl] *n* stile *m*; (*distinction*) eleganza, classe *f*; **stylish** *adj* elegante

stylus ['staɪləs] *n* (*of record player*) puntina

suave [swɑ:v] *adj* untuoso(a)

sub... [sʌb] *prefix* sub..., sotto...; ~**conscious** *adj* subcosciente ♦ *n* subcosciente *m*; ~**contract** *vt* subappaltare

subdue [səb'dju:] *vt* sottomettere, soggiogare; ~**d** *adj* pacato(a); (*light*) attenuato(a)

subject [*n* 'sʌbdʒɪkt, *vb* səb'dʒɛkt] *n* soggetto; (*citizen etc*) cittadino/a; (*SCOL*) materia ♦ *vt*: **to** ~ **to** sottomettere a; esporre a; **to be** ~ **to** (*law*) essere sottomesso(a) a; (*disease*) essere soggetto(a) a; ~**ive** [-'dʒɛktɪv] *adj* soggettivo(a); ~ **matter** *n* argomento; contenuto

sublet [sʌb'lɛt] *vt* subaffittare

submachine gun ['sʌbmə'ʃi:n-] *n* mitra *m inv*

submarine [sʌbmə'ri:n] *n* sommergibile *m*

submerge [səb'mɜ:dʒ] *vt* sommergere; immergere ♦ *vi* immergersi

submission [səb'mɪʃən] *n* sottomissione *f*; (*claim*) richiesta

submissive [səb'mɪsɪv] *adj* remissivo(a)

submit [səb'mɪt] *vt* sottomettere ♦ *vi* sottomettersi

subnormal [sʌb'nɔ:məl] *adj* subnormale

subordinate [sə'bɔ:dɪnət] *adj, n* subordinato(a)

subpoena [səb'pi:nə] *n* (*LAW*) citazione *f*, mandato di comparizione

subscribe [səb'skraɪb] *vi* contribuire; **to** ~ **to** (*opinion*) approvare, condividere; (*fund*) sottoscrivere a; (*newspaper*) abbonarsi a; essere abbonato(a) a; ~**r** *n* (*to periodical, telephone*) abbonato/a

subscription [səb'skrɪpʃən] *n* sottoscrizione *f*; abbonamento

subsequent ['sʌbsɪkwənt] *adj* successivo(a), seguente; conseguente; ~**ly** *adv* in seguito, successivamente

subside [səb'saɪd] *vi* cedere, abbassarsi; (*flood*) decrescere; (*wind*) calmarsi; ~**nce** [-'saɪdns] *n* cedimento, abbassamento

subsidiary [səb'sɪdɪərɪ] *adj* sussidiario(a); accessorio(a) ♦ *n* filiale *f*

subsidize ['sʌbsɪdaɪz] *vt* sovvenzionare

subsidy ['sʌbsɪdɪ] *n* sovvenzione *f*

subsistence [səb'sɪstəns] *n* esistenza; mezzi *mpl* di sostentamento; ~ **allowance** *n* indennità *f inv* di trasferta

substance ['sʌbstəns] *n* sostanza

substantial [səb'stænʃl] *adj* solido(a);

(amount, progress etc) notevole; *(meal)* sostanzioso(a)

substantiate [səb'stænʃɪeɪt] *vt* comprovare

substitute ['sʌbstɪtjuːt] *n (person)* sostituto/a; *(thing)* succedaneo, surrogato ♦ *vt*: **to ~ sth/sb for** sostituire qc/qn a

subterfuge ['sʌbtəfjuːdʒ] *n* sotterfugio

subterranean [sʌbtə'reɪnɪən] *adj* sotterraneo(a)

subtitle ['sʌbtaɪtl] *n (CINEMA)* sottotitolo; **~d** *adj* sottotitolato(a)

subtle ['sʌtl] *adj* sottile; **~ty** *n* sottigliezza

subtotal [sʌb'təutl] *n* somma parziale

subtract [səb'trækt] *vt* sottrarre; **~ion** [-'trækʃən] *n* sottrazione *f*

suburb ['sʌbəːb] *n* sobborgo; **the ~s** la periferia; **~an** [sə'bəːbən] *adj* suburbano(a); **~ia** *n* periferia, sobborghi *mpl*

subversive [səb'vəːsɪv] *adj* sovversivo(a)

subway ['sʌbweɪ] *n (US: underground)* metropolitana; *(BRIT: underpass)* sottopassaggio

succeed [sək'siːd] *vi* riuscire; avere successo ♦ *vt* succedere a; **to ~ in doing** riuscire a fare; **~ing** *adj (following)* successivo(a)

success [sək'sɛs] *n* successo; **~ful** *adj (venture)* coronato(a) da successo, riuscito(a); **to be ~ful (in doing)** riuscire (a fare); **~fully** *adv* con successo

succession [sək'sɛʃən] *n* successione *f*

successive [sək'sɛsɪv] *adj* successivo(a); consecutivo(a)

succumb [sə'kʌm] *vi* soccombere

such [sʌtʃ] *adj* tale; *(of that kind)*: **~ a book** un tale libro, un libro del genere; **~ books** tali libri, libri del genere; *(so much)*: **~ courage** tanto coraggio ♦ *adv* talmente, così; **~ a long trip** un viaggio così lungo; **~ a lot of** talmente *or* così tanto(a); **~ as** *(like)* come; **as ~** come *or* in quanto tale; **~-and-~** *adj* tale *(after noun)*

suck [sʌk] *vt* succhiare; *(breast, bottle)* poppare; **~er** *n (ZOOL, TECH)* ventosa; *(inf)* gonzo/a, babbeo/a

suction ['sʌkʃən] *n* succhiamento; *(TECH)* aspirazione *f*

sudden ['sʌdn] *adj* improvviso(a); **all of a ~**

improvvisamente, all'improvviso; **~ly** *adv* bruscamente, improvvisamente, di colpo

suds [sʌdz] *npl* schiuma (di sapone)

sue [suː] *vt* citare in giudizio

suede [sweɪd] *n* pelle *f* scamosciata

suet ['sʊɪt] *n* grasso di rognone

suffer ['sʌfə*] *vt* soffrire, patire; *(bear)* sopportare, tollerare ♦ *vi* soffrire; **to ~ from** soffrire di; **~er** *n* malato/a; **~ing** *n* sofferenza

suffice [sə'faɪs] *vi* essere sufficiente, bastare

sufficient [sə'fɪʃənt] *adj* sufficiente; **~ money** abbastanza soldi; **~ly** *adv* sufficientemente, abbastanza

suffocate ['sʌfəkeɪt] *vi (have difficulty breathing)* soffocare; *(die through lack of air)* asfissiare

sugar ['ʃʊgə*] *n* zucchero ♦ *vt* zuccherare; **~ beet** *n* barbabietola da zucchero; **~ cane** *n* canna da zucchero

suggest [sə'dʒɛst] *vt* proporre, suggerire; indicare; **~ion** [-'dʒɛstʃən] *n* suggerimento, proposta; indicazione *f*; **~ive** *(pej) adj* indecente

suicide ['sʊɪsaɪd] *n (person)* suicida *m/f*; *(act)* suicidio; *see also* **commit**

suit [suːt] *n (man's)* vestito; *(woman's)* completo, tailleur *m inv*; *(LAW)* causa; *(CARDS)* seme *m*, colore *m* ♦ *vt* andar bene a *or* per; essere adatto(a) a *or* per; *(adapt)*: **to ~ sth to** adattare qc a; **well ~ed** ben assortito(a); **~able** *adj* adatto(a); appropriato(a); **~ably** *adv (dress)* in modo adatto; *(impressed)* favorevolmente

suitcase ['suːtkeɪs] *n* valigia

suite [swiːt] *n (of rooms)* appartamento; *(MUS)* suite *f inv*; *(furniture)*: **bedroom/dining room ~** arredo *or* mobilia per la camera da letto/sala da pranzo

suitor ['suːtə*] *n* corteggiatore *m*, spasimante *m*

sulfur ['sʌlfə*] *(US) n* = **sulphur**

sulk [sʌlk] *vi* fare il broncio; **~y** *adj* imbronciato(a)

sullen ['sʌlən] *adj* scontroso(a); cupo(a)

sulphur ['sʌlfə*] *(US* **sulfur**) *n* zolfo

sultana [sʌl'tɑːnə] *n (fruit)* uva (secca)

sultanina

sultry ['sʌltrɪ] *adj* afoso(a)

sum [sʌm] *n* somma; (*SCOL etc*) addizione *f*; ~ **up** *vt, vi* riassumere

summarize ['sʌmǝraɪz] *vt* riassumere, riepilogare

summary ['sʌmǝrɪ] *n* riassunto

summer ['sʌmǝ*] *n* estate *f* ♦ *cpd* d'estate, estivo(a); ~ **holidays** *npl* vacanze *fpl* estive; **~house** *n* (*in garden*) padiglione *m*; **~time** *n* (*season*) estate *f*; ~ **time** *n* (*by clock*) ora legale (estiva)

summit ['sʌmɪt] *n* cima, sommità; (*POL*) vertice *m*

summon ['sʌmǝn] *vt* chiamare, convocare; ~ **up** *vt* raccogliere, fare appello a; **~s** *n* ordine *m* di comparizione ♦ *vt* citare

sump [sʌmp] (*BRIT*) *n* (*AUT*) coppa dell'olio

sumptuous ['sʌmptjuǝs] *adj* sontuoso(a)

sun [sʌn] *n* sole *m*; **~bathe** *vi* prendere un bagno di sole; **~block** *n* protezione *f* solare totale; **~burn** *n* (*painful*) scottatura; **~burnt** *adj* abbronzato(a); (*painfully*) scottato(a)

Sunday ['sʌndɪ] *n* domenica; ~ **school** *n* ≈ scuola di catechismo

sundial ['sʌndaɪǝl] *n* meridiana

sundown ['sʌndaʊn] *n* tramonto

sundry ['sʌndrɪ] *adj* vari(e), diversi(e); **all and** ~ tutti quanti; **sundries** *npl* articoli diversi, cose diverse

sunflower ['sʌnflaʊǝ*] *n* girasole *m*

sung [sʌŋ] *pp of* **sing**

sunglasses ['sʌnglɑ:sɪz] *npl* occhiali *mpl* da sole

sunk [sʌŋk] *pp of* **sink**

sun: **~light** *n* (luce *f* del) sole *m*; **~lit** *adj* soleggiato(a); **~ny** *adj* assolato(a), soleggiato(a); (*fig*) allegro(a), felice; **~rise** *n* levata del sole, alba; ~ **roof** *n* (*AUT*) tetto apribile; **~screen** *n* (*protective ingredient*) filtro solare; (*cream*) crema solare protettiva; **~set** *n* tramonto; **~shade** *n* parasole *m*; **~shine** *n* (luce *f* del) sole *m*; **~stroke** *n* insolazione *f*, colpo di sole; **~tan** *n* abbronzatura; **~tan lotion** *n* lozione *f* solare; **~tan oil** *n* olio solare

super ['su:pǝ*] (*inf*) *adj* fantastico(a)

superannuation [su:pǝrænju'eɪʃǝn] *n* contributi *mpl* pensionistici; pensione *f*

superb [su:'pǝ:b] *adj* magnifico(a)

supercilious [su:pǝ'sɪlɪǝs] *adj* sprezzante, sdegnoso(a)

superficial [su:pǝ'fɪʃǝl] *adj* superficiale

superhuman [su:pǝ'hju:mǝn] *adj* sovrumano(a)

superimpose ['su:pǝrɪm'pǝʊz] *vt* sovrapporre

superintendent [su:pǝrɪn'tɛndǝnt] *n* direttore/trice; (*POLICE*) ≈ commissario (capo)

superior [su'pɪǝrɪǝ*] *adj, n* superiore *m/f*; **~ity** [-'ɔrɪtɪ] *n* superiorità

superlative [su'pǝ:lǝtɪv] *adj* superlativo(a), supremo(a) ♦ *n* (*LING*) superlativo *m*

superman [su:pǝmæn] (*irreg*) *n* superuomo

supermarket ['su:pǝmɑ:kɪt] *n* supermercato

supernatural [su:pǝ'nætʃǝrǝl] *adj* soprannaturale ♦ *n* soprannaturale *m*

superpower ['su:pǝpaʊǝ*] *n* (*POL*) superpotenza

supersede [su:pǝ'si:d] *vt* sostituire, soppiantare

superstitious [su:pǝ'stɪʃǝs] *adj* superstizioso(a)

supertanker ['su:pǝtæŋkǝ*] *n* superpetroliera

supervise ['su:pǝvaɪz] *vt* (*person etc*) sorvegliare; (*organization*) soprintendere a; **supervision** [-'vɪʒǝn] *n* sorveglianza; supervisione *f*; **supervisor** *n* sorvegliante *m/f*; soprintendente *m/f*; (*in shop*) capocommesso/a

supine ['su:paɪn] *adj* supino(a)

supper ['sʌpǝ*] *n* cena

supplant [sǝ'plɑ:nt] *vt* (*person, thing*) soppiantare

supple ['sʌpl] *adj* flessibile; agile

supplement [*n* 'sʌplɪmǝnt, *vb* sʌplɪ'mɛnt] *n* supplemento ♦ *vt* completare, integrare; **~ary** [-'mɛntǝrɪ] *adj* supplementare

supplier [sǝ'plaɪǝ*] *n* fornitore *m*

supply [sǝ'plaɪ] *vt* (*provide*) fornire; (*equip*):

to ~ (with) approvvigionare (di); attrezzare (con) ♦ n riserva, provvista; (*supplying*) approvvigionamento; (*TECH*) alimentazione f; **supplies** npl (*food*) viveri mpl; (*MIL*) sussistenza; **~ teacher** (*BRIT*) n supplente m/f

support [sə'pɔːt] n (*moral, financial etc*) sostegno, appoggio; (*TECH*) supporto ♦ vt sostenere; (*financially*) mantenere; (*uphold*) sostenere, difendere; **~er** n (*POL etc*) sostenitore/trice, fautore/trice; (*SPORT*) tifoso/a

suppose [sə'pəuz] vt supporre; immaginare; **to be ~d to do** essere tenuto(a) a fare; **~dly** [sə'pəuzidli] adv presumibilmente; **supposing** conj se, ammesso che +sub

suppository [sə'pɔzitəri] n suppositorio

suppress [sə'prɛs] vt reprimere; sopprimere; occultare

supreme [su'priːm] adj supremo(a)

surcharge ['səːtʃɑːdʒ] n supplemento

sure [ʃuə*] adj sicuro(a); (*definite, convinced*) sicuro(a), certo(a); **~!** (*of course*) senz'altro, certo!; **~ enough** infatti; **to make ~ of sth/that** assicurarsi di qc/che; **~-footed** adj dal passo sicuro; **~ly** adv sicuramente; certamente

surf [səːf] n (*waves*) cavalloni mpl; (*foam*) spuma

surface ['səːfis] n superficie f ♦ vt (*road*) asfaltare ♦ vi risalire alla superficie; (*fig: news, feeling*) venire a galla; **~ mail** n posta ordinaria

surfboard ['səːfbɔːd] n tavola per surfing

surfeit ['səːfit] n: **a ~ of** un eccesso di; un'indigestione di

surfing ['səːfɪŋ] n surfing m

surge [səːdʒ] n (*strong movement*) ondata; (*of feeling*) impeto ♦ vi gonfiarsi; (*people*) riversarsi

surgeon ['səːdʒən] n chirurgo

surgery ['səːdʒəri] n chirurgia; (*BRIT: room*) studio or gabinetto medico, ambulatorio; (: *also:* **~ hours**) orario delle visite or di consultazione; **to undergo ~** subire un intervento chirurgico

surgical ['səːdʒikl] adj chirurgico(a); **~**

spirit (*BRIT*) n alcool m denaturato

surname ['səːneim] n cognome m

surpass [səː'pɑːs] vt superare

surplus ['səːpləs] n eccedenza; (*ECON*) surplus m inv ♦ adj eccedente, d'avanzo

surprise [sə'praiz] n sorpresa; (*astonishment*) stupore m ♦ vt sorprendere; stupire; **surprising** adj sorprendente, stupefacente; **surprisingly** adv (*easy, helpful*) sorprendentemente

surrender [sə'rɛndə*] n resa, capitolazione f ♦ vi arrendersi

surreptitious [sʌrəp'tiʃəs] adj furtivo(a)

surrogate ['sʌrəgit] n surrogato; **~ mother** n madre f provetta

surround [sə'raund] vt circondare; (*MIL etc*) accerchiare; **~ing** adj circostante; **~ings** npl dintorni mpl; (*fig*) ambiente m

surveillance [səː'veiləns] n sorveglianza, controllo

survey [n 'səːvei, vb səː'vei] n quadro generale; (*study*) esame m; (*in housebuying etc*) perizia; (*of land*) rilevamento, rilievo topografico ♦ vt osservare; esaminare; valutare; rilevare; **~or** n perito; geometra m; (*of land*) agrimensore m

survival [sə'vaivl] n sopravvivenza; (*relic*) reliquia, vestigio

survive [sə'vaiv] vi sopravvivere ♦ vt sopravvivere a; **survivor** n superstite m/f, sopravvissuto/a

susceptible [sə'sɛptəbl] adj: **~ (to)** sensibile (a); (*disease*) predisposto(a) (a)

suspect [adj, n 'sʌspɛkt, vb səs'pɛkt] adj sospetto(a) ♦ n persona sospetta ♦ vt sospettare; (*think likely*) supporre; (*doubt*) dubitare

suspend [səs'pɛnd] vt sospendere; **~ed sentence** n condanna con la condizionale; **~er belt** n reggicalze m inv; **~ers** npl (*BRIT*) giarrettiere fpl; (*US*) bretelle fpl

suspense [səs'pɛns] n apprensione f; (*in film etc*) suspense m; **to keep sb in ~** tenere qn in sospeso

suspension [səs'pɛnʃən] n (*gen AUT*) sospensione f; (*of driving licence*) ritiro

temporaneo; **~ bridge** *n* ponte *m* sospeso
suspicion [səs'pɪʃən] *n* sospetto
suspicious [səs'pɪʃəs] *adj* (*suspecting*)
sospettoso(a); (*causing suspicion*)
sospetto(a)
sustain [səs'teɪn] *vt* sostenere; sopportare;
(*LAW: charge*) confermare; (*suffer*) subire;
~able *adj* sostenibile; **~ed** *adj* (*effort*)
prolungato(a)
sustenance ['sʌstɪnəns] *n* nutrimento;
mezzi *mpl* di sostentamento
swab [swɔb] *n* (*MED*) tampone *m*
swagger ['swægə*] *vi* pavoneggiarsi
swallow ['swɔləu] *n* (*bird*) rondine *f* ♦ *vt*
inghiottire; (*fig: story*) bere; **~ up** *vt*
inghiottire
swam [swæm] *pt of* **swim**
swamp [swɔmp] *n* palude *f* ♦ *vt*
sommergere
swan [swɔn] *n* cigno
swap [swɔp] *vt*: **to ~ (for)** scambiare (con)
swarm [swɔ:m] *n* sciame *m* ♦ *vi* (*bees*)
sciamare; (*people*) brulicare; (*place*): **to be
~ing with** brulicare di
swastika ['swɔstɪkə] *n* croce *f* uncinata,
svastica
swat [swɔt] *vt* schiacciare
sway [sweɪ] *vi* (*tree*) ondeggiare; (*person*)
barcollare ♦ *vt* (*influence*) influenzare,
dominare
swear [swɛə*] (*pt* **swore**, *pp* **sworn**) *vi*
(*curse*) bestemmiare, imprecare ♦ *vt*
(*promise*) giurare; **~word** *n* parolaccia
sweat [swɛt] *n* sudore *m*, traspirazione *f*
♦ *vi* sudare
sweater ['swɛtə*] *n* maglione *m*
sweatshirt ['swɛtʃə:t] *n* felpa
sweaty ['swɛtɪ] *adj* sudato(a); bagnato(a) di
sudore
Swede [swi:d] *n* svedese *m/f*
swede [swi:d] (*BRIT*) *n* rapa svedese
Sweden ['swi:dn] *n* Svezia
Swedish ['swi:dɪʃ] *adj* svedese ♦ *n* (*LING*)
svedese *m*
sweep [swi:p] (*pt, pp* **swept**) *n* spazzata;
(*also:* **chimney ~**) spazzacamino ♦ *vt*
spazzare, scopare; (*current*) spazzare ♦ *vi*

(*hand*) muoversi con gesto ampio; (*wind*)
infuriare; **~ away** *vt* spazzare via;
trascinare via; **~ past** *vi* sfrecciare accanto;
passare accanto maestosamente; **~ up** *vt*,
vi spazzare; **~ing** *adj* (*gesture*) ampio(a);
circolare; **a ~ing statement**
un'affermazione generica
sweet [swi:t] *n* (*BRIT: pudding*) dolce *m*;
(*candy*) caramella ♦ *adj* dolce; (*fresh*)
fresco(a); (*fig*) piacevole; delicato(a),
grazioso(a); gentile; **~corn** *n* granturco
dolce; **~en** *vt* addolcire; zuccherare;
~heart *n* innamorato/a; **~ness** *n* sapore
m dolce; dolcezza; **~ pea** *n* pisello
odoroso
swell [swɛl] (*pt* **~ed**, *pp* **swollen**, **~ed**) *n* (*of
sea*) mare *m* lungo ♦ *adj* (*US: inf: excellent*)
favoloso(a) ♦ *vt* gonfiare, ingrossare;
aumentare ♦ *vi* gonfiarsi, ingrossarsi;
(*sound*) crescere; (*also:* **~ up**) gonfiarsi;
~ing *n* (*MED*) tumefazione *f*, gonfiore *m*
sweltering ['swɛltərɪŋ] *adj* soffocante
swept [swɛpt] *pt, pp of* **sweep**
swerve [swə:v] *vi* deviare; (*driver*) sterzare;
(*boxer*) scartare
swift [swɪft] *n* (*bird*) rondone *m* ♦ *adj*
rapido(a), veloce
swig [swɪg] (*inf*) *n* (*drink*) sorsata
swill [swɪl] *vt* (*also:* **~ out**, **~ down**)
risciacquare
swim [swɪm] (*pt* **swam**, *pp* **swum**) *n*: **to go
for a ~** andare a fare una nuotata ♦ *vi*
nuotare; (*SPORT*) fare del nuoto; (*head,
room*) girare ♦ *vt* (*river, channel*)
attraversare *or* percorrere a nuoto; (*length*)
nuotare; **~mer** *n* nuotatore/trice; **~ming**
n nuoto; **~ming cap** *n* cuffia; **~ming
costume** (*BRIT*) *n* costume *m* da bagno;
~ming pool *n* piscina; **~ming trunks**
npl costume *m* da bagno (da uomo);
~suit *n* costume *m* da bagno
swindle ['swɪndl] *n* truffa ♦ *vt* truffare
swine [swaɪn] (*inf!*) *n inv* porco (!)
swing [swɪŋ] (*pt, pp* **swung**) *n* altalena;
(*movement*) oscillazione *f*; (*MUS*) ritmo;
swing *m* ♦ *vt* dondolare, far oscillare; (*also:*
~ round) far girare ♦ *vi* oscillare, dondo-

lare; (*also*: ~ **round**: *object*) roteare;
(: *person*) girarsi, voltarsi; **to be in full ~**
(*activity*) essere in piena attività; (*party etc*)
essere nel pieno; ~ **door** (*US* ~**ing door**) *n*
porta battente

swingeing ['swɪndʒɪŋ] *adj* (*BRIT*: *defeat*)
violento(a); (: *cuts*) enorme

swipe [swaɪp] *vt* (*hit*) colpire con forza; dare
uno schiaffo a; (*inf*: *steal*) sgraffignare

swirl [swəːl] *vi* turbinare, far mulinello

Swiss [swɪs] *adj, n inv* svizzero(a)

switch [swɪtʃ] *n* (*for light, radio etc*)
interruttore *m*; (*change*) cambiamento ♦ *vt*
(*change*) cambiare; scambiare; ~ **off** *vt*
spegnere; ~ **on** *vt* accendere; (*engine,
machine*) mettere in moto, avviare;
~**board** *n* (*TEL*) centralino

Switzerland ['swɪtsələnd] *n* Svizzera

swivel ['swɪvl] *vi* (*also*: ~ **round**) girare

swollen ['swəulən] *pp of* **swell**

swoon [swuːn] *vi* svenire

swoop [swuːp] *n* incursione *f* ♦ *vi* (*also*: ~
down) scendere in picchiata, piombare

swop [swɔp] *n, vt* = **swap**

sword [sɔːd] *n* spada; ~**fish** *n* pesce *m*
spada *inv*

swore [swɔː*] *pt of* **swear**

sworn [swɔːn] *pp of* **swear** ♦ *adj* giurato(a)

swot [swɔt] *vi* sgobbare

swum [swʌm] *pp of* **swim**

swung [swʌŋ] *pt, pp of* **swing**

syllable ['sɪləbl] *n* sillaba

syllabus ['sɪləbəs] *n* programma *m*

symbol ['sɪmbl] *n* simbolo

symmetry ['sɪmɪtrɪ] *n* simmetria

sympathetic [sɪmpə'θetɪk] *adj* (*showing
pity*) compassionevole; (*kind*)
comprensivo(a); ~ **towards** ben
disposto(a) verso

sympathize ['sɪmpəθaɪz] *vi*: **to ~ with**
(*person*) compatire; partecipare al dolore
di; (*cause*) simpatizzare per; ~**r** *n* (*POL*)
simpatizzante *m/f*

sympathy ['sɪmpəθɪ] *n* compassione *f*;
sympathies *npl* (*support, tendencies*)
simpatie *fpl*; **in ~ with** (*strike*) per
solidarietà con; **with our deepest ~** con le

nostre più sincere condoglianze

symphony ['sɪmfənɪ] *n* sinfonia

symptom ['sɪmptəm] *n* sintomo; indizio

synagogue ['sɪnəgɔg] *n* sinagoga

syndicate ['sɪndɪkɪt] *n* sindacato

synopses [sɪ'nɔpsiːz] *npl of* **synopsis**

synopsis [sɪ'nɔpsɪs] (*pl* **synopses**) *n*
sommario, sinossi *f inv*

syntheses ['sɪnθəsiːz] *npl of* **synthesis**

synthesis ['sɪnθəsɪs] (*pl* **syntheses**) *n*
sintesi *f inv*

synthetic [sɪn'θetɪk] *adj* sintetico(a)

syphon ['saɪfən] *n, vb* = **siphon**

Syria ['sɪrɪə] *n* Siria

syringe [sɪ'rɪndʒ] *n* siringa

syrup ['sɪrəp] *n* sciroppo; (*also*: **golden ~**)
melassa raffinata

system ['sɪstəm] *n* sistema *m*; (*order*)
metodo; (*ANAT*) organismo; ~**atic** [-'mætɪk]
adj sistematico(a); metodico(a); ~ **disk** *n*
(*COMPUT*) disco del sistema; ~**s analyst** *n*
analista *m* di sistemi

T, t

ta [tɑː] (*BRIT*: *inf*) *excl* grazie!

tab [tæb] *n* (*loop on coat etc*) laccetto; (*label*)
etichetta; **to keep ~s on** (*fig*) tenere
d'occhio

tabby ['tæbɪ] *n* (*also*: ~ **cat**) (gatto) soriano,
gatto tigrato

table ['teɪbl] *n* tavolo, tavola; (*MATH, CHEM
etc*) tavola ♦ *vt* (*BRIT*: *motion etc*)
presentare; **to lay** *or* **set the ~**
apparecchiare *or* preparare la tavola;
~**cloth** *n* tovaglia; ~ **d'hôte** [tɑːbl'dəut]
adj (*meal*) a prezzo fisso; ~ **lamp** *n*
lampada da tavolo; ~**mat** *n* sottopiatto;
~ **of contents** *n* indice *m*; ~**spoon** *n*
cucchiaio da tavola; (*also*: ~**spoonful**: *as
measurement*) cucchiaiata

tablet ['tæblɪt] *n* (*MED*) compressa; (*of stone*)
targa

table: ~ **tennis** *n* tennis *m* da tavolo,
ping-pong ® *m*; ~ **wine** *n* vino da tavola

---
tabloid press
---

i *Il termine* **tabloid press** *si riferisce ai giornali popolari, che hanno un formato ridotto e pubblicano le notizie in modo sensazionalistico; vedi anche* **quality press**.

tacit ['tæsɪt] *adj* tacito(a)

tack [tæk] *n (nail)* bulletta; *(fig)* approccio ♦ *vt* imbullettare; imbastire ♦ *vi* bordeggiare

tackle ['tækl] *n* attrezzatura, equipaggiamento; *(for lifting)* paranco; *(FOOTBALL)* contrasto; *(RUGBY)* placcaggio ♦ *vt (difficulty)* affrontare; *(FOOTBALL)* contrastare; *(RUGBY)* placcare

tacky ['tækɪ] *adj* appiccicaticcio(a); *(pej)* scadente

tact [tækt] *n* tatto; **~ful** *adj* delicato(a), discreto(a)

tactical ['tæktɪkl] *adj* tattico(a)

tactics ['tæktɪks] *n, npl* tattica

tactless ['tæktlɪs] *adj* che manca di tatto

tadpole ['tædpəʊl] *n* girino

tag [tæg] *n* etichetta; **~ along** *vi* seguire

tail [teɪl] *n* coda; *(of shirt)* falda ♦ *vt (follow)* seguire, pedinare; **~ away** *vi* = **~ off**; **~ off** *vi (in size, quality etc)* diminuire gradatamente; **~back** *(BRIT) n (AUT)* ingorgo; **~ end** *n (of train, procession etc)* coda; *(of meeting etc)* fine *f*; **~gate** *n (AUT)* portellone *m* posteriore

tailor ['teɪlə*] *n* sarto; **~ing** *n (cut)* stile *m*; *(craft)* sartoria; **~-made** *adj (also fig)* fatto(a) su misura

tailwind ['teɪlwɪnd] *n* vento di coda

tainted ['teɪntɪd] *adj (food)* guasto(a); *(water, air)* infetto(a); *(fig)* corrotto(a)

take [teɪk] *(pt* **took**, *pp* **taken**) *vt* prendere; *(gain: prize)* ottenere, vincere; *(require: effort, courage)* occorrere, volerci; *(tolerate)* accettare, sopportare; *(hold: passengers etc)* contenere; *(accompany)* accompagnare; *(bring, carry)* portare; *(exam)* sostenere, presentarsi a; **to ~ a photo/a shower** fare una fotografia/una doccia; **I ~ it that** suppongo che; **~ after** *vt fus* assomigliare

a; **~ apart** *vt* smontare; **~ away** *vt* portare via; togliere; **~ back** *vt (return)* restituire; riportare; *(one's words)* ritirare; **~ down** *vt (building)* demolire; *(letter etc)* scrivere; **~ in** *vt (deceive)* imbrogliare, abbindolare; *(understand)* capire; *(include)* comprendere, includere; *(lodger)* prendere, ospitare; **~ off** *vi (AVIAT)* decollare; *(go away)* andarsene ♦ *vt (remove)* togliere; **~ on** *vt (work)* accettare, intraprendere; *(employee)* assumere; *(opponent)* sfidare, affrontare; **~ out** *vt* portare fuori; *(remove)* togliere; *(licence)* prendere, ottenere; **to ~ sth out of sth** *(drawer, pocket etc)* tirare qc fuori da qc; estrarre qc da qc; **~ over** *vt (business)* rilevare ♦ *vi:* **to ~ over from sb** prendere le consegne *or* il controllo da qn; **~ to** *vt fus (person)* prendere in simpatia; *(activity)* prendere gusto a; **~ up** *vt (dress)* accorciare; *(occupy: time, space)* occupare; *(engage in: hobby etc)* mettersi a; **to ~ sb up on sth** accettare qc da qn; **~away** *(BRIT) n (shop etc)* ≈ rosticceria; *(food)* pasto per asporto; **~off** *n (AVIAT)* decollo; **~out** *(US) n* = **~away**; **~over** *n (COMM)* assorbimento

takings ['teɪkɪŋz] *npl (COMM)* incasso

talc [tælk] *n (also:* **~um powder**) talco

tale [teɪl] *n* racconto, storia; **to tell ~s** *(fig: to teacher, parent etc)* fare la spia

talent ['tælnt] *n* talento; **~ed** *adj* di talento

talk [tɔːk] *n* discorso; *(gossip)* chiacchiere *fpl*; *(conversation)* conversazione *f*; *(interview)* discussione *f* ♦ *vi* parlare; **~s** *npl (POL etc)* colloqui *mpl*; **to ~ about** parlare di; **to ~ sb out of/into doing** dissuadere qn da/convincere qn a fare; **to ~ shop** parlare di lavoro *or* di affari; **~ over** *vt* discutere; **~ative** *adj* loquace, ciarliero(a); **~ show** *n* conversazione *f* televisiva, talk show *m inv*

tall [tɔːl] *adj* alto(a); **to be 6 feet ~** ≈ essere alto 1 metro e 80; **~ story** *n* panzana, frottola

tally ['tælɪ] *n* conto, conteggio ♦ *vi:* **to ~ (with)** corrispondere (a)

talon ['tælən] *n* artiglio

tambourine [tæmbə'ri:n] *n* tamburello

tame [teɪm] *adj* addomesticato(a); *(fig: story, style)* insipido(a), scialbo(a)

tamper ['tæmpə*] *vi*: **to ~ with** manomettere

tampon ['tæmpɔn] *n* tampone *m*

tan [tæn] *n (also:* **sun~**) abbronzatura ♦ *vi* abbronzarsi ♦ *adj (colour)* marrone rossiccio *inv*

tang [tæŋ] *n* odore *m* penetrante; sapore *m* piccante

tangent ['tændʒənt] *n*: **to go off at a ~** *(fig)* partire per la tangente

tangerine [tændʒə'ri:n] *n* mandarino

tangle ['tæŋgl] *n* groviglio; **to get into a ~** aggrovigliarsi; *(fig)* combinare un pasticcio

tank [tæŋk] *n* serbatoio; *(for fish)* acquario; *(MIL)* carro armato

tanker ['tæŋkə*] *n (ship)* nave *f* cisterna *inv*; *(truck)* autobotte *f*, autocisterna

tanned [tænd] *adj* abbronzato(a)

tantalizing ['tæntəlaɪzɪŋ] *adj* allettante

tantamount ['tæntəmaunt] *adj*: **~ to** equivalente a

tantrum ['tæntrəm] *n* accesso di collera

tap [tæp] *n (on sink etc)* rubinetto; *(gentle blow)* colpetto ♦ *vt* dare un colpetto a; *(resources)* sfruttare, utilizzare; *(telephone)* mettere sotto controllo; **on ~** *(fig: resources)* a disposizione; **~ dancing** *n* tip tap *m*

tape [teɪp] *n* nastro; *(also:* **magnetic ~**) nastro *(magnetico)*; *(sticky ~)* nastro adesivo ♦ *vt (record)* registrare (su nastro); *(stick)* attaccare con nastro adesivo; **~ deck** *n* piastra; **~ measure** *n* metro a nastro

taper ['teɪpə*] *n* candelina ♦ *vi* assottigliarsi

tape recorder *n* registratore *m* (a nastro)

tapestry ['tæpɪstrɪ] *n* arazzo; tappezzeria

tar [tɑ:*] *n* catrame *m*

target ['tɑ:gɪt] *n* bersaglio; *(fig: objective)* obiettivo

tariff ['tærɪf] *n* tariffa

tarmac ['tɑ:mæk] *n (BRIT: on road)* macadam *m* al catrame; *(AVIAT)* pista di decollo

tarnish ['tɑ:nɪʃ] *vt* offuscare, annerire; *(fig)*

macchiare

tarpaulin [tɑ:'pɔ:lɪn] *n* tela incatramata

tarragon ['tærəgən] *n* dragoncello

tart [tɑ:t] *n (CULIN)* crostata; *(BRIT: inf: pej: woman)* sgualdrina ♦ *adj (flavour)* aspro(a), agro(a); **~ up** *(inf) vt* agghindare

tartan ['tɑ:tn] *n* tartan *m inv*

tartar ['tɑ:tə*] *n (on teeth)* tartaro; **~(e) sauce** *n* salsa tartara

task [tɑ:sk] *n* compito; **to take to ~** rimproverare; **~ force** *n (MIL, POLICE)* unità operativa

taste [teɪst] *n* gusto; *(flavour)* sapore *m*, gusto; *(sample)* assaggio; *(fig: glimpse, idea)* idea ♦ *vi (sample)* assaggiare ♦ *vi*: **to ~ of** *or* **like** *(fish etc)* sapere *or* avere sapore di; **you can ~ the garlic (in it)** (ci) si sente il sapore dell'aglio; **in good / bad ~** di buon/cattivo gusto; **~ful** *adj* di buon gusto; **~less** *adj (food)* insipido(a); *(remark)* di cattivo gusto; **tasty** *adj* saporito(a), gustoso(a)

tatters ['tætəz] *npl*: **in ~** a brandelli

tattoo [tə'tu:] *n* tatuaggio; *(spectacle)* parata militare ♦ *vt* tatuare

tatty ['tætɪ] *adj* malridotto(a)

taught [tɔ:t] *pt, pp of* **teach**

taunt [tɔ:nt] *n* scherno ♦ *vt* schernire

Taurus ['tɔ:rəs] *n* Toro

taut [tɔ:t] *adj* teso(a)

tax [tæks] *n (on goods)* imposta; *(on services)* tassa; *(on income)* imposte *fpl*, tasse *fpl* ♦ *vt* tassare; *(fig: strain: patience etc)* mettere alla prova; **~able** *adj (income)* imponibile; **~ation** [-'seɪʃən] *n* tassazione *f*; tasse *fpl*, imposte *fpl*; **~ avoidance** *n* elusione *f* fiscale; **~ disc** *(BRIT) n (AUT)* ≈ bollo; **~ evasion** *n* evasione *f* fiscale; **~-free** *adj* esente da imposte

taxi ['tæksɪ] *n* taxi *m inv* ♦ *vi (AVIAT)* rullare; **~ driver** *n* tassista *m/f*; **~ rank** *(BRIT) n =* **~ stand**; **~ stand** *n* posteggio dei taxi

tax: **~ payer** *n* contribuente *m/f*; **~ relief** *n* agevolazioni *fpl* fiscali; **~ return** *n* dichiarazione *f* dei redditi

TB *n abbr* = **tuberculosis**

tea [ti:] *n* tè *m inv*; *(BRIT: snack: for children)*

merenda; **high ~** (*BRIT*) cena leggera (*presa nel tardo pomeriggio*); **~ bag** n bustina di tè; **~ break** (*BRIT*) intervallo per il tè

teach [tiːtʃ] (*pt, pp* **taught**) *vt*: **to ~ sb sth, ~ sth to sb** insegnare qc a qn ♦ *vi* insegnare; **~er** n insegnante *m/f*; (*in secondary school*) professore/essa; (*in primary school*) maestro/a; **~ing** n insegnamento

tea cosy n copriteiera *m inv*

teacup [ˈtiːkʌp] n tazza da tè

teak [tiːk] n teak *m*

tea leaves npl foglie *fpl* di tè

team [tiːm] n squadra; (*of animals*) tiro; **~work** n lavoro di squadra

teapot [ˈtiːpɔt] n teiera

tear[1] [teə*] (*pt* **tore**, *pp* **torn**) n strappo ♦ *vt* strappare ♦ *vi* strapparsi; **~ along** *vi* (*rush*) correre all'impazzata; **~ up** *vt* (*sheet of paper etc*) strappare

tear[2] [tiə*] n lacrima; **in ~s** in lacrime; **~ful** *adj* piangente, lacrimoso(a); **~ gas** n gas *m* lacrimogeno

tearoom [ˈtiːruːm] n sala da tè

tease [tiːz] *vt* canzonare; (*unkindly*) tormentare

tea set n servizio da tè

teaspoon [ˈtiːspuːn] n cucchiaino da tè; (*also:* **~ful**: *as measurement*) cucchiaino

teat [tiːt] n capezzolo

teatime [ˈtiːtaɪm] n ora del tè

tea towel (*BRIT*) n strofinaccio (per i piatti)

technical [ˈtɛknɪkl] *adj* tecnico(a); **~ college** (*BRIT*) n ≈ istituto tecnico; **~ity** [-ˈkælɪtɪ] n tecnicità; (*detail*) dettaglio tecnico; (*legal*) cavillo

technician [tɛkˈnɪʃən] n tecnico/a

technique [tɛkˈniːk] n tecnica

technological [tɛknəˈlɔdʒɪkl] *adj* tecnologico(a)

technology [tɛkˈnɔlədʒɪ] n tecnologia

teddy (bear) [ˈtɛdɪ-] n orsacchiotto

tedious [ˈtiːdɪəs] *adj* noioso(a), tedioso(a)

tee [tiː] n (*GOLF*) tee *m inv*

teem [tiːm] *vi*: **to ~ with** brulicare di; **it is ~ing (with rain)** piove a dirotto

teenage [ˈtiːneɪdʒ] *adj* (*fashions etc*) per giovani, per adolescenti; **~r** n adolescente *m/f*

teens [tiːnz] npl: **to be in one's ~** essere adolescente

tee-shirt [ˈtiːʃəːt] n = **T-shirt**

teeter [ˈtiːtə*] *vi* barcollare, vacillare

teeth [tiːθ] npl *of* **tooth**

teethe [tiːð] *vi* mettere i denti

teething ring [ˈtiːðɪŋ-] n dentaruolo

teething troubles [ˈtiːðɪŋ-] npl (*fig*) difficoltà *fpl* iniziali

teetotal [ˈtiːˈtəutl] *adj* astemio(a)

tele: **~conferencing** n teleconferenza; **~gram** n telegramma *m*; **~graph** n telegrafo; **~pathy** [təˈlɛpəθɪ] n telepatia

telephone [ˈtɛlɪfəun] n telefono ♦ *vt* (*person*) telefonare a; (*message*) comunicare per telefono; **~ booth** (*BRIT* **~ box**) n cabina telefonica; **~ call** n telefonata; **~ directory** n elenco telefonico; **~ number** n numero di telefono; **telephonist** [təˈlɛfənɪst] (*BRIT*) n telefonista *m/f*

telescope [ˈtɛlɪskəup] n telescopio

television [ˈtɛlɪvɪʒən] n televisione *f*; **on ~** alla televisione; **~ set** n televisore *m*

telex [ˈtɛlɛks] n telex *m inv* ♦ *vt* trasmettere per telex; **to ~ sb** contattare qn via telex

tell [tɛl] (*pt, pp* **told**) *vt* dire; (*relate: story*) raccontare; (*distinguish*): **to ~ sth from** distinguere qc da ♦ *vi* (*talk*): **to ~ (of)** parlare (di); (*have effect*) farsi sentire, avere effetto; **to ~ sb to do** dire a qn di fare; **~ off** *vt* rimproverare, sgridare; **~er** n (*in bank*) cassiere/a; **~ing** *adj* (*remark, detail*) rivelatore(trice); **~tale** *adj* (*sign*) rivelatore(trice)

telly [ˈtɛlɪ] (*BRIT*: *inf*) n abbr (= *television*) tivù *f inv*

temerity [təˈmɛrɪtɪ] n temerarietà

temp [tɛmp] n abbr (= *temporary*) segretaria temporanea

temper [ˈtɛmpə*] n (*nature*) carattere *m*; (*mood*) umore *m*; (*fit of anger*) collera ♦ *vt* (*moderate*) temperare, moderare; **to be in a ~** essere in collera; **to lose one's ~** andare in collera

temperament [ˈtɛmprəmənt] n (*nature*)

temperamento; **~al** [-'mɛntl] adj capriccioso(a)

temperate ['tɛmprət] adj moderato(a); (climate) temperato(a)

temperature ['tɛmprətʃə*] n temperatura; **to have** or **run a ~** avere la febbre

tempest ['tɛmpɪst] n tempesta

template ['tɛmplɪt] n sagoma

temple ['tɛmpl] n (building) tempio; (ANAT) tempia

temporary ['tɛmpərərɪ] adj temporaneo(a); (job, worker) avventizio(a), temporaneo(a)

tempt [tɛmpt] vt tentare; **to ~ sb into doing** indurre qn a fare; **~ation** [-'teɪʃən] n tentazione f; **~ing** adj allettante

ten [tɛn] num dieci

tenacity [tə'næsɪtɪ] n tenacia

tenancy ['tɛnənsɪ] n affitto; condizione f di inquilino

tenant ['tɛnənt] n inquilino/a

tend [tɛnd] vt badare a, occuparsi di ♦ vi: **to ~ to do** tendere a fare

tendency ['tɛndənsɪ] n tendenza

tender ['tɛndə*] adj tenero(a); (sore) dolorante ♦ n (COMM: offer) offerta; (money): **legal ~** moneta in corso legale ♦ vt offrire

tendon ['tɛndən] n tendine m

tenement ['tɛnəmənt] n casamento

tennis ['tɛnɪs] n tennis m; **~ ball** n palla da tennis; **~ court** n campo da tennis; **~ player** n tennista m/f; **~ racket** n racchetta da tennis; **~ shoes** npl scarpe fpl da tennis

tenor ['tɛnə*] n (MUS) tenore m

tenpin bowling ['tɛnpɪn-] n bowling m

tense [tɛns] adj teso(a) ♦ n (LING) tempo

tension ['tɛnʃən] n tensione f

tent [tɛnt] n tenda

tentative ['tɛntətɪv] adj esitante, incerto(a); (conclusion) provvisorio(a)

tenterhooks ['tɛntəhuks] npl: **on ~** sulle spine

tenth [tɛnθ] num decimo(a)

tent: ~ peg n picchetto da tenda; **~ pole** n palo da tenda, montante m

tenuous ['tɛnjuəs] adj tenue

tenure ['tɛnjuə*] n (of property) possesso; (of job) permanenza; titolarità

tepid ['tɛpɪd] adj tiepido(a)

term [tə:m] n termine m; (SCOL) trimestre m; (LAW) sessione f ♦ vt chiamare, definire; **~s** npl (conditions) condizioni fpl; (COMM) prezzi mpl, tariffe fpl; **in the short/long ~** a breve/lunga scadenza; **to be on good ~s with sb** essere in buoni rapporti con qn; **to come to ~s with** (problem) affrontare

terminal ['tə:mɪnl] adj finale, terminale; (disease) terminale ♦ n (ELEC) morsetto; (COMPUT) terminale m; (AVIAT, for oil, ore etc) terminal m inv; (BRIT: also: **coach ~**) capolinea m

terminate ['tə:mɪneɪt] vt mettere fine a

termini ['tə:mɪnaɪ] npl of **terminus**

terminus ['tə:mɪnəs] (pl **termini**) n (for buses) capolinea m; (for trains) stazione f terminale

terrace ['tɛrəs] n terrazza; (BRIT: row of houses) fila di case a schiera; **the ~s** npl (BRIT: SPORT) le gradinate; **~d** adj (garden) a terrazze

terracotta ['tɛrə'kɔtə] n terracotta

terrain [tɛ'reɪn] n terreno

terrible ['tɛrɪbl] adj terribile; **terribly** adv terribilmente; (very badly) malissimo

terrier ['tɛrɪə*] n terrier m inv

terrific [tə'rɪfɪk] adj incredibile, fantastico(a) (wonderful) formidabile, eccezionale

terrify ['tɛrɪfaɪ] vt terrorizzare

territory ['tɛrɪtərɪ] n territorio

terror ['tɛrə*] n terrore m; **~ism** n terrorismo; **~ist** n terrorista m/f

Terylene ® ['tɛrəli:n] n terital ® m, terilene ® m

test [tɛst] n (trial, check, of courage etc) prova; (MED) esame m; (CHEM) analisi f inv; (exam: of intelligence etc) test m inv; (: in school) compito in classe; (also: **driving ~**) esame m di guida ♦ vt provare; esaminare; analizzare; sottoporre ad esame; **to ~ sb in history** esaminare qn in storia

testament ['tɛstəmənt] n testamento; **the Old/New T~** il Vecchio/Nuovo testamento

testicle ['tɛstɪkl] n testicolo

testify ['testɪfaɪ] *vi* (*LAW*) testimoniare, deporre; **to ~ to sth** (*LAW*) testimoniare qc; (*gen*) comprovare or dimostrare qc

testimony ['testɪmənɪ] *n* (*LAW*) testimonianza, deposizione *f*

test match *n* (*CRICKET, RUGBY*) partita internazionale

test tube *n* provetta

tetanus ['tetənəs] *n* tetano

tether ['teðə*] *vt* legare ♦ *n*: **at the end of one's ~** al limite (della pazienza)

text [tekst] *n* testo; **~book** *n* libro di testo

textiles ['tekstaɪlz] *npl* tessuti *mpl*; (*industry*) industria tessile

texture ['tekstʃə*] *n* tessitura; (*of skin, paper etc*) struttura

Thames [temz] *n*: **the ~** il Tamigi

than [ðæn, ðən] *conj* (*in comparisons*) che; (*with numerals, pronouns, proper names*) di; **more ~ 10/once** più di 10/una volta; **I have more/less ~ you** ne ho più/meno di te; **I have more pens ~ pencils** ho più penne che matite; **she is older ~ you think** è più vecchia di quanto tu (non) pensi

thank [θæŋk] *vt* ringraziare; **~ you (very much)** grazie (tante); **~s** *npl* ringraziamenti *mpl*, grazie *fpl* ♦ *excl* grazie!; **~s to** grazie a; **~ful** *adj*: **~ful (for)** riconoscente (per); **~less** *adj* ingrato(a); **T~sgiving (Day)** *n* giorno del ringraziamento

┌─ **Thanksgiving (Day)** ─┐

ⓘ *Negli Stati Uniti ogni quarto giovedì di novembre ricorre il Thanksgiving (Day), festa in ricordo della celebrazione con cui i Padri Pellegrini, fondatori della colonia di Plymouth in Massachussets, ringraziarono Dio del buon raccolto del 1621.*

└──────────────────────────┘

┌─ *KEYWORD* ─┐

that [ðæt] (*pl* **those**) *adj* (*demonstrative*) quel(quell', quello) *m*; quella(quell') *f*; **~ man/woman/book** quell'uomo/quella donna/quel libro; (*not "this"*) quell'uomo/ quella donna/quel libro là; **~ one** quello(a) là

♦ *pron* **1** (*demonstrative*) ciò; (*not "this one"*) quello(a); **who's ~?** chi è?; **what's ~?** cos'è quello?; **is ~ you?** sei tu?; **I prefer this to ~** preferisco questo a quello; **~'s what he said** questo è ciò che ha detto; **what happened after ~?** che è successo dopo?; **~ is (to say)** cioè

2 (*relative*: *direct*) che; (: *indirect*) cui; **the book (~) I read** il libro che ho letto; **the box (~) I put it in** la scatola in cui l'ho messo; **the people (~) I spoke to** le persone con cui or con le quali ho parlato

3 (*relative*: *of time*) in cui; **the day (~) he came** il giorno in cui è venuto

♦ *conj* che; **he thought ~ I was ill** pensava che io fossi malato

♦ *adv* (*demonstrative*) così; **I can't work ~ much** non posso lavorare (così) tanto; **~ high** così alto; **the wall's about ~ high and ~ thick** il muro è alto circa così e spesso circa così

└──────────────────────────┘

thatched [θætʃt] *adj* (*roof*) di paglia; **~ cottage** *n* cottage *m inv* col tetto di paglia

thaw [θɔ:] *n* disgelo ♦ *vi* (*ice*) sciogliersi; (*food*) scongelarsi ♦ *vt* (*food*: *also*: **~ out**) (fare) scongelare

┌─ *KEYWORD* ─┐

the [ði:, ðə] *def art* **1** (*gen*) il(lo, l') *m*; la(l') *f*; i(gli) *mpl*; le *fpl*; **~ boy/girl/ink** il ragazzo/ la ragazza/l'inchiostro; **~ books/pencils** i libri/le matite; **~ history of ~ world** la storia del mondo; **give it to ~ postman** dallo al postino; **I haven't ~ time/money** non ho tempo/soldi; **~ rich and ~ poor** i ricchi e i poveri

2 (*in titles*): **Elizabeth ~ First** Elisabetta prima; **Peter ~ Great** Pietro il grande

3 (*in comparisons*): **~ more he works, ~ more he earns** più lavora più guadagna

└──────────────────────────┘

theatre ['θɪətə*] (*US* **theater**) *n* teatro; (*also:* **lecture ~**) aula magna; (*also:* **operating ~**)

sala operatoria; **~-goer** *n* frequentatore/trice di teatri

theatrical [θɪ'ætrɪkl] *adj* teatrale

theft [θeft] *n* furto

their [ðeə*] *adj* il(la) loro, *pl* i(le) loro; **~s** *pron* il(la) loro, *pl* i(le) loro; *see also* **my**; **mine**

them [ðem, ðəm] *pron* (*direct*) li(le); (*indirect*) gli, loro (*after vb*); (*stressed, after prep*: *people*) loro; (: *people, things*) essi(e); *see also* **me**

theme [θiːm] *n* tema *m*; **~ park** *n* parco di divertimenti (*intorno a un tema centrale*); **~ song** *n* tema musicale

themselves [ðəm'selvz] *pl pron* (*reflexive*) si; (*emphatic*) loro stessi(e); (*after prep*) se stessi(e)

then [ðen] *adv* (*at that time*) allora; (*next*) poi, dopo; (*and also*) e poi ♦ *conj* (*therefore*) perciò, dunque, quindi ♦ *adj*: **the ~ president** il presidente di allora; **by ~** allora; **from ~ on** da allora in poi

theology [θɪ'ɔlədʒɪ] *n* teologia

theorem ['θɪərəm] *n* teorema *m*

theoretical [θɪə'retɪkl] *adj* teorico(a)

theory ['θɪərɪ] *n* teoria

therapy ['θerəpɪ] *n* terapia

KEYWORD
---

there [ðeə*] *adv* **1**: **~ is, ~ are** c'è, ci sono; **~ are 3 of them** (*people*) sono in 3; (*things*) ce ne sono 3; **~ is no one here** non c'è nessuno qui; **~ has been an accident** c'è stato un incidente

2 (*referring to place*) là, lì; **up/in/down ~** lassù/là dentro/laggiù; **he went ~ on Friday** ci è andato venerdì; **I want that book ~** voglio quel libro là *or* lì; **~ he is!** eccolo!

3: **~, ~** (*esp to child*) su, su

thereabouts [ðeərə'bauts] *adv* (*place*) nei pressi, da quelle parti; (*amount*) giù di lì, all'incirca

thereafter [ðeər'ɑːftə*] *adv* da allora in poi

thereby [ðeə'baɪ] *adv* con ciò

therefore ['ðeəfɔː*] *adv* perciò, quindi

there's [ðeəz] = **there is**; **there has**

thermal ['θɜːml] *adj* termico(a)

thermometer [θə'mɔmɪtə*] *n* termometro

Thermos ® ['θɜːməs] *n* (*also*: **~ flask**) thermos ® *m inv*

thesaurus [θɪ'sɔːrəs] *n* dizionario dei sinonimi

these [ðiːz] *pl pron, adj* questi(e)

theses ['θiːsiːz] *npl of* **thesis**

thesis ['θiːsɪs] (*pl* **theses**) *n* tesi *f inv*

they [ðeɪ] *pl pron* essi(esse); (*people only*) loro; **~ say that ...** (*it is said that*) si dice che ...; **~'d** = **they had**; **they would**; **~'ll** = **they shall**; **they will**; **~'re** = **they are**; **~'ve** = **they have**

thick [θɪk] *adj* spesso(a); (*crowd*) compatto(a); (*stupid*) ottuso(a), lento(a) ♦ *n*: **in the ~ of** nel folto di; **it's 20 cm ~** ha uno spessore di 20 cm; **~en** *vi* ispessire ♦ *vt* (*sauce etc*) ispessire, rendere più denso(a); **~ly** *adv* (*spread*) a strati spessi; (*cut*) a fette grosse; (*populated*) densamente; **~ness** *n* spessore *m*; **~set** *adj* tarchiato(a), tozzo(a)

thief [θiːf] (*pl* **thieves**) *n* ladro/a

thieves [θiːvz] *npl of* **thief**

thigh [θaɪ] *n* coscia

thimble ['θɪmbl] *n* ditale *m*

thin [θɪn] *adj* sottile; (*person*) magro(a); (*soup*) poco denso(a) ♦ *vt*: **to ~ (down)** (*sauce, paint*) diluire

thing [θɪŋ] *n* cosa; (*object*) oggetto; (*mania*): **to have a ~ about** essere fissato(a) con; **~s** *npl* (*belongings*) cose *fpl*; **poor ~** poverino(a); **the best ~ would be to** la cosa migliore sarebbe di; **how are ~s?** come va?

think [θɪŋk] (*pt, pp* **thought**) *vi* pensare, riflettere ♦ *vt* pensare, credere; (*imagine*) immaginare; **to ~ of** pensare a; **what did you ~ of them?** cosa ne ha pensato?; **to ~ about sth/sb** pensare a qc/qn; **I'll ~ about it** ci penserò; **to ~ of doing** pensare di fare; **I ~ so/not** penso di sì/no; **to ~ well of** avere una buona opinione di; **~ out** *vt* (*plan*) elaborare; (*solution*) trovare; **~ over** *vt* riflettere su; **~ through** *vt* riflettere a fondo su; ~ **up** *vt* ideare; ~ **tank** *n* commissione *f* di esperti

third [θəːd] *num* terzo(a) ♦ *n* terzo/a; *(fraction)* terzo, terza parte *f*; *(AUT)* terza; *(BRIT: SCOL: degree)* laurea col minimo dei voti; **~ly** *adv* in terzo luogo; ~ **party insurance** *(BRIT)* *n* assicurazione *f* contro terzi; **~-rate** *adj* di qualità scadente; **the T~ World** *n* il Terzo Mondo

thirst [θəːst] *n* sete *f*; **~y** *adj* (person) assetato(a), che ha sete

thirteen [θəːˈtiːn] *num* tredici

thirty [ˈθəːtɪ] *num* trenta

KEYWORD
---

this [ðɪs] (*pl* **these**) *adj* (demonstrative) questo(a); ~ **man/woman/book** quest'uomo/questa donna/questo libro; (*not ''that''*) quest'uomo/questa donna/ questo libro qui; ~ **one** questo(a) qui ♦ *pron* (demonstrative) questo(a); (*not ''that one''*) questo(a) qui; **who/what is ~?** chi è/che cos'è questo?; **I prefer ~ to that** preferisco questo a quello; ~ **is where I live** io abito qui; ~ **is what he said** questo è ciò che ha detto; ~ **is Mr Brown** (*in introductions, photo*) questo è il signor Brown; (*on telephone*) sono il signor Brown ♦ *adv* (demonstrative): ~ **high/long** *etc* alto/lungo *etc* così; **I didn't know things were ~ bad** non sapevo andasse così male

---

thistle [ˈθɪsl] *n* cardo

thong [θɒŋ] *n* cinghia

thorn [θɔːn] *n* spina; **~y** *adj* spinoso(a)

thorough [ˈθʌrə] *adj* (search) minuzioso(a); (knowledge, research) approfondito(a), profondo(a); (person) coscienzioso(a); (cleaning) a fondo; **~bred** *n* (horse) purosangue *m/f inv*; **~fare** *n* strada transitabile; **''no ~fare''** ''divieto di transito''; **~ly** *adv* (search) minuziosamente; (wash, study) a fondo; (very) assolutamente

those [ðəuz] *pl pron* quelli(e) ♦ *pl adj* quei(quegli) *mpl*; quelle *fpl*

though [ðəu] *conj* benché, sebbene ♦ *adv*

comunque

thought [θɔːt] *pt, pp of* **think** ♦ *n* pensiero; (opinion) opinione *f*; **~ful** *adj* pensieroso(a), pensoso(a); (considerate) premuroso(a); **~less** *adj* sconsiderato(a); (behaviour) scortese

thousand [ˈθauzənd] *num* mille; **one ~** mille; **~s of** migliaia di; **~th** *num* millesimo(a)

thrash [θræʃ] *vt* picchiare; bastonare; (defeat) battere; ~ **about** *vi* dibattersi; ~ **out** *vt* dibattere

thread [θrɛd] *n* filo; (of screw) filetto ♦ *vt* (needle) infilare; **~bare** *adj* consumato(a), logoro(a)

threat [θrɛt] *n* minaccia; **~en** *vi* (storm) minacciare ♦ *vt*: **to ~en sb with/to do** minacciare qn con/di fare

three [θriː] *num* tre; **~-dimensional** *adj* tridimensionale; (film) stereoscopico(a); **~-piece suit** *n* completo (con gilè); **~-piece suite** *n* salotto comprendente un divano e due poltrone; **~-ply** *adj* (wool) a tre fili

threshold [ˈθrɛʃhəuld] *n* soglia

threw [θruː] *pt of* **throw**

thrifty [ˈθrɪftɪ] *adj* economico(a)

thrill [θrɪl] *n* brivido ♦ *vt* (audience) elettrizzare; **to be ~ed** (*with gift etc*) essere elettrizzato(a); **~er** *n* thriller *m inv*; **~ing** *adj* (book) pieno(a) di suspense; (news, discovery) elettrizzante

thrive [θraɪv] (*pt* **thrived**, *pp* **thrived**) *vi* crescere *or* svilupparsi bene; (business) prosperare; **he ~s on it** gli fa bene, ne gode; **thriving** *adj* fiorente

throat [θrəut] *n* gola; **to have a sore ~** avere (un *or* il) mal di gola

throb [θrɒb] *vi* palpitare; pulsare; vibrare

throes [θrəuz] *npl*: **in the ~ of** alle prese con; in preda a

thrombosis [θrɒmˈbəusɪs] *n* trombosi *f*

throne [θrəun] *n* trono

throng [θrɒŋ] *n* moltitudine *f* ♦ *vt* affollare

throttle [ˈθrɒtl] *n* (AUT) valvola a farfalla ♦ *vt* strangolare

through [θruː] *prep* attraverso; (time) per,

durante; (*by means of*) per mezzo di; (*owing to*) a causa di ♦ *adj* (*ticket, train, passage*) diretto(a) ♦ *adv* attraverso; **to put sb ~ to sb** (*TEL*) passare qn a qn; **to be ~** (*TEL*) ottenere la comunicazione; (*have finished*) essere finito(a); **"no ~ road"** (*BRIT*) "strada senza sbocco"; **~out** *prep* (*place*) dappertutto in; (*time*) per *or* durante tutto(a) ♦ *adv* dappertutto; sempre

throw [θrəʊ] (*pt* **threw**, *pp* **thrown**) *n* (*SPORT*) lancio, tiro ♦ *vt* tirare, gettare; (*SPORT*) lanciare, tirare; (*rider*) disarcionare; (*fig*) confondere; **to ~ a party** dare una festa; **~ away** *vt* gettare *or* buttare via; **~ off** *vt* sbarazzarsi di; **~ out** *vt* buttare fuori; (*reject*) respingere; **~ up** *vi* vomitare; **~away** *adj* da buttare; **~-in** *n* (*SPORT*) rimessa in gioco; **thrown** *pp of* **throw**

thru [θruː] (*US*) *prep, adj, adv* = **through**

thrush [θrʌʃ] *n* tordo

thrust [θrʌst] (*pt, pp* **thrust**) *vt* spingere con forza; (*push in*) conficcare

thud [θʌd] *n* tonfo

thug [θʌg] *n* delinquente *m*

thumb [θʌm] *n* (*ANAT*) pollice *m*; **to ~ a lift** fare l'autostop; **~ through** *vt fus* (*book*) sfogliare; **~tack** (*US*) *n* puntina da disegno

thump [θʌmp] *n* colpo forte; (*sound*) tonfo ♦ *vt* (*person*) picchiare; (*object*) battere su ♦ *vi* picchiare; battere

thunder ['θʌndə*] *n* tuono ♦ *vi* tuonare; (*train etc*): **to ~ past** passare con un rombo; **~bolt** *n* fulmine *m*; **~clap** *n* rombo di tuono; **~storm** *n* temporale *m*; **~y** *adj* temporalesco(a)

Thursday ['θəːzdɪ] *n* giovedì *m inv*

thus [ðʌs] *adv* così

thwart [θwɔːt] *vt* contrastare

thyme [taɪm] *n* timo

thyroid ['θaɪrɔɪd] *n* (*also*: **~ gland**) tiroide *f*

tiara [tɪ'ɑːrə] *n* (*woman's*) diadema *m*

Tiber ['taɪbə*] *n*: **the ~** il Tevere

tick [tɪk] *n* (*sound: of clock*) tic tac *m inv*; (*mark*) segno; spunta; (*ZOOL*) zecca; (*BRIT: inf*): **in a ~** in un attimo ♦ *vi* fare tic tac ♦ *vt* spuntare; **~ off** *vt* spuntare; (*person*) sgridare; **~ over** *vi* (*engine*) andare al

minimo; (*fig*) andare avanti come al solito

ticket ['tɪkɪt] *n* biglietto; (*in shop: on goods*) etichetta; (*parking ~*) multa; (*for library*) scheda; **~ collector** *n* bigliettaio; **~ office** *n* biglietteria

tickle ['tɪkl] *vt* fare il solletico a; (*fig*) solleticare ♦ *vi*: **it ~s** mi (*or gli etc*) fa il solletico; **ticklish** [-lɪʃ] *adj* che soffre il solletico; (*problem*) delicato(a)

tidal ['taɪdl] *adj* di marea; (*estuary*) soggetto(a) alla marea; **~ wave** *n* onda anomala

tidbit ['tɪdbɪt] (*US*) *n* (*food*) leccornia; (*news*) notizia ghiotta

tiddlywinks ['tɪdlɪwɪŋks] *n* gioco della pulce

tide [taɪd] *n* marea; (*fig: of events*) corso; **high/low ~** alta/bassa marea; **~ over** *vt* dare una mano a

tidy ['taɪdɪ] *adj* (*room*) ordinato(a), lindo(a); (*dress, work*) curato(a), in ordine; (*person*) ordinato(a) ♦ *vt* (*also*: **~ up**) riordinare, mettere in ordine

tie [taɪ] *n* (*string etc*) legaccio; (*BRIT: also*: **neck~**) cravatta; (*fig: link*) legame *m*; (*SPORT: draw*) pareggio ♦ *vt* (*parcel*) legare; (*ribbon*) annodare ♦ *vi* (*SPORT*) pareggiare; **to ~ sth in a bow** annodare qc; **to ~ a knot in sth** fare un nodo a qc; **~ down** *vt* legare; (*to price etc*) costringere ad accettare; **~ up** *vt* (*parcel, dog*) legare; (*boat*) ormeggiare; (*arrangements*) concludere; **to be ~d up** (*busy*) essere occupato(a) *or* preso(a)

tier [tɪə*] *n* fila; (*of cake*) piano, strato

tiger ['taɪgə*] *n* tigre *f*

tight [taɪt] *adj* (*rope*) teso(a), tirato(a); (*money*) poco(a); (*clothes, budget, bend etc*) stretto(a); (*control*) severo(a), fermo(a); (*inf: drunk*) sbronzo(a) ♦ *adv* (*squeeze*) fortemente; (*shut*) ermeticamente; **~s** (*BRIT*) *npl* collant *m inv*; **~en** *vt* (*rope*) tendere; (*screw*) stringere; (*control*) rinforzare ♦ *vi* tendersi; stringersi; **~-fisted** *adj* avaro(a); **~ly** *adv* (*grasp*) bene, saldamente; **~rope** *n* corda (da acrobata)

tile [taɪl] *n* (*on roof*) tegola; (*on wall or floor*) piastrella, mattonella; **~d** *adj* di tegole; **a piastrelle, a mattonelle**

till [tɪl] *n* registratore *m* di cassa ♦ *vt* (*land*) coltivare ♦ *prep, conj* = **until**

tiller ['tɪlə*] *n* (*NAUT*) barra del timone

tilt [tɪlt] *vt* inclinare, far pendere ♦ *vi* inclinarsi, pendere

timber [tɪmbə*] *n* (*material*) legname *m*

time [taɪm] *n* tempo; (*epoch: often pl*) epoca, tempo; (*by clock*) ora; (*moment*) momento; (*occasion*) volta; (*MUS*) tempo ♦ *vt* (*race*) cronometrare; (*programme*) calcolare la durata di; (*fix moment for*) programmare; (*remark etc*) dire (*or* fare) al momento giusto; **a long ~** molto tempo; **for the ~ being** per il momento; **4 at a ~ 4** per *or* alla volta; **from ~ to ~** ogni tanto; **at ~s** a volte; **in ~** (*soon enough*) in tempo; (*after some ~*) col tempo; (*MUS*) a tempo; **in a week's ~** fra una settimana; **in no ~** in un attimo; **any ~** in qualsiasi momento; **on ~** puntualmente; **5 ~s 5** 5 volte 5, 5 per 5; **what ~ is it?** che ora è?, che ore sono?; **to have a good ~** divertirsi; **~ bomb** *n* bomba a orologeria; **~less** *adj* eterno(a); **~ly** *adj* opportuno(a); **~ off** *n* tempo libero; **~r** *n* (*~ switch*) temporizzatore *m*; (*in kitchen*) contaminuti *m inv*; **~ scale** *n* periodo; **~-share** *adj*: **~-share apartment/villa** appartamento/villa in multiproprietà; **~ switch** (*BRIT*) *n* temporizzatore *m*; **~table** *n* orario; **~ zone** *n* fuso orario

timid ['tɪmɪd] *adj* timido(a); (*easily scared*) pauroso(a)

timing ['taɪmɪŋ] *n* (*SPORT*) cronometraggio; (*fig*) scelta del momento opportuno

timpani ['tɪmpənɪ] *npl* timpani *mpl*

tin [tɪn] *n* stagno; (*also: ~ plate*) latta; (*container*) scatola; (*BRIT: can*) barattolo (di latta), lattina; **~foil** *n* stagnola

tinge [tɪndʒ] *n* sfumatura ♦ *vt*: **~d with** tinto(a) di

tingle ['tɪŋgl] *vi* pizzicare

tinker ['tɪŋkə*]: **~ with** *vt fus* armeggiare intorno a; cercare di riparare

tinned [tɪnd] (*BRIT*) *adj* (*food*) in scatola

tin opener ['-əʊpnə*] (*BRIT*) *n* apriscatole *m inv*

tinsel ['tɪnsl] *n* decorazioni *fpl* natalizie (*argentate*)

tint [tɪnt] *n* tinta; **~ed** *adj* (*hair*) tinto(a); (*spectacles, glass*) colorato(a)

tiny ['taɪnɪ] *adj* minuscolo(a)

tip [tɪp] *n* (*end*) punta; (*gratuity*) mancia; (*BRIT: for rubbish*) immondezzaio; (*advice*) suggerimento ♦ *vt* (*waiter*) dare la mancia a; (*tilt*) inclinare; (*overturn: also: ~ over*) capovolgere; (*empty: also: ~ out*) scaricare; **~-off** *n* (*hint*) soffiata; **~ped** (*BRIT*) *adj* (*cigarette*) col filtro

Tipp-Ex ® ['tɪpeks] *n* correttore *m*

tipsy ['tɪpsɪ] *adj* brillo(a)

tiptoe ['tɪptəʊ] *n*: **on ~** in punta di piedi

tiptop ['tɪp'tɒp] *adj*: **in ~ condition** in ottime condizioni

tire ['taɪə*] *n* (*US*) = **tyre** ♦ *vt* stancare ♦ *vi* stancarsi; **~d** *adj* stanco(a); **to be ~d of** essere stanco *or* stufo di; **~less** *adj* instancabile; **~some** *adj* noioso(a); **tiring** *adj* faticoso(a)

tissue ['tɪʃuː] *n* tessuto; (*paper handkerchief*) fazzoletto di carta; **~ paper** *n* carta velina

tit [tɪt] *n* (*bird*) cinciallegra; **to give ~ for tat** rendere pan per focaccia

titbit ['tɪtbɪt] (*BRIT*) *n* (*food*) leccornia; (*news*) notizia ghiotta

title ['taɪtl] *n* titolo; **~ deed** *n* (*LAW*) titolo di proprietà; **~ role** *n* ruolo *or* parte *f* principale

TM *abbr* = **trademark**

KEYWORD

to [tuː, tə] *prep* **1** (*direction*) a; **to go ~ France/London/school** andare in Francia/a Londra/a scuola; **to go ~ Paul's/the doctor's** andare da Paul/dal dottore; **the road ~ Edinburgh** la strada per Edimburgo; **~ the left/right** a sinistra/destra

2 (*as far as*) (fino) a; **from here ~ London** da qui a Londra; **to count ~ 10** contare fino a 10; **from 40 ~ 50 people** da 40 a 50 persone

3 (with expressions of time): **a quarter ~ 5** le 5 meno un quarto; **it's twenty ~ 3** sono le 3 meno venti

4 (for, of): **the key ~ the front door** la chiave della porta d'ingresso; **a letter ~ his wife** una lettera per la moglie

5 (expressing indirect object) a; **to give sth ~ sb** dare qc a qn; **to talk ~ sb** parlare a qn; **to be a danger ~ sb/sth** rappresentare un pericolo per qn/qc

6 (in relation to) a; **3 goals ~ 2** 3 goal a 2; **30 miles ~ the gallon** ≈ 11 chilometri con un litro

7 (purpose, result): **to come ~ sb's aid** venire in aiuto a qn; **to sentence sb ~ death** condannare a morte qn; **~ my surprise** con mia sorpresa

♦ with vb 1 (simple infinitive): **go/eat** etc andare/mangiare etc

2 (following another vb): **to want/try/start ~ do** volere/cercare di/cominciare a fare

3 (with vb omitted): **I don't want ~** non voglio (farlo); **you ought ~** devi (farlo)

4 (purpose, result) per; **I did it ~ help you** l'ho fatto per aiutarti

5 (equivalent to relative clause): **I have things ~ do** ho da fare; **the main thing is ~ try** la cosa più importante è provare

6 (after adjective etc): **ready ~ go** pronto a partire; **too old/young ~ ...** troppo vecchio/giovane per ...

♦ adv: **to push the door ~** accostare la porta

toad [təʊd] n rospo; **~stool** n fungo (velenoso)

toast [təʊst] n (CULIN) pane m tostato; (drink, speech) brindisi m inv ♦ vt (CULIN) tostare; (drink to) brindare a; **a piece** or **slice of ~** una fetta di pane tostato; **~er** n tostapane m inv

tobacco [təˈbækəʊ] n tabacco; **~nist** n tabaccaio/a; **~nist's (shop)** n tabaccheria

toboggan [təˈbɒɡən] n toboga m inv

today [təˈdeɪ] adv oggi ♦ n (also fig) oggi m

toddler [ˈtɒdlə*] n bambino/a che impara a camminare

toe [təʊ] n dito del piede; (of shoe) punta; **to ~ the line** (fig) stare in riga, conformarsi; **~nail** n unghia del piede

toffee [ˈtɒfɪ] n caramella; **~ apple** n mela caramellata

toga [ˈtəʊɡə] n toga

together [təˈɡeðə*] adv insieme; (at same time) allo stesso tempo; **~ with** insieme a

toil [tɔɪl] n travaglio, fatica ♦ vi affannarsi; sgobbare

toilet [ˈtɔɪlət] n (BRIT: lavatory) gabinetto ♦ cpd (bag, soap etc) da toletta; **~ paper** n carta igienica; **~ries** npl articoli mpl da toletta; **~ roll** n rotolo di carta igienica; **~ water** n acqua di colonia

token [ˈtəʊkən] n (sign) segno; (substitute coin) gettone m; **book/record/gift ~** (BRIT) buono-libro/disco/regalo

told [təʊld] pt, pp of **tell**

tolerable [ˈtɒlərəbl] adj (bearable) tollerabile; (fairly good) passabile

tolerant [ˈtɒlərnt] adj: **~ (of)** tollerante (nei confronti di)

tolerate [ˈtɒləreɪt] vt sopportare; (MED, TECH) tollerare

toll [təʊl] n (tax, charge) pedaggio ♦ vi (bell) suonare; **the accident ~ on the roads** il numero delle vittime della strada

tomato [təˈmɑːtəʊ] (pl **~es**) n pomodoro

tomb [tuːm] n tomba

tomboy [ˈtɒmbɔɪ] n maschiaccio

tombstone [ˈtuːmstəʊn] n pietra tombale

tomcat [ˈtɒmkæt] n gatto

tomorrow [təˈmɒrəʊ] adv domani ♦ n (also fig) domani m inv; **the day after ~** dopodomani; **~ morning** domani mattina

ton [tʌn] n tonnellata (BRIT = 1016 kg; US = 907 kg; metric = 1000 kg); **~s of** (inf) un mucchio or sacco di

tone [təʊn] n tono ♦ vi (also: **~ in**) intonarsi; **~ down** vt (colour, criticism, sound) attenuare; **~ up** vt (muscles) tonificare; **~-deaf** adj che non ha orecchio (musicale)

tongs [tɒŋz] npl tenaglie fpl; (for coal) molle fpl; (for hair) arricciacapelli m inv

tongue [tʌŋ] n lingua; **~ in cheek** (say, speak) ironicamente; **~-tied** adj (fig) muto(a); **~-twister** n scioglilingua m inv

tonic ['tɒnɪk] n (MED) tonico; (also: **~ water**) acqua tonica

tonight [tə'naɪt] adv stanotte; (this evening) stasera ♦ n questa notte; questa sera

tonnage ['tʌnɪdʒ] n (NAUT) tonnellaggio, stazza

tonsil ['tɒnsl] n tonsilla; **~litis** [-'laɪtɪs] n tonsillite f

too [tuː] adv (excessively) troppo; (also) anche; **~ much** adv troppo ♦ adj troppo(a); **~ many** troppi(e)

took [tuk] pt of **take**

tool [tuːl] n utensile m, attrezzo; **~ box** n cassetta f portautensili

toot [tuːt] n (of horn) colpo di clacson; (of whistle) fischio ♦ vi suonare; (with car horn) suonare il clacson

tooth [tuːθ] (pl **teeth**) n (ANAT, TECH) dente m; **~ache** n mal m di denti; **~brush** n spazzolino da denti; **~paste** n dentifricio; **~pick** n stuzzicadenti m inv

top [tɒp] n (of mountain, page, ladder) cima; (of box, cupboard, table) sopra m inv, parte f superiore; (lid: of box, jar) coperchio; (: of bottle) tappo; (blouse etc) sopra m inv; (toy) trottola ♦ adj più alto(a); (in rank) primo(a); (best) migliore ♦ vt (exceed) superare; (be first in) essere in testa a; **on ~ of** sopra, in cima a; (in addition to) oltre a; **from ~ to bottom** da cima a fondo; **~ up** (US **~ off**) vt riempire; (salary) integrare; **~ floor** n ultimo piano; **~ hat** n cilindro; **~-heavy** adj (object) con la parte superiore troppo pesante

topic ['tɒpɪk] n argomento; **~al** adj d'attualità

top: ~less adj (bather etc) col seno scoperto; **~-level** adj (talks) ad alto livello; **~most** adj il(la) più alto(a)

topple ['tɒpl] vt rovesciare, far cadere ♦ vi cadere; traballare

top-secret adj segretissimo(a)

topsy-turvy ['tɒpsɪ'tɜːvɪ] adj, adv sottosopra inv

torch [tɔːtʃ] n torcia; (BRIT: electric) lampadina tascabile

tore [tɔː*] pt of **tear¹**

torment [n 'tɔːment, vb tɔː'ment] n tormento ♦ vt tormentare

torn [tɔːn] pp of **tear¹**

torpedo [tɔː'piːdəu] (pl **~es**) n siluro

torrent ['tɒrnt] n torrente m

torrid ['tɒrɪd] adj torrido(a); (love affair) infuocato(a)

tortoise ['tɔːtəs] n tartaruga; **~shell** ['tɔːtəʃel] adj di tartaruga

torture ['tɔːtʃə*] n tortura ♦ vt torturare

Tory ['tɔːrɪ] (BRIT: POL) adj dei tories, conservatore(trice) ♦ n tory m/f inv, conservatore/trice

toss [tɒs] vt gettare, lanciare; (one's head) scuotere; **to ~ a coin** fare a testa o croce; **to ~ up for sth** fare a testa o croce per qc; **to ~ and turn** (in bed) girarsi e rigirarsi

tot [tɒt] n (BRIT: drink) bicchierino; (child) bimbo/a

total ['təutl] adj totale ♦ n totale m ♦ vt (add up) sommare; (amount to) ammontare a

totally ['təutəlɪ] adv completamente

touch [tʌtʃ] n tocco; (sense) tatto; (contact) contatto ♦ vt toccare; **a ~ of** (fig) un tocco di; un pizzico di; **to get in ~ with** mettersi in contatto con; **to lose ~** (friends) perdersi di vista; **~ on** vt fus (topic) sfiorare, accennare a; **~ up** vt (paint) ritoccare; **~-and-go** adj incerto(a); **~down** n atterraggio; (on sea) ammaraggio; (US: FOOTBALL) meta; **~ed** adj commosso(a); **~ing** adj commovente; **~line** n (SPORT) linea laterale; **~y** adj (person) suscettibile

tough [tʌf] adj duro(a); (resistant) resistente; **~en** vt rinforzare

toupee ['tuːpeɪ] n parrucchino

tour ['tuə*] n viaggio; (also: **package ~**) viaggio organizzato or tutto compreso; (of town, museum) visita; (by artist) tournée f inv ♦ vt visitare; **~ guide** n guida turistica; **~ing** n turismo

tourism ['tuərɪzəm] n turismo

tourist ['tuərɪst] n turista m/f ♦ adv (travel) in classe turistica ♦ cpd turistico(a); **~ office** n pro loco f inv

tournament ['tuənəmənt] n torneo

tousled ['tauzld] adj (hair) arruffato(a)

tout [taut] vi: **to ~ for** procacciare, raccogliere; cercare clienti per ♦ n (also: **ticket ~**) bagarino

tow [təu] vt rimorchiare; **"on ~"** (BRIT), **"in ~"** (US) "veicolo rimorchiato"

toward(s) [tə'wɔ:d(z)] prep verso; (of attitude) nei confronti di; (of purpose) per

towel ['tauəl] n asciugamano; (also: **tea ~**) strofinaccio; **~ling** n (fabric) spugna; **~ rail** (US **~ rack**) n portasciugamano

tower ['tauə*] n torre f; **~ block** (BRIT) n palazzone m; **~ing** adj altissimo(a), imponente

town [taun] n città f inv; **to go to ~** andare in città; (fig) mettercela tutta; **~ centre** n centro (città); **~ council** n consiglio comunale; **~ hall** n ≈ municipio; **~ plan** n pianta della città; **~ planning** n urbanistica

towrope ['təurəup] n (cavo da) rimorchio

tow truck (US) n carro m attrezzi inv

toxic ['tɔksɪk] adj tossico(a)

toy [tɔɪ] n giocattolo; **~ with** vt fus giocare con; (idea) accarezzare, trastullarsi con; **~ shop** n negozio di giocattoli

trace [treɪs] n traccia ♦ vt (draw) tracciare; (follow) seguire; (locate) rintracciare; **tracing paper** n carta da ricalco

track [træk] n (of person, animal) traccia; (on tape, SPORT, path, gen) pista; (: of bullet etc) traiettoria; (: of suspect, animal) pista, tracce fpl; (RAIL) binario, rotaie fpl ♦ vt seguire le tracce di; **to keep ~ of** seguire; **~ down** vt (prey) scovare; snidare; (sth lost) rintracciare; **~suit** n tuta sportiva

tract [trækt] n (GEO) tratto, estensione f

tractor ['træktə*] n trattore m

trade [treɪd] n commercio; (skill, job) mestiere m ♦ vi commerciare ♦ vt: **to ~ sth (for sth)** barattare qc (con qc); **to ~ with/in** commerciare con/in; **~ in** vt (old car etc) dare come pagamento parziale; **~ fair** n fiera commerciale; **~mark** n marchio di fabbrica; **~ name** n marca, nome m depositato; **~r** n commerciante m/f;

~sman (irreg) n fornitore m; (shopkeeper) negoziante m; **~ union** n sindacato; **~ unionist** n sindacalista m/f

tradition [trə'dɪʃən] n tradizione f; **~al** adj tradizionale

traffic ['træfɪk] n traffico ♦ vi: **to ~ in** (pej: liquor, drugs) trafficare in; **~ circle** (US) n isola rotatoria; **~ jam** n ingorgo (del traffico); **~ lights** npl semaforo; **~ warden** n addetto/a al controllo del traffico e del parcheggio

tragedy ['trædʒədɪ] n tragedia

tragic ['trædʒɪk] adj tragico(a)

trail [treɪl] n (tracks) tracce fpl, pista; (path) sentiero; (of smoke etc) scia ♦ vt trascinare, strascicare; (follow) seguire ♦ vi essere al traino; (dress etc) strusciare; (plant) arrampicarsi; strisciare; (in game) essere in svantaggio; **~ behind** vi essere al traino; **~er** n (AUT) rimorchio; (US) roulotte f inv; (CINEMA) prossimamente m inv; **~er truck** (US) n (articulated lorry) autoarticolato

train [treɪn] n treno; (of dress) coda, strascico ♦ vt (apprentice, doctor etc) formare; (sportsman) allenare; (dog) addestrare; (memory) esercitare; (point: gun etc): **to ~ sth on** puntare qc contro ♦ vi formarsi; allenarsi; **one's ~ of thought** il filo dei propri pensieri; **~ed** adj qualificato(a); allenato(a); addestrato(a); **~ee** [treɪ'ni:] n (in trade) apprendista m/f; **~er** n (SPORT) allenatore/trice; (: shoe) scarpa da ginnastica; (of dogs etc) addestratore/trice; **~ing** n formazione f; allenamento; addestramento; **in ~ing** (SPORT) in allenamento; **~ing college** n istituto professionale; (for teachers) ≈ istituto magistrale; **~ing shoes** npl scarpe fpl da ginnastica

trait [treɪt] n tratto

traitor ['treɪtə*] n traditore m

tram [træm] (BRIT) n (also: **~car**) tram m inv

tramp [træmp] n (person) vagabondo/a; (inf: pej: woman) sgualdrina

trample ['træmpl] vt: **to ~ (underfoot)** calpestare

trampoline ['træmpəli:n] n trampolino

tranquil ['træŋkwɪl] *adj* tranquillo(a); **~lizer** *n* (*MED*) tranquillante *m*

transact [træn'zækt] *vt* (*business*) trattare; **~ion** [-'zækʃən] *n* transazione *f*

transatlantic ['trænzət'læntɪk] *adj* transatlantico(a)

transfer [*n* 'trænsfə*, *vb* træns'fə*] *n* (*gen, also SPORT*) trasferimento; (*POL: of power*) passaggio; (*picture, design*) decalcomania; (: *stick-on*) autoadesivo ♦ *vt* trasferire; passare; **to ~ the charges** (*BRIT: TEL*) fare una chiamata a carico del destinatario; **~ desk** *n* (*AVIAT*) banco *m* transiti *inv*

transform [træns'fɔ:m] *vt* trasformare

transfusion [træns'fju:ʒən] *n* trasfusione *f*

transient ['trænzɪənt] *adj* transitorio(a), fugace

transistor [træn'zɪstə*] *n* (*ELEC*) transistor *m inv*; (*also:* **~ radio**) radio *f inv* a transistor

transit ['trænzɪt] *n*: **in ~** in transito

transitive ['trænzɪtɪv] *adj* (*LING*) transitivo(a)

translate [trænz'leɪt] *vt* tradurre; **translation** [-'leɪʃən] *n* traduzione *f*; **translator** *n* traduttore/trice

transmission [trænz'mɪʃən] *n* trasmissione *f*

transmit [trænz'mɪt] *vt* trasmettere; **~ter** *n* trasmettitore *m*

transparency [træns'pɛərənsɪ] *n* trasparenza; (*BRIT: PHOT*) diapositiva

transparent [træns'pærnt] *adj* trasparente

transpire [træn'spaɪə*] *vi* (*happen*) succedere; (*turn out*): **it ~d that** si venne a sapere che

transplant [*vb* træns'plɑ:nt, *n* 'trænsplɑ:nt] *vt* trapiantare ♦ *n* (*MED*) trapianto

transport [*n* 'trænspɔ:t, *vb* træns'pɔ:t] *n* trasporto ♦ *vt* trasportare; **~ation** [-'teɪʃən] *n* (mezzo di) trasporto; **~ café** (*BRIT*) *n* trattoria per camionisti

trap [træp] *n* (*snare, trick*) trappola; (*carriage*) calesse *m* ♦ *vt* prendere in trappola, intrappolare; **~ door** *n* botola

trapeze [trə'pi:z] *n* trapezio

trappings ['træpɪŋz] *npl* ornamenti *mpl*; indoratura, sfarzo

trash [træʃ] (*pej*) *n* (*goods*) ciarpame *m*;

(*nonsense*) sciocchezze *fpl*; **~ can** (*US*) *n* secchio della spazzatura

trauma ['trɔ:mə] *n* trauma *m*; **~tic** [-'mætɪk] *adj* traumatico(a)

travel ['trævl] *n* viaggio; viaggi *mpl* ♦ *vi* viaggiare ♦ *vt* (*distance*) percorrere; **~ agency** *n* agenzia (di) viaggi; **~ agent** *n* agente *m* di viaggio; **~ler** (*US* **~er**) *n* viaggiatore/trice; **~ler's cheque** (*US* **~er's check**) *n* assegno turistico; **~ling** (*US* **~ing**) *n* viaggi *mpl*; **~ sickness** *n* mal *m* d'auto (*or* di mare *or* d'aria)

travesty ['trævəstɪ] *n* parodia

trawler ['trɔ:lə*] *n* peschereccio (a strascico)

tray [treɪ] *n* (*for carrying*) vassoio; (*on desk*) vaschetta

treacherous ['trɛtʃərəs] *adj* infido(a)

treachery ['trɛtʃərɪ] *n* tradimento

treacle ['tri:kl] *n* melassa

tread [trɛd] (*pt* **trod**, *pp* **trodden**) *n* passo; (*sound*) rumore *m* di passi; (*of stairs*) pedata; (*of tyre*) battistrada *m inv* ♦ *vi* camminare; **~ on** *vt fus* calpestare

treason ['tri:zn] *n* tradimento

treasure ['trɛʒə*] *n* tesoro ♦ *vt* (*value*) tenere in gran conto, apprezzare molto; (*store*) custodire gelosamente

treasurer ['trɛʒərə*] *n* tesoriere/a

treasury ['trɛʒərɪ] *n*: **the T~** (*BRIT*), **the T~ Department** (*US*) il ministero del Tesoro

treat [tri:t] *n* regalo ♦ *vt* trattare; (*MED*) curare; **to ~ sb to sth** offrire qc a qn

treatment ['tri:tmənt] *n* trattamento

treaty ['tri:tɪ] *n* patto, trattato

treble ['trɛbl] *adj* triplo(a), triplice ♦ *vt* triplicare ♦ *vi* triplicarsi; **~ clef** *n* chiave *f* di violino

tree [tri:] *n* albero; **~ trunk** *n* tronco d'albero

trek [trɛk] *n* escursione *f* a piedi; escursione *f* in macchina; (*tiring walk*) camminata sfiancante ♦ *vi* (*as holiday*) fare dell'escursionismo

trellis ['trɛlɪs] *n* graticcio

tremble ['trɛmbl] *vi* tremare

tremendous [trɪ'mɛndəs] *adj* (*enormous*) enorme; (*excellent*) meraviglioso(a), formidabile

tremor ['tremə*] *n* tremore *m*, tremito; (*also*: **earth ~**) scossa sismica

trench [trentʃ] *n* trincea

trend [trend] *n* (*tendency*) tendenza; (*of events*) corso; (*fashion*) moda; ~**y** *adj* (*idea*) di moda; (*clothes*) all'ultima moda

trespass ['trespəs] *vi*: **to ~ on** entrare abusivamente in; **"no ~ing"** "proprietà privata", "vietato l'accesso"

trestle ['tresl] *n* cavalletto

trial ['traɪəl] *n* (*LAW*) processo; (*test: of machine etc*) collaudo; ~**s** *npl* (*unpleasant experiences*) dure prove *fpl*; **on ~** (*LAW*) sotto processo; **by ~ and error** a tentoni; ~ **period** periodo di prova

triangle ['traɪæŋgl] *n* (*MATH, MUS*) triangolo

tribe [traɪb] *n* tribù *f inv*; ~**sman** (*irreg*) *n* membro di tribù

tribunal [traɪˈbjuːnl] *n* tribunale *m*

tributary ['trɪbjuːtərɪ] *n* (*river*) tributario, affluente *m*

tribute ['trɪbjuːt] *n* tributo, omaggio; **to pay ~ to** rendere omaggio a

trick [trɪk] *n* trucco; (*joke*) tiro; (*CARDS*) presa ♦ *vt* imbrogliare, ingannare; **to play a ~ on sb** giocare un tiro a qn; **that should do the ~** vedrai che funziona; ~**ery** *n* inganno

trickle ['trɪkl] *n* (*of water etc*) rivolo; gocciolio ♦ *vi* gocciolare

tricky ['trɪkɪ] *adj* difficile, delicato(a)

tricycle ['traɪsɪkl] *n* triciclo

trifle ['traɪfl] *n* sciocchezza; (*BRIT: CULIN*) ≈ zuppa inglese ♦ *adv*: **a ~ long** un po' lungo; **trifling** *adj* insignificante

trigger ['trɪgə*] *n* (*of gun*) grilletto; ~ **off** *vt* dare l'avvio a

trim [trɪm] *adj* (*house, garden*) ben tenuto(a); (*figure*) snello(a) ♦ *n* (*haircut etc*) spuntata, regolata; (*embellishment*) finiture *fpl*; (*on car*) guarnizioni *fpl* ♦ *vt* spuntare; (*decorate*): **to ~ (with)** decorare (con); (*NAUT: a sail*) orientare; ~**mings** *npl* decorazioni *fpl*; (*extras: gen CULIN*) guarnizione *f*

trinket ['trɪŋkɪt] *n* gingillo; (*piece of jewellery*) ciondolo

trip [trɪp] *n* viaggio; (*excursion*) gita, escursione *f*; (*stumble*) passo falso ♦ *vi* inciampare; (*go lightly*) camminare con passo leggero; **on a ~** in viaggio; ~ **up** *vi* inciampare ♦ *vt* fare lo sgambetto a

tripe [traɪp] *n* (*CULIN*) trippa; (*pej: rubbish*) sciocchezze *fpl*, fesserie *fpl*

triple ['trɪpl] *adj* triplo(a)

triplets ['trɪplɪts] *npl* bambini(e) trigemini(e)

triplicate ['trɪplɪkət] *n*: **in ~** in triplice copia

tripod ['traɪpɔd] *n* treppiede *m*

trite [traɪt] *adj* banale, trito(a)

triumph ['traɪʌmf] *n* trionfo ♦ *vi*: **to ~ (over)** trionfare (su)

trivia ['trɪvɪə] *npl* banalità *fpl*

trivial ['trɪvɪəl] *adj* insignificante; (*commonplace*) banale

trod [trɔd] *pt of* **tread**; ~**den** *pp of* **tread**

trolley ['trɔlɪ] *n* carrello; ~ **bus** *n* filobus *m inv*

trombone [trɔmˈbəun] *n* trombone *m*

troop [truːp] *n* gruppo; (*MIL*) squadrone *m*; ~**s** *npl* (*MIL*) truppe *fpl*; ~ **in/out** *vi* entrare/uscire a frotte; ~**ing the colour** *n* (*ceremony*) sfilata della bandiera

trophy ['trəufɪ] *n* trofeo

tropic ['trɔpɪk] *n* tropico; ~**al** *adj* tropicale

trot [trɔt] *n* trotto ♦ *vi* trottare; **on the ~** (*BRIT: fig*) di fila, uno(a) dopo l'altro(a)

trouble ['trʌbl] *n* difficoltà *f inv*, problema *m*; difficoltà *fpl*, problemi; (*worry*) preoccupazione *f*; (*bother, effort*) sforzo; (*POL*) conflitti *mpl*, disordine *m*; (*MED*): **stomach** *etc* ~ disturbi *mpl* gastrici *etc* ♦ *vt* disturbare; (*worry*) preoccupare ♦ *vi*: **to ~ to do** disturbarsi a fare; ~**s** *npl* (*POL etc*) disordini *mpl*; **to be in ~** avere dei problemi; **it's no ~!** di niente!; **what's the ~?** cosa c'è che non va?; ~**d** *adj* (*person*) preoccupato(a), inquieto(a); (*epoch, life*) agitato(a), difficile; ~**maker** *n* elemento disturbatore, agitatore/trice; (*child*) disloco/a; ~**shooter** *n* (*in conflict*) conciliatore *m*; ~**some** *adj* fastidioso(a), seccante

trough [trɔf] *n* (*also*: **drinking ~**) abbeveratoio; (*also*: **feeding ~**) trogolo, mangiatoia; (*channel*) canale *m*

trousers ['trauzəz] *npl* pantaloni *mpl*, calzoni *mpl*; **short ~** calzoncini *mpl*

trousseau ['tru:səu] (*pl* **~x** *or* **~s**) *n* corredo da sposa

trousseaux ['tru:səuz] *npl of* trousseau

trout [traut] *n inv* trota

trowel ['trauəl] *n* cazzuola

truant ['truənt] (*BRIT*) *n*: **to play ~** marinare la scuola

truce [tru:s] *n* tregua

truck [trʌk] *n* autocarro, camion *m inv*; (*RAIL*) carro merci aperto; (*for luggage*) carrello *m* portabagagli *inv*; **~ driver** *n* camionista *m/f*; **~ farm** (*US*) *n* orto industriale

true [tru:] *adj* vero(a); (*accurate*) accurato(a), esatto(a); (*genuine*) reale; (*faithful*) fedele; **to come ~** avverarsi

truffle ['trʌfl] *n* tartufo

truly ['tru:lɪ] *adv* veramente; (*truthfully*) sinceramente; (*faithfully*): **yours ~** (*in letter*) distinti saluti

trump [trʌmp] *n* (*also*: **~ card**) atout *m inv*

trumpet ['trʌmpɪt] *n* tromba

truncheon ['trʌntʃən] *n* sfollagente *m inv*

trundle ['trʌndl] *vt* far rotolare rumorosamente ♦ *vi*: **to ~ along** rotolare rumorosamente

trunk [trʌŋk] *n* (*of tree, person*) tronco; (*of elephant*) proboscide *f*; (*case*) baule *m*; (*US*: *AUT*) bagagliaio; **~s** *npl* (*also*: **swimming ~s**) calzoncini *mpl* da bagno

truss [trʌs] *vt*: **~ (up)** (*CULIN*) legare

trust [trʌst] *n* fiducia; (*LAW*) amministrazione *f* fiduciaria; (*COMM*) trust *m inv* ♦ *vt* (*rely on*) contare su; (*hope*) sperare; (*entrust*): **to ~ sth to sb** affidare qc a qn; **~ed** *adj* fidato(a); **~ee** [trʌs'ti:] *n* (*LAW*) amministratore(trice) fiduciario(a); (*of school etc*) amministratore/trice; **~ful** *adj* fiducioso(a); **~ing** *adj* = **~ful**; **~worthy** *adj* fidato(a), degno(a) di fiducia

truth [tru:θ, *pl* tru:ðz] *n* verità *f inv*; **~ful** *adj* (*person*) sincero(a); (*description*) veritiero(a), esatto(a)

try [traɪ] *n* prova, tentativo; (*RUGBY*) meta

♦ *vt* (*LAW*) giudicare; (*test*: *also*: **~ out**) provare; (*strain*) mettere alla prova ♦ *vi* provare; **to have a ~** fare un tentativo; **to ~ to do** (*seek*) cercare di fare; **~ on** *vt* (*clothes*) provare; **~ing** *adj* (*day*, *experience*) logorante, pesante; (*child*) difficile, insopportabile

tsar [zɑ:*] *n* zar *m inv*

T-shirt ['ti:-] *n* maglietta

T-square ['ti:-] *n* riga a T

tub [tʌb] *n* tinozza; mastello; (*bath*) bagno

tuba ['tju:bə] *n* tuba

tubby ['tʌbɪ] *adj* grassoccio(a)

tube [tju:b] *n* tubo; (*BRIT*: *underground*) metropolitana, metrò *m inv*; (*for tyre*) camera d'aria; **~ station** (*BRIT*) *n* stazione *f* della metropolitana

tubular ['tju:bjulə*] *adj* tubolare

TUC (*BRIT*) *n abbr* (= *Trades Union Congress*) confederazione *f* dei sindacati britannici

tuck [tʌk] *vt* (*put*) mettere; **~ away** *vt* riporre; (*building*): **to be ~ed away** essere in un luogo isolato; **~ in** *vt* mettere dentro; (*child*) rimboccare ♦ *vi* (*eat*) mangiare di buon appetito; abbuffarsi; **~ up** *vt* (*child*) rimboccare le coperte a; **~ shop** *n* negozio di pasticceria (*in una scuola*)

Tuesday ['tju:zdɪ] *n* martedì *m inv*

tuft [tʌft] *n* ciuffo

tug [tʌg] *n* (*ship*) rimorchiatore *m* ♦ *vt* tirare con forza; **~-of-war** *n* tiro alla fune

tuition [tju:'ɪʃən] *n* (*BRIT*) lezioni *fpl*; (: *private* ~) lezioni *fpl* private; (*US*: *school fees*) tasse *fpl* scolastiche

tulip ['tju:lɪp] *n* tulipano

tumble ['tʌmbl] *n* (*fall*) capitombolo ♦ *vi* capitombolare, ruzzolare; **to ~ to sth** (*inf*) realizzare qc; **~down** *adj* cadente, diroccato(a); **~ dryer** (*BRIT*) *n* asciugatrice *f*

tumbler ['tʌmblə*] *n* bicchiere *m* (*senza stelo*)

tummy ['tʌmɪ] (*inf*) *n* pancia; **~ upset** *n* mal *m* di pancia

tumour ['tju:mə*] (*US* **tumor**) *n* tumore *m*

tuna ['tjuːnə] *n inv* (*also:* ~ **fish**) tonno
tune [tjuːn] *n* (*melody*) melodia, aria ♦ *vt*
(*MUS*) accordare; (*RADIO, TV, AUT*) regolare,
mettere a punto; **to be in/out of** ~
(*instrument*) essere accordato(a)/
scordato(a); (*singer*) essere intonato(a)/
stonato(a); ~ **in** *vi:* **to** ~ **in (to)** (*RADIO, TV*)
sintonizzarsi (su); ~ **up** *vi* (*musician*)
accordare lo strumento; **~ful** *adj*
melodioso(a); **~r** *n:* **piano ~r** accordatore
m
tunic ['tjuːnɪk] *n* tunica
Tunisia [tjuːˈnɪzɪə] *n* Tunisia
tunnel ['tʌnl] *n* galleria ♦ *vi* scavare una
galleria
turban ['təːbən] *n* turbante *m*
turbulence ['təːbjuləns] *n* (*AVIAT*)
turbolenza
tureen [təˈriːn] *n* zuppiera
turf [təːf] *n* terreno erboso; (*clod*) zolla ♦ *vt*
coprire di zolle erbose; ~ **out** (*inf*) *vt*
buttar fuori
Turin [tjuəˈrɪn] *n* Torino *f*
Turk [təːk] *n* turco/a
Turkey ['təːkɪ] *n* Turchia
turkey ['təːkɪ] *n* tacchino
Turkish ['təːkɪʃ] *adj* turco(a) ♦ *n* (*LING*)
turco
turmoil ['təːmɔɪl] *n* confusione *f*, tumulto
turn [təːn] *n* giro; (*change*) cambiamento;
(*in road*) curva; (*tendency: of mind, events*)
tendenza; (*performance*) numero; (*chance*)
turno; (*MED*) crisi *f inv*, attacco ♦ *vt* girare,
voltare; (*change*): **to** ~ **sth into** trasformare
qc in ♦ *vi* girare; (*person: look back*) girarsi,
voltarsi; (*reverse direction*) girare; (*change*)
cambiare; (*milk*) andare a male; (*become*)
diventare; **a good** ~ un buon servizio; **it**
gave me quite a ~ mi ha fatto prendere
un bello spavento; **"no left** ~**"** (*AUT*)
"divieto di svolta a sinistra"; **it's your** ~
tocca a lei; **in** ~ a sua volta; a turno; **to**
take ~s (at sth) fare (qc) a turno; ~ **away**
vi girarsi (dall'altra parte) ♦ *vt* mandare via;
~ **back** *vi* ritornare, tornare indietro ♦ *vt*
far tornare indietro; (*clock*) spostare
indietro; ~ **down** *vt* (*refuse*) rifiutare;

(*reduce*) abbassare; (*fold*) ripiegare; ~ **in** *vi*
(*inf: go to bed*) andare a letto ♦ *vt* (*fold*)
voltare in dentro; ~ **off** *vi* (*from road*)
girare, voltare ♦ *vt* (*light, radio, engine etc*)
spegnere; ~ **on** *vt* (*light, radio etc*)
accendere; ~ **out** *vt* (*light, gas*) chiudere;
spegnere ♦ *vi* (*voters*) presentarsi; **to** ~ **out**
to be ... rivelarsi ..., risultare ...; ~ **over** *vi*
(*person*) girarsi ♦ *vt* girare; ~ **round** *vi*
girare; (*person*) girarsi ♦ *vt* girare; ~ **up** *vi* (*person*)
arrivare, presentarsi; (*lost object*) saltar fuori
♦ *vt* (*collar, sound*) alzare; **~ing** *n* (*in road*)
curva; **~ing point** *n* (*fig*) svolta decisiva
turnip ['təːnɪp] *n* rapa
turnout ['təːnaut] *n* presenza, affluenza
turnover ['təːnəuvə*] *n* (*COMM*) turnover *m*
inv; (*CULIN*): **apple** *etc* ~ sfogliatella alle
mele *ecc*
turnpike ['təːnpaɪk] (*US*) *n* autostrada a
pedaggio
turnstile ['təːnstaɪl] *n* tornella
turntable ['təːnteɪbl] *n* (*on record player*)
piatto
turn-up (*BRIT*) *n* (*on trousers*) risvolto
turpentine ['təːpəntaɪn] *n* (*also:* **turps**)
acqua ragia
turquoise ['təːkwɔɪz] *n* turchese *m* ♦ *adj*
turchese
turret ['tʌrɪt] *n* torretta
turtle ['təːtl] *n* testuggine *f*; **~neck**
(sweater) *n* maglione *m* con il collo alto
Tuscany ['tʌskənɪ] *n* Toscana
tusk [tʌsk] *n* zanna
tutor ['tjuːtə*] *n* (*in college*) docente *m/f*
(*responsabile di un gruppo di studenti*);
(*private teacher*) precettore *m*; **~ial** [-ˈtɔːrɪəl]
n (*SCOL*) lezione *f* con discussione (*a un
gruppo limitato*)
tuxedo [tʌkˈsiːdəu] (*US*) *n* smoking *m inv*
TV [tiːˈviː] *n abbr* (= *television*) tivù *f inv*
twang [twæŋ] *n* (*of instrument*) suono
vibrante; (*of voice*) accento nasale
tweed [twiːd] *n* tweed *m inv*
tweezers ['twiːzəz] *npl* pinzette *fpl*
twelfth [twelfθ] *num* dodicesimo(a)
twelve [twelv] *num* dodici; **at** ~ (**o'clock**)
alle dodici, a mezzogiorno; (*midnight*) a

mezzanotte

twentieth ['twεntɪθ] *num* ventesimo(a)

twenty ['twεntɪ] *num* venti

twice [twaɪs] *adv* due volte; **~ as much** due volte tanto; **~ a week** due volte alla settimana

twiddle ['twɪdl] *vt, vi*: **to ~ (with) sth** giocherellare con qc; **to ~ one's thumbs** (*fig*) girarsi i pollici

twig [twɪg] *n* ramoscello ♦ *vt, vi* (*inf*) capire

twilight ['twaɪlaɪt] *n* crepuscolo

twin [twɪn] *adj, n* gemello(a) ♦ *vt*: **to ~ one town with another** fare il gemellaggio di una città con un'altra; **~-bedded room** *n* stanza con letti gemelli; **~ beds** *npl* letti *mpl* gemelli

twine [twaɪn] *n* spago, cordicella ♦ *vi* attorcigliarsi

twinge [twɪndʒ] *n* (*of pain*) fitta; **a ~ of conscience/regret** un rimorso/rimpianto

twinkle ['twɪŋkl] *vi* scintillare; (*eyes*) brillare

twirl [twəːl] *vt* far roteare ♦ *vi* roteare

twist [twɪst] *n* torsione *f*; (*in wire, flex*) piega; (*in road*) curva; (*in story*) colpo di scena ♦ *vt* attorcigliare; (*ankle*) slogare; (*weave*) intrecciare; (*roll around*) arrotolare; (*fig*) distorcere ♦ *vi* (*road*) serpeggiare

twit [twɪt] (*inf*) *n* cretino(a)

twitch [twɪtʃ] *n* tiratina; (*nervous*) tic *m inv* ♦ *vi* contrarsi

two [tuː] *num* due; **to put ~ and ~ together** (*fig*) fare uno più uno; **~-door** *adj* (*AUT*) a due porte; **~-faced** (*pej*) *adj* (*person*) falso(a); **~-fold** *adv*: **to increase ~fold** aumentare del doppio; **~-piece (suit)** *n* due pezzi *m inv*; **~-piece (swimsuit)** *n* (costume *m* da bagno a) due pezzi *m inv*; **~some** *n* (*people*) coppia; **~-way** *adj* (*traffic*) a due sensi

tycoon [taɪˈkuːn] *n*: **(business) ~** magnate *m*

type [taɪp] *n* (*category*) genere *m*; (*model*) modello; (*example*) tipo; (*TYP*) tipo, carattere *m* ♦ *vt* (*letter etc*) battere (a macchina), dattilografare; **~-cast** *adj* (*actor*) a ruolo fisso; **~face** *n* carattere *m* tipografico; **~script** *n* dattiloscritto;

~writer *n* macchina da scrivere; **~written** *adj* dattiloscritto(a), battuto(a) a macchina

typhoid ['taɪfɔɪd] *n* tifoidea

typhoon [taɪˈfuːn] *n* tifone *m*

typical ['tɪpɪkl] *adj* tipico(a)

typify ['tɪpɪfaɪ] *vt* caratterizzare; (*person*) impersonare

typing ['taɪpɪŋ] *n* dattilografia

typist ['taɪpɪst] *n* dattilografo/a

tyrant ['taɪərnt] *n* tiranno

tyre ['taɪə*] (*US* tire) *n* pneumatico, gomma; **~ pressure** *n* pressione *f* (delle gomme)

tzar [zɑː*] *n* = **tsar**

U, u

U-bend ['juː'-] *n* (*in pipe*) sifone *m*

ubiquitous [juːˈbɪkwɪtəs] *adj* onnipresente

udder ['ʌdə*] *n* mammella

UFO ['juːfəu] *n abbr* (= *unidentified flying object*) UFO *m inv*

ugh [əːh] *excl* puah!

ugly ['ʌglɪ] *adj* brutto(a)

UHT *abbr* (= *ultra heat treated*) UHT *inv*, a lunga conservazione

UK *n abbr* = **United Kingdom**

ulcer ['ʌlsə*] *n* ulcera; (*also*: **mouth ~**) afta

Ulster ['ʌlstə*] *n* Ulster *m*

ulterior [ʌlˈtɪərɪə*] *adj* ulteriore; **~ motive** *n* secondo fine *m*

ultimate ['ʌltɪmət] *adj* ultimo(a), finale; (*authority*) massimo(a), supremo(a); **~ly** *adv* alla fine; in definitiva, in fin dei conti

ultrasound [ʌltrəˈsaund] *n* (*MED*) ultrasuono

umbilical cord [ʌmbɪˈlaɪkl-] *n* cordone *m* ombelicale

umbrella [ʌmˈbrεlə] *n* ombrello

umpire ['ʌmpaɪə*] *n* arbitro

umpteen [ʌmpˈtiːn] *adj* non so quanti(e); **for the ~th time** per l'ennesima volta

UN *n abbr* (= *United Nations*) ONU *f*

unable [ʌnˈeɪbl] *adj*: **to be ~ to** non potere, essere nell'impossibilità di; essere incapace di

unaccompanied [ʌnəˈkʌmpənɪd] *adj* (*child, lady*) non accompagnato(a)

unaccustomed [ʌnə'kʌstəmd] *adj*: **to be ~ to sth** non essere abituato a qc

unanimous [juː'nænɪməs] *adj* unanime; **~ly** *adv* all'unanimità

unarmed [ʌn'ɑːmd] *adj* (*without a weapon*) disarmato(a); (*combat*) senz'armi

unattached [ʌnə'tætʃt] *adj* senza legami, libero(a)

unattended [ʌnə'tɛndɪd] *adj* (*car, child, luggage*) incustodito(a)

unattractive [ʌnə'træktɪv] *adj* poco attraente

unauthorized [ʌn'ɔːθəraɪzd] *adj* non autorizzato(a)

unavoidable [ʌnə'vɔɪdəbl] *adj* inevitabile

unaware [ʌnə'wɛə*] *adj*: **to be ~ of** non sapere, ignorare; **~s** *adv* di sorpresa, alla sprovvista

unbalanced [ʌn'bælənst] *adj* squilibrato(a)

unbearable [ʌn'bɛərəbl] *adj* insopportabile

unbeknown(st) [ʌnbɪ'nəʊn(st)] *adv*: **~ to** all'insaputa di

unbelievable [ʌnbɪ'liːvəbl] *adj* incredibile

unbend [ʌn'bɛnd] (*irreg like* **bend**) *vi* distendersi ♦ *vt* (*wire*) raddrizzare

unbias(s)ed [ʌn'baɪəst] *adj* (*person, report*) obiettivo(a), imparziale

unborn [ʌn'bɔːn] *adj* non ancora nato(a)

unbreakable [ʌn'breɪkəbl] *adj* infrangibile

unbroken [ʌn'brəʊkən] *adj* intero(a); (*series*) continuo(a); (*record*) imbattuto(a)

unbutton [ʌn'bʌtn] *vt* sbottonare

uncalled for [ʌn'kɔːld-] *adj* (*remark*) fuori luogo *inv*; (*action*) ingiustificato(a)

uncanny [ʌn'kænɪ] *adj* misterioso(a), strano(a)

unceasing [ʌn'siːsɪŋ] *adj* incessante

unceremonious ['ʌnserɪ'məʊnɪəs] *adj* (*abrupt, rude*) senza tante cerimonie

uncertain [ʌn'sɜːtn] *adj* incerto(a); dubbio(a); **~ty** *n* incertezza

unchanged [ʌn'tʃeɪndʒd] *adj* invariato(a)

uncivilized [ʌn'sɪvɪlaɪzd] *adj* (*gen*) selvaggio(a); (*fig*) incivile, barbaro(a)

uncle ['ʌŋkl] *n* zio

uncomfortable [ʌn'kʌmfətəbl] *adj* scomodo(a); (*uneasy*) a disagio, agitato(a);

(*unpleasant*) fastidioso(a)

uncommon [ʌn'kɒmən] *adj* raro(a), insolito(a), non comune

uncompromising [ʌn'kɒmprəmaɪzɪŋ] *adj* intransigente, inflessibile

unconcerned [ʌnkən'sɜːnd] *adj*: **to be ~ (about)** non preoccuparsi (di or per)

unconditional [ʌnkən'dɪʃənl] *adj* incondizionato(a), senza condizioni

unconscious [ʌn'kɒnʃəs] *adj* privo(a) di sensi, svenuto(a); (*unaware*) inconsapevole, inconscio(a) ♦ *n*: **the ~** l'inconscio; **~ly** *adv* inconsciamente

uncontrollable [ʌnkən'trəʊləbl] *adj* incontrollabile; indisciplinato(a)

unconventional [ʌnkən'vɛnʃənl] *adj* poco convenzionale

uncouth [ʌn'kuːθ] *adj* maleducato(a), grossolano(a)

uncover [ʌn'kʌvə*] *vt* scoprire

undecided [ʌndɪ'saɪdɪd] *adj* indeciso(a)

under ['ʌndə*] *prep* sotto; (*less than*) meno di; al disotto di; (*according to*) secondo, in conformità a ♦ *adv* (al) disotto; **~ there** là sotto; **~ repair** in riparazione

under... ['ʌndə*] *prefix* sotto..., sub...; **~-age** *adj* minorenne; **~carriage** (*BRIT*) *n* carrello (d'atterraggio); **~charge** *vt* far pagare di meno a; **~clothes** *npl* biancheria (intima); **~coat** *n* (*paint*) mano *f* di fondo; **~cover** *adj* segreto(a), clandestino(a); **~current** *n* corrente *f* sottomarina; **~cut** *vt irreg* vendere a prezzo minore di; **~developed** *adj* sottosviluppato(a); **~dog** *n* oppresso/a; **~done** *adj* (*CULIN*) al sangue; (*pej*) poco cotto(a); **~estimate** *vt* sottovalutare; **~fed** *adj* denutrito(a); **~foot** *adv* sotto i piedi; **~go** *vt irreg* subire; (*treatment*) sottoporsi a; **~graduate** *n* studente(essa) universitario(a); **~ground** *n* (*BRIT*: *railway*) metropolitana; (*POL*) movimento clandestino ♦ *adj* sotterraneo(a); (*fig*) clandestino(a) ♦ *adv* sottoterra; **to go ~ground** (*fig*) darsi alla macchia; **~growth** *n* sottobosco; **~hand(ed)** *adj* (*fig*) furtivo(a), subdolo(a); **~lie** *vt irreg* essere

alla base di; **~line** *vt* sottolineare; **~mine**
vt minare; **~neath** [ʌndə'niːθ] *adv* sotto,
disotto ♦ *prep* sotto, al di sotto di; **~paid**
adj sottopagato(a); **~pants** *npl* mutande
fpl, slip *m inv*; **~pass** (BRIT) *n*
sottopassaggio; **~privileged** *adj* non
abbiente; meno favorito(a); **~rate** *vt*
sottovalutare; **~shirt** (US) *n* maglietta;
~shorts (US) *npl* mutande *fpl*, slip *m inv*;
~side *n* disotto; **~skirt** (BRIT) *n* sottoveste
f

understand [ʌndə'stænd] (*irreg: like* **stand**)
vt, vi capire, comprendere; **I ~ that ...**
sento che ...; credo di capire che ...; **~able**
adj comprensibile; **~ing** *adj*
comprensivo(a) ♦ *n* comprensione *f*;
(*agreement*) accordo

understatement [ʌndə'steitmənt] *n*:
that's an ~! a dire poco!

understood [ʌndə'stud] *pt, pp of*
understand ♦ *adj* inteso(a); (*implied*)
sottinteso(a)

understudy ['ʌndəstʌdɪ] *n* sostituto/a,
attore/trice supplente

undertake [ʌndə'teik] (*irreg: like* **take**) *vt*
intraprendere; **to ~ to do sth** impegnarsi a
fare qc

undertaker ['ʌndəteikə*] *n* impresario di
pompe funebri

undertaking [ʌndə'teikɪŋ] *n* impresa;
(*promise*) promessa

undertone ['ʌndətəun] *n*: **in an ~** a mezza
voce, a voce bassa

underwater [ʌndə'wɔːtə*] *adv* sott'acqua
♦ *adj* subacqueo(a)

underwear ['ʌndəwεə*] *n* biancheria
(intima)

underworld ['ʌndəwəːld] *n* (*of crime*)
malavita

underwriter ['ʌndəraitə*] *n* (INSURANCE)
sottoscrittore/trice

undesirable [ʌndɪ'zaɪərəbl] *adj* sgradevole

undies ['ʌndɪz] (*inf*) *npl* biancheria intima
da donna

undo [ʌn'duː] *vt irreg* disfare; **~ing** *n* rovina,
perdita

undoubted [ʌn'dautid] *adj* sicuro(a),

certo(a); **~ly** *adv* senza alcun dubbio

undress [ʌn'drεs] *vi* spogliarsi

undue [ʌn'djuː] *adj* eccessivo(a)

undulating ['ʌndjuleitɪŋ] *adj* ondeggiante;
ondulato(a)

unduly [ʌn'djuːlɪ] *adv* eccessivamente

unearth [ʌn'əːθ] *vt* dissotterrare; (*fig*)
scoprire

unearthly [ʌn'əːθlɪ] *adj* (*hour*) impossibile

uneasy [ʌn'iːzɪ] *adj* a disagio; (*worried*)
preoccupato(a); (*peace*) precario(a)

uneconomic(al) ['ʌniːkə'nɔmɪk(l)] *adj*
antieconomico(a)

unemployed [ʌnɪm'plɔɪd] *adj*
disoccupato(a) ♦ *npl*: **the ~** i disoccupati

unemployment [ʌnɪm'plɔɪmənt] *n*
disoccupazione *f*

unending [ʌn'εndɪŋ] *adj* senza fine

unerring [ʌn'əːrɪŋ] *adj* infallibile

uneven [ʌn'iːvn] *adj* ineguale; irregolare

unexpected [ʌnɪk'spεktɪd] *adj* inatteso(a),
imprevisto(a); **~ly** *adv* inaspettatamente

unfailing [ʌn'feilɪŋ] *adj* (*supply, energy*)
inesauribile; (*remedy*) infallibile

unfair [ʌn'fεə*] *adj*: **~ (to)** ingiusto(a) (nei
confronti di)

unfaithful [ʌn'feiθful] *adj* infedele

unfamiliar [ʌnfə'mɪlɪə*] *adj* sconosciuto(a),
strano(a); **to be ~ with** non avere
familiarità con

unfashionable [ʌn'fæʃnəbl] *adj* (*clothes*)
fuori moda; (*district*) non alla moda

unfasten [ʌn'faːsn] *vt* slacciare; sciogliere

unfavourable [ʌn'feivərəbl] (US
unfavorable) *adj* sfavorevole

unfeeling [ʌn'fiːlɪŋ] *adj* insensibile, duro(a)

unfinished [ʌn'fɪnɪʃt] *adj* incompleto(a)

unfit [ʌn'fɪt] *adj* (*ill*) malato(a), in cattiva
salute; (*incompetent*): **~ (for)** incompetente
(in); (: *work, MIL*) inabile (a)

unfold [ʌn'fəuld] *vt* spiegare ♦ *vi* (*story,
plot*) svelarsi

unforeseen ['ʌnfɔː'siːn] *adj* imprevisto(a)

unforgettable [ʌnfə'getəbl] *adj*
indimenticabile

unfortunate [ʌn'fɔːtʃnət] *adj* sfortunato(a);
(*event, remark*) infelice; **~ly** *adv*

sfortunatamente, purtroppo

unfounded [ʌnˈfaundɪd] *adj* infondato(a)

unfriendly [ʌnˈfrɛndlɪ] *adj* poco amichevole, freddo(a)

ungainly [ʌnˈgeɪnlɪ] *adj* goffo(a), impacciato(a)

ungodly [ʌnˈgɒdlɪ] *adj*: **at an ~ hour** a un'ora impossibile

ungrateful [ʌnˈgreɪtful] *adj* ingrato(a)

unhappiness [ʌnˈhæpɪnɪs] *n* infelicità

unhappy [ʌnˈhæpɪ] *adj* infelice; **~ about/ with** (*arrangements etc*) insoddisfatto(a) di

unharmed [ʌnˈhɑːmd] *adj* incolume, sano(a) e salvo(a)

unhealthy [ʌnˈhɛlθɪ] *adj* (*gen*) malsano(a); (*person*) malaticcio(a)

unheard-of [ʌnˈhɜːdɒv] *adj* inaudito(a), senza precedenti

unhurt [ʌnˈhɜːt] *adj* illeso(a)

uniform [ˈjuːnɪfɔːm] *n* uniforme *f*, divisa ♦ *adj* uniforme

uninhabited [ʌnɪnˈhæbɪtɪd] *adj* disabitato(a)

unintentional [ʌnɪnˈtɛnʃənəl] *adj* Involontario(a)

union [ˈjuːnjən] *n* unione *f*; (*also*: **trade ~**) sindacato ♦ *cpd* sindacale, dei sindacati; **U~ Jack** *n bandiera nazionale britannica*

unique [juːˈniːk] *adj* unico(a)

unit [ˈjuːnɪt] *n* unità *f inv*; (*section: of furniture etc*) elemento; (*team, squad*) reparto, squadra

unite [juːˈnaɪt] *vt* unire ♦ *vi* unirsi; **~d** *adj* unito(a); unificato(a); (*efforts*) congiunto(a); **U~d Kingdom** *n* Regno Unito; **U~d Nations (Organization)** *n* (Organizzazione *f* delle) Nazioni Unite; **U~d States (of America)** *n* Stati *mpl* Uniti (d'America)

unit trust (*BRIT*) *n* fondo d'investimento

unity [ˈjuːnɪtɪ] *n* unità

universal [juːnɪˈvɜːsl] *adj* universale

universe [ˈjuːnɪvɜːs] *n* universo

university [juːnɪˈvɜːsɪtɪ] *n* università *f inv*

unjust [ʌnˈdʒʌst] *adj* ingiusto(a)

unkempt [ʌnˈkɛmpt] *adj* trasandato(a); spettinato(a)

unkind [ʌnˈkaɪnd] *adj* scortese; crudele

unknown [ʌnˈnəun] *adj* sconosciuto(a)

unlawful [ʌnˈlɔːful] *adj* illecito(a), illegale

unleaded [ʌnˈlɛdɪd] *adj* (*petrol, fuel*) verde, senza piombo

unleash [ʌnˈliːʃ] *vt* (*fig*) scatenare

unless [ʌnˈlɛs] *conj* a meno che (non) +*sub*

unlike [ʌnˈlaɪk] *adj* diverso(a) ♦ *prep* a differenza di, contrariamente a

unlikely [ʌnˈlaɪklɪ] *adj* improbabile

unlisted [ʌnˈlɪstɪd] (*US*) *adj* (*TEL*): **to be ~** non essere sull'elenco

unload [ʌnˈləud] *vt* scaricare

unlock [ʌnˈlɒk] *vt* aprire

unlucky [ʌnˈlʌkɪ] *adj* sfortunato(a); (*object, number*) che porta sfortuna

unmarried [ʌnˈmærɪd] *adj* non sposato(a); (*man only*) scapolo, celibe; (*woman only*) nubile

unmistak(e)able [ʌnmɪsˈteɪkəbl] *adj* inconfondibile

unmitigated [ʌnˈmɪtɪgeɪtɪd] *adj* non mitigato(a), assoluto(a), vero(a) e proprio(a)

unnatural [ʌnˈnætʃrəl] *adj* innaturale; contro natura

unnecessary [ʌnˈnɛsəsərɪ] *adj* inutile, superfluo(a)

unnoticed [ʌnˈnəutɪst] *adj*: **(to go) ~ (passare) inosservato(a)**

UNO [ˈjuːnəu] *n abbr* (= *United Nations Organization*) ONU *f*

unobtainable [ʌnəbˈteɪməbl] *adj* (*TEL*) non ottenibile

unobtrusive [ʌnəbˈtruːsɪv] *adj* discreto(a)

unofficial [ʌnəˈfɪʃl] *adj* non ufficiale; (*strike*) non dichiarato(a) dal sindacato

unpack [ʌnˈpæk] *vi* disfare la valigia (or le valigie) ♦ *vt* disfare

unpalatable [ʌnˈpælətəbl] *adj* sgradevole

unparalleled [ʌnˈpærəleld] *adj* incomparabile, impareggiabile

unpleasant [ʌnˈplɛznt] *adj* spiacevole

unplug [ʌnˈplʌg] *vt* staccare

unpopular [ʌnˈpɒpjulə*] *adj* impopolare

unprecedented [ʌnˈprɛsɪdəntɪd] *adj* senza precedenti

unpredictable [ʌnprɪ'dɪktəbl] *adj* imprevedibile

unprofessional [ʌnprə'feʃənl] *adj* poco professionale

unqualified [ʌn'kwɔlɪfaɪd] *adj* (*teacher*) non abilitato(a); (*success*) assoluto(a), senza riserve

unquestionably [ʌn'kwestʃənəblɪ] *adv* indiscutibilmente

unravel [ʌn'rævl] *vt* dipanare, districare

unreal [ʌn'rɪəl] *adj* irreale

unrealistic [ʌnrɪə'lɪstɪk] *adj* non realistico(a)

unreasonable [ʌn'riːznəbl] *adj* irragionevole

unrelated [ʌnrɪ'leɪtɪd] *adj*: ~ **(to)** senza rapporto (con); non imparentato(a) (con)

unreliable [ʌnrɪ'laɪəbl] *adj* (*person, machine*) che non dà affidamento; (*news, source of information*) inattendibile

unremitting [ʌnrɪ'mɪtɪŋ] *adj* incessante

unreservedly [ʌnrɪ'zɜːvɪdlɪ] *adv* senza riserve

unrest [ʌn'rest] *n* agitazione *f*

unroll [ʌn'rəul] *vt* srotolare

unruly [ʌn'ruːlɪ] *adj* indisciplinato(a)

unsafe [ʌn'seɪf] *adj* pericoloso(a), rischioso(a)

unsaid [ʌn'sed] *adj*: **to leave sth ~** passare qc sotto silenzio

unsatisfactory ['ʌnsætɪs'fæktərɪ] *adj* che lascia a desiderare, insufficiente

unsavoury [ʌn'seɪvərɪ] (*US* **unsavory**) *adj* (*fig: person, place*) losco(a)

unscathed [ʌn'skeɪðd] *adj* incolume

unscrew [ʌn'skruː] *vt* svitare

unscrupulous [ʌn'skruːpjuləs] *adj* senza scrupoli

unsettled [ʌn'setld] *adj* (*person*) turbato(a); indeciso(a); (*weather*) instabile

unshaven [ʌn'ʃeɪvn] *adj* non rasato(a)

unsightly [ʌn'saɪtlɪ] *adj* brutto(a), sgradevole a vedersi

unskilled [ʌn'skɪld] *adj* non specializzato(a)

unspeakable [ʌn'spiːkəbl] *adj* (*indescribable*) indicibile; (*awful*) abominevole

unstable [ʌn'steɪbl] *adj* (*gen*) instabile;

(*mentally*) squilibrato(a)

unsteady [ʌn'stedɪ] *adj* instabile, malsicuro(a)

unstuck [ʌn'stʌk] *adj*: **to come ~** scollarsi; (*fig*) fare fiasco

unsuccessful [ʌnsək'sesful] *adj* (*writer, proposal*) che non ha successo; (*marriage, attempt*) mal riuscito(a), fallito(a); **to be ~** (*in attempting sth*) non avere successo

unsuitable [ʌn'suːtəbl] *adj* inadatto(a); inopportuno(a); sconveniente

unsure [ʌn'ʃuə*] *adj* incerto(a); **to be ~ of o.s.** essere insicuro(a)

unsuspecting [ʌnsə'spektɪŋ] *adj* che non sospetta nulla

unsympathetic [ʌnsɪmpə'θetɪk] *adj* (*person*) antipatico(a); (*attitude*) poco incoraggiante

untapped [ʌn'tæpt] *adj* (*resources*) non sfruttato(a)

unthinkable [ʌn'θɪŋkəbl] *adj* impensabile, inconcepibile

untidy [ʌn'taɪdɪ] *adj* (*room*) in disordine; (*appearance*) trascurato(a); (*person*) disordinato(a)

untie [ʌn'taɪ] *vt* (*knot, parcel*) disfare; (*prisoner, dog*) slegare

until [ʌn'tɪl] *prep* fino a; (*after negative*) prima di ♦ *conj* finché, fino a quando; (*in past, after negative*) prima che +*sub*, prima di +*infinitive*; **~ he comes** finché *or* fino a quando non arriva; **~ now** finora; **~ then** fino ad allora

untimely [ʌn'taɪmlɪ] *adj* intempestivo(a), inopportuno(a); (*death*) prematuro(a)

untold [ʌn'təuld] *adj* (*story*) mai rivelato(a); (*wealth*) incalcolabile; (*joy, suffering*) indescrivibile

untoward [ʌntə'wɔːd] *adj* sfortunato(a), sconveniente

unused [ʌn'juːzd] *adj* nuovo(a)

unusual [ʌn'juːʒuəl] *adj* insolito(a), eccezionale, raro(a)

unveil [ʌn'veɪl] *vt* scoprire; svelare

unwanted [ʌn'wɔntɪd] *adj* (*clothing*) smesso(a); (*child*) non desiderato(a)

unwavering [ʌn'weɪvərɪŋ] *adj* fermo(a),

incrollabile

unwelcome [ʌn'wɛlkəm] *adj* non gradito(a)

unwell [ʌn'wɛl] *adj* indisposto(a); **to feel ~** non sentirsi bene

unwieldy [ʌn'wiːldɪ] *adj* poco maneggevole

unwilling [ʌn'wɪlɪŋ] *adj*: **to be ~ to do** non voler fare; **~ly** *adv* malvolentieri

unwind [ʌn'waɪnd] (*irreg: like* **wind**[1]) *vt* svolgere, srotolare ♦ *vi* (*relax*) rilassarsi

unwise [ʌn'waɪz] *adj* poco saggio(a)

unwitting [ʌn'wɪtɪŋ] *adj* involontario(a)

unworkable [ʌn'wəːkəbl] *adj* (*plan*) inattuabile

unworthy [ʌn'wəːðɪ] *adj* indegno(a)

unwrap [ʌn'ræp] *vt* disfare, aprire

unwritten [ʌn'rɪtn] *adj* (*agreement*) tacito(a); (*law*) non scritto(a)

KEYWORD

up [ʌp] *prep*: **he went ~ the stairs/the hill** è salito su per le scale/sulla collina; **the cat was ~ a tree** il gatto era su un albero; **they live further ~ the street** vivono un po' più su nella stessa strada
♦ *adv* **1** (*upwards, higher*) su, in alto; **~ in the sky/the mountains** su nel cielo/in montagna; **~ there** lassù; **~ above** su in alto
2: **to be ~** (*out of bed*) essere alzato(a); (*prices, level*) essere salito(a)
3: **~ to** (*as far as*) fino a, **to now** finora
4: **to be ~ to** (*depending on*): **it's ~ to you** sta a lei, dipende da lei; (*equal to*): **he's not ~ to it** (*job, task etc*) non ne è all'altezza; (*inf: be doing*): **what is he ~ to?** cosa sta combinando?
♦ *n*: **~s and downs** alti e bassi *mpl*

---

upbringing ['ʌpbrɪŋɪŋ] *n* educazione *f*

update [ʌp'deɪt] *vt* aggiornare

upgrade [ʌp'greɪd] *vt* (*house, job*) migliorare; (*employee*) avanzare di grado

upheaval [ʌp'hiːvl] *n* sconvolgimento; tumulto

uphill [ʌp'hɪl] *adj* in salita; (*fig: task*) difficile
♦ *adv*: **to go ~** andare in salita, salire

uphold [ʌp'həuld] (*irreg: like* **hold**) *vt* approvare; sostenere

upholstery [ʌp'həulstərɪ] *n* tappezzeria

upkeep ['ʌpkiːp] *n* manutenzione *f*

upon [ə'pɔn] *prep* su

upper ['ʌpə*] *adj* superiore ♦ *n* (*of shoe*) tomaia; **~-class** *adj* dell'alta borghesia; **~ hand** *n*: **to have the ~ hand** avere il coltello dalla parte del manico; **~most** *adj* il(la) più alto(a); predominante

upright ['ʌpraɪt] *adj* diritto(a); verticale; (*fig*) diritto(a), onesto(a)

uprising ['ʌpraɪzɪŋ] *n* insurrezione *f*, rivolta

uproar ['ʌprɔː*] *n* tumulto, clamore *m*

uproot [ʌp'ruːt] *vt* sradicare

upset [*n* 'ʌpsɛt, *vb, adj* ʌp'sɛt] (*irreg: like* **set**) *n* (*to plan etc*) contrattempo; (*stomach ~*) disturbo ♦ *vt* (*glass etc*) rovesciare; (*plan, stomach*) scombussolare; (*person: offend*) contrariare; (*: grieve*) addolorare, sconvolgere ♦ *adj* contrariato(a); addolorato(a); (*stomach*) scombussolato(a)

upshot ['ʌpʃɔt] *n* risultato

upside down ['ʌpsaɪd-] *adv* sottosopra

upstairs [ʌp'stɛəz] *adv, adj* di sopra, al piano superiore ♦ *n* piano di sopra

upstart ['ʌpstɑːt] *n* parvenu *m inv*

upstream [ʌp'striːm] *adv* a monte

uptake ['ʌpteɪk] *n*: **he is quick/slow on the ~** è pronto/lento di comprendonio

uptight [ʌp'taɪt] (*inf*) *adj* teso(a)

up-to-date *adj* moderno(a), aggiornato(a)

upturn ['ʌptəːn] *n* (*in luck*) svolta favorevole; (*COMM: in market*) rialzo

upward ['ʌpwəd] *adj* ascendente; verso l'alto; **~(s)** *adv* in su, verso l'alto

urban ['əːbən] *adj* urbano(a); **~ clearway** *n* strada di scorrimento (in cui è vietata la sosta)

urbane [əː'beɪn] *adj* civile, urbano(a), educato(a)

urchin ['əːtʃɪn] *n* monello

urge [əːdʒ] *n* impulso; stimolo; forte desiderio ♦ *vt*: **to ~ sb to do** esortare qn a fare, spingere qn a fare; raccomandare a qn di fare

urgency ['əːdʒənsɪ] *n* urgenza; (*of tone*)

insistenza

urgent ['ɔːdʒənt] *adj* urgente; *(voice)* insistente

urinate ['juərɪneɪt] *vi* orinare

urine ['juərɪn] *n* orina

urn [əːn] *n* urna; *(also:* **tea ~)** bollitore *m* per il tè

us [ʌs] *pron* ci; *(stressed, after prep)* noi; *see also* **me**

US(A) *n abbr (= United States (of America))* USA *mpl*

usage ['juːzɪdʒ] *n* uso

use [*n* juːs, *vb* juːz] *n* uso; impiego, utilizzazione *f* ♦ *vt* usare, utilizzare, servirsi di; **in ~** in uso; **out of ~** fuori uso; **to be of ~** essere utile, servire; **it's no ~** non serve, è inutile; **she ~d to do it** lo faceva (una volta), era solita farlo; **to be ~d to** avere l'abitudine di; **~ up** *vt* consumare; esaurire; **~d** *adj (object, car)* usato(a); **~ful** *adj* utile; **~fulness** *n* utilità; **~less** *adj* inutile; *(person)* inetto(a); **~r** *n* utente *m/f*; **~r-friendly** *adj (computer)* di facile uso

usher ['ʌʃə*] *n* usciere *m*; **~ette** [-'rɛt] *n (in cinema)* maschera

USSR *n (HIST)*: **the ~** l'URSS *f*

usual ['juːʒuəl] *adj* solito(a); **as ~** come al solito, come d'abitudine; **~ly** *adv* di solito

utensil [juː'tɛnsl] *n* utensile *m*; **kitchen ~s** utensili da cucina

uterus ['juːtərəs] *n* utero

utility [juː'tɪlɪtɪ] *n* utilità; *(also:* **public ~)** servizio pubblico; **~ room** *n* locale adibito alla stiratura dei panni etc

utmost ['ʌtməust] *adj* estremo(a) ♦ *n*: **to do one's ~** fare il possibile *or* di tutto

utter ['ʌtə*] *adj* assoluto(a), totale ♦ *vt* pronunciare, proferire; emettere; **~ance** *n* espressione *f*; parole *fpl*; **~ly** *adv* completamente, del tutto

U-turn ['juː'təːn] *n* inversione *f* a U

V, v

v. *abbr* = **verse**; **versus**; **volt**; *(= vide)* vedi, vedere

vacancy ['veɪkənsɪ] *n (BRIT: job)* posto libero; *(room)* stanza libera; **"no vacancies"** "completo"

vacant ['veɪkənt] *adj (job, seat etc)* libero(a); *(expression)* assente

vacate [və'keɪt] *vt* lasciare libero(a)

vacation [və'keɪʃən] *(esp US)* vacanze *fpl*

vaccinate ['væksɪneɪt] *vt* vaccinare

vaccination [væksɪ'neɪʃən] *n* vaccinazione *f*

vacuum ['vækjum] *n* vuoto; **~ cleaner** *n* aspirapolvere *m inv*; **~ flask** *(BRIT) n* thermos ® *m inv*; **~-packed** *adj* confezionato(a) sottovuoto

vagina [və'dʒaɪnə] *n* vagina

vagrant ['veɪgrnt] *n* vagabondo/a

vague [veɪg] *adj* vago(a); *(blurred: photo, memory)* sfocato(a); **~ly** *adv* vagamente

vain [veɪn] *adj (useless)* inutile, vano(a); *(conceited)* vanitoso(a); **in ~** inutilmente, invano

valentine ['væləntaɪn] *n (also:* **~ card)** cartolina *or* biglietto di San Valentino; *(person)* innamorato/a

valet ['væleɪ] *n* cameriere *m* personale

valiant ['væliənt] *adj* valoroso(a), coraggioso(a)

valid ['vælɪd] *adj* valido(a), valevole; *(excuse)* valido(a)

valley ['vælɪ] *n* valle *f*

valour ['vælə*] *(US* **valor)** *n* valore *m*

valuable ['væljuəbl] *adj (jewel)* di (grande) valore; *(time, help)* prezioso(a); **~s** *npl* oggetti *mpl* di valore

valuation [vælju'eɪʃən] *n* valutazione *f*, stima

value ['væljuː] *n* valore *m* ♦ *vt (fix price)* valutare, dare un prezzo a; *(cherish)* apprezzare, tenere a; **~ added tax** *(BRIT) n* imposta sul valore aggiunto; **~d** *adj (appreciated)* stimato(a), apprezzato(a)

valve [vælv] *n* valvola

van [væn] n (AUT) furgone m; (BRIT: RAIL) vagone m
vandal ['vændl] n vandalo/a; **~ism** n vandalismo
vanilla [və'nɪlə] n vaniglia ♦ cpd (ice cream) alla vaniglia
vanish ['vænɪʃ] vi svanire, scomparire
vanity ['vænɪtɪ] n vanità
vantage ['vɑːntɪdʒ] n: **~ point** posizione f or punto di osservazione; (fig) posizione vantaggiosa
vapour ['veɪpə*] (US **vapor**) n vapore m
variable ['veərɪəbl] adj variabile; (mood) mutevole
variance ['veərɪəns] n: **to be at ~ (with)** essere in disaccordo (con); (facts) essere in contraddizione (con)
varicose ['værɪkəus] adj: **~ veins** vene fpl varicose
varied ['veərɪd] adj vario(a), diverso(a)
variety [və'raɪətɪ] n varietà f inv; (quantity) quantità, numero; **~ show** n varietà m inv
various ['veərɪəs] adj vario(a), diverso(a); (several) parecchi(e), molti(e)
varnish ['vɑːnɪʃ] n vernice f; (nail ~) smalto ♦ vt verniciare; mettere lo smalto su
vary ['veərɪ] vt, vi variare, mutare
vase [vɑːz] n vaso
Vaseline ® ['væsɪliːn] n vaselina
vast [vɑːst] adj vasto(a); (amount, success) enorme
VAT [væt] n abbr (= value added tax) I.V.A. f
vat [væt] n tino
Vatican ['vætɪkən] n: **the ~** il Vaticano
vault [vɔːlt] n (of roof) volta; (tomb) tomba; (in bank) camera blindata ♦ vt (also: **~ over**) saltare (d'un balzo)
vaunted ['vɔːntɪd] adj: **much-~** tanto celebrato(a)
VCR n abbr = **video cassette recorder**
VD n abbr = **venereal disease**
VDU n abbr = **visual display unit**
veal [viːl] n vitello
veer [vɪə*] vi girare, virare
vegan ['viːgən] n vegetaliano(a)
vegeburger ['vedʒɪbɜːgə*] n hamburger m

inv vegetariano
vegetable ['vedʒtəbl] n verdura, ortaggio ♦ adj vegetale
vegetarian [vedʒɪ'teərɪən] adj, n vegetariano(a)
vehement ['viːmənt] adj veemente, violento(a)
vehicle ['viːɪkl] n veicolo
veil [veɪl] n velo; **~ed** adj (fig: threat) velato(a)
vein [veɪn] n vena; (on leaf) nervatura
velvet ['velvɪt] n velluto ♦ adj di velluto
vending machine ['vendɪŋ-] n distributore m automatico
vendor ['vendə*] n venditore/trice
veneer [və'nɪə*] n impiallacciatura; (fig) vernice f
venereal [vɪ'nɪərɪəl] adj: **~ disease** malattia venerea
Venetian [vɪ'niːʃən] adj veneziano(a); **~ blind** n (tenda alla) veneziana
vengeance ['vendʒəns] n vendetta; **with a ~** (fig) davvero; furiosamente
Venice ['venɪs] n Venezia
venison ['venɪsn] n carne f di cervo
venom ['venəm] n veleno
vent [vent] n foro, apertura; (in dress, jacket) spacco ♦ vt (fig: one's feelings) sfogare, dare sfogo a
ventilate ['ventɪleɪt] vt (room) dare aria a, arieggiare; **ventilator** n ventilatore m
ventriloquist [ven'trɪləkwɪst] n ventriloquo/a
venture ['ventʃə*] n impresa (rischiosa) ♦ vt rischiare, azzardare ♦ vi avventurarsi; **business ~** iniziativa commerciale
venue ['venjuː] n luogo (designato) per l'incontro
verb [vɜːb] n verbo; **~al** adj verbale; (translation) orale
verbatim [vɜː'beɪtɪm] adj, adv parola per parola
verdict ['vɜːdɪkt] n verdetto
verge [vɜːdʒ] (BRIT) n bordo, orlo; **"soft ~s"** (BRIT: AUT) banchine fpl cedevoli; **on the ~ of doing** sul punto di fare; **~ on** vt fus rasentare

veritable ['vɛrɪtəbl] adj vero(a)
vermin ['vəːmɪn] npl animali mpl nocivi; (insects) insetti mpl parassiti
vermouth ['vəːməθ] n vermut m inv
versatile ['vəːsətaɪl] adj (person) versatile; (machine, tool etc) (che si presta) a molti usi
verse [vəːs] n versi mpl; (stanza) stanza, strofa; (in bible) versetto
version ['vəːʃən] n versione f
versus ['vəːsəs] prep contro
vertical ['vəːtɪkl] adj verticale ♦ n verticale m; ~ly adv verticalmente
vertigo ['vəːtɪgəu] n vertigine f
verve [vəːv] n brio; entusiasmo
very ['vɛrɪ] adv molto ♦ adj: **the ~ book which** proprio il libro che; **the ~ last** proprio l'ultimo; **at the ~ least** almeno; ~ **much** moltissimo
vessel ['vɛsl] n (ANAT) vaso; (NAUT) nave f; (container) recipiente m
vest [vɛst] n (BRIT) maglia; (: sleeveless) canottiera; (US: waistcoat) gilè m inv
vested interests ['vɛstɪd-] npl (COMM) diritti mpl acquisiti
vet [vɛt] n abbr (BRIT: = veterinary surgeon) veterinario ♦ vt esaminare minuziosamente
veteran ['vɛtərn] n (also: **war ~**) veterano
veterinary ['vɛtrɪnərɪ] adj veterinario(a); ~ **surgeon** (US **veterinarian**) n veterinario
veto ['viːtəu] (pl ~es) n veto ♦ vt opporre il veto a
vex [vɛks] vt irritare, contrariare; ~ed adj (question) controverso(a), dibattuto(a)
via ['vaɪə] prep (by way of) via; (by means of) tramite
viable ['vaɪəbl] adj attuabile; vitale
viaduct ['vaɪədʌkt] n viadotto
vibrant ['vaɪbrənt] adj (lively, bright) vivace; (voice) vibrante
vibrate [vaɪ'breɪt] vi: **to ~ (with)** vibrare (di); (resound) risonare (di)
vicar ['vɪkə*] n pastore m; ~**age** n presbiterio
vicarious [vɪ'kɛərɪəs] adj indiretto(a)
vice [vaɪs] n (evil) vizio; (TECH) morsa
vice- [vaɪs] prefix vice...

vice squad n (squadra del) buon costume f
vice versa ['vaɪsɪ'vəːsə] adv viceversa
vicinity [vɪ'sɪnɪtɪ] n vicinanze fpl
vicious ['vɪʃəs] adj (remark, dog) cattivo(a); (blow) violento(a); ~ **circle** n circolo vizioso
victim ['vɪktɪm] n vittima
victor ['vɪktə*] n vincitore m
Victorian [vɪk'tɔːrɪən] adj vittoriano(a)
victory ['vɪktərɪ] n vittoria
video ['vɪdɪəu] cpd video... ♦ n (~ film) video m inv; (also: ~ **cassette**) videocassetta; (also: ~ **cassette recorder**) videoregistratore m; ~ **tape** n videotape m inv; ~ **wall** n schermo m multivideo inv
vie [vaɪ] vi: **to ~ with** competere con, rivaleggiare con
Vienna [vɪ'ɛnə] n Vienna
Vietnam [vjɛt'næm] n Vietnam m; ~**ese** adj, n inv vietnamita m/f
view [vjuː] n vista, veduta; (opinion) opinione f ♦ vt (look at: also fig) considerare; (house) visitare; **on ~** (in museum etc) esposto(a); **in full ~ of** sotto gli occhi di; **in ~ of the weather/the fact that** considerato il tempo/che; **in my ~** a mio parere; ~**er** n spettatore/trice; ~**finder** n mirino; ~**point** n punto di vista; (place) posizione f
vigil ['vɪdʒɪl] n veglia
vigorous ['vɪgərəs] adj vigoroso(a)
vile [vaɪl] adj (action) vile; (smell) disgustoso(a), nauseante; (temper) pessimo(a)
villa ['vɪlə] n villa
village ['vɪlɪdʒ] n villaggio; ~**r** n abitante m/f di villaggio
villain ['vɪlən] n (scoundrel) canaglia; (BRIT: criminal) criminale m; (in novel etc) cattivo
vindicate ['vɪndɪkeɪt] vt comprovare; giustificare
vindictive [vɪn'dɪktɪv] adj vendicativo(a)
vine [vaɪn] n vite f; (climbing plant) rampicante m
vinegar ['vɪnɪgə*] n aceto
vineyard ['vɪnjɑːd] n vigna, vigneto

vintage ['vɪntɪdʒ] *n* (*year*) annata, produzione *f* ♦ *cpd* d'annata; ~ **car** *n* auto *f inv* d'epoca; ~ **wine** *n* vino d'annata

vinyl ['vaɪnl] *n* vinile *m*

violate ['vaɪəleɪt] *vt* violare

violence ['vaɪələns] *n* violenza

violent ['vaɪələnt] *adj* violento(a)

violet ['vaɪələt] *adj* (*colour*) viola *inv*, violetto(a) ♦ *n* (*plant*) violetta; (*colour*) violetto

violin [vaɪə'lɪn] *n* violino; ~**ist** *n* violinista *m/f*

VIP *n abbr* (= *very important person*) V.I.P. *m/f inv*

virgin ['və:dʒɪn] *n* vergine *f* ♦ *adj* vergine *inv*

Virgo ['və:gəu] *n* (*sign*) Vergine *f*

virile ['vɪraɪl] *adj* virile

virtually ['və:tjuəlɪ] *adv* (*almost*) praticamente

virtual reality ['və:tʃuəl -] *n* (*COMPUT*) realtà virtuale

virtue ['və:tju:] *n* virtù *f inv*; (*advantage*) pregio, vantaggio; **by ~ of** grazie a

virtuous ['və:tjuəs] *adj* virtuoso(a)

virus ['vaɪərəs] *n* (*also COMPUT*) virus *m inv*

visa ['vi:zə] *n* visto

vis-à-vis [vi:zə'vi:] *prep* rispetto a, nei riguardi di

visibility [vɪzɪ'bɪlɪtɪ] *n* visibilità

visible ['vɪzəbl] *adj* visibile

vision ['vɪʒən] *n* (*sight*) vista; (*foresight, in dream*) visione *f*

visit ['vɪzɪt] *n* visita; (*stay*) soggiorno ♦ *vt* (*person*: *US also*: ~ **with**) andare a trovare; (*place*) visitare; ~**ing hours** *npl* (*in hospital etc*) orario delle visite; ~**or** *n* visitatore/trice; (*guest*) ospite *m/f*; ~**or centre** *n* centro informazioni per visitatori di museo, zoo, parco ecc

visor ['vaɪzə*] *n* visiera

visual ['vɪzjuəl] *adj* visivo(a); visuale; ottico(a); ~ **aid** *n* sussidio visivo; ~ **display unit** *n* visualizzatore *m*

visualize ['vɪzjuəlaɪz] *vt* immaginare, figurarsi; (*foresee*) prevedere

visually-impaired ['vɪzjuəlɪ-] *adj* videoleso(a)

vital ['vaɪtl] *adj* vitale; ~**ly** *adv* estremamente; ~ **statistics** *npl* (*fig*) misure *fpl*

vitamin ['vɪtəmɪn] *n* vitamina

vivacious [vɪ'veɪʃəs] *adj* vivace

vivid ['vɪvɪd] *adj* vivido(a); ~**ly** *adv* (*describe*) vividamente; (*remember*) con precisione

V-neck ['vi:nek] *n* maglione *m* con lo scollo a V

vocabulary [vəu'kæbjulərɪ] *n* vocabolario

vocal ['vəukl] *adj* (*MUS*) vocale; (*communication*) verbale; ~ **cords** *npl* corde *fpl* vocali

vocation [vəu'keɪʃən] *n* vocazione *f*; ~**al** *adj* professionale

vociferous [və'sɪfərəs] *adj* rumoroso(a)

vodka ['vɔdkə] *n* vodka *f inv*

vogue [vəug] *n* moda; (*popularity*) popolarità, voga

voice [vɔɪs] *n* voce *f* ♦ *vt* (*opinion*) esprimere

void [vɔɪd] *n* vuoto ♦ *adj* (*invalid*) nullo(a); (*empty*): ~ **of** privo(a) di

volatile ['vɔlətaɪl] *adj* volatile; (*fig*) volubile

volcano [vɔl'keɪnəu] (*pl* ~**es**) *n* vulcano

volition [və'lɪʃən] *n*: **of one's own ~** di sua volontà

volley ['vɔlɪ] *n* (*of gunfire*) salva; (*of stones, questions etc*) raffica; (*TENNIS etc*) volata; ~**ball** *n* pallavolo *f*

volt [vəult] *n* volt *m inv*; ~**age** *n* tensione *f*, voltaggio

voluble ['vɔljubl] *adj* loquace, ciarliero(a)

volume ['vɔlju:m] *n* volume *m*

voluntarily ['vɔləntrɪlɪ] *adv* volontariamente; gratuitamente

voluntary ['vɔləntərɪ] *adj* volontario(a); (*unpaid*) gratuito(a), non retribuito(a)

volunteer [vɔlən'tɪə*] *n* volontario/a ♦ *vt* offrire volontariamente ♦ *vi* (*MIL*) arruolarsi volontario; **to ~ to do** offrire (volontariamente) di fare

voluptuous [və'lʌptjuəs] *adj* voluttuoso(a)

vomit ['vɔmɪt] *n* vomito ♦ *vt*, *vi* vomitare

vote [vəut] *n* voto, suffragio; (*cast*) voto; (*franchise*) diritto di voto ♦ *vt*: **to be ~d**

chairman *etc* venir eletto presidente *etc*; (*propose*): **to ~** approvare la proposta che ♦ *vi* votare; **~ of thanks** discorso di ringraziamento; **~r** *n* elettore/trice; **voting** *n* scrutinio

vouch [vautʃ]: **to ~ for** *vt fus* farsi garante di

voucher ['vautʃə*] *n* (*for meal, petrol etc*) buono

vow [vau] *n* voto, promessa solenne ♦ *vt*: **to ~ to do/that** giurare di fare/che

vowel ['vauəl] *n* vocale *f*

voyage ['vɔɪdʒ] *n* viaggio per mare, traversata

V-sign ['vi:-] (*BRIT*) *n* gesto volgare con le dita

vulgar ['vʌlgə*] *adj* volgare

vulnerable ['vʌlnərəbl] *adj* vulnerabile

vulture ['vʌltʃə*] *n* avvoltoio

W, w

wad [wɔd] *n* (*of cotton wool, paper*) tampone *m*; (*of banknotes etc*) fascio

waddle ['wɔdl] *vi* camminare come una papera

wade [weɪd] *vi*: **to ~ through** camminare a stento in; (*fig: book*) leggere con fatica

wafer ['weɪfə*] *n* (*CULIN*) cialda

waffle ['wɔfl] *n* (*CULIN*) cialda; (*inf*) ciance *fpl* ♦ *vi* cianciare

waft [wɔft] *vt* portare ♦ *vi* diffondersi

wag [wæg] *vt* agitare, muovere ♦ *vi* agitarsi

wage [weɪdʒ] *n* (*also*: **~s**) salario, paga ♦ *vt*: **to ~ war** fare la guerra; **~ earner** *n* salariato/a; **~ packet** *n* busta *f* paga *inv*

wager ['weɪdʒə*] *n* scommessa

wag(g)on ['wægən] *n* (*horse-drawn*) carro; (*BRIT: RAIL*) vagone *m* (merci)

wail [weɪl] *n* gemito; (*of siren*) urlo ♦ *vi* gemere; urlare

waist [weɪst] *n* vita, cintola; **~coat** (*BRIT*) *n* panciotto, gilè *m inv*; **~line** *n* (giro di) vita

wait [weɪt] *n* attesa ♦ *vi* aspettare, attendere; **to lie in ~ for** stare in agguato a; **to ~ for** aspettare; **I can't ~ to** (*fig*) non vedo l'ora di; **~ behind** *vi* rimanere (ad

aspettare); **~ on** *vt fus* servire; **~er** *n* cameriere *m*; **~ing** *n*: **"no ~ing"** (*BRIT*: *AUT*) "divieto di sosta"; **~ing list** *n* lista di attesa; **~ing room** *n* sala d'aspetto *or* d'attesa; **~ress** *n* cameriera

waive [weɪv] *vt* rinunciare a, abbandonare

wake [weɪk] (*pt* **woke**, **~d**, *pp* **woken**, **~d**) *vt* (*also*: **~ up**) svegliare ♦ *vi* (*also*: **~ up**) svegliarsi ♦ *n* (*for dead person*) veglia funebre; (*NAUT*) scia; **waken** *vt*, *vi* = **wake**

Wales [weɪlz] *n* Galles *m*

walk [wɔːk] *n* passeggiata; (*short*) giretto; (*gait*) passo, andatura; (*path*) sentiero; (*in park etc*) sentiero, vialetto ♦ *vi* camminare; (*for pleasure, exercise*) passeggiare ♦ *vt* (*distance*) fare *or* percorrere a piedi; (*dog*) accompagnare, portare a passeggiare; **10 minutes' ~ from** 10 minuti di cammino *or* a piedi da; **from all ~s of life** di tutte le condizioni sociali; **~ out** *vi* (*audience*) andarsene; (*workers*) scendere in sciopero; **~ out on** (*inf*) *vt fus* piantare in asso; **~er** *n* (*person*) camminatore/trice; **~ie-talkie** ['wɔːkɪ'tɔːkɪ] *n* walkie-talkie *m inv*; **~ing** *n* camminare *m*; **~ing shoes** *npl* pedule *fpl*; **~ing stick** *n* bastone *m* da passeggio; **W~man** ® ['wɔːkmən] *n* Walkman ® *m inv*; **~out** *n* (*of workers*) sciopero senza preavviso *or* a sorpresa; **~over** (*inf*) *n* vittoria facile, gioco da ragazzi; **~way** *n* passaggio pedonale

wall [wɔːl] *n* muro; (*internal, of tunnel, cave*) parete *f*; **~ed** *adj* (*city*) fortificato(a); (*garden*) cintato(a)

wallet ['wɔlɪt] *n* portafoglio

wallflower ['wɔːlflauə*] *n* violacciocca; **to be a ~** (*fig*) fare da tappezzeria

wallow ['wɔləu] *vi* sguazzare

wallpaper ['wɔːlpeɪpə*] *n* carta da parati ♦ *vt* (*room*) mettere la carta da parati in

wally ['wɔlɪ] (*inf*) *n* imbecille *m/f*

walnut ['wɔːlnʌt] *n* noce *f*; (*tree, wood*) noce *m*

walrus ['wɔːlrəs] (*pl* **~** *or* **~es**) *n* tricheco

waltz [wɔːlts] *n* valzer *m inv* ♦ *vi* ballare il valzer

wand [wɔnd] *n* (*also*: **magic ~**) bacchetta

(magica)

wander ['wɒndə*] vi (person) girare senza meta, girovagare; (thoughts) vagare ♦ vt girovagare per

wane [weɪn] vi calare

wangle [wæŋgl] (BRIT: inf) vt procurare con l'astuzia

want [wɒnt] vt volere; (need) aver bisogno di ♦ n: **for ~ of** per mancanza di; **~s** npl (needs) bisogni mpl; **to ~ to do** volere fare; **to ~ sb to do** volere che qn faccia; **~ed** adj (criminal) ricercato(a); **"~ed"** (in udverts) "cercasi"; **~ing** adj: **to be found ~ing** non risultare all'altezza

war [wɔː*] n guerra; **to make ~ (on)** far guerra (a)

ward [wɔːd] n (in hospital: room) corsia; (: section) reparto; (POL) circoscrizione f; (LAW: child: also: **~ of court**) pupillo/a; **~ off** vt parare, schivare

warden ['wɔːdn] n (of park, game reserve, youth hostel) guardiano/a; (BRIT: of institution) direttore/trice; (BRIT: also: **traffic ~**) addetto/a al controllo del traffico e del parcheggio

warder ['wɔːdə*] (BRIT) n guardia carceraria

wardrobe ['wɔːdrəub] n (cupboard) guardaroba m inv, armadio; (clothes) guardaroba; (CINEMA, THEATRE) costumi mpl

warehouse ['weəhaus] n magazzino

wares [weəz] npl merci fpl

warfare ['wɔːfeə*] n guerra

warhead ['wɔːhed] n (MIL) testata

warily ['weərɪlɪ] adv cautamente, con prudenza

warlike ['wɔːlaɪk] adj bellicoso(a)

warm [wɔːm] adj caldo(a); (thanks, welcome, applause) caloroso(a); (person) cordiale; **it's ~** fa caldo; **I'm ~** ho caldo; **~ up** vi scaldarsi, riscaldarsi ♦ vt scaldare, riscaldare; (engine) far scaldare; **~-hearted** adj affettuoso(a); **~ly** adv (applaud, welcome) calorosamente; (dress) con abiti pesanti; **~th** n calore m

warn [wɔːn] vt: **to ~ sb that/(not) to do/of** avvertire or avvisare qn che/di (non) fare/di; **~ing** n avvertimento; (notice) avviso;

(signal) segnalazione f; **~ing light** n spia luminosa; **~ing triangle** n (AUT) triangolo

warp [wɔːp] vi deformarsi ♦ vt (fig) corrompere

warrant ['wɒrnt] n (voucher) buono; (LAW: to arrest) mandato di cattura; (: to search) mandato di perquisizione

warranty ['wɒrəntɪ] n garanzia

warren ['wɒrən] n (of rabbits) tana; (fig: of streets etc) dedalo

warrior ['wɒrɪə*] n guerriero/a

Warsaw ['wɔːsɔː] n Varsavia

warship ['wɔːʃɪp] n nave f da guerra

wart [wɔːt] n verruca

wartime ['wɔːtaɪm] n: **in ~** in tempo di guerra

wary ['weərɪ] adj prudente

was [wɒz] pt of **be**

wash [wɒʃ] vt lavare ♦ vi lavarsi; (sea): **to ~ over/against sth** infrangersi su/contro qc ♦ n lavaggio; (of ship) scia; **to give sth a ~** lavare qc, dare una lavata a qc; **to have a ~** lavarsi; **~ away** vt (stain) togliere lavando; (subj: river) trascinare via; **~ off** vi andare via con il lavaggio; **~ up** vi (BRIT) lavare i piatti; (US) darsi una lavata; **~able** adj lavabile; **~basin** (US **~bowl**) n lavabo; **~cloth** (US) n pezzuola (per lavarsi); **~er** n (TECH) rondella; **~ing** n (linen etc) bucato; **~ing machine** n lavatrice f **~ing powder** (BRIT) n detersivo (in polvere)

Washington ['wɒʃɪŋtən] n Washington f

wash: ~ing up n rigovernatura, lavatura dei piatti; **~ing-up liquid** n detersivo liquido (per stoviglie); **~-out** (inf) n disastro; **~room** n gabinetto

wasn't ['wɒznt] = **was not**

wasp [wɒsp] n vespa

wastage ['weɪstɪdʒ] n spreco; (in manufacturing) scarti mpl; **natural ~** diminuzione f di manodopera (per pensionamento, decesso etc)

waste [weɪst] n spreco; (of time) perdita; (rubbish) rifiuti mpl; (also: **household ~**) immondizie fpl ♦ adj (material) di scarto; (food) avanzato(a); (land) incolto(a) ♦ vt sprecare; **~s** npl (area of land) distesa

desolata; ~ **away** *vi* deperire; ~ **disposal**
unit (*BRIT*) *n* eliminatore *m* di rifiuti; ~**ful**
adj sprecone(a); (*process*) dispendioso(a); ~
ground (*BRIT*) *n* terreno incolto *or*
abbandonato; ~**paper basket** *n* cestino
per la carta straccia; ~**pipe** *n* tubo di
scarico

watch [wɔtʃ] *n* (*also*: **wrist** ~) orologio (da
polso); (*act of watching, vigilance*)
sorveglianza; (*guard*: MIL, NAUT) guardia;
(*NAUT: spell of duty*) quarto ♦ *vt* (*look at*)
osservare; (*: match, programme*) guardare;
(*spy on, guard*) sorvegliare, tenere d'occhio;
(*be careful of*) fare attenzione a ♦ *vi*
osservare, guardare; (*keep guard*) fare *or*
montare la guardia; ~ **out** *vi* fare
attenzione; ~**dog** *n* (*also fig*) cane *m* da
guardia; ~**ful** *adj* attento(a), vigile;
~**maker** *n* orologiaio/a; ~**man** (*irreg*) *n*
see **night**; ~ **strap** *n* cinturino da orologio

water ['wɔːtə*] *n* acqua ♦ *vt* (*plant*)
annaffiare ♦ *vi* (*eyes*) lacrimare; (*mouth*): **to**
make sb's mouth ~ far venire l'acquolina
in bocca a qn; **in British** ~s nelle acque
territoriali britanniche; ~ **down** *vt* (*milk*)
diluire; (*fig: story*) edulcorare; ~ **cannon** *n*
idrante *m*; ~ **closet** (*BRIT*) *n* water *m inv*;
~**colour** *n* acquerello; ~**cress** *n* crescione
m; ~**fall** *n* cascata; ~ **heater** *n*
scaldabagno; ~**ing can** *n* annaffiatoio; ~
lily *n* ninfea; ~**line** *n* (*NAUT*) linea di
galleggiamento; ~**logged** *adj* saturo(a)
d'acqua; imbevuto(a) d'acqua; (*football
pitch etc*) allagato(a); ~ **main** *n* conduttura
dell'acqua; ~**melon** *n* anguria, cocomero;
~**proof** *adj* impermeabile; ~**shed** *n* (*GEO,
fig*) spartiacque *m*; ~**skiing** *n* sci *m*
acquatico; ~**tight** *adj* stagno(a); ~**way** *n*
corso d'acqua navigabile; ~**works** *npl*
impianto idrico; ~**y** *adj* (*colour*) slavato(a);
(*coffee*) acquoso(a); (*eyes*) umido(a)

watt [wɔt] *n* watt *m inv*

wave [weɪv] *n* onda; (*of hand*) gesto, segno;
(*in hair*) ondulazione *f*; (*fig: surge*) ondata
♦ *vi* fare un cenno con la mano; (*branches,
grass*) ondeggiare; (*flag*) sventolare ♦ *vt*
(*hand*) fare un gesto con; (*handkerchief*)

sventolare; (*stick*) brandire; ~**length** *n*
lunghezza d'onda

waver ['weɪvə*] *vi* esitare; (*voice*) tremolare

wavy ['weɪvɪ] *adj* ondulato(a); ondeggiante

wax [wæks] *n* cera ♦ *vt* dare la cera a; (*car*)
lucidare ♦ *vi* (*moon*) crescere; ~**works** *npl*
cere *fpl* ♦ *n* museo delle cere

way [weɪ] *n* via, strada; (*path, access*)
passaggio; (*distance*) distanza; (*direction*)
parte *f*, direzione *f*; (*manner*) modo, stile
m; (*habit*) abitudine *f*; **which ~? – this** ~
da che parte *or* in quale direzione? – da
questa parte *or* per di qua; **on the** ~ (*en
route*) per strada; **to be on one's** ~ essere
in cammino *or* sulla strada; **to be in the** ~
bloccare il passaggio; (*fig*) essere tra i piedi
or d'impiccio; **to go out of one's** ~ **to do**
(*fig*) mettercela tutta *or* fare di tutto per
fare; **under** ~ (*project*) in corso; **to lose**
one's ~ perdere la strada; **in a** ~ in un
certo senso; **in some** ~s sotto certi aspetti;
no ~! (*inf*) neanche per idea!; **by the** ~ ... a
proposito ...; **"~ in"** (*BRIT*) "entrata",
"ingresso"; **"~ out"** (*BRIT*) "uscita"; **the** ~
back la strada del ritorno; **"give ~"** (*BRIT:
AUT*) "dare la precedenza"

waylay [weɪ'leɪ] (*irreg: like* **lay**) *vt* tendere
un agguato a; attendere al passaggio

wayward ['weɪwəd] *adj* capriccioso(a);
testardo(a)

W.C. ['dʌblju'siː] (*BRIT*) *n* W.C. *m inv*,
gabinetto

we [wiː] *pl pron* noi

weak [wiːk] *adj* debole; (*health*) precario(a);
(*beam etc*) fragile; (*tea*) leggero(a); ~**en** *vi*
indebolirsi ♦ *vt* indebolire; ~**ling** ['wiːklɪŋ]
n smidollato/a; debole *m/f*; ~**ness** *n*
debolezza; (*fault*) punto debole, difetto; **to**
have a ~ness for avere un debole per

wealth [welθ] *n* (*money, resources*)
ricchezza, ricchezze *fpl*; (*of details*)
abbondanza, profusione *f*; ~**y** *adj* ricco(a)

wean [wiːn] *vt* svezzare

weapon ['wepən] *n* arma

wear [wɛə*] (*pt* **wore**, *pp* **worn**) *n* (*use*) uso;
(*damage through use*) logorio, usura;
(*clothing*): **sports/baby** ~ abbigliamento

sportivo/per neonati ♦ *vt* (*clothes*) portare; (*put on*) mettersi; (*damage: through use*) consumare ♦ *vi* (*last*) durare; (*rub etc through*) consumarsi; **evening ~** abiti *mpl* or tenuta da sera; **~ away** *vt* consumare; erodere ♦ *vi* consumarsi; essere eroso(a); **~ down** *vt* consumare; (*strength*) esaurire; **~ off** *vi* sparire lentamente; **~ out** *vt* consumare; (*person, strength*) esaurire; **~ and tear** *n* usura, consumo

weary ['wɪərɪ] *adj* stanco(a) ♦ *vi*: **to ~ of** stancarsi di

weasel ['wi:zl] *n* (ZOOL) donnola

weather ['wɛðə*] *n* tempo ♦ *vt* (*storm, crisis*) superare; **under the ~** (*fig: ill*) poco bene; **~-beaten** *adj* (*face, skin*) segnato(a) dalle intemperie; (*building*) logorato(a) dalle intemperie; **~cock** *n* banderuola; **~ forecast** *n* previsioni *fpl* del tempo, bollettino meteorologico; **~man** (*irreg inf*) *n* meteorologo; **~ vane** *n* = **~cock**

weave [wi:v] (*pt* **wove**, *pp* **woven**) *vt* (*cloth*) tessere; (*basket*) intrecciare; **~r** *n* tessitore/trice; **weaving** *n* tessitura

web [wɛb] *n* (*of spider*) ragnatela; (*on foot*) palma; (*fabric, also fig*) tessuto

wed [wɛd] (*pt, pp* **wedded**) *vt* sposare ♦ *vi* sposarsi

we'd [wi:d] = **we had**; **we would**

wedding ['wɛdɪŋ] *n* matrimonio; **silver/ golden ~ (anniversary)** *n* nozze *fpl* d'argento/d'oro; **~ day** *n* giorno delle nozze *or* del matrimonio; **~ dress** *n* abito nuziale; **~ ring** *n* fede *f*

wedge [wɛdʒ] *n* (*of wood etc*) zeppa; (*of cake*) fetta ♦ *vt* (*fix*) fissare con zeppe; (*pack tightly*) incastrare

Wednesday ['wɛdnzdɪ] *n* mercoledì *m inv*

wee [wi:] (SCOTTISH) *adj* piccolo(a)

weed [wi:d] *n* erbaccia ♦ *vt* diserbare; **~killer** *n* diserbante *m*; **~y** *adj* (*person*) allampanato(a)

week [wi:k] *n* settimana; **a ~ today/on Friday** oggi/venerdì a otto; **~day** *n* giorno feriale; (COMM) giornata lavorativa; **~end** *n* fine settimana *m or f inv*, weekend *m inv*; **~ly** *adv* ogni settimana, settimanalmente

♦ *adj* settimanale ♦ *n* settimanale *m*

weep [wi:p] (*pt, pp* **wept**) *vi* (*person*) piangere; **~ing willow** *n* salice *m* piangente

weigh [weɪ] *vt, vi* pesare; **to ~ anchor** salpare l'ancora; **~ down** *vt* (*branch*) piegare; (*fig: with worry*) opprimere, caricare; **~ up** *vt* valutare

weight [weɪt] *n* peso; **to lose/put on ~** dimagrire/ingrassare; **~ing** *n* (*allowance*) indennità; **~ lifter** *n* pesista *m*; **~y** *adj* pesante; (*fig*) importante, grave

weir [wɪə*] *n* diga

weird [wɪəd] *adj* strano(a), bizzarro(a); (*eerie*) soprannaturale

welcome ['wɛlkəm] *adj* benvenuto(a) ♦ *n* accoglienza, benvenuto ♦ *vt* dare il benvenuto a; (*be glad of*) rallegrarsi di; **thank you – you're ~!** grazie – prego!

weld [wɛld] *n* saldatura ♦ *vt* saldare

welfare ['wɛlfɛə*] *n* benessere *m*; **~ state** *n* stato assistenziale

well [wɛl] *n* pozzo ♦ *adv* bene ♦ *adj*: **to be ~** (*person*) stare bene ♦ *excl* allora!; ma!; ebbene!; **as ~** anche; **as ~ as** così come; oltre a; **~ done!** bravo(a)!; **get ~ soon!** guarisci presto!; **to do ~** andare bene; **~ up** *vi* sgorgare

we'll [wi:l] = **we will**; **we shall**

well: ~-behaved *adj* ubbidiente; **~-being** *n* benessere *m*; **~-built** *adj* (*person*) ben fatto(a); **~-deserved** *adj* meritato(a); **~-dressed** *adj* ben vestito(a), vestito(a) bene; **~-heeled** (*inf*) *adj* (*wealthy*) agiato(a), facoltoso(a)

wellingtons ['wɛlɪŋtənz] *npl* (*also*: **wellington boots**) stivali *mpl* di gomma

well: ~-known *adj* noto(a), famoso(a); **~-mannered** *adj* ben educato(a); **~-meaning** *adj* ben intenzionato(a); **~-off** *adj* benestante, danaroso(a); **~-read** *adj* colto(a); **~-to-do** *adj* abbiente, benestante; **~-wisher** *n* ammiratore/trice

Welsh [wɛlʃ] *adj* gallese ♦ *n* (LING) gallese *m*; **the ~** *npl* i Gallesi; **~man/woman** (*irreg*) *n* gallese *m/f*; **~ rarebit** *n* crostino al formaggio

went [wɛnt] *pt of* **go**

wept [wɛpt] *pt, pp of* **weep**

were [wə:*] *pt of* **be**

we're [wɪə*] = **we are**

weren't [wə:nt] = **were not**

west [wɛst] *n* ovest *m*, occidente *m*, ponente *m* ♦ *adj* (a) ovest *inv*, occidentale ♦ *adv* verso ovest; **the W~** l'Occidente *m*; **the W~ Country** (BRIT) *n* il sud-ovest dell'Inghilterra; **~erly** *adj* (*point*) a ovest; (*wind*) occidentale, da ovest; **~ern** *adj* occidentale, dell'ovest ♦ *n* (CINEMA) western *m inv*; **W~ Germany** *n* Germania Occidentale; **W~ Indian** *adj* delle Indie Occidentali ♦ *n* abitante *m/f* delle Indie Occidentali; **W~ Indies** *npl* Indie *fpl* Occidentali; **~ward(s)** *adv* verso ovest

wet [wɛt] *adj* umido(a), bagnato(a); (*soaked*) fradicio(a); (*rainy*) piovoso(a) ♦ *n* (BRIT: POL) politico moderato; **to get ~** bagnarsi; **"~ paint''** "vernice fresca''; **~ suit** *n* tuta da sub

we've [wiːv] = **we have**

whack [wæk] *vt* picchiare, battere

whale [weɪl] *n* (ZOOL) balena

wharf [wɔːf] (*pl* **wharves**) *n* banchina

wharves [wɔːvz] *npl of* **wharf**

---KEYWORD---

what [wɔt] *adj* 1 (*in direct/indirect questions*) che; quale; **~ size is it?** che taglia è?; **~ colour is it?** di che colore è?; **~ books do you want?** quali *or* che libri vuole?
2 (*in exclamations*) che; **~ a mess!** che disordine!
♦ *pron* 1 (*interrogative*) che cosa, cosa, che; **~ are you doing?** che *or* (che) cosa fai?; **~ are you talking about?** di che cosa parli?; **~ is it called?** come si chiama?; **~ about me?** e io?; **~ about doing ...?** e se facessimo ...?
2 (*relative*) ciò che, quello che; **I saw ~ you did/was on the table** ho visto quello che hai fatto/quello che era sul tavolo
3 (*indirect use*) (che) cosa; **he asked me ~ she had said** mi ha chiesto che cosa avesse detto; **tell me ~ you're thinking about** dimmi a cosa stai pensando
♦ *excl* (*disbelieving*) cosa!, come!

whatever [wɔt'ɛvə*] *adj*: **~ book** qualunque *or* qualsiasi libro +*sub* ♦ *pron*: **do ~ is necessary/you want** faccia qualunque *or* qualsiasi cosa sia necessaria/lei voglia; **~ happens** qualunque cosa accada; **no reason ~** *or* **whatsoever** nessuna ragione affatto *or* al mondo; **nothing ~** proprio niente

whatsoever [wɔtsəu'ɛvə*] *adj* = **whatever**

wheat [wiːt] *n* grano, frumento

wheedle ['wiːdl] *vt*: **to ~ sb into doing sth** convincere qn a fare qc (con lusinghe); **to ~ sth out of sb** ottenere qc da qn (con lusinghe)

wheel [wiːl] *n* ruota; (AUT: *also*: **steering ~**) volante *m*; (NAUT) (ruota del) timone *m* ♦ *vt* spingere ♦ *vi* (*birds*) roteare; (*also*: **~ round**) girare; **~barrow** *n* carriola; **~chair** *n* sedia a rotelle; **~ clamp** *n* (AUT) morsa che blocca la ruota di una vettura in sosta vietata

wheeze [wiːz] *vi* ansimare

---KEYWORD---

when [wɛn] *adv* quando; **~ did it happen?** quando è successo?
♦ *conj* 1 (*at, during, after the time that*) quando; **she was reading ~ I came in** quando sono entrato lei leggeva; **that was ~ I needed you** era allora che avevo bisogno di te
2 (*on, at which*): **on the day ~ I met him** il giorno in cui l'ho incontrato; **one day ~ it was raining** un giorno che pioveva
3 (*whereas*) quando, mentre; **you said I was wrong ~ in fact I was right** mi hai detto che avevo torto, quando in realtà avevo ragione

whenever [wɛn'ɛvə*] *adv* quando mai
♦ *conj* quando; (*every time that*) ogni volta che

where [wɛə*] *adv, conj* dove; **this is ~** è qui che; **~abouts** *adv* dove ♦ *n*: **sb's**

~**abouts** luogo dove qn si trova; ~**as** *conj*
mentre; ~**by** *pron* per cui; **wherever**
[-'evə*] *conj* dovunque +*sub*; (*interrogative*)
dove mai; ~**withal** *n* mezzi *mpl*
whet [wɛt] *vt* (*appetite etc*) stimolare
whether ['wɛðə*] *conj* se; **I don't know ~ to**
accept or not non so se accettare o no;
it's doubtful ~ è poco probabile che; ~
you go or not che lei vada o no

KEYWORD
---

which [wɪtʃ] *adj* 1 (*interrogative: direct,*
indirect) quale; ~ **picture do you want?**
quale quadro vuole?; ~ **one?** quale?; ~ **one**
of you did it? chi di voi lo ha fatto?
2: **in ~ case** nel qual caso
♦ *pron* 1 (*interrogative*) quale; ~ **(of these)**
are yours? quali di questi sono suoi?; ~ **of**
you are coming? chi di voi viene?
2 (*relative*) che; (: *indirect*) cui, il (la) quale;
the apple ~ you ate/~ is on the table la
mela che hai mangiato/che è sul tavolo;
the chair on ~ you are sitting la sedia
sulla quale *or* su cui sei seduto; **he said he**
knew, ~ is true ha detto che lo sapeva, il
che è vero; **after ~** dopo di che

---

whichever [wɪtʃ'evə*] *adj*: **take ~ book you**
prefer prenda qualsiasi libro che preferisce;
~ **book you take** qualsiasi libro prenda
whiff [wɪf] *n* soffio; sbuffo; odore *m*
while [waɪl] *n* momento ♦ *conj* mentre; (*as*
long as) finché; (*although*) sebbene +*sub*;
per quanto +*sub*; **for a** ~ per un po'; ~
away *vt* (*time*) far passare
whim [wɪm] *n* capriccio
whimper ['wɪmpə*] *n* piagnucolio ♦ *vi*
piagnucolare
whimsical ['wɪmzɪkl] *adj* (*person*)
capriccioso(a); (*look*) strano(a)
whine [waɪn] *n* gemito ♦ *vi* gemere;
uggiolare; piagnucolare
whip [wɪp] *n* frusta; (*for riding*) frustino; (*POL:*
person) capogruppo (*che sovrintende alla*
disciplina dei colleghi di partito) ♦ *vt*
frustare; (*cream, eggs*) sbattere; ~**ped**
cream *n* panna montata; ~**-round** (*BRIT*)

n colletta
whirl [wə:l] *vt* (*far*) girare rapidamente; (*far*)
turbinare ♦ *vi* (*dancers*) volteggiare; (*leaves,*
water) sollevarsi in vortice; ~**pool** *n*
mulinello; ~**wind** *n* turbine *m*
whirr [wə:*] *vi* ronzare; rombare; frullare
whisk [wɪsk] *n* (*CULIN*) frusta; frullino ♦ *vt*
sbattere, frullare; **to ~ sb away** *or* **off**
portar via qn a tutta velocità
whiskers ['wɪskəz] *npl* (*of animal*) baffi *mpl*;
(*of man*) favoriti *mpl*
whisky ['wɪskɪ] (*US, IRELAND* **whiskey**) *n*
whisky *m inv*
whisper ['wɪspə*] *n* sussurro ♦ *vt, vi*
sussurrare
whist [wɪst] *n* whist *m*
whistle ['wɪsl] *n* (*sound*) fischio; (*object*)
fischietto ♦ *vi* fischiare
white [waɪt] *adj* bianco(a); (*with fear*)
pallido(a) ♦ *n* bianco; (*person*) bianco/a; ~
coffee (*BRIT*) *n* caffellatte *m inv*; ~**-collar**
worker *n* impiegato; ~ **elephant** *n* (*fig*)
oggetto (*or* progetto) costoso ma inutile;
W~ House *n* Casa Bianca; ~ **lie** *n* bugia
pietosa; ~**ness** *n* bianchezza; ~ **paper** *n*
(*POL*) libro bianco; ~**wash** *n* (*paint*) bianco
di calce ♦ *vt* imbiancare; (*fig*) coprire
whiting ['waɪtɪŋ] *n inv* (*fish*) merlango
Whitsun ['wɪtsn] *n* Pentecoste *f*
whittle ['wɪtl] *vt*: **to ~ away**, ~ **down**
ridurre, tagliare
whizz [wɪz] *vi*: **to ~ past** *or* **by** passare
sfrecciando; ~ **kid** (*inf*) *n* prodigio

KEYWORD
---

who [hu:] *pron* 1 (*interrogative*) chi; ~ **is it?,**
~**'s there?** chi è?
2 (*relative*) che; **the man ~ spoke to me**
l'uomo che ha parlato con me; **those ~**
can swim quelli che sanno nuotare

---

whodunit [hu:'dʌnɪt] (*inf*) *n* giallo
whoever [hu:'evə*] *pron*: ~ **finds it**
chiunque lo trovi; **ask ~ you like** lo chieda
a chiunque vuole; ~ **she marries** chiunque
sposerà, non importa chi sposerà; ~ **told**
you that? chi mai gliel'ha detto?

whole [həʊl] *adj* (*complete*) tutto(a), completo(a); (*not broken*) intero(a), intatto(a) ♦ *n* (*all*): **the ~ of** tutto(a) il(la); (*entire unit*) tutto; (*not broken*) tutto; **the ~ of the town** tutta la città, la città intera; **on the ~, as a ~** nel complesso, nell'insieme; **~ food(s)** *n(pl)* cibo integrale; **~hearted** *adj* sincero(a); **~meal** *adj* (*bread, flour*) integrale; **~sale** *n* commercio *or* vendita all'ingrosso ♦ *adj* all'ingrosso; (*destruction*) totale; **~saler** *n* grossista *m/f*; **~some** *adj* sano(a); salutare; **~wheat** *adj* = **~meal**; **wholly** *adv* completamente, del tutto

whom [huːm] *pron* **1** (*interrogative*) chi; **~ did you see?** chi hai visto?; **to ~ did you give it?** a chi lo hai dato?
2 (*relative*) che, *prep* +il (la) quale (*check syntax of Italian verb used*); **the man ~ I saw/to ~ I spoke** l'uomo che ho visto/al quale ho parlato

whooping cough ['huːpɪŋ-] *n* pertosse *f*
whore [hɔː*] (*inf: pej*) *n* puttana

whose [huːz] *adj* **1** (*possessive: interrogative*) di chi; **~ book is this?, ~ is this book?** di chi è questo libro?; **~ daughter are you?** di chi sei figlia?
2 (*possessive: relative*): **the man ~ son you rescued** l'uomo il cui figlio hai salvato; **the girl ~ sister you were speaking to** la ragazza alla cui sorella stavi parlando ♦ *pron* di chi; **~ is this?** di chi è questo?; **I know ~ it is** so di chi è

why [waɪ] *adv, conj* perché ♦ *excl* (*surprise*) ma guarda un po'!; (*remonstrating*) ma (via)!; (*explaining*) ebbene!; **~ not?** perché no?; **~ not do it now?** perché non farlo adesso?; **that's not ~ I'm here** non è questo il motivo per cui sono qui; **the reason ~** il motivo per cui; **~ever** *adv* perché mai
wicked ['wɪkɪd] *adj* cattivo(a), malvagio(a);

maligno(a); perfido(a)
wickerwork ['wɪkəwəːk] *adj* di vimini ♦ *n* articoli *mpl* di vimini
wicket ['wɪkɪt] *n* (*CRICKET*) porta; area tra le due porte
wide [waɪd] *adj* largo(a); (*area, knowledge*) vasto(a); (*choice*) ampio(a) ♦ *adv*: **to open ~** spalancare; **to shoot ~** tirare a vuoto *or* fuori bersaglio; **~-angle lens** *n* grandangolare *m*; **~-awake** *adj* completamente sveglio(a); **~ly** *adv* (*differing*) molto, completamente; (*travelled, spaced*) molto; (*believed*) generalmente; **~n** *vt* allargare, ampliare; **~ open** *adj* spalancato(a); **~spread** *adj* (*belief etc*) molto *or* assai diffuso(a)
widow ['wɪdəʊ] *n* vedova; **~ed** *adj*: **to be ~ed** restare vedovo(a); **~er** *n* vedovo
width [wɪdθ] *n* larghezza
wield [wiːld] *vt* (*sword*) maneggiare; (*power*) esercitare
wife [waɪf] (*pl* **wives**) *n* moglie *f*
wig [wɪg] *n* parrucca
wiggle ['wɪgl] *vt* dimenare, agitare
wild [waɪld] *adj* selvatico(a); selvaggio(a); (*sea, weather*) tempestoso(a); (*idea, life*) folle; stravagante; (*applause*) frenetico(a); **~erness** ['wɪldənɪs] *n* deserto; **~life** *n* natura; **~ly** *adv* selvaggiamente; (*applaud*) freneticamente; (*hit, guess*) a casaccio; (*happy*) follemente; **~s** *npl* regione *f* selvaggia
wilful ['wɪlful] (*US* **willful**) *adj* (*person*) testardo(a), ostinato(a); (*action*) intenzionale; (*crime*) premeditato(a)

will [wɪl] (*pt, pp* **~ed**) *aux vb* **1** (*forming future tense*): **I ~ finish it tomorrow** lo finirò domani; **I ~ have finished it by tomorrow** lo finirò entro domani; **~ you do it? – yes I ~/no I won't** lo farai? – sì (lo farò)/no (non lo farò)
2 (*in conjectures, predictions*): **he ~** *or* **he'll be there by now** dovrebbe essere arrivato ora; **that ~ be the postman** sarà il postino
3 (*in commands, requests, offers*): **~ you be**

quiet! vuoi stare zitto?; **~ you come?** vieni anche tu?; **~ you help me?** mi aiuti?, mi puoi aiutare?; **~ you have a cup of tea?** vorrebbe una tazza di tè?; **I won't put up with it!** non lo accetterò!
♦ *vt*: **to ~ sb to do** volere che qn faccia; **he ~ed himself to go on** continuò grazie a un grande sforzo di volontà
♦ *n* volontà; testamento

willful ['wɪlful] (*US*) *adj* = **wilful**
willing ['wɪlɪŋ] *adj* volonteroso(a); **~ to do** disposto(a) a fare; **~ly** *adv* volentieri; **~ness** *n* buona volontà
willow ['wɪləu] *n* salice *m*
will power *n* forza di volontà
willy-nilly [wɪlɪ'nɪlɪ] *adv* volente o nolente
wilt [wɪlt] *vi* appassire
win [wɪn] (*pt, pp* **won**) *n* (*in sports etc*) vittoria ♦ *vt* (*battle, prize, money*) vincere; (*popularity*) conquistare ♦ *vi* vincere; **~ over** *vt* convincere; **~ round** (*BRIT*) *vt* convincere
wince [wɪns] *vi* trasalire
winch [wɪntʃ] *n* verricello, argano
wind[1] [waɪnd] (*pt, pp* **wound**) *vt* attorcigliare; (*wrap*) avvolgere; (*clock, toy*) caricare ♦ *vi* (*road, river*) serpeggiare; **~ up** *vt* (*clock*) caricare; (*debate*) concludere
wind[2] [wɪnd] *n* vento; (*MED*) flatulenza; (*breath*) respiro, fiato ♦ *vt* (*take breath away*) far restare senza fiato; **~ power** energia eolica; **~fall** *n* (*money*) guadagno insperato
winding ['waɪndɪŋ] *adj* (*road*) serpeggiante; (*staircase*) a chiocciola
wind instrument *n* (*MUS*) strumento a fiato
windmill ['wɪndmɪl] *n* mulino a vento
window ['wɪndəu] *n* finestra; (*in car, train*) finestrino; (*in shop etc*) vetrina; (*also:* **~ pane**) vetro; **~ box** *n* cassetta da fiori; **~ cleaner** (*person*) pulitore *m* di finestre; **~ envelope** *n* busta a finestra; **~ ledge** *n* davanzale *m*; **~ pane** *n* vetro; **~-shopping** *n*: **to go ~-shopping** andare a vedere le vetrine; **~sill** *n* davanzale *m*

windpipe ['wɪndpaɪp] *n* trachea
windscreen ['wɪndskriːn] *n* parabrezza *m inv*; **~ washer** *n* lavacristallo; **~ wiper** *n* tergicristallo
windshield ['wɪndʃiːld] (*US*) *n* = **windscreen**
windswept ['wɪndswept] *adj* spazzato(a) dal vento
windy ['wɪndɪ] *adj* ventoso(a); **it's ~** c'è vento
wine [waɪn] *n* vino; **~ bar** *n* enoteca (*per degustazione*); **~ cellar** *n* cantina; **~ glass** *n* bicchiere *m* da vino; **~ list** *n* lista dei vini; **~ merchant** *n* commerciante *m* di vini; **~ tasting** *n* degustazione *f* del vini; **~ waiter** *n* sommelier *m inv*
wing [wɪŋ] *n* ala; (*AUT*) fiancata; **~s** *npl* (*THEATRE*) quinte *fpl*; **~er** *n* (*SPORT*) ala
wink [wɪŋk] *n* ammiccamento ♦ *vi* ammiccare, fare l'occhiolino; (*light*) baluginare
winner ['wɪnə*] *n* vincitore/trice
winning ['wɪnɪŋ] *adj* (*team, goal*) vincente; (*smile*) affascinante; **~s** *npl* vincite *fpl*
winter ['wɪntə*] *n* inverno; **~ sports** *npl* sport *mpl* invernali
wintry ['wɪntrɪ] *adj* invernale
wipe [waɪp] *n* pulita, passata ♦ *vt* pulire (strofinando); (*erase: tape*) cancellare; **~ off** *vt* cancellare; (*stains*) togliere strofinando; **~ out** *vt* (*debt*) pagare, liquidare; (*memory*) cancellare; (*destroy*) annientare; **~ up** *vt* asciugare
wire ['waɪə*] *n* filo; (*ELEC*) filo elettrico; (*TEL*) telegramma *m* ♦ *vt* (*house*) fare l'impianto elettrico di; (*also:* **~ up**) collegare, allacciare; (*person*) telegrafare a
wireless ['waɪəlɪs] (*BRIT*) *n* (*set*) (apparecchio *m*) radio *f inv*
wiring ['waɪərɪŋ] *n* impianto elettrico
wiry ['waɪərɪ] *adj* magro(a) e nerboruto(a); (*hair*) ispido(a)
wisdom ['wɪzdəm] *n* saggezza; (*of action*) prudenza; **~ tooth** *n* dente *m* del giudizio
wise [waɪz] *adj* saggio(a); prudente; giudizioso(a)
...wise [waɪz] *suffix*: **time~** per quanto

riguarda il tempo, in termini di tempo
wish [wɪʃ] n (desire) desiderio; (specific desire) richiesta ♦ vt desiderare, volere; **best ~es** (on birthday etc) i migliori auguri; **with best ~es** (in letter) cordiali saluti, con i migliori saluti; **to ~ sb goodbye** dire arrivederci a qn; **he ~ed me well** mi augurò di riuscire; **to ~ to do/sb to do** desiderare or volere fare/che qn faccia; **to ~ for** desiderare; **~ful** adj: **it's ~ful thinking** è prendere i desideri per realtà
wishy-washy [ˈwɪʃɪˈwɒʃɪ] (inf) adj (colour) slavato(a); (ideas, argument) insulso(a)
wisp [wɪsp] n ciuffo, ciocca; (of smoke) filo
wistful [ˈwɪstful] adj malinconico(a)
wit [wɪt] n (also: **~s**) intelligenza; presenza di spirito; (wittiness) spirito, arguzia; (person) bello spirito
witch [wɪtʃ] n strega

KEYWORD

with [wɪð, wɪθ] prep 1 (in the company of) con; **I was ~ him** ero con lui; **we stayed ~ friends** siamo stati da amici; **I'll be ~ you in a minute** vengo subito
2 (descriptive) con; **a room ~ a view** una stanza con vista sul mare (or sulle montagne etc); **the man ~ the grey hat/blue eyes** l'uomo con il cappello grigio/gli occhi blu
3 (indicating manner, means, cause): **~ tears in her eyes** con le lacrime agli occhi; **red ~ anger** rosso dalla rabbia; **to shake ~ fear** tremare di paura
4: **I'm ~ you** (I understand) la seguo; **to be ~ it** (inf: up-to-date) essere alla moda; (: alert) essere sveglio(a)

withdraw [wɪθˈdrɔ:] (irreg: like **draw**) vt ritirare; (money from bank) ritirare; prelevare ♦ vi ritirarsi; **~al** n ritiro; prelievo; (of army) ritirata; **~al symptoms** (MED) crisi f di astinenza; **~n** adj (person) distaccato(a)
wither [ˈwɪðə*] vi appassire
withhold [wɪθˈhəuld] (irreg: like **hold**) vt (money) trattenere; (permission): **to ~ (from)** rifiutare (a); (information): **to ~**

(from) nascondere (a)
within [wɪðˈɪn] prep all'interno; (in time, distances) entro ♦ adv all'interno, dentro; **~ reach (of)** alla portata (di); **~ sight (of)** in vista (di); **~ a mile of** entro un miglio da; **~ the week** prima della fine della settimana
without [wɪðˈaut] prep senza; **to go ~ sth** fare a meno di qc
withstand [wɪθˈstænd] (irreg: like **stand**) vt resistere a
witness [ˈwɪtnɪs] n (person, also LAW) testimone m/f ♦ vt (event) essere testimone di; (document) attestare l'autenticità di; **~ box** (US **~ stand**) n banco dei testimoni
witticism [ˈwɪtɪsɪzm] n spiritosaggine f
witty [ˈwɪtɪ] adj spiritoso(a)
wives [waɪvz] npl of **wife**
wizard [ˈwɪzəd] n mago
wk abbr = **week**
wobble [ˈwɒbl] vi tremare; (chair) traballare
woe [wəu] n dolore m; disgrazia
woke [wəuk] pt of **wake**; **woken** pp of **wake**
wolf [wulf] (pl wolves) n lupo
wolves [wulvz] npl of **wolf**
woman [ˈwumən] (pl women) n donna; **~ doctor** n dottoressa; **women's lib** (inf) n movimento femminista
womb [wu:m] n (ANAT) utero
women [ˈwɪmɪn] npl of **woman**
won [wʌn] pt, pp of **win**
wonder [ˈwʌndə*] n meraviglia ♦ vi: **to ~ whether/why** domandarsi se/perché; **to ~ at** essere sorpreso(a) di; meravigliarsi di; **to ~ about** domandarsi di; pensare a; **it's no ~ that** c'è poco or non c'è da meravigliarsi che +sub; **~ful** adj meraviglioso(a)
won't [wəunt] = **will not**
wood [wud] n legno; (timber) legname m; (forest) bosco; **~ carving** n scultura in legno, intaglio; **~ed** adj boschivo(a); boscoso(a); **~en** adj di legno; (fig) rigido(a); inespressivo(a); **~pecker** n picchio; **~wind** npl (MUS): **the ~wind** i legni; **~work** n (craft, subject) falegnameria; **~worm** n tarlo del legno
wool [wul] n lana; **to pull the ~ over sb's**

eyes (fig) imbrogliare qn; **~len** (US **~en**) adj di lana; (industry) laniero(a); **~lens** npl indumenti mpl di lana; (fig: ideas) confuso(a)

word [wəːd] n parola; (news) notizie fpl ♦ vt esprimere, formulare; **in other ~s** in altre parole; **to break/keep one's ~** non mantenere/mantenere la propria parola; **to have ~s with sb** avere un diverbio con qn; **~ing** n formulazione f; **~ processing** n elaborazione f di testi, word processing m; **~ processor** n word processor m inv

wore [wɔː*] pt of wear

work [wəːk] n lavoro; (ART, LITERATURE) opera ♦ vi lavorare; (mechanism, plan etc) funzionare; (medicine) essere efficace ♦ vt (clay, wood etc) lavorare; (mine etc) sfruttare; (machine) far funzionare; (cause: effect, miracle) fare; **to be out of ~** essere disoccupato(a); **~s** n (BRIT: factory) fabbrica ♦ npl (of clock, machine) meccanismo; **to ~ loose** allentarsi; **~ on** vt fus lavorare a; (person) lavorarsi; (principle) basarsi su; **~ out** vi (plans etc) riuscire, andare bene ♦ vt (problem) risolvere; (plan) elaborare; **it ~s out at £100** fa 100 sterline; **~ up** vt: **to get ~ed up** andare su tutte le furie; eccitarsi; **~able** adj (solution) realizzabile; **~aholic** n maniaco/a del lavoro; **~er** n lavoratore/trice, operaio/a; **~force** n forza lavoro; **~ing class** n classe f operaia; **~ing-class** adj operaio(a); **~ing order** n: **in ~ing order** funzionante; **~man** (irreg) n operaio; **~manship** n abilità; **~sheet** n foglio col programma di lavoro; **~shop** n officina; (practical session) gruppo di lavoro; **~ station** n stazione f di lavoro; **~-to-rule** (BRIT) n sciopero bianco

world [wəːld] n mondo ♦ cpd (champion) del mondo; (power, war) mondiale; **to think the ~ of sb** (fig) pensare un gran bene di qn; **~ly** adj di questo mondo; (knowledgeable) di mondo; **~-wide** adj universale; **W~-Wide Web** n World Wide Web m

worm [wəːm] n (also: **earth~**) verme m

worn [wɔːn] pp of wear ♦ adj usato(a); **~-**

out adj (object) consumato(a), logoro(a); (person) sfinito(a)

worried ['wʌrɪd] adj preoccupato(a)

worry ['wʌrɪ] n preoccupazione f ♦ vt preoccupare ♦ vi preoccuparsi

worse [wəːs] adj peggiore ♦ adv, n peggio; **a change for the ~** un peggioramento; **~n** vt, vi peggiorare; **~ off** adj in condizioni (economiche) peggiori

worship ['wəːʃɪp] n culto ♦ vt (God) adorare, venerare; (person) adorare; **Your W~** (BRIT: to mayor) signor sindaco; (: to judge) signor giudice

worst [wəːst] adj il(la) peggiore ♦ adv, n peggio; **at ~** al peggio, per male che vada

worth [wəːθ] n valore m ♦ adj: **to be ~** valere; **it's ~ it** ne vale la pena; **it is ~ one's while (to do)** vale la pena (fare); **~less** adj di nessun valore; **~while** adj (activity) utile; (cause) lodevole

worthy ['wəːði] adj (person) degno(a); (motive) lodevole; **~ of** degno di

┌─────────────┐
│ **KEYWORD** │
└─────────────┘

would [wud] aux vb 1 (conditional tense): **if you asked him he ~ do it** se glielo chiedesse lo farebbe; **if you had asked him he ~ have done it** se glielo avesse chiesto lo avrebbe fatto

2 (in offers, invitations, requests): **~ you like a biscuit?** vorrebbe or vuole un biscotto?; **~ you ask him to come in?** lo faccia entrare, per cortesia; **~ you open the window please?** apra la finestra, per favore

3 (in indirect speech): **I said I ~ do it** ho detto che l'avrei fatto

4 (emphatic): **it WOULD have to snow today!** doveva proprio nevicare oggi!

5 (insistence): **she ~n't do it** non ha voluto farlo

6 (conjecture): **it ~ have been midnight** sarà stato mezzanotte; **it ~ seem so** sembrerebbe proprio di sì

7 (indicating habit): **he ~ go there on Mondays** andava lì ogni lunedì

would-be (*pej*) *adj* sedicente
wouldn't ['wudnt] = **would not**
wound¹ [waund] *pt, pp of* **wind¹**
wound² [wu:nd] *n* ferita ♦ *vt* ferire
wove [wəuv] *pt of* **weave; woven** *pp of*
weave
wrangle ['ræŋgl] *n* litigio
wrap [ræp] *vt* avvolgere; (*pack: also:* ~ **up**)
incartare; ~**per** *n* (*on chocolate*) carta;
(*BRIT: of book*) copertina; ~**ping paper** *n*
carta da pacchi; (*for gift*) carta da regali
wreak [ri:k] *vt* (*havoc*) portare, causare; **to ~**
vengeance on vendicarsi su
wreath [ri:θ, *pl* ri:ðz] *n* corona
wreck [rɛk] *n* (*sea disaster*) naufragio; (*ship*)
relitto; (*pej: person*) rottame *m* ♦ *vt*
demolire; (*ship*) far naufragare; (*fig*)
rovinare; ~**age** *n* rottami *mpl*; (*of building*)
macerie *fpl*; (*of ship*) relitti *mpl*
wren [rɛn] *n* (*ZOOL*) scricciolo
wrench [rɛntʃ] *n* (*TECH*) chiave *f*; (*tug*)
torsione *f* brusca; (*fig*) strazio ♦ *vt*
strappare; storcere; **to ~ sth from** strappare
qc a *or* da
wrestle ['rɛsl] *vi*: **to ~ (with sb)** lottare (con
qn); ~**r** *n* lottatore/trice; **wrestling** *n* lotta
wretched ['rɛtʃɪd] *adj* disgraziato(a); (*inf:
weather, holiday*) orrendo(a), orribile;
(: *child, dog*) pestifero(a)
wriggle ['rɪgl] *vi* (*also:* ~ **about**) dimenarsi;
(: *snake, worm*) serpeggiare, muoversi
serpeggiando
wring [rɪŋ] (*pt, pp* **wrung**) *vt* torcere; (*wet
clothes*) strizzare; (*fig*): **to ~ sth out of**
strappare qc a
wrinkle ['rɪŋkl] *n* (*on skin*) ruga; (*on paper
etc*) grinza ♦ *vt* (*nose*) torcere; (*forehead*)
corrugare ♦ *vi* (*skin, paint*) raggrinzirsi
wrist [rɪst] *n* polso; ~**watch** *n* orologio da
polso
writ [rɪt] *n* ordine *m*; mandato
write [raɪt] (*pt* **wrote,** *pp* **written**) *vt, vi*
scrivere; ~ **down** *vt* annotare; (*put in
writing*) mettere per iscritto; ~ **off** *vt* (*debt,
plan*) cancellare; ~ **out** *vt* mettere per
iscritto; (*cheque, receipt*) scrivere; ~ **up** *vt*
redigere; ~-**off** *n* perdita completa; ~**r** *n*

autore/trice, scrittore/trice
writhe [raɪð] *vi* contorcersi
writing ['raɪtɪŋ] *n* scrittura; (*of author*)
scritto, opera; **in ~** per iscritto; ~ **paper** *n*
carta da lettere
written ['rɪtn] *pp of* **write**
wrong [rɔŋ] *adj* sbagliato(a); (*not suitable*)
inadatto(a); (*wicked*) cattivo(a); (*unfair*)
ingiusto(a) ♦ *adv* in modo sbagliato,
erroneamente ♦ *n* (*injustice*) torto ♦ *vt* fare
torto a; **you are ~ to do it** ha torto a farlo;
you are ~ about that, you've got it ~ si
sbaglia; **to be in the ~** avere torto; **what's
~?** cosa c'è che non va?; **to go ~** (*person*)
sbagliarsi; (*plan*) fallire, non riuscire;
(*machine*) guastarsi; ~**ful** *adj* illegittimo(a);
ingiusto(a); ~**ly** *adv* (*incorrectly, by mistake*)
in modo sbagliato; ~ **number** *n* (*TEL*):
you've got the ~ number ha sbagliato
numero
wrote [rəut] *pt of* **write**
wrought iron [rɔːt-] *n* ferro battuto
wrung [rʌŋ] *pt, pp of* **wring**

X, x

Xmas ['ɛksməs] *n abbr* = **Christmas**
X-ray ['ɛksreɪ] *n* raggio X; (*photograph*)
radiografia ♦ *vt* radiografare
xylophone ['zaɪləfəun] *n* xilofono

Y, y

yacht [jɔt] *n* panfilo, yacht *m inv*; ~**ing** *n*
yachting *m*, sport *m* della vela
Yank [jæŋk] (*pej*) *n* yankee *m/f inv*
Yankee ['jæŋkɪ] (*pej*) *n* = **Yank**
yap [jæp] *vi* (*dog*) guaire
yard [jɑːd] *n* (*of house etc*) cortile *m*;
(*measure*) iarda (= 914 mm; 3 feet);
~**stick** *n* (*fig*) misura, criterio
yarn [jɑːn] *n* filato; (*tale*) lunga storia
yawn [jɔːn] *n* sbadiglio ♦ *vi* sbadigliare;
~**ing** *adj* (*gap*) spalancato(a)
yd. *abbr* = **yard(s)**

yeah [jɛə] (*inf*) *adv* sì

year [jɪə*] *n* anno; (*referring to harvest, wine etc*) annata; **he is 8 ~s old** ha 8 anni; **an eight-~-old child** un(a) bambino(a) di otto anni; **~ly** *adj* annuale ♦ *adv* annualmente

yearn [jəːn] *vi*: **to ~ for sth/to do** desiderare ardentemente qc/di fare

yeast [jiːst] *n* lievito

yell [jɛl] *n* urlo ♦ *vi* urlare

yellow ['jɛləʊ] *adj* giallo(a)

yelp [jɛlp] *vi* guaire, uggiolare

yeoman ['jəʊmən] *n*: **~ of the guard** guardiano della Torre di Londra

yes [jɛs] *adv* sì ♦ *n* sì *m inv*; **to say/answer ~** dire/rispondere di sì

yesterday ['jɛstədɪ] *adv* ieri ♦ *n* ieri *m inv*; **~ morning/evening** ieri mattina/sera; **all day ~** ieri per tutta la giornata

yet [jɛt] *adv* ancora; già ♦ *conj* ma, tuttavia; **it is not finished ~** non è ancora finito; **the best ~** finora il migliore; **as ~** finora

yew [juː] *n* tasso (*albero*)

yield [jiːld] *n* produzione *f*, resa; reddito ♦ *vt* produrre, rendere, (*surrender*) cedere ♦ *vi* cedere; (*US: AUT*) dare la precedenza

YMCA *n abbr* (= *Young Men's Christian Association*) Y.M.C.A. *m*

yoga ['jəʊgə] *n* yoga *m*

yog(h)ourt ['jəʊgət] *n* = **yog(h)urt**

yog(h)urt ['jəʊgət] *n* iogurt *m inv*

yoke [jəʊk] *n* (*also fig*) giogo

yolk [jəʊk] *n* tuorlo, rosso d'uovo

KEYWORD

you [juː] *pron* **1** (*subject*) tu; (*: polite form*) lei; (*: pl*) voi; (*: very formal*) loro; **~ Italians enjoy your food** a voi Italiani piace mangiare bene; **~ and I will go** tu ed io *or* lei ed io andiamo

2 (*object: direct*) ti; la; vi; loro (*after vb*); (*: indirect*) ti; le; vi; loro (*after vb*); **I know ~** ti *or* la *or* vi conosco; **I gave it to ~** te l'ho dato; gliel'ho dato; ve l'ho dato; l'ho dato loro

3 (*stressed, after prep, in comparisons*) te; lei; voi; loro; **I told YOU to do it** ho detto a *TE* (*or* a *LEI etc*) di farlo; **she's younger**

than **~** è più giovane di te (*or* lei *etc*)

4 (*impers: one*) si; **fresh air does ~ good** l'aria fresca fa bene; **~ never know** non si sa mai

you'd [juːd] = **you had**; **you would**

you'll [juːl] = **you will**; **you shall**

young [jʌŋ] *adj* giovane ♦ *npl* (*of animal*) piccoli *mpl*; (*people*): **the ~** i giovani, la gioventù; **~er** *adj* più giovane; (*brother*) minore, più giovane; **~ster** *n* giovanotto, ragazzo; (*child*) bambino/a

your [jɔː*] *adj* il(la) tuo(a), *pl* i(le) tuoi(tue); il(la) suo(a), *pl* i(le) suoi(sue); il(la) vostro(a), *pl* i(le) vostri(e); il(la) loro, *pl* i(le) loro; *see also* **my**

you're [jʊə*] = **you are**

yours [jɔːz] *pron* il(la) tuo(a), *pl* i(le) tuoi(tue); (*polite form*) il(la) suo(a), *pl* i(le) suoi(sue); (*pl*) il(la) vostro(a), *pl* i(le) vostri(e); (*: very formal*) il(la) loro, *pl* i(le) loro; *see also* **mine**; **faithfully**; **sincerely**

yourself [jɔːˈsɛlf] *pron* (*reflexive*) ti; si; (*after prep*) te; sé; (*emphatic*) tu stesso(a); lei stesso(a); **yourselves** *pl pron* (*reflexive*) vi; si; (*after prep*) voi; loro; (*emphatic*) voi stessi(e); loro stessi(e); *see also* **oneself**

youth [juːθ, *pl* juːðz] *n* gioventù *f*; (*young man*) giovane *m*, ragazzo; **~ club** *n* centro giovanile; **~ful** *adj* giovane; da giovane; giovanile; **~ hostel** *n* ostello della gioventù

you've [juːv] = **you have**

Yugoslav ['juːgəʊ'slɑːv] *adj*, *n* jugoslavo(a)

Yugoslavia ['juːgəʊ'slɑːvɪə] *n* Jugoslavia

yuppie ['jʌpɪ] (*inf*) *n*, *adj* yuppie *m/f inv*

YWCA *n abbr* (= *Young Women's Christian Association*) Y.W.C.A. *m*

Z, z

zany ['zeɪnɪ] *adj* un po' pazzo(a)

zap [zæp] *vt* (*COMPUT*) cancellare

zeal [ziːl] *n* zelo; entusiasmo

zebra ['ziːbrə] *n* zebra; **~ crossing** (*BRIT*) *n* (passaggio pedonale a) strisce *fpl*, zebre *fpl*

zero ['zɪərəu] *n* zero

zest [zɛst] *n* gusto; (*CULIN*) buccia

zigzag ['zɪgzæg] *n* zigzag *m inv* ♦ *vi* zigzagare

Zimbabwe [zɪm'bɑːbwɪ] *n* Zimbabwe *m*

zinc [zɪŋk] *n* zinco

zip [zɪp] *n* (*also*: ~ **fastener**, (*US*) **~per**) chiusura *f or* cerniera *f* lampo *inv* ♦ *vt* (*also*: ~ **up**) chiudere con una cerniera lampo; ~ **code** (*US*) *n* codice *m* di avviamento postale

zodiac ['zəudɪæk] *n* zodiaco

zombie ['zɔmbɪ] *n* (*fig*): **like a ~** come un morto che cammina

zone [zəun] *n* (*also MIL*) zona

zoo [zuː] *n* zoo *m inv*

zoology [zuː'ɔlədʒɪ] *n* zoologia

zoom [zuːm] *vi*: **to ~ past** sfrecciare; ~ **lens** *n* zoom *m inv*, obiettivo a focale variabile

zucchini [zuː'kiːnɪ] (*US*) *npl* (*courgettes*) zucchine *fpl*

ITALIAN VERBS

1 Gerundio *2* Participio passato *3* Presente *4* Imperfetto *5* Passato remoto *6* Futuro *7* Condizionale *8* Congiuntivo presente *9* Congiuntivo passato *10* Imperativo

andare *3* vado, vai, va, andiamo, andate, vanno *6* andrò *etc* *8* vada *10* va'!, vada!, andate!, vadano!

apparire *2* apparso *3* appaio, appari *o* apparisci, appare *o* apparisce, appaiono *o* appariscono *5* apparvi *o* apparsi, appparisti, apparve *o* apparì *o* apparse, apparvero *o* apparirono *o* apparsero *8* appaia *o* apparisca

aprire *2* aperto *3* apro *5* aprii *o* apersi, apristi *8* apra

AVERE *3* ho, hai, ha, abbiamo, avete, hanno *5* ebbi, avesti, ebbe, avemmo, aveste, ebbero *6* avrò *etc* *8* abbia *etc* *10* abbi!, abbia!, abbiate!, abbiano!

bere *1* bevendo *2* bevuto *3* bevo *etc* *4* bevevo *etc* *8* beva *etc* *9* bevessi *etc*

cadere *5* caddi, cadesti *6* cadrò *etc*

cogliere *2* colto *3* colgo, colgono *5* colsi, cogliesti *8* colga

correre *2* corso *5* corsi, corresti

cuocere *2* cotto *3* cuocio, cociamo, cuociono *5* cossi, cocesti

dare *3* do, dai, dà, diamo, date, danno *5* diedi *o* detti, desti *6* darò *etc* *8* dia *etc* *9* dessi *etc* *10* da'!, dia!, date!, diano!

dire *1* dicendo *2* detto *3* dico, dici, dice, diciamo, dite, dicono *4* dicevo *etc* *5* dissi, dicesti *6* dirò *etc* *8* dica, diciamo, diciate, dicano *9* dicessi *etc* *10* di'!, dica!, dite!, dicano!

dolere *3* dolgo, duoli, duole, dolgono *5* dolsi, dolesti *6* dorrò *etc* *8* dolga

dovere *3* devo *o* debbo, devi, deve, dobbiamo, dovete, devono *o* debbono *6* dovrò *etc* *8* debba, dobbiamo, dobbiate, devano *o* debbano

ESSERE *2* stato *3* sono, sei, è, siamo, siete, sono *4* ero, eri, era, eravamo, eravate, erano *5* fui, fosti, fu, fummo, foste, furono *6* sarò *etc* *8* sia *etc* *9* fossi, fossi, fosse, fossimo, foste, fossero *10* sii!, sia!, siate!, siano!

fare *1* facendo *2* fatto *3* faccio, fai, fa, facciamo, fate, fanno *4* facevo *etc* *5* feci, facesti *6* farò *etc* *8* faccia *etc* *9* facessi *etc* *10* fa'!, faccia!, fate!, facciano!

FINIRE *1* finendo *2* finito *3* finisco, finisci, finisce, finiamo, finite, finiscono *4* finivo, finivi, finiva, finivamo, finivate, finivano *5* finii, finisti, finì, finimmo, finiste, finirono *6* finirò, finirai, finirà, finiremo, finirete, finiranno *7* finirei, finiresti, finirebbe, finiremmo, finireste, finirebbero *8* finisca, finisca, finisca, finiamo, finiate, finiscano *9* finissi, finissi, finisse, finissimo, finiste, finissero *10* finisci!, finisca!, finite!, finiscano!

giungere *2* giunto *5* giunsi, giungesti

leggere *2* letto *5* lessi, leggesti

mettere *2* messo *5* misi, mettesti

morire *2* morto *3* muoio, muori, muore, moriamo, morite, muoiono *6* morirò *o* morrò *etc* *8* muoia

muovere *2* mosso *5* mossi, movesti

nascere *2* nato *5* nacqui, nascesti

nuocere *2* nuociuto *3* nuoccio, nuoci, nuoce, nociamo *o* nuociamo, nuocete, nuocciono *o* nuocevo *etc* *5* nocqui, nuocesti *6* nuocerò *etc* *7* nuoccia

offrire *2* offerto *3* offro *5* offersi *o* offrii, offristi *8* offra

parere *2* parso *3* paio, paiamo, paiono *5* parvi *o* parsi, paresti *6* parrò *etc* *8* paia, paiamo, paiate, paiano

PARLARE *1* parlando *2* parlato *3* parlo, parli, parla, parliamo, parlate, parlano *4* parlavo, parlavi, parlava, parlavamo, parlavate, parlavano *5* parlai, parlasti, parlò, parlammo, parlaste, parlarono *6* parlerò, parlerai, parlerà, parleremo, parlerete, parleranno *7* parlerei, parleresti, parlerebbe, parleremmo, parlereste, parlerebbero 8 parli, parli, parli, parliamo, parliate, parlino 9 parlassi, parlassi, parlasse, parlassimo, parlaste, parlassero 10 parla!, parli!, parlate!, parlino!

piacere 2 piaciuto 3 piaccio, piacciamo, piacciono 5 piacqui, piacesti 8 piaccia etc

porre 1 ponendo 2 posto 3 pongo, poni, pone, poniamo, ponete, pongono 4 ponevo etc 5 posi, ponesti 6 porrò etc 8 ponga, poniamo, poniate, pongano 9 ponessi etc

potere 3 posso, puoi, può, possiamo, potete, possono 6 potrò etc 8 possa, possiamo, possiate, possano

prendere 2 preso 5 presi, prendesti

ridurre 1 riducendo 2 ridotto 3 riduco etc 4 riducevo etc 5 ridussi, riducesti 6 ridurrò etc 8 riduca etc 9 riducessi etc

riempire 1 riempiendo 3 riempio, riempi, riempie, riempiono

rimanere 2 rimasto 3 rimango, rimangono 5 rimasi, rimanesti 6 rimarrò etc 8 rimanga

rispondere 2 risposto 5 risposi, rispondesti

salire 3 salgo, sali, salgono 8 salga

sapere 3 so, sai, sa, sappiamo, sapete, sanno 5 seppi, sapesti 6 saprò etc 8 sappia etc 10 sappi!, sappia!, sappiate!, sappiano!

scrivere 2 scritto 5 scrissi, scrivesti

sedere 3 siedo, siedi, siede, siedono 8 sieda

spegnere 2 spento 3 spengo, spengono 5 spensi, spegnesti 8 spenga

stare 2 stato 3 sto, stai, sta, stiamo, state, stanno 5 stetti, stesti 6 starò etc

8 stia etc 9 stessi etc 10 sta'!, stia!, state!, stiano!

tacere 2 taciuto 3 taccio, tacciono 5 tacqui, tacesti 8 taccia

tenere 3 tengo, tieni, tiene, tengono 5 tenni, tenesti 6 terrò etc 8 tenga

trarre 1 traendo 2 tratto 3 traggo, trai, trae, traiamo, traete, traggono 4 traevo etc 5 trassi, traesti 6 trarrò etc 8 tragga 9 traessi etc

udire 3 odo, odi, ode, odono 8 oda

uscire 3 esco, esci, esce, escono 8 esca

valere 2 valso 3 valgo, valgono 5 valsi, valesti etc 8 valga

vedere 2 visto o veduto 5 vidi, vedesti 6 vedrò etc

VENDERE 1 vendendo 2 venduto 3 vendo, vendi, vende, vendiamo, vendete, vendono 4 vendevo, vendevi, vendeva, vendevamo, vendevate, vendevano 5 vendei o vendetti, vendesti, vendé o vendette, vendemmo, vendeste, venderono o vendettero 6 venderò, venderai, venderà, venderemo, venderete, venderanno 7 venderei, venderesti, venderebbe, venderemmo, vendereste, venderebbero 8 venda, venda, venda, vendiamo, vendiate, vendano 9 vendessi, vendessi, vendesse, vendessimo, vendeste, vendessero 10 vendi!, venda!, vendete!, vendano!

venire 2 venuto 3 vengo, vieni, viene, vengono 5 venni, venisti 6 verrò etc 8 venga

vivere 2 vissuto 5 vissi, vivesti

volere 3 voglio, vuoi, vuole, vogliamo, volete, vogliono 5 volli, volesti 6 vorrò etc 8 voglia etc 10 vogli!, voglia!, vogliate!, vogliano!

VERBI INGLESI

present	pt	pp	present	pt	pp
arise	arose	arisen	feed	fed	fed
awake	awoke	awoken	feel	felt	felt
be (am, is, are; being)	was, were	been	fight	fought	fought
			find	found	found
bear	bore	born(e)	flee	fled	fled
beat	beat	beaten	fling	flung	flung
become	became	become	fly (flies)	flew	flown
begin	began	begun	forbid	forbade	forbidden
behold	beheld	beheld	forecast	forecast	forecast
bend	bent	bent	forego	forewent	foregone
beseech	besought	besought	foresee	foresaw	foreseen
beset	beset	beset	foretell	foretold	foretold
bet	bet, betted	bet, betted	forget	forgot	forgotten
bid	bid, bade	bid, bidden	forgive	forgave	forgiven
bind	bound	bound	forsake	forsook	forsaken
bite	bit	bitten	freeze	froze	frozen
bleed	bled	bled	get	got	got, (US) gotten
blow	blew	blown			
break	broke	broken	give	gave	given
breed	bred	bred	go (goes)	went	gone
bring	brought	brought	grind	ground	ground
build	built	built	grow	grew	grown
burn	burnt, burned	burnt, burned	hang	hung, hanged	hung, hanged
burst	burst	burst	have (has; having)	had	had
buy	bought	bought			
can	could	(been able)	hear	heard	heard
cast	cast	cast	hide	hid	hidden
catch	caught	caught	hit	hit	hit
choose	chose	chosen	hold	held	held
cling	clung	clung	hurt	hurt	hurt
come	came	come	keep	kept	kept
cost	cost	cost	kneel	knelt, kneeled	knelt, kneeled
creep	crept	crept			
cut	cut	cut	know	knew	known
deal	dealt	dealt	lay	laid	laid
dig	dug	dug	lead	led	led
do (3rd person:he/she/it does)	did	done	lean	leant, leaned	leant, leaned
			leap	leapt, leaped	leapt, leaped
draw	drew	drawn	learn	learnt, learned	learnt, learned
dream	dreamed, dreamt	dreamed, dreamt			
			leave	left	left
drink	drank	drunk	lend	lent	lent
drive	drove	driven	let	let	let
dwell	dwelt	dwelt	lie (lying)	lay	lain
eat	ate	eaten	light	lit, lighted	lit, lighted
fall	fell	fallen			

present	pt	pp	present	pt	pp
lose	lost	lost	spell	spelt, spelled	spelt, spelled
make	made	made	spend	spent	spent
may	might	—	spill	spilt, spilled	spilt, spilled
mean	meant	meant			
meet	met	met	spin	spun	spun
mistake	mistook	mistaken	spit	spat	spat
mow	mowed	mown, mowed	split	split	split
must	(had to)	(had to)	spoil	spoiled, spoilt	spoiled, spoilt
pay	paid	paid			
put	put	put	spread	spread	spread
quit	quit, quitted	quit, quitted	spring	sprang	sprung
			stand	stood	stood
read	read	read	steal	stole	stolen
rid	rid	rid	stick	stuck	stuck
ride	rode	ridden	sting	stung	stung
ring	rang	rung	stink	stank	stunk
rise	rose	risen	stride	strode	stridden
run	ran	run	strike	struck	struck, stricken
saw	sawed	sawn			
say	said	said	strive	strove	striven
see	saw	seen	swear	swore	sworn
seek	sought	sought	sweep	swept	swept
sell	sold	sold	swell	swelled	swollen, swelled
send	sent	sent			
set	set	set	swim	swam	swum
shake	shook	shaken	swing	swung	swung
shall	should	—	take	took	taken
shear	sheared	shorn, sheared	teach	taught	taught
shed	shed	shed	tear	tore	torn
shine	shone	shone	tell	told	told
shoot	shot	shot	think	thought	thought
show	showed	shown	throw	threw	thrown
shrink	shrank	shrunk	thrust	thrust	thrust
shut	shut	shut	tread	trod	trodden
sing	sang	sung	wake	woke	woken
sink	sank	sunk	waylay	waylaid	waylaid
sit	sat	sat	wear	wore	worn
slay	slew	slain	weave	wove, weaved	woven, weaved
sleep	slept	slept			
slide	slid	slid	wed	wedded, wed	wedded, wed
sling	slung	slung			
slit	slit	slit			
smell	smelt, smelled	smelt, smelled	weep	wept	wept
			win	won	won
sow	sowed	sown, sowed	wind	wound	wound
speak	spoke	spoken	wring	wrung	wrung
speed	sped, speeded	sped, speeded	write	wrote	written

I NUMERI

NUMBERS

uno(a)	1	one
due	2	two
tre	3	three
quattro	4	four
cinque	5	five
sei	6	six
sette	7	seven
otto	8	eight
nove	9	nine
dieci	10	ten
undici	11	eleven
dodici	12	twelve
tredici	13	thirteen
quattordici	14	fourteen
quindici	15	fifteen
sedici	16	sixteen
diciassette	17	seventeen
diciotto	18	eighteen
diciannove	19	nineteen
venti	20	twenty
ventuno	21	twenty-one
ventidue	22	twenty-two
ventitré	23	twenty-three
ventotto	28	twenty-eight
trenta	30	thirty
quaranta	40	forty
cinquanta	50	fifty
sessanta	60	sixty
settanta	70	seventy
ottanta	80	eighty
novanta	90	ninety
cento	100	a hundred, one hundred
cento uno	101	a hundred and one
duecento	200	two hundred
mille	1 000	a thousand, one thousand
milleduecentodue	1 202	one thousand two hundred and two
cinquemila	5 000	five thousand
un milione	1 000 000	a million, one million

primo(a), 1º		first, 1st
secondo(a), 2º		second, 2nd
terzo(a), 3º		third, 3rd
quarto(a)		fourth, 4th
quinto(a)		fifth, 5th
sesto(a)		sixth, 6th

I NUMERI

settimo(a)
ottavo(a)
nono(a)
decimo(a)
undicesimo(a)
dodicesimo(a)
tredicesimo(a)
quattordicesimo(a)
quindicesimo(a)
sedicesimo(a)
diciassettesimo(a)
diciottesimo(a)
diciannovesimo(a)
ventesimo(a)
ventunesimo(a)
ventiduesimo(a)
ventitreesimo(a)
ventottesimo(a)
trentesimo(a)
centesimo(a)
centunesimo(a)
millesimo(a)
milionesimo(a)

Frazioni etc

mezzo
terzo
due terzi
quarto
quinto
zero virgola cinque, 0,5
tre virgola quattro, 3,4
dieci per cento
cento per cento

Esempi

abita al numero dieci
si trova nel capitolo sette, a
  pagina sette
abita al terzo piano
arrivò quarto
scala uno a venticinquemila

NUMBERS

seventh
eighth
ninth
tenth
eleventh
twelfth
thirteenth
fourteenth
fifteenth
sixteenth
seventeenth
eighteenth
nineteenth
twentieth
twenty-first
twenty-second
twenty-third
twenty-eighth
thirtieth
hundredth
hundred-and-first
thousandth
millionth

Fractions etc

half
third
two thirds
quarter
fifth
(nought) point five, 0.5
three point four, 3.4
ten per cent
a hundred per cent

Examples

he lives at number 10
it's in chapter 7, on page 7

he lives on the 3rd floor
he came in 4th
scale 1:25,000

L'ORA

THE TIME

che ora è?, che ore sono?

what time is it?

è ..., sono ...

it is ...

mezzanotte	midnight, twelve p.m.
l'una (della mattina)	one o'clock (in the morning), one (a.m.)
l'una e cinque	five past one
l'una e dieci	ten past one
l'una e un quarto, l'una e quindici	a quarter past one, one fifteen
l'una e venticinque	twenty-five past one, one twenty-five
l'una e mezzo *or* mezza, l'una e trenta	half-past one, one thirty
le due meno venticinque, l'una e trentacinque	twenty-five to two, one thirty-five
le due meno venti, l'una e quaranta	twenty to two, one forty
le due meno un quarto, l'una e quarantacinque	a quarter to two, one forty-five
le due meno dieci, l'una e cinquanta	ten to two, one fifty
mezzogiorno	twelve o'clock, midday, noon
l'una, le tredici	one o'clock (in the afternoon), one (p.m.)
le sette (di sera), le diciannove	seven o'clock (in the evening), seven (p.m.)

a che ora?

at what time?

a mezzanotte	at midnight
all'una, alle tredici	at one o'clock
fra venti minuti	in twenty minutes
venti minuti fa	twenty minutes ago